Cook on Costs
2011

Cook on Costs
2011

A guide to legal remuneration in civil
contentious and non-contentious business

Michael J Cook

 LexisNexis®

Members of the LexisNexis Group worldwide

United Kingdom	LexisNexis Butterworths, a Division of Reed Elsevier (UK) Ltd, Halsbury House, 35 Chancery Lane, London, WC2A 1EL, and RSH, 1–3 Baxter's Place, Leith Walk Edinburgh EH1 3AF
Australia	LexisNexis Butterworths, Chatswood, New South Wales
Austria	LexisNexis Verlag ARD Orac GmbH & Co KG, Vienna
Benelux	LexisNexis Benelux, Amsterdam
Canada	LexisNexis Butterworths, Markham, Ontario
China	LexisNexis China, Beijing and Shanghai
France	LexisNexis SA, Paris
Germany	LexisNexis Deutschland GmbH, Munster
Hong Kong	LexisNexis Hong Kong, Hong Kong
India	LexisNexis India, New Delhi
Italy	Giuffrè Editore, Milan
Japan	LexisNexis Japan, Tokyo
Malaysia	Malayan Law Journal Sdn Bhd, Kuala Lumpur
New Zealand	LexisNexis NZ Ltd, Wellington
Poland	Wydawnictwo Prawnicze LexisNexis Sp, Warsaw
Singapore	LexisNexis Singapore, Singapore
South Africa	LexisNexis Butterworths, Durban
USA	LexisNexis, Dayton, Ohio

© Reed Elsevier (UK) Ltd 2010

Published by LexisNexis Butterworths

First published 1991   ISBN: 978 1 4057 4989 3

Printed and bound in Great Britain by William Clowes Ltd, Beccles, Suffolk

Visit LexisNexis UK at www.lexisnexis.co.uk

Preface

Welcome to the largest edition yet – I say that not with pride but regret. Like Topsy it just keeps growing. I hope it still fits in a brief case.

The publishers tell me the purpose of a Preface is to tell potential readers why they should buy the book. I shall risk incurring their wrath by giving you two reasons not to buy it this year. Do not purchase if you are expecting an exposition on Lord Justice Jackson's Review of Civil Litigation Costs or on Lord Young's report: *Common Sense: Common Safety* which deals with costs in the perceived compensation culture. I have summarised them both in two appendices, but this is a practical book about civil costs as they are – it is not about what costs law, practice and procedure might become, let alone what I think they ought to be. This time next year the Jackson/Young juggernaut may have changed the costs landscape, but in the meantime there have been more than enough developments to justify purchasing *Cook on Costs 2011*. That should keep the publishers happy.

I have always thought that a little of Mr Gradgrind goes a long way, and have tried to impart an understanding as well as a knowledge of costs. This book arose when after many years of speaking to the profession about costs I realised that my various talks amounted to half a book. Butterworths said if I would write the other half of the book they would be happy to publish it. So I did and they did nearly 20 years ago. I also took the view that in the same way that a speaker has a duty to his audience to keep them awake, an author has no less a duty to retain the interest of his readers and to apply sugar coating to the pill where needed.

This edition embraces two aspects of the changing costs scene. First, it is now increasingly difficult for any one person to have practical expertise in every aspect of civil costs. For example, I forget how many decades have passed since I last attended on a taxation of costs, as they then were, and Chapter 30 has for several years leant heavily on costs lawyer, as he now is, Harry Birks. I have now enlisted the help of five specialists in particular areas of costs. I acknowledge them on page xiii and thank them here.

The other sign of the times is that the chapter on conditional fees has now taken on a life of its own and become PART VII with no less than five user-friendly chapters thanks to David Chalk.

Through the wonders of modern publishing the law is as at I November 2010.

Michael Cook

Burwood Park

Guy Fawkes Night 2010

Foreword to the first annual edition

For litigation practitioners, the issue of costs used to be a relative afterthought. However, over the last decade the pendulum has swung to the point where the funding of litigation – whether the case can be funded and who pays what to whom at the end – has become a new and essential skill for litigators everywhere.

Fortunately *Cook on Costs* has been there in recent years to help the profession steer its way through the costs maze. But even Michael Cook, whose authorship on this complex subject has always kept us up-to-date, has appreciated that the current pace of change is so fast that an annual edition is now required. So that is what he has produced in the first annual edition of *Cook on Costs*. This is an indispensable text for every solicitor, whose own understanding of costs and the funding of litigation by conditional fees, the state or otherwise, is essential to the overriding need to ensure that costs issues are fully explained to and understood by the client.

Like my predecessor, Phillip Ely, who wrote the foreword to the excellent first edition, I am delighted to commend to all firms the timely arrival of *Cook on Costs 2000*.

Michael Napier

President

The Law Society

Foreword to the First Edition

It is my privilege as President of the Law Society to commend Michael Cook's very practical guide to all aspects of solicitors' costs (other than criminal costs).

He modestly suggests that the book does not contain any facts and figures that cannot be found elsewhere. Recognising the ultimate and total dependence of solicitors on the costs which they receive, he presents all those facts and figures with clarity borne of experience. This book adds to the major contribution which Michael Cook has already made to the profession on this vital topic.

It is also a clear response to the need for a definitive and manageable guide to an area which requires such practical and positive skills.

I hope that it will find a place in every solicitor's office.

October 1991

P T Ely

President

The Law Society

Preface to the First Edition

When the publishers asked me to write a preface I cavilled on the two grounds that no-one reads prefaces and they serve no useful purpose. I was told that the purpose is to explain the aims and intention of the work; in other words, why I have written the book and why you should read it. Fair enough. My late partner, Lionel Cranfield, at the end of some heavy litigation used to say, 'Now we come to the interesting part – the costs!'. In the quarter of a century since Lionel was killed in the hunting field, the profession has become increasingly aware that money is the life-blood of a solicitor's practice, but I continue to be perplexed that, in spite of this realisation, most solicitors and their clients lose out financially because of the profession's basic lack of understanding and interest in all aspects of costs. In a College of Law survey of the areas of skills on which solicitors wished the Law Society's new Legal Practice course to be based, costs did not even appear in the list.

And that is why I have written this book. It does not contain any facts and figures you cannot find elsewhere – apart from it being illustrated from my collection of unreported cases – but I have tried to write about costs in an interesting, coherent and digestible way. My aim in writing the book is therefore to impart to you the understanding of, and enthusiasm for, costs that Lionel Cranfield aroused in me all those years ago.

I much appreciate the kindness of Philip Ely in writing a foreword to the book in his year as President of the Law Society. I am seriously indebted to my old friend Master Michael Devonshire of the Supreme Court Taxing Office for reading the manuscript of the book and making many useful suggestions on the condition that I did not mention his name.

The law is stated as at 1 October 1991.

Michael Cook

Limpsfield
October 1991

Acknowledgments

I am grateful to the following for their contributions to this edition:

Assessment of costs

Harry Birks Costs Lawyer	Chapter 30 Detailed assessment

CPR Part 36

Dominic Regan of the City University	Chapter 14 Offers to Settle

Funding

Nicholas Bacon QC	Chapter 40 State-funded costs
Susan Dunn of Harbour Litigation Funding	Chapter 41 Third Party Funding
David Chalk of Winchester University	Part VII Conditional Fees

Many of the unreported cases first appeared in *The Litigation Letter* and are reproduced with the kind permission of the publishers, Informa plc

Extracts from the various Law Society publications and Legal Services Commission material are reproduced with the kind permission of the Law Society and Legal Services Commission.

Appendices

Appendix I
Summary of Lord Justice Jackson's Review of the Costs of Civil Litigation

The *Final Report* of the Review of the Costs of Civil Litigation published on 14 January 2010 consisted of 557 pages comprising 46 chapters, three annexes and ten appendices and incorporated the two volume Preliminary Report by means of cross-references.

A comprehensive package

The Report proposes a comprehensive coherent package of inter-dependent reforms designed to reduce litigation costs and to promote access to justice. Lord Justice Jackson is confident that if it is implemented in full it will improve access to justice, provide a more effective legal and court system, control excesses in litigation as well as costs and yield substantial savings in legal costs for both the litigant and the taxpayer. The proposals are contained in the following extracts from the executive summary.

Success fees and ATE insurance premiums should cease to be recoverable

I recommend that success fees and ATE insurance premiums should cease to be recoverable from unsuccessful opponents in civil litigation. If this recommendation is implemented, it will lead to significant costs savings, whilst still enabling those who need access to justice to obtain it. It will be open to clients to enter into 'no win, no fee' (or similar) agreements with their lawyers, but any success fee will be borne by the client, not the opponent. (2.2)

Increase in general damages

In order to ensure that claimants are properly compensated for personal injuries, and that the damages awarded to them (which may be intended to cover future medical care) are not substantially eaten into by legal fees, I recommend as a complementary measure that awards of general damages for pain, suffering and loss of amenity be increased by 10%, and that the maximum amount of damages that lawyers may deduct for success fees be capped at 25% of damages (excluding any damages referable to future care or future losses). In the majority of cases, this should leave successful claimants no worse off than they are under the current regime, whilst at the same time ensuring that unsuccessful defendants only pay normal and proportionate legal costs to successful claimants. It will also ensure that claimants have an interest in the costs being incurred on their behalf. (2.4)

Referral fees

It is a regrettably common feature of civil litigation, in particular personal injuries litigation, that solicitors pay referral fees to claims management companies, before-the-event ('BTE') insurers and other organisations to 'buy' cases. Referral fees add to the costs of litigation, without adding any real value to it. I recommend that lawyers should not be permitted to pay referral fees in respect of personal injury cases. (2.5)

Qualified one way costs shifting

ATE insurance premiums add considerably to the costs of litigation. Litigation costs can be reduced by taking away the need for ATE insurance in the first place. This can occur if qualified one way costs shifting is introduced, at least for certain categories of litigation in which it is presently common for ATE insurance to be taken out. By 'qualified' one way costs shifting I mean that the claimant will not be required to pay the defendant's costs if the claim is unsuccessful, but the defendant will be required to pay the claimant's costs if it is successful. . . . I can certainly see the benefit of there being qualified one way costs shifting in personal injuries litigation.

It seems to me that a person who has a meritorious claim for damages for personal injuries should be able to bring that claim, without being deterred by the risk of adverse costs. The same could be said of clinical negligence, judicial review and defamation claims. There may be other categories of civil litigation where qualified one way costs shifting would be beneficial. (2.6–2.7)

Sir Rupert has explained he has in mind protecting vulnerable claimants by provisions similar to those afforded to state funded litigants by section 11 of the Access to Justice Act 1999.

Overall result

If the package of proposed reforms summarised above is introduced, there will be five consequences:

- Most personal injury claimants will recover more damages than they do at present, although some will recover less.
- Claimants will have a financial interest in the level of costs which are being incurred on their behalf.
- Claimant solicitors will still be able to make a reasonable profit.
- Costs payable to claimant solicitors by liability insurers will be significantly reduced.
- Costs will also become more proportionate, because defendants will no longer have to pay success fees and ATE insurance premiums. (2.8)

Fixed costs in fast track litigation

Cases in the fast track are those up to a value of £25,000, where the trial can be concluded within one day. A substantial proportion of civil litigation is conducted in the fast track. I recommend that the costs recoverable for fast track personal injury cases be fixed. For other types of case I recommend that there be a dual system (at least for now), whereby costs are fixed for certain types of case, and in other cases there is a financial limit on costs recoverable (I propose that £12,000 be the limit for pre-trial costs). The ideal is for costs to be fixed in the fast track for all types of claim. (2.9)

Costs Council

If a fixed costs regime is adopted for the fast track, the costs recoverable for the various types of claim will need to be reviewed regularly to make sure that they are reasonable and realistic. I propose that a Costs Council be established to undertake the role of reviewing fast track fixed costs, as well as other matters. (2.11)

In announcing the creation of an Advisory Committee on Civil Costs the Ministry of Justice minister said it was 'in response to a recommendation from the Civil Justice Council [in its report Improved Access to Justice – Funding Options and Proportionate Costs in 2005], but the Committee's terms of reference were not what the CJC had in mind and Sir Rupert recommends that it is replaced.

BTE insurance

BTE insurance (or 'legal expenses insurance') is insurance cover for legal expenses taken out before an event which gives rise to civil litigation. It is under-used in England and Wales. If used more widely, it could produce benefits for small and medium enterprises ('SMEs') and individuals who may become embroiled in legal disputes. (3.1)

Contingency fees

It is my recommendation that lawyers should be able to enter into contingency fee agreements with clients for contentious business, provided that:

- the unsuccessful party in the proceedings, if ordered to pay the successful party's costs, is only required to pay an amount for costs reflecting what would be a conventional amount, with any difference to be borne by the successful party; and
- the terms on which contingency fee agreements may be entered into are regulated, to safeguard the interests of clients. (3.2)–(3.3)

Contingency Legal Aid Fund ('CLAF') and Supplementary Legal Aid Scheme ('SLAS') (chapter 13)

CLAFs and SLASs are self-funding and usually not-for-profit forms of litigation funding. The information I have reviewed during the Costs Review does not provide any strong indication of financial viability. I would, nevertheless, recommend that the use of CLAFs and SLASs as a form of legal funding for civil litigation be kept under review. (3.4)

Assessment of general damages for pain, suffering and loss of amenity for personal injury

During the Costs Review I explored the possibility of producing a transparent and 'neutral' calibration of existing software systems to assist in calculating general damages, which could encourage the early settlement of personal injury claims for acceptable amounts. I believe that this is indeed possible, and suggest that a working group be set up consisting of representatives of claimants, defendants, the judiciary and others to take this matter further (4.1)–(4.2)

Process and procedure

I recommend that the new process for handling personal injury claims arising out of road traffic accidents where the amount in dispute is up to £10,000 and liability is admitted be monitored, to see whether it leads to costs being kept proportionate, or whether costs in fact increase due to satellite litigation. I also encourage a productive engagement, under the aegis of the Civil Justice Council, between claimant and defendant representatives to see whether a similar procedure can be applied in other fast track personal injuries litigation. (4.3)

Hope triumphs over experience.

Clinical negligence

One of the principal complaints that was made during the Costs Review about clinical negligence actions was that pre-action costs were often being racked up to disproportionately high levels. There may be a number of reasons for this (which I mention in chapter 23). The recommendations I have made here include increasing the response time for defendants to pre-action letters from three months to four months (to give more time for a thorough investigation of the claim), and that where the defendant is proposing to deny liability it should obtain independent expert evidence on liability and causation within that period. I also recommend that case management directions for clinical negligence claims be harmonised across England and Wales and that costs management of clinical negligence cases be piloted. (4.4)

Intellectual property litigation

To reduce the costs of IP litigation, and particularly the cost to SMEs, I recommend that the Patents County Court (the 'PCC'), which deals with lower value IP disputes, be reformed to provide a cost-effective environment for IP disputes. These reforms include:
(i)   allowing costs to be recovered from opponents according to cost scales; and
(ii)   capping total recoverable costs to £50,000 in contested actions for patent infringement, and £25,000 for all other cases. I also recommend that there be a fast track and a small claims track in the PCC. (5.1)

Small business disputes

It is important that the litigation environment for such cases is streamlined, accessible to non-lawyers and cost-effective. (5.2

Large commercial claims

Much large commercial litigation is conducted in the Commercial Court. The feedback that I received during the Costs Review indicated that there was a strong general level of satisfaction amongst court users with the current workings of the Commercial Court, . . . though I have made certain recommendations in relation to disclosure, the use of lists of issues as a case management tool and docketing of cases to judges. (5.5)

Chancery litigation

I make a number of specific recommendations in relation to chancery litigation. One is that CPR Part 8 should be amended to enable actions to be assigned to the fast track at any time. This would enable smaller value chancery cases to be dealt with under the economical model that applies in the fast track. Another recommendation is that there should be developed a scheme of benchmark costs for routine bankruptcy and insolvency cases. (5.6)

Technology and Construction Court litigation

Litigation in the Technology and Construction Court (the 'TCC') is often conducted in a proportionate manner, and I make only modest recommendations concerning the operation of that court. I do, however, recommend that there be a fast track in the TCC.(5.7)

Defamation and related claims

I have recommended that lawyers' success fees and ATE insurance premiums should cease to be recoverable for all types of civil litigation. If this recommendation is adopted, it should go a substantial distance to ensuring that unsuccessful defendants in such proceedings are not faced with a disproportionate costs liability. However, such a measure could also reduce access to justice for claimants of slender means.

To overcome this potential problem, I recommend complementary measures for defamation and related proceedings, namely:

- increasing the general level of damages in defamation and breach of privacy proceedings by 10%; and
- introducing a regime of qualified one way costs shifting, under which the amount of costs that an unsuccessful claimant may be ordered to pay is a reasonable amount, reflective of the means of the parties and their conduct in the proceedings. (5.10)–(5.11)

At the launch of the Final Report, Sir Rupert gave the example an unsuccessful media defendant paying a fourfold increase of reasonable and proportionate costs: (1) their own costs (2) the claimant's costs (3) a 100% success fee and (4) an ATE insurance premium of up to 100%.

Collective actions

My recommendation is that costs shifting should remain for collective actions (with the exception of personal injury collective actions), but that the court should have a discretion to order otherwise if this will better facilitate access to justice. (5.12)

Pre-action protocols

I recommend that the ten pre-action protocols for specific types of litigation be retained, albeit with certain amendments to improve their operation (and to keep pre-action costs proportionate).

The Practice Direction – Pre-Action Conduct, which was introduced in 2009 as a general practice direction for all types of litigation, is unsuitable as it adopts a 'one size fits all' approach, often leading to pre-action costs being incurred unnecessarily (and wastefully). I recommend that substantial parts of this practice direction be repealed. (6.1)–(6.2).

Alternative dispute resolution

There should be a serious campaign to ensure that all litigation lawyers and judges are properly informed of how ADR works, and the benefits that it can bring.

The public and small businesses who become embroiled in disputes are also made aware of the benefits of ADR.

Nevertheless ADR should not be mandatory for all proceedings. The circumstances in which it should be used (and when it should be used) will vary from case to case, and much will come down to the judgment of experienced practitioners and the court. (6.3)

Disclosure

Disclosure can be an expensive exercise (particularly in higher value, complex cases), and it is therefore necessary that measures be taken to ensure that the costs of disclosure in civil litigation do not become disproportionate.

E-disclosure in particular has emerged as a new and important facet of disclosure generally, and I recommend that solicitors, barristers and judges alike be given appropriate training on how to conduct e-disclosure efficiently.

I also recommend that there be a 'menu' of disclosure options available for large commercial and similar claims, where the costs of standard disclosure are likely to be disproportionate. I would, however, exclude large personal injury and clinical negligence claims from this 'menu' option, as standard disclosure usually works satisfactorily in those cases. (6.4), (6.5), (6.6)

Witness statements and expert evidence

There is nothing fundamentally wrong with the manner in which evidence is currently adduced in civil litigation, by way of witness statements and expert reports. The only substantial complaint which is made is that in some cases the cost of litigation is unnecessarily increased because witness statements and expert reports are unduly long. I recommend two measures (in appropriate cases) for curbing litigants' over-enthusiasm for prolixity, being (i) case management measures to place controls on the content or length of statements; and (ii) cost sanctions. (6.7)

Sir Rupert also recommends that volunteers should pilot the procedure of both experts giving oral evidence concurrently or, because the practice emanates from Australia, 'hot tubbing'.

Case management

Effective case management means:

- where practicable allocating cases to judges who have relevant expertise;
- ensuring that, so far as possible, a case remains with the same judge;
- standardising case management directions; and
- ensuring that case management conferences and other interim hearings are used as effective occasions for case management, and do not become formulaic hearings that generate unnecessary cost (eg where directions could easily have been given without a hearing). (6.8)–(6.9)

Costs management

Costs management is an adjunct to case management, whereby the court, with input from the parties, actively attempts to control the costs of cases before it. The primary means by which costs management is effected is for the parties to provide budgets of their own costs, with those budgets being updated from time to time and submitted for approval to the court. The court then formulates the directions and orders which it makes with a view to ensuring that costs do not become disproportionate. It may do this, for example, by limiting disclosure, or limiting the number of witnesses. (6.10)

Part 36 offers

In order to provide greater incentives for defendants to accept settlement offers, I recommend that where a defendant fails to beat a claimant's offer, the claimant's recovery should be enhanced by 10%. (6.12)

Sensational! A 10% increase, not of the costs, but of the claim. He also recommends that the decision in *Carver v BAA* should be reversed, which would restore some sanity and certainty to the process.

Summary and detailed assessments

The procedure for the summary assessment of costs generally works well, and should be retained. I do, however, recommend a number of specific improvements to the process. For detailed assessments, I recommend that a new format for bills of costs be developed. I also recommend the streamlining of the procedure for detailed assessment through the use of IT. (6.14)

The government has issued a 100 page consultation paper on those proposals which require primary legislation to implement with responses due by St Valentine's Day 2011.

Appendix II
Common Sense: Common Safety

Lord Young of Graffham was appointed by the prime minister personally to advise on health and safety and in particular to review what he called 'the damaging compensation culture'. Lord Young's report, *Common Sense: Common Safety*, published on 15 October 2010 recommends:

- Introduce a simplified claims procedure for personal injury claims similar to that for road traffic accidents under £10,000 on a fixed costs basis. Explore the possibility of extending the framework of such a scheme to cover low value medical negligence claims which may greatly simplify the claims process, reduce the time taken to agree damages and result in reduced costs for all parties.
- Examine the option of extending the upper limit for road traffic accident personal injury claims to £25,000. Many millions of pounds would be diverted from legal costs to health delivery annually if we do this right. One of the incidental but important advantages of the adoption of this scheme will be the vastly reduced scope for advertising that a scale fee system will deliver.
- Introduce as soon as possible the recommendations in Lord Justice Jackson's review of civil litigation costs that CFA success fees and ATE insurance premiums should cease to be recoverable from the losing party in litigation; that lawyers should be able to enter into contingency fee agreements, also known as damages based agreements (DBAs) and extend BTE insurance. Lord Young recommends the practicability of a national scheme should be investigated. 'Extending BTE insurance might be a fair solution to the problem of access to justice. I propose consulting with the insurance industry on developing stand-alone BTE policies suitable for individuals, as well as on how to best develop policies for small businesses.'
- The claims management company regulations do not go far enough: they allow companies and personal injury lawyers to advertise in such a way that encourages individuals to believe that they can easily claim compensation for the most minor of incidents. The system needs to go further and do more to control both the volume of advertising that such companies produce and also the content of these adverts.
- Restrict the operation of referral agencies and personal injury lawyers and control the volume and type of advertising. It is not right that some people should be led to believe that they can absolve themselves from any personal responsibility for their actions, that financial recompense can make good any injury, or that compensation should be a cash cow for lawyers and referral agencies.
- Clarify (through legislation if necessary) that people will not be held liable for any consequences due to well-intentioned voluntary acts on their part. People who seek to do good in our society should not fear litigation as a result of their actions.

Contents

Contents

Contents

Contents

Contents

Contents

Contents

Contents

Contents

Table of Statutes

References in the right-hand column are to paragraph numbers. Paragraph references printed in **bold** type indicate where the statute is set out in part or in full.

Table of Statutory Instruments

References in the right-hand column are to paragraph numbers. Paragraph references printed in **bold** type indicate where the statutory instrument is set out in part or in full.

Table of Civil Procedure Rules

References in the right-hand column are to paragraph numbers. Paragraph references printed in **bold** type indicate where the CPR is set out in part or in full.

Table of Practice Directions

References in the right-hand column are to paragraph numbers. Paragraph references printed in **bold** type indicate where the Section is set out in part or in full.

Table of Non-Statutory Provisions

References in the right-hand column are to paragraph numbers. Paragraph references printed in **bold** type indicate where the Provisions are set out in part or in full.

Table of Cases

A

Table of Cases

C

Table of Cases

D

E

F

G

H

Table of Cases

K

L

N

O

Table of Cases

S

T

Table of Cases

X

Y

Z

PART I

SOLICITOR AND CLIENT

CHAPTER 1

THE RETAINER

A CAUTIONARY TALE

[1.1]

Let us start with a story. It arose when I was sitting as chairman of the Solicitors' Disciplinary Tribunal, so it is a horror story. The applicant, in person, complained that the respondent had been guilty of conduct unbefitting a solicitor. The applicant's wife wished to sue her former employers, HM Government, over pension rights. In his search for justice on behalf of his wife, the applicant had been to no fewer than 22 firms of solicitors in London – a circumstance he regarded as reflecting criticism on the legal profession and not on himself. The respondent was his twenty-third solicitor. The respondent agreed to instruct counsel to see the applicant in conference and thereafter to give his opinion in writing. The applicant paid the respondent £150 on account of costs. The conference was a disaster. It lasted for over three hours and broke up in confusion. There was no doubt that it was agreed that the applicant would provide counsel with further papers through his solicitor. On receipt of the further papers, the solicitor rendered a bill to the applicant for £450 plus £250 counsel's fees, requesting immediate payment together with a further sum of £2,000 generally on account of costs before he would deliver the papers to counsel. The client demurred. He wrote to the solicitor saying that the sum of £150 that he had paid was an all-in fee. When he heard nothing he wrote to the solicitor with detailed complaints and enquiries, to which he again received no reply. The solicitor issued a writ against the applicant and his wife for his and counsel's fees. He obtained summary judgment. On appeal the judgment was set aside and the action transferred to the county court. In the middle of the trial before the judge in the county court the applicant sought an adjournment, which unlikely request was granted only upon the condition that the applicant paid the full amount of money claimed into court. He failed to do this and judgment was entered once again. Although the applicant again appealed, the Court of Appeal refused permission to appeal. The solicitor issued a bankruptcy petition. On the hearing of the petition the applicant disputed the judgment on which the petition was based, but again he failed. He and his wife were adjudicated bankrupt. The applicant reported the solicitor to the Professional Purposes Committee (as it then was) of the Law Society, who declined to take any action. He then applied personally to the Solicitors' Disciplinary Tribunal, who held there was no *prima facie* case against the solicitor. The applicant appealed from that decision to the Court of Appeal who said that on his version of events there was a case for the solicitor to answer and directed the Disciplinary Tribunal to hear the application. That is where I came in. I am not going to tell you what happened because that is not the point of the story. The point I wish to make is that in my opinion that solicitor was not entitled to render a bill at all and therefore there should have been no writ, no judgment and no bankruptcy. When you have read this chapter I hope you will agree with me.

A CONTRACT

[1.2]

The giving of instructions by a client to a solicitor constitutes the solicitor's retainer by the client. It is a contract. It creates the solicitor's right to be paid. The rights and liabilities of the parties are governed by the ordinary law of contract, but the relationship is also subject to the special statutory provisions which govern contracts between a solicitor and his client. It is an implied term of the contract that the client will pay the solicitor's charges and disbursements. The retainer need not be in writing but, if the true construction of an arrangement is that the solicitor's costs are guaranteed by a third party, then, of course, the requirement that a guarantee must be in writing applies to the arrangement between the solicitor and the third party. For example, in *Manches LLP v Carl Freer* [2006] EWHC 991 (QB), [2006] All ER (D) 428 (Nov) solicitors claimed payment of their outstanding fees from the defendant for work done for a company of which he was a director. The solicitors claimed that the defendant was personally liable because of a provision in their terms of business that stated the directors would be directly liable for fees and disbursements if the company failed to pay them. The defendant accepted that he had signed the engagement letter but said it was on behalf of the company and not so as to make him personally liable. The court agreed with the defendant and held that for the defendant to be personally liable as a guarantor he had to have signed the letter both as a director and in his personal capacity, or preferably he should have signed two letters. I suspect the reaction of many solicitors to this decision was 'There but for the Grace of God go I'.

Where there is a dispute between a solicitor and his client about the terms of an oral retainer, the word of the client is to be preferred to the word of the solicitor, or, at least, more weight is to be given to it. The reason is plain. It is because the client is ignorant and the solicitor is, or should be, learned in the law. If the solicitor does not take the precaution of getting a written retainer, he has only himself to blame for being at variance with his client over it and must take the consequences. The onus is on the solicitor to establish the terms of the retainer and in the absence of persuasive evidence the court should prefer the client's version. 'It is up to the solicitor to take the appropriate steps to clarify precisely the extent of his retainer' (*Gray v Buss Merton (a firm)* [1999] PNLR 882 & 892) 'because the client, through ignorance of the correct terminology, may not be able to express his instructions clearly' (*Sibley & Co v Reachbyte Ltd (1) and Kris Motor Spares Ltd (2)* [2008] EWHC 2665, [2008] All ER (D) 15 (Nov)).

TERMINATION OF THE RETAINER

(a) Other than by the solicitor

[1.3]

The client may terminate a retainer at any time for any reason.

The retainer may also be terminated by the effluxion of time if it was for a fixed period, or by the death, bankruptcy or insanity of the solicitor or the client (or both!), or if its continuance becomes unlawful.

The client may have the right to cancel under the Cancellation of Contracts made in a Consumer's Home or Place of Work etc Regulations 2008. See para [5.48].

The Guidance (para 69 iii) to Rule 2.0 of the Solicitors Code of Conduct 2007 ('The Guidance') recommends: 'If your client loses mental capacity after you have started to act, the law will automatically end the contractual relationship. However, it is important that the client, who is in a very vulnerable situation, is not left without legal representation. Consequently, you should notify an appropriate person (eg the Court of Protection), or you may look for someone legally entitled to provide you with instructions, such as an attorney under an enduring power of attorney, or take the appropriate steps for such a person to be appointed, such as a receiver or a litigation friend. This is a particularly complex legal issue and you should satisfy yourself as to the law before deciding on your course of action.'

(b) By the solicitor

(i) For good cause

[1.4]

There is an implied term that the solicitor may terminate the retainer upon reasonable notice for good cause, such as a failure to provide funds for disbursements or give adequate instructions; the client requiring the solicitor to behave unlawfully or unethically; obstructing the solicitor, or preventing him from dealing with the matter, and where there is a serious breakdown in confidence between them.

The main issue in *Richard Buxton (Solicitors) v Mills-Owens* [2008] EWHC 1831 (QB); [2008] All ER (D) 356 (Jul) was whether a solicitor had 'good reason', pursuant to r 12.12 of the Rules and the Solicitors' Code of Conduct 2007, r 2.01(2), for terminating a retainer if a client insisted on his putting forward a case and instructing counsel to argue a case that was 'doomed to disaster' or which the solicitor believed was 'bound to fail'.

There is no comprehensive definition of what amounts to a 'good reason' to terminate in the Rules or the Solicitors Code of Conduct 2007, because it is a fact-sensitive question. It was wrong to restrict the circumstances in which a solicitor could lawfully terminate his retainer to those in which he was instructed to do something improper. Solicitors should not lightly be able lawfully to terminate their retainers, but the desirability of protecting a client from an arbitrary and unreasonable termination was not a sufficient justification for a narrow interpretation of the phrase 'good reason'.

It would be improper in a statutory planning appeal to advance an argument based on the merits of the decision by the planning inspector, which was hopeless and not genuinely arguable. As the client had insisted that such arguments be advanced, the solicitors had good reason for terminating the retainer. The retainer was an entire contract that had not been completed, but as it had been terminated for good reason the solicitors were entitled to their proper costs and disbursements for work done prior to the termination.

The Guidance (para 6(b) to Rule 2.01) recommends: 'Before taking on a new matter, you must consider whether your firm has the resources – including knowledge, qualifications, expertise, time, sufficient support staff and, where appropriate, access to external expertise such as agents and counsel – to provide the support required to represent the client properly. The obligation is a continuing one, and you must ensure that an appropriate or agreed level of service can be delivered even if circumstances change.'

Lack of resources would include a solicitor having insufficient time, experience or skill to deal with the instructions. Although it would be unethical for the solicitor to continue to act in these circumstances it would not be a 'good cause' for terminating the retainer and the solicitor would be in breach of it, thereby disentitling him to any payment for work done (see 'An entire contract', below). He could also be liable for any damage the client may suffer as a result of the termination.

Paragraph 9 of the Guidance reads: 'If there is good reason to cease acting, you must give reasonable notice to the client. What amounts to reasonable notice will depend on the circumstances. For example, it would normally be unreasonable to stop acting for a client immediately before a court hearing where it is impossible for the client to find alternative representation. In such a case, if there is no alternative but to cease acting immediately, you should attend and explain the circumstances to the court – see rule 11 (Litigation and advocacy). There may be circumstances where it is reasonable to give no notice.'

(ii)   Under the Solicitors Act 1974, s 65(2)

[1.5]

In respect of contentious costs only, the Law Society secured in the Solicitors Act 1974, s 65(2) an important concession for solicitors. Where a solicitor requests a client to pay a reasonable sum of money on account of costs incurred and to be incurred in respect of contentious business, if the client fails to make that payment within a reasonable time, this shall be a good cause upon which the solicitor may, on giving reasonable notice to the client, terminate the retainer.

AN ENTIRE CONTRACT

[1.6]

A retainer is normally an entire contract under which the solicitor is to do certain work for the client and under the law of contract in the absence of agreement, or a request from the client for a final bill, he cannot seek any remuneration until that work has been completed or the retainer has been terminated in some other way. Subject to the provisions of the Solicitors Act 1974, s 65(2) (above) in respect of contentious business, and to any special agreement entered into with a client covering contentious or non-contentious business, a solicitor is not entitled to any payment on account of his costs other than disbursements. If the solicitor wrongfully terminates the retainer he is not entitled to any payment at all for the work he has done, either on a *quantum meruit* or any other basis (*Wild v Simpson* [1919] 2 KB 544, CA). In *Wong v Vizards (a firm)* [1997] 2 Costs LR 46, QBD, where solicitors declined to represent their client at a hearing unless he made a substantial payment on account of a disputed bill it was held that because the amount claimed by the solicitors was unreasonable they had wrongfully terminated the retainer on the grounds of non-payment and were therefore not entitled to any payment at all for the work they had done in preparation for the hearing.

INTERIM BILLS

[1.7]

Even though the Solicitors Act 1974, s 65(2) is limited to contentious business, solicitors have always been free to agree the terms of their retainer with their clients in respect of both non-contentious and contentious business. It was only in recent years that solicitors realised what has long been appreciated in every other walk of life, that without stage payments by the client the entire burden of financing the work falls upon he who is doing it. Litigation in particular can be protracted, complicated and lingering, as can some non-contentious work. An agreement with a client that the firm will render interim bills at monthly, three-monthly or six-monthly intervals will transform a firm's cash flow. I know that there are problems in preparing detailed interim bills during the currency of an active matter, but any basic system of time recording and costing will enable simple interim bills to be produced based on time spent and hourly rates. Any anomalies or inequities can be rectified in the final bill. The clients will be grateful. Solicitors live in fear of offending their clients with requests for payments on account of costs and disbursements, but it is nothing compared with the fear of the clients of the ever-growing size of an unknown bill which they know they will inevitably receive. Clients welcome knowing the amount of costs they have incurred to date, even if it may mean them crying 'Halt!' before any more costs are incurred; they will also welcome the opportunity of making stage payments. Furthermore, clients appreciate that a solicitor who is efficient in the conduct of his own affairs is likely to be no less efficient in looking after theirs.

There are two kinds of interim bill, and the difference between them is crucial.

(a) Interim statute bills

(i) *Self-contained final bills*

[1.8]

These are called statute bills because they comply with all the requirements of the Solicitors Act 1974 and result in all the consequences which flow from such compliance – the solicitor can enforce payment by suing the client, the client can obtain an order for a Solicitors Act assessment and the various time limits relating to the client's rights to an assessment run from the date of their delivery. Although they are interim bills they are also final bills in respect of the work covered by them. There can be no subsequent adjustment in the light of the outcome of the business. They are complete self-contained bills of costs to date. Interim statute bills during the currency of the retainer can arise in only two ways: by natural break or agreement.

(ii) *Natural break*

[1.9]

There is authority for the rendering of an interim statute bill at a natural break in protracted litigation. There is, however, little authority for identifying what is a natural break. In *Chamberlain v Boodle & King (a firm)* [1982] 3 All ER 188, CA, Lord Denning said: 'It is a question of fact whether there are natural breaks in the work done by a solicitor so that each portion of it can and should be treated as a separate and distinct part in itself, capable of and rightly being charged separately and taxed separately'. In that case the Court of Appeal held that there had been no natural breaks justifying treating a series of accounts rendered during litigation as final accounts and that they should accordingly be treated as one bill all of which could be assessed. (The case is also memorable for the claimant being a gentleman who lived in New Orleans rejoicing in the name of Bartlett Beardslee Chamberlain III.) In *Wilson v William Sturges & Co* [2006] EWHC 792 (QB), [2006] 16 EG 146 (CS) a bill delivered at the end of the first stage of proceedings was held to be a statute bill. Even though the court held it to be 20% in excess of the proper amount, the solicitors' insistence on it being paid before proceeding further did not terminate the retainer and disentitle the solicitors to their reasonable costs. The Law Society's advice is not to rely on the 'natural break' principle as a ground for delivering an interim statute bill except in the clearest circumstances.

(iii) *Agreement*

[1.10]

'Before a solicitor is entitled to require a bill to be treated as a complete self-contained bill of costs to date, he must make it plain to the client expressly or by implication that that is the purpose of his sending in that bill for that amount at that time. Then of course one looks to see what the client's reaction is. If the client's reaction is to pay the bill in its entirety without demur, it is not difficult to infer an agreement that the bill is to be treated as a self-contained bill of costs to date.'

That was how Roskill LJ put it in *Davidsons v Jones-Fenleigh* (1980) 124 Sol Jo 204, CA. In that case the court found that each of four bills delivered was complete and final in its own right and that the time for challenging three of them had expired. In *Abedi v Penningtons (a firm)* [2000] NLJR 465, CA, the solicitors had not agreed with their client that they could deliver interim bills and there were no natural breaks in the litigation, but the solicitors did in fact deliver bills on a monthly basis, each purporting to be a final bill for the period in question. The client at first paid regularly, but then stopped, leaving five bills unpaid and four bills partially paid. The client then alleged that she had been overcharged and sought a detailed assessment under the Solicitors Act. She was so long out of time in making her application that if each of the bills was treated as a final bill she was not entitled to have any of them assessed under the Act. The Court of Appeal upheld the award of summary judgment to the solicitors on the grounds that the possibility of interim bills being statute bills could arise by virtue of an inferred as well as an express agreement. The client, far from disputing the bills, had paid them regularly and had promised to pay the outstanding bills. The case was distinguished from *Re Romer & Haslam* [1893] 2 QB 286, CA, because in that case the solicitors had never asked for payment of any of their bills, but merely sought and obtained payment on account.

In *Adams v Mackinnes* SCCO Case No 13 of 2001 the retainer commenced in 1990 with a client care letter, no copy of which survived. In August 1994 the solicitors sent a further client care letter, which was available, stating they would apply an uplift for care and conduct but probably not until the end of the action, when they could decide what mark-up was merited. However, they did not change the format of their bills until May 1996, when they bore a prominent message that the bill was an interim bill. Prior to then the bills were drawn in a way which made them look like final bills. They set out exactly what work had been done, the rate being charged and the period covered by the bill, and each carried a notice informing the client of his rights to detailed assessment under the Solicitors Act. In these circumstances the solicitors were not entitled to any uplift for care and conduct prior to their client care letter of August 1994. It was not mentioned in this short report, but on the face of it, it would be arguable that the format of the bills until May 1996 resulted in them being final bills on which no mark-up could subsequently be claimed.

The Law Society advises practitioners to make it expressly clear in their terms of business letter that they propose to deliver interim statute bills in the event of protracted work.

(b) Interim bills on account

(i) Request for payment on account

[1.11]

We have seen that the Solicitors Act 1974, s 65(2) provides that in respect of contentious business a solicitor may request the client to pay a reasonable sum on account of costs and that the refusal or failure to make such a payment shall be deemed to be a good cause whereby the solicitor may, upon giving reasonable notice to the client, withdraw from the retainer. It is vital to differentiate between a request for payment under s 65(2), which is usually known as a 'bill on account', and an interim statute bill, particularly as both are often described as 'interim' bills.

(ii) Not enforceable by action

[1.12]

A bill on account is really nothing more than a request for payment on account in fancy dress. Not being a statute bill it cannot be sued on by the solicitor, the client cannot apply for a detailed assessment of it and, of course, the time limits for applying for a detailed assessment do not run. In *Turner & Co v Palomo SA* [2000] 1 WLR 37, CA, five bills rendered during the course of litigation had been headed 'on account of charges and disbursements incurred or to be incurred'. It was held these could not be construed as final or statute bills in respect of the work covered by them, and accordingly the time limits for applying for a detailed assessment under the Solicitors Act had not started to run. If the client does not pay a bill on account the solicitor should give him the 'reasonable notice' required by s 65(2), that unless payment is made within a stipulated (reasonable) time, the solicitor will withdraw from the retainer. If the client regards the amount requested on account as excessive he can invite the solicitor to render a statute bill which he may then have assessed. If the solicitor fails to render a statute bill the client can obtain an order from the court that he should do so, pursuant to the Solicitors Act 1974, s 68.

(iii) May be increased

[1.13]

One advantage to the solicitor of rendering a bill on account is that it need not be the final quantification of all the work included in it, but is merely the minimum amount of his charges to date. It also avoids the risk of limiting any between-the-parties costs recoverable in respect of this period to the amount of the bill on account under the indemnity principle and any risk of appearing to charge by results. For this reason it is important to make it clear to the client that the bill on account is simply a request for payment on account of the statute bill which will be delivered later. Wording on the following lines will achieve this:

> 'There is statutory provision for various discretionary factors to be taken into account when calculating solicitors' fees, some of which cannot be assessed until all the work is completed; these will be taken into account in our final bill when we shall be able to make an overall evaluation of the matter.'

The position is also covered in the precedent terms of business letter at para [2.38].

(iv) Payable into the office account

[1.14]

A bill on account constitutes a written intimation to the client of the amount of costs incurred to date and therefore entitles a solicitor to transfer from his client account into his office account money received from the client in accordance with the Solicitors' Accounts Rules 1991. Such a transfer is restricted to the amount of costs already incurred and must not cover anticipated future costs. A bill on account must therefore be restricted to costs incurred. Any request for money on account of future costs must, in respect of contentious business, comply with the requirements of the Solicitors Act 1974, s 65(2) and in respect of non-contentious costs must be pursuant to an agreement with the client.

THE SIX HURDLES

[1.15]

We can now see where the solicitor in the story at the beginning of this chapter went wrong. The business had not been completed, the retainer had not been terminated, there had been no agreement that a statute bill could be delivered and there was no natural break – they were in mid-conference. Even on the solicitor's own version – rejecting the suggestion he had agreed an all-in fee of £150 – this 'bill' was at best a request for payment on account pursuant to the Solicitors Act 1974, s 65(2). Before the solicitor could issue a writ there had to be six stages:

(a) A request for a reasonable amount on account.
(b) Failure to pay that amount.
(c) Reasonable notice by the solicitor of his intention to terminate the retainer.
(d) Termination of the retainer.
(e) Delivery of a statute bill.
(f) The expiration of one month.

The solicitor got over none of these hurdles. Even assuming the request for a further payment was reasonable (the Tribunal found that it was not), and accepting that this was contentious business and the client had failed to pay the amount requested, the solicitor had not given notice of his intention to terminate the retainer, had not in fact terminated it and was not entitled to deliver a statute bill. You will be relieved to know that the Tribunal did not regard the improper delivery of the account as amounting to professional misconduct – not only did the solicitor think he was entitled to do so, a Queen's Bench master, a High Court judge, a county court judge, a bankruptcy registrar and the Court of Appeal (twice) saw nothing wrong with it either. I told you it was a horror story.

POSTSCRIPT

[1.16]

For the client there was a semi-happy ending. The solicitor's insurers settled the claim for £200,000 and £50,000 costs, but it was three years after the death of his wife.

CHAPTER 2

AGREEMENTS WITH CLIENTS

COSTS INFORMATION

Pre-1 July 2007

[2.1]

The conduct of solicitors before 1 July 2007 was governed by the Solicitors Practice Rules 1990, Rule 15 (Costs information and client care) of which provided in respect of costs:

Solicitors shall:
(a)   give information about costs and other matters, and
(b)   operate a complaints handling procedure,

in accordance with a Solicitors' Costs Information and Client Care Code made from time to time by the Council of the Law Society with the concurrence of the Master of the Rolls, but subject to the notes.

Notes
(i)   A serious breach of the code, or persistent breaches of a material nature, will be a breach of the rule, and may also be evidence of inadequate professional services under section 37A of the Solicitors Act 1974.
(ii)   Material breaches of the code which are not serious or persistent will not be a breach of the rule, but may be evidence of inadequate professional services under section 37A.
(iii) The powers of the Law Society on a finding of inadequate professional services include:
(a)   disallowing all or part of the solicitor's costs; and
(b)   directing the solicitor to pay compensation to the client up to a limit of £15,000.
(iv) Non-material breaches of the code will not be a breach of the rule, and will not be evidence of inadequate professional services under section 37A.

Further explanation was provided in the Guide to the Professional Conduct of Solicitors 1999. The Solicitors' Costs Information and Client Care Code is now to be found on the Law Society website (http://www.lawsociety.org.uk). It required information to be given in plain English at the outset of, and at appropriate stages throughout, the matter, with information given orally being confirmed in writing as soon as possible. At the outset the solicitor had to give the client the best information possible about the likely overall costs, including a breakdown between fees, VAT and disbursements, including the basis upon which the fees are to be calculated and whether an estimate, quotation or other indication of costs was not intended to be fixed. The solicitor was required to discuss with the client how, when and by whom any costs are were to be met, including consideration of Community Legal Service funding, legal expenses insurance, after-the-event insurance to cover another party's costs, and whether a client's liability for costs might be payable by another person such as an employer or trade union. Costs-benefit and risk must be discussed; CLS-funded clients must be advised about the statutory charge, their liability to the CLS and liability to their opponents, whereas privately paying clients were similarly to be advised as to their liability for paying their opponent's costs and that solicitor and client costs might exceed those recoverable in the event of success. Solicitors were required to tell the client, unless otherwise agreed, how much the costs were at regular intervals, not less than six months, and in appropriate cases to deliver interim bills at agreed intervals. They must also explain to the client any changes of circumstances which were likely to affect (i) the amount of costs, (ii) the degree of risk involved and (iii) the costs-benefit to the client of continuing with the matter. Although the Code and Guidance have been replaced they still contain sound advice as to good practice.

The Solicitors' Code of Conduct 2007

[2.2]

The Solicitors' Code of Conduct 2007 came into force on 1 July 2007. It is not the *Law Society's* Code but the *Solicitors'* Code because it is prescribed not by the Law Society but by the Solicitors' Regulation Authority. The Code contains 25 rules, with Rule 2 - promoted from 15 - dealing with client relations, including information about the cost in Rule 2.03. Here it is together with relevant extracts from the accompanying Guidance, which it is emphasised is not part of the Code and is not mandatory:

[2.3]

2.03 Information about the cost

(1)   You must give your client the best information possible about the likely overall cost of a matter both at the outset and, when appropriate, as the matter progresses. In particular you must:
(a)   advise the client of the basis and terms of your charges;
(b)   advise the client if charging rates are to be increased;
(c)   advise the client of likely payments which you or your client may need to make to others;
(d)   discuss with the client how the client will pay, in particular:
    (i)   whether the client may be eligible and should apply for public funding; and
    (ii)   whether the client's own costs are covered by insurance or may be paid by someone else such as an employer or trade union;
(e)   advise the client that there are circumstances where you may be entitled to exercise a lien for unpaid costs;
(f)   advise the client of their potential liability for any other party's costs; and
(g)   discuss with the client whether their liability for another party's costs may be covered by existing insurance or whether specially purchased insurance may be obtained.
(2)   Where you are acting for the client under a conditional fee agreement, (including a collective conditional fee agreement) in addition to complying with

2.03(1) above and 2.03(5) and (6) below, you must explain the following, both at the outset and, when appropriate, as the matter progresses:

(a)   the circumstances in which your client may be liable for your costs and whether you will seek payment of these from the client, if entitled to do so;

(b)   if you intend to seek payment of any or all of your costs from your client, you must advise your client of their right to an assessment of those costs; and

(c)   where applicable, the fact that you are obliged under a fee sharing agreement to pay to a charity any fees which you receive by way of costs from the client's opponent or other third party.

(3)   Where you are acting for a publicly funded client, in addition to complying with 2.03(1) above and 2.03(5) and (6) below, you must explain the following at the outset:

(a)   the circumstances in which they may be liable for your costs;

(b)   the effect of the statutory charge;

(c)   the client's duty to pay any fixed or periodic contribution assessed and the consequence of failing to do so; and

(d)   that even if your client is successful, the other party may not be ordered to pay costs or may not be in a position to pay them.

(4)   Where you agree to share your fees with a charity in accordance with 8.01(k) you must disclose to the client at the outset the name of the charity.

(5)   Any information about the cost must be clear and confirmed in writing.

(6)   You must discuss with your client whether the potential outcomes of any legal case will justify the expense or risk involved including, if relevant, the risk of having to pay an opponent's costs.

(7)   If you can demonstrate that it was inappropriate in the circumstances to meet some or all of the requirements in 2.03(1) and (5), you will not breach 2.03.

It is unfortunate that the Code throughout uses the word 'advise' as a synonym for 'inform' or 'explain'

[2.4]

GUIDANCE EXTRACTS (NOT PART OF THE CODE AND NOT MANDATORY)

General

2. It is not envisaged or intended that a breach of 2.02, 2.03 or 2.05 should invariably render a retainer unenforceable. As noted in the introduction to this rule, the purpose of 2.02 and 2.03 is to ensure that clients are given the information necessary to enable them to make appropriate decisions about if and how their matter should proceed. These parts of the rule together with 2.05 require you to provide certain information to your client. Sub-rules 2.02(3), 2.03(7) and 2.05(2) recognise that it is not always necessary to provide all this information to comply with the underlying purpose of the rule. Similarly, the information you are required to give to your client varies in importance both inherently and in relation to the individual client and the retainer. Consequently, the rule will be enforced in a manner which is proportionate to the seriousness of the breach. For example, if you were to fail to tell your client that they would be liable to pay another party's costs in breach of 2.03(1)(f), this is likely to be treated as a more serious breach than your failure to advise your client about your right to exercise a lien for unpaid costs in breach of 2.03(1)(e).

Ceasing to act

11   When you cease acting for a client, you will need to consider what should be done with the paperwork. You must hand over the client's files promptly on request

15

subject to your right to exercise a lien in respect of outstanding costs. You should try to ensure the client's position is not prejudiced, and should also bear in mind his or her rights under the Data Protection Act 1998. Undertakings to secure the costs should be used as an alternative to the exercise of a lien if possible. There may be circumstances where it is unreasonable to exercise a lien, for example, where the amount of the outstanding costs is small and the value or importance of the matter is very great. In any dispute over the ownership of documents you should refer to the law. Further advice about the law of lien or the ownership of documents can be found in *Cordery on Solicitors* or other reference books on the subject.

Information about the cost – 2.03

27.   The purpose of 2.03 is to ensure that the client is given relevant costs information and that this is clearly expressed. Information about costs must be worded in a way that is appropriate for the client. All costs information must be given in writing and regularly updated.

28.   Subrule 2.03 recognises that there may be circumstances where it would be inappropriate to provide any or all of the information required. It will be for you to justify why compliance was not appropriate in an individual matter. For example, your firm may regularly do repeat work for the client on agreed terms and the client might not need the costs information repeated. However, the client should be informed, for example, of any changes in a firm's charging rates.

29.   If you are an in-house solicitor or REL, much of 2.03 will be inappropriate if you are acting for your employer.

30.   This guidance does not deal with the form a bill can take, final and interim bills, when they can be delivered and when and how a firm can sue on a bill. All these matters are governed by complex legal provisions, and there are many publications that provide help to firms and clients. Advice on some aspects of costs is available from the Law Society's Practice Advice Service.

31.   You will usually be free to negotiate the cost and the method of payment with your clients. It will not normally be necessary for the client to be separately advised on the cost agreement. Different cost options may have different implications for the client – for example, where the choice is between a conditional fee agreement and an application for public funding. In those circumstances clients should be made aware of the implications of each option.

32.   The rule requires you to advise the client of the circumstances in which you may be entitled to exercise a lien for unpaid costs. For more information see note 11 above.

33.   Clients may be referred to you at a stage when they have already signed a contract for a funding arrangement – see also rule 9 (Referrals of business). You should explain the implications of any such arrangement fully including the extent to which the charges associated with such an arrangement may be recovered from another party to the proceedings.

34.   There may be some unusual arrangements, however, where it should be suggested that the client considers separate advice on what is being proposed – for example, where you are to receive shares in a new company instead of costs. See also rule 3 (Conflict of interests) and 9.02(g) for details about your obligations to clients who have been referred to you.

35.   Sub-rule 2.03 does not cover all the different charging arrangements possible or the law governing them. However, it does require that the chosen option is explained as fully as possible to the client. It also requires that if you have agreed to pay all, or part, of your fees to a charity in accordance with rule 8 (Fee sharing) the client must be informed at the outset of the name of that charity.

36.   It is often impossible to tell at the outset what the overall cost will be. Sub-rule 2.03 allows for this and requires that you provide the client with as much information as possible at the start and that you keep the client updated. If a precise figure cannot be given at the outset, you should explain the reason to the client and agree a ceiling figure or review dates.

37.   Particular information will be of relevance at particular stages of a client's matter. You should, for example, ensure that clients understand the costs implications of any offers of settlement. Where offers of settlement are made,

clients must be fully informed of the amount to be deducted in respect of costs and how this figure is calculated. You should advise clients of their rights to assessment of your costs in such circumstances.

38.   When a potential client contacts you with a view to giving you instructions you should always, when asked, try to be helpful in providing information on the likely costs of their matter.

Best information possible

[2.5]

The former requirement to provide the client with the 'best information possible about the likely overall cost' both at the outset and, when appropriate, as the matter progresses is retained in Rule 2.03(1), but the definition of what *is* 'the best information possible' in the former Practice Rule 4 has gone, as have the requirements to specify the 'time likely to be spent' and to update cost information 'at least every six months'.

Rule 2.03(1)(a) simply requires the solicitor to advise the client of 'the basis and terms of your charges'. The former requirement to 'inform the client as soon as it appears that an estimate may or will be exceeded' is replaced, by the less precise but more flexible provision that advice should be given 'when appropriate, as the matter progresses'.

Increases

[2.6]

Rule 2.03(1)(b) is oddly worded. It requires the client to be advised 'if charging rates are to be increased'. But for charging rates to be increased the solicitor must have reserved the contractual right to do so in the retainer – it has nothing to do with the Code of Conduct. So does the sub-rule mean that the solicitor must specifically draw the attention of the client to any provision in the retainer to this effect? Or does it simply mean that where the solicitor does have the right to increase his hourly charging rate he must inform the client of his intention to exercise it, which he must of course do in any event under the retainer? Either way, the provision seems on the face of it an unnecessary precaution.

Payments to others

[2.7]

The requirement in Rule 2.03(1)(c) to advise the client about payments which may have to be made to others presumably refers to future disbursements and not to adverse costs orders which appear later.

Funding

[2.8]

Rule 2.03(1)(d) confirms the duty of a solicitor to consider with the client whether they are eligible and if so should apply for public funding. A disastrous consequence of not so doing is at [42.1]. Similarly the rule reminds the solicitor of his or her duty to consider whether the client's costs may covered by an existing before-the-event (BTE) insurance policy, perhaps as part of a house or car policy, or if they may be payable by a third party such as an employer or trade union.

Lien

[2.9]

There is a requirement in Rule 2.03(1)(e) to notify the client that in certain circumstances the solicitor may have a right to a lien for unpaid costs. I consider this in the section on lien in Chapter 6.

Adverse Costs Orders

[2.10]

Rule 2.03(1)(f) and (g) requires the client to be warned of any possibility of an adverse costs order in litigation and about BTE and after-the-event (ATE) insurance

In writing

[2.11]

Sub-rule (5) confirms that any information about the cost must be clear and confirmed in writing.

Payment in kind

[2.12]

Paragraph 34 of the Guidance contains the intriguing suggestion that a solicitor may receive shares in a new company instead of costs; is this the city equivalent of country solicitors being paid in pheasants or rabbits?

Escape clause

[2.13]

Sub-Rule 2.03(7) provides an escape clause: if the solicitor can demonstrate that it was inappropriate in the circumstances to meet some or all of the requirements in 2.03(1) and (5), he will not breach 2.03. The circumstances will be very rare and in any event the escape clause applies only to breaches of the code and will not remedy any deficiencies in the contractual retainer
The Guidance is in Paragraph 28:

> 'It will be for you to justify why compliance was not appropriate in an individual matter. For example, your firm may regularly do repeat work for the client on agreed terms and the client might not need the costs information repeated.'

But, beware of the warning by the Court of Appeal in *Darby v Law Society* [2003] EWHC 2270 (Admin), [2003] All ER (D) 210 (Oct):

> 'There is . . . a heavy onus on a solicitor to establish that his client is so sophisticated [about costs] that the rule may be disregarded.'

Other exceptions are where compliance may be insensitive or impractical, such as the taking of instructions for a deathbed will and emergencies. While an emergency might be a sufficient reason for not giving costs information at the outset of the retainer and before work is started, it does not excuse complete failure to give any information at any stage. Where solicitors took over the conduct of proceedings from another firm only five days before the final hearing, they inadvertently overlooked the matter of costs information. This may have been understandable, but unfortunately the retainer continued for a further 18 months, during which time the client was given no information as to costs nor were any interim bills rendered. The outcome was that the solicitors were ordered to pay compensation to the client amounting to almost one-fifth of their fees (*Law Society Gazette*, 25 April 2002).

Sanctions

[2.14]

What will be the consequences of breaking the Code? Will the solicitor be struck off the Roll or made to take the Solicitors Final Examination again, or simply be unable to recover any costs from the client?

In Rule 2.03 the word 'must' has replaced the word 'should' in the previous code. However, in interpreting rules relating to costs it is a mistake to think that the word 'must' means that the rule is mandatory! It is not always. In the present context we have the guidance of *Garbutt v Edwards* [2005] EWCA Civ 1206, [2006] 1 All ER 553 which held that the requirement in Solicitor's Practice Rule 15 that a solicitor 'shall' give to the client the information prescribed in the Costs Code was not mandatory, and failure to comply with it did not render the retainer unlawful.

So what is the position under the new code if the client is not at the outset given the 'best information possible about the likely overall cost of the matter'? Help – of a sort - is at hand in paragraph 2 of the Guidance:

> 'It is not envisaged or intended that a breach of rule 2.03 should invariably render a retainer unenforceable. ... Subrules 2.02(3), 2.03(7) and 2.05(2) recognise that it is not always necessary to provide all this information to comply with the underlying purpose of the rule. Similarly, the information you are required to give to your client varies in importance both inherently and in relation to the individual client and the retainer. Consequently, the rule will be enforced in a manner which is proportionate to the seriousness of the breach.

In *Garbutt* the Court of Appeal was at pains to emphasise that the rules were not designed to relieve paying parties of their obligations but to protect clients. Might the court therefore have taken a different view if the dispute had not been between the parties to litigation been between a solicitor and client? In the words of the Guidance the sanction for breach will depend in future on what is perceived to be 'the underlying purpose of the rule' that has been broken.

QUOTATIONS AND ESTIMATES

[2.15]

The new Code, as did the previous provisions, encourages the use of fixed or agreed fees ('quotations') but does so implicitly not explicitly, stating in paragraph 36 of the Guidance: 'If a precise figure cannot be given at the outset, you should explain the reason to the client and agree a ceiling figure or review dates'. Accordingly, the requirement that an explanation be given to the client why it was not possible to fix a fee or give a realistic estimate of the costs is still there but it has been relegated to mere guidance. Although the 2007 Code does not anywhere use the words 'quotation' and 'estimate' they continue to be traps for the unwary.

Quotations

[2.16]

Do you really know the difference between a quotation and an estimate in respect of solicitors' costs? A quotation is a fixed price for doing the work which cannot be exceeded in any circumstances except with the freely given consent of the client.

Estimates

[2.17]

Estimates have a chameleon quality. They have a tendency to turn into quotations when you are not looking. An unqualified estimate, for example, is for all practical purposes a fixed price quotation. This was demonstrated in a decision of the Office for the Supervision of Solicitors (now replaced by the Legal Ombudsman), reported in the Law Society Gazette, 20 February 2003, where a firm of solicitors had informed the client at the outset of his matrimonial proceedings that he could expect a bill in the region of £2,500. The firm regularly rendered interim bills, the penultimate one leaving the total cost just a little short of the original estimate. Nine months later, after the fee earner who had dealt with the client had left the firm, the solicitors sent the client an additional bill that took his costs £750 above the estimate he had been given originally. The OSS adjudication panel ordered the firm to refund to the client the costs in excess of the estimate.

Anthony (John) v Ellis & Fairbairn (a firm) (Case No 9 of 2000) unreported, SCCO is a cautionary tale. The sting here was that the estimate was specifically restricted to an early settlement and there was no early settlement, but the judge still held this did not justify the solicitors delivering a bill for two-and-a-half times the amount of their estimate without giving the client prior warning that it would be exceeded.

In *Reynolds v Stone Rowe Brewer (a firm)* [2008] EWHC 497 (QB) the claimant instructed the defendant solicitors to represent her in a dispute with a building contractor and they informed her that the estimated cost of taking the matter forward and through to trial would be in the region of £10,000-£18,000 plus VAT. Throughout the course of the litigation, the defendants rendered a number of invoices and they then wrote to the claimant saying that their estimate of the likely cost of the case had to be revised to around £30,000 plus VAT. The court upheld the finding of the costs judge that the revised estimate had been an attempt to correct an 'earlier under-estimate' and was not attributable to any change in the facts. The solicitors were not saved by the provision in their client care letter 'This is only of course an estimate which could be increased depending on how strenuously the matter is defended'. There had been no significantly unusual developments before the revised estimate such as to explain the difference between the £18,000 estimate and the £30,000 revised estimate.

Qualified estimates

[2.18]

Even a qualified estimate is not *carte blanche*. A qualified estimate is an indication of price which is qualified by a statement that the solicitor may have to charge more if the matter involves more work than he expects. There are circumstances in which what started out in life as a qualified estimate can finish up as binding on the solicitor as a quotation. Paragraph 13.02(1)(*e*) of the Law Society's *Guide to the Professional Conduct of Solicitors 1999* provided: 'The solicitor should make it clear at the outset if an estimate, quotation or other indication of cost is not intended to be fixed'. The *Guide* continued that the solicitor should 'inform the client in writing as soon as it appears that a costs estimate or agreed upper limit may or will be exceeded' and 'oral estimates should be confirmed in writing and clients should be informed immediately if it appears that the estimate will be, or is likely to be, exceeded. In most cases this should happen before undertaking the work that exceeds the estimate'. In other words, the final amount payable should not vary substantially from the estimate unless there has been a change in circumstances of which the client has been informed. The qualified estimate should state the circumstances which might give rise to an increase and the client should be informed when any of those circumstances arise. The fact that the solicitor has seriously underestimated the work or disbursements involved will not necessarily be a changed circumstance – indeed it could be a strong indication of negligence on the part of the solicitor in preparing the original estimate. A factor in considering whether any upward revision of an estimate is reasonable is whether the client instructed the solicitor after shopping around and taking the lowest estimate he had been given.

In *Mastercigars Direct Ltd v Withers LLP* [2007] EWHC 2733 (Ch), [2008] 3 All ER 417 a qualified estimate did not turn into a quotation. The relevant wording of Withers' qualified estimate is worth quoting: 'When you instruct us we will do our best to tell you the likely level of our fees. Unless we tell you otherwise, this will be an estimate only, not a fixed quotation. If you ask for a fixed quotation we will try to provide one. However it may not be possible to predict the amount of time we will need to deal with the matter. You may set an upper limit on our costs. We will not do any work that will take our fees over this limit without your permission . . . '. The SCCO master had held that in the circumstances Withers had failed to update their estimate and were bound by it but Withers' appeal was allowed. The judge held that their estimate was not a fixed quotation, nor was it an upper limit on costs, nor did it define the work to be done. The retainer was subject to the Supply of Goods and Services Act 1982, s 15 and it was therefore an implied term that the solicitors would be paid reasonable remuneration for their services. Although the solicitors had given a contractual promise to update the costs estimate, that was not a condition precedent to them recovering any sum in addition to the sums set out in the estimate. He held that where a costs estimate is given but the costs subsequently claimed exceeded the estimate, it does not follow that the solicitor would be restricted to recovering the sum in the estimate. The question was 'What, in all the circumstances, is it reasonable for the client to be expected to pay?' And the estimate was one, but only one, of those circumstances. As explained in *Leigh v Michelin Tyre plc* [2003] EWCA Civ 1766, [2004] 2 All ER 175 the court could have regard to the estimate and it was a factor to be taken into consideration as a yardstick in determining what was reasonable. The greater the difference between an estimate and the final bill, the greater the explanation called for. However, if there is a satisfactory explanation of the difference an estimate may cease to be a useful yardstick. Reliance on the estimate by the client is another factor. It was not necessary to imply into the contract of retainer a term that the solicitors had to comply with the Solicitors Costs Information and Client Care Code in respect of updating costs information.

There are two postscripts. First, the judge directed the costs judge to decide whether the client had in fact relied on the estimate and, if so, how this should be reflected in the amount allowed. Master Simons held that Mastercigars had relied on the estimate and that in the circumstances Withers's costs could only exceed it by 20%. On appeal back to the judge ([2009] EWHC 651 (Ch), [2009] 1 WLR 881) he found that the costs judge's reasons for selecting a 20% margin were inadequate and gave the appearance of being arbitrary. (I consider margins at para **[2.19]**). The judge had been sitting with assessors, including the senior costs judge, and the judge asked him to prepare a report, which would enable the court to decide the questions, which were outstanding.

The second postscript is further guidance on reliance on an estimate. When refusing permission to appeal ([2009] EWCA Civ 1526, 7 December) the Court of Appeal endorsed paragraph 54 of the second judgment in *Mastercigars* which read: 'In my judgment, the legal process involved in a case where a client contends that its reliance on an estimate should be taken into account in determining the figure which it is reasonable for the client to pay is as follows. The court should determine whether the client did rely on the estimate. The court should determine how the client relied on the estimate. The court should try to determine the above without conducting an elaborate and detailed investigation. The court should decide whether the costs claimed should be reduced by reason of its findings as to reliance and, if so, in what way and by how much. Whether there should be a reduction, and if so to what extent, is a matter of judgment. Specific deductions can be made from the costs otherwise recoverable to reflect the impact which an erroneous and uncorrected estimate had on the conduct of the client. Such an approach requires the court to form an assessment of the impact of the estimate on the conduct of the client. The court should consider the deductions which are needed in order to do justice between the parties. It is not the proper function of the court to punish the solicitor for providing a wrong estimate or for failing to keep it up to date as events unfolded. In terms of the sequence of the decisions to be made by the court, it has been suggested that the court should determine whether, and if so how, it will reflect the estimate in the detailed assessment before carrying out the detailed assessment. The suggestion as to the sequence of decision making may not always be appropriate. The suggestion is put forward as practical guidance rather than as a legal imperative. The ultimate question is as to the sum which it is reasonable for the client to pay, having regard to the estimate and any other relevant matter

The judge did not agree with my summary in earlier editions, but I shall risk another. On a solicitor and client assessment of costs which have not been fixed (are not a quotation) the court will pay significant attention to any estimate relied upon by a client. The client does not need to have acted to its it detriment but merely show it was 'deprived . . . of an opportunity of acting differently' The estimate, while an important factor is not to be considered by the court in isolation but taking into account any other important matter and the reasons why it has been exceeded: solicitors are not to be penalised if they can show good reasons for any excess.

However, if the estimate has only been exceeded because it was too low in the first place, the solicitor is likely to get short shrift.

15% margin

[2.19]

In *Wong v Vizards (a firm)* [1997] 2 Costs LR 46, QBD, the solicitors in a letter to their client allowed for profit costs of £9,955 (*sic*) stating 'the fee proposal hopefully sets out the fullest extent of your liability to this firm for costs likely to be incurred in the future'. Although this did not amount to a binding agreement that in no circumstances would the solicitors' fees exceed their fee proposal, it was a clear and considered indication of the maximum, upon which the client was likely to rely and did rely. The solicitors in fact delivered bills exceeding £45,000. In considering whether a reasonable amount for the work done should exceed what the fee-payer had been led to believe was a worst case assessment, regard should be had to any explanation of the divergence. It had not been suggested there was any unexpected development between the date of the solicitors' letter and the date of trial, and no satisfactory explanation had been given why the solicitors should be entitled to profit costs exceeding the amount put forward as their worst case assessment. The judge limited the solicitors' costs to £9,955.

But, there was more . . . The trial had taken two days less than estimated by the solicitors at a charge of £660 a day. The client argued that the estimate should therefore be reduced by the resultant saving of £1,320. This was about 15% of the total estimate and the judge thought it not unreasonable to give the solicitors the benefit of this margin and therefore allowed them to recover the full amount of their estimate. And it is from this that the myth has arisen that *Wong v Vizards* is authority for the proposition that solicitors may exceed their estimates by a margin of 15%. It is much more an authority that solicitors cannot exceed their estimate by 350%!

The judge in *Mastercigars* confirmed there is no 15% margin, while the judge in *Reynolds* said it was not possible to say that the sum he would have allowed represented any particular margin over the estimates. However, in at least two SCCO cases costs judges have found it helpful to apply it, and this was one of the matters on which the assessors disagreed with the judge in

Mastercigars. On appeal from the costs judge, who had applied a 20% margin, the High Court judge addressed margins in these terms: 'The adoption of an approach which involves adding a margin, usually expressed as a percentage, to the estimate as the conventional approach and the majority of cases would pay scant, if any, regard to that legal process. While there are advantages to the margin approach, it should not be systematically endorsed. The adoption of a margin approach greatly simplifies the steps which a costs judge needs to take when carrying out a detailed assessment of the bill which has been proceeded by a lower estimate. If the margin approach became the permissible conventional approach, then the costs of the detailed assessment could be reduced and the outcome would be more predictable. But even where a court had followed the proper assessment process, it can never be right for costs to be expressed by reference to a margin.'

Criminal offence

[2.20]

An estimate can, however, turn really nasty. The Consumer Protection Act 1987, ss 20 and 21, apply to the supply of services as well as to the supply of goods. These sections make it a criminal offence to obtain business by giving a misleading price indication to a consumer. For example, if an estimate reasonably led the client to understand it to be inclusive of VAT and disbursements, any attempt to increase the estimate by adding VAT and disbursements could amount to an offence. Similarly, when an estimate is based upon expense rates which include postage, telephone calls, faxes and other incidentals, it would probably be an offence under the Act as well as a breach of the retainer to seek to claim additional disbursements in respect of these items.

Failure to give an estimate

[2.21]

Garbutt v Edwards [2005] EWCA Civ 1206, [2006] 1 All ER 553 was concerned with the effect of the indemnity principle between the parties. It decided that the requirement in Solicitor's Practice Rule 15 that a solicitor '*shall*' give to the client the information prescribed in the Costs Code was not mandatory, and failure to comply with it did not render the retainer unlawful. Between the parties, failure to give an estimate was merely a matter for the costs judge, who should consider whether this has in any way increased the costs over what they would have been if an estimate had been given.

Between solicitor and client, the position appears to be that if a solicitor gives a costs estimate he is bound by it, but if he breaches the Solicitors Code of Conduct 2007 and fails to provide the client with the 'best information possible about the likely overall cost' there is no restriction on what he may charge, and there is still no effective sanction for breaching the rule. If so, solicitors who provide estimates which prove to be inaccurate are still in a worse position than those who provide no estimates at all!'

Costs estimates between the parties

(a)   CPR

[2.22]

Section 6 of the CPR Costs Practice Direction provides for detailed costs estimates to be provided not only to the court and the other parties on the filing of the allocation questionnaire and any pre-trial check list but also to the client (see Chapter 10). These are potentially dangerous documents and should carry a solicitor and client costs warning. If they are too high, in order to cover every possible eventuality so as to maximise the between-the-parties costs recoverable, they might scare the client off the litigation completely. On the other hand, if they are too low, while they are not at present binding between the parties, it could well be the basis of a complaint by the client if the final bill substantially exceeded a CPR estimate. The remedy is to explain to the client either that the estimate is probably too high because it covers every eventuality (and is intended to frighten off the opposition?) or that the solicitor and client costs are likely to exceed it. It is also important to remember that although the CPR do not require updated estimates to be filed and served, the client must be informed of any increase on the CPR estimate and the reason for it.

(b)   Family

[2.23]

Costs estimates are even more dangerous in family proceedings, because while in civil proceedings the between-the-parties costs estimate is on the party and party basis in family proceedings the between-the-parties estimate in Form H is of the solicitor and client costs incurred by the party filing it. It would be very difficult for a solicitor to justify charging the client more than the costs disclosed in Form H.

NON-CONTENTIOUS BUSINESS AGREEMENTS

[2.24]

The Solicitors Act 1974, s 57 as amended by the Courts and Legal Services Act 1990, s 98, provides that a solicitor and his client may before, after or in the course of non-contentious business, make an agreement about the solicitor's remuneration. It must be in writing in a single document signed by the client or his agent. It must show all the terms of the bargain (*Chamberlain v Boodle & King (a firm)* [1982] 3 All ER 188, CA). It is a binding contract if all of these conditions are satisfied, but s 57(5) provides that if the solicitor relies on it and the client objects to it as being unfair or unreasonable, a costs officer may inquire into the facts and certify them to the court. If from that certificate it appears to the court that the agreement should be set aside, or the amount payable under it reduced, the court may so order. The court may also give such consequential directions as it thinks fit, such as directing that an itemised bill be delivered and assessed (*Rutter v Sheridan-Young* [1958]

2 All ER 13, CA). Although the court requires only prima facie evidence of unfairness or unreasonableness in order to intervene, in the opinion of Mustill J in *Walton v Egan* [1982] QB 1232, QBD 'from a practical point of view the agreement of the client is the strongest evidence that the fee is reasonable'. Section 57(2) enacts that the agreement may provide for remuneration by a gross sum, a commission, a percentage, a salary or otherwise. An important amendment introduced by the Courts and Legal Services Act 1990, s 98 permits an agreement to be by reference to an hourly rate. Section 98 provides that if, on the assessment of any costs, an agreement by reference to an hourly rate is relied on by the solicitor and the client objects to the total of the costs (but is not alleging that the agreement is unfair or unreasonable), then the amount of the hourly rate will be binding on the client, but the costs officer may inquire into (a) the number of hours worked by the solicitor, and (b) whether the number of hours worked by him or her was excessive. The agreement may include all or any disbursements made by the solicitor in respect of searches, plans, travelling, postage, fees or other matters.

An advantage to the solicitor of a non-contentious business agreement is that the provisions of the Solicitors' (Non-Contentious Business) Remuneration Order 1994 do not apply to it and therefore the client is precluded from applying for a remuneration certificate (*Walton v Egan* above)

CONTENTIOUS BUSINESS AGREEMENTS

Solicitors Act 1974, s 59

[2.25]

A solicitor may make an agreement with his client as to his remuneration in respect of any contentious business before, after or during doing the work pursuant to the Solicitors Act 1974, s 59(1). As with non-contentious business agreements, it must be in writing, signed by the client or his agent and show all the terms of the bargain. Also as with non-contentious business agreements, the Courts and Legal Services Act 1990 permits a contentious business agreement to be by reference to an hourly rate. This means, unlike where work is to be done for a fixed sum, the client is not able to calculate how much he is being asked to pay, because neither he nor anyone else knows how long the litigation will last.

The agreement must not give the solicitor any interest in the proceedings; ie it must not be champertous or on a contingency basis. It may, however, contain a conditional fee agreement stipulating for payment only in the event of success (with or without a fee uplift), provided it complies with the rules and regulations relating to conditional fee agreements (see Chapter 42). The effect of a contentious business agreement is to preclude a Solicitors Act assessment of the costs as between the solicitor and the client except in respect of agreements by reference to hourly rates when the same provisions apply as for non-contentious business agreements. The agreement itself does not give a cause of action. Before a solicitor can rely on it he must apply to the court for leave to enforce the agreement; equally, the client may apply to the court to set it aside (Solicitors Act 1974, s 61(1)). Where the agreement relates to an action the client may also apply under s 61(3) to a costs judge or district judge who may either allow the agreement or require the opinion of the court to be taken on it. Both applications are made under CPR Part 8. The outcome will depend on whether or not the court is of the opinion that the agreement is fair and reasonable. Applications in respect of bills less than £25,000 must be made in the county court (Courts and Legal Services Act 1990, s 3). An application may be made at any time before the bill is paid, before or after the work has been done. The Solicitors Act 1974, s 61(5), provides that the court may re-open the agreement within 12 months of payment or longer if there are special circumstances.

Precedent application under Solicitors Act 1974, s 61(1)

[2.26]

Claim Form N208 CPR Part 8

Details of claim

1. A declaration that the written agreement entered into between the applicants and the respondent on [date], a copy of which is attached, is a valid contentious business agreement within the meaning of the Solicitors Act 1974, s 59.

2. A declaration that the agreement is valid in all respects and may be enforced.

3. Such order or orders for further or other relief as may be necessary for the enforcement of the agreement.

4. The respondent may be ordered to pay the applicants' costs of and incidental to this application.

5. The grounds for this application are:

    (a) the agreement is a valid contentious business agreement within the meaning of s 59 of the Act;

    (b) the business described or referred to in the agreement has been properly and fully done by the applicants for the respondent;

    (c) the respondent, despite demands made upon him by the applicants, has refused or failed to pay the amount due under the agreement;

    (d) the agreement should therefore be enforced.

Statement of truth

CPR Rule 48.8

[2.27]

It is important to distinguish between a formal contentious business agreement and the effect of the provisions of CPR Rule 48.8 and its supplemental Practice Direction, which preserves the freedom of the solicitor and client to make whatever agreement they desire. Rule 48.8(2)(*a*) and (*b*) provide that all costs incurred with the express or implied approval of the client shall be presumed to have been reasonably incurred and, where the amount has been expressly or impliedly approved by the client, to be reasonable in amount. This is subject to the provision of Rule 48.8(2)(*c*) that costs of an unusual nature or amount shall be presumed to have been unreasonably incurred, unless the solicitor expressly warned his client that he might not recover all of those costs from the other party. There is no requirement that the approval of the client shall be in writing or signed by him, and indeed the client's agreement may be implied. There is also no provision for setting aside such approval however unfair and unreasonable the resultant costs may be. It appears that the only way in which the agreement could be upset would be by the client commencing an action to have it set aside on the grounds of undue influence, or perhaps negligence, by the solicitor in not advising him to obtain independent advice from another solicitor before entering into the agreement. However, for the client to be bound by the presumption, his approval must be 'informed'. It must have been secured after a full and fair exposition of the relevant factors: *MacDougall v Boote Edgar Esterkin* (2001) 1 Costs LR 118. Although the presumptions under Rule 48.8 are rebuttable, while those in respect of hourly rates introduced as a result of the Courts and Legal Services Act 1990, s 98 into non-contentious and contentious business agreements are irrebuttable, the apparent advantage of this to the solicitor appears to be far outweighed by the stringent and complicated provisions relating to the formation and enforcement of non-contentious and contentious business agreements.

Differences between a contentious business agreement and CPR 48.8

[2.28]

The differences between a contentious business agreemetn and CPR 48.8 are as follows:

(1)
    (a)   Under Rule 48.8 there is a presumption that hourly rates expressly or impliedly approved by the client are reasonable. The presumption is rebuttable (Costs Practice Direction 54.2).

    (b)   Hourly rates in a valid CBA are binding on the client and cannot be the subject of a Solicitors Act assessment, although the *number* of hours spent and the reasonableness of those hours may be challenged. Further, a CBA cannot be enforced without the permission of the court, which will not be granted if it takes the view that *any* aspect of the CBA is unfair or unreasonable. The court may set aside the agreement and proceed as though it had never been made.

(2)

(a)   Under Rule 48.8 there is a presumption that costs are unreasonably incurred if they are of an unreasonable amount or of an
unusual nature and the solicitor did not warn the client that they
may not be recoverable between the parties.

(b)   There is no such presumption with a CBA, although failure to
give such advice might amount to negligence.

(3)

(a)   Rule 48.8 does not appear to apply to an agreement to conduct
litigation for a fixed fee.

(b)   A CBA is appropriate for a fixed fee agreement.

THE FUTURE

[2.29]

Do non-contentious and contentious business agreements still have a role to
play in these days of consumer protection embodied in the costs information
requirements and the client care provisions of the Solicitors' Code of Conduct
2007? It is difficult to envisage circumstances in which terms fair to the client
would not be enforced by the court whether or not they were embodied in an
agreement which complied with the requirements of section 57 or 59 of the
Solicitors Act 1974, and it is equally difficult to envisage the court enforcing
unfair terms even if they were embodied in an agreement compliant with the
Act, by reference, if necessary, to the considerations of unfairness, unreasonableness, undue influence and negligence mentioned above. Two examples of
CBAs are where a client agreed to pay the solicitor excessive fees for work the
solicitor did not wish to do and where a public company requested the solicitor
to charge modestly for a property transaction in return for high hourly rates in
substantial litigation. In both cases the solicitors protected their high hourly
rates in CBAs, but did they really need to?

COUNTY COURT

The Between-the-Parties Cap

[2.30]

The Solicitors Act 1974, s 74(3) provides: 'the amount which may be allowed
on the taxation [*assessment*] of any costs or bill of costs in respect of any item
relating to the proceedings in a county court shall not, except in so far as
rules of court may otherwise provide, exceed the amount which could have
been allowed in respect of that item as between the parties in those proceedings, having regard to the nature of the proceedings and the amount of the
claim and of any counterclaim'.

Opting Out

[2.31]

At the last minute, it was realised that the Civil Procedure Rules made no exception to the provision that solicitor and client costs may not exceed the amount recoverable between the parties with the result that they could not exceed the fixed costs on the fast track. The operation of s 74(3) also appears to preclude a solicitor from charging a client a disproportionate amount where the between-the-parties costs have been restricted on the grounds they were disproportionate to the issues, even though the proportionality rule does not apply as between solicitor and client. Further, in spite of the wording of the Conditional Fee Agreements Regulations and Rules, payment of an irrecoverable success fee could also be said to offend against s 74(3). Accordingly a new sub-rule (1A) was inserted into Rule 48.8 as follows:

> 'Section 74(3) of the Solicitors Act 1974 applies unless the solicitor and client have entered into a written agreement which expressly permits payment to the solicitor of an amount of costs greater than which the client could have recovered from another party to the proceedings.'

Discretionary costs

[2.32]

The decision in *Lynch v Paul Davidson Taylor (a firm)* [2004] EWHC 89 (QB), [2004] 1 WLR 1753, distinguished between fixed and discretionary costs. The client contended that the effect of s 74(3) was that where costs had been assessed between the parties the amount allowed constituted a cap on the amount the solicitor could charge the client. Not so. The costs are limited to the amount which 'could have been allowed' between the parties – and on a detailed assessment the Court *could* have allowed any amount! When the Section was introduced there were scales of costs in the county court and the Section was designed to limit the solicitor and client costs to the maximum in those scales. Those scales having gone, there is now no limit.

Fixed costs

[2.33]

The reference to s 74(3) in CPR rule 48.8(1A) above shows that the section does not simply survive, but it is intended still to bite wherever there are fixed costs, as increasingly there are on the fast track and on the small claims track. Accordingly, in all county court work it is prudent for the solicitor at the outset of litigation to identify the probability of a shortfall to the client as the result of fixed costs or the proportionality test, and to obtain the client's signature to an agreement that the solicitor and client costs may exceed those recoverable between the parties.

CONDITIONAL FEES

[2.34]

See Part VII – Conditional Fees.

CLIENT CARE

[2.35]

Rule 2.02 of the Solicitors' Code of Conduct 2007 provides:
(1)   You must:
    (a)   identify clearly the client's objectives in relation to the work to be done for the client;
    (b)   give the client a clear explanation of the issues involved and the options available to the client;
    (c)   agree with the client the next steps to be taken; and
    (d)   keep the client informed of progress, unless otherwise agreed.
(2)   You must, both at the outset and, as necessary, during the course of the matter:
    (a)   agree an appropriate level of service;
    (b)   explain your responsibilities;
    (c)   explain the client's responsibilities;
    (d)   ensure that the client is given, in writing, the name and status of the person dealing with the matter and the name of the person responsible for its overall supervision; and
    (e)   explain any limitations or conditions resulting from your relationship with a third party (for example a funder, fee sharer or introducer) which affect the steps you can take on the client's behalf.
(3)   If you can demonstrate that it was inappropriate in the circumstances to meet some or all of these requirements, you will not breach 2.02.

[2.36]

The importance of complying with the predecessor to sub-rule 2.02(2)(d) was dramatically illustrated in *Pilbrow v Pearless De Rougemont & Co (a firm)* [1999] 3 All ER 355, CA, where the court upheld the client's refusal to pay his solicitor's bill on the grounds that he had asked for an appointment with a solicitor but it transpired that the person to whom he was referred by the receptionist was neither a solicitor nor a qualified legal executive. Although the work done was up to the standard of a competent solicitor the contract was one to provide legal services by a solicitor and therefore the firm did not perform that contract at all. No legal services were provided by any solicitor. The situation was not to be equated with where a drinker asks for a pint of one make of bitter but was mistakenly provided with a pint of another make and did not discover the difference until he had drunk the glass dry. The firm should have trained its receptionist when faced with a request to see a solicitor to do one of the following:
(i)   refer the client to a solicitor;
(ii)   refer the client to someone who was not a solicitor but inform the client that that person was not a solicitor; or

(iii)   refer the client to someone who the receptionist knew was not a solicitor, refrain from telling the client that fact and alert the referee to the fact that the client had asked for a solicitor.

If the last course were adopted then it would be the duty of the referee straight away to make clear to the client that he was not a solicitor.

The compliance with this provision in the client care letter is therefore as much for the protection of the solicitor as for the client. It is also important to note that the term 'legal executive' is restricted to Fellows of the Institute of Legal Executives. Alternatives to 'Legal Executive' are: executive; clerk; manager; secretary; paralegal and trainee solicitor.

Pilbrow v Pearless was followed in *Adrian Allen Ltd v Fuglers* SCCO Case No 13 of 2003 where a struck-off solicitor was employed by the defendant firm of solicitors with the permission of the Law Society. He informed the claimant, who was a client of the firm, that he was a solicitor and that he could assist in the litigation in which it was engaged. The claimant instructed him, but he proved to be incompetent, and subsequently disappeared. The solicitors were not entitled to any payment for the work done because the terms of the retainer were for the work to be done by a solicitor.

TERMS AND CONDITIONS OF RETAINER

[2.37]

I suggest the lesson to be learned from this chapter is that it is as much in the interests of the solicitor as the client to agree the terms of the retainer with each client in respect of both non-contentious and contentious work. The terms can be incorporated in a terms of business letter, which may be standard, or specifically selected for a particular client from a prepared menu of provisions. My own view is that you should not aspire to achieving a contentious or non-contentious business agreement unless the work is such that both you and the client are able to agree a fee in advance. In spite of the amendment allowing reference to hourly rates, the requirements of the Solicitors Act 1974, ss 57–63 are so forbidding and stringent that it is very difficult to produce a binding agreement, and even if that were possible, the agreement would always be subject to the risk of the statutory right of challenge.

The client should be supplied with an extra copy of the letter or agreement with a request to countersign it and return it, although this is not essential to make the letter binding on the client. In litigation, another advantage from the solicitor's point of view is that the letter constitutes express authority from the client in respect of the matters contained in it and these agreed terms are therefore, pursuant to CPR Rule 48.8, presumed to be reasonable. Whatever the view of the costs officer may be as to the agreement, on a Solicitors Act assessment of costs the client is bound by it.

Precedent terms of business letter

[2.38]

This precedent is based on that produced by Tony Girling Training Ltd for Litigation and Family matters. A selection of precedents for contentious and non contentious work, including various types of CFA, are available for a modest fee from Tony Girling Training Ltd. Contact tonygirling@lineone.net. I am grateful for permission to use it.

Our Aim
- We aim to offer our clients quality legal advice with a personal service at a fair cost. As a start, we hope it is helpful to you to set out in this statement the basis on which we will provide our professional services.

Our Hours of Business
- The normal hours of opening at our offices are between [ ] am and [ ] pm on weekdays. Messages can be left on the answerphone outside those hours and appointments can be arranged at other times when this is essential.

People Responsible for your Work
- The person who will deal with your work will be [ ] who is a [solicitor/ legal executive/trainee solicitor]. [ ] is an [assistant/secretary] who may be able to deal with your queries and who will be pleased to take any message from you. We will try to avoid changing the people who handle your work but if this cannot be avoided, we will tell you promptly of any change and why it may be necessary.
- [ ] is the partner of this firm with final responsibility for work done in this department.

Charges and Expenses

[Insert here all the information required by rule 2.03 of the Solicitors Code of Conduct in order to provide the client with 'the best information possible about the likely overall costs', in particular setting out any agreed fee or a realistic estimate or forecast within a range of costs or explanation why this is not possible].
- Our charges will be calculated mainly by reference to the time actually spent by the solicitors and other staff in respect of any work which they do on your behalf. This may include meetings with you and perhaps others; reading, preparing and working on papers; making and receiving telephone calls, emails, faxes and text messages; preparation of any detailed costs estimates, schedules and bills; attending at court; and time necessarily spent travelling away from the office. From time to time we may arrange for some of this work to be carried out by persons not directly employed by us; such work will be charged to you at the hourly rate which would be charged if we had done the work ourselves.
- Routine letters, e-mails and texts that we send and routine telephone calls that we make and receive are charged at one tenth of the hourly rate. Routine letters, e-mails and texts received are not charged for, however, all letters, e-mails and calls whether sent or received which take longer than six minutes to deal with are charged on a time spent basis.

- The current hourly rates are set out below. We will add VAT to these at the rate that applies when the work is done. At present, VAT is 17.5%.
£

Partners and Consultants
Solicitors
Fellows of Inst. of Legal Executives, Senior Executives
Executives
Trainee Solicitors
Junior Executives/Personal Assistants

- These hourly rates have to be reviewed periodically to reflect increases in overhead costs and inflation. Normally the rates are reviewed with effect from 1 January each year. If a review is carried out before this matter has been concluded, we will inform you of any variation in the rate before it takes effect.

- In addition to the time spent, we may take into account a number of factors including any need to carry out work outside our normal office hours, the complexity of the issues, the speed at which action has to be taken, any particular specialist expertise which the case may demand. An increase in the rates may be applied to reflect such factors. In property transactions, in the administration of estates and in matters involving a substantial financial value or benefit to a client, a charge reflecting, for example, the price of the property, the size of the estate, or the value of the financial benefit may be considered. It is not always possible to indicate how these aspects may arise but on present information we would expect them to be sufficiently taken into account in the rates which we have quoted. Where an increase in the rates or a charge reflecting any value element is to be added we will explain this to you.

- Solicitors have to pay out various other expenses on behalf of clients ranging from Land or Probate Registry fees, court fees, experts' fees, and so on. We have no obligation to make such payments unless you have provided us with the funds for that purpose. VAT is payable on certain expenses. We refer to such payments generally as 'disbursements'.

Payment Arrangements

- It is our normal practice to ask clients to pay interim bills and sums of money from time to time on account of the charges and expenses which are expected in the following weeks or months. We find that this helps clients in budgeting for costs as well as keeping them informed of the legal expenses which are being incurred. If such requests are not met with prompt payment, delay in the progress of a case may result. In the unlikely event of any bill or request for payment not being met, this firm must reserve the right to stop acting for you further.

- Payment is due to us within 28 days of our sending you a bill. Interest will be charged on a daily basis at 4% over Lloyds TSB Bank Plc's base rate from time to time from the date of the bill in cases where payment is not made within 28 days of delivery by us of the bill.

- The common law entitles us to retain any money, papers or other property belonging to you which properly come into our possession pending payment of our costs, whether or not the property is acquired in connection with the matter for which the costs were incurred. This is known as a "general lien". We are not entitled to sell property held under a lien but we are entitled to hold property, other than money, even if the value of it greatly exceeds the amount due to us in respect of costs.

- If we are conducting litigation for you, we have additional rights in any property recovered or preserved for you whether it is in our possession or not and in respect of all costs incurred, whether billed or unbilled. We also have a right to ask the court to make a charging order in our favour for any assessed costs.
- We do not accept payments to us in cash in excess of £200. Monies due to you from us will be paid by cheque or bank transfer, but not in cash, and will not be made payable to a third party.

Costs Payable by a Third Party

- In some cases and transactions a client may be entitled to payment of costs by some other person. It is important that you understand that in such circumstances, the other person may not be required to pay all the charges and expenses which you incur with us. An example is that our charges are on what is known as the indemnity basis while costs awarded in litigation are usually on the standard basis which is more restricted. We shall be happy to explain this further if you so wish. In any event, you have to pay our charges and expenses in the first place and any amounts which can be recovered will be a contribution towards them. If the other party is in receipt of legal aid no costs are likely to be recovered.
- If you are successful and a court orders another party to pay some or all of your charges and expenses, interest can be claimed on them from the other party from the date of the court order. We will account to you for such interest to the extent that you have paid our charges or expenses on account, but we are entitled to the rest of that interest.
- You will also be responsible for paying our charges and expenses of seeking to recover any costs that the court orders the other party to pay to you.

Other Parties' Charges and Expenses

- A client who is unsuccessful in a court case may be ordered to pay the other party's legal charges and expenses. That money would be payable in addition to our charges and expenses. Arrangements can be made to take out insurance to cover liability for such legal expenses. Please discuss this with us if you are interested in this possibility.

Interest Payment

- Any money received on your behalf will be held in our Client Account. Subject to certain minimum amounts and periods of time set out in the Solicitors' Accounts Rules 1998, interest will be calculated and paid to you at the rate from time to time payable on Lloyds TSB Bank Plc's Designated Client Accounts. The period for which interest will be paid will normally run from the date(s) on which funds are received by us until the date(s) of issue of any cheque(s) from our Client Account.
- Where a client obtains borrowing from a lender in a property transaction, we will ask the lender to arrange that the loan cheque is received by us a minimum of 4 working days prior to the completion date. If the money can be telegraphed, we will request that we receive

it the day before completion. This will enable us to ensure that the necessary funds are available in time for completion. Such clients need to be aware that the lender may charge interest from the date of issue of their loan cheque or the telegraphing of the payment.

Papers and Documents

- In addition to any lien, as explained under 'Payment arrangements above, we will keep your file of papers for you in storage for not less than 1 year. After that, storage is on the clear understanding that we have the right to destroy it after such period as we consider reasonable or to make a charge for storage if we ask you to collect your papers and you fail to do so. We will not of course destroy any documents such as Wills, Deeds, and other securities, which you ask us to hold in safe custody. No charge will be made to you for such storage unless prior notice in writing is given to you of a charge to be made from a future date which may be specified in that notice.
- If we retrieve papers or documents from storage in relation to continuing or new instructions to act in connection with your affairs, we will not normally charge for such retrieval. However, we may make a charge based on time spent at the junior executive hourly rate for producing stored papers or documents to you or another at your request. We may also charge for reading, correspondence or other work necessary to comply with your instructions.

Financial Services and Insurance Contracts

- If, while we are acting for you, you need advice on investments, we may have to refer you to someone who is authorised by the Financial Services Authority, as we are not. However, as we are regulated by the Law Society, we may be able to provide certain limited investment services where these are closely linked to the legal work we are doing for you.
- We are not authorised by the Financial Services Authority. However, we are included on the register maintained by the Financial Services Authority so that we can carry on insurance mediation activity, which is broadly the advising on, selling and administration of insurance contracts. Insurance mediation activities and investment services, including arrangements for complaints or redress if something goes wrong, are regulated by The Law Society. The register can be accessed via the Financial Services Authority website at www.fsa.gov.uk/register.

Termination

- You may terminate your instructions to us in writing at any time but we will be entitled to keep all your papers and documents while there is money owing to us for our charges and expenses. If at any stage you do not wish us to continue doing work and/or incurring charges and expenses on your behalf, you must tell us this clearly in writing.
- If we decide to stop acting for you, for example if you do not pay an interim bill or comply with the request for a payment on account, we will tell you the reason and give you notice in writing.
- Under the Consumer Protection (Distance Selling) Regulations 2000, for some non-business instructions, you may have the right to withdraw, without charge, within 7 working days of the date on which you asked us to act for you. However, if we start work with your

consent within that period, you lose that right to withdraw. Your acceptance of these terms and conditions of business will amount to such a consent. If you seek to withdraw instructions, you should give notice by telephone, email or letter to the person named in these terms of business as being responsible for your work. The Regulations require us to inform you that the work involved is likely to take more than 30 days.

Limited Companies

• When accepting instructions to act on behalf of a limited company, we may require a Director and/or controlling shareholder to sign a form of personal guarantee in respect of the charges and expenses of this firm. If such a request is refused, we will be entitled to stop acting and to require immediate payment of our charges on an hourly basis and expenses as set out earlier.

Tax Advice

• Any work that we do for you may involve tax implications or necessitate the consideration of tax planning strategies. We may not be qualified to advise you on the tax implications of a transaction that you instruct us to carry out, or the likelihood of them arising. If you have any concerns in this respect, please raise them with us immediately. If we can undertake the research necessary to resolve the issue, we will do so and advise you accordingly. If we cannot, we may be able to identify a source of assistance for you.

Identity, Disclosure and Confidentiality Requirements

• We are entitled to refuse to act for you if you fail to supply appropriate proof of identity for yourself or for any principal whom you may represent. We may arrange to carry out an electronic verification of your identity if we consider that a saving of time and cost will be achieved by doing so. The cost of any such search will be charged to you. If the amount is in excess of £10 including VAT, we will seek your prior agreement.

• Solicitors are under a professional and legal obligation to keep the affairs of the client confidential. This obligation, however, is subject to a statutory exception: Legislation on money laundering and terrorist financing has placed solicitors under a legal duty in certain circumstances to disclose information to the Serious and Organised Crime Agency. Where a solicitor knows or suspects that a transaction on behalf of a client involves money laundering, the solicitor may be required to make a disclosure. If, while we are acting for you, it becomes necessary to make such a disclosure, we may not be able to inform you that it has been made, or of the reasons for it, because the law prohibits 'tipping-off'. Where the law permits us, we will tell you about any potential money laundering problem and explain what action we may need to take.

• Our firm may be subject to audit or quality checks by external firms or organisations. We may also outsource work. This might be for example typing or photocopying or costings, or research and preparation to assist with your matter. Information from your file may therefore be made available in such circumstances. We will always aim to obtain a confidentiality agreement with the third party.

37

- In order to comply with court and tribunal rules, all documentation relevant to any issues in litigation, however potentially damaging to your case, have to be preserved and may be required to be made available to the other side. This aspect of proceedings is known as "disclosure". Subject to this, we will not reveal confidential information about your case except as provided by these terms of business and where, for example, your opponent is ordered to pay your costs, we have to meet obligations to reveal details of the case to them and to the court.

Communication Between You and Us
- Our aim is to offer all our clients an efficient and effective service at all times. We are proud that we hold the accreditation of Investor in People and our clients and our staff are of first importance to us. We hope that you will be pleased with the work we do for you. However, should there be any aspect of our service with which you are unhappy, please raise your concern in the first place with [insert fee earner name]. If you still have queries or concerns, please contact our [ ] who is the Client Care Partner to whom any final difficulty can be reported.
- We will aim to communicate with you by such a method as you may request. We may need to virus check discs or email. Unless you withdraw consent, we will communicate with others when appropriate by email or fax but we cannot be responsible for the security of correspondence and documents sent by email or fax.
- The Data Protection Act requires us to advise you that your particulars are held on our database. We may, from time to time, use these details to send you information which we think might be of interest to you.
- Where we act for two or more clients jointly it is on the clear understanding that we are authorised to act on instructions from either, both or any of them.

Terms and Conditions of Business
- Unless otherwise agreed, and subject to the application of then current hourly rates, these Terms and Conditions of Business shall apply to any future instructions given by you to this firm.
- Although your continuing instructions in this matter will amount to an acceptance of these Terms and Conditions of Business, it may not be possible for us to start work on your behalf until one copy of them has been signed and returned to us for us to keep on our file.

I confirm I have read and understood, and I accept, these Terms and Conditions of Business.

Signed . . . .

Date . . . .

Client care letter deficiencies

Mark-up

[2.39]

The *Law Society Gazette* of 3 June 1998 summarised two cases before the Compliance and Supervision Committee of the Office for the Supervision of Solicitors (now the Consumer Complaints Service). In the first case the client received a client care letter which made no reference to a mark-up on the firm's charges. The client did not question the standard of work or service given but he did object to the unexpected mark-up on the bill. The bill was reduced from £1,600 to £1,100 plus VAT to reflect the solicitors' failure to inform.

No information

[2.40]

In the second case no client care letter was sent to a client in respect of non-contentious business. The client asked the solicitors to obtain a remuneration certificate. In the absence of costs information, the certificate was issued reducing the bill from £5,400 to £4,500 plus VAT.

Hourly rates

[2.41]

In *Wong v Vizards (a firm)* [1997] 2 Costs LR 46, QBD the solicitors informed the client that he would be charged hourly rates of £125 for a partner and £110 for an assistant solicitor, both rates to be subject to review. That was in June 1991. In November 1993 the solicitors wrote to the client with an estimate of costs showing the assistant solicitor's time at £110 per hour. However, their final bill charged rates of £140 an hour for the partner and £125 an hour for the assistant solicitor after 30 November 1993. No indication was ever given to the client of a proposed increase in the hourly rates and accordingly the solicitors were bound by their original figures.

Reliance on costs to be recovered

[2.42]

The Law Society's Gazette of 30 October 2003 reported the case of a solicitor who was, perhaps justifiably, so convinced that his client would win against an insured defendant he was prepared to accept whatever costs he recovered from the defendant's insurers. Unfortunately the solicitor failed to meet his client's expectations and the client changed solicitors. What was the solicitor to do? He was advised to come to some arrangement with the new firm about payment of his costs when the matter was finally concluded.

CHAPTER 3

FORM AND CONTENT OF A BILL

FORM

[3.1]

The formalities governing the delivery of a bill are surprisingly few. The Solicitors Act 1974 is silent as to the form of a bill for non-contentious work and in respect of contentious business s 64 merely prescribes that the bill of costs may, at the option of the solicitor, be either a bill containing detailed items or a gross sum bill. Section 64(2) provides that the party chargeable may, before he is served with proceedings and within three months of the date on which the bill was delivered to them (whichever is the earlier), require the solicitor to deliver a bill containing detailed items in lieu of the original bill. This has the dramatic effect that the gross sum bill is of no effect. Accordingly, the solicitor is no longer bound by the amount of the gross sum bill and he is free to deliver a detailed bill for a higher amount if his new calculations justify this (*Polak v Marchioness of Winchester* [1956] 2 All ER 660, CA).

What amounts to a 'requirement' of a solicitor to deliver a detailed bill for the purpose of triggering s 64(2)? Even though the client does not quote the section and is unaware of its provisions this does not prevent it being triggered by a request for details. *Carlton v Theodore Goddard & Co* [1973] 2 All ER 877, ChD decided that a letter from the client saying that he wanted the costs taxed [*assessed*] was not a sufficient request – the letter did not 'contain a word about "a bill containing detailed items"'. However, in *Penningtons (a firm) v Brown* (30 April 1998, unreported, CA) the Court of Appeal upheld the judge's view that a letter from a client requesting 'a full breakdown of your firm's bill' with a view to having the gross sum bill delivered taxed [*assessed*] was a s 64(2) request. In view of this decision it would be prudent when receiving such a letter to write to the client explaining the provisions of s 64(2) and ascertaining precisely what the client wants. It would do no harm to point out that the replacement detailed bill could exceed the amount of the gross sum bill. The Court of Appeal was particularly influenced by the fact that the request was from a layman who was unlikely to appreciate the implications and consequences of his request. So, beware. Section 64(2) gives the client the additional right to an order for the detailed assessment of a gross sum bill if requested within a month of the service of proceedings. Where proceedings are commenced on a gross sum bill, s 64(2) entitles the costs officer to require such further details of the costs as are necessary for the purposes of a detailed assessment.

CONTENT

(a) Amount

(i)   Gross not net

[3.2]

It is fundamental to an understanding of costs to appreciate that there are only two sources from which a solicitor can be remunerated – by their own client under contract or out of the Legal Aid or Legal Services Commission Fund under statute. All other costs arise out of the client's rights against other persons or funds, and they belong not to the solicitor but to the client. Even costs awarded out of central funds in criminal matters belong in theory to the client. However, fundamental principles are not impervious to the dictates of state funding and solicitors can have an interest in costs awarded between the parties where their clients are legally aided.

The trustee looks to a trust fund for reimbursement, a successful party in litigation can expect an order for costs against the loser, the landlord may provide in the lease that his legal costs be paid by the tenant, but none of this affects the solicitor and client relationship between the trustee, the successful litigant or the landlord and their respective solicitors. The solicitor on behalf of his client seeks to recover money due to the client from the trust fund, the unsuccessful litigant or the tenant, but he does not have any personal relationship with them. The solicitor looks to his client for payment of the costs whether or not the client is reimbursed by a third party. The solicitor must therefore deliver a bill to his client for the whole of his costs and give credit for any sum that has been received. He must not treat the costs recovered as his own and merely render an account to his client for any additional payment he requires. This was dramatically illustrated as long ago as 1908 in *Cobbett v Wood* [1908] 2 KB 420, CA, when the Court of Appeal held that a bill of costs which excluded the between the parties' items and simply referred to the excess chargeable as between solicitor and own client was not a proper bill. The VAT ramifications of this principle, also dramatic, are set out in Chapter 12.

(ii)   Interim bills

[3.3]

Where interim bills on account have been rendered pursuant to s 65(2) of the Solicitors Act 1974 these should be ignored for the purposes of the final bill and treated as requests for payment of money on account. The final bill should therefore be for the total amount of the solicitor's charges and disbursements with any additional mark-up (or mark-down) on the interim bills and give credit for all payments received as a result of bills on account. If pursuant to an agreement with your client you have been rendering interim statute bills each bill is a self-contained account for the work done during the period which it covers.

(b) Narrative

[3.4]

A bill of costs must contain sufficient particulars to enable the client to judge the fairness of the charges. There are a number of decisions relating to this and surprisingly the most succinct warning of the dangers of computer printouts is *Haigh v Ousey* (1857) 7 E & B 578, which held the bill ought to be drawn so as to enable the client to judge its fairness, a solicitor to advise on it and a taxing officer to judge the propriety of the various items of which it is composed. It was held 121 years later in *Re Kingsley* (1978) 122 Sol Jo 457 that a bill merely stating 'for professional services' was void as inadequate. Although details of hours spent and letters written are not essential, a bill requires at least a sufficient summary of the work done. In my view a bill showing no more than the hours spent would be treated by the court as not being a properly delivered bill, and I also think that any client who understandably requested more details of such a bill may well not be regarded as having made a formal request justifying the delivery of a detailed itemised account for a larger amount pursuant to the Solicitors Act, s 64(3), despite *Penningtons v Brown* (see para [3.1]).

In respect of bills for contentious business it is arguable that the provisions of the Solicitors Act, s 64 for substituting a gross sum bill with a detailed bill made the decisions in *Haigh v Ousey* and other nineteenth century cases obsolete. In respect of non-contentious business, since the Solicitors Remuneration Order 1953, a solicitor has been entitled to such sum as may be fair and reasonable having regard to all the circumstances of the case, and the client has been entitled to apply to the Law Society to certify what this amount should be (see Chapter 5). Lord Denning in *Re a Solicitor* [1955] 2 QB 252, CA interpreted the position as being that the solicitor could deliver:

'a lump sum as before, but whereas previously the client could afterwards insist on a detailed bill of charges, he now has no right to have the lump sum split up into items. He is however given a valuable new right. He can require the solicitor to put the bill before the Law Society, so that the Law Society can see whether the sum charged is fair and reasonable. If it is fair and reasonable, they will certify accordingly; or if not they will say what the proper sum should be . . . Such being the effect of the new Order the question is; what must a solicitor's bill for non-contentious business now contain? It need not contain detailed charges as it used to do before 1920. Nor need it contain all of the details which the solicitor will have to give, if required, to the Law Society or the taxing master [*costs judge*]. But I think that it must contain a summarised statement of the work done, sufficient to tell the client what it is for which he is asked to pay. A bare account for "professional services" between certain dates, or for "work done in connection with your matrimonial affairs" would not do. The nature of the work must be stated, such as, advising on such and such a matter, instructing counsel to do so and so, drafting such and such a document and so forth.'

Paragraph 30 of the Guidance to Rule 2.03 of the Solicitors' Code of Conduct 2007 neatly side-steps this and related issues in these words: 'This guidance does not deal with the form a bill can take, final and interim bills, when they can be delivered and when and how a firm can sue on a bill. All these matters are governed by complex legal provisions, and there are many publications that provide help to firms and clients. Advice on some aspects of costs is available from the Law Society's Practice Advice Service' (which recommends this book and you're already there!).

Even in *Haigh v Ousey* (para [3.4]) Lord Chief Justice Campbell said:

> 'I do not think that the legislature intended to throw on a solicitor the burthen (*sic*) of preparing a bill such that another solicitor on looking at it should without any further statement, see on the face of the bill all information requisite to enable him to say if the charges were reasonable . . . If we required in respect of every item a precise exactness of form, we should go beyond the words and meaning of the statute, and should give facilities to dishonest clients to defeat just claims upon a defence of a defect of form, in respect of which they have no real interest.'

And Erle J said:

> 'No man, unless there were interminable prolixity in the bill, could tell from the bill alone what is a fair charge for matters depending on the quantum meruit, that is for almost everything except mere steps in a cause . . . The bill should give reasonable information; if the client wants more, he may demand it.'

The safety net in respect of non-contentious business is the client's right to obtain a certificate as to reasonableness from the Law Society. The safety net in respect of contentious business is the client's right to request a detailed bill (see above). I am grateful to Jeremy Morgan, of counsel, for drawing to my attention the judgment of CS Clarke QC sitting as a High Court judge in *Re a Solicitor* (10 May 1994, unreported, QBD), which is a 27-page comprehensive survey of the history of the provision. The solicitor's action for the unpaid balance of their costs was met with a defence that their bill did not satisfy the law's requirements for a solicitor's bill in that it did not contain sufficient information to enable the defendant to obtain advice as to whether or not he should tax it, based on *Haigh v Ousey*. The judge in *Re a Solicitor* held that the option given to a solicitor of submitting a gross sum bill conferred by s 64 of the Act was not available at the time of *Haigh v Ousey*, nor at that time did the clients have the rights conferred in s 64(2)–(4). He continued:

> 'In my judgment Parliament did not intend to oblige a solicitor submitting a gross sum bill for contentious business to include any more than, in the words of Lord Denning, "a summarised statement of the work done sufficient to tell the client what it is which he is asked to pay". Parliament intended to give to the solicitor the option of submitting, in contentious business, the same form of bill as was already permitted in non-contentious business. Any further obligation would render the provision wholly ineffective. Section 64 was intended to recognise that, in many cases, the client is content to accept a gross sum bill but to provide safeguards for a client who, for any reason, was not.'

He concluded:

> 'a bill which, to use Lord Denning's example, simply said "to professional services" would not, of course, be sufficient since such a document would leave it wholly unclear what the client would be paying for, if he paid it, or in respect of what the solicitor might or might not, after payment, be able to make a further claim. If such a document is a bill at all, it is certainly not a bill contemplated by the Act.'

Why should lack of information make a bill 'invalid', and not, for example, merely unenforceable? The concept of invalidity for lack of particularity is judge-made.

No doubt a bill which does not even attain the modest aspirations of Law Society's Practice Rule 14.07 ought to be void on the ground that it is not really a bill at all, but should not any other deficiency merely result in the bill being unenforceable until the basic information has been supplied? The law was reviewed by the Court of Appeal in *Ralph Hume Garry (a firm) v Gwillim* [2002] EWCA Civ 1500, [2003] 1 All ER 1038. A balance must be struck between protection of the client's right to seek a Solicitors Act assessment and the solicitor's right to payment not being defeated by 'opportunist resort to technicality'. To establish that a bill was not in 'bona fide compliance' with the Act, a client must establish (i) it contained no sufficient narrative to identify what he was being charged for; and (ii) he did not have sufficient knowledge from documents in his possession, or from what he had been told, to take advice about challenging the bill. The more the client knows, the less the need for the bill to spell it out. These 'unseemly disputes' could be avoided if the bill were accompanied by a computer print-out showing the time spent, with the rate charged and some description of the work done.

A totally inadequate bill for contentious business (for example one not giving any information as to how the amount charged was calculated) cannot be saved by a request by the client for further details.

A full narrative could include details embarrassing to the client who wishes to use the bill as a VAT invoice and there are various methods of preserving this confidentiality, the most usual being to set out the narrative either on a separate sheet or on a tear-off portion at the end of the bill.

(c) Unpaid disbursements

[3.5]

The bill may include unpaid disbursements, but only if they are described in the bill as not yet paid; the defect is fatal to these items if they are challenged on a subsequent assessment. The only remedy would be to ask the costs judge for an adjournment, apply to the court for leave to withdraw the entire bill, re-deliver it (at the risk of being ordered to pay all the costs thrown away) and then start again (Solicitors Act 1974, s 67). However, in *Tearle & Co v Sherring* (29 October 1993, unreported, QBD), Wright J held that where a solicitor has acted in good faith but by inadvertence has omitted to describe disbursements as unpaid, the court not only had power to give him leave to withdraw his bill and deliver another one, to save costs it could in an appropriate case give leave to amend his bill by adding the words 'unpaid'. He tentatively expressed the view that a costs officer might have the same powers.

(d) Cash account

[3.6]

It is the duty of a solicitor when delivering a bill of costs also to deliver a cash account detailing the receipts and payments made on behalf of the client. It is important to know what disbursements should appear in the bill itself and what should be charged in the cash account. Many solicitors lose money on assessments of costs by regarding as cash account items payments which should have been included in the bill as disbursements. Disbursements have been defined as 'such payments as the solicitor in the due discharge of his duty is bound to make whether his client furnishes him with money for the purpose, with money on account, or not, as for example court fees, counsel's fees, expenses of witnesses, agents and stationers'. All of these items should appear in the bill. Other items which the solicitor is not bound by law or custom to make, such as purchase money, interest, sums paid into court, or damages, costs paid to an opponent, estate duty and Land Registry fees, are properly charged in the cash account (*Re Remnant* (1849) 11 Beav 603; *Re Buckwell and Berkeley* [1902] 2 Ch 596, CA; *Browne v Barber* [1913] 2 KB 553, CA).

(e) VAT

[3.7]

A solicitor's bill of costs must comply with the VAT regulations which apply to his services. The bill must of course contain the solicitor's VAT registration number, but there are other provisions which are so misunderstood and surprising that I have devoted the next chapter to them.

(f) Signature

[3.8]

Although not essential to the validity of the bill, a solicitor may not sue for his costs unless he has complied with the requirements of the Solicitors Act 1974, s 69 as to signature.

Until 7 March 2008, s 69 of the Solicitors Act 1974 provided that solicitor's bill of costs to the client must be signed by the solicitor or one of his partners, either in his own name or in the name of the firm or be accompanied by a letter which is so signed and refers to the bill. For bills delivered after 7 March 2008, The Legal Services Act 2007 amended s 69 to require a bill to be signed by the solicitor or on his behalf by an employee of the solicitor authorised by him to sign. A commonly used abbreviation of the firm's name will suffice (*Bartletts de Reya v Byrne* (1983) 127 Sol Jo 69, CA). A signature impressed by means of a rubber stamp suffices (*Goodman v J Eban Ltd* [1954] 1 QB 550, CA). In these days of delegation it is important to ensure that this provision is complied with. Some firms instruct their accounts department not to issue or enter a bill unless it bears an authorised signature.

The practical difference between a bill which is valid but unenforceable by court proceedings because it is not signed and an invalid bill, is that the former entitles a solicitor to appropriate money paid on account in settlement of the bill or to exercise a lien until the bill is paid, while the latter is of no effect for any purpose. However, if an action on a defective bill gets before the court, the judge has the discretion in appropriate circumstances to give leave for the bill to be withdrawn and replaced without commencing fresh proceedings (*Zuliani v Veira* [1994] 1 WLR 1149, PC).

(g) Delivery

[3.9]

The Solicitors Act 1974, s 69(2)(*b*) also provides that the bill must be delivered to the party to be charged either personally or by being sent to him by post to, or left for him at, his place of business, dwelling house or last known place of abode.

CHAPTER 4

SOLICITOR AND CLIENT VAT

CHARGEABILITY

[4.1]

A solicitor's services to his client are subject to VAT at the standard rate unless the solicitor is not registered for VAT or the services are zero-rated.

VAT Chargeability Chart

Service Rendered by Solicitors	Capacity of Client (See Note 1)	Residence of Client (See Note 2)	VAT Chargeability
1. General legal services other than those below	Private or	UK	Full
		EEC (Non UK)	Full
		World (Non EEC)	Zero
	Business	UK	Full
		EEC (Non UK)	Zero
		World (Non EEC)	Zero
2. Services relating to land outside UK	Private or	UK	Zero
		World (Non UK)	Zero
	Business		
3. Services relating to land inside UK	Private or	UK	Full
		World (Non UK)	Full
ie: conveyancing, litigation and advice associated with land	Business		

Note 1.	Capacity of client
	It should be clearly established in every case whether a client gives instructions in a private or in a business capacity.
Note 2.	Residence of client
	Private individuals: country where they are usually resident.

Business client with premises: the country where it has any business establishment including a branch or agency. If this would give it more than one country or residence then it is to be treated as resident in the country where its establishment is located which is most directly concerned with the services rendered.

Business client without premises: for corporate clients, the country or incorporation or legal constitution; for individual clients the country of the individual's usual residence.

THE TAX POINT

[4.2]

I said in the last chapter that the effect of some of the regulations is surprising.

The basic rule is that the tax point for services is the date on which their performance is completed. VAT becomes payable on that date irrespective of when the bill is delivered.

For solicitors there is a minor exception. If a tax invoice is issued within three months of the basic tax point, the date of the invoice becomes the actual tax point. VAT is therefore payable by a solicitor when the work is completed or when his bill is delivered provided that this is within three months of the completion of the work (HM Customs and Excise Notice No 700 (Notice 700) and the Value Added Tax Act 1994, s 6(6)). This provision has the force of law and it is therefore an offence for a solicitor not to quantify his charges within three months of completing a matter for the purposes of calculating and paying VAT.

This is NOT a VAT invoice: One effect of Notice 700 is to make unlawful and ineffective the practice of a solicitor writing to a client informing him of his proposed fees but not issuing a VAT invoice until payment has been received. This erroneous philosophy was set out in the *Architect's Journal* as follows:

'If VAT registered it can pay to liaise with the client and give a note of what the total bill will be and not actually issue an invoice until the date the cheque arrives. This is because once an invoice for VAT is issued you are liable to pay the VAT over to HM Customs and Excise regardless of whether or not you are paid. To ensure that you keep your own cash intact, rather than having to pay it over before it reaches you from the client, you can issue your statements headed with the wording: "This is not a VAT invoice. An authenticated invoice for VAT will be sent on receipt of your cheque".'

The creation of the basic tax point cannot be circumvented by any such device.

DISBURSEMENTS

(a) VAT

[4.3]

In respect of which litigation disbursements should a client be charged VAT? The simple answer is 'none'. Unfortunately this gives rise to the much more complicated question 'what is a disbursement?'. The answer is to be found in the VAT *Guide* (HM Customs and Excise Notice 700), which sets out eight criteria. The test is whether the goods or services are supplied to the solicitor to enable him to render his service to the client, in which event they are not a disbursement and VAT is chargeable. For example, postage, telephone calls, travelling and hotel expenses are not disbursements and VAT must be charged on them. A disbursement is a payment which relates to goods or services supplied to the client, even if it is, in the first place, paid for by the solicitor. Examples are oath and court fees. A method of avoiding VAT on a payment which would not otherwise attract VAT, such as an air fare, is for the client to pay for it direct. The solicitor need not then include it in his account. An example of the importance of this was recently drawn to my attention by Simon Young of Veitch Penny. Their VAT inspector contended that all the medical reports, notes or records they had obtained in personal injury cases were obtained for their benefit and not the clients' (ie they were primarily to enable the solicitors to do their job) and as such formed part of their services to their clients, who should have been charged VAT on those items. The correspondence ended happily with HM Customs and Excise accepting that the payments satisfied the conditions of para 10.8 of Notice 700 and were true disbursements.

(b) Counsel's fees

[4.4]

The fees of counsel are part of the service rendered by the solicitor and should therefore be included in the solicitor's bill and attract VAT even if the barrister is not registered for VAT. However, there is a long-standing concession under which HM Customs and Excise permit solicitors to re-address counsel's fee notes to the lay client, who then makes payment direct (or is requested by the solicitor to return the fee note to him with a separate cheque payable to counsel) so that counsel's fees do not pass through the solicitor's books at all. Where this is done the fees of the unregistered barrister do not attract VAT, and the solicitor avoids incurring VAT liability on counsel's fees because he need not include them in his VAT quarterly return.

RECOVERY OF VAT

[4.5]

If the client is registered for VAT and the legal services supplied to him are for the purposes of his business he may recover the tax charged, either out of VAT received by him from his customers or by reclaiming it from HM Customs and Excise. It is therefore important for the solicitor to distinguish between a client's personal matters and his business affairs and to render separate accounts in respect of them.

AGREED FEES

[4.6]

The Solicitors' Costs Information and Client Care Code, para 4, requires a solicitor to give the client a breakdown between fees, VAT and disbursements in advance. If the solicitor fails to do this, the implication will be that an agreed fee included VAT (see also 'Criminal Offence' at para [2.20]). Where a VAT inclusive fee has been agreed the solicitor must nevertheless account to HM Customs and Excise for the VAT element (for VAT at 17.5%, the magic formula is 17/74ths) and provide a VAT invoice to the client if he requests one.

VAT ON FIXED COSTS RECOVERED

[4.7]

Fixed costs recovered under CPR Rule 45, RSC Order 62 and CCR Order 38 contain no element of VAT. The solicitor may either charge the client an amount equal to the fixed costs or charge on the normal solicitor and client basis, in both cases giving credit for the sum recovered. By either method he must charge the client VAT in addition to the fixed costs. VAT is recoverable on fast track trial fixed costs under CPR Rule 46 provided the client is not registered for VAT (see [4.5], above).

INSURANCE CLAIMS

(a) Policy holder can recover VAT

[4.8]

If the insurance relates to the client's business and it is VAT registered the client will be able to take a full input tax credit for the VAT on the solicitor's bill. In these circumstances the insurers will only be responsible to their policy holder for the amount of the solicitor's bill exclusive of VAT.

(b) Policy holder cannot recover VAT

[4.9]

Where the client is partly exempt, or the insurance does not relate to his business, or he is not VAT registered, the solicitor's bill must still be addressed to the client and include VAT. In the circumstances there is no objection to the client sending the entire bill to the insurers for payment, as previously. If, for internal accounting purposes, the insurers wish solicitors to issue invoices directly to them, this may be done but the invoice so delivered will not be a VAT invoice.

(c) The Lloyd's Underwriters, ILU and AIOA scheme

[4.10]

There may be cases in which the amount equivalent to the VAT payable by an insured party proves difficult or impossible to recover. The Law Society has negotiated a scheme with Lloyd's Underwriters, ILU and AIOA to cover this situation. Other insurers will usually be members of the Association of British Insurers, who have advised their members of the statement, but when dealing with these companies it is necessary for solicitors to confirm directly with them that they accept the scheme.

[4.11]

Here is the Law Society's summary of the scheme:

LLOYD'S UNDERWRITERS, ILU AND AIOA SCHEME

(1)   In indemnity/liability claims, underwriters will expect to pay the solicitor's bill exclusive of the VAT equivalent when it is rendered by the solicitor. Solicitors will send the VAT invoice direct to assureds who are registered for VAT with a request for payment by them to the solicitors of the VAT equivalent. Solicitors are to use their best endeavours to obtain payment by the assured of the VAT equivalent. Underwriters will indemnify solicitors for any of the VAT equivalent remaining unpaid if, after a period of 90 days, solicitors are unable to obtain payment. In any event, solicitors will not seek to recover the VAT equivalent direct from assureds, where the amount per invoice is less than £50, and this will therefore be a cost to underwriters. If an assured pays the VAT equivalent to a solicitor after the 90-day period, the solicitor will reimburse underwriters for that amount.

(2)   In subrogation cases, underwriters will expect to pay the solicitor's bill inclusive of the VAT element when it is rendered by solicitors. However, solicitors are to use their best endeavours to obtain payment by the assured of the VAT equivalent. If successful, solicitors will reimburse underwriters. In any event, underwriters will not ask solicitors to pursue the payment of the VAT equivalent from assureds where the amount per invoice is less than £50. This will therefore be a cost to underwriters.

(3)   Nothing shall prevent an underwriter adopting a different method of invoicing for VAT purposes should any particular circumstances require such a method, save that they are not to be more onerous upon solicitors than described above.

The Law Society understands that, generally, Customs will allow solicitors to rely on underwriters' and insurers' knowledge when deciding whether their bill is entitled to zero-rating: in any case of doubt, solicitors should consult their local VAT office before treating their services as zero-rated in whole or in part. In reference to VAT invoicing generally, attention is drawn to the requirements of the relevant regulations which are now in the Value Added Tax (General) Regulations 1985 (SI 1985/886).

INSURANCE COMMISSIONS

[4.12]

The Law Society's view is that VAT is assessable on the full amount of the bill, disregarding any reduction for insurance commission set-off. Furthermore, VAT is still payable on the full amount of what the bill would have been, even if no bill at all is rendered. If this is because of offset insurance commission, the amount that the bill would have been is presumably equivalent to the whole of the commission. In the Law Society's opinion, solicitors who treat VAT in any other way in such circumstances are putting themselves at considerable risk because of the likelihood of a subsequent claim by HM Customs and Excise.

CLAIMS HANDLING SERVICES

[4.13]

In an article in the *New Law Journal* of 8 April 2005 the costs team at Kings Chambers drew attention to the decision of the European Court of Justice (First Chamber) C-472/03 on 3 March 2005 in *Staatssecretaris Van Financien v Arthur Andersen and Co*. The ECJ held that 'back-office' functions performed by a firm of accountants under a contractual arrangement with an insurance company were services that were chargeable to VAT. The authors suggested that the case has important implications for firms of solicitors who provide a claims handling service on behalf of firms of insurers. At present such a service is not chargeable to VAT because the solicitors are acting as intermediaries. However, domestic law may well be changed in the light of this decision.

RATE CHANGE

[4.14]

The standard rate of VAT was reduced from 17.5 per cent to 15 per cent as of 1 December 2008. This rate applied until 31 December 2009, after which it reverted to 17.5 per cent on 1 January 2010. Matters completed before 1 December 2008 are to be charged at the old rate of 17.5 per cent and matters completed on or after 1 December 2008 at the new rate of 15 per cent. The Chancellor of the Exchequer has announced that the standard rate will increase to 20 per cent with effect from 4 January 2011. At least it will make the arithmetic easier.

A VAT invoice is normally raised when the service is completed. However, in circumstances where work is yet to be completed, the rate of VAT to be charged will depend on the date at which the supply of service, the tax point, occurs.

CHAPTER 5

THE CLIENT'S RIGHTS

FORMAL DEFECTS

[5.1]

If the formalities (see Chapter 3) that are a prerequisite to a solicitor commencing proceedings for the recovery of his costs have not been complied with, his bill is nevertheless valid. Accordingly, although the solicitor cannot sue on his bill, the client can only ignore it with impunity if the solicitor has no funds of the client that he can set off against the bill and no property of the client over which he can exercise a lien.

REMUNERATION CERTIFICATES

[5.2]

Until 11 August 2009 the Solicitors' (Non-Contentious Business) Remuneration Order 1994 set out the requirements applying when a solicitor delivered a bill for non-contentious business. An important part of this process was the right of the client to request the solicitor to obtain a remuneration certificate from the Legal Complaints Service if the client disputed the amount of the bill.

Article 6 of the Order made it a condition precedent to bringing proceedings for the recovery of non-contentious costs that the solicitor informed any entitled person, in writing, of:
(i)   their right to a remuneration certificate;
(ii)   their right to assessment by the court; and
(iii)   the solicitor's right to charge interest on a bill.

[5.3]

However, the Solicitors' (Non-Contentious Business) Remuneration Order 2009 which came into effect on 11 August 2009 abolished remuneration certificates from that date. The new order did not contain any information requirements for clients, but on 1 March 2010 some of the information requirements about challenging a solicitor's bill were carried over into rule 2.05 of the Solicitors Code of Conduct 2007 as follows:

2.05 Complaints handling

(1) If you are a recognised body, a manager of a recognised body or a recognised sole practitioner you must ensure:

(a) that the firm has a written complaints procedure and that complaints are handled promptly, fairly and effectively in accordance with it;

(b) that the client is told, in writing, at the outset (or in the case of existing clients, at the next appropriate opportunity):

(i) that, in the event of a problem, the client is entitled to complain; and

(ii) how and to whom the client should complain;

(iii) that this could include a complaint about the firm's bill;

(iv) that the firm has a complaints procedure, a copy of which is available on request;

(v) of their right to complain to the Legal Ombudsman at the conclusion of your complaint process, the timeframe for doing so and full details of how to contact the Legal Ombudsman;

(vi) that there may also be a right to object to the bill by applying to the court for an assessment of the bill under Part III of the Solicitors Act 1974; and

(vii) that if all or part of a bill remains unpaid the firm may be entitled to charge interest;

(c) that the client is given a copy of the complaints procedure on request; and

(d) that once a complaint has been made, the person complaining is told in writing:

(i) how the complaint will be handled; and

(ii) within what timescales they will be given an initial and/or substantive response;

(e) that at the conclusion of the firm's complaints process the client is told of their right to complain to the Legal Ombudsman, the timeframe for doing so and full details of how to contact the Legal Ombudsman.

(2) If you can demonstrate that it was inappropriate in the circumstances to meet some or all of these requirements, you will not breach 2.05.

(3) You must not charge your client for the cost of handling a complaint.

Guidance

47. The purpose of 2.05 is to encourage complaints to be properly and openly dealt with. There are huge benefits in terms of time, money and client satisfaction if complaints can be dealt with effectively at firm level.

48. The content of your firm's complaints handling procedure is a matter for the firm, but the procedure must be in writing, clear and unambiguous. If a complaint is made to the Legal Complaints Service (LCS) or the Solicitors Regulation Authority the firm will need to be able to demonstrate compliance. Everyone in the firm will need to know about this obligation to ensure that clients know who to contact if they have a problem, the information to give the client when a complaint is made, and the importance of recording the stages of the complaint and the final outcome. When you acknowledge the complaint, your letter should contain details of the LCS, with the post and web addresses of that organisation. You should also explain that the client(s) can ask the LCS to become involved at the end of the firm's own complaints

procedure if they are unhappy with the outcome. It is important to advise of the time limit, which can be checked by looking at the LCS website or by telephoning the LCS.

49. Your firm's arrangements for dealing with complaints must be fair and effective. Any investigation must be handled within an agreed timescale. Any arrangements must also comply with rule 6 (Equality and diversity).

49A. Where your client is unhappy with your bill you should treat this like any other complaint about your service. In such circumstances it may be helpful, when responding to the complaint, to provide a detailed narrative of your bill so that your client can clearly understand how the costs were incurred. You may be required to provide the Legal Complaints Service with such a narrative where a complaint about your bill is referred to them.

49B. In some circumstances it will be appropriate for your firm to remind the client at a later stage whom they should approach under the firm's complaints handling procedure if they want to complain about the bill (or for your firm to inform the client of this at a later stage if the client has not been told at the outset). This will be appropriate if:

(a)   the client is particularly vulnerable;

(b)   the client is a private client and you are delivering a bill more than two years after the original information was given;

(c)   you are taking your costs from money held on client account, and have not previously supplied the information; or

(d)   you are suing on the bill, and have not previously supplied the information.

Where you or your firm are, in effect, the client – for example, as the executors administering a deceased's estate or as the trustees of a trust – you should consider whether information on complaining about a bill should be given to any person likely to be affected by the bill.

50. Rule 2.05(3) prevents you charging your client for the cost of handling a complaint. Dealing properly with complaints is an integral part of any professional business. The associated costs are part of the firm's overheads, and complainants must not be charged separately.

51. Rule 2.05(2) allows for situations where it may be inappropriate to give all the information required.

Note that this guidance applies to both contentious and non-contentious costs.

ENTITLED THIRD PARTIES

[5.5]

The Solicitors' (Non-Contentious Business) Remuneration Order 1994 gave rights to an 'entitled third party' who it defined as:

> '... a residuary beneficiary absolutely and immediately (and not contingently) entitled to an inheritance, where a solicitor has charged the estate for his professional costs for acting in the administration of the estate, and either: (a) the only personal representatives are solicitors (whether or not acting in a professional capacity); (b) the only personal representatives are solicitors acting jointly with partners or employees in a professional capacity.'

The effect of this was that a residuary beneficiary of an estate where there is at least one lay executor is not an entitled third party. A residuary beneficiary of an estate in which all the personal representatives are solicitors was able to ask the solicitor billing the estate to obtain a remuneration certificate. Not only did the Solicitors' (Non-Contentious Business) Remuneration Order 2009 abolish remuneration certificates but entitled third parties appear to have gone with them.

New guidance

[5.6]

The new paragraph 49B (see [5.4] above) inserted in the Guidance Notes to the Solicitors Code of Conduct 2007 on 1 March 2010 provides that where the solicitor is the client, for example as executor of an estate, 'you should consider whether information on complaining about a bill should be given to any person likely to be affected by the bill'. The Legal Complaints Service investigated complaints from residuary beneficiaries immediately entitled and presumably the Legal Ombudsman as its successor will do the same.

DETAILED ASSESSMENT

[5.7]

In *Barrett v Rutt-Field (1) Mathews (2) Marshall Sutton Jones (3)* [2006] W TLR 1505; NLJ 16 February p 255 Wendy Barrett was the sole residuary beneficiary of her late aunt's estate. The first and second defendants were the executors. The third defendant was a firm of solicitors of which the second defendant was a partner and which had been instructed by the executors to carry out the administration of the estate. The claimant sought a detailed assessment of the solicitors' accounts. She lost because the first defendant was a priest! The claimant could claim only if she were an entitled third party and there can only be an entitled third party if all the executors are solicitors. The claimant then argued that she was a quasi-client. She said the solicitors had acknowledged this by treating her as a client. They had kept her fully supplied with all the information about the firm's practice and its fees to which a client is entitled. Again she was wrong. The solicitors had only kept her informed as a matter of good practice because she was the residuary beneficiary and not because she was their client. On the strict definitions set out in the Order the claimant was neither a client nor could she be treated as a client even though she has been entitled to make an application under section 71 of the Solicitors Act 1974, that definition being different from the definition in the Order. Perhaps the solicitors had over-done it but that could not turn the claimant into a quasi-client because there is no such thing. You are either a client or you are not. And she was not.

APPLICATION FOR DELIVERY OF A BILL

[5.8]

Section 68 of the Solicitors Act 1974 empowers the court on an application by the client to order the solicitor to deliver a bill. The jurisdiction in the High Court extends to all cases, including those in which no business has been done by the solicitor in the High Court, while the county court has similar jurisdiction where the bill of costs relates wholly or partly to contentious business done by the solicitor in that county court. There are two usual circumstances which may give rise to such an application. The first is where the solicitor attempts to retain money paid on account without having delivered an adequate bill. The second is where the solicitor makes what the client regards as an excessive demand for an interim payment on account.

(a) Precedent originating application to deliver bill of costs

[5.9]

Claim Form N208 CPR Part 8

Details of claim

The claimant seeks an order that within . . . days the defendant delivers to the claimant or to his solicitor a bill of costs in all cases and matters in which he is concerned for the claimant and give credit in them for all money received by him for or on account of the claimant.

(b) Precedent order for delivery of bill of costs (CPR Schedule of Costs Precedent K)

[5.10]

CPR Schedule of Costs: Precedent K

Solicitor's Act: order for delivery of bill

DATED the [DATE]   **[Claim No]**

IN THE HIGH COURT OF JUSTICE
[DIVISION]
[JUDGE TYPE] [JUDGE NAME]

                                      [CLAIMANT]

BETWEEN: **Claimant**

                                      – and –

                                      [DEFENDANT]

                                                                        Defendant

UPON THE APPLICATION OF THE PARTY
[the parties and their representatives who attended]
AND UPON HEARING
AND UPON READING the documents on the Court File

IT IS ORDERED THAT
(1)   The [PARTY]   must within [NUMBER OF DAYS] deliver to the [PARTY]   or to his so-licitor, a bill of costs in all causes and matters in which he has been con-cerned for the [PARTY]

61

(2)   The [PARTY]   must give credit in that bill for all money
       received by him from or on account of the   [PARTY]

REQUEST A DETAILED BILL

[5.11]

In respect of contentious business, within three months of the delivery of a
gross sum bill and before service of a claim for the recovery of the costs, the
client may require the solicitor to deliver a bill containing detailed items.

APPLY TO SET ASIDE A CONTENTIOUS BUSINESS AGREEMENT

[5.12]

Such an application may be made on the grounds that it is unfair or
unreasonable, either when the solicitor applies for leave to enforce the
agreement or by an application by the client.

SUE FOR NEGLIGENCE

[5.13]

If the client alleges that he or she has suffered loss because of the solicitor's negligence, the client may sue the solicitor for damages and for a return
of costs paid. A solicitor cannot charge costs for negligent work if the result of
that negligence was to render the work wholly fruitless. To succeed in a claim
for damages there must be proof of actual damage, but, although the court
does not have the power to award exemplary damages as a mark of its
disapproval of a solicitor's conduct, Peter Birts QC suggests it may be possible
to claim damages for injury to feelings on the grounds that a main purpose of
the solicitor's retainer was to give peace of mind and that his negligence has
caused the client vexation etc (*Heywood v Wellers (a firm)* [1976] QB 446,
[1976] 1 All ER 300). If you ever succeed with that argument, please let Peter
Birts or me know!

   On a solicitor and client assessment, while the costs officer can disallow
items unreasonably incurred by virtue of the solicitor's negligence, a costs
officer cannot disallow the entire bill because he cannot try an action for
negligence.

WAIT UNTIL SUED

[5.14]

The client may wait until the solicitor institutes proceedings and then defend and counterclaim for negligence, seek a detailed assessment, or seek a quantum meruit (see *Watts (Thomas) & Co (a firm) v Smith* and *Turner & Co (a firm) v O Palomo SA*, at para [5.20]). In respect of proceedings commenced on a gross sum bill, s 64(3) of the Solicitors Act 1974 requires the court to order an assessment if the party chargeable so requests within a month of the commencement of proceedings.

(a) In the High Court

[5.15]

Where the solicitor sues in the High Court, if the client disputes only the amount of the bill, usually on an application for summary judgment, the order will direct that the bill be referred to a costs judge and that the solicitor be entitled to sign judgment for the costs as assessed, together with the costs of the action. The client can also obtain such an order by making an application in the action under CPR Part 23.

(b) Precedent application for a detailed assessment after action brought

[5.16]

Application notice (Form N244)

I [name of client] the defendant intend to apply for an order that the claimant's bills of costs and charges [and disbursements if disputed] delivered to the defendant for the recovery of which this action is brought be referred to a costs officer to be assessed, and that the claimant give credit for all sums of money received by him from or on account of the defendant, and that the costs officer assess the costs of the reference, and certify the amount due to or from either party in respect of the bill and of the costs of the reference (according to the statute), and that the claimant be restrained from prosecuting this action pending the reference, and that upon payment of what (if anything) is found to be due to the claimant, together with the costs of this action also to be assessed and paid, all further proceedings to be stayed.

Because I dispute that the claimant is entitled to the charges [and disbursements] in his bill of costs.

I rely on section 70 of the Solicitors Act 1974.

Statement of truth

(c) In the county court

[5.17]

If the solicitor has sued in the county court, the county court may only assess the solicitor's bill where:
(a)   the bill relates wholly or in part to contentious business done in a county court;

(b)   part of that work was done in the county court in which the application to assess is brought;

(c)   the bill does not exceed £5,000.

(Solicitors Act 1974, s 69(3).)

Where the defendant client cannot apply for an order for a Solicitors Act assessment, there are various courses which may be adopted:

(a)   Transfer the action to the High Court under the County Courts Act 1984, s 42. The court may then make a '*Smith v Edwardes Order*' based on *Smith v Edwardes* (1888) 22 QBD 10, CA which provides:

> 'It is ordered that the bill of costs on which this action is brought be referred to the costs judge/district judge pursuant to the Solicitors Act 1974, s 69, and that the claimant give credit at the time of the assessment for all sums of money received by him from or on account of the defendant and that the claimant be at liberty to sign judgment for the amount of the cost judge's/district judge's certificate on the said assessment together with costs to be assessed.'

(b)   Order that if the client issues an originating application in the High Court for an assessment of the costs within a fixed period the solicitor shall have leave to sign judgment for the amount to be found due on assessment or, if the client fails to institute proceedings within the requisite time, for the amount claimed.

(c)   Refer to a costs judge, with his and the parties' consent, as a referee under the County Courts Act 1984, s 5(1)(c).

(d)   Make a similar reference to a district judge for enquiry and report.

(e)   Adopt the course followed by the High Court in *Lumsden v Shipcote Land Co* [1906] 2 KB 433, CA where the registrar [*district judge*] ascertained the proper amount to be paid, just as in the case of any other action for work and labour done.

These orders are, of course, subject to the client satisfying the court that he still has the right to apply for an assessment (see the Solicitors Act 1974, s 70 at para [5.20]).

However, a frequent condition imposed by the court is that the full amount claimed by the solicitor be paid into court by the client. The solicitor should also consider applying for an interim payment (see para [6.10]).

REQUEST THE SOLICITOR TO HAVE HIS COSTS ASSESSED

[5.18]

Frequently a client asks the solicitor to have his costs assessed. Although a solicitor may issue an application to assess his own costs, it is an invitation that should be declined unless there are some very unusual circumstances. Section 70(9) provides that if a solicitor issues an application to assess his own costs, unless the client attends on the assessment or the costs judge certifies there are special circumstances, there will be no order for the costs of the proceedings. Another objection is that on the face of it the order made on the application cannot include an order for payment of the assessed costs by the client, but since the introduction of the Civil Procedure Rules the judges of the Supreme Court Costs Office (now the Senior Courts Costs Office) have included such an order in all final costs certificates whether the application was made by the solicitor or the client. Section 56.19 of the Costs Practice Direction states that a final certificate will include an order for payment unless the court provides otherwise. It is certainly a practical solution because otherwise if the client does not pay, the solicitor must institute separate proceedings for payment. Nevertheless, if a client wishes the costs to be assessed, the solicitor should advise him to make his own application. If, in spite of my advice, you do apply to assess your own costs, and it appears that many solicitors do, this is the order you will get:

[5.19]

CPR Schedule of costs: Precedent M

Order on Solicitor's Application for Assessment Under the Solicitor's Act 1974 Part III

Upon hearing . . . upon reading
. . .

IT IS ORDERED THAT

(1) A detailed assessment must be made of the bill dated [ ] delivered to the defendant by the claimant.

(2) If the defendant attends the detailed assessment the court making that assessment must also assess the costs of these proceedings and certify what is due to or from either party in respect of the bill and the costs of these proceedings.

(3) Until these proceedings are concluded the claimant must not commence or continue any proceedings against the defendant in respect of the bill mentioned above.

(4) Upon payment by the defendant of any sum certified as due to the claimant in these proceedings the claimant must deliver to the defendant all the documentation in the claimant's possession or control which belong to the defendant.

OBTAIN AN ORDER FOR THE COSTS TO BE ASSESSED

(a) Solicitors Act 1974, s 70

[5.20]

The Solicitors Act 1974, s 70 provides:

(i) Where the application is made within one month of the delivery of the bill the High Court shall make an unconditional order that the bill be taxed [*assessed*] and that no action be commenced on it until the taxation [*assessment*] is completed.

(ii) After one month has expired the court may make the same order, subject to such directions and such conditions as it thinks fit.

(iii) Where 12 months have expired from the delivery of the bill or after a judgment has been obtained or where the bill has been paid within 12 months of the application, no order shall be made except in special circumstances. Such a circumstance could be where a client has paid the bill (perhaps to enable his new solicitor to obtain the papers) reserving his right to assess the bill if so advised. In *Re Norman* (1886) 16 QBD 673, CA the Court of Appeal held that special circumstances are not limited to overcharging so extreme as to amount to fraud or where there has been undue pressure on the client. In *Kralj v Birkbeck Montague* (18 February 1988, unreported, CA) the Court of Appeal found special circumstances where the solicitors had dissuaded their client from having their costs taxed [*assessed*] and had charged her substantially more than was recovered between the parties, including such items as time spent with law reporters. In *A v BCD (a firm)* (5 June 1997, unreported), QBD, the court observed that the word used was 'special' and not 'exceptional'. In this case the client had exercised his right to request the solicitors to obtain a remuneration certificate but the assessment was not made until four days after the anniversary of the rendering of the bill. The court regarded this as a special circumstance even though (unfortunately) it was not exceptional. Any other course would devalue the remuneration certificate procedure (abolished from 11 August 2009) and discourage the use of it. The court also discounted the practice of a client paying a bill in full while unilaterally 'reserving the right' to have the bill assessed. Although the solicitor could, by agreement in return for payment, waive the right to resist an order for taxation [*assessment*] out of time, the most the client could do is to pay under protest and deploy the protest as a special circumstance if possible. More recently, the court held in *Arrowfield Services v BP Collings* SCCO Case No 15 of 2003 that it is difficult to conceive of a more powerful special circumstance for assessing a bill out of time than where the solicitor has agreed to such an assessment, because by his agreement that the assessment should take place, he has apparently agreed that the protection given to him by the time limits should not apply. In *Kundrath (Silvia) v Harry Kwatia & Gooding (a firm)* [2004] EWHC 2852 (QB), [2004] All ER (D) 181 (Dec) when the client queried the solicitors' bill and requested that it be taxed pursuant to the Solicitors Act 1974, s 70 the solicitors replied that it was for the client to apply for assessment and, astonishingly, that because a month had passed since they had delivered the bill, any order for assessment would be subject to her paying 40% of it into court. Eleven months after delivery of the bill the solicitors served a statutory demand for payment. The court held that the purpose of the letter was to induce payment. It was not merely inaccurate and a misrepresentation, but, given the inequality of the parties, exerted such pressure that it amounted to special circumstances justifying an assessment of costs, despite the client's delay.

(iv) The court has no power to order an assessment of an application by the party chargeable with the bill after the expiration of 12 months from the payment of the bill. It is important to remember that this provision also affects third parties liable to meet the solicitor's bill to his client, such as mortgagors and lessors. This cannot be circumvented by resort to the inherent jurisdiction of the court: *Harrison v Tew* [1990] 2 AC 523, HL, where the House of Lords held that the Solicitors Act 1974, s 70(4), displaced the court's inherent jurisdiction to order the taxation [*assessment*] of a solicitor's bill of costs in cases where the application to tax [*assess*] had been made more than a year after the bill had been paid. The court said the claimants would have had a more attractive-looking case if it had been made to appear that, in the absence of inherent jurisdiction, a client who had been grossly overcharged would have no remedy once he had been careless or unfortunate enough to fall foul of the 12-month limit. However in some cases the solicitor would have deducted his costs from the money received on the client's behalf, in which case the client could sue under the ordinary jurisdiction described in *Re Park* (1889) 41 Ch D 326, CA. In some other cases the client could, by making a complaint, set in motion disciplinary proceedings. While the onus of proof would lie on the complainant, the bill could be referred to the costs judge and the court could order a refund in appropriate cases. In *Re Metal Distributors (UK) Ltd* [2004] EWHC 2535 (Ch), [2004] All ER (D) 486 (Jul) it was held that the refusal of solicitors to provide a breakdown of their costs, whether or not it this was good client management, did not amount to special circumstances justifying an application being made after the expiration of the 12-month period.

(v) In *A v BCD* (see above) the court held that, whether payment in full had been made under protest or not, s 70(4) put an absolute bar on obtaining an order for taxation after the expiration of 12 months after payment. However, in *Watts (Thomas) & Co (a firm) v Smith* [1998] 2 Costs LR 59, CA) the Court of Appeal held that even 12 months after payment all was not lost. Where the solicitors sued for their costs they could not simply ask the court, without any further investigation, to underwrite the amount they had chosen to claim. In such a case where solicitors are applying for payment of their bill, the situation is analogous to one in which a claimant is applying for an unquantified sum which has to be quantified by a judicial process before judgment can be awarded for the appropriate amount. This is common in damages claims. Judgment for damages to be assessed is a very common form of order under an application for summary judgment. In a quantum meruit claim for work done, the benefit of which has been obtained under a contract where the contract sum had not been agreed, there may be an order for judgment to be entered for the claimant with the quantum to be assessed. If the court is to be asked to make an order for payment by the client of the amount claimed by the solicitors, a process of judicial assessment must first take place. A costs judge should carry out the judicial assessment. It is the costs judges who have the requisite expertise for that purpose. The court should not simply leave the client liable to pay the sum the solicitors have chosen, perhaps rightly chosen, but which has not been tested, to include in their bills. The defendant should have leave to defend by making representations on quantum as to the amount claimed in the solicitor's bill. In *Watts* the court ordered that the amount that ought to be paid by the defendant client to the claimant's solicitors was to be assessed by a costs judge and judgment entered for the amount so assessed. *Turner & Co (a firm) v O Palomo SA* [1999] 4 All ER 353, CA was an attempt to obtain a declaration that *Watts* was wrongly decided. It backfired. The court confirmed the decision and held that the prohibition of a detailed assessment in s 70 did not take away the need for a solicitor suing for his fees to prove that they were reasonable if challenged, in the absence of any express agreement as to what they should be. If the hourly rate is agreed the solicitor must still prove the reasonableness of the hours spent. Although the procedure provided by the Act is convenient and advantageous for the client, perhaps for both parties, it does not take away the client's common law rights to raise the unreasonable amount of the charges as a defence if the solicitor sues on his bill. The bill was ordered to be sent for assessment (but not for detailed assessment) by a costs judge.

(vi)   Where funds are transferred by a solicitor from the account of an estate into his office account in satisfaction of his bill, the account is paid for the purposes of s 70(4) when the payers know and consent to the transfer: *Gough v Chivers & Jordan (a firm)* [1996] 26 LS Gaz R 20, CA.

(b) Application

[5.21]

The application is under the Solicitors Act 1974, s 70 and is made by using the claim form in accordance with CPR Part 8 if it is an originating application or CPR Part 23 in existing proceedings. *Szekeres v Alan Smeath & Co* [2005] EWHC 1733 (Ch), [2005] 4 Costs LR 707, [2005] 32 LS Gaz R 31 demonstrated that the court is concerned with substance not form. Although there were defects in the claim form seeking the detailed assessment of eight bills of costs it had been sufficient to commence the proceedings within one month: its effect had been to convey to the solicitor the message that the client had wanted the bills to be assessed within the statutory period. Accordingly the costs judge had been in error by refusing to make an order for detailed assessment of the bills because of the formal deficiencies. Part III of the Solicitors Act 1974 was not affected by the Civil Procedure Rules and it still refers to 'taxations', although CPR Rules 48.8 and 48.10 prescribing the procedure uses the word 'assessment' and the practice is now to refer to 'Solicitors Act assessments'.

(c) Application in the county court

(i)   Jurisdiction

[5.22]

Under the provisions of the Solicitors Act 1974, s 69(3) and (4), where a solicitor's bill of costs relates wholly or partly to contentious business done in a county court and the amount of the bill does not exceed £5,000, then the powers of the court relating to assessment of the solicitor's bill under the Solicitors Act 1974, ss 70 and 71 may be exercised and performed by the county court. Otherwise the assessment must be in the Supreme Court Costs Office (now the Senior Courts Costs Office). The fact that the solicitor has applied for a charging order under s 73 of the Solicitors Act 1974 does not disapply the jurisdictional provisions of s 69 (*Jones v Twinsectra Ltd* [2002] EWCA Civ 668, [2002] All ER (D) 87 (Apr)).

By CCR Order 49, r 18 an application under s 69(3) may be heard and determined by a district judge. The proceedings must be brought in a county court in which part of the work was done.

(ii) Limit

[5.23]

Unless the solicitor and client have entered into a written agreement pursuant to CPR Rule 48.8(1A) expressly permitting payment to a solicitor of an amount of costs greater than that which the client could have recovered from another party in the proceedings, the Solicitors Act 1974, s 74(3), limits the solicitor's entitlement to that amount.

(d) Precedent originating application by client for Solicitors Act assessment

[5.24]

Details of claim

The claimant seeks an order that the bill of charges and disbursements delivered to the claimant by the defendants be referred to a costs judge to be assessed and that the defendant give credit for all sums of money received by him on account of the claimant, and that he refund anything that on such assessment may appear to have been overpaid.

And it is further ordered that the costs judge do assess the costs of the assessment, and certify what is due to or from either party in respect of the bill and of the costs of the assessment.

And it is further ordered that the solicitors do not prosecute or continue to prosecute any action against the claimant in respect of the said bill pending the reference.

And it is further ordered upon payment by the claimant of anything that may appear to be due to the defendants, the defendants deliver up to the claimant or as he may direction all deeds, books, papers, and writings, in the defendants' possession, custody, or power, belonging to the claimant.

Statement of truth

(e) Precedent order on client's application for detailed assessment of solicitor's bill (CPR Schedule of Costs Precedent L)

[5.25]

CPR Schedule of costs: Precedent L

Order on Client's Application for Detailed Assessment of Solicitor's Bill

DATED the [DATE]
IN THE HIGH COURT OF JUSTICE   **[Claim No]**

[DIVISION]
[JUDGE TYPE] [JUDGE NAME]

[CLAIMANT]

BETWEEN: **Claimant**

– and –

[DEFENDANT]

Defendant

UPON THE APPLICATION OF THE PARTY
[the parties and their representatives who attended]
AND UPON HEARING
AND UPON READING the documents on the Court File

(1)   A detailed assessment must be made of the bill dated [
] delivered to the claimant by the   defendant

(2)   On making the detailed assessment, the court must also assess the costs of these proceedings and certify what is due to or from either party in respect of the bill and the costs of these proceedings.

(3)   Until these proceedings are concluded the defendant must not commence or continue any proceedings against the claimant in respect of the bill mentioned above.

(4)   Upon payment by the claimant of any sum certified as due to the defendant in these proceedings the defendant must deliver to the claimant all the documentation in the defendant's possession or control which belong to the claimant.

(f) Detailed assessment

[5.26]

CPR Rule 48.8: Basis of detailed assessment of solicitor and client costs

(1)   This rule applies to every assessment of a solicitor's bill to his client except a bill which is to be paid out of the Community Legal Service Fund under the Legal Aid Act 1988 or the Access to Justice Act 1999.

(1A)   Section 74 (3) of the Solicitors Act 1974 applies unless the solicitor and client have entered into a written agreement which expressly permits payment to the solicitor of an amount of costs greater than that which the client could have recovered from another party to the proceedings.

(2)   Subject to paragraph (1A), costs are to be assessed on the indemnity basis but are to be presumed—

    (a)   to have been reasonably incurred if they were incurred with the express or implied approval of the client;

    (b)   to be reasonable in amount if their amount was expressly or impliedly approved by the client;

    (c)   to have been unreasonably incurred if—

        (i)   they are of an unusual nature or amount; and

        (ii)   the solicitor did not tell his client that as a result he might not recover all of them from the other party.

The remainder of this section concerns CFAs and is at para [44.54].

[5.27]

CPD Section 54 Basis of detailed assessment of solicitor and client costs: Rule 48.8

54.1   A client and his solicitor may agree whatever terms they consider appropriate about the payment of the solicitor's charges for his services. If however, the costs are of an unusual nature (either in amount or in the type of costs incurred) those costs will be presumed to have been unreasonably incurred unless the solicitor satisfies the court that he informed the client that they were unusual and, where the costs relate to litigation, that he informed the client they might not be allowed on an assessment of costs between the parties. That information must have been given to the client before the costs were incurred.

54.2

> (1)   Costs as between a solicitor and client are assessed on the indemnity basis as defined by rule 44.4.
>
> (2)   Attention is drawn to the presumptions set out in rule 48.8(2). These presumptions may be rebutted by evidence to the contrary.

54.3   Rule 48.10 and Section 56 of this Practice Direction deal with the procedure to be followed for obtaining the assessment of a solicitor's bill pursuant to an order under Part III of the Solicitors Act 1974.

54.4   If a party fails to comply with the requirements of rule 48.10 concerning the service of a breakdown of costs or points of dispute, any other party may apply to the court in which the detailed assessment hearing should take place for an order requiring compliance with rule 48.10. If the court makes such an order, it may—

> (a)   make it subject to conditions including a condition to pay a sum of money into court; and
>
> (b)   specify the consequences of failure to comply with the order or a condition.

The remainder of this section concerns CFAs and is at para [44.55].

(g) Assessment procedure

[5.28]

CPR Rule 48.10: Assessment procedure

(1)   This rule sets out the procedure to be followed where the court has made an order under Part III of the Solicitors Act 1974 for the assessment of costs payable to a solicitor by his client.

(2)   The solicitor must serve a breakdown of costs within 28 days of the order for costs to be assessed.

(3)   The client must serve points of dispute within 14 days after service on him of the breakdown of costs.

(4)   If the solicitor wishes to serve a reply, he must do so within 14 days of service on him of the points of dispute.

(5)   Either party may file a request for a hearing date—

> (a)   after points of dispute have been served; but
>
> (b)   no later than 3 months after the date of the order for the costs to be assessed.

(6)   This procedure applies subject to any contrary order made by the court.

[5.29]

CPD Section 56 Procedure on Assessment of Solicitor and Client Costs: CPR Rule 48.10

56.1   The paragraphs in this section apply to orders made under Part III of the Solicitors Act 1974 for the assessment of costs. In these paragraphs 'client' includes any person entitled to make an application under Part III of that Act.

56.2   The procedure for obtaining an order under Part III of the Solicitors Act 1974 is by the alternative procedure for claims under Part 8, as modified by rule 67.3 and the Practice Direction supplementing Part 67. Precedent J of the Schedule of Costs Precedents annexed to this Practice Direction is a model form of claim form. The application must be accompanied by the bill or bills in respect of which assessment is sought, and, if the claim concerns a conditional fee agreement, a copy of that agreement. If the original bill is not available a copy will suffice.

56.3   Model forms of order, which the court may make, are set out in Precedents K, L and M of the Schedule of Costs Precedents annexed to this Practice Direction.

56.4   Attention is drawn to the time limits within which the required steps must be taken: ie the solicitor must serve a breakdown of costs within 28 days of the order for costs to be assessed, the client must serve points of dispute within 14 days after service on him of the breakdown, and any reply must be served within 14 days of service of the points of dispute.

56.5   The breakdown of costs referred to in rule 48.10 is a document which contains the following information:

    (a)   details of the work done under each of the bills sent for assessment; and

    (b)   in applications under Section 70 of the Solicitors Act 1974, an account showing money received by the solicitor to the credit of the client and sums paid out of that money on behalf of the client but not payments out which were made in satisfaction of the bill or of any items which are claimed in the bill.

56.6   Precedent P of the Schedule of Costs Precedents annexed to this Practice Direction is a model form of breakdown of costs. A party who is required to serve a breakdown of costs must also serve—

    (1)   copies of the fee notes of counsel and of any expert in respect of fees claimed in the breakdown, and

    (2)   written evidence as to any other disbursement which is claimed in the breakdown and which exceeds £250.

56.7   The provisions relating to default costs certificates (rule 47.11) do not apply to cases to which rule 48.10 applies.

56.8   Points of dispute should, as far as practicable, be in the form complying with paragraphs 35.1 to 35.7.

56.9   The time for requesting a detailed assessment hearing is within 3 months after the date of the order for the costs to be assessed.

56.10   The form of request for a hearing date must be in Form N258C. The request must be accompanied by copies of—

    (a)   the order sending the bill or bills for assessment;

    (b)   the bill or bills sent for assessment;

    (c)   the solicitor's breakdown of costs and any invoices or accounts served with that breakdown;

    (d)   a copy of the points of dispute, annotated as necessary in order to show which items have been agreed and their value and to show which items remain in dispute;

(e)   as many copies of the points of dispute so annotated as there are other parties to the proceedings to whom the court should give details of the assessment hearing requested;

(f)   a copy of any replies served;

(g)   a statement signed by the party filing the request or his legal representative giving the names and addresses for service of all parties to the proceedings.

56.11   The request must include an estimate of the length of time the detailed assessment hearing will take.

56.12   On receipt of the request for a detailed assessment hearing the court will fix a date for the hearing or if the costs judge or district judge so decides, will give directions or fix a date for a preliminary appointment.

56.13

(1)   The court will give at least 14 days notice of the time and place of the detailed assessment hearing to every person named in the statement referred to in paragraph 56.10(g) above.

(2)   The court will when giving notice, give all parties other than the party who requested the hearing a copy of the points of dispute annotated by the party requesting the hearing in compliance with paragraph 56.10(e) above.

(3)   Attention is drawn to rule 47.14(6) and (7): apart from the solicitor whose bill it is, only those parties who have served points of dispute may be heard on the detailed assessment unless the court gives permission, and only items specified in the points of dispute may be raised unless the court gives permission.

56.14

(1)   If a party wishes to vary his breakdown of costs, points of dispute or reply, an amended or supplementary document must be filed with the court and copies of it must be served on all other relevant parties.

(2)   Permission is not required to vary a breakdown of costs, points of dispute or a reply but the court may disallow the variation or permit it only upon conditions, including conditions as to the payment of any costs caused or wasted by the variation.

56.15   Unless the court directs otherwise the solicitor must file with the court the papers in support of the bill not less than 7 days before the date for the detailed assessment hearing and not more than 14 days before that date.

56.16   Once the detailed assessment hearing has ended it is the responsibility of the legal representative appearing for the solicitor or, as the case may be, the solicitor in person to remove the papers filed in support of the bill.

56.17

(1)   Attention is drawn to rule 47.15 (power to issue an interim certificate).

(2)   If, in the course of a detailed assessment hearing of a solicitor's bill to his client, it appears to the costs judge or district judge that in any event the solicitor will be liable in connection with that bill to pay money to the client, he may issue an interim certificate specifying an amount which in his opinion is payable by the solicitor to his client. Such a certificate will include an order to pay the sum it certifies unless the court orders otherwise.

56.18

(1)   Attention is drawn to rule 47.16 which requires the solicitor to file a completed bill within 14 days after the end of the detailed

assessment hearing. The court may dispense with the requirement to file a completed bill.

    (2)   After the detailed assessment hearing is concluded the court will—

        (a)   complete the court copy of the bill so as to show the amount allowed;

        (b)   determine the result of the cash account;

        (c)   award the costs of the detailed assessment hearing in accordance with Section 70(8) of the Solicitors Act 1974; and

        (d)   issue a final costs certificate showing the amount due following the detailed assessment hearing.

56.19   A final costs certificate will include an order to pay the sum it certifies unless the court orders otherwise.

(h) Costs of the assessment

[5.30]

The costs of the assessment are paid according to the outcome. If one-fifth of the amount of the bill is disallowed, the solicitor pays the costs, if not, the party chargeable pays (Solicitors Act 1974, s 70(9)). With this provision in mind the party chargeable may think it prudent to exercise his right when obtaining an order for assessment to limit the order to the profit costs only if there are substantial disbursements which he does not wish to challenge or, conversely, limited to counsel's or expert's fees if these are all that he wishes to challenge (s 70(6)). If non-contentious costs are reduced by more than half, the costs officer is under an obligation to refer the matter to the Law Society by the Solicitors' (Non-Contentious Business) Remuneration Order 1994, art 5. Rule 10.01 of the Solicitors' Code of Conduct 2007 prescribes: 'You must not use your position to take unfair advantage of anyone either for your own benefit or for another person's benefit'. This replaces the provision that 'A solicitor must not take unfair advantage of the client by overcharging for work done or to be done' in para 14.12, the Law Society's *Guide to the Professional Conduct of Solicitors 1999*). Although less specific, the new rule will doubtless be regarded as having the same effect.

(i) Gross sum bills

[5.31]

Where the bill being assessed is a gross sum bill which has not been replaced by a detailed bill following a request by the client under the Solicitors Act 1974, s 69(3) the costs officer may nevertheless for the purposes of the assessment direct the solicitor to provide a detailed breakdown of his bill showing how the gross sum is calculated or justified. It is important to appreciate that such a breakdown is for the purposes of the assessment only and that it is still the original gross sum bill delivered to the client which is being assessed and which at the end of the assessment will be either upheld or reduced. Accordingly, although the detailed breakdown may quite properly justify a figure considerably higher than the amount of the gross sum bill, it is of assistance only in considering the reasonableness of the gross sum bill and is of no relevance to the question of whether or not the gross sum bill has been reduced by one-fifth.

(j) Order made in proceedings

[5.32]

Many orders for solicitor and client costs to be assessed arise after the solicitors have commenced proceedings for their recovery, in either the High Court or the county court and the defence merely challenges the amount of the solicitor's bill. The procedure is set out in para [5.16].

SHODDY WORK

[5.33]

Schedule 1A inserted into the Solicitors Act 1974 by the Courts and Legal Services Act 1990 reads as follows (the text was repealed by the Legal Services Act 2007, from a date to be appointed):

[5.34]

SCHEDULE 1A INADEQUATE PROFESSIONAL SERVICES

Circumstances in which Council's powers may be exercised

1

(1)   The Council may take any of the steps mentioned in paragraph 2 ('the steps') with respect to a solicitor where it appears to them that the professional services provided by him in connection with any matter in which he or his firm have been instructed by a client have, in any respect, not been of the quality which it is reasonable to expect of him as a solicitor.

(2)   The Council shall not take any of the steps unless they are satisfied that in all the circumstances of the case it is appropriate to do so.

(3)   In determining in any case whether it is appropriate to take any of the steps, the Council may—

    (a)   have regard to the existence of any remedy which it is reasonable to expect to be available to the client in civil proceedings; and

    (b)   where proceedings seeking any such remedy have not been begun by him, have regard to whether it is reasonable to expect him to begin them.

[5.35]

2 **Directions which may be given**

(1)   The steps are—

    (a)   determining that the costs to which the solicitor is entitled in respect of his services ('the costs') are to be limited to such amount as may be specified in the determination and directing him to comply, or to secure compliance, with such one or more of the permitted requirements as appear to the Council to be necessary in order for effect to be given to their determination;

    (b)   directing him to secure the rectification, at his expense or at that of his firm, of any such error, omission or other deficiency arising in connection with the matter in question as they may specify;

(c)   directing him to pay such compensation to the client as the Council sees fit to specify in the direction;

(d)   directing him to take, at his expense or at that of his firm, such other action in the interests of the client as they may specify.

(2)   The 'permitted requirements' are—

(a)   that the whole or part of any amount already paid by or on behalf of the client in respect of the costs be refunded;

(b)   that the whole or part of the costs be remitted;

(c)   that the right to recover the costs be waived, whether wholly or to any specified extent.

(3)   The power of the Council to take any such steps is not confined to cases where the client may have a cause of action against the solicitor for negligence.

[5.36]

3 Compensation

(1)   The amount specified in a direction by virtue of paragraph 2(1)(c) shall not exceed £5,000.

(2)   The Secretary of State may by order made by statutory instrument amend sub-paragraph (1) by substituting for the sum of £1,000 such other sum as he considers appropriate.

(3)   Before making any such order the Secretary of State shall consult the Law Society.

(4)   Any statutory instrument made under this paragraph shall be subject to annulment in pursuance of a resolution of either House of Parliament.

[5.37]

4 Taxation of costs

(1)   Where the Council have given a direction under paragraph 2(1)(a), then—

(a)   for the purposes of any taxation of a bill covering the costs, the amount charged by the bill in respect of them shall be deemed to be limited to the amount specified in the determination; and

(b)   where a bill covering the costs has not been taxed, the client shall, for the purposes of their recovery (by whatever means and notwithstanding any statutory provision or agreement) be deemed to be liable to pay in respect of them only the amount specified in the determination.

(2)   Where a bill covering the costs has been taxed, the direction shall, so far as it relates to the costs, cease to have effect.

[5.38]

5 Failure to comply with direction

(1)   If a solicitor fails to comply with a direction given under this Schedule, any person may make a complaint in respect of that failure to the Tribunal; but no other proceedings whatever shall be brought in respect of it.

(2)   On the hearing of such a complaint the Tribunal may, if it thinks fit (and whether or not it makes any order under section 47(2)), direct that the direction be treated, for the purpose of enforcement, as if it were contained in an order made by the High Court.

[5.39]

6 Fees

(1)   The Council may, by regulations made with the concurrence of the Secretary of State and the Master of the Rolls, make provision for the payment, by any client with respect to whom the Council are asked to consider whether to take any of the steps, of such fee as may be prescribed.

(2)   The regulations may provide for the exemption of such classes of client as may be prescribed.

(3)   Where a client pays the prescribed fee it shall be repaid to him if the Council take any of the steps in the matter with respect to which the fee was paid.

(4)   In this paragraph 'prescribed' means prescribed by the regulations.

[5.40]

7 Costs

Where the Council take any of the steps with respect to a solicitor they may also direct him to pay to the Council—

(a)   the amount of the fee payable by the Council to the client under paragraph 6(3); and

(b)   an amount which is calculated by the Council as the cost to them of dealing with the complaint, or which in their opinion represents a reasonable contribution towards that cost.

[5.41]

8 Duty of tribunal

Where the Tribunal—

(a)   is considering, or has considered, an application or complaint with respect to a solicitor; and

(b)   is of the opinion that the Council should consider whether to take any of the steps with respect to that solicitor, it shall inform the Council.

[5.42]

9

The Council's powers under this Schedule are exercisable in relation to a person even though his name has been removed from, or struck off, the roll and references to a solicitor in this Schedule, so far as they relate to the exercise of those powers, shall be construed accordingly.

[5.43]

How it works in practice is that the Council of the Law Society has delegated its disciplinary powers to the Legal Complaints Service (LCS). Accordingly all references in the Schedule to 'the Council' may in practice be regarded as references to the LCS. When the LCS receives a complaint of shoddy work the solicitor is required to produce his file, which is considered by two report writers. If they disagree, the opinion of a third report writer is obtained. Where shoddy work is found, the solicitor's observations are invited and he can request further consideration by a review panel of practising solicitors. If it is decided that there is no evidence of shoddy work, the complainant may require the file to be referred to the Compliance and Supervision Committee. If the Compliance and Supervision Committee agree that there is no evidence of shoddy work, that is the end of the matter, subject to the right of complaint to the Legal Services Ombudsman. If an allegation of shoddy work is substantiated, the matter goes before the Adjudication Committee, which may take one or more of the following actions:

(a)   Limit the costs which the solicitor may recover for the services, and require a refund of all or part of the costs.

(b)   Require the solicitor to put right any error, omission or deficiency caused by the shoddy work.

(c)   Direct the solicitor to pay compensation to the client of up to £1,000.

(d)   Direct the solicitor to take some other action in the interests of the client.

(e)   Direct the solicitor to pay to the Council of the Law Society any fee repaid to the complainant on the filing of the complaint.

(f)   Direct the solicitor to pay the Council of the Law Society a sum representing the costs of dealing with the complaint, or a contribution towards those costs.

DISPUTING COUNSEL'S FEES

(a) Solicitor's duty to challenge

[5.44]

The solicitor has a duty to his client to challenge any counsel's fee which he considers to be unreasonable. Paragraph 8 of the Terms of Work agreed by the Bar Council and The Law Society provides that any challenge by a solicitor to counsel's fees giving rise to an issue of competence or a dispute on quantum must be made within three months of the receipt by the solicitor of the itemised fee note.

(b) Joint tribunal

[5.45]

Disputes as to counsel's fees may be referred to a joint tribunal consisting of a member of the Council of the Law Society and a Queen's Counsel nominated respectively by the President of the Law Society and the Chairman of the Bar. It is an informal body which may or may not involve an oral hearing. The parties are required to undertake to abide by the decision and failure to comply with an award is unbefitting conduct. Surprisingly the new Code does not reproduce the previous provision: 'Except in legal aid cases, solicitors are personally liable as a matter of professional conduct for the payment of counsel's proper fees, whether or not they have been placed in funds by the client.'

As the etiquette of the Bar precludes suing a solicitor for unpaid fees, the reporting of a defaulting solicitor for professional misconduct to the Law Society is a valuable recourse for the Bar and it is to be hoped that the omission was not intended to be of any significance.

(c) Solicitors Act assessment

[5.46]

Section 67 of the Solicitors Act 1974 also prescribes that counsel's fees are to be paid before assessment is completed. Under the Code of Conduct of the Bar 1990, brief fees need no longer have to be agreed in advance or marked on the brief, but a prudent solicitor will agree counsel's brief and refresher fees in advance, not only with counsel but also with his client.

(d) Last-minute settlements

[5.47]

Last-minute settlements are another area of difficulty. Where the brief has been delivered, counsel is entitled to the full fee. However, counsel may accept no fee, or less than the agreed fee and in these circumstances the solicitor has a duty to seek to renegotiate it. If the solicitor fails to seek to renegotiate the fee he is bound to pay counsel's fee in full but will not be able to recover from his client any reduction of the fee made by the court on a Solicitors Act assessment.

CANCELLATION

[5.48]

Since 1 October 2008 the seven day cooling-off period for contracts made at a consumer's home or place of work has been extended to legal services by the Cancellation of Contracts made in a Consumer's Home or Place of Work etc Regulations 2008, SI 2008/1816. This applies even where the retainer is entered into at the solicitor's office following a visit to the client's home or place of work. Where the regulations apply, Regulation 7(5) requires the client to be notified in writing of the right to cancel 'set out in a separate box with the heading *Notice of the Right to Cancel*'. Unlike termination of the retainer by the client, cancellation has the effect of the retainer being treated as if it had never existed which may be a deterrent to a solicitor carrying out any work or making any disbursement during the cooling off period. However in a case of urgency the client care letter may include a provision that the client accepts liability for any costs or disbursements incurred during the cooling off period.

CHAPTER 6

RECOVERY OF COSTS

PROCEEDINGS

(a) Prerequisites

(i) Final bill

[6.1]

It is essential that a final bill in the form and content described in Chapter 3 has been delivered. Where there has been a series of interim bills on account no proceedings may be commenced until the delivery of a final statute bill. This bill should be for the entirety of the work done and disbursements incurred throughout, either at the agreed charging rate or the direct cost with an appropriate mark-up in light of all the factors including the outcome of the matter, giving credit for payments received.

(ii) Elapse of one month

[6.2]

One month must have elapsed since the delivery of the bill unless the party chargeable is about to: quit England and Wales; to become bankrupt or to compound with his creditors or do any other act which tends to prevent or delay the solicitor obtaining payment. In these circumstances the solicitor can seek leave to issue proceedings within a month (Solicitors Act 1974, s 69(1)). Service of a statutory demand for payment of a solicitor's costs does not constitute the bringing of an action for the purposes of s 69(1) and may therefore be served within a month without leave. If the statutory demand is not complied with within 21 days of service the solicitor may present a bankruptcy petition, but because this is an action within the meaning of s 69, a petition may not be issued within a month without leave (*Re A Debtor (No 88 of 1991)* [1993] Ch 286, [1992] 4 All ER 301).

(iii) No application or order for a detailed assessment

[6.3]

The client must not have either made an application to the court for a detailed assessment of the costs within one month of delivery of the bill or obtained an order for the bill to be assessed, in either of which events no action may be commenced on the bill or proceeded with until the assessment is completed: Solicitors Act 1974, s 70(1), (2).

(iv) Solicitors' Code of Conduct 2007 Rule 2.08 Information on challenging a bill

[6.4]

For Complaints handling see paras [5.4]-[5.5].

(v) Limitation Act 1980

[6.5]

Proceedings must be commenced within six years from the day after the cause of action arose (*Marren v Dawson Bentley & Co Ltd* [1961] 2 QB 135, [1961] 2 All ER 270) which is when the solicitor becomes entitled to his fees under the retainer whether or not they have been quantified and irrespective of the requirement that one month must have expired since the bill was delivered before proceedings may be commenced unless the debt has been acknowledged since the cause of action arose. A solicitor's lien on the other hand cannot become statute barred (*Higgins v Scott* (1831) 2 B & Ad 413).

[6.6]

For entitled third parties see para [5.7].

(b) High Court or county court?

[6.7]

The Practice Direction supplementing CPR Part 7 provides that proceedings may be started in either the High Court or a county court, except that in order to qualify for the High Court a claim must exceed £25,000. Proceedings which include a claim for damages in respect of personal injuries must not be started in the High Court unless the value of the claim is £50,000 or more.

CPR Rule 26.2 provides that, where the defendant is an individual, if a defence is filed the court will transfer the proceedings to the defendant's home court which, in High Court proceedings, means the district registry for the district in which the defendant's address for service is situated, and in the county court, the court whose jurisdiction covers the defendant's address for service.

(c) Precedent statement of case

[6.8]

Claim form N1 CPR Part 7

The claimant's claim is for work done and disbursements incurred as a solicitor on behalf of the defendant at the defendant's request for which [a bill] [bills] of costs [has] [have] been delivered to the defendant pursuant to the provisions of the Solicitors Act 1974.

Particulars

20 June 2009	To bill of costs number 1234
re Fagin v Yourself	£94,250
Less paid on account	£30,000
	£64,250

AND the claimant claims:

1.   £64,250.

2.   Interest pursuant to [Section 35A of the Supreme Court (now Senior Courts) Act 1981] [Section 69 of the County Courts Act 1984] on the said sum of £64,250 to the date hereof amounting to £ [ ] being interest at the rate of [not to exceed the amount payable on judgment debts] per annum from 20 June 2009 to the date of issue hereof.

3.   Continuing interest pursuant to [Section 35A of the Supreme Court (now Senior Courts) Act 1981] [Section 69 of the County Courts Act 1984] on the said sum of £ [ ] at the rate of [not to exceed the rate payable on judgment debts] per annum being a daily rate of £ [ ], from the date of issue hereof until judgment or sooner payment.

The statement that a bill or bills have been delivered 'pursuant to the provisions of the Solicitors Act 1974', refers to the prerequisites to instituting proceedings set out at the beginning of this chapter.

(d) Non-contentious and contentious business agreements

[6.9]

The main difference between a solicitor relying on a non-contentious and a contentious business agreement is that he must obtain the permission of the court to enforce the latter. There is a view, to which I do not subscribe, that this provision precludes a solicitor who has entered into a contentious business agreement from suing for his costs without first applying for permission to enforce the agreement. The reason I disagree is that, in my view, it is only if the solicitor wishes to rely on the contentious business agreement that he needs permission to proceed. There is nothing to prevent the solicitor commencing proceedings in the usual way in the hope of obtaining judgment by default or a summary judgment. If, and only if, the matter is disputed and the solicitor wishes to rely on the contentious business agreement need he, at that stage, apply for permission to enforce it. I see no point in anticipating trouble by incurring the expense of obtaining permission to enforce an agreement until the need to rely on it arises. If the need should arise the solicitor can make an application in the proceedings for permission, similar to an application to come off the record.

(e) Interim payment

[6.10]

Where the client does not dispute liability but merely alleges that the charges are too high, for whatever reason, and therefore all that is in dispute is the amount of the costs, the solicitor should apply under CPR Rules 25.6 and 25.7

for an interim payment of the minimum amount he must eventually recover, even if the client were to succeed on all his objections to the bill. Disputes over quantum are often exercises in putting off the inevitable, and an order for an interim payment of a substantial amount has been known to result in the client deciding the outstanding balance was not worth incurring the expense of continuing to dispute it. The application should be supported by written evidence filed and served at least three days before the hearing. This should include an attempted quantification of all of the client's objections at their maximum and deducting these from the amount of the outstanding costs. The balance is the amount to be claimed as an interim payment.

(f) Interest

(i) Non-contentious

[6.11]

Article 5 of the Solicitors' (Non-Contentious Business) Remuneration Order 2009 provides:

[6.12]

5 Interest

(1) A solicitor may charge interest on the unpaid amount of his costs plus any paid disbursements and value added tax, subject to the remainder of this article.

(2) Where an entitlement to interest arises under paragraph (1), and subject to any agreement made between a solicitor and client, the period for which interest may be charged runs from one month after the date of delivery of a bill.

(3) Subject to any agreement made between a solicitor and client, the rate of interest must not exceed the rate for the time being payable on judgment debts.

(4) Interest charged under this article must be calculated, where applicable, by reference to—

    (a) the amount specified in a determination of costs by the Law Society under Schedule 1A to the Solicitors Act 1974;

    (b) the amount ascertained on taxation if an application has been made for the bill to be taxed.

[6.13]

See paragraphs [5.3] and [5.4] in Chapter 5 for details of the complaints information prescribed by rule 2.05 of the Solicitors' Code of Conduct 2007 since 1 March 2010.

(ii) Contentious

[6.14]

Although in contentious matters a solicitor has no statutory or professional duty to inform a client about his right to assessment, the Law Society strongly advises solicitors to do so before beginning recovery proceedings. This avoids confusion and may prevent the case being adjourned for an assessment. There is no right to claim interest. However, pursuant to the Supreme Court (now Senior Courts) Act 1981, s 35A, and the County Courts Act 1984, s 69(1), where proceedings are instituted, the court has power to award interest from the date when payment was due.

In addition, interest runs at the prescribed rate on judgment debts including all judgments in the county court since 1 November 1998. By these means interest may be recovered on contentious costs.

(g) Effect of writing off costs

[6.15]

In *Slatter v Ronaldsons (a firm)* SCCO Case No 2 of 2002, [2001] All ER (D) 251 (Dec), ChD the defendant solicitors had acted for the claimant in matrimonial proceedings for which they had outstanding costs. When the claimant became unemployed they concluded that it would be uneconomic to pursue him for the balance of their costs and accordingly 'wrote them off', obtaining the appropriate VAT refund. Subsequently the client instructed other solicitors who wrote to the defendants requesting delivery up of all relevant papers which the defendants refused to do, contending that they had a lien over the papers until their bills were discharged in full. The judge, on appeal, upheld the lien. The contractual liability to pay the balance of the bills survived their 'writing off' and there was no evidence that the claimant acted to his detriment entitling him to promissory estoppel, on the basis that the balance of the bills had been written off.

LIEN

[6.16]

Rule 2.03(1)(e) of the Solicitors Code of Conduct 2007 requires the solicitor to advise the client that there are circumstances where the solicitor may be entitled to exercise a lien for unpaid costs. I am not happy with the advice in paragraph 11 of the Guidance to the Solicitors Code of Conduct 2007 (para [2.4]):

> 'You should try to ensure the client's position is not prejudiced, . . . There may be circumstances where it is unreasonable to exercise a lien, for example, where the amount of the outstanding costs is small and the value or importance of the matter is very great.'

But, I always thought that the whole purpose of a lien was to prejudice the client so that they paid up, and that the very best sort of lien is where the value of the documents to the client is very great and the amount of costs they owe is by comparison very small! What on earth is the purpose of exercising a lien over documents a former client neither wants or needs?

(a) Acquisition of lien

(i) Retaining lien

[6.17]

A solicitor has, at common law, a general lien to retain any money, papers or other property belonging to his client which properly come into his possession until payment of his costs, whether or not the property was acquired in connection with the matter for which the costs were incurred. The solicitor may retain, until payment of his costs, property other than money to any value even if it greatly exceeds the amount due, but he cannot hold money in excess of the amount due. A solicitor is not entitled to sell property held under a lien or to transfer it into his ownership without an order from the court.

(ii) Property recovered

[6.18]

A solicitor also has at common law a particular lien on property recovered or preserved by him in litigation which extends to all costs incurred, both billed and unbilled. Unlike the general lien, a particular lien covers property not in the solicitor's possession and gives him an equitable right to have the property transferred into his possession.

(iii) Solicitors Act Charging Order

[6.19]

The lien on property recovered is in effect extended by the Solicitors Act 1974, s 73, which provides that any court in which a solicitor has been employed to prosecute or defend any suit, matter or proceeding may at any time:

(a)   declare the solicitor entitled to a charge on any property recovered or preserved through his instrumentality for his assessed costs in relation to that suit, matter or proceedings; and

(b)   make such orders for the assessment of those costs and for raising money to pay or for paying them out of the property recovered or preserved as the court thinks fit. In *Fairfold Properties Ltd v Exmouth Docks Co Ltd (No 2)* [1993] Ch 196, ChD the claimant, in proceedings in which they were substantially successful, obtained an order that the defendant should bear their costs. Before the costs were assessed the claimant had become a dormant company with no assets other than the order for costs. The claimant's solicitors now sought a charging order under s 73 of the Solicitors Act 1974 on any costs recoverable by the claimant from the defendant and, pending such recovery, a charge on the benefit of the order. The court had jurisdiction to make such an order. Although a charging order had necessarily, by virtue of s 73(1)(a) of the Act, to be expressed as one for the solicitors' assessed costs, the court was not bound to order that the costs in question be assessed as between solicitor and client. It seemed impossible that the between the parties costs could exceed the same costs assessed as between solicitor and client. Nevertheless, the judge gave liberty to the solicitors to apply for an order for their costs to be assessed.

A Solicitors Act Charging Order differs from a general lien in two particular ways. First, it applies to real as well as personal property and, second, it does not apply where the claim for costs is statute-barred. The application is made under the alternative procedure prescribed by CPR Part 8 and is made pursuant to RSC Order 106 which was preserved by Schedule 1 of the CPR. Here are the precedents:

1. Precedent application for Solicitor's Charging Order (RSC Order 106)

[6.20]

Claim Form N208 CPR Part 8

Details of claim

The claimant applies for an order that he shall have a charge upon [here specify the nature and amount of the property sought to be charged] for his costs, charges and expenses of this action and that in the meantime the [property or funds, or as may be] do stand charged as stated.

The grounds of the application are [here set out the facts on which the claim is based].

Statement of truth

---

2. Precedent Charging Order, solicitor's costs (RSC Order 106)

[6.21]

Upon hearing and upon reading the affidavit of, sworn the [ ] day of [ ] 20 [ ], and It is ordered that shall have a charge upon for his costs, charges, and expenses of this action.

Dated the [ ] day of [ ] 20 [ ].

(iv) Accounts rules

[6.22]

The Solicitors' Accounts Rules 1991 (Rule 29) specifically provide that nothing in those rules shall deprive a solicitor of any recourse or right, whether by way of lien, set off, counterclaim, charge or otherwise, against moneys standing to the credit of a client account.

(b) Loss of lien

[6.23]

A solicitor may lose his lien in the following ways:

(i) Security for costs

[6.24]

The Solicitors' (Non-Contentious Business) Remuneration Order 2009, art 4 provides that in non-contentious business a solicitor may take from his client security for the payment of any remuneration including the amount of any interest to which the solicitor may become entitled under art 5.

The Solicitors Act 1974, s 65(1) states: 'a solicitor may take security from his client for costs, to be ascertained by taxation [*assessment*] or otherwise, in respect of any contentious business to be done by him.' If a solicitor does take security from his client for costs this will preclude him from claiming a lien over subsequent money, property or documents in his possession unless that lien has been expressly reserved.

(ii) Payment into court

[6.25]

CPR 25.1(1)(*m*) provides that where the defendant to a claim for the recovery of personal property does not dispute the title of the party making the claim but claims to be entitled to retain the property by virtue of a lien, the court may make an order permitting the defendant to pay money into court pending the outcome of the proceedings and directing that if he does so, the property shall be given up to him.

(iii) Waiver

[6.26]

If at any stage the solicitor takes alternative security from a client with the intention of satisfying his claim for fees by this alternative means his lien will have been waived:

> 'Whether a lien is waived or not by taking a security depends upon the intention expressed or to be inferred from the position of the parties and all the circumstances of the case . . . It appears to me that in each case the question whether the lien is waived by taking security must be decided according to the particular circumstances. I do not mean to say that taking a security necessarily imports an abandonment of the lien; but if there are circumstances in the taking of the security which are inconsistent with the continuance of the old security, it is to be inferred that the solicitor intended to abandon his lien.'

(*Re Taylor, Stileman, and Underwood, Re ex p Payne Collier* [1891] 1 Ch 590, 60 LJ Ch 525, CA.)

From this and other authorities it is clear that if a solicitor takes security for costs generally and that security is inconsistent with his lien and the solicitor does not in so doing reserve the lien then, on the face of it, he will be taken to have abandoned it. In *A v B* [1984] 1 All ER 265, QBD, [1983] Com LR 226(Comm Ct) it was held that the solicitors' arrest of a vessel owned by their clients was in no way inconsistent with their lien and that no intention to waive the lien could be inferred from the fact of that arrest. Where the clients executed a legal charge over their property in favour of their solicitors securing their costs of a legal action it was not inconsistent with a possessory lien or a solicitor's right to apply for a charge on the sum recovered under the terms of the settlement. It is at least seriously arguable that the grant of the legal charge is not inconsistent or incompatible with the exercise by the claimant of the right to apply for a charge under s 73 of the Solicitors Act 1974 and that therefore the taking of the charge did not amount to a waiver: *Clifford Harris & Co (a firm) v Solland International Ltd* [2004] EWHC 2488 (ChD), [2004] All ER (D) 40 (Nov).

(iv)   Discharge of the retainer

1.   Discharge by client

[6.27]

If the retainer is terminated by the client other than for misconduct by the solicitor, the solicitor's lien is virtually absolute. He cannot be required to hand over or produce for inspection any papers in his possession and he is entitled to keep them until his costs have been paid (*Abse (Leo) & Cohen v Evan G Jones (Builders) Ltd* (1984) 128 Sol Jo 317, [1984] LS Gaz R 1684, CA).

2.   Discharge by solicitor

[6.28]

(a) *Serving the interests of justice.* Where during litigation a solicitor discharges himself, the usual practice of the court is to order him to hand over the client's papers to the new solicitor against an undertaking by the new solicitor to preserve the lien of the original solicitor, even if that renders the lien worthless. However, this is not automatic and the court exercises its discretion. In approaching the matter, the overriding principle is that the order made should be that which would best serve, or at least not frustrate, the interests of justice. The principle that a litigant should not be deprived of material relevant to the conduct of his case and so driven from the judgment seat is to be weighed against the principle that litigation should be conducted with due regard to the interests of the court's own officers, who should not be left without payment for what was justly due to them. Where the solicitors have behaved impeccably and of whose conduct there has been no criticism, whilst their clients, without any excuse, have not paid the costs and there is a default judgment against them, the balance of hardship would be far greater on the solicitors if the lien were not enforced, because they would then probably recover nothing, whereas it was open to the clients to preserve their position by paying the solicitor's costs (*A v B*, para [6.26]).

(b) *Undertakings.* Unless there are exceptional circumstances the fact that the solicitors had reasonable cause to discharge themselves would not justify modifying the overriding principle that a solicitor discharging himself should not be allowed to exert his lien so as to interfere with the course of justice and he has therefore only a qualified lien on the papers. He is, however, entitled to the following undertakings from the new solicitors:

(i)   To hold all papers and documents delivered subject to his lien for costs.
(ii)   To afford him reasonable access to the papers and documents for the purpose of preparing his bill of costs.
(iii)   To prosecute or defend the action in an active manner.
(iv)   To redeliver the papers and documents after the conclusion of the action (*Gamlen Chemical Co (UK) Ltd v Rochem Ltd* [1980] 1 All ER 1049, [1980] 1 WLR 614, CA).

(v)   Rights of third parties

[6.29]

A solicitor cannot obtain by his lien a better title to property than that of his client. Accordingly, the solicitor of a company cannot in the exercise of his lien refuse to hand over papers to an administrative receiver seeking an order under the Insolvency Act 1986, s 236 or in defiance of a court order against the client.

(vi)   State funding

[6.30]

As a matter of law, a solicitor's lien arises in respect of costs due for work done on the instructions of the client, for which the client has undertaken personal liability. Pre-certificate costs and disbursements (apart from those covered by legal help) will fall within this category, and this lien is protected by the Civil Legal Aid (General) Regulations 1989, reg 103. However, once a funding certificate has been issued the situation is altered, since the assisted person's solicitor has a statutory right to be paid out of the fund, and may not take any payment other than from the fund (Legal Aid Act 1988, s 31; Civil Legal Aid (General) Regulations 1989, reg 64).

When a funding certificate is amended to enable a new solicitor to have the conduct of an assisted person's case the Council of the Law Society considers, therefore, that no lien arises in respect of costs and disbursements payable under a funding certificate, and that it is misleading to use the word 'lien' in relation to such costs and disbursements. The Law Society takes the view that a solicitor's costs are secured by an order for assessment or certificate and it follows that it would be inappropriate to call for a professional undertaking from the successor solicitor to pay the costs except in respect of any outstanding pre-certificate costs. A solicitor should not part with the papers on a community-funded matter until the certificate is transferred to the successor solicitor, although the papers should be made available for inspection in the meantime or copies provided. In respect of costs due from the fund it is permissible to ask for an undertaking requiring the successor solicitor to:

(a)   return the papers promptly on completion to enable a bill of costs to be drawn up; or

(b)   have the first solicitor's costs included in the successor solicitor's bill, collect those costs and pay them to the first solicitor.

Accordingly, where, under a community funding certificate, a change of solicitor is authorised, subject to (a) there being no lien in respect of pre-certificate costs and disbursements, and (b) an undertaking being given by the new solicitor as to the eventual assessment of costs, there is no reason why the papers should not be expeditiously transferred to the new solicitor.

(c) Documents to be handed over

[6.31]

What papers should be handed over by a solicitor on the termination of his retainer and lien?

Annex 12A of the Law Society's *Guide to the Professional Conduct of Solicitors 1999* gave the following guidance:

[6.32]

Is the client entitled to the whole file once the retainer is terminated?

Not necessarily. Most files will contain some documents which belong to you, some which belong to the client and possibly others belonging to a third party. Documents in existence before the retainer, held by you as agent for and on behalf of the client or a third party, must be dealt with in accordance with the instructions of the client or third party (subject to your lien). Documents coming into existence during the retainer fall into four broad categories (see also Cordery on Solicitors):

(a)   Documents prepared by you for the benefit of the client and which have been paid for by the client, either directly or indirectly, belong to the client.
        Examples: instructions and briefs; most attendance notes; drafts; copies made for the client's benefit of letters received by you; copies of letters written by you to third parties if contained in the client's case file and used for the purpose of the client's business. There would appear to be a distinction between copies of letters written to the client (which may be retained by you) and copies of letters written to third parties.

(b)   Documents prepared by you for your own benefit or protection, the preparation of which is not regarded as an item chargeable against the client, belong to you.
        Examples: copies of letters written to the client; copies made for your own benefit of letters received by you; copies of letters written by you to third parties if contained only in a filing system of all letters written in your office; tape recordings of conversations; inter-office memoranda; entries in diaries; time sheets; computerised records; office journals; books of account.

(c)   Documents sent to you by the client during the retainer, the property in which was intended at the date of despatch to pass from the client to you, belong to you.
        Examples: letters, authorities and instructions written or given to you by the client.

(d) Documents prepared by a third party during the course of the retainer and
sent to you (other than at your expense) belong to the client.
Examples: receipts and vouchers for disbursements made by you on behalf
of the client; medical and witness reports; counsel's advice and opinion;
letters received by you from third parties.

Writing in the Solicitors Journal of 17 February 2006 Thomas Braithwaite
criticised this guidance as being 'unprincipled, incomplete and, in some
important respects, wrong'. He observed that no authority is given for the four
'somewhat haphazard and arbitrary categorisations' and although there is a
reference to *Cordery on Solicitors*, *Cordery* says attendance notes usually
belong to the solicitor but the Law Society says they belong to the client. Mr
Braithwaite concluded: 'It appears that when the new Code of Conduct comes
into force, the Law Society proposes not to preserve Annex 12A. Instead,
solicitors will be told that at the end of a retainer they must hand over 'the
client's files' and will be referred to *Cordery* to work out what this means (see
draft guidance note 11 to Rule 2). While this will have the benefit of removing
the contradictions between Annex 12A and *Cordery* it does not address the
shortcomings in the current approach to the question of title. That approach
is incomplete in its analysis, unduly mechanistic in its categorisations and gives
undue prominence to the question of payment.' Mr Braithwaite's prognosis
was accurate. Here is paragraph 11 of the Guidance to Rule 2 of the
Solicitors' Code of Conduct 2007:

'When you cease acting for a client, you will need to consider what should be done
with the paperwork. You must hand over the client's files promptly on request
subject to your right to exercise a lien in respect of outstanding costs. You should try
to ensure the client's position is not prejudiced, and should also bear in mind his or
her rights under the *Data Protection Act* 1998. Undertakings to secure the costs
should be used as an alternative to the exercise of a lien if possible. There may be
circumstances where it is unreasonable to exercise a lien, for example, where the
amount of the outstanding costs is small and the value or importance of the matter
is very great. In any dispute over the ownership of documents you should refer to the
law. Further advice about the law of lien or the ownership of documents can be
found in *Cordery on Solicitors* or other reference books on the subject.'

It is advice with which I am not happy. I always thought that the whole
purpose of a lien was to prejudice the client so that they paid up, and that the
very best sort of lien is where the value of the documents to the client is very
great and the amount of costs they owe is by comparison very small! What is
the purpose of exercising a lien over documents the former client neither needs
nor wants?

(d) Client's remedy

[6.33]

Where there is a valid and enforceable lien, the only practical remedy for the
client who wishes to obtain without delay documents on which his previous
solicitor is claiming a lien is to pay his costs. Sometimes the solicitor is willing
to agree to the money being paid into a joint account to await the outcome of
a Solicitors Act assessment. If not, the client should obtain either the original
solicitor's consent to a Solicitors Act assessment or an order from the court

before making the payment, as otherwise the court might not order an assessment. This course not only has the advantage of securing the immediate release of the papers, but it also enables the new solicitors to inspect and consider them at their leisure in order to advise whether the costs should be challenged – and, if so, on what grounds – before proceeding with the assessment.

STATUTORY DEMAND

[6.34]

Service of a statutory demand for payment of a solicitor's costs does not constitute the bringing of an action for the purposes of the Solicitors Act 1974, s 69(1) which prohibits solicitors from bringing any action to recover costs within one month of delivery of their bill without special leave of the court. The consequences to which a statutory demand leads, if not complied with, is a presumption that the debtor is unable to pay the debt in question. This, in turn, enables the creditor to present a bankruptcy petition. In general the court should exercise its discretion to set aside the statutory demand if, but only if, it would not be just for those consequences to apply in the circumstances. Arguments based on s 69 do not amount to sufficient grounds for setting aside the demand. Accordingly, a solicitor may serve a statutory demand for payment of his costs before the expiration of a month from the date of delivery of his bill of costs (*Re A Debtor (No 88 of 1991)* [1993] Ch 286, [1992] 4 All ER 301). In an article in the *New Law Journal* Angharad Start, counsel for the unhappy debtor, considered that unless the courts do set aside such demands as a matter of policy, or there is a new rule of professional conduct or an amendment to s 69 of the Solicitors Act, the Insolvency Act of 1986 will have to all intents and purposes amended legislation which has been in place for over 250 years.

The Law Society recommends that solicitors should be wary of following this course of action because of the power to set aside a statutory demand on the grounds of injustice (*Re A Debtor (No 88 of 1991)* [1993] Ch 286, [1992] 4 All ER 301). Another reason for caution is that the decision in *Turner & Co (a firm) v O Palomo SA* [1999] 4 All ER 353, [2000] 1 WLR 37, CAcould be interpreted as precluding statutory demands based on a solicitor's bill because the amount of the bill is always open to challenge in proceedings brought to recover it even after the time limit for a detailed assessment has expired and therefore it is not a liquidated demand. In any event although a bankruptcy petition may be issued 21 days after non-compliance with a statutory demand, a petition is an 'action' within the meaning of s 69 of the Solicitors Act 1974 and cannot be issued within one month of delivery of the bill.

BANKRUPTCY PETITION

[6.35]

In *Truex v Toll* [2009] EWHC 396 (Ch), [2009] 1 WLR 2121, [2009] 2 FLR 250 the defendant client presented a list of perceived complaints about the solicitor's services in respect of her matrimonial proceedings. The solicitor served a statutory demand for his outstanding fees and followed it up with a bankruptcy petition. It was held on appeal that as the costs did not form the subject of a judgment, assessment or agreement, they were not a liquidated sum for the purpose of founding a bankruptcy petition; the bill as a whole was capable of challenge as to quantum and was thus for an un-liquidated sum. It was not possible to say that any part of the work done by the solicitor had been quantified, or was quantifiable by the bankruptcy court as a mere matter of arithmetic. The sum claimed only became a liquidated sum once the fees had been assessed by a costs judge, determined in an action, or agreed. Whether a sum is liquidated and whether there is a defence to the claim are separate issues, and the first must be determined before the second is addressed.

CHAPTER 7

THE SOLICITOR AND THIRD PARTIES

INSTRUCTIONS

[7.1]

Where instructions are received not from a client but from a third party purporting to represent that client, it is prudent for the solicitor to obtain written instructions from the client that he or she wishes him or her to act. Rule 2.01(1)(c) of the Solicitors' Code of Conduct 2007 provides: 'Where instructions are given by someone other than the client, or by only one client on behalf of others in a joint matter, you must not proceed without checking that all clients agree with the instructions given'.

WHO IS THE CLIENT?

[7.2]

It is a wise solicitor who knows his own client! Is the client the trade union or its member? The driver of the car or his insurers? The employer or his insurers? The insured or the legal expenses insurers? The limited company or its director personally? A husband and wife or just one of them? The solicitor who does not ascertain clearly at the outset who his client is may repent at leisure if it transpires he has taken instructions from the wrong person or finds his bill rejected by the person to whom he renders it.

WARRANTY OF AUTHORITY

[7.3]

Solicitors in commencing proceedings warrant no more than that they have authority from their client to do so. A firm of solicitors instituted proceedings, including obtaining a freezing injunction, on behalf of a client whom they were unaware was an undischarged bankrupt. A bankrupt is not entitled to bring an action relating to his property, the cause of action having vested in his trustee in bankruptcy. Nevertheless, a bankrupt has the capacity and authority to retain solicitors, and solicitors acting for him without knowledge of his bankruptcy were saying no more than that they had a client and that the client had authorised the proceedings. In those circumstances there had been no breach by them of their duty to the court, nor had they been negligent, and thus the court should exercise its discretion in their favour when considering an application for costs against them personally by the defendant (*Nelson v Nelson* [1997] 1 All ER 970, CA).

THIRD PARTY FUNDING

[7.4]

Between-the-parties costs are awarded on the basis of the paying party reimbursing to the receiving party costs which he is liable to pay to his solicitors. In other words, it is on the principle of indemnifying him up to the amount of the charges he must pay his own solicitor. Where the receiving party is not liable to pay costs to his own solicitor (see Chapter 17, where, in *Gundry v Sainsbury* [1910] 1 KB 645, CA, the solicitor had agreed to act for nothing) the receiving party does not need, and is not entitled to, an indemnity. There is a danger of this argument being put forward where a client has the financial backing of a third party, such as his trade union or an insurance company. To succeed in this argument the paying party would have to show that the receiving party had no liability to his solicitor for costs – when this argument has been raised it has invariably been held that there is a dual liability or a primary liability on the client, thus entitling him to an order for between-the-parties costs. See, for example, *R v Miller (Raymond)* [1983] 3 All ER 186, QBD and more recently, *Ilangaratne v British Medical Association* [2007] EWHC 920 (Ch) in which the claimant had been the unsuccessful litigant in a negligence action against the defendants. The defendants had defended the claim through insurers who had instructed solicitors and the claimant alleged that there was therefore no retainer between the defendant and the solicitors, which was a breach of the indemnity principle.

There was, however, a standing arrangement between the insurers and the solicitors as to costs contained in a letter. Although the letter itself was not a written contract or retainer it evidenced that there was a standing arrangement that any instructions to the solicitors on behalf of the insurer's customers would give rise to a retainer between the customer and the solicitor on terms already advised and agreed. The solicitors' retainer included by way of incorporation the charging rate previously agreed by the insurers.

Nevertheless, where in contentious business the client is being funded by a third party, solicitors should expressly incorporate in the terms of their retainer the right to look to the client for their costs whatever the outcome of the litigation.

NO BILL TO THIRD PARTY

[7.5]

I emphasised at para [3.2] that all costs receivable from a third party belong to the client and not to the solicitor. The solicitor must therefore deliver a bill to his own client and give credit for any money recovered from a third party. In no circumstance may a solicitor render a bill to someone who is not his client. Misunderstandings about this arise frequently when a third party who is paying the client's costs wishes to have an invoice on which he can recover the VAT. These problems are addressed in Chapter 12.

LANDLORD AND TENANT

[7.6]

It is not improper for a landlord to request an undertaking from the tenant to pay his costs. However, a solicitor who requests an undertaking for costs should also provide a cap on the amount to be covered by the undertaking.

It has become common to include in a lease a clause providing that the landlord should be 'compensated fully' or 'indemnified' for costs and expenses incurred as a result of the tenant's breach of the lease. Similar clauses appear in most mortgage deeds. The Court of Appeal decided in *Gomba Holdings UK Ltd v Minories Finance Ltd (No 2)* [1993] Ch 171, CA, that mortgagees were entitled to recover costs on the indemnity basis following a review of the meaning of 'indemnity costs' clauses. The Court of Appeal in *Church Comrs for England v Ibrahim* [1997] 1 EGLR 13, CA, confirmed that the principles in *Gomba Holdings* are not confined to mortgage cases. It held that in general the landlord is not to be deprived of a contractual right to indemnity costs. Although the court always retains a discretion on costs, that discretion should be used to reflect the contractual agreement between the landlord and the tenant unless the landlord's conduct is improper or unreasonable. This decision clarifies the landlord's position on costs and should make it easier in the future either to negotiate or obtain from the court adequate compensation for the costs of litigation against defaulting tenants. However, the wording of the indemnity clause must be clear and a claim to costs should be fully pleaded in the particulars of claim.

(a) Landlord and tenant

[7.7]

When a solicitor is acting for a landlord, whether a lease is being granted or a licence has been applied for, the client on whose behalf the relevant costs have been incurred is the landlord. Where the tenant is liable to pay those costs and they are in dispute the device of the landlord applying for a remuneration certificate is no longer available since their abolition with effect from 11 August 2009.

(b) Detailed assessment

[7.8]

There is judicial authority for saying that an undertaking to pay reasonable costs means costs to be assessed if not agreed (*Zaniewski v Scales* (1969) 113 Sol Jo 525). If the landlord is unwilling to give his consent to an application for a remuneration certificate, the tenant is entitled to apply to the High Court for an assessment of the bill under the Solicitors Act 1974, s 71. The client should be warned of the estimated expense of such an application and as to whether such expense might be disproportionate to the amount of the bill in dispute. Further, the client's attention should be drawn to the provisions of s 70(9) relating to payment of the costs of the assessment proceedings (Statement of the Law Society Council, *Law Society Gazette*, 19 December 1984, pp 3556–3557). A third party should be aware of the risk of losing their right to an assessment as the result of the provision in the Solicitors Act 1974, s 70(4) that no order for assessment can be made if 12 months have elapsed since the date of payment of the bill (see *Harrison v Tew*, para [5.24]). If a mortgagee has paid his solicitor's costs in respect of possession proceedings which resulted in a suspended order, and added those costs to the mortgage debt, the mortgagor may not discover this until long after the 12-month period has expired. It would therefore be prudent for the mortgagor after any such litigation to ascertain the amount of the mortgagee's solicitor's costs so that an application for an assessment may be made within the requisite time. However, the warnings given above in respect of the assessment of a landlord's costs by the tenant apply equally here.

SOLICITORS ACT 1974, SECTION 71

[7.9]

Section 71(1) of the Solicitors Act 1974 provides:

(1)   Where a person other than the party chargeable with the bill for the purposes of section 70 has paid, or is or was liable to pay, a bill either to the solicitor or to the party chargeable with the bill, that person, or his executors, administrators or assignees may apply to the High Court for an order for the taxation [*assessment*] of the bill as if he were the party chargeable with it, and the court may make the same order (if any) as it might have made if the application had been made by the party chargeable with the bill.

The effect of this provision is 'that if a person who is not chargeable thinks fit to pay the bill it is open to him to do so, and if he does so, he should be entitled to have that bill assessed as the party chargeable therewith might himself have done' (*Re Newman* (1867) 2 Ch App 707, per Rolt LJ). Although the assessment must be conducted as between the solicitor and his own client, a third party does not, by obtaining an order to assess, increase his liability to the solicitor's client. For example, if a mortgagor has the costs of the mortgagee's solicitor assessed, items which the mortgagor would not be liable to pay as between himself and the mortgagee will be disallowed even if the solicitor is entitled to charge them against his client, the mortgagee (*Re Longbotham & Sons* [1904] 2 Ch 152, CA).

ENTITLED THIRD PARTIES

[7.10]

The Solicitors' (Non-Contentious Business) Remuneration Order 2009 omitted the rights previously given to a class of beneficiaries to certain estates. See paras [5.3] and [5.4].

NO PROTECTION AGAINST CONSTRUCTIVE TRUST

[7.11]

In *United Mizrahi Bank Ltd v Doherty* [1998] 2 All ER 230, ChD, a provision in a freezing order permitted the defendants to use assets otherwise frozen, for reasonable legal expenses. Such a provision merely prevented the use of the assets in this way from being a breach of the order and a contempt of court. It was no advance guarantee that, if at the trial the claimant was successful in establishing a proprietary claim against the defendant, such that the money so expended turned out to have been the claimant's, the solicitors acting for the defendant could avoid a claim of constructive trust for knowing receipt being raised against them. The claimant bank was bringing an action against the first defendant for breach of his duty to the bank in which it alleged that he wrongfully obtained money from customers which had ended up in the hands of his wife and servant companies and had been used for the purchase of properties including the properties the subject matter of the application. The bank thus had a claim for breach of trust against him and in constructive trust and tracing against the other defendants. The first defendant and his solicitors had issued a notice of motion effectively seeking in advance the court's determination that the expenditure on the costs allowed by the freezing order would deprive the bank of any such claim of constructive trust. This was not a case where the court could or should say, in advance, that there would be no breach of trust by the expenditure of those moneys in legal costs.

COUNSEL

[7.12]

The Solicitors' Code of Conduct 2007 omits the previous rule that except in publicly funded cases, solicitors are personally liable as a matter of professional conduct for the payment of counsel's proper fees, whether or not they had been placed in funds by the client. Indeed, rule 10.07 states: '(1) if in the course of practice you instruct a lawyer of another jurisdiction you must, as a matter of professional conduct, pay the lawyer's proper fees unless the lawyer is practising as a solicitor or barrister of England and Wales'. When I took this up with the Law Society they unsurprisingly denied that this implied that solicitors have *carte blanche* to ignore paying English counsel's fees! Although the specific conduct obligation has gone the Law Society would still take action against persistent non payers under rule 1 (integrity). What has gone wrong is that the new Code was drafted on the assumption that new contractual terms of work would have been negotiated between the Bar Council and the Law Society in time for concurrent publication. The negotiations have gone on for years and are still going on. Historically, the etiquette of the bar precluded barristers suing for their fees because they were honoraria but this had little practical consequence because solicitors were bound by their rules to pay counsel, whether or not they were in funds. Barristers are now permitted in their Code of Conduct to enter into contractual relationships with the solicitors instructing them and since the professional duty on solicitors has gone it appears it would be prudent for barristers to now enter into contracts with their instructing solicitors to pay them personally, whatever the arrangement with the lay client. In the absence of an agreed fee or an engagement letter, it appears that counsel must resort to claiming on a *quantum meruit*.

It has also been suggested that even if a solicitor takes the precaution of obtaining money on account of disbursements from the client and on the strength of this incurs counsel's fees the client can subsequently instruct the solicitor not to use the money to pay counsel. This would of course undermine the purpose of obtaining payment on account of disbursements and be a matter of serious consequence to the conduct of litigation. My understanding is that the payment of money on account of disbursements gives the solicitor irrevocable authority to use it to discharge any liability for disbursements, including counsel's fees, he incurs in reliance on the money in his client account.

Part II

Between the Parties

CHAPTER 8

SYNOPSIS

1605–1978

[8.1]

Solicitors have been required to deliver detailed bills of costs since 1605. When I first encountered costs they were prescribed for the High Court in Appendix N to the Rules of the Supreme Court 1883. It contained no less than 204 items, with fixed minima and maxima. The result was a scale which, in the words of the Evershed Committee, was 'derogatory of the dignity and standing of a profession no less distinguished, learned and reputable than any of the other professions which charge on the basis of the real value of the skill and industry involved'. Nevertheless, the scale was not amended until the Supreme Court (Costs) Rules 1959 introduced Appendix 3 to RSC Ord 62, which, although it contained a mere 100 items, resulted in an even more complicated form of bill, requiring not only a skilled specialist to draw it, but someone of equal skill to check, read and assess it. The negotiations over the next 20 years comprised long periods of stagnation interspersed with short bursts of feverish activity which eventually resulted in the introduction of a new Appendix 2 on 24 April 1979. In the county court there continued to be a variety of scales depending on the amount recovered or claimed.

1979

[8.2]

The new High Court scale, which reduced the number of items to 12, for the first time distinguished between routine ('mechanical') work and skilled and experienced ('thinking') work which was clearly analogous to the work of non-fee earners and fee earners. The individual items in the scale related to mechanical work, while thinking work was concentrated in the instructions item. The philosophy behind it was simple and consistent with the Law Society's *The Expense of Time*, which divided the members of a solicitors' firm into the two categories of fee earner and non-fee earner and provided formulae for calculating the hourly expense of fee earners by apportioning the overheads of the firm between them. Nevertheless, the then Chief Taxing Master described the scale as a 'half-way house', while other appellations were less polite.

The new scale perpetuated some of the unfairness of the previous scale, created its own illogicalities and did not materially simplify the drawing of bills.

1986

[8.3]

On 28 April 1986 all the complaints about High Court costs were swept away in the culmination of the Law Society's campaign for an all-discretionary bill of costs. The fixed limits had gone. The daily rate had gone. There was a profit mark-up on all interlocutory work. In the county court there were still four scales until July 1991 and three afterwards.

However, discretion is a two-edged sword – it can be exercised both for and against – it does not automatically confer benefits. Under the old scale with fixed minimum amounts, however low the figures may have been, they were negotiated by the Law Society on behalf of all solicitors. In a discretionary regime, every solicitor must fend for himself and justify his own charges.

1999

[8.4]

On 26 April 1999, the Civil Procedure Rules 1998 saw the achievement of another long cherished ideal – the abolition of the difference between High Court and county court costs by the introduction of one unified regime. I accept that it was part of the equally cherished unification and simplification of all the rules and codes of procedure in the civil courts, but unification was particularly welcome in respect of costs. All that was good in the former RSC Ord 62 and the CCR Ord 38 was incorporated in Parts 43–48 of the CPR, which also include much of the codified principles and practice that were applied in the past but were not part of the Rules. They were supplemented by a Costs Practice Direction which is integral to Parts 43-48 and which together with them has had no less than 54 statutory updates. The new Rules were not a mere codification of what was already there. They introduced a new philosophy and approach to costs. In the past, the court had been concerned only to decide whether or not to award costs to one party or the other at the end of a hearing, with any costs awarded being quantified at the end of the proceedings if the parties could not agree them. Now costs permeate every aspect of civil litigation: the courts are charged with the responsibility of managing cases to ensure that the work undertaken by the parties (and therefore the costs they incur) are proportionate to the issues, while costs orders may be made as sanctions to ensure that the conduct of the parties (both before and during the proceedings) is in compliance with the new procedural code. As well as seeking to achieve proportionality and using costs orders as sanctions, the new regime also aims to make the amount of costs more predictable by requiring the parties to provide estimates of their costs at various stages of the litigation, and for costs on the fast track to be fixed, initially for the trial only, but eventually for the entire action.

Two innovations which had an immediate dramatic impact on civil litigation were the provision for the summary assessment of costs by the judge after an interim hearing or a hearing lasting not more than one day and for those costs to be paid within 14 days (which has apparently substantially reduced the number of interim applications), and the provision in Part 36 that a *claimant* may make an offer to settle with possible favourable financial consequences if the claimant subsequently recovers more than the amount of his offer. The concepts of proportionality and of the winner of litigation no longer virtually automatically receiving all, or indeed any, of his costs, also brought about fundamental changes in the conduct of litigation.

2000

[8.5]

Part 2 of the Access to Justice Act 1999 in April 2000 allowed the recoverability of additional liabilities in the form of success fee premiums and after-the-event insurance premiums thereby triggering the satellite litigation known as the costs wars.

CHAPTER 9

VOCABULARY

[9.1]

CPR Rule 43.2: Definitions and application

(1)   In Parts 44 to 48, unless the context otherwise requires—

(a)   'costs' includes fees, charges, disbursements, expenses, remuneration, reimbursement allowed to a litigant in person under rule 48.6, any additional liability incurred under a funding arrangement and any fee or reward charged by a lay representative for acting on behalf of a party in proceedings allocated to the small claims track;

(b)   'costs judge' means a taxing master of the Senior Courts;

(ba)   'Costs Office' means the Senior Courts Costs Office;

(c)   'costs officer' means—

(i)   a costs judge;

(ii)   a district judge; and

(iii)   an authorised court officer;

(d)   'authorised court officer' means any officer of—

(i)   a county court;

(ii)   a district registry;

(iii)   the Principal Registry of the Family Division; or

(iv)   the Costs Office, whom the Lord Chancellor has authorised to assess costs.

(e)   'fund' includes any estate or property held for the benefit of any person or class of person and any fund to which a trustee or personal representative is entitled in that capacity;

(f)   'receiving party' means a party entitled to be paid costs;

(g)   'paying party' means a party liable to pay costs;

(h)   'assisted person' means an assisted person within the statutory provisions relating to legal aid;

(i)   'LSC funded client' means an individual who receives services funded by the Legal Services Commission as part of the Community Legal Service within the meaning of Part I of the Access to Justice Act 1999;

(j)   'fixed costs' means the amounts which are to be allowed in respect of solicitors' charges in the circumstances set out in Part 45.

(k)   'funding arrangement' means an arrangement where a person has—

(i)   entered into a conditional fee agreement or a collective conditional fee agreement which provides for a success fee within the meaning of section 58(2) of the Courts and Legal Services Act 1990;

(ii)   taken out an insurance policy to which section 29 of the Access to Justice Act 1999 (recovery of insurance premiums by way of costs) applies; or

(iii)   made an agreement with a membership organisation to meet that person's legal costs;

(l) 'percentage increase' means the percentage by which the amount of a legal representative's fee can be increased in accordance with a conditional fee agreement which provides for a success fee;

(m) 'insurance premium' means a sum of money paid or payable for insurance against the risk of incurring a costs liability in the proceedings, taken out after the event that is the subject matter of the claim;

(n) 'membership organisation' means a body prescribed for the purposes of section 30 of the Access to Justice Act 1999 (recovery where body undertakes to meet costs liabilities);

(o) 'additional liability' means the percentage increase, the insurance premium, or the additional amount in respect of provision made by a membership organisation, as the case may be;

(p) 'free of charge' has the same meaning as in section 194(10) of the Legal Services Act 2007;

(q) 'pro bono representation' means legal representation provided free of charge; and

(r) 'the prescribed charity' has the same meaning as in section 194(8) of the Legal Services Act 2007.

(2) The costs to which Parts 44 to 48 apply include—

(a) the following costs where those costs may be assessed by the court—

(i) costs of proceedings before an arbitrator or umpire;

(ii) costs of proceedings before a tribunal or other statutory body; and

(iii) costs payable by a client to his solicitor; and

(b) costs which are payable by one party to another party under the terms of a contract, where the court makes an order for an assessment of those costs.

(3) Where advocacy or litigation services are provided to a client under a conditional fee agreement, costs are recoverable under Parts 44 to 48 notwithstanding that the client is liable to pay his legal representative's fees and expenses only to the extent that sums are recovered in respect of the proceedings, whether by way of costs or otherwise.

(4) In paragraph (3), the reference to a conditional fee agreement is to an agreement which satisfies all the conditions applicable to it by virtue of section 58 of the Courts and Legal Services Act 1990.

THE COSTS PRACTICE DIRECTION

[9.2]

This Practice Direction supplements CPR Parts 43 to 48.

Section 1: Introduction

1.1   *This Practice Direction supplements Parts 43 to 48 of the Civil Procedure Rules. It applies to all proceedings to which those Parts apply.*
1.2   *Paragraphs 57.1 to 57.9 of this Practice Direction deal with various transitional provisions affecting proceedings about costs.*
1.3   *Attention is drawn to the powers to make orders about costs conferred on the Senior Courts and any county court by Section 51 of the Senior Courts Act 1981.*
1.4   *In these Directions:*
   'counsel' means a barrister or other person with a right of audience in relation to proceedings in the High Court or in the County Courts in which he is instructed to act.
   'LSC' means Legal Services Commission.
   'solicitor' means a solicitor of the Senior Courts or other person with a right of audience in relation to proceedings, who is conducting the claim or defence (as the case may be) on behalf of a party to the proceedings and, where the context admits, includes a patent agent.
1.5   *In respect of any document which is required by these Directions to be signed by a party or his legal representative the Practice Direction supplementing Part 22 will apply as if the document in question was a statement of truth. (The Practice Direction supplementing Part 22 makes provision for cases in which a party is a child, a protected party or a company or other corporation and cases in which a document is signed on behalf of a partnership.)*

[9.3]

The CPR were designed so that they are easier to understand. This approach resulted in old and familiar words being replaced by words which were perceived to be more user-friendly. The first word to go was 'taxation' which smacked too much of the Inland Revenue for modern ears. There were various candidates to replace it, the eventual selection being 'assessment'.

The terms 'the paying party' and the 'receiving party' could not be in plainer English but it was proposed at one time that even they should be replaced with some gobbledygook, but this was happily abandoned. Another semantic triumph was the abolition of the archaic term 'solicitor and own client' costs and its replacement with 'solicitor and client' costs, it being at last accepted that a solicitor is unlikely with any prospect of success to render a bill to someone who is not his own client! The recovery of success fees and after-the-event insurance premiums introduced the compendium description 'additional liability' to embrace either or both of them.

[9.4]

CPR Rule 43.3: Meaning of summary assessment
'Summary assessment' means the procedure by which the court, when making an order about costs, orders payment of a sum of money instead of fixed costs or 'detailed assessment'.

[9.5]

CPD Section 3 Model Forms for Claims for Costs
Rule 43.3 Meaning of Summary Assessment
3.1 *Rule 43.3 defines summary assessment. When carrying out a summary assessment of costs where there is an additional liability the court may assess the base costs alone, or the base costs and the additional liability.*
3.2 *Form N260 is a model form of Statement of Costs to be used for summary assessments. 3.3 Further details about Statements of Costs are given in paragraph 13.5 below.*

[9.6]

CPR Rule 43.4: Meaning of detailed assessment
'Detailed assessment' means the procedure by which the amount of costs is decided by a costs officer in accordance with Part 47.

[9.7]

CPD Section 3 Meaning of detailed assessment
3.4 *Rule 43.4 defines detailed assessment. When carrying out a detailed assessment of costs where there is an additional liability the court will assess both the base costs and the additional liability, or, if the base costs have already been assessed, the additional liability alone.*
3.5 *Precedents A, B, C and D in the Schedule of Costs Precedents annexed to this Practice Direction are model forms of bills of costs to be used for detailed assessments.*
3.6 *Further details about bills of costs are given in the next section of these Directions and in paragraphs 28.1 to 49.1, below.*
3.7 *Precedents A, B, C and D in the Schedule of Costs Precedents and the next section of this Practice Direction all refer to a model form of bill of costs. The use of a model form is not compulsory, but is encouraged. A party wishing to rely upon a bill which departs from the model forms should include in the background information of the bill an explanation for that departure.*
3.8 *In any order of the court (whether made before or after 26 April 1999) the word 'taxation' will be taken to mean 'detailed assessment' and the words 'to be taxed' will be taken to mean 'to be decided by detailed assessment' unless in either case the context otherwise requires.*

[9.8]

Here is an alphabetical list of some of the other changes over the years in the litigation vocabulary.

Old	New
Anton Piller	Search order
Calderbank offer	Part 36 offer
Cause	Case
Contingency fee	Damages based agreement
Discovery	Disclosure

Old	New
Ex parte	Without notice
Further and better particulars	Further information
Guardian ad litem	Litigation friend
In camera	In private
Infant	Child
Interlocutory	Interim
Inter partes	With notice
Leave of the court	Permission of the court
Listing questionnaire	Pre-trial checklist
Mareva	Freezing order
Medical negligence	Clinical negligence
Minor	Child
Next friend	Litigation friend
Party and party	Between the parties
Party under a disability	Protected party or child
Payment into court	Part 36 payment
Plaintiff	Claimant
Pleading	Statement of case
Third party proceedings	Additional claim
Writ	Claim form

CPR GLOSSARY

[9.9]

This glossary is a guide to the meaning of certain legal expressions as used in these Rules, but it does not give the expressions any meaning in the rules which they do not otherwise have in law.

Expression	Meaning
Affidavit	A written, sworn statement of evidence.
Alternative dispute resolution	Collective description of methods of resolving disputes otherwise than through the normal trial process.
Base rate	The interest rate set by the Bank of England which is used as the basis for other banks' rates.
Contribution	A right of someone to recover from a third person all or part of the amount which he himself is liable to pay.

Expression	Meaning
Counterclaim	A claim brought by a defendant in response to the claimant's claim, which is included in the same proceedings as the claimant's claim.
Cross-examination (and see 'evidence in chief')	Questioning of a witness by a party other than the party who called the witness.
Damages	A sum of money awarded by the court as compensation to the claimant.
Aggravated damages	Additional damages which the court may award as compensation for the defendant's objectionable behaviour.
Exemplary damages	Damages which go beyond compensating for actual loss and are awarded to show the court's disapproval of the defendant's behaviour
Defence of tender before claim	A defence that, before the claimant started proceedings, the defendant unconditionally offered to the claimant the amount due or, if no specified amount is claimed, an amount sufficient to satisfy the claim.
Evidence in chief (and see 'cross-examination')	The evidence given by a witness for the party who called him.
Indemnity	A right of someone to recover from a third party the whole amount which he himself is liable to pay.
Injunction	A court order prohibiting a person from doing something or requiring a person to do something.
Joint liability (and see 'several liability')	Parties who are jointly liable share a single liability and each party can be held liable for the whole of it.
Limitation period	The period within which a person who has a right to claim against another person must start court proceedings to establish that right. The expiry of the period may be a defence to the claim.
List	Cases are allocated to different lists depending on the subject matter of the case. The lists are used for administrative purposes and may also have their own procedures and judges.
Official copy	A copy of an official document, supplied and marked as such by the office which issued the original.
Practice form	Form to be used for a particular purpose in proceedings, the form and purpose being specified by a practice direction.

Expression	Meaning
Pre-action protocol	Statements of understanding between legal practitioners and others about pre-action practice and which are approved by a relevant practice direction.
Privilege	The right of a party to refuse to disclose a document or produce a document or to refuse to answer questions on the ground of some special interest recognised by law.
Seal	A seal is a mark which the court puts on a document to indicate that the document has been issued by the court.
Service	Steps required by rules of court to bring documents used in court proceedings to a person's attention.
Set aside	Cancelling a judgment or order or a step taken by a party in the proceedings.
Several liability (and see 'joint liability')	A person who is severally liable with others may remain liable for the whole claim even where judgment has been obtained against the others.
Stay	A stay imposes a halt on proceedings, apart from taking any steps allowed by the Rules or the terms of the stay. Proceedings can be continued if a stay is lifted.
Strike out	Striking out means the court ordering written material to be deleted so that it may no longer be relied upon.
Without prejudice	Negotiations with a view to a settlement are usually conducted 'without prejudice' which means that the circumstances in which the content of those negotiations may be revealed to the court are very restricted.

THE SUPREME COURT COSTS OFFICE GUIDE 2006

[9.10]

(The 'Supreme Court Costs Office' is now the 'Senior Courts Costs Office'.)

Additional liability	Items of costs which are recoverable in certain circumstances: that part of a success fee (defined below) under a conditional fee agreement (also defined below) which is recoverable from a paying party (defined below) and/or a reasonable sum in respect of a relevant insurance premium (also defined below) and/or an additional amount which is sometimes recoverable in respect of 'self insurance' notionally incurred by a litigant whose case is funded by a trade union or similar body. These three forms of additional liability are the items about which the paying party should have received a notice of funding (defined below).
Applications clerk	The clerk to whom all papers and enquiries should be directed concerning the issue of claim forms and application notices: the applications clerk's office is currently located in Room 2.13.
Appropriate office	The office in which a request for a detailed assessment hearing should be filed: it is the County Court Office or District Registry for the court in which the order for costs was made or, in all other cases, the Supreme Court Costs Office (SCCO). Where the SCCO is the appropriate office for the request, it is also the appropriate office for any request or application made earlier in the detailed assessment proceedings, eg, a request for a default costs certificate, a request or application to set aside such a certificate and applications for extension of time and sanctions for delay.
Central Funds	Money provided by Parliament out of which may be paid the costs of defendants in criminal cases in respect of which a 'defendants costs order' has been made.
Clerk of Appeals	The clerk to whom all papers and enquiries should be directed which relate to SCCO work concerning criminal fee appeals. The Clerk of Appeal's office is currently located in Room 2.13.
Conditional fee agreement	An agreement with a legal representative which provides for the payment of fees or part of them only in specified circumstances. A party who wishes to recover a success fee payable under the agreement from his opponent should serve a notice of funding on the opponent at the outset of the claim.

Costs between the parties	Costs payable by one litigant to another litigant under the terms of an order made by the court. The expression is used in order to distinguish these costs from 'solicitor and client costs' (costs payable by a client to a solicitor under the terms of a contract made between them) and 'LSC only costs' (costs payable by the Legal Services Commission to a solicitor or barrister).
Costs Judges	Judges sitting in the SCCO (also known as Taxing Masters and as Masters of the SCCO). Costs Judges also act as District Judges of the Principal Registry of the Family Division, and as District Judges of the County Court when assessing costs from those courts.
Costs Officers	Authorised court officers who assess most bills for sums not exceeding certain amounts specified from time to time. From their decisions, appeals lie as of right to the Costs Judges.
Costs-only proceedings	The procedure to be followed where, before court proceedings are commenced, the parties to a dispute reach an agreement on all issues, including which party is to pay costs, but are unable to agree the amount of those costs.
Counsel	One or more barristers acting for a litigant. Very senior barristers are awarded the title 'Queen's Counsel'.
CPD	The Costs Practice Direction, supplementing the CPR (defined below).
CPR	The Civil Procedure Rules which, supplemented by the CPD (defined above) govern the procedure to be followed in most civil cases brought in the SCCO. The text of the CPR and the CPD are set out in practitioner's books such as the White Book Service and the Civil Court Practice. Most of the relevant texts are also included on the SCCO page of the Court Service website (as to which, see para 1.10, below).
Detailed assessment	The judicial process under which bills of costs are checked as to their reasonableness; the court may allow or disallow any items claimed in a bill or may vary any figures claimed in respect of them.
Determining officer	The court officer in criminal cases (only) who first assesses the costs payable to a defendant out of Central Funds (defined above) or payable by the LSC to solicitors and counsel under criminal legal aid orders. Costs Judges have jurisdiction to hear appeals from the decisions of Determining Officers.

Disbursements	Sums of money, eg, court fees, counsel's fees and witness expenses which are paid or payable by a 'receiving party' (defined below) which cannot and do not include any element of profit for that party or for the solicitor acting for him. A special meaning is given to this term in the case of litigants in person (see para 22.2, below).
Form N252 and other N forms	Court forms which are referred to in the CPD (defined above). Copies of the forms for use in the SCCO can be obtained from the SCCO itself or from the SCCO page of the Court Service Website (as to which, see para 1.10, below).
Funding arrangement	An arrangement made by a litigant which gives rise to an additional liability (defined above).
Insurance premium	The sum paid or payable by a litigant who has taken out an 'after the event' insurance policy taken out in respect of particular litigation and covering against the risk of losing that litigation.
Litigant in person	A party to any proceedings who does not have a solicitor or other legal representative duly authorised to represent him or her in those proceedings.
LSC	The Legal Services Commission, which is the body set up by Parliament to provide financial help as to the costs of legal services provided to litigants in civil claims and defendants in criminal cases who come within certain eligibility criteria.
LSC funded client	A litigant who has been granted financial help by the Legal Services Commission.
Notice of Funding	A notice (usually in Form N251) by which one party warns another of any additional liability (defined above) which may later be recoverable.
Offer to settle	An offer in writing made by one party to another in detailed assessment proceedings proposing the payment of a specific sum of money thereby avoiding the need for any further delay or expense. If the offer is not accepted and the costs in question are later subject to detailed assessment, neither party is allowed to reveal the existence of the offer to the Costs Judge or Costs Officer until the detailed assessment has been completed. The letter containing the offer should include the words 'without prejudice save as to the costs of the detailed assessment' or words to that effect.
Part 23 application	Applications made by any party which relate to existing or intended detailed assessment proceedings. The notice of application should be in Form N244 (as to which, see above).

Part 36 offer or payment	An offer in writing made by one litigant to another during the proceedings preceding the detailed assessment proceedings, proposing to settle those proceedings on specified terms. After proceedings have started an offer by a defendant to settle a money claim should be supported by a payment into court of the specific sum offered.
Paying party	The party to detailed assessment proceedings who is liable to pay the costs which are the subject of the assessment. The opposing party is referred to as the 'receiving party' which is defined below.
Points of dispute	A written statement made by the paying party identifying the areas of disagreement as to the costs to be assessed. In respect of each item of costs which is disputed the statement should outline the reason for disputing it and, where a reduction is sought, should suggest the reduced figure.
Profit costs	Costs paid or payable in respect of work done by a solicitor which are not 'disbursements' (defined above).
Provisional assessment	An assessment of costs made without a hearing. Subsequently the court notifies the receiving party of the sum proposed to be allowed and requires the receiving party to so inform the court office within 14 days if he wishes a hearing to be convened.
RCJ	The Royal Courts of Justice the postal address of which is Strand, London, WC2A 2LL.
Receiving party	A party to detailed assessment proceedings who is entitled to recover from another party the costs which are the subject of the assessment. In the case of 'costs between the parties' (defined above) the receiving party is the person in whose favour the court's order for costs was made or the solicitor or other legal representative acting for such a person. In the case of 'solicitor and client costs' (which is defined below) the receiving party is the solicitor.
Regional Costs Judge	A Regional Costs Judge is a District Judge who has been appointed to sit in both the County Court and the District Registry of the High Court to carry out detailed assessments in larger and more difficult cases.
SCCO	The Supreme Court Costs Office the postal address of which is Clifford's Inn, Fetter Lane, London, EC4A 1DQ.

Sitting Master	Each day the Master so nominated for that day deals with any applications in matters not yet assigned to other Masters and is also available to give guidance on points of practice to the Judges of the Supreme Court and other courts throughout the country and (via his clerk) to any litigants or lawyers seeking his help.
Solicitor and client costs	See 'costs between the parties' above.
Statement of truth	A statement to be included in any claim form, application notice or witness statement which confirms that the facts stated therein are true. The statement of truth must be signed by the litigant, or his litigation friend or legal representative or witness as the case may be.
Success fees	An additional fee which is payable in certain circumstances under the terms of a conditional fee agreement. The success fee must be expressed as a percentage of the other profit costs payable under the agreement.
Summary assessment	The procedure by which the court, when making an award of costs, immediately calculates and specifies the sum of costs it allows.
Wasted costs order	An order against a legal representative which disallows, or, as the case may be, orders the legal representative to meet, the whole or any part of costs found to have been incurred as a result of improper, unreasonable or negligent acts or omissions on the part of the legal representative or any consequential costs.

CHAPTER 10

COSTS CONTROL

ESTIMATES

(a) Costs Practice Direction

[10.1]

CPD Section 6: Estimates of costs

6.1 *This section sets out certain steps which parties and their legal representatives must take in order to keep the parties informed about their potential liability in respect of costs and in order to assist the court to decide what, if any, order to make about costs and about case management.*
6.2
(1) *In this section an 'estimate of costs' means—*
    (a) *an estimate of costs of—*
        (i) *base costs (including disbursements) already incurred; and*
        (ii) *base costs (including disbursements) to be incurred,*
    which a party, if successful in the proceedings, intends to seek to recover from any other party under an order for costs; or
    (b) *in proceedings where the party has pro bono representation and intends, if successful in the proceedings, to seek an order under section 194(3) of the Legal Services Act 2007, an estimate of the sum equivalent to—*
        (i) *the base costs (including disbursements) that the party would have already incurred had the legal representation provided to that party not been free of charge; and*
        (ii) *the base costs (including disbursements) that the party would incur if the legal representation to be provided to that party were not free of charge.*
    ('Base costs' are defined in paragraph 2.2 of this Practice Direction.)
    (c) *A party who intends to recover an additional liability (defined in rule 43.2) need not reveal the amount of that liability in the estimate.*
6.3 *The court may at any stage in a case order any party to file an estimate of base costs and to serve copies of the estimate on all other parties. The court may direct that the estimate be prepared in such a way as to demonstrate the likely effects of giving or not giving a particular case management direction which the court is considering, for example a direction for a split trial or for the trial of a preliminary issue. The court may specify a time limit for filing and serving the estimate. However, if no time limit is specified the estimate should be filed and served within 28 days of the date of the order.*
6.4
(1) *When—*
    (i) *a party to a claim which is outside the financial scope of either the small claims track or the fast track, files an allocation questionnaire; or*

(ii)   a party to a claim which is being dealt with on the fast track or the multi track files a pre-trial check list (listing questionnaire),
that party must also file an estimate of costs and serve a copy of it on every other party, unless the court otherwise directs. Where a party is represented, that party's legal representative must in addition serve a copy of the estimate on that party.

(2)   Where a party who is required to file and serve a new estimate of costs in accordance with Rule 44.15(3) is represented, the legal representative must in addition serve the new estimate on that party.

(3)   This paragraph does not apply to litigants in person.

6.5   An estimate of base costs should be substantially in the form illustrated in Precedent H in the Schedule of Costs Precedents annexed to the Practice Direction.

6.5A

(1)   If there is a difference of 20% or more between the base costs claimed by a receiving party on detailed assessment and the costs shown in an estimate of costs filed by that party, the receiving party must provide a statement of the reasons for the difference with his bill of costs.

(2)   If a paying party –
(a)   claims that he reasonably relied on an estimate of costs filed by a receiving party; or
(b)   wishes to rely upon the costs shown in the estimate in order to dispute the reasonableness or proportionality of the costs claimed,
the paying party must serve a statement setting out his case in this regard in his points of dispute.

('Relevant person' is defined in paragraph 32.10(1) of the Costs Practice Direction)

6.6

(1)   On an assessment of the costs of a party the court may have regard to any estimate previously filed by that party, or by any other party in the same proceedings. Such an estimate may be taken into account as a factor among others, when assessing the reasonableness of any costs claimed.

(2)   In particular, where –
(a)   there is a difference of 20% or more between the base costs claimed by a receiving party and the costs shown in an estimate of costs filed by that party; and
(b)   it appears to the court that –
(i)   the receiving party has not provided a satisfactory explanation for that difference; or
(ii)   the paying party reasonably relied on the estimate of costs; the court may regard the difference between the costs claimed and the costs shown in the estimate as evidence that the costs claimed are unreasonable or disproportionate.

Where a claim is outside the financial scope of the small claims track, a party (other than a litigant in person) filing an allocation questionnaire is required to file an estimate of costs and serve a copy of it on every other party and the client. A further estimate is required on the filing of the pre-trial checklist; again the estimate must be served on every other party and the client. The estimate should follow the form of Precedent H annexed to the Practice Direction. Here it is, but be warned — the amounts are now ten years out of date:

(b) Precedent H

[10.2]

Schedule of Costs Precedents:
Precedent H

IN THE HIGH COURT OF JUSTICE   2000-B-9999
QUEEN'S BENCH DIVISION
BRIGHTON DISTRICT REGISTRY
BETWEEN

AB	Claimant
– and –	
CD	Defendant

ESTIMATE OF CLAIMANT'S COSTS DATED 12th APRIL 2001

The claimant instructed E F & Co under a conditional fee agreement dated 8th July 2000 in respect of which the following hourly rates are recoverable as base costs

Partner – £180 per hour plus VAT

Assistant Solicitor – £140 per hour plus VAT

Other fee earners – £85 per hour plus VAT

Item No.	Description of work done	V.A.T.	Disburse-ments	Profit Costs
	PART 1: BASE COSTS ALREADY INCURRED			
	8th July 2000 – EF & Co in-structed			
	7th October 2000 Claim issued			
1	Issue fee	—	£400.00	
	21st October 2000 – Particu-lars of			
	claim served			
	25th November 2000 – Time for			
	service of defence extended by			
	agreement to 14th January 2001			
2	Fee on allocation	—	£80.00	
	20th January 2001 – case allocated to multi-track			
	9th February 2001 – Case			

Item	Description of work done	V.A.T.	Disburse-ments	Profit
No.				Costs
	management conference at which costs were awarded to the claimant and the base costs were summarily assessed at £400			
	(paid on 24th February 2001) –			
	23rd February 2001 – Claimant's list of documents			
	ATTENDANCES, COMMUNICATIONS AND WORK DONE			
	Claimant			
3	0.75 hours at £180			£135.00
4	4.4 hours at £140			£616.00
	To Summary	£ —	£480.00	£751.00
	Witnesses of Fact			
5	3.8 hours at £140			£532.00
6	Paid travelling on 9th October 2000	£4.02	£22.96	
	Medical expert (Dr. IJ)			
7	1.5 hours at £140			£210.00
8	Dr. IJ's fee for report		£350.00	
	Defendant and his solicitor			
9	2.5 hours at £140			£350.00
	Court (communications only)			
10	0.4 hours at £140			£56.00
	Documents			
11	0.75 hours at £180 and 22.25 hours at £140			£3,250.00
	Negotiations			
12	2.75 hours at £140			£385.00
13	VAT on solicitor's base fees	£968.45		
	To Summary	£972.47	£372.96	£4,783.00
	PART 2: BASE COSTS TO BE INCURRED			
14	**Fee on listing**		£400.00	
	Attendance at pre-trial review			
15	5 hours at £140			£700.00
16	Counsel's base fee for pre-trial review		£750.00	
	Attendance at trial			
17	20 hours at £140			£2,800.00

Item	Description of work done	V.A.T.	Disburse-ments	Profit
No.				Costs
18	Counsel's base fee for trial including refresher		£3,000.00	
19	Fee of expert witness (Dr. IJ)	—	£1,000.00	
20	Expenses of witnesses of fact	—	£150.00	
	ATTENDANCES, COMMUNICATIONS AND WORK TO BE DONE			
	Claimant			
21	1 hour at £180			£180.00
22	8 hours at £140			£1,120.00
	Witnesses of fact			
23	5 hours at £140			£700.00
	Medical expert (Dr. IJ)			
24	1 hour at £140			£140.00
	Defendant and his solicitor			
25	2 hours at £140			£280.00
	To Summary	£ —	£5,300.00	£5,920.00
	Court (communications only)			
26	1 hour at £140			£140.00
	Counsel (communications only)			
27	3 hours at £140			£420.00
	Documents			
28	1 hour at £180, 25 hours at £140 and 15 hours at £85			£4,995.00
	Negotiations			
29	5 hours at £140			£700.00
	Other work			
30	5 hours at £140			£700.00
31	VAT on solicitor's base fees	£2,253.13		
	To Summary	£2,253.13	£ —	£6,955.00
	SUMMARY			
	Part 1			
	Page 1	£ —	£480.00	£751.00
	Page 2	£972.47	£372.96	£4,783.00
	Total base costs already incurred	£972.47	£852.96	£5,534.00
	Part 2			
	Page 2	£ —	£5,300.00	£5,920.00
	Page 3	£2,253.13	£ —	£6,955.00
	Total base costs to be incurred	£2,253.13	£5,300.00	£12,875.00
	Total of base costs	£3,225.60	£6,152.96	£18,409.00
	Grand total			£27,787.56

(c) Allocation questionnaire

[10.3]

Although the estimate of costs required to accompany the allocation question-naire does not act as a limit to the amount of costs which may be claimed, it may be taken into account on a detailed or summary assessment and, if an estimate is substantially exceeded, this will provide ammunition for an opponent when those costs come to be assessed. When preparing the estimate for the allocation questionnaire it is not necessary to do more than enter a figure on the questionnaire but that figure must have been worked out carefully and it is advisable to be in a position to back up the estimated figure with a breakdown showing how it has been arrived at.

(d) Pre-trial checklist

[10.4]

The costs estimate accompanying the pre-trial checklist must be accurate in respect of costs incurred to date, and there is no reason why it should not be. With regard to the future costs it should be possible to be more accurate than at the allocation stage, since the litigation will by that time have taken on a definite pattern. Again, an estimate which is exceeded, while not limiting the amount of costs which can be claimed, may be taken into account and will provide an opponent with the opportunity to attack the figures sought.

(e) Additional liabilities

[10.5]

Because of the desire to preserve confidentiality, additional liabilities (success fees and after-the-event insurance premiums) have been excluded from esti-mates. There is concern that this exclusion defeats the object of estimates and costs transparency.

(f) Exceeding the estimate

[10.6]

There is continuing consultation with the profession as to whether estimates of between-the-parties costs should result in a limit on the recoverable costs which cannot be exceeded without a reasonable explanation. Since September 2005 section 6.5A of the Costs Practice Direction provides that if there is a difference of 20% or more between the base costs claimed and the costs shown in its estimate, the receiving party must on a detailed assessment provide in the bill of costs a statement of the reasons for the difference. The Civil Jus-tice Council has taken this further and recommends that the Practice Direction should now be amended to ensure that the giving of an estimate carries a sanction if the estimate is departed from significantly.

This seems unlikely in respect of the allocation questionnaire because the figure given is simply the best that can be arrived at on the information available. The estimate accompanying the pre-trial checklist will provide an opportunity for revising the figures, but if there is a change of circumstance, resulting in the estimate being substantially wrong, it will probably be in the party's interests to inform the court and the opposing parties of the new figures as soon as possible.

Another question to be decided is whether a judge is entitled to exercise discretion to exceed the estimate and in what circumstances. The allocation estimate is less likely to influence the judges than the pre-trial checklist estimate, although both estimates should be as accurate as circumstances permit.

(g) Revision

[10.7]

As costs estimates assume greater significance it is not only important that they should be as accurate as possible, but also to remember that a revised estimate may be served at any time if it transpires that the original estimate was too low.

(h) Guidance

[10.8]

Although the Court of Appeal in *Leigh v Michelin Tyre plc* [2003] EWCA Civ 1766, [2004] 2 All ER 175, agreed with the district judge that despite the claimant's estimate of costs being wholly inadequate it had not prejudiced the paying party and therefore the amount of costs eventually claimed should not be reduced, it deprecated the circuit judge's description of costs estimates as being 'damp squibs'. The court gave the following guidance:

First, the estimates made by solicitors of the overall likely costs of the litigation should usually provide a useful yard-stick by which the reasonableness of the costs finally claimed may be measured. If there is a substantial difference between the estimated costs and the costs claimed, that difference calls for an explanation. In the absence of a satisfactory explanation, the court may conclude that the difference itself is evidence from which it can conclude that the costs claimed are unreasonable.

Second, the court may take the estimated costs into account if the other party shows that it relied on the estimate in a certain way. An obvious example would be where A shows that he relied on the relatively low estimate given by B not to make an offer of settlement, but carried on with the litigation on the basis that his potential liability for costs was likely to be of the order indicated in B's estimate.

Third, the court may take the estimate into account in cases where it decides that it would probably have given different case management directions if a realistic estimate had been given. It might, for example, have trimmed the number of experts who could be called, and taken other steps to slim down the complexity of the litigation in the interests of controlling costs in a reasonable and proportionate manner.

It would not be a correct use of the power conferred by Costs Practice Direction paragraph 6.6 to hold a party to his estimate simply in order to penalise him for providing an inadequate estimate. Thus, if (a) the paying party did not rely on the estimate in any way, (b) the court concludes that, even if the estimate had been close to the figure ultimately claimed, its case management directions would not have been affected, and (c) the costs claimed are otherwise reasonable and proportionate, it would be wrong to reduce the costs claimed simply because they exceed the amount of the estimate. That would be tantamount to treating a costs estimate as a costs cap, in circumstances where the estimate does not purport to be a cap.

COSTS CAPPING

(a) Court control

[10.9]

A primary objective of the CPR was to restrict the costs through case management, with the court controlling the work to be done by the parties to ensure it was proportionate to the issues. For various reasons, including the front-loading of work by the CPR regime, this approach has had limited, if any, success. The other side of the coin is to limit the work by restricting costs in advance. On the small claims track this is achieved by not awarding between-the-parties profit costs. Both parties know at the outset what, in normal circumstances, the recoverable costs will be, whatever the outcome of the litigation. On the fast track, control is gradually being achieved by the court by fixed trial costs, the predictable costs scheme for road traffic pre-action costs and continuing research into fixed pre-trial costs. On the multi-track an increasingly important development in court control of costs is costs capping, which a former Master of the Rolls called 'rough justice; which has to be contemplated to rein in costs'. Costs capping is an acknowledgement of the failure of the judiciary to restrict the costs at the start of the proceedings through case management and at the end of the proceedings by failing to award between the parties only those costs which are reasonable and proportionate. To continue the equestrian analogy, the bridle and the bit are there, but the horse has bolted.

(b) Jurisdiction

(i)   Legislation

[10.10]

Pioneering work on costs capping was done by District Judge Lethem in the Tunbridge Wells County Court. His philosophy is that the difficulty with the present regime is that the assessment of costs takes place *ex post facto*. So the judge retrospectively assessing the costs of the successful party is not assisting the solicitor in the budgeting exercise contemplated in *Jefferson* (see para [11.38]) but is simply penalising him to the extent the judge thinks he got it wrong. Costs capping orders are a bespoke solution tailored to each particular case based on considering the costs estimates filed with the allocation questionnaires.

District Judge Lethem founds his jurisdiction not only on paragraph 6 of the Costs Practice Direction but also on s 51(3) of the Supreme Court (now Senior Courts) Act 1981 which provides: 'The court shall have full power to determine by whom and to what extent costs are to be paid' without specifying that this shall be done at any particular stage of the proceedings. He receives further support from CPR 3.1(2)(*m*) which empowers the court to 'take any other step or make any other order for the purpose of managing the case and furthering the overriding objective'. However this is subject to the provision 'except where these rules provide otherwise' and CPR 44.3 provides that the court must have regard to Part 36 offers and the conduct of the parties neither of which can be done until after the conclusion of the proceedings. Accordingly the requirements of CPR 3.1(2) are infringed unless the cost capping order permits both prospective and retrospective variation on these lines:

> 'The base costs of the Claimant shall not, without the permission of the court, exceed the sum of £x [or such sum as the Regional Costs Judge shall determine at the adjourned hearing referred to below] and those of the Defendant shall not exceed £y [or such sum as the Regional Costs Judge shall determine at the adjourned hearing referred to below] save that any costs awarded in favour of a party on any interim application shall not count towards the said costs limit unless the court orders otherwise. Either party may apply without notice to increase the costs limit and, unless otherwise ordered, any such application shall be supported by a statement addressing the need for the increase and a revised costs estimate calculated to trial.'

Costs capping orders being bespoke and not off-the-peg, adjustments can be made where appropriate in each case, for example the costs of both parties need not be capped and there does not have to be a further hearing to fix the cap in every case.

(ii) The cases

[10.11]

Griffiths v Solutia UK Ltd [2001] EWCA Civ 736, [2001] All ER (D) 196 (Apr). The court said that although the CPR did not confer upon the court an express power to place an advance limit on the costs which would be recoverable for all or part of the litigation (equivalent to the power in the Arbitration Act 1996, s 65), case management powers surely allowed a judge to exercise the power of limiting costs, either indirectly or even directly, so that they are proportionate to the amount involved. Judges conducting cases should make full use of their powers under section 6 of the Costs Practice Direction to obtain estimates of costs and to exercise their powers in respect of costs and case management to keep costs within the bounds of the proportionate in accordance with the overriding objective.

AB v Leeds Teaching Hospital NHS Trust [2003] EWHC 1034 (QB), [2003] 3 Costs LR 405. Having referred to s 51 of the Supreme Court (now Senior Courts) Act 1981, to the various parts of the CPR which deal with costs, and giving full effect to the overriding objective of the CPR, the judge was not only satisfied the court has power to make a costs cap order, but that it should do so in group litigation in which the desirability of ensuring that costs are kept within bounds makes it unnecessary for the court to require exceptional circumstances to be shown before exercising its discretion to make a costs cap order, as has been suggested in the administrative field. After considering the four component parts of solicitors' costs, experts' fees, counsels' fees and other disbursements in the light of a probable recovery of £10 to £15 million, the judge imposed a costs cap on the claimants to the end of the trial in the sum of £500,000.

1. In favour

[10.12]

Various Ledward Claimants v Kent and Medway Health Authority and East Kent Hospitals NHS Trust [2003] EWHC 251 (QB), [2004] 1 Costs LR 101. A group litigation order had been made by eight lead claimants in respect of 59 claims alleging rape or sexual assault by a consultant gynaecologist when the claimants were patients in care and he was employed by the defendants. The parties agreed that there was a need for a costs cap on the generic case and the eight lead cases which should be in respect of the base costs only, and not take into account any CFA success fee. The claimants' solicitors' analysis of work to be done contained gross overestimates which the court reduced by 50%. The claimants' cost to the end of the trial were capped at £215,000, being made up of 740 grade A hours at £150, 265 grade B hours at £135 and 745 grade D hours at £85. It was appropriate to award leading counsel £250 an hour for 75 hours of pre-trial work, a brief fee of £50,000 and refreshers of £1,750 per day. Junior counsels' fees were allowed at half of these amounts. The outcome of the application was that the claimants' costs were capped at £395,000 and defendants' costs at £460,000.

Laybourne v Mills Tunbridge Wells County Court (2003), unreported. Speaking at the IBC Annual Costs Conference, District Judge Lethem said that it was not in his experience that the approach contemplated in *Smart* (para [10.13]) would be required. For example, in his own case of *Laybourne v Mills*, which was a fast-track case, he was faced at the allocation stage with a costs estimate of £22,000 to recover £13,000. Could it really be right that in these circumstances a court should sit idly by? Equally, issues of proportionality might be highly relevant in lower level multi-track trials. He considered that a case can be made out for such control on all major and significant litigation. Generally, the costs estimate found in or attached to the allocation questionnaire will suggest whether or not the case is one where the court ought to consider a costs capping order.

King v Telegraph Group Ltd [2004] EWCA Civ 613, (2004) Times, 21 May. Although the subject matter of this action was defamation the principles enunciated in the judgment can be applied to any substantial litigation. The claimant was funded under a conditional fee agreement but had no insurance to cover the defendant's costs if he lost. The court referred to the obvious unfairness of a defendant in libel proceedings having to pay very high costs even if successful because an impecunious client, without insurance protection, was funded under a CFA. Otherwise the existing system was bound to have a chilling effect upon those seeking to exercise their right to freedom of expression as a result, as in this case, of the extravagant claimant's costs. The claimant's solicitors had written a letter before action in a vituperative tone, calculated to raise the temperature and to inflate the parties' legal costs in a manner that entirely conflicted with the philosophy underlying the Civil Justice Reforms. There were three weapons available to a party concerned about extravagant conduct by the other side, or the risk of it: a prospective costs-capping order; a retrospective assessment of costs conducted in accordance with the principles of the CPR; and a wasted costs order. Recourse to the first of those weapons should be the court's response when a concern was raised by defendants of the type being considered. The court had power to impose a costs-capping order in the appropriate case, as was clear from s 51 of the Supreme Court (now Senior Courts) Act 1981 and CPR rule 3.1(2)(m) and, moreover, in deciding what order to make, the court should take the principles set out in CPR rule 44.3 governing the retrospective assessment of costs as an important point of reference. In such a case a High Court master should at the allocation stage make an order analogous to an order under s 65(1) of the Arbitration Act 1996; and in the ordinary course of things such order would cover the costs of the litigation. Further, when making a costs-capping order the court should prescribe a total amount of recoverable costs, which would be inclusive so far as a CFA funded party was concerned, of any additional liability. If the introduction of such a novel costs-capping regime meant that a claimant's lawyers might be reluctant to accept instructions on a CFA basis unless they assess the chances of success as significantly greater than evens, that was a small price to pay in contrast to the price that was potentially to be paid if the present state of affairs were allowed to continue. In future, if a claimant's solicitors agreed to act under a CFA without insurance cover in a defamation action they would have to bear in mind from the time they were first instructed the requirement to assess the likely value of the claim, its importance and complexity and the necessary work appropriate to each of the stages in bringing the action to trial, as well as the likely overall cost. For further thoughts see 'CFAs and costs-capping' in Chapter 42.

In *Sheppard v Mid Essex Strategic Health Authority* [2006] 1 Costs LR 8, it was held that the courts are moving towards a system of pre-emptive strikes in order to avoid the costs of litigation spiralling out of control and becoming unreasonable or disproportionate. It was far better for the court to attempt to control and budget for costs where appropriate, than to allow costs to be incurred and then submitted to detailed assessment after the event. The idea of a costs capping order was to exercise some kind of control, even over the most experienced and respected firms of solicitors. Any solicitor had to act with the best interests of their client at heart. With the best intentions there was a risk that in certain cases, without some kind of control by the court, there may be an unreasonable or disproportionate expenditure of limited resources. It was significant in the instant case that both sides were publicly funded. Public funds were scarce and it was the duty of the court to play its part in ensuring they were expended properly and effectively. The estimate of the claimant's costs was substantial for an action in clinical negligence, even with two claimants. On the facts it was appropriate for the master to have made the capping order since there was a real risk that, without control, the already substantial costs would become disproportionate or unreasonable. The most effective way of exercising control was by having a budget imposed by an experienced costs judge.

During the hearing of *AB v Leeds Teaching Hospital* (above para [10.11]), the Senior Costs Judge made it clear that the purpose of the cap was to fix a maximum sum a party could recover at the conclusion of the case; he commented this would obviate the need for a detailed assessment. This gave rise to conjecture whether costs budgeting and costs-capping may eventually lead to the end of detailed assessments, not only in group litigation but in cases on the multi-track generally.

2.   Against

[10.13]

Smart v East Cheshire NHS Trust [2003] EWHC 2806 (QB), 80 BMLR 115. Although the Queen's Bench judge acknowledged the legality of costs capping by the procedural judge he was less than enthusiastic about it, saying that the costs cap is not of universal application, he continued 'In my judgement, the court should only consider making a costs cap order in such cases where the applicant shows by evidence that there is a real and substantial risk that without such an order costs will be disproportionately or unreasonably incurred; and that this risk may not be managed by conventional case management and a detailed assessment of costs after a trial and it is just to make an order. It seems to me that it is unnecessary to ascribe to such a test the general heading of exceptional circumstances. I would expect that in the run of ordinary actions it will be rare for this test to be satisfied but it is impossible to predict all the circumstances in which it may be said to arise'.

Petursson v Hutchison 3G UK Ltd [2004] EWHC 2609 (TCC) 28 October held that a costs cap should normally be prospective and a retrospective cap would be wholly exceptional; indeed District Judge Lethem finds it hard to envisage any circumstances in which the court could make a fair retrospective order. A party should know in advance if its costs are to be capped so that it can tailor its case accordingly. It would be unjust for the court to order parties to comply with directions and then to impose a retrospective cap. In *Petursson* the defendant had complied with court directions, and indeed had probably spent more time on the action than might otherwise be the case as a result of the claimants' failures to comply with orders. Both sides have the right to a fair hearing. To impose a retrospective limit on costs would have amounted to a breach of the defendant's right to a fair hearing. It would be a wholly exceptional case where it was appropriate to order a cap retrospectively. The appropriate time to consider a costs cap is at the early stage of an action when the parties and the court can together plan the steps needed to bring the matter to trial, the costs implications of those steps and whether a cap is appropriate. The judge also added, controversially in the light of *AB v Leeds Teaching Hospital* (above), that to justify a cap there must be a risk that the future costs which would be incurred would be disproportionately or unreasonably incurred or could not be managed by conventional case management and a detailed assessment of costs after trial.

In *Knight v Beyond Properties Pty Ltd* [2006] EWHC 1242 (Ch), [2006] NLJR 989, the court refused to make a costs capping order solely on the grounds the claimant was instructing solicitors under a conditional fee agreement and he did not have after-the-event insurance cover. Lord Justice

Brooke's remarks in *King v Telegraph Group Ltd* (above) were made in the context of a defamation action. He was not laying down wider principles applicable to all litigation. The court would only consider making a cost-capping order where it was established on evidence that there was a real risk of disproportionate or unreasonable costs being incurred and that risk could not satisfactorily be provided for by more conventional means, such as the usual costs assessment after the trial. Retrospective judgments were likely to be more reliable than prospective ones.

In *Henry v BBC* [2005] EWHC 2503 (QB), [2006] 1 All ER 154 the judge having refused a costs capping order on the grounds the application was too late and an order could not be retrospective, went on to say that another reason why he would not make a cost-capping order was that did not feel qualified to determine without assistance from a costs judge the amount of the brief fees, the charging rates and how much work between the application and the end of the trial would be reasonable and proportionate. The exercise was more suitable for a costs judge, or at least a judge sitting with a costs judge.

Sayers v Smithkline Beecham plc [2004] EWHC 1899 (QB), [2004] All ER (D) 607 (Jul). Mr Justice Keith: 'Without wishing to lay down a hard and fast rule, it seems to me that a prospective order limiting the amount of costs which one party to group litigation may recover from another party should only be contemplated where there are grounds for believing that a party may incur excessive legal costs, i.e. costs which are not justified by the scale of the litigation or the complexity of the issues which it raises, or which are disproportionate to the sums of money at stake, and where the risk that excessive legal costs are being incurred unnecessarily will not be picked up by the court when exercising case management functions or when conducting a detailed assessment of the costs after the trial. It has not been suggested that that can be said to apply to this case up to now. Whether it could be said to apply to the case in the future will depend on the form which the case takes. But cost capping is a relatively dramatic course to take, and it will only be ordered on cogent evidence'.

(c) The future

[10.14]

These decisions demonstrated that not all of the senior judiciary share the enthusiasm of District Judge Lethem and the Senior Costs Judge for judicial costs control on the multi-track by, in effect, acting as costs judges in advance of the litigation and that the difference of judicial opinions needed resolution. It was confidently expected and intended that in *Willis v Nicolson* [2007] EWCA Civ 199, 152 Sol Jo LB 394, 13 March the Court of Appeal would give general guidance on costs capping.. Lord Justice Buxton said:

'The very high costs of civil litigation in England and Wales is a matter of concern not merely to the parties in a particular case, but for the litigation system as a whole. One element in the high cost of litigation was undoubtedly the expectation as to annual income of the professionals who conducted it. The costs system could not do anything about that, because it assessed the proper charge for work on the basis of the market rates charged by professionals. It had been hoped when the CPR came into force that that practice might change. However, no change has occurred. The reasonable amount per hour of a professional's time continues to be determined by the market. Therefore, the focus of costs limitation has to be on the way in which the professionals intended to conduct the case, because the amount recoverable on assessment was fixed, as to rates, by the standard amounts allowed. To limit the way in which professionals intended to conduct a case was a delicate matter. The court would have to be careful to select the right moment in the litigation process for the consideration of a costs cap.'

To limit the way in which the professionals intend to conduct the case is indeed a delicate matter. If there is to be a cap in any case, the party capped is likely to be required to alter its conduct in relation to costs, if that were not part of the intent behind the cap then there would probably be no point in having a cap.

The court will therefore need to be careful before imposing such a restriction, particularly when those restricted are, as in the present case, acting for a claimant who has suffered catastrophic injuries.

And further reasons why the exercise of costs capping should not be entered upon lightly are that the amount of the cap has to be determined by a costs judge, a scarce resource; and if the exercise is to be done properly it is likely, as in effect a substitute for final assessment, to be as expensive and time-consuming as a final assessment itself.

With all these factors in mind we drafted a comprehensive set of principles to be applied in personal injury cases, which are the most obvious candidates for costs capping; which could also be considered for application to other types of case.'

Hurrah! That is what we were waiting for. But Lord Justice Buxton continued:

> 'However, further discussion with members of the court, including the Master of the Rolls and the Deputy Head of Civil Justice, has demonstrated that, despite the terms in which permission to appeal was granted in this case and the observations in this court, there remain serious doubts as to whether further guidance on costs capping, if it is to be given at all, should emanate from a constitution of the court as opposed to being formulated by the Civil Procedure Rules Committee, after extensive consultation. We are bound to recognise the imperative of that view. We therefore do not pursue the question further. It will be for the Rules Committee to decide whether, and if so with what degree of urgency, to take up the issues that we have identified earlier in this judgment.'

With the greatest respect we already knew the issues – what we wanted and expected were some answers – but they were vetoed from on high.

The only conclusions to be drawn from the judgments are that the earlier an application for a costs cap is made the better, and that the judges at the coal-face in the High Court are less attracted to costs capping than those sitting in the Court of Appeal

It may be that benchmarking or a predictable matrix requiring no, or minimal, judicial input is the immediate way ahead.

The Civil Justice Council recommends that in multi track cases where the value exceeds £1 million, in all group actions and in other complex proceedings there should be a rebuttable presumption requiring the parties to present budgets, supervised by the Court at appropriate stages to ensure compliance with the proportionality provisions of the overriding objective of the CPR. It also recommends that where the parties have agreed or the court has approved an estimate or budget and/or cap, both the receiving party and the paying party should be entitled to apply for detailed assessment but only at a costs risk if a significant increase/reduction in the amount claimed is not achieved.

(d) Costs Capping Rules

[10.15]

With commendable alacrity the Civil Procedure Rules Committee (CPRC) drafted amendments to CPR Part 44 and the Costs Practice Direction on which it invited comments. Less encouraging was the accompanying statement that the proposals 'are drawn from current case law' and 'do not propose new policy' when the 'current case law' is in conflict and there appears to be no 'present policy'. I understand the problem was that the members of the committee were no more able to reach agreement than were the judiciary and rather than resolve their opposing views settled on an anodyne approach based on the following guidelines:

- the court has jurisdiction to make costs capping orders;
- the approach to such orders should be conservative and such orders should only be made in exceptional circumstances when there is a particular reason for doing so, not as a matter of course; and
- costs capping orders should generally be made on application.

The rules which were introduced into the Civil Procedure Rules by the Civil Procedure (Amendment No 3) Rules 2008 on 6 April 2009 are:

44.18 Costs capping orders – General

(1)   A costs capping order is an order limiting the amount of future costs (including disbursements) which a party may recover pursuant to an order for costs subsequently made.

(2)   In this rule, "future costs" means costs incurred in respect of work done after the date of the costs capping order but excluding the amount of any additional liability.

(3)   This rule does not apply to protective costs orders.

(4)   A costs capping order may be in respect of—

(a)   the whole litigation; or

(b)   any issues which are ordered to be tried separately.

(5)   The court may at any stage of proceedings make a costs capping order against all or any of the parties, if—

    (a)   it is in the interests of justice to do so;

    (b)   there is a substantial risk that without such an order costs will be disproportionately incurred; and

    (c)   it is not satisfied that the risk in sub-paragraph (b) can be adequately controlled by—

        (i)   case management directions or orders made under Part 3; and

        (ii)   detailed assessment of costs.

(6)   In considering whether to exercise its discretion under this rule, the court will consider all the circumstances of the case, including—

    (a)   whether there is a substantial imbalance between the financial position of the parties;

    (b)   whether the costs of determining the amount of the cap are likely to be proportionate to the overall costs of the litigation;

    (c)   the stage which the proceedings have reached; and

(d)　the costs which have been incurred to date and the future costs.

(7)　A costs capping order, once made, will limit the costs recoverable by the party subject to the order unless a party successfully applies to vary the order. No such variation will be made unless—

　(a)　there has been a material and substantial change of circumstances since the date when the order was made; or

　(b)　there is some other compelling reason why a variation should be made.

44.19 Application for a costs capping order

(1)　An application for a costs capping order must be made on notice in accordance with Part 23.

(2)　The application notice must—

　(a)　set out—

　　(i)　whether the costs capping order is in respect of the whole of the litigation or a particular issue which is ordered to be tried separately; and

　　(ii)　why a costs capping order should be made; and

　(b)　be accompanied by an estimate of costs setting out—

　　(i)　the costs (and disbursements) incurred by the applicant to date; and

　　(ii)　the costs (and disbursements) which the applicant is likely to incur in the future conduct of the proceedings.

(3)　The court may give directions for the determination of the application and such directions may—

　(a)　direct any party to the proceedings—

　　(i)　to file a schedule of costs in the form set out in the Practice Direction supplementing this rule;

　　(ii)　to file written submissions on all or any part of the issues arising;

　(b)　fix the date and time estimate of the hearing of the application;

　(c)　indicate whether the judge hearing the application will sit with an assessor at the hearing of the application; and

　(d)　include any further directions as the court sees fit.

44.20 Application to vary a costs capping order

An application to vary a costs capping order must be made by application notice pursuant to Part 23.

At the same time a new Section 23A was inserted into the Costs Practice Direction as follows:

CPD Section 23A Costs capping orders

When to make an application

23A.1　*The court will make a costs capping order only in exceptional circumstances.*

23A.2　*An application for a costs capping order must be made as soon as possible, preferably before or at the first case management hearing or shortly afterwards. The stage which the proceedings have reached at the time of the application will be one of the factors the court will consider when deciding whether to make a costs capping order.*

Estimate of costs

23A.3 The estimate of costs required by rule 44.19 must be in the form illustrated in Precedent H in the Schedule of Costs Precedents annexed to this Practice Direction.

Schedule of costs

23A.4   The schedule of costs referred to in rule 44.19(3)—
(a)   must set out—
   (i)   each sub-heading as it appears in the applicant's estimate of costs (column 1);
   (ii)   alongside each sub-heading, the amount claimed by the applicant in the applicant's estimate of costs (column 2); and
   (iii) alongside the figures referred to in sub-paragraph (ii) the amount that the respondent proposes should be allowed under each sub-heading (column 3); and
   must be supported by a statement of truth.

Assessing the quantum of the costs cap

23A.5   When assessing the quantum of a costs cap, the court will take into account the factors detailed in rule 44.5 and the relevant provisions supporting that rule in this Practice Direction. The court may also take into account when considering a party's estimate of the costs they are likely to incur in the future conduct of the proceedings a reasonable allowance on costs for contingencies.

A triumph for the *Smart v East Cheshire NHS Trust* (para [10.13]) school of thought. Costs capping is virtually dead in the water. Costs capping orders can now be made only in exceptional cases where (i) it is in the interests of justice to do so, (ii) there is a substantial risk that without a cap disproportionate costs will be incurred and (iii) where conventional case management and a detailed assessment are not sufficient to control costs adequately. That these are virtually insuperable hurdles was demonstrated by Coulson J in *Barr v Biffa Waste Services Ltd* [2009] EWHC 2444 (TCC), [2009] NLJR 1513, [2009] All ER (D) 176 (Oct) and Eady J in *Peacock v MGN Ltd* [2009] EWHC 769 (QB), [2009] All ER (D) 88 (Apr). In the words of Coulson J, 'It would be a very unusual case in which a High Court judge did not feel able to utilise one or both of [the tools of case management and detailed assessment] to control disproportionate costs. That is, after all, what they are there for'.

An application for a costs capping order should be made as soon as possible and one of the factors that the court will consider when deciding whether to make an order is the stage that the proceedings have reached when the application is made.

The provisions provide that the estimate of costs must be in a designated form. It also indicates the way in which the schedule of costs must be set out and that a statement of truth must support the schedule. Finally, the proposed provisions set out the factors that the court will take into account when assessing the quantum of the costs cap and clarifies that this may include a reasonable allowance on costs for contingencies.

In limited circumstances rule 44.18(7) permits an application to vary the cap, but only if there has been a material and substantial change of circumstances or for some other 'compelling reason', which is not easy to envisage.

The rules do not apply to protective costs orders, nor do they apply to solicitor and client costs and therefore they do not restrict the amount a party may wish to spend on the litigation. They are not retrospective and apply only to future costs as defined by rule 44.18(2).

Whether the guidance in the new rule and practice direction will generate more enthusiasm in the judiciary for costs capping remains to be seen.

PROTECTIVE COSTS ORDERS

[10.16]

Do you mean what I mean when we talk about protective, protected, pre-emptive and prospective costs orders? Or as the judge in *R (on the application of the Campaign for Nuclear Disarmament) v Prime Minister* [2002] EWHC 2777 (Admin), [2003] 3 LRC 335, DC put it: 'Counsel describes his application as seeking a "protective costs order", but I prefer the adjective "pre-emptive".' Until then *pre-emptive costs orders* were a rare species living in the tropical jungle of the Chancery Division, emerging into the daylight only when a trustee or personal representative sought an advance assurance that win or lose they could take their costs out of the property in dispute. For more than a hundred years they have been known as *'Beddoe applications'* (see para [36.4]). Call me old-fashioned, but I would prefer to leave it that way.

'Prospective costs orders' is a useful portmanteau description of costs-capping orders in all their forms. It is however a term appropriated by the Vice-Chancellor of the Chancery Division in 2001 in a Practice Statement: 'Trust Proceedings; Prospective Costs Orders' relating to obtaining authority to make future payments of costs to parties out of a fund. Perhaps we can share the designation.

That leaves *protective costs orders* (sometimes called protected costs orders, but not, so far as I am aware, by the rules or the judiciary).

The first case was *R (on the application of the Campaign for Nuclear Disarmament) v Prime Minister* (above) in which the Campaign for Nuclear Disarmament (CND) sought permission to apply for a declaration that the United Nations Security Council Resolution 1441, on the basis of which weapons inspectors had gone to Iraq, did not authorise the use of force in the event of there being a breach, and that a further Security Council resolution would be required to authorise such force. In the course of proceedings CND applied for and obtained an order that in the event of costs being awarded against it in the High Court such costs be limited to £25,000, on the grounds that CND's modest resources were such that if they were not given the comfort sought by the order they would be unable to proceed with the challenge.

The authorities and philosophy of protective costs orders were considered in *R (on the application of Corner House Research) v Secretary of State for Trade and Industry* [2005] EWCA Civ 192, [2005] 4 All ER 1. They will only be made in exceptional cases. The governing principles are:
(1)

(i) A protective costs order may be made at any stage of the proceedings, on such conditions as the court thinks fit, provided that the court is satisfied that
    (a) the issues raised are of general public importance;
    (b) the public interest requires that those issues should be resolved;
    (c) the applicant has no private interest in the outcome of the case;
    (d) having regard to the financial resources of the applicant and the respondent and to the amount of costs that are likely to be involved it is fair and just to make the order;
    (e) if the order were not made the applicant would probably discontinue the proceedings and would be acting reasonably in so doing.

(ii) If those acting for the applicant were doing so *pro bono* that would be likely to enhance the merits of the application for a protective costs order.

(iii) It is for the court, in its discretion, to decide whether it is fair and just to make the order in the light of the above considerations: *R v Lord Chancellor, ex p Child Povery Action Group; R v DPP, ex p Bull* [1999] 1 WLR 347 approved, save in respect of the second guideline which set too high a test on the prospects of success required.

(2) A protective costs order can take a number of different forms and the choice of form is an important aspect of the judge's discretion. Where an applicant is seeking an order for costs, if it is successful the court should prescribe by way of a capping order a total amount of the recoverable costs, which allows for modest legal representation (*King v Telegraph Ltd* above applied).

(3) A claimant should apply for a protective costs order in his claim form, which should include a schedule of the claimant's future costs, of and incidental to, the full judicial review application. A defendant should set out any reasons for resisting an order in its acknowledgment of service.

R (on the application of Compton) v Wiltshire Primary Care Trust [2008] EWCA Civ 749 confirmed that the principles for making a protective costs order set out in *Corner House* are to be followed in the court of first instance and in the Court of Appeal. The criterion that the issues raised had to be of 'general' public importance did not mean that they had to be of interest to all the public nationally. In the present case it had been open to the judge to find that there was a public interest in the resolution of issues as to the closure of parts of a hospital that affected a wide community and that the issues were therefore of general public importance. 'Exceptionality' was not an additional criterion but a prediction of the effect of applying the principles of *Corner House*.

Procedurally, if the recipient of the protective costs order in the court below wished to appeal, an application for an order should be lodged with an application for permission. The respondent should have an opportunity of providing written reasons why an order was appropriate. The decision would be taken on paper by the single Lord Justice. If an order was refused the applicant could apply orally. If it was granted then a respondent would need compelling reasons to set it aside. Appeals from the refusal to grant an order, or against an order, should be dealt with by a single Lord Justice on paper with the normal order being no order for costs.

In *R (on the application of Buglife, The Invertebrate Conservation Trust) v Thurrock Thames Gateway Development Corpn* [2008] EWCA Civ 1209, [2008] 45 EG 101 (CS), (2008) Times, 18 November the applicant Conservation Trust applied for a protective costs order (pco) capping its liability in costs in a dispute with the respondent local planning authority, who in turn applied for an order capping their own liability in costs to the applicant. The Court of Appeal stressed that the courts should do their utmost to dissuade the parties from engaging an expensive satellite litigation on the question whether pcos and cost capping orders should be made. In *Buglife* the guidelines had not been followed. The local authority's case was not put before the court on paper before the applicants for permission to appeal and for a pco were considered by the judge. It was of great importance that issues relating to permission to appeal and to a pco and a consequent cost capping order should all be considered at the same time and on paper. In the present case, because the claimant had been granted permission to appeal, it should have some protection but it would be unfair for it to have total protection especially given the fact that there was a significant risk that it would lose. The just order was to limit the claimant's costs in the Court of Appeal to a further £10,000 making its potential total liability £20,000. It was right to cap the authority's liability to the claimant in an appropriate sum, which was also £10,000.

The Master of the Rolls said: "In the rare case in which it is necessary to have an oral hearing, it should last a short time as contemplated in *Corner House* and it should take place in good time before the hearing of the substantive application for judicial review, so that the parties may know the position as to their potential liabilities for costs in advance of incurring the costs."

[10.17]

Subsequent decisions have demonstrated the difficulty in satisfying the dual requirements of there being a public interest but there being no private interest. In *R (on the application of Goodson) v HM Coroner for Bedfordshire and Luton* [2004] EWHC 2931 (Admin), (2005) TLR 1 November although there was an issue of general importance the applicant had an undoubted private interest in the proceedings and the public interest in having the issues decided was not so great as to require a decision from the Appeal Court at the inevitable expense to the Luton and Dunstable Hospital NHS Trust, the second respondent, as to its own costs. In *Weir v Secretary of State for Transport* [2005] EWHC 2192 (Ch), [2005] All ER (D) 160 (Oct) 14 October the claimant, a member of the Railtrack private shareholders action group who had commenced proceedings against the Secretary of State alleging misfeasance in public office and breach of the European Convention on Human Rights, failed to obtain a protective costs order limiting his costs liability to £1.35 million because he personally was seeking compensation

R (on the application of Ministry of Defence) v Wiltshire and Swindon Coroner [2005] EWHC 889 (Admin), [2005] 4 All ER 40, QBD demonstrated that a protective costs order can be made in favour of a defendant, The court granted an application by the Ministry of Defence that the Coroner for Wiltshire and Swindon produce digital recordings of his summing up at an inquest, but refused the application of the defendant coroner for a protective costs order because, provided he acted reasonably, he would be indemnified by the council as his active involvement in the case was reasonable. Therefore a protective costs order was inappropriate.

In *Eweida v British Airways Plc* [2009] EWCA Civ 1025, 153 Sol Jo (no 40) 37, [2009] All ER (D) 161 (Oct), the claimant failed to obtain either a protective costs order or a cap. She worked for the employer on its check-in desks and complained of not having been allowed to wear a cross denoting her Christian faith in such a way as to be visible outside her uniform. The tribunal rejected all aspects of the claim and the EAT dismissed her appeal. When she obtained permission to appeal to the Court of Appeal she applied for a protective costs order but her application was refused not only because this was not public law litigation but also the employee's private interest was too significant to make an order appropriate even if it were public law litigation. Her alternative of a costs capping order was also refused on the grounds that the rates proposed to be charged were not unreasonable and there was no reason to suppose that any risk of disproportionality could not be adequately controlled by the costs judge on the detailed assessment.

The future

[10.18]

The Civil Justice Council recommends building on the protective costs order as explained in *Corner House Research* (above) to permit access to justice in public law cases by further consideration being given to the wider import of the judgment (*Recommendation 12*). However, in *R (A) (Disputed Children) v Secretary of State for the Home Department* [2007] EWHC 2494 (Admin) while the Court accepted that the issues raised were of general importance and that the public interest required them to be resolved, it did not accept that the public interest required them to be resolved on terms that exposed the Secretary of State to a substantial costs order if she failed but prevented her from recovering her costs if she were successful. Although the Secretary of State's pocket was deep, her resources were not unlimited and money spent on litigation was money which could otherwise be spent on her ordinary operations.

On the other hand, in *Baker v (1) Quantum Clothing Group Ltd. (2) Meridian (3) Pretty Polly* [2008] EWCA Civ 823, CA, 11 June when the claimant appealed against the dismissal of her claim against her employer for damages for industrial injury suffered by her in the course of her employment it was apparent that Meridian and Pretty Polly could be affected by the judgment on appeal and they were joined as parties to the proceedings. The claimant had after-the-event insurance which covered the first defendant's costs but not those of the added defendants. Accordingly, the claimant applied for an order that the 2nd and 3rd defendant companies should bear the burden of their own costs of her appeal in any event. Unless the application were granted, the claimant would be unable to pursue her appeal. The costs that would be incurred on the appeal were, by comparison with the costs liabilities accrued in the case to date, relatively small and it was important that those prior costs should not have been incurred pointlessly by bringing the matter to a premature end. In those circumstances and in the interests of justice, the fact that the claimant's appeal would be stifled if her application was refused outweighed the injustice that would be caused to Meridian and Pretty Polly in compelling them to bear the burden of their own costs of the appeal. Accordingly the court made a protective costs order.

BUDGETING

(a) Project management

[10.19]

One of the first mentions of budgeting was by AAS Zuckerman in a paper annexed to the Access to Justice Report under the heading 'Prospective Budget Setting'. It read: 'One option to be considered is replacing retrospective taxation (*assessment*) with prospective budget setting. Under this regime budgets would be set in advance so that the process would have to conform to budgetary constraints, rather than the costs following the process as at present'. The paper was not well received by the profession. In fact the Civil Justice Inquiry went so far as to say 'The paper occasioned a general outcry from the legal profession. Prospective budget-setting was seen as unworkable, unfair and likely to be abused by the creation of inflated budgets. The ability of judges to be involved in the hard details of matters such as costs was generally doubted because the system was an open-ended procedural activity and, therefore, could not have a budget attached to it.'

Because at that time Lord Woolf was not persuaded that either fixed fees on the one hand, or budgeting on the other, were feasible, he concluded that costs should be controlled by judicial case management of the amount of work the parties were permitted to do, and it is because this attempt has failed that the courts are revisiting the control of costs by means of budgeting – and, of course, estimates, capping, fixed costs, predictable costs and benchmark costs. Lord Woolf distinguished between estimates and budgeting as follows: 'Estimates need not go into detail and would, therefore, not disclose confidential information which might be of tactical value to an opponent. They would fall short of the radical proposals set out by Adrian Zuckerman in the issues paper. The estimates would be an indication to help the procedural judge decide the best course of action, rather than budgets which limited what parties could recover.'

A perceived impediment to costs budgeting was that it might result in unacceptable disclosure of a party's tactics, which may be legitimate even in these days in which cards on the table have replaced trial by ambush. The most colourful description of budgeting was by Professor John Peysner in a comprehensive and erudite article 'Predictability and Budgeting' in the Civil Justice Quarterly which is available on the Civil Justice Council website. He likened budgeting to a walk in inclement weather in which the walker is the claimant and the weather the defendant! He wrote: 'Post CPR a completely unpredictable piece of litigation is as unlikely as a completely predictable one. Like a country walk in inclement weather (let the walker be the claimant and the weather be the defendant) there will be a limit to the amount of predictability that can be created by planning. One route might appear to be passable but good planning will have a contingency element so that another route can be used if necessary. The ideal route is one which takes account of as many contingencies as possible and chooses a way forward which is likely to be passable in all possible conditions. Thus, one takes into account that the perfect can be the enemy of the good.'

Budgeting is no more than project management as carried out by most commercial enterprises, in common with both commercial and publicly funded litigation. It involves the assessment and costing of a project to be carried out by one or more people, made up of a series of activities or steps, both consecutive and concurrent, each involving time and money. Budgeting need be no more sophisticated than costing the various stages (eg pre-action allocation questionnaire, case management conference and pre-trial check list) which litigators now undertake wittingly or unwittingly, in case management under the CPR. It involves considering the issues, the procedural steps, the time each is likely to take, the levels of fee earner, their hourly rates and a margin, of say 15%, for Professor Peysner's really inclement weather.

(b) The Benefits

[10.20]

Budgeting will benefit the solicitor by enabling him to produce a realistic forecast of his costs for the purposes of estimates between the parties and to his client as required by Solicitors' Practice Rule 15. It will better enable him to resist attacks on his figures from either source at any stage and enable him to make an informed proposal in any application for a costs-capping order. The client will not only appreciate a solicitor who provides a budget at the outset; clients will increasingly expect a solicitor to conduct his business with the same discipline with which they conduct their own.

The Law Society recommends budgeting, its spokesman being quoted as saying that prospective budgeting is a practical way forward, although it is likely to be more appropriate for the larger cases in the multi-track. It would bring more realism to costs issues and enable clients to make informed decisions, as well as making it easier for the courts to test proportionality. He continued: 'Budgeting should not have any great effect on the level of costs, but it should make the costs more transparent, which is good. It will cause more work for solicitors and courts in the early stages of a case – this is bad – but this should be offset by the savings in time in dealing with costs at the end of the case – also good.'

Speaking at the Annual Conference of the Association of Law Costs Draftsmen, Tony Guise said: 'The provision of a budget is a tool to inform decisions about strategy and tactics. In this way, it is invaluable in determining the cost/benefit analysis of any particular action. Budgets provide a sound basis for accurate costs estimates for the court at allocation questionnaire and pre-trial checklist stages. They also ensure that one avoids attacks by paying parties arising out of the indemnity principle. Above all, failure to budget will seriously damage your wealth.'

(c) The pilots

On budgetting and costs management the future is already with us in London, Manchester and Birmingham.

1. *Royal Courts of Justice and Manchester District Registry*

[10.21]

Although Practice Direction 51D is entitled 'Defamation Proceedings Costs Management Scheme' and operates only in the Royal Courts of Justice and the Manchester District Registry, it is in fact a blueprint for costs budgetting for all types of litigation.

Although the scheme is mandatory, the costs estimates required are less detailed than those needed for a costs capping order and should not require much more than the level of information that solicitors are already obliged to provide their clients.

The aim of costs budgeting is that the court will manage the costs of the litigation as well as the case itself in a way which is proportionate to the value of the claim and the reputational issues at stake. The parties are required to monitor costs against the budget and to update each other on the position. The court may also call regular costs management conferences (by telephone where possible). At each hearing the court considers and records its approval or disapproval of each party's budget, after representations where necessary. The court will also take account of the additional costs of each procedural step when giving case management directions. Directions orders produced at the end of case management conferences and/or costs management conferences must be given to the parties on each side by their respective lawyers, together with copies of the budgets which the court has approved or disapproved.

Solicitors must liaise monthly to check that the budget is not being exceeded. In the event that the budget is exceeded, either party may apply to the court to fix a costs management conference.

And here is the sting - the judge conducting a detailed or summary assessment will have regard to the budget estimates of the receiving party and to any view previously expressed by the court. Unless there has been a significant change in circumstances the judge will approve as reasonable and proportionate any costs claimed which fall within the last previously approved budget. Only in exceptional circumstances the judge will not approve as reasonable and proportionate any costs claimed which do not fall within the last previously approved budget.

The Birmingham Mercantile Court

[10.22]

The Mercantile Court in Birmingham under His Honour Judge Simon Brown QC is running a pilot scheme whereby detailed budgets are submitted to the Court at the outset and are thoroughly scrutinised by the judge who believes that the Court has a duty to actively manage cases rather than taking a passive approach. He considers, for example, whether there are issues which could conveniently be dealt with so as to save time and money. Split trials, summary judgment and the identification of preliminary points are his forte. He is also adept at electronic disclosure having delivered the important decision in *Earles v Barclays Bank* [2009] EWHC 2500 (QB), (2009) Times, 20 October.

Professor Dominic Regan has recently been appointed by the Master of the Rolls and Lord Justice Jackson to oversee the pilot and to consider how it might well be extended to other areas of multi-track work.

Professor Regan is to report by the end of November 2010. He informs me that he is an utter convert to the process but its success very much depends upon the judge managing the case. Soundings he has taken from practitioners show that they welcome the intervention of an experienced judge setting the parties off at the outset on the right, sensible and proportionate path. In one case Judge Brown identified pointless proposed expenditure on experts who would add nothing to the knowledge of the court and in another he curbed proposed expenditure on international accountants where a Birmingham firm could do the job competently for a fraction of the price.

There is of course no reason why only mercantile matters should be managed in this way.

CHAPTER 11

GENERAL RULES ABOUT COSTS (CPR PART 44)

[11.1]

Part 44 contains the general or core costs rules. Here it is with the supplemental Practice Direction:

Part 44: General rules about costs

Contents of this part

[11.2]

CPR Rule 44.1: Scope of this part

This Part contains general rules about costs, entitlement to costs and orders in respect of pro bono representation.

(The definitions contained in Part 43 are relevant to this Part)

[11.3]

CPR Rule 44.2: Solicitor's duty to notify client

Where—

(a)   the court makes a costs order against a legally represented party; and

(b)   the party is not present when the order is made,

the party's solicitor must notify his client in writing of the costs order no later than 7 days after the solicitor receives notice of the order.

CPD Section 7 Solicitor's Duty To Notify Client: Rule 44.2

[11.4]

7.1   *For the purposes of rule 44.2 'client' includes a party for whom a solicitor is acting and any other person (for example, an insurer, a trade union or the LSC) who has instructed the solicitor to act or who is liable to pay his fees.*
7.2   *Where a solicitor notifies a client of an order under that rule, he must also explain why the order came to be made.*
7.3   *Although rule 44.2 does not specify any sanction for breach of the rule the court may, either in the order for costs itself or in a subsequent order, require the solicitor to produce to the court evidence showing that he took reasonable steps to comply with the rule.*

[11.5]

Rule 44.2 requires a solicitor to notify his client within seven days of a costs order being made against him if the client was not present when it was made. This is in place of the original proposal that the client should attend every interim hearing to ensure he is aware of what costs are being incurred. Early drafts of this rule even included the draconian sanction that a solicitor who failed to comply with the rule should pay the costs personally. Now, no sanction is prescribed for non-compliance with this much watered-down provision, although the Practice Direction provides the sop that the court may order the solicitor to produce evidence that he has taken reasonable steps to comply with the rule, which sounds like a slap with a limp wrist.

[11.6]

CPR Rule 44.3: Court's discretion and circumstances to be taken into account when exercising its discretion as to costs
(1)   The court has discretion as to—
    (a)   whether costs are payable by one party to another;
    (b)   the amount of those costs; and
    (c)   when they are to be paid.
(2)   If the court decides to make an order about costs—
    (a)   the general rule is that the unsuccessful party will be ordered to pay the costs of the successful party; but
    (b)   the court may make a different order.
(3)   The general rule does not apply to the following proceedings—
    (a)   proceedings in the Court of Appeal on an application or appeal made in connection with proceedings in the Family Division; or
    (b)   proceedings in the Court of Appeal from a judgment, direction, decision or order given or made in probate proceedings or family proceedings.
(4)   In deciding what order (if any) to make about costs, the court must have regard to all the circumstances, including—
    (a)   the conduct of all the parties;

    (b)   whether a party has succeeded on part of his case, even if he has not been wholly successful; and

    (c)   any payment into court or admissible offer to settle made by a party which is drawn to the court's attention, and which is not an offer to which costs consequences under Part 36 apply.

(5)   The conduct of the parties includes—

    (a)   conduct before, as well as during, the proceedings, and in particular the extent to which the parties followed the Practice Direction (Pre-action Conduct) or any relevant pre-action protocol;

    (b)   whether it was reasonable for a party to raise, pursue or contest a particular allegation or issue;

    (c)   the manner in which a party has pursued or defended his case or a particular allegation or issue; and

    (d)   whether a claimant who has succeeded in his claim, in whole or in part, exaggerated his claim.

(6)   The orders which the court may make under this rule include an order that a party must pay—

    (a)   a proportion of another party's costs;

    (b)   a stated amount in respect of another party's costs;

    (c)   costs from or until a certain date only;

    (d)   costs incurred before proceedings have begun;

    (e)   costs relating to particular steps taken in the proceedings;

    (f)   costs relating only to a distinct part of the proceedings; and

    (g)   interest on costs from or until a certain date, including a date before judgment.

(7)   Where the court would otherwise consider making an order under paragraph (6)(f), it must instead, if practicable, make an order under paragraph (6)(a) or (c).

(8)   Where the court has ordered a party to pay costs, it may order an amount to be paid on account before the costs are assessed.

(9)   Where a party entitled to costs is also liable to pay costs the court may assess the costs which that party is liable to pay and either—

    (a)   set off the amount assessed against the amount the party is entitled to be paid and direct him to pay any balance; or

    (b)   delay the issue of a certificate for the costs to which the party is entitled until he has paid the amount which he is liable to pay.

CPD Section 8 Court's Discretion And Circumstances To Be Taken Into Account When Exercising Its Discretion As To Costs: Rule 44.3

[11.7]

8.1   *Attention is drawn to the factors set out in this rule which may lead the court to depart from the general rule stated in rule 44.3(2) and to make a different order about costs.*

8.2   *In a probate claim where a defendant has in his defence given notice that he requires the will to be proved in solemn form (see paragraph 8.3 of the Practice Direction 57), the court will not make an order for costs against the defendant unless it appears that there was no reasonable ground for opposing the will. The term 'probate claim' is defined in rule 57.1(2).*

8.3

(1)   *The court may make an order about costs at any stage in a case.*

(2)   *In particular the court may make an order about costs when it deals with any application, makes any order or holds any hearing and that order about costs may relate to the costs of that application, order or hearing.*

(3)   *Rule 44.3A(1) [at para [29.11]] provides that the court will not assess any additional liability until the conclusion of the proceedings or the part of the proceedings to which the funding arrangement relates. (Paragraphs 2.4 and 2.5 above explain when proceedings are concluded. As to the time when detailed assessment may be carried out see paragraph 28.1, below.)*

8.4   *In deciding what order to make about costs the court is required to have regard to all the circumstances including any payment into court or admissible offer to settle made by a party which is drawn to the court's attention, and which is not an offer to which costs consequences under Part 36 apply.*

8.5   *There are certain costs orders which the court will commonly make in proceedings before trial. The following table sets out the general effect of these orders. The table is not an exhaustive list of the orders which the court may make.* [This table is set out and considered in Chapter 16.]

8.6   *Where, under rule 44.3(8), the court orders an amount to be paid before costs are assessed—*

(1)   *the order will state that amount, and*

(2)   *if no other date for payment is specified in the order rule 44.8 (Time for complying with an order for costs) will apply.*

Fees of counsel

[11.8]

8.7

(1)   *This paragraph applies where the court orders the detailed assessment of the costs of a hearing at which one or more counsel appeared for a party.*

(2)   *Where an order for costs states the opinion of the court as to whether or not the hearing was fit for the attendance of one or more counsel, a costs officer conducting a detailed assessment of costs to which that order relates will have regard to the opinion stated.*

(3)   *The court will generally express an opinion only where:*

    (a)   *the paying party asks it to do so;*

    (b)   *more than one counsel appeared for a party or,*

    (c)   *the court wishes to record its opinion that the case was not fit for the attendance of counsel.*

Fees payable to conveyancing counsel appointed by the court to assist it

[11.9]

8.8

(1)   *Where the court refers any matter to the conveyancing counsel of the court the fees payable to counsel in respect of the work done or to be done will be assessed by the court in accordance with rule 44.3.*

(2)   *An appeal from a decision of the court in respect of the fees of such counsel will be dealt with under the general rules as to appeals set out in Part 52. If the appeal is against the decision of an authorised court officer, it will be dealt with in accordance with rules 47.20 to 47.23.*

[11.10]

Rule 44.3 preserves the court's discretion as to costs and retains the rebuttable presumption that the loser pays the winner's costs. However, in deciding what order, if any, to make about costs the court must have regard to all the circumstances including:

(a)   the conduct of the parties;

(b)   whether a party has been partly, if not wholly, successful;
(c)   any payment into court or any admissible offer to settle.
Consideration of the conduct of the parties is now an integral part of the philosophy of the costs of litigation. It includes:
(a)   conduct *before*, as well as *during* the proceedings including compliance with any relevant pre-action protocol;
(b)   whether it was *reasonable* for a party to raise, pursue or contest a particular allegation or issue;
(c)   the *manner* in which a party has pursued or defended his case or a particular allegation or issue; and
(d)   whether a claimant has *exaggerated* his claim in whole or in part.
Under CPR Rule 44.3(2)(b) the discretion exists to depart from the ordinary approach of costs following the event, having regard to the overriding objective. This was demonstrated in *Re Peninsular and Oriental Steam Navigation Co* [2006] EWHC 3279 (Ch), [2006] All ER (D) 82 (Oct).

Prior to the CPR, special rules had been developed in cases concerning company schemes of arrangement that displaced the ordinary approach to costs of the unsuccessful party paying the costs of the successful party. The considerations that had led the court to develop special rules in the schemes of arrangement cases prior to the CPR were equally applicable when it came to giving effect to the overriding objective under the CPR and therefore the authorities were of continuing assistance in deciding how the court's power to award costs should be exercised. The authorities establish that the courts do not generally make costs orders against objecting shareholders or creditors in shareholders' or creditors' schemes when their objections were not frivolous and had been of assistance to the court.

The two long-established exceptions to the normal rule that costs follow the event which survived the introduction of the Civil Procedure Rules in respect of contentious probate actions are:
(1)   where a testator had been the cause of the litigation, costs should come out of the estate; and
(2)   where the circumstances led reasonably to an investigation of the matter, costs should be borne by both sides.
In *Kostic v Chaplin* [2007] EWHC 2909 (Ch), [2008] 2 Costs LR 271, [2007] All ER (D) 119 (Dec) the testator had left his estate worth £8 million to the local Conservative Party Association at a time when he suffered from delusions, which were so far-reaching that a challenge to his testamentary capacity after his death was all but inevitable. The claimant successfully challenged the validity of the will on the ground of lack of testamentary capacity. Under the normal costs rule, the defendants would bear the costs of both parties. However, in the circumstances the Conservative Party Association was fully justified in investigating the issue of testamentary capacity once the challenge to the will was advanced on a formal basis, so that their costs of the investigation were ordered to come out of the estate down to the stage where a realistic assessment of the merits of the claim could be made. Each party was ordered to bear its own costs during an intermediate period of the proceedings up to the date on which expert reports were exchanged, whereafter costs followed the event.

THE PHILOSOPHY

[11.11]

Although Rule 44.3(2)(a) preserves the general rule that costs follow the event, the remainder of the rule prescribes the discretionary exceptions. In *Straker v Tudor Rose* [2007] EWCA Civ 368 Lord Justice Waller gave this helpful guidance on the approach to between-the-parties costs:

- First, is it appropriate to make an order for costs?
- Second, if so, the general rule is that the unsuccessful party will pay the costs of the successful party.
- Next, identify the successful party.
- Then, consider whether there are reasons for departing from the general rule in whole or in part. If so the judge should make clear findings of the factors justifying costs not following the event.

A helpful test is 'Who gets the cheque?' (see para [11.17]).

[11.12]

(i) Partial success A party who has ignored or been cavalier about a pre-action protocol, or who has raised every possible allegation in his statement of case and failed in all but one or two minor matters, or who has claimed grossly exaggerated damages may be deprived of all or part of his costs. Previously the philosophy was that if a claimant succeeded in recovering any part of a disputed claim he was entitled to his costs because it had been necessary for him to come to court to recover anything. In *Re Elgindata Ltd (No 2)* [1993] 1 All ER 232, CA the Court of Appeal had held that the general rule that costs should follow the event did not cease simply because the successful party raised an issue or made allegations that failed. The winner now no longer takes all. If a party only succeeds partially, they may recover only a proportionate amount of their costs. Indeed, they can be ordered to pay all or some of the 'loser's' costs, as happened in *Phoenix Finance Ltd v Federation Internationale de l'Automobile* [2002] EWHC 1028 (Ch), [2002] All ER (D) 347 (May), where the Vice-Chancellor ordered the claimants to pay the defendants' costs on the indemnity basis because they had not sent a letter before action. In *Reid v Capita Group* [2005] EWHC 2448 (Ch), [2005] All ER (D) 180 (Oct) 17 October, the premature issuing of proceedings without a letter before action resulted in the claimant being ordered to pay the defendant's costs.

In *Islam v Ali* [2003] EWCA Civ 612 the Court of Appeal allowed the defendant's appeal against an order for costs on the basis that although there had been judgment against her in the sum of £12,746.41, she had won the case in principle, a factor to which the trial judge had failed to have due regard. In the principal judgment Lord Justice Auld said: 'The general rule is that an unsuccessful party should pay the successful party's costs; see Civil Procedure Rules, rule 44.3(2)(a). The trial judge, however, has a wide discretion in furtherance of the overriding objective of justice and fairness to make a different order; see Civil Procedure Rules, rule 44.3(2)(b). In exercise of that discretion the judge should have regard to all the circumstances, including the conduct of the parties, for example, how they have respectively pitched and pursued their cases and whether a party has succeeded on part, if not all, of his case and to any payment in or offer made'.

There is no automatic rule requiring reduction of a successful party's costs if he loses on one or more issues. In any litigation, particularly complex litigation such as the present case had been, any winning party was likely to fail on one or more issues in the case (*HLB Kidsons (a firm) v Lloyds Underwriters* [2007] EWHC 2699 (Comm)).

A judge cannot cut down the costs of a successful party under CPR r 44.3(4) merely because he had not done as well as he had hoped. In *Hall v Stone* [2007] EWCA Civ 1354, 18 December 2008 there was no conduct by the claimants which was of such consequence as to warrant any reduction in their entitlement to costs. The initial exaggeration of their claims had no real effect on the costs of the action. The defendant did not enjoy any partial success to entitle her to an abatement of those costs. Nor should the claimants suffer any abatement on account of their attitude to the early offers which had been made at too early a stage and which had not been held open until after they had obtained medico-legal advice. The three defendants were the successful parties and entitled to their full costs.

In *Aspin v Metric Group Ltd* [2007] EWCA Civ 922 the judge was wrong to have deprived the claimant of his costs on the global grounds that his most substantial claims had been dismissed. Those claims had not been exaggerated in that if he had established them his claims for damage were not unrealistic. The order for costs should have been issues based. That did not mean cross-orders for costs which were usually time-consuming and inconvenient but an order that one party pays and the other receives a proportion of the whole costs of the proceedings. On this basis the claimant was awarded 50% of his costs to the conclusion of the trial and all his costs after that.

My suggestion in the previous edition (page 127 - para [11.12]) 'Although exaggeration of a claim cannot of itself deprive the claimant of his entitlement to costs, it is relevant to consider whether the exaggeration has caused costs to be incurred which would not have been incurred had there been a more realistic evaluation of the claim' was quoted with approval by Lord Justice Ward in *Widlake v BAA Ltd* [2009] EWCA Civ 1256, 153 Sol Jo (no 45) 29, [2009] All ER (D) 246 (Nov), in which he also dramatically observed 'Lies are told in litigation every day'. In that case the court distinguished between a concocted claim and an exaggerated one, holding that there is no general rule that dishonest exaggeration of a genuine claim would result in the dismissal of the whole claim. The exaggeration had put the defendant to unnecessary costs but the defendant had failed to protect itself by an increased Part 36 offer therefore the right order was no order for costs. In *Sulaman v Axa Insurance Plc* [2009] EWCA Civ 1331, (2009) Times, 25 January, [2009] All ER (D) 116 (Dec), the Court of Appeal upheld the trial judge's decision to award the claimant her costs on the indemnity basis but to reduce them by two thirds because she had lied twice when giving evidence. If she had lied three times would she have got any costs at all?

'A claimant should prima facia be entitled to his full costs of preparing and presenting his claim. The Board of Assessment's discretion to reduce the award from the payment of full costs should be exercised judicially. If it holds that the claim was grossly excessive, it is necessary for the Board then to enquire whether the exaggeration gave rise to an obvious and substantial escalation in the costs over and above those which it was reasonable for the claimant to incur. If it is satisfied that this was the case, then it is open to the Board to exercise its discretion to deprive the claimant of part of his costs. The amount of departure from full payment of the payment's costs should be proportionate, having regard to the waste of time and costs properly attributable to the claimant's acts or omissions.' (*Blakes Estates Ltd v Government of Montserrat* [2005] UKPC 46, [2006] 1 WLR 297). The judgment in *Blakes Estates* expressly approved the decision in *Purfleet Farms Ltd v Secretary of State for Transport* [2001] EWLands ACQ_108_2000 (10 April 2001) in which the Lands Tribunal found that the claimants' value was assessed at a particularly high figure and this should result in a reduction in costs. The claimants' entitlement to the recovery of their costs was reduced to three-quarters.

In *Earl of Malmesbury v Strutt and Parker (a partnership)* [2008] EWHC 424 (QB) the court considered the issue of exaggeration, saying it accorded with the authorities to take account of how the exaggeration of the claim had come about. 'Exaggeration' meant no more than that the claimant only recovered a fraction of the claim advanced. The worst case was deliberate and dishonest exaggeration. Unreasonable conduct came next. Finally, exaggeration might occur without fault. But even where that was so, it might be appropriate to reflect in the order for costs the fact that the claimant had only recovered a fraction of his claim. The appropriate order depended on the circumstances and the court has to seek a solution which did justice between the parties. In the present case, the claim was initially put too high because of the advice the claimants received. As the action proceeded, the claimants' belief in their claim for damages at the highest level should have diminished until by the trial they should have realised that it had no real chance of success. Because of the exaggeration, the claimants were rewarded only 70% of their costs. (see also para [11.20])

[11.13]

(ii) Issues based The issues based approach to costs was explained by Lord Woolf in *Phonographic Performance Ltd v AEI Rediffusion Music Ltd* [1999] 1 WLR 1507: as follows:

> 'The most significant change of emphasis of the new Rules is to require courts to be more ready to make separate orders which reflect the outcome of different issues. In doing this the new Rules are reflecting a change of practice which has already started. It is now clear that too robust an application of the "follow the event principle" encourages litigants to increase the costs of litigation, since it discourages litigants from being selective as to the points they take. If you recover all your costs as long as you win, you are encouraged to leave no stone unturned in your effort to do so.'

It was first applied in *Bank of Credit and Commerce International SA (in liquidation) v Ali* [1999] 2 All ER 1005, Ch D, Lightman J said that under the CPR, the straitjacket imposed by *Elgindata* had gone and that success was not now a technical term but a result in real life, the question of who had succeeded being a matter for the exercise of common sense. Before the CPR, in a group action, complainants who established a breach of contract but could prove no loss would have been ordered to pay the defendant's costs. However, in this case that was only half the picture; although test case employees had lost, the judgment opened the door to possible successful claims by other employees. Accordingly, the judge held that the proper course was to make no order for costs. In *Gwembe Valley Development Co Ltd v Koshy* [2000] 11 LS Gaz R 38, Ch D, Mr Justice Rimer held that even before the CPR came into force, the principle that costs should follow the event was merely the starting point from which the court could readily depart. The CPR did not alter the nature of the court's discretion so much as introduce a change of emphasis requiring the courts to be more ready to make separate orders reflecting the outcome of different issues. However, a successful party should not have to pay costs to an unsuccessful party unless the points taken by the successful party or the manner in which they were taken, or both were unreasonable. In this case, the defendant was ordered to pay 70% of the costs. In *Liverpool City Council v Rosemary Chavasse Ltd* (18 August 1999, unreported, Ch D), before the commencement of proceedings the claimant council had stuck its head in the sand and had only half-heartedly attempted negotiations; after proceedings had commenced it had left everything to the last minute and the matter could have been dealt with more quickly and cheaply if, among other things, the pressure of time had not been so great. CPR Rule 44.3 requires the court, when deciding what order to make about costs, to have regard to all the circumstances including the conduct of the parties before, as well as during, the proceedings. Applying these criteria the court awarded the successful claimant only half its costs of the proceedings with only five eighths of their costs of preparing the bundles because they had included excessive documents.

Kastor Navigation Co Ltd v AGF MAT (No 2) [2004] EWCA Civ 277 [2004] 2 Lloyd's Rep 119, demonstrated that it is not longer a prerequisite that the party who is successful overall in the litigation should only pay the costs of the other party of a particular issue on which the successful party had failed if it were shown that the successful party had acted unreasonably or improperly. The claim arose out of the loss of a vessel caused by fire in which the court held the claimants were not entitled to recover the actual total loss caused by the fire, as initially pleaded, but only for indemnity in respect of the constructive total loss of the vehicle, as introduced by an amendment to the pleadings. The making and pursuit of the claim for the actual loss substantially lengthened and increased the costs both of the action.

The provision in CPR 44.3(2)(a) that 'the general rule is that the unsuccessful party will be ordered to pay the costs of the successful party', is a reference to the party successful in the litigation as a whole, not the party successful on any particular issue. In commercial litigation about money the winner is the party who receives money. The trial judge could not be faulted for adopting an issue by issue approach, nor was there anything wrong in principle with an order which resulted in the successful party having to pay the unsuccessful party a substantial proportion of its costs. However the question in this case was whether the judge was right to apply the issue by issue approach so rigorously ('logically' as he put it) to the exclusion of any other factors. Although that approach may be entirely justified in some cases it was not justified in this case. On the issues basis one party would have recovered 70% of their costs, but on the 'Who got the money?' test the other party would have recovered 100% of their costs. Where there are factors pulling either way, it is necessary to look at the range of available orders, to consider the strength

153

of the factors pulling in each direction and adjust the result accordingly. Where possible it is preferable to make a single net order, rather than cross-orders. The court cut the Gordian knot by making no order for costs.

This approach was also adopted in *Stocking v Montila* [2007] EWHC 26 (Ch), [2007] All ER (D) 213 (Jan), 26 January where although the various considerations pointed to a complicated issues based order (with orders both ways) of the nature contemplated by CPR 44.3(6)(f) this would in the circumstances have lead to more expense and delay. Accordingly, the just disposal of the issues as to costs was to make no order.

In *Somnez v Kebabery Wholesale Ltd* [2009] CA (Civ) 22 October 2009 the claimant employee suffered serious injuries which the employer alleged had been contributed to by the claimant's own negligence. Prior to the trial of a preliminary issue on the question of contributory negligence, the claimant made a Part 36 offer in respect of liability which was 100% in his favour. The defendant made a counter offer to settle on a two thirds basis which was rejected by the claimant. The claimant made a further offer to settle at 75% to 25% in his favour which offer was refused. At the trial the claimant was held to have been 20% contributorily negligent. Accordingly the judge had been in error in ordering the claimant to pay the defendant's costs. Nevertheless the court had to consider whether the costs should be reduced because of the claimant's conduct. It found that his conduct did not fall within that envisaged in CPR Rule 44.3(5) and accordingly the order of the judge was reversed. The defendant was ordered to pay the claimant's costs of the trial of the preliminary issue.

[11.14]

Further examples

(a) *Clark v Devon County Council* (2005) Times, 22 April, CA. The claimant claimed damages for negligence for failure to diagnose his learning difficulties, but the allegations of negligence against headteachers of two schools and two out of three educational psychologists failed or were withdrawn, and the claim succeeded only in respect of the negligence of one psychologist. In those circumstances it would be wrong to award the claimant all his costs in relation to wholly discrete issues on which he had failed. In order to reflect this in the order for costs the claimant was awarded only 70% of his costs.

(b) *Apotex Europe Ltd v Smithkline Beecham plc* [2004] EWHC 964 (Ch). Judgment extract:

> 'The starting point is the general rule set out in CPR 44.3(2), that generally the unsuccessful party will be ordered to pay the costs of the successful parties. The rules specifically contemplate that in exercising its discretion in making an order for costs, the court will have regard to all the circumstances and in particular the matters set out in CPR 44.3(4) as explained in 44.3(5) and authorise the types of order listed in 44.3(6). Where the court wishes to make an order under 44.3(6)(f), that is, an order for costs relating only to a distinct part of the proceeding, it is encouraged by 44.3(7) to reflect its assessment of the value of that distinct part of the proceeding by an order for payment of a stated proportion of another party's costs.
>
> In patent actions the practice has been to make an "issue based" costs order for some years. If it is decided to make an order for costs that is based upon the parties' successes on specific issues, there are two questions to be decided. The first is whether, notwithstanding its overall success, the success-

ful party should not recover some and if so what part of the costs it has incurred; and, in relation to those matters on which it fails to recover its costs, whether it should not also pay the costs of the unsuccessful party. When the question of recoverability has been determined in principle in this manner, it is usually comparatively straightforward to convert the conclusion into an award of costs based upon a percentage recovery so as to comply with the principle articulated in CPR 44.3(7).

Apotex, successful on the issue of infringement, had raised arguments of non-infringement upon which they failed. These issues took a substantial amount of time at the trial and represent 14% of the total costs of Apotex. Accordingly, there should be a 14% deduction from their overall costs'.

The defendants also succeeded on a separate issue resulting in a further deduction from the claimant's costs of 10%, the overall result being that the defendants were ordered to pay 76% of the claimant's costs.

(c)   *Secretary of State for Education & Skills v Frontline Technology Ltd* [2004] EWHC 1563 (Ch). The court found for the claimant on two patent claims and for the defendant on another. The court adopted an issue-based approach, relating the issues to the percentage of time taken at trial, applying the same apportionment to the pre-trial costs. The question was how one categorised who was the successful party. Even by the standards of patent actions there had been serious overloading on the grounds of attack by the claimant with little attempt to limit the issues. After considering the evidence and the issues individually the claimant was ordered to pay 80% of the defendant's costs.

(d)   *Shore v Sedgwick Financial Services Ltd* [2007] EWHC 3054 (QB), 20 December. The claim was eventually dismissed on the issue of limitation and so it was clear that the defendants were the successful party. However, the main issue in the case was whether the defendants were in breach of their duty and they failed on that issue. The issues in the case had been intertwined to an extent. Applying the ordinary principles, in the circumstances of the case, a reduction should be made from the costs awarded to the defendant. Taking into account the time taken at trial in dealing with the explanations of the transaction given to the claimant, the warnings given about the risks and considering whether regulatory rules had been breached, using a broad brush approach, the appropriate deduction was 25%. Accordingly the claimant was ordered to pay 75% of the defendants' costs.

(e)   In *'Krysia' Maritime Inc v Intership Ltd* [2008] EWHC 1880 (Admlty), [2008] All ER (D) 12 (Aug), NLJ 8 August 2008, p 1148 the defendant contended that although the claimant was the party that 'had really won at trial' on the issue of liability, it was inappropriate for the court to adopt the general rule in CPR r 44.3(2)(a) of costs following the event and award the claimant the entirety of its costs first because of the claimant's 30% contributory negligence and second, applying the Merchant Shipping Act 1995, s 187(1) and s 187(2) the longstanding practice in the Admiralty Court was that costs should reflect the court's decision on the degree of blame which attached to each of the parties.

The court held that the claimant having really won at the trial the general rule in CPR r 44.3(2)(a) had to apply unless there was a good reason why it should not do so. If the general rule was not followed, a judge might often follow an 'issues based' approach to costs and if this were done, then it had to be justified. The judge had to show which of the relevant factors indicated in the rule he had taken into account. He had to similarly justify adopting any other approach permitted by the rule. None of the authorities established any rule or principle, applicable to collision cases or analogous types of case in the Admiralty Court, where there was no counterclaim, that a claimant who was found at fault under s 187(1) and s 187(2) of the 1995 Act should recover its costs in proportion to the percentage of liability of the defendant. Moreover the fact that the claimant had recovered only 70% of its claim was not a sufficient reason to reduce its costs and there was no other basis on which it was legitimate to make an 'issues based' or other costs order.

(f)   In patent litigation in *Actavis UK Ltd v Novartis AG* [2009] EWHC 502 (Ch), [2009] All ER (D) 205 (Mar) the claimant had established the invalidity of the defendant's patent and sought its costs on the basis of costs following the event. However, to reflect the fact that the claimant had only succeeded on one narrow point it was deprived of 50% of its costs and had a further 5% costs disallowed in relation to infringement and prior art relied on by the claimant but abandoned a few days before the exchange of expert evidence. The disallowance was pitched at a level to reflect the court's view that the claimant should not only be deprived of its own costs but should meet the defendant's costs on a pure issue-based approach. Accordingly the defendant was ordered to pay 45% of the claimant's costs

THE PRINCIPLES

[11.15]

In *Johnsey Estates (1990) Ltd v Secretary of State for the Environment, Transport and the Regions* [2001] EWCA Civ 535, [2001] 2 EGLR 128, the court summarised the principles applicable as follows: (i) costs cannot be recovered except under an order of the court; (ii) the question of whether to make any order as to costs – and if so, what – is a matter entrusted to the discretion of the trial judge; (iii) the starting point for the exercise of discretion is that costs should follow the event; nevertheless, (iv) the judge may make different orders for costs in relation to discrete issues – and, in particular, should consider doing so where a party has been successful on one issue but unsuccessful on another issue and, in that event, may make an order for costs against a party who has been generally successful in the litigation; and (v) the judge may deprive a party of costs of an issue on which he has been successful if satisfied that the party has acted unreasonably in relation to that issue.

Spiers v English [1907] P 122, established the principle that in contested proceedings as to the validity of a will the judge could make an alternative order to costs following the event where the testator or those interested in the residue had been the cause of the litigation, or if the circumstances led reasonably to an investigation.

In *Re Good* [2002] EWHC 640 (Ch), [2002] 23 LS Gaz R 27 the testator was a disabled elderly woman who left most of her £1.5 million estate to her housekeeper and her housekeeper's husband who had cared for her for more than 20 years. There were grounds for suspecting undue influence and the defendants were entitled to test their case. Nevertheless, the claimant had shown that the deceased knew and approved of the contents of the will and had succeeded in defending an unpleasant allegation of undue influence. In the circumstances the defendants were ordered to pay one-half of the claimant's costs.

Hackney London Borough Council v Campbell (2005) Solicitor's Journal 6 May, CA confirmed the basic rule that costs should follow the event, but the judge failed to follow that approach. If a court is to reflect the success or failure on individual issues it should do so by expressing that success or failure in the form of a proportion of the costs.

The principle that costs orders are very much in the discretion of the judge was illustrated by two cases in which the Court of Appeal upheld the differing approaches of the judges. The first was *Alan Williams Entertainment Ltd v Hurd* [2006] EWCA Civ 1637, 150 Sol Jo LB 1464, 2 November in which the defendant contended that the judge should not have made any order for costs after a hearing on liability until the quantum of damages had been decided. The Court of Appeal held that under CPR Rule 1.4(2)(i) a court has to deal with as many aspects of a case as possible in one hearing. It is not a rule that the successful party is ascertained on a monetary basis. On the other hand, in *Shepherds Investments Ltd v Walters* [2007] EWCA Civ 292, [2007] All ER (D) 40 (Apr), 3 April, the Court of Appeal dismissed the claimant's appeal against an order reserving the issue of costs until after the outcome of an account of profits in its claim against the defendants, holding that a judge is not required by the CPR to make an immediate decision on costs and has a discretion to postpone it until quantum had been finally determined.

THE MENU OF ORDERS

[11.16]

Rule 44.3(6) sets out a menu of the various orders the court may make giving a successful party less than the whole of its costs. Rule 44.3(6)(*a*) to (*f*) are in descending order of desirability for the purposes of ease of a summary judgment. Rule 43.3(7) states that (*f*) is to be avoided if it is possible to order either (*a*) or (*c*). The judge will probably start with (*a*) and try *not* to work his way down. An example of this approach in practice was in *Grupo Torras SA v Sheikh Fahad Mohammed Al-Sabah* [1999] CLC 1469, QBD (Comm Ct). In three cases involving allegations of conspiracy to defraud and dishonest assistance, the defendants had succeeded. The judge rejected the claimant's submissions that as the defendants had only achieved a 'narrow success' they should not be awarded their costs. However, he found that the defendants had been guilty of backdating documents, deceiving the claimant's auditors and were in dereliction of their duties as directors of the claimants, so that the claimants had been justified in bringing and continuing the proceedings. Under CPR Rule 44.3(2)(*b*) the court had power to deviate from the general rule that costs follow the event and he awarded the defendants only half of their costs in one case and only one-third of their costs in the other two cases. The new thinking was also demonstrated by Park J in the Chancery Division on 10 February 1999 (before the introduction of the

CPR) in the unreported case of *Frayling Furniture Ltd v Premier Uphol-stery Ltd*. In consolidated actions involving four parties with various claims and cross-claims the judge regarded the various complaints about the behaviour of the parties as cancelling themselves out in respect of the award of costs. After weighing up all the factors he declined to make separate orders for costs, which would require two payments in opposite directions and awarded Premier, the party that had won significantly more than it had lost, three-fifths of its costs against Frayling and two-fifths of its costs against 3-D Designs. He also ordered 3-D Designs to pay one-half of Premier's costs of the third party proceedings and ordered Premier to pay Mr Hewson one-half of the aggregate costs of Mr Hewson and 3-D Designs of the third party proceedings or (if lower) the whole of Mr Hewson's own costs of the third party proceedings. There is clearly no limit to the number of permutations of costs orders where there are a number of parties and third parties.

In *Verrechia (t/a Freightmaster Commercials) v Metropolitan Police Comr* [2002] EWCA Civ 605, [2002] 3 All ER 385, the court emphasised that the CPR require that an order which allows or disallows costs by reference to certain issues should be made only if other forms of order cannot be made which sufficiently reflect the justice of the case (CPR Rule 44.3(7)). There are good reasons for this rule. An order which allows or disallows costs on certain issues creates difficulties at the stage of the detailed assessment of costs because the costs judge would have to master the issue in detail to understand what costs were properly incurred in dealing with it, and then analyse the work done by the receiving party's legal advisers to determine whether or not it was attributable to the issue the costs of which have been disallowed. All this adds to the cost of detailed assessment and to the amount of time absorbed in dealing with costs on this basis. The costs incurred on assessment may thus be disproportionate to the benefit gained. In all the circumstances, contrary to what might be thought to be the case, a 'percentage' order under CPR Rule 44.3(6)(a) made by the judge who heard the application will often produce a fairer result than a 'distinct parts' order under CPR Rule 44.3(6)(f). Moreover such an order is consistent with the overriding objective of the CPR.

These considerations will in most cases lead to the conclusion that a 'distinct parts' order is not to be made. Wherever practicable, the judge should endeavour to form a view as to the percentage of costs to which the winning party should be entitled, or alternatively, whether justice would be sufficiently done by awarding costs from or until a particular date only, as suggested by CPR Rule 44.3(6)(c).

In *Budgen v Andrew Gardner Partnership* [2002] EWCA Civ 1125, [2002] 39LS Gaz R 37 the trial judge ordered the defendant to pay only 75% of the claimant's costs of the action because the claimant had lost on one issue, which had taken up a substantial amount of the trial. The defendant's appeal against the judge's refusal to make a 'distinct parts' order in its favour was dismissed.

CLAIM AND COUNTERCLAIM

[11.17]

Rule 44.3(9) is aimed at the situation where the claimant succeeds on the whole or on part in his claim and the defendant succeeds on the whole or on part on his counterclaim. It is infinitely preferable for there to be only one order for costs adjusted appropriately by allowing a proportion or some other partial order as to costs in favour of one party rather than making cross-orders for costs in favour of the successful claimant and the successful defendant on his counterclaim. If not, it appears that even under the new rules the lengthy, tedious and often unfair investigation of the costs attributable to the claim and those attributable to the counterclaim prescribed in the case of *Medway Oil and Storage Co Ltd v Continental Contractors Ltd* [1929] AC 88, 98 LJKB 148, HL will still apply. Under this approach the counterclaim will have attributed to it only the increase in the costs which it had brought about so that the result will be that the balance of the costs will almost certainly be in favour of the claimant and be unfair to the defendant. Similarly, where there is no counterclaim but the claimant only recovers 80% of his claim, implying that the defendant has been 20% successful, instead of awarding the defendant 20% of his costs the judge could consider reducing the award of costs to the claimant from 80% to perhaps 60% or 70% to compensate the defendant for that part of the claim in which he had been successful but had not been awarded any costs.

However *Amin v Amin and 17 others (costs)* [2007] EWHC 827 (Ch D) decided that where the costs on each side are very large it is not safe to carry out an exercise of setting-off by reference to percentages of one side's costs against the other. Instead, it is appropriate to ascertain a percentage of each side's costs which is payable to the other and leave the parties to turn those percentages into money amounts and to effect set-off at that level. The litigation concerned two actions concerning a partnership dispute and an unfair prejudice petition against a company in which the court decided that overall 35% of each side's total costs were to be attributed to the company action, and 65% to the partnership action. After making reductions the court held that V and X were liable for 33% of U and B's costs of the company action while V and U were ordered to pay 25% of each other's costs of the partnership actions. Although it was not appropriate to set off these figures against each other because of the disparity, the parties were of course free to agree to such a set-off should they wish to do so.

Dyson Technology Ltd v Strutt [2007] EWHC 1756 (Ch), [2007] 4 Costs LR 597, [2007] All ER (D) 381 (Jul) confirmed that where the costs of the action are awarded to one party with the exception of costs relating to a particular matter or issue, the party in whose favour the costs of that issue were awarded is not entitled to recover anything except the extra costs generated by that issue and not to costs that were incurred and were equally attributable to both elements of the claim. This demonstrates the importance of time records distinguishing between work done on the claim and work done on the counterclaim in cases where *Medway Oil* (above) may still be applied. It also confirms there is much to be said for keeping to the simple formula of orders for a stated proportion of the costs or a stated amount of costs in cases where recognition of a limited degree of success by one or the other party is called for.

Although the modern tendency is at least to consider the award of costs on an issue by issue basis, the judge in *Burchell v Bullard* [2005] EWCA Civ 358 had been correct to dismiss this approach because of the difficulty in the preparation of the bill of costs and the enormous complication of the process of detailed assessment in this building dispute. However, he had not found another way but had resorted to costs following the event, ordering the defendants to pay the costs of the claim and the claimant to pay the defendant's costs of the counterclaim. In doing so he had fallen into the error of fettering his discretion and not considering what alternatives were available. The most obvious and frequently most desirable option is that in CPR 44.3(6)(a), that of ordering a proportion of the party's costs to be paid. Costs following the event was the general rule and in this kind of litigation, the event was determined by establishing who had written the cheque at the end of the case. In this case the defendants had done so and they therefore were the unsuccessful party. The starting point was that the claimant was entitled to the costs of the proceedings, claim and counterclaim taken together. The specific aspects of conduct identified in CPR 44.3(5) had then to be taken into account when considering a departure from the general rule. This approach resulted in the Court of Appeal ordering the defendants to pay 60% of the claimant's costs of the claim, counterclaim and the Part 20 proceedings and 60% of the claimant's liability to pay the Part 20 defendant's costs.

In *Square Mile Partnership Ltd v Fitzmaurice McCall Ltd* [2006] EWHC 236 (Ch), [2006] All ER (D) 84 (Jan) 18 January the claimant had to issue proceedings to get the defendant to admit its claim and had to come to court in order to recover the moneys it obtained. However, most of the evidence and pre-trial work went to the main issue of the counterclaim upon which the defendant had been successful. Accordingly, both parties could be said to have succeeded in accordance with CPR rule 44.3(4). To award the claimant a significant proportion of its costs would not be just, as it would fail to reflect the defendant's successful counterclaim. To give the defendant its costs would be harsh, as the claimant had succeeded in getting significant moneys out of the defendant despite losing on the counterclaim. Taking all the factors into account, the appropriate order was no order as to costs. However, in *Day v Day* [2006] EWCA Civ 415, [2006] All ER (D) 184 (Mar) 14 March the judge was wrong to have called it a draw and to make no order for costs on the grounds that his judgment was the same as the identical fallback positions of each party. Applying the 'Who wrote the cheque?' test there was no doubt that the defendant was the loser, he had refused to pay anything to the claimant and had failed to make a payment into court. Accordingly costs should have followed the event.

Following a road traffic accident, both parties had intended to issue personal injury claims, however, the claimant did so first. The parties formally agreed that the issue of liability would be determinative of the claimant's claim and of the defendant's intended claim, without the need for the defendant to issue separate proceedings or a counterclaim. The judge determined that the claimant should recover 35% of the value of his claim and that the defendant 65% of the value of his. The claimant appealed against the judge's decision that he should recover only 35% of his costs in line with the ruling on liability, submitting that it was not open to the judge to consider the notional cross-claim as there was no real evidence of it before him save for the defendant's fleeting reference to having 'a claim by the wayside', and that, as liability had been established in the claimant's favour, albeit in a reduced fashion, he was entitled to all of his costs. The defendant conceded that if the reduction had been made solely because of the claimant's contributory negligence, the decision was wrong.

The Court of Appeal held that although there was no explicit reference in the judge's determination to the cross-claim it was clear from his decision to apportion costs in the same proportion as liability that he had had it in mind. The judge had correctly exercised his discretion and it was clear that he had had proper regard to the claim and notional cross-claim when making the order for costs.

Following *Medway Oil* (above) it might have been right to make no order as to costs, which would be more just than costs of the claim and counterclaim, however, the claimant had made Part 36 offers on liability and the defendant had made none, and so the claimant should not be deprived of all his costs.

NO WINNER OR LOSER

[11.18]

Shirley v Caswell [2002] Lloyd's Rep PN 955, CA was an action for damages against a barrister. The judge found that the barrister had given negligent advice on some issues, but he rejected other allegations. The judge ordered the defendant barrister to pay 60% of the claimant's costs and ordered the claimant to pay 40% of the defendant's costs on the basis that the claimant had abandoned various issues before trial after the defendant had incurred costs in preparation to those matters. The Court of Appeal held that, although the judge had been entitled to exercise his discretion in making the order for costs, the order he made exposed the claimant to the risk of being doubly penalised in respect of the costs relating to the abandoned issues because those costs would be considered on a detailed assessment in any event. The appropriate order was that the defendant should pay all of the claimant's costs and the claimant should pay 40% of the defendant's costs. The judgment referred to the decision in *Phonographic Performance Ltd v AEI Rediffusion Music Ltd* [1999] 2 All ER 299, CA, an appeal from an order for costs by the Copyright Tribunal, in which the Court of Appeal held that the Tribunal had erred in principle by seeking to find a winner and a loser and that in reality neither side had won. Accordingly, there should be no order for costs. Cross-orders for costs, either arising out of a successful claim and a successful counterclaim or, as in the present case, where the parties succeed on some points and lose on others, can give rise to serious difficulties on a detailed assessment. If, therefore, the judge is able to reach an overall decision on costs and either make no order for costs, or perhaps in the present case, have awarded the claimant, say, 50% of his costs with no award to the defendant, the assessment of costs is considerably simplified and the requirements of justice are met.

A decision with which I am not entirely happy is *Stocznia Gdanska SA v Latvian Shipping Co (No 2)* [1999] 3 All ER 822, QBD (Comm Ct). The claimant abandoned two of the three distinct parts of its claim in tort. The claimants submitted that the court should not take into account the fact that a party had failed on an issue unless it was unreasonable for the party to have raised, pursued or contested the particular allegation or issue. This was a misapprehension. It was clear that under Rule 44.3(4)(*b*) the reasonableness of the party taking a particular point or bringing a part of the case was not necessarily relevant to the award of costs. This sub-paragraph is quite distinct from the conduct of the parties referred to in Rule 44.3(4)(*a*) and defined in Rule 44.3(5). The reasonableness of raising an issue did not necessarily have to be taken into account in applying Rule 44.3(4)(*b*), the purpose of which was to encourage litigants to be selective as to the points they took, thus decreasing the costs of litigation. The defendant was treated as having succeeded on two parts of the claim under Rule 44.3(4)(*b*) and therefore entitled to the costs of those parts. The claimant was entitled, in all the circumstances, to 38% of the overall costs of the action. Although the logic of the award was impeccable, it did result in a detailed assessment of bills of costs from both parties, perhaps with some element of overlap, particularly as the defendants were to recover the whole of the costs in respect of two parts of the claim and the claimant to recover 38% of the overall costs of the action. Rule 44.3(9) envisages that in circumstances such as these, or where there is a successful claim and a successful counterclaim, the judge may make a broad brush order setting off the costs of one party against the other, resulting in a one-way order for costs at an appropriate percentage, or, as is happening with increasing frequency, a decision that the cross-entitlements to costs cancel each other out, resulting in the judge making no order for between-the-parties costs.

The preferred approach was exemplified in *Verrechia (t/a Freightmaster Commercials) v Metropolitan Police Comr* [2001] All ER (D) 173 (Mar), QBD where the claimant sought damages of £141,500 plus aggravated and exemplary damages under the Torts (Interference with Goods) Act 1977 in respect of 65 items which the police had failed to return to him. The claimant had offered to settle for £98,000 which was followed by a payment into court by the police of the sum of £5,500 in full settlement of the whole of the claimant's claim. The judge awarded damages in the sum of £37,300 plus interest with the result that neither party succeeded to the extent of their prior offers. The judge clearly thought the action had resulted in a 'draw'. Although when the case started there were some 65 items, by the time of closing speeches, there were only 40 items in issue. The appellant won in respect of half in number of these items. There were no criticisms relevant to costs in the conduct of either party. The appellant had won one-half of his case and lost on the rest. The police as well as the appellant had come to court to win that part of the case in which they succeeded. To this extent the judge is entitled to take the view that each side was to that extent the winner. Alternatively, it was open to the judge, in the light of the wide powers conferred by the CPR, to conclude that, in any event, the appellant should only have part of his costs as he had been successful in part only of his case, and that the police should have the cost of the part of the case on which they had been successful. On either basis the judge could properly conclude that the proportion of costs which each party should receive was 50% and that the net result was nil when these two percentages were set against each other.

The Court of Appeal emphasised that the CPR require that an order which allows or disallows costs by reference to certain issues should be made only if other forms of order cannot be made which sufficiently reflect the justice of the case (CPR Rule 44.3(7)). There are good reasons for this rule. An order which allows or disallows costs on certain issues creates difficulties at the stage of the detailed assessment of costs because the costs judge would have to master the issue in detail to understand what costs were properly incurred in dealing with it, and then analyse the work done by the receiving party's legal advisers to determine whether or not it was attributable to the issue, the costs of which have been disallowed. All this adds to the cost of detailed assessment and to the amount of time absorbed in dealing with costs on this basis. The costs incurred on assessment may thus be disproportionate to the benefit gained. In all the circumstances, contrary to what might be thought to be the case, a 'percentage' order under Rule 44.3(6)(*a*) made by the judge who heard the application will often produce a fairer result than an 'issues-based' order under Rule 44.3(6)(*f*). Moreover such an order is consistent with the overriding objective of the CPR.

In *R (on the application of Mendes) v Southwark London Borough Council* (2009) Times, 7 April, [2009] All ER (D) 231 (Mar) the Court of Appeal warned judges against being tempted too readily to adopt the fall-back position of 'no order for costs' where judicial review claims are withdrawn on settlement and confirmed that costs can and should in appropriate cases be awarded in favour of publicly funded claimants where claims are settled outside of court.. The judge had been wrong to make no order as to costs where clearly the claimant had strong prospects of success and the decision to bring proceedings had been a reasonable one in the face of the defendant's refusal to withdraw its incorrect decision before proceedings were commenced.

COUNSEL

[11.19]

The former requirement that the costs of counsel attending an interim hearing would not be allowed unless the judge certified that counsel's attendance was reasonable has gone. It was replaced by para 8.7(2) of the Practice Direction which envisages that the judge might express an opinion to which the costs officer should have regard. This provision led to some confusion and was resolved by para 8.7(3) which sets out the only circumstances in which the court will generally express an opinion as to whether or not a hearing was fit for the attendance of counsel.

FAILURE TO MEDIATE

(i) Costs sanction

[11.20]

In *Dunnett v Railtrack plc (in railway administration)* [2002] EWCA Civ 303, [2002] 2 All ER 850, on granting the claimant permission to appeal against the dismissal of his action for damages for negligence by Railtrack, the judge told both parties they should attempt alternative dispute resolution, but Railtrack refused to do so, on the grounds that they were not prepared to make any further payment to the claimant and were confident that they would succeed on the appeal. Railtrack did succeed in having the appeal dismissed, but the Court of Appeal demonstrated its displeasure at their outright refusal to consider ADR by depriving them of their costs, noting that parties and their lawyers should ensure that they are aware that it is one of their duties fully to consider ADR, especially when the court has suggested it, and not merely to flatly turn it down. To flatly turn down ADR could place the party doing so at risk of adverse consequences in costs.

The decision was welcomed by the Centre for Effective Dispute Resolution as the decision which the mediation industry had been expecting and waiting for. Its director, Tony Allen, said: 'It makes clear that the Court of Appeal views mediation and related processes as at the heart of the overriding objective. The legal profession and its clients must take mediation seriously or face the consequences'.

Failure to mediate had similar consequences in *Royal Bank of Canada Trust Corpn Ltd v Secretary of State for Defence* [2003] EWHC 1479 (Ch), [2004] 1 P & CR 448, where in a lease dispute the Ministry of Defence refused to mediate because the dispute turned on a point of law, was between commercial parties and (unlike previous ADR cases involving costs penalties) the matter was not one where emotions played a significant part in the case. The MoD won but was deprived of its costs because it had ignored the Government's ADR pledge (given by the Lord Chancellor's Department in March 2001) that ADR would be considered and used in all suitable cases wherever the other party accepts it. The judge said that the MoD's reasons did not make the matter unsuitable for mediation.

In *Virani Ltd v Manuel Revert y Cia SA* [2003] EWCA Civ 1651, [2004] 2 Lloyd's Rep 14, the Court of Appeal ordered an unsuccessful appellant to pay costs on the indemnity basis because he refused the offer of its mediation service on being granted permission to appeal and failed to negotiate or enter into any form of mediation or ADR.

A party who agrees to mediation, but then causes the mediation to fail by reason of his unreasonable position in the mediation is in reality in the same position as a party who unreasonably refused to mediate. It is something which the court could and should take account of in the costs order. In *Earl of Malmesbury v Strutt and Parker* (para [11.12]) had the claimants made an offer which better reflected their true position, the mediation might have succeeded. The judge said 'It would be wrong to say more', presumably because he could only say what he did because both parties waived privilege for the mediation. Taking account of unreasonable conduct in privileged mediation is not easy. He reduced the claimant's costs to 80% to reflect their unreasonable attitude in the mediation.

(ii) No costs sanction

[11.21]

Hurst v Leeming [2002] EWHC 1051 (Ch), [2003] 1 Lloyd's Rep 379, Ch D was the first of a series of cases where the court refused to penalise failure to mediate. Mr Leeming was held to have been justified in taking the view that mediation was not appropriate because it had no realistic prospect of success. It was plain that Mr Hurst had been so seriously disturbed by the tragic course of events resulting from the dissolution of his partnership that he was incapable of a balanced evaluation of the facts. He was out to obtain a substantial sum in the mediation process and was not likely to accept any mediation which did not achieve that result, although his claim plainly entitled him to nothing.

In *Firle Investments Ltd v Datapoint International Ltd* [2001] EWCA Civ 1106, [2001] All ER (D) 258 (Jun), the claimant had undoubtedly been at fault in being unwilling to negotiate and by persisting with hopeless issues, thereby lengthening the trial, but ultimately it had beaten the payments in and had succeeded by a substantial amount in the period up to a second payment in. The claimant recovered all of its costs up to the date of the second payment and 70% of its costs thereafter. The judge retained a discretion under CPR Rule 44.3(6)(*a*) to disapply the normal rule relating to costs and could take into account such factors as payments in, offers to settle, the conduct of the parties and whether a party had lost an issue. However, the judge should refrain from speculating on whether hypothetical offers to settle would have been accepted.

Société Internationale de Telecommunications Aeronautiques SC v Wyatt Co (UK) Ltd (Maxwell Batley (a firm), Part 20 defendant) [2002] EWHC 2401 (Ch), (2003) 147 Sol Jo LB 27, was another case in which the court refused to impose a sanction for refusing to mediate. The judge refused on a number of grounds to deprive Maxwell Batley of any of their costs because of their refusal to mediate. First, the only reason why Watson Wyatt wanted Maxwell Batley to take part in the mediation was so that pressure could be brought on them to make a large contribution to whatever Société Internationale was willing to accept from Watson Wyatt. Second, the purpose of the invitation to mediate was not with a view to resolving the liability of Maxwell Batley without litigation: there was no suggestion that, with influence by the mediator, Watson Wyatt might not pursue their claim against Maxwell Batley. Third, Watson Wyatt had tried to browbeat and bully Maxwell Batley into the mediation in a manner which the judge found disagreeable and off-putting; they had even suggested that Maxwell Batley's solicitor's reputation would suffer as a result of the way in which they were conducting the claim. Finally, Watson Wyatt told Maxwell Batley that the mediator had told them that they could get $10 million from Maxwell Batley and that he was 'motoring' against them. The judge found that to be an astonishing way of trying to persuade Maxwell Batley to join the mediation. The invitation, or rather demand, of Watson Wyatt to Maxwell Batley to participate in the mediation had been self-serving and it would be a grave injustice to Maxwell Batley to deprive them of any part of their costs because they had not done so.

In *Valentine v Allen* [2003] EWCA Civ 915, [2003] All ER (D) 79 (Jul), the claimant lost his proceedings seeking to restrain alleged trespass by his neighbours over his land and he lost his appeal. He endeavoured to resist an order that he should pay the costs of the appeal because the defendants had refused his offers to mediate before the trial. The court held that the defendants had made reasonable and generous offers to resolve the matter but these were refused by the claimant who was seeking a settlement by way of payment of a large sum by the respondents. In these circumstances, the respondents had not acted unreasonably by refusing the offer to mediate, and in any event the claimant had been refused permission to appeal the judge's order as to costs, in which the mediation issue had been dealt with.

In *Halsey v Milton Keynes General NHS Trust; Steel v Joy* [2004] EWCA Civ 576, [2004] All ER (D) 125 (May). the court went even further, holding, contrary to previous beliefs, that there is no presumption that a party to a dispute should agree to mediation or other alternative dispute resolution processes. The general rule is that costs of litigation should follow the event. Refusal to agree to ADR does not justify departure from the general rule, unless it is shown that the successful party acted unreasonably in refusing to do so. To oblige truly unwilling parties to refer their disputes to mediation would be to impose an unacceptable obstruction on their right to access the court, and indeed a court order to mediate could itself be a violation of article 8 of the European Convention on Human Rights. The unsuccessful party must show that the mediation had a reasonable chance of success. Other factors relevant to the question of whether a party unreasonably refused ADR include, but are not limited to: the nature of the dispute; the merits of the case; the extent to which other settlement methods had been attempted; whether the costs of the ADR would have been disproportionately high; whether any delay in setting up and attending the ADR would have been prejudicial; and whether the ADR should result in a cost penalty. Compulsory mediation, therefore, continues to be a contradiction in terms. The pendulum has swung from the assumption that it is unreasonable to refuse to mediate, to the assumption that such refusal is reasonable unless the other party can demonstrate otherwise. ADR is to be achieved by persuasion and encouragement from the court and not force. On the other hand, the message is that parties should routinely consider whether their disputes are suitable for ADR and appreciate that if the unsuccessful party can demonstrate that the refusal to mediate was unreasonable this could rebut the presumption that costs follow the event.

In *Burchell v Bullard* [2005] EWCA Civ 358, [2005] NLJR 593, the Court of Appeal endorsed *Halsey* saying that the case made it plain there was a high rate of success achieved by mediation and also established its importance as a track to a just result running parallel with that of the court system. The court had given its stamp of approval for mediation and it was now the legal profession which had to become fully aware of and acknowledge its value. The profession could no longer with impunity shrug aside reasonable requests to mediate. Claimants and defendants alike in the future could expect little sympathy if they blithely battle on regardless of the alternatives. In particular, a party could not ignore a proper request to mediate simply because it had been made before the claim had been issued.

Despite the warnings in *Halsey* and *Burchall* they were followed by another three cases in which a refusal to mediate was upheld: *Daniels v Metropolitan Police Comr* [2005] EWCA Civ 1312, [2005] 44 LS Gaz R 30, 20 Oct (it was reasonable for a public body to contest what it reasonably considered to be an unfounded claim in order to deter similarly unfounded claims); *Wethered Estate Ltd v Davis* [2005] EWHC 1903 (Ch), [2005] 39 LS Gaz R 29 (it was not unreasonable to refuse mediation until the true nature of the dispute had been defined) and *Hickman v Blake Lapthorn* [2006] EWHC 12 (QB), [2006] All ER (D) 67 (Jan) (a barrister who was not prepared to compromise a negligence claim against him had legitimately and reasonably refused to mediate). In *Hickman* the court gave the following guidance:

'(a)   A party cannot be ordered to submit to mediation as that would be contrary to article 6 of the European Convention on Human Rights.

(b)   The burden is on the unsuccessful party to show why the general rule of costs following the event should not apply, and it must be shown that the successful party acted unreasonably in refusing to agree to mediation.

(c)   A party's reasonable belief that he has a strong case is relevant to the reasonableness of his refusal, otherwise the fear of costs sanctions may be used to extract unmerited settlements.

(d)   Where a case is evenly balanced . . . a party's belief that he would win should be given little or no weight in considering whether a refusal was reasonable . . . his belief must be unreasonable.

(e)   The costs of mediation is a relevant factor.

(f)   Whether the mediation had a reasonable prospect of success is relevant to the reasonableness of a refusal to agree to mediation.

(g)   In considering whether the refusal to agree to mediation was unreasonable, it is for the unsuccessful party to show that there was a reasonable prospect that the mediation would have been successful.

(h)   Where a party refuses to take part in mediation despite encouragement from the court to do so, that is a factor to be taken into account.

(i)   Public bodies are not in a special position.'

PRE-ACTION PROTOCOL AND DISCLOSURE

[11.22]

Section 51(1) of the Supreme Court (now Senior Courts) Act 1981 provides that the costs 'of and incidental to all proceedings' shall be in the discretion of the court. *McGlinn v Waltham Contractors Ltd* [2005] EWHC 1419 (TCC), [2005] 3 All ER 1126 held that costs incurred in complying with any pre-action protocol are capable of being costs 'incidental to' any proceedings which are subsequently commenced. However, only in exceptional circumstances could costs incurred by a defendant at the stage of a pre-action protocol, in dealing with and responding to issues which were subsequently dropped from the action when the proceedings were commenced be costs 'incidental to' those proceedings. It would be contrary to the whole purpose of the pre-action protocols if claiming parties were routinely penalised if they decided not to pursue claims in court which they had originally included in their protocol claim letters. The whole purpose of pre-action protocol procedure was to narrow issues and to allow a prospective defendant, wherever possible, to demonstrate to a prospective claimant that a particular claim was doomed to failure. It would be wrong in principle to penalise a claimant for abandoning claims which the defendant had demonstrated were not going to succeed because to do so would be to penalise the claimant for doing the very thing which the protocol was designed to achieve. Even so, the defendant in *McGlinn* was £20,000 out of pocket by complying with the protocol and responding to claims which did not subsequently form part of the proceedings. In the light of this decision prospective defendants may not comply with the pre-action protocol too assiduously.

In *SES Contracting Ltd v UK Coal plc* [2007] EWCA Civ 791, 26 July the claimant made a successful application for pre-action disclosure against the first named defendant under CPR Rule 31.16. The application had been opposed and the judge ordered the first named defendant to pay the costs of the application. The Court of Appeal held the judge had failed to have sufficient regard to the general rule that the respondent to such an application was normally entitled to his costs. There was ample material to justify a departure from the general rule in this case, but not to the extent of ordering the first defendant to pay the whole of the claimant's costs. In the circumstances, the right order was no order as to costs.

LATE AMENDMENT

[11.23]

In *Professional Information Technology Consultants Ltd v Jones* [2001] EWCA Civ 2103, [2001] All ER (D) 90 (Dec) the claimant succeeded in the action as a result of being given permission to make a substantial last-minute amendment. The trial judge was satisfied that had the defendant known the claimant's case in its amended form from the outset she would have settled. Accordingly the judge awarded the claimant only two-thirds of her costs. The court rejected the defendant's contention that as a matter of principle she should be awarded her costs up to the date of the amendment. CPR Rule 44.3(6) empowers the court to order a party to pay a proportion of the costs and the one-third discount was an acceptable method of reflecting the amendment.

MISLEADING CONDUCT

[11.24]

In *Douglas v Hello! Ltd (No 7)* [2004] EWHC 63 (Ch), [2004] EMLR 230, the three claimants had each succeeded in their claims under the law of confidence. An award that simply looked at the number of issues won and lost would not fairly reflect the realities of the case. While they lost a good many issues, it was not unreasonable, particularly in light of the first three defendants' misleading conduct, for the claimants to have raised the issues that they did. Overall the claimants were winners of the liability hearing. If an award were to be made issue by issue, there would undoubtedly be a disproportionate amount of time taken up and it was preferable to mark the degree to which time and money were spent unnecessarily or disproportionately by awarding the claimants only a proportion of their costs of the liability hearing. That appropriate proportion was 75%.

UNATTRACTIVE BEHAVIOUR

[11.25]

In *Base Metal Trading Ltd v Shamurin (No 3)* [2003] EWHC 2606 (Comm), [2003] All ER (D) 79 (Nov), the defendant succeeded at the trial but had raised unsuccessful defences or issues which extended the length of the trial by 14 days and caused the claimant to incur significant expenditure. It would not therefore be appropriate that the defendant should recover all of his costs. There needs to be encouragement to litigants to be selective as to the points they take and an incentive for responsible behaviour. Both parties had behaved unattractively. The claimant had not established a cause of action and the proceedings had been brought in a deliberate attempt to divert and deplete the defendant's resources. In those circumstances, making no order as to costs achieved the closest approximation to the modern issues-based approach. In *Gil v Baygreen Properties Ltd (in liquidation)* [2004] EWHC 2029 (Ch), [2004] All ER (D) 108 (Aug) the successful claimant's unwillingness to negotiate and her fabrication of documents had to be reflected in the costs order in her favour. Her costs were reduced by £20,000.

However, in *Lawal v Northern Spirit Ltd* [2004] EWCA Civ 208, [2004] All ER (D) 319 (Feb), a litigant in person's offensive and intemperate language in correspondence did not amount to misconduct under CPR rule 44.3(4)(a) such as to entitle his opponent to costs.

In *Strachey v Ramage* [2008] EWCA Civ 804 16 July the claimant paid the price of her solicitors' aggressive conduct.

In a boundary dispute which the claimant won on appeal the defendant contended there should be no order as to costs in respect of either the claim or the appeal on the grounds that the claimant had pursued the claim aggressively and unreasonably and made no serious attempt to compromise the parties' differences. The Court of Appeal regarded the opening letter from the claimant's solicitors as aggressive and unjustifiably heavy-handed. A letter of that sort written to the other side's solicitors is one thing: they can explain its exaggeration to the client. Such a letter written to the individual direct is another matter. It would be calculated to cause immediate worry and concern, much of which would be unjustified. After proceedings had been commenced, the defendant's solicitors offered to concede the claim and make a contribution of £2500 to the claimant's cost. The offer was not accepted because the appellant's costs were by then more than £16,000, disclosure and the exchange of witness statements having taken place. For the appellant to have run up costs of that order by then was, on the face of it, disproportionate. At the case management conference, the district judge made a strong mediation recommendation, which the defendant solicitors also took up on the same day. There was no positive response from the claimant. There was nothing to show the claimant made any reasonable response to the respondent's overtures to concede her claim; and the overt aggression with which the appellant had run her case to date suggests that it is unlikely that she did. Although the successful appellant was in principle entitled to have costs of the claim, they were limited to 66% to reflect the solicitors' unreasonable conduct.

TRIAL JUDGE OR COSTS JUDGE?

[11.26]

Aaron v Shelton [2004] EWHC 1162 (QB), [2004] 3 All ER 561, [2004] NLJR 853, held that where a losing party considers that he should not be liable to pay the whole of the costs of the action by reason of the opposing party's conduct, he should make an application to the trial judge when he is considering what orders as to costs should be made under CPR rule 44.3.

However, in *Northstar Systems Ltd v Fielding* [2006] EWCA Civ 1660, [2007] 2 All ER 983 it was held that the principle stated in *Aaron v Shelton* was too broadly worded.

Where the paying party had not sought an order from the judge reflecting the dishonest misconduct of the receiving party, that should not deprive the paying party from referring to it on the assessment of costs, or prevent the assessing judge from considering whether the costs incurred by the dishonest party were reasonable. Consideration of a party's conduct should normally take place both when the trial judge was considering what order for costs he should make, and then when the costs judge was assessing costs. The court would want to ensure that dishonesty was penalised, but that the dishonest party was not placed in double jeopardy. Ultimately, the question was one of the proper construction of the order made by the judge.

Accordingly, it is important for the judge who is asked to take dishonesty into account at the end of the trial when considering the order as to costs, to consider what was likely to occur on the assessment. Where dishonest conduct was being reflected in an order made by the trial judge, it must be wise for him to make clear whether he was making the order on the basis that on the assessment the paying party would still be entitled to raise the dishonesty in arguing that costs incurred in supporting the particular dishonesty were unreasonably incurred. Judges might also want to consider whether to make an order under the misconduct provisions of CPR 44.14, and it would be wise to do that before considering precisely what order to make in relation to the cost of a trial generally.

If a judge ordered a reduction by 20% without more, the natural construction of such an order, unless the contrary was expressly stated, was that the party guilty of dishonesty should not be entitled to say on assessment that his costs incurred in seeking to make a dishonest case could be taken as reasonably incurred because the judge had made a reduction. If the dishonest party was entitled to succeed on such an argument, he would hardly suffer any penalty at all. The judge had not misdirected himself in making a reduction to reflect a finding of dishonesty against the receiving parties, but this did not mean that the costs judge must treat the costs incurred in the dishonesty as having been reasonably incurred.

In *Wright v HSBC Bank plc* [2006] EWHC 1473 (QB), 150 Sol Jo LB 887, 23 June the claim failed but the trial judge found some aspects of the defendant's conduct throughout the litigation had not been commendable, particularly in relation to disclosure. Accordingly, it was appropriate to disallow the defendant the costs which it had incurred in relation to disclosure of its documents. Furthermore, it was lamentable that the defendant had allowed the claimant in person to proceed on an incorrect basis. It was appropriate to disallow £5,000 from the defendant's costs on that ground.

In *Three Rivers District Council v Governor and Company of the Bank of England* [2006] EWHC 816 (Comm), [2006] All ER (D) 175 (Apr) the trial judge not only awarded indemnity costs to the defendants but offered to give the costs judge such assistance as he reasonably could, including answering his written questions and sitting with him on the assessment if necessary!

Drew v Whitbread plc [2010] EWCA Civ 53, [2010] 1 WLR 1725, [2010] NLJR 270, was allocated to the multi-track but the claimant only recovered damages well within the limits of the fast track. The judge awarded him his costs to be assessed on the standard basis. At the assessment, the costs judge ruled that the claimant could never have recovered the damages he was claiming, and that the claim should be treated as if it were a fast track in order to ensure that costs were proportionate. The claimant appealed, contending that the costs judge did not have the power to impose fast track costs, as in effect that rescinded the award of standard basis costs by the trial judge. The Court of Appeal held that the costs judge was not entitled simply to rule that she was going to assess the costs of trial as if the case were on the fast track. That would be to rescind the trial judge's order. The permissible approach was to assess the costs on the standard basis taking into account that the case should have been allocated to the fast track. A costs judge is entitled, as part of the process of assessment, to hold that a case should, if reasonably presented, have been allocated to the fast track, and to assess costs accordingly. The fact this point was not raised at trial did not preclude it. The approach in *Aaron v Shelton* was too narrow, and was disapproved. There might be some points which could not be raised at an assessment, because it would in effect require the costs judge to re-try the case. But that did not mean there was a general rule that a failure to raise a matter at trial for the purposes of CPR 44.3 precluded the raising of the matter at assessment for CPR 44.5 purposes. CPR 44.3 and 44.5 were intended to work in harmony and it was intended that the parties' conduct might have to be considered under both. It was legitimate for a costs judge considering 'all the circumstances of the case' to consider whether the case was in reality a fast track.

In *O'Beirne v Hudson* [2010] EWCA Civ 52, [2010] 1 WLR 1717 the consent order provided: 'The defendant do pay the claimant's reasonable costs and disbursements on the standard basis, to be subject to detailed assessment if not agreed.' The defendants argued that had the matter proceeded to allocation it would have been allocated to the small claims track and therefore only fixed costs under CPR 27 should be allowed. The Court of Appeal held that although a costs judge cannot vary a costs order he, or in this case she, could exercise her discretion in considering whether costs were reasonably incurred, and whether it was reasonable for the paying party to pay more than would have been recoverable in the case that should have been allocated to the small claims track. Therefore a costs judge must question whether, for example, it is reasonable that the paying party should pay for the cost of the receiving party having a lawyer? A costs judge cannot simply apply small claims track costs, but this would still be a highly material circumstance in considering what by way of assessment should be payable.

The costs judge is entitled to take into account all of the circumstances of the case under CPR Rule 44.5(1) including the fact that the case would almost certainly been allocated to the small claims track. In so doing the district judge would have regard to what could or could not be recovered if the case had been so allocated. Nicholas Bacon QC observed that this case is a warning to anyone settling a low value personal injury claim to agree a figure for costs.

PAYMENT ON ACCOUNT

[11.27]

Rule 44.3(8) is aimed at deterring the paying party from seeking a detailed assessment in order to delay parting with his money. Where a detailed assessment is ordered the court will usually order a substantial payment on account.

CPR Rule 44.3(8) (see para [11.6] contains the important provision that if the trial judge does order a detailed assessment he may order a payment on account. The attraction of a detailed assessment to a paying party is the delay before he has to part with his money. An order for an interim payment removes that attraction. Statements of costs will be available to help the judge order a realistic amount. A robust example of this was in *Mars UK Ltd v Teknowledge Ltd* [1999] 2 Costs LR 44, Ch D. It is a judgment of Jacob J, who with Laddie J pioneered summary assessment of costs for some years before their introduction in the Civil Procedure Rules. He confirmed that in general an interim order for costs on account should be made. However, in exercising its discretion the court had to take into account all the circumstances, one of which might be an unsuccessful party's wish to appeal; other considerations were the relative financial position of each party and the court's overriding objective to deal with cases justly. Jacob J ordered the defendants to make an interim payment of £80,000 but he allowed the money to be paid in instalments of £30,000 within the first month and five monthly sums of £10,000 each thereafter so as not to preclude the defendants from being able to afford an appeal against his decision. In estimating the amount at which the costs might eventually be assessed the court took into account the claimant's pre-action heavy-handedness and misconduct during the proceedings as a result of which the judge thought it unlikely that on a detailed assessment the claimant would recover more than 40% of their solicitor and client costs.

In *Days Healthcare UK Ltd v Pihsiang Machinery Manufacturing Co Ltd* [2006] EWHC 1444 (QB), [2006] 4 All ER 233 16 June the defendant had failed to comply with an order to make an interim costs payment of £2 million plus interest and the claimant applied for an order that unless the payment was made, a final costs certificate should be issued in the amount it had claimed. Quite apart from any specific rule, the court has an inherent jurisdiction to control its own processes sufficiently enough to enable it to make the order sought. CPR rule 3.1(1) expressly preserves the inherent powers of the court, while rule 3.1(3)(a) provides that where the court makes an order in the course of its general powers of management, it can do so subject to conditions, including a condition to pay a sum of money into court. However, points of dispute having been properly served, the order should provide for there to be an assessment but the defendants should not be permitted to participate further unless they made the interim payment.

Conditional orders will never be made if the effect would be to stifle the litigant's access to the court and will usually only be made against a litigant without assets in England and against whom enforcement is likely to be difficult or impossible. This paragraph was considered in *Hextalls (a firm) v Al-Sami* [2009] EWHC 3678 (QB) in which the costs judge described it as 'an unwarranted gloss', but on appeal the High Court judge expressly endorsed it. The costs judge had observed there was no authority for this passage. There is now!

NO PAYMENT ON ACCOUNT

[11.28]

In *Dyson Ltd v Hoover Ltd* [2003] EWHC 624 (Ch), [2003] 2 All ER 1042, the claimant obtained judgment for damages to be assessed for infringement of its registered patent by the defendant. Two weeks before the hearing of an enquiry into damages the claimant accepted a payment into court of £4 million. The payment in was more advantageous than the claimant's own Part 36 offer and the judge awarded the claimant the cost of the enquiry to be assessed on the standard basis. Before the costs had been assessed the claimant applied to another judge for an order under CPR Rule 44.3(8) that an amount be paid on account of its costs before they were assessed. The application was opposed on the grounds that because the court had not had the benefit of hearing the full trial or of hearing the enquiry, there was no normal rule applicable and the court was ill-placed to make any order for an interim payment. The court agreed, saying it had to exercise particular caution when invited to make an interim payment in these circumstances, because the judge was blind to the issues between the parties and the sums of money in dispute were considerable. It was important to bear in mind that the costs judge was empowered under CPR Rule 47.15 to issue an interim costs certificate at any time after the receiving party had filed a request for a detailed assessment hearing. This provision operated on the basis that the costs judge's power to order interim costs had been preceded by steps placing him in the position to make an accurate assessment and be able to decide whether an interim payment was appropriate and, if so, how much it should be.

Blackmore v Cummings (CA Civ Div, 10 June 2009, unreported) held there is no legal presumption that a party is entitled to realise the benefit of a costs order in his favour by having an interim payment on account. A costs order is simply one factor to be taken into account by a judge in the exercise of his wide discretion under the CPR Rule 44.3. The idea that a party should not be kept from money to which he had become entitled by virtue of a costs order was not a rule that had the status of a presumption. There was no dispute that once the costs were assessed the paying party would be able to meet any liability, the receiving party was not in any financial difficulty had delayed commencing the costs proceedings by some 29 months.

[11.29]

CPR Rule 44.3A: Costs orders relating to funding arrangements
See Chapter 44.

[11.30]

CPR Rule 44.3B: Limits on recovery under funding arrangements
See Chapter 44.

PRO BONO

[11.31]

Legal Services Act 2007 Section 194: Payments in respect of pro bono representation

(1)   This section applies to proceedings in a civil court in which—

(a)   a party to the proceedings ("P") is or was represented by a legal representative ("R"), and

(b)   R's representation of P is or was provided free of charge, in whole or in part.

(2)   This section applies to such proceedings even if P is or was also represented by a legal representative not acting free of charge.

(3)   The court may order any person to make a payment to the prescribed charity in respect of R's representation of P (or, if only part of R's representation of P was provided free of charge, in respect of that part).

(4)   In considering whether to make such an order and the terms of such an order, the court must have regard to—

(a)   whether, had R's representation of P not been provided free of charge, it would have ordered the person to make a payment to P in respect of the costs payable to R by P in respect of that representation, and

(b)   if it would, what the terms of the order would have been.

(5)   The court may not make an order under subsection (3) against a person represented in the proceedings if the person's representation was at all times within subsection (6).

(6)   Representation is within this subsection if it is—

(a)   provided by a legal representative acting free of charge, or

(b)   funded by the Legal Services Commission as part of the Community Legal Service.

(7)   Rules of court may make further provision as to the making of orders under subsection (3), and may in particular—

(a)   provide that such orders may not be made in civil proceedings of a description specified in the rules;

(b)   make provision about the procedure to be followed in relation to such orders;

    (c)   specify matters (in addition to those mentioned in subsection (4)) to which the court must have regard in deciding whether to make such an order, and the terms of any order.

(8)   "The prescribed charity" means the charity prescribed by order made by the Lord Chancellor.

(9)   An order under subsection (8) may only prescribe a charity which—

    (a)   is registered in accordance with section 3A of the Charities Act 1993, and

    (b)   provides financial support to persons who provide, or organise or facilitate the provision of, legal advice or assistance (by way of representation or otherwise) which is free of charge.

(10)   In this section—

"legal representative", in relation to a party to proceedings, means a person exercising a right of audience or conducting litigation on the party's behalf;

"civil court" means the civil division of the Court of Appeal, the High Court, or any county court;

"free of charge" means otherwise than for or in expectation of fee, gain or reward.

(11)   The court may not make an order under subsection (3) in respect of representation if (or to the extent that) it is provided before this section comes into force.

[11.32]

A problem with *pro bono* work is that because of the indemnity principle even when it succeeds the loser cannot be ordered to pay costs to the winner or his lawyers because by definition the lawyers were working for nothing. But since Section 194 of the Legal Services Act 2007 came into force on 1 October 2007 the unsuccessful opponent of a litigant who has been represented pro-bono can be ordered to pay costs and the indemnity principle abrogated. However, payment is not to the winner but to the Access to Justice Foundation, a charity specially created to receive money recovered under pro bono orders and funnelled through a network of six regional support trusts for distribution to local advice charities and pro-bono communities.

The provisions were incorporated in a new CPR Rule 44.3C and costs practice direction as follows:

[11.33]

CPR Rule 44.3C: Orders in respect of pro bono representation

(1)   In this rule, 'the 2007 Act' means the Legal Services Act 2007.

(2)   Where the court makes an order under section 194(3) of the 2007 Act—

    (a)   the court may order the payment to the prescribed charity of a sum no greater than the costs specified in Part 45 to which the party with pro bono representation would have been entitled in accordance with that Part and in respect of that representation had it not been provided free of charge; or

    (b)   where Part 45 does not apply, the court may determine the amount of the payment (other than a sum equivalent to fixed costs) to be made by the paying party to the prescribed charity by—

        (i)   making a summary assessment; or

        (ii)   making an order for detailed assessment,

of a sum equivalent to all or part of the costs the paying party would have been ordered to pay to the party with pro bono representation in respect of that representation had it not been provided free of charge.

(3) Where the court makes an order under section 194(3) of the 2007 Act, the order must specify that the payment by the paying party must be made to the prescribed charity.

(4) The receiving party must send a copy of the order to the prescribed charity within 7 days of receipt of the order.

(5) Where the court considers making or makes an order under section 194(3) of the 2007 Act, Parts 43 to 48 apply, where appropriate, with the following modifications—

    (a)   references to 'costs orders', 'orders about costs' or 'orders for the payment of costs' are to be read, unless otherwise stated, as if they refer to an order under section 194(3);

    (b)   references to 'costs' are to be read, as if they referred to a sum equivalent to the costs that would have been claimed by, incurred by or awarded to the party with pro bono representation in respect of that representation had it not been provided free of charge; and

    (c)   references to 'receiving party' are to be read, as meaning a party who has pro bono representation and who would have been entitled to be paid costs in respect of that representation had it not been provided free of charge.

[11.34]

CPD Section 10A Orders In Respect Of Pro Bono Representation: CPR Rule 44.3C

10A.1 Rule 44.3C(2) sets out how the court may determine the amount of payment when making an order under section 194(3) of the Legal Services Act 2007. Paragraph 13.2 of this Practice Direction provides that the general rule is that the court will make a summary assessment of costs in the circumstances outlined in that paragraph unless there is good reason not to do so. This will apply to rule 44.3C(2)(b) with the modification that the summary assessment of the costs is to be read as meaning the summary assessment of the sum equivalent to the costs that would have been claimed by the party with pro bono representation in respect of that representation had it not been provided free of charge.

10A.2 Where an order under section 194(3) of the Legal Services Act 2007 is sought, to assist the court in making a summary assessment of the amount payable to the prescribed charity, the party who has pro bono representation must prepare, file and serve in accordance with paragraph 13.5(2) a written statement of the sum equivalent to the costs that party would have claimed for that legal representation had it not been provided free of charge.

Costs orders both ways

[11.34A]

In an article in the Law Society Gazette of 13 November 2009, Jeremy Morgan, QC drew attention to a practical issue which needs careful consideration:

'What happens in the case where there is a series of cost orders going either way. If the first order is made in favour of the Foundation and the second made in favour of the opponent, it will not be possible to direct a set-off of these orders, as they lack the mutuality essential for ordering set-offs. As a later court has no general power to revoke an earlier order, both will stand and be enforceable. There is an obvious unfairness about such a result. The solution is to invite the court in pro-bono cases to reserve costs until the trial or other final hearing, preferably with a note on the court file to indicate the order which would have been made but for this problem. The court conducting the final hearing can then make a single order, one way or the other, which reflects the justice of the case overall including the interlocutory successes and failures.'

[11.35]

CPR Rule 44.4: Basis of assessment

(1)   Where the court is to assess the amount of costs (whether by summary or detailed assessment) it will assess those costs—

    (a)   on the standard basis; or

    (b)   on the indemnity basis,

but the court will not in either case allow costs which have been unreasonably incurred or are unreasonable in amount.

(Rule 48.3 sets out how the court decides the amount of costs payable under a contract)

(2)   Where the amount of costs is to be assessed on the standard basis, the court will—

    (a)   only allow costs which are proportionate to the matters in issue; and

    (b)   resolve any doubt which it may have as to whether costs were reasonably incurred or reasonable and proportionate in amount in favour of the paying party.

(Factors which the court may take into account are set out in rule 44.5)

(3)   Where the amount of costs is to be assessed on the indemnity basis, the court will resolve any doubt which it may have as to whether costs were reasonably incurred or were reasonable in amount in favour of the receiving party.

(4)   Where—

    (a)   the court makes an order about costs without indicating the basis on which the costs are to be assessed; or

    (b)   the court makes an order for costs to be assessed on a basis other than the standard basis or the indemnity basis,

the costs will be assessed on the standard basis.

(5)   [Revoked.]

(6)   Where the amount of a solicitor's remuneration in respect of non-contentious business is regulated by any general orders made under the Solicitors Act 1974, the amount of the costs to be allowed in respect of any such business which falls to be assessed by the court will be decided in accordance with those general orders rather than this rule and rule 44.5.

THE TWO BASES

[11.36]

To appreciate fully the two bases for the assessment of costs it is necessary to go back into history before RSC Ord 62 was introduced in 1986. In those far off days judges could make any costs orders they wished. Examples were 'the defendant do indemnify the plaintiff as to costs', 'the defendant to pay all costs', and, my favourite, 'the defendant to pay the utmost costs'. No one knew what they meant but the judge felt a lot better for having made them! These orders could in theory mean that the loser had to pay whatever costs the winner claimed, however unreasonable his costs and however unreasonable his disbursements. So when RSC Ord 62 was re-drafted some prohibitory words were inserted to make the rules judge proof. Similar words are alive and well in the new Rule 44.4(4) which provides that if the court makes an order for costs to be assessed other than on the standard or indemnity basis, or makes an order which does not indicate the basis on which the costs are to be assessed the costs will be assessed on the standard basis. Both bases allow costs reasonably incurred and of a reasonable amount. Prior to the CPR the only difference between the two bases was in respect of the burden of proof of reasonableness. On the standard basis any doubt as to reasonableness is to be resolved in favour of the paying party, whilst on the indemnity basis any doubt is to be resolved in favour of the receiving party. As former Chief Taxing Master Matthews put it: 'If there is no doubt, there is no difference'. It had nothing whatsoever to do with hourly rates, profit mark-up or the scope of the work. In other words, it was not the modern equivalent of 'the utmost costs'. This distinction remains.

PROPORTIONALITY

[11.37]

However, under Rule 44.4(2) there is now another important difference. On the standard basis the court will only allow costs which are not only reasonable but are also 'proportionate to the matters in issue'. 'What is proportionality?' is a conundrum the courts are still trying to solve.

(a) CPR Rule 1.1(2)

[11.38]

We start with Rule 1.1(2) which explains that 'proportionate' refers to (i) the amount of money involved; (ii) the importance of the case; (iii) the complexity of the issues; and (iv) the financial position of each party. The last provision arises out of the avowed aim of the CPR of equalising any disparity between the parties.

(b) Practice Direction

[11.39]

Section 11 of the Costs Practice Direction makes a further stab at defining 'proportionality' by saying what it *isn't*.

[11.40]

CPD Section 11 Factors to be taken into account in deciding the amount of costs: Rule 44.5

11.1 *In applying the test of proportionality the court will have regard to rule 1.1(2)(c). The relationship between the total of the costs incurred and the financial value of the claim may not be a reliable guide. A fixed percentage cannot be applied in all cases to the value of the claim in order to ascertain whether or not the costs are proportionate.*

11.2 *In any proceedings there will be costs which will inevitably be incurred and which are necessary for the successful conduct of the case. Solicitors are not required to conduct litigation at rates which are uneconomic. Thus in a modest claim the proportion of costs is likely to be higher than in a large claim, and may even equal or possibly exceed the amount in dispute.*

11.3 *Where a trial takes place, the time taken by the court in dealing with a particular issue may not be an accurate guide to the amount of time properly spent by the legal or other representatives in preparation for the trial of that issue.*

11.4 *Where a party has entered into a funding arrangement the costs claimed may, subject to rule 44.3B include an additional liability.*

11.5 *In deciding whether the costs claimed are reasonable and (on a standard basis assessment) proportionate, the court will consider the amount of any additional liability separately from the base costs.*

11.6 *In deciding whether the base costs are reasonable and (if relevant) proportionate the court will consider the factors set out in rule 44.5.*

11.7 *Subject to paragraph 17.8(2), when the court is considering the factors to be taken into account in assessing an additional liability, it will have regard to the facts and circumstances as they reasonably appeared to the solicitor or counsel when the funding arrangement was entered into and at the time of any variation of the arrangement.*

11.8

(1) *In deciding whether a percentage increase is reasonable relevant factors to be taken into account may include:—*

    (a) *the risk that the circumstances in which the costs, fees or expenses would be payable might or might not occur;*

    (b) *the legal representative's liability for any disbursements;*

    (c) *what other methods of financing the costs were available to the receiving party.*

(2) *Omitted*

11.9 *A percentage increase will not be reduced simply on the ground that, when added to base costs which are reasonable and (where relevant) proportionate, the total appears disproportionate.*

11.10 *In deciding whether the cost of insurance cover is reasonable, relevant factors to be taken into account include:*

(1) *where the insurance cover is not purchased in support of a conditional fee agreement with a success fee, how its cost compares with the likely cost of funding the case with a conditional fee agreement with a success fee and supporting insurance cover;*

(2) *the level and extent of the cover provided;*

(3) *the availability of any pre-existing insurance cover;*

(4) *whether any part of the premium would be rebated in the event of early settlement;*

(5) *the amount of commission payable to the receiving party or his legal representatives or other agents.*

11.11 *Where the court is considering a provision made by a membership organisation, rule 44.3B(1) (b) provides that any such provision which exceeds the likely cost to the receiving party of the premium of an insurance policy against the risk of incurring a liability to pay the costs of other parties to the proceedings is not recoverable. In such circumstances the court will, when assessing the additional liability, have regard to the factors set out in paragraph 11.10 above, in addition to the factors set out in rule 44.5.*

[11.41]

Paragraph 11.1 emphasises that a fixed percentage cannot be applied in all cases to the value of the claim in order to ascertain whether or not the costs are proportionate. This provision was inserted because there was gathering support for a school of thought that proportionality could be reduced to a formula that the costs should not, for example, exceed 20% or 33.3% of the claim. Paragraph 11.2 explains why this approach is erroneous. In all proceedings there will be an unavoidable base of costs and of course the lower the claim the higher the base of costs will be proportionately to the amount of the claim. Similarly, para 11.3 emphasises that the length of time taken by the court to deal with a particular issue is not necessarily relevant to the amount of time properly spent on preparing for the trial of that issue.

(c) Assessment at outset

[11.42]

Judicial guidance was first given by Lord Woolf when the Court of Appeal sat in Newcastle-upon-Tyne in *Jefferson v National Freight Carriers plc* [2001] EWCA Civ 2082, [2001] 2 Costs LR 313. He said:

'Proportionality is a very important feature of the assessment of costs on the standard basis. This is particularly true in relation to the fast track and if a claimant is going to seek to recover a sum which is substantially in excess of the amount recovered, as was being sought to be recovered in this case, the legal representatives of the claimant at the hearing have to be in a position to help the judge further than was the case here. They first must bear in mind that if they are going to conduct litigation of a modest nature of the sort which was being conducted here, where the likely sum which was to be recovered, even on their own Part 36 offer, was a sum below £3000, they are under a heavy duty to conduct that litigation in as economical manner as possible. There is no decision which has been placed before this court indicating precisely what approach should be adopted in exercising the jurisdiction which the judge was exercising. However, we have been shown the decision of the Birmingham County Court on the 22nd June last year, when Judge Alton dealt with the issue in a manner which I regard as of considerable assistance. The judge said in particular "In modern litigation, with the emphasis on proportionality, it is necessary for the parties to make an assessment at the outset of the likely value of the claim and its importance and complexity and then to plan in advance the necessary work, the appropriate level of person to carry out the work, the overall time which it would be necessary and appropriate to spend on the various stages in bringing the action to trial and the likely overall cost. While it was not unusual for costs to exceed the amount in issue, it was, in the context of modern litigation, such as the present case, one reason for seeking to curb the amount of work done and the cost by reference to the need for proportionality." I would respectfully endorse every word of those comments of Judge Alton.'

In considering overall proportionality at the outset, fresh from reading the documents and the advocates' submissions, it is neither reasonable nor necessary to expect an experienced costs judge to go through the seven factors prescribed in rule 44.5(3). The costs judge need not pedantically rehearse them (*Ortwein v Rugby Managements Ltd* [2003] EWHC 2077 (Ch), [2003] All ER (D) 457 (Jul), and *Young v JR Smart (Builders) Ltd* [2004] EWHC 103 (QB), [2004] All ER (D) 83 (Jan); RCJ 15 January.

(d) Reasonable or necessary?

[11.43]

Lownds v Home Office [2002] EWCA Civ 365, [2002] 4 All ER 775 gave Lord Woolf a further opportunity to consider the application of the principle of proportionality to between-the-parties costs. It is ironic that in its search for clarity the Court of Appeal has disinterred the old concept of necessity which was buried by the introduction of the CPR.

(i)   Central role in CPR

[11.44]

He described the principle of proportionality as having a direct bearing on the policy on which the effectiveness of the Civil Procedure Rules depends. He continued:

> 'Because of the central role that proportionality should have in the resolution of civil litigation, it is essential that courts should attach the appropriate significance to the requirement of proportionality when making orders for costs and when assessing the amount of costs. What has, however, caused practitioners and the members of the judiciary who have to assess costs difficulty is how to give effect to requirements of proportionality. In particular there is uncertainty as to the relationship between the requirement of reasonableness and the requirement of proportionality. Where there is a conflict between reasonableness and proportionality does one requirement prevail over the other and, if so, which requirement is it that takes precedence? There is also the question of whether the proportionality test is to be applied globally or on an item-by-item basis, or both globally and on an item-by-item basis. These are the questions which directly arise on this appeal and explain why this judgment is so important.'

(ii)   Necessary

[11.45]

Quoting para 11.2 of the Costs Practice Direction, Lord Woolf confirmed that solicitors are not required to conduct litigation at rates which are uneconomic and that in a modest claim the proportion of costs is likely to be higher than in a large claim, and 'may even equal or possibly exceed the amount in dispute'. The court held that the words 'which are necessary' are the key to how judges in assessing costs should give effect to the requirement of proportionality. If the appropriate conduct of the proceedings makes costs necessary then the requirement of proportionality does not prevent all the costs being recovered either on an item-by-item approach or on a global approach. Where an item of costs is necessarily incurred then a reasonable amount for the item should normally be allowed. Any item that is not necessary should be disallowed.

Although when costs are disproportionate it is necessary to determine what was necessary, the court emphasised that a sensible standard of necessity has to be adopted which takes fully into account the need to make allowances for the different judgments which those responsible for litigation can sensibly come to as to what is required. The danger of setting too high a standard with the benefit of hindsight has to be avoided. While the threshold required to meet necessity is higher than that of reasonableness, it is still a standard that a competent practitioner should be able to achieve without undue difficulty. When a practitioner incurs expenses which are reasonable but not necessary, he may be able to recover his fees and disbursements from his client, but extra expense which results from conducting litigation in a disproportionate manner cannot be recovered from the other party.

In deciding what is necessary the conduct of the other party is highly relevant. The other party, by co-operation, can reduce costs; by being uncooperative can increase costs. If he is unco-operative that may render necessary costs which would otherwise be unnecessary and that he should pay the costs for the expense which he has made necessary is perfectly acceptable. Access to justice would be impeded if lawyers felt they could not afford to do what is necessary to conduct the litigation. Giving appropriate weight to the requirements of proportionality and reasonableness will not make the conduct of litigation uneconomic if on the assessment there is allowed a reasonable sum for the work carried out which was necessary.

(iii) Two-stage approach

[11.46]

There has to be a global approach and an item-by-item approach. The global approach will indicate whether the total sum claimed is or appears to be disproportionate having particular regard to the considerations which CPR Rule 44.5(3) states are relevant. If the costs as a whole are not disproportionate according to that test, then all that is normally required is that each item should have been reasonably incurred and the costs for that item are reasonable. If, on the other hand, the costs as a whole appear disproportionate then the court will want to be satisfied that the work in relation to each item was necessary and, if necessary, that the costs of the item are reasonable. If, because of lack of planning or due to other causes, the global costs are disproportionately high, then the requirement that the costs should be proportionate means that no more should be payable than would have been payable if the litigation had been conducted in a proportionate manner. This in turn means that reasonable costs will only be recovered for the items which were necessary if the litigation had been conducted in a proportionate manner. The fact that the litigation had been conducted in an insufficiently rigorous manner to meet the requirement of proportionality does not mean that no costs are recoverable. It means that only those costs which would have been recoverable if the litigation had been appropriately conducted will be recovered. No greater sum can be recovered than that which would have been recoverable item-by-item if the litigation had been conducted proportionately.

(iv)   Proportionality

[11.47]

In a case where proportionality is likely to be an issue, a preliminary judgment as to the proportionality of the costs as a whole must be made at the outset. This will ensure that the costs judge applies the correct approach to the detailed assessment. In considering that question, the costs judge will have regard to whether the appropriate level of fee earner or counsel has been deployed, whether offers to settle have been made, whether unnecessary experts have been instructed and the other matters set out in Rule 44.5(3). Once a decision is reached as to proportionality of costs as a whole, the judge will be able to proceed to consider the costs, item-by-item, applying the appropriate test of reasonableness or necessity to each item.

In considering overall proportionality at the outset of a detailed assessment, fresh from a reading of the documents and the advocates' submissions, it is not necessary or reasonable to expect an experienced costs judge to go through the seven items under CPR Rule 44.5(3). *Ortwein v Rugby Managements Ltd* [2003] EWHC 2077 (Ch), [2003] All ER (D) 457 (Jul) made it clear that the costs judge need not pedantically rehearse the list of 7 items under Rule 44.5(3). Such a structured approach is not necessary (*Young v J R Smart (Builders) Ltd* [2004] EWHC 103 (QB), [2004] All ER (D) 83 (Jan); RCJ 15 January).

(v)   The amounts claimed and recovered

[11.48]

The proportionality of the costs incurred by the claimant should be determined having regard to the sum that it was reasonable for him to believe that he might recover at the time he made the claim. He should be allowed to claim the costs necessary to pursue a reasonable claim, but not allowed to recover costs increased or incurred by putting forward an exaggerated claim.

The proportionality of the costs incurred by the defendant should be determined having regard to the sum that it was reasonable for him to believe that the claimant might recover should his claim succeed. This is likely to be the amount that the claimant has claimed, for a defendant will normally be entitled to take a claim at its face value. A defendant should not be prejudiced if he assumes the claim which was made was one which was reasonable and he incurs costs in contesting the claim on this assumption.

(vi)   Not inexpensive

[11.49]

Lord Woolf concluded by conceding that this approach will not make litigation inexpensive but it should help to ensure that costs are kept within proper bounds. Costs assessed in the way indicated will also underline the advantages to a claimant, before embarking on litigation, of making a formal offer to settle which will avoid the risks of litigation if the offer is accepted, or provide a real prospect of obtaining an indemnity order for costs if the offer is rejected.

(e) Unprincipled ceiling

[11.50]

In *SCT Finance Ltd v Bolton* [2002] EWCA Civ 56, [2003] 3 All ER 434 the judge made an order for costs to be ascertained by detailed assessment on the standard basis, but limited the amount to £15,000 because the costs were disproportionate to the amount at stake and because of the paying party's limited means. The judge had already ordered that three sets of the costs of the successful party were to be ascertained by detailed assessment, so the principal effect of the judge's decision to impose a ceiling was to require the costs assessor to disallow costs which, on an overall rather than mechanical view, were disproportionate to the matters in issue and indeed to disallow them if he remained in doubt on the point. The ceiling of £15,000 imposed by the judge was unprincipled. It purported to make allowance for the perceived lack of proportionality of the amount of costs in circumstances where his orders for assessments on the standard basis had already made full allowance for any such lack of proportion. The ceiling would have effect only to the extent of requiring the costs assessor to disallow costs exceeding £15,000 which he had been satisfied were proportionate to the matters in issue. The effect of the ceiling would in that event be to excise from Mr Bolton's liability the excess element of the proportionate costs and would thus be contrary to the judge's primary reason for imposing it. Furthermore, the extent to which it was proper to have regard to Mr Bolton's perceived lack of means, was a factor which would also in any event figure in the assessor's appraisal of proportionality.

Lord Woolf said the costs 'may even equal or possibly exceed the amount in dispute', but if the man-in-the-street were asked if he thought this was proportionate, I doubt that he would agree. However, perhaps this may now be the benchmark – a rebuttable presumption that costs which exceed the amount in dispute are disproportionate.

(f) Seat of the pants

[11.51]

A practical aid to considering reasonableness and necessity in the context of proportionality is to consider the costs incurred by the paying party. What, for example, was their level of fee earner, charging rate, seniority of counsel and the amount of time spent? If the paying party has increased the stakes by using a senior partner, leading counsel and a fashionable expert, is it disproportionate for the receiving party to have done likewise? Is the pot calling the kettle black?

[11.52]

CPR Rule 44.5 Factors to be taken into account in deciding the amount of costs
See Chapter 21.

THE INDEMNITY BASIS

(a) Culpability and abuse of process

[11.53]

The requirement that the costs must be proportionate does not apply to costs on the indemnity basis, as a result of which an order for costs on the indemnity basis has the potential to hit a paying party much harder than before. Traditionally costs on the indemnity basis have been awarded only where there has been some culpability or abuse of process such as:

(a)   deceit or underhandedness;
(b)   abuse of the courts procedure;
(c)   not coming to court with open hands;
(d)   tenuous claims;
(e)   unjustified defences;
(f)   voluminous and unnecessary evidence; or
(g)   extraneous motives for the litigation.

If indemnity costs are sought, the court must decide whether there is something in the conduct of the action, or the circumstances of the case in question, which takes it out of the norm in a way which justifies an order for indemnity costs (*Noorani v Calver* [2009] EWHC 592 (QB), 153 Sol Jo (no 13) 27, [2009] All ER (D) 274 (Mar)).

Examples

[11.54]

Cooper v P&O Stena Line Ltd [1999] 1 Lloyd's Rep 734, QBD (Admiralty Ct). In an action for personal injuries, an allegation of malingering is a serious allegation of fraud and has to be pleaded. If the defendant had undertaken a proper investigation it was unlikely they would have defended on liability at all and in terms of quantum there never had been sufficient material on which to base the allegation of fraud. The unusual circumstances of the case justified the award of costs on the indemnity basis.

Griffiths v British Coal Corpn QBD. There were two broad generic issues, namely medical and liability. After taking into account that not all the generic medical costs had been unreasonably incurred and that only some of the liability costs would have been unreasonably incurred, the judge ordered the whole of the costs of the generic medical issues to be paid on the indemnity basis and the costs in respect of liability to be on the standard basis.

Amoco (UK) Exploration Co v British American Offshore Ltd (No 2) [2002] BLR 135, QBD (Comm Ct). The claimant sought to avoid a contract which had become unprofitable by putting pressure on the defendant to renegotiate and, when this failed, terminating the contract. The grounds of termination were different to those subsequently put forward at the trial. The claimant lost heavily and was ordered to pay costs on the indemnity basis because it had conducted itself throughout on the basis that its commercial interests took precedence over the rights and wrongs of the matter, and had then sought to justify its stance by a constantly changing case.

In *Re Satellite (2003) Ltd* (17 November 2003, unreported), Ch D, the petitioning creditor served a number of statutory demands on the company seeking sums allegedly due from the company. The company not only denied that the sums were due, but had a cross-claim. Nevertheless, the creditor presented a winding-up petition, which was dismissed. The winding-up jurisdiction should not be used as a means of debt collection. There was no evidence of the company's insolvency or any proper basis for the presentation of a petition. Accordingly, the petitioning creditor was ordered to pay the company's costs on the indemnity basis.

Phoenix Finance Ltd v Federation International de l'Automobile [2002] EWHC 1028 (Ch), [2003] CP Rep 1. It is not the law that an indemnity costs order will only be made if the conduct complained of has increased the costs that are recoverable. The question is the reasonableness or otherwise of the conduct and is not dependent upon whether the conduct, whether reasonable or unreasonable, has increased the costs payable. Letters before action are required in all proper cases and if letters before action are not written and if in the event the claimant loses then he can hardly complain if he ends up paying indemnity costs, particularly in the circumstances of this case where the evidence suggested strongly that there was no justification for interlocutory relief in the first place.

Lifeline Gloves Ltd v Richardson [2005] EWHC 1524 (Ch), [2005] All ER (D) 36 (Jul). The defendants successfully opposed the claimant's application for summary judgment with the costs being reserved. The defendants then withdrew their defence. The claimants were awarded their costs on the indemnity basis on the grounds that the defendants' conduct and the lack of merit in their defence amounted to unreasonable behaviour under CPR 44.3(4)(a) justifying an award of indemnity costs.

Wates Construction Ltd v HGP Greentree Allchurch Evans Ltd [2005] EWHC 2174 (TCC), [2006] BLR 45, 10 October. The claimant informed the defendant on the day of the trial that it was discontinuing its claim and accepted in accordance with CPR rule 38.6 that it had to pay the defendant's costs. The defendant contended that the claimant's conduct of the case had been so unreasonable that the court should award the defendant all its costs on the indemnity basis, alternatively on the indemnity basis from the time of exchange of witness statements, when it was apparent that the claimant's claim was hopeless.

The court agreed. The witness statements and in particular an agreement reached between the experts, made it clear beyond doubt that the claimant had no case against the defendant and should have discontinued its claim at that stage. From then on its conduct was so unreasonable that it justified an order for costs on the indemnity basis.

A v B (No 2) [2007] EWHC 54 (Comm), [2007] 1 All ER (Comm) 633, [2007] 1 Lloyd's Rep 358, sub nom *A v AJ* [2007] All ER (D) 157 (Jan). Provided that it can be established by a successful application for a stay, or an anti-suit injunction, as a remedy for breach of an arbitration or jurisdiction clause that the breach had caused the innocent party reasonably to incur legal costs, then those costs should normally be recoverable on the indemnity basis. If costs were confined to the standard basis, there would be necessarily part of the successful applicant's costs of the application which had been properly incurred but could not recover by such an order because of the restricted process of assessment.

That unidentified portion of costs would then be a loss which could only be recoverable as damages for breach of the jurisdiction or arbitration agreement, if such a damages claim were permissible. Authority suggested it would not be, which would be a fundamentally unjust situation. There is no policy argument which precludes a rule that costs in the circumstances should be on the indemnity basis.

National Westminster Bank plc v Rabobank Nederland [2007] EWHC 1742 (Comm) QBD, 19 July held that the minimum nature of the conduct required to justify an order for costs on the indemnity basis was, except in very rare cases, that there had been a significant level of unreasonableness or otherwise inappropriate conduct in its widest sense in relation to that party's pre-litigation dealings with the winning party or in relation to the commencement or conduct of the litigation itself. The conduct must be looked at in the context of the entire litigation and a view taken as to whether the level of unreasonableness or inappropriateness is in all the circumstances high enough to engage such an order. In this case the entire underlying foundation of the defendant's core allegation of fraudulent design by senior officials of the claimant bank showed itself from the very commencement of the counterclaim to be deeply flawed and the allegation involved an assumption so improbable as to be far fetched. The defendants had vigorously pursued claims of dishonesty throughout a long trial despite the fact that such allegations were highly speculative, if not doomed from the start. The defendants had crossed the frontier by conducting litigation in a manner so unreasonable or so unsatisfactory as to justify an order for costs against it on the indemnity basis in respect of its counterclaim.

In *Franses (Ian) v Al Assad* [2007] EWHC 2442 (Ch), [2007] All ER (D) 415 (Oct) the claimant obtained a freezing order improperly without notice, there were severe procedural flaws (including insufficient documentary evidence and a defective affidavit), and the duty of full and frank disclosure was breached in two respects. The injunction was discharged. The award of costs on the indemnity basis will not be justified unless the conduct of the paying party can be said in some respects to have been unreasonable. In this case the decision to make the application without notice was unreasonable, and at least some of the procedural deficiencies were serious matters of which the court should mark its disapproval. These features taken together were sufficient to remove the case from the ordinary run, or to take it 'out of the norm'.

In *Digicel (St Lucia) Ltd (a company registered under the laws of St Lucia) v Cable & Wireless plc* [2010] EWHC 888, Ch D, [2010] All ER (D) 166 (Apr), the claimants had alleged bad faith and conspiracy, which were allegations of serious wrongdoing. The claims were very wide, which meant that the defendants had to respond to allegations that virtually everything they had done was unlawful. The claimants' witness statements had not confined themselves to evidence of facts within the witness' own knowledge. The claimants had significantly overstated the quantum of their claim. On the basis of those findings, it was just that the successful defendants should recover their costs, provided they were reasonably incurred and reasonable in amount, without being subject to the possibility that some part of those costs should be disallowed on the grounds of proportionality, as would be the case under the standard basis. There was no injustice in denying the claimants the benefit of an assessment on a proportionate basis when they had showed no interest in proportionality by casting their claim disproportionately wide and requiring the defendants to meet such a claim. The claimants had also forfeited their right to the benefit of the doubt on reasonableness.

(b) No culpability or abuse of process

Examples

[11.55]

Reid Minty (a firm) v Taylor [2001] EWCA Civ 1723, [2002] 2 All ER 150: A party can be ordered to pay costs on the indemnity basis under CPR Rule 44.3 even though there had been no moral lack of probity or conduct deserving of moral condemnation on its part. The provision included a discretion to decide whether some or all of the costs awarded should be on the standard or indemnity basis. If costs were awarded on the indemnity basis, in many cases there would be some implicit expression of disapproval of the way in which the litigation had been conducted, but that would not necessarily be so in every case. Litigation could be conducted in a way which was unreasonable and which justified an award of costs on the indemnity basis, but which could not properly be regarded as lacking moral probity or deserving moral condemnation. It would not be right, however, that every defendant in every case could put themselves in the way of claiming indemnity costs simply by inviting the claimant at an early stage to give up and pay the defendant's costs. It might be different if the defendant offered to move some way towards the claimant's position and the result was more favourable to the defendant than that.

   Re Continental Assurance Co of London plc (in liquidation) (13 June 2001, unreported): Park J expressly disavowed his disapproval of some of the conduct of the liquidators as being the reason for his award of costs against them being on the indemnity basis. He did take into account what the consequences of the choice would be and where it would be appropriate for the benefit of any doubt to lie. There is a prima facie steer in the CPR that in the normal case costs should be awarded on the standard basis so that the benefit of any doubt should go to the paying party. However, this was not a normal, but a wholly exceptional case where it would be wrong and unacceptable for matters to be resolved against the respondents. The liquidators had pursued all issues at full length and right to the end, with the result that the amount of costs incurred must have been enormous. It was appropriate the costs of the successful respondents should be assessed on the indemnity basis so that they, and not the liquidators, received the benefit of any doubts.

In future it will be interesting to see if a new line of awards on the indemnity basis emerges on the grounds that, although the costs were disproportionate to the matters in issue, there nevertheless were good reasons for incurring them and therefore the award should be on the indemnity basis, to avoid the risk of reduction on the ground of disproportionality on the detailed assessment.

In *Kiam v MGN Ltd (No 2)* [2002] EWCA Civ 66, [2002] 2 All ER 242 the claimant had been awarded £105,000 damages in a jury libel case against which the defendant appealed. Before the appeal was heard the claimant's solicitors wrote 'without prejudice save as to costs' offering to accept £75,000 and to return to the defendant £30,000 plus appropriate interest, an offer which the defendant simply ignored. When the appeal was dismissed the claimant sought costs on the indemnity basis under the court's general discretion under CPR Part 44. Where litigation was conducted in a way that was unreasonable, even though the conduct could not properly be regarded as lacking moral probity or deserving moral condemnation, CPR Rule 44.3(4) required the court when deciding what order to make about costs, to have regard to all the circumstances, including any admissible offer to settle made by a party.

The court held it would be a rare case where a refusal of a settlement offer would attract, under CPR Part 44, not merely an adverse order for costs, but an order on the indemnity rather than on the standard basis. Although conduct falling short of misconduct deserving of moral condemnation could be so unreasonable as to justify an order for indemnity costs, such conduct would need to be unreasonable to a high degree, not merely wrong or misguided in hindsight. An indemnity costs order made under Part 44, unlike one made under Part 36, did carry at least some stigma. It should not be understood that under the CPR it was now generally appropriate to condemn in indemnity costs those who declined reasonable settlement offers. In the instant case, it was quite impossible to regard the defendant's refusal of the claimant's offer as unreasonable, let alone unreasonable to so pronounced a degree as to merit an award of indemnity costs.

(c) Part 36 offer

[11.56]

Costs on the indemnity basis may also be awarded as the result of a Part 36 offer. See Chapter 14.

(d) Indemnity costs refused

[11.57]

In *John v Pricewaterhouse Coopers (formerly Price Waterhouse)* [2002] 1 WLR 953, Ch D the defendants had successfully resisted the claimant's claim arising out of their conduct as auditors of the claimant companies. The defendants sought an order for costs on the indemnity basis on the grounds that as auditors they were entitled to be indemnified out of the assets of the companies against all their costs under the provisions of Table A. It was held that in their role of litigants the defendants were entitled only to an order for costs on the standard basis. There was nothing to prevent the auditors from seeking to recover the difference between standard costs and indemnity costs in separate proceedings to enforce the relevant contractual terms.

In *Simms v Law Society* [2005] EWCA Civ 849, [2005] NLJR 1124, the judge fell into error. After making a between-the-parties order for costs on the indemnity basis against the claimant, the judge rejected the claimant's attack on the proportionality of the Law Society's response to his application to the High Court, which he claimed had generated 'enormous costs', saying the matter could be dealt with on the detailed assessment. On the indemnity basis lack of proportionality is of no relevance and the judge's response was therefore inconsistent with the order he had made. On appeal the order was varied to the standard basis.

In *Zissis v Lukomski* [2006] EWCA Civ 341, [2006] 1WLR 2778 the district judge had awarded costs on the indemnity basis on the ground that if parties litigate only as to costs, then it seemed to him that they must bear a greater risk that if they are unsuccessful they will be ordered to pay costs on the indemnity basis. In allowing an appeal against the order, the Court of Appeal held that there is no reason why parties litigating over costs alone should be at any greater risk of an award of indemnity costs than those litigating over other matters.

In *Balmoral Group Ltd v Borealis (UK) Ltd* [2006] EWHC 2531 (Comm), [2006] All ER (D) 183 (Oct), 17 October 2006 the successful defendants contended that the claimant's behaviour had been so unreasonable both before and during the proceedings, including the presentation of a grossly exaggerated claim, unreasonable failure to make efforts to settle and by the character of the technical evidence adduced that costs should be awarded on the indemnity basis.

The judge held that justice does not demand that a resounding defeat should always carry with it an award of indemnity costs. The claimants' pre-action activity had not over-stepped the mark and although the claim for damages (loss of profits) was put very high and the explanation given by the claimant rested more on wishful thinking than evidential support, the court was not persuaded that continuing with the claim was so unreasonable that costs should be awarded on the indemnity basis. However, the deficient expert evidence adduced by the claimant had lead to unnecessary costs incurred by the defendant and accordingly the costs incurred by the defendant in that respect were awarded on the indemnity basis.

A claimant's rejection of a Part 36 offer does not take the case out of the norm even though, in light of the outcome of the case, it was wrong to reject it. In complex commercial litigation of the present kind it could not be said that it was unreasonable to have rejected the offer. For indemnity costs to be awarded there needed to be some conduct or circumstance taking the case out of the norm. The costs were ordered to be paid on the standard basis. (*HLB Kidsons (a firm) v Lloyds Underwriters subscribing to Lloyd's Policy No. 621/PKIDOO101* [2007] EWHC 2699 (Comm), [2007] All ER (D) 341 (Nov)).

Although the claims in *Webster v Ridgeway Foundation School* [2010] EWHC 318 (QB), [2010] All ER (D) 97 (Mar) failed, they, except one in respect of which indemnity costs were awarded, were not hopeless. Although a collateral purpose in pursuing the proceedings was to bring the defendants to book, there was nothing improper in pursuing litigation for this purpose. A desire to obtain compensation can often co-exist with a wish to demonstrate that the defendant has been at fault. It is only where an over-zealous claimant engages in unreasonable conduct that indemnity costs are justified.

(e) Public funding

[11.58]

In *Brawley v Marczynski (No 2)* [2002] EWCA Civ 1453, [2002] 4 All ER 1067 costs were awarded on the indemnity basis to a publicly funded party in order to penalise the losing party's unreasonable conduct in the case. It is no impediment to an award of indemnity costs that the only beneficiaries of penalising the defendant's solicitors would be the claimant's lawyers.

[11.59]

CPR Rule 44.6: Fixed Costs
A party may recover the fixed costs specified in Part 45 in accordance with that Part.
See Chapter 25 for Part 45 with the relevant Practice Direction and narrative.

[11.60]

CPR Rule 44.7: Procedure for assessing costs
Where the court orders a party to pay costs to another party (other than fixed costs) it may either—
    (a)   make a summary assessment of the costs; or
    (b)   order detailed assessment of the costs by a costs officer,
unless any rule, practice direction or other enactment provides otherwise.
(The Costs Practice Direction sets out the factors which will affect the court's decision under this rule)

[11.61]

CPD Section 12 Procedure for Assessing Costs: Rule 44.7
12.1 *Where the court does not order fixed costs (or no fixed costs are provided for) the amount of costs payable will be assessed by the court. This rule allows the court making an order about costs either*
(a)   *to make a summary assessment of the amount of the costs, or*
(b)   *to order the amount to be decided in accordance with Part 47 (a detailed assessment).*
12.2 *An order for costs will be treated as an order for the amount of costs to be decided by a detailed assessment unless the order otherwise provides.*
12.3 *Whenever the court awards costs to be assessed by way of detailed assessment it should consider whether to exercise the power in rule 44.3(8) (Courts Discretion as to Costs) to order the paying party to pay such sum of money as it thinks just on account of those costs.*

[11.62]

See Chapter 29 for summary assessment and Chapter 30 for detailed assessment with the relevant Practice Directions and narrative.

[11.63]

> **CPR Rule 44.8: Time for complying with an order for costs**
> A party must comply with an order for the payment of costs within 14 days of—
>
> (a)   the date of the judgment or order if it states the amount of those costs;
>
> (b)   if the amount of those costs (or part of them) is decided later in accordance with Part 47, the date of the certificate which states the amount; or
>
> (c)   in either case, such later date as the court may specify.
>
> (Part 47 sets out the procedure for detailed assessment of costs)

REVOLUTIONARY

[11.64]

CPR Rule 44.8 contains the revolutionary requirement that all orders for costs, both interim and final, must be paid within 14 days of assessment. Hitherto, the rules precluded the assessment of interim costs until the conclusion of the action and therefore the order for costs had no immediate consequences. Indeed if the action were subsequently settled, interim orders for costs were invariably subsumed in the overall agreement. However, now not only is it expected that interim costs will be assessed at the end of the hearing, but they are to be paid within 14 days. Clients realise that their lawyers have lost a battle and they will have to put their hands in their pockets and part with their money at an early stage of the proceedings. The provision appears to have resulted in a marked reduction in the number of interim applications, and certainly concentrates minds on costs at an early stage in the proceedings.

CONDITIONAL FEES

[11.65]

If the party who has been ordered to pay the costs of an interim hearing is funded under a conditional fee agreement such an order could have serious consequences. Most indemnity insurance policies in respect of orders to pay the other party's costs, exclude orders for payment of interim costs. The result will be that either the client, or his solicitors on his behalf, will have to pay the costs.

NON-PAYMENT

[11.66]

On 12 March 1999 the Vice-Chancellor wrote to all judges suggesting that if there were a conditional fee agreement the judge should consider staying any order for costs until the end of the action, and consider not requiring a payment on account if he orders a detailed assessment. Why should this particular method of funding be given preferential treatment over a party who is funding the litigation himself, perhaps with a bank overdraft or by selling investments? He too will have to put his hand in his, or his funder's, pocket because his legal representative has fought and lost a battle. If it is thought unfair that the receiving party should have to wait to the end of the litigation before receiving his costs, it will not be any less unfair because his adversary has chosen one method of funding in preference to another.

The Supreme Court Costs Office *Guide to the Summary Assessment of Costs* used to advise:

> '28 Before deciding to defer payment of costs where the paying party has agreed conditional fee terms with his solicitor the court should consider:
>
> (i)   whether such orders should also be made in the case of those litigants of modest means who do not agree no win no fee terms with their solicitors. Such litigants would, on the face of it, be ordered to pay the amount of any summarily assessed costs within 14 days in the normal way.
>
> (ii) Whether an order for payment of the costs forthwith might bring the action to an end and whether this would be just in all the circumstances.'

It now contents itself with:

> '33 As a general rule a paying party should be ordered to pay the amount of any summarily assessed costs within 14 days. Before making such an order the court should consider whether an order for payment of the costs might bring the action to an end and whether this would be just in all the circumstances.'

What happens if the costs are not paid within 14 days? Rule 3.1(2)(*a*) provides that the court may extend any time prescribed by the rules and therefore if a party ordered to pay interim costs is unable to do so within 14 days he should apply to the judge conducting the hearing for an extension. Although the courts are concerned that an order to pay interim costs should not stifle meritorious litigation, an application for an extension must be supported by adequate evidence: *Pepin v Watts* [2000] All ER (D) 1262, CA. It is intended that such extensions will not readily be granted. It appears that the order will be enforceable as a civil debt after the expiration of 14 days but it will not preclude the defaulting party from continuing with the proceedings. In *Stevens v School of Oriental and African Studies* (2001) Times, 2 February, Ch D where an earlier action had been struck out with an order for costs, it was held to be reasonable to stay further proceedings arising out of the same facts until the costs of the first action had been paid.

[11.67]

CPR Rule 44.9: Costs on the small claims track and fast track

See Chapter 26.

[11.68]

CPR Rule 44.10: Limitation on amount court may allow where a claim allocated to the fast track settles before trial

See Chapter 27.

[11.69]

CPR Rule 44.11: Costs following allocation and re-allocation

(1)   Any costs orders made before a claim is allocated will not be affected by allocation.

(2)   Where—

(a)   a claim is allocated to a track; and

(b)   the court subsequently re-allocates that claim to a different track,

then unless the court orders otherwise, any special rules about costs applying—

(i)   to the first track, will apply to the claim up to the date of re-allocation; and

(ii)   to the second track, will apply from the date of re-allocation.

(Part 26 deals with the allocation and re-allocation of claims between tracks)

[11.70]

CPD Section 16 Costs following Allocation and Re-allocation: Rule 44.11

16.1   *This paragraph applies where the court is about to make an order to reallocate a claim from the small claims track to another track.*

16.2   *Before making the order to re-allocate the claim, the court must decide whether any party is to pay costs to any other party down to the date of the order to re-allocate in accordance with the rules about costs contained in Part 27 (The Small Claims Track).*

16.3   *If it decides to make such an order about costs, the court will make a summary assessment of those costs in accordance with that Part.*

[11.71]

CPR Rule 44.12: Cases where costs orders deemed to have been made

(1)   Where a right to costs arises under—

(a)   rule 3.7 (defendant's right to costs where claim struck out for non-payment of fees);

(b)   rule 36.10(1) or (2) (claimant's right to costs where a Part 36 offer is accepted);

(c)   . . . ; or

(d)   rule 38.6 (defendant's right to costs where claimant discontinues),

a costs order will be deemed to have been made on the standard basis.

(1A)   Where such an order is deemed to be made in favour of a party with pro bono representation, that party may apply for an order under section 194(3) of the Legal Services Act 2007.

(2)   Interest payable pursuant to section 17 of the Judgments Act 1838 or section 74 of the County Courts Act 1984 on the costs deemed to have been ordered under paragraph (1) shall begin to run from the date on which the event which gave rise to the entitlement to costs occurred.

COSTS ONLY PROCEEDINGS

[11.72]

CPR Rule 44.12A: Costs-only proceedings

(1)   This rule sets out a procedure which may be followed where—

    (a)   the parties to a dispute have reached an agreement on all issues (including which party is to pay the costs) which is made or confirmed in writing; but

    (b)   they have failed to agree the amount of those costs; and

    (c)   no proceedings have been started.

(1A)   *Revoked with effect from 1 April 2005 by SI 2004/3419.*

(Rule 21.10 makes provision for compromise etc. by or on behalf of a child or patient.)

(2)   Either party to the agreement may start proceedings under this rule by issuing a claim form in accordance with Part 8.

(3)   The claim form must contain or be accompanied by the agreement or confirmation.

(4)   Except as provided in paragraph (4A) (and subject to rule 44.12B), in proceedings to which this rule applies the court—

    (a)   may

        (i)   make an order for costs to be determined by detailed assessment; or

        (ii)   dismiss the claim; and

    (b)   must dismiss the claim if it is opposed.

(4A)   In proceedings to which Section II or Section VI applies, the court shall assess the costs in the manner set out in that Section.

(5)   Rule 48.3 (amount of costs where costs are payable pursuant to a contract) does not apply to claims started under the procedure in this rule. (Rule 7.2 provides that proceedings are started when the court issues a claim form at the request of the claimant.)

(Rule 8.1(6) provides that a practice direction may modify the Part 8 procedure).

[11.73]

CPD Section 17 Costs-only proceedings: Rule 44.12A

17.1   *A claim form under this rule should not be issued in the High Court unless the dispute to which the agreement relates was of such a value or type that had proceedings been begun they would have been commenced in the High Court.*

17.2   *A claim form which is to be issued in the High Court at the Royal Courts of Justice will be issued in the Supreme Court Costs Office.*

17.3   *Attention is drawn to rule 8.2 (in particular to paragraph (b)(ii)) and to rule 44.12A(3). The claim form must:*

(1)   *identify the claim or dispute to which the agreement to pay costs relates;*

(2)   *state the date and terms of the agreement on which the claimant relies;*

(3)   *set out or have attached to it a draft of the order which the claimant seeks;*

(4)   *state the amount of the costs claimed; and,*

(5)   state whether the costs are claimed on the standard or indemnity basis. If no basis is specified the costs will be treated as being claimed on the standard basis.

17.4   The evidence to be filed and served with the claim form under Rule 8.5 must include copies of the documents on which the claimant relies to prove the defendant's agreement to pay costs.

17.5   A costs judge or a district judge has jurisdiction to hear and decide any issue which may arise in a claim issued under this rule irrespective of the amount of the costs claimed or of the value of the claim to which the agreement to pay costs relates. A costs officer may make an order by consent under paragraph 17.7, or an order dismissing a claim under paragraph 17.9 below.

17.6   When the time for filing the defendant's acknowledgement of service has expired, the claimant may by letter request the court to make an order in the terms of his claim, unless the defendant has filed an acknowledgement of service stating that he intends to contest the claim or to seek a different order.

17.7   Rule 40.6 applies where an order is to be made by consent. An order may be made by consent in terms which differ from those set out in the claim form.

17.8

(1)   An order for costs made under this rule will be treated as an order for the amount of costs to be decided by a detailed assessment to which Part 47 and the practice directions relating to it apply. Rule 44.4(4) (determination of basis of assessment) also applies to the order.

(2)   In cases in which an additional liability is claimed, the costs judge or district judge should have regard to the time when and the extent to which the claim has been settled and to the fact that the claim has been settled without the need to commence proceedings.

17.9

(1)   For the purposes of rule 44.12A(4)(b)—

     (a)   a claim will be treated as opposed if the defendant files an acknowledgment of service stating that he intends to contest the making of an order for costs or to seek a different remedy; and

     (b)   a claim will not be treated as opposed if the defendant files an acknowledgment of service stating that he disputes the amount of the claim for costs.

(2)   An order dismissing the claim will be made as soon as an acknowledgment of service opposing the claim is filed. The dismissal of a claim under rule 44.12A(4) does not prevent the claimant from issuing another claim form under Part 7 or Part 8 based on the agreement or alleged agreement to which the proceedings under this rule related.

17.10

(1)   Rule 8.9 (which provides that claims issued under Part 8 shall be treated as allocated to the multi-track) shall not apply to claims issued under this rule. A claim issued under this rule may be dealt with without being allocated to a track.

(2)   Rule 8.1(3) and Part 24 do not apply to proceedings brought under rule 44.12A.

17.11   Nothing in this rule prevents a person from issuing a claim form under Part 7 or Part 8 to sue on an agreement made in settlement of a dispute where that agreement makes provision for costs, nor from claiming in that case an order for costs or a specified sum in respect of costs.

[11.74]

From 3 July, 2000 the Civil Procedure (Amendment No 3) Rules 2000 introduced Rule 44.12A which contains a useful procedure to be followed where parties to a dispute have reached an agreement on all issues, including which party is to pay the costs, but have failed to agree the amount of the costs where no proceedings have been started. Previously the only possible course was to institute proceedings based upon the agreement seeking an order that the costs be assessed and paid pursuant to the agreement. In these circumstances, either party may start proceedings by issuing a claim form in accordance with Part 8. The claim form must contain or be accompanied by the agreement or confirmation. The court may either make an order for costs or dismiss the claim. It must dismiss the claim if the application is opposed.

Practice Direction 17.11 confirms that this rule does not prevent a party from issuing a claim form under Part 7 or Part 8 to sue on an agreement made in settlement of a dispute where that agreement makes provision for costs, nor from claiming in that case an order for costs or a specified sum in respect of costs. Indeed if the paying party does not consent to a costs-only application, the receiving party has no other course.

[11.75]

Senior Costs Judge Peter Hurst gave guidance to the Designated Civil Judges as follows:

'CPR Rule 44.12A was introduced with effect from 3 July 2000 to provide a procedure enabling parties who have settled the substantive dispute between them to resolve any outstanding question relating to costs.

The new procedure appears to be being misused by both claimants and defendants in breach of the overriding objective. This misuse has given rise to difficulties for District Judges. It appears that solicitors acting on behalf of claimants, having settled the amount of damages, are saying to defendants' insurers: "Our costs are £x and if this figure is not agreed/paid within 14 days costs-only proceedings will be commenced". In one court there has been a bulk issue of 800 applications.

Defendants' representatives for their part make unreasonably low offers in respect of pre-proceedings costs and in some cases accompany the offer with a statement that the offer is made for the purpose of negotiation only and that they do not agree to the matter being resolved by use of the costs only procedure.

If a claimant is forced to commence proceedings under Part 7, rather than costs only proceedings under Part 8, defendants will find themselves having to pay, not only the reasonable and proportionate costs of the claim itself, but also the costs of the Part 7 proceedings and any related assessment proceedings. If the defendant has acted unreasonably in compelling the commencement of Part 7 proceedings, consideration should be given to making an order for costs on the indemnity basis.

Two distinct steps are required: firstly the Part 8 application seeking an order for costs; and secondly detailed assessment of those costs.

The intention is that the proceedings should effectively be brought with the consent of both parties as a convenient means of resolving the dispute over costs. If the acknowledgement of service indicates that the application is not opposed the court may make an order for costs without a hearing. (It is recognised that at present Form N210 makes no provision for indicating that the claim is not opposed. This is being addressed.)

Paragraph (9) sets out the circumstances in which the court may dismiss the application without a hearing.

The procedure under Rule 44.12A is intended to be cheap and straightforward.

The steps are as follows:

(1)   The parties must have reached an agreement on all the issues including which party is to pay the costs.

(2)   That agreement must be made or confirmed in writing.

(3)   No proceedings must have been started and the parties (after a proper attempt at agreement) must have failed to agree the amount of the costs.

(4)   Either party may start costs-only proceedings under Rule 44.12A.

(5)   The Part 8 claim form must:

    (a)   identify the claim or dispute to which the agreement to pay costs relates;

    (b)   state the date and terms of the agreement on which the claimant relies:

    (c)   set out a draft of the order sought;

    (d)   state the amount of the costs claimed: and

    (e)   state whether costs are claimed on the standard or the indemnity basis

(6)   The evidence filed in support of the claim must include copies of the documents on which the claimant relies to prove the defendant's agreement to pay the costs.

(7)   The matter should not be listed before the District Judge until an acknowledgment of service has been filed. If the defendant agrees that the order should be made, or a consent order is filed, the court will make the order without the necessity of a hearing.

(8)   If the time for filing acknowledgement of service expires, the claimant may request the court by letter to make an order in the terms of the claim. If the defendant files an acknowledgement of service out of time but before the court has made an order in the terms of the claim, paragraph (9) applies.

(9)   The court may (i) make an order for costs; or, (ii) dismiss the claim. The court must dismiss the claim if it is opposed. A claim is treated as opposed if the defendant states in the acknowledgement of service that it intends to consent the proceedings or to seek a different remedy. The court will then dismiss the claim without a hearing.

(10)   The court may make an order by consent in terms which differ from those set out in the claim form. The order is treated as an order or the amount of costs to be decided by detailed assessment.

In no circumstances should a District Judge or Costs Judge attempt to hear the application and then immediately embark upon a summary assessment of the costs in dispute. Arguments that the District Judge/Costs Judge should do so are incorrect, since a summary assessment is an assessment made by a Judge who has decided the substantive issue. In costs only proceedings the only issue decided by the Judge is whether or not there should be an assessment of the costs.

It is accepted that for bills of modest size detailed assessment may be unnecessarily cumbersome and consideration is being given to introducing either a disposal procedure or a short form of bill in order to overcome this problem.'

[11.76]

CPR Rule 44.12B: Costs-only proceedings – costs in respect of insurance premium in publication cases

(1)   If in proceedings to which rule 44.12A applies it appears to the court that—

    (a)   if proceedings had been started, they would have been publication proceedings;

    (b)   one party admitted liability and made an offer of settlement on the basis of that admission;

    (c)   agreement was reached after that admission of liability and offer of settlement; and

    (d)   either—

        (i)   the party making the admission of liability and offer of settlement was not provided by the other party with the information about an insurance policy as required by the Practice Direction (Pre-Action Conduct); or

    (ii)   that party made the admission of liability and offer of settlement before, or within 42 days of, being provided by the other party with that information,

no costs may be recovered by the other party in respect of the insurance premium.

(2)   In this rule, "publication proceedings" means proceedings for—

    (a)   defamation;

    (b)   malicious falsehood; or

    (c)   breach of confidence involving publication to the public at large.

[11.77]

Since 1 October 2009 this provision, relating only to publication proceedings, precludes the recovery of adverse costs insurance premiums in the four circumstances specified.

[11.78]

CPR Rule 44.12C: Costs-only application after a claim is started under Part 8 in accordance with Practice Direction 8B

(1)   This rule sets out the procedure where—

    (a)   the parties to a dispute have reached an agreement on all issues (including which party is to pay the costs) which is made or confirmed in writing; but

in relation to that order; but

    (b)   they have failed to agree the amount of those costs; and

    (c)   proceedings have been started under Part 8 in accordance with Practice Direction 8B.

(2)   Either party may make an application for the court to determine the costs.

(3)   Where an application is made under this rule the court will assess the costs in accordance with rule 45.34 or rule 45.37.

(4)   Rule 48.3 (amount of costs where costs are payable pursuant to a contract) does not apply to an application under this rule.

(Practice Direction 8B sets out the procedure for a claim where the parties have followed the Pre-Action Protocol for Low Value Personal Injury Claims in Road Traffic Accidents.)

[11.78A]

CPR Rule 44.13: Special situations

(1)   Where the court makes an order which does not mention costs—

    (a)   subject to paragraphs (1A) and (1B), the general rule is that no party is entitled—

        (i)   to costs; or

        (ii)   to seek an order under section 194(3) of the Legal Services Act 2007,

in relation to that order; but

    (b)   this does not affect any entitlement of a party to recover costs out of a fund held by that party as trustee or personal representative, or pursuant to any lease, mortgage or other security.

(1A)   Where the court makes

    (a)   an order granting permission to appeal;

(b)   an order granting permission to apply for judicial review; or

(c)   any other order or direction sought by a party on an application without notice,

and its order does not mention costs, it will be deemed to include an order for applicant's costs in the case.

(1B)   Any party affected by a deemed order for costs under paragraph (1A) may apply at any time to vary the order.

(2)   The court hearing an appeal may, unless it dismisses the appeal, make orders about the costs of the proceedings giving rise to the appeal as well as the costs of the appeal.

(3)   Where proceedings are transferred from one court to another, the court to which they are transferred may deal with all the costs, including the costs before the transfer.

(4)   Paragraph (3) is subject to any order of the court which ordered the transfer.

Paragraph 1 confirms that the rights of a party against a fund are not affected by the absence of an order for costs.

[11.79]

CPR Rule 44.14: Court's powers in relation to misconduct
See Chapter 33.

[11.80]

CPR Rule 44.15: Providing information about funding arrangements
See Chapter 44.

[11.81]

CPR Rule 44.16: Adjournment where legal representative seeks to challenge disallowance of any amount of percentage increase
See Chapter 44.

[11.82]

CPR Rule 44.17: Application of costs rules
See Chapter 19.

[11.83]

CPR Rule 44.18: Costs capping orders – general
See Chapter 10.

[11.84]

CPR Rule 44.19: Application for a costs capping order
See Chapter 10.

[11.85]

CPR Rule 44.20: Application to vary a costs capping order
See Chapter 10.

THE SUPREME COURT RULES 2009

[11.86]

Part 7 deals with fees and costs in the Supreme Court accompanied by Practice Direction No 13 on Costs.

Costs may be awarded on either the standard or the indemnity basis with the same definitions as in the CPR. There is provision for the paying party to file and serve points of dispute and for the receiving party to respond.

So, what differs from the provisions of the Civil Procedure Rules 1998?

[11.87]

Rule 47 Submissions as to costs

(1)　If a party wishes to defer making submissions as to costs until after judgment, the Court must be informed of this not later than at the close of the oral argument.

(2)　If the Court accedes to the request it will give such directions as appear appropriate and it may, in particular, give directions—

　　(a)　for the hearing of oral submissions as to costs immediately after judgment;

　　(b)　for the simultaneous or sequential filing of written submissions as to costs within a specified period after judgment;

　　(c)　for the hearing of oral submissions after the filing of written submissions.

Under Rule 47 submissions as to costs must be made before judgment unless an application to which the court accedes is made by the close of oral argument.

[11.88]

Rule 49 Assessment of costs

(1)　Every detailed assessment of costs shall be carried out by two costs officers appointed by the President and—

　　(a)　one costs officer must be a Costs Judge (a Taxing Master of the Senior Courts), and

　　(b)　the second may be the Registrar.

(2)　A disputed assessment shall be dealt with at an oral hearing.

(3)　An assessment may provide for the costs of the assessment procedure.

(4)　The Registrar will give the receiving party and the paying party written notice of the date of the assessment.

(5)　Where one of the parties so requests or in the circumstances specified in the relevant practice direction, the Registrar may make a provisional assessment of costs without the attendance of the parties.

(6)　The Registrar must inform the parties in writing of the outcome of a provisional assessment and, if a party is dissatisfied with the outcome, or if points of disagreement cannot be resolved in correspondence, the Registrar shall appoint a date for an oral hearing.

(7)　Any request for an oral hearing following a provisional assessment of costs must be made within 14 days of the receipt of the Registrar's decision on the assessment.

Under rule 49 either party may request a *provisional assessment* of costs by the Registrar. If either or both parties are dissatisfied with the provisional assessment the registrar will try to resolve it in correspondence.

If that fails he will appoint an oral hearing before two costs officers, one of whom will be a taxing master and the other an appointee of the President – probably the Registrar.

Practice Direction 13: Costs

[11.89]

Practice Direction 13 provides that the assessment of costs is governed by the relevant provisions of the Supreme Court Rules supplemented by this and the other Practice Directions issued by the President. To the extent that the Supreme Court Rules and Practice Directions do not cover the situation, the Rules and the Practice Directions which supplement Parts 43 to 48 of the Civil Procedure Rules are applied by analogy at the discretion of the Costs Officers, with appropriate modifications for appeals from Scotland and Northern Ireland. The legal principles applied are those also applicable to assessments between parties in the High Court and Court of Appeal in England and Wales.

It sets out in detail the practice and procedure to be followed on a detailed assessment, including guideline rates.

Enquiries about costs should be made to the Costs Clerk (tel: 020-7960 1990).

Enquiries about fees should be made to the Registry (tel: 020-7960 1991, 1992).

Drafts and cheques for fees, including assessment fees, should be made payable to 'The Supreme Court of the United Kingdom'.

Drafts and cheques for security money only should be made payable to 'UK Supreme Court Security Fund Account'.

CHAPTER 12

VAT BETWEEN THE PARTIES

THE SOLICITOR AND CLIENT BILL

[12.1]

In litigation the court may order one party to the action to pay costs to the other party, usually the winner, or the parties may settle the action on the basis that one party will pay the agreed or assessed costs of the other party. The winner's solicitors must nevertheless deliver to their own client a full solicitor and client bill, including VAT.

WINNER NOT REGISTERED

[12.2]

Where the winner is not registered for VAT or the legal services are not supplied in connection with his business, he cannot recover the VAT payable on his solicitor and client costs. An amount equal to VAT at the current rate should therefore be added to the between-the-parties costs. This is not a payment of VAT but is to indemnify the winner for the VAT he will pay on the proportionate part of his solicitor and client costs. The winner's solicitors have not supplied any kind of service to the loser and there is therefore no question of the loser reclaiming or deducting VAT in respect of those costs. Because it is not a payment of VAT by the loser, he is not entitled to a VAT invoice for the between the parties costs, nor is he entitled to recoup the payment even if he is registered for VAT. Indeed, the Law Society recommends that the paying party should receive a note of the other party's costs in such terms that it cannot be mistaken for a tax invoice. This may be done, for example by clearly marking the copy of the bill sent to the paying party with the words 'this is not a tax invoice' or – if acceptable to the paying party – by issuing a summary of the bill without a VAT registration number and without the tax element identified.

WINNER REGISTERED

(a) **Fully registered**

[12.3]

Where the winner is registered for VAT and the legal services are supplied in the course of his business, he will be entitled to an input tax credit and therefore able to recover the VAT paid to his solicitor. In such a case the receiving party does not need indemnifying and should not claim VAT on his profit costs or disbursements, including counsel's fees, as between the parties. On an assessment of between-the-parties costs the onus is on the paying party to object to the inclusion of an indemnity for VAT.

(b) Partly exempt

[12.4]

Where the solicitor's client is a partly exempt registered taxable person he is not entitled to be indemnified for VAT to the extent that he can obtain credit for input tax.

NO RECOVERY

[12.5]

The SCCO Guide helpfully lists the following additional circumstances in which the receiving party cannot recover the VAT on costs payable by the paying party:
(a) receiving party domicile outside the European Union
(b) receiving party domiciled within the European Union but outside the UK and received the legal services for the purpose of his business
(c) receiving party is a legal representative representing himself (the 'self supply' exception to VAT)

SECTION 5: PRACTICE DIRECTION SUPPLEMENTING CPR PART 43

[12.6]

Section 5 of the Costs Practice Direction, 'Special Provisions Relating to VAT' (set out below) incorporates the provision of the Supreme Court Taxing Office Practice Direction of 1994. Its provisions have been agreed between HM Customs and Excise, the Lord Chancellor's Department, the Legal Aid Board (now Legal Services Commission), the Law Society and the Supreme Court Costs Office (now the Senior Courts Costs Office).

[12.7]

Section 5: Special Provisions Relating to VAT

5.1 *This section deals with claims for value added tax (VAT) which are made in respect of costs being dealt with by way of summary assessment or detailed assessment.*

[12.8]

VAT Registration Number

5.2   *The number allocated by HM Customs and Excise to every person registered under the Value Added Tax Act 1983 (except a Government Department) must appear in a prominent place at the head of every statement, bill of costs, fee sheet, account or voucher on which VAT is being included as part of a claim for costs.*

[12.9]

Entitlement to VAT on costs

5.3   *VAT should not be included in a claim for costs if the receiving party is able to recover the VAT as input tax. Where the receiving party is able to obtain credit from HM Customs and Excise for a proportion of the VAT as input tax, only that proportion which is not eligible for credit should be included in the claim for costs.*

5.4   *The receiving party has responsibility for ensuring that VAT is claimed only when the receiving party is unable to recover the VAT or a proportion thereof as input tax.*

5.5   *Where there is a dispute as to whether VAT is properly claimed the receiving party must provide a certificate signed by the solicitors or the auditors of the receiving party substantially in the form illustrated in Precedent F in the Schedule of Costs Precedents annexed to this Practice Direction. Where the receiving party is a litigant in person who is claiming VAT, reference should be made by him to HM Customs and Excise and wherever possible a Statement to similar effect produced at the hearing at which the costs are assessed.*

5.6   *Where there is a dispute as to whether any service in respect of which a charge is proposed to be made in the bill is zero rated or exempt, reference should be made to HM Customs and Excise and wherever possible the view of HM Customs and Excise obtained and made known at the hearing at which the costs are assessed. Such application should be made by the receiving party. In the case of a bill from a solicitor to his own client, such application should be made by the client.*

[12.10]

Form of bill of costs where VAT rate changes

5.7   *Where there is a change in the rate of VAT, suppliers of goods and services are entitled by ss 88(1) and 88(2) of the VAT Act 1994 in most circumstances to elect whether the new or the old rate of VAT should apply to a supply where the basic and actual tax points span a period during which there has been a change in VAT rates.*

5.8   *It will be assumed, unless a contrary indication is given in writing, that an election to take advantage of the provisions mentioned in paragraph 5.7 above and to charge VAT at the lower rate has been made. In any case in which an election to charge at the lower rate is not made, such a decision must be justified to the court assessing the costs.*

[12.11]

Apportionment

5.9   *All bills of costs, fees and disbursements on which VAT is included must be divided into separate parts so as to show work done before, on and after the date* or dates from which any change in the rate of VAT takes effect. Where, however, a lump sum charge is made for work which spans a period during which there has been a change in VAT rates, and paragraphs 5.7 and 5.8 above do not apply, reference should be made to paragraphs 8 and 9 of Appendix F of Customs' Notice 700 (or any revised edition of that notice), a copy of which should be in the possession of every registered trader. If necessary, the lump sum should be apportioned. The totals of profit costs and disbursements in each part must be carried separately to the summary.

5.10   Should there be a change in the rate between the conclusion of a detailed assessment and the issue of the final costs certificate, any interested party may apply for the detailed assessment to be varied so as to take account of any increase or reduction in the amount of tax payable. Once the final costs certificate has been issued, no variation under this paragraph will be permitted.

[12.12]

Disbursements

5.11   Petty (or general) disbursements such as postage, fares etc which are normally treated as part of a solicitor's overheads and included in his profit costs should be charged with VAT even though they bear no tax when the solicitor incurs them. The cost of travel by public transport on a specific journey for a particular client where it forms part of the service rendered by a solicitor to his client and is charged in his bill of costs, attracts VAT.

5.12   Reference is made to the criteria set out in the VAT Guide (Customs and Excise Notice 700 – 1st August 1991 edition paragraph 83, or any revised edition of that Notice), as to expenses which are not subject to VAT. Charges for the cost of travel by public transport, postage, telephone calls and telegraphic transfers where these form part of the service rendered by the solicitor to his client are examples of charges which do not satisfy these criteria and are thus liable to VAT at the standard rate.

[12.13]

Legal AID/LSC funding

(1)   VAT will be payable in respect of every supply made pursuant to a legal aid/ LSC certificate where –
    (a)   the person making the supply is a taxable person; and
    (b)   the assisted person/ LSC funded client –
        (i)   belongs in the United Kingdom or another member state of the European Union; and
        (ii)   (ii) is a private individual or receives the supply for non-business purposes.
(2)   Where the assisted person/LSC funded client belongs outside the European Union, VAT is generally not payable unless the supply relates to land in the United Kingdom.
(3)   For the purpose of sub-paragraphs (1) and (2), the place where a person belongs is determined by section 9 of the Value Added Tax Act 1994.
(4)   Where the assisted person/LSC funded client is registered for VAT and the legal services paid for by the LSC are in connection with that person's business, the VAT on those services will be payable by the LSC only.

5.14   Any summary of costs payable by the LSC must be drawn so as to show the total VAT on Counsel's fees as a separate item from the VAT on other disbursements and the VAT on profit costs.

[12.14]

Tax invoice

5.15   *A bill of costs filed for detailed assessment is always retained by the Court. Accordingly if a solicitor waives his solicitor and client costs and accepts the costs certified by the court as payable by the unsuccessful party in settlement, it will be necessary for a short statement as to the amount of the certified costs and the VAT thereon to be prepared for use as the tax invoice.*

[12.15]

Vouchers

5.16   *Where receipted accounts for disbursements made by the solicitor or his client are retained as tax invoices a photostat copy of any such receipted account may be produced and will be accepted as sufficient evidence of payment when disbursements are vouched.*

[12.16]

Certificates

5.17   *In a costs certificate payable by the LSC, the VAT on solicitor's costs, Counsel's fees and disbursements will be shown separately.*

[12.17]

Litigants acting in person

5.18   *Where a litigant acts in litigation on his own behalf he is not treated for the purposes of VAT as having supplied services and therefore no VAT is chargeable in respect of work done by that litigant (even where, for example, that litigant is a solicitor or other legal representative).*

5.19   *Consequently in the circumstances described in the preceding paragraph, a bill of costs presented for agreement or assessment should not claim any VAT which will not be allowed on assessment.*

[12.18]

Government departments

5.20   *On an assessment between parties, where costs are being paid to a Government Department in respect of services rendered by its legal staff, VAT should not be added.*

[12.19]

Payment pursuant to an order under section 194(3) of the Legal Services Act 2007

5.21   *Where an order is made under section 194(3) of the Legal Services Act 2007 any bill presented for agreement or assessment pursuant to that order must not include a claim for VAT.*

INSURANCE COMPANIES

[12.20]

Where the bill to be assessed relates to proceedings taken in the name of an insured by his insurance company, usually arising out of a road traffic accident, the fact that the insurance company is not liable for VAT is irrelevant in deciding whether or not VAT is recoverable. The question of whether or not the VAT is recoverable is answered by the lay client's VAT position and not that of the insurance company (*Law Society Gazette*, 15 January 1986, vol 83, p 90).

EMPLOYED SOLICITORS

[12.21]

Where costs have been awarded to a party, some of whose work has been done by a solicitor employee, there has been no supply of services attracting VAT and there is therefore no necessity for him to seek indemnity in respect of VAT on those legal expenses from the paying party.

DISPUTES

[12.22]

If there is a dispute about whether or not a party is liable for VAT or able to reclaim VAT and the matter cannot be resolved by agreement, the court will direct the party whose bill it is to obtain a certificate, either from HM Customs and Excise or from their accountants, as to the correct VAT position.

CHAPTER 13

SECURITY FOR COSTS

GENERALLY

[13.1]

One party to litigation may be ordered to provide security for the costs of the other party in the very limited circumstances prescribed by the Companies Act 1985, s 726(1), CPR Rules 25.12–25.15 and the Arbitration Act 1996, s 38. Only under the Arbitration Act 1996 might an individual party resident in the UK be ordered to give security.

AGAINST A LIMITED COMPANY

(a) Companies Act 1985, s 726(1)

[13.2]

'Where in England a limited company is plaintiff [*claimant*] in an action or other legal proceeding, the court having jurisdiction in the matter may, if it appears by credible testimony that there is reason to believe that the company will be unable to pay the defendant's costs if successful in his defence, require sufficient securities to be given for those costs, and may stay all proceedings until the security is given.'

The phrase 'other legal proceedings' refers to any matter in which the jurisdiction of the court is invoked and accordingly an application for security for costs can be made against a company which brings a petition under the Companies Act 1985, s 459 (*Re Unisoft Group Ltd* [1993] BCLC 528, ChD (Companies Ct)). The section also empowers the court to grant security for costs against a company which has been granted leave to move by way of judicial review (*R v Westminster City Council, ex p Residents' Association of Mayfair* [1991] COD 182, QBD).

(b) Inability to pay

[13.3]

The fact that a company is in liquidation is, on the face of it, evidence that it is unable to pay the defendant's costs unless evidence to the contrary is given (*Northampton Coal, Iron and Waggon Co v Midland Waggon Co* (1878) 7 Ch D 500, CA). Otherwise, an application for security must be supported by an affidavit which credibly and reasonably shows the inability of the company to pay the costs if the defendant were successful. The mere issuing of a debenture charging all the company's assets is not a sufficient reason to order security. Where a company's accountant deposed to there being sufficient cash-flow to meet an order for costs despite a shortage of assets the court accepted this in the absence of expert evidence to the contrary (*Kim Barker Ltd v Aegon Insurance Co (UK) Ltd* (1989) Times, 9 October, CA).

In *Automotive Latch Systems Ltd v Honeywell International Inc* [2006] EWHC 2340 (Comm), [2006] All ER (D) 121 (Sep), 26 September the court rejected the claimant's submission that in respect of orders for security for costs, CPR Rule 25.13(2)(c) looked to the ability to pay costs at the time an order to pay was made and that as a matter of jurisdiction, the defendant could not show that in two years' time or so when any litigation would be likely to be the subject of a judgment and a costs order that the claimant's finances would not be such as to enable it to pay the defendants' costs. The court also rejected the claimant's submission that the defendant had caused its financial difficulties because to do so would be pre-judge one of the major issues in dispute in the proceedings.

(c) Discretion

[13.4]

In *Sir Lindsay Parkinson & Co Ltd v Triplan Ltd* [1973] QB 609, CA, Lord Denning identified the following circumstances which the court might take into account in exercising its discretion:

(i)   Whether the claimant's claim is bona fide and not a sham.

(ii)   Whether the claimant has a reasonably good prospect of success.

(iii)   Whether there is an admission by the defendant on the pleadings or elsewhere that the money is due.

(iv)   Whether there is a substantial payment into court or an 'open offer' of a substantial amount.

(v)   Whether the application for security is being used oppressively, eg so as to stifle a genuine claim.

(vi)   Whether the claimant's want of means is being brought about by any conduct by the defendants, such as delay in payment or in doing their part of the work.

(vii) Whether the application for security is made at a late stage of the proceedings.

(d) No order if oppressive

[13.5]

Where an order for security for costs against the claimant company might result in oppression in that the claimant company would be forced to abandon a claim which had a reasonable prospect of success, the court is entitled to refuse to make that order notwithstanding that the claimant company, if unsuccessful, will be unable to pay the defendant's costs (*Aquila Design (GRP Products) Ltd v Cornhill Insurance plc* [1988] BCLC 134, CA). It is not necessary for the company to produce evidence of its inability to pursue the proceedings if the order is made for the application to be dismissed; it is sufficient if the company shows that there is a probability that it will be unable to pursue the proceedings. Unless it is clearly demonstrable one way or the other it is not appropriate to go into the merits of the claim in such an application (*Trident International Freight Services Ltd v Manchester Ship Canal Co* [1990] BCLC 263, CA). *Europa Holdings Ltd v Circle Industries*

(UK) plc [1993] BCLC 320, CA was another example. The claimants were a small company operating on a limited turnover with a net deficit in a time of great depression. It was a solvent and prudently managed company with a genuine claim for payments for work done. It would be oppressive to force the claimant to abandon its claim by ordering it to give security for costs. Again, in *Edmund Murray Ltd v BSP International Foundations Ltd* (1992) 33 Con LR 1, CA in which the Court of Appeal set aside an order for security for costs on the ground that the claimants were simply unable to meet it and would be forced to abandon their claim, which was acknowledged to be a credible one, and thus denied justice. The detriment to the claimant would be worse if the order was made than to the defendant if it were not, and the order was quashed. On the other hand in *Automotive Latch Systems Ltd v Honeywell International Inc* (above) the court observed that it was a common, if not inevitable, feature of any order for security that the paying party would expect to find a better use for the money if it did not have to pay it as security.

On a company limited by guarantee being granted leave to move by way of judicial review the respondents applied for security for costs. The Companies Act 1985, s 726(1) empowered the court to enquire into a limited company's financial position and to stay proceedings until sufficient security for costs is provided. The application for security was granted, the court finding that in the circumstances an order for security for costs would not stifle the litigation as those behind the application would be able to find the resources if they wished the matter to proceed (*R v Westminster City Council, ex p Residents' Association of Mayfair* [1991] COD 182, QBD). See also 'Amount' at para [13.30].

(e) Northern Ireland company

[13.6]

In *Raeburn v Andrews* (1874) LR 9 QB 118, QBD it was held that security for costs should no longer be ordered against a claimant resident in another part of the UK; there was no reason to discriminate against the claimant by treating him differently from a claimant similarly placed but resident in England. In *DSQ Property Co Ltd v Lotus Cars Ltd (No 2)* (1990) Times, 28 June, CA, the claimant company, which was incorporated and resident in Northern Ireland, was in receivership and liquidation. If the company were resident in England, security for costs could have been ordered under the Companies Act 1985, s 726 and there was no reason in principle why security for costs should not be ordered against the claimant. To order otherwise would mean that an insolvent company incorporated and resident in Northern Ireland would be in a uniquely favourable position enjoyed by no other insolvent company incorporated anywhere in the world, in or out of the UK.

(f) Co-claimant

[13.7]

Where the defendants obtained an order for security for costs against a claimant company which was not complied with, this did not entitle them to an order for security against an individual claimant as a condition of him being joined in the proceedings. The law offered the defendants no protection against costs which could not be paid by impoverished personal claimants (*Eurocross Sales Ltd v Cornhill Insurance plc* [1995] 4 All ER 950, CA). Similarly, where a claimant company had failed to comply with an order to provide security but had executed a deed of assignment of its equitable interests in the claims to a shareholder justifying his joinder as a party under CPR rule 19.2 an order for security for costs could not be made against the shareholder under the guise of a condition imposed on joinder, except to the extent of security for any additional costs caused by or wasted as a result of his joinder: *Compagnie Noga d'Importation et d'Exportation SA v Australia and New Zealand Banking Group Ltd* [2004] EWHC 2601 (Comm).

(g) No assignment to avoid giving security

[13.8]

In *Hendry v Chartsearch Ltd* [1998] CLC 1382, CA, the claimant company was in financial difficulties and could not afford to give security for costs. Accordingly, it transferred and assigned its causes of action to its chairman and majority shareholder who commenced proceedings. The contract precluded assignment without the prior consent of the defendants, which was not to be unreasonably refused. The Companies Act 1985 gave the defendant a statutory right which protected them from being sued by an impecunious limited company without security for their costs. It could not be regarded as unreasonable for the defendant to insist upon that statutory right and refuse consent to assignment. If the individual assignee were willing to provide security on the same terms as if he were the company then the defendant could not reasonably refuse its consent on that ground. But that was not the position in this case.

(h) Pre-action costs

[13.9]

In *Lobster Group Ltd v (1) Heidelberg Graphic Equipment Ltd (2) Close Asset Finance Ltd* [2008] EWHC 413 (TCC) lengthy pre-action mediation had failed and the first defendant sought security for the costs of the mediation from the claimant, which was now in administration. The court held that although as a matter of principle pre-action costs can be the subject of an application for security (*Gibson's Settlement Trusts, Re* (1981) Ch 179, Ch D and *McGlinn v Waltham Contractors Ltd* [2005] EWHC 1419 (TCC), [2005] 3 All ER 1126) the court should be slow to exercise its discretion in favour of an applicant as there was a risk that if the pre-action period was lengthy the costs could be extensive and any subsequent attempt to obtain security might become penal in nature. Under the terms of the mediation the parties had agreed to bear their own costs. The costs of the mediation were unlikely to be recoverable in the subsequent proceedings and, even if they were, they should not form part of the security ordered. Costs of separate pre-action mediation were not 'costs of and incidental to the proceedings'. Both the course of the mediation and the reasons for its unsuccessful outcome were privileged matters and, as a matter of general principle, the costs incurred in respect of such procedure were not recoverable under the Supreme Court (now Senior Courts) Act 1981, s 51. The pre-action period was very prolonged covering a period of over two years and to order the claimant to provide security for costs incurred during that period would be Draconian. The claimant was ordered to provide security for costs from the commencement of proceedings up until the exchange of witness statements.

CIVIL PROCEDURE RULES

[13.10]

RSC Order 23, Rule 1 and CCR Order 13, Rule 8 were preserved by the Schedules to the CPR but these were revoked in March 2000 and replaced by CPR Rules 25.12–25.15. Here they are:

[13.11]

CPR Rule 25.12: Security for costs
(1)   A defendant to any claim may apply under this Section of this Part for security for his costs of the proceedings.
(Part 3 provides for the court to order payment of sums into court in other circumstances. Rule 20.3 provides for this Section of this Part to apply to Part 20 claims)
(2)   An application for security for costs must be supported by written evidence.
(3)   Where the court makes an order for security for costs, it will—
    (a)   determine the amount of security; and
    (b)   direct—
          (i)   the manner in which; and
          (ii)   the time within which
the security must be given.

[13.12]

CPR Rule 25.13: Conditions to be satisfied
(1)   The court may make an order for security for costs under rule 25.12 if—
    (a)   it is satisfied, having regard to all the circumstances of the case, that it is just to make such an order; and
    (b)
          (i)   one or more of the conditions in paragraph (2) applies, or
          (ii)   an enactment permits the court to require security for costs.
(2)   The conditions are—
    (a)   the claimant is—
          (i)   resident out of the jurisdiction; but
          (ii)   not resident in a Brussels Contracting State, a Lugano Contracting State or a Regulation State, as defined by section 1(3) of the Civil Jurisdiction and Judgments Act 1982;
    (b)   . . .
    (c)   the claimant is a company or other body (whether incorporated inside or outside Great Britain) and there is reason to believe that it will be unable to pay the defendant's costs if ordered to do so;

(d) the claimant has changed his address since the claim was commenced with a view to evading the consequences of the litigation;

(e) the claimant failed to give his address in the claim form, or gave an incorrect address in that form;

(f) the claimant is acting as a nominal claimant, other than as a representative claimant under Part 19, and there is reason to believe that he will be unable to pay the defendant's costs if ordered to do so;

(g) the claimant has taken steps in relation to his assets that would make it difficult to enforce an order for costs against him.

(Rule 3.4 allows the court to strike out a statement of case and Part 24 for it to give summary judgment)

[13.13]

CPR Rule 25.14: Security for costs other than from the claimant

(1) The defendant may seek an order against someone other than the claimant, and the court may make an order for security for costs against that person if—

(a) it is satisfied, having regard to all the circumstances of the case, that it is just to make such an order; and

(b) one or more of the conditions in paragraph (2) applies.

(2) The conditions are that the person—

(a) has assigned the right to the claim to the claimant with a view to avoiding the possibility of a costs order being made against him; or

(b) has contributed or agreed to contribute to the claimant's costs in return for a share of any money or property which the claimant may recover in the proceedings; and

is a person against whom a costs order may be made.

(Rule 48.2 makes provision for costs orders against non-parties)

[13.14]

CPR Rule 25.15: Security for costs of an appeal

(1) The court may order security for costs of an appeal against—

(a) an appellant;

(b) a respondent who also appeals,

on the same grounds as it may order security for costs against a claimant under this Part.

(2) The court may also make an order under paragraph (1) where the appellant, or the respondent who also appeals, is a limited company and there is reason to believe it will be unable to pay the costs of the other parties to the appeal should its appeal be unsuccessful.

(a) Residence abroad

[13.15]

Rule 25.13 provides that where the court is satisfied having regard to all the circumstances of the case, it is 'just' to do so, it may order an individual claimant or company ordinarily resident out of the jurisdiction in a country which is not a party to the Brussels or Lugano Conventions, to give such security for the defendant's costs of the action or the proceedings. The test of whether or not a corporation is ordinarily resident outside the jurisdiction requires the court to locate its central management and control (*Re Little Olympian Each Ways Ltd* [1994] 4 All ER 561, ChD).

(b) Philosophy

[13.16]

The basic underlying principle is that it is, on the face of it, unjust that a foreign claimant, who by virtue of his foreign residence is more or less immune to the consequences of a costs order against him, should be allowed to proceed without making funds available within the jurisdiction against which such an order should be executed (*Corfu Navigation Co v Mobil Shipping Co Ltd* [1991] 2 Lloyd's Rep 52, CA). In *Okotcha v Voest Alpine Intertrading GmbH* [1993] BCLC 474, CA the claimants were a man and a Nigerian company wholly owned by him who were seeking commission allegedly due under an agreement. Although there was no ground for requiring the individual claimant to give security for costs, the fact that the company would not be able to meet the funds required was not a reason for refusing to order that it should give security. Nor was it right to refuse to order the company to give security on the grounds that the action would go ahead with the individual claimant anyway. The defendant should not be required to resist an action by a foreign claimant without such security as would enable them to enforce any orders for costs they obtained.

(c) Factors

(i) Residence abroad not enough

[13.17]

Although residence abroad is a condition precedent to the application, this alone is not sufficient to justify an order for security (*Berkeley Administration Inc v McClelland* [1990] 2 QB 407, CA). Such an approach would be discriminatory and contrary to art 14 of the European Convention for the Protection of Human Rights. The court has now moved to a more flexible approach and the discretion should be exercised on objectively justified grounds relating to obstacles to or the burden of enforcement in the context of the particular country concerned (*Nasser v United Bank of Kuwait* [2002] EWCA Civ 556, [2002] 1 All ER 401).

(ii) Poverty

[13.18]

The claimant's poverty alone is not a ground for ordering security but the financial viability of the claimant is a relevant factor.

(iii) Prospect of success

[13.19]

If it can clearly be demonstrated that the claimant has a very high probability of success, that is a matter that can properly be weighed in the balance. Similarly, if it can be shown that there is a very high probability that the defendant will succeed that also is a matter that can be weighed. The court deplores attempts to go into the merits of the case, unless it can be clearly demonstrated one way or the other that there is a high degree of probability of success or failure (*Porzelack KG v Porzelack (UK) Ltd* [1987] 1 All ER 1074, ChD).

This approach was confirmed in *Al-Koronsky v Time Life Entertainment Group Ltd* [2005] EWHC 1688 (QB), [2005] All ER (D) 457 (Jul) which also held that a defendant should not be denied security merely because the claimant had succeeded in previous litigation.

(iv) Admission

[13.20]

If a defendant admits so much of the claim as would be equal to the amount for which security would have been ordered, the court may refuse him security, for he can secure himself by paying the admitted amount into court (*Hogan v Hogan (No 2)* [1924] 2 IR 14).

(v) Summary judgment

[13.21]

The issuing of a summons for judgment under Part 24 does not in any way inhibit an application for security against a foreign claimant or an insolvent company, although the court will be concerned to ensure that there is a defence to the claim before granting security *(Gottlieb v Geiger* (3 July 1905, unreported), CA).

(vi) Discretion

[13.22]

In *Sir Lindsay Parkinson & Co Ltd v Triplan Ltd* [1973] 2 All ER 273, CA, Lord Denning identified the circumstances which the court might take into account in exercising its discretion. They are listed at pp 129–130 of the judgment.

(vii)   Negotiations

[13.23]

A defendant should not be adversely affected in seeking security merely because he has attempted to reach a settlement. Evidence of negotiations conducted 'without prejudice', should not be admitted without their consent (*Simaan General Contracting Co v Pilkington Glass Ltd* [1987] 1 All ER 345, CA).

(viii)   EC claimant

[13.24]

Data Delecta AB v MSL Dynamics Ltd: C-43/95 [1996] All ER (EC) 961, ECJ, held that a provision that security could be ordered against an individual claimant resident in the EC, even if there were cogent evidence of substantial difficulty in enforcing the judgment, was discriminatory. There is therefore now no basis upon which an order can be made against an individual claimant who resides in the EC on the grounds of his residence abroad. However, the fact that the claimant, a Dutch national residing in Florida, had assets in Holland and Switzerland did not protect him from an order for security for costs under CPR Rule 25.13(2)(*a*)(ii) as being 'a person against whom a claim [could] be enforced under the Brussels Conventions or the Lugano Convention'. The rule is aimed at the juridical characteristics of the claimant, regardless of the assets that he owned or where those assets might be situated. A claimant who was not ordinarily resident in the UK or a Convention state could not escape liability to give security for costs merely by placing an asset in a Convention state (*De Beer v Kanaar & Co (a firm)* [2001] EWCA Civ 1318, [2002] 3 All ER 1020).

The position in respect of insolvent limited companies is not affected by EC residence.

(ix)   Convention claimant

[13.25]

Where the claimant resides outside the EC but in a country which is a member of either the Brussels or Lugano Conventions the ease of enforcement of the judgment for costs is a sufficient ground for denying the defendant an order for security for costs (*Thune v London Properties Ltd* [1990] 1 All ER 972, CA).

(x)   English co-claimants

[13.26]

There is no settled rule of practice that no order will be made against a foreign claimant if there are co-claimants resident in England (*Slazengers Ltd v Seaspeed Ferries International Ltd* [1987] 3 All ER 967, CA).

(xi)   Appeal

[13.27]

In *Antonelli v Allen* [2001] EWCA Civ 1563 the claimant paid £100,000 to her solicitor, who had subsequently been struck off the roll of solicitors, in dubious circumstances. She retrieved £70,000 of the money but lost her claim for the balance of £30,000 from the solicitor's partner. On the claimant obtaining permission to appeal, the defendant sought an order for security for costs under CPR 25.13(2)(*a*) (residence outside the jurisdiction) and CPR 25.13(2)(*g*) (against a claimant who 'has taken steps in relation to his assets that would make it difficult to enforce an order for costs against him'). At the time of proceedings the claimant was living in Israel, but had now moved to New York, which made the case for security stronger, because there is no reciprocal enforcement of judgments between this country and the United States. Because a claimant had failed to respond to any questions about the fate of the £70,000 she had recovered, there was an inference that she had dealt with that sum in such a way as to put it beyond the reach of creditors. The respondent to the appeal was therefore entitled to security. The court was not prepared to assume in the absence of evidence that the costs of enforcing a judgment against the claimant in New York would not be substantial and would not, for the most part, be irrevocable. In these circumstances the court fixed the amount of security at £10,000 with a provision that if payment was not made by a fixed date the appeal would be struck out automatically and that the appeal be stayed in the meantime.

Whether and when orders for security for costs should be made has always been a matter of practice rather than of substantive law; the court deplored a semantic dissection of judicial reasoning in an endeavour to demonstrate that there is still a rule of practice that it was only where it was certain, or virtually so, that the English claimant would become liable for all the costs if the defendant succeeded that an order for security would be made (*Corfu Navigation Co v Mobil Shipping Co Ltd* [1991] 2 Lloyd's Rep 52, CA).

CPR RULE 3.1

[13.28]

CPR Rule 3.1 provides:
>   (2)   . . . the court may –
>   ...
>
>   (f)   stay the whole of part of any proceedings or judgment either generally or until a specified date or event . . .
>   (ll)   order any party to file and serve an estimate of costs;
>   (m)   take any other steps or make any other order for the purpose of managing the case and furthering the overriding objective.
>   (3)   When the court makes an order, it may—
>   (a)   make it subject to conditions, including a condition to pay a sum of money into court; and
>   (b)   specify the consequence of failure to comply with the order or a condition.

(4)　. . .

(5)　The court may order a party to pay a sum of money into court if that party has, without good reason, failed to comply with a rule, practice direction or a relevant pre-action protocol.

(6)　When exercising its power under paragraph (5) the court must have regard to—

(a)　the amount in dispute; and

(b)　the costs which the parties have incurred or which they may incur.

[13.29]

In *Olatawura v Abiloye* [2002] EWCA Civ 998, [2002] 4 All ER 903 the Court of Appeal held that paras (4) and (5) of the Practice Direction to Rule 24 contemplated the making of orders akin to security for costs on the hearing of applications for summary judgment. However, before ordering security for costs in any case, whether or not within Rule 25, the court should be alert and sensitive to the risk that by making such an order it might be denying the party concerned the right to access to the court.

It was right also to bear in mind that under the new rules it was not just the claimant against whom an order for security for costs could be made; it could also be made against the defendant.

If, as a condition of pursuing an unpromising defence, it was appropriate to secure the claim, why not also the claimant's costs of advancing the claim? And if that, why was it not at least as appropriate to require someone advancing an unpromising claim to secure the defendant's costs?

There is a substantial difference between an application for payment into court as security for the costs of an application set aside, and an application for payment of past costs as a condition of being allowed to pursue an application to set aside a default judgment. The principle established in security for costs applications, that the court could take into account not only what a party possessed, but also what it might raise from other sources, might be inappropriate in an application in respect of past costs. There might be injustice in requiring an applicant wishing to set aside a judgment to make a payment into court in respect of past costs as a condition of being allowed to proceed with such an application. The court should not do so in the absence of good faith on the part of the party against whom the order was sought. That consideration was reinforced by the greater significance, since the Human Rights Act 1998 came into force, which the court attaches to not impeding access to justice (*CIBC Mellon Trust Co v Mora Hotel Corpn NV* [2002] EWCA Civ 1688, [2003] 1 All ER 564).

Pursuant to CPR rules 3.1(2)(f) and 3.1(2)(m), the court has power to grant a stay until a specified event, namely a payment into court to secure costs of future proceedings, independent of its power under rule 3.2(5) to order the payment in of a sum of money if a party had without good reason failed to comply with a rule, practice direction or pre-action protocol. However, it would only be in an exceptional case, if ever, that a court would order security for costs if the order would stifle a claim or an appeal. In any event (1) an order should not normally be made unless the party concerned could be shown to have been regularly flouting court procedures or otherwise to be demonstrating a want of good faith, which was to be taken to consist of a will to litigate a genuine case as economically and expeditiously as reasonably possible, and (2) an order would not be appropriate in every case where the party concerned had a weak case, and the weakness of a party's case would ordinarily only be relevant where he had no real prospect of success (*Ali v Hudson (t/a Hudson Freeman Berg (a firm))* [2003] EWCA Civ 1793, [2003] All ER (D) 225 (Dec)).

The difference between rule 3.1 and rule 25.15 was further illustrated in *Great Future Ltd v Sealand Housing Corpn* [2003] EWCA Civ 682, [2003] All ER (D) 365 (May). The defendants, who had not complied with interim orders to pay £1 million on account of costs, sought permission to appeal against the judgment. The claimant sought orders that the interim orders be complied with and for security for their costs of the appeal before the application was heard. Although they could not rely on CPR rule 25.15, because there was no appeal until permission was granted, the Court of Appeal could exercise case management powers under rule 3.1. There was no evidence that making the order sought would stifle the appeal and accordingly the orders were made.

AMOUNT

[13.30]

The application should be supported by a skeleton bill of costs showing the amount of costs incurred to date and the estimated future costs. In considering the costs the court may well discount the sum claimed against the prospects of the settlement or the reduction of costs on assessment. However, the former 'conventional approach' that only two-thirds of the estimated costs should be awarded as security was discredited in *Procon (GB) Ltd v Provincial Building Co Ltd* [1984] 2 All ER 368, CA. An application for security for costs under the Companies Act 1985, s 726 does not have to be determined on an all-or-nothing basis. The court has power to order security in a sum less than the total potential order for costs. A balancing exercise is required (*Re Unisoft Group (No 2)* [1993] BCLC 532, ChD (Companies Ct). As we have seen, the court will not make an order which would prevent a claimant from proceeding with a legitimate claim. An example of this was *Innovare Displays plc v Corporate Broking Services Ltd* [1991] BCC 174, CA, where the Court of Appeal held that 'sufficient security' for costs does not mean complete security, but security of a sufficiency in all the circumstances of the case as to be just. Accordingly, although the defendant sought to obtain an order for security of costs in the sum of £147,655, which it estimated would be its costs, the court held that a sum of £10,000 would be appropriate! A state-funded claimant cannot be ordered to give greater security than the amount he would be likely to be ordered to pay if the defence were to succeed (*Wyld v Silver (No 2)* [1962] 2 All ER 809, CA).

COUNTERCLAIM

[13.31]

Although there can be no order for security for costs against a defendant who is exercising his right to defend himself, even though resident out of the jurisdiction, there may be such an order in respect of a counterclaim. As a general rule, where a counterclaim could properly be relied upon as a set-off and where it arose out of the same subject matter as the claim, the counter-claiming defendant ought not to be required to give security for costs of that counterclaim unless there are exceptional circumstances (*Ashworth v Berkeley-Walbrood Ltd* (1989) Independent, 9 October, CA).

A counterclaim is more than a mere defence to a claim: it is a claim which has a 'vitality of its own' is how it was put in *Jones v Environcom Ltd* [2009] EWHC 16 (Comm), [2009] All ER (D) 115 (Jan). The inference that the defendant has a claim which has a vitality of its own can de drawn where (i) the defendant would have issued proceedings itself and it was a matter of chance which party issued proceedings first and (ii) the defendant would continue with the proceedings pursuing its own claim if the claimant discontinued its claim.

Security against a defendant was refused where the counterclaim raised the same issues as the claim in *BJ Crabtree (Insulation) Ltd v GPT Communications Systems Ltd* (1990) 59 BLR 43, CA. The marked discrepancy in size between the amount claimed in the action and the very much greater amount claimed by the counterclaim is relevant to an application by the claimant for security for costs in considering whether the counterclaim is a mere defence or a cross-claim in its own right which might well stand and be proceeded with even though the original claim were abandoned (*Hutchison Telephone (UK) Ltd v Ultimate Response Ltd* [1993] BCLC 307, CA). Another example was in *L/M International Construction Inc v Circle Partnership Ltd* [1995] CLY 4010, CA where the claimants' claim for costs and fees of about £1 million was met with a counterclaim for breach of contract totalling £15 million. The court was of the view that the amount of the counterclaim put the defendants in the character of a claimant and they ought to be ordered to give security irrespective of the defence to the original action. The court can make such an order even in the absence of exceptional circumstances. However, in *Petromin SA v Secnav Marine Ltd* [1995] 1 Lloyd's Rep 603, QBD where both parties in a case involving a counterclaim were making substantial claims based on the same facts, the order for security for costs of the counterclaim in favour of the claimant was for the full amount of those costs and not merely for the amount by which the claimant's costs were increased in defending the counterclaim. The defendant was entitled to be secured in respect of costs no less fully than if it were merely defendant to the claim advanced in the counterclaim and not also claimant in the action. In *Flender Werft AG v Aegean Maritime Ltd* [1990] 2 Lloyd's Rep 27, QBD it was held that obtaining a freezing injunction against the claimant in an arbitration as security for a counterclaim did not preclude the defendants obtaining an order for security for costs of the counterclaim. The freezing of the funds relating to the counterclaim was not relevant to the issue of security for costs in the main action in respect of which the defendants were entitled to a separate security in the event that the claimant's claims against them failed.

The defendants had offered to provide security for the costs of their counter-claim. In the circumstances it was fairer to make an order to the effect that each side should secure the other, rather than to make no order as to security at all. Neither party should be at risk in costs if successful. There is no jurisdiction to order a defendant seeking an enquiry as to damages arising out of the claimant's interim injunction to provide security for the claimant's costs arising from the defendant's application (*CT Bowring & Co (Insurance) Ltd v Corsi & Partners Ltd* [1995] 1 BCLC 148, CA).

FUNDING BY THIRD PARTY

[13.32]

In *Condliffe v Hislop* [1996] 1 All ER 431, CA, Kennedy LJ observed that if the circumstances suggested that if the litigating party were to lose, an order for costs would be difficult to enforce against a maintainer of that party, even though there was no power to order security for costs against the maintained party (who did not fall within RSC Ord 23 (now CPR Rules 25.12–25.15) or the Companies Act 1985, s 726) nevertheless a stay of the proceedings could be ordered.

In *Abraham v Thompson* [1997] 4 All ER 362, CA, the Court of Appeal disagreed. The right of a claimant to bring a properly pleaded and constituted action in good faith took precedence over the interest of a defendant who might be unable to recover costs against an impecunious claimant. It was preferable that a successful defendant should suffer the injustice of irrecoverable costs than that a claimant with a genuine claim should be prevented from pursuing it. The defendant's application for an order requiring the claimant to disclose details of any funding he was receiving from third parties to enable the defendants to make an application for an order for security for costs on the grounds that it might be difficult to enforce an order for costs against the funder was rejected.

The question of making orders for costs against the maintainer of litigation under the Supreme Court (now Senior Courts) Act 1981, s 51 is considered at Chapter 34. However, under CPR Rule 25.14 an order may be sought against someone to whom a claim has been assigned with a view to avoiding an order for costs or who has contributed or agreed to contribute to the costs in exchange for an interest in the proceedings.

OTHER GROUNDS

[13.33]

CPR Rule 25.13 gives the court a discretion to order security for costs in the following circumstances:

(a) Change of address

[13.34]

That the claimant has changed his address during the course of the proceedings with a view to evading the consequences of litigation. This rule applies not only to a change of address from that given on the claim form but to second or subsequent changes. 'The consequences of the litigation' are not confined to an order for the payment by the claimant of the defendant's costs at the end of the proceedings, but were also aimed at a claimant who sought to go to ground to avoid his obligations. They also include the possibility of being ordered to provide security for the defendant's costs and the various other consequences arising out of bringing proceedings in England (*Aoun v Bahri* [2002] EWHC 29 (Comm), [2002] 3 All ER 182).

(b) No, or wrong, address

[13.35]

That the claimant's address is not stated in the claim form or other originating process or is incorrectly stated therein, provided there shall be no such order if the claimant satisfies the court that the failure to state his address or the misstatement thereof was made innocently and without intention to deceive.

(c) Nominal claimant

[13.36]

That the claimant (not being a claimant who is suing in a representative capacity) is a nominal claimant who is suing for the benefit of some other person and that there is reason to believe that they will be unable to pay the costs of the defendant if ordered to do so. In *Envis v Thakkar* [1997] BPIR 189, CA the claimant was in financial difficulties when he began his action, but if he succeeded he would be able to discharge his liabilities. His creditors would benefit but so would he. Before a person could be branded a 'nominal claimant' there had to be some element of deliberate duplicity or window-dressing operating to the detriment of the defendant. In this case the claimant could not be regarded simply as a nominal claimant suing for the benefit of some other person.

(d) Dealing with assets

[13.37]

The claimant has taken steps that would make it difficult to enforce an order for costs against his assets (Rule 25.13(2)(g)). The rule is not concerned with the claimant's motivation for the disposal of an asset (*Aoun v Bahri*, [13.33] above). There does not have to be a subjective intention; it is sufficient that a claimant has taken steps in relation to his assets that would make it difficult to enforce a costs order against him (*Harris v Wallis* [2006] EWHC 630 (Ch), (2006) Times, 12 May).

ARBITRATION

[13.38]

The Arbitration Act 1996, s 38(3) provides:

> 'The Tribunal may order a claimant to provide security for the costs of the arbitration. This power shall not be exercised on the ground that the claimant is:
>
> (a)   An individual ordinarily resident outside the United Kingdom, or
> (b)   A corporation or association incorporated or formed under the law of a country outside the United Kingdom, or whose central management and control is exercised outside the United Kingdom.'

The Arbitration Bill limited the arbitrator's discretion to the circumstances covered by the Companies Act 1985, s 726(1) and RSC Ord 23 but this limitation was omitted from the Act. This gives to the arbitrator a wide general discretion, which he must nevertheless exercise judicially – especially as the 'costs of the arbitration' include his own fees and expenses! No doubt the various factors relevant to applications for security for costs in other litigation will be taken into account by arbitrators. Also still of relevance is the decision in *K/S A/S Bani v Korea Shipbuilding and Engineering Corpn* [1987] 2 Lloyd's Rep 445, CA, in which it was held that where an international arbitration is of a type regularly conducted in London for many years and is not a one-off arbitration, security for costs should be ordered; all the more so if the litigation costs are very high.

Another practical difference between security for costs in arbitration and in other litigation is the tradition in litigation that applications for security for costs are not heard by the trial judge, because privileged and prejudicial matters, such as offers for settlement, may have to be considered on the application. Parliament must have taken the view that arbitrators are made of sterner stuff and can more readily put such matters out of their minds, because arbitrators themselves deal with applications for security.

Where a party is challenging the enforcement of a foreign arbitration award, it is right for the court to treat that party as a defendant, with the consequence that the court has jurisdiction to grant security for costs against the holder of the award (*Dardana Ltd v Yukos Oil Co* [2002] EWCA Civ 543, [2002] 1 All ER (Comm) 819).

Section 70(6) of the Act empowers the court to order the applicant or appellant in an appeal against an award to provide security for the costs of the application or appeal, although such an order cannot be made on the grounds of residence outside the United Kingdom.

Section 75 empowers an arbitrator to make the same declarations and orders as the court charging property recovered with the payment of the solicitor's costs under s 73 of the Solicitors Act 1974

ORDER

(a) Time limit

[13.39]

The Court of Appeal in *Clive Brooks & Co Ltd v Baynard* (1998) Times, 30 April, CA criticised an order for security of costs which provided no time limit within which the security was to be given, and although it stayed the action in the meantime, it did not provide that the action should be dismissed if security was not given. It ruled that orders should specify a time within which security is to be given, stay all further proceedings until security is given and provide for the action or appeal to be dismissed without further order if security was not given within the time specified. A President Direction of 30 March 1998 prescribed the following form:

> It is ordered that the claimant by . . . . p.m. on 200
> . . . . give security for the defendant's costs in the sum of £.
> . . . . [by payment into court of the same] [by lodging with the defendant's solicitors] a . . . . (here describe the form of banker's draft etc.)]
> [in such manner as to the satisfaction of the Master] and that all further proceedings be stayed until security is given. In default of such security being given, the action is struck out with judgment for the defendant and his costs to be taxed if not agreed.

(b) 'Unless' order

[13.40]

It is very doubtful whether an 'unless' order is appropriate for an order for security for costs. The obtaining of an order for security for cost is a special form of order intended to give a claimant a proper choice as to whether to put up the security and continue with his action or whether to withdraw it. There is a difference in practice between the Masters' corridor and the Commercial Court, perhaps because in the latter substantial sums are involved, which take longer to raise. Even if an unless order is made as part of the first order, the period for compliance should be generous. The making of an order is not intended to be a weapon by which a defendant can obtain a speedy summary judgment without trial (*Radu v Houston* [2006] EWCA Civ 1575, [2006] NLJR 1847).

VARIATION

[13.41]

In *Gordano Building Contractors Ltd v Burgess* [1988] 1 WLR 890, CA, the claimant was ordered to give £20,000 security for the defendant's costs with 'liberty to both parties to apply'. Subsequently, the claimants obtained a letter from their bank stating that it would be willing to lend the claimants £20,000 to pay the costs if required. The claimants applied to have the order set aside but the judge held he had no jurisdiction to hear the application.

It was held on appeal that there were two questions: Can a claimant return if he can show a material change of circumstances? Can a claimant return if he produces fresh evidence as to the state of affairs extant at the date of the original order? The answer to the second question is 'No'. If a claimant wishes to have an opportunity to produce new evidence he should, no doubt at some penalty as to costs, apply for an adjournment. The answer to the first question must be that it is open to a claimant to apply to get an order for security set aside or varied in the light of changed circumstances. In the present case the judge had not considered whether there was a material change of circumstances and, if so, what as a matter of discretion he would do about it. The appeal was allowed to the extent of remitting the matter to the judge for reconsideration. In an application for relief under the Arbitration Act 1996 where the parties had agreed £30,000 security for costs and had also agreed that it would not be increased even if there were a material change of circumstances, the court still retained a residual discretion to vary the agreement if there were wholly exceptional circumstances. In the present case, there were such circumstances and accordingly the judge had been wrong to refuse to order further security for costs (*Republic of Kazakhstan v Istil Group Inc* [2005] EWCA Civ 1468, [2006] 1 All ER (Comm) 26, 9 November).

COURT OF APPEAL

[13.42]

The principles of applications for security for costs from appellants to the Court of Appeal are the same as in the court of first instance. CPR Rule 25.15, no doubt with an eye to the forthcoming Human Rights Act, removed the former fundamental difference that the impecuniosity of the appellant *was* a ground for ordering security for the costs of the appeal.

Nasser v United Bank of Kuwait [2001] EWCA Civ 556, [2002] 1 All ER 401 confirmed that the provision in Rule 25.15(1) enabling the court to make an order for security for costs of an appeal in respect of parties outside the jurisdiction of the Brussels and Lugano Conventions is not discriminatory under Schedule 1, Part 1, s 14 of the Human Rights Act 1998, because the court retains a discretion and there is no assumption that such a party should be ordered to provide security as a matter of course. The Court of Appeal has an unfettered discretion and is unlikely to shut out a meritorious appeal by an order for security which would stifle it.

Rule 52.9 provides: '(1) The appeal court may (a) strike out the whole or part of an appeal notice; (b) set aside permission to appeal in whole or in part; (c) impose or vary conditions upon which an appeal may be brought. (2) The court will only exercise its powers under paragraph (1) where there is a compelling reason for doing so.'

In *Bell Electric Ltd v Aweco Appliance Systems GmbH & Co KG* [2002] EWCA Civ 1501, [2003] 1 All ER 344, the defendants appealed against a judgment ordering them to pay to Bell within 14 days £100,000 by way of interim damages and £35,000 on account of costs. Aweco was in deliberate breach of the order to pay the judgment sum and their application for a stay had been refused. The failure or delay in making the payment was due not to any financial difficulty but was cynically based upon the practical difficulties for the respondent in seeking enforcement in a foreign jurisdiction. Accordingly there was a compelling reason for the Court of Appeal to order that the appeal be stayed unless within 14 days Aweco paid into court £135,000 to abide its outcome.

UK SUPREME COURT

[13.43]

Rule 36 of the Supreme Court Rules 2009 states that orders for security for costs will be made sparingly in the Supreme Court. The Supreme Court may, on the application of the respondent, order an appellant to give security for the costs of the appeal, and will set out the amount of the security and the manner in which it must be given. Security for costs will not generally be required for appellants who have been granted state funding, for Ministers or Government departments, or where the appeal is under the Child Abduction and Custody Act 1985. No security for costs is required in cross-appeals. Failure to provide security as required will result in the appeal being struck out by the Registrar although the appellant may apply to reinstate the appeal.

HOW TO GIVE SECURITY

(a) Payment into court

[13.44]

Payment into court may be either as the result of an order of the court or an agreement to give security, the latter being effected by completing Pay Office Form 2 and having it sealed by a High Court master or a district judge.

(b) Solicitor's undertaking

[13.45]

If the solicitor has sufficient faith in his client, or preferably sufficient funds in his client or other account under his control, he may give an undertaking that costs in the agreed or awarded amount will be paid, in respect of which he would of course be personally liable (*A Ltd v B Ltd* [1996] 1 WLR 665, ChD).

(c) Bond

[13.46]

Another way of avoiding an unattractive investment in the court deposit account is to obtain an order or agreement that the claimant shall give security by banker's bond in a form to be agreed by the parties or settled by the court.

(d) ATE

[13.47]

The fact that a claimant has a conditional fee agreement with his solicitors backed by after-the-event (ATE) insurance is not in itself a sufficient reason for not making an order for security for costs. Nearly all ATE policies contain wide terms enabling an insurer to repudiate if a claim fails because of the insured's own conduct. In the present case, if the claimant lost at the trial, it was likely that it would be on grounds that would render their ATE insurance policy ineffective (*Al-Koronky v Time-Life Entertainment Group Ltd* [2006] EWCA Civ 1123, [2006] All ER (D) 447 (Jul)).

CHAPTER 14

OFFERS TO SETTLE

CPR PART 36

(a) Good for the money

[14.1]

NHS Trusts developed a practice to avoid paying substantial sums of money into court of making written offers under the provisions of Parts 36 and 44 by reference to which they hoped to persuade courts to make the same order for costs in their favour as if they had made a payment into court. They contended that as the Trust was bound to be good for the money their letter was as sound as a payment-in and should be so treated. In *Crouch v Kings Healthcare NHS Trust and Murry v Blackburn Hyndburn and Ribble Valley Healthcare NHS Trust* [2004] EWCA Civ 1332, (2004) Times, 9 November the Court of Appeal held that there was no reason why a defendant might not during the currency of proceedings take an offer letter to the court and seek a direction that it should be treated as a Part 36 payment with all the consequences which flowed from that. Further, in exercising its discretion as to costs under Rule 44.3(4) the court must have regard to any admissible offer to settle which is drawn to its attention whether or not made in accordance with Part 36. The court doubted whether there was any real difference in exercising the discretion under Rule 44.3 as opposed to Part 36 because the court would have regard to all the circumstances and ask itself whether it was right to apply the presumption or make some different order depending on the circumstances of the case. Accordingly, because the Trust was bound to be good for the money, the court should treat such an offer in the same way as a payment-in.

[14.2]

This decision was followed in *Trustees of Stokes Pension Fund v Western Power Distribution (South West) plc* [2005] EWCA Civ 854, [2005] All ER (D) 107 (Jul), (which for some obscure reason is invariably referred to as 'Western Power') in which the Court of Appeal regretted that although the CPR provide that the court can order that an offer is to have the same costs consequences as a Part 36 payment into court they gave no guidance as to how the discretion to do so should be exercised. The court held that an offer by a clearly solvent defendant to settle a money claim should usually be treated as having the same effect as a payment into court if the offer was expressed in clear terms, was open for acceptance for at least 21 days and otherwise accorded with the substance of a *Calderbank* offer, was a genuine offer and if the defendant was good for the money when the offer was made. To the extent that any of those conditions was not satisfied the offer should be given less weight than a payment into court for the purposes of a decision as to the incidence of costs. Where none of the conditions was satisfied it was likely that the court would hold that the offer afforded the defendant no costs protection at all.

(b) Reform

[14.3]

Following these decisions the Department for Constitutional Affairs published a consultation paper '*Part 36 of the Civil Procedure Rules: Offers to settle and payments into court*' inviting comments on issues arising from them, including the meaning of 'good for the money' and the need for certain categories of defendant (Government and health service bodies and insured defendants) to make payments into court in settlement of their cases. This paper aimed to build on these judgments and to promote Part 36 as a means of encouraging early settlement of cases. Other issues raised were:

(a)   whether parties should be able to accept or withdraw offers after the time limit for acceptance without the need for the court's permission;
(b)   whether the court or the offeror should be able to extend the time limit for acceptance;
(c)   whether defendants should be entitled to indemnity costs or enhanced interest if a claimant fails to beat his or her own offer.

There was broad support for the proposal to reform along the lines set out in *Stokes v Western Power* (above), and very few objections to the proposed approach to defining the categories of defendant who could be deemed 'good for the money', subject to the need to ensure prompt payment.

Nevertheless, the proposal was criticised for not going far enough and thereby creating unfairness. The London Solicitors Litigation Association observed that it seemed perverse for the rules to be changed so that, in terms, those who can afford to pay into court do not have to do so, whereas those who cannot demonstrate financial security have to pay in. Its members expressed a strong preference for all defendants to be permitted to make offers rather than payments into court. Lord Justice Dyson, the then Deputy Head of Civil Justice and chairman of the Civil Procedure Rule Committee, said he thought payments into court should go in their entirety. They were intended to encourage settlement, not to provide security for the claimant. The fact that a defendant had little money was a reason for settling before heavy costs were incurred. Not only gilt-edged defendants should be exempted from payments-in.

The criticism was accepted and with effect from 6 April 2007 the Civil Procedure (Amendment No 3) Rules 2006 introduced a new CPR Part 36 to replace in its entirety the former Part 36, and in particular dispensing with the requirement that a defendant's offer of settlement be accompanied by a payment into court. Here is the new CPR Part 36 as amended:

CPR Part 36: Offers to settle
  Rule 36.1: Scope of this Part
  Rule 36.2: Form and content of a Part 36 offer
  Rule 36.3: Part 36 offers—general provisions
  Rule 36.4: Part 36 offers—defendants' offers

Rule 36.5: Personal injury claims for future pecuniary loss
Rule 36.6: Offer to settle a claim for provisional damages
Rule 36.7: Time when a Part 36 offer is made
Rule 36.8: Clarification of a Part 36 offer
Rule 36.9: Acceptance of a Part 36 offer
Rule 36.10: Costs consequences of acceptance of a defendant's Part 36 offer
Rule 36.11: The effect of acceptance of a Part 36 offer
Rule 36.12: Acceptance of a Part 36 offer or a Part 36 payment made by one or more, but not all, defendants
Rule 36.13: Restriction on disclosure of a Part 36 offer
Rule 36.14: Costs consequences following judgment
Rule 36.15: Deduction of benefits and lump sum payments

[14.5]

CPR Rule 36.A1: Scope of this Part

(1)   This Part contains rules about—
   (a)   offers to settle; and
   (b)   the consequences where an offer to settle is made in accordance with this Part.
(2)   Section I of this Part contains rules about offers to settle other than where Section II applies.
(3)   Section II of this Part contains rules about offers to settle where the parties have followed the Pre-Action Protocol for Low Value Personal Injury Claims in Road Traffic Accidents ("the RTA Protocol") and have started proceedings under Part 8 in accordance with Practice Direction 8B.

[14.5A]

Section I Part 36 Offers to SettleCPR Rule 36.1: Scope of this Section

(1)   This Section does not apply to an offer to settle to which Section II of this Part applies.
(2)   Nothing in this Section prevents a party making an offer to settle in whatever way he chooses, but if the offer is not made in accordance with rule 36.2, it will not have the consequences specified in rules 36.10, 36.11 and 36.14.
(Rule 44.3 requires the court to consider an offer to settle that does not have the costs consequences set out in this Section in deciding what order to make about costs)

[14.6]

It is important to note that Rule 36.1(2) provides that a party may make an offer to settle in whatever way he chooses, but if the offer is not made in accordance with Part 36 it will not have the costs consequences specified in rules 36.10, 36.11 and 36.14. It emphasises that in deciding what order to make about costs Rule 44.3 requires the court to have regard to any offer whether it has been made in accordance with Part 36 or not. See para [14.42].

[14.7]

CPR Rule 36.2: Form and content of a Part 36 offer

(1)   An offer to settle which is made in accordance with this rule is called a Part 36 offer.
(2)   A Part 36 offer must—

(a)   be in writing;

(b)   state on its face that it is intended to have the consequences of Section I of Part 36;

(c)   specify a period of not less than 21 days within which the defendant will be liable for the claimant's costs in accordance with rule 36.10 if the offer is accepted;

(d)   state whether it relates to the whole of the claim or to part of it or to an issue that arises in it and if so to which part or issue; and

(e)   state whether it takes into account any counterclaim.

(Rule 36.7 makes provision for when a Part 36 offer is made)

(3)   Rule 36.2(2)(c) does not apply if the offer is made less than 21 days before the start of the trial.

(4)   In appropriate cases, a Part 36 offer must contain such further information as is required by rule 36.5 (Personal injury claims for future pecuniary loss), rule 36.6 (Offer to settle a claim for provisional damages), and rule 36.15 (Deduction of benefits).

(5)   An offeror may make a Part 36 offer solely in relation to liability.

[14.8]

For an offer to have Part 36 consequences it must not only be in writing but must actually state it is intended to have those consequences, be open for at least 21 days, accept liability for costs and be clear. For example it must state whether or not it takes into account any counterclaim and whether it is in respect of the whole claim or only a specified part of it. The requirement in 36.2(2)(c) for the defendant to accept liability for costs appears to overlook that the offer may in fact have been made by the claimant. Indeed, Part 36 nowhere specifically states that an offer may be made by either party, presumably on the basis it is not necessary to make explicit that which is implicit.

[14.9]

Rule 36.3: Part 36 offers—general provisions

(1)   In this Part—

(a)   the party who makes an offer is the "offeror";

(b)   the party to whom an offer is made is the "offeree"; and

(c)   "the relevant period" mans—

    (i)   in the case of an offer made not less than 21 days before trial, the period stated under rule 36.2(2)(c) or such longer period as the parties agree;

    (ii)   otherwise, the period up to end of the trial or such other period as the court has determined.

(2)   A Part 36 offer—

(a)   may be made at any time, including before the commencement of proceedings; and

(b)   may be made in appeal proceedings.

(3)   A Part 36 offer which offers to pay or offers to accept a sum of money will be treated as inclusive of all interest until—

(a)   the date on which the period stated under rule 36.2(2)(c) expires; or

(b)   if rule 36.2(3) applies, a date 21 days after the date the offer was made.

(4)   A Part 36 offer shall have the consequences set out in this Section only in relation to the costs of the proceedings in respect of which it is made, and not in relation to the costs of any appeal from the final decision in those proceedings.

(5)   Before expiry of the relevant period, a Part 36 offer may be withdrawn or its terms changed to be less advantageous to the offeree, only if the court gives permission.

(6)   After expiry of the relevant period and provided that the offeree has not previously served notice of acceptance, the offeror may withdraw the offer or change its terms to be less advantageous to the offeree without the permission of the court.

(7)   The offeror does so by serving written notice of the withdrawal or change of terms on the offeree.

(Rule 36.14(6) deals with the costs consequences following judgment of an offer that is withdrawn)

[14.10]

Prior to 6 April 2007 although a payment into court could not be withdrawn or reduced within the specified period without the permission of the court, an offer could be withdrawn at any time before it was accepted under the general contractual law of offer and acceptance. Under the new regime an offer is equated to a payment into court.

If an offer has been made before the commencement of proceedings it survives the commencement of proceedings. There is no need to repeat it or do anything. It will last until it is withdrawn or accepted.

As with the previous rule, an offer to settle before the commencement of proceedings may still have costs consequences. This provision was dramatically illustrated in *Walker Residential Ltd v Davis* [2005] All ER (D) 160 (Dec) 9 December, where prior to the commencement of proceedings, the defendant offered the claimant £85,000 in settlement of the claimant's prospective claim. The claimant rejected the offer and issued proceedings. On service of the claim form, the defendant paid £85,000 into court, which the claimant accepted. The defendants had not made the CPR Part 36 payment within the requisite time period under rule 36.10 and had not sought an extension before the claimant accepted the payment. Those facts could not be changed by the deputy master purporting to extend the defendant's time: he could not change the automatic provision for costs under CPR rule 44.12(1)(b).

An offer may not be withdrawn within 21 days without permission from the court. In *Flynn v Scougal* [2004] EWCA Civ 873 without waiting for a medical report on the claimant the defendant paid £24,500 into court. Six days later the report arrived saying that the claimant's injuries were not as serious as had been thought. The defendant applied for permission to withdraw £14,500, leaving only £10,000. The application was refused. There had been no material unforeseen change in circumstances. The defendant had taken a risk in making an early payment-in and it would not be justice to deprive the claimant of his right to accept the payment within 21 days. After 21 days an offer may be withdrawn or reduced without permission.

In *Wakefield (t/a Wills Probate and Trusts of Weybridge) v Ford* [2009] EWHC 122 (QB), [2009] All ER (D) 242 (Jan) in defamation proceedings, the defendant made an offer to pay the claimants' costs to date provided he withdrew his complaint of malice. Following further disclosure several months later, the claimant purported to accept the defendants' offer and applied for permission to accept it. He was too late. The offer to settle no longer remained by the time the claimant purported to accept it. The offer had been clear that the defendant was prepared to pay the 'costs to date' and that if the offer was not accepted, the demands of the claimant would be correspondingly greater as the costs built up towards trial. It was therefore untenable to construe that the offer was to continue indefinitely into the future, so that the claimant could accept it at any time.

Offers are made when they are received. The fastest way to make a written offer or acceptance under the rules is by fax. A fax message sent before 4.30 pm is deemed to be served on that very same day.

Unlike in the law of contract, a counter-offer does not terminate the original offer which will still exist if the counter-offer is refused and may be accepted at any time before it is withdrawn.

An offer may be accepted at any time before the trial starts. After the trial has started it may only be accepted with the permission of the court.

If an offer is accepted after 21 days, the claimant pays the defendant's costs from the expiry of the 21 day period to the date of acceptance UNLESS the court orders otherwise – which it might do if there was late disclosure by the defendant preventing an informed decision on the offer by the claimant.

Huck v Robson [2002] EWCA Civ 398, [2002] 3 All ER 263 concerned a road traffic accident in which it was likely the finding on liability would be either 50/50 or 100%, the claimant made a pre-action offer to accept a 95%–5% split on liability. The defendant rejected the offer and the trial judge refused to take it into account in his award of costs on the grounds that the apportionment was 'illusory'. The Court of Appeal disagreed. Although a judge would be entitled to exercise his discretion and refuse indemnity costs where an offer was purely tactical, for example, to settle for 99.9% of the full value of the claim, that could not be said of the claimant's offer. The reduction of 5% provided the defendant with a real opportunity of settlement and did not represent the court's probable decision on liability. After applying the prescribed factors the court, by a majority, awarded the claimant her costs on the indemnity basis. I find the concept of a 'purely tactical' offer difficult. All Part 36 offers are tactical, and they are none the worse for it.

Rule 36.3(3), like its predecessor, provides that claimants' offers and defendants' payments are to be treated as inclusive of interest. For example, in *Blackham v Entrepose UK* [2004] EWCA Civ 1109, (2004) 148 Sol Jo LB 945 the trial judge was wrong to have regarded his award of £40,854 including interest to the date of judgment as beating the claimant's Part 36 offer of £40,000 made two years earlier. The damages element of the offer was £39,644, the balance being interest, which exceeded the damages element of the judgment. The claimant was therefore entitled to his costs, presumably on the indemnity basis. Unlike its predecessor Rule 36.3(3) is not subject to the offer stating that it excludes interest.

Rule 36.3 (4) limits an offer to the proceedings in respect of which it was made and excludes appeals. In *East West Corpn v Dampskibsselsabet AF, 1912, A/S (a body corporate)* [2003] EWCA Civ 174, [2003] 1 Lloyd's Rep 265n and *KR v Bryn Alyn Community (Holdings) Ltd (in liquidation)* [2003] EWCA Civ 383, [2003] PIQR P562, the claimants had made offers to settle before the trial under the previous Part 36 which were not accepted by the defendants. The defendants were unsuccessful at the trial and the trial judge ordered that they should pay the claimants' costs on the indemnity basis. After the defendants' unsuccessful appeal, the claimants sought a similar order in respect of their costs of the appeal. However, they had made no further Part 36 offer in respect of the appeal. There was no hint that the rule-makers ever considered that the claimant might make a portmanteau offer which would provide him with protection both at first instance and on a subsequent appeal. If a claimant wanted to protect himself as to the costs of an appeal, he had to make a further offer on the appeal proceedings. It is now in the rule.

[14.11]

CPR Rule 36.4: Part 36 offers—defendants' offers

(1)   Subject to rule 36.5(3) and rule 36.6(1), a Part 36 offer by a defendant to pay a sum of money in settlement of a claim must be an offer to pay a single sum of money.

(2)   But, an offer that includes an offer to pay all or part of the sum, if accepted, at a date later than 14 days following the date of acceptance will not be treated as a Part 36 offer unless the offeree accepts the offer.

Rule 36.4 provides that an offer must be for a single lump sum which is payable within 14 days; if it is not it is not effective for the purposes of Part 36 unless the offer is accepted.

[14.12]

CPR Rule 36.5: Personal injury claims for future pecuniary loss

(1)   This rule applies to a claim for damages for personal injury which is or includes a claim for future pecuniary loss.

(2)   An offer to settle such a claim will not have the consequences set out in rules 36.10, 36.11 and 36.14 unless it is made by way of a Part 36 offer under this rule.

(3)   A Part 36 offer to which this rule applies may contain an offer to pay, or an offer to accept—

    (a)   the whole or part of the damages for future pecuniary loss in the form of—

        (i)   a lump sum; or

        (ii)   periodical payments; or

        (iii)   both a lump sum and periodical payments;

    (b)   the whole or part of any other damages in the form of a lump sum.

(4)   A Part 36 offer to which this rule applies—

    (a)   must state the amount of any offer to pay the whole or part of any damages in the form of a lump sum;

    (b)   may state—

        (i)   what part of the lump sum, if any, relates to damages for future pecuniary loss; and

        (ii)   what part relates to other damages to be accepted in the form of a lump sum;

    (c)   must state what part of the offer relates to damages for future pecuniary loss to be paid or accepted in the form of periodical payments and must specify—

        (i)   the amount and duration of the periodical payments;

> (ii)   the amount of any payments for substantial capital purchases and when they are to be made; and
>
> (iii)   that each amount is to vary by reference to the retail prices index (or to some other named index, or that it is not to vary by reference to any index); and

(d)   must state either that any damages which take the form of periodical payments will be funded in a way which ensures that the continuity of payment is reasonably secure in accordance with section 2(4) of the Damages Act 1996 or how such damages are to be paid and how the continuity of their payment is to be secured.

(5)   Rule 36.4 applies to the extent that a Part 36 offer by a defendant under this rule includes an offer to pay all or part of any damages in the form of a lump sum.

(6)   Where the offeror makes a Part 36 offer to which this rule applies and which offers to pay or to accept damages in the form of both a lump sum and periodical payments, the offeree may only give notice of acceptance of the offer as a whole.

(7)   If the offeree accepts a Part 36 offer which includes payment of any part of the damages in the form of periodical payments, the claimant must, within 7 days of the date of acceptance, apply to the court for an order for an award of damages in the form of periodical payments under rule 41.8.

(Practice Direction 41B contains information about periodical payments under the Damages Act 1996)

[14.13]

CPR Rule 36.6: Offer to settle a claim for provisional damages

(1)   An offeror may make a Part 36 offer in respect of a claim which includes a claim for provisional damages.

(2)   Where he does so, the Part 36 offer must specify whether or not the offeror is proposing that the settlement shall include an award of provisional damages.

(3)   Where the offeror is offering to agree to the making of an award of provisional damages the Part 36 offer must also state—

(a)   that the sum offered is in satisfaction of the claim for damages on the assumption that the injured person will not develop the disease or suffer the type of deterioration specified in the offer;

(b)   that the offer is subject to the condition that the claimant must make any claim for further damages within a limited period; and

(c)   what that period is.

(4)   Rule 36.4 applies to the extent that a Part 36 offer by a defendant includes an offer to agree to the making of an award of provisional damages.

(5)   If the offeree accepts the Part 36 offer, the claimant must, within 7 days of the date of acceptance, apply to the court for an order for an award of provisional damages under rule 41.2.

[14.14]

CPR Rule 36.7: Time when a Part 36 offer is made

(1)   A Part 36 offer is made when it is served on the offeree.

(2)   A change in the terms of a Part 36 offer will be effective when notice of the change is served on the offeree.

(Rule 36.3 makes provision about when permission is required to change the terms of an offer to make it less advantageous to the offeree)

[14.15]

CPR Rule 36.8: Clarification of a Part 36 offer

(1)   The offeree may, within 7 days of a Part 36 offer being made, request the offeror to clarify the offer.

(2)   If the offeror does not give the clarification requested under paragraph (1) within 7 days of receiving the request, the offeree may, unless the trial has started, apply for an order that he does so.

(Part 23 contains provisions about making an application to the court)

(3)   If the court makes an order under paragraph (2), it must specify the date when the Part 36 offer is to be treated as having been made.

[14.16]

Although a party is not entitled to interrogate their opponent as to the thinking behind a Part 36 offer (other than to clarify the precise scope of the offer) the court has power to make an order for the early disclosure of admissible documents. This could enable the offeree to have additional material with which to consider the offer. The general rule that a party who fails to beat an offer paid the costs after the offer should have been accepted, should not apply when the other party has failed properly to disclose documents or information. In *R v Secretary of State for Transport, ex p Factortame (No 7)* [2001] 1 WLR 942, (2001) Butterworths Costs Service Bulletin, January, QBD (TCC) the claimants should have had an opportunity to consider expert and other evidence not previously available and therefore the government was ordered to pay their costs until the date by which it would have been reasonable for them to have had this opportunity. Similarly, in *Ford v GKR Construction Ltd* [2000] 1 All ER 802, CA, although the claimant failed to beat a Part 36 payment, she still received her costs after the payment in because the defendants had waited until during the trial to obtain video evidence undermining her evidence as to the extent of her symptoms, depriving her of a real opportunity to deal with their allegations of dishonesty. Judges should consider whether or not the parties had conducted the litigation in accordance with a system designed to enable them to make informed decisions at the earliest possible stage.

[14.17]

CPR Rule 36.9: Acceptance of a Part 36 offer

(1)   A Part 36 offer is accepted by serving written notice of the acceptance on the offeror.

(2)   Subject to rule 36.9(3), a Part 36 offer may be accepted at any time (whether or not the offeree has subsequently made a different offer) unless the offeror serves notice of withdrawal on the offeree.

(Rule 21.10 deals with compromise etc. by or on behalf of a child or protected party)

(3)   The court's permission is required to accept a Part 36 offer where—

   (a)   rule 36.12(4) applies;

   (b)   rule 36.15(3)(b) applies, the relevant period has expired and further deductible amounts have been paid to the claimant since the date of the offer;

   (c)   an apportionment is required under rule 41.3A; or

(d)   the trial has started.

(Rule 36.12 deals with offers by some but not all of multiple defendants)

(Rule 36.15 defines 'deductible amounts')

(Rule 41.3A requires an apportionment in proceedings under the Fatal Accidents Act 1976 and Law Reform (Miscellaneous Provisions) Act 1934)

(4)   Where the court gives permission under paragraph (3), unless all the parties have agreed costs, the court will make an order dealing with costs, and may order that the costs consequences set out in rule 36.10 will apply.

(5)   Unless the parties agree, a Part 36 offer may not be accepted after the end of the trial but before judgment is handed down.

[14.18]

Rule 36.9(2) provides that an offeree may accept an offer at any time unless it has been withdrawn whether or not he has previously rejected the offer or made a counter-offer. The law of contract whereby a counter-offer or a rejection kills an offer completely does not apply to Rule 36. *Sampla v Rushmoor Borough Council and Crowley* [2008] EWHC 2616 (TCC), [2008] All ER (D) 335 (Oct)was a dramatic illustration. Mr Crowley settled the claim and sought a 20% contribution from his co-defendant (RBC). This was robustly refused but in the course of a two day hearing RBC offered a contribution of 33.5% which Mr Crowley rejected. RBC then accepted his original offer of 20% which had not been withdrawn. The lesson is clear: specifically withdraw any offer which the offeror no longer wishes to be accepted. For example, if after making an offer based on his own culpability the defendant obtains a very favourable expert's report, if he does not withdraw his offer before disclosing the report the claimant may still accept the offer.

In the consolidated appeals of *Gibbon v Manchester City Council : LG Blower Specialist Bricklayer Ltd v Reeves* [2010] EWCA Civ 726, [2010] 1 WLR 2081, [2010] 27 EG 84 (CS) the claimant in Gibbon had made a Part 36 offer of £2,500. Though the local authority had initially made lower offers, it eventually offered the full £2,500. The claimant by then had raised her sights and rejected that offer without withdrawing her Part 36 offer, which the local authority then formally accepted. The judge found that the local authority had been entitled to accept the offer and was entitled to its costs from the date of the offer. In dismissing the appeal the Court of Appeal held: (1) Part 36 is a self-contained code, prescribing the manner in which an offer might be made and the consequences flowing from accepting or failing to accept it. Although basic concepts of offer and acceptance clearly underpinned Part 36, it was not to be understood as incorporating all the rules governing the formation of contracts. Indeed, it was not desirable that it should so do. Certainty was to be commended in a procedural code which had to be understood by ordinary citizens, and it was with that in mind that Part 36 had been drafted. It was to be read and understood according to its terms without importing other rules derived from the general law, save where that was clearly intended. (2) The claimant's arguments could not be reconciled with the clear language of Part 36, which clearly stated how an offer could be withdrawn and did not provide for an offer to lapse or to become incapable of acceptance upon rejection by the offeree. Rather, it proceeded on the footing that the offer was available for acceptance until withdrawn. There were good reasons for that, and to import into Part 36 the common law rule that an offer lapsed on rejection by the offeree would undermine that element of the scheme. Nor was there any room for the concept of implied withdrawal of an offer, CPR r 36.3(7) required express notice in writing in clear terms. Such notice has, for the avoidance of uncertainty, to include an express reference to the date and terms of the offer and has to make it clear that it was being withdrawn. In *Blower* it was explained, obiter, it was possible for several Part 36 offers to exist at the same time and for any one of them to be accepted until withdrawn and that in comparing an offer with a judgment the interest element in the offer (CPR 36.3(3)) must be stripped out.

Rule 36.9(5) enshrines the decision in *Hawley v Luminar Leisure plc* [2006] EWCA Civ 18, [2006] Lloyd's Rep 307, 24 January in which after the judge had reserved judgment the defendant purported to accept a Part 36 offer the claimant had made earlier in the proceedings and had not withdrawn. The court held that an offer was probably only open for acceptance until the hearing commenced and certainly could not be accepted after the court had reserved judgment.

[14.19]

CPR Rule 36.10: Costs consequences of acceptance of a Part 36 offer

(1) Subject to paragraph (2) and paragraph (4)(a), where a Part 36 offer is accepted within the relevant period the claimant will be entitled to the costs of the proceedings up to the date on which notice of acceptance was served on the offeror.

(2) Where—

    (a) a defendant's Part 36 offer relates to part only of the claim; and

    (b) at the time of serving notice of acceptance within the relevant period the claimant abandons the balance of the claim,

the claimant will be entitled to the costs of the proceedings up to the date of serving notice of acceptance unless the court orders otherwise.

(3) Costs under paragraphs (1) and (2) of this rule will be assessed on the standard basis if the amount of costs is not agreed.

(Rule 44.4(2) explains the standard basis for assessment of costs)

(Rule 44.12 contains provisions about when a costs order is deemed to have been made and applying for an order under section 194(3) of the Legal Services Act 2007.)

(4) Where—

    (a) a Part 36 offer that was made less than 21 days before the start of trial is accepted; or

    (b) a Part 36 offer is accepted after expiry of the relevant period,

if the parties do not agree the liability for costs, the court will make an order as to costs.

(5) Where paragraph (4)(b) applies, unless the court orders otherwise—

    (a) the claimant will be entitled to the costs of the proceedings up to the date on which the relevant period expired; and

    (b) the offeree will be liable for the offeror's costs for the period from the date of expiry of the relevant period to the date of acceptance.

(6) The claimant's costs include any costs incurred in dealing with the defendant's counterclaim if the Part 36 offer states that it takes into account the counterclaim.

[14.20]

Where a Part 36 offer is accepted in time the claimant is entitled to the costs of the proceedings up to the date on which notice of acceptance was served. A party may seek indemnity costs in one of two ways, either because there is a presumption that such costs apply, for example under CPR Rule 36.14 or because it could demonstrate the necessary evidence of conduct under CPR Rule 44.3. In *Fitzpatrick Contractors Ltd v Tyco Fire and Integrated Solutions (UK) Ltd (formerly Wormald Ansul (UK) Ltd) (No 3)* [2009] EWHC 274 (TCC), 123 ConLR 69, [2009] BLR 144 it was held there is no basis under the CPR which would allow the court to order indemnity costs for any other reason or on any other basis.

An indemnity costs presumption should not be imported into r.36.10. There was a right to claim recovery of indemnity costs but no rebuttable presumption that such costs would be recovered. Whilst the case was complex, the parties' approach to it was generally reasonable on both sides and a settlement three months before trial, at a figure that represented about half of the claim, was an unexceptional result. It was impossible to say that there was any basis on which the claimant could be entitled to have its costs assessed on the indemnity basis under Rule 44.3. However, the defendant had taken almost a year to accept the claimant's reasonable Part 36 offer during which period the claimant incurred considerable further costs. In all the circumstances it was appropriate to order interest on costs at one per cent over base rate

Where a Part 36 offer made less than 21 days before the start of trial is accepted, or a Part 36 offer is accepted after expiry of the relevant period, the court will decide the liability for costs if the parties cannot agree

In *Lahey v Pirelli Tyres Ltd* [2007] EWCA Civ 91, [2007] NLJR 294, [2007] All ER (D) 165 (Feb) the claimant accepted a CPR Part 36 payment by the defendant and thereby became entitled to his costs of the proceedings up to the date of serving notice of acceptance. However, at the outset of the detailed assessment, the defendant asked the district judge to order, before embarking on the detailed assessment, that the claimant should be only awarded 25% of the assessed costs. The defendant contended that in determining whether costs had been 'unreasonably incurred or are unreasonable in amount' (within the meaning of CPR 44.4(1)), the court was not constrained only to look at items of cost individually. It might conclude that a whole stage of the proceedings was unreasonable. It could look at the conduct of the parties in the round and not only by reference to specific items of costs. The district judge held he had no jurisdiction to order any such reduction, he was upheld by the judge on appeal and again by the Court of Appeal. The effect of the CPR is that, upon acceptance of a Part 36 payment, 'a costs order is deemed to have been made on the standard basis'. That meant the claimant was entitled to 100% of the assessed costs, those being the amount that the cost judge decided was payable at the conclusion of the detailed assessment. The district judge had no power to vary that order. The power to vary or revoke an order given by CPR 3.1(7) is only exercisable in relation to an order that the court has previously made, and not to an order that is deemed to be made by operation of the rules.

[14.21]

CPR Rule 36.11: The effect of acceptance of a Part 36 offer

(1)   If a Part 36 offer is accepted, the claim will be stayed$^{(GL)}$.

(2)   In the case of acceptance of a Part 36 offer which relates to the whole claim the stay$^{(GL)}$ will be upon the terms of the offer.

(3)   If a Part 36 offer which relates to part only of the claim is accepted—

      (a)   the claim will be stayed$^{(GL)}$ as to that part upon the terms of the offer; and

      (b)   subject to rule 36.10(2), unless the parties have agreed costs, the liability for costs shall be decided by the court.

(4)   If the approval of the court is required before a settlement can be binding, any stay$^{(GL)}$ which would otherwise arise on the acceptance of a Part 36 offer will take effect only when that approval has been given.

(5)   Any stay$^{(GL)}$ arising under this rule will not affect the power of the court—

      (a)   to enforce the terms of a Part 36 offer;

      (b)   to deal with any question of costs (including interest on costs) relating to the proceedings.

(6)   Unless the parties agree otherwise in writing, where a Part 36 offer by a defendant that is or that includes an offer to pay a single sum of money is accepted, that sum must be paid to the offeree within 14 days of the date of—

      (a)   acceptance; or

      (b)   the order when the court makes an order under rule 41.2 (order for an award of provisional damages) or rule 41.8 (order for an award of periodical payments), unless the court orders otherwise.

(7)   If the accepted sum is not paid within 14 days or such other period as has been agreed the offeree may enter judgment for the unpaid sum.

(8)   Where—

      (a)   a Part 36 offer (or part of a Part 36 offer) which is not an offer to which paragraph (6) applies is accepted; and

      (b)   a party alleges that the other party has not honoured the terms of the offer,

that party may apply to enforce the terms of the offer without the need for a new claim.

[14.22]

The effect of Rule 36.11 is that if an offer is accepted, unless the offeror pays the money within 14 days he risks the double sanction of judgment being entered against him for the amount of the offer and losing the Part 36 costs protection unless the offeree agrees otherwise. It is therefore important not only to ensure the money will be in place before making the offer but to remember that a cheque takes several days to be cleared. A cheque on the 14th day is not payment within the rule.

[14.23]

CPR Rule 36.12: Acceptance of a Part 36 offer made by one or more, but not all, defendants

(1)   This rule applies where the claimant wishes to accept a Part 36 offer made by one or more, but not all, of a number of defendants.

(2)   If the defendants are sued jointly or in the alternative, the claimant may accept the offer if—

(a)   he discontinues his claim against those defendants who have not made the offer; and

(b)   those defendants give written consent to the acceptance of the offer.

(3)   If the claimant alleges that the defendants have a several liability (GL) to him, the claimant may—

(a)   accept the offer; and

(b)   continue with his claims against the other defendants if he is entitled to do so.

(4)   In all other cases the claimant must apply to the court for an order permitting him to accept the Part 36 offer.

[14.24]

CPR Rule 36.13: Restriction on disclosure of a Part 36 offer

(1)   A Part 36 offer will be treated as 'without prejudice except as to costs'.

(2)   The fact that a Part 36 offer has been made must not be communicated to the trial judge or to the judge (if any) allocated in advance to conduct the trial until the case has been decided.

(3)   Paragraph (2) does not apply—

(a)   where the defence of tender before claim has been raised;

(b)   where the proceedings have been stayed under rule 36.11 following acceptance of a Part 36 offer; or

(c)   where the offeror and the offeree agree in writing that it should not apply.

[14.25]

Rule 36.13 prohibits in mandatory terms disclosure of a Part 36 offer or payment to any judge hearing an appeal until all issues have been determined. In *Garratt v Saxby* [2004] EWCA Civ 341, [2004] 1 WLR 2152, the claimant's claim for damages was heard by a judge in the county court and on his appeal to a High Court judge his solicitors inadvertently included in the appeal bundle references to the defendant's Part 36 offer. The claimant's appeal succeeded, subject to a finding of 40% contributory negligence. The Court of Appeal dismissed the defendant's appeal on the grounds that the judge had made no reference to the offer, which she would doubtless have had done had she seen it, and therefore the defendant had not shown there to have been a serious procedural irregularity. Accordingly, the interests of fairness and justice did not require the appeal to be reheard before a different judge. If the judge had been aware of the offer she would have had to decide whether or not to recuse herself, and in making this decision would have been entitled to take into account the additional time, cost and difficulty involved if the hearing were to be aborted.

But what is the position where there is split trial between liability and quantum and the claimant succeeds on liability where there is a Part 36 offer? Under the previous rule if the claimant applied for costs at that stage the judge could be told there was a Part 36 payment which invariably resulted in the costs being reserved. The new rule includes no such provision. It could well be wrong that a claimant who subsequently fails to beat a Part 36 offer should have been awarded his costs of the liability hearing. Either the old rule needs restoring or the claimant's costs on a split trial should always be reserved until all the issues have been resolved.

Support for this approach came in *Shepherds Investments Ltd v Walters* [2007] EWCA Civ 292, [2007] All ER (D) 40 (Apr), 3 April, where the Court of Appeal dismissed the claimant's appeal against an order reserving the issue of costs until after the outcome of an account of profits in its claim against the defendants, holding that a judge is not required by the CPR to make an immediate decision on costs and has a discretion to postpone it until quantum had been finally determined (see para [11.15]).

[14.26]

CPR Rule 36.14: Costs consequences following judgment

(1)   This rule applies where upon judgment being entered—

    (a)   a claimant fails to obtain a judgment more advantageous than a defendant's Part 36 offer; or

    (b)   judgment against the defendant is at least as advantageous to the claimant as the proposals contained in a claimant's Part 36 offer.

(2)   Subject to paragraph (6), where rule 36.14(1)(a) applies, the court will, unless it considers it unjust to do so, order that the defendant is entitled to—

    (a)   his costs from the date on which the relevant period expired; and

    (b)   interest on those costs.

(3)   Subject to paragraph (6), where rule 36.14(1)(b) applies, the court will, unless it considers it unjust to do so, order that the claimant is entitled to—

    (a)   interest on the whole or part of any sum of money (excluding interest) awarded at a rate not exceeding 10% above base rate for some or all of the period starting with the date on which the relevant period expired;

    (b)   his costs on the indemnity basis from the date on which the relevant period expired; and

    (c)   interest on those costs at a rate not exceeding 10% above base rate.

(4)   In considering whether it would be unjust to make the orders referred to in paragraphs (2) and (3) above, the court will take into account all the circumstances of the case including—

    (a)   the terms of any Part 36 offer;

    (b)   the stage in the proceedings when any Part 36 offer was made, including in particular how long before the trial started the offer was made;

    (c)   the information available to the parties at the time when the Part 36 offer was made; and

    (d)   the conduct of the parties with regard to the giving or refusing to give information for the purposes of enabling the offer to be made or evaluated.

(5)   Where the court awards interest under this rule and also awards interest on the same sum and for the same period under any other power, the total rate of interest may not exceed 10% above base rate.

(6)   Paragraphs (2) and (3) of this rule do not apply to a Part 36 offer—

    (a)   that has been withdrawn;

    (b)   that has been changed so that its terms are less advantageous to the offeree, and the offeree has beaten the less advantageous offer;

    (c)   made less than 21 days before trial, unless the court has abridged the relevant period.

(Rule 44.3 requires the court to consider an offer to settle that does not have the costs consequences set out in this Section in deciding what order to make about costs)

[14.27]

Under rule 36.14(3) a claimant who obtains a judgment at least as advantageous as his offer is entitled to interest at a rate not exceeding 10% above base rate, his costs on the indemnity basis and interest on the costs also at a rate not exceeding 10% above base rate.

Rule 36.14(2) makes no similar provision for a defendant who has made an offer which is not beaten. For a defendant to obtain costs on the indemnity basis there must be circumstances which take the case out of the norm (*Excelsior Commercial and Industrial Holdings Ltd v Salisbury Hamer Aspden & Johnson (a firm)* [2002] EWCA Civ 879, [2002] All ER (D) 39 (Jun)). In *Société Internationale de Telecommunications Aeronautiques* (above, para [11.21]), Maxwell Batley had made a token Part 36 payment into court of £1,000 and, because they had wholly succeeded in the action, sought their costs on the indemnity basis. It could be argued that it is anomalous that a defendant who, after his payment into court is refused, is only partly successful at trial gets some costs benefit from having made the payment in, whereas a defendant who is wholly successful at trial gets no costs benefit from his payment in (unless the court disapproves of some aspects of how the claimant conducted the litigation): the wholly successful defendant who made the payment into court will recover his costs assessed on the standard basis, which is exactly what he would have done if he had not made the payment in at all. However, whether that is anomalous or not, it is the effect of the Court of Appeal's decision in *Excelsior*. For Maxwell Batley to have had a good claim for indemnity costs it would have been necessary for them to show not just that Watson Wyatt refused their Part 36 offer, but also that there was some respect in which Watson Wyatt's conduct of the litigation should be disapproved. Watson Wyatt had pursued the claim with determination, but there was nothing wrong in that. Watson Wyatt also pursued the claim scrupulously, fairly and without any impropriety. In those circumstances it was not appropriate to award indemnity costs.

Whether or not a Part 36 offer was valid, if the parties had treated it as such, then so should the court. If a party did not raise a technical point about a Part 36 offer at the time, then that party should not be able to take that point later (*J Murphy & Sons Ltd v Johnston Precast Ltd (formerly Johnston Pipes Ltd)* [2008] EWHC 3104 (TCC), [2008] All ER (D) 14 (Dec)).

In *Painting v University of Oxford* [2005] EWCA Civ 161, (2005) Times, 15 February judgment had been entered for the claimant in her personal injury claim but within a week of paying £184,000 into court the University became aware of video surveillance taken of the claimant which showed she was able to walk normally without aid and was able to bend and straighten herself looking at display items in shops. The University obtained permission to withdraw all the money in court save for £10,000 and contested that the claimant had been exaggerating her claim. On the assessment of damages the judge found the claimant had indeed exaggerated her claim and awarded her only £22,000 but also her costs on the basis that she had beaten the payment into court. The Court of Appeal held that the judge should have taken into account the provisions of CPR Rule 44.3. The judge had only taken into account the inadequacy of the Part 36 payment. The University was the real winner and accordingly the court ordered the claimant to pay the costs of the action from the date of the reduced payment into court. Which would not leave her much of her £22,000.

Under the previous rule, to qualify for costs a party had to obtain a judgment which 'bettered' a Part 36 offer or payment. The requirement for a claimant now is to obtain a judgment 'at least as advantageous' as their offer. It was generally thought that the purpose of the new wording was to merely simplify Part 36 and to avoid penalising a claimant who gets his offer exactly right, as would have happened in *Read v Edmed* [2004] EWHC 3274 (QB), (2004) Times, 13 December had not the judge resorted to exercising his discretion under CPR rule 44.3. However, in *Carver v BAA plc* [2008] EWCA Civ 412, [2008] 3 All ER 911, (2008) Time, 4 June the Court of Appeal held that the change in words signified a change of approach and requires the same broad approach as for claims which include a non-money element. Previously if a claimant beat a payment of money into court by a modest amount, even £1, they had bettered the judgment and were entitled to costs. Is the Court now entitled to look at all the circumstances of the case in deciding where the balance of advantage lies? Miss Carver was an air hostess injured in the course of her occupation who after protracted negotiations and litigation recovered £4,520, a mere £51 more than the money in court. In non-money claims where there is no yardstick of pounds and pence by which to make the comparison, all the circumstances of the case have to be taken into account. Under the new Part 36, money claims and non-money claims are to be treated in the same way, and therefore:

> " 'more advantageous' is, an open-textured phrase. It permits a more wide-ranging review of all the facts and circumstances of the case in deciding whether the judgment, which is the fruit of the litigation, was worth the fight. The Civil Procedure Rules, and Part 36 in particular, encourage both sides to make offers to settle. Compromise is seen as an object worthy of promotion, for compromise is better than contest, both for the litigants concerned, for the court and for the administration of justice as a whole. Litigation is time consuming and it comes at a cost, emotional as well as financial. Those are, therefore, appropriate factors to take into account in deciding whether the battle was worth it. Money is not the sole governing criterion."

The judge was correct in looking at the case broadly. He was entitled to take into account that the extra £51 gained was more than offset by the irrecoverable cost incurred by the claimant in continuing to contest the case for as long as she did. He was entitled to take into account the added stress to her as she waited for the trial and the stress of the trial process itself. No reasonable litigant would have embarked upon this campaign for a gain of £51. Accordingly, the judge was entitled to order the claimant to pay the defendant's costs after the time to accept the payment-in had expired.

So, what does 'more advantageous' mean in the context of any individual case? The court saw force in the argument that a pure monetary comparison produces clarity and avoids placing value upon subjective elements such as the stress and anxiety involved in protracted, risky litigation, but nevertheless it said 'so be it'. The approach must now be subjective as well as objective. The test is no longer just simple arithmetic. What percentage of financial benefit will suffice to offset the emotional factors? How often will claimants like Miss Carver now pay the price for their own stress and anxiety?

In contrast, in *Morgan v UPS* [2008] EWCA Civ 1476 the claimant had reduced his claim from £200,000 to £91,000 on being confronted with video evidence that he was malingering. His eventual award of £44,329.12 beat the payment into court by only £629.10. Nevertheless the Court of Appeal upheld the judge's order that the defendants paid the claimant's costs. The claimant's reduced offer, although too high, was not wholly unreasonable and the defendants had unsuccessfully argued that an operation on the claimant had been unnecessary. Accordingly the trial had not been caused by the malingering.

I still feel sorry for Miss Carver and I am not alone. The decision has been criticised by many commentators, including Lord Justice Jackson in his Review of Civil Litigation Costs, Final Report, on the grounds that it introduces an unwelcome degree of uncertainty into the operation of Part 36 and by Lord Justices Moore-Bick and Carnwarth in *Gibbon v Manchester City Council : LG Blower Specialist Bricklayer Ltd v Reeves* [2010] EWCA Civ 726, [2010] 1 WLR 2081, [2010] 27 EG 84 (CS) (see also para [14.18]) who held that it should be recognised that what may be more important than the factors to be taken into account is the weight that is to be attached to them, which remains a matter for the judge in each case. Moreover, when deciding how much weight to attach to any particular factor it is important to see things from the litigant's perspective rather than to be too ready to impose the court's own view of what is and is not to his advantage. That is particularly important when dealing with money claims, both because to recover judgment for more than what was offered is legitimately regarded as success, and because a party faced with a Part 36 offer ought to be entitled to evaluate it by reference to a rational assessment of his own case. In a case where the offer has been beaten by a very small amount and there is clear evidence that the successful party has suffered serious adverse consequences as a result of pursuing the case to judgment those factors may be sufficient to outweigh success in pure financial. However, in most cases obtaining judgment for an amount greater than the offer is likely to outweigh all other factors. Carver should not be interpreted as opening the way to a wide ranging investigation of emotional and other factors in every case.

The judge in *Multiplex Constructions (UK) Ltd v Cleveland Bridge UK Ltd (2) Cleveland Bridge Dorman Long Engineering Ltd (No 6)* [2008] EWHC 2280 (TCC), 122 ConLR 88, [2008] all ER (D) 04 (Oct) confirmed that *Carver v BAA Plc* [2008] EWCA Civ 412 is not restricted to personal injury cases. It set out how the court ought to approach the matter in circumstances where: (a) one party has made an offer which was nearly but not quite sufficient; and (b) the other party has rejected that offer outright without any attempt to negotiate.

From a comprehensive review of the authorities the judge in *Multiplex* derived the following eight principles:

(i)   In commercial litigation where each party has claims and asserts that a balance is owing in its own favour, the party which ends up receiving payment should generally be characterised as the overall winner of the entire action.

(ii)   In considering how to exercise its discretion the court should take as its starting point the general rule that the successful party is entitled to an order for costs.

(iii)   The judge must then consider what departures are required from that starting point, having regard to all the circumstances of the case.

(iv)   Where the circumstances of the case require an issues-based costs order, that is what the judge should make. However, the judge should hesitate before doing so, because of the practical difficulties which this causes and because of the steer given by rule 44.3(7).

(v)   In many cases the judge can and should reflect the relative success of the parties on different issues by making a proportionate costs order.

(vi)   In considering the circumstances of the case the judge will have regard not only to any part 36 offers made but also to each party's approach to negotiations (insofar as admissible) and general conduct of the litigation.

(vii)   If (a) one party makes an order offer under part 36 or an admissible offer within rule 44.3(4)(c) which is nearly but not quite sufficient, and (b) the other party rejects that offer outright without any attempt to negotiate, then it might be appropriate to penalise the second party in costs.

(viii) In assessing a proportionate costs order the judge should consider what costs are referable to each issue and what costs are common to several issues. It will often be reasonable for the overall winner to recover not only the costs specific to the issues which he has won but also the common costs.

D Pride and Partners (a firm) v Institute for Animal Health [2009] EWHC 1617 (QB), [2009] All ER (D) 84 (Jul) also considered the meaning of 'more advantageous'.

The claimants were livestock farmers who sought damages from the defendants (H, M and the Secretary of State) for losses alleged to have been suffered during an outbreak of foot and mouth disease which originated in H and M's laboratories. H and M sought an order that the claimants pay their costs of the proceedings from the last date for acceptance of the Part 36 offers made by H and M until the conclusion of the proceedings by a settlement.

It could be inferred that the claimants might have obtained by the settlement higher compensation than they would have been awarded on an assessment by the court. If the claims advanced and settled in full were greater than the entitlement in law of each claimant, then that was not an advantage contemplated by CPR Rule 36.14 in the phrase 'a judgment more advantageous'. The overriding objective was for the court to deal with cases justly. There might be cases where a claimant was able to persuade a defendant to pay him more than his legal entitlement, or to pay his legal entitlement more quickly than he would otherwise do, in circumstances where the cost of contesting that entitlement would not be worth incurring. Part 36 should be construed as designed to protect defendants from claims being pursued on such a basis, and not to reward, in costs, claimants who pursued their claims on such a basis. Given the information that was available to H and M at the time, the offer they made was the best offer that they could have made. It would be unjust not to make the order for costs sought by H and M. The claimants were ordered to pay the costs of H and M in respect of the proceedings other than those costs provided for in the settlement agreement.

In *(1) Diageo North America Inc (2) Diageo Great Britain Ltd v (1) Intercontinental Brands (LCB) Ltd (2) Intercontinental Brands (Holdings) Ltd (3) Incorporated Beverages (Jersey) Ltd (Costs)* [2010] EWHC 172 (Pat), 2 February, Diageo, the producers of Smirnoff vodka, had obtained in a passing off action damages and an injunction against the producers of VODKAT, a mixture of vodka and fermented alcohol. Relying on a CPR Part 36 offer made by it, Diageo sought an order for costs to be assessed on the indemnity basis. Although the damages awarded were clearly in excess of those it had been willing to accept, there was an issue as to whether the injunction it obtained was more or less advantageous to it than what it had proposed.

In considering whether a judgment was 'as least as advantageous' to a claimant as the proposals contained in its Part 36 offer, the guidance given in Carver (above) was applicable *mutatis mutandis*. The concept of advantageousness was a broad one and had to be viewed in the light of all the circumstances of the case. Strict monetary comparison was not the governing criterion. It was also important to bear in mind that CPR r 36.14 was designed as an incentive to encourage claimants to make, and defendants to accept, appropriate offers of settlement. It was too simplistic merely to say that the judgment of the court was not as advantageous to Diageo as its Part 36 offer because the injunction granted was a qualified one. Even though the injunction was a qualified one, the defendant would still have a small mountain to climb to be able to continue to use the name VODKAT in relation to a product that was not vodka and still comply with the injunction. Looking at the matter broadly, the injunction was, in terms of its practical effect, little short of that which Diageo had sought in its offer. The defendant could have protected itself as to costs by making a counter offer agreeing to submit to a qualified injunction, but it had not done so and had instead fought and lost. Overall, the judgment obtained was as advantageous as the proposals contained in the Part 36 offer. Costs were ordered on the indemnity basis from the date of expiry of the offer and interest on those costs was to run at the enhanced rate.

A defendant who has paid money into court cannot argue that if the claimant had been more reasonable he would have offered more. A defendant has the remedy in his own hands where a claimant is being intransigent. He is able to protect himself from costs by offering whatever he wishes and whatever he does offer must be regarded as his best offer unless he increases it.

The judge having awarded damages that exceeded a Part 36 payment into court was wrong to refuse to award any costs on the basis of the claimant's failure to engage in negotiations, which was a failure to comply with the pre-action protocol. The judge had already discounted the claimant's costs because he had failed on one of two issues and there should have been no further reduction (*Straker v Tudor Rose (a firm)* [2007] EWCA Civ 368, [2007] All ER (D) 224 (Apr)).

It is not unjust that interest should be paid on costs awarded on the indemnity basis. The purpose is to redress the perceived unfairness arising from the general rule that interest is not allowed on costs incurred before judgment. There may be cases where evidence will demonstrate actual dates when clients have put up funds and from which interest will run. Without such evidence the court can do no more than make the interest run from the date when the work was done or the liability for disbursements was incurred. The rate of interest should reflect (albeit generously) the cost of money at, say, 4%

over base rate. If it were questioned why there should be a difference between the rate of interest on costs and on the damages, the answer would be that the rate on damages compensates also for the general impact of proceedings. There must not be double compensation for the impact and the provisions of Rule 36.21 are not intended to be penal. The position should be no different where the receiving party is publicly funded (*KR v Bryn Alyn Community (Holdings) Ltd (in liquidation)* [2003] EWCA Civ 383, [2003] PIQR P562).

[14.28]

CPR Rule 36.15: Deduction of benefits and lump sum payments

(1) In this rule and rule 36.9—

(a) "the 1997 Act" means the Social Security (Recovery of Benefits) Act 1997;

(b) "the 2008 Regulations" means the Social Security (Recovery of Benefits)(Lump Sum Payments) Regulations 2008;

(c) "recoverable amount" means—

(i) "recoverable benefits" as defined in section 1(4)(c) of the 1997 Act; and

(ii) "recoverable lump sum payments" as defined in regulation 4 of the 2008 Regulations;

(d) "deductible amount" means—

(i) any benefits by the amount of which damages are to be reduced in accordance with section 8 of, and Schedule 2 to the 1997 Act ("deductible benefits"); and

(ii) any lump sum payment by the amount of which damages are to be reduced in accordance with regulation 12 of the 2008 Regulations ("deductible lump sum payments"); and

(e) "certificate"—

(i) in relation to recoverable benefits is construed in accordance with the provisions of the 1997 Act; and

(ii) in relation to recoverable lump sum payments has the meaning given in section 29 of the 1997 Act as applied by regulation 2 of, and modified by Schedule 1 to the 2008 Regulations.

(2) This rule applies where a payment to a claimant following acceptance of a Part 36 offer would be a compensation payment as defined in section 1(4)(b) or 1A(5)(b) of the 1997 Act.

(3) A defendant who makes a Part 36 offer should state either—

(a) that the offer is made without regard to any liability for recoverable amounts; or

(b) that it is intended to include any deductible amounts.

(4) Where paragraph (3)(b) applies, paragraphs (5) to (9) of this rule will apply to the Part 36 offer.

(5) Before making the Part 36 offer, the offeror must apply for a certificate.

(6) Subject to paragraph (7), the Part 36 offer must state—

(a) the amount of gross compensation;

(b) the name and amount of any deductible amount by which the gross amount is reduced; and

(c) the net amount of compensation.

(7)   If at the time the offeror makes the Part 36 offer, the offeror has applied for, but has not received a certificate, the offeror must clarify the offer by stating the matters referred to in paragraphs (6)(b) and (6)(c) not more than 7 days after receipt of the certificate.

(8)   For the purposes of rule 36.14(1)(a), a claimant fails to recover more than any sum offered (including a lump sum offered under rule 36.5) if the claimant fails upon judgment being entered to recover a sum, once deductible amounts identified in the judgment have been deducted, greater than the net amount stated under paragraph (6)(c).

(Section 15(2) of the 1997 Act provides that the court must specify the compensation payment attributable to each head of damage. Schedule 1 to the 2008 Regulations modifies section 15 of the 1997 Act in relation to lump sum payments and provides that the court must specify the compensation payment attributable to each or any dependant who has received a lump sum payment.)

(9)   Where—

   (a)   further deductible benefits have accrued since the Part 36 offer was made; and

   (b)   the court gives permission to accept the Part 36 offer,

the court may direct that the amount of the offer payable to the offeree shall be reduced by a sum equivalent to the deductible amounts paid to the claimant since the date of the offer.

(Rule 36.9(3)(b) states that permission is required to accept an offer where the relevant period has expired and further deductible amounts have been paid to the claimant)

[14.28A]

Section II RTA Protocol offers to settleCPR Rule 36.16: Scope of this Section

(1)   Where this Section applies Section I does not apply.

(2)   This Section applies to an offer to settle where the parties have followed the RTA Protocol and started proceedings under Part 8 in accordance with Practice Direction 8B ('the Stage 3 Procedure').

(3)   A reference to the 'Court Proceeding Pack Form' is a reference to the form used in the RTA Protocol.

(4)   Nothing in this Section prevents a party making an offer to settle in whatever way that party chooses, but if the offer is not made in accordance with this Section, it will not have any costs consequences.

CPR Rule 36.17: Form and content of an RTA Protocol offer

(1)   An offer to settle which is made in accordance with this rule is called an RTA Protocol offer.

(2)   An RTA Protocol offer must –

   (a)   be set out in the Court Proceedings Pack (Part B) Form; and

   (b)   contain the final total amount of the offer from both parties.

CPR Rule 36.18: Time when an RTA Protocol offer is made

The RTA Protocol offer is deemed to be made on the first business day after the Court Proceedings Pack (Part A and Part B) Form is sent to the defendant.

CPR Rule 36.19: General provisions

An RTA Protocol offer –

   (a)   is treated as exclusive of all interest; and

(b)   has the consequences set out in this Section only in relation to the fixed costs of the Stage 3 Procedure as provided for in rule 45.29, and not in relation to the costs of any appeal from the final decision of those proceedings.

CPR Rule 36.20: Restrictions on disclosure of an RTA Protocol offer

(1)   The amount of the RTA Protocol offer must not be communicated to the court until the claim is determined.

(2)   Any other offer to settle must not be communicated to the court at all.

(3)   Once the claim is determined, the court will examine the RTA Protocol offer.

CPR Rule 36.21: Costs consequences following judgment

(1)   This rule applies where, on the determination by the court, the claimant obtains judgment against the defendant for an amount of damages that is –

    (a)   less than or equal to the amount of the defendant's RTA Protocol offer;

    (b)   more than the defendant's RTA Protocol offer but less than the claimant's RTA Protocol offer; or

    (c)   equal to or more than the claimant's RTA Protocol offer.

(2)   Where paragraph (1)(a) applies, the court will order the claimant to pay –

    (a)   the fixed costs in rule 45.38; and

    (b)   interest on those fixed costs from the first business day after the deemed date of the RTA Protocol offer under rule 36.18.

(3)   Where paragraph (1)(b) applies, the court will order the defendant to pay the fixed costs in rule 45.32.

(4)   Where paragraph (1)(c) applies, the court will order the defendant to pay –

    (a)   interest on the whole of the damages awarded at a rate not exceeding 10% above base rate for some or all of the period starting with the date specified in rule 36.18;

    (b)   the fixed costs in rule 45.32; and

    (c)   interest on those costs at a rate not exceeding 10% above base rate.

CPR Rule 36.22: Deduction of benefits

For the purposes of rule 36.21(1)(a) the amount of the judgment is less than the RTA Protocol offer where the judgment is less than that offer once deductible amounts identified in the judgment are deducted.

('Deductible amount' is defined in rule 36.15(1)(d).)

Glossary

[14.29]

The glossary to the Civil Procedure Rules is a guide to the meaning of certain legal expressions as used in the Rules, but it does not give the expressions any meaning in the Rules which they do not otherwise have in the law. The following extracts are referred to in Part 36:

Several liability	A person who is severally liable with others may remain liable for the whole claim even where judgment has been obtained against the others.

Stay

A stay imposes a halt on proceedings, apart from taking any steps allowed by the Rules or the terms of the stay. Proceedings can be continued if a stay is lifted.

FIXED FEES

[14.30]

In *Lamont v Burton* [2007] EWCA Civ 429, [2007] All ER 173 the claimant in a road traffic accident claim was represented under a conditional fee agreement but although liability was admitted he failed to beat a Part 36 payment. Accordingly, the claimant was awarded his costs up until the latest date on which the Part 36 payment could have been accepted. When those costs were assessed he claimed a 100% success fee under CPR 45.16 on the ground that the claim had been concluded at trial. The defendant argued that although Rule 45.16 did not itself give the court jurisdiction to allow a different percentage increase, it contained a lacuna in that it did not deal with situations in which a claimant failed at trial to better a Part 36 payment, which could be remedied by the court exercising its discretion under Rule 44.3 to award a success fee no greater that it would have been under Rule 45.16 had the offer been accepted, namely 12.5%. The court held the 100% success fee to be mandatory in all cases. There was no discretion to award the claimant a success fee of less than 100%, CPR Part 44 was excluded by the very words used. It would be a matter for the Rules Committee and the Civil Justice Council whether to amend Part 45 to make special provision to deal with the Part 36 issue.

[14.31]

PRACTICE DIRECTION SUPPLEMENTING CPR PART 36

Formalities of Part 36 offers and other notices under this Part

1.1   *A Part 36 offer may be made using Form N242A.*
1.2   *Where a Part 36 offer, notice of acceptance or notice of withdrawal or change of terms is to be served on a party who is legally represented, the document to be served must be served on the legal representative.*

[14.32]

Application for permission to withdraw a Part 36 Offer

2.1   *Rule 36.3(4) provides that before expiry of the relevant period a Part 36 offer may only be withdrawn or its terms changed to be less advantageous to the offeree with the permission of the court.*

2.2   *The permission of the court must be sought-*

(1)   *by making an application under Part 23, which must be dealt with by a judge other than the judge (if any) allocated in advance to conduct the trial, unless the parties agree that such judge may hear the application;*

(2)   *at a trial or other hearing, provided that it is not to the trial judge or to the judge (if any) allocated in advance to conduct the trial, unless the parties agree that such judge may hear the application.*

[14.33]

Acceptance of a Part 36 offer

3.1   *Where a Part 36 offer is accepted in accordance with rule 36.9(1) the notice of acceptance must be served on the offeror and filed with the court where the case is proceeding.*

3.2   *Where the court's permission is required to accept a Part 36 offer, the permission of the court must be sought-*

(1)   *by making an application under Part 23, which must be dealt with by a judge other than the judge (if any) allocated in advance to conduct the trial, unless the parties agree that such judge may hear the application;*

(2)   *at a trial or other hearing, provided that it is not to the trial judge or to the judge (if any) allocated in advance to conduct the trial, unless the parties agree that such judge may hear the application.*

3.3   *Where rule 36.9(3)(b) applies, the application for permission to accept the offer must-*

(1)   *state-*

   (a)   *the net amount offered in the Part 36 offer;*

   (b)   *the deductible amounts that had accrued at the date the offer was made;*

   (c)   *the deductible amounts that have subsequently accrued; and*

(2)   *be accompanied by a copy of the current certificate.*

OFFERS AND PAYMENTS BEFORE 6 APRIL 2007

[14.34]

Rule 7 of the Civil Procedure (Amendment No 3) Rules 2006 contained provisions that dealt with how the rules are to apply to offers and payments into court made before 6 April 2007. Practice Direction 36B (there is no Practice Direction 36A!) prescribes how those provisions operate.

[14.35]

Offers and Payments made before 6th April 2007

1.1   *Paragraph (2) of rule 7 provides that where a Part 36 offer or Part 36 payment was made before 6th April 2007, if it would have had the consequences set out in* the rules of court contained in Part 36 as it was in force immediately before 6th April 2007, it will have the consequences set out in rules 36.10, 36.11 and 36.14 after that date.

1.2 This provision makes clear that a Part 36 offer or Part 36 payment that was valid before 6th April 2007, will continue to be a valid Part 36 offer under the rules in force from 6th April 2007, and will have the consequences set out in those rules, specifically in relation to costs and the effect of acceptance.

[14.36]

Permission of the court

2.1 Paragraph (3) of rule 7 provides that where a Part 36 offer or Part 36 payment was made before 6th April 2007, the permission of the court is required to accept that offer or payment, if permission would have been required under the rules of court contained in Part 36 as it was in force immediately before 6th April 2007.

2.2 This provision preserves the requirement to obtain the permission of the court to accept an offer as it existed under the rules in force immediately before 6th April 2007. Therefore, if permission would have been required before 6th April 2007, it will be required after that date. But, if permission would not have been required because the parties have been able to agree liability for costs, or if a further offer has been made triggering a new period for acceptance, permission will not be required after 6th April 2007.

[14.37]

Payments into court made before 6th April 2007

3.1 Paragraph (4) of rule 7 provides that rule 37.3 will apply to a Part 36 payment made before 6th April 2007 as if that payment into court had been made under a court order.

3.2 Rule 37.3 applies to all payments under Part 37, including payments into court under order, and permission is required to take the money out of court.

3.3 By applying rule 37.3 to payments into court made before 6th April 2007, this provision preserves in particular the requirement that permission be obtained to withdraw such payment.

3.4 But, rule 37.3 also provides that money may be taken out of court without the court's permission where a Part 36 offer (including an offer underlying a Part 36 payment) is accepted without needing the permission of the court and the defendant agrees that the sum may be paid out in satisfaction of the offer. Paragraph 3.4 of the Practice Direction to Part 37 makes provision about how to take money out of court.

3.5 This exception to the permission requirement preserves the right under rule 37.2, as it was in force immediately before 6th April 2007, to treat a payment into court made under order or by way of a defence of tender before claim as a Part 36 payment.

3.6 This provision has the effect that a Part 36 payment made before 6th April 2007 may be taken out of court simply by filing a request for payment if the offer underlying the Part 36 payment is accepted without needing permission. In those circumstances, it may be assumed that the defendant agrees to the money being used in satisfaction of the sum offered, and the requirement in paragraph 3.4 of the Practice Direction to Part 37 to file a Form 202 will not apply.

[14.38]

Offers remaining open for acceptance

4.1   *Paragraph (5) of rule 7 provides that the rules of court contained in Part 36 as it was in force immediately before 6th April 2007 shall continue to apply to a Part 36 offer or Part 36 payment made less than 21 days before 6th April 2007.*

4.2   *This provision preserves those rules in their entirety in relation to offers and payments made less than 21 days before 6th April 2007 for the period that they are expressed to remain open for acceptance.*

4.3   *Paragraph (6) of rule 7 provides that paragraph (5) ceases to apply at the expiry of 21 days from the date that the offer or payment was made, unless the trial has started within that period.*

4.4   *This provision has the effect that once the 21 day period has expired, the new regime (including the modifications at paragraphs (2), (3) and (4) of rule 7) will apply to the offer or payment.*

4.5   *If the trial has started within the 21 day period, the rules that were in force before 6th April 2007 will continue to apply to the offer or payment.*

[14.39]

Offers made before commencement of proceedings

5.1   *Paragraph (7) of rule 7 deals with the position where, before 6th April 2007, a person made an offer to settle before commencement of proceedings which complied with the provisions of rule 36.10 as it was in force immediately before 6th April 2007.*

5.2   *The court will take that offer into account when making any order as to costs. This preserves the discretion of the court to take into account an offer made before commencement of proceedings as it existed before 6th April 2007.*

5.3   *The permission of the court will be required to accept such an offer after proceedings have been commenced. This preserves the position under rule 36.10(4) as it was in force immediately before 6th April 2007.*

5.4   *If proceedings are commenced after 6th April 2007, the requirement to pay money into court in respect of a defendant's money offer under rule 36.10(3)(a) (as it was in force before 6th April 2007) will not an apply to a defendant's money offer made before the proceedings were commenced.*

OTHER OFFERS

[14.40]

CPR Part 36 is only half of the story of offers to settle. It is important to remember that rule 36.1(2) (see para [14.5]) provides that a party may make an offer to settle in whatever way he chooses, but if the offer is not made in accordance with Part 36 it will not have the costs consequences specified in rules 36.10, 36.11 and 36.14. It emphasises that in deciding what order to make about costs rule 44.3(4)(c) (see para [11.6]) requires the court to have regard to any admissible offer which does not have the costs consequences of Part 36.

Calderbank letters

[14.41]

Since 1975 a frequently used alternative to a payment into court has been an offer contained in a *Calderbank* letter even though it may not have had the same costs consequences. It is called *'Calderbank'* because it is a form of offer first approved by the Court of Appeal in *Calderbank v Calderbank* [1975] 3 All ER 333, and this is still a useful description. It is an offer made 'Without prejudice save as to costs'. The magic words are 'save as to costs' as was demonstrated in *Reed Executive plc v Reed Business Information Ltd* [2004] EWCA Civ 887. The defendants had made offers in privileged meetings and in 'without prejudice' correspondence on which they sought to rely on the question of costs. Disaster! The court could not look at the correspondence. In its judgment the Court of Appeal said: 'Parties may negotiate in the faith and expectation that the negotiations cannot be used against them even on the question of costs unless the negotiations are expressly stated to be 'without prejudice save as to costs'. Magic words indeed.

Even though offers no longer have to be accompanied by a payment into court there are still many circumstances in which a defendant may consider it advantageous to make a *Calderbank* offer rather than one which complies with Part 36. Some of these are:

– if the defendant cannot raise the money in a single sum or within the prescribed 14 days;
– to make a walk-away offer, or what I am assured is known as a 'Mexican Stand-off';
– to make a package of proposals;
– to offer to do remedial work;
– to make an apology;
– to offer to do further business; and
– in a multi-party action.

Cases

[14.42]

The approach of the court is still illustrated by cases decided before 6 April 2007

Farag v Metropolitan Police Comr [2006] CA Solicitors Journal 27 January was a claim for damages for wrongful arrest, false imprisonment, malfeasance in public office and for assaults. The defendant had made an offer to settle the matter in 1997 at a stage when minimal costs had been incurred. The offer was withdrawn two years before the trial. The judge had failed to exercise his discretion on costs correctly because he had failed to give any reasons for not taking the offer into consideration when awarding costs. He should have had regard to the offer at the time of the trial and after the coming into force of the CPR. An offer made by letter in appropriate circumstances is be taken into account and treated as a CPR Part 36 offer and the fact that it was withdrawn did not deprive it of effect.

In *Codent Ltd v Lyson Ltd* [2005] EWCA Civ 1835, [2005] All ER (D) 138 (Dec) 8 December the defendant company made a *Calderbank* offer of £100,000 in full and final settlement of the claim, offered to waive its counterclaim of £81,000 and to pay the costs of the action. The claimant refused the offer and although successful in its claim recovered substantially less then the defendant's offer. The costs judge was wrong to rule that the defendant should get no benefit from its offer because it could have made a Part 36 payment in to court. He had been in error to proceed on the basis that either the offer had full effect or no effect at all. He did not consider whether an intermediate position was possible and as such he erred in principle. Account had to be taken of the fact that the offer was not made more than 21 days before the trial and that it was not left open for 21 days. The correct order in light of the offer was that the claimant should have 70% of its costs of the action up to the first day of the trial and the defendant have its costs thereafter.

In *Jackson v Ministry of Defence* [2006] EWCA Civ 46, [2006] All ER (D) 14 (Jan) the claimant had issued proceedings for personal injury against the MoD for injury suffered during a training exercise. He advanced substantial claims for damages for future loss of earnings and for specially adapted accommodation based on his account of his residual disability. The medical evidence did not support the claim of residual disability and those claims were eventually abandoned, reducing his claim from over £1 million to £240,000. The MoD made a CPR Part 36 payment into court in the sum of £150,000. Damages of £155,000 were awarded and the Court of Appeal upheld the judge's reduction of the claimant's costs by 25% to reflect the fact that the award had only just beaten the payment into court and the fact the claimant had exaggerated his evidence. The reduction that the judge made in costs and the likely reduction at the detailed assessment were likely to act as a disincentive to claimants who sought to make exaggerated claims. The order made was well within the judge's wide discretion.

E Ivor Hughes Educational Foundation v Leach [2005] EWHC 1317 (Ch), [2005] All ER (D) 127 (Jun) demonstrated the disadvantage of not being able to make a Part 36 offer and payment with a denial of liability. The defendant was accused, among other things, of fiddling his expenses to the tune of £87,000, which he denied but paid £5,000 into court in order to dispose of this head of claim. The claimant accepted the offer but the judge directed that the employment tribunal in the defendant's claim for wrongful dismissal could construe the payment as an admission of liability in relation to making false expenses claims. Sarah Murray in the New Law Journal of 14 October 2005 suggested that this could justify making a *Calderbank* offer with a denial of liability rather than a payment-in, while in the Solicitor's Journal of 20 January 2006, Jonathan Brogden agreed with her but conjectured how the judge could have equated a payment into court with an admission of liability – especially as Lord Devlin in *A Martin French v Kingswood Hill Ltd* [1961] 1 QB 96 had said it wasn't!

In *Amber v Stacey* [2001] 2 All ER 88, CA, after the commencement of proceedings, the defendant wrote offering £4,000 plus costs but made no payment into court. In August 1998, the defendant paid in £2,000 and this was topped up to £3,000 in January 1999. At the trial in April 1999, the claimant was awarded £2,300. The judge concluded the claimant had acted unreasonably in refusing the original offer of £4,000 and awarded the defendant his costs from that date. The Court of Appeal held that the judge was wrong to award the defendant his full costs of the period before the payment into court of £3,000. He had ignored the important difference between a Part 36 offer and a Part 36 payment. Nevertheless, because of the claimant's unreasonableness, it was appropriate to award the defendant half his costs for the period before the payment in. The court identified the following advantages of payments into court: (a) genuineness; (b) the offeror's ability to pay; (c) whether the offer is open or without prejudice and (d) the terms on which the dispute can be settled. Simon Brown LJ said: 'They are clearly to be encouraged, and written offers, although obviously relevant, should not be treated as precise equivalents'. Commenting on the decision, Jeremy Morgan QC observed that despite extolling the virtues of payments into court, the decision in fact eroded the difference between an offer and a payment in. He wrote 'It is certainly not safe for a claimant's solicitor to ignore an offer in a situation where a payment could have been made, and advise his client to wait until there is a payment in'. Prophetic words.

SMALL CLAIMS TRACK

[14.43]

Although Part 36 does not apply to the small claims track (Rule 27.2) there is no reason why a party to a small claim should not make an offer which could be taken into account when awarding costs and disbursements.

EMPLOYMENT TRIBUNALS

[14.44]

An offer is a factor that the Employment Tribunal may take into account in deciding whether to make a costs order in accordance with Rule 14 of the Employment Tribunals Rules of Procedure, but failure to achieve an award in excess of the offer is not conclusive. The Employment Tribunal must also be satisfied that the conduct of the applicant in rejecting the offer was unreasonable (*Kopel v Safeway Stores plc* [2003] IRLR 753, EAT).

CHAPTER 15

FAMILY PROCEEDINGS

CIVIL PROCEDURE RULES

[15.1]

For many weeks during the spring of 1999 it appeared that from 26 April, where there had previously been provision for costs in family proceedings there would just be a gaping hole, because from that date RSC Ord 62 and CCR Ord 38 would be replaced by the Civil Procedure Rules 1998 which did not apply to family proceedings. We were confident that, as in all good B movies, we should be rescued at the stroke of midnight, and of course we were, but not in the way that most of us expected. Instead of the existing costs provisions for family proceedings (The Matrimonial Causes (Costs) Rules 1988) being preserved whilst there was a period of consultation preparatory to the introduction of a regime of costs tailor-made for family proceedings, they were revoked and the costs provisions of the CPR were simply superimposed onto family work, with one inspirational adaptation. Wherever the CPR used the word 'claimant' or 'defendant', this was to be treated as a reference to petitioner, applicant or respondent. Just think of the midnight oil that must have been burnt in devising that!

THE FAMILY PROCEEDINGS (MISCELLANEOUS AMENDMENTS) RULES 1999

[15.2]

This is how it was done. Parts 43 to 48 of the CPR were applied to family proceedings with these exceptions:
(a)   *Rule 44.3(2)* (The general rule that costs follow the event, but see below)
(b)   *Rules 44.9–44.11* (Relating to the small claims and fast tracks which of course do not apply in family proceedings)
(c)   *Rule 44.12* (Costs orders deemed to have been made, such as where notice of discontinuance is served or money in court is accepted. Again, not appropriate for family proceedings)
(d)   *Part 45* (Fixed costs)
(e)   *Part 46* (Fast track trial costs)

DIRECTIONS

[15.3]

The new costs rules were accompanied by a Practice Direction of 22 April 1999 ([1999] 3 All ER 192, Fam). Here it is:

[15.4]

PRACTICE DIRECTION (FAMILY DIVISION: ALLOCATION OF CASES: COSTS)

It is directed that upon the coming into force on 26 April 1999 of the Civil Procedure Rules (CPR) and the Family Proceedings (Miscellaneous Amendments) Rules 1999, SI 1999/1012:

(a)   [Not relevant to costs]
(b)   The Practice Direction about costs supplementing CPR, Pts 43 to 48 (the costs direction) shall apply to family proceedings to which the Family Proceedings Rules 1991, SI 1991/1247, apply and to proceedings in the Family Division. References in the costs direction to 'claimant' and 'defendant' are to be read as references to the equivalent terms used in family proceedings and other terms and expressions used in the costs direction shall be similarly treated. References to procedural steps and to other parts of the CPR which have not yet been applied to family proceedings are to be read as referring to equivalent or similar procedures under the rules applicable to family proceedings, as the context may permit. The previous practice in relation to 'costs reserved' will no longer be followed and such an order will have the effect specified in the costs direction. It should also be noted that the period for commencing detailed assessment proceedings will be as specified in CPR, r 47.7 (three months) in substitution for the period of six months previously applicable.

Issued with the approval and concurrence of the Lord Chancellor.

Sir Stephen Brown

[15.5]

It applied to family proceedings all of the Practice Directions supplementing CPR Parts 43 to 48; as previously noted, it substituted the family equivalent for 'claimant' and 'defendant'; at long last the term 'costs reserved' was given the same meaning as in civil proceedings (see para [16.8]) and there was further unification by the substitution of 'three months' for the period in which a detailed assessment must be commenced for the previous 'six months' in family proceedings.

The 1999 Direction was supplemented on 24 July 2000 as follows:

[15.6]

PRACTICE DIRECTION (FAMILY DIVISION: COSTS: CIVIL PROCEDURE RULES 1998)

The President's Practice Direction (Family Division: allocation of cases: costs) ([1999] 3 All ER 192, [1999] 1 WLR 1128) dated 22 April 1999 applied the (Civil Procedure) Practice Direction about costs supplementing Parts 43 to 48 of the Civil Procedure Rules (the costs direction) to family proceedings (within the Family Proceedings Rules 1991, SI 1991/1247) and to proceedings in the Family Division. A further edition of the costs direction (effective from 3 July 2000) has been published and it is hereby directed that the further edition (and all subsequent editions as and when they are published and come into effect) shall extend to family proceedings and to proceedings in the Family Division in the same way as did the costs direction and to the extent applicable to such proceedings.

The further edition of the costs direction includes provisions applicable to proceedings following changes in the manner in which legal services are funded pursuant to the Access to Justice Act 1999. It should be noted that although the costs of the premium in respect of legal costs insurance (s 29), and all the costs of funding by a prescribed membership organisation (s 30) may be recoverable, family proceedings (within s 58A(2) of the Courts and Legal Services Act 1990) cannot be the subject of an enforceable conditional fee agreement.

Issued with the approval of the Lord Chancellor.

Dame Elizabeth Butler-Sloss

COSTS FOLLOWING THE EVENT

(a) Costs do not follow the event

[15.7]

As we have seen, the Family Proceedings (Miscellaneous Amendment) Rules 1999 provide that CPR Rule 44.3(2) shall not apply in family proceedings. This covers both the costs of the suit and the costs of ancillary proceedings. A between-the-parties order for costs of the suit may be inappropriate when the petition is based on two years' separation and consent or five years' separation. In a consent petition the petitioner often claims costs, or half of the costs. If the respondent agrees, there is no problem. If the respondent is not willing to pay the costs claimed, he or she should refuse to consent until the claim for costs is withdrawn or agreed. In other petitions a helpful device is to include a prayer for costs 'only if the suit is defended'.

(b) The cases

[15.8]

Nevertheless, in *Gojkovic v Gojkovic (No 2)* [1992] Fam 40, CA it was held that even in the Family Division the starting point has to be that costs on the face of it follow the event, although the presumption might be more easily displaced and in circumstances which did not apply in other Divisions of the High Court. One important example was that it was unusual to order costs in Children Act cases. Indeed, in family matters it is often difficult to identify an 'event' which costs might follow.

However, there does not have to be an identifiable event to justify an award of costs. In *Hurley v Hurley* [1998] 2 FCR 14, CA the Court of Appeal held that the judge had misdirected himself in refusing to order a respondent husband to pay the costs of his mother-in-law who had intervened in order to preserve her alleged beneficial interest in the matrimonial home. When the husband conceded that the home should not be sold and that the petitioner could continue to live there, it was no longer necessary for the mother-in-law to pursue her claim because her daughter was happy for her to continue living with her. The judge took the view that as the mother-in-law had not pursued her claim to adjudication, she had neither won nor lost and therefore there was no event in respect of which the court could found an order for costs against the husband. He was wrong: he should have approached the matter on the basis of whether it was reasonable in the circumstances for the intervener to intervene and, if so, whether she unnecessarily or unreasonably added to the costs of the proceedings? The judge had greatly fettered the exercise of his judicial discretion by propounding a principle for which there was no authority. I hope it will not undermine your confidence in this book when I confess that I was the judge.

Three more cases illustrate the approach of the courts. In *Re G (a child) (costs: child case)* [1999] 3 FCR 463, CA the Court of Appeal held that 'it was unusual to order costs in a family case, although it would be appropriate to order costs where a parent, even a litigant in person, went beyond the limit of what was reasonable to pursue the application before the court'. Even though the judge had found the father's case to be hopeless, the court held that hopelessness and unreasonableness were not necessarily the same thing. Furthermore, a greater degree of generosity might be appropriate in ruling that pursuing an application had become unreasonable where the litigant was acting in person rather than where he was receiving legal advice. In *Re W (a child)* (26 August 2000, unreported), CA on the father's application to vary an order for residence with the mother, the judge confirmed the existing arrangements, extended staying contact and ordered the father to pay the costs, commenting that the proceedings had been long and protracted and that the mother had been the successful party. In allowing the father's appeal against the order for costs, the court said the judge had not criticised the father's motives or provided any other readily discernible reason for departing from the normal rule in private family law cases that each party should pay its own costs. It is essential that between-the-parties costs orders should only ever be made in exceptional cases where a party had been guilty of manipulating the litigation for their own ends rather than advancing a case which they genuinely believed to be in the best interests of the child. The third case, *Re B (costs)* [1999] 3 FCR 586, CA demonstrated that although it is rare to make costs orders in Children Act cases, the rule is not invariable. The mother had suffered from a serious manic depressive illness as a result of which the child resided with the father, who opposed the mother's application for staying contact because of his fear the mother might have a relapse which could put the child at risk. The mother produced evidence from a psychiatric consultant that the child would not be at any risk, but the father was unwilling to accept this even when a psychiatrist instructed by him agreed with the mother's psychiatrist. The Court of Appeal held the judge was right to take the view that from the date that the two psychiatrists reached agreement the father should have withdrawn his opposition to staying contact and therefore ordered him to pay the mother's costs from that date, and that the judge was also correct in assessing the costs of the father's continued and unjustified opposition at 80% of the costs of the hearing. If I now reveal that I was also the judge in that case I hope it may restore some of your confidence in me!

ANCILLARY RELIEF

(a) Duty to negotiate

[15.9]

*Gojkovic (above)*also established that where the assets are substantial and where an order for costs, if appropriate, could be made, negotiations which might lead to a settlement were to be encouraged by the courts. For a *Calderbank* offer (a 'without prejudice' offer to settle) to be effective it required teeth and 'it was incumbent on the recipient of an offer to accept or reject it and, if the latter, to make (her) position clear and indicate in figures what (she) is asking for (a counter-offer). It is incumbent on both parties to negotiate if possible and at least make an attempt to settle the case'.

(b) False teeth

[15.10]

With a view to 'giving teeth' to *Calderbank* offers, CCR Order 11 rule 10, which related to *Calderbank* offers in civil proceedings, was applied to ancillary relief by a new FPR 2.69 in October 1992. On 5 June 2000 in the light of eight years' experience the procedure was codified and expanded in new FPR 2.69A to E. Whether because of defects in the new rules or the way in which they were applied, or perhaps because they highlighted underlying flaws in the system itself, they have not worked. In the words of Thorpe LJ: 'The innovation was not well received and did not stand up to hard wear and tear'. Nicholas Mostyn QC did not believe 'these rules say what we intended them to say'. In *GW v RW* [2003] EWHC 611 (Fam), [2003] 2 FCR 289, Mr Mostyn, sitting as a deputy High Court judge, held that the rules were incomprehensible and that where both parties had made *Calderbank* offers, became unworkable. He identified two problems in particular. The first was the destabilising effect that costs can have on financial settlements that have been carefully constructed by the court. Having considered the facts and circumstances of a case the court arrives at a settlement that, in its judgment, does justice between the parties. At the conclusion of some cases it is revealed to the court that one party has failed to 'beat' a *Calderbank* offer, the consequences of which could undermine completely the substantive order for ancillary relief that the court had just made. This stems from *Calderbank* offers not being brought to the attention of the court until all matters have been determined and the court is considering the issue of costs. The second problem identified by Mr Mostyn was that the system of closed offers had introduced a degree of procedural gamesmanship which lead to uncertainty and had introduced an undesirable element of gambling into ancillary relief proceedings. *Calderbank* offers had been likened to a form of spread betting. The result could be disproportionate and produce unfairness not only in big money cases but also where modest sums were involved.

(c) The Senior Costs Judge writes

[15.11]

The view that the approach of the courts in family financial matters needed reconsideration was reinforced by a letter to the President from the Senior Costs Judge shortly after the SCCO took over the assessment of costs in family proceedings. He wrote: "It is apparent that whereas in non-family civil proceedings the resolution of the substantive dispute frequently takes the heat out of any animosity between the parties, and enables settlement of the costs to be achieved in a significant number of cases, in family proceedings that animosity, which is in any event likely to be at a very high level, continues unabated during the assessment proceedings. The successful spouse on one side vows to bleed the other dry of every penny if at all possible, whilst the paying spouse goes out of his or her way to deny the other the possibility of any recovery. The number of settlements in assessments arising out of family proceedings is very low . . . It may be worth giving serious thought to doing away with fee shifting in family proceedings. The Family Proceedings (Miscellaneous Amendment) Rules 1991 disapply CPR 44.3(2) (costs follow the event). It is therefore a relatively short step to providing that in family proceedings no order for costs will be made unless a particular party has behaved in such an unreasonable manner that the court feels that a sanction should be imposed."

(d) The matrimonial pot

[15.12]

In October 2004, the Department for Constitutional Affairs, in collaboration with the President's Ancillary Relief Advisory Group published a Consultation Paper *Costs in Ancillary Relief Proceedings and Appeals in Family Proceedings*. The Consultation Paper included a draft statutory instrument making amendments to FPR, r 2.69 on offers to settle and inserting a new FPR, r 2.71 on costs in ancillary relief proceedings. The principal objective was to establish a clear general rule in ancillary relief proceedings that the court should make no order for costs, unless there had been "unreasonable conduct" in relation to the proceedings, by one of the parties. It was envisaged that as a result, the role of *Calderbank* offers in ancillary relief proceedings would be ended. The new philosophy was to move the costs regime in ancillary relief proceedings further away from the classic 'costs follow the event' approach in civil litigation and to enable the court to include consideration of costs as part of the overall settlement of the parties' financial affairs. Justice would be better served by dealing with costs as part of the substantive application rather than treating costs as a separate issue. Absent misconduct, costs would be paid out of the matrimonial 'pot' and the court would then divide the remainder between the parties. The new regime was introduced by the Family Proceedings (Amendment) Rules 2006 on 3 April 2006.

(e) Two regimes

[15.13]

The new regime applies only where the application for ancillary relief is made on or after 3 April 2006. Where a petition for divorce filed before 3 April contains an application for ancillary relief and the respondent applies for ancillary relief on or after 3 April the old regime will apply. However, where an application is made on or after 3 April 2006 for a variation order in relation to an order made prior to 3 April 2006, the new regime will apply. Accordingly in this edition of the book it is necessary to deal with both the old and the new.

(f) Pre-3 April 2006

[15.14]

The Family Proceedings (Amendment No 2) Rules 1999, which came into force on 5 June 2000, amended the Family Proceedings Rules 1991 in respect of the costs of ancillary relief proceedings. They contained some surprising provisions about the costs consequences of offers to settle. Rule 2.69 is replaced and followed by new Rules 2.69A–2.69D relating to costs. Rule 2.69 provides:

[15.15]

FPR Rule 2.69: Offers to settle
(1)   Either party to the application may at any time make a written offer to the other party which is expressed to be 'without prejudice except as to costs' and which relates to any issue in the proceedings relating to the application.
(2)   Where an offer is made under paragraph (1), the fact that such an offer has been made shall not be communicated to the court, except in accordance with rule 2.61E(3), until the question of costs falls to be decided.

[15.16]

Nothing surprising there. Rule 2.69B provides:

[15.17]

FPR Rule 2.69B: Judgment or order more advantageous than an offer made by the other party
(1)   This rule applies where the judgment or order in favour of the applicant or respondent is more advantageous to him than an offer made under rule 2.69(1) by the other party.
(2)   The court must, unless it considers it unjust to do so, order that other party to pay any costs incurred after the date beginning 28 days after the offer was made.

[15.18]

There are some curious omissions. Rule 2.69B penalises a party who does not do as well as his own without prejudice offer but does not confer any corresponding benefit on that party if he does as well or better than his offer. He (or, of course, she) is on a hiding to nothing. The rule appears to deter the making of offers rather than to encourage them. Another omission is any provision requiring there to be a response to an offer, either by accepting it or making a counter-offer, in accordance with the principles laid down in *Gojkovic*

[15.19]

FPR Rule 2.69C: Judgment or order more advantageous than offers made by both parties

This rule introduced the surprising concept in ancillary relief proceedings that where both parties had made an offer and one party obtained an order better than both offers (ie had beaten their own offer) the court could award them enhanced interest on their claim and order costs to be paid on the indemnity basis. The practical consequence was the reverse of what was no doubt intended, not only was the rule too complicated and complex, but unless a wife was supremely confident about the amount she would receive, she was unwise to respond to any offer and thereby incur the risk of triggering the sanctions under the rule. It was accepted that rule 2.69C did not work and on 24 February 2003 it was removed, together with the superfluous rule 2.69A. Rule 2.69D provides:

[15.20]

FPR Rule 2.69D: Factors for court's consideration under Rule 2.69b

In considering whether it would be unjust, or whether it would be just, to make the orders referred to in rule 2.69B, the court must take into account all the circumstances of the case, including—

    (a)   the terms of any offers made under rule 2.69(1);

    (b)   the stage in the proceedings when any offer was made;

    (c)   the information available to the parties at the time when the offer was made;

    (d)   the conduct of the parties with regard to the giving or refusing to give information for the purposes of enabling the offer to be made or evaluated; and

    (e)   the respective means of the parties.

[15.21]

Making an offer is one of the factors prescribed in rule 2.69D as being relevant to an award of costs, as indeed it is in CPR Rule 44.3(4). Family practitioners now have to take into account two costs regimes when advising whether or not a Calderbank offer should be made or responded to and at what level it should be pitched. The provisions appear unnecessarily to undermine and confuse the culture of negotiation and settlement which had operated so successfully in family matters from long before the introduction of the Woolf reforms in civil litigation. Nevertheless the Court of Appeal has said that by applying CPR Rule 44.3 where there is no Calderbank offer and integrating FPR 2.69 into it where there is one, the remaining rules 2.69B and 2.69D are 'not unworkable'.

Rule 2.69E provides:

[15.22]

FPR Rule 2.69E: Open proposals

(1) Not less than 14 days before the date fixed for the final hearing of an application for ancillary relief, the applicant must (unless the court directs otherwise) file with the court and serve on the respondent an open statement which sets out concise details, including the amounts involved, of the orders which he proposes to ask the court to make.

(2) Not more than 7 days after service of a statement under paragraph (1), the respondent must file with the court and serve on the applicant an open statement which sets out concise details, including the amounts involved, of the orders which he proposes to ask the court to make.

[15.23]

Although rule 2.69E requires the parties to make open offers, there are conflicting decisions (such as *Singer v Sharegin* [1984] FLR 114, CA; *H v H* [1998] 2 FCR 27, Fam and *Leadbeater v Leadbeater* [1985] FLR 789, CA) as to whether the court should decide on the award and amount of costs before making its final decision about the family assets.

A PRACTICAL APPROACH

[15.24]

In *C v C (costs: ancillary relief)* [2003] EWHC 2321 (Fam), [2004] 1 FLR 291, Mr Justice Charles gave guidance on a 'practical approach' to costs in ancillary relief cases as follows:

(1) Ask who would or should have paid the costs if agreement had been reached at an early stage, and why this was so. The answer to this question will often identify who should be regarded as the paying party or the person who should prima facie be liable for costs. Also the answer to this may often support the view that up to a certain point, prima facie, one party should pay the costs of the other.

(2) Identify the issues that are not in dispute at trial and the issues that have prevented an agreement being reached, and consider their impact on the question of costs:
    (i)   their nature and whether the reality is that one party is going to be paying the other or whether there is a division of the assets;
    (ii)   the time taken in resolving the disputed issues;
    (iii) who won on such issues.

(3) Consider the *Calderbank* offers, and therefore apply FPR 1991 rule 2.69.

(4) Consider the matters referred to in CPR Rule 44.3 (which include open offers).

(5) Consider how the costs of both parties have been affected by the disputed issues.

(6) Remember that the court has a judicial discretion.

(g) On and after 3 April 2006

(i) The Family Proceedings (Amendment) Rules 2006

[15.25]

The new rules sought to attain the objectives of the consultation paper by rescinding FPR 2.69, 2.69B and 2.69D and replacing them with a new Rule 2.71 as follows:

[15.26]

FPR 2.71

(1)   CPR rule 44.3(1) to (5) shall not apply to ancillary relief proceedings.

(2)   CPR rules 44.3(6) to (9) apply to an order made under this rule as they apply to an order made under CPR rule 44.3.

(3)   In this rule "costs" has the same meaning as in CPR rule 43.2(I)(a) and includes the costs payable by a client to his solicitor.

(4)

(a)   The general rule in ancillary relief proceedings is that the court will not make an order requiring one party to pay the costs of another party; but

(b)   the court may make such an order at any stage of the proceedings where it considers it appropriate to do because of the conduct of a party in relation to the proceedings (whether before or during them).

(5)   In deciding what order (if any) to make under paragraph (4)(b), the court must have regard to—

(a)   any failure by a party to comply with these Rules, any order of the court or any practice direction which the court considers relevant;

(b)   any open offer to settle made by a party;

(c)   whether it was reasonable for a party to raise, pursue or contest a particular allegation or issue;

(d)   the manner in which a party has pursued or responded to the application or a particular allegation or issue;

(e)   any other aspect of a party's conduct in relation to the proceedings which the court considers relevant; and

(f)   the financial effect on the parties of any costs order.

(6)   No offer to settle which is not an open offer to settle shall be admissible at any stage of the proceedings, except as provided by rule 2.61 E.

(ii) President's Practice Direction

[15.27]

The new provisions were helpfully summarised in the President's accompanying practice direction:

[15.28]

1.   The Family Proceedings (Amendment) Rules 2006 make significant changes to the court's power to make costs orders in ancillary relief proceedings. The new rules will come into force on 3rd April 2006. They will apply to an application for ancillary relief contained in a petition or answer filed on or after 3rd April 2006, or to such an application which has not been made in a petition or answer but is made

in Form A on or after that date. The rules will also apply to an application under s 10(2) of the Matrimonial Causes Act 1973 or under s 48(2) of the Civil Partnership Act 2004 made in Form B on or after that date. They do not however apply to such applications if they are to be heard by the court with an application which was made before that date.

2. Under the new rules the court will only have power to make a costs order in ancillary relief proceedings when this is justified by the litigation conduct of one of the parties (see new rule 2.71 of the Family Proceedings Rules 1991). When determining whether and how to exercise this power the court will be required to take into account the list of factors set out in the rules. The court will no longer be able to take into account any offers to settle expressed to be "without prejudice" or "without prejudice save as to costs" in deciding what, if any, costs order to make.

3. The new rules require the completion of Forms H and H1 (see rule 2.61 F of the Family Proceedings Rules 1991, as amended). Form H is to be used at interim hearings so that the court has available to it a realistic estimate of the costs incurred to date. Form H1 is for use at a final hearing to provide the court with accurate details of the costs which each party has incurred, or expects to incur, in relation to the ancillary relief proceedings. The purpose of this form is to enable the court to take account of the impact of each party's costs liability on their financial situations. Parties should ensure that the information contained in these forms is as full and accurate as possible and that any sums already paid in respect of a party's ancillary relief costs are clearly set out. Where relevant, any liability arising from the costs of other proceedings between the parties should continue to be referred to in the appropriate section of a party's Form E; any such costs should not be included in Forms H or H1.

4. Parties who intend to seek a costs order against another party in proceedings to which rule 2.71 of the Family Proceedings Rules 1991 applies should ordinarily make this plain in open correspondence or in skeleton arguments before the date of the hearing. In any case where summary assessment of costs awarded under rule 2.71 of the Family Proceedings Rules 1991 would be appropriate parties are under an obligation to file a statement of costs in CPR Form N260 (see CPR Practice Direction supplementing Parts 43 to 48 (Costs), Section 13 and paragraph 6 below).

5. An order for maintenance pending suit which includes an element to allow a party to deal with legal fees (see *A v A (maintenance pending suit: provision for legal fees)* [2001] 1 WLR 605; *G v G (maintenance pending suit: costs)* [2002] EWHC 306 (Fam), [2002] 3 FCR 339; *McFarlane v McFarlane, Parlour v Parlour* [2004] EWCA Civ 872, [2005] Fam 171; *Moses-Taiga v Taiga* [2005] EWCA Civ 1013, [2006] 1 FLR 1074) is an order made pursuant to s 22 of the Matrimonial Causes Act 1973, and is not a "costs order" within the meaning of rule 2.71 of the Family Proceedings Rules 1991.

6. The President's Direction: Civil Procedure Rules 1998: Allocation of Cases: Costs dated 22nd April 1999 (as supplemented by the President's Direction: Costs: Civil Procedure Rules 1998 dated 24th July 2000) makes provision in relation to the application of the (Civil Procedure) Practice Direction about costs (Supplementing Parts 43 to 48 of the Civil Procedure Rules) to family proceedings to which the Family Proceedings Rules 1991 apply. Those President's Directions apply to a costs order made under new rule 2.71 of the Family Proceedings Rules 1 991 as though the reference to the (Civil Procedure) Practice Direction was a reference to that direction excluding Section 6, Paragraphs 8.1 to 8.4 and Sections 15 and 16.

20 February 2006

[15.29]

Did the new rules in fact abolish *Calderbank* offers and between-the-parties costs orders?

The answer to both questions is 'no'.

(iii) *Calderbank* offers

[15.30]

Although rule 2.71 makes inadmissible offers which are not open, it permits their admission on Financial Dispute Resolution hearings under rule 2.61E. They carry no costs sanction and therefore if privilege is sought the mere heading 'Without Prejudice' will suffice. The district judge is able to comment on the privileged offers, and to observe perhaps, that a wholly inappropriate open offer to settle may result in a departure from the general rule of no costs order. At this stage, and indeed during any subsequent proceedings, there may be two separate strands of negotiation with more generous proposals contained in privileged correspondence which will be admissible before the district judge at the FDR hearing but not before any other judge. Parties may therefore continue to make privileged offers in negotiations more favourable than those known to the court but if settlement is not reached, the offers will have no costs consequences.. However, the fundamental change was that at the final hearing all the cards are on the table, with the parties' total liability for costs and the offers they have made being known to the judge before deciding what financial orders to make.

(iv) *Between-the-parties costs orders*

[15.31]

On the face of it between-the-parties costs orders have also gone. Paragraph (4)(a) of Rule 2.71 says so.
But the sting is in paragraph (4)(b):

> 'The court may make an order between the parties at any stage of the proceedings where it considers it appropriate to do because of the conduct of a party in relation to the proceedings (whether before or during them).'

1. *No misconduct*

[15.32]

If there is no litigation misconduct the costs are governed by paragraph (4)(a). So, does the court look at the total solicitor and client costs of each party, add them both together, deduct their total from the family assets and then proceed to share between the parties what the lawyers have left for them?
There are two schools of thought.

[15.33]

(a) Costs out of the pot. In the red corner is the consultation paper on *Costs in Ancillary Relief Proceedings* which it is important to remember was produced not only by the Department for Constitutional Affairs but also by

the illustrious President's Ancillary Relief Advisory Group and its Costs sub-committee. Paragraph 27 is unambiguous: 'The purpose of applying a 'no order for costs' principle in ancillary relief proceedings is to stress to the parties, and to their legal advisers, that running up costs in litigation will serve only to reduce the resources that the parties will have left to support them in their new lives apart. The proposed amendments to the costs rules are designed to establish the principle that, in the absence of litigation misconduct, the normal approach of the court to costs in ancillary relief proceedings should be to treat them as part of the parties' reasonable financial needs and liabilities. *Costs will have to paid from the matrimonial 'pot' and the court will then divide the remainder between the parties.* (My italics)

On this approach there are problems:

– there is no control over the costs a party could claim out of the matrimonial pot. Solicitor and client costs are on the indemnity basis to which the test of proportionality does not apply and if the client accepts their solicitor's costs, those costs cannot be challenged on the grounds of being unreasonable. The client is contractually bound to pay them. So how could they be reduced even if either the court or the other party objects to the amount claimed coming out of the pot?

– where is the incentive for a party to control their legal costs if half are in effect to be paid by the other spouse?

– what if one party is economical and the other is not ? Should the economical party have to subsidise the other? David Burrows in *The New Ancillary Relief Costs Regime* gives the example of family assets of £1 million, with the husband having incurred costs of £100,000 and the wife £50,000. If the costs are deducted before the net assets of £850,000 are divided 50/50, the wife will pay £25,000 of the husband's costs. And if the wife is to receive 60% of the assets she will on this basis pay £40,000 of the husband's costs.

– is there any incentive for a party to act in person to reduce costs if the other party has legal representation paid out of the pot?

– each of these factors gives rise to what have been described as 'back-door adverse costs orders' and 'standing justice on her head'. Only if you adopt what has been called the *Leadbetter* technique – Mr Justice Balcombe in *Leadbetter v Leadbetter* [1989] Family Law Reports 789 – and deal with the gross assets – notionally writing back any costs already paid – do you arrive at the position of each party paying their own costs out of their share of the assets.

[15.34]

(b) Individual debts. In the blue corner we have Judge Martin Cardinal and District Judge Simon Middleton in the second edition of *Matrimonial Costs* who quote Lord Justice Wilson that the proper treatment of liabilities for costs under the new regime will generally be that they are debts to which the judge should have regard in making his substantive award. In other words, the court must first apply the s 25 criteria to all the available assets and it is then for each party to discharge their own costs together with any other debts out of their share of the family assets, subject, of course, to the court taking into account all of a party's liabilities in determining what is a fair division of the family assets according to traditional practice.

But even this approach has its difficulties. If a party's liability for costs is to be taken out of the equation altogether and treated as a personal debt to be paid out of their share of the assets, this can drive a coach and horses through a needs-based order. Cardinal and Middleton give the example of a mother who needs £150,000 to re-house herself and her two children but has a costs liability of £20,000. Does she get the £170,000 she needs? If she does it is another back-door order for costs in the guise of a needs based asset division.

If liability for costs is to be taken into account as a debt in sharing the assets, what if one party has incurred twice the costs of the other? Should the court look behind the solicitor and client screen and hold a mini Solicitors Act assessment and for the purposes of s 25 ignore any costs above the amount it regards as reasonable – perhaps the amount of the costs of the other party? If so we are into retrospective costs capping.

[15.35]

(c) Half-way house? There is, I suggest, a possible halfway house between the two positions of either the costs of both parties being deducted from the family assets before applying the s 25 factors on the one hand and on the other hand applying the s 25 factors to the whole of the assets, leaving each party to pay their legal fees out of their own share. At the outset of the proceedings the court could give an indication of (or the parties might even agree) the amount of costs each party is likely to receive out of the pot before the remaining assets are shared between them. In that way, the parties and their legal advisers would know from the start how much of their costs they will recover out of the pot and that any costs above that amount will have to come out of their share of the family assets.

This approach could even lead to a matrix of predictable or benchmark costs to be charged against the matrimonial assets for each stage of the ancillary relief proceedings. The amount could be geared to the value of the matrimonial assets and the complexity of the issues, leaving each party free to incur additional solicitor and client costs out of their own share of the assets if they so choose.

Until the Court of Appeal declares the red corner or the blue corner or some half-way house to be the winner, the 'no order for costs' principle should be treated with great caution.

2. Misconduct in the proceedings

[15.36]

The starting presumption identified in *Gojkovic* (above) that even in matrimonial matters costs follow the event having been replaced by the general rule the court will not order costs between the parties (Rule 2.71(4)(a)), what difference will this make in practice? Paragraph (b) of the rule provides that the court may make such an order if it considers the conduct of a party in relation to the proceedings (litigation, not matrimonial, misconduct), both before (for example failure to comply with the pre-action protocol) and during them, makes it appropriate to do so. It then lists the matters to which the court must have regard in deciding whether to make an order and they look remarkably like the usual suspects under the old regime – including offers to settle, failure to comply with the rules, practice direction or court order, and unreasonably raising, pursuing, contesting or responding to any particular allegation or issue. Furthermore, the new rule preserves the menu of possible costs orders under CPR rules 44.3(6)(a)-(g). On the face of it, it is difficult to distinguish between the provisions of the CPR regime for civil costs based on the general rule of between-the-parties orders for costs, and the relevant factors under this new matrimonial regime based on a general rule of no between-the-parties orders for costs. They appear to be the opposite sides of the same coin.

RH v RH (Costs) (Adjustment for Gross Disparity) [2008] EWHC 347 (Fam), [2008] All ER (D) 67 (Apr) was a rare report of a decision under the new costs rules which permit the court under r 2.71 FPR 1991 to make a between-the-parties costs order based on litigation misconduct.

In protracted ancillary relief proceedings brought by the husband, the wife had argued that her £1.55m inheritance should be disregarded from the calculation, while the husband sought the equalisation of their capital situation. The husband further contended that in light of the wife's conduct in attempting to conceal the ownership of several properties he was entitled to more than half.

The husband formulated an offer whereby settlement would be reached through a property exchange in his favour, or a £750,000 payment being made to him. The wife neither accepted nor rejected the husband's offer. The court rejected the respective arguments of the wife in relation to the disregarding of the inheritance, and of the husband in respect of entitlement to more than a half share. In awarding the husband £670,000, the court had had regard to the considerable disparity in the costs that each side had run up. At the date of the award the wife's costs were £265,000 and the husband's £486,000. Accordingly, the court adjusted the assets subject to division by, in effect, writing back £225,000 of the husband's costs. The husband appealed and contended that the judge erred in discounting £225,000 and that the award payable should have been £782,500 to achieve parity. On appeal the court ruled that the husband's offer of 9 February represented a genuine offer that the wife should have accepted. However, the husband had been unreasonable to expend so much more than the wife in litigating the case. As such, the husband should not recoup more than that which was reasonable for the wife to pay and the wife should pay the husband's costs in the fixed sum of £150,000.

In *M v M* [2009] EWHC 1941 (Fam), [2010] 1 FLR 256, [2009] Fam Law 1029 a complete change of tack by the wife only weeks before the trial necessitated the whole focus of the husband's trial preparation to shift, only to shift again a matter of days before the trial when the wife abandoned her attempt to have the shares in the husband's company transferred to her and instead claimed periodical payments. In the witness box the wife admitted that the inflated budget annexed to her Form E was devised 'in revenge' and her expert's report was disclosed only on the first day of the hearing. She was ordered to pay £175,000 to the husband which represented about 20% of his costs.

3. Maintenance Pending Suit

[15.37]

Where does Rule 2.71(4)(a) leave costs allowances under the quaintly named Maintenance Pending Suit provisions? The President in his Practice Direction and Lord Justice Wilson in *Currey v Currey* [2006] EWCA Civ 1338, [2007] 1 FLR 946 confirmed that the principle of no between- the-parties costs orders is not breached by an order for maintenance pending suit containing an element to finance the receiving party's legal costs – a costs allowance as it is called – because technically it is not an order for costs – a technicality which might well evoke from the paying party the retort: 'Well, you could have fooled me'. And indeed it will fool the 'no-order for costs' principle if those payments on account of costs do not eventually stand to the credit of the party who paid them.

Nevertheless, the belief that maintenance pending suit orders may be a back, or even a front, door route for recovering between-the-parties costs may result in an increase in applications for maintenance pending suit orders containing a costs allowance. The President helpfully set out some of the authorities in paragraph 5 of his Practice Direction.

In *Moses-Taiga v Taiga* [2005] EWCA Civ 1013, [2006] 1 FLR 1074, Lord Justice Thorpe identified three criteria for including a costs allowance in an order for maintenance pending suit:

(1) No assets
(2) No security for borrowing
(3) No certainty of outcome which would enable the applicant to enter into a *Sears Tooth* agreement (*Sears Tooth (a firm) v Payne Hicks Beach (a firm)* [1997] 2 FLR 116) with his or her solicitor to pay their costs out of their eventual share of the family assets.

He might have added inability to find a solicitor willing to enter into a *Sears Tooth* agreement.

But what he did add was that a costs allowance would only be given in exceptional circumstances. What did he mean by 'exceptional'? The ubiquitous Nicholas Mostyn sitting in *TL v ML* [2005] EWHC 2860 (Fam), [2006] 1 FCR 465 thought he meant no more than that the three criteria Lord Justice. Thorpe had identified did themselves amount to exceptional circumstances. Mr Justice Hedley in *C v C* [2006] 2 FLR 1207 disagreed and thought the criteria were 'illustrative' and not 'definitive' of 'exceptional' and made a costs allowance even though the wife not only did have available security to raise a loan for her costs but had in fact already done so. Mr Justice Singer and Mr Justice Mumby followed suit in *L-K v K* [2006] EWHC 153 (Fam), [2006] 2 FLR 1113 and *Re B* [2006] EWHC 1834 (Fam), [2007] 1 FLR 1674.

And then in *Currey* (above) Lord Justice Wilson (after a linguistically valiant attempt to demonstrate that when Lord Justice Thorpe said 'exceptional', he did not mean 'exceptional') explained that the initial, overarching enquiry is into whether the applicant for a costs allowance can demonstrate that she (or he) cannot *reasonably* procure legal advice and representation by any other means. And on this approach he added a fourth criterion to Lord Justice Thorpe's three, namely, that the court needs also to be satisfied that there is no public funding available to the applicant.

In these days when fairness is equated to equality in family finance, fairness must surely extend to equality of arms in financing legal advice and representation. It is a simple question of cash-flow. If all the liquid assets are under the control of one of the parties, funds should be made equally available to both parties for paying the lawyers during the proceedings, whatever the final distribution of the family assets may be.

4. Pound for pound

[15.38]

In *Mubarak v Mubarak* [2006] EWHC 1260 (Fam), [2007] 1 WLR 271 where there was a serious inequity in the financial resources of the parties and the husband had behaved disgracefully throughout the proceedings. Mr Justice Mumby innovatively directed that for each one pound the recalcitrant husband paid to his own lawyers for preparation, representation or advice in respect of the wife's forthcoming applications he should pay one pound into a joint account in the names of the parties' respective solicitors. The money lodged was to be held to the order of the court to be paid out to the wife's solicitors at the conclusion of the hearing unless otherwise ordered. The terms were not intended to punish or penalise the husband, but to achieve the legitimate aim of trying to create a fair hearing for both parties. The order sought to moderate the husband's ability to continue to employ a Rolls-Royce legal team while simultaneously failing to pay the wife any of the monies owed to her and leaving her reliant on credit in trying to achieve enforcement of the court orders with which the husband had not complied.

5. Appeals

[15.39]

In *Judge v Judge* (2008) EWCA Civ 1458 19 December, the wife failed in an application to set aside ancillary relief orders and resisted the husband's claim for costs his costs under the general rule in FPR 2.71(4)(a) was that the court will not make an order requiring one party to pay the costs of another party in ancillary relief proceedings. The Court of Appeal held FPR 2.71(4)(a) is limited to occasions when the court is dividing up the matrimonial assets and own costs are treated as a liability for the purposes of calculating the substantive award. Accordingly an application to set aside an ancillary relief order is not ancillary relief proceedings. However, the court also rejected the husband's argument that the proceedings were governed by CPR 44.3(2)(a), which provides that as a general rule the loser pays the successful party's costs. The CPR did not apply because the proceedings were still family proceedings. There was therefore no general rule. The trial judge had awarded the husband half his costs and the Court of Appeal found that he had enough material to depart from the position that the losing party should pay all the costs. Both parties' appeals were therefore dismissed.

(v) The matrimonial pot

[15.40]

A fundamental difference between civil and matrimonial litigation, is that in civil litigation no order for costs means each party must pay its own costs out of its own resources, but in matrimonial litigation there are no outside resources and the costs of both parties must come out of the family assets. Abolishing between-the-parties costs orders does not alter the basic fact that all the costs must come out of the matrimonial pot, nor does it answer the basic question of how the costs are to be allocated fairly between the parties. An immediate consequence of the abolition of costs orders will be that many aspects of costs which have hitherto been dealt with on a detailed assessment by a costs judge must now be considered by the judge conducting the final hearing before he or she can make an order. Two aspects of costs in particular must be resolved before a partisan order can be made: quantum and penalties for litigation misconduct.

(vi) Quantification

[15.41]

Under the new regime the judge at the final hearing must first decide if there has been litigation misconduct, and if so, presumably quantify the costs of both parties arising out of the misconduct, and then order that the total of those costs be paid out of the share of the offending party, otherwise the sanction has no teeth.

The judge must also decide whether a costs order should be on the standard or the indemnity basis, there are different kinds and levels of what may be called litigation misconduct in family matters, not all of them justifying the award of indemnity costs.

And because the costs have to be quantified before the family assets can be apportioned, this will again involve the family judge in a task which hitherto has been undertaken by a costs judge on a detailed assessment.

(vii) Compensation or Sanction?

[15.42]

A second area of difficulty arises out of the dual role of costs as both compensation and as a sanction for litigation misconduct.

A fee shifting order in a big money case where the family assets exceed the aggregate needs of the family creates no problem, but what about the great majority of cases where there is simply not enough money to go round to start with? Take Cardinal and Middleton's example of a wife who needs £150,000 to re-house herself and the children but has £20,000 solicitor and client costs. What if the court finds she has been guilty of litigation misconduct causing the husband to incur £5,000 of costs? If you do not increase her award by £20,000 to pay her solicitor and client costs and you also order her to pay the husband £5,000 between-the-parties costs, she is £25,000 short of her needs. Where does that leave her and the children? Out in the street?

The dilemma arises whenever a between-the-parties costs order for litigation misconduct would result in the needs of one of the parties not being met. A fee-shifting order could in most cases upset the delicate balance between meeting the needs of both parties and meeting the needs of only one of them.

Which is to take priority – the *needs* of a party or *punishing* them for litigation misconduct? The new Rule 2.71, para 5(f) requires the court to have regard to the financial effect on the parties of making a costs order. If a party's and the children's needs are in any event going to over-ride the making of a between-the-parties costs order then what is the point of investigating misconduct in the proceedings in the first place?

(viii) Wasted costs

[15.43]

There is one way for an order for costs based on litigation misconduct not to be met out of the matrimonial pot – that is an order that the solicitors pay them personally. CPR Rule 44.14 which enables the court to order the legal representative of one party to pay the costs of the other for misconduct has not been disapplied from ancillary relief proceedings nor have the wasted costs provisions of s 51(7) of Supreme Court (now Senior Courts) Act 1981. Shall we now have a spate of applications for wasted costs orders against solicitors similar to those against solicitors who have acted for unsuccessful publicly funded claimants? Will it be another addition to the catalogue of satellite costs litigation? I have a fantasy of both parties getting together and agreeing each to claim wasted costs against the other's solicitors in order to preserve the matrimonial pot!

(ix) Satellite litigation

[15.44]

FPR 2.71 and CPR 44.3 (6) appear to be charters for satellite costs litigation before the hearing judge which the presumption of no order for costs will do nothing to abate. Costs reform has always been a triumph of hope over experience and despite the consultation and consideration given to these reforms at the highest level, the Supreme Court Costs Office (now the Senior Courts Costs Office) may well emerge as the main beneficiary of the new regime.

(x) No security

[15.45]

In ancillary relief proceedings, the wife was ordered to make a lump sum payment to the husband accompanied by a clean break order. The husband successfully appealed against the clean break order, which prepared the way for him to make an application for interim periodical payments. The judge dismissed the wife's application for security for costs on the grounds that there was no jurisdiction to make such an order, but did grant a stay of execution of the payment of the lump sum until the determination of the application for periodical payments in order to protect the wife from costs orders yet to be made. The Court of Appeal found the judge's reasoning was unsupportable. He recognised that he had no power to make an order for security for costs, but reasoned he would grant a stay on the basis it would act to protect the wife against cost orders yet to be made. The judge had failed to deal with the crucial question of how the application for a stay could be correct in law when it expressly achieved security for costs by the back door. Whatever happened in the application for periodical payments, the husband was entitled to the lump sum and the stay had been granted erroneously. The husband's appeal was allowed (*Bradley v Bradley* [2008] EWCA Civ 629, [2008] Fam Law 832).

ESTIMATES

[15.46]

The importance of knowing the amount of the costs of each party was emphasised by a Practice Direction of 28 March 1988, requiring each party to provide an estimate of their costs incurred and expected.

Although the practice direction has not been revoked it is in effect incorporated in FPR Rule 2.61F:

[15.47]

FPR Rule 2.61F: Costs

(1)   Subject to paragraph (2), at every hearing or appointment each party must produce to the court an estimate in Form H of the costs incurred by him up to the date of that hearing or appointment.

(2)   Not less than 14 days before the date fixed for the final hearing of an application for ancillary relief, each party must (unless the court directs otherwise) file with the court and serve on each other party a statement in Form H1 giving full particulars of all costs in respect of the proceedings which he has incurred or expects to incur, to enable the court to take account of the parties' liabilities for costs when deciding what order (if any) to make for ancillary relief.

CURBING COSTS

(a) Guidelines

[15.48]

Concern over increasingly heavy legal costs was also expressed by Booth J in *Evans v Evans* [1990] 2 All ER 147, Fam when she said that the court was at times unable to make appropriate provision orders for wives and children because of the liability for costs. She issued the following general guidelines to family law practitioners in the preparation of substantial ancillary relief cases:

'(1)   Affidavit evidence should be confined to relevant facts and should not be prolix or diffuse. Each party should normally file one substantive affidavit dealing with matters to which the court should have regard under s 25 of the Matrimonial Causes Act 1973 [as substituted by s 3 of the Matrimonial and Family Proceedings Act 1984] and matters which are material to the application. If any further affidavit is necessary it should be confined to matters as answering a serious allegation made by the other party dealing with any serious allegation made by the other party dealing with any serious issue raised or setting out any material change of circumstances.

(2)   Inquiries made under [rule 2.62 of the Family Proceedings Rules 1991] should, as far as possible, be contained in one comprehensive questionnaire and should not be made piecemeal at different times.

(3)   Wherever possible valuations of properties should be obtained from a valuer jointly instructed by both parties. Where each party instructs a valuer then reports should be exchanged and the valuers should meet in an attempt to resolve any differences between them or otherwise to narrow the issues.

(4)   While it may be necessary to obtain a broad assessment of the value of a shareholding in a private company it is inappropriate to undertake an expensive and meaningless exercise to achieve a precise valuation of a private company which will not be sold: see *P v P (financial provision)* [1989] 2 FLR 241.

(5)   All professional witnesses should be careful to avoid a partisan approach and should maintain proper professional standards.

(6)   Care should be taken in deciding what evidence, other than professional evidence, should be adduced and emotive issues which are not material should be avoided. Where affidavit evidence is filed the deponents must be available for cross-examination on notice from the other side.

(7)   Solicitors on both sides should together prepare bundles of documents for use at the hearing and should reach agreement as to what should be included and what excluded; duplication of documents should always be avoided. [This is now covered by Practice Direction (family proceedings: court bundles) [2000] 2 All ER 287, Fam.]

(8)   A chronology of material facts should be agreed and made available to the court.

(9)   In a substantial case it might be desirable to have a pre-trial review to explore the possibility of settlement and to define the issues and to ensure readiness for hearing if a settlement cannot be reached.

(10)   Solicitors and counsel should keep their clients informed of the costs at all stages of the proceedings and, where appropriate, should ensure that they understand the implications of the legal aid charge: the court will require an estimate of the approximate amount of the costs on each side before it can make a lump sum award (see Practice Direction [1982] 2 All ER 800).

(11)   The desirability of reaching a settlement should be borne in mind throughout the proceedings. While it is necessary for the legal advisers to have sufficient knowledge of the financial situation of both parties before advising their client on a proposed settlement, the necessity to make further inquiries must always be balanced by a consideration of what they are realistically likely to achieve and the increased costs which are likely to be incurred by making them.'

(b) Practice Note: case management

[15.49]

On 31 January 1995 the President took matters further by issuing the *Practice Note: Case Management* [1995] 1 All ER 586; Fam. Here it is:

[15.50]

(1) The importance of reducing the cost and delay of civil litigation makes it necessary for the court to assert greater control over the preparation for the

conduct of hearings than has hitherto been customary. Failure by practitioners to conduct cases economically will be visited by appropriate orders for costs, including wasted costs orders.

(2)   The court will accordingly exercise its discretion to limit—
(a)   discovery;
(b)   the length of opening and closing oral submissions;
(c)   the time allowed for the examination and cross-examination of witnesses;
(d)   the issues on which it wishes to be addressed;
(e)   reading aloud from documents and authorities.

(3)   Unless otherwise ordered, every witness statement or affidavit shall stand as the evidence in chief of the witness concerned. The substance of the evidence which a party intends to adduce at the hearing must be sufficiently detailed, but without prolixity; it must be confined to material matters of fact, not (except in the case of the evidence of professional witnesses) of opinion; and if hearsay evidence is to be adduced, the source of the information must be declared or good reason given for not doing so.

(4)   It is a duty owed to the court both by the parties and by their legal representatives to give full and frank disclosure in ancillary relief applications and also in all matters in respect of children. The parties and their advisers must also use their best endeavours—
(a)   to confine the issues and the evidence called to what is reasonably considered to be essential for the proper presentation of their case;
(b)   to reduce or eliminate issues for expert evidence;
(c)   in advance of the hearing to agree which are the issues or the main issues.

(5)   Unless the nature of the hearing makes it necessary, and in the absence of specific directions, bundles should be agreed and prepared for use by the court, the parties and the witnesses, and shall be in A4 format where possible, suitably secured. The bundles for use by the court shall be lodged with the court (the Clerk of the Rules in matters in the RCJ in London) at least two clear days before the hearing. Each bundle should be paginated, indexed, wholly legible and arranged chronologically. Where documents are copied unnecessarily or bundled incompetently, the cost will be disallowed.

(6)   In cases estimated to last for five days or more and in which no pre-trial review has been ordered, application should be made for a pre-trial review. It should when practicable be listed at least three weeks before the hearing and be conducted by the judge or district judge before whom the case is to be heard, and should be attended by the advocates who are to represent the parties at the hearing. Whenever possible, all statements or evidence and all reports should be filed before the date of the review and in good time for them to have been considered by all parties.

(7)   Whenever practicable, and in any matter estimated to last five days or more, each party should, not less than two clear days before the hearing, lodge with the court, or the Clerk of the Rules in matters in the RCJ in London, and deliver to other parties, a chronology and a skeleton argument concisely summarising that party's submissions in relation to each of the issues, and citing the main authorities relied upon. It is important that skeleton arguments should be brief.

(8)   In advance of the hearing upon request, and otherwise in the course of their opening, parties should be prepared to furnish the court, if there is no core bundle, with a list of documents essential for a proper understanding of the case.

(9)   The opening speech should be succinct. At its conclusion other parties may be invited briefly to amplify their skeleton arguments. In a heavy case the court may in conjunction with final speeches require written submissions, including the findings of fact for which each party contends.

(10)   This Practice Direction, which follows the directions handed down by the Lord Chief Justice and the Vice-Chancellor to apply in the Queen's Bench and

Chancery Divisions, shall apply to all family proceedings in the High Court and in all Care Centres, Family Hearing Centres and divorce county courts.

(11) Issued with the concurrence of the Lord Chancellor.

(c) Estate agents' and auctioneers' fees

[15.51]

1. The charges of estate agents and auctioneers selling freehold or leasehold property pursuant to orders of the Chancery Division, Family Division, the Court of Protection, or divorce county courts will normally be considered reasonable by the Court if they do not exceed the rate of commission which that agent would normally charge on a sole agency basis, and they do not exceed 2½ per cent of the sale price, exclusive of Value Added Tax.

2. These charges are to include all commission, valuations, expenses and other disbursements, including making affidavits, the cost of advertising, and all other work except surveys. The allowance for a survey will be at the Court's discretion.

3. If—
(a)   an agent's charges do not fall within the limits set out in paragraph 1; or
(b)   there is a sale of any investment property, business property, or farm property, or
(c)   a property is sold in lots or by valuation,
an application must be made to the court to authorise the fee, to be charged.

4. The limits set out in paragraphs 1 and 2 above do not apply to sales of property for patients of the Court of Protection where an agreement has been concluded with the estate agent before the jurisdiction of the court has been invoked.

5. In matrimonial cases, either where the party who has been condemned in these costs has not agreed to the increased rate, or where the costs fall to be paid out of the Legal Aid Fund, the higher charges will be subject to the discretion of the Taxing Officer.

6. This Practice Direction applies to all instructions for sale which are placed with estate agents and auctioneers after 1 January 1983.

Practice Direction (estate agents' and auctioneers' fees) [1972] 3 All ER 256, 1 WLR 1431 and *Practice Direction (family division: sale of land)* [1972] 3 All ER 910, [1972] 1 WLR 1471 are hereby revoked.

(By Direction of the Vice-Chancellor and the President of the Family Division and with the concurrence of the Lord Chancellor, 22 December 1982.) [1983] 1 All ER 160, [1983] 1 WLR 86.

SUMMARY ASSESSMENT

(a) No presumption of detailed assessment

[15.52]

The general rule in para 13.2 of the Practice Direction in Part 44 of the CPR did not imply a general rule requiring detailed assessment of costs in hearings lasting longer than a day. On the contrary, the exercise of the power to make a summary assessment must be considered in every case. In family cases in particular, the aggravation of detailed assessment ran counter to the satisfactory resolution of disputes (*Q v Q (Family Division costs: summary assessment)* [2002] 2 FLR 668, Fam).

(b) Discrete issues

[15.53]

Because so many aspects of family matters, such as the divorce, children and ancillary relief, are dealt with at the same time, often in the same attendance, telephone call or letter, it is particularly important to be able to distinguish between them for the purposes of the summary assessment of the costs of an interim application. Otherwise, there is the risk that the statement of costs may include either more or less than the work done for that particular hearing. In substantial matters you should therefore consider having separate folders or dividers within the file, or even separate files, relating to each aspect, or to a specific hearing such as an application for maintenance pending suit. Where appropriate, separate letters should be written on each aspect of the matter, with the time spent on attendances and telephone calls being similarly apportioned. By these means you will be able to satisfy the judge that you are not over-charging – and yourself that you are charging enough.

ENFORCEMENT

(a) Statutory demand

[15.54]

Rule 12.3 of the Insolvency Rules 1986 provides:

> (1) Subject as follows, in bankruptcy . . . all claims by creditors are provable as debts against . . . the bankrupt . . . The following are not provable – (a) in bankruptcy, any fine imposed for an offence and any obligation arising under an order made in family proceedings or under a maintenance assessment made under the Child Support Act 1991 . . .

On this basis, Mr Levy, who was a bankrupt, applied to set aside a statutory demand served by the Legal Aid Board, now the Legal Services Commission, claiming £62,732 costs incurred by his former wife in her family proceedings. Although there was jurisdiction to make a bankruptcy order on a petition based upon a non-provable debt, the jurisdiction was discretionary and would not be exercised except in special circumstances. It was puzzling that s 382(1) contemplated that a non-provable debt might be regarded as a bankruptcy debt, but it was difficult to conceive of any circumstances where that would occur (*Levy v Legal Services Commission* [2001] 1 All ER 895, CA).

(b) Judgment summons

[15.55]

Schedule 8 to the Administration of Justice Act 1990, which prescribes the matrimonial orders enforceable by judgment summons, does not specifically mention orders for costs, but rule 7.4 of the Family Proceedings Rules 1991 contemplates enforcement of costs orders by judgment summons by providing that on the hearing of a judgment summons the judge may make a new order for payment of the amount due where the original order is for a lump sum provision or costs.

However, in *Murbarak v Murbarak* [2001] 1 FCR 193, CA, the Court of Appeal held that the existing judgment summons procedure under s 5 of the Debtors Act 1869 was not human rights compliant. Judgment summons proceedings for contempt are classified as criminal proceedings and the requirement that the debtor shall attend before the court to show cause why he should not be sent to prison amounts to an unacceptable reversal of the burden of proof and removes the protection against self-incrimination. Accordingly rule 7.4(1) was amended so that instead of the judgment debtor being ordered 'to appear and be examined on oath as to his means' he is now simply ordered 'to attend court'. A new rule 7.4(3A) requires the judgment creditor to file with the request, copies of all written evidence on which he (in practice, invariably 'she') intends to rely. A new rule 7.4(7B) provides:

> 'No person may be committed on an application for a judgment summons unless—(a) where the proceedings are in the High Court, the court has summoned the debtor to attend, he has failed to do so, and he has also failed to attend the adjourned hearing; (b) where the proceedings are in the county court, an order is made under section 110(2) of the County Courts Act 1984; or (c) the judgment creditor proves that the debtor— (i) has or has had since the date of the order the means to pay the sum in respect of which he is made default; and (ii) has refused or neglected, or refuses or neglects, to pay that sum.'

And for the avoidance of doubt, a new rule 7.4(7C) provides that the debtor may not be compelled to give evidence.

(c) Bankruptcy

[15.56]

The Insolvency (Amendment) Rules 2005 which came into force on 1 April 2005 provided that lump sum orders and costs orders made in family proceedings are now provable in bankruptcy in respect of bankruptcy orders made on or after that date. Arrears of periodical payments and under child support assessments are still not provable.

CHILDREN

Schedule 1 applications

[15.57]

Schedule 1 of the Children Act 1989 provides three forms of financial relief for a child: (1) a maintenance order, settlement and transfer of property order to be made in favour of a child against either or both of its parents; (2) a periodical payments order and lump sum order to be made in favour of a child who has reached 18; and (3) the court may vary a maintenance agreement containing financial arrangements for the child either during the lifetime of the parent or after the death of one of them. The application may be made by a parent or guardian or the child itself if over 18. The costs provisions of the Family Proceedings Rules do not apply to Schedule 1 applications and therefore although the applicant is at the risk of a between-the-parties costs order he or she, usually she, is still able to protect their costs position by making a 'Calderbank' offer. Furthermore, the prohibition against interim lump sum orders in divorce proceedings in section 23(5) of the Matrimonial Causes Act 1973 does not apply to Schedule 1 applications and the applicant may be able to obtain funding in this way, as appears to have been done in *MT v T* [2006] EWHC 2494 (Fam), [2007] 2 FLR 925.

(b) Costs order in child abduction

[15.58]

In an application under the Child Abduction and Custody Act 1985 the mother had been unreasonable in the conduct of the case through her persistent pursuit of uncorroborated false allegations of abduction and serious dishonesty involving the forgery of documents. At the conclusion of the hearing the father, a man of limited means who was bringing up the parties' child on his own without any financial support from the mother and who had been wholly successful in the outcome of the proceedings, had asked for his costs against the mother. The mother, who was publicly funded, contended there should be no order for costs in view of Article 26 of the Convention on the Civil Aspects of International Child Abduction 1980 and that as a matter of public policy, so as not to deter genuine abduction applicants or the acceptance of instructions by solicitors from the Child Abduction Unit of the Official Solicitor's Office. The court held It would be inconsistent to say that the rules generally and the costs rules in particular applied to the 1985 Act but that they should not have effect because the power to make a costs order against a claimant was not expressly set out on the face of the Hague Convention. There was nothing inimical to the operation of the Hague Convention in the application of ordinary funding costs principles against an unsuccessful claimant. Accordingly there was jurisdiction to make a costs order against a claimant in proceedings under the 1985 Act. Deliberate and persistent falsification of a case in an attempt to deprive a child of his habitual residence or to render ineffective the custody, access and Article 8 rights of the child and the other parent were relevant when exercising the court's discretion as to costs. Accordingly, since in each case where a costs application was made there should be a costs enquiry on the merits, having regard to the statutory test in s 11 of the Access to Justice Act 1999, it was appropriate to make an order for costs against the mother and adjourn for detailed assessment on the standard basis by a costs judge (*EC-L v DM (child abduction: costs)* [2005] EWHC 588 (Fam), [2005] 2 FLR 772, [2005] Fam Law 606).

(b) Costs against recalcitrant mother

[15.59]

Although after a fact-finding hearing the judge found that the mother with whom the child resided need have no concerns about the child's contact with its father the mother remained obdurate and made further unfounded allegations against the necessitating a total of four hearings. There is a limit to which allowance could be made for a parent who deliberately and unreasonably obstructs contact and the Court of Appeal upheld the judge's order that the mother should pay the costs of all four hearings (*Re T (a child)(order for costs)* [2005] EWCA Civ 311, [2005] 1 FCR 625).

(c) Joint-report costs

[15.60]

The apportionment of the costs of obtaining jointly commissioned expert's reports in care proceedings is a matter for the discretion of the court, but a pragmatic half and half apportionment is out of step with the rationale and conventional use of costs orders. If the work would normally be undertaken by the local authority as part of its core preparation it would almost certainly be required to pay the whole of the cost. The judgment gives detailed guidance on the approach to be adopted. In the present case there were three respondents as well a the local authority and it was appropriate that each party should pay a quarter, resulting in the Legal Services Commission paying three-quarters of the costs (*Calderdale Metropolitan Borough Council v S* [2004] EWHC 2529 (Fam), [2005] 1 FLR 751, [2005] Fam Law 353).

(d) Costs of residential assessment

[15.61]

The question in *Lambeth London Borough Council v S* [2005] EWHC 776 (Fam), [2005] 2 FLR 1171, [2005] Fam Law 685 was whether the approach in *Calderdale* applied to the cost of a residential assessment in child care proceedings or whether the cost should be borne solely by the local authority. Section 38 of the Children Act 1989 provides '(6) Where the court makes an interim care order or interim supervision order, it may give such directions (if any) as it considers appropriate with regard to the medical or psychiatric examination or other assessment of the child . . . '. Such an assessment was not part of the local authority's case, it was a power in the court to direct its own process within inquisitorial proceedings for the benefit of the child. A s 38(6) direction was no more made against the local authority than it was against any other relevant party: the importation of the language of the adversarial contest into children proceedings was unhelpful. There was an obligation on the parties in child proceedings to help the court further the over-riding objective; a process which was inextricably linked to the obligation on the court to ensure within its process an exploration rather than the inclusion of expert assessment and opinion that might negate the state's case for the child's permanent removal from his parents. There is no relevant distinction in principle between funding of a jointly-instructed expert report and a s 38(6) assessment. The plain meaning of s 22(4) of the Access to Justice Act 1999, which provides the court should not make any different order or exercise its discretion in any different way because a party had the benefit of public funding suggested that the normal practice in children proceedings was to be followed. That would be to make no order as to costs absent exceptional circumstances. On a joint instruction that would involve an equal apportionment of the overall cost between the parties, funded or otherwise. That was precisely what the *Calderdale* criteria provided for, just as they provided for the circumstances where the local authority should take a greater or full share of the costs because of the circumstances of the case. Accordingly the cost of the residential assessment in child care proceedings does not have to be borne solely by the local authority which had brought the care proceedings and can be apportioned between the parties. The Legal Services Commission has power to fund such an assessment. This approach was confirmed in *Sheffield City Council v V; LSC intervening* [2006] EWHC 1861 (Fam), (2006) Times, 25 August, which set out the factors to be taken into account and the steps to be taken.

APPEAL

[15.62]

Costs are much more likely to be awarded on an appeal than at first instance. At first instance nobody knows what the judge is going to find. On an appeal both parties have the chance to take stock and make an offer. In *Re M* [2009] EWCA Civ 311 the Court of Appeal refused permission to appeal from the High Court judge's order that the husband should pay the wife's costs of her successful appeal from the district judge. The husband through his counsel had opposed the appeal 'root and branch' and announced that he intended to apply for costs if the appeal were successfully opposed. Such a litigant, if he lost as here, could not complain when the judge took the view that he should contribute to or pay, the appellant's costs.

SOLICITOR AND CLIENT

[15.63]

The Conditional Fee Agreement Rules and Regulations (see Section VII) precludes solicitors entering into conditional fee agreements in respect of matrimonial matters. A SCCO costs judge was in error when he found that a client care letter in matrimonial proceedings sent to the wife by her solicitor containing the clause 'we have agreed that a claim for costs will not be made until money is received at the end of the case' was a conditional fee agreement which did not comply with the regulations, and was therefore unenforceable. The Court, on appeal, was satisfied that the letter taken as a whole showed that the wife was to be liable for her own costs and the phrase meant that the solicitor agreed not to claim his costs until the conclusion of the case, a position wholly in line with the manner in which family proceedings were often undertaken (*Denton v Denton* [2004] EWHC 1308 (Fam), [2004] 2 FLR 594, [2005] Fam Law 353).

Similarly, an agreement by a wife to pay her solicitor's fees in divorce proceedings out of such sums as the court might award her in the proceedings was not champertous and invalid (*Sears Tooth (a firm) v Payne Hicks Beach (a firm)* [1997] 2 FLR 116).

CHAPTER 16

GETTING THE RIGHT ORDER – AND THE ORDER RIGHT

[16.1]

At the end of a hearing the judge's mind is turning towards his next case. The advocates are busy endorsing and tying up their papers. Emotions are high – someone has won and someone has lost, and dealing with costs is a sordid anti-climax. Nevertheless, the fruits of victory can be soured if the proper orders are not made for costs.

It is equally important to make proper provision for costs in any terms of compromise.

NO AGREEMENT AS TO COSTS

[16.2]

It is surprising how often the parties reach agreement on all issues except the question of costs.

(a) No proceedings

[16.3]

Where proceedings have not been instituted and agreement cannot be reached over costs, the position is clear: there is no agreement. The matter has not been settled. Sometimes, particularly when negotiating with insurance companies, one party agrees to pay the other's costs but there is no agreement of the amount. The agreement may say 'Costs to be ascertained by detailed assessment if not agreed', but there are no proceedings in which the machinery for a detailed assessment can be set in motion. Until recently, the only possible course was to institute proceedings based upon the agreement seeking an order that the costs be assessed and paid pursuant to the agreement. This incurred the expense of instituting proceedings, which is the very thing the compromise was intended to avoid. However, the dilemma was resolved by the Civil Procedure (Amendment No 3) Rules 2000 which introduced CPR Rule 44.12A (see para [11.68]) containing the procedure to be followed where the parties to a dispute have reached an agreement on all issues, including which party is to pay the costs, but have failed to agree the amount of the costs where no proceedings have been started. In these circumstances, either party may start proceedings by issuing a claim form in accordance with Part 8. The court may either make an order for costs or dismiss the claim. It must dismiss the claim if the application is opposed. Otherwise it is vital to grasp the nettle and agree the quantum of costs when compromising a dispute in respect of which proceedings have not been commenced.

(b) Proceedings

[16.4]

If the parties have agreed who will pay the costs but have not agreed the amount then, of course, they have reached agreement and there is no difficulty about the court ordering a detailed assessment of the costs. But what if the parties are agreed on everything but the incidence of costs: can they ask the court to resolve the issue?

In *Booker Belmont Wholesale Ltd v Ashford Developments Ltd* (18 July 2000, unreported), CA, the parties reached an agreement whereby the fourth party should 'pay such proportion of the [claimant's] costs of the action as the court shall determine and the reasonable costs of the [claimant's] expert . . . '. The judge was held to have been wrong to refuse to make an order determining the proportion of costs to be paid by the fourth party on the grounds that both as a matter of construction and jurisdiction he had no power to do so. As a matter of construction, this was a valid order for costs in a proportion to be fixed by the court. As a matter of jurisdiction, the court always had jurisdiction to decide the costs of an action. The correct approach for the judge would have been to determine the extent to which having regard to the degree of lack of success of the claimant, there should be some reduction in the amount of costs awarded.

Boxall v Waltham Forest London Borough [2000] All ER (D) 2445, Admin deduced the following principles where a judicial review was resolved without a hearing:

(a)   the court has power to make a costs order when the substantive proceedings have been resolved without a trial but the parties have not agreed about costs;

(b)   it will ordinarily be irrelevant that the claimant is legally aided;

(c)   the overriding objective is to do justice between the parties without incurring unnecessary court time and consequently additional cost;

(d)   at each end of the spectrum there will be cases where it is obvious which side would have won had the substantive issues been fought to a conclusion. In between, the position will, in differing degrees, be less clear. How far the court will be prepared to look into the previously unresolved substantive issues will depend upon the circumstances of the particular case, not least the amount of costs at stake and the conduct of the parties;

(e)   in the absence of a good reason to make any other order, the fall-back is to make no order as to costs;

(f)   the court should take care to ensure that it does not discourage parties from settling judicial review proceedings, for example by a local authority making a concession at an early stage.

Boxall was followed in *Rambus Inc v Hynx Semiconductor UK Ltd* [2004] EWHC 2313 (Pat), [2004] All ER (D) 587 (Jul) which was resolved by ADR in which the claimants claimed to have won on some issues although they had lost on others. The court's discretion was wide enough to make an issues based costs order even where there had been no trial, but the circumstances of this case did not justify doing so.

Brawley v Marczynski [2002] EWCA Civ 756, [2002] 4 All ER 1060 confirmed there is no tradition of there being no order as to costs where without judicial intervention, a dispute is settled except as to costs. A note of caution was sounded in *BCT Software Solutions Ltd v C Brewer & Sons Ltd* [2003] EWCA Civ 939, [2003] 35 LS Gaz R 35 where shortly after the commencement of the trial, the claimant agreed to accept £10,000 in full settlement of its substantial claim, save as to costs, which the parties requested the trial judge to determine based on their minute of compromise. The first question was whether the Court was in a position to make an order about costs under CPR Rule 44.3(2), in the absence of agreed or adjudicated facts on which to decide the question. In litigation in which all other issues had been compromised without a full trial, a judge should be cautious before making an order for costs, and could even decline an invitation to exercise his discretion under s 51(1) of the Supreme Court (now Senior Courts) Act 1981. However, where the parties had invited the judge to exercise his discretion, it was not open to them to complain that the judge set out to do what both parties had invited him to do. In *Promar International v Philip Clarke* [2006] EWCA Civ 332, [2006] All ER (D) 35 (Apr) before the trial the claimant accepted the defendant's offer of an undertaking and abandoned its claim for damages, but the costs were disputed. The judge at first awarded the claimant 75% of its costs but on having *BCT Software v Brewer* (above) brought to his attention decided there was no way of telling which party would have succeeded at a trial and made no order for costs.

In *R (on the application of G) v Worcestershire County Council* [2005] EWHC 2332 (Admin), [2005] All ER (D) 111 (Oct); APIL PI Focus November the claimants brought judicial review proceedings, but prior to the substantive hearing engaged in mediation, which lead to an agreement on all issues except costs. The judge declined to determine the issue of costs on the grounds that, on the face of it, it had been reasonable for the claimants to institute proceedings for judicial review, but it was impossible to say that it was obvious that either party would have won and in those circumstances it was inappropriate to make any order as to costs.

CHILDREN AND PROTECTED PARTY SETTLEMENTS

[16.5]

There must not only be a detailed assessment of the costs awarded to a child or a protected party, but also of any adult who is a claimant – both their between-the-parties and solicitor and client costs. However, the Practice Direction supplementing CPR Rule 48.5 enables this to be avoided where costs are agreed between the parties and the solicitor waives any further solicitor and client costs, but only if this is specifically provided for in the order. For the full provision see 'Costs where money is payable by or to a child or protected party' at para [37.3]. The Supreme Court Costs Office (now the Senior Courts Costs Office) takes the view that the words 'costs to be assessed if not agreed' are not a sufficient waiver to avoid a detailed assessment.

STATE FUNDING

[16.6]

The only way in which the solicitor for a funded client in litigation can avoid having a detailed assessment of his costs is if they are under £2,500 (including counsel's fees and disbursements, but not VAT) which costs may be assessed by the Area Director. Otherwise, their costs must be approved by the court. However, where the assisted person's solicitor is able to agree the costs to be paid by the other party which he and counsel are willing to accept in full satisfaction of their claim against the fund, the solicitor may avoid a detailed assessment by submitting the amount of the costs, with supporting documents, for assessment by the Area Director. It is quick, efficient and free!

In the context of legal aid costs, remember the statutory charge. It is negligent not to advise a client that all of the assisted person's costs will be deducted out of the proceeds of a consent judgment if you do not also recover costs from the other party.

GLOSSARY

[16.7]

Section 8.5 of the Practice Direction supplementing CPR Rule 44.3 provides a useful table of the most commonly made interim orders for costs setting out the general effect of these orders. It makes no claim to be exhaustive. Here it is:

[16.8]

CPD Section 8: Court's discretion and circumstances to be taken into account when exercising its discretion as to costs: rule 44.3

8.5

Term	Effect
• Costs or Costs in any event	The party in whose favour an order is made is entitled to the costs in respect of the part of the proceedings to which the order relates, whatever other costs orders are made in the proceedings.
• Costs in the case or Costs in the application	The party in whose favour the court makes an order for costs at the end of the proceedings is entitled to his costs of the part of the proceedings to which the order relates.
• Costs reserved	The decision about costs is deferred to a later occasion, but if no later order is made the costs will be costs in the case.

- Claimant's/defendant's costs in the case/application

  If the party in whose favour the costs order is made is awarded costs at the end of the proceedings, that party is entitled to his costs of the part of the proceedings to which the order relates. If any other party is awarded costs at the end of the proceedings, the party in whose favour the final costs order is made is not liable to pay the costs of any other party in respect of the part of the proceedings to which the order relates.

- Costs thrown away

  Where, for example, a judgment or order is set aside, the party in whose favour the costs order is made is entitled to the costs which have been incurred as a consequence. This includes the costs of—

  a) preparing for and attending any hearing at which the judgment or order which has been set aside was made;

  b) preparing for and attending any hearing to set aside the judgment or order in question;

  c) preparing for and attending any hearing at which the court orders the proceedings or the part in question to be adjourned;

  d) any steps taken to enforce a judgment or order which has subsequently been set aside.

- Costs of and caused by

  Where, for example, the court makes this order on an application to amend a statement of case, the party in whose favour the costs order is made is entitled to the costs of preparing for and attending the application and the costs of any consequential amendment to his own statement of case.

- Costs here and below

  The party in whose favour the costs order is made is entitled not only to his costs in respect of the proceedings in which the court makes the order but also to his costs of the proceedings in any lower court. In the case of an appeal from a Divisional Court the party is not entitled to any costs incurred in any court below the Divisional Court.

- No order as to costs or

  Each party to pay his own costs

  Each party is to bear his own costs of the part of the proceedings to which the order relates whatever costs order the court makes at the end of the proceedings.

[16.9]

The orders and definitions in the Practice Direction are basically the same as before the CPR, with the helpful addition of 'costs thrown away'. This has always sounded good and although everyone thought they knew what it meant, they did not always think that it meant the same thing. The detailed definition should save much confusion. In fact, there should be little prospect of orders for costs thrown away being made because, except in the most unusual circumstances, there should be a summary assessment at the end of the hearing.

SILENCE

(a) No costs

[16.10]

Silence on the question of costs in a final judgment or order, or terms of compromise, has always been construed as meaning that each party will bear their own costs. In respect of interim hearings the glossary confirms that 'no order as to costs' continues to mean that each party bears their own costs of that application in any event. But what about silence? What if the court in fact makes no orders for costs, in other words it is silent on the subject. Prior to 26 April 1999, those costs would be included in the final order for costs and go to the receiving party. However, CPR Rule 44.13(1) provides that if the judge says nothing about costs, no party shall in any event be entitled to the costs relating to that order. It will be the same as if the judge had actually uttered the words 'no order as to costs'. This was demonstrated in *Griffiths v Metropolitan Police Comr* [2003] EWCA Civ 313, [2003] All ER (D) 32 (Mar) when the court held not only that where an interim order was silent, no party was entitled to their costs, but also that the trial judge had no jurisdiction to vary that order. There may be a remedy under the slip rule – or just hope that on the detailed assessment no-one notices the omission!

(b) Judicial review

[16.11]

Matters are different in the Administrative Court. A *Practice Statement (Judicial Review: costs)* QBD (2004) Times, 20 May provides: 'In judicial review claims it is necessary to obtain permission to proceed and it has sometimes been suggested that a successful claimant could not recover the costs of obtaining permission unless the court had made a specific order. It has never been the practice in the Administrative Court or its predecessor, the Crown Office, to make any costs order in granting permission because it was assumed that those costs would be costs in the case. To avoid any argument, a grant of permission to pursue a claim for judicial review, whether made on paper or after oral argument, would be deemed to contain an order that costs be costs in the case. Any different order made by the judge must be reflected in the court order granting permission.'

APPEALS

(a) Interim

[16.12]

If either party appeals against an interim order, then the winner of the appeal is likely to be awarded their costs of that appeal in any event.

(b) Final

[16.13]

A frequent ground for applying for permission to appeal from an award of costs is the failure of the judge to give adequate reasons. This was addressed by the Court of Appeal in *English v Emery Reimbold & Strick Ltd* [2002] EWCA Civ 605, [2002] 3 All ER 385, in which it held:

(1)   Where an application for permission to appeal on the ground of lack of reasons is made to the judge of first instance, he should consider whether his judgment is defective for lack of reasons, adjourning for that purpose if necessary. If he concludes that it was, then he should remedy the defect by providing additional reasons, and then refuse permission to appeal. If he concludes that his reasons were adequate, then he should refuse permission to appeal.

(2)   Where an application for permission to appeal on the ground of lack of reasons is made to an appellate court, and it appears to that court that the application is well-founded, it should consider adjourning the application and remitting the case to the trial judge with an invitation to provide reasons, or additional reasons. Where the appellate court is in doubt as to the adequacy of reasons, it may be appropriate to adjourn the application to an oral hearing on notice to the respondent.

(3)   Where permission to appeal is granted on the ground of inadequate reasons, the appellate court should review the judgment in the light of the evidence and submissions at trial in order to determine whether it was apparent why the judge had reached the decision he did. If the reason is apparent and valid, the appeal would be dismissed. If the reasons were still not apparent the appeal court would have to consider whether to proceed to a rehearing or direct a new trial.

(4)   If the reasons for a judge's order as to costs are plain, as where costs followed the event, there was no need for the judge to give reasons for a costs order. However, the CPR sometimes require a more complex approach to costs, and judgments dealing with costs will more often need to identify the provisions of the rules which have been in play and why these have led to the order made. Where no express reason for a costs order is given the appeal court will approach the material facts on the assumption that the judge has a good reason for the order made, and where there is a perfectly rational explanation for the order the appeal court is likely to draw the inference that this is what motivated the judge in making the order. Accordingly it was only in cases where an order for costs was made with neither reasons nor any obvious explanation for the order that it is likely to be appropriate to give permission to appeal on the ground of lack of reasons.

(5)   In the costs decision under consideration on this appeal, the judge had made no order as to costs without giving any reasons. However, analysis of the judgment showed that the judge thought that the action had resulted in a draw, a conclusion which was open to the judge. That appeal would therefore be dismissed.

(6)   The court confirmed what was said in CPR Rule 44.3(7), namely that a trial court should ordinarily not make an order for the costs of issues, and should only make such an order if other forms of order could not be made which adequately reflected the justice of the case.

(This summary is from Butterworths Costs Service Bulletin 12, by Jeremy Morgan QC, to whom I am grateful.)

In *Lavelle v Lavelle* [2004] EWCA Civ 223, [2004] 2 FCR 418, at the end of the hearing, the judge concluded that there should only be a modest departure from the usual rule that costs follow the event, but no note was kept of the judge's reasons for the order he had made. The costs were dealt with at the end of a long day and the reasons were perfunctory. Costs are important, particularly where they are disproportionate to what is at stake. Judges have to be sure that their reasons for costs orders are clear: they should not be left to inference, albeit it is often possible to infer the reasons.

JUDICIAL REVIEW

[16.14]

The practice direction to CPR Part 54 on judicial review provides:

> '8.5   Neither the defendant nor any other interested party need attend a hearing on the question of permission unless the court directs otherwise.
>
> 8.6   Where the defendant or any party does attend a hearing, the court will not generally make an order for costs against the claimant.'

In *R (Leach) v Comr for Local Administration* [2001] EWHC Admin 455, [2001] 4 PLR 28, the judge had awarded a successful defendant at the permission stage his costs of filing an acknowledgement of service. The proper approach to the award of costs against an unsuccessful claimant is as follows:

- The effect of *Leach*, certainly in a case to which the pre-action protocol applied and where a defendant or other interested party had complied with it, was that a successful defendant or other party at the permission stage who had filed an acknowledgement of service pursuant to rule 54.8 should generally recover the costs of doing so from the claimant whether or not he attended any permission hearing.
- The effect of paragraph 8.6 read with paragraph 8.5 of the Practice Direction is that a defendant who attended and successfully resisted the grant of permission at a renewal hearing should not generally recover from the claimant his costs of, and occasioned by, doing so.
- Only in exceptional circumstances should such costs be awarded.
- The court has a broad discretion to determine whether there are exceptional circumstances.
- Such circumstances might include the hopelessness of the claim; the claimant's persistence in making a hopeless claim after being alerted to its hopelessness; the extent to which the claimant was abusing the process of judicial review for collateral ends and whether the unsuccessful claimant had by the deployment of full argument and documentary evidence at the application stage, secured the advantage of an early substantive hearing.
- The unsuccessful claimant's resources might be relevant.
- The appeal court should be slow to interfere with the broad discretion exercised by the lower court.

(*R (Mount Cook Land Ltd) v Westminster City Council* [2003] EWCA Civ 1346, [2004] 2 P & CR 405).

APPLICATIONS 'NOT ON NOTICE'

[16.15]

If a claimant expressly or tacitly invites the defendant to be present on the hearing of a 'not on notice' application, either to give evidence or to disclose his line of argument and the motion or summons is dismissed, the court can order the claimant to pay the defendant's costs, either in the case or in any event, even though the application was not on formal notice.

PITFALLS

(a) Costs reserved

[16.16]

Any interim costs which have been reserved will automatically be awarded to the winner of the action unless the trial judge orders otherwise.

(b) Costs in any event

[16.17]

Where an action is settled, unless the terms of settlement say otherwise, any costs which have been awarded to one of the parties 'in any event' will still be recoverable. Such costs will even survive the termination of proceedings on the basis 'record withdrawn – no costs on either side'!

(c) Third parties

[16.18]

It is important to ensure that the final order makes provision for the costs of a third party against whom proceedings have been stayed at an earlier stage.

(d) Bullock and Sanderson orders

[16.19]

These orders arise where an action founded on either contract or tort against two separate defendants is successful against one and unsuccessful against the other. The court has a discretion (see *Mayer v Harte* [1960] 2 All ER 840, CA for the principles upon which such discretion is exercised) to order the unsuccessful defendant to pay the successful defendant's costs. This can be done in one of two ways:

(i) An order that the unsuccessful defendant pay directly to the successful defendant the latter's costs (known as a Sanderson order because it was first made in *Sanderson v Blyth Theatre Co* [1903] 2 KB 533, CA).

(ii) An order that the claimant pay the successful defendant's costs, permitting the claimant to add them to the costs ordered to be paid to him by the unsuccessful defendant (a Bullock order – *Bullock v London General Omnibus Co* [1907] 1 KB 264, CA).

Where the claimant has no means, then, subject to the court's discretion, the Sanderson order (ie (i) above) is the fairer way of dealing with the justice of the case. Neither order is appropriate in favour of a claimant who has sued both defendants because of a doubt as to the law as opposed to the facts, or where the causes of action against each are quite distinct, nor where the respective claims are not alternative or are based upon quite distinct sets of facts.

Irvine v Metropolitan Police Comr [2005] EWCA Civ 1293 confirmed that the jurisdiction to make a Sanderson order survived the introduction of the CPR. The exercise of discretion in deciding whether to make such a costs order has to be guided by the overriding objective and CPR Part 44 and it had to be recognised that it was capable of working injustice against a successful defendant. The court had a wide discretion over costs. In determining whether to order an unsuccessful defendant to pay the costs of a successful defendant the relevant factors included whether the claim against the successful defendant had been made 'in the alternative', whether the causes of action had been connected with those on which the claimant had been successful and whether it had been reasonable for the claimant to join and pursue a claim against the successful defendant. A significant factor was likely to be whether one defendant blamed another, but whether it had been reasonable to join that defendant and pursue the claim would depend on the facts of the case and whether the claimant could in fact sustain such a claim. Although the claimant had succeeded against the first defendant he had failed to establish a sustainable claim against the second defendant and in relation to the third defendant it was only sued in the alternative 15 months after the proceedings had started: the claimant had produced no cogent evidence in support of his claim against it. Accordingly, the judge had been entitled to conclude that although the first defendant should pay the costs of the claimant, the claimant should pay the costs of the two defendants against which his claims in negligence had failed.

Moon v Garrett [2006] EWCA Civ 1121, (2006) Times, 1 September confirmed the decision in *Irvine* (above) that there are no hard and fast rules as to when it is appropriate to make a *Bullock* or a *Sanderson* order. If a claimant has acted reasonably in suing two defendants, it will be harsh if he ends up paying the costs of suing the defendant against whom he has failed. Whether one defendant has blamed another will always be a factor. The fact that claims are not truly alternative does not mean that the court does not have the power to order one defendant to pay the costs of another.

Only in truly exceptional circumstances could a claimant who has lost against two separate defendants recover the costs of pursuing one defendant from the other. Where claims made by the claimant against both the second and fourth defendants had failed a *Bullock* order was not appropriate and the fourth defendants' costs were ordered to be borne by the claimant. It had been unreasonable for the claimant to pursue the fourth defendants but, even if it had been reasonable, it would be unjust to make the second defendant pay the costs of the unsuccessful pursuit of allegations against the fourth defendant where the second defendant had not blamed the fourth defendant or encouraged pursuit of the fourth defendant by the claimant (*McGlinn v (1) Waltham Contractors Ltd. (2) Huw Thomas Associates (3) DJ Hartigan & Associates Ltd. (4) Wilson Large & Partners (5)* [2007] EWHC 698 (TCC), 112 Con LR 148).

(e) Consent orders

[16.20]

In *Richardson Roofing & Co Ltd v Ballast Plc* [2009] CA (Civ Div) 13 February under a consent order the claimant was to pay a fourth party's costs incurred and thrown away by the adjournment of the trial. Three years later, the fourth party served a draft bill of cost for its entire costs until the hearing ordering a preliminary issue. The fourth party issued proceedings seeking an order that the costs judge dealing with the assessment should be directed that the costs included the fourth party's preparation for trial because there was no prospect that the claim would be revived. The judge made an order directing the costs judge to carry out the assessment using the guidance set out in six specified paragraphs of his judgment.

The Court of Appeal thought it highly debatable whether the judge had had any jurisdiction to hear the application. The order in dispute was a consent order with no application to vary it. As the jurisdiction point had not been fully argued before the Court of Appeal, the point could not be decided and the court therefore assumed jurisdiction, despite its serious reservations. Even if the judge had jurisdiction, he should not have exercised it because the matter would ordinarily go before a costs judge for a detailed assessment. It was undesirable for judges to make this sort of order referring to guidance set out in their judgment, which was extremely diffuse. Judgments provide the reasons for the subsequent orders and any order made at the end of a judgment should stand on its own. The judge had failed to answer the issue in relation to the construction of the consent order and his consequent order was of no assistance to a costs judge. Accordingly, his order could not stand.

In *Newall v Lewis* [2008] EWHC 910 (Ch), [2008] 4 Costs LR 626, [2008] All ER (D) 426 (Apr) the SCCO master decided that all that the parties had meant by 'incidental costs' in a consent order were the investigative costs pre-issue, which would be subject to detailed assessment and referral to a judge, and that all costs claimed post-issue, including incidental ones, were potentially recoverable and did not need to be referred to a judge. On appeal it was held, contrary to the master's conclusion, the order imposed the requirement on the costs judge of separating into distinct categories the costs of the Part 8 proceedings and the costs incidental to them. The correct approach was that if disputes on which costs had been expended pre-issue were relevant to the eventual proceedings and the other party's attitude had made it reasonable to expect them to be included in the litigation, those costs should be recoverable, *Re Gibson's Settlement Trusts* [1981] Ch 179. [1981] 1 All ER 233 applied. The matter was one of fact and legal analysis rather than discretion

(f) State funding

[16.21]

Where you are acting for two or more parties, some, but not all of whom are in receipt of state funding, ensure that the order adequately protects the claim against the fund. Otherwise the costs recoverable against the fund will be divided by the number of parties for whom you act – with a disastrous (for you) decrease in the costs payable under the funding certificate.

(g) VAT between the parties

[16.22]

This subject is so important and gives rise to so much misunderstanding that I devote Chapter 12 to it.

VARYING AND REVOKING

[16.23]

Prior to the introduction of the CPR, once an order had been made and entered by the court neither the judge who made it nor another judge of co-ordinate jurisdiction had any jurisdiction to vary it unless the order itself contained a power permitting an application to vary. The only remedy was to appeal. However, CPR Rule 3.1(7) provides 'the power of the court under these rules to make an order includes the power to vary or revoke the order'. It will be interesting to see to what extent judges are prepared to exercise their jurisdiction under Rule 3.1(7) in respect of orders for costs. Rule 40.9 provides that even a person who is not a party but who is directly affected by a judgment or order may apply to have the judgment or order set aside or varied.

DISCONTINUANCE

[16.24]

CPR rule 38.6 provides:
    (1)   Unless the court orders otherwise, a claimant who discontinues is liable for the costs which a defendant against whom the claimant discontinues incurred on or before the date on which notice of discontinuance was served on the defendant.
    (2)   If proceedings are only partly discontinued –
    (a)   the claimant is liable under paragraph (1) for costs relating only to the part of the proceedings which he is discontinuing; and
    (b)   unless the court orders otherwise, the costs which the claimant is liable to pay must not be assessed until the conclusion of the rest of the proceedings.
    (3)   This rule does not apply to claims allocated to the small claims track.
(Rule 44.12 provides for the basis of assessment where the right to costs arises on discontinuance and contains provisions about when a costs order is deemed to have been made and applying for an order under section 194(3) of the Legal Services Act 2007.)

Where claimants deleted a claim by amendments to the particulars of claim this was in effect a discontinuance of that claim with the same costs consequences (*Isaac v Isaac* [2005] EWHC 435 (Ch), [2005] All ER (D) 379 (Mar). The burden is on a claimant who seeks to avoid the costs consequences of discontinuance to persuade the court that some other order is appropriate, perhaps because of some unavoidable and unforeseeable change of circumstance (*Walker v Walker* [2005] EWCA Civ 247, [2006] 1 All ER 272, [2006] 1 WLR 2194). An example might be where the defendant had rendered the claimant's claim worthless, say by embarking on some other unsuccessful proceedings which lead to bankruptcy. Changing circumstances are part and parcel of litigation. It is difficult to see how any change in circumstances could amount to good reason unless connected with some conduct on the part of the defendant which deserved to result in costs against them. A change of circumstances was simply the beginning of the enquiry, not the end of it. The context for the court's mandatory consideration of all the circumstances under CPR Rule 44.3 was therefore the determination of whether there was good reason to depart from the presumption imposed by rule 38.6 (*Teasdale v HSBC Bank plc* [2010] EWHC 612 (QB), [2010] NLJR 878, [2010] All ER (D) 34 (Jun)).

In *Messih v McMillan Williams* [2010] EWCA Civ 844, 22 July the claimant brought proceedings against two firms of solicitors alleging different causes of action arising out of his tenancy of commercial premises. The proceedings against the first solicitors were settled on the terms that the solicitors paid damages and the claimant's costs. The claimant wished to discontinue against the second firm of solicitors on the basis that each party would pay their own costs, but the solicitors would not agree. Accordingly the claimant served notice of discontinuance and applied for an order under CPR Rule 38.6(1) that he should not be required to pay the second firm's costs. The judge made the order requested against which the defendant appealed.

The Court of Appeal held that the judge was wrong. If CPR Rule 38.6 had been intended to create a general discretion as to costs on discontinuance it would have said so. The rule made it clear that the defendant started from the position of being entitled to his costs and it was for the claimant to justify the making of some other order. Accordingly the claimant was ordered to pay the second solicitors' cost up to the date of discontinuance.

THE SLIP RULE

[16.25]

Let us end on a note of comfort. Clerical mistakes in judgments, or orders or errors arising therein from any accidental slip or omission, may at any time be corrected by the court (Rule 40.12). A party may apply for a correction without notice. The Practice Direction supplementing Part 40 provides as follows:

[16.26]

PRACTICE DIRECTION SUPPLEMENTING CPR PART 40

Correction of errors in judgments and orders

4.1 Where a judgment or order contains an accidental slip or omission a party may apply for it to be corrected.

4.2 The application notice (which may be an informal document such as a letter) should describe the error and set out the correction required. An application may be dealt with without a hearing:

(1) where the applicant so requests,

(2) with the consent of the parties, or

(3) where the court does not consider that a hearing would be appropriate.

4.3 The judge may deal with the application without notice if the slip or omission is obvious or may direct notice of the application to be given to the other party or parties.

4.4 If the application is opposed it should, if practicable, be listed for hearing before the judge who gave the judgment or made the order.

4.5 The court has an inherent power to vary its own orders to make the meaning and intention of the court clear.

[16.27]

The power arises where the clearly expressed judgment of the judge has been wrongly recorded in the judgment or order. The error may be rectified on the application of either party or on the initiative of the court itself. Apart from this provision of the rules, the court has an inherent power to vary its own orders so as to carry out its own meaning and to make its meaning plain (*Thynne v Thynne* [1955] P 272, CA). The power to correct clerical mistakes extends not only to those made by an administrative officer of the court but also to those made by a party or his advisors (*Navimpex Centrala Navala v George Moundreas & Co SA* (1983) 127 Sol Jo 392, CA). However, the slip rule cannot be invoked to rehear or amend an order for costs which correctly reflects the judge's order (*Preston Banking Co v William Allsup & Sons* [1895] 1 Ch 141, CA) or where there has been a misunderstanding as to the effect of a conventional costs order (*Mölnlycke AB v Procter & Gamble Ltd (No 6)* [1993] FSR 154, ChD). It can be used where the judge was not asked to make an order which he would have done had he been asked (*Re Inchcape (Earl) Craigmyle v Inchcape* [1942] Ch 394, [1942] 2 All ER 157). There is no time limit for such an application.

It is important to note that not every failure of an order to give effect to the court's intention can be corrected under the slip rule which is limited to accidental omissions.

It is common for the court to encourage parties to agree matters of detail in the drawing up of its order with the proviso that the parties might mention the matter again to the court in the event of disagreement. Matters deliberately included by the parties in an order drawn up and sealed by the court do not constitute accidental slips or omissions within the rule and cannot be corrected under the slip rule unless the error had an unintended effect which was inconsistent with the court's intention: *Leo Pharma A/S v Sandoz Ltd* (2010) Times, 6 October, ChD.

CHAPTER 17

THE INDEMNITY PRINCIPLE

NOT A FULL INDEMNITY

[17.1]

In England and Wales it is usual for the loser in litigation to be ordered to pay the winner's costs or, as CPR Rule 44.3(2)(*a*) puts it, 'the general rule is that the unsuccessful party will be ordered to pay the costs of the successful party'. Costs are awarded to indemnify the successful party for the costs and expenses he has incurred in the litigation. Although this is called an indemnity it is not a full indemnity (as we shall see in Chapter 22) for a variety of reasons: the winner (the receiving party) may have agreed an unreasonable charging rate with his solicitors; unreasonable or disproportionate work may have been done; the work may have been done by the wrong level of fee earner or counsel and unnecessary disbursements may have been incurred. All of these are matters over which the loser (the paying party) had no control and it would be wrong for the receiving party to be indemnified for them.

NO PROFIT

[17.2]

Although it is unusual for costs ordered between the parties to be as much as the receiving party's solicitor and client costs, what is certain is that costs between the parties can *never exceed* the solicitor and client costs. The receiving party is entitled only to be indemnified for his liability to his solicitor – he cannot make a profit out of the costs recovered from the other party. The first record of this principle being expounded was in *Harold v Smith* (1860) 5 H & N 381 in these terms:

> 'Costs as between party and party are given by the law as an indemnity to the person entitled to them: they are not imposed as a punishment on the party who pays them, nor given as a bonus to the party who receives them. Therefore, if the extent of the indemnification can be found out, the extent to which costs ought to be allowed is also ascertained.'

PITFALLS

(a) Impecunious client

[17.3]

We now come to the pitfalls. Let us start with an easy one. If the solicitor agrees to work for nothing, the client has no liability for costs to his solicitor and therefore has no need for or entitlement to an indemnity from the other party if he succeeds in the litigation.

The seminal case is *Gundry v Sainsbury* [1910] 1 KB 645, CA in which the Court of Appeal held that to award costs to a client whose solicitor had agreed not to charge costs would have been giving a bonus to the party receiving them. That was contrary to justice and to common sense and also to the law as laid down in *Harold v Smith* (above). It is understandable that a solicitor may agree to act on the basis that he will make no charge unless the action succeeds. Indeed, in practice, this is often the case when a solicitor is acting for an impoverished non-state funded client, but why, you might ask, would a solicitor agree to act on the basis that he would not be paid whatever the outcome of the litigation? I know of only two such reported cases. The first was *Gundry v Sainsbury* itself, in which the client was a labourer suing for injuries caused by being bitten by a dog and who in the course of the cross-examination said: 'I could not pay costs and I had arranged with my solicitor not to pay the costs of the action'. The solicitor disagreed that those were in fact the terms of the retainer but he was precluded from giving evidence to this effect by the Attorneys and Solicitors Act 1870, s 4! As Buckley LJ said in the Court of Appeal, it was a matter of some regret that the solicitor was not allowed to go into the box and state the real facts relating to the agreement. It was for this reason that the public-spirited solicitor was deprived of the between-the-parties costs of the successful litigation. A more recent example arose in *British Waterways Board v Norman* (1993) 26 HLR 232, QBD, in which the court held that where solicitors agreed to act for a client whose financial circumstances were such that there was no prospect of the client paying the solicitors' costs unless the action succeeded, in the absence of a specific agreement to the contrary, the court concluded there must have been an understanding between the solicitors and the client that they would not look to her for costs if she lost. This appears to be a reversal of the usual basis of a contract that either party is entitled to enforce it unless there is an express prohibition against them doing so. This case is often referred to as having been overruled by *Thai Trading Co (a firm) v Taylor* [1998] QB 781, CA (see p520). But *Thai Trading* was concerned about the lawfulness of a 'no win, no fee' agreement and it was only this aspect of the judgment in *British Waterways Board v Norman* that was overruled by *Thai Trading*. The basic tenet remains that, if a solicitor expressly or impliedly agrees that he will not in any circumstances charge his client, no costs are recoverable from the other party.

Two subsequent cases in which the question of impecuniosity was invoked were *Leeds City Council v Carr* and *Wells v Barnsley Metropolitan Borough Council* (1999) 32 HLR 753, QBD DC, in which the local authorities sought to avoid paying costs ordered against them on the grounds that private prosecutions in respect of defective properties were funded by the solicitors on the basis that their clients would not be liable to pay any costs to them, win or lose, and that any purported agreement to the contrary was a sham. In both cases the court found there was no sufficient basis for the allegation.

In *Burstein v Times Newspapers Ltd (No 2)* [2002] EWCA Civ 1739, [2003] 03 LS Gaz R 31, CA the claimant was awarded his costs of his successful libel action against the defendants. The defendants contended that when the claimant's solicitors became aware that their client was no longer able to pay their costs, the agreement in their retainer that he would pay their costs became a sham and unenforceable. Accordingly, the defendants contended that the claimant had no liability towards his own solicitors for costs. The judge and the Court of Appeal rejected that argument, holding that the material produced by the defendants did not undermine the evidence of the claimant's solicitors that the agreements were proper. The defendants' proposition that a retainer was, or became, champertous and therefore unlawful and unenforceable if a solicitor became aware at any time that their client could not have afforded to pay his costs, was a proposition which could not on the authorities be supported.

(b) Pro bono

[17.4]

A topical example of working for no fee, whatever the outcome of the litigation, are the professional pro bono groups. In its consultation paper, 'Costs Recovery in Pro Bono Assisted Cases', the Department for Constitutional Affairs (now the Ministry of Justice) said: 'Pro bono work is an important adjunct to the main strands of the provision of legal services. However, there is an injustice caused by the fact that costs cannot be recovered from the losing party if the successful party is represented pro bono, even though a pro bono assisted party would be liable for his opponent's costs if his opponent won. In such cases, the opponent is aware that if he loses, he will not be asked to pay the other party's costs because that party is represented pro bono. It is intended that the sums recovered will go, not to those providing the representation but, to a prescribed charitable body that will administer and distribute monies received to voluntary organisations that provide free legal support to the community.' The result was section 194 of the Legal Services Act 2007 (see para [11.30A]) and the abrogation of the indemnity principle in pro bono assisted cases.

(c) Payment by a third party

[17.5]

Litigation is increasingly being funded under arrangements whereby the solicitor's costs are to be paid by a third party, perhaps a trade union or an insurance company. In order to recover costs from another party it must be shown that the client had a primary, or dual, liability for his solicitor's costs, as he was able to do in *R v Miller (Raymond)* [1983] 3 All ER 186, CA. It is therefore important expressly to incorporate in the client care letter the right to look to the client for payment of the solicitor and client costs if the case is won, and, indeed, if it is lost, unless there is a valid conditional fee agreement.

Otherwise, on the basis of *British Waterways Board v Norman*, it may be argued that there is an implication to the contrary and that the client has no liability to his solicitor for which he is entitled to be indemnified between the parties.

In *Ilangaratne v British Medical Association* [2007] EWHC 920 (Ch) the insurers of the BMA, who were successful in the action, had instructed the solicitors and the claimant alleged there was therefore no retainer between the defendant and the solicitors – another breach of the indemnity principle. However, there was a standing arrangement between the insurers and the solicitors, as to costs evidenced by a letter between them. Although the letter itself was not a written contract or retainer it was evidence of a standing arrangement that any instructions to the solicitors on behalf of the insurer's customers would give rise to a retainer between the customer and the solicitor on terms already advised and agreed, including the charging rate previously agreed with the insurers. There was therefore a retainer.

(d) Fixed fee

[17.6]

Where a solicitor agrees to work for a fixed fee, that is the maximum amount that can be recovered from another party.

(e) Interim bill

[17.7]

If during the course of litigation the solicitor delivers a bill to the client for work done to date – a stage payment – if that bill is a statute bill and not merely a request for payment on account (see para [1.8]) then the solicitor has fixed his costs at that amount for the work done during the period covered by the bill and cannot recover a higher amount from another party for that period.

(f) Item-by-item

[17.8]

A dramatic development in the application of the indemnity principle was the decision of the Court of Appeal in *General of Berne Insurance Co v Jardine Reinsurance Management Ltd* [1998] 2 All ER 301, CA. Two Supreme Court Taxing Office masters (now costs judges) had reached conflicting decisions on whether the application of the indemnity principle should be on an item-by-item basis, or whether it only provides a global cap, so that the receiving party may recover on assessment uplifted hourly expense rates which are judged to be reasonable, even if they exceed the rates that the solicitors were entitled to receive from their client under a contentious business agreement, provided that the total amount allowed between the parties did not exceed the total amount the solicitors were entitled to recover from their client. There were arguments both ways and, in the words of the Court of Appeal, 'each of the parties' cases has its problems'. The court came down in favour of the item-by-item approach, even though it accepted that examples could arise where complicated and painstaking reductions could be required, commenting 'taxation [*assessment*] of costs can be a laborious procedure in any event, and can be expensive in taxing [*assessing*] fees'. No one would quarrel with that. *Nederlandse Reassurantie Groep Holding NV v Bacon & Woodrow* ([1998] 2 Costs LR 32, QBD), a review of a taxation [*detailed assessment*] by Tucker J, confirmed that the *General of Berne v Jardine* interpretation of the indemnity principle applied to all retainers, whether or not a formal contentious business agreement was in place.

The full consequences of these decisions are still emerging, for example: where interim costs have been awarded against the receiving party or where parts of the receiving party's costs have been excluded; if the receiving party's solicitor was acting for a fixed fee, there cannot be an item-by-item comparison; if the retainer provides that the solicitor will not charge the client more than the amount of costs recovered between the parties what is the amount for which the client is entitled to be indemnified? Nil? Or perhaps the solicitor should agree not to charge the client *less* than the amount recovered between the parties! How is a retainer for a fixed expense rate with a flexible mark-up to be compared between the parties? How does the indemnity principle apply where there is a financial limit on the funding certificate? How does the amount of the success fee under a conditional fee agreement affect the application of the indemnity principle? How does the principle apply where a party is entitled to fixed costs? In any event, the Law Society recommends the inclusion of a 'slip clause' when acting on an hourly charge-out basis to permit an additional percentage in the final bill in certain circumstances to cover the item-by-item approach if necessary.

(g) Disclosure

[17.9]

A matter which has bedevilled assessments of costs for some years is how is the paying party to discover the terms of the retainer to ascertain the level of the indemnity to which the receiving party is entitled? For some time I have expressed the view that solicitors for a paying party could be negligent if they fail to obtain this information and, indeed, that the onus should be on the receiving party to satisfy the costs officer that the terms of the retainer entitle him to the indemnity for costs he is seeking. This view received support in *Bailey v IBC Vehicles Ltd* [1998] 3 All ER 570, CA, in which the court held that in future, any client care letter setting out the terms of the client's financial obligations to the solicitors should be attached to the bill of costs together with any contentious business agreement or other relevant documents. However, Henry LJ suggested that the signing of the between-the-parties bill of costs by the solicitor as an officer of the court was effectively a certificate that the receiving party's solicitors were not seeking to recover in relation to any item more than they had agreed to charge their client. There was a presumption of trust and any breach of that trust should be treated as a most serious disciplinary offence. This suggestion was rejected by the Court of Appeal in *Hollins v Russell* [2003] EWCA Civ 718, [2003] 4 All ER 590, in respect of challenges to conditional fee agreements, which it distinguished from conventional challenges, as in *Bailey*. In *Bailey* the paying party was not saying that there was no liability at all to pay any costs to the receiving party, but was challenging the hourly rate and mark-up being applied. The challenge to a bill of costs moved several ratchets up the scale once the challenge changed from a challenge to the figures produced to a challenge to the principle of paying anything at all. The conditional fee agreement (CFA) regulations introduced a new level of complexity. The solicitor's certificate as to accuracy may not be sufficient where the quality and quantity of the information served on the paying party about the success fee is less than would be made available in respect of the other aspects of the bill in the case of an assessment where there is no additional liability claimed. The question of whether the CFA complies with the Courts and Legal Services Act 1990 is principally a matter of law, while challenges to conventional bills are generally questions of fact. It is not appropriate to impose on costs judges the responsibility of acting as a filter to see that the regulations are complied with in every respect. *Bailey* should not be extended to CFAs, but limited to challenges to conventional bills. It should therefore become normal practice for a CFA to be disclosed for the purpose of costs proceedings in which a success fee is claimed, subject to the provision in para 40.14 of the Costs Practice Direction that the judge may ask the receiving party to elect whether to disclose the CFA to the paying party in order to rely on it or whether to decline disclosure and instead rely on other evidence. If the CFA contains confidential information relating to other proceedings, it may be suitably redacted before disclosure takes place. Attendance notes and other correspondence should not ordinarily be disclosed, but the judge conducting the assessment may require the disclosure of material of this kind if a genuine issue is raised. A genuine issue is one in which there is a real chance that the CFA is unenforceable as a result of failure to satisfy the applicable conditions.

This approach has been exemplified in both the Supreme Court Costs Office's *Guide to the Summary Assessment of Costs* and in the case of *Hazlett v Sefton Metropolitan Borough Council* [2000] 4 All ER 887, QBD DC in which it was held that for the purpose of making an order for costs between the parties, there is a presumption that the client would be personally liable for her solicitor's costs and it would not normally be necessary for the client to have to adduce evidence to that effect. However, where there was a genuine issue raised by the paying party as to whether the receiving party had properly incurred costs in the proceedings, the position would be different. If it were alleged that the receiving party was not liable to pay her solicitor's costs, whether because she had entered into an unlawful and an unenforceable CFA with her solicitor or for any other reasons, she would be at risk if she continued to rely upon the presumption that she was liable for her solicitor's costs. If she did not then adduce evidence to prove that she had properly incurred costs in the proceedings or that the paying party could show by evidence or argument that she had not, she would be most unlikely to succeed in recovering her costs. The need for a claimant to give evidence to prove her entitlement to costs rather than relying upon the presumption in her favour would not, however, arise if the paying party simply put the claimant to proof of her entitlement to costs. Then the claimant would be justified in relying on the presumption in her favour. The SCCO *Guide* quotes the words of Henry LJ in *Bailey v IBC Vehicles* and suggests that the signature of a statement of costs (or a bill for detailed assessment) by a solicitor is, in normal circumstances, sufficient to enable the court to be satisfied that the indemnity principle has not been breached.

Dickinson (t/a Dickinson Equipment Finance) v Rushmer (t/a FJ Associates) [2002] NLJR 58, ChD was an appeal from a detailed assessment by a costs judge to Rimer J sitting with assessors. On the detailed assessment the paying party (the defendant) invoked the indemnity principle, asserting that the receiving party (the claimant) could not have assumed a personal responsibility to pay costs of the amount claimed in his solicitor's bills. The claimant's solicitors produced to the costs judge documents to prove the terms of the retainer and demonstrate there was no breach of the indemnity principle. The costs judge refused to allow the defendant to see the documents on the grounds they were privileged. It was held that the costs judge was wrong. It is one of the most basic principles of natural justice that each side is entitled to know what the other side's case is and to see the documentary material on which he is relying. The receiving party, without producing any documents, could ask the costs judge to direct whether he regarded the paying party as having raised a genuine issue which needed to be met by evidence, or if he accepted the signification on the bill of costs that the indemnity principle had not been offended. If the receiving party pre-empts any such decision by the costs judge by producing the documents, the paying party is entitled to see them, even though they are privileged.

In *South Coast Shipping Co Ltd v Havant Borough Council* [2002] 3 All ER 779, ChD the costs judge had been shown documents which the paying party had not been allowed to see on the grounds that they were privileged. The appeal raised human rights issues, in particular the conflict between the right to privilege and the right to a fair trial. If the costs judge, having seen the documents in question, required the receiving party to elect between giving secondary evidence of the retainer and waiving the privilege, there was no incompatibility with the principles articulated by the European Convention for Human Rights. That was not intended to suggest that the costs judge should put the receiving party to its election in respect of every document relied on, regardless of its degree of relevance. In the great majority of cases the paying party would be content to agree that the costs judge alone should see privileged documents. Only where it was necessary and proportionate should the receiving party be put to his election. The redaction and production of privileged documents, or the adducing of further evidence, would lead to additional delay and increase costs.

Where solicitors go on the record for a party there is a *prima facie* inference on the balance of probabilities that there exists a relationship whereby the solicitors can look to the party for payment of their costs. It is for the paying party to prove otherwise. The presumption in favour of the paying party in CPR 44.4(2)(b) applies only to questions of reasonableness and proportionality and not to the issue of the existence or otherwise of the retainer (*Bulmer v Owlett* [2007] Ch D. 17 May RCJ).

(h) Unlawful retainer

[17.10]

Worst of all, if a solicitor enters into an invalid retainer with the client – a champertous agreement or a conditional fee agreement which does not comply with the regulations – it is unenforceable against the client and the client can therefore recover nothing from the other party. For disastrous examples see Chapter 42.

(i) Fixed costs

[17.11]

In *Butt v Nizami* [2006] EWHC 159 (QB) (9 February), sometimes reported as *Nizami v Butt*, the claimants both suffered whiplash injuries when the car they were travelling in was hit by the defendant's car. Their claims were settled, but costs could not be agreed. They commenced costs-only proceedings under CPR Part 8 claiming fixed recoverable costs under CPR Rule 45.9, disbursements under Rule 45.10 and a fixed success fee under Rule 45.11. The defendants alleged that the claimants' solicitors had failed to make appropriate enquiries about the availability of before-the-event insurance and sought a direction for the solicitors to certify compliance with the Conditional Fee Agreement Regulations 2000. The costs judge held that the claimants' entitlement to costs depended not on the existence of a valid and enforceable conditional fee agreement, but on their entitlement under the fixed recoverable costs rule. He was upheld on appeal.

The intention underlying CPR 45.7–45.14 is to provide an agreed scheme of recovery that is certain and easily calculated by providing fixed levels of remuneration, which might over-reward in some cases and under-reward in others, but which were regarded as fair when taken as a whole. There was a change in the law effected by the amendment to s 51(2) of the Supreme Court (now Senior Courts) Act 1981 which significantly modified the indemnity principle and permitted changes in the rules to give effect to the modification.

It was clear that it was intended that the indemnity principle should not apply to the figures that were recoverable, and accordingly there was little reason why the indemnity principle should have any application to Rules 45.9 and 45.11, and good reasons why it should not. The CPR had successfully disapplied the indemnity principle in relation to the predictable costs scheme.

This decision illustrates that whether or not solicitors are acting under a conditional fee agreement, it is implicit in all fixed costs regimes that the indemnity principle is disapplied. CPR Part 45 covers two kinds of fixed costs. In Section I, Table I gives the fixed costs on commencement, Table II costs on entry of judgment and Table III miscellaneous fixed costs, which are concerned mainly with service of documents. The prescribed amounts are payable without any enquiry into the terms of the retainer between the receiving party and their solicitor. Section II is concerned with predictable costs in road traffic accident claims and this decision confirms that it is inappropriate to enquire into the terms of the receiving party's retainer. A further form of fixed costs is the fixed trial costs on the fast track under CPR Part 46, Rule 46.2 (2) of which prescribes that the court shall not award less than the amount shown in the table. This clearly precludes an investigation into the terms of the successful party's retainer and, for example, it is accepted that the amount of counsel's brief fee is of no relevance, even if it is substantially less than the prescribed amount of the fixed costs. At the recent Civil Justice Council's Cost Forum, it was generally agreed that in road traffic accident cases it would be helpful to make progress towards a predictable costs regime for the pre-trial costs. The attraction of the certainty and consistency of fixed, or predictable costs, would be undermined if they were subject to the indemnity principle. Fixed costs are an incentive to efficiency and a sanction against inefficiency.

THE FUTURE OF THE INDEMNITY PRINCIPLE

[17.12]

In a previous edition, I wrote:

> 'It seems to me that the indemnity principle, first identified in *Harold v Smith* nearly 140 years ago, has outlived its usefulness: its application in modern times is causing horrendous and virtually insoluble problems. Why should the amount payable by the loser in litigation be influenced by the winner's liability to his own solicitor? Why should a successful litigant not be able to recover a reasonable and proportionate amount for the costs of the action irrespective of his financial arrangement with his solicitor and the method by which the litigation is being funded? At a time when reforms are aimed at achieving proportionality between costs and the subject matter of the litigation, it is ironic that the satellite litigation of drawing and assessing bills should itself be incurring costs disproportionate to the costs themselves.'

In May 1999 the Lord Chancellor produced a consultation paper entitled 'Controlling Costs and the Future of the Indemnity Principle'. The paper said it was clear that the application of the indemnity principle had become increasingly marginalised by the changes which had taken place in recent years and the question therefore arose as to whether there was any merit in its retention. The paper continued:

> 'However, whilst the principle is being observed as much in the breach, it does continue to have a central position in costs law and is inextricably linked to the general presumption that the successful party is entitled to be indemnified by his opponent for his legal costs. It is argued that the indemnity principle operates to place some limit on the sums that can be recovered, and generally acts to keep the costs no greater than the liability of the client to his solicitor. Whilst minded to accept the thrust of the argument for the abolition of the remaining vestiges of the principle, the Lord Chancellor is concerned that its removal should not lead to an increase in legal costs being awarded by the courts over time. The indemnity principle provides a cap on the costs which can be recovered from the losing party. Without it solicitors will be technically free to claim costs without bounds, subject to assessment by the court.'

The government's conclusions following consultation on the Lord Chancellor's Department's consultation paper on 'Collective Conditional Fees' are not everyone's idea of a good bedtime read, but tucked away at the end were the glad tidings that the indemnity principle is to be disapplied in respect of the assessment of costs. Respondents had commented overwhelmingly that the indemnity principle no longer served any useful purpose and should be abolished in full. The principle did not act in anyone's interest and had no impact on overall costs, given the introduction of proportionality. The government recognised the heavy burden of current work on the Civil

Procedure Rules Committee would dictate the date at which any rules could be made, but recommended that the Committee considered the early introduction of any necessary rules. Here is the government's explanation of policy, giving the original paragraph numbers:

'30.   The Government recognises that a constraint on an organisation or legal representative's ability to enter into a completely transparent relationship with their client concerning costs, is the threat of the opponent arguing on assessment that the indemnity principle had been breached.

31.   Although there have been many changes in law which have had the effect of diluting the impact of the indemnity principle, whether in terms of Legal Aid changes, the introduction of conditional fee agreements or the growing body of case law, the indemnity principle continues to exert a major influence on the assessment of costs. By invoking the indemnity principle, paying parties have argued against any liability for costs in cases where a client has entered into an agreement where a solicitor has agreed to waive any fees if the case is unsuccessful and, if successful, seek to recover what the court allows from the paying party, without setting out the charging rate they will seek to recover. This is a particular issue where the client is indemnified for their costs by a third party. In these cases it is argued by the paying party that the client has no actual obligation to his solicitor and therefore neither do they.

32.   To ensure that they do not fall victim to the indemnity principle, providers enter into agreements which set out the charging rate to be applied in the event of a successful case, even though it is clear to the providers that the charging rate will rarely apply and should they win, and not recover the full amount billed, they will not recover the excess from their clients. In third party funded cases lawyers have drawn up agreements which regard both the organisation and client as being liable to pay, thereby avoiding the indemnity principle.

33.   The Government recognises that clients are not always versed in legal proceedings and misconstrue the agreements they have entered into. The client having been told that they have no liability whatever the outcome of the case does not understand why the agreement states that there is a liability. This is a particular concern in cases funded by trade unions or membership organisations. The Government believes that it is in the interests of all concerned for there to be complete clarity in the provision of these services. The operation of the indemnity principle clearly inhibits clarity. Although the introduction of CCFA regulations under s 58 of the Courts and Legal Services Act 1990 (as amended) abrogates the indemnity principle for CCFAs, the Government is persuaded that there is no longer any justification for the operation of the principle when assessing costs no matter how funded.

34.   Section 31 of the Access to Justice Act 1999 (when commenced) amends s 51 of the Supreme Court Act 1981 to provide that the amount recovered by way of costs may not be limited to 'what would have been payable by him (the client) to them (his lawyers) if he had not been awarded costs.'

[17.13]

The implementation of s 51 would allow rules of court to be drawn up which provide, beyond any doubt, that the receiving party can receive reasonable and proportionate costs irrespective of the terms of the agreement, in cases where an additional liability is claimed.

The method of financing litigation should be a privileged matter between the client and the solicitor. Funding may or may not be under a conditional fee agreement, which itself may be 'no win, no fee' or 'no win, lesser fee' or some other formula, it may be by a trade union or a maiden aunt and it may involve after-the-event insurance or be covered by legal expenses insurance ('before-the-event' insurance), none of which should be of concern to the court or other party.

Costs recoverable between the parties should be such sum as is reasonable and proportionate having regard to the subject matter of the litigation regardless of the terms under which those services have been provided.

In his inaugural lecture as a professor, John Peysner of Nottingham Law School said that 'the long and baffling' existence of the indemnity principle, which has no place in the modern world of litigation, should be brought to a humane end by comprehensive abolition; not only was it contrary to the basis of risk management and sound business principles, it also acted as a bar to progress on introducing fixed or capped fees as a means of bringing certainty to fast track costs. David Hartley, then head of the Law Society's remuneration team added to the call for abolition, saying: 'We no longer believe that the indemnity principle serves any useful purpose. It will need to go to ensure that collective conditional fee agreements will work properly.'

The Civil Justice Council's working party on predictable costs almost unanimously agreed that the indemnity principle should be abolished, a view which has since been endorsed by Lord Phillips, then Master of the Rolls, and May J, then Deputy Head of Civil Justice. Unfortunately there is no unanimity as to how this may be achieved, and, in particular, whether primary legislation is necessary. In previous editions I wrote: 'Surely what is required is the implementation of s 31 of the Access to Justice Act 1999 which amends s 51 of the Supreme Court Act 1981'. It has been implemented with effect from 2 June 2003. The prevailing view, for reasons too arcane to pursue here, is that primary legislation is necessary for the outright abolition of the indemnity principle (which I concede would first have to be defined and identified before it could be shot) therefore stop-gap measures have been taken by disapplying the indemnity principle to simple no win, no fee, no deductions agreements ('CFA-lites') which are more fully considered in Section VII. However, the mischief of the indemnity principle remains in respect of all other methods of litigation funding. The Civil Justice Council has set up a working group to consider implementation of abolishing the indemnity principle. If it is still considered that abolition requires primary legislation, the group will investigate the use of the Civil Procedure Rules to achieve this. Unfortunately, the indemnity principle survived the revocation of the CFA Regulations on 1 November 2005 (see Section VII). In his Review of the Costs of Civil Litigation Lord Justice Jackson identified seven reasons for its abrogation.

CHAPTER 18

INTEREST ON COSTS

STATUTES

[18.1]

Section 35A of the Supreme Court (now Senior Courts) Act, sub-s (1), provides:

> ' . . . subject to rules of court, in proceedings (whenever instituted) before the High Court for the recovery of a debt or damages there may be included in any sum for which judgment is given simple interest, at such rate as the court thinks fit or as rules of court may provide, on all or any part of the debt or damages in respect of which judgment is given, or payment is made before judgment, for all or any part of the period between the date when the cause of action arose . . . '

Section 74(1) of the County Courts Act 1984 is similar:

> ' . . . the Lord Chancellor may by order made with the concurrence of the Treasury provide any sums to which this subsection applies shall carry interest at such rate in between such time as may be prescribed by the order.'

Section 17(1) of the Judgments Act 1838 continues the provision:

> ' . . . every judgment debt shall carry interest at the rate of . . . from such time as shall be prescribed by rules of court until the same shall be satisfied, and such interest may be levied under a writ of execution on such judgment.'

The Judgments Act 1838, s 17 provides for the recovery of interest on costs in the High Court, whilst the County Court (Interest on Judgment Debts) Order 1991, made under the County Courts Act 1984, s 74, provides for interest to be paid on 'relevant judgments'. A relevant judgment is one for not less than £5,000 or in respect of a 'qualifying debt' as defined by the Late Payment of Commercial Debts (Interest) Act 1998, into which we shall not delve.

THE INCIPITUR RULE

[18.2]

The dispute as to the date from which interest on costs runs from went all the way up to the House of Lords where, in *Hunt v R M Douglas (Roofing) Ltd* [1990] 1 AC 398, it was held that interest on costs ran from the date on which judgment is pronounced and not from the date of the costs officer's certificate. The former is known as the *incipitur rule* and the latter as the *allocatur rule*. Neither rule is entirely satisfactory but it was held that the balance of justice favoured the incipitur rule because the unsuccessful party had unnecessarily caused the costs to be incurred and that as neither rule covers costs incurred before the judgment the application of the allocatur rule, generally speaking, does greater injustice than the operation of the incipitur rule, even though this meant the successful party would recover interest on disbursements before they were made and costs after judgment before they were incurred. This has now been enshrined in CPR Rule 40.8(1) as follows:

'(1) Where interest is payable on a judgment pursuant to section 17 of the Judgments Act 1838 or section 74 of the County Courts Act 1984, the interest shall begin to run from the date that judgment is given unless—

(a)   a rule in another Part or a Practice Direction makes different provision; or
(b)   the court orders otherwise.

(2) The court may order that interest shall begin to run from a date before the date that judgment is given.'

ORDERS DEEMED TO HAVE BEEN MADE

[18.3]

CPR Rule 44.12(2) provides that interest payable pursuant to of the Judgments Act 1838, s 17 or the County Courts Act 1984, s 74 on costs deemed to have been ordered (where a Part 36 payment or offer is accepted or where a claimant discontinues) shall begin to run from the date on which the event which gave rise to the entitlement to costs occurred.

ENHANCED INTEREST

[18.4]

CPR Rule 36.21 provides that where at trial a defendant is held liable for more, or the judgment against a defendant is more advantageous to a claimant than the proposals contained in a claimant's Part 36 offer, the court may order that the claimant is entitled to their costs on the indemnity basis and interest on those costs at a rate not exceeding 10% above base rate. For an example of this in practice, see p156.

BACKDATING

[18.5]

Where the costs judge had made various orders for the costs of the receiving party during the course of the assessment, the interest on those costs also ran from the date of the order for costs to be assessed under the incipitur rule not from the dates of the costs officer's certificates (*Ross v Owners of the ship 'Bowbelle'* [1997] 1 WLR 1159, CA). Similarly, in *Electricity Supply Nominees Ltd v Farrell* [1997] 2 All ER 498, CA, where a consent order provided that the costs 'shall be taxed [*assessed*] upon the standard basis if not agreed and *such costs when taxed* [assessed] *or agreed shall be paid* by the defendants' it did not operate as a genuine postponement until after assessment of the obligation to pay the costs so as to avoid interest running from the date of the order pursuant to the rule in *Hunt v RM Douglas (Roofing) Ltd* [1990] 1 AC 398, HL. The words in italics were probably verbiage derived from a precedent and were no more than a recitation of what in fact was to occur. Although it is open to the parties to a consent order to make a side agreement as to interest or to take account of the effect of the court's order on interest, altering the wording of costs orders is unlikely to achieve the desired result. It was doubtful if even in a consent order the court could directly alter the incidence of interest on the judgment because that is governed by the Act and rules of court.

In *Nykredit Mortgage Bank plc v Edward Erdman Group Ltd (No 2)* [1998] 1 All ER 305, HL the House of Lords said that the Court of Appeal had been 'lured into error' when in *Kuwait Airways Corpn v Iraqi Airways Co (No 2)* [1995] 1 All ER 790, CA it held that the Rules of the Supreme Court empowered it to backdate its order for costs to enable interest to run from the original judgment. Statute apart, courts have no power to award interest on costs, however desirable it might be for the court to have power to order the payment of interest on costs from a date earlier than the date on which the court gave judgment. However, although the court had no general inherent power to order the payment of interest, the result of the appeal had been that orders in the courts below should not have been made and that some of the money previously paid by the defendants to the plaintiffs as damages and costs pursuant to orders of the trial judge and the Court of Appeal had fallen to be repaid to them. This could have been an idle exercise unless the court was able to make consequential orders that achieved, as near as reasonably practicable, the necessary restitution which included interest on the money to be repaid. The power to do so was derived from the inherent jurisdiction of the House of Lords, which was also possessed by the Court of Appeal. To enable lesser mortals to do the same, the Civil Procedure (Modification of Enactments) Order 1998 amended the Judgments Act 1838, s 17(1) to provide that interest will run from such time as is prescribed by rules of court. The resultant rule is CPR Rule 44.3(6)(g) which empowers any court to award 'interest on costs from or until a certain date, including a date *before* judgment'.

In a clinical negligence claim on behalf of a child who suffered severe brain damage soon after birth, liability was admitted and judgment entered by consent in April 1994. The damages were not assessed until June 2001, when there was an award of £2,175,000. The claim for interest on the costs almost exceeded the amount of the bill itself, being dated back to April 1994. The delay had arisen from uncertainly about the medical prognosis rather than any sloth on the part of the claimant or his lawyers. The defendants contended that interest should run from June 2001, the date of the actual assessment of the quantum of damages. On the assumption that these were the only two dates available to him, the costs judge ordered interest from the date of the judgment rather than the date of the quantification of damages. In overturning the costs judge the Court of Appeal noted that neither party had referred the costs judge to Rule 44.3(6)(g) which gave him discretion to select any date which fitted the justice of the case (*Powell v Herefordshire Health Authority* [2002] EWCA Civ

1786, [2003] 3 All ER 253). In *Amoco (UK) Exploration Co v British American Offshore Ltd (No 2)* [2002] BLR 135, QBD (Comm Ct) the judge said:

> 'For my part, I think it may well be appropriate for at least in substantial proceedings involving commercial interests of significant importance both in balance sheet and reputational terms, that the court should award interest on costs under CPR r 44.3(6)(g) where substantial sums have inevitably been expended perhaps a year or more before the award of costs is made and interest begins to run on it under the general rule.'

In *Amec Process and Energy Ltd v Stork Engineers and Contractors BV (No 3)* [2002] All ER (D) 48 (Apr), QBD (TCC), it was held that the 'fairest way of awarding interest is to adopt a broad brush and award interest on the whole of the costs but for half of the period . . . at a composite rate of 6 per cent'.

DISCRETION

[18.6]

'There may even be good reasons for having a fixed and constant judgment debt rate. It gives certainty and clarity and in some cases it will provide an incentive for paying sooner rather than later' (*Schlumberger Holdings Ltd (a company incorporated in the British Virgin Islands) v Electromagnetic Geoservices AS (a company incorporated in Norway)* [2009] EWHC 773 (Pat)).

In *Colour Quest Ltd v Total Downstream UK plc* [2009] EWHC 823 (Comm), [2009] All ER (D) 152 (Apr) the unusual nature of the case and the substantial costs involved justified an order that interest should only run from six months after the judgment.

'The ability of the High Court to depart from the incipitur rule was conferred in order that the court could take account of the fact that money would often be expended before any judgment, Conversely, where money has not been expended, for example where the bulk of the costs have been paid at a date long after the relevant judgment, justice requires that the date of commencement of the interest is postponed beyond the date of that judgment' (*Fattal v Walbrook Trustees (Jersey) Ltd* [2009] EWHC 1674 (Ch), [2009] All ER (D) 190 (Jul).

When it was argued before SCCO Master Rogers that because the claimant was represented under a conditional fee agreement and he would never have to pay any costs he was not entitled to any interest on the costs he would never pay, the master prudently held that a decision with such far reaching consequences was for a court far higher than his.

THE RATE

[18.7]

Since April 1993 the rate of interest on judgment debts has been 8%, as prescribed by the Judgment Debts (Rate of Interest) Order 1993. This is despite the reduction of interest rates on funds invested in court to 7% on the special account and 5.25% on the basic account with effect from 1 August 1999. It therefore remains good investment – provided the judgment and costs are eventually paid. However, in respect of county court judgments where the judgment creditor applies to enforce payment of the judgment by execution or some other means, interest will not accrue if the enforcement process is wholly or partly successful (County Court (Interest on Judgment Debts) Order 1991, art 4). Presumably, this provision was made because, if the enforcement process is wholly successful the judgment will have been satisfied, whilst if it is only partly successful it will be too complicated to calculate the interest on the various amounts outstanding from time to time.

CHAPTER 19

COSTS OF SUCCESSFUL NON-STATE FUNDED PARTIES

PROCEDURE

[19.1]

From 1 April 2000 the Legal Aid Board was replaced by the Legal Services Commission (LSC) for all civil matters commencing on or after that date and the funding of assisted persons or 'clients' (as those who receive funded services are now called), has been provided through the Community Legal Service. I deal with the present regime, including its vocabulary, in Chapter 41. Although for some years to come there will be litigation involving parties funded under the old regime, since 5 June 2001 regs 127–130 and 134–147 of the Civil Legal Aid (General) Regulations 1989 have no longer applied resulting in the amount of the liability of all state-funded parties together with applications for costs against the state, in the form of the Legal Aid Board or the Legal Services Commission, all being now decided under the Community Legal Service (Costs) Regulations 2000.

There are therefore two forms of public funding of litigation: under Legal Aid Certificates, granted before 1 April 2000 by the Legal Aid Board; and, after 1 April 2000, under Community Legal Service certificates, funded by the Legal Services Commission which replaced the Legal Aid Board. 'Public funding certificate' is a useful portmanteau description covering both forms of funding.

COSTS AGAINST A STATE-FUNDED PARTY

(a) Liability for costs

[19.2]

The award of between-the-parties costs is uninfluenced by the fact that either or both of the parties is funded by the state. Awards of costs are determined by the factors prescribed in CPR Rule 44.3. For these purposes the funding certificate is ignored. However, a party who is in receipt of legal aid is protected by the Legal Aid Act 1988, s 17, while an LSC-funded litigant has the protection of the Access to Justice Act 1999, s 11.

(b) Cost protection

(i) Legal aid funded

[19.3]

Where proceedings have been concluded in which an assisted person is liable or would have been liable for costs if he had not been an assisted person, no costs attributable to the period during which his certificate was in force shall be recoverable from him until the court has determined the amount of his liability in accordance with the Legal Aid Act 1988, s 17(1) which provides as follows:

[19.4]

17 Limit on costs against assisted party

(1) The liability of a legally assisted party under an order for costs made against him with respect to any proceedings shall not exceed the amount (if any) which is a reasonable one for him to pay having regard to all the circumstances, including the financial resources of all the parties and their conduct in connection with the dispute.

(2) Regulations shall make provision as to the court, tribunal or person by whom that amount is to be determined and the extent to which any determination of that amount is to be final.

(3) None of the following, namely, a legally assisted person's dwelling house, clothes, household furniture and the tools and implements of his trade shall—

    (a)   be taken into account in assessing his financial resources for the purposes of this section, or

    (b)   be subject to execution or any corresponding process in any part of the United Kingdom to enforce the order,

except so far as regulations may prescribe.

In *Mohammadi v Shellpoint Trustees Ltd* [2009] EWHC 1098 (Ch), [2009] NLJR 823, [2009] 23 EG 92 (CS) in protracted litigation the claimant had obtained public funding over a period of 12 years by means of several overlapping legal aid certificates, during which time she had instructed several solicitors. With each change of solicitors, her legal aid certificate was discharged and then reinstated. During the intervening periods she was without legal representation. The question arose 'Was the claimant a "legally assisted party" within the meaning of s 17 of The Legal Aid Act 1988 or was she a litigant in person?' If she were the former, she would get substantial protection from liability to pay her opponent's costs. The court held it could not be right that the other litigants, once informed that the previously legally assisted person had ceased to be in receipt of legal advice and representation, were none the less kept in suspense until the outcome of any investigation as to their opponent's motivation, or the outcome of any subsequent application to reinstate the legal aid certificate in question. When a legally assisted person's solicitors have ceased to act without another firm being retained under a legal aid certificate, and that fact has been communicated to the opposing party, then from the moment of that communication the litigant ceases to be a legally assisted person even though she was actively seeking to reinstate the provision to her of legal advice, assistance and representation.

This was the plain meaning of s 2(11) of the Legal Aid Act 1988. She was not therefore protected from adverse costs orders being enforced in respect of those periods.

[19.5]

Where the assisted person's certificate does not relate to, or has been amended so that it no longer relates to the whole of the proceedings, the court shall nevertheless make a determination under s 17(1) of the Act in respect of that part of the proceedings to which the certificate relates.

The amount of an assisted person's liability for costs shall be determined by the court which tried or heard the proceedings (Civil Legal Aid (General) Regulations 1989, reg 124).

Where a claimant has been granted legal aid limited to cover specific procedural steps, the certificate is spent once those steps have been accomplished. Accordingly even though the legal aid certificate has not been discharged, the assisted person is not protected from liability for costs under the Legal Aid Act 1988, s 17 in respect of any step taken outside the scope of the certificate (*Turner v Plasplugs Ltd* [1996] 2 All ER 939, CA).

(ii) *Community Legal Service funded*

[19.6]

The Community Legal Service (Cost Protection) Regulations 2000 define 'costs protection' as the limit on costs awarded against a client set out in the Access to Justice Act 1999, s 11(1), a 'client' being defined as an individual who receives funded services.

Section 11 of the Access to Justice Act 1999 provides:

[19.7]

11 Costs in funded cases

(1) Except in prescribed circumstances, costs ordered against an individual in relation to any proceedings or part of proceedings funded for him shall not exceed the amount (if any) which is a reasonable one for him to pay having regard to all the circumstances including—

    (a)   the financial resources of all the parties to the proceedings, and

    (b)   their conduct in connection with the dispute to which the proceedings relate;

and for this purpose proceedings, or a part of proceedings, are funded for an individual if services relating to the proceedings or part are funded for him by the Commission as part of the Community Legal Service.

(2) In assessing for the purposes of subsection (1) the financial resources of an individual for whom services are funded by the Commission as part of the Community Legal Service, his clothes and household furniture and the tools and implements of his trade shall not be taken into account, except so far as may be prescribed.

(3) Subject to subsections (1) and (2), regulations may make provision about costs in relation to proceedings in which services are funded by the Commission for any of the parties as part of the Community Legal Service.

(4) The regulations may, in particular, make provision—

(a) specifying the principles to be applied in determining the amount of any costs which may be awarded against a party for whom services are funded by the Commission as part of the Community Legal Service,

(b) limiting the circumstances in which, or extent to which, an order for costs may be enforced against such a party,

(c) as to the cases in which, and extent to which, such a party may be required to give security for costs and the manner in which it is to be given,

(d) requiring the payment by the Commission of the whole or part of any costs incurred by a party for whom services are not funded by the Commission as part of the Community Legal Service,

(e) specifying the principles to be applied in determining the amount of any costs which may be awarded to a party for whom services are so funded,

(f) requiring the payment to the Commission, or the person or body by which the services were provided, of the whole or part of any sum awarded by way of costs to such a party, and

(g) as to the court, tribunal or other person or body by whom the amount of any costs is to be determined and the extent to which any determination of that amount is to be final.

[19.8]

The protection of s 11(1) does not cover a person who has obtained public funding founded upon fraudulent claims (*Jones v Congregational and General Insurance plc* [2003] EWHC 1027 (QB), [2003] 1 WLR 3001).

The Community Legal Service (Cost Protection) Regulations 2000 (SI 2000/824) provide:

[19.9]

3 Cost protection

(1) Cost protection shall not apply in relation to such parts of proceedings, or prospective proceedings, as are funded for the client by way of:

(a) Help at Court . . . ;

(b) . . .

(c) subject to paragraph (2), Legal Help;

(d) General Family Help and Help with Mediation in family proceedings;

(e) Legal Representation in family proceedings.

(2) Subject to paragraph (4), where the client receives Legal Help, but later receives Legal Representation or General Family Help or Help with Mediation in respect of the same dispute, other than Legal Representation in family proceedings or General Family Help or Help with Mediation in family proceedings, cost protection shall apply, both in respect of:

(a) the costs incurred by the receiving party before the commencement of proceedings which, as regards the client, are funded proceedings by virtue of the client's receipt of Legal Help, and

(b) the costs incurred by the receiving party in the course of proceedings which, as regards the client, are funded proceedings by virtue of the client's receipt of Legal Representation, General Family Help or Help with Mediation.

(3)　Subject to paragraph (4), cost protection shall apply only to costs incurred by the receiving party in relation to proceedings which, as regards the client, are funded proceedings, and:

    (a)　where work is done before the issue of a certificate, cost protection shall (subject to paragraphs (2) and (5)) apply only to costs incurred after the issue of the certificate;

    (b)　where funding is withdrawn by discharging the client's certificate, cost protection shall apply only to costs incurred before the date when funded services under the certificate ceased to be provided.

(4)　Where funding is withdrawn by revoking the client's certificate, cost protection shall not apply, either in respect of work done before or after the revocation.

(5)　Cost protection shall apply to work done immediately before the grant of an emergency certificate, other than an emergency certificate granted in relation to family proceedings, if:

    (a)　no application for such a certificate could be made because the Commission's office was closed; and

    (b)　the client's solicitor applies for an emergency certificate at the first available opportunity, and the certificate is granted.

[19.10]

4　Enforcement of costs order against client

Where, in a case where costs protection applies, for the purpose of enforcing a costs order against a client (alone or together with any other judgment or order), a charging order under section 1 of the Charging Orders Act 1979 is made in respect of the client's interest in the main or only dwelling in which he resides:

    (a)　that charging order shall operate to secure the amount payable under the costs order (including, without limitation, any interest) only to the extent of the amount (if any) by which the proceeds of sale of the client's interest in the dwelling (having deducted any mortgage debts) exceed £100,000; and

    (b)　an order for the sale of the dwelling shall not be made in favour of the person in whose favour the charging order is made.

(iii)　The costs rules

[19.11]

CPR Rule 44.17: Application of costs rules

This Part and Part 45 (fixed costs), Part 46 (fast track trial costs), Part 47 (procedure for detailed assessment of costs and default provisions) and Part 48 (special cases), do not apply to the assessment of costs in proceedings to the extent that—

    (a)　section 11 of the Access to Justice Act 1999, and provisions made under that Act, or

    (b)　regulations made under the Legal Aid Act 1988,

make different provision. (The Costs Practice Direction sets out the procedure to be followed where a party was wholly or partially funded by the Legal Services Commission).

[19.12]

CPD Section 21: Application of costs rules: Rule 44.17

21.1   Rule 44.17(b) excludes the costs rules to the extent that regulations under the Legal Aid Act 1988 make different provision. The primary examples of such regulations are the regulations providing prescribed rates (with or without enhancement).

21.2   Rule 44.17(a) provides that the procedure for detailed assessment does not apply to the extent that section 11 of the Access to Justice Act 1999 and provisions made under that Act make different provision.

21.3   Section 11 of the Access to Justice Act 1999 provides special protection against liability for costs for litigants who receive funding by the LSC (Legal Services Commission) as part of the Community Legal Service. Any costs ordered to be paid by a LSC funded client must not exceed the amount which is reasonable for him to pay having regard to all the circumstances including:

(a)   the financial resources of all the parties to the proceedings, and

(b)   their conduct in connection with the dispute to which the proceedings relate.

21.4   In this Practice Direction

"cost protection" means the limit on costs awarded against a LSC funded client set out in Section 11(1) of the Access to Justice Act 1999.

"partner" has the meaning given by the Community Legal Service (Costs) Regulations 2000.

21.5   Whether or not cost protection applies depends upon the "level of service" for which funding was provided by the LSC in accordance with the Funding Code approved under section 9 of the Access to Justice Act 1999. The levels of service referred to are:

(1)   Legal Help – advice and assistance about a legal problem, not including representation or advocacy in proceedings.

(2)   Help at Court – advocacy at a specific hearing, where the advocate is not formally representing the client in the proceedings.

(3)   Family Mediation.

(4)   Legal Representation – representation in actual or contemplated proceedings. Legal Representation can take the form of Investigative Help (limited to investigating the merits of a potential claim) or Full Representation.

(5)   General Family Help and Help with Mediation.

21.6   Levels of service (4) and (5) are provided under a certificate (similar to a legal aid certificate). The certificate will state which level of service is covered. Where there are proceedings, a copy of the certificate will be lodged with the court.

21.7   Cost protection does not apply where:

(1)   The LSC funded client receives Help at Court;

(2)   The LSC funded client receives Legal Help only i.e. where the solicitor is advising, but not representing a litigant in person. However, where the LSC funded client receives Legal Help e.g. to write a letter before action, but later receives Legal Representation or General Family Help or Help with Mediation in respect of the same dispute, other than in family proceedings, cost protection does apply to all costs incurred by the receiving party in the funded proceedings or prospective proceedings;

(3)   The LSC funded client receives General Family Help or Help with Mediation in family proceedings;

(4)   The LSC funded client receives Legal Representation in family proceedings.

21.8   Where cost protection does not apply, the court may award costs in the normal way.

21.9   Where work is done before the issue of a certificate, cost protection does not apply to those costs, except where:

(1)   *pre-action Legal Help is given and the LSC funded client subsequently receives Legal Representation or General Family Help or Help with Mediation in respect of the same dispute, other than in family proceedings; or*

(2)   *where urgent work is undertaken immediately before the grant of an emergency certificate, other than in family proceedings, when no emergency application could be made as the LSC's offices were closed, provided that the solicitor seeks an emergency certificate at the first available opportunity and the certificate is granted.*

21.10   *If a LSC funded client's certificate is revoked, costs protection does not apply to work done before or after revocation.*

21.11   *If a LSC funded client's certificate is discharged, costs protection only applies to costs incurred before the date on which funded services ceased to be provided under the certificate. This may be a date before the date on which the certificate is formally discharged by the LSC (Burridge v Stafford: Khan v Ali [2000] 1 WLR 927, [1999] 4 All ER 660 C.A.).*

21.11A   *Where an LSC funded client has costs protection, the procedure described in sections 22 and 23 of this Practice Direction applies. However that procedure does not apply in relation to costs claimed during any periods in the proceedings when the LSC funded client did not have cost protection, and the procedure set out in CPR Parts 45 to 47 will apply (as appropriate) in relation to those periods.*

(Continued at para [19.22])

(iv)   Three stages

[19.13]

First, the judge makes an order that the state-funded party do pay the costs of the receiving party either assessed at a specified sum (if he has summarily assessed them) or to be ascertained by detailed assessment.

That is stage one. That is the procedure for determining the full costs which a state-funded party would pay if he were not in receipt of state funding.

Stage two is the determination of the amount the state-funded party will actually have to pay under the costs protection scheme. The usual order is: 'The amount of the costs payable under section 17(1) of the Legal Aid Act or section 11 of the Access to Justice Act to be determined'. That determination will not be carried out by the trial judge, but by a costs or district judge.

However, if the trial judge is satisfied that he is in a position there and then to determine the amount payable, perhaps to be set off against an earlier award of costs in favour of the funded party, or against his damages, or even as was approved in *Williams v Walkett* [1994] CLY 3587, an order to pay the assessed costs by monthly instalments, the judge may make what is not very imaginatively called 'an order specifying the costs payable'.

There is one further action the judge may take if he is so minded when making an order for costs to be determined. Paragraph 22.6 of the Practice Direction provides he may 'make findings of fact, e.g., concerning the conduct of all the parties which are to be taken into account by the court in the subsequent determination proceedings'.

The third stage is for the receiving party to take the appropriate steps to have the costs determined within three months, although he may apply at any time within six years to vary that determination if the funded party wins the pools, the lottery or *Who Wants to be a Millionaire?*

(v)   Interim

[19.14]

Neither s 17 of the Legal Aid Act 1989 nor reg 124 of the Civil Legal Aid (General) Regulations 1989 prevents the court at an interim stage making an order for costs in favour of the other party directing that those costs be set off against either any damages or costs to which the legally-aided party had or could in future become entitled in the action. The operation of the set-off did not place the person whose chose in action was thereby reduced or extinguished under an obligation to pay. The operation of the set-off in respect of the liability of the assisted person under an order for costs did not require him to pay anything: it did not lead to any costs being recoverable against the legally aided person. Such an order would in general in equity impeach the right of the claimant to recover from the defendant the costs of the action ordered to be paid by the defendant (*Lockley v National Blood Transfusion Service* [1992] 2 All ER 589, CA).

COSTS AGAINST THE STATE

(a) Against the Legal Aid Board

[19.15]

Where one party is legally aided ('the assisted party') and the other is not ('the unassisted party') and the proceedings between them are finally decided in favour of the unassisted party, the court may, subject to the following conditions being satisfied, order the whole or, part of the costs of the unassisted party in those proceedings to be paid by the Legal Aid Board.

There can be such final decision even though it may not have been wholly in favour of the unassisted party (*Kelly v London Transport Executive* [1982] 2 All ER 842, CA).

(i)   The conditions

[19.16]

An order under the Legal Aid Act 1988, s 18 in respect of any costs may only be made if:
(1)   an order for costs would be made in the proceedings apart from this Act, as respects the costs incurred in a court of first instance, those proceedings were instituted by the assisted party and the court is satisfied that the unassisted party will suffer severe financial hardship unless the order is made; and
(2)   in any case, the court is satisfied that it is just and equitable in all the circumstances of the case that provision for the costs should be made out of public funds.

In *Din v Wandsworth London Borough Council (No 2)* [1982] 1 All ER 1022, HL it was held that it is not just and equitable to make a provisional order, as a *matter of course* when an unassisted party has succeeded, that he should have his costs out of the legal aid fund, reserving to The Law Society (now the Legal Aid Board) the opportunity to make representations with regard thereto.

K v K (legal aid: costs) [1995] 2 FCR 189, CA illustrated dramatically the provision in s 18(4) that an order against the Legal Aid Board may only be made if an order for costs would have been made in the proceedings apart from the Act. The wife incurred substantial costs as a result of the husband's proceedings in respect of the children, which proceedings were finally decided in her favour. It was unusual to make a between-the-parties order for costs between the parties in respect of proceedings concerning the children and the wife's liability to her solicitors for costs was a factor which would be taken into account when considering ancillary relief. Although the pre-condition of s 18(4) was reasonable in the context of conventional civil litigation, where costs on the face of it followed the event, it precluded the award of costs against the Legal Aid Board cases involving children because such an order is unusual.

In *Aire Property Trust v Treeweek* [1989] 1 EGLR 61, CA, a successful respondent to an appeal which should never have been made (because there was no right of appeal without leave) and in respect of which legal aid should never have been granted was entitled to an order for his costs against the legal aid fund.

In *Adams v Riley* [1988] QB 372, QBD, in making an order against the legal aid fund under the Legal Aid Act 1974, s 13(1) the court held it should determine the proportion of the costs the successful party could pay without suffering hardship and order that he recover only the excess. It was not a question of a successful party who had got across the threshold recovering everything: he recovered only the difference between the actual costs and that sum which would have just failed to get him over the threshold.

In *O'Sullivan v Herdmans Ltd (No 2)* [1988] 1 WLR 1373, HL, the legally-aided claimant with a nil contribution had successfully resisted an order for disclosure before the master and judge but failed before the Court of Appeal and the House of Lords. The House of Lords proposed ordering that the defendant's costs be paid out of the legal aid fund but it was suggested that the effect of this order would be that the amount of costs so paid would be a charge on any damages the claimant might recover. Accordingly, the House adjourned to enable representations to be made. On the restored hearing it was confirmed that the order for costs out of the legal aid fund would not give rise to a charge on any sum eventually recovered by the claimant against the defendants. The House of Lords accordingly affirmed the provisional order previously made. In the event, the argument was only over the sum of £1,000, because that is the amount for which the claimant settled her claim!

(ii) 'Financial hardship'

[19.17]

If his costs, if he is left to bear them himself, will so bear heavily on the unassisted person, a possible claim for hardship may be made out. The financial hardship used to have to be 'severe' but on 3 December 2001 the test of severity was removed. A limited company or body corporate is capable of suffering financial hardship so that an order may, in an appropriate case, be made in its favour. No appeal lies from a court order for payment of the costs of an unassisted party out of the fund, or a refusal to make such an order, if only a question of fact is involved. It would seem that a finding as to financial hardship or as to its absence is such a question of fact. When the unassisted party is concerned only in a representative, fiduciary or official capacity, the court is not to have regard to his personal resources, but *must* take into account the value of the property estate or fund out of which he is entitled to be indemnified and *may* have regard to the resources of the persons, including, where appropriate, the unassisted party, beneficially interested (reg 135).

The provision that it is only an unassisted person who can claim against the Legal Aid Board can cause hardship to a successful assisted person. In *Almond v Miles* (1992) Times, 4 February, ChD the claimant claimed a share of the equity in a flat in which the defendant lived. The defendant successfully resisted her claim. Both parties were in receipt of legal aid. The claimant's own flat was sacrosanct under the legal aid provision in respect of the costs awarded against her but the Legal Aid Board had a charge for their costs over the defendant's property as being property preserved by the proceedings. The court regretted that in these circumstances it could not order the defendant's costs to be paid by the Legal Aid Board and called for urgent reconsideration of the legislation. In *Re H (minors) (No 2) (abduction: custody rights)* [1992] 2 AC 303, HL the House of Lords was faced with a similar situation but in that case the unsuccessful party had previously been unassisted. The fact that he was assisted at the time of the making of the order did not preclude the court from ordering payment by the Legal Aid Board of such part of the successful party's costs as had been incurred while he was unassisted.

(b) Against the Legal Services Commission

(i) The Community Legal Service (Cost Protection) Regulations 2000 (SI 2000/824)

[19.18]

These Regulations provide (at regs 5–7):

[19.19]

5 Costs order against commission
(1) The following paragraphs of this regulation apply where:
   (a) funded services are provided to a client in relation to proceedings;
   (b) those proceedings are finally decided in favour of a non-funded party; and

(c)   cost protection applies.

(2)   The court may, subject to the following paragraphs of this regulation, make an order for the payment by the Commission to the non-funded party of the whole or any part of the costs incurred by him in the proceedings (other than any costs that the client is required to pay under a section 11(1) costs order).

(3)   An order under paragraph (2) may only be made if all the conditions set out in sub-paragraphs (a), (b), (c) and (d) are satisfied:

(a)   a section 11(1) costs order is made against the client in the proceedings, and the amount (if any) which the client is required to pay under that costs order is less than the amount of the full costs;

(b)   unless there is a good reason for the delay, the non-funded party makes a request under regulation 10(2) of the Community Legal Service (Costs) Regulations 2000 within three months of the making of the section 11(1) costs order;

(c)   as regards costs incurred in a court of first instance, the proceedings were instituted by the client, the non-funded party is an individual, and the court is satisfied that the non-funded party will suffer financial hardship unless the order is made; and

(d)   in any case, the court is satisfied that it is just and equitable in the circumstances that provision for the costs should be made out of public funds.

(3A)   An order under paragraph (2) may be made—

(a)   in relation to proceedings in the Supreme Court, by such officers as may be appointed by the President;

(b)   in relation to proceedings in the Court of Appeal, High Court or a county court, by a costs judge or a district judge;

(c)   in relation to proceedings in a magistrates' court, by a single justice or by the justices' clerk;

(d)   in relation to proceedings in the Employment Appeal Tribunal, by the Registrar of that tribunal.

(4)   Where the client receives funded services in connection with part only of the proceedings, the reference in paragraph (2) to the costs incurred by the non-funded party in the relevant proceedings shall be construed as a reference to so much of those costs as is attributable to the part of the proceedings which are funded proceedings.

(5)   Where a court decides any proceedings in favour of the non-funded party and an appeal lies (with or without permission) against that decision, any order made under this regulation shall not take effect:

(a)   where permission to appeal is required, unless the time limit for applications for permission to appeal expires without permission being granted;

(b)   where permission to appeal is granted or is not required, unless the time limit for appeal expires without an appeal being brought.

(6)   Subject to paragraph (7), in determining whether the conditions in paragraph (3)(c) and (d) are satisfied, the court shall have regard to the resources of the non-funded party and of his partner.

(7)   The court shall not have regard to the resources of the partner of the non-funded party if the partner has a contrary interest in the funded proceedings.

(8)   Where the non-funded party is acting in a representative, fiduciary or official capacity and is entitled to be indemnified in respect of his costs from any property, estate or fund, the court shall, for the purposes of paragraph (3), have regard to the

value of the property, estate or fund and the resources of the persons, if any, including that party where appropriate, who are beneficially interested in that property, estate or fund.

[19.20]

6 Orders for costs against commission—litigation support

(1) Paragraph (2) applies where:

    (a)   the client receives Litigation Support and the certificate is not revoked;

    (b)   the client has effected insurance against liability in respect of costs in the proceedings, or has made other arrangements, approved by the Commission as being equivalent to such insurance;

    (c)   the amount of liability insured under that insurance (or covered by those other arrangements) is subject to a maximum which has been approved by the Commission; and

    (d)   a costs order has been made against the client in favour of a non-funded party and the actual amount of the client's liability in respect of costs under that costs order exceeds the maximum referred to in sub-paragraph (c).

(2) Where this paragraph applies, the amount of the excess referred to in paragraph (1)(d) shall, subject to paragraph (3), be paid by the Commission, not by the client, and the court shall order accordingly.

(3) The amount of the Commission's liability under this regulation shall not exceed the reasonable costs of the non-funded party incurred during the period in which Litigation Support was provided.

(Regulation 6 is revoked by SI 2005/2006 with effect from July 2006, except in relation to certificates for Litigation Support granted before that date.)

[19.21]

7 Effect of these regulations

(1) No order to pay costs in favour of a non-funded party shall be made against the Commission in respect of funded proceedings except in accordance with these Regulations, and any costs to be paid under such an order shall be paid out of the Community Legal Service Fund.

(2) Nothing in these Regulations shall be construed, in relation to proceedings where one or more parties are receiving, or have received, funded services, as:

    (a)   requiring a court to make a costs order where it would not otherwise have made a costs order; or

    (b)   affecting the court's power to make a wasted costs order against a legal representative.

(ii)   CPD Section 21 continued from para [19.12]

[19.22]

Assessing a LSC Funded Client's Resources

21.12   The first £100,000 of the value of the LSC funded client's interest in the main or only home is disregarded when assessing his or her financial resources for the purposes of s 11 and cannot be the subject of any enforcement process by the receiving party. The receiving party cannot apply for an order to sell the LSC funded client's home, but could secure the debt against any value exceeding £100,000 by way of a charging order.

21.13 The court may only take into account the value of the LSC funded client's clothes, household furniture, tools and implements of trade to the extent that it considers that having regard to the quantity or value of the items, the circumstances are exceptional.

21.14 The LSC funded client's resources include the resources of his partner, unless the partner has a contrary interest in the dispute in respect of which funded services are provided.

Party acting in a Representative, Fiduciary or Official Capacity

21.15 (1) Where a LSC funded client is acting in a representative, fiduciary or official capacity, the court shall not take the personal resources of the party into account for the purposes of either a Section 11 order or costs against the Commission, but shall have regard to the value of any property or estate or the amount of any fund out of which the party is entitled to be indemnified, and may also have regard to the resources of any persons who are beneficially interested in the property, estate or fund.

(2) Similarly, where a party is acting as a litigation friend to a client who is a child or a protected party, the court shall not take the personal resources of the litigation friend into account in assessing the resources of the client.

(3) The purpose of this provision is to ensure that any liability is determined with reference to the value of the property or fund being used to pay for the litigation, and the financial position of those who may benefit from or rely on it.

Costs against the LSC

21.16 Regulation 5 of the Community Legal Service (Cost Protection) Regulations 2000 governs when costs can be awarded against the LSC. This provision only applies where cost protection applies and the costs ordered to be paid by the LSC funded client do not fully meet the costs that would have been ordered to be paid by him if cost protection did not apply.

21.17 In this Section and the following two Sections of this Practice Direction 'non-funded party' means a party to proceedings who has not received LSC funded services in relation to these proceedings under a legal aid certificate or a certificate issued under the LSC Funding Code other than a certificate which has been revoked.

21.18 The following criteria set out in Regulation 5 must be satisfied before the LSC can be ordered to pay the whole or any part of the costs incurred by a non-funded party:

(1) the proceedings are finally decided in favour of a non-funded party;
(2) unless there is good reason for delay the non-funded party provides written notice of intention to seek an order against the LSC within three months of the making of the section 11(1) costs order;
(3) the court is satisfied that it is just and equitable in the circumstances that provision for the costs should be made out of public funds; and
(4) where costs are incurred in a court of first instance, the following additional criteria must also be met:
   (i) the proceedings were instituted by the LSC funded client;
   (ii) the non funded party is an individual; and
   (iii) the non-funded party will suffer financial hardship unless the order is made.

('Section 11(1) costs order' is defined in paragraph 22.1, below).

21.19 In determining whether conditions (3) and (4) are satisfied, the court shall take into account the resources of the non-funded party and his partner, unless the partner has a contrary interest.

21.19A An order under Regulation 5 may be made in relation to proceedings in the Court of Appeal, High Court or a county court, by a costs judge or a district judge.

Effect of Appeals

21.20 *(1) An order for costs can only be made against the LSC when the proceedings (including any appeal) are finally decided. Therefore, where a court of first instance decides in favour of a non-funded party and an appeal lies, any order made against the LSC shall not take effect unless:*

(a)   *where permission to appeal is required, the time limit for permission to appeal expires, without permission being granted;*

(b)   *where permission to appeal is granted or is not required, the time limit for appeal expires without an appeal being brought.*

(2) Accordingly, if the LSC funded client appeals, any earlier order against the LSC can never take effect. If the appeal is unsuccessful, an application can be made to the appeal court for a fresh order.

(iii)   Guidance

[19.23]

In the tragic case of *Re Wyatt (a child) (medical treatment: continuation of order) (costs)* [2006] EWCA Civ 529, [2006] 20 EG 293 (CS) 3 May Mr and Mrs Wyatt were in dispute with Portsmouth Hospital NHS about life and death decisions concerning the treatment of their daughter Charlotte born on 21 October 2003. After extensive court proceedings in which the Wyatts were publicly funded they sought permission to appeal against the judge's refusal to discharge declarations he had made concerning Charlotte's treatment. He also gave them permission to appeal against his decision that his declarations should remain in force without time limit. The Court of Appeal had dismissed both the application for permission to appeal and the appeal.

The Wyatts were impecunious and therefore the Trust wished to obtain an order for costs against the Legal Services Commission pursuant to The Community Legal Service (Costs Protection) Regulations 2000. Although the Trust had made it clear that it had no wish to seek any payment from the Wyatts and that the order sought against them was solely to enable a claim to be made against the LSC, the application, to the expressed surprise of the Court of Appeal, was vigorously opposed by counsel for the Wyatts.

Accordingly it was necessary for the Court of Appeal to consider the various stages of obtaining an order against the Legal Services Commission as follows:

(1)   The provision in regulation 5, which precludes orders against the LSC where the proceedings were not commenced by the assisted party does not apply to appeals.

(2)   An order for costs must have been made against the assisted party under s 11 of the Access to Justice Act 1999.

(3)   The Court of Appeal itself was unable to make a costs order against the Trust following the surprising decision in *R (on the application of Gunn) v Secretary of State for the Home Dept* [2001] EWCA Civ 891, [2001] 3 All ER 481, that the CPR costs regime is not compatible with the court's former practice of and that an order against the LSC can be made only by a costs or district judge.

(4)   The regulations involve a two-stage process in relation to the recovery of costs in cases to which s 11(1) of the 1999 Act applies. The procedure to be followed is primarily to be derived from the costs regulations.

[19.24]

The first stage involves the trial court dealing with the substance of the dispute as follows:

(i)   To decide whether to make an order for costs against a funded litigant (the client) (reg 9(1)).

(ii)   To decide whether it is in a position to specify the amount, if any, to be paid by the client (reg 9(2)).

(iii)   To make a costs order against the client which either (a) specifies the amount, if any, to be paid by the client and states the amount of the full costs, or (b) does not specify the amount to be paid by the client (reg 9(3) and (4)). The order is described in the regulations as a 's 11(1) costs order' and is defined in both sets of regulations as a 'costs order against a client where costs protection applies'. 'Costs protection' means 'the limit set on costs awarded against a client set out in s 11(1) of the Act'.

(iv)   Where the order does not specify the amount to be paid by the client, to make, if it sees fit, findings of fact, as to the parties' conduct in the proceedings or otherwise, relevant to the determination of the amount (reg 9(6)).

[19.25]

Stage 2 is for the district or costs judge. It consists of the procedure to be followed to ascertain the amount of costs to be paid by the client against whom the trial court has made an order that does not specify the amount. It also includes the procedure for determining whether an order for costs should be made against the Commission.

The first limb

[19.26]

Regulation 9(1) of the Costs Regulations provides: 'Where the court is considering whether to make a section 11(1) costs order, it shall consider whether, but for cost protection, it would have made a costs order against the client and, if so, whether it would, on making the costs order, have specified the amount to be paid under that order.'

Applied to the facts of this case the first limb of that question became: 'Had the Wyatts not been publicly funded, would the court have made an order for costs against them at the conclusion of their application for permission to appeal, and of the appeal itself?' The court was of the clear view that the answer to that question was "Yes". Such a conclusion had nothing to do with the need for there to have been reprehensible behaviour on the Wyatts' part, or any preconceived determination of the manner in which judicial discretion has to be exercised under CPR Order 44.3. It had everything to do with the proper exercise of a judicial discretion to make orders for costs following the outcome of proceedings in the Court of Appeal.

The second limb

[19.27]

Were it not for the costs protection would the court have specified the amount under regulation 9(1)? Regulation 9(3) provides:

[19.28]

> (3) If the court considers that it would have made a costs order against the client, and that it would have specified the amount to be paid under it, the court shall, when making the section 11(1) costs order:
> > (a) specify the amount (if any) that the client is to pay under that order if, but only if, it considers that it has sufficient information before it to decide what amount is, in that case, a reasonable amount for the client to pay, in accordance with section 11(1) of the Act;
> > (b) otherwise, it shall not specify the amount the client is to pay under the . . . costs order.
> (4) Any order made under paragraph (3) shall state the amount of the full costs.

[19.29]

In the circumstances it was open to the court to say that it did have sufficient information to decide what amount the Wyatts should pay. Section 11(1) of the 1999 Act requires that the amount "shall not exceed the amount (if any) which is a reasonable one for (them) to pay". The court was entitled to accept the Trust's assertion that the Wyatts were impecunious. It was self-evident that if the court were to determine the full costs there and then, they would be no more than nothing. In those circumstances, it was open to the court to specify that the amount the Wyatts should pay under the costs order is nothing. Accordingly the court made an for costs against the assisted parties assessed at nothing.

The Court of Appeal observed that the whole exercise could have been avoided by a sensible recognition that, in a case of this nature, the Trust was entitled to ask that the LSC reimburse it a relatively small proportion of the costs it has expended on this case overall. The point should not have been contentious. Whether or not the Trust succeeded against the Legal Services Commission was not a matter for the Court of Appeal nor was it of any personal financial interest to Mr and Mrs Wyatt.

ASSESSMENT OF LIABILITY

(i) The Community Legal Service (Costs) Regulations 2000 (SI 2000/441)

[19.30]

These regulations prescribe the procedure for assessing the amount of liability under the Access to Justice Act 1999, s 11(1). The relevant regulations are as follows:

PART II   COSTS ORDERS AGAINST CLIENT AND AGAINST COMMISSION

[19.31]

5. Application of regulations 6 to 13
Regulations 6 to 13 apply only where the cost protection applies.

[19.32]

6. Security for costs
Where in any proceedings a client is required to give security for costs, the amount of that security shall not exceed the amount (if any) which is a reasonable one having regard to all the circumstances, including the client's financial resources and his conduct in relation to the dispute to which the proceedings relate.

[19.33]

7. Assessment of resources
(1)   The first £100,000 of the value of the client's interest in the main or only dwelling in which he resides shall not be taken into account in having regard to the client's resources for the purposes of section 11(1) of the Act.

(2)   Where, but only to the extent that, the court considers that the circumstances are exceptional, having regard in particular to the quantity or value of the items concerned, the court may take into account the value of the client's clothes and household furniture, or the tools and implements of his trade, in having regard to the client's resources for the purposes of section 11(1) of the Act.

(3)   Subject to paragraph (4), in having regard to the resources of a party for the purposes of section 11(1) of the Act, the resources of his partner shall be treated as his resources.

(4)   The resources of a party's partner shall not be treated as that party's resources if the partner has a contrary interest in the dispute in respect of which the funded services are provided.

(5)   Where a party is acting in a representative, fiduciary or official capacity, the court shall not take the personal resources of the party into account for the purposes of section 11(1) of the Act, but shall have regard to the value of any property or estate, or the amount of any fund out of which he is entitled to be indemnified, and may also have regard to the resources of the persons, if any, including that party where appropriate, who are beneficially interested in that property, estate or fund.

(6)   For the purposes of section 11(1) of the Act, where a party is acting as a litigation friend to a client who is a child or a patient, the court shall not take the personal resources of the litigation friend into account in assessing the resources of the client.

[19.34]

8. Statements of resources
(1)   Any person who is a party to proceedings in which another party is a client may make a statement of resources, and file it with the court.

(2)   A person making and filing a statement of resources under paragraph (1) shall serve a copy of it on the client.

(3)   Where a copy of a statement of resources has been served under paragraph (2) not less than seven days before the date fixed for a hearing at which

the amount to be paid under a section 11(1) costs order falls, or may fall, to be decided, the client shall also make a statement of resources, and shall produce it at that hearing.

[19.35]

9. Procedures for ordering costs against client and commission

(1)   Where the court is considering whether to make a section 11(1) costs order, it shall consider whether, but for cost protection, it would have made a costs order against the client and, if so, whether it would, on making the costs order, have specified the amount to be paid under that order.

(2)   If the court considers that it would have made a costs order against the client, but that it would not have specified the amount to be paid under it, the court shall, when making the section 11(1) costs order:

  (a)   specify the amount (if any) that the client is to pay under that order if, but only if:

    (i)   it considers that it has sufficient information before it to . decide what amount is, in that case, a reasonable amount for the client to pay, in accordance with section 11(1) of the Act; and

    (ii)   it is satisfied that, if it were to determine the full costs at that time, they would exceed the amount referred to in sub-paragraph (i);

  (b)   otherwise, it shall not specify the amount the client is to pay under the . . . costs order.

(3)   If the court considers that it would have made a costs order against the client, and that it would have specified the amount to be paid under it, the court shall, when making the section 11(1) costs order:

  (a)   specify the amount (if any) that the client is to pay under that order if, but only if, it considers that it has sufficient information before it to decide what amount is, in that case, a reasonable amount for the client to pay, in accordance with section 11(1) of the Act;

  (b)   otherwise, it shall not specify the amount the client is to pay under the . . . costs order.

(4)   Any order made under paragraph (3) shall state the amount of the full costs.

(5)   The amount (if any) to be paid by the client under an order made under paragraph (2)(b) or paragraph (3)(b), and any application for a costs order against the Commission, shall be determined in accordance with regulation 10, and at any such determination following an order made under paragraph (2)(b), the amount of the full costs shall also be assessed.

(6)   Where the court makes a section 11(1) costs order that does not specify the amount which the client is to pay under it, it may also make findings of fact, as to the parties' conduct in the proceedings or otherwise, relevant to the determination of that amount, and those findings shall be taken into consideration in that determination.

[19.36]

10.

(1)   The following paragraphs of this regulation apply where the amount to be paid under a section 11(1) costs order, or an application for a costs order against the Commission, is to be determined under this regulation, by virtue of regulation 9(5).

(2)   The receiving party may, within three months after a section 11(1) costs order is made, request a hearing to determine the costs payable to him.

(3)   A request under paragraph (2) shall be accompanied by:

(a)   if the section 11(1) costs order does not state the full costs, the receiving party's bill of costs, which shall comply with any requirements of relevant rules of court relating to the form and content of a bill of costs where the court is assessing a party's costs;

(b)   unless the conditions set out in paragraph (3A) are satisfied, a statement of resources; and

(c)   if the receiving party is seeking, or, subject to the determination of the amount to be paid under the section 11(1) costs order, may seek, a costs order against the Commission, written notice to that effect.

(3A)   The conditions referred to in paragraph (3)(b) above are that

(a)   the court is determining an application for a costs order against the Commission;

(b)   the costs were not incurred in a court of first instance.

(4)   The receiving party shall file the documents referred to in paragraph (3) with the court and at the same time serve copies of them:

(a)   on the client, if a determination of costs payable under section 11(1) of the Act is sought; and

(b)   on the . . . Director, if notice has been given under paragraph (3)(c).

(5)   Where documents are served on the client under paragraph (4)(a), the client shall make a statement of resources.

(6)   The client shall file the statement of resources made under paragraph (5) with the court, and serve copies of it on the receiving party and, if notice has been given under paragraph (3)(c), on the . . . Director, not more than 21 days after the client receives a copy of the receiving party's statement of resources.

(7)   The client may, at the same time as filing and serving a statement of resources under paragraph (6), file, and serve on the same persons, a statement setting out any points of dispute in relation to the bill of costs referred to in paragraph (3)(a).

(8)   If the client, without good reason, fails to file a statement of resources in accordance with paragraph (6), the court shall determine the amount which the client shall be required to pay under the section 11(1) costs order (and, if relevant, the full costs), having regard to the statement made by the receiving party, and the court need not hold an oral hearing for such determination.

(9)   If the client files a statement of resources in accordance with paragraph (6), or the period for filing such notice expires, or if the costs payable by the client have already been determined, the court shall set a date for the hearing and, at least 14 days before that date, serve notice of it on:

(a)   the receiving party;

(b)   the client (unless the costs payable by the client have already been determined); and

(c)   if a costs order against the Commission is or may be sought, the . . . Director.

(10)   The court's functions under this regulation may be exercised:

(a)   in relation to proceedings in the Supreme Court, by such officers as may be appointed by the President;

(b)   in relation to proceedings in the Court of Appeal, High Court or a county court, a costs judge or a district judge;

(c)   in relation to proceedings in a magistrates' court, by a single justice or by the justices' clerk;

(d)   in relation to proceedings in the Employment Appeal Tribunal, by the Registrar of that Tribunal.

(11)   The amount of costs to be determined under this regulation may include the costs incurred in relation to a request made under this regulation.

[19.37]

10A.

(1)   Subject to paragraph (2), where the court makes a section 11(1) costs order but does not specify the amount which the client is to pay under it, the court may order the client to pay an amount on account of the costs which are the subject of the order.

(2)   The court may order a client to make a payment on account of costs under this regulation only if it has sufficient information before it to decide the minimum amount which the client is likely to be ordered to pay on a determination under regulation 10.

(3)   The amount of the payment on account of costs shall not exceed the minimum amount which the court decides that the client is likely to be ordered to pay on such a determination.

(4)   Where the court orders a client to make a payment on account of costs—

(a)   it shall order the client to make the payment into court; and

(b)   the payment shall remain in court unless and until the court—

(i)   makes a determination under regulation 10 of the amount which the client should pay to the receiving party under the section 11(1) costs order, and orders the payment on account or part of it to be paid to the receiving party in satisfaction or part satisfaction of the client's liability under that order; or

(ii)   makes an order under paragraph (5)(b) or (5)(c) of this regulation that the payment on account or part of it be repaid to the client.

(5)   Where a client has made a payment on account of costs pursuant to an order under paragraph (1) of this regulation—

(a)   the receiving party shall request a hearing under regulation 10 to determine the amount of costs payable to him;

(b)   if the receiving party fails to request such a hearing within the time permitted by regulation 10(2), the payment on account shall be repaid to the client;

(c)   if upon the hearing under regulation 10 the amount of costs which it is determined that the client should pay is less than the amount of the payment on account, the difference shall be repaid to the client.

[19.38]

11. Appeals, etc

(1)   Subject to the following paragraphs of this regulation, and to regulation 12, any determination made under regulation 9 or regulation 10 shall be final.

(2)   Any party with a financial interest in an assessment of the full costs may appeal against that assessment, if and to the extent that that party would, but for these Regulations, be entitled to appeal against an assessment of costs by the court in which the relevant proceedings are taking place.

(3)　Where, under regulation 9(2)(a), the court has specified the amount which a client is required to pay under a section 11(1) costs order, the client may apply to the court for a determination of the full costs and if, on that determination, the amount of the full costs is less than the amount which the court previously specified under regulation 9(2)(a), the client shall instead be required to pay the amount of the full costs.

(4)　The receiving party or the Commission may appeal, on a point of law, against the making of a costs order against the Commission (including the amount of costs which the Commission is required to pay under the order), or against the court's refusal to make such an order.

[19.39]

12. Variation and late determination of amount of costs

(1)　The following paragraphs of this regulation apply where the court makes a section 11(1) costs order.

(2)　Where the amount (if any) which the client is required to pay under the section 11(1) costs order, together with the amount which the Commission is required to pay under any costs order against the Commission, is less than the full costs, the receiving party may, on the ground set out in paragraph (4)(a), apply to the court for an order varying the amount which the client is required to pay under the section 11(1) costs order.

(3)　Where the court has not specified the amount to be paid under the section 11(1) costs order, and the receiving party has not, within the time limit in regulation 10(2), applied to have that amount determined in accordance with regulation 10, the receiving party may, on any of the grounds set out in paragraph (4), apply for a determination of the amount that the client is required to pay.

(4)　The grounds referred to in paragraphs (2) and (3) are the grounds that:

- (a)　there has been a significant change in the client's circumstances since the date of the order;
- (b)　material additional information as to the client's financial resources is available, and that information could not with reasonable diligence have been obtained by the receiving party in time to make an application in accordance with regulation 10; or
- (c)　there were other good reasons justifying the receiving party's failure to make an application within the time limit in regulation 10(2).

(5)　Any application under paragraph (2) or (3) shall be made by the receiving party within six years from the date on which the section 11(1) costs order is first made.

(6)　On any application under paragraph (2), the order may be varied as the court thinks fit, but the amount of costs ordered (excluding any costs ordered to be paid under paragraph (9)) shall not exceed the amount of the full costs as stated in any previous order of the court.

(7)　When the amount which the client is required to pay under the section 11(1) costs order has been determined under regulation 9(2)(a), and the receiving party applies under paragraph (2) for an order varying that amount:

- (a)　the receiving party shall file with the application under paragraph (2) his bill of costs, which shall comply with any requirements of relevant rules of court relating to the form and content of a bill of costs where the court is assessing a party's costs; and
- (b)　the court shall, when determining the application, assess the full costs.

(8) Where the receiving party has received funded services in relation to the proceedings, the Commission may make an application under paragraph (2) or paragraph (3), and:

    (a) when making the application the Commission shall file with the court a statement of the receiving party's costs or, if those costs have not been assessed, the receiving party's bill of costs; and

    (b) paragraphs (4) to (6) shall apply to that application as if 'the Commission' were substituted for 'the receiving party' in those paragraphs.

(9) The amount of costs to be determined under this regulation may include the costs incurred in relation to an application made under this regulation.

[19.40]

13. Rights to appear

(1) The . . . Director may appear at:

    (a) any hearing in relation to which notice has been given under regulation 10(3)(c);

    (b) the hearing of any appeal under regulation 11(4); or

    (c) the hearing of any application under regulation 12(8).

(2) The . . . Director may, instead of appearing under paragraph (1), give evidence in the form of a written statement to the court, verified by a statement of truth.

(3) The . . . Director shall file with the court any statement under paragraph (2), and serve a copy on the receiving party, not less than seven days before the hearing to which it relates.

(ii) The Costs Practice Direction

[19.41]

See para [19.22] for sections 21.12 to 21.20 of the Costs Practice Direction.

[19.42]

CPD Section 22 Orders for costs to which Section 11 of the Access to Justice Act 1999 applies

22.1 *In this Practice Direction:*

'order for costs to be determined' means an order for costs to which Section 11 of the Access to Justice Act 1999 applies under which the amount of costs payable by the LSC funded client is to be determined by a costs judge or district judge under Section 23 of this Practice Direction.

'order specifying the costs payable' means an order for costs to which Section 11 of the Act applies and which specifies the amount which the LSC funded client is to pay.

'full costs' means, where an order to which Section 11 of the Act applies is made against a LSC funded client, the amount of costs which that person would, had cost protection not applied, have been ordered to pay.

'determination proceedings' means proceedings to which paragraphs 22.1 to 22.10 apply.

'Section 11(1) costs order' means an order for costs to be determined or an order specifying the costs payable other than an order specifying the costs payable which was made in determination proceedings.

'statement of resources' means

(1)   a statement, verified by a statement of truth, made by a party to proceedings setting out:

    (a)   his income and capital and financial commitments during the previous year and, if applicable, those of his partner;

    (b)   his estimated future financial resources and expectations and, if applicable, those of his partner ('partner' is defined in paragraph 21.4, above);

    (c)   a declaration that he and, if applicable, his partner, has not deliberately foregone or deprived himself of any resources or expectations;

    (d)   particulars of any application for funding made by him in connection with the proceedings; and,

    (e)   any other facts relevant to the determination of his resources; or

(2)   a statement, verified by a statement of truth, made by a client receiving funded services, setting out the information provided by the client under Regulation 6 of the Community Legal Service (Financial) Regulations 2000, and stating that there has been no significant change in the client's financial circumstances since the date on which the information was provided or, as the case may be, details of any such change.

'Regional Director' means any Regional Director appointed by the LSC and any member of his staff authorised to act on his behalf.

22.2   Regulations 8 to 13 of the Community Legal Service (Costs) Regulations 2000 as amended set out the procedure for seeking costs against a funded client and the LSC. The effect of these Regulations is set out in this section and the next section of this Practice Direction.

22.3   As from 5 June 2000, Regulations 9 to 13 of the Community Legal Service (Costs) Regulations 2000 as amended also apply to certificates issued under the Legal Aid Act 1988 where costs against the assisted person fall to be assessed under Regulation 124 of the Civil Legal Aid (General) Regulations 1989. In this section and the next section of this Practice Direction the expression 'LSC funded client' includes an assisted person (defined in rule 43.2).

22.4   Regulation 8 of the Community Legal Service (Costs) Regulations 2000 provides that a party intending to seek an order for costs against a LSC funded client may at any time file and serve on the LSC funded client a statement of resources. If that statement is served 7 or more days before a date fixed for a hearing at which an order for costs may be made, the LSC funded client must also make a statement of resources and produce it at the hearing.

22.5   If the court decides to make an order for costs against a LSC funded client to whom cost protection applies it may either:

(1)   make an order for costs to be determined, or

(2)   make an order specifying the costs payable.

22.6   If the court makes an order for costs to be determined it may also

(1)   state the amount of full costs, or

(2)   make findings of facts, eg concerning the conduct of all the parties which are to be taken into account by the court in the subsequent determination proceedings.

22.7   The court will not make an order specifying the costs payable unless:

(1)   it considers that it has sufficient information before it to decide what amount is a reasonable amount for the LSC funded client to pay in accordance with Section 11 of the Act, and

(2)   either

    (a)   the order also states the amount of full costs, or

    (b)   the court considers that it has sufficient information before it to decide what amount is a reasonable amount for the LSC funded client to pay in accordance with Section 11 of the Act and is satisfied that, if it were to determine the full costs at that time, they would exceed the amounts specified in the order.

22.8   Where an order specifying the costs payable is made and the LSC funded client does not have cost protection in respect of all of the costs awarded in that order, the order must identify the sum payable (if any) in respect of which the LSC funded client has cost protection and the sum payable (if any) in respect of which he does not have cost protection.

22.9   The court cannot make an order under Regulations 8 to 13 of the Community Legal Service (Costs) Regulations 2000 as amended except in proceedings to which the next section of this Practice Direction applies.

[19.43]

CPD Section 23 Determination proceedings and similar proceedings under the Community Legal Service (Costs) Regulations 2000

23.1 This section of this Practice Direction deals with
(1)   proceedings subsequent to the making of an order for costs to be determined,
(2)   variations in the amount stated in an order specifying the amount of costs payable and
(3)   the late determination of costs under an order for costs to be determined.
(4)   appeals in respect of determination.
23.2   In this section of this Practice Direction 'appropriate court office' means:
(1)   the district registry or county court in which the case was being dealt with when the Section 11(1) order was made, or to which it has subsequently been transferred; or
(2)   in all other cases, the Costs Office.
(1)   This paragraph applies where the appropriate office is any of the following county courts:
Barnet, Bow, Brentford, Bromley, Central London, Clerkenwell, Croydon, Edmonton, Ilford, Kingston, Lambeth, Mayors and City of London, Romford, Shoreditch, Uxbridge, Wandsworth, West London, Willesden and Woolwich.
(2)   Where this paragraph applies:–
        (i)   a receiving party seeking an order specifying costs payable by an LSC funded client and/or by the Legal Services Commission under this section must file his application in the Costs Office and, for all purposes relating to that application, the Costs Office will be treated as the appropriate office in that case; and
        (ii)   unless an order is made transferring the application to the Costs Office as part of the High Court, an appeal from any decision made by a costs judge shall lie to the Designated Civil Judge for the London Group of County Courts or such judge as he shall nominate. The appeal notice and any other relevant papers should be lodged at the Central London Civil Justice Centre.
(1)   A receiving party seeking an order specifying costs payable by an LSC funded client and/or by the LSC may within 3 months of an order for costs to be determined, file in the appropriate court office an application in Form N244 accompanied by
        (a)   the receiving party's bill of costs (unless the full costs have already been determined);
        (b)   the receiving party's statement of resources (unless the court is determining an application against a costs order against the LSC and the costs were not incurred in the court of first instance); and
        (c)   if the receiving party intends to seek costs against the LSC, written notice to that effect.
(2)   If the LSC funded client's liability has already been determined and is less than the full costs, the application will be for costs against the LSC only. If the LSC funded client's liability has not yet been determined, the receiving party

must indicate if costs will be sought against the LSC if the funded client's liability is determined as less than the full costs.

(The LSC funded client's certificate will contain the addresses of the LSC funded client, his solicitor, and the relevant Regional Office of the LSC.)

23.4   The receiving party must file the above documents in the appropriate court office and (where relevant) serve copies on the LSC funded client and the Regional Director. In respect of applications for funded services made before 3 December 2001 a failure to file a request within the 3 months time limit specified in Regulation 10(2) is an absolute bar to the making of a costs order against the LSC. Where the application for funded services was made on or after 3 December 2001 the court does have power to extend the 3 months time limit, but only if the applicant can show good reason for the delay.

23.8   Determination proceedings will be listed for hearing before a costs judge or district judge. The determination of the liability on the LSC funded client will be listed as a private hearing.

23.9   Where the LSC funded client does not have cost protection in respect of all of the costs awarded, the order made by the costs judge or district judge must in addition to specifying the costs payable, identify the full costs in respect of which cost protection applies and the full costs in respect of which cost protection does not apply.

23.10   The Regional Director may appear at any hearing at which a costs order may be made against the LSC. Instead of appearing, he may file a written statement at court and serve a copy on the receiving party. The written statement should be filed and a copy served, not less than 7 days before the hearing.

[19.44]

Variation of an order specifying the costs payable

(1)   This paragraph applies where the amount stated in an order specifying the costs payable plus the amount ordered to be paid by the LSC is less than the full costs to which cost protection applies.

(2)   The receiving party may apply to the court for a variation of the amount which the LSC funded client is required to pay on the ground that there has been a significant change in the client's circumstances since the date of the order.

23.12   On an application under paragraph 23.11, where the order specifying the costs payable does not state the full costs

(1)   the receiving party must file with his application the receiving party's state-ment of resources and bill of costs and copies of these documents should be served with the application.

(2)   The LSC funded client must respond to the application by making a statement of resources which must be filed at court and served on the receiving party within 21 days thereafter. The LSC funded client may also file and serve written points disputing the bill within the same time limit.

(3)   The court will, when determining the application assess the full costs identifying any part of them to which cost protection does apply and any part of them to which cost protection does not apply.

23.13   On an application under paragraph 23.11 the order specifying the costs payable may be varied as the court thinks fit. That variation must not increase:

(1)   the amount of any costs ordered to be paid by the LSC, and

(2)   the amount payable by the LSC funded client,

to a sum which is greater than the amount of the full costs plus the costs of the application.

(1)   Where an order for costs to be determined has been made but the receiving party has not applied, within the three month time limit under para-graph 23.2, the receiving party may apply on any of the following grounds for a determination of the amount which the funded client is required to pay:

(a)   there has been a significant change in the funded client's circum-stances since the date of the order for costs to be determined; or

(b) material additional information about the funded client's financial resources is available which could not with reasonable diligence have been obtained by the receiving party at the relevant time; or

(c) there were other good reasons for the failure by the receiving party to make an application within the time limit.

(2) An application for costs payable by the LSC cannot be made under this paragraph.

(1) Where the receiving party has received funded services in relation to the proceedings, the LSC may make an application under paragraphs 23.11 and 23.14 above.

(2) In respect of an application under paragraph 23.11 made by the LSC, the LSC must file and serve copies of the documents described in paragraph 23.12(1).

23.16 An application under paragraph 23.11, 23.14 and 23.15 must be commenced before the expiration of 6 years from the date on which the court made the order specifying the costs payable, or (as the case may be) the order for costs to be determined.

23.17 Applications under paragraphs 23.11, 23.14 and 23.15 should be made in the appropriate court office and should be made in Form N244 to be listed for a hearing before a costs judge or district judge.

Appeals

(1) Save as mentioned above any determination made under Regulation 9 or 10 of the Costs Regulations is final (Regulation 11(1)). Any party with a financial interest in the assessment of the full costs, other than a funded party, may appeal against that assessment in accordance with CPR Part 52 (Regulation 11(2) and CPR rule 47.20).

(2) The receiving party or the Commission may appeal on a point of law against the making of a costs order against the Commission, against the amount of costs the Commission is required to pay or against the court's refusal to make such an order (Regulation 11(4)).

WASTED COSTS ORDER

[19.45]

In care proceedings, the judge granted continuous staying contact with the grandparents and suspended contact with the father. On appeal it was conceded that the judge's orders had been made without jurisdiction. The local authority applied for costs, indicating that it was indifferent as to whether they were awarded against the Board or against the grandparents' legal advisers under the wasted costs jurisdiction. An order against the grandparents would have no effect because they had no assets. The court laid down the following guidelines to be adopted in similar applications:

(1) Were there circumstances justifying:

(a) an order for costs against the assisted party if that party had not been legally aided, or

(b) a wasted costs order against that party's legal representatives?

(2) If circumstances could justify (a), such an application should be made.

(3) If it were appropriate to apply for (b), that application should be made.

(4) If the court considered it appeared to be so clear a case for making a wasted costs order against the legal representatives that it would not be just and equitable to make an order nisi against the Board, the court should adjourn the application against the Board and proceed to take

the steps necessary to establish that a wasted costs order was necessary. If such an order were made in respect of all the relevant costs, there would ordinarily be no reason to proceed further against the Board.

(5) If the application against the Board was not adjourned:

   (a) the court should ascertain whether the requirements of the Legal Aid Act 1988, s 18 were met, and if so make any order against the legally aided party and, if justified, an order nisi against the Board. In addition, if the court considered that there was a real possibility that a wasted costs order would be made, it should direct that that should be drawn to the Board's attention;

   (b) the lawyers representing the legally-aided litigant should regard it as their responsibility to draw to the court's attention any matters relevant in determining whether the requirements of s 18 had been met;

   (c) if the Board objected to an order, it could raise any contention it wished to pursue in respect of a wasted costs order.

(6) If an application against the Board was adjourned pending the investigation of an application for a wasted costs order and no such order was made, the application against the Board could be restored and determined.

In cases involving children, the position was complicated by the fact that the court did not attach the same significance to which party was successful, recognising that as its primary concern was the child's welfare, it was frequently inappropriate to determine questions of costs by merely asking who had won. On appeal, the approach was similar, but subject to an important qualification: that those who participate in litigation in the Court of Appeal involving the future of children had to be prepared for the appellate court to take the view that while it was reasonable for them to play an active part in proceedings at first instance, it was not so on appeal. If that was the position, they had to be prepared for an order for costs to be made against them (*Re O (a minor) (costs: liability of Legal Aid Board)* [1997] 1 FCR 159, CA).

CHAPTER 20

ARBITRATION

ARBITRATION ACT 1996

[20.1]

The law relating to arbitration is contained in the Arbitration Act 1996 which was greeted with universal acclaim as a model statute in both form and content when it came into force on 1 January 1997. Sections 59–65 relate to costs. Here they are:

[20.2]

59 Costs of the arbitration
    (1)   References in this Part to the costs of the arbitration are to—
        (a)   the arbitrators' fees and expenses,
        (b)   the fees and expenses of any arbitral institution concerned, and
        (c)   the legal or other costs of the parties.
    (2)   Any such reference includes the costs of or incidental to any proceedings to determine the amount of the recoverable costs of the arbitration (see section 63).

[20.3]

Section 28 of the Act makes the parties jointly and severally liable for such of the arbitrator's reasonable fees and expenses as are appropriate in the circumstances. It also makes provision for the parties to agree with the arbitrator his fees and expenses, including capping and restrictions, or to apply to the court for them to be considered and adjusted.

Section 37(2) provides that the arbitrator's expenses include the fees and expenses of any expert, legal adviser or assessor appointed by the tribunal.

[20.4]

60 Agreement to pay costs in any event
    An agreement which has the effect that a party is to pay the whole or part of the costs of the arbitration in any event is only valid if made after the dispute in question has arisen.

[20.5]

Section 60 of the Act preserves the unusual prohibition in respect of arbitrations that the parties may not in the arbitration agreement provide that each party shall pay their own costs in any event, and extends the prohibition to agreements that one party shall pay the other party's costs whatever the outcome of the arbitration. The purpose is to try to create a level playing field between large contractors and small contractors, and not deter a party from commencing arbitration proceedings because he will be liable for his own costs in any event. This consideration does not apply to any post-dispute agreement the parties may wish to enter into.

[20.6]

61 **Award of costs**

(1)   The tribunal may make an award allocating the costs of the arbitration as between the parties, subject to any agreement of the parties.

(2)   Unless the parties otherwise agree, the tribunal shall award costs on the general principle that costs should follow the event except where it appears to the tribunal that in the circumstances this is not appropriate in relation to the whole or part of the costs.

[20.7]

Section 61 of the Act empowers the arbitrator to award the whole or part of the costs of the arbitration to either party, subject to the general principle that costs follow the event except where it appears to the tribunal that in the circumstances this is not appropriate in relation to the whole or part of the costs. Matters such as exaggeration, conduct, failure on particular issues, reasonableness, proportionality and sealed offers were relevant to the award of arbitration costs long before these concepts were introduced into civil litigation by the Civil Procedure Rules 1998. CPR 43.2(2) applies the CPR rules Parts 44 to 48 to the costs of arbitration proceedings and to this extent the practice has been codified in the CPR both in respect of the principles on which costs are both awarded and quantified. but also in respect of offers to settle. CPR Part 62, and its supplementary practice direction, applies to arbitration proceedings but does not specifically mention costs. If a sealed offer is made in arbitration, being the arbitral equivalent of a payment into court, a respondent is normally entitled to payment of costs from the date of the offer if the award in respect of the claim and interest is less than the offer. The arbitrator is not entitled to take into account whether an award of costs would be made in favour of the claimant because that would require the claimant to assess not only the likelihood of achieving an award on his claim and interest exceeding the offer, but also, if there was a risk of an order that the claimant pay the respondent's costs, the chance of obtaining an award greater than the offer and the respondent's costs. Such a result would hinder settlement and introduce complications inconsistent with the principle that the costs should follow the event (*Everglade Maritime Inc v Schiffahrtsgesellschaft Detlef von Appen mbH* [1993] QB 780, CA).

As it is customary for an award to deal at one and the same time both with the parties' claims and with the question of costs, the existence of a sealed offer has to be brought to the attention of the arbitrator before he has reached a decision. However, it should remain sealed at that stage and it would be wholly improper for the arbitrator to look at it before he has reached a final decision on the matters in dispute other than as to costs, or to revise that decision in the light of the terms of the sealed offer when he sees them. There are arbitrators and umpires who feel that this procedure is not satisfactory. They take the view that respondents will feel that their defence is weakened if the arbitrator knows that they have made a sealed offer, even if the figure is concealed. If this is so, respondents may be deterred from making a sealed offer. The solution to the problem is if an arbitrator or umpire thinks it appropriate, he can always invite, and possibly require, the respondents to give him at the end of the hearing a sealed envelope which is to contain either a statement that no sealed offer has been made or the sealed offer itself. If this procedure is adopted, the existence of a sealed offer is hidden from the tribunal until the moment at which it has to consider that part of the award which relates to costs, the delivery of a sealed envelope of itself being devoid of all significance (*Tramountana Armadora SA v Atlantic Shipping Co SA* [1978] 2 All ER 280).

FAIRNESS

[20.8]

An arbitrator's power to award costs under s 61 of the Act or under the applicable procedural rules is subject to the general duty under s 33(1)(a) of the Act to act fairly and impartially as between the parties. Accordingly, if the arbitrator had been troubled by matters not raised by the parties and on which he had relied in making his order as to costs, he ought to have brought them to the attention of the parties before so doing so that the applicants could have dealt with them, and his failure to do so constituted a serious irregularity within the meaning of s 68(2)(a) of the Act (*Ghangbola v Smith & Sherriff Ltd* [1998] 3 All ER 730).

[20.9]

62 Effect of agreement or award about costs

Unless the parties otherwise agree, any obligation under an agreement between them as to how the costs of the arbitration are to be borne, or under an award allocating the costs of the arbitration, extends only to such costs as are recoverable.

[20.10]

63 The recoverable costs of the arbitration

(1) The parties are free to agree what costs of the arbitration are recoverable.

(2) If or to the extent there is no such agreement, the following provisions apply.

(3) The tribunal may determine by award the recoverable costs of the arbitration on such basis as it thinks fit.

If it does so, it shall specify—

(a) the basis on which it has acted, and

(b) the items of recoverable costs and the amount referable to each.

(4) If the tribunal does not determine the recoverable costs of the arbitration, any party to the arbitral proceedings may apply to the court (upon notice to the other parties) which may—

(a) determine the recoverable costs of the arbitration on such basis as it thinks fit, or

(b) order that they shall be determined by such means and upon such terms as it may specify.

(5) Unless the tribunal or the court determines otherwise—

    (a)   the recoverable costs of the arbitration shall be determined on the basis that there shall be allowed a reasonable amount in respect of all costs reasonably incurred, and

    (b)   any doubt as to whether costs were reasonably incurred or were reasonable in amount shall be resolved in favour of the paying party.

(6)   The above provisions have effect subject to section 64 (recoverable fees and expenses of arbitrators).

(7)   Nothing in this section affects any right of the arbitrators, any expert, legal adviser or assessor appointed by the tribunal, or any arbitral institution, to payment of their fees and expenses.

[20.11]

Ahead of the Civil Procedure Rules 1998 arbitrators were empowered and encouraged to assess costs themselves where possible and otherwise to refer them to the court, subject to the right of the parties to agree what costs are recoverable. Costs were in effect on the standard basis as it was defined before 26 April 1999 unless the arbitrator ordered otherwise, but the application of the CPR 1998 now incorporates the specific additional test of proportionality. Section 63(3) of the Act permits the arbitrator to award costs on such basis 'as he thinks fit'. Where costs awarded between the parties are to be determined by the court the effect of sections 63(4) and (5) is they are assessed on the standard basis as it was defined before the introduction of the CPR unless the arbitrator orders otherwise, namely costs of a reasonable amount, reasonably incurred. However CPR rule 43.2(2) requires the court to apply CPR rules 44–48 to arbitration proceedings and these include the principle of proportionality. We therefore appear to have the unsatisfactory, and no doubt unintentional, position that the arbitrator may, if he thinks fit, ignore the test of proportionality but the court must apply it.

Where a party is represented in an arbitration by a person who is not qualified as a barrister or solicitor, but who provides similar services, and an award is made providing for payment of that party's costs by the other party or for such costs to be assessed in the High Court if not agreed, the court has power to allow the costs of the unqualified person in relation to the conduct of the arbitration. The prohibition in s 25(1) of the Solicitors Act 1974 against the recovery of costs in respect of anything done by any unqualified person 'acting as a solicitor' does not apply to an unqualified person representing a party in an arbitration since an unqualified person does not 'act as a solicitor' within the meaning of s 25(1) merely by doing acts of a kind commonly done by solicitors. Acts prohibited by s 25(1) are limited to acts which are lawful only for a qualified solicitor to do and which only a solicitor may perform, or acts purportedly done in that capacity. They do not include acts commonly done by a solicitor but which do not involve a representation that the person so acting is acting as a solicitor. A person acting as an advocate for a party in arbitration proceedings who is not qualified as a barrister or solicitor and does not hold himself out as such is not acting as a barrister or solicitor and accordingly the party employing him is not precluded from entitlement to payment of his costs (*Piper Double Glazing Ltd v DC Contracts (1992) Ltd* [1994] 1 All ER 177).

RECOVERABILITY

[20.12]

Section 63 provides three methods of resolving the question of costs recoverability:

(1)   Agreement
(2)   Determination by the tribunal. In which case the tribunal shall specify the basis on which it has acted, the items of recoverable costs and the amount of each item.
(3)   In the absence of either of the above either party may apply to the court.

Does an award of costs 'to be agreed or taxed in default of agreement' permit the arbitrator to determine the costs, or does it amount to either a reference to the court or to a failure to determine the costs, enabling the receiving party to apply to the court?

In *M/S Alghanim Industries Inc v Skandia International Insurance Corpn* [2001] 2 All ER (Comm) 30 it was held that the phrase is not to be construed as a determination of the proceedings with a reference of taxation to the court in the event that the parties could not agree. The arbitrators had not expressly declined to tax and settle the costs, requiring the matter to go to the court. An award of costs to be agreed or taxed in default of an agreement was not a refusal to tax but was neutral in its language, it left open the possibility of an application by either party to the arbitrators. This was consistent with the spirit of the Act that as far as possible matters should be resolved by arbitration rather than application to the court.

[20.13]

64 Recoverable fees and expenses of arbitrators

(1)   Unless otherwise agreed by the parties, the recoverable costs of the arbitration shall include in respect of the fees and expenses of the arbitrators only such reasonable fees and expenses as are appropriate in the circumstances.

(2)   If there is any question as to what reasonable fees and expenses are appropriate in the circumstances, and the matter is not already before the court on an application under section 63(4), the court may on the application of any party (upon notice to the other parties)—

(a)   determine the matter, or
(b)   order that it be determined by such means and upon such terms as the court may specify.

(3)   Subsection (1) has effect subject to any order of the court under section 24(4) or 25(3)(b) (order as to entitlement to fees or expenses in case of removal or resignation of arbitrator).

(4)   Nothing in this section affects any right of the arbitrator to payment of his fees and expenses.

[20.14]

Section 28 of the Act makes the parties jointly and severally liable for such of the arbitrator's reasonable fees and expenses as are appropriate in the circumstances. It also makes provision for the parties to agree with the arbitrator his fees and expenses, including capping and restrictions, or to apply to the court for them to be considered and adjusted.

The definition of costs in the Arbitration Act 1996, s 59 includes the arbitrator's fees and expenses, which are defined in s 64(1) as 'such reasonable fees and expenses as are appropriate in the circumstances', while s 37(2) provides that 'expenses' may include the fees and expenses of experts, legal advisers and assessors appointed by the arbitrator, so for these to be recoverable, they too must be reasonable. Section 64(1) is subject to any order made under ss 24 and 25 of the Act on the removal or resignation of an arbitrator.

Any dispute about the reasonableness of an arbitrator's fees and expenses may be resolved by the court under s 64(2). However, this is subject to the right of the parties and the arbitrator to agree the amount of his fees and expenses at the outset, creating a contract with which the court cannot interfere (Arbitration Act 1996, s 64(4)). If the agreement relates only to hourly or daily rates, the court can investigate the reasonableness of the time spent, but not the agreed amounts.

It is not improper for a party appointing an arbitrator to agree his fees before appointment since the appointing party and the proposed arbitrator are respectively free to appoint someone else or not to accept the appointment if the terms are not acceptable. However, once an appointment had been made it is contrary to the arbitrator's quasi-judicial status for him to bargain unilaterally with only one party for his fees and any agreement made without the consent of the other party between the appointing party and his arbitrator or a third arbitrator after they had accepted appointment for the payment of any fees to either arbitrator probably constitutes misconduct, and is in any event liable to render the arbitrator vulnerable to the imputation of bias. Although it is not improper for an arbitrator to stipulate at the time of his appointment for a commitment fee to be made payable in any event even if the arbitration did not take place, once appointed an arbitrator is not entitled unilaterally to change the terms of his contract by demanding a commitment fee unless there is a significant and substantial change in the commitment required of him which justifies the payment of a further fee (*Norjarl K/S A/S v Hyundai Heavy Industries Co Ltd* [1992] 1 QB 863, [1991] 3 All ER 211

Section 56 empowers the tribunal to refuse to deliver an award unless the arbitrator's fees and expenses are paid in full.

Section 28(2) also makes provision for the court to order that the amount of an arbitrator's fees and expenses shall be considered and adjusted by such means and upon such terms as it may direct. This course was successfully adopted by the paying party in *Agrimex Ltd v Tradigrain SA* [2003] EWHC 1656 (Comm), [2003] 2 Lloyd's Rep 537, in respect of the fees of a legal draftsman employed by the arbitrators to assist them in drafting the award. The draftsman was a solicitor of only three years' post-qualification experience, but charged £9,300 out of total costs of under £20,000. After deprecating the use of legal draftsmen except in very special circumstances, the court held that the charges were disproportionate and that no competent lawyer could have spent the amount of time claimed for. The solicitor's fee was allowed at £5,000 — which would have been lower had not this been the amount proposed by the paying party!

[20.15]

65 Power to limit recoverable costs

(1)   Unless otherwise agreed by the parties, the tribunal may direct that the recoverable costs of the arbitration, or of any part of the arbitral proceedings, shall be limited to a specified amount.

(2)   Any direction may be made or varied at any stage, but this must be done sufficiently in advance of the incurring of costs to which it relates, or the taking of any steps in the proceedings which may be affected by it, for the limit to be taken into account.

[20.16]

Again ahead of the radical philosophy of the Civil Procedure Rules, the Arbitration Act 1996, s 65 empowers the arbitrator, unless the parties have agreed otherwise, to limit the costs recoverable in the arbitration either as a whole or in respect of a specified part. This enables the arbitrator either on his own initiative or, more likely, on the application of one of the parties to specify the maximum liability for costs of the arbitration. It will not of course prevent either party spending a disproportionate amount on costs, but it will put a cap on the amount they can recover from the other party. It would be helpful to support an application with a schedule of the estimate of costs, which it may not be possible to prepare until directions have been given as to the format of the arbitration.

Writing in the *New Law Journal*, 9 April 1999, Francis Miller considered the impact of a limitation of costs under s 65 on a conditional fee agreement between the claimant and their legal advisers. He suggested this could result in the actual recoverable costs from the respondent, in the event of the claimant winning, being limited to an amount which was a great deal less than the actual costs incurred by the claimant. In this event, recourse might be had to the safeguard in s 65(2) which provides:

> 'Any direction may be made or varied at any stage, but this must be done sufficiently in advance of the incurring of costs to which it relates, or the taking of any steps in the proceedings which may be affected by it, for the limit to be taken into account.'

CORRECTING A COSTS AWARD

[20.17]

Under s 57(3)(*a*) of the 1996 Act, an arbitrator has the default power to 'correct an award so as to remove any clerical mistake or error arising from an accidental slip or omission'. In *Gannet Shipping Ltd v Eastrade Commodities Inc* [2002] 1 All ER (Comm) 297, QBD (Comm Ct) Langley J held that the arbitrator also had jurisdiction to vary the costs order at the same time. The costs error was an error 'arising from' the 'accidental slip' in the amount awarded, and accordingly it could be corrected. Furthermore, the costs award could also have been amended under the jurisdiction to intervene conferred by both s 62(2)(*a*) (failure by the tribunal to comply with the natural justice principle in s 33 of the 1996 Act) and s 62(2)(*i*) (irregularity in the conduct of the proceedings or in the award which is admitted by the tribunal). The only limiting factor was the need to show substantial injustice.

FAILURE TO GIVE REASONS

[20.18]

Under s 52(3) of the Arbitration Act 1996 an award 'shall contain reasons for the award'. There is no sanction in s 53(3) for a failure to include reasons, and a failure to include reasons for a costs award does not render the award void but simply allows a party to seek reasons by means of an application to the court under s 68 of the 1996 Act on the basis that the arbitrators have failed to comply with the requirements as to the form of the award (s 68(2)(*b*); *Ridler v Walter* [2001] TASSC 98, Supreme Court of Tasmania).

APPLICATIONS TO THE COURT

[20.19]

Matters relating to costs which are subject to applications to the court include:
(1) applications under section 28(2) to have the amount of the arbitrator's fees and expenses considered and adjusted;
(2) applications under section 56(2) for a review of the arbitrator's fees and expenses;
(3) applications under section 63(4) of the Arbitration Act 1996 to determine the recoverable costs of the arbitration;
(4) applications under section 64(2) to determine the reasonable fees and expenses of the arbitrator;
(5) applications under section 68 on the grounds of a serious irregularity;
(6) appeals under section 69 on the grounds of a serious error of law in the award as to costs;
(7) applications under section 70(4) for an order that the arbitrator provides proper reasons for his award as to costs.

CIVIL PROCEDURE RULES

[20.20]

When the CPR were introduced, rule 49(2) included arbitration claims in a list of specialist proceedings with a practice direction applying to those proceedings. On 25 March 2002 arbitration claims were removed from the list and received their own rules in Part 62 and supplementary practice direction.

COSTS OF ENFORCEMENT

[20.21]

Enforcement of an award involves an application under CPR 62.18 for permission to enforce the award as a judgment with the option of entering judgment in the terms of the award. The application should be for costs to be included in the order giving permission and if judgment is to be obtained 'for the costs of any judgment to be entered'

SECURITY FOR COSTS

[20.22]

See Chapter 13.

Part III

Quantification

CHAPTER 21

WHAT IS THE DIFFERENCE?

CONTENTIOUS AND NON-CONTENTIOUS

(a) Vive la difference?

[21.1]

Most approaches to costs start by distinguishing between contentious and non-contentious work, solicitors tending to identify themselves with one or the other, thereby not only relieving themselves from the responsibility of having any knowledge of the other species of costs but enabling them to say with complacent self-disparagement 'of course I don't know anything about contentious costs' (or 'non-contentious costs' as the case may be) as though they were some alien discipline. I do not in any way wish to minimise the difference between contentious and non-contentious costs – as between sexes there are differences and they are important; on the other hand, again as with the sexes, the similarities are much greater than the differences and I think that the best approach is to treat solicitors' costs as an entity, considering the differences only when they arise.

Non-contentious business is defined by the Solicitors Act 1974 as 'any business done as a solicitor which is not contentious business', and if you find that less than helpful you will also find in the Solicitors Act contentious business defined as being 'business done whether as solicitor or advocate in or for the purposes of proceedings begun before a Court or before an arbitrator appointed under the Arbitration Act 1950 other than non-contentious probate business'. The key word there is 'begun'. If you take instructions for divorce proceedings but before you present the petition the parties are reconciled that, contrary to all the appearances, was non-contentious work. Similarly debt collection is non-contentious business until proceedings are begun, as are all disputes, but the catch is that if proceedings are started the work becomes retrospectively contentious from the beginning. Another trap for the unwary is that someone who can never have visited an Employment Tribunal has classified it (and all other tribunals except the Lands Tribunal) as non-contentious business, even though an appeal from an Employment Tribunal to the Employment Appeal Tribunal takes its rightful place as contentious business. That is because the Lands Tribunal and the EAT are statutory superior courts of record.

An argument that whatever the position may have been before, since 1990 an employment tribunal has been a court as defined by s 119 of the Courts and Legal Services Act of that year was disposed of in *Tel-Ka Talk v Revenue And Customs Comrs (PTH 0904822)* (17 June 2010, unrepoerted), SCCO in which the Law Society intervened. Senior Costs Master Hurst held that a contingency fee agreement (whereby a lawyer is paid a percentage of what his client recovers) entered into between a solicitor and his client for the former to represent the latter before the VAT and Duties Tribunal was lawful because it was it was specifically made lawful by s 57 of the Solicitors Act 1974 in a non contentious business agreement. The Tribunal was not a 'court' within the purview of s 87 of that Act. The business of the tribunal was non contentious and there was no evidence that parliament intended to enlarge the meaning of 'court' to include tribunals or that proceedings before a tribunal were contentious business. The Senior Master observed 'Failure to comply with the Damages Based Agreement Regulations 2010 (see para [42.3A]) may render an agreement unenforceable. It seems likely that in future legal representatives in the employment tribunal will rely on conditional fee agreements which are no longer regulated and which can be drafted in such a way as to produce the same result as a contingency fee agreement'.

The definitions were considered in *Bilkus v Stockler Brunton (A Firm)* [2010] EWCA Civ 101, [2010] 3 All ER 64, [2010] NLJR 311, 16 February. The words 'in or for the purposes of proceedings' in s 87(1) should be construed as a composite whole. Business (or work) 'in ... proceedings begun before a court' referred to the work done in the actual litigation. Work 'for the purposes of proceedings' could be carried out before the proceedings were begun (taking instructions, writing a letter before claim, obtaining evidence and so on) or during the proceedings. Obtaining a witness statement could be regarded as done for the purposes of proceedings, even if the witness statement was not ultimately served or used; the filing and service of a witness statement was work done in the proceedings. The phrase 'for the purposes of' required the proceedings to be contemporaneous with the work in question or to be in the future. Work done after the completion of proceedings was done not for the purpose of those proceedings, but in consequence of those proceedings. Steps taken to enforce a judgment through the courts were clearly themselves proceedings. In this case, the work carried out by the solicitors in connection with the independent valuation was contentious business. The valuation of the share in the company was carried out under a court order and pursuant to directions given by the court. It was not possible to distinguish this case from the costs of the solicitor who wrote to the other side following a judgment to obtain payment of a sum ordered by the court to be paid to his client. That work was done for the purpose of the proceedings, in that it could not sensibly be distinguished from those proceedings.

(b) The prescribed factors

(i) Non-contentious

[21.2]

A solicitor's remuneration for non-contentious business is governed by the Solicitors' (Non-Contentious Business) Remuneration Order 2009, art 3 (which came into force on 11 August 2009 and applies to all non-contentious business for which bills are delivered on or after that date.

The Solicitors' (Non-Contentious Business) Remuneration Order 1994 was revoked except in its application to non-contentious business for which bills were delivered before this Order came into force):

> (3) A solicitor's costs must be fair and reasonable having regard to all the circumstances of the case and in particular to—

(a)   the complexity of the matter or the difficulty or novelty of the questions raised;

(b)   the skill, labour, specialised knowledge and responsibility involved;

(c)   the time spent on the business;

(d)   the number and importance of the documents prepared or considered, without regard to length;

(e)   the place where and the circumstances in which the business or any part of the business is transacted;

(f)   the amount or value of any money or property involved;

(g)   whether any land involved is registered land within the meaning of the Land Registration Act 2002;

(h)   the importance of the matter to the client; and

(i)   the approval (express or implied) of the entitled person or the express approval of the testator to:—

    (i)   the solicitor undertaking all or any part of the work giving rise to the costs or

    (ii)   the amount of the costs.

(ii)   Contentious

[21.3]

The quantification of contentious costs is governed by CPR Rule 44.5.

[21.4]

CPR Rule 44.5: Factors to be taken into account in deciding the amount of costs

(1)   The court is to have regard to all the circumstances in deciding whether costs were—

(a)   if it is assessing costs on the standard basis—

    (i)   proportionately and reasonably incurred; or

    (ii)   were proportionate and reasonable in amount, or

(b)   if it is assessing costs on the indemnity basis—

    (i)   unreasonably incurred; or

    (ii)   unreasonable in amount.

(2)   In particular the court must give effect to any orders which have already been made.

(3)   The court must also have regard to—

(a)   the conduct of all the parties, including in particular—

    (i)   conduct before, as well as during, the proceedings; and

    (ii)   the efforts made, if any, before and during the proceedings in order to try to resolve the dispute;

(b)   the amount or value of any money or property involved;

(c)   the importance of the matter to all the parties;

(d)   the particular complexity of the matter or the difficulty or novelty of the questions raised;

(e)   the skill, effort, specialised knowledge and responsibility involved;

(f)   the time spent on the case; and

(g)   the place where and the circumstances in which work or any part of it was done.

(Rule 35.4 (4) gives the court power to limit the amount that a party may recover with regard to the fees and expenses of an expert)

(c) The bases

[21.5]

Let us dispose of another difference which is more apparent than real between contentious and non-contentious costs. There are two bases for the assessment of costs, the standard basis and the indemnity basis, and on neither basis will the court allow costs which have been unreasonably incurred or are unreasonable in amount (Rule 44.4(1)). They are therefore fundamentally the same. Non-contentious costs are always to be assessed on the indemnity basis (Rule 48.8(2)) while Rule 44.4 prescribes that contentious costs may be awarded on either basis. There are two differences between the standard and the indemnity basis: (a) the benefit of any doubt is resolved in favour of the paying party on the standard basis and in favour of the receiving party on the indemnity basis and (b) on the standard basis costs have to be proportionate to the matters in issue (Rule 44.4(2); see para [11.30]). These two exceptions apart, there is no difference between the prescribed principles governing the quantification of non-contentious and contentious business.

(d) The paying party

[21.6]

An apparent difference between contentious and non-contentious costs is that in contentious work the costs are frequently ordered to be paid by somebody other than the person who ordered the work to be done. In litigation they will probably be paid by the loser, while if it is a legal aid matter, the costs may be paid out of the legal aid fund. Therefore, in litigation it is necessary much more frequently than in non-contentious business to protect the interests of a paying party who was not privy to the incurring of the costs he has to pay. But this is not a crucial difference. In non-contentious work one sees with increasing frequency provision in leases and other commercial documents for costs to be paid by someone other than the client.

(e) Value

[21.7]

More imagination has been shown in applying the prescribed factors in non-contentious work than contentious. Various formulae or yardsticks have been tried – financial bands, regressive scales, the adrenalin factor, percentage service increments, time plus 25% plus half the value, time plus an overall uplift – together with a variety of ways of assessing the value of different types of non-contentious work, such as leases, options and probate. In comparison, litigation costs have become increasingly hypnotised with time – an obsession which has now led to prescribed hourly rates for summary assessments which are professed to take into account, or rather to circumscribe, all of the factors required to be taken into account by Rule 44.5.

The main reason for this divergence is no doubt because in non-contentious work the value element is more readily identifiable and ascertainable than in much contentious work. What, for example, is the value element in a divorce suit or a criminal matter? Who can put a value on the liberty of the subject, whether the freedom be from a spouse or a prison? On the other hand the reverse also applies, there is often a very substantial value element identifiable in litigation while in some non-contentious work the value element may be unquantifiable or so small as to be only a minor factor in charging. What, for example, is the value of a will to the *client* as distinct from the beneficiaries?

(f) Conclusion

[21.8]

There are no inherent distinctions of principle necessitating different approaches to the quantification of contentious and non-contentious costs. In his judgment in *Jemma Trust Ltd v Liptrott* [2003] EWCA Civ 1476, [2004] 1 All ER 510, Lord Justice Mance supported this view. He found 'the distinction, which at present apparently exists between contentious and non-contentious work is difficult fully to rationalise' and he thought the primary reason for the different approaches was that in non-contentious work it was more feasible to identify value. Much of contentious and non-contentious work was distinguished by practical considerations. He did not find the question why non-contentious work should, in the absence of any agreement about basic fees, be any different from contentious work an easy question to answer. Neither do I.

SOLICITOR AND CLIENT AND BETWEEN-THE-PARTIES.

(a) Definition

[21.9]

Whatever happened to Solicitor and Client costs? I recently came across one of my earlier works – *A Guide to the Simplification of The Taxation of Contentious Costs*, published in 1979. This was to introduce the brand new all-singing all-dancing new Appendix 2 to Order 62 of the RSC. The 'simplification' of taxations! – we were innocent babes in those days. The book starts with the definition of between-the-parties costs by Vice-Chancellor Malins in 1875 in *Smith v Buller* (1875) L.R. 19 Eq. which was:

> 'It is of great importance to litigants who are unsuccessful that they should not be oppressed by having to pay an excessive amount of costs. The costs chargeable under a taxation (*assessment*) between party and party are all that are necessary to enable the adverse party to conduct the litigation, and no more. Any charges merely for conducting litigation more conveniently may be called luxuries, and must be paid for by the party incurring them.'

Some years later the *Esher Report* considered whether successful parties should recover the whole of their costs – be 'harmless as to costs' as it is sometimes succinctly put – and the report came down firmly against full recoverability on the grounds that large and wealthy litigants would run up substantial and disproportionate costs in order to frighten poorer litigants into submission and costs generally would escalate out of control. In other words, *Smith v Buller* had got it right.

(b) The standard basis

[21.10]

In *The Taxation of Legal Costs*, published in 1986 introducing another brand new Order 62 and Appendix 2, I summarised the first of the changes thus:

> 'The abolition of the party and party basis of taxation. It is replaced by the common fund basis, which in turn is renamed "the standard basis". The effect of this reform is that the successful party in litigation will recover more costs from the loser: he should, therefore, receive a smaller solicitor and client bill.'

There was no suggestion that the client would not receive *any* solicitor and client bill.

(c) Solicitor and client

[21.11]

Then we had the Benson Report. Benson, Lord Benson as he became, was an accountant, and Mr Justice Templeman, Lord Templeman as he became, told me that when Benson had asked him what was the difference between solicitor and client costs and party and party costs he had replied: '33 1/3'. And he was about right. But what should Lord Templeman reply today? Or to pose the question in modern terms, in the vast majority of cases what is the difference between costs on the indemnity basis and on the standard basis? What is wrong with a successful client making a reasonable additional payment to his solicitor above the amount recovered between the parties, especially in these days of prescribed, fixed and predictable costs. Even the sound-bite 'No win – no fee' implies if there is a win there is a fee. The assumption that a successful litigant should be harmless as to costs is the result of the profession being taken in by its own propaganda. One of the great disadvantages of the recoverability of CFA additional liabilities is that the client has no incentive to keep a check on the amount of costs being incurred by his solicitor because he or she will never have to pay them. The result was summarised by Jeremy Rawkins, President of the Association of District Judges, in the Law Society's Gazette of 30 June 2005: 'It should not be the role of the court to interfere with the legitimate contractual relationship between solicitor and client, much less to dictate the rate of financial reward, but it is the court's duty to regulate the extent of costs recovery for the victor from the vanquished. The valuable demarcation between solicitor/client costs and party/party costs has been eroded so that there is no practical distinction.' It is time that the profession regained its confidence to distinguish between the two.

CHAPTER 22

TIME

COSTING TIME

[22.1]

Time is relevant in a solicitor's practice in two distinct ways. First, it is his raw material, his stock in trade. Some years ago the young partners in an old and venerable firm were trying to persuade their elders to bring the firm into the twentieth century. One of the senior partners remonstrated with them: 'The trouble with your generation is you are trying to run the practice like a business'. In the same way that businesses keep control over materials and stock, a solicitor should keep control over his own and his employees' time. The first relevance of time is therefore to the good running and management of a solicitor's practice. Could the time be put to better use?

The second relevance of time is to charging. Not only is time one of the prescribed factors for both contentious and non-contentious business, and in routine matters it is the most important, it also runs like a thread through the other factors. The importance and complexity of the matter, the difficulty or novelty of questions raised can all affect the amount of time spent. An hourly cost rate applied to recorded time, in the words of Donaldson J:

' . . . if calculated accurately, informs a solicitor of the minimum figure which he must charge, if he is not to make an actual loss on the transaction. Second, it gives him an idea of the relationship between the overheads attributable to the transaction and the profit accruing to him. This latter point is plainly relevant in the broad sense that the nature of some transactions will justify much larger profits than others of a more routine type. But we must stress that it is only one of a number of cross-checks on the fairness and reasonableness of the final figure. The final figure will result from an exercise in judgment, not arithmetic, whatever arithmetical cross-checks may be employed.'

(*Treasury Solicitor v Regester* [1978] 2 All ER 920, QBD.)

Together with value, time is one of the only two factors that are quantifiable, and if a solicitor is not able to quantify it, it is going to cast considerable doubt on his ability to quantify the other, less tangible, factors.

ALTERNATIVES TO COSTING TIME

(a) For management

(i) Budget

[22.2]

You can prepare a budget of expenses for the next year. You can divide that by 12. You now know that if in each month you do not bill at least that amount you are running at a loss. You can take it a stage further by adding to your budgeted expenses for the forthcoming year the profit you hope to make during that period and dividing that total by 12. This gives you a total target figure for bills delivered. Having calculated the figure for bills to deliver during the year, it can be apportioned among the fee earners so that the total targets of the fee earners equals your overall target. If each fee earner accepts his target as realistic, you know you should reach your overall target for the year. As a result of monthly checks you will have an early warning if any fee earner is falling behind his target. Each month you will know whether you are on, ahead of or behind your target.

(ii) Employees

[22.3]

There is no point in one solicitor (the principal) employing another solicitor or legal executive (the assistant), paying him a salary, supplying him free of charge with accommodation, secretarial services and all the other tools of his profession, unless that assistant either makes a profit for his principal or relieves the principal of routine work, thereby enabling the principal to undertake more profitable work. A rough formula which has stood the test of time is that a fee earner's share of the overheads is not less than one-and-a-half times his salary. An assistant with a salary of £40,000 a year will have a share of the overheads of £60,000 a year, meaning that he must bill £100,000, or two-and-a-half times his salary, to break even. If to this is added a modest profit of half his salary, this produces a target of £120,000, or three times his salary. I was interested to discover that a survey of surveyors had identified what they called a factor of 2.7–3.0; they had reached the same conclusion – that unless an assistant earns at least three times his salary, his employment must be justified by some means other than the profit he is making for the firm.

These two aspects of management control depend solely upon the calculation of expenses and projected profit. They do not require any recording or costing of time.

(b) For charging

[22.4]

There is a variety of ways in which solicitors' charges could be calculated, other than on the basis of time. Examples are according to value, scale, commission, salary, fixed fees, a contingency basis, and a quantum meruit.

Not only does time not enter into any of these bases, the less time a solicitor takes to do the work where time is not the basis of calculation, the bigger the profit he makes because he has more time to spend on other work.

In an article in *The Lawyer*, Anne Gallagher considered various methods of charging in the United States. She identified four basic billing methods: hourly, fixed-fee and contingency, all of which determine in advance the billing method that will be used, and 'value billing', where the lawyer retrospectively determines what the fee will be, based upon either subjective or agreed-upon criteria. Variations of billing methods included:

(i)	*Blended hourly rate*	All services are charged at a common hourly rate whether for a senior partner, junior partner or associate.
(ii)	*Fixed fee plus hourly rate*	Certain defined services are charged on a fixed-fee basis, while the remainder of the time expended is billed on an hourly basis.
(iii)	*Hourly rate plus premium*	The established hourly rate is standard or lower than standard with a bonus paid if certain results are achieved.
(iv)	*Percentage fees*	The actual amount of the fee depends on the value of the total transaction.
(v)	*Unit charges*	For a defined segment of service, a unit charge is established, usually in combination with hourly billing.
(vi)	*Relative value fees*	A fee is established based on the relative value of the activity. For example, time spent answering correspondence may be assigned a lower value than time spent in research or negotiation.
(vii)	*Availability only retainer*	No services are included in this arrangement, which is established to ensure that legal counsel will be available when needed and not available to represent an adverse party. Fees are then paid as rendered.

THE EXPENSE OF TIME

(a) Profit and loss

[22.5]

Time recording and time costing were introduced back in the days when it was slowly dawning on the solicitors' branch of the profession that solicitors were no longer certain to make a profit simply by working all hours that God sent and charging as much as the matter or client would stand (subject to the time honoured exceptions that Lady So-and-So would be mortally offended if we were to send her a reminder if she did not deign to pay our bill, and of course we would not dream of charging the little old lady around the corner who had no money anyway). It was becoming increasingly clear that not all work was profitable. It was for that reason that the profession introduced time costing – to see what work was being run at a profit and at a loss. It had nothing to do with charging – indeed conveyancing was still on a fixed scale but conveyancers were exhorted to cost their time to see what profit, if any, they were making. The object, therefore, was to check whether work which was being charged on a scale or some other basis was in fact being done at a profit. As a result many Central London firms stopped doing domestic conveyancing. In the present climate of competitive charging in both non-contentious and contentious work, with costs for the latter being increasingly restricted by being fixed, capped or subject to a predictable matrix (see Chapter 27), it is as important as ever for a solicitor to know what each area of work is costing and whether it can be charged for at a profit.

For the system to work you have to know how much each job costs and to do this you have to calculate the cost to the firm of each fee earner in reasonable units of time. There was a variety of different methods of costing work but the method suggested by the Law Society in its booklet *The Expense of Time* seemed to most firms using it simple and satisfactory. In the contemporary words of *The Solicitors' Journal*, 'It recommends a simplified system suitable for near innumerate solicitors. It is a triumph that so many firms have put its provisions into practice'.

I shall not set it out here. *The Expense of Time* is now in its fifth edition and includes a simplified back-of-an-envelope approach upon which I cannot improve. Basically, it divides the firm into fee earners and non-fee earners and then divides the projected overheads of the firm, including the salaries of the non-fee earners, between the fee earners, after building in various adjustments such as notional salaries for partners, deduction of interest on the client account and applying the retail price index and the estimated rate of inflation.

(b) Big brother

[22.6]

It was also appreciated that if fee earners recorded non-chargeable time under various categories as well as chargeable time and the time records were fed into a computer, the partners would have an overall picture of each fee earner's day and could identify how he spent his time. This 'big brother' aspect of time recording did not commend itself to everyone, although no one could gainsay Tom Woodcock, the father of *The Expense of Time*, when he talked about the 'benefits flowing effortlessly and virtually gratuitously from computerised time recording'. His message was that the difficult part was the discipline of recording time. You could of course record time on the back of old envelopes then put them in the file. To record time on time sheets involved the fee earner in no more work, but the benefits to the firm in management control were substantial. It really is a question of what turns you on. Many partners, when they see the voluminous weekly print-outs from their computerised time recording system have a reaction similar to that of the little girl in the James Thurber story, who was set the task for her homework of reading a book about penguins and then writing an essay on the subject. Her essay started, 'This book told me more about penguins than I wanted to know'!

USING TIME FOR CHARGING

(a) The dangers

(i)   The expense of time

[22.7]

We have seen that the recording and costing of time was introduced for the purpose of knowing whether work was being done at a profit or a loss and that it had the additional advantage of affording management control information for those who desired it. It was not intended as a basis of charging. What then happened was that costs judges applying the rules for the assessment of costs, those responsible for devising those rules, and indeed the profession itself, all realised that the cost of doing the work was a useful method of quantifying both contentious and non-contentious work, particularly in routine matters.

Nevertheless, this was using time costing for a purpose for which it was never intended, so it was not really surprising when complaints began to ring out that the formula was too unreliable and too unsophisticated to bear the burden that had been imposed on it. As an aid to business efficiency, the costing of time was a matter of only domestic concern to each firm costing its work. If the formula they used, or their arithmetic, was wrong, it was only they who were misled into thinking they were making a bigger or smaller profit than they really were. Arithmetical sums are clearly unacceptable as a basis of charging.

(ii)   The painful plodder's charter

[22.8]

Another objection to time charging is the same as the objection to the historical quantitative methods of assessment. We now laugh at the thought of payment calculated in relation to the height of the file or the weight of papers, but payment by the metre, the kilo or the hour are all equally flawed: they all relate to quantity not quality. Payment based on time means that the longer a solicitor takes to do the work, the more he is paid. The greater his skill and expertise, the greater his expedition, the less time he will record and the less will be his reward. Where a solicitor brings to bear years of experience, or has a flash of inspiration, it happens so quickly that he does not have time to make even a mark on his time sheet. High quality work which should be encouraged is in fact severely penalised in any system of charges based solely on time. Charges based on the time spent reward the painful plodder for his slowness and inefficiency while penalising the speed and efficiency of others. In contending that this basis of charging is against the client's interests an American commentator referred to the 'misaligned interests of the hourly rate'. In the words of an old catch-phrase 'Don't mind the quality, feel the width'. Former Chief Taxing Master Jimmy Matthews used a golfing analogy. He did not expect a solicitor to be a duffer learning at the client's expense but neither did he expect every solicitor to play off scratch. He applied the concept of the 12-handicap solicitor.

(iii)   Outdated

[22.9]

The chief executive of the Legal Complaints Service, Deborah H Evans, has described the system of charging by billable hours as 'outdated' and recommended firms to look at 'new and interesting ways of charging'. She continued 'Less efficient lawyers will bill more than more efficient ones and there's no benchmark for the consumer. Some people are getting a Rolls-Royce service when they really don't need one and it would be far better to think about what the work is worth to the client and agree a figure at the start.'

(b) Cost plus profit

(i)   The basis of assessment

[22.10]

The approach to assessment was explained nearly 30 years ago by Brightman J in *Re Eastwood, Lloyds Bank v Eastwood* [1975] Ch 112, ChD, in the following extract from his judgment:

> 'During the hearing of the argument I was given certain advice by the assessors as to the manner in which a taxation proceeds at the present day . . . The advice given to me is this: "At the present day, on the taxation of a bill of costs of a firm of solicitors in private practice which has been engaged in litigation on behalf of a client . . . the taxation invariably proceeds on the following basis. The firm informs the taxing master of the period of time that has been spent by any partner or employee of the firm on any 'relevant' aspect of the case: the word 'relevant' is intended to exclude time spent on a part of the case for which there is a fixed charge prescribed by statute or rule. The firm submits (a) what is the proper cost per hour of the time so spent, having regard to a reasonable estimate of the overhead expenses of the solicitors' firm including (if the time spent is that of an employee) the reasonable salary of the employee or (if the time spent is that of a partner) a notional salary. The firm will also submit (b) what is a proper additional sum to be allowed over and above (a) by way of further profit costs."'

(ii)   'A' and 'B' identified

[22.11]

This philosophy was further expounded in *Leopold Lazarus Ltd v Secretary of State for Trade and Industry* (1976) 120 Sol Jo 268, QBD in which Kerr J promoted '(a)' and '(b)' to 'A' and 'B' and ever since they have been known as the A factor and the B factor. This was also the first time that the expression 'direct cost' was used:

> 'In his Answer the master helpfully summarised the practice concerning the computation of Item 26 in cases such as this. Having considered the weight of the proceedings and the responsibility and skill involved, the practice is then to arrive at a total figure consisting of two elements which are referred to as A and B in the judgment of the Court of Appeal in *Eastwood*'s case.
>
> The computation of the A figure involves an assessment of the reasonable direct cost, that is to say the grade of person (senior solicitor, assistant solicitor, legal executive,

etc) whom it was reasonable to employ at each stage; an approximation of the cost of employment of each individual by considering the number of hours for each of them to be reasonably engaged; and assessing a rate per hour sufficient to cover the salary and the appropriate share of the general overheads of each such person. The assessment of the appropriate rate per hour would be based on the taxing master's knowledge and experience of the average solicitor or executive employed by the average firm in the area concerned. The total hours of each person multiplied by an approximate cost per hour, together with an allowance for letters, telephone calls and telex messages, then produces what the Court of Appeal referred to as the A figure. The B figure is then conventionally assessed by adding a percentage to the A figure which is appropriate in all circumstances to cover matters which cannot be calculated on an hourly basis, that is to say supervision and other indirect expenses, together with what the master referred to in his Answer as "imponderables", which reflect the degree of skill, responsibility and the other factors set out in [*CPR Rule 44.5*]. As mentioned above, the increase for the B figure claimed in the present case was just under 50 per cent, which would be perfectly normal and certainly not excessive in cases of this type. This is the figure which, in the case of an independent firm of solicitors, is expected to make a contribution to the profits of the firm. The appropriateness of the total of A and B, arrived at in this way, is then considered against the background of the proceedings as a whole and rounded off to a convenient sum which appears right in all the circumstances.'

[22.12]

The A factor was therefore identified as the hourly expense rate, and the B factor as the profit, A and B together giving the hourly charging rate. The A factor is arrived at by ascertaining the amount and cost of the time spent, whilst the B factor is arrived at by the application of the factors prescribed in the Solicitors' (Non-Contentious Business) Remuneration Order 1994, art 3 or in CPR Rule 44.5. The greatest danger with the present obsession with time is that it not only may over-reward the quantity of time spent ('The Painful Plodder's Charter'), it may even result in the other factors being lost sight of altogether, with the result that time costing becomes time charging. That is what is increasingly happening to the costs of civil litigation.

(c) Ascertaining the direct cost

(i) Solicitor and client

[22.13]

As I have said, time costing was introduced to enable solicitors to see what work was being run at a profit and what at a loss. You will not obtain this information by basing your rates on what other firms are charging or by adopting the going rates being allowed on between-the-parties assessments of costs. There is no satisfactory substitute for each firm of solicitors undertaking the *Expense of Time* calculation at least annually, not only for their own benefit but, as we shall see, for the benefit of the profession as a whole. On an assessment of costs between a solicitor and his or her client in both contentious and non-contentious costs, the costs officer starts with the retainer. If this is silent as to hourly expense rates, the costs officer must consider the actual cost to the firm of doing the work and whether that cost is reasonable in the context of the nature of the work. (If, as it should, the retainer makes express provision for hourly rates, the position is as explained in Chapter 2.)

(ii)   Between the parties

[22.14]

Although you may have calculated your hourly expense rate meticulously in accordance with *The Expense of Time* it does not follow that this amount will be allowed between the parties. If you choose to be a prestigious firm with luxurious offices and expensive cars – as you are perfectly entitled to do – and your client chooses you and your firm – as he is perfectly entitled to do – it is not reasonable that the loser in litigation should have to pay your above-average expense rates because of your sybaritic lifestyle. Between-the-parties costs on the standard basis must be both reasonable and proportionate.

How are judges to decide what the hourly cost rate should be? I used to say that costs judges fixed the rate by pulling open the third drawer down on the right hand side of their desk and looking at a bit of paper showing the 'hourly going rate' for a particular class of work but no one knew where it had come from. A costs judge took issue with me: interestingly enough, he did not disagree that costs judges had bits of paper in the third drawer down but he said that they knew where they came from: they wrote them themselves, based on information learned from assessments. 'Sitting day in and day out, hearing other solicitors disputing or accepting them, we form a view as to market rates. We do not lay down the rates. We adjudicate on the opposing contentions of the parties.' In other words, costs judges do not fix rates, they merely reflect them.

Guidance on hourly cost rates was given in two cases:

[22.15]

Extract from the decision of Hirst J *Stubbs v Board of Governors of the Royal National Orthopaedic Hospital* [1997] Costs LR 117, QBD:

'Stress is placed on the average cost of the average solicitor or legal executive – in the particular area concerned . . .   In arriving at a figure, the essence of the exercise was an appropriate apportionment of the estimated overhead expenses of the solicitors' firm having regard to the position, status, and likely rate of remuneration of the persons who were employed on the case under consideration. This is of its very nature suitable for assessment by the taxing master in the light of his very wide experience; it is also a matter which is properly approached by reference to averages since it is unlikely that there will be a very wide divergence between comparable firms of solicitors operating in similar fields of work in similar geographical areas.'

[22.16]

Although the judgment in *Finley v Glaxo Laboratories Ltd* [1997] Costs LR 106, QBD was not in open court the judge, Hobhouse J, directed a tape recording of it to be made and he authorised publication of the following passages from the transcript:

' . . .   The next point – and it is the one which formed the main part of the argument before me – is the rate per hour which should be allowed. It is clear that the rate which should be allowed is the actual cost, assessed on an objective basis. In other words, it is not answered merely by reference to what has been the cost to the solicitor in question of doing the relevant work on an hourly basis. It has to be assessed on an objective basis having regard to what is reasonable. Therefore, one must consider the position of other solicitors in question. One has to consider whether it is the appropriate level of fee earner that is claimed for. In the present matter it has been accepted, and I accept, that the appropriate level of fee earner for a case of this character was a senior litigation partner; and the solicitor concerned matched that description.'

(d) Charging rates

(i) Profit is not a four-letter word

[22.17]

So far we have been concerned only with the cost of doing the work (the A factor), to which must, of course, be added the solicitor's reasonable profit (the B factor) to ascertain the hourly charging rate. This is an exercise in evaluating the prescribed factors other than time (the remaining six pillars of wisdom). These are so important I have devoted the next chapter to them. There is however a complication: at the behest of a former Lord Chancellor solicitors have fallen into line with the rest of the world and no longer disclose how their hourly rate is calculated between overheads and profit – expense rate plus profit mark-up, but use a composite charging rate. The introduction of a charging rate was not as revolutionary as might at first appear. It is proper commercial practice for a business to calculate the cost of doing the work in terms of time and materials and then to add on a profit. The profit element is still there whether the client or the paying party is told what it is or not. Hitherto the courts and the parties have had the advantage of knowing what it was, and what was revolutionary is that with guideline charging rates not distinguishing between the cost of doing the work and the profit, it is not possible to know how the figures were arrived at – what represents expense and what profit – with the consequence that the CPR Rule 44.5 factors (the seven pillars of wisdom) must be applied to the total figure. Otherwise there would be no facility to enable a judge carrying out an assessment to reward skill, effort, specialised knowledge and responsibility or for him to acknowledge the importance, complexity, difficulty or novelty of the matter. The provisions of Rule 44.5 would be negated. In calculating going charging rates it is therefore necessary to calculate the expense rate and add a profit percentage, which in routine matters is generally accepted as 50%, in other words, one-third of the charging rate. In a non-routine case the receiving party can seek an increased charging rate because of the B factor, and indeed the paying party could seek a reduction of the profit element.

(ii) The fallacy

[22.18]

The introduction of hourly charging rates has given rise to the fallacy that the A and B factors have been abolished. Of course they have not been abolished. Every butcher, baker, plumber and tradesman from Al Fayed to a market stall holder knows what the product cost him and what profit he is seeking to make – the A factor and the B factor. The legal profession did not invent them. The fallacy was demonstrated in The Lord Chancellor's Department's consultation paper 'Controlling Costs' which included the astonishing proposition: 'Solicitors will be required to provide an inclusive charging basis, *thereby abolishing the uplift for care and conduct element claimed in a bill of costs*'. As I have said, the care and conduct element is the profit and one has only to substitute the word 'profit' for 'care and conduct' in the proposition to demonstrate its fallacy. Solicitors cannot be expected to work for their overheads alone: the proposal would not abolish profit (care and conduct) but merely conceal it. The premise that profit could in this way be abolished demonstrates that both the proposal and its objective are fundamentally flawed. Far from controlling costs a charging rate in fact remove all those controls, checks and balances built into between-the-parties costs over the years and carefully preserved in the CPR. A combined rate in no way reduces the amount of costs, it merely makes the calculation less transparent. Whether or not the A and B factors are identified or concealed in a charging rate, they are still there. Any commercial enterprise must base its prices and charges on costs plus profit and it is naive to think that the legal profession could operate in some other way. In *Cox v MGN* [2006] EWHC 1235 (QB), [2006] All ER (D) 396 (May) the judge quoted this passage from *Cook on Costs 2006* saying it was an observation that it is important to keep in mind.

(iii)   The Seven Pillars of Wisdom

[22.19]

If the legendary visitor from Mars and the man on the Clapham omnibus were to visit a detailed assessment they would be astounded to learn that time spent on a matter is only one of seven prescribed factors in the quantification of solicitors' costs, both in contentious and non-contentious work and as between solicitor and client or party and party. They could be forgiven for thinking that ascertaining the amount of time spent and the amount of time which should have been spent was the be-all and end-all of solicitors' remuneration. The complexity of the matter, the novelty of the questions raised; the skill, labour, specialised knowledge and responsibility involved; the number and importance of the documents prepared and perused; the place where and the circumstance in which the work was done; the amount or value of any money or property involved and the importance of the matter to all the parties are unlikely to have had even a passing mention. The quantification of costs has taken a giant stride from being a judicial function to becoming a bureaucratic exercise. Rule 44.5 might as well never have been written. It should also be remembered that the B factor is not solely concerned with profit, it also covers such matters as unrecordable time and supervision which would otherwise be unremunerated. The Civil, Family and Criminal Legal Aid Regulations all embrace the concept of profit mark-up, and it would be unfortunate if, in respect of non-funded civil litigation, judges and costs officers were to be deprived of the flexibility, which the CPR rightly regard as essential to the assessment of reasonable and proportionate costs, afforded by the application of the A and B factors. Solicitors are entitled to calculate and justify their charges, both to their clients and between the parties in whatever manner is fair and reasonable, and there is nothing in the CPR which requires them to abandon a system which has served so well in the past. If charging is based on hourly rates, these can only be calculated on the basis of reasonable cost plus profit and, whether the rate is shown as expense-plus-profit or as a charge combining both, the relevant factors must still be applied in the quantification of costs. The correct approach was explained in *Cox v MGN* [22.17]: 'The court is required to take into account all the circumstances including, in particular, the factors listed at CPR Part 44.5(3), which are sometimes referred to as the 'Seven Pillars of Wisdom'. It is necessary to have regard to the solicitor's particular skill, effort, specialised knowledge and responsibility. Obviously, also, the case in hand must be assessed for importance, complexity, difficulty or novelty. All the while the court will apply the test of proportionality.'

(iv)   The A and B test

[22.20]

Further confirmation that the A and B factors are alive and well came in the tragic case of *Higgs v Camden and Islington Health Authority* [2003] EWHC 15 (QB), (2003) 72 BMLR 95 in which the nine-year-old claimant was awarded £3.5 million damages for inadequate care during the first 35 minutes of his life, resulting in severe, acquired, hypoxic brain injury; dyskinetic quadriplegic cerebral palsy causing major and permanent motor disabilities, but no intellectual impairment. He would be dependent for his, probably lengthy, lifetime for all daily activities, such as eating, toileting, washing and dressing. It was held that the SCCO Guide had only limited significance in circumstances such as these, given in particular that brain damage at birth is a particularly sensitive subject matter for litigation and that the specific demands placed upon solicitors by clients and litigation friends will vary widely from case to case. The Guide itself is aimed at providing assistance in relation to assessing costs at the end of hearings lasting not more than one day. The guideline figures at Appendix 2 to the Guide are broad approximations and it is expressly stated that costs and fees exceeding the guidelines 'may well be justified' in an appropriate case at the discretion of the court. Further, the guideline figures were not supposed to replace the experience and knowledge of those familiar with the local area and the field generally. Accordingly, the guideline figures were not of great value in this instance. It is expressly recognised in the Guide that costs and fees exceeding the guidelines may well be justified in an appropriate case as an exercise of discretion. The paying party criticised the costs judge for carrying out an old 'A plus B' calculation as used before the introduction of the CPR in order to test the reasonableness of the rate charged by the partner. However, the bill of costs did in fact claim an inclusive rate of £300 per hour and the costs judge did no more than use the A plus B method as one of the measures and indicators to ensure that he was able to gauge the propriety or otherwise of a figure of £300 per hour. He used the A plus B type analysis to inform his consideration of the reasonableness of the inclusive rate sought; he had in mind the solicitor's expense rate and he took the seven pillars of wisdom (the CPR Rule 44.5 factors) into account in reaching the final figure. The court upheld the award of £300 an hour which represented £150 an hour with a 100% mark-up. It could, of course, have been £200 an hour with a 50% mark-up.

(d) Assessing the hourly cost

(i) Time spent

[22.21]

The costs officer must be satisfied that the amount of time claimed was actually spent. Properly kept and detailed time records are helpful in support of a bill provided they explain the nature of the work as well as recording the time involved. In *JemmaTrust Co Ltd v Liptrott & Forrester (No 2)* [2003] EWCA Civ 1476, [2004] 1 All ER 510 the court held that there is no obligation on a solicitor to keep attendance notes in respect of either contentious or non-contentious work. The true position is that in both kinds of work the burden is on the solicitor not only to show that the time claimed has been spent, but that it had been reasonable to spend that time. The keeping of an attendance note is one way, but not the only way, in which this can be demonstrated. The failure to keep such notes exposes the solicitor to the risk of being unable to prove the reasonableness of the time spent. In the present case the costs judge after examining all the files was satisfied that the time recorded as spent had been reasonably spent.

While the absence of records could result in the disallowance or diminution of the charges claimed, the records themselves will not be accepted as conclusive evidence that the time recorded either has been spent, or if spent, is 'reasonably' or 'proportionately' chargeable. Always keep in mind the words of Payne J in *Re Kingsley* (1978) 122 Sol Jo 457:

'I ought to add that this case illustrates the dangers which are present if reliance is placed on a modern system of recording, without at the same time retaining the old and well tried practice of keeping attendance notes showing briefly the time taken and the purport of the work done day by day. It may be that this case will invite attention to the importance of appreciating the limits to which the computer system can be used in cases where taxation of costs must follow litigation and to the necessity of preserving as well the use of the traditional systems.'

The stage is never going to be reached of producing a computer print-out as incontrovertible evidence of the number of hours spent.

Letters received and copies of letters sent, instructions to counsel, statements of case, proofs of evidence and all other documents are tangible records and evidence of the work involved. All other work, such as attendances on the client, counsel, court and witnesses, telephone conversations, perusals, considering the facts and law, does not automatically create records of itself and a solicitor must be able to prove that he has done work of this nature. The best way is to create and keep records of it. Inferences can be drawn and oral evidence given but it is in the solicitor's interests to have available on assessment the best possible evidence of work done, and this can most easily be provided by making contemporaneous records. However, here are some words of comfort:

'The right to charge cannot depend upon the question whether discussions are recorded or unrecorded. It must depend, initially, upon whether they in fact took place and occupied the time claimed. If they are recorded in attendance notes this will no doubt ordinarily be accepted as sufficient evidence of those facts. If they are not so recorded it may well be that the claimant is unable to satisfy the taxing (costs) officer or master (costs judge) as to the facts. But neither the presence nor the absence of an attendance note is conclusive. It may well be for example that it is wholly impractical in some instances to keep such notes. In an exceptionally complex case, such as this which is occupying two fee earners there may be short but important discussions in respect of which it would be wholly unreasonable to expect attendance notes to be kept. In such cases an estimate of the time involved is inevitable. The question which then arises for decision is whether the estimate given is reasonable. This is a matter wholly for the taxing authorities. In general, however, all such discussions involving any substantial period of time should be recorded and an estimated addition should only be allowed for short discussions which it would be impracticable to record.'

(Parker J in *Re Frascati (in chambers)* (2 December 1981, unreported, QBD).)

[22.22]

A number of points arise:
(1) We are dealing here with time which could have been recorded but for some reason was not, and not with unrecordable time, such as supervision, which is covered by general care and attention (see [23.10]).
(2) How the time was recorded does not, for these purposes, matter. It can be on the most sophisticated computer system or on the back of old envelopes. If the latter contains greater detail of the work which was done it is preferable to the former. The problem with most computer systems is that they do not provide a sufficient narrative. A separate file note is essential. With a mark-up for care and control on all contentious work it is not only the time but also the quality of the work that needs to be recorded. A printed form of memorandum with a panel in which to indicate the relevant CPR Rule 44.5 factors for mark-up could be invaluable.
(3) Experience shows that many solicitors have now trained themselves adequately to record the time spent on attendances but they are not so well disciplined in respect of time spent on the preparation and perusal of documents such as pleadings, instructions to counsel and, particularly in long actions, refreshing their memory from the statements of case, affidavits, attendance notes, correspondence and opinions. These are the danger areas.
(4) Time spent considering the law and procedure is usually non-chargeable – and the higher the expense rate, the more law and procedure the fee earner is expected to know. In a review of criminal costs it was held that leading and junior counsel can be assumed to be fully up-to-date with the law in the field in which they hold themselves out as practising in and they will not be paid for researching the law unless the case is unusual or infrequent (*Perry v Lord Chancellor* (1994) Times, 26 May, QBD). The same principle of course applies to civil work and to solicitors.
(5) Where there has been an omission to record time, the costs draftsman – and the costs officer – must rely on their own experience to assess from the documents in the file what time a competent solicitor would have spent on their preparation and perusal. The documents prove the work has been done but someone has to put a time and value on that work.

(6)   In *Johnson v Reed Corrugated Cases Ltd* [1992] 1 All ER 169, QBD
        Evans J was less enthusiastic about giving credit for unrecorded time,
        saying:

> 'In my judgment, the submission that there were unrecorded occasions when
> chargeable time was spent on these cases must be rejected. This leaves the
> registrar's decision that in practice not all time will be fully recorded, even for
> those items of work in respect of which a claim is made. The claims
> invariably are for global figures, mostly to the nearest five minutes. No doubt
> there were some occasions when the periods spent were slightly more, others
> when it was slightly less. There is no evidence that any substantial items were
> not recorded at all. In my judgment, therefore, this item must be disallowed.'

(ii)   Was the time reasonably, proportionately and relevantly spent?

[22.23]

This is an objective test between the parties. Was it reasonable to do all the
work that was done and was it done within a reasonable time? If on the
standard basis, was it proportionate to the matters in issue? If it was
excessive or irrelevant it will be unreasonable or disallowed. In contentious
costs on the standard basis any doubt as to reasonableness will be resolved
in favour of the paying party. Between a solicitor and his client the same
objective tests apply, together with, in respect of contentious work, the
express and implied subjective assumptions prescribed by CPR Rule 48.8(2)
(see para [5.30]). Because solicitor and client costs are on the indemnity
basis, any doubt will be resolved in favour of the solicitors.

(iii)   The level of fee earner

[22.24]

Has a senior partner done work which could have been done by a legal
executive? If so only the expense rate of a legal executive can be allowed. Has
a legal executive done the work of a senior partner? Again only the expense
rate of a legal executive can be allowed. However, in both examples, the hourly
rate can be appropriately adjusted by the application of the other prescribed
factors – perhaps to award the partner for his expertise and expedition and the
legal executive for punching above his weight. See the next chapter.

(iv)   Hourly rate too high

[22.25]

As I have said, rates above the going rate can be claimed on the basis of the
prescribed factors other than time, but there are other circumstances in which
the going rate for a particular court may be exceeded on a detailed assessment.
    In *Jones v Secretary of State for Wales* [1997] 2 All ER 507, QBD, because
a provincial firm of solicitors was more specialised than the norm for the area,
an assessment of costs made in relation to its work was calculated at a higher
hourly rate than the local norm. Pitmans of Reading were in effect a London
firm who had moved to Reading and were doing work that only a London firm

could do. The judge was of the view that it would be odd and undesirable if the higher London rate could be recovered by a London firm, but not the somewhat lower rate claimed by Pitmans for doing a case which otherwise would probably have to be handled by a London firm. This approach was followed by SCCO Master Wright in *Wood v Worthing and Southlands Hospitals NHS Trust* (9 July 2004, unreported), when in a complex clinical negligence case he allowed London rates for the specialist partner in the Hampstead office of a national firm on the grounds that it would be inappropriate to apply the rates recoverable if the work had been done by a small Hampstead firm. A note of caution about this approach was sounded in *Cox v MGN* [22.17]: "If you wish to take yourself out of the norm you have to provide the court with evidence to enable you to do so. You may have a niche practice, and you may be able to persuade celebrities that you are the solicitor to go to at whatever rate you choose to charge them, but without evidence that your overheads are out of the ordinary there is no basis for holding that a Jones (*Jones v Secretary of State for Wales* [1997] 2 All ER 507) increase should apply".

In *Truscott v Truscott, Wraith v Sheffield Forgemasters Ltd* [1998] 1 All ER 82, CA and *Sullivan v Co-operative Insurance Society Ltd* ([1999] 2 Costs LR 158, CA, the Court of Appeal addressed the question of whether the liability of an unsuccessful party ordered to pay costs should be restricted to what a reasonably competent solicitor practising in the area of the court (or in the area where the successful party lived) might have been expected to charge, or whether the successful party should be entitled to recover the sums claimed by the solicitor who was in fact instructed to act on his behalf. The court held that a costs judge had to consider whether, having regard to all the relevant considerations, the successful party had acted reasonably in instructing the particular solicitors. In *Truscott* the claimant had been ill-served by local solicitors in the Brighton County Court and had instructed London solicitors who rectified the matter and obtained a wasted costs order against the original solicitors. The court held that it was reasonable for a London firm to have been instructed in these circumstances and that as their charges were reasonable by London standards they were allowed. The same principles applied in *Wraith* but in that case the only reason why the work went to London solicitors was that the claimant's trade union had adopted the practice of sending all their work to these solicitors. The action was proceeding in the Sheffield District Registry and the court was satisfied there were firms of solicitors in Sheffield or Leeds well qualified to do the work. The trade union knew, or ought to have known, what sort of legal fees it would have to expend to obtain competent services and their connection with one firm of solicitors in London was of limited relevance. *Sullivan* applied the same test over the Pennines, holding there were in Manchester, and in many other centres outside London, legal practitioners who conducted cases of substantially greater weight and complexity than the present case, every day of their working lives. Although the fact that a trade union or other organisation habitually used a particular firm of solicitors was a relevant factor, it was of limited relevance in an individual case. There were no weighty factors in the context of costs justifying the trade union in employing London solicitors to conduct litigation in Manchester. Subjectively the choice may have been entirely reasonable, but between the parties the various circumstances had to be balanced objectively.

Wraith was followed in *A v Chief Constable of South Yorkshire Police* [2008] EWHC 1658 (QB), [2008] All ER (D) 226 (Jul) where in proceedings in Sheffield the court disallowed the costs of specialist London solicitors on the grounds that a reasonable person in the position of the claimant would have enquired about solicitors in Sheffield with experience of bringing claims against the police. Such enquiries would have brought to his attention a law firm in Sheffield that undertook police misconduct cases. He would have appreciated that there was a substantial difference in rates and would have instructed the Sheffield firm.

In *Ryan v Tretol Group Ltd* [2002] EWHC 1956 (QB), [2002] All ER (D) 156 (Jul) the claimant in an asbestosis claim instructed local solicitors, but after the legal executive dealing with the matter left the firm, the claimant was dissatisfied with the service he was receiving. The claim was legally and factually complex and in the circumstances it was reasonable for the claimant to change his legal representatives to a London firm with considerable asbestosis experience in the absence of other firms with similar experience in the claimant's locality.

Subjective factors also applied in *Higgins v Ministry of Defence* [2010] EWHC 654 (QB), 153 Sol Jo (no 14) 28, [2010] All ER (D) 281 (Mar). At the age of 82 the claimant, who lived in Broadstairs in Kent, was diagnosed with asbestosis by a local consultant who told Mr Higgins that his condition was advanced and there was no treatment. By this time Mr Higgins was able to walk very little, and his daughter had moved in to care for him. The consultant mentioned a firm of solicitors in Central London, Field Fisher Waterhouse (FFW), who had experience in these matters and whom the claimant consulted.

The claimant had been exposed to asbestos during the course of his work for the Ministry of Defence in Davenport and the solicitors were able to reach a settlement, but could not agree the costs. The solicitors claimed an hourly rate of £345 while the defendants argued that according to the guidelines for summary assessment the recoverable hourly rate would have been up to £200 for Kent and up to £250 for outer London firms. The judge could find no point of principle saying: 'It is not in dispute that a reasonable litigant would normally be expected to investigate the hourly rates of solicitors whom we might instruct, and that he will normally be expected to consider a number of other factors, including the time and costs associated with geographical location, before choosing whom to instruct and to take advice on these and other matters before he does so'. It would not be objectively reasonable to expect an 82 year old man who had just been informed that he was incurably ill, to undertake a trawl of local solicitors, in circumstances where an experienced consultant had given him the name of FFW as solicitors who specialised in this field. None of the alternative firms whose names were put forward were markedly more accessible from Broadstairs than is London. The costs judge had considered all the relevant factors including the claimant's age and the urgency of the case before deciding it reasonable for Mr Higgins to have instructed FFW and it would not be appropriate for the court to interfere with his decision on appeal.

Gazley v Wade [2004] EWHC 2675 (QBD), [2004] All ER (D) 291 (Nov) went the other way, holding that it is not always necessary to instruct London specialist solicitors in order to have the necessary or proportionate expertise available. The appellant appealed against a decision that he should recover costs from the respondents on the basis of rates applicable to fee earners in the Norwich area although his solicitors were London libel specialists. The costs judge was not wrong to find that it was not reasonable for the appellant to instruct London libel specialists rather than a local firm in Norwich in respect of his defamation claim against a national newspaper even though he erred in deciding that the case 'was obviously a Norfolk case'. The fact that the claimant was from Norfolk did not make it a Norfolk case. At the relevant time the likelihood was that the hearing would have been in London. Moreover, it was a grave libel published nationwide by defendants based in London. However, it was important to recognise that in order to have the necessary or proportionate expertise available, it was not always necessary to instruct London specialist solicitors. An important factor was that any competent litigation solicitor in the country could call upon specialist members of the Bar at very short notice. The costs judge's conclusion of the unreasonableness of instructing London solicitors was based on the particular facts of the case, in the light of his very wide experience of litigation generally, including the role of specialist practitioners.

That the nature of the work is relevant to the level of fees was demonstrated by the senior costs judge in *King v Telegraph Group Ltd* [2004] EWCA Civ 613, [2004] All ER (D) 242 (May). City rates for City solicitors are recoverable only where the City solicitor is undertaking City work, which is normally heavy commercial or corporate work. Defamation is not in that category, and, particularly given the reduction in damages awards for libel, is never likely to be. A City firm which undertakes work, which could be competently handled by a number of Central London solicitors, is acting unreasonably and disproportionately if it seeks to charge City rates. Newspapers and insurers control defendants' lawyer's fees and are not prepared to pay the level of fees which the lawyers may wish to charge.

(e) The SCCO Guide to Summary Assessment

Hourly rates

[22.26]

The Supreme Court Costs Office (now the Senior Courts Costs Office) Guide to the Summary Assessment of Costs includes guideline hourly rates for different levels of fee earner in different parts of the country. It is not the fault of the *Guide* that the profession and the judiciary ignore its title and most of its content, and focus entirely on the tables of hourly rates. As the title and the content state, the *Guide* is specifically limited to summary assessments of costs and is intended to provide a simple collation of hourly rates applicable for routine costs to be assessed summarily at the end of a hearing which has lasted no more than a day. It has nothing to do with detailed assessments which are considered in Chapter 30.

Increasingly the *Guide* is treated as if it prescribes hourly rates: it does not, it merely collates them. To regard these rates as a substitute for solicitors calculating their own rates is to put the cart before the horse – the figures in the *Guide* are no more than a simple collation of figures that individual firms of solicitors *have* calculated. The original figures for each locality were arrived at through a framework of local co-ordinators based on civil trial centres set up by the Law Society to assist in the agreement of local rates. The co-ordinators were responsible for liaising with local law societies and district judges and thereafter with the designated civil judge for each trial centre to ensure consistency across the group. The figures were then communicated to the SCCO for publication on its website and in the *Guide*.

In 2005 the *Guide* ceased to give hourly rates approved for each court. It massaged the rates into three groups for the entire country plus London. As a result the rates are no longer approved by any member of the judiciary, do not refer to any particular court and to that extent have become a bureaucratic and not a judicial exercise.

Advisory Committee on Civil Costs

[22.27]

In its report *Improved Access to Justice – Funding Options and Proportionate Costs* in 2005, the Civil Justice Council recommended the creation of a Costs Council 'to oversee the introduction, implementation and monitoring of the reforms we recommend and in particular to establish and review annually the recoverable fixed fees in the fast track and guideline hourly rates between the parties in the multi-track'.

In 2008 the Ministry of Justice transferred the task of collating hourly rates to an Advisory Committee on Civil Costs under the chairmanship of Professor Stephen Nickell. In announcing the Advisory Committee the Ministry of Justice minister said it was 'in response to a recommendation from the Civil Justice Council', but it was not quite the response the Council expected. Professor Nickell wrote to the Master of the Rolls on 9 December 2008 in the following terms:

"The Advisory Committee on Civil Costs recommends the attached Table of Guideline Hourly Rates to apply from 1st January, 2009. As you know these guideline rates are broad approximations to be used only as a starting point for judges carrying out summary assessment. These rates are interim in nature in the sense that there remain some unresolved issues which are made clear in the enclosed document entitled "The Derivation of New Guideline Hourly Rates", from which you will understand that at least one member was pressing for an immediate reduction in rates. The unresolved issues include the extent of work done by solicitors outside the region in which they are located and the extent to which referral fees can account for the gap between the hourly rates charged by claimants', as opposed to defendants', solicitors. We hope to have looked at these specific issues by 2010.

Our new interim Guideline Hourly Rates are based on data collected in a survey of solicitors and other interested parties as well as both written and oral evidence provided by representatives of the main interest groups and others. The information collected refers to the calendar year 2007 and, as last year, we have used the rise in the ONS Average Earnings Index (AEI) for Private Sector Service industries, excluding bonuses, seasonally adjusted, from 2006 Q3 to 2008 Q3 to uprate the 2007 numbers.

I should emphasise that the Committee sees this as unfinished business and that when the outstanding issues have been resolved, we shall revisit the question."

The committee was concerned that the figures were skewed because an increasing number of firms have offices both in London and the provinces and by the payment of referral fees.

The Master of the Rolls accepted the recommendation of the Advisory Committee that the guideline hourly rates for Summary Assessment should be increased in line with inflation by 1.7% with effect from 1 April 2010. The rates for London 3, Bands A and B are presented as ranges which are said to go some way towards reflecting the wide range of work types transacted in these areas.

(f) Guideline Hourly Rates from 1 April 2010

Bands of fee earner

[22.28]

What were previously grades of fee earners became Bands.

The grades of fee earner were agreed between representatives of the Supreme Court Costs Office (now the Senior courts Costs Office), the Association of District Judges and the Law Society. The categories are as follows:

(A)   Solicitors with over eight years post qualification experience including at least eight years litigation experience.

(B)   Solicitors and legal executives with over four years post qualification experience including at least four years litigation experience.

(C)   Other solicitors and legal executives and fee earners of equivalent experience.

(D)   Trainee solicitors, para legals and other fee earners.

Note: 'legal executive' means a Fellow of the Institute of Legal Executives.

An hourly rate in excess of the guideline figures may be appropriate for Band A fee earners in substantial and complex litigation where other factors, including the value of the litigation, the level of complexity, the urgency or importance of the matter as well as any international element would justify a significantly higher rate to reflect higher average costs.

Localities

[22.29]

What were previously Bands have become National Regions.

Until 31 December 2008 the guideline figures showed Bands One, Two and Three outside the London Area, and a further three localities within the London area. The difference in the rates between Bands Two and Three were perceived to be so small that Band Three was promoted to the same level as Band Two and the bands re-titled National 1 and National 2

Tables

[22.30]

National Region 1 from 1 April 2010

BAND	A**	B	C	D
GUIDELINE RATES	217	192	161	118

Aldershot, Farnham, Bournemouth (including Poole)

Birmingham Inner

Cambridge City, Harlow

Canterbury, Maidstone, Medway and Tunbridge Wells

Cardiff (Inner)

Chelmsford South, Essex and East Suffolk

Fareham, Winchester

Hampshire, Dorset, Wiltshire, Isle of Wight

Kingston, Guildford, Reigate, Epsom

Leeds Inner (within 2 kilometres radius of the City Art Gallery)

Lewes

Liverpool, Birkenhead

Manchester Central

Newcastle City Centre (within a 2-mile radius of St Nicholas Cathedral)

Norwich City

Nottingham City

Oxford, Thames Valley

Southampton, Portsmouth

Swindon, Basingstoke

Watford

National Region 2 from 1 April 2010

BAND	A**	B	C	D
GUIDELINE RATES	201	177	146	111

Birmingham (Outer), Bradford (Dewsbury, Halifax, Huddersfield, Keighley & Skipton), Bath, Cheltenham and Gloucester, Taunton, Yeovil

Bury

BAND	A**	B	C	D
GUIDELINE RATES	201	177	146	111

Chelmsford North, Cambridge County, Peterborough, Bury St Edmunds, Norfolk, Lowestoft

Chester and North Wales

Coventry, Rugby, Nuneaton, Stratford and Warwick, Cumbria, Devon, Cornwall

Exeter, Plymouth, Grimsby, Skegness

Hull (City), Hull (Outer), Kidderminster

Leeds (Outer), Wakefield & Pontefract

Leigh

Lincoln

Luton, Bedford, St Albans, Hitchin, Hertford

Manchester (Outer), Oldham, Bolton, Tameside

Newcastle (other than City Centre), Northampton & Leicester, Nottingham & Derbyshire

Scarborough & Ripon

Sheffield, Doncaster and South Yorkshire

Stafford, Stoke, Tamworth

St Helens, Shrewsbury, Telford, Ludlow, Oswestry, South & West Wales, Southport

Stockport, Altrincham, Salford, Swansea, Newport, Cardiff (Outer)

Teesside

Wigan

Wolverhampton, Walsall, Dudley and Stourbridge, Worcester, Hereford, Evesham and Redditch

York, Harrogate

[22.31]

London from 1 April 2010

LONDON				
Bands	A**	B	C	D
London 1 EC1, EC2, EC3, EC4	409	296	226	138
London 2 W1, WC1, WC2, SW1	317	242	196	126

LONDON

Bands	A**	B	C	D
London 3 All other London post-codes: W, NW, N, E, SE, SW and Bromley, Croydon, Dartford, Gravesend and Uxbridge	229–267	172–229	165	121

Level of fee earner

[22.32]

Note that the word 'partner' does not appear. The bands are based upon experience, not status. 'Legal executive' means a Fellow of the Institute of Legal Executives. Although fee earners of an equivalent experience may be entitled to similar rates it must be borne in mind that Fellows of the Institute of Legal Executives generally spend two years in a solicitor's office before passing their Part 1 general examinations, a further two years before passing the Part 2 specialist examinations and then complete a further two years in practice before being able to become fellows. They have therefore acquired considerable practical and academic experience. It is semantically unfortunate that lesser beings, although they are members of the Institute of Legal Executives, may not call themselves legal executives and must be described by some other name such as, fee earner, clerk or paralegal and treated as being in the bottom grade unless the court is satisfied they have the equivalent experience. The *Guide* adds:

[22.33]

Many High Court cases justify fee earners at a senior level. However the same may not be true of attendance at pre-trial hearings with counsel. The task of sitting behind counsel should be delegated to a more junior fee earner in all but the most important pre-trial hearings. As with hourly rates the costs estimate supplied by the paying party may be of assistance. What grade of fee earner did they use?

In some proceedings solicitors appear as advocates more frequently than they used to. It must be borne in mind that, especially in substantial hearings, it may be more economical if the advocacy is conducted by counsel rather than a solicitor. In all cases the court should consider whether the decision whether or not to instruct counsel has led to an increase in costs and whether that increase is justifiable.

Using the guide

[22.34]

The following extracts from the guide are important to its application:
- The *Guide* is specifically limited to summary assessments of costs and is intended to provide a simple collation of hourly rates incorporating a 50% profit mark-up appropriate for routine costs to be assessed summarily at the end of a hearing which has lasted no more than a day. It has nothing to do with detailed assessments
- The rates, in the words of the *Guide*, 'are broad approximations only'. They are not prescribed by the SCCO. They are not a scale. They may be amended

locally at any time by the Designated Civil Judge. They are not carved in stone. As Sir Rupert Jackson put it in his Final Report, 'As their name suggests, the Guideline Hourly Rates can only be guidelines or starting points. The judge doing the summary assessment should move up or down from those rates, as appropriate' (Chapter 44, para 3.13).

- The guideline figures have been grouped according to locality by way of general guidance only. Although many firms may be comparable with others in the same locality, some of them will not be. For example, a firm located in the City of London which specialises in fast track personal injury claims may not be comparable with other firms in that locality and vice versa.
- In any particular case the hourly rate it is reasonable to allow should be determined by reference to the rates charged by comparable firms. For this purpose the costs estimate supplied by the paying party may be of assistance. The rate to allow should not be determined by reference to locality or postcode alone.
- An hourly rate in excess of the guideline figures may be appropriate for Band A fee earners in substantial and complex litigation where other factors, including the value of the litigation, the level of complexity, the urgency or importance of the matter as well as any international element would justify a significantly higher rate to reflect higher average costs.
- The guideline rates for solicitors provided here are broad approximations only. In any particular area the Designated Civil Judge may supply more exact guidelines for rates in that area. Also the costs estimate provided by the paying party may give further guidance if the solicitors for both parties are based in the same locality

The future

[22.35]

In its report *Improved Access to Justice – Funding Options and Proportionate Costs* in 2005, the Civil Justice Council recommended the creation of a Costs Council 'to oversee the introduction, implementation and monitoring of the reforms we recommend and in particular to establish and review annually the recoverable fixed fees in the fast track and guideline hourly rates between the parties in the multi-track'. I said at the time that it was important to remember that the award of costs is a matter of judicial discretion, which includes hourly rates. If the purpose of the Council was simply to collate hourly rates for approval by the local judiciary that would be an acceptable extension of the present role of the Supreme Court Costs Office (now the Senior Courts Costs Office). However, any attempt to impose hourly rates from on high would be unacceptable.

Professor Stephen Nickell has been quoted as saying the Advisory Committee on Civil Costs will 'collect information on the rates that solicitors charge at various levels for a variety of activities ahead of making a "sensible and defensible" decision. These will not necessarily be only the activities to which the Summary Assessment Guideline rates apply, but also related activities, such as employment tribunal work. The committee will also recommend methods of up-rating the figures.'

The reference to costs in employment tribunals is interesting because between-the-parties costs are rarely awarded and solicitor and client costs are usually on a contingency basis.

In announcing the Advisory Committee the Ministry of Justice minister said it was 'in response to a recommendation from the Civil Justice Council', but I suspect it was not quite the response the Council expected.

In his Final Report Sir Rupert Jackson recommended that the Advisory Committee be disbanded and replaced by a Costs Council tasked with the annual setting of guideline hourly rates for summary assessments; reviewing the matrices of fast track fixed costs and reviewing the overall upper limit for fast track costs.

(g) Counsel's Fees

[22.36]

The following table sets out figures based on Supreme Court Costs Office (now the Senior Courts Costs Office) statistics dealing with run of the mill proceedings in the Queens Bench and Chancery Division and in the Administrative Court. The table gives figures for cases lasting up to an hour and up to half a day, in respect of counsel up to five years call, up to ten years call and over ten years call. It is emphasised that these figures are not recommended rates but it is hoped that they may provide a helpful starting point for judges when assessing counsel's fees. The appropriate fee in any particular case may be more or less than the figures appearing in the table, depending upon the circumstances.

The table does not include any figures in respect of leading counsel's fees since such cases would self evidently be exceptional. Similarly, no figures are included for the Commercial Court or the Technology & Construction Court.

Table of Counsel's Fees

QUEENS BENCH	1 hour hearing	½ day hearing
Junior up to 5 years call	£259	£450
Junior 5–10 years call	£386	£767
Junior 10+ years call	£582	£1,164

CHANCERY DIVISION	1 hour hearing	½ day hearing
Junior up to 5 years call	£291	£56
Junior 5–10 years call	£497	£931
Junior 10+ years call	£757	£1,397

ADMINISTRATIVE COURT	1 hour hearing	½ day hearing
Junior up to 5 years call	£381	£582
Junior 5–10 years call	£698	£1,164
Junior 10+ years call	£989	£1,746

[22.37]

If the paying parties were represented by counsel, the fee paid to their counsel is an important factor but not a conclusive one on the question of fees payable to the receiving party's counsel.

In deciding upon the appropriate fee for counsel the question is not simply one of counsel's experience and seniority but also of the level of counsel which the particular case merits.

Counsel's fees should not be allowed in cases in which it was not reasonable to have instructed counsel, but it must be borne in mind that, especially in substantial hearings, it may be more economical if the advocacy is conducted by counsel rather than a solicitor. In all cases the court should consider whether or not the decision to instruct counsel has led to an increase in costs and whether that increase is justifiable.

(h) Brief fees

[22.38]

Although the time spent is a relevant factor in assessing a brief fee it is not appropriate to determine a brief fee by having regard to an hourly rate. Leading counsel had been required to prepare large amounts of material, and to undertake complex cross-examinations which required highly specialised skills. It could not be said that his brief fee was unreasonable (*XYZ v Schering Health Care* SCCO Costs Appeal No 9 of 2004).

CHAPTER 23

THE OTHER FACTORS

[23.1]

Let us now consider the art 3 (Solicitors' (Non-Contentious Business) Remuneration Order 1994) and CPR Rule 44.5 factors other than time on the basis, not of non-contentious and contentious, but of routine and non-routine.

NON-ROUTINE

[23.2]

' . . . it is wrong always to start by assessing the direct and indirect expense to the solicitor, represented by the time spent on the business. This must always be taken into account, but it is not necessarily, or even usually, a basic factor to which all others are related. Thus, although the labour involved will usually be directly related to, and reflected by, the time spent, the skill and specialised knowledge involved may vary greatly for different parts of that time. Again not all time spent on a transaction necessarily lends itself to being recorded, although the fullest possible records should be kept.

This error is compounded if, as an invariable rule, the figure representing the expense of recorded time spent on the transaction is multiplied by another figure to reflect the other factors. The present case provides an illustration of this error. The responsibility and value of the property involved were linked factors, but neither was affected by whether the recorded time spent was 30 hours or 60 hours. Yet the application of a multiplier would double the responsibility/value factor, if the recorded time spent had happened to be 60 rather than 30 hours.

In my judgment the proper approach is to start by taking a broad look at "all the circumstances of the case" and in particular the general nature of the business. This should be followed by a systematic consideration of the factors specified in the paragraphs of art 2 [now art 3] of the order.'

(*Property and Reversionary Investment Corpn Ltd v Secretary of State for the Environment* [1975] 2 All ER 436, QBD, per Donaldson J.)

'The magnetic attraction of [time] as a foundation for assessment of fair and reasonable remuneration is that in the absence of an approved scale applied to value, it is the only figure which is readily calculable. It is an attraction which must be sternly resisted in cases of this sort where one or more of the other factors is such as to dwarf it into insignificance.'

(Donaldson J, in my own firm's case of *Treasury Solicitor v Regester* [1978] 2 All ER 920, QBD.)

(a) What are the factors which may 'dwarf time into insignificance'?

(i) Value

[23.3]

There is no escape from Donaldson J. In *Treasury Solicitor v Regester* he said:

> 'Turning now to value, we remind ourselves that scale fees have been abolished. Nevertheless, it is reasonable and fair to the client that the remuneration should not be disproportionate to the value of the property involved. It was therefore useful to employ a yardstick to assess that relationship. Various yardsticks, with a regressive basis, can be suggested, and an example will be found in the Oyez Practice Notes [No 20, 6th edn, at p 31]. The author correctly stresses that this is only an example and each case will have to be considered on its own merits. The fact is that there is no right yardstick, although some may be wrong. For our part, we would consider that 1/2% on the first £250,000 in a major transaction, and thereafter regressing, provides a reasonable method of assessment.'

The yardstick to which Donaldson J was giving cautious approval followed the bands suggested by Donaldson J himself in the *Property and Reversionary* case. The Council of the Law Society suggested revised bands in 1980 and took the opportunity to make further adjustments in July 1987 in their *An Approach to Non-Contentious Costs*, as follows (revised in 1994):

Band	£ Percentage
Up to £400,000	1/2% (0.5%)
On next £600,000 (maximum total value £1,000,000)	3/8% (0.375%)
On next £1,500,000 (maximum total value £2,500,000)	1/4% (0.25%)
On next £2,500,000 (maximum total value £5,000,000)	1/4% (0.125%)
On next £5,000,000 (maximum total value £10,000,000)	1/10% (0.1%)

What the Law Society booklet does not tell you, and what you must be desperate to know, is that Donaldson J suggested a percentage charge of 0.05% for values of over £10,000,000!

Do not however assume that this provides the profession with a yardstick, because Donaldson J continued:

> 'We must also make it clear that we disagree with the suggestion in the Oyez Notes that the purpose of a scale is to arrive at remuneration for the responsibility/risk element, which is then to be added to the remuneration for the other elements. This is not the case. Remuneration has to be assessed for all the circumstances taken together, and the purpose of a regressing yardstick is, as we have said, to check that the provisional figure bears a reasonable relationship to the value of the property. This is not only reasonable but also fair to both parties and in particular to the client.'

(ii) Adrenalin

[23.4]

In *Treasury Solicitor v Regester*, Donaldson J identified a ninth factor. He said:

'We then looked at the eight factors and asked ourselves, what was the factor or factors, if any, which distinguished this transaction from the general run of such transactions? The answer was clearly "the adrenalin factor". By this, we mean that the solicitor had not only to work fast but had absolutely no margin for error. The transaction had to be completed by 31 July come what might, or their client had lost not only this deal but all possibility of avoiding the effects of the development land tax. In a different case we might have found that there was plenty of time and that the transaction was very similar to one with which the solicitors had previously been concerned for the same client. This would have caused us to look in the reverse direction . . . recorded time does not provide an arithmetical basis for a charge in cases such as this. Its relevance is to check whether the provisional figures for remuneration bear a reasonable relationship to the overheads attributable to the transaction. In this case, the figures which we had in mind did not seem to bear an unusual relationship to the overheads in a transaction of this type, and we therefore obtained no positive assistance from considering this factor.'

(iii) Skill, etc

[23.5]

It is the same where a solicitor brings to bear great skill and experience far in excess of that of the average solicitor, or where one of the other factors such as complexity, documents, place, title or importance to the client result in the amount of time spent being an irrelevance.

Although the *Property and Reversionary* and *Treasury Solicitor v Regester* cases dealt with non-contentious commercial matters, there is no reason why there should not be an identical approach in non-routine contentious matters, where the value, the adrenalin or another factor overwhelms the time involved. A gross sum bill to the client can be calculated on these principles. Should the client request a detailed bill or details be ordered on a Solicitors Act assessment the solicitor will be expected to produce a breakdown in terms of hourly rates. Even if the rates appear to be ludicrously high, the overall total can be justified on the approach of *Property and Reversionary* and *Treasury Solicitor v Regester*.

(b) The dangers

[23.6]

With an approach based upon factors other than time, there is always the danger that someone will come along and divide the end product by the number of hours and proclaim that the solicitors have been paid hundreds of pounds an hour. In *Treasury Solicitor v Regester*, Edward John Parris, writing in the *Estates Gazette*, by getting his figures and arithmetic wrong, calculated that my own firm had been paid £270 an hour in 1978, while in 1975 Geoffrey Bindman in the *LAG Bulletin* interpreted the *Property and Reversionary* case as allowing £375 an hour reduced to £183, and described as 'grotesque and nonsensical' the hourly rate he calculated we had received. This sort of criticism misses the point and arises out of a fixation about time. We are dealing here with matters in which the time is irrelevant to the fee. How much an hour does a brain or heart surgeon charge? Who cares?

The most effective way of avoiding such misunderstandings is, whenever possible, to agree a fixed fee with the client in advance, and where this is not possible, to agree the basis of charging and to discuss and endeavour to agree the amount of your charges before rendering a bill.

ROUTINE

[23.7]

Here, time is the starting point. What should be added for the remaining factors? As I said in the previous chapter, no-one has suggested any way of applying the factors prescribed in CPR Rule 44.5 other than by using them to quantify the profit element to be added to a solicitor's direct costs.

(a) The B factor in contentious costs

[23.8]

'Why should I pay £100 an hour to my lawyers and then have to pay a 50% surcharge for them to give my matter care and attention?' 'Mark-up', 'profit element', 'service increment', 'care, skill and attention', 'personal care and conduct', the 'B factor', and simply 'profit' are some of the words for it. What it means is the factors prescribed in art 3 and Rule 44.5 other than the time expended in doing the work. It includes unrecordable time, supervision and other indirect expenses.

(b) Unrecordable time

[23.9]

Time not capable of being recorded and not included in the A factor, was described by Walton J in *Maltby v DJ Freeman & Co (a firm)* [1978] 2 All ER 913, ChD:

> 'No professional man, or senior employee of a professional man, stops thinking about the day's problems the minute he lifts his coat and umbrella from the stand and sets out on the journey home. Ideas, often very valuable ideas, occur in the train or car home, or in the bath, or even whilst watching television. Yet nothing is ever put down on a time sheet, or can be put down on a time sheet adequately to reflect this out of hours devotion of time.'

This enabled Mr Parris (whom we met at para [23.6]), to write that solicitors were now to be paid for having baths and watching television! This was echoed by a report in the *Sun* newspaper quoting a firm of solicitors who were claiming £7,500 'thinking time' as saying 'this was a very big case which tied up one of our people for 24 hours a day. Sometimes some of our best ideas come when we are at home or in the car'.

(c) Supervision

[23.10]

We saw in *Re Frascati* ([22.20]) that time which should have been recorded but wasn't, should be taken into account in the A factor. What sort of time are we dealing with here? Supervision is one example.

R v Sandhu (29 November 1984, reported in the Lord Chancellor's Department's *Taxing Compendium*) identified three categories of supervision:

(i)   The ordinary day-to-day supervision which is part of the overheads of the firm reflected in the basic mark-up – or indeed in the partners' non-chargeable time.

(ii)   Supervision where a senior fee earner takes a direct hand in the case, in which event he should record his time and charge for it in the direct costs in the A factor.

(iii)   Where a junior fee earner competently conducts the case with the assistance of regular but unquantified supervision from a senior fee earner whose time is not charged in the direct cost. This supervision is covered by the B factor.

(d) Applying the factors

(i)   Add or subtract

[23.11]

One must either add or subtract from the direct cost the other factors. Where someone has made a meal or a mess of a case, the percentage increase for care and conduct for that work could be nothing. In other cases, it could be much higher than average. For example, where a legal executive has done work which could justifiably have been done by a senior partner he may be rewarded with a 200% mark-up for care and conduct on his hourly expense rate. Similarly, if someone has been brilliant, or had extraordinary responsibility, or has been very expeditious, this is the place to take it into account – otherwise the fee earner will be penalised by his own expedition. Twenty years ago, in *The Taxation of Contentious Costs*, I gave the true example of a solicitor friend with vast experience in personal injury matters who conducted two cases for injured workmen and, without going to counsel, negotiated substantial (in those days) settlements of £40,000 and £50,000. His recorded time was but a fraction of the time that would have been recorded had the matter been dealt with by a solicitor who was competent but who lacked my friend's expertise and who would also, quite properly, have incurred substantial counsel's fees. On the taxation of his costs my friend was quite rightly allowed a 200% profit mark-up on the time he had spent on the matter.

In neither of these examples would the paying party be penalised. The legal executive with a £60 an hour expense rate who is given a 200% mark-up receives no more than would a solicitor with a £120 an hour expense rate and a 50% mark-up. Similarly, my friend, who did all the work himself quickly and without using counsel, even with a 200% mark-up, cost the paying party no more than if the average solicitor had taken an average length of time and incurred average counsel's fees. A solicitor who is expeditious and efficient is entitled to benefit from, and not be penalised by, the lack of time he has spent on the matter. The result is reward for merit – and that is the difference between time-costing and time-charging.

Just one caveat to that. The higher the level of fee earner, the more he is expected to know. Therefore the higher the expense rate the lower the mark-up – you cannot expect to be rewarded twice.

(ii)   75%

[23.12]

There was consideration of mark-up in *Finley v Glaxo* (see [22.16]), where Hobhouse J said:

'The solicitor claimed 125%. The Registrar allowed 85% so as to give a composite figure of £65 per hour in conjunction with the £35 per hour rate.

The solicitor was, at the material times, effectively a sole practitioner. He had another solicitor with him for part of the time but that is not material to the present case. He had a special experience and knowledge of vaccine and similar matters. He brought to the consideration of the plaintiff's case a familiarity with the subject matter and a measure of expertise appropriate to a lawyer dealing with that class of case. It must also be borne in mind that he had acted for the plaintiff previously in the tribunal matter, so that he was aware of the background through that source. He is a practitioner in Newcastle . . .   That takes me to the second half of the calculation, which is the question of uplift and the "B" factor. One of the matters on which the district registrar was criticised in relation to the "A" factor, in my judgment correctly, was that he got too much involved, in considering the cost assessment, with questions of profit and with the question of the uplift that he was later going to apply. The simplest way to illustrate this point is by referring to the concluding passage in his reasons, where he said:

"I cannot see, on the evidence before me, any compelling reasons why I should on this evidence increase the currently allowed hourly rate. The allowed rate is £35 per hour. This plus an 85% mark-up gives a remuneration of £65 per hour, which I consider to be both fair and reasonable having regard to the weight of the case and Mr Deas' seniority."

The district registrar is quite right that at the end of any assessment of this kind he should stand back for a moment and consider the implications and the overall picture presented by his decision on the detail. That is what he is doing there. But it also shows that there is a relationship between the percentage that he chose to allow and the hourly rate. There are many other passages in his reasons where he allows the overall profit assessment to colour his views about the hourly rate. I consider – and counsel has not sought to argue to the contrary – that, having substantially altered the hourly rate, it is appropriate and proper for me to reconsider the uplift that has been allowed.

The uplift factor was a subject that was referred to Kerr J in the *Leopold Lazarus* case at page 4 of the transcript. In view of the hour I will not read out what he says. He refers to Appendix 2 to Order 62 in the earlier version, which is now a slightly different version in the current Appendix. That requires the court, and indeed the taxing officer, in assessing the costs, to take into account, among other things, the complexity of the item or of the cause or matter in which it arises; the difficulty or novelty of the questions involved; the skills, specialised knowledge and responsibility required; the time and labour expended by the solicitor; the number and importance of documents; the importance of the cause or matter to the client; the amount of money involved, and soon.

This present case did involve matters of responsibility for the solicitor, because he was taking upon himself the responsibility of assessing the evidence that was available on a preliminary basis and advising the client. He advised against the continuation of proceedings and, far from his deserving to be marked down for that, he deserves credit for taking upon himself that responsibility and also being prepared to say, of his own judgment, that the proceedings should not continue as to do so would not be in the interests of the client and would, indeed, be a waste of time and money. It was an important case for the client. It potentially involved a very large sum of money. But the medical issues were ones which, although complicated and technical, were not outside the expertise of the solicitor; and it is because of this expertise that the matter was being dealt with by a senior partner.

One must also bear in mind that this case was at a very early stage: it was at a stage of, essentially, perusal and advice. The solicitor was not involved in the preparation of complicated documents, nor was he involved in the conduct of any negotiations. Still less was he actually involved in the conduct of any litigation. All those factors might have put this case in a different light.

I have to consider what is the appropriate uplift for a senior partner in the conduct of a case of this character at the stage which it had reached. The starting point for this exercise is 50%; that is the advice I received, and it is also the practice in the North East. If one is concerned with a High Court or potential High Court action, that is the appropriate starting point for the uplift. Likewise I am satisfied that 125% was far too high for a case of this kind. One of the reasons, I suspect, why 125% was even being considered by the solicitor is the too low figure that he might have feared he was going to be allowed as an hourly rate. As I have already made clear, I would not lend support to the adoption of an unduly low hourly rate and then seeking to put it right by applying a higher uplift percentage. The right approach is that which I have emphasised, namely to adopt a realistic approach to the hourly rate to reflect the actual cost of the fee earner involved, and then to apply an appropriate but not excessive uplift.

The advice that I have had from my assessors in this matter is that no more than 75% is the maximum justifiable uplift in a case of this character, at the stage that it was at, and involving the work which it did involve at that stage. I am advised, and I have also formed the view, that 85% is too high and cannot be supported.'

(iii)   75% again

[23.13]

Evans J also dealt with mark-up in *Johnson v Reed Corrugated* (para [22.21]) as follows:

' . . .   the range for normal, ie non-exceptional cases, starts at 50%   . . .   an appropriate figure for "run-of-the-mill" cases. The figure increases above 50% so as to reflect a number of possible factors—including the complexity of the case, any particular need for special attention to be paid to it, and any additional responsibilities which the solicitor may have undertaken towards the client, and others, depending upon the circumstances—but only a small percentage of accident cases results in an allowance of over 70%. To justify a figure of 100% or even one closely approaching 100% there must be some combination of factors which mean that the case approaches the exceptional.'

He too allowed 75%.

(iv)   125%

[23.14]

Before you get too excited about a 125% mark-up I must emphasise that this was the major test case of *Loveday v Renton (No 2)* [1992] 3 All ER 184, QBD relating to the whooping cough vaccine. The action ran between 1982 and 1988 and culminated in a 300-page judgment which took two days to read. The trial itself lasted for 65 working days. The documentation ran to some 100 lever arch files and The Wellcome Foundation had prepared a 'library' of some 50 files containing literature on the subject. The case was truly exceptional in terms of weight, complexity and responsibility. In delivering his judgment Hobhouse J emphasised that the court deplored any artificially depressed rates being compensated for by artificially inflated mark-up figures. He continued:

'To justify an uplift in excess of 100% it is necessary, as has recently been re-stated by Evans J in *Johnson v Reed Corrugated Cases Ltd* to demonstrate that the case is exceptional. There has been a tendency among some firms of solicitors to put forward grossly inflated percentages by way of uplift and a failure to appreciate that to justify an uplift even as high as 100% requires the demonstration that the case is exceptional. In the present case, having regard to the features to which I have referred, I am satisfied (not without some hesitation) that the taxing master was wrong to alter his own original assessment on bill A of an uplift of 125%. I consider that 125% is at the top end of the bracket of uplift which would be proper for this case overall and I would not have interfered with a figure which lay somewhere between 125% and 100%. But I do accept the solicitors' submission before me that 100% was too low for bill A and I therefore shall reinstate the original allowance of 125%.'

(iv)   Up-to-date

[23.15]

For a more recent example of applying the Rule 44.5 factors (the seven pillars of wisdom) see *Higgs v Camden and Islington Health Authority* in para [22.20].

(v)   Message

[23.16]

Solicitors cannot expect to obtain mark-ups in excess of 75% except in the heaviest and most complex cases and probably only those which involve a contested hearing. The message to costs officers is also clear: they should not use the mark-up as an adjuster for allowing an unreasonably low hourly expense rate.

(e) Non-contentious guidance

[23.17]

The assessment of fair and reasonable remuneration is an art not a science. It is arrived at by a commonsense feel of the matter – not by the application of a rigid formula by a computer. The Law Society, in its publication *Non-Contentious Costs* (May 2005), gives guidance on how the quantification of costs for various categories will work. Reference should be made to this booklets, but the approach may be summarised as follows.

(i) No value element

[23.18]

Where there is no readily ascertainable value element, such as in simple wills, administration of trusts and all other routine non-contentious matters, the approach is the hourly cost plus a mark-up. The mark-up will rarely be less than 35%, usually 50% and, as we have seen, can be substantially higher. Each of the prescribed factors should be examined to see how they should be reflected.

(ii) Value element

1. Domestic conveyancing

[23.19]

The Law Society used to suggest either a 50% mark-up on the cost of the time or adding 1/2% of the value up to £400,000, whichever was the greater, using the regressive yardstick (para [23.3]) for higher values. However, the Law Society now recommends one of two methods:

Method (i): Charge an hourly expense rate and add a value element calculated as follows

Value band	Percentage
Up to £400,000	0.5
On next £600,000 (maximum total value £1 million)	0.375
On next £1,500,000 (maximum total value £2.5 million)	0.25
On next £2,500,000 (maximum total value £5 million)	0.125
On next £5,000,000 (maximum total value £10 million)	0.1

Method (ii): Take a broad look at the circumstances of the transaction' and calculate 'a single charging figure incorporating the time spent and what is fair and reasonable in all the circumstances. This single charging figure may comprise a fixed fee or an estimate.' This is also where time costing for management comes into play – if, in order to attract conveyancing work, you are cutting your charges below what is profitable, it is as well that you should know this.

2. Leases

[23.20]

To find the value
(i)   take one-half of the yearly rent;
(ii)   multiply it by the unexpired term of the lease with a maximum of 20 years;
(iii)   add any premium payable by the lessee and deduct any premium payable by the lessor to or from the capitalised value or deduct any reverse premium; and
(iv)   apply to the value the regressive scale at [23.19] above.

3. Mortgages

[23.21]

The Law Society suggests the following guideline charges where the solicitor is acting only for the lender:

Advance not exceeding	Without assignment of life policy	With assignment of life policy
Up to £15,000	£120	Plus flat rate £25 where there is an assignment/deposit of life policy irrespective of the number of policies or companies.
£15,001–£20,000	£121–£129	
£20,001–£25,000	£136.50	
£25,001–£30,000	£141	
£30,001–£60,000	£150	
£60,001–£100,000	£189	

Where the advance exceeds

£100,000	add £188 for each £10,000 or part thereof	

[23.22]

In other cases the Law Society suggests the following percentages of value:

Acting for purchaser/mortgagor $^1/_4$%
Acting for purchaser/mortgagor and mortgagee $^1/_4$%
Acting for mortgagee alone $^1/_2$%
Acting for mortgagor alone $^1/_2$%

4. Probates and administrations

[23.23]

Charge an inclusive figure of the fee earner's expense rate with an uplift of 25–33% for care and conduct plus a value element calculated as follows:

Non-solicitor executor	1%	of gross value less residence
	0.5%	of residence
Solicitor not an executor but acting for corporate executor with general conduct of matter	0.5%	gross value less residence
	0.25%	of residence
Solicitor not an executor but acting for corporate executor making probate application only	0.06%	of gross value less residence
	0.12%	of residence
Solicitor executor (sole or with non corporate executor)	1.5%	of gross value less residence
	0.75%	of residence
Solicitor joint executor with corporate executor	0.75%	of gross value less residence
	0.375%	of residence

The Law Society recommends that the value of deceased's home be reduced by half the value of the deceased's interest in the property before applying the guideline percentage, ie if the property is solely owned by the deceased, the percentage will apply to half the value of the property. If the property is jointly owned, the percentage will apply to only a quarter of the value of the property.

In *Jemma Trust Co Ltd v Liptrott* [2003] All ER (D) 164 (Sep), Costs Judge Peter Rogers had held that a solicitor's charges for administering a large estate should no longer be based on both hourly rates and an additional element in respect of value. The estate in question was worth nearly £10 million for the administration of which the solicitor had elected to charge on the basis of an hourly rate for work carried out and in addition he charged 1.5% of the gross value of the estate (save for the house, which was charged at 0.5%) as a value element. This resulted in a value element of £227,000 in addition to the hourly rate charges of £386,000, totalling some £613,000 plus VAT. The master concluded that now hourly rates are calculated invariably on the basis of sophisticated time recording material, it is anachronistic and wrong to include an additional element in respect of value.

The Court of Appeal held that he was wrong on two counts. First, it is still appropriate for solicitors administering an estate and charging the time spent on administration to charge a separate fee based on the value of the estate, provided of course it is fair and reasonable remuneration in the light of all the circumstances. Second, by disallowing a charge based on the value element and only allowing a miserly hourly rate, the costs judge had in effect failed to have any regard to the value element. However, the Law Society's advice in its 1995 publication 'An Approach to Non-Contentious costs', and its subsequent 1999 booklet, that in high value estates 'consideration should be given to reducing the value element percentage' was insufficiently firm. The regressive scale adopted in *Maltby v DJ Freeman & Co* should be used, resulting, when updated for inflation, in the following figures for work done in 2003:

(1)	Up to £1 million	1.5%
(2)	Over £1 million up to £4 million	$\frac{1}{2}$%
(3)	Over £4 million up to £8 million	$\frac{1}{6}$%
(4)	Over £8 million up to £12 million	$\frac{1}{12}$%

The Court of Appeal gave this guidance:

'(1)   Much the best practice is for a solicitor to obtain prior agreement as to the basis of his charges not only from the executors but also, where appropriate, from any residuary beneficiary who is an entitled third party under the 1994 Order. This is encouraged in the 1994 booklet and letter 8 of Appendix 2 to the 1999 booklet provides a good working draft of such agreement. We support that encouragement;

(2)   in any complicated administration, it will be prudent for solicitors to provide in their terms of retainer for interim bills to be rendered for payment on account; this is, of course, subject to the solicitor's obligation to review the matter as a whole at the end of the business so as to ensure that he has claimed no more than is fair and reasonable, taking into account the factors set out in the 1994 Order;

(3)   there should be no hard and fast rule that charges cannot be made separately by reference to the value of the estate; value can, by contrast, be taken into account as part of the hourly rate; value can also be taken into account partly in one way and partly in the other. What is important is that:
    (a)   it should be transparent on the face of the bill how value is being taken into account; and
    (b)   in no case should it be taken into account more than once;

(4)   in many cases, if a charge is separately made by reference to the value of the estate, it should usually be on a regressive scale. The bands and percentages will be for the costs judge in each case; the suggestions to the costs judge set out in paragraph 30 may be thought by him to be appropriate for this case but different bands and percentages will be appropriate for other cases and figures set out in paragraph 30 cannot be any more than a guideline;

(5)   it may be helpful at the end of the business for the solicitor or, if there is an assessment, for the costs judge, when a separate element of the bill is based on the value of the estate, to calculate the number of hours that would notionally be taken to achieve the amount of the separate charge. That may help to determine whether overall the remuneration claimed or assessed is fair and reasonable within the terms of the 1994 Order;

(6)   it may also be helpful to consider the Law Society's Guidance in cases where there is no relevant and ascertainable value factor which is given in the 1994 booklet at paragraph 13.4. If the time spent on the matter is costed out at the solicitor's expense rate (which should be readily ascertainable from the Solicitor's Expense of Time calculations) the difference between

that sum (the cost to the solicitor of the time spent on the matter) and the final figure claimed will represent the mark-up. The mark-up (which should take into account the factors specified in the 1994 Order including value) when added to the cost of the time spent must then be judged by reference to the requirement that this total figure must represent "such sum as may be fair and reasonable to both solicitor and entitled person".'

5.   Other matters

[23.24]

In all other routine non-contentious matters, where there is an ascertainable value element, consider whether the non-value factors are subsumed by value. It used to be only in exceptional circumstances that there would be a mark-up expressed as a percentage of time in addition to the value factor. However, the fall in the value of money since the value yardsticks were set means that there are now probably fewer cases where a value factor in itself is sufficient. If there is a value factor the usual mark-up on time might be less, perhaps between 25% and 33% in matters other than routine domestic conveyancing, or none at all following *Jemma Trust Co Ltd v Liptrott*, above.

CHAPTER 24

VALUE JUDGEMENT

[24.1]

Let Donaldson J, as he then was, have the final word on the approach to the quantification of costs:

> 'Each case will always have to be considered on its merits . . . various figures will no doubt come to mind. They can be tested relative to the remuneration generally accepted or previously held to be fair and reasonable in comparable transactions, due allowance being made for all distinctions . . . in the end it is a value judgement based on discretion and experience. We have had to make a value judgement. Our figure may not be *the* right figure, and indeed such a figure probably does not exist, but we hope that it will be *a* right figure.'

(*Property and Reversionary Investment Corpn Ltd v Secretary of State for the Environment* [1975] 2 All ER 436, QBD.)

CHAPTER 25

FIXED COSTS UNDER SECTION I CPR PART 45

[25.1]

There are now two kinds of fixed costs covered by Part 45. Costs fixed by Section I (this chapter) must be distinguished from the fixed or predictable costs on the fast track in Sections II to VI (Chapter 27).

The fixed costs dealt with in Section I are the fixed costs on default and summary judgment and fixed commencement costs where payment is made in full within 14 days of service.

The fixed costs provisions of Section I apply only where the claim is for a specified sum of money and the circumstances set out in the rule apply; or the only claim is one where the court gives a fixed date for the hearing when it issues the claim and judgment is given for the delivery of goods. In either case the value of the claim must exceed £25.

Although it is not mentioned specifically in Part 45, Rule 27.14 limits the costs payable on the small claims track to the fixed costs attributable to issuing the claim (there are other circumstances in which the court may order costs on the small claims track, as to which see Chapter 26).

The amount of costs payable is set out in the tables to the rules. Table 1 gives the fixed costs on commencement, Table 2 costs on entry of judgment and Table 3 miscellaneous fixed costs, which are largely to do with service documents. In addition to the fixed costs, any appropriate court fee will be allowed.

Here is Section I of Part 45 and its supporting Practice Direction:

[25.2]

I FIXED COSTS

CPR Rule 45.1: Scope of this section

(1)   This Section sets out the amounts which, unless the court orders otherwise, are to be allowed in respect of solicitors' charges in the cases to which this Part applies.

(The definitions contained in Part 43 are relevant to this Part)

(2)   This Section applies where—

    (a)   the only claim is a claim for a specified sum of money where the value of the claim exceeds £25 and—

        (i)   judgment in default is obtained under rule 12.4(1);

        (ii)   judgment on admission is obtained under rule 14.4(3);

        (iii)   judgment on admission on part of the claim is obtained under rule 14.5(6);

        (iv)   summary judgment is given under Part 24;

        (v)   the court has made an order to strike out[(GL)] a defence under rule 3.4(2)(a) as disclosing no reasonable grounds for defending the claim; or

        (vi)   rule 45.3 applies; or

(b)   the only claim is a claim where the court gave a fixed date for the hearing when it issued the claim and judgment is given for the delivery of goods and the value of the claim exceeds £25;

(c)   the claim is for the recovery of land, including a possession claim under Part 55, whether or not the claim includes a claim for a sum of money and the defendant gives up possession, pays the amount claimed, if any, and the fixed commencement costs stated in the claim form;

(d)   the claim is for the recovery of land, including a possession claim under Part 55, where one of the grounds for possession is arrears of rent, for which the court gave a fixed date for the hearing when it issued the claim and judgment is given for the possession of land (whether or not the order for possession is suspended on terms) and the defendant—

    (i)   has neither delivered a defence, or counterclaim, nor otherwise denied liability; or

    (ii)   has delivered a defence which is limited to specifying his proposals for the payment of arrears of rent;

(e)   the claim is a possession claim under Section II of Part 55 (accelerated possession claims of land let on an assured shorthold tenancy) and a possession order is made where the defendant has neither delivered a defence, or counterclaim, nor otherwise denied liability;

(f)   the claim is a demotion claim under Section III of Part 65 or a demotion claim is made in the same claim form in which a claim for possession is made under Part 55 and that demotion claim is successful; or

(g)   a judgment creditor has taken steps under Parts 70 to 73 to enforce a judgment or order.

(Practice Direction 7B sets out the types of case where a court will give a fixed date for a hearing when it issues a claim)

(3)   Any appropriate court fee will be allowed in addition to the costs set out in this Section.

(4)   The claim form may include a claim for fixed commencement costs.

[25.3]

CPR Rule 45.2: Amount of fixed commencement costs in a claim for the recovery of money or goods

(1)   The amount of fixed commencement costs in a claim to which rule 45.1(2)(a) or (b) applies—

(a)   shall be calculated by reference to Table 1; and

(b)   the amount claimed, or the value of the goods claimed if specified, in the claim form is to be used for determining the band in Table 1 that applies to the claim.

The amounts shown in Table 4 are to be allowed in addition, if applicable.

[25.4]

Rule 45.2A: Amount of fixed commencement costs in a claim for the recovery of land or a demotion claim

(1)   The amount of fixed commencement costs in a claim to which rule 45.1(2)(c), (d) or (f) applies shall be calculated by reference to Table 2.

(2)   The amounts shown in Table 4 are to be allowed in addition, if applicable.

Table 1 Fixed costs on commencement of a claim

Relevant Band	Where the claim form is served by the court or by any method other than personal service by the claimant	Where the claim form is served personally by the claimant; and there is only one defendant	Where there is more than one defendant, for each additional defendant personally served at separate addresses by the claimant
Where— the value of the claim exceeds £25 but does not exceed £500	£50	£60	£15
Where— the value of the claim exceeds £500 but does not exceed £1,000	£70	£80	£15
Where— the value of the claim exceeds £1,000 but does not exceed £5,000; or the only claim is for delivery of goods and no value is specified or stated on the claim form	£80	£90	£15
Where— the value of the claim exceeds £5,000	£100	£110	£15

Table 2 Fixed costs on commencement of a claim for the recovery of land or a demotion claim

Where the claim form is served by the court or by any method other than personal service by the claimant	Where— —the claim form is served personally by the claimant; and —there is only one defendant	Where there is more than one defendant, for each additional defendant personally served at separate addresses by the claimant
£69.50	£77.00	£15.00

[25.5]

CPR Rule 45.3: When defendant only liable for fixed commencement costs
Where—
(a)   the only claim is for a specified sum of money; and
(b)   the defendant pays the money claimed within 14 days after service of particulars of claim on him, together with the fixed commencement costs stated in the claim form,

the defendant is not liable for any further costs unless the court orders otherwise.
(2) . . .

[25.5A]

In an article in the New Law Journal, Francis Davey considered the effect of 'unless the court orders otherwise' in rule 45.3. He suggested that provided a tenancy agreement has a properly drafted clause requiring the tenant to pay the landlord's costs, the court ought normally to award the landlord's reasonable costs and not fixed costs, even on the indemnity basis if the clause so provides. However, he observed, a landlord can never recover more than reasonable costs, whatever the tenancy agreement might say to the contrary.

[25.6]

CPR Rule 45.4: Costs on entry of judgment in a claim for the recovery of money or goods
Where—
    (a)   the claimant has claimed fixed commencement costs under rule 45.2; and
    (b)   judgment is entered in a claim to which rule 45.1(2)(a) or (b) applies in the circumstances specified in Table 3, the amount to be included in the judgment for the claimant's solicitor's charges is the total of—
        (i)   the fixed commencement costs; and
        (ii)   the relevant amount shown in Table 3.

[25.7]

Rule 45.4A: Costs on entry of judgment in a claim for the recovery of land or a demotion claim
(1)   Where—
    (a)   the claimant has claimed fixed commencement costs under rule 45.2A; and
    (b)   judgment is entered in a claim to which rule 45.1(2)(d) or (f) applies, the amount to be included in the judgment for the claimant's solicitor's charges is the total of—
        (i)   the fixed commencement costs; and
        (ii)   the sum of £57.25.
(2)   Where an order for possession is made in a claim to which rule 45.1(2)(e) applies, the amount allowed for the claimant's solicitor's charges for preparing and filing—
    (a)   the claim form;
    (b)   the documents that accompany the claim form; and
    (c)   the request for possession,
is £79.50.

Table 3 Fixed costs on entry of judgment in a claim for the recovery of money or goods

	Where the amount of the judgment exceeds £25 but does not exceed £5,000	Where the amount of the judgment exceeds £5,000

Where judgment in default of an acknowledgment of service is entered under rule 12.4 (1) (entry of judgment by request on claim for money only)	£22	£30
Where judgment in default of a defence is entered under rule 12.4 (1) (entry of judgment by request on claim for money only)	£25	£35
Where judgment is entered under rule 14.4 (judgment on admission), or rule 14.5 (judgment on admission of part of claim) and claimant accepts the defendant's proposal as to the manner of payment	£40	£55
Where judgment is entered under rule 14.4 (judgment on admission), or rule 14.5 (judgment on admission on part of claim) and court decides the date or times of payment	£55	£70
Where summary judgment is given under Part 24 or the court strikes out a defence under rule 3.4 (2)(a), in either case, on application by a party	£175	£210
Where judgment is given on a claim for delivery of goods under a regulated agreement within the meaning of the Consumer Credit Act 1974 and no *other entry in this table applies*	£60	£85

[25.8]

CPR Rule 45.5: Miscellaneous fixed costs
Table 4 shows the amount to be allowed in respect of solicitor's charges in the circumstances mentioned.

Table 4 Miscellaneous fixed costs

For service by a party of any document required to be served personally including preparing and copying a certificate of service for each individual served	£15
Where service by an alternative method or at an alternative place is permitted by an order under rule 6.15 for each individual served	£53.25
Where a document is served out of the jurisdiction—	
(a) in Scotland, Northern Ireland, the Isle of Man or the Channel Islands	£68.25
(b) in any other place	£77

[25.9]

CPR Rule 45.6: Fixed enforcement costs
Table 5 shows the amount to be allowed in respect of solicitors' costs in the circumstances mentioned. The amounts shown in Table 4 are to be allowed in addition, if applicable.

Table 5 Fixed enforcement costs

For an application under rule 70.5(4) that an award may be enforced as if payable under a court order, where the amount outstanding under the award:	
exceeds £25 but does not exceed £250	£30.75
exceeds £250 but does not exceed £600	£41.00
exceeds £600 but does not exceed £2,000	£69.50
exceeds £2,000	£75.50
On attendance to question a judgment debtor (or officer of a company or other corporation) who has been ordered to attend court under rule 71.2 where the questioning takes place before a court officer, including attendance by a responsible representative of the solicitor:	for each half-hour or part, £15.00
	(When the questioning takes place before a judge, he may summarily assess any costs allowed.)
On the making of a final third party debt order under rule 72.8(6)(a) or an order for the payment to the judgment creditor of money in court under rule 72.10(1)(b):	
if the amount recovered is less than £150	one-half of the amount recovered
	£98.50
On the making of a final charging order under rule 73.8(2)(a):	£110.00
	The court may also allow reasonable disbursements in respect of search fees and the registration of the order.
Where a certificate is issued and registered under Schedule 6 to the Civil Jurisdiction and Judgments Act 1982, the costs of registration	£39.00
Where permission is given under RSC Order 45, rule 3 to enforce a judgment or order giving possession of land and costs are allowed on the judgment or order, the amount to be added to the judgment or order for costs—	
(a) basic costs	£42.50
(b) where notice of the proceedings is to be to more than one person, for each additional person	£2.75
Where a writ of execution as defined in the RSC Order 46, rule 1, is issued against any party	£51.75

Where a request is filed for the issue of a warrant of execution under CCR Order 26, rule 1, for a sum exceeding £25	£2.25
Where an application for an attachment of earnings order is made and costs are allowed under CCR Order 27, rule 9 or CCR Order 28, rule 10, for each attendance on the hearing of the application	£8.50

[25.10]

CPD Section 24 Fixed costs in small claims

24.1   *Under Rule 27.14 the costs which can be awarded to a claimant in a small claims track case include the fixed costs payable under Part 45 attributable to issuing the claim.*
24.2   *Those fixed costs shall be the sum of*
(a)   *the fixed commencement costs calculated in accordance with Table 1 of Rule 45.2 and;*
(b)   *the appropriate court fee or fees paid by the claimant.*

[25.11]

CPD Section 24A Claims to which Part 45 does not apply
24A   *In a claim to which Part 45 does not apply, no amount shall be entered on the claim form for the charges of the claimant's solicitor, but the words "to be assessed" shall be inserted.*

[25.12]

CPD Section 25 Fixed costs on the issue of a default costs certificate
25.1   *Unless paragraph 24.2 applies or unless the court orders otherwise, the fixed costs to be included in a default costs certificate are £80 plus a sum equal to any appropriate court fee payable on the issue of the certificate.*
25.2   *The fixed costs included in a certificate must not exceed the maximum sum specified for costs and court fee in the notice of commencement.*

[25.13]

Where a default costs certificate is issued (see para [30.57]) the receiving party is entitled to recover the amount for fixed costs specified in the Practice Direction supplementing Part 45, at present £80, and the court fee for issuing the certificate. The amount recoverable is fixed unless the court makes a different order and in any event may not exceed the maximum sum specified for costs and court fees in the notice of commencement.

The following additional fixed costs provisions have been preserved in the CPR Schedules.

[25.14]

RSC ORDER 62: COSTS

APPENDIX 3

Fixed costs
The scale of costs set out in this Appendix shall apply in the cases to which the Appendix refers.

[25.15]

Part II Costs on judgment without trial for possession of land
1.
   (1)   Where the claim is for the possession of land, and the claimant obtains judgment—
   (a)   under CPR Part 12 (default judgment); or
   (c)   under CPR Part 24 (summary judgment),

   for possession of the land and costs, then, subject to sub-paragraph (2), there shall be allowed the costs prescribed by paragraph 2 of this Part of this Appendix.
   (2)   Where the claimant is also entitled under the judgment to damages to be assessed, or where the plaintiff claims any remedy of the nature specified in Order 45, rule 3(2), this Part of this Appendix shall not apply.

2.   The costs to be allowed under this Part of this Appendix shall be £143.75, together with any court fee, and additional costs where appropriate set out in the Table below.

Additional costs	Amount to be allowed
(1) Where there is more than one defendant, in respect of each additional defendant served	£13.75
(2) Where service by an alternative method is ordered and effected, in respect of each defendant served	£53.25
(3) Where service out of the jurisdiction is ordered and effected, in the case of service:	
(a) in Scotland, Northern Ireland, the Isle of Man or the Channel Islands	£68.25
(b) in any other place out of the jurisdiction	£77.00
(4) In the case of default judgment under CPR Part 12 or summary judgment under CPR Part 24 the claimant makes an affidavit of service for the purpose of a judgment where the defendant failed to respond to the claim form (the allowance to include the search fee)	£20.50
(5) In the case of summary judgment under CPR Part 24 where an affidavit of service of the Part 23 application is required	£20.50
(6) In the case of summary judgment under CPR Part 24 for each adjournment of the application	£20.50

This Part shows the amount to be allowed in respect of enforcement costs.

[25.16]

Part III **Miscellaneous**

---

2. Where a certificate in respect of money provisions contained in a judgment is registered in the High Court in the Register of United Kingdom judgments under Schedule 6 to the Civil Jurisdiction and Judgments Act 1982, there shall be allowed:

Costs of registration	£39.00

2A. Where costs are allowed under the following paragraphs of this Part, the appropriate court fees shall be allowed in addition

3. Where, upon the application of any person who has obtained a judgment or order against a debtor for the recovery or payment of money, a garnishee order is made under Order 49, rule 1, against a garnishee attaching debts due or accruing due from the debtor, the following costs shall be allowed:

(a)	to the garnishee to be deducted by him from any debt due by him as aforesaid before payment to the applicant	£23.00
(b)	to the applicant, to be retained, unless the Court otherwise orders, out of the money recovered by him under the garnishee order and in priority to the amount of the debt owing to him under the judgment or order:	

(i)	Basic costs	one half of the amount recovered

If the amount recovered by the applicant from the garnishee is:

less than £150

not less than £150	£98.50

(ii) Additional costs

Where the garnishee fails to attend the hearing of the application and an affidavit of service is required	£18.00

4. Where a charging order is granted and made absolute there shall be allowed:

Basic costs	£110.00
Additional costs where an affidavit of service is required	£18.00
together with such reasonable disbursements	
in respect of search fees and the registration	
of the order as the Court may allow	£18.00

5. Where leave is given under Order 45, rule 3, to enforce a judgment or order for the giving of possession of land by writ of possession, if the costs are allowed on the judgment or order there shall be allowed the following costs, which shall be added to the judgment or order:

Basic costs	£42.50
Where notice of the proceedings has been given to more than one person, in respect of each additional person	£2.75

6. Where a writ of execution within the meaning of Order 46, rule 1, is issued against any party, there shall be allowed:

Costs of issuing execution	£51.75

[25.17]

Note: Paragraphs 3 and 4 above were revoked by SI 2001/4015, r 34 with effect from 25 March 2002 (except in relation to fixed costs to be awarded in enforcement proceedings which are issued before that date): see SI 2001/4015, rr 1(c), 43(2).

[25.18]

CCR ORDER 38: COSTS

Order 38, Rule 18 Fixed costs
(1)   Appendix B shall effect for the purpose of showing the total amount which, in the several cases to which Appendix B applies, shall be allowed to the solicitor for the claimant as fixed costs without assessment (whether by the summary or the detailed procedure), unless the court otherwise orders.

(2)   In a claim to which Appendix B or CPR Part 45 does not apply no amount shall be entered on the claim form for the charges of the claimant's solicitor, but the words 'to be assessed' shall be inserted.

[25.19]

APPENDIX B

PART I CLAIMS FOR THE RECOVERY OF PROPERTY

Directions
1.   The Tables in this Part of this Appendix show the amount to be entered on the claim form or application in respect of solicitors' charges—

    (a)   in a claim for the recovery of property, including land, with or without a claim for a sum of money (other than a claim to which CPR Part 45 applies), for the purpose of Part II of this Appendix or of fixing the amount which the plaintiff may receive in respect of solicitors' charges without assessment whether by the detailed or summary procedure in the event of the defendant giving up possession and paying the amount claimed, if any, and costs.

2.   In addition to the amount entered in accordance with the relevant Table the appropriate court fees shall be entered on the application.

3.   In the Tables the expression 'claim' means—

    (a)   the sum of money claimed, or

    (b)   in relation to a claim for the recovery of land (with or without a claim for a sum of money), a sum exceeding £600 but not exceeding £2,000;

    (c)   in relation to a claim for the recovery of property other than money or land, the value of the property claimed or in the case of goods supplied under a hire purchase agreement, the unpaid balance of the total price.

4.   The Tables do not apply where the application or the claim form is to be served out of England and Wales or where service by an alternative method is ordered.

Tables of fixed costs

Where claim exceeds £25 but does not exceed £250

Amount of charges:

(a) Where service is not by solicitor	£30.75
(b) Where service is by solicitor	£35.00

Where claim exceeds £250 but does not exceed £600
Amount of charges:

(a) Where service is not by solicitor	£41.00
(b) Where service is by solicitor	£48.50

Where claim exceeds £600 but does not exceed £2,000
Amount of charges:

(a) Where service is not by solicitor	£69.50
(b) Where service is by solicitor	£77.00

Where claim exceeds £2,000
Amount of charges:

(a) Where service is not by solicitor	£75.50
(b) Where service is by solicitor	£82.00

[25.20]

PART II JUDGMENTS

Directions

Where an amount in respect of solicitors' charges has been entered on the claim form under Part I of this Appendix and judgment is given in the circumstances mentioned in paragraph (d) in column 1 of the following Table, the amount to be included in the judgment in respect of the solicitors' charges shall be the amount entered on the application or the claim form together with the amount shown in column 2 of the Table under the sum of money by reference to which the amount entered on the application or the claim form was fixed. Where judgment is given for a sum less than the amount claimed or for the delivery of goods of which the value or the balance of the total price is a sum less than the amount claimed, the foregoing paragraph shall, unless the court otherwise directs, have effect as if the amount entered on the application or the claim form had been fixed by reference to that sum.

Fixed costs on judgments

Column 1	Column 2 Sum of money		
	A	B	C
	exceeding £25 but not exceeding £600	exceeding £600 but not exceeding £3000	exceeding £3000
(d) Where judgment is given in a fixed date action for:			
(i) delivery of goods where goods are not subject to a regulated agreement; or			

(ii)	possession of land, where one of the grounds for possession is arrears of rent (whether or not the order for possession is suspended on terms) and the defendant has neither delivered a defence, admission or counterclaim, nor otherwise denied liability	£38.50 £57.25 £70.75	

(Delivery of goods claims subject to a regulated agreement are dealt with by CPR Part 45)

[25.21]

MISCELLANEOUS PROCEEDINGS

Amount to be allowed

3. For filing a request for the issue of a warrant of execution for a sum exceeding £25 — £2.25

4. For service of any document required to be served personally (other than an application for an attachment of earnings order or a judgment summons unless allowed under Order 27, rule 9(1)(a), or Order 28, rule 10(2)(a)(i)), including copy and preparation of certificate of service — £8.50

5. For service by an alternative method, including attendances, making appointments to serve claim forms, preparing and attending to swear and file affidavits and to obtain order, and the fees paid for oaths — £25.00

6. For each attendance on the hearing of an application for an attachment of earnings order of a judgment summons where costs are allowed under Order 27, rule 9, or Order 28, rule 10 — £8.50

7. For the costs of the judgment creditor when allowed in garnishee proceedings or an application under Order 30, rule 12:

    (a) where the money recovered is less than £70.00 — one half of the amount recovered

    (b) where the money recovered is not less than £70.00 — £46.50

8. For the costs of the judgment creditor when allowed on an application for a charging order — £71.00

9. For obtaining a certificate of judgment where costs allowed under Order 35, rule 5(3)(d) — £8.00

10. Where an order for possession is made under rule 6 or rule 6A of Order 49 [Part II of CPR Part 55 (Possession claims)] without the attendance of the claimant, for preparing and filing the application, the documents attached to the application and the request for possession — £79.50

11. On examination of a witness under CCR Order 25,   £15.00
rule 3 where any responsible representative of the
solicitor attends, for each half-hour or part thereof

[25.22]

Notes: Paragraphs 7, 8, 11 above were revoked by SI 2001/4015, r 42(c) with effect from 25 March 2002: see SI 2001/4015, r 1(c).

In paragraph 10 in column 2, the words 'Section II of CPR Part 55 (Possession claims)' in square brackets were substituted by SI 2001/256, r 29 with effect from 15 October 2001 (except in relation to claim forms issued before that date): see SI 2001/256, rr 1(d), 31.

Schedules 1 and 2 to the Civil Procedure Rules set out with modification certain provisions previously contained in the Rules of the Supreme Court 1965 and the County Court Rules 1981. The schedules preserve certain fixed costs provisions not covered by Part 45, they are set out above.

CHANCERY AND QUEEN'S BENCH DIVISIONS

[25.23]

On 1 May 2003, the Chief Chancery Master and the Senior Queen's Bench Master approved a table of fixed costs replacing the table approved on 1 November 2000. It contains nothing new, but it is a convenient compilation of CPR Part 45 and Schedule 1 to Part 50 of the CPR (RSC Order 62) and the Supreme Court Fees Order 1999. It came into operation on 1 April 2003. There is no VAT addition to this table of costs. The table sets out the amounts which, unless the court orders otherwise, are to be allowed in respect of solicitors' charges together with the court fee, where appropriate. Here it is:

[25.24]

**HIGH COURT OF JUSTICE
CHANCERY AND QUEEN'S DIVISIONS**

A. Fixed commencement costs on claim form

The following apply to all claim forms for a specified sum of money only Where the claim form is served by the court or by any other method other than personal service by the claimant and:	
the sum claimed exceeds £15,000 but does not exceed £50,000	£400.00
the sum claimed exceeds £50,000 but does not exceed £100,000	£700.00
the sum claimed exceeds £100,000 but does not exceed £150,000	£800.00
the sum claimed exceeds £150,000	£900.00

Where the claim form is served personally by the claimant and where there is more than one defendant and:	
the sum claimed exceeds £15,000 but does not exceed £50,000	£510.00
the sum claimed exceeds £50,000 but does not exceed £100,000	£710.00
the sum claimed exceeds £100,000 but does not exceed £150,000	£810.00
the sum claimed exceeds £150,000	£910.00
(the fee is included in the above figures)	
Additional costs	
Where the claim form is served personally by the claimant and where there is more than one defendant, for each additional defendant personally served at separate addresses by the claimant	£15.00
For service by a party of any document required to be served personally including preparing and copying a certificate of service for each individual served	£15.00*
Where service by an alternative method is permitted by an order under rule 6.8 for each individual served	£25.00*
Where a document is served out of the jurisdiction:	
(a) in Scotland, Northern Ireland, the Isle of Man or in the Channel Islands	£65.00*
(b) in any other place	£75.00*
* Add application fee if appropriate	

[25.25]

B. Fixed costs on entry of judgment

The following are to be added to the fixed commencement costs	
Where judgment in default of an acknowledgment of service is entered under rule 12.4(1) (entry of judgment by request on claim for money only)	£30.00
Where judgment in default of a defence is entered under rule 12.4(1) (entry of judgment by request on claim for money only)	£35.00
Where judgment is entered under rule 14.4 (judgment on admission of part of claim) and claimant accepts the defendant's proposal as to the manner of payment	£55.00
Where judgment is entered under rule 14.4 (judgment on admission) or rule 14.5 (judgment on admission on part of a claim) and court decides the dates or times of payment	£70.00
Where summary judgment is given under Part 24 or the court strikes out a defence under rule 3.4(2)(a), in either case, on application by a party	£270.00

[25.26]

C. Costs on judgment without trial for possession of land

This section does not apply where the claimant is also entitled under the judgment to damages to be assessed, or where the plaintiff claims any remedy of the nature specified in Order 88 rule 1 (mortgage claims)

Where the claim is for the possession of land, and the claimant obtains judgment under CPR Part 12 (default judgment) under CPR Part 24 (summary judgment) for possession of land and costs

£143.75 together with any court fee and additional costs (see Table below) where appropriate

Additional costs

Where there is more than one defendant, in respect of each defendant served	£13.75
Where service by an alternative method is ordered and effected, in respect of each defendant served	£53.25*
Where service out of the jurisdiction is ordered and effected, in the case of service—	
(a) in Scotland, Northern Ireland, the Isle of Man or the Channel Islands	£68.25*
(b) in any other place out of the jurisdiction	£77.00*
In the case of default judgment under CPR Part 12 or summary judgment under CPR Part 12 or summary judgment under CPR Part 24 the claimant makes an affidavit of service for the purpose of a judgment where the defendant failed to respond to the claim form (the allowance to include the search fee)	£20.50
In the case of summary judgment under CPR Part 24 where an affidavit of service of the summons is required	£20.50
In the case of summary judgment under CPR Part 24 for each adjournment of the application	£20.50

*   Add application fee if appropriate

[25.27]

D. Enforcement costs

The following apply only where an amount in respect of solicitor's charges has been entered on the claim form under CPR Part 45 (see sections A and B above) or Schedule I (RSC O62) (see section C above).

Scottish and Northern Ireland money judgments

Where a certificate in respect of money provisions contained in a judgment is registered in the High Court in the Register of United Kingdom judgments under Schedule 6 to the Civil Jurisdiction and Judgments Act 1982

Costs of registration	£39.00

Recovery of Award

For an application under rule 70.5(4) that an award may be enforced as if payable under a court order, where the amount outstanding under the award:

exceeds £25 but does not exceed £250	£30.75
exceeds £250 but does not exceed £600	£41.00
exceeds £600 but does not exceed £2,000	£69.50
exceeds £2,000	£75.50

Orders to obtain information

On attendance to question a judgment debtor (or officer of a company or other organisation) who has been ordered to attend court under rule 71.2 where the questioning takes place before a court officer, including attendance by a responsible representative of the solicitor

For each half hour or part, £15.00 (when the questioning takes place before a judge, he may summarily assess any costs allowed) plus fee of £40.00

Third party Debt Orders and Money in Court to credit of Judgment Debtor

On the making of a final third party debt order under rule 72.8(6)(a) or an order for the payment to the Judgment creditor of money in court under rule 72.10(1)(b):

If the amount recovered is less than £150	one half of the amount recovered plus fee of £50
Otherwise (including fee)	£148.50

Charging Order

On the making of a final charging order under	£160.00. The court may also
Rule 73.8(2)(a)	allow reasonable disbursements in respect of search fees and the registration of the order.

Writ of possession

Where leave is given under Order 45 rule 3 to enforce a judgment or order for the possession of land by writ of possession of land by writ of possession, if the costs are allowed on the judgment or order there shall be allowed the following costs, which shall be added to the judgment or order—

Basic costs (including fee)	£72.50
Where notice of the proceedings has been given to more than one person, in respect of each additional person	£2.75

Writ of execution

Where a writ of execution within the meaning of Order 46 rule 1 is issued against any party, there shall be allowed—

Costs of issuing execution (including fee)	£81.75

CHAPTER 26

SMALL CLAIMS TRACK

[26.1]

CPR Rule 26.6 provides that general claims for not more than £5,000, claims for damages for personal injuries of not more than £1,000 and certain claims made by tenants against landlords shall be allocated to the small claims track. 'Damages for personal injuries' are defined as meaning damages claimed as compensation for pain, suffering and loss of amenity and does not include any other damages which are claimed.

Rule 27.14 and its supplementary Practice Direction provide:

[26.2]

CPR Rule 27.14: Costs on the small claims track

(1)   This rule applies to any case which has been allocated to the small claims track unless paragraph (5) applies.

(Rules 44.9 and 44.11 make provision in relation to orders for costs made before a claim has been allocated to the small claims track)

(2)   The court may not order a party to pay a sum to another party in respect of that other party's costs, fees and expenses, including those relating to an appeal, except–

- (a)   the fixed costs attributable to issuing the claim which–
  - (i)   are payable under Part 45; or
  - (ii)   would be payable under Part 45 if that Part applied to the claim;
- (b)   in proceedings which included a claim for an injunction or an order for specific performance a sum not exceeding the amount specified in Practice Direction 27 for legal advice and assistance relating to that claim;
- (c)   any court fees paid by that other party;
- (d)   expenses which a party or witness has reasonably incurred in travelling to and from a hearing or in staying away from home for the purposes of attending a hearing;
- (e)   a sum not exceeding the amount specified in Practice Direction 27 for any loss of earnings or loss of leave by a party or witness due to attending a hearing or to staying away from home for the purposes of attending a hearing;
- (f)   a sum not exceeding the amount specified in Practice Direction 27 for an expert's fees;
- (g)   such further costs as the court may assess by the summary procedure and order to be paid by a party who has behaved unreasonably; and
- (h)   the Stage 1 and, where relevant, the Stage 2 fixed costs in rule 45.29 where:
  - (i)   the claim was within the scope of the Pre-Action Protocol for Low Value Personal Injury Claims in Road Traffic Accidents ("the RTA Protocol");

(ii) the claimant reasonably believed that the claim was valued at more than the small claims track limit in accordance with paragraph 4.1(4) of the RTA Protocol; and

(iii) the defendant admitted liability under the process set out in the RTA Protocol; but

(iv) the defendant did not pay those Stage 1 and, where relevant, Stage 2 fixed costs.

(2A) A party's rejection of an offer in settlement will not of itself constitute unreasonable behaviour under paragraph (2)(d) but the court may take it into consideration when it is applying the unreasonableness test.

(3) The court may also order a party to pay all or part of—

(a) any court fees paid by another party;

(b) expenses which a party or witness has reasonably incurred in travelling to and from a hearing or in staying away from home for the purposes of attending a hearing;

(c) a sum not exceeding the amount specified in the relevant practice direction for any loss of earnings or loss of leave by a party or witness due to attending a hearing or to staying away from home for the purpose of attending a hearing; and

(d) a sum not exceeding the amount specified in the relevant practice direction for an expert's fees.

(4) The limits on costs imposed by this rule also apply to any fee or reward for acting on behalf of a party to the proceedings charged by a person exercising a right of audience by virtue of an order under section 11 of the Courts and Legal Services Act 1990 (a lay representative).

(5) Where—

(a) the financial value of a claim exceeds the limit for the small claims track; but

(b) the claim has been allocated to the small claims track in accordance with rule 26.7(3),

the small claims track costs provisions will apply unless the parties agree that the fast track costs provisions are to apply.

(6) Where the parties agree that the fast track costs provisions are to apply, the claim will be treated for the purposes of costs as if it were proceeding on the fast track except that trial costs will be in the discretion of the court and will not exceed the amount set out for the value of claim in rule 46.2 (amount of fast track trial costs).

[26.3]

PRACTICE DIRECTION SUPPLEMENTING CPR PART 27

7.1 Attention is drawn to Rule 27.14 which contains provisions about the costs which may be ordered to be paid by one party to another.

7.2 The amount which a party may be ordered to pay under rule 27.14(2)(b) (for legal advice and assistance in claims including an injunction or specific performance) is a sum not exceeding £260.

7.3 The amounts which a party may be ordered to pay under rule 27.14(3)(c) (loss of earnings) and (d) (expert's fees) are:

(1) for the loss of earnings of each party or witness due to attending a hearing or staying away from home for the purpose of attending a hearing, a sum not exceeding £50 per day for each person, and

(2)   *for expert's fees, a sum not exceeding £200 for each expert.*

(As to recovery of pre-allocation costs in a case in which an admission by the defendant has reduced the amount in dispute to a figure below £5,000, reference should be made to paragraph 7.4 of the Practice Direction supplementing CPR Part 26 and to paragraph 5.1(3) of the Costs Directions relating to CPR Part 44)

[26.4]

Rule 27.14 refers to Rules 44.9 and 44.11. Here is Rule 44.9 with its supplementary Practice Direction:

[26.5]

CPR Rule 44.9: Costs on the small claims track and fast track
(1)   Part 27 (Small claims) and Part 46 (Fast track trial costs) contain special rules about—
(a)   liability for costs;
(b)   the amount of costs which the court may award; and
(c)   the procedure for assessing costs.
(2)   Once a claim is allocated to a particular track, those special rules shall apply to the period before, as well as after, allocation except where the court or a practice direction provides otherwise.

[26.6]

CPD Section 15 Costs on the small claims track and fast track: Rule 44.9
15.1
(1)   *Before a claim is allocated to one of those tracks the court is not restricted by any of the special rules that apply to that track.*
(2)   *Where a claim has been allocated to one of those tracks, the special rules which relate to that track will apply to work done before as well as after allocation save to the extent (if any) that an order for costs in respect of that work was made before allocation.*
(3)
(i)   *This paragraph applies where a claim, issued for a sum in excess of the normal financial scope of the small claims track, is allocated to that track only because an admission of part of the claim by the defendant reduces the amount in dispute to a sum within the normal scope of that track.*
       (See also paragraph 7.4 of Practice Direction 26)
(ii)   *On entering judgment for the admitted part before allocation of the balance of the claim the court may allow costs in respect of the proceedings down to that date.*

In *Lee v Birmingham City Council* [2008] EWCA Civ 891, [2008] NLJR 1180, [2008] All ER (D) 423 (Jul) the secure tenant's solicitors had sent to the local authority a letter of claim in respect of disrepair, invoking the Pre-action Protocol for Housing Disrepair Cases. Most of the repairs were carried out and the council offered a global sum for damages and costs. It was agreed any action would have been allocated to the small claims track as it was for less than £5,000 and there was no claim for specific performance. However since the promulgation of the protocol, it was no longer the position that a claim was only made when litigation was begun. The protocol included a warning that there was likely to be a costs penalty if a claim was not first pursued in accordance with its terms. This clearly demonstrated that its object was to achieve settlement of disrepair claims without recourse to litigation. If the effect of the claim was to get the work done, then providing that the landlord was liable for the disrepair, the tenant should recover the reasonable cost of achieving that result. Under CPR Rule 44.11, pre-allocation costs orders were unaffected by allocation. The court's powers were unrestricted in relation to pre-allocation costs. It was perfectly proper to make an order in relation to them under Rule 44.9(2) if to do so was necessary to ensure that the protocol did not operate to prevent recovery of cost reasonably incurred in achieving the repair. The tenant was entitled to an order for the costs of the protocol period up to the date the repair work was done on the fast track basis. Nicholas Bacon suggests the case may well have wider implication in respect of claims for costs arising out of the protocol period where the 'loser' refuses to pay cost to the 'winner' and where proceedings are not in fact issued.

[26.7]

Rule 44.11 refers to costs following allocation and reallocation. Here it is with its Practice Direction:

[26.8]

CPR Rule 44.11: Costs following allocation and re-allocation
(1)   Any costs orders made before a claim is allocated will not be affected by allocation.
(2)   Where—
    (a)   a claim is allocated to a track; and
    (b)   the court subsequently re-allocates that claim to a different track,
then unless the court orders otherwise, any special rules about costs applying—
        (i)   to the first track, will apply to the claim up to the date of re-allocation; and
        (ii)   to the second track, will apply from the date of re-allocation.
(Part 26 deals with the allocation and re-allocation of claims between tracks)

[26.9]

Section 16: Practice Direction Supplementing CPR Rule 44.11

16.1 *This paragraph applies where the court is about to make an order to re-allocate a claim from the small claims track to another track.*
16.2 *Before making the order to re-allocate the claim, the court must decide whether any party is to pay costs to any other party down to the date of the order to re-allocate in accordance with the rules about costs contained in Part 27 (The Small Claims Track).*
16.3 *If it decides to make such an order about costs, the court will make a summary assessment of those costs in accordance with that Part.*

ALLOCATION

[26.10]

The restrictions on costs recoverable apply only to cases which have been allocated to the small claims track. There is no automatic allocation of a case to the small claims track, and although Rule 44.9(2) provides that the limitation on costs applies both before and after the matter has been allocated to the small claims track, Rule 44.11(1) provides that if a party obtains an order for costs before a claim has been allocated to a track that order will not be affected by subsequent allocation to the small claims track. Accordingly if either party makes an application for summary judgment prior to allocation, the court may make an order awarding the costs of the application to one of the parties. Where the parties consent to a case being allocated to the small claims track even though it exceeds the limit for that track, the costs restrictions do not apply and are replaced by the rules applying to the fast track contained in Part 46 (see Chapter 27). These provisions have a number of practical consequences. It would be a mistake for anyone, litigant in person or not, to commence a claim within the jurisdiction of the Small Claims Track (£5,000, unless personal injury or against a landlord for disrepair) to assume they were immune against being ordered to pay any of the other party's costs. They are not. If the defendant applies for summary judgment the application will be heard before allocation. If the defendant's application succeeds he may expect to obtain an order for his costs, both in the application and of the action. Even in cases where the claimant realises that his claim is misconceived at an early stage, or the court of its own initiative strikes it out before allocation, the defendant is not precluded from claiming the costs he has incurred. The message to defendants of no-hope Small Claims Track claims is therefore to ensure that any application for summary judgment or other relief is made before allocation.

Is this what the Woolf Reforms intended? If not, the remedy would appear to be a rule requiring a case to be allocated to the Small Claims Track before it is dismissed either on application or on the court's own initiative, or before an order for costs has been made.

NOT CONCLUSIVE

[26.11]

In *Voice and Script International Ltd v Alghafar* [2003] EWCA Civ 736, [2003] All ER (D) 86 (May) default judgment was entered for £9,140. On the hearing of an application to set aside the judgment the claimant's solicitors apologised for what they described as 'an element of double entry' which reduced the claim to £5,320. During the course of examining the documents produced by the claimant the defendant discovered that an item for $3,850 had been shown as £3,850. This resulted in a further reduction of the claim to £4,002. On any view, that represented the fullest possible value of the claim. When the defendant, acting in person, pointed out that this amount came 'under the small claims' the district judge rejected any such point in the very brief observation 'No, because it was never allocated to a track because a judgment was entered'. By treating the absence of allocation to a track as conclusive, the district judge misdirected himself. The omission may have meant that the small claims costs regime did not follow as a virtually automatic starting point, but it did not preclude the court even from considering whether it would be reasonable to make an assessment consistent with the small claims costs regime or, for that matter, to apply the regime to a claim which should never have exceeded and never was anything more than a small claim. If that approach is not expressly stated in the CPR, it follows from two essential principles: first, the discretionary nature of costs orders and, second, the overriding requirement of proportionality in civil litigation generally, and also as an essential ingredient for consideration when any question of costs arises. In the absence of any specific factors suggesting otherwise, in a case like this where, if sought, an allocation would have been made to the small claims track, the normal rule should be that the small claims costs regime for costs should apply.

[26.12]

Sometimes there may be a claim which exceeds the financial limit for the small claims track but which may be factually straightforward and which the parties agree should nonetheless proceed on the small claims track. When this happens the claim will be treated, for the purposes of costs, as if it were proceeding on the fast track. The court is given discretion in respect of the trial costs but they may not exceed the relevant amount of fast track trial costs.

[26.13]

Both the small claims track and the fast track have their own costs rules but those special rules do not apply until a claim is allocated to a particular track. Before allocation the court is not restricted by any of the special rules. Once the claim has been allocated any special rules will apply to work done before allocation as well as that done after it. If, however, the court has made an order for costs in respect of work before allocation (and assessed the costs) the special rules will not affect that order.

[26.14]

The Rule Committee, in considering how to deal with costs before and after allocation, were aware that a defendant might make an admission of part of a claim, thereby reducing the amount in dispute to a lower track. It was recognised that this could operate unfairly and the Practice Direction therefore provides that, where judgment is entered for the admitted part of the claim before allocation, the court may allow costs in respect of the proceedings down to that date, ie, without being restricted by any special rules.

COSTS RECOVERABLE

[26.15]

The only costs recoverable are:

(a) fixed costs attributable to issuing the claim;
(b) in proceedings which include a claim for an injunction or an order for specific performance, the cost of obtaining legal advice and assistance relating to the claim not exceeding £260;
(c) loss of earnings by a party or witnesses due to attending a hearing or to staying away from home for the purpose of attending a hearing not exceeding £50 per day for each person;
(d) experts' fees not exceeding £200 each;
(e) all court fees; and
(f) costs to be summarily assessed against a party who has behaved unreasonably.

What is unreasonable conduct must depend upon each case and little help is to be gained from the authorities prior to 26 April 1999. It has been held that abandoning a defence at the last minute was unreasonable, as was the fabrication of an untruthful defence or a gross overstatement of the amount of damages claimed.

COSTS LIMITATION IN APPEALS AND TRANSFERS

[26.16]

Until 6 October 2006 the costs restriction in rule 27.14 did not apply to appeals where liability for costs was potentially unlimited. The risk of having to pay the costs of an appeal against any judgment they obtained could have deterred potential litigants and therefore paragraph (6) was amended to extend the costs restriction to appeals. The same potential difficulty arises when the claim is transferred to the fast track (where fixed costs apply) or the multi-track (where costs are unlimited). In those circumstances the costs of the higher track will apply. This open exposure to costs is a potential disincentive to bringing or pursuing a claim, particularly where a litigant brings an action against a large corporation, which is legally represented, and whose eventual costs might exceed the value of the claim. This is incompatible with the overall concept of the small claims track, which is designed to provide a simple and informal way of resolving disputes; nor is it likely to be proportionate. Although the exemption of appeals from the restriction has been implemented the proposal that either a costs cap of £1,000 be imposed on transfers from small claims or that the small claims costs protection be extended to them has not

PERSONAL INJURY CLAIMS

[26.17]

A debate raged over whether or not the small claims limit for personal injury claims should be raised, and, if so, to what amount. At one stage the proposed figure was £5,000; by March 2005 the Lord Chancellor was of the view that 'the factors point to not raising the limit' and then, to add to the confusion, he announced in November 2005: 'Let me be clear about one thing – the present system cannot continue.' Matters were brought to a head in January 2006 by a report of the Constitutional Affairs Committee, an all-party committee of MPs, – *The Courts: Small Claims* – which recommended raising the small claims limit for PI claims to £2,500. The CAC denied that PI claims being subjected to the no-costs regime of the small claims track would impede access to justice or disadvantage litigants, and the Lord Chancellor contended that it would provide redress more efficiently and in a less adversarial manner. Their protagonists, lead by the Law Society, the Civil Justice Council and the Association of Personal Injury Lawyers, say the starting point for PI claims below £5,000 should remain at £1,000. Raising the threshold would undoubtedly impede access to justice for injured claimants who would be deprived of compensation if they could not recover the costs of being legally represented. They emphasise that evaluating the quantum of damage for personal injury is not to be equated with debt recovery. Personal injury cases usually involve complex issues of causation, liability and evidence and are too complex for most people to handle without help from a solicitor. Defendants will usually be represented by an insurance company receiving expert advice. Many claimants will not pursue the matter because the evidence is complex, and an insurance company may be pressuring them to drop a claim or settle.

To the surprise of many, a DCA (now the Ministry of Justice) report following a consultation paper, '*Case track limits and the claims process for personal injury claims*' concluded that the present limit of £1,000 should remain. It proposed that the small claims limit of £5,000 should remain for all other cases.

Lord Justice Jackson in the preliminary report to his Review of Civil Litigation Costs re-opened the debate by inviting submissions on addressing disproportionate costs in lower value personal injury claims. However in his Final Report he too thought the limit should not be reviewed and specifically made no recommendation for raising it.

CHAPTER 27

FAST TRACK

[27.1]

The fast track is the normal track for any claim exceeding £5,000 and not exceeding £25,000 (£15,000 before 6 April 2009), provided it is not likely to last for more than one day. Expert witnesses may be limited to one for each party in each field of expertise, there being not more than two such fields (CPR Rule 26.6).

SIMPLICITY

[27.2]

The fast track was one of the great innovations of the Woolf reforms. In the past the choice was between the informality and palm-tree justice of a small claims arbitration or the full Monty of the lengthy and expensive practice and procedure prescribed in both the Rules of the Supreme Court and the County Court Rules for all claims irrespective of their amount or subject matter. The idea of the fast track is to enable simple matters to be dealt with simply.

FIXED COSTS

(a) Pre-trial

[27.3]

Two basic tenets of the fast track were that hearings were to last no more than one day and the costs were to be fixed so that each party knew what costs it would have to pay if it lost and what costs it might recover if it won. The one-day hearing has happened – if we ignore the 'cheating' of split trials (the eminently sensible costs-saving practice, of, one day being allocated for deciding liability and another day for the quantification of damages if the case gets that far). Fixed fast track costs have not yet happened, except for fast track trials. That is unsurprising. The Access to Justice Report contained a suggested costs scale or matrix, taking into account the weight and complexity of the case and the stage it had reached, and it was met with almost universal condemnation. Various pilot schemes threw out widely-differing results, serving only to highlight the difficulty in obtaining the necessary data and translating it into a regime of fixed costs in respect of a practice and procedure yet to be implemented. The Lord Chancellor therefore postponed the introduction of fixed fast track pre-trial costs until the fast track had been running long enough for the amount of work involved in it to be ascertained and evaluated. The failure to implement this integral part of the Woolf reforms has been the worst track of all – the back track! The certainty of fixed costs was at the heart of Lord Woolf's proposals and, although the costs must of course be fixed at the right level and regularly reviewed, the giving of any discretion to the court would undermine the value of the regime by introducing the uncertainty they are intended to avoid – the costs would no longer be fixed and the dispute as to whether or not the discretion should be exercised would move the litigation from its subject matter to the costs. The primary objectives of fast track fixed costs should be certainty, simplicity and proportionality to the amount in dispute. Lord Justice Jackson and his panel of assessors were unanimously of the view that they should try to achieve a fixed costs system in all fast track cases, and in the Executive Summary of his Final Report he recommended:

'2.9 . . . that the costs recoverable for fast track personal injury cases be fixed. For other types of case I recommend that there be a dual system (at least for now), whereby costs are fixed for certain types of case, and in other cases there is a financial limit on costs recoverable (I propose that £12,000 be the limit for pre-trial costs). The ideal is for costs to be fixed in the fast track for all types of claim.

2.10 There are several advantages to the fixing of costs in lower value litigation. One is that it gives all parties certainty as to the costs they may recover if successful, or their exposure if unsuccessful. Secondly, fixing costs avoids the further process of costs assessment, or disputes over recoverable costs, which can in themselves generate further expense. Thirdly, it ensures that recoverable costs are proportionate. There is a public interest in making litigation costs in the fast track both proportionate and certain.

2.11 Costs Council. If a fixed costs regime is adopted for the fast track, the costs recoverable for the various types of claim will need to be reviewed regularly to make sure that they are reasonable and realistic. I propose that a Costs Council be established to undertake the role of reviewing fast track fixed costs, as well as other matters.'

(b) Trial

[27.4]

Uncertainty was not perceived to be an obstacle to introducing fixed costs for preparation for and the conduct of the final hearing, which would not be fundamentally altered by the CPR, and accordingly fast track trial fixed costs were introduced on 26 April 1999. Despite many forebodings and the fact that they have not been increased since that date, there has been little criticism of the fast track fixed costs.

Provision is made in CPR Part 46 as follows:

[27.5]

CPR PART 46: FAST TRACK TRIAL COSTS

CPR Rule 46.1: Scope of this Part
(1)   This Part deals with the amount of costs which the court may award as the costs of an advocate for preparing for and appearing at the trial of a claim in the fast track (referred to in this rule as 'fast track trial costs').
(2)   For the purposes of this Part—

(a)   'advocate' means a person exercising a right of audience as a representative of, or on behalf of, a party;

(b)   'fast track trial costs' means the costs of a party's advocate for preparing for and appearing at the trial, but does not include—

(i)   any other disbursements; or

(ii)   any value added tax payable on the fees of a party's advocate; and

(c)   'trial' includes a hearing where the court decides an amount of money or the value of goods following a judgment under Part 12 (default judgment) or Part 14 (admissions) but does not include—

(i)   the hearing of an application for summary judgment under Part 24; or

(ii)   the court's approval of a settlement or other compromise under rule 21.10.

(Part 21 deals with claims made by or on behalf of, or against, children and protected parties)

[27.6]

CPD Section 26 Scope of Part 46: Rule 46.1

26.1   *Part 46 applies to the costs of an advocate for preparing for and appearing at the trial of a claim in the fast track.*

26.2   *It applies only where, at the date of the trial, the claim is allocated to the fast track. It does not apply in any other case, irrespective of the final value of the claim.*

26.3   *In particular it does not apply to:*

(a)   *the hearing of a claim which is allocated to the small claims track with the consent of the parties given under rule 26.7(3); or*

(b)   *a disposal hearing at which the amount to be paid under a judgment or order is decided by the court (see paragraph 12.8 of the Practice Direction which supplements Part 26 (Case Management – Preliminary Stage)).*

[27.7]

Cases which settle before trial

26.4   *Attention is drawn to rule 44.10 (limitation on amount court may award where a claim allocated to the fast track settles before trial).*

[27.8]

CPR Rule 46.2: Amount of fast track trial costs

(1)   The following table shows the amount of fast track trial costs which the court may award (whether by summary or detailed assessment).

Value of the claim	Amount of fast track trial costs which the court may award
No more than £3,000	£485

Value of the claim	Amount of fast track trial costs which the court may award
More than £3,000 but not more than £10,000	£690
More than £10,000 but not more than £15,000	£1,035
For proceedings issued on or after 6th April 2009, more than £15,000	£1,650

    (2)   The court may not award more or less than the amount shown in the table except where—

        (a)   it decides not to award any fast track trial costs; or

        (b)   rule 46.3 applies;

but the court may apportion the amount awarded between the parties to reflect their respective degrees of success on the issues at trial.

[27.9]

Rule 46.2(3), (4), (5) and (6) are in para [27.14].

[27.10]

CPR Rule 46.3: Power to award more or less than the amount of fast track trial costs

(1)   This rule sets out when a court may award—

        (a)   an additional amount to the amount of fast track trial costs shown in the table in rule 46.2 (1); and

        (b)   less than those amounts.

(2)   If—

        (a)   in addition to the advocate, a party's legal representative attends the trial;

        (b)   the court considers that it was necessary for a legal representative to attend to assist the advocate; and

        (c)   the court awards fast track trial costs to that party,

the court may award an additional £345 in respect of the legal representative's attendance at the trial.

(Legal representative is defined in rule 2.3)

(2A)   The court may in addition award a sum representing an additional liability

(The requirements to provide information about a funding arrangement where a party wishes to recover any additional liability under a funding arrangement are set out in the Costs Practice Direction)

('Additional liability' is defined in rule 43.2)

(3)   If the court considers that it is necessary to direct a separate trial of an issue then the court may award an additional amount in respect of the separate trial but that amount is limited in accordance with paragraph (4) of this rule.

(4)   The additional amount the court may award under paragraph 2A must not exceed two-thirds of the amount payable for that claim, subject to a minimum award of £485.

(5)   Where the party to whom fast track trial costs are to be awarded is a litigant in person, the court will award—

        (a)   if the litigant in person can prove financial loss, two thirds of the amount that would otherwise be awarded; or

(b)   if the litigant in person fails to prove financial loss, an amount in respect of the time spent reasonably doing the work at the rate specified in the Costs Practice Direction.

(6)   Where a defendant has made a counterclaim against the claimant, and—

(a)   the claimant has succeeded on his claim; and

(b)   the defendant has succeeded on his counterclaim,

the court will quantify the amount of the award of fast track trial costs to which—

(i)   but for the counterclaim, the claimant would be entitled for succeeding on his claim; and

(ii)   but for the claim, the defendant would be entitled for succeeding on his counterclaim,

and make one award of the difference, if any, to the party entitled to the higher award of costs.

(7)   Where the court considers that the party to whom fast track trial costs are to be awarded has behaved unreasonably or improperly during the trial, it may award that party an amount less than would otherwise be payable for that claim, as it considers appropriate.

(8)   Where the court considers that the party who is to pay the fast track trial costs has behaved improperly during the trial the court may award such additional amount to the other party as it considers appropriate.

[27.11]

CPD Section 27 Power to award more or less than the amount of fast track trial costs: Rule 46.3

27.1   *Rule 44.15 (providing information about funding arrangements) sets out the requirement to provide information about funding arrangements to the court and other parties. Section 19 of this Practice Direction sets out the information to be provided and when this is to be done.*

27.2   *Section 11, of this Practice Direction explains how the court will approach the question of what sum to allow in respect of additional liability.*

27.3   *The court has the power, when considering whether a percentage increase is reasonable, to allow different percentages for different items of costs or for different periods during which costs were incurred.*

(See also Part 47.)

[27.12]

The amounts prescribed are those that the court must award – or as the rule somewhat quaintly puts it 'the court may not award more or less' than those amounts – except for the £345 increase where both an advocate and a legal representative are necessary and the minimum additional payment of £485 for a split trial. When is it necessary for a legal representative to attend? The guidance to Rule 11 of the Solicitors' Code of Conduct 2007 provides:

'8.   Whenever you instruct an advocate – whether counsel or a solicitor advocate – you will need to decide whether it is in the interests of your client and the interests of justice for you, or a responsible representative of your firm, to attend the proceedings. In reaching this decision you will need to consider what is necessary for the proper conduct of the case, taking into account the nature and complexity of the case and the capacity of the client to understand the proceedings. For example, you, or your representative, should normally attend:

(a) where the client is charged with an offence classified pursuant to section 75(2) of the Supreme Court Act 1981 as class 1 or 2 (such as murder, manslaughter or rape);
(b) in cases of complex or serious fraud;
(c) where the client may have difficulty in giving or receiving instructions or in understanding the proceedings, for example if the client is a child, has inadequate knowledge of English, or suffers from a mental illness or some other disability;
(d) where the client is likely to disrupt proceedings if the advocate appears alone;
(e) where the advocate is representing more than one party to the hearing;
(f) where there are a substantial number of defence documents at a trial;
(g) where there are a large number of witnesses in the case;
(h) on the day on which the client is to be sentenced, particularly where the client is likely to receive a custodial sentence; or
(i) where issues are likely to arise which question the client's character or your conduct of the case.

9. Where you decide that an advocate should not be attended you should inform the advocate and deliver a full and detailed brief sufficiently early for the advocate to consider the papers and to decide whether it would be appropriate for the advocate to attend alone. You should also inform the client that the advocate will be unattended and how instructions may be given.'

[27.13]

It is an anomaly that there is no restriction on the costs of an advocate appearing on an interim hearing on the fast track. Presumably, it was thought these would not happen on the fast track, but they do and brief fees are sometimes claimed in excess of the trial limit! Rule 46.3(6) specifically exempts from fast track trials the awarding of amounts to both the claimant and the defendant. This is done by deciding what the entitlement would be for succeeding on the claim or the counterclaim and taking one figure from the other and making an award for the difference to the party with the higher entitlement. The decision in *Medway Oil and Storage Co Ltd v Continental Contractors Ltd* [1929] AC 88, HL does not apply to fast track trial costs.

Unreasonable or improper behaviour may be penalised by either awarding one party less than would otherwise have been payable to it or the other party may be awarded an additional amount. It is important to appreciate that where a fast track trial is adjourned to another day the costs limitations in respect of fast track trial costs still apply, irrespective of the length of the trial, and accordingly no additional fast track trial costs can be awarded in respect of the adjournment.

[27.14]

CPR Rule 46.2: Valuing the claim for the purposes of quantifying fast track trial costs (continued from para [27.8])
(3) Where the only claim is for the payment of money—
    (a) for the purpose of quantifying fast track trial costs awarded to a claimant, the value of the claim is the total amount of the judgment excluding—
        (i) interest and costs; and
        (ii) any reduction made for contributory negligence;

(b)   for the purpose of quantifying fast track trial costs awarded to a defendant, the value of the claim is—

  (i)   the amount specified in the claim form (excluding interest and costs);

  (ii)   if no amount is specified, the maximum amount which the claimant reasonably expected to recover according to the statement of value included in the claim form under rule 16.3; or

  (iii)   more than £15,000, if the claim form states that the claimant cannot reasonably say how much is likely to be recovered.

(4)   Where the claim is only for a remedy other than the payment of money the value of the claim is deemed to be more than £3,000 but not more than £10,000, unless the court orders otherwise.

(5)   Where the claim includes both a claim for the payment of money and for a remedy other than the payment of money, the value of the claim is deemed to be the higher of—

(a)   the value of the money claim decided in accordance with paragraph (3); or

(b)   the deemed value of the other remedy decided in accordance with paragraph (4),

unless the court orders otherwise.

(6)   Where—

(a)   a defendant has made a counterclaim against the claimant;

(b)   the counterclaim has a higher value than the claim; and

(c)   the claimant succeeds at trial both on the claim and the counterclaim,

for the purpose of quantifying fast track trial costs awarded to the claimant, the value of the claim is the value of the defendant's counterclaim calculated in accordance with this rule.

[27.15]

If costs are awarded to the claimant, the value of the claim is the total amount of the judgment, excluding interest and costs and excluding any reduction for contributory negligence. If costs are awarded to the defendant, the value of the claim is the amount specified in the claim form excluding interest and costs or, if no amount is specified, the maximum amount according to the statement of value in the claim form. For non-money claims the value is to be taken as more than £3,000 but not more than £10,000 unless the court decides otherwise.

[27.16]

CPR Rule 46.4: Fast track trial costs where there is more than one claimant or defendant

(1)   Where the same advocate is acting for more than one party—

(a)   the court may make only one award in respect of fast track trial costs payable to that advocate; and

(b)   the parties for whom the advocate is acting are jointly entitled to any fast track trial costs awarded by the court.

(2)   Where—

(a)   the same advocate is acting for more than one claimant; and

(b)   each claimant has a separate claim against the defendant,

the value of the claim, for the purpose of quantifying the award in respect of fast track trial costs is to be ascertained in accordance with paragraph (3).

(3)   The value of the claim in the circumstances mentioned in paragraph (2) is—
    (a)   where the only claim of each claimant is for the payment of money—
        (i)   if the award of fast track trial costs is in favour of the claimants, the total amount of the judgment made in favour of all the claimants jointly represented; or
        (ii)   if the award is in favour of the defendant, the total amount claimed by the claimants,

and in either case, quantified in accordance with rule 46.2 (3);
    (b)   where the only claim of each claimant is for a remedy other than the payment of money, deemed to be more than £3,000 but not more than £10,000; and
    (c)   where claims of the claimants include both a claim for the payment of money and for a remedy other than the payment of money, deemed to be—
        (i)   more than £3,000 but not more than £10,000; or
        (ii)   if greater, the value of the money claims calculated in accordance with sub paragraph (a) above.

(4)   Where—
    (a)   there is more than one defendant; and
    (b)   any or all of the defendants are separately represented,
the court may award fast track trial costs to each party who is separately represented.

(5)   Where—
    (a)   there is more than one claimant; and
    (b)   a single defendant,
the court may make only one award to the defendant of fast track trial costs, for which the claimants are jointly and severally liable(GL).

For the purpose of quantifying the fast track trial costs awarded to the single defendant under paragraph (5), the value of the claim is to be calculated in accordance with paragraph (3) of this rule.

[27.17]

Where the same advocate is acting for more than one party there will be only one award of costs to be apportioned between the receiving parties. However, if defendants are separately represented the court may award costs to each defendant. The rule sets out how the value of a claim is to be ascertained where the same advocate is acting for more than one claimant and each claimant has a separate claim against the defendant.

[27.18]

CPR Rule 44.10: Limitation on amount court may allow where a claim allocated to the fast track settles before trial

(1)   Where the court—
    (a)   assesses costs in relation to a claim which—
        (i)   has been allocated to the fast track; and
        (ii)   settles before the start of the trial; and
    (b)   is considering the amount of costs to be allowed in respect of a party's advocate for preparing for the trial,

it may not allow, in respect of those advocate's costs, an amount that exceeds the amount of fast track trial costs which would have been payable in relation to the claim had the trial taken place.

(2)   When deciding the amount to be allowed in respect of the advocate's costs, the court shall have regard to—

(a)   when the claim was settled; and

(b)   when the court was notified that the claim had settled.

(3)   In this rule, 'advocate' and 'fast track trial costs' have the meanings given to them by Part 46.

(Part 46 sets out the amount of fast track trial costs which may be awarded)

[27.19]

Where a fast track case settles before the start of the trial the court will have to consider the amount of costs to be allowed in respect of the successful party's advocate for preparing for trial. The amount may not of course exceed the prescribed amount.

BENCHMARK COSTS

[27.20]

The name is new, the concept is not. For example, prior to 26 April 1999, many courts had a going rate for possession summonses which was the amount awarded by judges and accepted, usually without demur, by practitioners. In his Final Report, Lord Woolf said:

'there are, however, some multi-track proceedings in which further steps could be taken to assist the parties and the courts. These are proceedings which have a limited and fairly constant procedure. Here the court with the assistance of user groups and the information available to them (the SCCO), should over time be able to produce figures indicating a standard of guideline costs or a range of costs for a class of proceedings. An obvious candidate for this approach will be cases which did not substantially turn on issues of fact . . .   judicial review is . . .   a possible example. The steps taken in the majority of cases are standard.'

Although Lord Woolf there referred to multi-track, the same approach can be applied to the fast track pending the introduction of fixed costs, which are themselves a form of benchmark costs. The object of benchmark costs is to set a figure, or perhaps a bracket of figures, for the amount of costs normally awarded for particular kinds of cases or applications. This is the amount the receiving party may accept without further investigation or assessment, or which the receiving party may seek to have increased by summary or detailed assessment if he can justify it, or which the paying party could seek to have reduced. Some of the advantages of benchmark costs are the avoidance of the necessity of preparing a written statement of costs, the avoidance of summary assessments and getting away from a system of payment by reward based on the length of time spent rather than the skill and expertise with which the work was done. Provided that benchmark costs are a guide and are not simply fixed costs in Woolf's clothing, are of realistic amounts and revised regularly, then they are to be welcomed. They are a halfway-house between summary assessment and fixed costs. The SCCO prepared a preliminary paper on benchmark costs indicating various Queen's Bench Division and insolvency applications and proceedings which might be susceptible of benchmarking. The Family Division also undertook consultation. However there has been so much slippage of time and opposition both in principle and detail that the prospect of benchmarks has receded. The impetus is now with predictable costs.

PREDICTABLE COSTS

(a) Costs forum

[27.21]

When it became increasingly clear that problems in relation to costs were impeding the access to justice, spawning what the Master of the Rolls described as a cottage industry of costs, the Civil Justice Council held a Costs Forum in November 2001 which included representatives of the litigation and insurance industries. As well as supporting the abolition of the indemnity principle the Forum recommended the Council should initiate further work to try to make costs more certain, controlled and transparent, particularly on the fast track, using the description 'predictable' rather than 'fixed'.

As a result, a Civil Justice Council's Predictable Costs Working Party was set up which held its first meeting in June 2002, when everyone concerned with litigation costs was either present or represented.

The meeting underwent a surprising sea-change when it transpired that the majority of those attending were not so much concerned about pre-trial costs or even the recoverability of conditional fee agreement (CFA) success fees and after-the-event (ATE) premiums, as they were about pre-issue costs, which, it appears, constitute 95% of between-the-parties costs.

(b) Road Traffic Accidents (RTA)

(i)   Industrial agreement

[27.22]

In the days when I negotiated with the Lord Chancellor's Department on behalf of the Law Society, the government consulted and then decided (at least I hoped it was in that order), but costs are now so sensitive that the government facilitates negotiations between the two sides of the costs industry and is grateful for any agreement that emerges, however modest. The second Civil Justice Costs Forum, in December 2002, at which pre-issue costs were again perceived to be the major problem, in the end achieved more provisional agreement on predictable costs than at one stage seemed probable, although considerably less than at the outset some of us had hoped possible

(ii)   The scheme

[27.23]

There was general agreement that:

- A predictable costs model should cover RTA personal injury cases with a value above the small claims track up to the sum of £10,000 (including general and special damages and interest, but not VAT) settled without the issuing of proceedings.
- There should be regional variations, at least between London and outside London ('London weighting'), with an uplift applied to the total overall costs recovered. To qualify, the claimant must live or work in London and the solicitors practise in London as defined by the SCCO Guide.
- The receiving party should have the right to opt out ('the escape clause') of the predictable costs matrix by applying for an assessment under CPR Rule 14.22 (known as Part 8 applications), subject to two sanctions: if on assessment the receiving party is not awarded at least 20% more than the matrix figure, he will (i) not receive more than the matrix figure, and (ii) pay the costs of the Part 8 application.
- The base costs in the matrix should have index-linked annual increases.
- The scheme should be reviewed after two years, during which time it would be monitored and data collected from receivers, payers and, it was hoped, the Court Service.
- Solicitor and client costs would be unaffected.

(iii)   The figures

[27.24]

Considerable collation and analysis of data had been undertaken by two university economists, Paul Fenn and Neil Rickman, on the level of costs paid in respect of pre-issue settlements, but as their work had not been completed and further data was awaited, it was possible only to draw general conclusions rather than identify exact figures. Nonetheless, a sufficient pattern emerged for various models to be produced and discussed by the Forum with some confidence that they would be supported by the final report.

- There were provisional indications that there had been an increase in agreed pre-issue costs over the past 18 months of a staggering 50%, with an increase of some 15% to 25% in litigated costs over the same period.
- Profit costs appeared to increase with the damages by a ratio of some 20%, reducing to 15% for higher awards.
- CFA success fees would generally be 5%. This would be a simple additional payment within the scheme.
- ATE insurance premiums would not be included in the scheme.

(iv)   The new rule

[27.25]

The Civil Justice Council made recommendations to the Lord Chancellor based on the provisional agreement, which he approved and passed to the Civil

Procedure Rules Committee for implementation. The only alteration of substance was the reduction of the London weighting allowance to 12.5% from the 25% sought by the Association of Personal Injury Lawyers. It was introduced on 6 October 2003 by a new Section II to CPR Part 45.

[27.26]

II ROAD TRAFFIC ACCIDENTS – FIXED RECOVERABLE COSTS

CPR Rule 45.7: Scope and interpretation
(1)   This Section sets out the costs which are to be allowed in
    (a)   costs-only proceedings under the procedure set out in rule 44.12A; or
    (b)   proceedings for approval of a settlement or compromise under rule 21.21(2), in cases to which this Section applies.
(2)   This Section applies where—
    (a)   the dispute arises from a road traffic accident;
    (b)   the agreed damages include damages in respect of personal injury, damage to property, or both;
    (c)   the total value of the agreed damages does not exceed £10,000; and
    (d)   if a claim had been issued for the amount of the agreed damages, the small claims track would not have been the normal track for that claim.
(3)   This Section does not apply where the claimant is a litigant in person.
(Rule 2.3 defines 'personal injuries' as including any disease and any impairment of a person's physical or mental condition)
(Rule 26.6 provides for when the small claims track is the normal track)
(4)   In this Section—
    (a)   'road traffic accident' means an accident resulting in bodily injury to any person or damage to property caused by, or arising out of, the use of a motor vehicle on a road or other public place in England and Wales;
    (b)   'motor vehicle' means a mechanically propelled vehicle intended for use on roads; and
    (c)   'road' means any highway and any other road to which the public has access and includes bridges over which a road passes.

[27.27]

CPR Rule 45.8: Application of fixed recoverable costs
Subject to rule 45.12, the only costs which are to be allowed are—
    (a)   fixed recoverable costs calculated in accordance with rule 45.9;
    (b)   disbursements allowed in accordance with rule 45.10; and
    (c)   a success fee allowed in accordance with rule 45.11.
(Rule 45.12 provides for where a party issues a claim for more than the fixed recoverable costs).

[27.28]

CPR Rule 45.9: Amount of fixed recoverable costs
(1)   Subject to paragraphs (2) and (3), the amount of fixed recoverable costs is the total of—
    (a)   £800;
    (b)   20% of the damages agreed up to £5,000; and

      (c)   15% of the damages agreed between £5,000 and £10,000.

(2)   Where the claimant—

      (a)   lives or works in an area set out in the Costs Practice Direction; and

      (b)   instructs a solicitor or firm of solicitors who practise in that area,

the fixed recoverable costs shall include, in addition to the costs specified in paragraph (1), an amount equal to 12.5% of the costs allowable under that paragraph.

(3)   Where appropriate, value added tax (VAT) may be recovered in addition to the amount of fixed recoverable costs and any reference in this Section to fixed recoverable costs is a reference to those costs net of any such VAT.

[27.29]

CPR Rule 45.10: Disbursements

(1)   The court—

      (a)   may allow a claim for a disbursement of a type mentioned in paragraph (2); but

      (b)   must not allow a claim for any other type of disbursement.

(2)   The disbursements referred to in paragraph (1) are—

      (a)   the cost of obtaining—

            (i)   medical records;

            (ii)   a medical report;

            (iii)   a police report;

            (iv)   an engineer's report; or

            (v)   a search of the records of the Driver Vehicle Licensing Authority;

      (b)   the amount of an insurance premium or, where a membership organisation undertakes to meet liabilities incurred to pay the costs of other parties to proceedings, a sum not exceeding such additional amount of costs as would be allowed under section 30 in respect of provision made against the risk of having to meet such liabilities;

      (c)   where they are necessarily incurred by reason of one or more of the claimants being a child or protected party as defined in Part 21—

            (i)   fees payable for instructing counsel; or

            (ii)   court fees payable on an application to the court;

      (d)   any other disbursement that has arisen due to a particular feature of the dispute.

('insurance premium' is defined in rule 43.2)

[27.30]

CPR Rule 45.11: Success fee

(1)   A claimant may recover a success fee if he has entered into a funding arrangement of a type specified in rule 43.2(1)(k)(i).

(2)   The amount of the success fee shall be 12.5% of the fixed recoverable costs calculated in accordance with rule 45.9(1), disregarding any additional amount which may be included in the fixed recoverable costs by virtue of rule 45.9(2).

In *Kilby v Gawith* (2008) CA 19 May, (2008) Times, 13 June, the claimant issued costs proceedings and the defendant contended that the court had a discretion whether or not to allow a success fee and at what level. The defendant accepted that if a success fee were payable, the amount was fixed by

Part 45, but argued that the language of the rules was flexible enough to enable the court to disallow a success fee in principle if to allow it would be to allow the recovery of a cost unreasonably incurred. In this case the claimant had before-the-event insurance and therefore did not need a CFA with a success fee. The Court of Appeal held that the provision in CPR rule 45.11(2) that the amount of the success fee 'shall be' 12.5%, meant that where a success fee was recovered it had to be 12.5%. If the draftsman had intended there to be a discretion to grant a success fee he would not have fettered that discretion by specifying the amount. On its true construction the language of Part 45 Section II meant that there was no discretion to disallow the success fee where a CFA had been entered into. The purpose of the rules was to provide fixed levels of remuneration. The decision gave rise to much speculation that claimant's solicitors may now increase the profit costs by 12.5% by the simple expedient of entering into a CFA whether it is needed or not.

[27.31]

CPR Rule 45.12: Claims for an amount of costs exceeding fixed recoverable costs
(1)   The court will entertain a claim for an amount of costs (excluding any success fee or disbursements) greater than the fixed recoverable costs but only if it considers that there are exceptional circumstances making it appropriate to do so.
(2)   If the court considers such a claim appropriate, it may—
    (a)   assess the costs; or
    (b)   make an order for the costs to be assessed.
(3)   If the court does not consider the claim appropriate, it must make an order for fixed recoverable costs only.

[27.32]

CPR Rule 45.13: Failure to achieve costs greater than fixed recoverable costs
(1)   This rule applies where—
    (a)   costs are assessed in accordance with rule 45.12(2); and
    (b)   the court assesses the costs (excluding any VAT) as being an amount which is less than 20% greater than the amount of the fixed recoverable costs.
(2)   The court must order the defendant to pay to the claimant the lesser of—
    (a)   the fixed recoverable costs; and
    (b)   the assessed costs.

[27.33]

CPR Rule 45.14: Costs of the costs-only proceedings
Where—
    (a)   the court makes an order for fixed recoverable costs in accordance with rule 45.12(3); or
    (b)   rule 45.13 applies,

    the court must—
        (i)   make no award for the payment of the claimant's costs in bringing the proceedings under rule 44.12A; and

       (ii)   order that the claimant pay the defendant's costs of defending those proceedings.

[27.34]

III FIXED PERCENTAGE INCREASE IN ROAD TRAFFIC ACCIDENT CLAIMS
See Section VII.

[27.35]

IV FIXED PERCENTAGE INCREASE IN EMPLOYER'S LIABILITY CLAIMS
See Section VII.

[27.36]

V FIXED RECOVERABLE SUCCESS FEES IN EMPLOYER'S LIABILITY DISEASE CLAIMS
See Section VII.

LOW VALUE RTA CLAIMS

(a) Pre-Action Protocol for Low Value Personal Injury Claims in Road Traffic Accidents

[27.37]

The protocol describes the behaviour the court will normally expect of the parties prior to the start of proceedings where a claimant claims damages valued at no more than £10,000 as a result of a personal injury sustained in a road traffic accident. Its aim is to ensure that:

(1)   the defendant pays damages and costs without the need for proceedings;

(2)   damages are paid within a reasonable time; and

(3)   the claimant's legal representative receives the fixed costs at the end of each of the three stages in the protocol.

The protocol applies where:

(1)   a claim for damages arises from a road traffic accident occurring on or after 30th April 2010;

(2)   the claim includes damages in respect of personal injury;

(3)   the claimant values the claim at not more than £10,000 on a full liability basis including pecuniary losses but excluding interest ('the upper limit'); and

(4)   if proceedings were started the small claims track would not be the normal track for that claim.

A claim may include vehicle related damages but these are excluded for the purposes of valuing the claim

(b) Stage 1

(i) Claim Notification Form (CNF)

[27.38]

The claimant must complete and send a CNF to the defendant and his insurer.

(ii)   Response

[27.39]

The defendant must send to the claimant an electronic acknowledgment the next day after receipt of the CNF.

The defendant must respond within 15 days.

The claim will no longer continue under the protocol where the defendant:
(1)   makes an admission of liability but alleges contributory negligence (other than in relation to the claimant's admitted failure to wear a seat belt);
(2)   does not complete and send the CNF response;
(3)   does not admit liability; or
(4)   notifies the claimant that the defendant considers that:
    (a)   there is inadequate mandatory information in the CNF; or
    (b)   if proceedings were issued, the small claims track would be the normal track for that claim.

(iii)   Stage 1 Costs

[27.40]

Fixed recoverable costs of £400 are to be paid within a further 10 days at the end of Stage 1 where liability is admitted, (whether or not contributory negligence is alleged). Under a CFA a fixed 12.5% success fee will also applies.

(c) Stage 2

(i)   Medical Report

[27.41]

On receipt of an admission of liability the claimant's solicitor will obtain a medical report.

If the insurer having seen the medical report questions or denies causation the claim will leave the process.

(ii)   Agreement

[27.42]

The Claimant's solicitor is to prepare settlement pack within 15 days to which the defendant's Insurer must respond within 15 days in default of which the claim exits the Protocol.

The parties have a further 20 days for consideration and negotiation which may be extended by agreement.

Whether or not agreement is reached, Stage 2 ends.

(iii)   Stage 2 Costs

[27.43]

Fixed recoverable costs of £800 apply to all claims taken forward under this process from the beginning to the end of Stage 2. This attracts a 12.5% CFA success fee uplift, where the case settles.

(d) Stage 3

[27.44]

Where quantum has not been agreed it will be determined by the court.

(i)   Stage 3 Costs

[27.45]

CPR Part 36 applies to the final offers made by parties in the Stage 3 Settlement Pack to be submitted to court.

(ii)   Claimant

[27.46]

There are separate fixed recoverable costs for Stage 3 of the process for paper hearings (£250) and oral hearings (£500). There is a fixed CFA success fee of 100%, which will only apply where the claimant has won at a trial. Where an offer is made and settlement is reached between the issue of the claim and before the trial commences fixed recoverable costs of £250 will apply and there will be a fixed CFA success fee of 12.5%. The agreed damages and fixed costs should be paid within 10 days of settlement being reached.

(iii)   Defendant

[27.47]

The defendant's recoverable costs are fixed in Stage 3 only with £250 for paper hearings and £500 for an oral hearing. This provides certainty to the claimant solicitor advising a client on the merits of an offer and the risks of proceeding to Stage 3.

(e) Review

[27.48]

The Government agreed it is vital that the costs are fixed in an independent and transparent way and regularly reviewed and/or increased. The Advisory Committee on Civil Costs arrived at the prescribed figures after lengthy consultation with the relevant stakeholders to identify the processes that need to be followed, the level of fee earner that should carry out the work and the amount of time it should take. Although the figures agreed could result in a 33% reduction of costs in a maximum claim with a 53% reduction where quantum is agreed, the work has also been reduced and simplified and the costs paid without delay. There is also provision for two medical reports where appropriate and an additional £500 in cases involving a child. The Advisory Committee will also consider the arrangements for reviewing or increasing the fixed recoverable costs on a regular basis.

[27.49]

VI PRE-ACTION PROTOCOL FOR LOW VALUE PERSONAL INJURY CLAIMS IN ROAD TRAFFIC ACCIDENTS

CPR Rule 45.27: Scope and interpretation
(1)　This Section applies to claims that have been or should have been started under Part 8 in accordance with Practice Direction 8B ("the Stage 3 Procedure").
(2)　Where a party has not complied with the RTA Protocol rule 45.36 will apply.
(3)　"RTA Protocol" means the Pre-Action Protocol for Personal Injury Claims in Road Traffic Accidents.
(4)　A reference to "Claim Notification Form" is a reference to the form used in the RTA Protocol.

[27.50]

CPR Rule 45.28: Application of fixed costs, disbursements and success fee
The only costs allowed are—
　　(a)　　fixed costs in rule 45.29;
　　(b)　　disbursements in accordance with rule 45.30; and
　　(c)　　a success fee in accordance with rule 45.31.

[27.51]

CPR Rule 45.29: Amount of fixed costs
(1)　Subject to paragraph (4), the amount of fixed costs is set out in Table 1.
(2)　In Table 1—
　　(a)　　"Type A fixed costs" means the legal representative's costs;
　　(b)　　"Type B fixed costs" means the advocate's costs; and
　　(c)　　"Type C fixed costs" means the costs for the advice on the amount of damages where the claimant is a child.
(3)　Advocate has the same meaning as in rule 46.1(2)(a).
(4)　Subject to rule 45.36(2) the court will not award more or less than the amounts shown in Table 1.
(5)　Where the claimant—
　　(a)　　lives or works in an area set out in the Costs Practice Direction; and
　　(b)　　instructs a legal representative who practices in that area,
the fixed costs will include, in addition to the costs set out in Table 1, an amount equal to 12.5% of the Stage 1 and 2 and Stage 3 Type A fixed costs.
(6)　Where appropriate, value added tax (VAT) may be recovered in addition to the amount of fixed costs and any reference in this Section to fixed costs is a reference to those costs net of any such VAT.

TABLE 1—FIXED COSTS IN RELATION TO THE RTA PROTOCOL

Stage 1 fixed costs	£400
Stage 2 fixed costs	£800
Stage 3–	
Type A fixed costs	£250
Type B fixed costs	£250
Type C fixed costs	£150

[27.52]

CPR Rule 45.30: Disbursements

(1) The court—

　　(a) may allow a claim for a disbursement of a type mentioned in paragraph (2); but

　　(b) must not allow a claim for any other type of disbursement.

(2) The disbursements referred to in paragraph (1) are—

　　(a) the cost of obtaining—

　　　　(i) medical records;

　　　　(ii) a medical report or reports as provided for in the RTA Protocol;

　　　　(iii) an engineer's report;

　　　　(iv) a search of the records of the—

　　　　　　(aa) Driver Vehicle Licensing Authority;

　　　　　　(bb) Motor Insurance Database;

　　(b) the amount of the insurance premium or, where a membership organisation undertakes to meet liabilities incurred to pay the costs of other parties to proceedings, a sum not exceeding such additional amount of costs as would be allowed under section 30 of the Access to Justice Act 1999 in respect of provision made against the risk of having to meet such liabilities;

　　(c) court fees as a result of Part 21 being applicable;

　　(d) court fees payable where proceedings are started as a result of a limitation period that is about to expire;

　　(e) court fees in respect of the Stage 3 Procedure;

　　(f) any other disbursement that has arisen due to a particular feature of the dispute.

(Insurance premium is defined in rule 43.2(1)(m).)

(Membership organisation is defined in rule 43.2(1)(n).)

[27.53]

CPR Rule 45.31: Success fee

(1) A party who has entered into a funding arrangement of a type specified in rule 43.2(1)(k)(i) in respect of any element of the fixed costs in rule 45.29 may recover a success fee on that element of the fixed costs.

(2) A reference to a success fee in this Section is a reference to a success fee in accordance with paragraph (1).

(3) Where the court—

　　(a) determines the claim at a Stage 3 hearing or on the papers; and

      (b)   awards an amount of damages that is more than the defendant's RTA Protocol offer,

the amount of the claimant's success fee is—

      (i)   12.5% of the Stage 1 and 2 fixed costs; and

      (ii)   100% of the relevant Stage 3 fixed costs.

(RTA Protocol offer is defined in rule 36.17.)

(4)   Where the court—

      (a)   determines the claim at a Stage 3 hearing or on the papers; and

      (b)   awards an amount of damages that is equal to or less than the defendant's RTA Protocol offer,

the amount of the defendant's success fee is 100% of the relevant Stage 3 fixed costs.

(5)   Where the claimant is a child and the court—

      (a)   does not approve a settlement at a settlement hearing;

      (b)   determines the claim at a Stage 3 hearing; and

      (c)   awards an amount of damages that is more than the amount of the settlement considered by the court at the first settlement hearing;

the amount of the claimant's success fee is—

      (i)   12.5% of the Stage 1 and 2 fixed costs; and

      (ii)   100% of the relevant Stage 3 fixed costs.

(6)   Where paragraphs (3) to (5) do not apply the success fee is—

      (a)   12.5% of the Stage 1 and 2 fixed costs; and

      (b)   12.5% of the relevant Stage 3 fixed costs.

(7)   The amount of the success fee set out in paragraphs (3) to (6) will be calculated without regard to any additional amount which may be included in the fixed costs by virtue of rule 45.29(5).

[27.54]

CPR Rule 45.32: Where the claimant obtains judgment for an amount more than the defendant's RTA Protocol offer

(1)   Where rule 36.21(1)(b) or (c) applies, the court will order the defendant to pay—

      (a)   where not already paid by the defendant, the Stage 1 and 2 fixed costs;

      (b)   where the claim is determined—

            (i)   on the papers, Stage 3 Type A fixed costs;

            (ii)   at a Stage 3 hearing, Stage 3 Type A and B fixed costs; or

            (iii)   at a Stage 3 hearing and the claimant is a child, Type A, B and C fixed costs;

      (c)   disbursements allowed in accordance with rule 45.30; and

      (d)   a success fee in accordance with rule 45.31(3).

[27.55]

CPR Rule 45.33: Settlement at Stage 2 where the claimant is a child

(1)   This rule applies where—

      (a)   the claimant is a child;

      (b)   there is a settlement at Stage 2 of the RTA Protocol; and

      (c)   an application is made to the court to approve the settlement.

(2)   Where the court approves the settlement at a settlement hearing it will order the defendant to pay—

    (a)   the Stage 1 and 2 fixed costs;

    (b)   the Stage 3 Type A, B and C fixed costs;

    (c)   disbursements allowed in accordance with rule 45.30; and

    (d)   a success fee in accordance with rule 45.31(6).

(3)   Where the court does not approve the settlement at a settlement hearing it will order the defendant to pay the Stage 1 and 2 fixed costs.

(4)   Paragraphs (5) and (6) apply where the court does not approve the settlement at the first settlement hearing but does approve the settlement at a second settlement hearing.

(5)   At the second settlement hearing the court will order the defendant to pay—

    (a)   the Stage 3 Type A and C fixed costs for the first settlement hearing;

    (b)   disbursements allowed in accordance with rule 45.30;

    (c)   the Stage 3 Type B fixed costs for one of the hearings; and

    (d)   a success fee in accordance with rule 45.31(6) on the Stage 1 and 2 fixed costs and the Stage 3 Type A, B and C fixed costs.

(6)   The court in its discretion may also order—

    (a)   the defendant to pay—

        (i)   an additional amount of either or both the Stage 3—

            (aa)   Type A fixed costs;

            (bb)   Type B fixed costs; and

        (ii)   a success fee in accordance with rule 45.31(6) on the additional Stage 3 fixed costs in sub-paragraph (a)(i); or

    (b)   the claimant to pay an amount equivalent to either or both the Stage 3—

        (i)   Type A fixed costs;

        (ii)   Type B fixed costs.

[27.56]

CPR Rule 45.34: Settlement at Stage 3 where the claimant is a child

(1)   This rule applies where—

    (a)   the claimant is a child;

    (b)   there is a settlement after proceedings are started under the Stage 3 Procedure;

    (c)   the settlement is more than the defendant's RTA Protocol offer; and

    (d)   an application is made to the court to approve the settlement.

(2)   Where the court approves the settlement at the settlement hearing it will order the defendant to pay—

    (a)   the Stage 1 and 2 fixed costs;

    (b)   the Stage 3 Type A, B and C fixed costs;

    (c)   disbursements allowed in accordance with rule 45.30; and

    (d)   a success fee in accordance with rule 45.31(6).

(3)   Where the court does not approve the settlement at the settlement hearing it will order the defendant to pay the Stage 1 and 2 fixed costs.

(4)   Paragraphs (5) and (6) apply where the court does not approve the settlement at the first settlement hearing but does approve the settlement at the Stage 3 hearing.

(5)   At the Stage 3 hearing the court will order the defendant to pay—

    (a)   the Stage 3 Type A and C fixed costs for the settlement hearing;

    (b)   disbursements allowed in accordance with rule 45.30;

    (c)   the Stage 3 Type B fixed costs for one of the hearings; and

      (d)   a success fee in accordance with rule 45.31(6) on the Stage 1 and 2 fixed costs and the Stage 3 Type A, B and C fixed costs.

  (6)   The court in its discretion may also order—

      (a)   the defendant to pay—

          (i)   an additional amount of either or both the Stage 3—

             (aa)   Type A fixed costs;

             (bb)   Type B fixed costs; and

          (ii)   a success fee in accordance with rule 45.31(6) on the additional Stage 3 fixed costs in sub-paragraph (a)(i); or

      (b)   the claimant to pay an amount equivalent to either or both the Stage 3—

          (i)   Type A fixed costs;

          (ii)   Type B fixed costs.

  (7)   Where the settlement is not approved at the Stage 3 hearing the court will order the defendant to pay the Stage 3 Type A fixed costs.

[27.57]

CPR Rule 45.35: Where the court orders the claim is not suitable to be determined under the Stage 3 Procedure and the claimant is a child

Where—

      (a)   the claimant is a child; and

      (b)   at a settlement hearing or the Stage 3 hearing the court orders that the claim is not suitable to be determined under the Stage 3 Procedure,

the court will order the defendant to pay—

      (i)   the Stage 1 and 2 fixed costs;

      (ii)   the Stage 3 Type A, B and C fixed costs;

[27.58]

CPR Rule 45.36: Failure to comply or electing not to continue with the RTA Protocol—costs consequences

  (1)   This rule applies where the claimant—

      (a)   does not comply with the process set out in the RTA Protocol; or

      (b)   elects not to continue with that process,

and starts proceedings under Part 7.

  (2)   Where a judgment is given in favour of the claimant but—

      (a)   the court determines that the defendant did not proceed with the process set out in the RTA Protocol because the claimant provided insufficient information on the Claim Notification Form;

      (b)   the court considers that the claimant acted unreasonably—

          (i)   by discontinuing the process set out in the RTA Protocol and starting proceedings under Part 7;

         (ii)   by valuing the claim at more than £10,000, so that the claimant did not need to comply with the RTA Protocol; or

         (iii)   except for paragraph (2)(a), in any other way that caused the process in the RTA Protocol to be discontinued; or

      (c)   the claimant did not comply with the RTA Protocol at all despite the claim falling within the scope of the RTA Protocol;

the court may order the defendant to pay no more than the fixed costs in rule 45.29 together with the disbursements allowed in accordance with rule 45.30 and success fee in accordance with rule 45.31(3).

(3) Where the claimant starts proceedings under paragraph 7.22 of the RTA Protocol and the court orders the defendant to make an interim payment of no more than the interim payment made under paragraph 7.14(2) or (3) of that Protocol the court will, on the final determination of the proceedings, order the defendant to pay no more than—

    (a)   the Stage 1 and 2 fixed costs;

    (b)   the disbursements allowed in accordance with rule 45.30; and

    (c)   a success fee in accordance with rule 45.31(3).

[27.59]

CPR Rule 45.37: Where the parties have settled after proceedings have started

(1) This rule applies where an application is made under rule 44.12C (costs-only application after a claim is started under Part 8 in accordance with Practice Direction 8B).

(2) Where the settlement is more than the defendant's RTA Protocol offer the court will order the defendant to pay—

    (a)   the Stage 1 and 2 fixed costs where not already paid by the defendant;

    (b)   the Stage 3 Type A fixed costs;

    (c)   disbursements allowed in accordance with rule 45.30; and

    (d)   a success fee in accordance with rule 45.31(6).

(3) Where the settlement is less than or equal to the defendant's RTA Protocol offer the court will order the defendant to pay—

    (a)   the Stage 1 and 2 fixed costs where not already paid by the defendant;

    (b)   disbursements allowed in accordance with rule 45.30; and

    (c)   a success fee in accordance with rule 45.31(6).

(4) The court may, in its discretion, order either party to pay the costs of the application.

[27.60]

CPR Rule 45.38: Where the claimant obtains judgment for an amount equal to or less than the defendant's RTA Protocol offer

Where rule 36.21(1)(a) applies, the court will order the claimant to pay—

    (a)   where the claim is determined—

        (i)   on the papers, Stage 3 Type A fixed costs; or

        (ii)   at a hearing, Stage 3 Type A and B fixed costs;

    (b)   disbursements allowed in accordance with rule 45.30; and

    (c)   a success fee in accordance with rule 45.31(4).

[27.61]

Rule 45.39: Adjournment

Where the court adjourns a settlement hearing or a Stage 3 hearing it may, in its discretion, order a party to pay—

    (a)   an additional amount of the Stage 3 Type B fixed costs; and

    (b)   any court fee for that adjournment.

[27.62]

CPR Rule 45.40: Account of payment of Stage 1 fixed costs

Where a claim no longer continues under the RTA Protocol the court will, when making any order as to costs including an order for fixed recoverable costs under Section II of this Part, take into account the Stage 1 fixed costs together with any success fee on those costs that have been paid by the defendant.

OUTSOURCING

[27.63]

In *Woollard v Fowler* [2005] EWHC 90051 (Costs) the claimants had succeeded in their RTA claim and were entitled to fixed costs under Part II of CPR 45. Their solicitors had obtained medical reports and medical records through the agency of Mobile Doctors Limited. Were the solicitors entitled to recover the fees of MDL as a disbursement in addition to the fixed costs? Yes, held the Senior Costs Judge. The use of medical agencies has been widespread for a number of years. In cases outside the predictable costs regime the system had operated without undue difficulty, provided the fees claimed have been reasonable and proportionate. Those fees had, by general and established custom, been treated as disbursements. The advent of the predictable costs regime did not mean that the court's approach to such fees should alter, so that they are treated in a different way under the predictable costs regime. To hold otherwise would create the difficulty that until a case has been settled it would not be known whether or not the predictable costs regime would apply. The decision caused some consternation because treating outsourcing as a disbursement could drive a coach and horses through predictable costs. On this basis the solicitors could recover all their fixed costs leaving the paying party to pay someone else for doing work covered by the fixed costs.

The decision was appealed on a variety of grounds, but the hearing was stayed while the parties attempted mediation through the Civil Justice Council which, on 9 May 2007, resulted in 10 major insurance companies and eight major medical reporting agencies signing an agreement putting in place capped costs for obtaining medical reports in most personal injury cases under £15,000 in value. The agreement established upper limits on the amounts recoverable for medical reports where those reports are obtained from General Practitioners, Orthopaedic Consultants, and Accident and Emergency Consultants. Rates are specified for reports, obtaining medical records, and reviewing medical notes. The rates do not affect individual bilateral agreements between medical reporting organisations and liability insurers, who may agree figures different to those contained in this agreement. Separate rates were agreed for invoices that are paid promptly (within 90 days) and those where payment is delayed. The figures, including administrative charges made by medical reporting organisations, are:

	Rate A Paid within 90 days of receipt of the Applicable Invoice and Required Information	Rate B Paid after 90 days of receipt of the Applicable Invoice and Required Information
General practitioner Report - No notes	£195	£220
Review notes by General Practitioner	£50	£55
Orthopaedic Report - Including review of notes	£425	£465
Accident and Emergency report - Including review of notes	£375	£410
Addendum	Cost + £25	Cost + £30
Cost of obtaining each set of medical records	Cost charged by data provider + £25	Cost charged by data provider + £30

The agreement applied to existing claims, and will remain in force until 1 April 2009. Other liability insurers or medical report providers may also join the agreement.

Although mediation is to be commended it is disappointing to be deprived of a decision of the Court of Appeal on such an important and contentious issue, especially based on a judgment which was so at odds with all previous decisions at the same level. The decision of a costs judge is of no precedent value and the agreement reached is binding only on the parties to it and on any other insurers and providers who may subsequently subscribe to it. Nor does the agreement apply to reports other than medical reports or claims for damages exceeding £15,000. In the Solicitors Journal of 1 June 2007 Kerry Underwood accused the Court of Appeal of abdicating responsibility by allowing a stay for mediation resulting in what he described as a 'non-binding fudge between two different representatives of big business'. He cited the 'sunshine in litigation' principle in many states in the US, which precludes private settlements and litigation confidentiality clauses to prevent rich people and corporations buying off bad publicity.

Neither *Woollard v Fowler* nor this agreement affect the series of contrary decisions commencing with *Earle v Centrica* (Ipswich County Court Lawtel 5 October 2005) that solicitors should not seek to circumvent the restrictions on their profit costs by delegating matters that would normally be viewed as solicitors' work to third parties who could claim as disbursements that which the solicitor would normally have been expected to perform within the predictable fee structure. It is to be hoped the Rules Committee will not import the terms of this agreement into the Civil Procedure Rules without full consultation on this retrograde erosion of the certainty and predictability which are the purpose of fixed costs. The decision appears to have been seriously undermined by the decision in *Crane v Canons Leisure Centre* (see para [30.36]) that the work of independent costs draftsmen is solicitor's work and can be charged as such, including a success fee. Surely what is outsource for the goose is outsource for the gander?

(v) The Practice Direction

[27.64]

The new Rule was accompanied by the following new Section 25A of the Costs Practice Direction.

CPD Section 25A: Road traffic accidents: Fixed recoverable costs in costs-only proceedings

Scope

25A.1   *Section II of Part 45 ('the Section') provides for certain fixed costs to be recoverable between parties in respect of costs incurred in disputes which are settled prior to proceedings being issued. The Section applies to road traffic accident disputes as defined in rule 45.7(4)(a), where the accident which gave rise to the dispute occurred on or after 6th October 2003.*

25A.2   *The Section does not apply to disputes where the total agreed value of the damages is within the small claims limit or exceeds £10,000. Rule 26.8(2) sets out how the financial value of a claim is assessed for the purposes of allocation to track.*

25A.3   *Fixed recoverable costs are to be calculated by reference to the amount of agreed damages which are payable to the receiving party. In calculating the amount of these damages—*

(a)   *account must be taken of both general and special damages and interest;*

(b)   *any interim payments made must be included;*

(c)   *where the parties have agreed an element of contributory negligence, the amount of damages attributed to that negligence must be deducted;*

(d)   *any amount required by statute to be paid by the compensating party directly to a third party (such as sums paid by way of compensation recovery payments and National Health Service expenses) must not be included.*

25A.4   *The Section applies to cases which fall within the scope of the Uninsured Drivers Agreement dated 13 August 1999. The section does not apply to cases which fall within the scope of the Untraced Drivers Agreement dated 14 February 2003.*

[27.65]

Fixed recoverable costs formula

25A.5   *The amount of the fixed costs recoverable is calculated by totalling the following—*

(a)   *the sum of £800;*

(b)   *20% of the agreed damages up to £5,000; and*

(c)   *15% of the agreed damages between £5,000 and £10,000.*

For example, agreed damages of £7,523 would result in recoverable costs of £2178.45 i.e.

£800 + (20% of £5,000) + (15% of £2,523).

[27.66]

Additional costs for work in specified areas

25A.6   *The areas referred to in rules 45.9(2) and 45.29(5) are (within London) the county court districts of Barnet, Bow, Brentford, Central London, Clerkenwell, Edmonton, Ilford, Lambeth, Mayors and City of London, Romford, Shoreditch,*

Wandsworth, West London, Willesden and Woolwich and (outside London) the county court districts of Bromley, Croydon, Dartford, Gravesend and Uxbridge.

[27.67]

Multiple claimants

25A.7   *Where there is more than one potential claimant in relation to a dispute and two or more claimants instruct the same solicitor or firm of solicitors, the provisions of the section apply in respect of each claimant.*

[27.68]

Information to be included in the claim form

25A.8   *Costs only proceedings are commenced using the procedure set out in rule 44.12A. A claim form should be issued in accordance with Part 8. Where the claimant is claiming an amount of costs which exceed the amount of the fixed recoverable costs he must include on the claim form details of the exceptional circumstances which he considers justifies the additional costs.*

25A.9   *The claimant must also include on the claim form details of any disbursements or success fee he wishes to claim. The disbursements that may be claimed are set out in rule 45.10(1). If the disbursement falls within 45.10(2)(d) (disbursements that have arisen due to a particular feature of the dispute) the claimant must give details of the particular feature of the dispute and why he considers the disbursement to be necessary.*

[27.69]

Disbursements and success fee

25A.10   *If the parties agree the amount of the fixed recoverable costs and the only dispute is as to the payment of, or amount of, a disbursement or as to the amount of a success fee, then proceedings should be issued under rule 44.12A in the normal way and not by reference to Section II of Part 45.*

(vi) Agreed damages

[27.70]

What is the amount of the 'damages agreed' where the solicitors were instructed only in respect of general damages and a tiny claim for special damage, the cost of repairs and replacement car hire having been agreed between the insurers before the solicitors were instructed? The solicitors calculated their costs on the basis of the total amount of the agreed damages. 'Oh no you can't', said Judge Harris in the Oxford County Court in *Swatton v Smithurst* on 3 February 2005, 'You cannot use the predictable costs formula to obtain remuneration for work you have not been engaged to do and which you did not do'.

(vii) Ready reckoner

[27.71]

The costs agreement on which the fixed recoverable costs formula in Practice Direction 25A was based provides a useful ready reckoner:

Damages	Costs	Description
Up to £1,000	£1,000	£800 + 20% (of damages)
£2,000	£1,200	£800 + 20%
£3,000	£1,400	£800 + 20%
£4,000	£1,600	£800 + 20%
£5,000	£1,800	£800 + 20%
£6,000	£1,950	£800 + 20% to 5k, 15% thereafter
£7,000	£2,100	£800 + 20% to 5k, 15% thereafter
£8,000	£2,250	£800 + 20% to 5k, 15% thereafter
£9,000	£2,400	£800 + 20% to 5k, 15% thereafter
£10,000	£2,550	£800 + 20% to 5k, 15% thereafter

(c) Fixed success fees

[27.72]

The Civil Procedure (Amendment) Rules 2004 introduced a new Section III to CPR Part 45, with effect from 1 June 2004, implementing a further industrial agreement in respect of CFA fixed success fees in RTA cases commenced since 5 October 2003, where the predictable costs provisions do not apply. Conditional fee agreement fixed success fees were extended to the estimated 48,000 annual claims brought for accidents at work from 1 October 2004 by the Civil Procedure (Amendment No 2) Rules 2004 which introduced new CPR rules 45.20-45.22. A similarly structured agreement in respect of employers' liability disease CFA success fees was implemented on 3 October 2005. The rules incorporating these three agreements are in Chapter 42.

NO MEAT IN THE SANDWICH

[27.73]

Before there is predictability on the fast track, three further steps have to be taken. First, the Forum jibbed at extending the predictable costs matrix to £15,000, lest it should be thought to be lock-stepped to the fast track limit (now £25,000). But, surely, that is precisely what the Woolf reforms envisaged! Second, the question of the post-issue, pre-trial costs (described as the meat in the sandwich) remains to be addressed. These costs, surprisingly, were not seen as a problem; but only when they have been quantified (perhaps as a result of the Fenn and Rickman researches) will the objectives of predictability, control, and transparency have been achieved. And, finally, the matrix must be extended to cover all cases on the fast track. A substantial additional bonus would be the virtual elimination of the summary assessment of costs on the fast track. The euphoria and relief which has greeted this meatless sandwich should not obscure the fact that there is still a long way to go.

Lord Justice Jackson and his panel of assessors were unanimously of the view that they should try to achieve a fixed costs system in all fast track cases (see para [27.3]).

CHAPTER 28

MULTI-TRACK AND SUPREME COURT

[28.1]

The multi-track is the normal track for any claim for which the small claims track (see Chapter 26) or the fast track (see Chapter 27) is not the normal track (CPR Rule 26.6(6)). Although claims on the other two tracks will always be in a county court, claims on the multi-track may be in either the High Court or a county court. There are no specific costs rules relating only to the multi-track and therefore Parts 43, 44, 47 and 48 all apply.

The Civil Justice Council's recommendations are;

Recommendation 7

[28.2]

In multi track cases where the value exceeds £1 million, in all group actions and in other complex proceedings there should be a rebuttable presumption requiring the parties to present budgets, supervised by the Court at appropriate stages to ensure compliance with the proportionality provisions of the overriding objective of the CPR.

Recommendation 8

Where the parties have agreed or the court has approved an estimate or budget and/or cap, both the receiving party and the paying party should be entitled to apply for detailed assessment but only at a costs risk if a significant increase/reduction in the amount claimed is not achieved.

Recommendation 9

Benchmark Costs (see para [27.20])
In all multi track cases benchmark costs should be provided for pre-action protocol work.

THE SUPREME COURT

[28.3]

The Supreme Court has its own Practice Directions which replace the Civil, Criminal and Taxation Practice Directions and standing orders of the Appellate Committee of the House of Lords.

Part 7 of the Supreme Court Rules 2009 deals with costs and is accompanied by Practice Direction No 13. They are to be found at http://www.supremecourt.gov.uk/procedures/practice-directions.html.

Costs may be awarded on either the standard or the indemnity basis with the same definitions as in the CPR. There is provision for the paying party to file and serve points of dispute and for the receiving party to respond.

What is different?

[28.4]

Rule 47 provides that submissions as to costs will be made before judgment unless before the close of oral argument a party applies to defer making submissions until after judgment. The court could direct oral submissions immediately after judgment, or the simultaneous or sequential filing of written submissions or written submissions followed by oral submissions.

Under rule 49 either party may request a provisional assessment of costs by the Registrar. If either or both parties are dissatisfied with the provisional assessment the registrar will try to resolve it in correspondence. If that fails he will appoint an oral hearing before two costs officers, one of whom will be a SCCO master and the other an appointee of the President – probably the Registrar.

CHAPTER 29

SUMMARY ASSESSMENT

[29.1]

Since 26 April 1999, the general rule is that at the end of any trial of a case that is being dealt with on the fast track and at the conclusion of any other hearing which has lasted not more than one day, the court will make a summary assessment of the costs unless there is good reason not to do so. What is the authority for that proposition? There is nothing in the rules. You might have thought that something so revolutionary as summary assessment by the trial judge would have been in the rules. But it is not. It is in the Practice Direction supplementing CPR Rule 44.7.

Here are the rule and the Practice Direction:

[29.2]

CPR Rule 44.7: Procedure for assessing costs
Where the court orders a party to pay costs to another party (other than fixed costs) it may either—
  (a)   make a summary assessment of the costs; or
  (b)   order detailed assessment of the costs by a costs officer,
unless any rule, practice direction or other enactment provides otherwise.
(The costs practice direction sets out the factors which will affect the court's decision under this rule)

[29.3]

CPD SECTION 13: SUMMARY ASSESSMENT: GENERAL PROVISIONS

13.1   *Whenever a court makes an order about costs which does not provide for fixed costs to be paid the court should consider whether to make a summary assessment of costs.*

13.2   *The general rule is that the court should make a summary assessment of the costs:*
(1)   *at the conclusion of the trial of a case which has been dealt with on the fast track, in which case the order will deal with the costs of the whole claim, and*
(2)   *at the conclusion of any other hearing, which has lasted not more than one day, in which case the order will deal with the costs of the application or matter to which the hearing related. If this hearing disposes of the claim, the order may deal with the costs of the whole claim;*
(3)   *in hearings in the Court of Appeal to which Paragraph 14 of the Practice Direction supplementing Part 52 (Appeals) applies;*

unless there is good reason not to do so eg where the paying party shows substantial grounds for disputing the sum claimed for costs that cannot be dealt with summarily or there is insufficient time to carry out a summary assessment.

13.3   *The general rule in paragraph 13.2 does not apply to a mortgagee's costs incurred in mortgage possession proceedings or other proceedings relating to a* mortgage unless the mortgagee asks the court to make an order for his costs to be paid by another party. Paragraphs 50.3 and 50.4 deal in more detail with costs relating to mortgages.

13.4   Where an application has been made and the parties to the application agree an order by consent without any party attending, the parties should agree a figure for costs to be inserted in the consent order or agree that there should be no order for costs. If the parties cannot agree the costs position, attendance on the appointment will be necessary but, unless good reason can be shown for the failure to deal with costs as set out above, no costs will be allowed for that attendance.

(1)   It is the duty of the parties and their legal representatives to assist the judge in making a summary assessment of costs in any case to which paragraph 13.2 above applies, in accordance with the following paragraphs.

(2)   Each party who intends to claim costs must prepare a written statement of the costs he intends to claim showing separately in the form of a schedule:

(a)   the number of hours to be claimed,

(b)   the hourly rate to be claimed,

(c)   the grade of fee earner;

(d)   the amount and nature of any disbursement to be claimed, other than counsel's fee for appearing at the hearing,

(e)   the amount of solicitor's costs to be claimed for attending or appearing at the hearing,

(f)   the fees of counsel to be claimed in respect of the hearing, and

(g)   any value added tax (VAT) to be claimed on these amounts.

(3)   The statement of costs should follow as closely as possible Form N260 and must be signed by the party or his legal representative. Where a litigant is an assisted person or is a LSC funded client or is represented by a solicitor in the litigant's employment the statement of costs need not include the certificate appended at the end of Form N260.

(4)   The statement of costs must be filed at court and copies of it must be served on any party against whom an order for payment of those costs is intended to be sought. The statement of costs should be filed and the copies of it should be served as soon as possible and in any event not less than 24 hours before the date fixed for the hearing.

(5)   Where the litigant is or may be entitled to claim an additional liability the statement filed and served need not reveal the amount of that liability.

13.6   The failure by a party, without reasonable excuse, to comply with the foregoing paragraphs will be taken into account by the court in deciding what order to make about the costs of the claim, hearing or application, and about the costs of any further hearing or detailed assessment hearing that may be necessary as a result of that failure.

13.7   If the court makes a summary assessment of costs at the conclusion of proceedings the court will specify separately

(1)   the base costs, and if appropriate, the additional liability allowed as solicitor's charges, counsel's fees, other disbursements and any VAT; and

(2)   the amount which is awarded under Part 46 (Fast Track Trial Costs).

13.8   The court awarding costs cannot make an order for a summary assessment of costs by a costs officer. If a summary assessment of costs is appropriate but the court awarding costs is unable to do so on the day, the court must give directions as to a further hearing before the same judge.

13.9   The court will not make a summary assessment of the costs of a receiving party who is an assisted person or LSC funded client.

13.10   A summary assessment of costs payable by an assisted person or LSC funded client is not by itself a determination of that person's liability to pay those costs (as to which see rule 44.17 and paragraphs 21.1 to 23.17 of this Practice Direction).

(1)   *The court will not make a summary assessment of the costs of a receiving party who is a child or protected party within the meaning of Part 21 unless the solicitor acting for the child or protected party has waived the right to further costs (see paragraph 51.1 below).*

(2)   *The court may make a summary assessment of costs payable by a child or protected party.*

(1)   *Attention is drawn to rule 44.3A which prevents the court from making a summary assessment of an additional liability before the conclusion of the proceedings or the part of the proceedings to which the funding arrangement relates. Where this applies, the court should nonetheless make a summary assessment of the base costs of the hearing or application unless there is a good reason not to do so.*

(2)   *Where the court makes a summary assessment of the base costs all statements of costs and costs estimates put before the judge will be retained on the court file.*

13.13   *The court will not give its approval to disproportionate and unreasonable costs. Accordingly:*

(a)   *When the amount of the costs to be paid has been agreed between the parties the order for costs must state that the order is by consent.*

(b)   *If the judge is to make an order which is not by consent, the judge will, so far as possible, ensure that the final figure is not disproportionate and/or unreasonable having regard to Part 1 of the CPR. The judge will retain this responsibility notwithstanding the absence of challenge to individual items in the make-up of the figure sought. The fact that the paying party is not disputing the amount of costs can however be taken as some indication that the amount is proportionate and reasonable. The judge will therefore intervene only if satisfied that the costs are so disproportionate that it is right to do so.*

WHAT IS COVERED?

[29.4]

The general rule applies to all hearings that have lasted – the word is 'lasted', not 'listed', so the test is hindsight not foresight – not more than one day. It is not limited to fast track trials and interim hearings; 'other hearings' include multi-track trials and appeals in the Court of Appeal which do not last more than a day. Although the general rule applies to cases that last no more than one day it was held in *Q v Q (Family Division: costs: summary assessment)* [2002] 2 FLR 668 (Fam) that there is no presumption against summary assessment in relation to costs where hearings last more than one day. Indeed para 13.1 of the Costs Practice Direction requires summary assessment to be considered in every case. Section 6.4.4 of the Technology and Construction Court Guide provides that if the hearing of an application has to be adjourned because of delays by one or other of the parties in serving evidence, the court is likely to order that party to pay the costs straight away, and to make a summary assessment of those costs.

EXCEPTIONS TO THE GENERAL RULE

[29.5]

What is a 'good reason' for not carrying out a summary assessment? Paragraph 13.2 gives as examples of good reasons where the paying party shows substantial grounds for disputing the sum claimed for costs that cannot be dealt with summarily, or where there is insufficient time to carry out a summary assessment. 'Insufficient time' is not a complete bar to a summary assessment because, although paragraph 13.8 prohibits delegation to a costs officer, it also envisages the trial judge postponing his summary assessment to another date. In *Mahmood v Penrose* [2002] EWCA Civ 457, [2002] All ER (D) 227 (Mar) the Court explained the reasoning behind paragraph 13.8 was that only the person who has actually heard the case and knows about it is in a position to make a summary assessment.

Another reason for not having a summary assessment could be legal arguments which could not properly be dealt with on a summary assessment. In *R v Cardiff City Council, ex p Brown* (11 August 1999, unreported, QBD) it was alleged that the hourly rate claimed was in breach of the indemnity principle because the work had been done by the receiving party's own legal department and the hourly cost of doing the work could not have been as much as the rate claimed between the parties. The issue required a consideration of the legal department's costings and the various relevant authorities, which Harrison J concluded was not a suitable exercise for a summary assessment.

In *Neil v Stephenson* (2000) CLW, 8 December, QBD although the claimant, acting in person, had his action struck out, he had been awarded his costs of an interim hearing. When the claim was struck out, the judge acceded to the claimant's request for a detailed assessment to give him an opportunity to demonstrate that he should be entitled to recover the value of a contract which his business had allegedly lost as a result of his attendance at the interim hearing. The fairest course was to order an expedited detailed assessment of the costs of both parties to give the litigant in person the opportunity to consider his arguments and put the case before an experienced costs judge.

Paragraph 13.3 disapplies the general rule to the mortgagee's costs of mortgage possession proceedings.

The former paragraph 4.4(3) provided that generally there would be no summary assessment of costs if an order has been made for costs in the case. However, I contended that as both parties have gone to the trouble and expense of preparing statements of costs there would appear to be a benefit in summarily assessing the costs of each party of that hearing to await the final outcome of the proceedings. The restriction was removed.

ADMIRALTY AND COMMERCIAL COURTS

[29.5A]

Paragraph F14.2 of the Admiralty and Commercial Courts Guide provides 'active consideration will generally be given by the court to adopting the

468

summary assessment procedure in all cases where the schedule of costs of the successful party is no more than £100,000, but the parties should always be prepared for the court to assess costs summarily even where the costs exceed this amount'. There is further guidance in the next two paragraphs:

F14.3   In carrying out a summary assessment of costs, the court may have regard amongst other matters to:

(i)   advice from a Commercial Costs Judge or from the Chief Costs Judge on costs of specialist solicitors and counsel;

(ii)   any survey published by the London Solicitors Litigation Association showing the average hourly expense rate for solicitors in London;

(iii)   any information provided to the court at its request by one or more of the specialist associations (referred to at section A4.2) on average charges by specialist solicitors and counsel.

F14.4   Reference should also be made to CPR44.3(8). Active consideration will generally be given by the court to making an order for a payment on account of costs if they are not assessed summarily.

[29.6]

Paragraph 13.4 avoids the need for a summary assessment or the attendance of the parties, provided they have either agreed the amount of the costs or agreed that there shall be no order for costs. They cannot agree to a detailed assessment. The then Master of the Rolls and Vice-Chancellor were anxious that the court should not be seen to be endorsing disproportionate and unreasonable costs and accordingly the Practice Direction was amended to provide that when the amount of the costs to be paid has been agreed, the order should make it clear that it was made by consent; where the order is not by consent the judge has a responsibility to ensure that even those items which are not challenged are reasonable and proportionate (paragraph 13.13), although he will only intervene if the costs are clearly unreasonable or disproportionate.

Paragraph 13.10 provides that where one of the parties is in receipt of state funding there cannot be a summary assessment of any costs ordered to be paid to them by the other party, because the Legal Aid Act 1988 and Legal Service Commission regulations require those costs to be the subject of a detailed assessment. It is the same for a child or a protected party, unless their solicitor agrees not to make any further charge to his client (paragraph 13.11). The judge may, however, assess costs ordered to be paid by a legally assisted person, a child or a protected party, although you might think that in most cases that would be an academic exercise. In any event, the summary assessment of costs payable by an assisted person or LSC-funded client is not by itself determination of the assisted person's liability to pay those costs for the purposes of the Legal Aid Act 1988, s 17 or the Access to Justice Act 1999, s 11 (see Chapter 19).

The summary assessment at the end of a fast track trial will deal with the costs of the whole of the claim, remembering that the advocacy costs of the trial are fixed, and bearing in mind that there may already have been one or more summary assessments of the costs of an interim application. A summary assessment at the end of an interim application will deal with the costs of the application or matter to which it related.

WRITTEN STATEMENT OF COSTS

[29.7]

Paragraph 13.5 prescribes that any party intending to claim costs must prepare a written statement of the costs he intends to claim particularising the information specified in the Practice Direction, following as closely as possible Form N260 signed by the party or his legal representative. Here it is:

FORM N260

Statement of Costs
(summary assessment)

In the	
	Court
Case Reference	

Judge/Master

Case Title

[Party]'s Statement of Costs for the hearing on *(date)*   **(interim application/fast track trial)**

Description of fee earners*

(a) *(name) (grade) (hourly rate claimed)*	
(b) *(name) (grade) (hourly rate claimed)*	
(c) *(name) (grade) (hourly rate claimed)*	
(d) *(name) (grade) (hourly rate claimed)*	

Attendances on *(party)*

(a) *(number)*		hours at £		£	
(b) *(number)*		hours at £		£	
(c) *(number)*		hours at £		£	
(d) *(number)*		hours at £		£	

Attendances on opponents

(a) *(number)*		hours at £		£	
(b) *(number)*		hours at £		£	
(c) *(number)*		hours at £		£	
(d) *(number)*		hours at £		£	

Attendance on others

(a) *(number)*		hours at £		£	
(b) *(number)*		hours at £		£	
(c) *(number)*		hours at £		£	
(d) *(number)*		hours at £		£	

Site inspections etc

(a) *(number)*		hours at £		£	
(b) *(number)*		hours at £		£	
(c) *(number)*		hours at £		£	
(d) *(number)*		hours at £		£	

N260 Statement of Costs (summary assessment) (06.09)
© Crown Copyright. Reproduced by permission of the Controller of Her Majesty's Stationery Office. Published by LexisNexis.

Work done on negotiations

    (a) *(number)* ☐   hours at £ ☐   £ ☐

    (b) *(number)* ☐   hours at £ ☐   £ ☐

    (c) *(number)* ☐   hours at £ ☐   £ ☐

    (d) *(number)* ☐   hours at £ ☐   £ ☐

Other work, not covered above

    (a) *(number)* ☐   hours at £ ☐   £ ☐

    (b) *(number)* ☐   hours at £ ☐   £ ☐

    (c) *(number)* ☐   hours at £ ☐   £ ☐

    (d) *(number)* ☐   hours at £ ☐   £ ☐

Work done on documents

    (a) *(number)* ☐   hours at £ ☐   £ ☐

    (b) *(number)* ☐   hours at £ ☐   £ ☐

    (c) *(number)* ☐   hours at £ ☐   £ ☐

    (d) *(number)* ☐   hours at £ ☐   £ ☐

Attendance at hearing

    (a) *(number)* ☐   hours at £ ☐   £ ☐

    (b) *(number)* ☐   hours at £ ☐   £ ☐

    (c) *(number)* ☐   hours at £ ☐   £ ☐

    (d) *(number)* ☐   hours at £ ☐   £ ☐

    (a) *(number)* ☐   hours travel and waiting time £ ☐   £ ☐

    (b) *(number)* ☐   hours travel and waiting time £ ☐   £ ☐

    (c) *(number)* ☐   hours travel and waiting time £ ☐   £ ☐

    (d) *(number)* ☐   hours travel and waiting time £ ☐   £ ☐

Sub Total £ ☐

472

Brought forward £ [   ]

Counsel's fees *(name) (year of call)* [   ]

Fee for [advice/conference/documents] £ [   ]

Fee for hearing £ [   ]

Other expenses

[court fees] £ [   ]

Others
*(give brief
description)* £ [   ]

Total £ [   ]

Amount of VAT claimed

on solicitors and counsel's fees £ [   ]

on other expenses £ [   ]

Grand Total £ [   ]

The costs stated above do not exceed the costs which the *(party)* [   ]
(party) is liable to pay in respect of the work which this
statement covers. Counsel's fees and other expenses have
been incurred in the amounts stated above and will be paid to
the persons stated.

Dated [   ] Signed [   ]

Name of firm of solicitors
[partner] for the *(party)* [   ]

* 4 grades of fee earner are suggested:

(A) Solicitors with over eight years post qualification experience including at least eight years litigation experience.

(B) Solicitors and legal executives with over four years post qualification experience including at least four years litigation experience.

(C) Other solicitors and legal executives and fee earners of equivalent experience.

(D) Trainee solicitors, para legals and other fee earners.

"Legal Executive" means a Fellow of the Institute of Legal Executives. Those who are not Fellows of the Institute are not entitled to call themselves legal executives and in principle are therefore not entitled to the same hourly rate as a legal executive.

In respect of each fee earner communications should be treated as attendances and routine communications should be claimed at one tenth of the hourly rate.

The statement must be filed at court and copies served on any party against whom an order for payment is intended to be sought not less than 24 hours before the date of the hearing (not the time of the hearing). The beauty of this procedure is that when the solicitor is filling in his statement of costs he does not know whether his client is going to be the receiving or the paying party, which should assist him to take a balanced view of the exercise. Paragraph 13.6 says failure to comply will be taken into account in the decision-making process and the defaulter will be at the risk of an order for costs if his failure necessitates an adjournment or a detailed assessment. Even worse, he might not get any costs at all because the Practice Direction makes the lodging and serving of a statement of costs a condition precedent to applying for costs.

However, in *MacDonald v Taree Holdings Ltd* [2001] 06 LS Gaz R 45, ChD it was held that, despite the use of the word 'must', the provision is not mandatory and a deputy district judge had been wrong to refuse the successful party's application for summary assessment of his costs on the grounds that he had not served a statement of costs upon the respondent 24 hours in advance. The court has a wide discretion when deciding whether or not to award costs under Part 44 and in applications for summary judgment for costs, the failure to serve a schedule of costs was often being used for grounds for depriving a party of his costs or for curtailing a party's costs. Where, however, the only factor against awarding costs was merely a failure to serve a schedule without aggravating factors, a party should not be deprived of all his costs. The court should take the matter into account but its reaction should be proportionate. The question the court should ask itself was what, if any, prejudice there had been to the paying party and how should that prejudice be dealt with. The court should consider: first, whether it would be appropriate to have a brief adjournment for the paying party to consider the schedule and then proceed to a summary assessment of the costs. In that event, the judge should err in favour of awarding a lighter figure; secondly, whether the matter should be stood over for a detailed assessment; thirdly, whether the matter should be stood over for a summary assessment at a later date or for summary assessment to be dealt with in writing.

Where there is an adjournment for a summary assessment at a later date or an order for a detailed assessment, the receiving party will, of course, be at the risk of paying the consequential additional costs.

Note it is called a 'statement' not a schedule as it is so frequently miss-called. However, a schedule giving a detailed breakdown of the figures attached to the statement is very much to be commended.

QUANTIFICATION

(a) Factors to be taken into account in deciding the amount of costs

[29.8]

The factors to be taken into account in deciding the amount of costs are not affected by whether the method of assessment is summary or detailed. They are in Chapter 10. The Supreme Court Costs Office (now the Senior Courts Costs Office) Guide to the Summary Assessment of Costs contains the following advice:

[29.9]

23.   Rule 44.5 (Appendix 1) sets out the factors to be taken into account. Those factors include: the conduct of all the parties, including in particular, conduct before as well as during the proceedings and the efforts made, if any, before and during the proceedings in order to try to resolve the dispute.

24.   In deciding whether the costs claimed are reasonable and (on the standard basis) proportionate, the court will consider the amount of any additional liability separately from the base costs.

25.   The Judge, before commencing a summary assessment on the standard basis should, in accordance with the guidance in *Lownds v Home Office* [2002] EWCA Civ 365, [2002] 4 All ER 775, [2002] 1 WLR 2450 (see paragraph 16 above), step back and consider the proportionality of the costs claimed. If the costs claimed overall appear proportionate they may be assessed applying a test of reasonableness. If on the other hand the costs appear to be disproportionate then the more stringent test of necessity should be applied. If previous orders for summarily assessed costs have been made then the Judge should, subject to paragraph 27, consider the proportionality of the total costs of the proceedings.

26.   In considering what is necessary, a sensible standard of necessity has to be adopted. This is a standard which takes fully into account the need to make allowances for the different judgements which those responsible for litigation can sensibly come to as to what is required. The danger of setting too high a standard with the benefit of hindsight has to be avoided. The threshold required to meet 'necessity' is higher than that of 'reasonableness' but it is still a standard that a competent practitioner should be able to achieve without undue difficulty. In deciding what is necessary the conduct of the other party is highly relevant. A party who is unco-operative may render necessary costs which would otherwise be unnecessary. It is acceptable that that party should pay the costs for the expense which he has made necessary.

27.   In arriving at a final figure the Judge should not reduce the costs of the receiving party on account of the costs awarded to that party under a previous summary assessment. To do so would impugn the decision of the earlier Judge. Where however the amount of costs previously ordered to be paid has been agreed by the parties with no judicial assessment there is nothing to prevent the court taking these figures into account when considering proportionality.

(b) Hourly Rates

[29.10]

The *SCCO Guide* contains a table of guideline hourly rates which is set out in full and considered in Chapter 22.

ADDITIONAL LIABILITIES

[29.11]

CPR rule 44.3A: Costs order relating to funding arrangements

(1)   The court will not assess any additional liability until the conclusion of the proceedings, or the part of the proceedings, to which the funding arrangement relates.

('Funding arrangement' and 'additional liability' are defined in rule 43.2)

(2)   At the conclusion of the proceedings, or the part of the proceedings, to which the funding arrangement relates the court may—

(a)   make a summary assessment of all the costs, including any additional liability;

(b)   make an order for detailed assessment of the additional liability but make a summary assessment of the other costs; or

(c)   make an order for detailed assessment of all the costs.

(Part 47 sets out the procedure for the detailed assessment of costs)

[29.12]

CPD SECTION 9 COSTS ORDERS RELATING TO FUNDING ARRANGEMENTS: RULE 44.3A

9.1   *Under an order for payment of 'costs' the costs payable will include an additional liability incurred under a funding arrangement.*

(1)   *If before the conclusion of the proceedings the court carries out a summary assessment of the base costs it may identify separately the amount allowed in respect of: solicitors' charges; counsels' fees; other disbursements; and any value added tax (VAT). (Sections 13 and 14 of this Practice Direction deal with summary assessment.)*

(2)   *If an order for the base costs of a previous application or hearing did not identify separately the amounts allowed for solicitor's charges, counsel's fees and other disbursements, a court which later makes an assessment of an additional liability may apportion the base costs previously ordered.*

[29.13]

This provision is necessary because the barrister and the solicitor may have agreed different success fees. Even where there is not an additional liability it is good practice for the judge to separately assess the barrister's and solicitor's awards, so that it is clear what has been allowed to each.

[29.14]

CPD SECTION 14: SUMMARY ASSESSMENT WHERE COSTS CLAIMED INCLUDE AN ADDITIONAL LIABILITY

Orders made before the conclusion of the proceedings

14.1   *The existence of a conditional fee agreement or other funding arrangement within the meaning of rule 43.2 is not by itself a sufficient reason for not carrying out a summary assessment.*
14.2   *Where a legal representative acting for the receiving party has entered into a conditional fee agreement the court may summarily assess all the costs (other than any additional liability).*
14.3   *Where costs have been summarily assessed an order for payment will not be made unless the court has been satisfied that in respect of the costs claimed, the receiving party is at the time liable to pay to his legal representative an amount equal to or greater than the costs claimed. A statement in the form of the certificate appended at the end of Form N260 may be sufficient proof of liability. The giving of information under rule 44.15 (where that rule applies) is not sufficient.*
14.4   *The court may direct that any costs, for which the receiving party may not in the event be liable, shall be paid into court to await the outcome of the case, or shall not be enforceable until further order, or it may postpone the receiving party's right to receive payment in some other way.*

[29.15]

Orders made at the conclusion of the proceedings

14.5   *Where there has been a trial of one or more issues separately from other issues, the court will not normally order detailed assessment of the additional liability until all issues have been tried unless the parties agree.*
14.6   *Rule 44.3A(2) sets out the ways in which the court may deal with the assessment of the costs where there is a funding arrangement. Where the court makes a summary assessment of the base costs:*
(1)   *The order may state separately the base costs allowed as (a)solicitor's charges, (b) counsel's fees, (c) any other disbursements and (d) any VAT;*
(2)   *the statements of costs upon which the judge based his summary assessment will be retained on the court file.*
14.7   *Where the court makes a summary assessment of an additional liability at the conclusion of proceedings, that assessment must relate to the whole of the proceedings; this will include any additional liability relating to base costs allowed by the court when making a summary assessment on a previous application or hearing.*
14.8   *Paragraph 13.13 applies where the parties are agreed about the total amount to be paid by way of costs, or are agreed about the amount of the base costs that will be paid. Where they disagree about the additional liability the court may summarily assess that liability or make an order for a detailed assessment.*
14.9   *In order to facilitate the court in making a summary assessment of any additional liability at the conclusion of the proceedings the party seeking such costs must prepare and have available for the court a bundle of documents which must include—*
(1)   *a copy of every notice of funding arrangement (Form N251) which has been filed by him;*
(2)   *a copy of every estimate and statement of costs filed by him;*
(3)   *a copy of the risk assessment prepared at the time any relevant funding arrangement was entered into and on the basis of which the amount of the additional liability was fixed.*

[29.16]

An additional liability is either a conditional fee agreement success fee or an after-the-event insurance premium, and usually both. They are considered fully in Chapter 42.

On an interim hearing, the existence of an additional liability is not a reason for not carrying out a summary assessment, but the judge may only assess the base costs – he is precluded from assessing the additional liability. That is the combined effect of section 14.1 of the Costs Practice Direction and Rule 44.3A. If the judge does assess the base costs he may not make an order for them to be paid, because if the action is lost the receiving party will have no liability to his solicitor, unless he is satisfied that the receiving party is in any event liable to pay his solicitor the amount claimed. The judge may, however, order the costs to be paid into court pending the outcome of the proceedings, or that the order shall not be enforced without permission or fetter the receiving party in some other way.

After a final hearing, Rule 44.3A gives three options:
(1)   summary assessment of all the costs;
(2)   summary assessment of the base costs only. Sending the additional liability for detailed assessment; or
(3)   detailed assessment of all the costs.

The January 2005 revision of the SCCO *Guide to the Summary Assessment of Costs* gives the following advice on the summary assessment of additional liabilities:

[29.17]

SUMMARY ASSESSMENT WHERE COSTS CLAIMED INCLUDE AN ADDITIONAL LIABILITY

19.   Rule 44.3A deals with costs orders relating to funding arrangements. An order for payment of 'costs' includes an additional liability incurred under a funding arrangement. Where the court carries out a summary assessment of base costs before the conclusion of proceedings it is helpful if the order identifies separately the amount allowed in respect of: solicitors' charges; counsel's fees; other disbursements; and any value added tax. If this is not done, the court which later makes an assessment of an additional liability, will have to apportion the base costs previously assessed.

20.   Rule 44.3B sets out the limits on recovery under funding arrangements. The court will consider the amount of any additional liability separately from the base costs and when considering the factors to be taken into account under rule 44.5 in assessing an additional liability the court will have regard to the facts and circumstances as they reasonably appeared to the solicitor or counsel when the funding arrangement was entered into and at the time of any variation of the arrangement.

21.   Where an order for costs is made before the conclusion of the proceedings and a legal representative for the receiving party has entered into a conditional fee agreement the court may summarily assess the base costs. An order for payment of those costs will not be made unless the court is satisfied that the receiving party is at the time liable to pay to his legal representative an amount equal to or greater than the costs claimed. If the court is not so satisfied it may direct that any costs,

for which the receiving party may not in the final event be liable, be paid into court to await the outcome of the case or shall not be enforceable until further order, or the court may postpone the receiving party's right to receive payment in some other way.

Orders Made at the Conclusion of Proceedings

22.   Where the court makes a summary assessment of an additional liability at the conclusion of the proceedings, that assessment must relate to the whole of the proceedings; this will include any additional liability relating to base costs allowed by the court when making a summary assessment on a previous application or hearing.

Conditional Fee Agreements with a Success Fee

28   The factors to be taken into account when deciding whether a percentage increase is reasonable may include:
(a)   the risk that the circumstances in which the costs, fees or expenses would be payable might or might not occur;
(b)   the legal representative's liability for any disbursements;
(c)   what other methods of financing the costs were available to the receiving party.

The court has the power to allow different percentages for different items of costs or for different periods during which costs were incurred (CPD 11.8(2)). The court should have regard to the facts and circumstances as they reasonably appeared to the solicitor or counsel when the funding arrangement was entered into, and at the time of any variation of the agreement (CPD 11.7).

29.   A percentage increase should not be reduced simply on the ground that, when added to base costs which are reasonable and (where relevant) proportionate, the total appears disproportionate (CPD 11.9).

In road traffic accident claims where the accident occurred on or after 6 October 2003 the percentage increase to be allowed as a success fee is fixed by rules: see CPR 45, Section III.

Insurance Premiums

30.   Relevant factors to be taken into account when deciding whether the cost of insurance cover is reasonable include:
(a)   where the insurance cover is not purchased in support of a conditional fee agreement with a success fee, how its cost compares with the likely cost of funding the case with a conditional fee agreement with a success fee and supporting insurance cover;
(b)   the level and extent of the cover provided;
(c)   the availability of any pre-existing insurance cover;
(d)   whether any part of the premium would be rebated in the event of early settlement;
(e)   the amount of commission payable to the receiving party or his legal representatives or other agents.

Membership Organisation – Additional Amount

31.   When considering a provision made by a membership organisation the court should not allow a provision which exceeds the likely cost to the receiving party of the premium of an insurance policy against the risk of incurring a liability to pay the costs of other parties to the proceedings. In those circumstances the court will have regard to the factors set out in paragraph 26 above in addition to the factors set out in rule 44.5 (Appendix 1).

Success Fee Diputes Between Legal Representative and Client: Procedure Following the Summary Assessment

32.   A court which has made a summary assessment which disallows or reduces a legal representative's percentage increase may then and there decide the issue whether the disallowed amount should continue to be payable. The court may do this if:

(a)   the receiving party and all parties to the relevant agreement consent to the court doing so;

(b)   the receiving party (or, if corporate, a duly authorised officer) is present in court; and

(c)   the court is satisfied that the issue can be fairly decided then and there.

33.   In any other case the court will give directions to enable an application to be made by the legal representative for the disallowed amount to be payable by his client, including if appropriate a direction that the application will be determined by a Costs Judge or District Judge of the court dealing with the case.

PROPORTIONALITY

[29.18]

In Chapter 11, I considered the requirement of Rule 44.4 that costs shall be proportionate to the matters in issue and the various attempts to define proportionality. The SCCO *Guide to the Summary Assessment of Costs* deals with proportionality on summary assessment after a final hearing in the light of the decision in *Lownds v Home Office* (para [11.39]) as follows:

[29.19]

Proportionality

14.   'Proportionality' is not defined in the rules or the Practice Direction. Section 11 of the Costs Practice Direction indicates, however, that in applying the test of proportionality the court will have regard to rule 1.1(2)(c) by, so far as practicable, dealing with the case in ways which are proportionate:

(i)   to the amount of money involved;

(ii)   to the importance of the case;

(iii)   to the complexity of the issues; and

(iv)   to the financial position of each party.

15.   Paragraphs 11.1 to 11.3 of the Practice Direction give the following warnings as to the test of proportionality.

(i)   The relationship between the total costs incurred and the financial value of the claim may not be a reliable guide. A fixed percentage cannot be applied in all cases to the value of the claim in order to ascertain whether or not the costs are proportionate.

(ii)   In any proceedings, there will be costs which will inevitably be incurred and which are necessary for the successful conduct of the case. Solicitors are not required to conduct litigation at rates which are uneconomic. Thus in a modest claim the proportion of costs is likely to be higher than in a large claim and may even equal or possibly exceed the amount in dispute.

(iii)   Where a trial takes place the time taken by the court in dealing with the particular issue may not be an accurate guide to the amount of time properly spent by the legal or other representatives in preparation for the trial of that issue.

16.   The Court of Appeal has given guidance on the correct approach to proportionality when assessing costs:

'what is required is a two stage approach. There has to be a global approach and an item by item approach. The global approach will indicate whether the total sum claimed is or appears to be disproportionate having particular regard to the considerations which Part 44.5(3) states are relevant. If the costs as a whole are not disproportionate according to that test then all that is normally required is that each item should have been reasonably incurred and the costs for that item should be reasonable. If on the other hand the costs as a whole appear disproportionate then the court will want to be satisfied that the work in relation to each item was necessary, and, if necessary, the cost of the item was reasonable'

(*Home Office v Lownds* [2002] EWCA Civ 365; [2002] 4 All ER 775, [2002] 1 WLR 2450).
The text of rule 44.5(3) is included in Appendix 1 to this Guide.
17.   The relevant costs for consideration at the first stage are the base costs only before VAT is added (CPD 11.5 and *Giambrone v JMC Holidays* [2003] 2 Costs LR 189).
18.   The fact that, at the first stage, the costs as a whole appear to be proportionate does not prevent the court from finding individual items are dispro-portionate and applying the test of necessity to them alone (*Giambrone*).

[29.20]

An important message is that on a summary judgment a judge cannot regard previous costs awards as mere water under the bridge but must look at the totality of the awards in considering proportionality overall.

THE INDEMNITY PRINCIPLE

[29.21]

Until the indemnity principle is disapplied, a party in whose favour an order for costs has been made may not recover more than he is liable to pay to his own solicitors (see Chapter 17). The written statement of costs (Form N260) contains the statement 'the costs estimated above do not exceed the costs which the party is liable to pay in respect of the work which this estimate covers'. The SCCO *Guide to the Summary Assessment of Costs* summarises the position as follows:

The Indemnity Principle
34.   A party in whose favour an order for costs has been made may not recover more than he is liable to pay his own solicitors. See *Harold v Smith* [1865] 5 H&N 381, 385; and *Gundry v Sainsbury* [1910] 1 KB 645 CA. There are exceptions to the principle, notably costs funded by the Legal Services Commission and fees payable under certain types of conditional fee agreement.
35.   The statement of costs put before the court for summary assessment must be signed by the party or its legal representative. That form contains the statement: "The costs estimated above do not exceed the costs which the [party] is liable to pay in respect of the work which this estimate covers."
36.   Following the decision of Lord Justice Henry in *Bailey v IBC Vehicles Ltd* [1998] 3 All ER 570, CA, the signature of a statement of costs (or a bill for detailed assessment) by a solicitor is, in normal circumstances, sufficient to enable the court to be satisfied that the indemnity principle has not been breached. A solicitor is an officer of the court and as Henry LJ stated:

'In so signing he certifies that the contents of the bill are correct. That signature is no empty formality. The bill specifies the hourly rates applied . . . If an agreement between the receiving solicitor and his client . . . restricted (say) the hourly rate payable by the client that hourly rate is the most that can be claimed or recovered on [assessment] . . . The signature of the bill of costs . . . is effectively the certificate of an officer of the court that the receiving party's solicitors are not seeking to recover in relation to any item more than they have agreed to charge their client . . . '

(See *Hazlett v Sefton Metropolitan Borough Council* at para [17.8] for an example in practice.) Paragraph 14.3 of the Practice Direction confirms that the signed statement may be sufficient proof of liability.

PAYMENT DEFERRED

[29.22]

As we have seen, Rule 44.8 requires an order for costs to be paid within 14 days. If a party funded under a conditional fee agreement (CFA) has an after-the-event costs indemnity insurance policy it will usually exclude paying interim costs awarded to the other side. Who then is to pay them – the solicitor, the client or who? CFAs are so regarded as the panacea for the funding of litigation that the problem has caused much concern in high places. On 12 March 1999 the Vice-Chancellor wrote to all judges suggesting that if there is a CFA the judge should consider staying any order for costs until the end of the action and also consider not requiring a payment on account if he orders a detailed assessment. This gave rise to the question why a party who chose a particular method of funding should be given preferential treatment over a party who is funding the litigation himself, perhaps by mortgaging his home, or by means of a bank overdraft or by selling investments at a loss? It is in any event wrong to assume that someone who has entered into a CFA is impecunious, much commercial litigation is now financed in this way (see Chapter 42). It also raises the question why the receiving party should have to wait until the end of the litigation before receiving interim costs just because his adversary has chosen one method of funding in preference to another. Paragraph 33 of the SCCO *Guide to the Summary Assessment of Costs* suggests:

37. As a general rule a paying party should be ordered to pay the amount of any summarily assessed costs within 14 days. Before making such an order the court should consider whether an order for payment of the costs might bring the action to an end and whether this would be just in all the circumstances.

The indemnity principle could also result in deferment. The court must be satisfied that the receiving party is in fact liable to pay his own solicitor at that stage of the proceedings the costs of an interim hearing equal to the amount ordered between the parties. If not, payment of the between the parties costs must be deferred until he is liable, probably at the conclusion of the proceedings.

COUNSEL'S FEES

[29.23]

The following table sets out figures based on SCCO statistics dealing with run of the mill proceedings in the Queens Bench and Chancery Division and in the Administrative Court. The table gives figures for cases lasting up to an hour and up to half a day, in respect of counsel up to five years call, up to ten years call and over ten years call. It is emphasised that these figures are not recommended rates but it is hoped that they may provide a helpful starting point for judges when assessing counsel's fees. The appropriate fee in any particular case may be more or less than the figures appearing in the table, depending upon the circumstances. They have not been increased since 2005.

The table does not include any figures in respect of leading counsel's fees since such cases would self evidently be exceptional. Similarly, no figures are included for the Commercial Court or the Technology & Construction Court.

Table of counsel's fees

Queen's Bench	1 hour hearing	½ day hearing
Junior up to 5 years' call	£259	£450
Junior 5–10 years' call	£386	£767
Junior 10+ years' call	£582	£1,164
Chancery Division	1 hour hearing	½ day hearing
Junior up to 5 years' call	£291	£556
Junior 5–10 years' call	£497	£931
Junior 10+ years' call	£757	£1,397
Administrative Court	1 hour hearing	½ day hearing
Junior up to 5 years' call	£381	£582
Junior 5–10 years' call	£698	£1,164
Junior 10+ years' call	£989	£1,746

If the paying parties were represented by counsel, the fee paid to their counsel is an important factor but not a conclusive one on the question of fees payable to the receiving party's counsel.

In deciding upon the appropriate fee for counsel the question is not simply one of counsel's experience and seniority but also of the level of counsel which the particular case merits.

Counsel's fees should not be allowed in cases in which it was not reasonable to have instructed counsel, but it must be borne in mind that, especially in substantial hearings, it may be more economical if the advocacy is conducted by counsel rather than a solicitor. In all cases the court should consider whether or not the decision to instruct counsel has led to an increase in costs and whether that increase is justifiable.

The Statement of Costs Form footnote states that routine communications should be charged at one-tenth of the fee earner's hourly rate, which is of course a six-minute unit. This should cover reading an incoming letter as well as writing the reply and routine telephone calls. Any exchange of letters or telephone call taking longer than six minutes should be timed and charged accordingly.

ADVOCACY FEES

(a) Solicitors

[29.24]

The SCCO *Guide* provides:

Solicitor Advocates

40.　Remuneration of solicitor advocates is based on the normal principles for remuneration of solicitors. It is not therefore appropriate to seek a brief fee and refreshers as if the advocate were a member of the Bar. If the cost of using a solicitor advocate is more than the cost of instructing counsel, the higher cost is unlikely to be recovered. The figures properly recoverable by solicitor advocates should reflect the amount of preparation undertaken, the time spent in court and the weight and gravity of the case.

41.　Where the solicitor advocate is also the solicitor who does the preparation work, the solicitor is entitled to charge normal solicitors' rates for that preparation, but once the solicitor advocate starts preparation for the hearing itself the fees recoverable should not exceed those which would be recoverable in respect of counsel.

42.　It is clearly wrong for the fees of a solicitor acting as a junior counsel to exceed the fee appropriate for the leading counsel.

(b) Counsel

[29.25]

The SCCO *Guide* quotes from the judgment of Pennycuick J in *Simpsons Motor Sales (London) Ltd v Hendon Corpn* [1964] 3 All ER 833, ChD:

A proper measure for counsel's fees . . . was to estimate what fee a hypothetical counsel, cap-able of conducting the case effectively, but unable or unwilling to insist on the higher fees sometimes demanded by counsel of pre-eminent reputation, would be content to take on the brief: but there is no precise standard of measurement and the judge must, using his or her knowledge and experience, determine the proper figure.'

CONDUCTING THE ASSESSMENT

[29.26]

Solicitors and counsel should be aware that the summary assessment of costs at the end of the hearing will be dealt with by the advocate who conducted the hearing. If counsel has been briefed, counsel will have to either justify his client's statement of costs if he succeeds or to attack the other side's statement if he loses. When I spoke to young barristers on behalf of the Bar Council I told them they must become costs experts. Solicitors might forgive them for losing a case, but they will never forgive them for making a mess of the costs! I advise solicitors that counsel must be fully briefed on how to justify their own statement of costs or attack that of the other side depending on the outcome.

It is, for example, helpful to have available a detailed breakdown of how the figures in the statement of costs were arrived at. The absence of the solicitor's file can also cause difficulty if a query arises as to the number, length or content of documents.

DUPLICATION

[29.27]

On the summary assessment of costs of an interim hearing, the bill will inevitably include a claim for work which often has a dual purpose, being both costs of the application and costs in the main action. If a judge disallows an element of the claim he should give his reasons for doing so. He should distinguish between disallowing costs because the work was not done or was unreasonable or disproportionate and between disallowances of costs of the main action: *Sterling Publications Ltd v Burroughs* [2000] 2 Costs LR 155, QBD.

NO TARIFF

[29.28]

Pending the introduction of benchmark costs, the court must be careful not to use summary assessment as a 'vehicle for the introduction of a scale of judicial tariffs for different categories of case'. In *1–800 Flowers Inc v Phone-names Ltd* [2001] EWCA Civ 721, [2001] IP & T 839, the Court of Appeal said it was of the essence of a summary assessment of costs that the court should focus on the detailed breakdown of costs actually incurred by the party in question as shown in its statement of costs; and that it should carry out the assessment by reference to the items appearing in that statement. In so doing the court might find it helpful to draw to a greater or lesser extent on its own experience of summary assessment of costs in what it considered to be comparable cases. Equally, having dealt with the costs by reference to the detailed items in the statement of costs which was before it, the court might find it helpful to look at the total sum at which it had arrived in order to see whether that sum fell within the bounds of what it considered reasonable and proportionate. If the court considered the total sum to be unreasonable or disproportionate, it might wish to look again at the various detailed items in order to see what further reductions should be made. Such an approach was wholly unobjectionable. However, the judge in this case did not appear to have focused at all on the detailed items in the opponent's statement of costs. Rather, having concluded that the total of the detailed items was unreasonably high he then proceeded to apply his own tariff, which appeared to have been derived primarily from a case in which the opponent had not been involved and about which it and its advisers knew nothing. However general the approach which the court chose to adopt when assessing costs summarily, and however broad the brush which the court chose to use, the assessment must be directed to and focused upon the detailed breakdown of costs contained in the receiving party's statement of costs.

COURT OF APPEAL

[29.29]

The SCCO *Guide* describes the regime as follows:

[29.30]

Summary assessment of costs in the court of appeal

53.   The Practice Direction supplementing CPR Part 52 identifies five types of hearing at which costs are likely to be assessed by way of summary assessment and states that parties attending any of those hearings should be prepared to deal with the summary assessment. The Costs Practice Direction (Section 13 paragraph 13.5) places a duty on the parties and their legal representatives to file and serve a statement of any costs they intend to claim in respect of such hearings.
54.   In this Guide the term 'counsel' includes a solicitor-advocate who is instructed by another solicitor.

Contested Directions Hearings; Applications for Permission to Appeal at which the Respondent is Present; and Appeals from Case Management Decisions

55.   The guidance given below in relation to contested directions hearings, applications for permission to appeal at which the respondent is present and appeals from case management decisions relates to hearings which, although important, are not difficult or complex and are not of general public importance and are listed either for a hearing not exceeding one hour or for a hearing not exceeding one half day.
56.   If these hearings are attended by solicitor and counsel the number of hours which it is reasonable to presume that the solicitor will undertake (in respect of preparation, attendance, travel in Central London and waiting) is 4 hours for a one hour appointment and 7.5 hours for a half day appointment. It is reasonable to presume that counsel who has between 5 and 10 years' experience merits a fee of approximately £500 (exclusive of VAT) for a one hour appointment and merits a fee of approximately £800 (exclusive of VAT) for a half day appointment.
57.   If these hearings were attended by a solicitor without counsel it is reasonable to presume that the total number of hours the solicitor will spend (in respect of preparation, attendance, travel in Central London and waiting) is 5 hours for a one hour appointment and 10 hours for a half day appointment.
58.   If these hearings are attended by a litigant in person it is reasonable to presume that the total number of hours the litigant in person will spend (in respect of preparation, attendance and waiting) is 9 hours for a one hour appointment and 14 hours for a half day appointment. In each case a further allowance should be made for time and expense in travelling to the appointment.

(3) Dismissal List Hearings at which the Respondent is Present

59.   The guidance given below in relation to dismissal list hearings in the Court of Appeal at which the respondent is present, relates to cases which are listed for less

than one hour and are of significantly less weight than the contested directions hearings, applications for permission to appeal and appeals from case management decisions described above.

60.   If the hearing is attended by solicitor and counsel (for the appellant or the respondent), it is reasonable to presume that the total number of hours to allow the solicitor (in respect of preparation, attendance, travel in Central London and waiting) is 2 hours, and it is reasonable to presume that counsel who has between 5 and 10 years' experience merits a fee of approximately £350 (exclusive of VAT).

61.   If an appeal is dismissed and costs are awarded to the respondent, it will probably be appropriate to allow further costs in respect of work previously done in responding to the appeal. Consideration should be given to whether it is in fact appropriate to carry out a summary assessment, depending on the amount of work done by the respondent.

62.   Subject to paragraph 56 if the hearing is attended by a solicitor without counsel it is reasonable to presume that the total number of hours to allow the solicitor (in respect of preparation, attendance, travel in Central London and waiting) is 3 hours.

63.   Subject to paragraph 56, if the hearing is attended by a litigant in person it is reasonable to presume that the total number of hours to allow the litigant in person (in respect of preparation, attendance and waiting) is 6 hours with a further allowance for time and expense in travelling to the appointment.

(5) Appeals Listed for One Day or Less

64.   Appeals listed for one day or less vary enormously as to weight, complexity and importance. Thus, it is not at present possible to give guidance as to the number of hours reasonably spent by solicitors (in respect of preparation, attendances, travel and waiting) in such appeals. However, after research and consultation, it may be possible in future to give such guidance in relation to particular types of general and specialist appeals. Pending such research and consultation, the only guidance which can be given is as follows.

(1)   It may not be appropriate to carry out a summary assessment if a case lasts more than half a day or involves leading counsel since in those circumstances the case is likely to be complex and weighty. It will often be unwise for the court to assess summarily costs in a matter which is not simple and straightforward, unless the difference between the parties is comparatively small, or unless the correct allowance appears clear.

(2)   The reasonable fees of counsel are likely to exceed the reasonable fees of the solicitor.

(3)   The fact that the same counsel appeared in the lower court does not greatly reduce the reasonable fee unless, for example, the lower court dealt with a great many more issues than are raised on the appeal. It is reasonable for counsel to spend as much time preparing issues for the Court of Appeal hearing as he spent preparing those issues for the lower court hearing.

(4)   If the case merits leading counsel it may merit also the instruction of a junior to assist him. The junior's fees should be allowed at one half of the leader's fees unless:

    (a)   the junior is a senior junior and the case merited both a leader and a senior junior.

    (b)   The junior took a responsibility which was equal to or larger than that taken by the leader.

    (c)   The junior undertook work not covered by the brief.

(5)   In many cases the largest element in the solicitors' reasonable fees for work in the Court of Appeal concerns instructing counsel and preparing the appeal bundles. Time spent by the solicitor in the development of legal submissions will only be allowed where it does not duplicate work done by counsel and is claimed at a rate the same or lower than the rate counsel would have claimed.

(6)   Although the solicitor may have spent many hours with the client, the client should have been warned that little of this time is recoverable against a

losing party. Reasonable time spent receiving instructions and reporting events should not greatly exceed the time spent on attending the opponents.

(7)   Given that the case will be presented by a barrister or a solicitor advocate there is usually no reason for any other solicitor to spend many hours perusing papers. A large claim for such perusal probably indicates that a new fee earner was reading in. Reading in fees are not normally recoverable from an opponent.

(8)   Although it is usually reasonable to have a senior fee earner sitting with counsel in the Court of Appeal, it is not usually reasonable to have two fee earners. The second fee earner may be there for training purposes only.

(9)   In most appeals it will be appropriate to make an allowance for copy documents. The allowance for copying which is included in the solicitor's hourly rates will have already been used up or exceeded in the lower court. An hourly rate charge is appropriate for selecting and collating documents and dictating the indices. If the paperwork is voluminous much of this should be delegated to a trainee. Note that:

    (a)   For the copying itself, a fair allowance is 10p per page, i.e. £100 per 1,000 sheets. This includes an allowance for checking the accuracy of the copying.

    (b)   Time spent standing at the photocopier and time spent taking the papers to a local photocopy shop is not recoverable. Such work is not fee earner work; it is secretarial.

(10)   It must be borne in mind that skeleton arguments will have been lodged at an early stage, and, in respect of floating appeals, the case may have come into and out of the list. In those circumstances it may be necessary to change counsel which would inevitably increase the costs. New counsel may decide to submit a different skeleton argument. Where this has occurred, detailed assessment is to be preferred.

Solicitors Charges

65.   Although many appointments in the Court of Appeal merit the attendance of a senior fee earner familiar with the case, the most minor appointments may not. For example, on an application in the dismissal list in a case tried in Newcastle, if counsel who was briefed for the trial attends it may be unreasonable for a solicitor familiar with the case to travel from Newcastle to attend also. In order to arrive at a notional figure to represent the instruction of and costs of an agent, it may be appropriate to disallow most of the travel time and travelling expenses claimed by the solicitor.

66.   The Court of Appeal has stated that it is the duty of litigators (particularly unions and insurers) to keep down the cost of litigation. This means that if they instruct London solicitors who charge London rates for a case which has no obvious connection with London and which does not require expertise only to be found there, they will, even if successful, recover less than the solicitors have charged (see *Wraith v Sheffield Forgemasters Ltd* [1998] 1 WLR 132 CA).

67.   In relation to the first four types of hearing appropriate for summary assessment in the Court of Appeal, some guidance is given above suggesting the number of hours which may be reasonable for the solicitor to spend. That guidance should be used as a starting point only. The court should also have regard to the number of hours actually claimed.

Counsel's Fees in the Court of Appeal

68.   Counsel's fees depend upon the seniority of counsel which it was reasonable to instruct and the market price for the item of work in question. It is not appropriate to specify an hourly rate for counsel and to remunerate them at a multiple of that rate according to the number of hours reasonably spent. Such an approach would reward the indolent and penalise the expeditious.

69.   In previous paragraphs (paragraphs 51 and 55), figures were suggested for brief fees for counsel who has between 5 and 10 years' experience. For less experienced counsel it may be appropriate to reduce these figures; for more

experienced counsel it may be appropriate to increase these figures. The guideline figures are a starting point only and the Court has the discretion to allow fees appropriate to the particular circumstances of the appeal.

Conditional Fee Agreements with Success Fees

70. Although not common for appellants to enter into such agreements, it is common for respondents (the successful party at first instance) whose claim or defence was conducted under a conditional fee agreement: such agreements usually also cover appeals brought by the opponent.

71. Attention is drawn to paragraph 3 of this Guide dealing with summary assessment of an additional liability at the conclusion of proceedings.

72. Paragraphs 24 and 25 set out the factors to be taken into account when deciding whether a percentage increase is reasonable.

Costs Awarded to Litigants in Person

73. Attention is drawn to paragraphs 38 to 40 of this Guide.

APPEALS AGAINST SUMMARY ASSESSMENT

[29.31]

See Chapter 31.

THE END OF SUMMARY ASSESSMENTS?

(a) Association of Law Costs Draftsmen

[29.32]

The Council of the Association of Law Costs Draftsmen recommends that the summary assessment procedures should be withdrawn, subject to the right of any party at the conclusion of an interim application to seek summary assessment of the costs relating to that application and the right of the court in straightforward cases to summarily assess costs. Their proposal is based on the 'enormous' variations arising from some summary assessments: assessments appearing to have been carried out arbitrarily; the procedure increasing rather than reducing costs; preparation of statements of costs resulting in unnecessary work for solicitors; solicitors being ill-able to afford to release papers for the preparation of a statement of costs at a time when they are preparing for a hearing; there being often insufficient time for a summary assessment to be carried out satisfactorily and there being a variety of exceptions to the requirement for summary assessment. The proposal is in conjunction with the Association's proposal for revised procedures for detailed assessment, based on two pilot schemes, one for lower-value claims where the profit costs do not exceed £10,000 and there is no disputed fact, and the second applying to assessments where the profit costs exceed £10,000. It is claimed that the proposed procedures would be fairer and more workable than the present summary assessment, judicial time would be reduced and the courts freed for more essential business at the end of a trial. The receiving party would be able to produce a claim for costs that is better explained than the existing model form used for summary assessment, while the paying party would be provided with more detail of the claim and better able to identify what costs claimed or items of costs claimed may reasonably be challenged. The court would be afforded cogent written reasons summarising the disputes to assist it in its requirement that the parties be proactive before any assessment in trying to resolve disputes and limiting the issues to be determined by the court. In particular, dispute resolution and mediation should be considered in appropriate cases.

(b) Litigation Funding

[29.33]

Here are my views as expressed in an article in the Law Society's excellent publication, *Litigation Funding*:

> 'It is a truth universally acknowledged that the costs provisions are the least successful part of the Civil Procedure Rules, and that the least successful part of the costs provisions is summary assessment. That is because summary assessment has imposed on the judiciary a function that Lord Woolf never intended it to perform. The linchpin of Lord Woolf's proposals was a fast track with fixed costs. We have the fast track, but not the fixed costs, except for the trial itself. As a result, at the end of an exhausting fast track hearing there is often the pantomime of two barristers addressing a former barrister (the trial judge), who has had a one-hour JSB crash course on costs, on matters of which none of them has any practical experience, in circumstances where even the most experienced costs judge or costs draftsman would flounder. There is a one-page statement (why do people persist in calling it a 'schedule'?) of costs containing no information other than the time spent on various activities and the amount claimed. It has usually been prepared by someone who is not present in court, and relates to a file of papers which is also conspicuous by its absence. The judge has to choose between two sets of figures apparently plucked from the air, or arrive at his own by the same route. Because the whole exercise is based on hourly rates, without any enhancement for care, skill and attention as previously, we now have a painful plodder's charter with the rewards going to the slowest, least able and most imaginative. Is it any wonder that instead of costs being controlled and certain, as was envisaged for the fast track, costs for both interim and final hearings have spiralled out of all recognition? Instead of certainty we have a lottery. The answer is simple and not as Draconian as may at first sight appear: abolish summary assessments. There are no summary assessments on the small claims track because only exceptionally are between-the-parties costs awarded. It is unusual for costs to be summarily assessed after a multi-track trial, which usually lasts for more than one day, and are sent for detailed assessment. There is no summary assessment of the costs of a fast track trial, which are fixed. There is no summary assessment of additional liabilities after an interim hearing and after a final hearing the judge has the option of sending additional liabilities, together with the basic costs, for detailed assessment. Accordingly, there is no necessity for a summary assessment where the receiving party is funded under a CFA with recoverable additional liabilities. This leaves pre-trial costs on the fast track and the costs of interim hearings. Even here there are many exceptions to the requirement for a summary assessment; these include: orders for 'costs in the case'; where there is insufficient time; where there are arguments about the law, the calculations or the retainer; mortgagee's costs; where the receiving party is state funded, a child or a patient and, of course, where the costs are agreed. As for the remainder, fixed or predictable pre-trial costs for all fast track actions should be introduced as a matter

of urgency, with provision for an additional prescribed amount for the costs of any interim application necessitated by the unreasonable conduct of one of the parties. All multi-track trial costs should go for detailed assessment, with benchmark costs for interim hearings. The introduction of fixed pre-trial costs on the fast track was delayed to enable the government to monitor fast track proceedings and collect and collate data. It is unfortunate that this was not done.'

JACKSON RECOMMENDATIONS (FINAL REPORT — CHAPTER 44)

[29.34]

Jackson LJ included the following recommendations in his review of costs:
(1)   If any judge at the end of a hearing within Costs PD paragraph 13.2 considers that he or she lacks the time or the expertise to assess costs summarily (either at that hearing or on paper afterwards), then the judge should order a substantial payment on account of costs and direct detailed assessment.
(2)   A revised and more informative version of Form N260 should be prepared for use in connection with summary assessments at the end of trials or appeals.

CHAPTER 30

DETAILED ASSESSMENT

[30.1]

CPR Rule 44.7 (see para [11.56]) provides that the amount of any costs ordered to be paid by one party to another shall be ascertained either by summary assessment by the judge at the end of a hearing (Chapter 29) or by a costs officer by a detailed assessment. The provisions for detailed assessment are contained in CPR Part 47.

[30.2]

CPR PART 47

SECTION I GENERAL RULES ABOUT DETAILED ASSESSMENT

CPR Rule 47.1: Time when detailed assessment may be carried out
The general rule is that the costs of any proceedings or any part of the proceedings are not to be assessed by the detailed procedure until the conclusion of the proceedings but the court may order them to be assessed immediately.
(The costs practice direction gives further guidance about when proceedings are concluded for the purpose of this rule)

[30.3]

CPD Section 28 Time when assessment may be carried out: Rule 47.1

(1)   *For the purposes of rule 47.1, proceedings are concluded when the court has finally determined the matters in issue in the claim, whether or not there is an appeal.*
(2)   *For the purposes of this rule, the making of an award of provisional damages under Part 41 will be treated as a final determination of the matters in issue.*
(3)   *The court may order or the parties may agree in writing that, although the proceedings are continuing, they will nevertheless be treated as concluded.*
(4)
    (a)   *A party who is served with a notice of commencement (see paragraph 32.3 below) may apply to a costs judge or a district judge to determine whether the party who served it is entitled to commence detailed assessment proceedings.*
    (b)   *On hearing such an application the orders which the court may make include: an order allowing the detailed assessment proceedings to continue, or an order setting aside the notice of commencement.*
(5)   *A costs judge or a district judge may make an order allowing detailed assessment proceedings to be commenced where there is no realistic prospect of the claim continuing.*

[30.4]

The purpose of this Rule in the past was to ensure that all costs were assessed by the same person at the same time, but its usefulness and importance were eroded by the introduction of summary assessments at the end of interim hearings which have lasted not more than one day. The Rule does, however, exclude detailed assessments of interim orders for costs in any event, unless the judge making the order has been persuaded to order an immediate detailed assessment. Paragraph 28.1(5) contains the useful provision that where there has been an order for a detailed assessment of interim costs, presumably against the claimant, and there is no prospect of the claim continuing, a costs judge or district judge may authorise the commencement of detailed assessment proceedings.

[30.5]

CPR Rule 47.2: No stay of detailed assessment where there is an appeal
Detailed assessment is not stayed pending an appeal unless the court so orders.

[30.6]

CPD Section 29 No stay of detailed assessment where there is an appeal: Rule 47.2
(1)   *Rule 47.2 provides that detailed assessment is not stayed pending an appeal unless the court so orders.*
(2)   *An application to stay the detailed assessment of costs pending an appeal may be made to the court whose order is being appealed or to the court who will hear the appeal.*

[30.7]

How refreshing to find a Rule which means what it says and says what it means. Previously there was a widespread misapprehension that an appeal acted as a stay in respect of orders for costs.

[30.8]

CPR Rule 47.3: Powers of an authorised court officer
(1)   An authorised court officer has all the powers of the court when making a detailed assessment, except—
    (a)   power to make a wasted costs order as defined in rule 48.7;
    (b)   power to make an order under—
        (i)   rule 44.14 (powers in relation to misconduct)
        (ii)   rule 47.8 (sanction for delay in commencing detailed assessment proceedings);
        (iii)   paragraph (2) (objection to detailed assessment by authorised court officer); and
    (c)   power to make a detailed assessment of costs payable to a solicitor by his client, unless the costs are being assessed under rule 48.5 (costs where money is payable to a child or protected party).
(2)   Where a party objects to the detailed assessment of costs being made by an authorised court officer, the court may order it to be made by a costs judge or a district judge.
(The Costs Practice Direction sets out the relevant procedure)

[30.9]

CPD Section 30 Powers of an authorised court officer: Rule 47.3

(1) *The court officers authorised by the Lord Chancellor to assess costs in the Costs Office and the Principal Registry of the Family Division are authorised to deal with claims for costs not exceeding £30,000 (excluding VAT) in the case of senior executive officers, or their equivalent and £75,000 (excluding VAT) in the case of principal officers.*

(2) *In calculating whether or not a bill of costs is within the authorised amounts, the figure to be taken into account is the total claim for costs including any additional liability.*

(3) *Where the receiving party, paying party and any other party to the detailed assessment proceedings who has served points of dispute are agreed that the assessment should not be made by an authorised court officer, the receiving party should so inform the court when requesting a hearing date. The court will then list the hearing before a costs judge or a district judge.*

(4) *In any other case a party who objects to the assessment being made by an authorised court officer must make an application to the costs judge or district judge under Part 23 (General Rules about Applications for Court Orders) setting out the reasons for the objection and if sufficient reason is shown the court will direct that the bill be assessed by a costs judge or district judge.*

[30.10]

An authorised court officer is defined in CPR Rule 43.2(1)(*d*) as any officer of (i) a county court; (ii) a district registry; (iii) the Principal Registry of the Family Division; or (iv) the Senior Courts Costs Office whom the Lord Chancellor has authorised to assess costs. When Lord Hailsham, as Lord Chancellor, sought to introduce a similar provision in the 1986 Rules, there was rioting in the streets and the solicitor and barrister members of the Supreme Court Rules Committee refused to sign the new Order 62. The objection was that the assessment of costs is a judicial function not an administrative act and that officers of district registries and county courts are not lawyers, most have never worked in a solicitor's office and are equipped neither by training nor experience to exercise judicial discretion. A twelfth-hour compromise resulted in RSC Ord 62r19(4)(b) providing that authorisation was limited to principal or senior executives of (i) the Supreme Court Costs Office (now the Senior Courts Costs Office), or a principal or a senior executive of (ii) a district registry who had previously served in either of such capacities for at least two years in the Supreme Court Costs Office or in one of the Birmingham, Bristol, Cardiff, Leeds, Liverpool or Manchester District Registries. The CPR contain no such provision but following the Lord Chancellor's assurance that he would follow the previous criteria, para 30.1 of the Practice Direction provides that the only authorised court officers are to be found in the SCCO and in the Principal Registry of the Family Division with financial limits on their jurisdiction. In fact there are none in the Principal Registry. A further safeguard is that the parties may agree that the detailed assessment should not be dealt with by an authorised court officer; if one party only objects he may make an application under Part 23 to a costs judge or district judge and, because a party is entitled to have a dispute resolved by a qualified judge, it is difficult to envisage any ground on which the application could be refused. Authorised court officers do not have the penal powers of a costs judge or district judge and this could be a reason for one of the parties objecting to them – or preferring them!

[30.11]

CPR Rule 47.4: Venue for detailed assessment proceedings

(1)   All applications and requests in detailed assessment proceedings must be made to or filed at the appropriate office.

(The Costs Practice Direction sets out the meaning of 'appropriate office' in any particular case)

(2)   The court may direct that the appropriate office is to be the Costs Office.

(3)   A county court may direct that another county court is to be the appropriate office.

(4)   A direction under paragraph (3) may be made without proceedings being transferred to that court.

(Rule 30.2 makes provision for any county court to transfer the proceedings to another county court for detailed assessment of costs)

[30.12]

CPD Section 31 Venue for detailed assessment proceedings: Rule 47.4

31.1 For the purposes of rule 47.4(1) the 'appropriate office' means

(1)   the district registry or county court in which the case was being dealt with when the judgment or order was made or the event occurred which gave rise to the right to assessment, or to which it has subsequently been transferred;

(1A)   where a tribunal, person or other body makes an order for the detailed assessment of costs, a county court (subject to paragraph 31.1A(1)); or

(2)   in all other cases, including Court of Appeal cases, the Costs Office.

(1)   This paragraph applies where the appropriate office is any of the following county courts:

Barnet, Bow, Brentford, Bromley, Central London, Clerkenwell and Shoreditch, Croydon, Edmonton, Ilford, Kingston, Lambeth, Mayors and City of London, Romford, Uxbridge, Wandsworth, West London, Willesden and Woolwich.

(2)   Where this paragraph applies:-

  (i)   the receiving party must file any request for a detailed assessment hearing in the Costs Office and, for all purposes relating to that detailed assessment (other than the issue of default costs certificates and applications to set aside default costs certificates), the Costs Office will be treated as the appropriate office in that case;

  (ii)   default costs certificates should be issued and applications to set aside default costs certificates should be issued and heard in the relevant county court; and

  (iii)   unless an order is made under rule 47.4(2) directing that the Costs Office as part of the High Court shall be the appropriate office, an appeal from any decision made by a costs judge shall lie to the Designated Civil Judge for the London Group of County Courts or such judge as he shall nominate. The appeal notice and any other relevant papers should be lodged at the Central London Civil Justice Centre.

(1)   A direction under rule 47.4(2) or (3) specifying a particular court, registry or office as the appropriate office may be given on application or on the court's own initiative.

(2)   *Before making such a direction on its own initiative the court will give the parties the opportunity to make representations.*

(3)   *Unless the Costs Office is the appropriate office for the purposes of Rule 47.4(1) an order directing that an assessment is to take place at the Costs Office will be made only if it is appropriate to do so having regard to the size of the bill of costs, the difficulty of the issues involved, the likely length of the hearing, the cost to the parties and any other relevant matter.*

[30.13]

Detailed assessments will generally take place at the court in which the case was proceeding, subject to the ability of the court to direct the detailed assessment to take place at another county court or district registry, presumably for the convenience of the parties or if one court has a serious backlog of work. In the latter event the transfer would no doubt only be with the prior agreement of the receiving court. However, the Senior Costs Judge, Peter Hurst, has announced that the SCCO is able to accept bills at all levels. Bills below £75,000 will usually be given a hearing date four to six weeks ahead, above that figure, the hearing date is likely to be three to four months ahead. The SCCO is able to deal with all bills from the Court of Appeal, High Court, Principal Registry of the Family Division, divorce county courts and other county courts. Transfer to the SCCO can be achieved by a simple direction to this effect. A case which is of high value, complex, or which is going to take a considerable time to assess is clearly suitable for transfer. The same may be true of a low-value bill containing a novel or complex point of principle.

The parties must, of course, be given the opportunity to make representations as to whether or not the case should be transferred. The first and most obvious criterion is the cost of requiring the parties to attend the SCCO in London as against the actual amount in dispute in the bill. Rule 31.1A(1) permanently implements the pilot scheme whereby detailed assessments in proceedings in any London county court are heard in the Senior Courts Costs Office. In non-London cases the time and cost of attending the SCCO may be a significant factor. Where the cost of transporting the papers and the travel and hotel expenses of those involved in what will inevitably be a lengthy hearing become disproportionate, it may be possible to arrange for a costs judge or costs officer to sit outside the SCCO in order to deal with the matter.

A proposal by the Association of District Judges that some of their members with a special interest and expertise in costs should be made available to deal with the larger assessments of costs was supported by the Lord Chancellor and members of the senior judiciary. The result was the appointment of 22 district judges authorised to sit as regional costs judges on all circuits outside London. The scheme, launched on 14 November 2005, applies where (i) the estimated duration of the detailed assessment is more than one day, and/or (ii) the total amount claimed in the bill of costs exceeds £50,000, and/or (iii) complex arguments on points of law or an issue affecting a group of similar cases are identified in the points of dispute or reply, or are referred to in argument at a detailed assessment hearing. When a request for detailed assessment in Form N258 is filed, it is referred to a district judge who decides whether it satisfies one or more of the criteria for reference to a regional costs judge. If it does, the bill will be referred to the appropriate regional costs judge who will decide whether or not to accept it and, if so, give any necessary directions, including as to listing. Delay can be avoided if the parties themselves agree that the case fulfils the requirements for reference to a regional costs judge and say so, with supporting written submissions if necessary, when the request for a detailed assessment hearing is lodged. If possible, the parties should agree the reference to a regional costs judge, any directions and the venue. The file need not be transferred to the regional costs judge's court, so enquiries may continue at the originating court. Although the new scheme does not preclude transfer of a detailed assessment to the SCCO in accordance with CPR 47.4(2), or the possibility of a costs judge from the SCCO having an away day, the need for either of these steps should be significantly reduced.

Requests for detailed assessment of the costs of proceedings in the Court of Protection should be directed to the Senior Courts Costs Office. The fee payable is £200. A Practice Direction dated 11 May 2004 introduced a new 'short form' bill of costs for assessment where the amount of costs involved does not exceed £3,000, excluding VAT and disbursements. The precedent appears below. In such cases, a reduced assessment fee of £100 is payable. The SCCO will normally deal with Court of Protection assessments on a provisional basis by post. If the solicitor is not satisfied with the assessment, the costs officer must be informed within 14 days of receipt of the provisional assessment. The SCCO will then fix a date for hearing. In practice the costs officer will deal with any enquiries by telephone or letter.

Model Short Form Bill

IN THE COURT OF PROTECTION

Case No: - ....

SCCO reference ....
(to be completed by the court)

IN THE MATTER OF

.... (A patient)

Short form bill of costs of the Receiver of*(e.g.) General Management for the period* ....
to be assessed pursuant to the First General Order dated .... *and General Direction dated* **19/11/82**

Summary of work carried out

Fee earner category .... Rate claimed ....

Work done:-   **Charge:-**

Time spent in personal attendances
e.g. 22/9/02   45mins   Upon patient   ....

Time spent in travel ....

Letters Sent ....

Telephone Calls ....

Time spent on documents ....

Other work *(give details)*
....
....

                                                    Sub Total   ....
                                                    V.A.T.   ....
Disbursements (list below)
....
....   Disbursements   ....
                                                    V.A.T.   ....

                                                    Grand Total   ....

I certify that this bill is both accurate and complete.

.... (name and position)

**Short form bill of costs for use in Court of Protection assessments
where the total costs claimed do not exceed £3000
excluding VAT and disbursements**

Name, address and reference of person filing bill

[30.14]

SECTION II COSTS PAYABLE BY ONE PARTY TO ANOTHER – COMMENCEMENT OF DETAILED ASSESSMENT PROCEEDINGS

CPR Rule 47.5: Application of this section
This section of Part 47 applies where a cost officer is to make a detailed assessment of:

- (a)   costs which are payable by one party to another; or
- (b)   the sum which is payable by one party to the prescribed charity pursuant to an order under section 194(3) of the Legal Services Act 2007.

[30.15]

CPR Rule 47.6: Commencement of detailed assessment proceedings
(1)   Detailed assessment proceedings are commenced by the receiving party serving on the paying party—

- (a)   notice of commencement in the relevant practice form; and
- (b)   a copy of the bill of costs.

(Rule 47.7 sets out the period for commencing detailed assessment proceedings)

(2)   The receiving party must also serve a copy of the notice of commencement and the bill on any other relevant persons specified in the costs practice direction.

(3)   A person on whom a copy of the notice of commencement is served under paragraph (2) is a party to the detailed assessment proceedings (in addition to the paying party and the receiving party).

(The Costs Practice Direction deals with:

other documents which the party must file when he requests detailed assessment; the court's powers where it considers that a hearing may be necessary; the form of a bill; and the length of notice which will be given if a hearing date is fixed)

[30.16]

CPD Section 32 Commencement of detailed assessment proceedings: Rule 47.6
32.1   *Precedents A, B, C and D in the Schedule of Costs Precedents annexed to this Practice Direction are model forms of bills of costs for detailed assessment. Further information about bills of costs is set out in Section 4.*

32.2   *A detailed assessment may be in respect of:*
- (1)   *base costs, where a claim for additional liability has not been made or has been agreed;*
- (2)   *a claim for additional liability only, base costs having been summarily assessed or agreed;*
        or
- (3)   *both base costs and additional liability.*

32.3   *If the detailed assessment is in respect of costs without any additional liability, the receiving party must serve on the paying party and all the other relevant persons the following documents:*
- (a)   *a notice of commencement;*
- (b)   *a copy of the bill of costs;*
- (c)   *copies of the fee notes of counsel and of any expert in respect of fees claimed in the bill;*
- (d)   *written evidence as to any other disbursement which is claimed and which exceeds £500;*

(e)   a statement giving the name and address for service of any person upon whom the receiving party intends to serve the notice of commencement.

32.4   If the detailed assessment is in respect of an additional liability only, the receiving party must serve on the paying party and all other relevant persons the following documents:

(a)   a notice of commencement;
(b)   a copy of the bill of costs;
(c)   the relevant details of the additional liability;
(d)   a statement giving the name and address of any person upon whom the receiving party intends to serve the notice of commencement.

32.5   The relevant details of an additional liability are as follows:

(1)   In the case of a conditional fee agreement with a success fee:

    (a)   a statement showing the amount of costs which have been summarily assessed or agreed; and the percentage increase which has been claimed in respect of those costs;

    (b)   where the conditional fee agreement was entered into before 1st November 2005, a statement of the reasons for the percentage increase given in accordance with regulation 3(1)(a) of the Conditional Fee Agreements Regulations 2000 or regulation 5(1)(c) of the Collective Conditional Fee Agreements Regulations 2000 [Both sets of regulations were revoked by the Conditional Fee Agreements (Revocation) Regulations 2005 but continue to have effect in relation to conditional fee agreements and collective conditional fee agreements entered into before 1st November 2005.];

    (c)   where the conditional fee agreement was entered into on or after 1st November 2005 (except in cases where the percentage increase is fixed by CPR Part 45, sections II to V), either a statement of the reasons for the percentage increase or a copy of the risk assessment prepared at the time that the conditional fee agreement was entered into;

    (d)   if the conditional fee agreement is not disclosed (and the Court of Appeal has indicated that it should be the usual practice for a conditional fee agreement, redacted where appropriate, to be disclosed for the purpose of costs proceedings in which a success fee is claimed), a statement setting out the following information contained in the conditional fee agreement so as to enable the paying party and the court to determine the level of risk undertaken by the solicitor –

        (i)   the definition of 'win' and, if applicable, 'lose';
        (ii)   details of the receiving party's liability to pay costs if that party wins or loses; and
        (iii) details of the receiving party's liability to pay costs if that party fails to obtain a judgment more advantageous than a Part 36 offer.

(2)   If the additional liability is an insurance premium, a copy of the insurance certificate showing –

    (a)   whether the policy covers:
        (i)   the receiving party's own costs;
        (ii)   the receiving party's opponent's costs;
        (iii) the receiving party's own costs and opponent's costs; and
    (b)   the maximum extent of that cover; and
    (c)   the amount of the premium paid or payable.

(3)   If the receiving party claims an additional amount under section 30 of the Access to Justice Act 1999, a statement setting out the basis upon which the receiving party's liability for the additional amount is calculated.

32.6   Attention is drawn to the fact that the additional amount recoverable pursuant to section 30 of the Access to Justice Act 1999 in respect of a membership organisation must not exceed the likely cost of the premium of an insurance policy against the risk of incurring a liability to pay the costs of other parties to the proceedings as provided by the Access to Justice (Membership Organisation) Regulations 2000 Regulation 4.(for the purposes of arrangements entered into before 1st November 2005) and the Access to Justice (Membership

Organisation) Regulations 2005 Regulation 5 (for the purposes of arrangements entered into on or after 1st November 2005).

32.7   If a detailed assessment is in respect of both base costs and an additional liability, the receiving party must serve on the paying party and all other relevant persons the documents listed in paragraph 32.3 and the documents giving relevant details of an additional liability listed in paragraph 32.5.

(1)   *The Notice of Commencement should be in Form N252.*

(2)   *Before it is served, it must be completed to show as separate items;*

    (a)   *the total amount of the costs claimed in the bill;*

    (b)   *the extra sum which will be payable by way of fixed costs and court fees if a default costs certificate is obtained.*

(1)   *This paragraph applies where the notice of commencement is to be served outside England and Wales.*

(2)   *The date to be inserted in the notice of commencement for the paying party to send points of dispute is a date (not less than 21 days from the date of service of the notice) which must be calculated by reference to Section IV of Part 6 as if the notice were a claim form and as if the date to be inserted was the date for the filing of a defence.*

(1)   *For the purposes of rule 47.6(2) a 'relevant person' means:*

    (a)   *any person who has taken part in the proceedings which gave rise to the assessment and who is directly liable under an order for costs made against him;*

    (b)   *any person who has given to the receiving party notice in writing that he has a financial interest in the outcome of the assessment and wishes to be a party accordingly;*

    (c)   *any other person whom the court orders to be treated as such.*

(2)   *Where a party is unsure whether a person is or is not a relevant person, that party may apply to the appropriate office for directions.*

(3)   *The court will generally not make an order that the person in respect of whom the application is made will be treated as a relevant person, unless within a specified time he applies to the court to be joined as a party to the assessment proceedings in accordance with Part 19 (Parties and Group Litigation).*

(1)   *This paragraph applies in cases in which the bill of costs is capable of being copied onto a computer disk.*

(2)   *If, before the detailed assessment hearing, a paying party requests a disk copy of a bill to which this paragraph applies, the receiving party must supply him with a copy free of charge not more than 7 days after the date on which he received the request.*

[30.17]

The commencement of detailed assessment proceedings by serving documents on the paying party rather than filing them at court was entirely new. Notice of commencement must be served on Form N252.

Rule 47.6(2) requires service to be on the 'paying party and on any other relevant persons' who are defined in para 32.10 of the Practice Direction. Where there is any doubt as to who is a relevant person, para 32.10(2) provides for there to be an application to the court for directions, which should be made in accordance with CPR Part 23. The importance of service where the paying parties are jointly and severally liable was emphasised in *Mainwaring v Goldtech Investments Ltd (No 2)* [1999] 1 All ER 456, CA where the receiving party delayed for about six years in serving a bill of costs on one of two paying parties. The first paying party's assessment had been completed and a certificate issued. When the second party successfully applied to set aside the certificate and had the costs against them disallowed in their entirety because of the delay the first paying party succeeded in having the costs award against her also set aside in its entirety, because there could not be two certificates in different amounts arising from a single costs order imposing joint and several liability. There was only one bill and there could therefore be only one penalty.

Paragraph 32.3 provides that the notice of commencement must be accompanied by: a copy of the bill of costs; copies of the fee notes of counsel and of any expert in respect of fees claimed in the bill; written evidence as to any other disbursement which is claimed which exceeds £250; a statement giving the name and address for service of any person on whom the receiving party intends to serve the notice of commencement. Writing in the New Law Journal, Costs Judge John O'Hare pointed out that although failing to serve copies of the fee notes of counsel and of any expert did not nullify the notice of commencement they do make irregular both the notice and any default costs certificate obtained in respect of it. Another common mistake made by receiving parties is to fail to take account of the correct date of service, as specified by Rule 6.7, thus allowing paying parties less than the prescribed 21-day period for serving points of dispute. If the notice of commencement is served by first class post or Document Exchange, it is deemed to be served on the second day after it was posted. A receiving party who obtains a default costs certificate while ignoring a request for relevant fee notes, or who obtains a default costs certificate earlier than he should have done, may expect his certificate to be set aside with costs payable by him, such costs to be set off against any costs payable under the bill for assessment.

PROVISIONAL ASSESSMENT

[30.18]

Despite Sir Rupert Jackson's proposal (Jackson, Ch 45, 5.17) that 'It would be sensible to defer this pilot until after the proposed fixed costs regime for the fast track has been introduced', a pilot scheme for provisional assessment without an oral hearing where the base costs are under £25,000 was introduced on 1 October 2010 in the Leeds, York and Scarborough County Courts. It is contained in a new Practice Direction 51E as follows:

[30.18A]

Practice Direction 51E – County Court Provisional Assessment Pilot Scheme

(1) *This Practice Direction is made under rule 51.2. It provides for a pilot scheme (the County Court Provisional Assessment Pilot Scheme) to—*
   (i) *operate from the 1 October 2010 to 30 September 2011;*
   (ii) *operate in the Leeds, York and Scarborough County Courts;*
   (iii) *apply to detailed assessment proceedings—*
   (a) *which are commenced on or after 1 October 2010; and*
   (b) *in which the base costs claimed are £25,000 or less.*

(2)   Under this pilot scheme CPR Part 47 will apply with modifications. The following provisions of Part 47 and the Costs Practice Direction will continue to apply—

    (i)   rules 47.1, 47.2, 47.4 to 47.13, 47.14 (except paragraphs (6) and (7)), 47.15, 47.16, 47.18 and 47.19; and

    (ii)   sections 28, 29, 31 to 39, 40 (with the exception of paragraphs 40.5 to 40.7, 40.9, 40.11 and 40.16), 41, 42, 45 and 46 of the Costs Practice Direction.

(3)   In cases falling within the scope of this pilot scheme, when the receiving party files the request for a detailed assessment hearing, that party must not only file the request in Form N258 together with the documents set out at paragraph 40.2 of the Costs Practice Direction but must also file with them an additional copy of the bill and a statement of the costs claimed in respect of the detailed assessment drawn on the assumption that (unless any of the following paragraphs apply) no party will subsequently request an oral hearing following a provisional assessment.

(4)   On receipt of the request for detailed assessment and the supporting papers, the court will within 6 weeks undertake a provisional assessment based on the information contained in the bill and supporting papers and the contentions set out in the points of dispute and any reply. No party will be permitted to attend the provisional assessment.

(5)   If, having commenced a provisional assessment, the court takes the view that the matter is unsuitable for a provisional assessment, the court will direct that the matter must be listed for hearing and thereafter the pilot scheme will cease to apply to it.

(6)   If the court completes a provisional assessment, it will send a copy of the bill as provisionally assessed to each party with a notice stating that either party may request the court to list the matter for full argument on any aspect of the provisional assessment within 21 days of receipt of the notice.

(7)   Unless paragraph 9 applies, either party may, within 21 days of receipt of the notice and provisionally assessed bill, request the court by letter to list the matter for an oral hearing. On receipt of a request for an oral hearing the court will fix a date for the hearing and give at least 14 days notice of the time and place of the detailed assessment hearing to all parties who are entitled to be heard.

(8)   Unless the court otherwise orders the costs of and incidental to an oral hearing convened under paragraph 8 above, shall be awarded as follows.

    (i)   Costs may be awarded to a paying party if the amount allowed is reduced to a sum which is 80% or less than the sum which had been provisionally assessed (excluding costs of the provisional assessment), or if the oral hearing was requested by a receiving party only and the amount allowed is not increased to a sum which is 120% or more than the sum which had been provisionally assessed (excluding costs of the provisional assessment).

    (ii)   Costs may be awarded to a receiving party, if the amount allowed is increased to a sum which is 120% or more than the sum which had been provisionally assessed (excluding costs of the provisional assessment), or if the oral hearing was requested by a paying party only and the amount allowed is not reduced to a sum which is 80% or less than the sum which had been provisionally assessed (excluding costs of the provisional assessment).

    (iii)   Where requests for an oral hearing are made by a receiving party and also by a paying party no order for the costs of and incidental to the oral hearing will be made if the amount allowed is greater than 80%

> *but less than 120% of the sum which had been provisionally assessed (excluding costs of the provisional assessment).*

(9) *If a party wishes to be heard only as to the amount provisionally assessed in respect of the receiving party's costs of the provisional assessment, the court will invite each side to make written submissions and the amount of the costs of the provisional assessment will be finally determined without a hearing.*

[30.19]

CPR Rule 47.7: Period for commencing detailed assessment proceedings

The following table shows the period for commencing detailed assessment proceedings.

SOURCE OF RIGHT TO DETAILED AS- SESSMENT	TIME BY WHICH DETAILED ASSESS- MENT PROCEEDINGS MUST BE COM- MENCED
Judgment, direction, order, award or other determination	3 months after the date of the judgment etc.
	Where detailed assessment is stayed pending an appeal, 3 months after the date of the order lifting the stay.
Discontinuance under Part 38	3 months after the date of service of notice of discontinuance under rule 38.3; or 3 months after the date of the dismissal of application to set the notice of discontinuance aside under rule 38.4.
Acceptance of an offer to settle un- der Part 36	3 months after the date when the right to costs arose.

[30.20]

CPD Section 33 Period for commencing detailed assessment proceedings: Rule 47.7

33.1 *The parties may agree under rule 2.11 (Time limits may be varied by parties) to extend or shorten the time specified by rule 47.7 for commencing the detailed assessment proceedings.*

33.2 *A party may apply to the appropriate office for an order under rule 3.1(2)(a) to extend or shorten that time.*

33.3 *Attention is drawn to rule 47.6(1). The detailed assessment proceedings are commenced by service of the documents referred to.*

33.4 *Permission to commence assessment proceedings out of time is not required.*

[30.21]

CPR Rule 47.8: Sanction for delay in commencing detailed assessment proceedings

(1) Where the receiving party fails to commence detailed assessment proceedings within the period specified—

    (a)   in rule 47.7; or

    (b)   by any direction of the court,

the paying party may apply for an order requiring the receiving party to commence detailed assessment proceedings within such time as the court may specify.

(2)   On an application under paragraph (1), the court may direct that, unless the receiving party commences detailed assessment proceedings within the time specified by the court, all or part of the costs to which the receiving party would otherwise be entitled will be disallowed.

(3)   If—

(a)   the paying party has not made an application in accordance with paragraph (1); and

(b)   the receiving party commences the proceedings later than the period specified in 47.7,

the court may disallow all or part of the interest otherwise payable to the receiving party under—

(i)   section 17 of the Judgments Act 1838; or

(ii)   section 74 of the County Courts Act 1984,

but must not impose any other sanction except in accordance with rule 44.14 (powers in relation to misconduct).

(4)   Where the costs to be assessed in a detailed assessment are payable out of the Community Legal Service Fund, this rule applies as if the receiving party were the solicitor to whom the costs are payable and the paying party were the Legal Services Commission.

[30.22]

CPD Section 34 Sanction for delay in commencing detailed assessment proceedings: Rule 47.8

(1)   *An application for an order under rule 47.8 must be made in writing and be issued in the appropriate office.*

(2)   *The application notice must be served at least 7 days before the hearing.*

DELAY

[30.23]

In other words, the period for commencing detailed assessment proceedings is three months after the event giving rise to the right of assessment.

Before the CPR if a receiving party did not get on with the assessment proceedings the paying party was able to do so. Now, if the receiving party does not commence detailed assessment proceedings within the time prescribed by the Rules or any direction of the court, the paying party's remedy is to make an application using the Part 23 procedure for an order under Rule 47.8 that unless the receiving party commences proceedings within a specified period all or part of the costs will be disallowed. Where the paying party has not obtained such an order there is nothing to prevent the receiving party from commencing the assessment proceedings at any time, the only sanction being the court's power to disallow interest under Rule 47.8(3)(*b*). Some costs officers require justification of the delay in writing when considering whether or not to disallow interest.

The paying party may also have recourse to Rule 44.14(2)(*a*) and (*b*) which empowers the court to disallow all or part of the costs where there has been misconduct. The case law does not hold out much hope for applications under Rule 44.14 based on costs delays.

In *Botham v Khan* and *Lamb v Khan* [2004] EWHC 2602 (QB) 12 November the court held that the sanction of disallowance pursuant to r 44.14 on the ground of misconduct would be disproportionate. Although there was culpable delay by the defendant the claimants had not availed themselves of the right to apply under CPR rule 47.8(1) for an order requiring the defendant to commence detailed assessment within a specified period. The delay had not prevented a fair assessment of the defendant's costs although the process would be more difficult than if it had been carried out on a timely basis.

In *Less v Benedict* [2005] EWHC 1643 (Ch), [2005] All ER (D) 355 (Jul) the claimants were ordered to pay the defendant's costs to be ascertained by detailed assessment and the defendant served notice of commencement of assessment. The notice was served within the time limit specified in CPR rule 47.7 but as a result of confusion and oversight it was not until three and half years later that the defendant re-served the notices on the claimants at their last known addresses. The claimants submitted their right to a hearing within a reasonable time under Article 6 of the European Convention on Human Rights would be breached if the costs assessment was allowed to continue; the excessive and unreasonable delay without explanation was an abuse of process; the claimants could not have a fair hearing as they no longer had access to the relevant files. The court held there had been no violation of the claimant's rights under Article 6 because CPR Part 47 provided a mechanism for the claimants to bring the matter to the attention of the court to obtain a hearing within a reasonable time. If a party failed to take advantage of that mechanism it could not be said that he had thereby been deprived of his rights under Article 6. The court would not, by proceeding to a hearing, be sanctioning a continuance of a breach of any rights, but would be taking remedial action to correct the consequences of such a breach.

The paying party was equally unsuccessful under Rule 44.4 in *Haji-Ioannou v Frangos* [2006] EWCA Civ 1663, [2007] 3 All ER 938, even though the delay was for more than five years. Although Rules 47.8 and 44.14 are not inconsistent there was no case for imposing upon the defendants the further sanction of disallowing any part of their costs under Rule 44.14 in addition to loss of interest under Rule 47.8(3). Their delay was not deliberate or wilful and the claimant had not himself been a model of expedition. Where the relevant rule not only gave the paying party the option of preventing further delay by himself taking the initiative but also spelt out the normal sanction for such delay, the court should be hesitant to impose further penalties by way of reducing otherwise allowable costs.

The message is clear. Paying parties may be understandably reluctant to stir up receiving parties by making an application under Rule 47.8, but if the sleeping dog does eventually awake, the sanction is likely to be deprivation of interest alone and not of costs as well.

PUBLIC FUNDING

[30.24]

The Official Receiver v Dobson, Re Homes Assured Corpn plc; Sampson v Wilson [2002] 1 Costs LR 71, ChD were appeals from detailed assessments to Park J sitting with assessors. In the first case, under the Civil Legal Aid (General) Regulations 1989 the assisted party's solicitors' bill should have been lodged for assessment within three months, but it was lodged four years out-of-time. In the absence of any adequate explanation for the delay, the deputy costs judge, after assessing the profit costs at £29,500, disallowed them in their entirety, under regulation 109 and rule 44.14. On appeal it was held on the authorities relating to delay that the court was not confronted with the stark choice between a reprimand but no sanction, on the one hand, and a total striking-out on the other. The court can graduate the penalty between these two extremes. There is the built-in sanction in delay in lodging a public funding bill that no interest is payable on the outstanding costs and it is only the solicitors who are prejudiced by the delay. The delay is positively beneficial to the Legal Services Commission who suffer no discernible prejudice, while the delay in no way impeded the normal and efficient assessment of the bill. The delay was such that the deputy costs judge had been right to impose a sanction, but it should have been a reduction of 30%, not 100%.

In the second case, the costs judge also disallowed the profit costs in their entirety, but did not assess them. The bill when first lodged for assessment was only five months out-of-time, but by the time the solicitors had corrected various errors of omission and got the fee right, it was 17 months overdue. After some further months had elapsed the SCCO informed the solicitors that the costs judge had in mind disallowing the whole of their costs, to which the solicitors responded that as the matter was still ongoing they were withdrawing their legal aid bill from assessment at that stage. There then followed months of communications in which the solicitors demonstrated, contrary to the suspicions of the costs judge, not malice but muddle. The costs judge gave as his reason for disallowing the whole of the profit costs claimed by the solicitors, of some £58,000, 'the way that they have dealt with the whole of this matter' and in particular referred to 'the long delay in lodgement' and 'because you withdrew the bills of costs lodged'. The costs judge had misinterpreted regulation 109(1) in considering it authorised him to disallow costs because he disapproved of the firm's conduct of the assessment. Whether an item of costs in a bill was wasted or not must depend on circumstances as they existed when the item was incurred. That was not a good reason for disallowing any profit costs in this matter. The delay could not justify a disallowance of all the profit costs by way of penalty, which was disproportionate to such an extent that it went beyond the acceptable limits for the exercise of the costs judge's discretion.

The purpose of rule 47.8(4) is to enable the Legal Services Commission to put pressure on a solicitor who has delayed commencing detailed assessment proceedings. Solicitors who have received payment on account, particularly, as sometimes happens, if it exceeds the ultimate amount of the bill, have no incentive to commence detailed assessment proceedings, which causes difficulty for counsel who remain unpaid but cannot themselves commence detailed assessment proceedings.

FORM AND CONTENTS OF BILLS OF COSTS

[30.25]

The Schedule of Costs Precedents annexed to the Costs Practice Direction provides four model forms of bills of costs for detailed assessment. Before we look at the models it is necessary to revert to the Practice Direction supplementing Part 43 which prescribes the form and contents of bills of costs.

[30.26]

CPD Section 4 Form and contents of bills of costs

4.1   *A bill of costs may consist of such of the following sections as may be appropriate:—*
(1)   *title page;*
(2)   *background information;*
(3)   *items of costs claimed under the headings specified in paragraph 4.6;*
(4)   *summary showing the total costs claimed on each page of the bill;*
(5)   *schedules of time spent on non-routine attendances; and*
(6)   *the certificates referred to in paragraph 4.15.*
4.2   *Where it is necessary or convenient to do so, a bill of costs may be divided into two or more parts, each part containing sections (2), (3) and (4) above. Circumstances in which it will be necessary or convenient to divide a bill into parts include:—*

(1)   *Where the receiving party acted in person during the course of the proceedings (whether or not the party also had a legal representative at that time) the bill must be divided into different parts so as to distinguish between;*
     (a)   *the costs claimed for work done by the legal representative; and*
     (b)   *the costs claimed for work done by the receiving party in person.*
(1A)   *Where the receiving party had pro bono representation for part of the proceedings and an order under section 194(3) of the Legal Services Act 2007 has been made, the bill must be divided into different parts so as to distinguish between:*
     (a)   *the sum equivalent to the costs claimed for work done by the legal representative acting free of charge; and*
     (b)   *the costs claimed for work done by the legal representative not acting free of charge.*
(2)   *Where the receiving party was represented by different solicitors during the course of the proceedings, the bill must be divided into different parts so as to distinguish between the costs payable in respect of each solicitor.*
(3)   *Where the receiving party obtained legal aid or LSC funding in respect of all or part of the proceedings the bill must be divided into separate parts so as to distinguish between;*
     (a)   *costs claimed before legal aid or LSC funding was granted;*
     (b)   *costs claimed after legal aid or LSC funding was granted; and*
     (c)   *any costs claimed after legal aid or LSC funding ceased.*
(4)   *Where value added tax (VAT) is claimed and there was a change in the rate of VAT during the course of the proceedings, the bill must be divided into separate parts so as to distinguish between;*
     (a)   *costs claimed at the old rate of VAT; and*
     (b)   *costs claimed at the new rate of VAT.*
(5)   *Where the bill covers costs payable under an order or orders under which there are different paying parties the bill must be divided into parts so as to deal separately with the costs payable by each paying party.*
(6)   *Where the bill covers costs payable under an order or orders, in respect of*

which the receiving party wishes to claim interest from different dates, the bill must be divided to enable such interest to be calculated.

4.3 Where a party claims costs against another party and also claims costs against the LSC only for work done in the same period, the costs claimed against the LSC only can be claimed either in a separate part of the bill or in additional columns in the same part of the bill. Precedents C and D in the Schedule of Costs Precedents annexed to this Practice Direction show how bills should be drafted when costs are claimed against the LSC only.

4.4 The title page of the bill of costs must set out:—
(1)   the full title of the proceedings;
(2)   the name of the party whose bill it is and a description of the document showing the right to assessment (as to which see paragraph 40.4, below);
(3)   if VAT is included as part of the claim for costs, the VAT number of the legal representative or other person in respect of whom VAT is claimed;
(4)   details of all legal aid certificates, LSC certificates and relevant amendment certificates in respect of which claims for costs are included in the bill.

4.5 The background information included in the bill of costs should set out:—
(1)   a brief description of the proceedings up to the date of the notice of commencement;
(2)   a statement of the status of the solicitor or solicitor's employee in respect of whom costs are claimed and (if those costs are calculated on the basis of hourly rates) the hourly rates claimed for each such person.

It should be noted that 'legal executive' means a Fellow of the Institute of Legal Executives.

Other clerks, who are fee earners of equivalent experience, may be entitled to similar rates. It should be borne in mind that Fellows of the Institute of Legal Executives will have spent approximately 6 years in practice, and taken both general and specialist examinations. The Fellows have therefore acquired considerable practical and academic experience.

Clerks without the equivalent experience of legal executives will normally be treated as being the equivalent of trainee solicitors and para-legals.
(3)   a brief explanation of any agreement or arrangement between the receiving party and his solicitors, which affects the costs claimed in the bill.

4.6 The bill of costs may consist of items under such of the following heads as may be appropriate:—
(1)   attendances on the court and counsel up to the date of the notice of commencement;
(2)   attendances on and communications with the receiving party;
(3)   attendances on and communications with witnesses including any expert witness;
(4)   attendances to inspect any property or place for the purposes of the proceedings;
(5)   attendances on and communications with other persons, including offices of public records;
(6)   communications with the court and with counsel;
(7)   work done on documents: preparing and considering documentation, including documentation necessary to comply with Practice Direction (Pre-Action Conduct) or a relevant pre-action protocol where appropriate, work done in connection with arithmetical calculations of compensation and/or interest and time spent collating documents;
(8)   work done in connection with negotiations with a view to settlement if not already covered in the heads listed above;
(9)   attendances on and communications with London and other agents and work done by them;
(10)   other work done which was of or incidental to the proceedings and which is not already covered in the heads listed above.

4.7 In respect of each of the heads of costs:—
(1)   'communications' means letters out, e-mails out and telephone calls;
(2)   communications, which are not routine communications, must be set out in chronological order;

(3)   *routine communications must be set out as a single item at the end of each head;*

4.8   *Routine communications are letters out, e mails out and telephone calls which because of their simplicity should not be regarded as letters or e mails of substance or telephone calls which properly amount to an attendance.*

4.9   *Each item claimed in the bill of costs must be consecutively numbered.*

4.10   *In each part of the bill of costs which claims items under head (1) (attendances on court and counsel) a note should be made of:*

(1)   *all relevant events, including events which do not constitute chargeable items;*

(2)   *any orders for costs which the court made (whether or not a claim is made in respect of those costs in this bill of costs).*

4.11   *The numbered items of costs may be set out on paper divided into columns. Precedents A, B, C and D in the Schedule of Costs Precedents annexed to this Practice Direction illustrate various model forms of bills of costs.*

4.12   *In respect of heads (2) to (10) in paragraph 4.6 above, if the number of attendances and communications other than routine communications is twenty or more, the claim for the costs of those items in that section of the bill of costs should be for the total only and should refer to a schedule in which the full record of dates and details is set out. If the bill of costs contains more than one schedule each schedule should be numbered consecutively.*

4.13   *The bill of costs must not contain any claims in respect of costs or court fees which relate solely to the detailed assessment proceedings other than costs claimed for preparing and checking the bill.*

4.14   *The summary must show the total profit costs and disbursements claimed separately from the total VAT claimed. Where the bill of costs is divided into parts the summary must also give totals for each part. If each page of the bill gives a page total the summary must also set out the page totals for each page.*

4.15   *The bill of costs must contain such of the certificates, the texts of which are set out in Precedent F of the Schedule of Costs Precedents annexed to this Practice Direction, as are appropriate.*

4.16   *The following provisions relate to work done by solicitors:*

(1)   *Routine letters out, routine e-mails out and routine telephone calls will in general be allowed on a unit basis of 6 minutes each, the charge being calculated by reference to the appropriate hourly rate. The unit charge for letters out and e-mails out will include perusing and considering the relevant letters in or e-mails in and accordingly no separate charge is to be made for in-coming letters or e-mails.*

(2)   *The court may, in its discretion, allow an actual time charge for preparation of electronic communications other than e-mails sent by solicitors, which properly amount to attendances provided that the time taken has been recorded.*

(3)   *Local travelling expenses incurred by solicitors will not be allowed. The definition of 'local' is a matter for the discretion of the court. While no absolute rule can be laid down, as a matter of guidance, 'local' will, in general, be taken to mean within a radius of 10 miles from the court dealing with the case at the relevant time. Where travelling and waiting time is claimed, this should be allowed at the rate agreed with the client unless this is more than the hourly rate on the assessment.*

(4)   *The cost of postage, couriers, out-going telephone calls, fax and telex messages will in general not be allowed but the court may exceptionally in its discretion allow such expenses in unusual circumstances or where the cost is unusually heavy.*

(5)   *The cost of making copies of documents will not in general be allowed but the court may exceptionally in its discretion make an allowance for copying in unusual circumstances or where the documents copied are unusually numerous in relation to the nature of the case. Where this discretion is invoked the number of copies made, their purpose and the costs claimed for them must be set out in the bill.*

(6)   *Agency charges as between principal solicitors and their agents will be dealt with on the principle that such charges, where appropriate, form part of the*

> *principal solicitor's charges. Where these charges relate to head (1) in paragraph 4.6 (attendances at court and on counsel) they must be included in their chronological order in that head. In other cases they must be included in head (9) (attendances on London and other agents).*
>
> (1) *Where a claim is made for a percentage increase in addition to an hourly rate or base fee, the amount of the increase must be shown separately, either in the appropriate arithmetic column or in the narrative column. (For an example see Precedent A or Precedent B.)*
>
> (2) *Where a claim is made against the LSC only and includes enhancement and where a claim is made in family proceedings and includes a claim for uplift or general care and conduct, the amount of enhancement uplift and general care and conduct must be shown, in respect of each item upon which it is claimed, as a separate amount either in the appropriate arithmetic column or in the narrative column. (For an example, see Precedent C.)*
>
> *'Enhancement' means the increase in prescribed rates which may be allowed by a costs officer in accordance with the Legal Aid in Civil Proceedings (Remuneration) Regulations 1994 or the Legal Aid in Family Proceedings (Remuneration) Regulations 1991.*
>
> *4.18 A claim may be made for the reasonable costs of preparing and checking the bill of costs.*

This section of the Costs Practice Direction helpfully incorporates all of those aspects of practice directions and decisions under the previous costs regime which apply equally to the present. It is a mine of practice and procedure.

Paragraph 4.6(10) of the Costs Practice Direction confirms that an order for costs includes work 'of or incidental to the proceedings' while *Roach v Home Office; Matthews v Home Office* [2009] EWHC 312 (QB) [2009] 3 All ER 510, [2009] NLJR 474 demonstrated that under ss 51(1) and (2) of the Supreme Court (now Senior Courts) Act 1981 not only were pre-action costs recoverable but also the costs of and incidental to other proceedings, such as an inquest, are covered.

(a) Six-minute unit

[30.27]

Paragraph 4.16 is a particularly useful guide on various matters which have caused problems in the past.

It is important to understand that the six-minute unit (one-tenth of the fee earner's hourly rate) referred to in para 4.16 applies not only to letters but also routine telephone calls and emails sent. An amendment to the Practice Direction acknowledges that relevant text messages may be chargeable on the same basis.

If an exchange of letters or a telephone call which replaces a personal attendance and materially progresses the matter exceeds six minutes, the time should be recorded and charged (*Bwanaoga v Bwanaoga* [1979] 2 All ER 105, Fam, in which I, for the first and last time, represented the Lord Chancellor).

(b) Travelling and waiting

[30.28]

I deal with the use of expense rates and mark-up as opposed to charge-out rates in Chapter 22. It is, however, worth noting that a windfall to solicitors arising out of the use of charge-out rates, both on summary and detailed assessments, is in respect of travelling and waiting times. Under the old regime the solicitor recovered his expense rate but no profit mark-up. Now, if the retainer does not differentiate between the rates chargeable for preparation and for travelling and waiting, there will be no difference in the amount recoverable from the other party if it is reasonable and proportionate. If the agreement with the client provides for a reduced rate for travelling and waiting, then under the indemnity principle only the reduced rate is recoverable from the paying party. However, old habits die hard – one costs officer reduces the rate by half if travelling by train on the basis that the fee earner can do other work on the train. Assuming of course that he can get a seat and it is a mobile phone-free compartment.

(c) Counsel's fees

(i) *Practice Note: Brief fees*

[30.29]

The Practice Note: Brief Fees is set out below:

(1)   Counsel's brief (or, where appropriate, refresher) fee includes (a) remuneration for taking a note of the judgment of the court, (b) having the note transcribed accurately, (c) submitting the note to the judge for approval where appropriate, (d) revising it if so requested by the judge, and (e) providing any copies required for the Court of Appeal, instructing solicitors and lay client. Accordingly, save in exceptional circumstances, there can be no justification for charging any additional fee for such work.

(2)   When required to attend on a later day to take a judgment not delivered at the end of the hearing, counsel will, subject to the rules of the court, ordinarily be entitled to a further fee for such attendance. This note is not intended to affect that entitlement.

(3)   This practice note, in which the General council of the Bar concurs, replaces the practice note of 9 May 1989 ([1989] 2 All ER 288, [1989] 1 WLR 605, CA).

(Issued by the Master of the Rolls, [1994] 1 All ER 96, [1994] 1 WLR 74, CA.)

(ii) *Skeleton arguments*
Hornsby v Clark Kenneth Leventhal (a firm) [2000] 4 All ER 567, QBD

[30.30]

Following an unsuccessful appeal to the Court of Appeal, leading counsel claimed a fee of £30,000 for settling the skeleton argument and a further fee of £30,000 on the brief, but was allowed on assessment only £6,000 on each. Junior counsel claimed £6,650 for drafting the skeleton argument and a brief fee of £20,000. He was allowed £3,000 on each.

The correct approach for assessing fees for skeleton arguments and briefs in the Court of Appeal is in three stages. In the first stage, the fee for the skeleton argument should be assessed, usually by reference to the amount of time which counsel had reasonably and proportionately devoted to reading the documents, researching the law and drafting the skeleton argument. The second stage is assessing the brief fee, bearing in mind there is an overlap between the work covered by the skeleton argument fee and the work covered by the brief fee. Where the skeleton argument was drafted shortly before the hearing, then the overlap is greater than it would have been if the skeleton argument had been drafted far in advance of the hearing. This exercise involves considering both the amount of time properly spent and the various factors in CPR Rule 44.5. The guidance given in *Loveday v Renton (No 2)* [1992] 3 All ER 184 at 195, QBD is still effective. The third stage, having arrived at an appropriate skeleton argument fee and brief fee, is a cross-check. The two figures should be aggregated to see whether the total appears too large or too small for the overall conduct of the case in the Court of Appeal. In the present case, counsel had spent some 150 hours in relation to the skeleton argument. That was the equivalent of 20 days or four working weeks. It was not reasonable or proportionate. Half that time would have been reasonable and accordingly the appropriate fee was £15,000. In reaching his figure of £6,000, the costs judge had erred by placing considerable reliance on the fees charged by leading junior counsel for the other appellants. First, counsel for the other appellants would have been able to adopt and rely upon many of the submissions made on behalf of the first and second appellants. Second, as a matter of principle, the fees charged by other counsel in a case is only one of the relevant factors and it should not have been given disproportionate weight. Having regard to the time spent by junior counsel and all the circumstances of the case, his proper fee was £5,000. Turning to the brief fee, leading counsel had spent 103 hours preparing for the hearing, excluding time relating to the skeleton argument. His proper brief fee was £25,000. Junior counsel had taken an active role and in all the circumstances his fee should have been 60% of leading counsel's brief fee, namely £15,000. The cross-check gave leading counsel £40,000 of fees and junior counsel £20,000. Those figures were reasonable and proportionate remuneration.

Although this appeal related to an appeal to the Court of Appeal, the approach would appear to be appropriate in all cases where counsel charges a separate fee for preparing a skeleton argument.

(iii) Junior counsel's brief fee

[30.31]

In a routine road traffic accident claim, leading counsel claimed a brief fee of £10,000, which had not been negotiated, and junior counsel claimed £5,000, being 50% of that claimed by his leader. On a between-the-parties detailed assessment the leader's brief fee was allowed at £8,000 and accordingly junior counsel's brief fee was reduced to £4,000. Junior counsel appealed, arguing that he should still be allowed £5,000 even though his leader had not appealed. He criticised the costs judge for not taking into account the allowances made in, what he said was, a similar case, and for making comparison of his fees for the claimant with those of the defendant's counsel.

On appeal to Garland J sitting with assessors it was held that the proper approach was to look at the time spent and the work actually carried out. Because these were not negotiated fees, and junior counsel's fee had been submitted at 50% of his leader's fee it was impossible to criticise the costs judge's approach, and therefore no increase would be granted on the brief fee allowed to junior counsel (*Matthews v Dorkin* [2000] All ER (D) 1584, QBD).

Under the Code of Conduct of the Bar 1990, brief fees no longer have to be agreed in advance or marked on the brief, but it is surprising in this case that they do not appear to have been agreed even before the detailed assessment. If the client has not negotiated and agreed his liability to counsel, how is he to know the amount for which he is seeking to be indemnified by the paying party? Or is the agreement, express or implied, that counsel will be paid whatever is allowed between party and party? That would appear to leave it open to the paying party to argue that nothing should be awarded in respect of counsel's fee with the result that the receiving party would owe nothing to counsel, and thereby be fully indemnified! Although the judge held that the proper approach was to look at the time spent and the work actually carried out, the Bar Council has been concerned to ensure that it is not seen to be advocating remuneration for barristers upon the basis of an hourly rate. It supports the practice of barristers being paid for each item of work which involves taking into account all the relevant factors as well as the time spent. This is a principle which solicitors, with increasing lack of success, have been fighting to preserve for many years and this decision is an indication that barristers are now joining solicitors on the slippery slope to payment based on time spent and hourly rates alone. This and other aspects of counsel's remuneration are now covered comprehensively in Division J of *Butterworths Costs Service*, edited by Peter Birts QC. See also the table of counsel's fees in the SCCO *Guide to the Summary Assessment of Costs* at para [29.23].

(iv)   Justifying counsel's fees

[*30.32*]

On an appeal against the reduction of counsel's fees on a detailed assessment it is doubtful whether the appellant may be entitled to rely on material which had not been put before the costs judge. Where substantial counsel's fees are being assessed on a detailed assessment under a funding certificate evidence should be provided that the fees were appropriate. Counsel should prepare a short note commenting on their fees which should be submitted to the court together with the relevant fee notes (*Armitage v Nurse (Assessment of Costs)* [2000] 2 Costs LR 231, ChD).

(v)   Settlement

[*30.33*]

Martin v Holland & Barrett Ltd [2002] 3 Costs LR 530, QBD was an appeal to Holland J (presumably no relation) sitting with assessors. A personal injury trial had been fixed for 28 October. On 14 October counsel advised in conference following a further payment into court. The brief was delivered on 15 October and agreement was reached on 16 October. Counsel's brief fee was £3,500 plus VAT. On the detailed assessment the district judge accepted that counsel was fully prepared for the hearing. She allowed £2,350 plus VAT to cover both the conference and the brief. On appeal the judge and assessors agreed that a brief fee of £3,500 would have been reasonable if the case had proceeded. However, given the proximity of the conference on 14 October and delivery of the brief on 15 October, with settlement on 16 October the brief fee allowed by the district judge was too high. It exceeded the generous ambit within which reasonable disagreement was possible. A reasonable discounted brief fee, to include the conference and to reflect the early settlement, was £1,500 plus VAT.

(vi)   Apportioning counsel's fees

[30.34]

In *Miller v Hales* [2006] EWHC 1529 (QB), [2006] All ER (D) 67 (Jul) although the claimant was the successful party, he was only awarded his costs after a certain date as a penalty because of costs thrown away. Briefs had been delivered to counsel before that date, but the trial was after it. In apportioning the brief fee, the judge made the following observations:

> 'The old, the very old, rule was that when a brief was delivered the full fee was payable whatever happened thereafter. Many years ago, it became common for agreement to be reached between the solicitor and counsel's clerk in large cases as to the dates on which a proportion of the brief fee would become payable in advance of the trial. There are two elements to be reflected there: the work counsel would put in on the brief as the trial approaches, which would be regarded as the main element, and the fact that counsel has been booked for the trial and so will have a gap in his diary if the case settles, which may be difficult to fill at short notice. I would not expect today that where no particular terms have been agreed, counsel would require to be paid his full brief fee where the brief had been delivered well in advance of the trial and the case settled soon after delivery. In short, it is today appropriate to take a realistic and practical approach rather than to apply rigidly the old rule that a brief fee becomes payable on the delivery of the brief.'

(vii)   No brief fee

[30.35]

The Lawyer reported that counsel instructed in the Princess Diana inquest took the unusual step of not agreeing a brief fee but being paid on an hourly basis because 'everything about the inquest was so uncertain – when it would start and how long it would take'. Their hourly rate was £575.

(d) Costs drafting

[30.36]

Solicitors cannot charge for the cost of preparing a bill to their own client any more than can any supplier of goods or services. However, in civil litigation, before a successful party can recover costs from a paying party, the rules require him to prepare a detailed statement or bill of costs. Paragraph 4.18 of the Practice Direction belatedly recognised that the preparation and checking of a statement or bill of costs is as much a part of the costs of conducting litigation as any other work done in the course of proceedings. It is fee-earning work and the person who does it is therefore a fee earner. There are four categories of fee earner and the inescapable logic is that a costs draftsman must fall into one of these and be paid the appropriate hourly rate for the time he has spent. All the problems and anomalies which arise from treating law costs draftsmen as some alien race outside the recognised categories of fee earners disappear if they are classified as fee earners. The costs must of course be reasonable and not, for example, include putting a file into the order in which it should have been kept, and, on the standard basis, the costs of preparing the bill must be proportionate to the matters in issue. The status of costs draftsmen as fee earners was confirmed in *Crane v Canons Leisure Centre* [2007] EWCA Civ 1352, 19 December 2007, (2008) Times, 10 January in which the court held that under a conditional fee agreement with a single rate success fee that rate applied as much the work of a costs draftsman as to any other fee earner. There was no reason of principle or policy that compelled the court to require parties who have entered into a CFA to address separately at the outset, the risk of costs proceedings, by way of a different success fee. The fact that a single success fee was normally carried through into costs proceedings highlighted the underlying fact that success fees are mainly to compensate lawyers for other cases that they had lost, and thus encourage them to take the risk of receiving no fee in cases that they may lose. First, there was a wider interest than the individual case. Further, at the outset the solicitors have to face a risk that their clients claim would fail, but they may have to conduct costs assessment proceedings on a costs order in favour of the other party for which they would receive no payment. It made general sense for CFAs not to be over-complicated. The case also addressed the use of independent costs draftsmen which I consider below under 'Outsourcing'.

[30.37]

Having established that costs draftsmen are fee earners, it is then necessary to decide into which category they fall. A conference of the Designated Civil Judges published a paper 'Guidance in Relation to the Fees of Costs Draftsmen' which, after making some derogatory and inaccurate remarks about the nature of a costs draftsman's work (do remember that I am a past honorary president of the Association of Law Costs Draftsmen), concluded that in the vast majority of cases, the appropriate rate would be that of a Grade 3 (now Grade D) fee earner based in the locality in which the receiving party's solicitor works. They were clearly unaware of the exacting standards and experience necessary to qualify as an Associate or Fellow of the Association. Grade D is only the equivalent of a trainee solicitor and although this might be acceptable for routine bills, the preparation of substantial bills and advocacy on detailed assessments is at least the equivalent of the work done by Grade C or B fee earners. This was raised at a meeting of the Costs Practitioners' Group at the Senior Courts Costs Office whose view was that while Grade D fee earners might be able to draw straightforward bills of under £10,000, all other bills ought to be drafted by a Grade C fee earner, since costs are a technical matter, and matters such as the operation of the indemnity principle need more experience than a Grade D fee earner is likely to possess. In bills which are not entirely straightforward, a Grade C costs draftsman is often used for the advocacy before the costs officer and it was arguable that the bill should be prepared by the costs draftsman who was going to argue it. (I would add, that in heavy bills involving amounts considerably in excess of the fast track jurisdiction of £15,000, in which Grade A or B fee earners are regularly engaged, the use of a Grade A or B costs draftsman, for example a Fellow of the ALCD, would be reasonable and proportionate, especially if his status has been enhanced by the grant of a right of audience (see para [30.71].) In *Crane* (above) Lord Justice May emphasised that drawing a bill of costs was solicitor's work for which the solicitor may charge 'the proper amount which he, and not the sub-contractor, would charge'. The SCCO Costs Practitioners' Group also commented that the lower the grade of fee earner who prepared the bill, the longer the time that would have to be spent by a partner checking it, to enable him to comply with the stringent requirement that he should approve and sign it.

(e) Outsourcing

(i) Litigation support

[30.38]

An increasing number of solicitors, rather than incur the overheads and liabilities of employing fee earners, use outside agencies to do work for them. In a bill of between-the-parties costs should the charges of an outside agency be treated as a disbursement or are the solicitors entitled to treat the work done by their agents as though it had been done by their own fee earner and charge on this basis?

An understandable initial reaction might be – why should a solicitor make a profit out of someone else's work? The answer is that solicitors, as with most commercial enterprises, professional or otherwise, do it all the time. They make a profit out of those they employ. Otherwise, what would be the point or purpose of having employees? Most firms of solicitors employ qualified or unqualified fee earners for whose work they make an hourly charge to their clients, usually calculated on the cost of the fee earner to the firm, including his share of the overheads, together with an appropriate profit margin. It is a practice which has long been recommended and supported by the Law Society in its publication *The Expense of Time*. An historic example of a solicitor charging as though he had done work actually done by someone else is where a firm of solicitors pay counsel for his advice out of their own pockets, but charge the client as though they themselves had given the advice. Another long-standing practice is enshrined in paragraph 4.16(6) of the Costs Practice Direction which provides:

> 'Agency charges as between a principal solicitor and his agent will be dealt with on the principle that such charges, where appropriate, form part of the principal solicitor's charges.'

The various threads of this philosophy were drawn together in the judgment of Hallett J in the case of *Smith Graham* (see para [30.35]), when she held that a retired police officer, who was not an employee of the firm of solicitors who instructed him to carry out investigative work, was not excluded from the definition of 'fee earner'. She rejected the contention of the defendant that the police officer as an independent contractor should be treated as a disbursement and not a fee earner. That case concerned the assessment of costs under a legal aid certificate in criminal proceedings, but the principle and philosophy are of equal application to privately-funded civil work.

(ii)   Independent costs draftsmen

[30.39]

In *Crane v Canons Leisure Centre* [2007] EWCA Civ 1352, 19 December 2007, (2008) Times, 10 January, the underlying dispute was compromised and costs only proceedings were commenced. A collective conditional fee agreement had distinguished between charges for work done by or on behalf of the solicitors and expenses that the solicitors had incurred on the client's behalf. It was a distinction between the charges by the solicitors themselves for work they themselves did or were directly responsible for and expenses that they incurred for the client, some of which were for other people's work for which the solicitor was not directly responsible and which they simply passed on to the client at cost. On the detailed assessment, the solicitors instructed a firm of costs consultants. The work carried out by the costs consultants was undoubtedly solicitor's work. It was the type of work that the solicitors were retained to do. The solicitors may have chosen to delegate the work, but they never relinquished control of and responsibility for it. The classification of the work carried out could not sensibly depend on whether the solicitors did the work themselves or whether they delegated it to another solicitor or whether they delegated it to costs draftsmen who were not solicitors. Accordingly, the costs consultant's work was properly described as work done 'on behalf of the solicitors' and the consultant's fees were properly described as base costs within the terms of the CCFA attracting a success fee.

Whether the solicitor pays an independent costs draftsman an hourly rate or a percentage of the bill as drawn or assessed is irrelevant – provided the client has agreed to pay for the preparation of the bill at no lower rate than is claimed from the paying party in order to comply with the indemnity principle.

Tony Girling emphasises the importance of solicitors charging the fees of external costs draftsmen to their nominal ledger and not as a disbursement in the client account in order to demonstrate that the costs draftsman was performing the work for the solicitor. He also suggests the retainer should include a provision that outsourced work will be charged at the same hourly rate as if it had been done by the solicitors themselves.

(iii)   Medical agencies

[30.40]

In routine personal injury cases, where a medical report is required, it has become common practice to instruct a medical agency to arrange a medical examination of the claimant; undertake the collation and obtaining of relevant medical reports; arrange the appointment with the medical expert and the claimant; deal with any cancellations or rearrangements and deliver the resultant medical report to the solicitors. Because of the specialisation, experience, expertise and contacts of the medical agency they are able to do this administrative work at least as efficiently, expeditiously and economically as most firms of solicitors using their own fee earners. There can be no objection in principle to the fees of the medical agency being recoverable between the parties, provided it is demonstrated that their charges do not exceed the reasonable and proportionate costs of the work if it had been done by the solicitors. Where the invoice, or 'fee note', from the medical agency shows the medical consultant's fees and their own charges separately, it is possible for the costs officer to assess them both. A practice of some concern is where a medical agency charges a composite fee, without differentiating between the amount of the medical consultant's fee and their own charges. The medical fees and the agency's charges should be shown separately, with the latter being sufficiently particularised to enable the costs officer to be satisfied they do not exceed the reasonable and proportionate cost of a solicitor's fee earner doing the work.

This section is based on a judgment delivered by me in *Stringer v Copley* in the Kingston-upon-Thames County Court on 17 May 2002.

(f) Work done by employees

[30.41]

Admiral Management Services Ltd v Para-Protect Europe Ltd [2002] EWHC 223 (Ch), [2003] 2 All ER 1017: the reasonable costs of the claimant's expert employees in investigating, formulating and presenting claims against the defendants (after the claimant had formed the suspicion of wrongdoing by the defendants) which, if done by someone who was not an employee, would have been recoverable between the parties, could qualify for a costs order. In *Re Nossen's Patent* [1969] 1 All ER 775, ChD, it was held that the costs of expert employees investigating a claim of wrongful use of intellectual property was an exception to the general rule that the work of a party's employees in investigating, formulating and prosecuting a claim by legal proceedings did not qualify for an order for the payment of costs of, and incidental to, those proceedings. There is no reason why a different principle in regard to the recoverability of costs should apply to intellectual property as against other claims.

(g) Partitioning the bill

[30.42]

Paragraph 4.2 of the Practice Direction sets out the usual circumstances in which it is necessary or convenient to divide a bill of costs into separate parts, one being where the receiving party is represented by different solicitors during the course of the proceedings. Parties who, having instructed two firms of solicitors, commenced detailed assessment proceedings with the bill of one firm alone, were given a bitter pill to swallow by the court in *Harris v Moat Housing Group South Ltd* [2007] EWHC 3092 (QB). The appellants ('either oblivious or heedless of the provisions of the practice direction,' said Christopher Clarke J) failed to include the costs of their previous solicitors in their bill of costs, and the costs of their second solicitors were compromised by agreement with the paying party. If the appellants had, either in their notice of commencement or in the bills or otherwise, made clear that the amount claimed was only part of their claim to costs and that they would be claiming later in respect of the work of their first solicitors; and the agreement was that the respondents would pay a sum in respect of the costs claimed, recognising that the costs in respect of the first solicitors were still to be dealt with, the appellants would not have been prevented from making a claim in respect of those costs. There would have been a failure to comply with the Practice Direction, but subject to any sanction that the court thought fit to impose there would be no reason in principle why the court should not assess the remaining costs in dispute. However, the position here was different, because what had been settled was the amount of the receiving parties' costs pursuant to particular orders. If they had left out of their bill part of what they should have claimed and there had been a settlement of the bill, they could not recover more than the amount agreed. The omission was their misfortune.

(h) Narrative

[30.43]

Paragraph 4.5 twice uses the word 'brief' in regard to the background information to be included in a bill of costs. It may be worth recalling the wording of the pre-CPR Practice Direction:

> 'The bill should commence with a brief narrative indicating the issues and the relevant circumstances. This narrative should be short and succinct; the assessment of allowances which depend partly on arithmetical computation and partly on judgments of value is not assisted by prolixity.'

Let us now look at the four precedent model bills, but note that the figures are ten years old:

(i)   Precedent A is the suggested form of bill for a case conducted under a CFA where both the solicitor's base costs and the success fee are to be assessed. It also includes counsel's success fee under a CFA.

(ii)   Precedent B deals with the same case, but assumes that base costs have been summarily assessed. The bill therefore suggests the format for claiming success fees only. Both Precedents A and B are similar in layout to the old 'three-column' bill except that the 'taxed off' column has disappeared.

(iii)   Precedent C illustrates the situation in which the receiving party is publicly-funded and also benefits from an order for costs between parties. It is similar in layout to the old 'six-column' bill.

(iv)   Precedent D is the original model bill suggested in the first Costs Practice Direction published in April 1999. In the words of Harry Birks:

> 'It provoked great controversy in the costs drafting profession, most draftsmen expressing strong opposition to the change, along the lines of "if it ain't broke, don't fix it". An enlightened minority looked beyond the immediate effects of change and saw benefits for lay clients in the easier-to-follow format and for themselves in the potential to apply computer technology to bills of costs, both in the drafting process and after detailed assessment. They were out-voted.'

[30.44]

Costs Practice Direction: Schedule A
Schedule of Costs Precedents
Precedent A

IN THE HIGH COURT OF JUSTICE	2000 – B – 9999

QUEEN'S BENCH DIVISION
BRIGHTON DISTRICT REGISTRY
BETWEEN

	AB	Claimant
	– and –	
	CD	Defendant

CLAIMANT'S BILL OF COSTS TO BE ASSESSED
PURSUANT TO THE ORDER DATED 26th JULY
2000

V.A.T. No. 33 4404 90

In these proceedings the claimant sought compensation for personal injuries and other losses suffered in a road accident which occurred on Friday 1st January 1999 near the junction between Bolingbroke Lane and Regency Road, Brighton, East Sussex. The claimant had been travelling as a front seat passenger in a car driven by the defendant. The claimant suffered severe injuries when, because of the defendant's negligence, the car left the road and collided with a brick wall.

The defendant was later convicted of various offences arising out of the accident including careless driving and driving under the influence of drink or drugs.

In the civil action the defendant alleged that immediately before the car journey began the claimant had known that the defendant was under the influence of alcohol and therefore consented to the risk of injury or was contributorily negligent as to it. It was also alleged that, immediately before the accident occurred, the claimant wrongfully took control of the steering wheel so causing the accident to occur.

The claimant first instructed solicitors, E F & Co, in this matter in July 2000. The claim form was issued in October 2000 and in February 2001 the proceedings were listed for a two day trial commencing 25th July 2001. At the trial the defendant was found liable but the compensation was reduced by 25% to take account of contributory negligence by the claimant. The claimant was awarded a total of £78,256.83 plus £1,207.16 interest plus costs.

The claimant instructed E F & Co under a conditional fee agreement dated 8th July 2000 which specifies the following base fees and success fees.

Partner – £180 per hour plus VAT

Assistant Solicitor – £140 per hour plus VAT

Other fee earners – £85 per hour plus VAT

Success fees exclusive of disbursement funding costs: 40%

Success fee in respect of disbursement funding costs: 7.5% (not claimed in this bill)

Except where the contrary is stated the proceedings were conducted on behalf of the claimant by an assistant solicitor, admitted November 1999.

E F & Co instructed Counsel (Miss GH, called 1992) under a conditional fee agreement dated 5th June 2001 which specifies a success fee of 75% and base fees, payable in various circumstances, of which the following are relevant

Fees for interim hearing whose estimated duration is up to 2 hours: £600

Brief for trial whose estimated duration is 2 days: £2,000

Fee for second and subsequent days: £650 per day

Item No.	Description of work done	V.A.T.	Disburse-ments	Profit Costs
	8th July 2000 – EF & Co in-structed			
	22nd July 2000 – AEI with Eastbird Legal Protection Ltd			
1	Premium for policy	£ —	£120.00	
	7th October 2000 – Claim issued			
2	Issue fee	£ —	£400.00	
	21st October 2000 – Par-ticulars of claim served			
	25th November 2000 – Time for service of defence ex-tended by agreement to 14th January 2001			
3	Fee on allocation	£ —	£80.00	
	20th January 2001 – case allocated to multi-track			
	9th February 2001 – Case management conference at which costs were awarded to the claimant and the base costs were summarily as-sessed at £400 (paid on 24th February 2001)			
	23rd February 2001 – Claim-ant's list of documents			
	12th April 2001 – Payment into court of £25,126.33			
	13th April 2001 – Filing pre-trial checklist			
4	Fee on listing	£ —	£400.00	
	28th June 2001 – Pre trial review: costs in case En-gaged 1.5 hours £210.00			

Item No.	Description of work done	V.A.T.	Disburse-ments	Profit Costs
	Travel and waiting 2.00 hours £280.00			
5	Total solicitor's base fee for attending			£490.00
6	Counsel's base fee for pre trial review (Miss GH)		£600.00	
	25th July 2001 – Attending first day of trial: adjourned part heard			
	Engaged in Court 5.00 hours £700.00			
	Engaged in conference 0.75 hours £105.00			
	Travel and waiting 1.5 hours £210.00			
7	Total solicitor's base fee for attending			£1,015.00
8	Counsel's base fee for trial (Miss GH)		£2,000.00	
9	Fee of expert witness (Dr. IJ)	£ —	£850.00	
10	Expenses of witnesses of fact	£ —	£84.00	
	26th July 2001 – Attending second day of trial when judgment was given for the claimant in the sum of £78,256.53 plus £1207.16 interest plus costs			
	Engaged in Court 3.00 hours £420.00			
	Engaged in conference 1.5 hours £210.00			
	Travel and waiting 1.5 hours £210.00			
11	Total solicitor's base fee for attending			£840.00
12	Counsel's base fee for sec-ond day (Miss GH)		£650.00	
	To Summary	£ —	£5,184.00	£2,345.00
13	**Claimant**			£135.00
	8th July 2000 – First instruc-tions: 0.75 hours by Partner: base fee			
	Other timed attendances in person and by telephone – see Schedule 1			
14	Total base fee for Schedule 1 – 7.5 hours			£1,050.00

Item No.	Description of work done	V.A.T.	Disburse-ments	Profit Costs
15	Routine letters out and tele-phone calls – 29 (17 + 12) total base fee			£406.00
	Witnesses of Fact			
	Timed attendances in per-son, by letter out and by telephone – see Schedule 2			
16	Total base fee for Schedule 2 – 5.2 hours			£728.00
17	Routine letters out, e mails and telephone calls – 8 (4 + 2 + 2) total base fee			£112.00
18	Paid travelling on 9th Octo-ber 2000	£4.02	£22.96	
	Medical expert (Dr. IJ)			
19	11th September 2000 – long letter out 0.33 hours: base fee			£46.20
20	30th January 2001 – long letter out 0.25 hours base fee			£35.00
21	23rd May 2001 – telephone call 0.2 hours base fee			£28.00
22	Routine letters out and tele-phone calls – 10 (6 + 4) to-tal base fee			£140.00
23	Dr. IJ's fee for report	£ —	£350.00	
	Defendant and his solicitor			
24	8th July 2000 – timed letter sent 0.5 hours: base fee			£70.00
25	19th February 2001 – tele-phone call 0.25 hours: base fee			£35.00
26	Routine letters out and tele-phone calls – 24 (18 + 6) total base fee			£336.00
	Communications with the court			
27	Routine letters out and tele-phone calls – 9 (8 + 1) total base fee			£126.00
	Communications with Coun-sel			
28	Routine letters out, e mails and telephone calls – 19 (4 + 7 + 8) total base fee			£266.00
	Work done on documents			
	Timed attendances – see Schedule 3			

Item No.	Description of work done	V.A.T.	Disburse-ments	Profit Costs
29	Total base fees for Schedule 3 – 0.75 hours at £180, 44.5 hours at £140, 12 hours at £85			£7,385.00
	Work done on negotiations			
	23rd March 2001 – meeting at offices of Solicitors for the Defendant			
	Engaged – 1.5 hours £210.00			
	Travel and waiting – 1.25 hours £175.00			
30	Total base fee for meeting			£385.00
	Other work done			
	Preparing and checking bill			
	Engaged: Solicitor – 1 hour £140.00			
	Engaged: Costs Draftsman – 4 hours £340.00			
31	Total base fee on other work done			£480.00
	To summary	£4.02	£372.96	£11,763.20
32	Success fee on solicitor's base fee on interim orders which were summarily assessed (40% of £400) plus VAT at 17.5%	£28.00		£160.00
33	VAT on solicitor's other base fees (17.5% of £14,108.20)	£2,468.94		
34	Success fee on solicitor's other base fees (40% of £14,108.20) plus VAT at 17.5%	£987.58		£5,643.28
35	VAT on Counsel's base fees (17.5% of £3,250)	£568.75		
36	Success fee on Counsel's base fee (75% of £3,250) plus VAT at 17.5%	£426.57	£2,437.50	
	To Summary	£4,479.84	£2,437.50	£5,803.28
	SUMMARY			
	Page 3	£ —	£5,184.00	£2,345.00
	Page 4	£4.02	£372.96	£11,763.20
	Page 5	£4,479.84	£2,437.50	£5,803.28
	Totals	£4,483.86	£7,994.46	£19,911.48
	Grand total			£32,389.80

[30.45]

Costs Practice Direction: Precedent B
Schedule of Costs Precedents
Precedent B

IN THE HIGH COURT OF JUSTICE   2000 – B –
                                            9999
QUEEN'S BENCH DIVISION
BRIGHTON DISTRICT REGISTRY
BETWEEN

	AB	Claimant
	– and –	
	CD	Defendant

CLAIMANT'S BILL OF COSTS TO BE ASSESSED
PURSUANT TO THE ORDER DATED 26th JULY
2000

V.A.T. No. 33 4404 90

In these proceedings the claimant sought compensation for personal injuries and other losses suffered in a road accident which occurred on Friday 1st January 1999 near the junction between Bolingbroke Lane and Regency Road, Brighton, East Sussex. The claimant had been travelling as a front seat passenger in a car driven by the defendant. The claimant suffered severe injuries when, because of the defendant's negligence, the car left the road and collided with a brick wall.

The defendant was later convicted of various offences arising out of the accident including careless driving and driving under the influence of drink or drugs.

In the civil action the defendant alleged that immediately before the car journey began the claimant had known that the defendant was under the influence of alcohol and therefore consented to the risk of injury or was contributorily negligent as to it. It was also alleged that, immediately before the accident occurred, the claimant wrongfully took control of the steering wheel so causing the accident to occur.

The claimant first instructed solicitors, E F & Co, in this matter in July 2000. The claim form was issued in October 1999 and in February 2000 the proceedings were listed for a two day trial commencing 25th July 2001. At the trial the defendant was found liable but the compensation was reduced by 25% to take account of contributory negligence by the claimant. The claimant was awarded a total of £78,256.83 plus £1,207.16 interest plus costs, and the base costs were summarily assessed

The claimant instructed E F & Co under a conditional fee agreement dated 8th July 2000 which specifies the following base fees and success fees.

Partner – £180 per hour plus VAT

Assistant Solicitor – £140 per hour plus VAT

Other fee earners – £85 per hour plus VAT

Success fees exclusive of disbursement funding costs: 40%

Success fee in respect of disbursement funding costs: 7.5% (not claimed in this bill)

Except where the contrary is stated the proceedings were conducted on behalf of the claimant by an assistant solicitor, admitted November 1999.

E F & Co instructed Counsel (Miss GH, called 1992) under a conditional fee agreement dated 5th June 2001 which specifies a success fee of 75% and base fees, payable in various circumstances, of which the following are relevant.

Fees for interim hearing whose estimated duration is up to 2 hours: £600

Brief for trial whose estimated duration is 2 days: £2,000

Fee for second and subsequent days: £650 per day

Item No.	Description of work done	V.A.T.	Disburse-ments	Profit Costs
	8th July 2000 – EF & Co in-structed			
	22nd July 2000 – AEI with Eastbird Legal Protection Ltd			
1	Premium for policy	£ —	£120.00	
	9th February 2001 – Case management conference at which costs were awarded to the Claimant and the base costs were summarily as-sessed at £400			
2	Success fee on costs of case management confer-ence (40% of £400) plus VAT	£28.00		£160.00
	28th June 2001 – Pre trial review: costs in the case (base costs included base costs at trial)			
	25th July 2001 – First day of trial			
	26th July 2001 – Second day of trial at which judg-ment was given for the claimant as follows:			
	Compensation: £78,256.83 Interest thereon: £1,207.16			
	Base costs to trial			
	Solicitor's fees: £12,500.00 plus £2187.50 VAT thereon			
	Counsel's fees: £3,200.00 plus £560.00 VAT thereon			
	Other disbursements: £2,300.00 plus £4.02 VAT thereon			

Item No.	Description of work done	V.A.T.	Disbursements	Profit Costs
3	Success fee on solicitor's base costs awarded at trial (40% of £12,500) plus VAT	£875.00		£5,000.00
4	Success fee on Counsel's base costs awarded at trial (75% of £3,200) plus VAT	£420.00	£2,400.00	
	Other work done			
	Preparing and checking bill Engaged: Solicitor – 0.25 hours £35.00			
	Engaged: Costs draftsman – 1.75 hours £148.75			
5	Total base fee for other work done plus VAT	£32.16		£183.75
6	Success fee for other work done (40% of £183.75) plus VAT	£12.87		£73.50
	Totals:	£1,368.03	£2,520.00	£5,417.25
	Profit Costs s			£5,417.25
	Disbursement			£2,520.00
	VAT			£1,368.03
	Grand total:			£9,305.28

[30.46]

Costs Practice Direction: Precedent C
Schedule of Costs Precedents
Precedent C

IN THE HIGH COURT OF JUSTICE   1999 – B – 9999

QUEEN'S BENCH DIVISION
BRIGHTON DISTRICT REGISTRY
BETWEEN

AB	Claimant
– and –	
CD	Defendant

CLAIMANT'S BILL OF COSTS TO BE ASSESSED PURSUANT TO THE ORDER DATED 26th JULY 2000 AND IN ACCORDANCE WITH REGULATION 107A OF THE CIVIL LEGAL AID (GENERAL) REGULATIONS 1989

Legal Aid Certificate No. 01. 01. 99. 32552X issued on 9th September 1999.

V.A.T. No. 33 4404 90

In these proceedings the claimant sought compensation for personal injuries and other losses suffered in a road accident which occurred on Friday 1st January 1999 near the junction between Bolingbroke Lane and Regency Road, Brighton, East Sussex. The claimant had been travelling as a front seat passenger in a car driven by the defendant. The claimant suffered severe injuries when, because of the defendant's negligence, the car left the road and collided with a brick wall.

The defendant was later convicted of various offences arising out of the accident including careless driving and driving under the influence of drink or drugs.

In the civil action the defendant alleged that immediately before the car journey began the claimant had known that the defendant was under the influence of alcohol and therefore consented to the risk of injury or was contributorily negligent as to it. It was also alleged that, immediately before the accident occurred, the claimant wrongfully took control of the steering wheel so causing the accident to occur.

The claimant first instructed solicitors, E F & Co, in this matter in July 1999. The claim form was issued in October 1999 and in February 2000 the proceedings were listed for a two day trial commencing 25th July 2000. At the trial the defendant was found liable but the compensation was reduced by 25% to take account of contributory negligence by the claimant. The claimant was awarded a total of £78,256.83 plus £1,207.16 interest plus costs.

The proceedings were conducted on behalf of the claimant by an assistant solicitor, admitted November 1998. The bill is divided into two parts.

Part 1 Costs payable by the defendant to the date of grant of legal aid

This covers the period from 8th July 1999 to 8th September 1999. In this part the solicitor's time is charged at £140 per hour (including travel and waiting time) and letters out and telephone calls at £14.00 each.

Part 2 Costs payable by the defendant and L.S.C. from the date of grant of legal aid

This part covers the period from 9th September 1999 to the present time, the client having the benefit of a legal aid certificate covering these proceedings. In this part, solicitor's time in respect of costs payable by the defendant has been charged as in Part 1 plus costs draftsman's and trainee's time charged at £85 per hour. Solicitor's time in respect of costs payable by the LSC only are charged at the prescribed hourly rates plus enhancement of 50%.

Preparation: £74

Attending counsel in conference or at court: £36.40

Travelling and waiting: £32.70

Routine letters out: £7.40

Routine telephone calls: £4.10

Item No	Description of work done	Payable by L.S.C. only V.A.T.	Disbursements	Profit Costs	Payable by Defendant V.A.T.	Disbursements	Profit Costs
	Part 1: COSTS TO DATE OF GRANT OF LEGAL AID						
	Claimant						
1	8th July 1999 – First Instructions – 0.75 hours:						£105.00
2	Routine Letters out – 3						£42.00
	Witnesses of Fact						
3	Routine Letters out – 2						£28.00
	The Defendant						
4	8th July 1999 – Timed letter sent – 0.5 hours						£70.00
5	VAT on total profit costs (17.5% of £245)				£42.88		
	To Summary				£42.88	£ —	£245.00
	Part 2: COSTS FROM DATE OF GRANT OF LEGAL AID						
	7th October 1999 – Claim issued						
6	Issue fee					£400.00	
	21st October 1999 – Particulars of claim served						
	25th November 1999 – Time for service of defence extended by agreement to 14th January 2000						
	17th January 2000 – Filing allocation questionnaire						
7	Fee on allocation					£80.00	

Description of work done Item No	Payable by L.S.C. only			Payable by Defendant		
	V.A.T.	Disbursements	Profit Costs	V.A.T.	Disbursements	Profit Costs
Part 1: COSTS TO DATE OF GRANT OF LEGAL AID						
20th January 2000 – Case allocated to multi-track						
9th February 2000 – Case management conference						
Engaged 0.75 hours £105.00						
Travel and waiting 2.00 hours £280.00						
8 Total solicitor's fee for attending						£385.00
23rd February 2000 – Claimant's list of documents						
12th April 2000 – Payment into court of £25,126.33						
13th April 2000 – Filing pre-trial check list						
9 Fee on listing					£400.00	
28th June 2000 – Pre-trial review						
Engaged 1.5 hours £210.00						
Travel and waiting 2.00 hours £280.00						
10 Total solicitor's fee for attending						£490.00
11 Counsel's brief fee for attending pre-trial review (Miss GH)				£105.00	£600.00	
To Summary	£ —	£ —	£ —	£105.00	£1,480.00	£875.00
25th July 2000 – Attending first day of trial: Adjourned part heard						

Description of work done / Item No	Payable by L.S.C. only			Payable by Defendant		
	V.A.T.	Disbursements	Profit Costs	V.A.T.	Disbursements	Profit Costs
Part 1: COSTS TO DATE OF GRANT OF LEGAL AID						
Engaged in court 5.00 hours £700.00						
Engaged in conference 0.75 hours £105.00						
Travelling and waiting 1.5 hours £210.00						
12 Total solicitor's fee for attending						£1,015.00
13 Counsel's brief fee for trial (Miss GH)				£350.00	£2,000.00	
14 Fee of expert witness (Dr IJ)					£850.00	
15 Expenses of witnesses of fact				—	£84.00	
26th July 2000 Attending second day of trial when judgment was given for the claimant in the sum of £78,256.83 plus £1,207.16 interest plus costs						
Engaged in court 3.00 hours £420.00						
Engaged in conference 1.5 hours £210.00						
Travel and waiting 1.5 hours £210.00						
16 Total solicitor's fee for attending						£840.00
17 Counsel's fee for second day (Miss GH)				£113.75	£650.00	

Item No	Description of work done	Payable by L.S.C. only V.A.T.	Disbursements	Profit Costs	Payable by Defendant V.A.T.	Disbursements	Profit Costs
	Part 1: COSTS TO DATE OF GRANT OF LEGAL AID						
	Claimant – (1) Payable by Defendant Timed attendances in person and by telephone – see Schedule 1						
18	Total fees for Schedule 1 – 7.50 hours						£1,050.00
19	Routine letters out and telephone calls – 26 (14 + 12)						£364.00
	Claimant – (2) Payable by LSC only 11th September 1999 – telephone call						
	Engaged 0.25 hours £18.50						
	Enhancement 50% £9.25						
20	Total solicitor's fee			£27.75			
	10th April 2000 – telephone call						
	Engaged 0.1 hours £4.10						
	Enhancement 50% £2.05						
21	Total solicitor's fee			£6.15			
	Witnesses of fact						
	Timed attendances in person, by letter out and by telephone – see Schedule 2						
22	Total fees for Schedule 2 – 5.2 hours						£728.00
23	Routine letters out (including e mails) and telephone calls – 6 (4 + 2)						£84.00
24	Paid travelling on 9th October 1999				£4.02	£22.96	

Description of work done Item No	Payable by L.S.C. only			Payable by Defendant		
	V.A.T.	Disbursements	Profit Costs	V.A.T.	Disbursements	Profit Costs
To Summary	£ —	£ —	£33.90	£467.77	£3,606.96	£4,081.00
Medical expert (Dr IJ)						
25 11th September 1999 – long letter out 0.33 hours						£46.20
26 30th January 2000 – long letter out 0.25 hours						£35.00
27 23rd May 2000 – telephone call 0.2 hrs						£28.00
28 Routine letters out and telephone calls – 10 (6 + 4)						£140.00
29 Dr IJ's fee for report				£ —	£350.00	
Solicitors for the defendant						
30 19th February 2000 – telephone call 0.25 hours						£35.00
31 Routine letters out and telephone calls – 24 (18 + 6)						£336.00
Communications with the court						
32 Routine letters out and telephone calls – 9 (8 + 1)						£126.00
Communications with Counsel						
33 Routine letters out (including e mails) and telephone calls – 19 (11 + 8)						£266.00
Legal Aid Board and LSC – Payable by LSC only						
2nd August 2000 – Report on case						

Part 1: COSTS TO DATE OF GRANT OF LEGAL AID

Description of work done / Item No	Payable by L.S.C. only			Payable by Defendant		
	V.A.T.	Disbursements	Profit Costs	V.A.T.	Disbursements	Profit Costs
Part 1: COSTS TO DATE OF GRANT OF LEGAL AID						
Engaged 0.5 hours £37.00						
Enhancement 50% £18.50						
34 Total solicitor's fee			£55.50			
Routine letters out and telephone calls Letters out – 2 £14.80						
Telephone calls – 4 £16.40						
35 Total solicitor's fee			£31.20			
Work done on documents						
Timed attendances – see Schedule 3						
36 Total fees for Schedule 3 – 45.25 hours at £140 + 12 hours at £85						£7,355.00
Work done on negotiations						
23rd March 2000 – meeting at offices of solicitors for the Defendant						
Engaged – 1.5 hours £210.00						
Travel and waiting – 1.25 hours £175.00						
37 Total solicitor's fee for meeting						£385.00
Other work done – (1) Payable by Defendant						
Preparing and checking bill						
Engaged: Solicitor – 1 hour £140.00						
Engaged: Costs Draftsman 4 hours £340.00						

Item No	Description of work done	Payable by L.S.C. only			Payable by Defendant		
		V.A.T.	Disbursements	Profit Costs	V.A.T.	Disbursements	Profit Costs
	Part 1: COSTS TO DATE OF GRANT OF LEGAL AID						
38	Total on other work done (1)						£480.00
	To Summary	£ —	£ —	£86.70		£350.00	£9,232.20
	Other work done – (2)						
	Payable by LSC only						
	Preparing and checking bill						
	Engaged: Solicitor – no claim						
	Engaged: Costs Draftsman – 1 hour £74.00						
39	Total on other work done (2)			£74.00			
40	VAT on total profit costs payable by Defendant (17.5% of £14,176.20)				£2,480.84		
41	VAT on total profit costs payable by LSC only (17.5% of £205.60)	£35.98					
	To Summary	£35.98	£ —	£74.00	£2,480.84	£ —	£ —
	SUMMARY						
	Part 1 – Pre Legal Aid						
	Page 3	£ —			£42.88	£ —	£245.00
	Part 2 – Costs since grant of legal aid						
	Page 3	£ —	£ —	£ —	£105.00	£1,480.00	£875.00
	Page 4	£ —	£ —	£33.90	£467.77	£3,606.96	£4,081.00

537

Description of work done Item No	Payable by L.S.C. only			Payable by Defendant		
	V.A.T.	Disbursements	Profit Costs	V.A.T.	Disbursements	Profit Costs
Part 1: COSTS TO DATE OF GRANT OF LEGAL AID						
Page 5	£ —	£ —	£86.70	£ —	£350.00	£9,232.20
Page 6	£35.98	£ —	£74.00	£2,480.84	£ —	£ —
Totals	£35.98	£ —	£194.60	£3,096.49	£5,436.96	£14,433.20
Grand totals						
Costs payable by Defendant						£22,966.65
Costs payable by LSC only						£230.58
Grand total:						£23,197.23

[30.47]

Costs Practice Direction: Precedent D
Schedule of Costs Precedents
Precedent D

IN THE HIGH COURT OF JUSTICE

1999 – B –
9999

QUEEN'S BENCH DIVISION
BRIGHTON DISTRICT REGISTRY
BETWEEN

	AB	Claimant
	– and –	
	CD	Defendant

CLAIMANT'S BILL OF COSTS TO BE ASSESSED
PURSUANT TO THE ORDER DATED 26th JULY
2000 AND IN ACCORDANCE WITH REGULATION
107A OF THE CIVIL LEGAL AID (GENERAL) REGU-
LATIONS 1989

Legal Aid Certificate No. 01. 01. 99. 32552X issued on 9th September 1999.

V.A.T. No. 33 4404 90

In these proceedings the claimant sought compensation for personal injuries and other losses suffered in a road accident which occurred on Friday 1st January 1999 near the junction between Bolingbroke Lane and Regency Road, Brighton, East Sussex. The claimant had been travelling as a front seat passenger in a car driven by the defendant. The claimant suffered severe injuries when, because of the defendant's negligence, the car left the road and collided with a brick wall.

The defendant was later convicted of various offences arising out of the accident including careless driving and driving under the influence of drink or drugs.

In the civil action the defendant alleged that immediately before the car journey began the claimant had known that the defendant was under the influence of alcohol and therefore consented to the risk of injury or was contributorily negligent as to it. It was also alleged that, immediately before the accident occurred, the claimant wrongfully took control of the steering wheel so causing the accident to occur.

The claimant first instructed solicitors, E F & Co, in this matter in July 1999. The claim form was issued in October 1999 and in February 2000 the proceedings were listed for a two day trial commencing 25th July 2000. At the trial the defendant was found liable but the compensation was reduced by 25% to take account of contributory negligence by the claimant. The claimant was awarded a total of £78,256.83 plus £1,207.16 interest plus costs.

The proceedings were conducted on behalf of the claimant by an assistant solicitor, admitted November 1998. The bill is divided into three parts.

Part 1 Costs payable by the defendant to the date of grant of legal aid: This covers the period from 8th July 1999 to 8th September 1999. In this part the solicitor's time is charged at £140 per hour (including travel and waiting time) and letters out and telephone calls at £14.00 each.

Part 2 Costs payable by the defendant from the date of grant of legal aid: This part covers the period from 9th September 1999 to the present time, the client having the benefit of a legal aid certificate covering these proceedings. In this part, solicitor's time in respect of costs payable by the defendant has been charged as in Part 1 plus costs draftsman's and trainee's time charged at £85 per hour.

Part 3 Costs payable by the LSC only: This part covers the same period as Part 2. In this part solicitor's time in respect of costs payable by the LSC only are charged at the prescribed hourly rates plus enhancement of 50%.

Preparation: £74

Attending counsel in conference or at court: £36.40

Travelling and waiting: £32.70

Routine letters out: £7.40

Routine telephone calls: £4.10

Item No.	Item	Amount claimed	VAT	Amount allowed	VAT
	Part 1: COSTS PAYABLE BY THE DEFENDANT				
	Claimant				
1	8th July 1999 – First Instructions – 0.75 hours	£105.00	£18.38		
2	Routine Letters out – 3	£42.00	£7.35		
	Witnesses of Fact				
3	Routine Letters out – 2	£28.00	£4.90		
	The Defendant				
4	8th July 1999 – Timed letter sent – 0.5 hours	£70.00	£12.25		
	To Summary	£245.00	£42.88		
	Part 2: COSTS PAYABLE BY THE DEFENDANT				
	7th October 1999 – Claim issued				
5	Issue fee	£400.00	£ —		
	21st October 1999 – Particulars of claim served				
	25th November 1999 – Time for service of defence extended by agreement to 14th January 2000				
	17th January 2000 – Filing allocation questionnaire				

6	Fee on allocation	£80.00	£ —
	20th January 2000 – Case allocated to multi-track		
	9th February 2000 – Case management conference		
	Engaged 0.75 hours £105.00		
	Travel and waiting 2.00 hours <u>£280.00</u>		
7	Total solicitor's fee for attending	£385.00	£67.38
	23rd February 2000 – Claimant's list of documents		
	12th April 2000 – Payment into court of £25,126.33		
	13th April 2000 – Filing pre-trial check list		
8	Fee on listing	£400.00	
	28th June 2000 – Pre-trial review		
	Engaged 1.5 hours £210.00		
	Travel and waiting 2.00 hours £280.00		
9	Total solicitor's fee for attending	£490.00	£85.75
10	Counsel's brief fee for attending pre-trial review (Miss GH)	£600.00	£105.00
	25th July 2000 – Attending first day of trial: adjourned part heard		
	Engaged in court 5.00 hours £700.00		
	Engaged in conference 0.75 hours £105.00		
	Travel and waiting 1.5 hours <u>£210.00</u>		
11	Total solicitor's fee for attending	£1,015.00	£177.63
12	Counsel's brief fee for trial (Miss GH)	£2,000.00	£350.00
13	Fee of expert witness (Dr IJ)	£850.00	

14	Expenses of witnesses of fact	£84.00	
	26th July 2000 – Attending second day of trial when judgment was given for the claimant in the sum of 78,256.83 plus £1,207.16 interest plus costs		
	Engaged in court 3.00 hours £420.00		
	Engaged in conference 1.5 hours £210.00		
	Travel and waiting 1.5 hours £210.00		
15	Total solicitor's fee for attending	£840.00	£147.00
16	Counsel's fee for second day (Miss GH)	£650.00	£113.75
	Claimant		
	Timed attendances in person and by telephone – see Schedule 1		
17	Total fees for Schedule 1 – 7.50 hours	£1,050.00	£183.75
18	Routine letters out and telephone calls – 26 (14 + 12)	£364.00	£63.70
	Witnesses of fact		
	Timed attendances in person, by letter out and by telephone – see Schedule 2		
19	Total fees for Schedule 2 – 5.2 hours	£728.00	£127.40
20	Routine letters out (including e mails) and telephone calls – 6 (4 + 2)	£84.00	£14.70
21	Paid travelling on 9th October 1999	£22.96	£4.02
	Medical expert (Dr IJ)		
22	11th September 1999 – long letter out 0.33 hours	£46.20	£8.09
23	30th January 2000 – long letter out 0.25 hours	£35.00	£6.13
24	23rd May 2000 – telephone call 0.2 hours	£28.00	£4.90
25	Routine letters out and telephone calls – 10 (6 + 4)	£140.00	£24.50
26	Dr IJ's fee for report	£350.00	£ —
	Solicitors for the defendant		
27	19th February 2000 – telephone call 0.25 hours	£35.00	£6.13

28	Routine letters out and tele-phone calls – 24 (18 + 6)	£336.00	£58.80

Communications with the court

29	Routine letters out and tele-phone calls – 9 (8 + 1)	£126.00	£22.05

Communications with Counsel

30	Routine letters out (includ-ing e mails) and telephone calls – 19 (11 + 8)	£266.00	£46.55

Work done on documents

Timed attendances – see Schedule 3

31	Total fees for Schedule 3 – 45.25 hours at £140 + 12 hours at £85	£7,355.00	£1,287.13

Work done on negotiations

23rd March 2000 – meeting at offices of solicitors for the Defendant

Engaged – 1.5 hours £210.00

Travel and waiting – 1.25 hours £175.00

32	Total solicitor's fee for meeting	£385.00	£67.38
33	**Other work done**		

Preparing and checking bill

Engaged: Solicitor – 1 hour £140.00

Engaged: Costs Draftsman 4 hours £340.00

	Total on other work done	£480.00	£84.00
	To Summary	£19,625.16	£3,055.70

Part 3: COSTS PAYABLE
BY LSC ONLY

Claimant

11th September 1999 – telephone call

Engaged 0.25 hours £18.50

Enhancement 50% £9.25

34	Total solicitor's fee	£27.75	£4.86

10th April 2000 – telephone call

Engaged 0.1 hours £4.10

Enhancement 50% £2.05

35	Total solicitor's fee	£6.15	£1.08
	Legal Aid Board and LSC		
	2nd August 2000 – Report on case		
	Engaged 0.5 hours £37.00		
	Enhancement 50% <u>£18.50</u>		
36	Total solicitor's fee	£55.50	£9.71
	Routine letters out and telephone calls		
	Letters out – 2 £14.80		
	Telephone calls – 4 <u>£16.40</u>		
37	Total solicitor's fee	£31.20	£5.46
	Other work done		
	Preparing and checking bill		
	Engaged: Solicitor – no claim		
	Engaged: Costs Draftsman – 1 hour <u>£74.00</u>		
38	Total on other work done	£74.00	£12.95
	To Summary	£194.60	£34.06
	SUMMARY		
	Costs payable by the Defendant		
	Part 1	£245.00	£42.88
	Part 2	£19,625.16	£3,055.70
	Total costs payable by the Defendant	£19,870.16	£3,098.58
	Costs payable by LSC only		
	Part 3	£194.60	£34.06
	Grand Totals		
	Costs payable by the Defendant	£19,870.16	£3,098.58
	Costs payable by LSC only	£194.60	£34.06
	Grand total	£20,064.76	£3,132.63

[30.48]

As I have indicated, the original model bill caused more difficulty than almost any other aspect of the CPR costs Rules and Practice Direction. Not only was there understandable criticism of various aspects of the bill but there was also confusion arising out of the wording of the Practice Direction supplementing Part 43 as to whether use of the 'model' form of bill was compulsory and, if not, why the previous form of bill could not continue to be used. Some district judges insisted on no deviation from the model form, whilst others were more relaxed. This led to the Vice-Chancellor in September 1999 writing to all designated civil judges:

'A number of district judges have interpreted [para 3.5] of the practice direction as imposing a mandatory obligation upon the parties to use the new form of bill. This was never the intention. The model form of bill is an attempt to improve upon the form previously used. It had, however, never been tried before and there are clearly some situations in which it would not be appropriate.'

This was followed up by an amendment of para 3.7 to make it clear that the use of the model form of bill is not compulsory. Although para 3.5 of the Practice Direction still says that the model bills of costs are 'to be used for detailed assessments', para 3.7 makes it clear that they are not mandatory.

The way in which a bill must be drawn is not prescribed except that according to para 4.1 of the Practice Direction there may be a title page, background information, the items of costs claimed, a summary showing the total costs claimed on each page with schedules of time spent and the relevant certificates as in Precedent F, which you will find at the end of this section. The Legal Services Commission complained to the Court Service that it is too much work for them to cross-check completed bills without individual page totals. As a result the Court Service HQ sent letters to all the court managers indicating that any bills lodged for assessment certificates without individual page totals should be returned to the solicitors. One court even returned a between-the-parties bill on this ground! There is no such power and the requirement was withdrawn. Bills prepared using computer software are usually accurate; I suspect that errors creep in when bills are made up in solicitors' offices following provisional assessment. The prudent course is to ask the costs draftsman to make up the bill – he or she has probably included an allowance for checking and completing the bill, in any event. Paragraph 4.12 provides that if the number of attendances and communications other than routine communications is 20 or more the claim for costs of those items in that section of the bill of costs should be for the total only and should refer to a schedule in which the full record of dates and details is set out. This number was increased by amendment from the original figure of five.

In practice, costs draftsmen have produced a variety of formats, based upon the precedents and incorporating their own particular preferences. One inevitable result of the changes is that modern technology has largely taken over from the former practice of typing an original 'red line' bill on pre-printed stationery, most bills now being generated by word processors. When combined with the use of spreadsheets, the process of 'casting' a bill has become at once simpler and less prone to errors. Commercially available software now enables costs draftsmen to produce bills of costs at their PCs without needing the support of an audio-typist. Sophisticated programs allow data, rates, enhancement, etc to be entered via the keyboard, the bill then being automatically generated for printing.

Whether draftsmen produce their own computer-generated bills or use commercial software, the old information technology adage 'GIGO' still prevails – garbage in, garbage out. Whatever format or software is used, accuracy and clarity are obviously paramount. With the increasing variety of situations to be covered, including partial costs orders, summary assessment of interim costs, conditional fees, VAT rate changes and the enhancement provisions in family proceedings, to name but a few, bills of costs are often not the easiest of documents to follow, particularly for the lay client. Clear and careful presentation of the bill in a manner which assists the parties and the costs officer is a factor to be taken into account in deciding the reasonable costs of preparing the bill.

Sir Rupert Jackson has now added his voice to the criticism of post-CPR bills. In his final report (Jackson, Ch 45, 2.2), he says: 'The present format of bills did not attract favourable comment. The concerns expressed include the following. The bill is expensive and cumbersome to draw. It does not make use of the available technology. It is not easy for the reader of a bill to digest its import. The bill does not contain all necessary information.' He singled out the 'Documents' item for particular criticism: 'Bills usually give insufficient information to enable the reader or the costs judge to determine how much time was properly spent in considering and dealing with documents.'

The solution, Sir Rupert suggests, lies in modern technology. He envisages a world in which all solicitors will use the same software that will capture relevant information as work proceeds and automatically generate bills of costs at different levels of generality, as required: either a user-friendly synopsis, or a detailed bill with all the information needed for a detailed assessment, or an intermediate document with more explanation than a synopsis but less than a detailed bill. Sir Rupert concedes that developing such software will be expensive, but the savings generated would include 'the huge costs of drafting bills of costs'. These proposals undoubtedly raise some difficult questions. Who will pay for the development of the new software? How will the contract to develop this software be awarded? Will solicitors be expected to write-off their substantial investment in existing software systems? Is Sir Rupert confident that the government, if it decides to proceed with these recommendations, could avoid the debacle of previous attempts to implement new software such as, for example, the ongoing problems experienced with the replacement of paper-based records in the NHS?

A cheaper and more realistic target might be to tighten up the current required format for bills of costs. For example, if it is generally accepted that dividing the bill into five "phases" (Jackson, Ch 45, 5.6) would simplify detailed assessment, the Costs Practice Direction could be amended to make this prescriptive, with sanctions on costs of assessment for parties who failed to comply.

For the reasons given in the chapter on the indemnity principle (Chapter 17) the certificate of the receiving party's solicitors that the indemnity principle has not been breached is important. It is also important for the court to ensure that there is no double recovery of costs as a result of costs of interim hearings which have already been summarily assessed. Accordingly, the Rules prescribe certificates in respect of these and other matters which must be signed as appropriate. They are in Precedent F:

[30.49]

Costs Practice Direction: Precedent F
Schedule of Costs Precedents
Precedent F

Certificates for inclusion in bill of costs
- Appropriate certificates under headings (1) and (2) are required in all cases. The appropriate certificate under (3) is required in all cases in which the receiving party is an assisted person or a LSC funded client. Certificates (4), (5) and (6) are optional. Certificate (6) may be included in the bill, or, if the dispute as to VAT recoverability arises after service of the bill, may be filed and served as a supplementary document amending the bill under paragraph 39.10 of this Practice Direction.
- All certificates must be signed by the receiving party or by his solicitor. Where the bill claims costs in respect of work done by more than one firm of solicitors, certificate (1), appropriately completed, should be signed on behalf of each firm.

(1) Certificate as to accuracy

I certify that this bill is both accurate and complete [and]
- (where the receiving party was funded by legal aid/LSC) [in respect of Part(s) . . . of the bill] all the work claimed was done pursuant to a certificate issued by the Legal Aid Board/Legal Services Commission granted to [the assisted person] [the LSC funded client].
- (where costs are claimed for work done by an employed solicitor) [in respect of Part(s) . . . of the bill] the case was conducted by a solicitor who is an employee of the receiving party.
- (other cases where costs are claimed for work done by a solicitor) [in respect of Part(s) . . . of the bill] the costs claimed herein do not exceed the costs which the receiving party is required to pay me/my firm.

(2) Certificate as to interest and payments

I certify that:
- No rulings have been made in this case which affects my/the receiving party's entitlement (if any) to interest on costs.

or
- The only rulings made in this case as to interest are as follows:
  [give brief details as to the date of each ruling, the name of the Judge who made it and the text of the ruling]

and
- No payments have been made by any paying party on account of costs included in this bill of costs.

or
- The following payments have been made on account of costs included in this bill of costs:
  [give brief details of the amounts, the dates of payment and the name of the person by or on whose behalf they were paid]

547

(3) Certificate as to interest of assisted person/LSC funded client pursuant to regulation 119 of the Civil Legal Aid (General) Regulations 1989

I certify that the assisted person/LSC funded client has no financial interest in the detailed assessment.

or

I certify that a copy of this bill has been sent to the assisted person/LSC funded client pursuant to Regulation 119 of the Civil Legal Aid General Regulations 1989 with an explanation of his/her interest in the detailed assessment and the steps which can be taken to safeguard that interest in the assessment. He/she has/has not requested that the costs officer be informed of his/her interest and has/has not requested that notice of the detailed assessment hearing be sent to him/her.

(4) Consent to the signing of the certificate within 21 days of detailed assessment pursuant to regulations 112 and 121 of the Civil Legal Aid (General) Regulations 1989

I certify that notice of the fees reduced or disallowed on detailed assessment has been given in writing to counsel on [date].

or

I certify that: there having been no reduction or disallowance of counsel's fees it is not necessary to give notice to counsel.

I/we consent to the final costs certificate being issued immediately.

(5) Certificate in respect of disbursements not exceeding £500

I hereby certify that all disbursements listed in this bill which individually do not exceed £500 (other than those relating to counsel's fees) have been duly discharged.

(6) Certificate as to recovery of VAT

With reference to the pending assessment of the [claimant's/defendant's] costs and disbursements herein which are payable by the [claimant/defendant] we the under-signed [solicitors to] [auditors of] the [claimant/defendant] hereby certify that the [claimant/defendant] on the basis of its last completed VAT return [would/would not be entitled to recover would/be entitled to recover only percent of the] Value Added Tax on such costs and disbursements, as input tax pursuant to Section 14 of the Value Added Tax Act 1983.

[30.50]

CPR Rule 47.9: Points of dispute and consequence of not serving
(1)   The paying party and any other party to the detailed assessment proceedings may dispute any item in the bill of costs by serving points of dispute on—
    (a)   the receiving party; and
    (b)   every other party to the detailed assessment proceedings.
(2)   The period for serving points of dispute is 21 days after the date of service of the notice of commencement.
(3)   If a party serves points of dispute after the period set out in paragraph (2) he may not be heard further in the detailed assessment proceedings, unless the court gives permission.

(The Costs Practice Direction sets out requirements about the form of points of dispute)

(4) The receiving party may file a request for a default costs certificate if—

    (a) the period set out in rule 47.9 (2) for serving points of dispute has expired; and

    (b) he has not been served with any points of dispute.

(5) If any party (including the paying party) serves points of dispute before the issue of a default costs certificate the court may not issue the default costs certificate.

(Section IV of this Part sets out the procedure to be followed after points of dispute have been filed)

[30.51]

CPD Section 35 Points of dispute and consequences of not serving: Rule 47.9

35.1 *The parties may agree under rule 2.11 (Time limits may be varied by parties) to extend or shorten the time specified by rule 47.9 for service of points of dispute. A party may apply to the appropriate office for an order under rule 3.1(2)(a) to extend or shorten that time.*

35.2 *Points of dispute should be short and to the point and should follow as closely as possible Precedent G of the Schedule of Costs Precedents annexed to this Practice Direction.*

35.3 *Points of dispute must—*

(1) *identify each item in the bill of costs which is disputed,*

(2) *in each case, state concisely the nature and grounds of dispute,*

(3) *where practicable suggest a figure to be allowed for each item in respect of which a reduction is sought, and*

(4) *be signed by the party serving them or his solicitor.*

35.4

(1) *The normal period for serving points of dispute is 21 days after the date of service of the notice of commencement.*

(2) *Where a notice of commencement is served on a party outside England and Wales the period within which that party should serve points of dispute is to be calculated by reference to Section IV of Part 6 as if the notice of commencement was a claim form and as if the period for serving points of dispute were the period for filing a defence.*

35.5 *A party who serves points of dispute on the receiving party must at the same time serve a copy on every other party to the detailed assessment proceedings, whose name and address for service appears on the statement served by the receiving party in accordance with paragraph 32.3 or 32.4 above.*

35.6

(1) *This paragraph applies in cases in which Points of Dispute are capable of being copied onto a computer disk.*

(2) *If, within 14 days of the receipt of the Points of Dispute, the receiving party requests a disk copy of them, the paying party must supply him with a copy free of charge not more than 7 days after the date on which he received the request.*

35.7

(1) *Where the receiving party claims an additional liability, a party who serves points of dispute on the receiving party may include a request for information about other methods of financing costs which were available to the receiving party.*

(2)   Part 18 (further information) and the Practice Direction supplementing that part apply to such a request.

[30.52]

Paragraph 35.1 is a reminder that under CPR Rule 2.11 the parties may agree to extend (or shorten) the 21-day time limit for service of points of dispute. If there is no agreement the paying party may also apply under Rule 3.1(2)(*a*) for an extension of the time for service of points of dispute, the application being made in accordance with Part 23. The receiving party may also apply to shorten the time although it is not easy to imagine the circumstances in which such an application would succeed, or, in many courts, when the application would even be heard before the 21-day time limit had expired. This provision is the nub of the new detailed assessment regime. If points of dispute are not served, the receiving party may request a default costs certificate for the full amount of the bill without any other judicial intervention. If points of dispute are served the judicial intervention will be limited to the points identified. It is, in effect, the voluntary pilot scheme run for several years in the Supreme Court Costs Office (now the Senior Courts Costs Office) and which is now embodied in the Rules. If points of dispute are not served within the time limit and no extension has been agreed between the parties or ordered by the court, all is not lost. Service of points of dispute out of time will prevent the issue of a default costs certificate necessitating a hearing at which the points in dispute must be taken into account, whether or not the costs officer is prepared to hear argument on behalf of the paying party. Setting aside a default certificate is covered by Rule 47.12 (para [30.62]).

The frequency and extent of Part 18 requests in detailed assessment proceedings has increased in recent years as paying parties seek to find new challenges to claims for costs, in particular where additional liabilities are involved. In *Hutchings v British Transport Police Authority* [2006] EWHC 90064 (Costs), the senior costs judge, sitting as a recorder, gave guidance on requests for further information under para 35.7 of the Practice Direction. The starting point is the overriding objective, and in particular the requirement of proportionality. The court should not willingly do anything which is likely to promote further satellite litigation. The defendant's Part 18 request originally ran to 13 questions all of which the deputy district judge refused on the grounds it was a fishing expedition. On appeal the senior costs judge described the application as a brash and ill-considered attempt to uncover information which would enable the defendant to challenge the claimant's bill on a technical point but he allowed three of the requests as being reasonable and proportionate. The other questions could be raised as part of the points of dispute and argued on the assessment.

The purpose of paragraph 35.6(2) of the Practice Direction is to enable paying parties to add their replies in an additional column alongside the relevant points of dispute – see Precedent G at para [30.53]. Information technology having moved on since this direction was drafted, this objective is more commonly achieved by requesting the points of dispute as an email attachment, thus complying with the spirit if not the letter of the Practice Direction. Regrettably, the use of the procedure afforded by paragraph 35.6(2), whether by disk or by email, seems to remain the exception rather than the norm.

Points of dispute should be in Precedent G of the Schedule of Costs forms to the Costs Practice Direction. Here it is:

[30.53]

Costs Practice Direction: Precedent G
Schedule of Costs Precedents
Precedent G

IN THE HIGH COURT OF JUSTICE   2000 – B –
                                                            9999

QUEEN'S BENCH DIVISION
BRIGHTON DISTRICT REGISTRY
BETWEEN

AB		Claimant
– and –		
CD		Defendant

POINTS OF DISPUTE SERVED BY THE DEFEN-
DANT

Item	Dispute	Claimant's Comments
General point	Base rates claimed for the assistant solicitor and other fee earners are excessive. Reduce to £100 and £70 respectively plus VAT. Each item in which these rates are claimed should be recalculated at the reduced rates.	
(1)	The premium claimed is excessive. Reduce to £95.	
(14)	The claim for timed attendances on claimant (Schedule 1) is excessive. Reduce to 4 hours ie. £400 at reduced rates.	
(29)	The total claim for work done on documents by the assistant solicitor is excessive. A reasonable allowance in respect of documents concerning court and counsel is 8 hours, for documents concerning witnesses and the expert witness, 6.5 hours, for work done on arithmetic, 2.25 hours and for other documents, 5.5 hours. Reduce to 22.25 hours ie. £2,225 at reduced rates (£3,380 in total).	
(31)	The time claimed is excessive. Reduce solicitor's time to 0.5 hours ie. to £50 at reduced rates and reduce the costs draftsman's time to three hours ie. £210 (£260 in total).	
(32)	The success fee claimed is excessive. Reduce to 25% ie. £100 plus VAT of £17.50.	
(33)	The total base fees when recalculated on the basis of the above points amounts to £7,788, upon which VAT is £1,362.90.	

> (34)   The success fee claimed is excessive. Reduce to 25% of £7,788 ie. £1,947.50 plus VAT of £340.73.
>
> (36)   The success fee claimed is excessive. Reduce to 50% ie. £1,625 plus VAT of £284.38.

Served on . . . . [date] by . . . . [name] [solicitors for] the Defendant.

[30.53A]

In his final report Sir Rupert Jackson observed: 'Points of dispute are said to be overlong, therefore expensive to read and expensive to reply to. Points of reply are similarly prolix. Both of these pleadings are in large measure formulaic and are built up from standard paragraphs held by solicitors on their databases. In addition, there are lengthy passages in the points of dispute and the points of reply dealing with time spent on documents.' (Ch 45, 2.7) Only those negotiators who deserve Andrew Twambley's epithet 'costs muppets' would disagree with Sir Rupert's conclusion that there should be no need to plead to every individual item in a bill of costs, nor to reply to every paragraph in the points of dispute (Jackson, Ch 45, 5.11). However, this practice stems from CPR 47.14(7): 'Only items specified in the points of dispute may be raised at the hearing, unless the court gives permission.' If this rule were revoked, we could end up back in the bad old days of hatchet jobs by ambush – resulting in shorter pleadings, but longer hearings.

[30.54]

CPR Rule 47.10: Procedure where costs are agreed

(1)   If the paying party and the receiving party agree the amount of costs, either party may apply for a costs certificate (either interim or final) in the amount agreed. (Rule 47.15 and Rule 47.16 contain further provisions about interim and final costs certificates respectively)

(2)   An application for a certificate under paragraph (1) must be made to the court which would be the venue for detailed assessment proceedings under rule 47.4.

[30.55]

CPD Section 36 Procedure where costs are agreed: Rule 47.10

36.1   Where the parties have agreed terms as to the issue of a costs certificate (either interim or final) they should apply under rule 40.6 (Consent judgments and orders) for an order that a certificate be issued in terms set out in the application. Such an application may be dealt with by a court officer, who may issue the certificate.

36.2   Where in the course of proceedings the receiving party claims that the paying party has agreed to pay costs but that he will neither pay those costs nor join in a consent application under paragraph 36.1, the receiving party may apply under

Part 23 (General Rules about Applications for Court Orders) for a certificate either interim or final to be issued.

36.3   An application under paragraph 36.2 must be supported by evidence and will be heard by a costs judge or a district judge. The respondent to the application must file and serve any evidence he relies on at least two days before the hearing date.

36.4   Nothing in rule 47.10 prevents parties who seek a judgment or order by consent from including in the draft a term that a party shall pay to another party a specified sum in respect of costs.

36.5

(1)   The receiving party may discontinue the detailed assessment proceedings in accordance with Part 38 (Discontinuance).

(2)   Where the receiving party discontinues the detailed assessment proceedings before a detailed assessment hearing has been requested, the paying party may apply to the appropriate office for an order about the costs of the detailed assessment proceedings.

(3)   Where a detailed assessment hearing has been requested the receiving party may not discontinue unless the court gives permission.

(4)   A bill of costs may be withdrawn by consent whether or not a detailed assessment hearing has been requested.

[30.56]

If the costs are agreed there will be no need to trouble the court if they are to be paid without delay. If the costs are agreed before the final judgment or order the agreed amount may be included in the judgment or order (paragraph 36.4). If a certificate is to be obtained, the agreement may relate to only part of the costs, in which event it will be an interim certificate, or to the whole of the costs, when it will be a final certificate.

An application may be made either before or after the court has become involved in the detailed assessment proceedings. If the agreement is after the commencement of detailed assessment proceedings the application will be to the 'appropriate office' as specified in Rule 47.4, otherwise it will be to the court where the judgment or order was made. Paragraph 36.5 makes provision for discontinuance of detailed assessment proceedings and for withdrawal of a bill of costs by consent.

[30.57]

SECTION III   COSTS PAYABLE BY ONE PARTY TO ANOTHER – DEFAULT PROVISIONS

CPR Rule 47.11: Default costs certificate

(1)   Where the receiving party is permitted by rule 47.9 to obtain a default costs certificate, that party does so by filing a request in the relevant practice form.

(The costs practice direction deals with the procedure by which the receiving party may obtain a default costs certificate)

(2)   A default costs certificate will include an order to pay the costs to which it relates.

(3)   Where a receiving party obtains a default costs certificate, the costs payable to that party for the commencement of detailed assessment proceedings shall be the sum set out in the Costs Practice Direction.

(4)   A receiving party who obtains a default costs certificate in detailed assessment proceedings pursuant to an order under section 194(3) of the Legal Services Act 2007 must send a copy of the default costs certificate to the prescribed charity.

[30.58]

CPD Section 37 Default costs certificate: Rule 47.11

37.1
(1)   *A request for the issue of a default costs certificate must be made in Form N254 and must be signed by the receiving party or his solicitor.*
(2)   *The request must be accompanied by a copy of the document giving the right to detailed assessment. (Section 40.4 of the Costs Practice Direction identifies the appropriate documents).*
37.2   *The request must be filed at the appropriate office.*
37.3   *A default costs certificate will be in Form N255.*
37.4   *Attention is drawn to Rules 40.3 (Drawing up and Filing of Judgments and Orders) and 40.4 (Service of Judgments and Orders) which apply to the preparation and service of a default costs certificate. The receiving party will be treated as having permission to draw up a default costs certificate by virtue of this Practice Direction.*
37.5   *The issue of a default costs certificate does not prohibit, govern or affect any detailed assessment of the same costs which are payable out of the Community Legal Service Fund.*
37.6   *An application for an order staying enforcement of a default costs certificate may be made either—*
(1)   *to a costs judge or district judge of the court office which issued the certificate; or*
(2)   *to the court (if different) which has general jurisdiction to enforce the certificate.*
37.7   *Proceedings for enforcement of default costs certificates may not be issued in the Costs Office.*
37.8   *The fixed costs payable in respect of solicitor's charges on the issue of the default costs certificate are £80.*

[30.59]

The ability to obtain a default costs certificate is a continuation of the philosophy of not involving the court until it is clear that there is a dispute for the court to resolve. Again the Rules impose tight time limits. We have seen that points of dispute must be served within 21 days of service of the notice of commencement, and that because a default costs certificate includes an order to pay, the provisions of Rule 44.8 mean that it must be paid within 14 days. To further expedite these matters para 37.4 of the Practice Direction allows the receiving party to draw up the default costs certificate. See Forms N254 and N255 at paras [30.60] and [30.61] below. Receiving parties should be aware, however, of potential pitfalls in rushing to obtain a default costs certificate if their houses are not completely in order. See para [30.17] above.

Form N255 (HC) is the same form for the High Court, without the reference to the Register of County Court Judgments. In view of the strict time limits, parties faced with orders to pay large sums may consider applying for a stay of enforcement under para 37.6 of the Practice Direction or for an extension of time for payment under CPR 44.8. Paragraph 37.7 points out that although the Senior Courts Costs Office can grant a stay of enforcement, enforcement proceedings themselves may not be issued in the Senior Courts Costs Office.

[30.60]

FORM N254

Request for a Default Costs Certificate

In the	
Claim No.	
Claimant (include Ref.)	
Defendant (include Ref.)	

I certify that (1) notice of commencement (2) the bill of costs and (3) a copy of the document giving the right to detailed

assessment, were served on the paying party . . . .

(*and give details of any other party served with the notice*)

on . . . . (*insert date*)

Copies of (1) and (3) are attached.

I also certify that I have not received any points of dispute and that the time for receiving them has now elapsed.

I now request the court to issue a certificate for the amount of the bill of costs plus such fixed costs and court fees as are appropriate in this case.

Signed . . . . **Date** . . . .
       (Claimant)(Defendant)('s Solicitor)

The court office at

is open between 10 am and 4 pm Monday to Friday. When corresponding with the court, please address forms or letters to the Court Manager and quote the claim number.

N254 Request for a Default Costs Certificate (07.02)   *The Court Service Publications Branch*

[30.61]

FORM N255

Default costs certificate

Name of court		Claim No.
Name of Claimant (including ref.)		
Name of Defendant (including ref.)		
[Defendant's][Claimant's] date of birth		
Date		

To [Claimant][Defendant]['s Solicitor]

As you have not raised any points of dispute on the [defendant's][claimant's] bill of costs, the costs of the claim have been allowed and the total sum of £   is now payable.

You must pay this amount to the [defendant][claimant] [within 14 days from the date of this order]

[on or before [   ]]

The date from which any entitlement to interest under this certificate is to run is:-

1. as to the amount of the bill as assessed excluding the costs of assessment, [the date of the order]

2. and as to [£   ] being the fixed costs of assessment, the date of this certificate.

--- **Take Notice** ---

To the defendant (claimant)

If you do not pay in accordance with this order your goods may be removed and sold or other enforcement proceedings may be taken against you. If your circumstances change and you cannot pay, ask at the court office about what you can do

Further interest may be added if judgment has been given for £5,000 or more or is in respect of a debt which attracts contractual or statutory interest for late payment.

If you do not pay as ordered, this judgment may be registered on the Register of Judgments, Orders and Fines. This may make it difficult for you to get credit. **If you then pay in full within one month** you can ask the court to cancel the entry on the Register. You will need to give proof of payment. You can (for a fee) also obtain a Certificate of Cancellation from the court. If you pay the debt in full after one month you can ask the court to mark the entry on the Register as satisfied and (for a fee) obtain a Certificate of Satisfaction to prove that the debt has been paid.

--- **Address for Payment** ---

--- **How to Pay** ---

- **PAYMENT(S) MUST BE MADE to the person named at the address for payment quoting their reference and the court case number.**
- **DO NOT bring or send payments to the court. THEY WILL NOT BE ACCEPTED.**
- You should allow at <u>least 4</u> days for your payment to reach the claimant (defendant) or his representative.
- Make sure that you keep records and can account for all payments made. Proof may be required if there is any disagreement. It is not safe to send cash unless you use registered post.
- A leaflet giving further advice about payment can be obtained from the court.
- If you need more information you should contact the claimant (defendant) or his representative.

The court office at

is open between 10 am and 4 pm Monday to Friday. Address all communications to the Court Manager quoting the claim number

N255 Default costs certificate

[30.62]

CPR Rule 47.12: Setting aside default costs certificate

(1)   The court must set aside a default costs certificate if the receiving party was not entitled to it.

(2)   In any other case, the court may set aside or vary a default costs certificate if it appears to the court that there is some good reason why the detailed assessment proceedings should continue.

(3)   Where—

    (a)   the receiving party has purported to serve the notice of commencement on the paying party;

    (b)   a default costs certificate has been issued; and

    (c)   the receiving party subsequently discovers that the notice of commencement did not reach the paying party at least 21 days before the default costs certificate was issued,

the receiving party must—

        (i)   file a request for the default costs certificate to be set aside; or

        (ii)   apply to the court for directions.

(4)   Where paragraph (3) applies, the receiving party may take no further step in

    (a)   the detailed assessment proceedings; or

    (b)   the enforcement of the default costs certificate,

until the certificate has been set aside or the court has given directions.

(5)   Where the court sets aside or varies a default costs certificate in detailed assessment proceedings pursuant to an order under section 194(3) of the Legal Services Act 2007, the receiving party must send a copy of the order setting aside or varying the default costs certificate to the prescribed charity.

(The Costs Practice Direction contains further details about the procedure for setting aside a default costs certificate and the matters which the court must take into account)

[30.63]

CPD Section 38 Setting aside the default costs certificate: Rule 47.12

38.1

(1)   *A court officer may set aside a default costs certificate at the request of the receiving party under rule 47.12(3).*

(2)   *A costs judge or a district judge will make any other order or give any directions under this rule.*

38.2

(1)   *An application for an order under rule 47.12(2) to set aside or vary a default costs certificate must be supported by evidence.*

(2)   *In deciding whether to set aside or vary a certificate under rule 47.12(2) the matters to which the court must have regard include whether the party seeking the order made the application promptly.*

(3)   *As a general rule a default costs certificate will be set aside under rule 47.12(2) only if the applicant shows a good reason for the court to do so and if he files with his application a copy of the bill and a copy of the default costs certificate, and a draft of the points of dispute he proposes to serve if his application is granted.*

38.3

(1)   *Attention is drawn to rule 3.1(3) (which enables the court when making an order to make it subject to conditions) and to rule 44.3(8) (which enables*

the court to order a party whom it has ordered to pay costs to pay an amount on account before the costs are assessed).

(2)   A costs judge or a district judge may exercise the power of the court to make an order under rule 44.3(8) although he did not make the order about costs which led to the issue of the default costs certificate.

38.4   If a default costs certificate is set aside the court will give directions for the management of the detailed assessment proceedings

[30.64]

If, for whatever reason, the receiving party was not entitled to a default costs certificate, perhaps because the paying party did not have 21 days' notice, or had served points of dispute within this time, the court must set aside the certificate: it has no discretion. Rule 47.12(3) contains the unusual provision making it obligatory on a *receiving* party who discovers that the notice of commencement did not reach the paying party at least 21 days before the default costs certificate was issued to either file a request for the certificate to be set aside or to apply to the court for directions. Where a valid default costs certificate has been obtained it is for the paying party to establish that there is some good reason why the assessment proceedings should continue. The application is to be made in accordance with CPR Part 23, supported by evidence and will be unlikely to succeed unless it is accompanied by a draft of the points of dispute. It should be made promptly. If the court does set aside the certificate it can impose conditions, including ordering the paying party to make a payment on account.

[30.65]

SECTION IV   COSTS PAYABLE BY ONE PARTY TO ANOTHER – PROCEDURE WHERE POINTS OF DISPUTE ARE SERVED

CPR Rule 47.13: Optional reply

(1)   Where any party to the detailed assessment proceedings serves points of dispute, the receiving party may serve a reply on the other parties to the assessment proceedings.

(2)   He may do so within 21 days after service on him of the points of dispute to which his reply relates.

(The Costs Practice Direction sets out the meaning of reply)

[30.66]

CPD Section 39: Optional reply: Rule 47.13

(1)   A receiving party wishing to serve a reply to some or all of the points of dispute must also serve a copy on every other party to the detailed assessment proceedings. The time for doing so is within 21 days after service of the points of dispute.

(2)   A reply means:—
(a)   a separate document prepared by the receiving party; or
(b)   the receiving party's written comments added to the points of dispute.

(3)   A reply must be signed by the party serving it or his solicitor.

39.2   Where there is a dispute about the insurance premium in a staged policy (which has the same meaning as in paragraph 19.4(3A)) it will normally be sufficient *for the receiving party to set out in any reply the reasons for choosing the particular insurance policy and the basis on which the insurance premium is rated whether block rated or individually rated.*

[30.67]

Although a reply is not obligatory (yet some district judges purport to make it so by directing that a reply be filed and served by a certain date), it is probably tactically advisable except in the simplest of cases. It could also be relevant when the court considers its order in respect of the costs of the detailed assessment proceedings. Paragraph 39.1(2) of the Practice Direction defines a reply as either a separate document prepared by the receiving party or the receiving party's comments added to the points of dispute. It is usually easier at an assessment hearing for the parties' representatives and the costs officer to refer to a single document containing both points of dispute and replies. I have referred at para [30.17] to the mechanism for facilitating this procedure.

[30.68]

CPR Rule 47.14: Detailed Assessment Hearing
(1) Where points of dispute are served in accordance with this Part, the receiving party must file a request for a detailed assessment hearing.
(2) He must file the request within 3 months of the expiry of the period for commencing detailed assessment proceedings as specified—
    (a) in rule 47.7; or
    (b) by any direction of the court.
(3) Where the receiving party fails to file a request in accordance with paragraph (2), the paying party may apply for an order requiring the receiving party to file the request within such time as the court may specify.
(4) On an application under paragraph (3), the court may direct that, unless the receiving party requests a detailed assessment hearing within the time specified by the court, all or part of the costs to which the receiving party would otherwise be entitled will be disallowed.
(5) If—
    (a) the paying party has not made an application in accordance with paragraph (3); and
    (b) the receiving party files a request for a detailed assessment hearing later than the period specified in paragraph (2),
the court may disallow all or part of the interest otherwise payable to the receiving party under—
    (i) section 17 of the Judgments Act 1838; or
    (ii) section 74 of the County Courts Act 1984,
but must not impose any other sanction except in accordance with rule 44.14 (powers in relation to misconduct).
(6) No party other than—
    (a) the receiving party;
    (b) the paying party; and
    (c) any party who has served points of dispute under rule 47.9,
may be heard at the detailed assessment hearing unless the court gives permission.
(7) Only items specified in the points of dispute may be raised at the hearing, unless the court gives permission.

(The Costs Practice Direction specifies other documents which must be filed with the request for hearing and the length of notice which the court will give when it fixes a hearing date)

[30.69]

CPD Section 40 Detailed assessment hearing: Rule 47.14

40.1   *The time for requesting a detailed assessment hearing is within 3 months of the expiry of the period for commencing detailed assessment proceedings.*

40.2   *The request for a detailed assessment hearing must be in Form N258. The request must be accompanied by:*

(a)   *a copy of the notice of commencement of detailed assessment proceedings;*

(b)   *a copy of the bill of costs,*

(c)   *the document giving the right to detailed assessment (see paragraph 40.4 below);*

(d)   *a copy of the points of dispute, annotated as necessary in order to show which items have been agreed and their value and to show which items remain in dispute and their value;*

(e)   *as many copies of the points of dispute so annotated as there are persons who have served points of dispute;*

(f)   *a copy of any replies served;*

(g)   *a copy of all orders made by the court relating to the costs which are to be assessed;*

(h)   *copies of the fee notes and other written evidence as served on the paying party in accordance with paragraph 32.3 above;*

(i)   *where there is a dispute as to the receiving party's liability to pay costs to the solicitors who acted for the receiving party, any agreement, letter or other written information provided by the solicitor to his client explaining how the solicitor's charges are to be calculated;*

(j)   *a statement signed by the receiving party or his solicitor giving the name, address for service, reference and telephone number and fax number, if any, of–*

   (i)   *the receiving party;*

   (ii)   *the paying party;*

   (iii)   *any other person who has served points of dispute or who has given notice to the receiving party under paragraph 32.10(1)(b) above;*

   and giving an estimate of the length of time the detailed assessment hearing will take;

(k)   *where the application for a detailed assessment hearing is made by a party other than the receiving party, such of the documents set out in this paragraph as are in the possession of that party;*

(l)   *where the court is to assess the costs of an assisted person or LSC funded client—*

   (i)   *the legal aid certificate, LSC certificate and relevant amendment certificates, any authorities and any certificates of discharge or revocation;*

   (ii)   *a certificate, in Precedent F(3) of the Schedule of Costs Precedents;*

   (iii)   *if the assisted person has a financial interest in the detailed assessment hearing and wishes to attend, the postal address of that person to which the court will send notice of any hearing;*

   (iv)   *if the rates payable out of the LSC fund are prescribed rates, a schedule to the bill of costs setting out all the items in the bill which are claimed against other parties calculated at the legal aid prescribed rates with or without any claim for enhancement: (further information as to this schedule is set out in Section 48 of this Practice Direction);*

   (v)   *a copy of any default costs certificate in respect of costs claimed in the bill of costs.*

40.3

(1)   This paragraph applies to any document described in paragraph 40.2(i) above which the receiving party has filed in the appropriate office. The document must be the latest relevant version and in any event have been filed not more than 2 years before filing the request for a detailed assessment hearing.

(2)   In respect of any documents to which this paragraph applies, the receiving party may, instead of filing a copy of it, specify in the request for a detailed assessment hearing the case number under which a copy of the document was previously filed.

40.4   'The document giving the right to detailed assessment' means such one or more of the following documents as are appropriate to the detailed assessment proceedings:

(a)   a copy of the judgment or order of the court giving the right to detailed assessment;

(b)   a copy of the notice served under rule 3.7 (sanctions for non-payment of certain fees) where a claim is struck out under that rule;

(c)   a copy of the notice of acceptance where an offer to settle is accepted under Part 36 (Offers to settle);

(d)   a copy of the notice of discontinuance in a case which is discontinued under Part 38 (Discontinuance);

(e)   a copy of the award made on an arbitration under any Act or pursuant to an agreement, where no court has made an order for the enforcement of the award;

(f)   a copy of the order, award or determination of a statutorily constituted tribunal or body;

(g)   in a case under the Sheriffs Act 1887, the sheriff's bill of fees and charges, unless a court order giving the right to detailed assessment has been made;

(h)   a notice of revocation or discharge under Regulation 82 of the Civil Legal Aid (General) Regulations 1989;

(i)   in the county courts certain Acts and Regulations provide for costs incurred in proceedings under those Acts and Regulations to be assessed in the county court if so ordered on application. Where such an application is made, a copy of the order.

40.5   On receipt of the request for a detailed assessment hearing the court will fix a date for the hearing, or, if the costs officer so decides, will give directions or fix a date for a preliminary appointment.

40.6

(1)   The court will give at least 14 days notice of the time and place of the detailed assessment hearing to every person named in the statement referred to in paragraph 40.2(j) above.

(2)   The court will when giving notice, give each person who has served points of dispute a copy of the points of dispute annotated by the receiving party in compliance with paragraph 40.2(d) above.

(3)   Attention is drawn to rule 47.14(6)&(7): apart from the receiving party, only those who have served points of dispute may be heard on the detailed assessment unless the court gives permission, and only items specified in the points of dispute may be raised unless the court gives permission.

40.7

(1)   If the receiving party does not file a request for a detailed assessment hearing within the prescribed time, the paying party may apply to the court to fix a time within which the receiving party must do so. The sanction, for failure to commence detailed assessment proceedings within the time specified by the court, is that all or part of the costs may be disallowed (see rule 47.8(2)).

(2)   Where the receiving party commences detailed assessment proceedings after the time specified in the rules but before the paying party has made an application to the court to specify a time, the only sanction which the court may impose is to disallow all or part of the interest which would otherwise be

payable for the period of delay, unless the court exercises its powers under rule 44.14 (court's powers in relation to misconduct).

40.8   If either party wishes to make an application in the detailed assessment proceedings the provisions of Part 23 (General Rules about Applications for Court Orders) apply.

40.9

(1)   This paragraph deals with the procedure to be adopted where a date has been given by the court for a detailed assessment hearing and

    (a)   the detailed assessment proceedings are settled; or

    (b)   a party to the detailed assessment proceedings wishes to apply to vary the date which the court has fixed; or

    (c)   the parties to the detailed assessment proceedings agree about changes they wish to make to any direction given for the management of the detailed assessment proceedings.

(2)   If detailed assessment proceedings are settled, the receiving party must give notice of that fact to the court immediately, preferably by fax.

(3)   A party who wishes to apply to vary a direction must do so in accordance with Part 23 (General Rules about Applications for Court Orders).

(4)   If the parties agree about changes they wish to make to any direction given for the management of the detailed assessment proceedings—

    (a)   they must apply to the court for an order by consent; and

    (b)   they must file a draft of the directions sought and an agreed statement of the reasons why the variation is sought; and

    (c)   the court may make an order in the agreed terms or in other terms without a hearing, but it may direct that a hearing is to be listed.

40.10

(1)   If a party wishes to vary his bill of costs, points of dispute or a reply, an amended or supplementary document must be filed with the court and copies of it must be served on all other relevant parties.

(2)   Permission is not required to vary a bill of costs, points of dispute or a reply but the court may disallow the variation or permit it only upon conditions, including conditions as to the payment of any costs caused or wasted by the variation.

40.11   Unless the court directs otherwise the receiving party must file with the court the papers in support of the bill not less than 7 days before the date for the detailed assessment hearing and not more than 14 days before that date.

40.12   The following provisions apply in respect of the papers to be filed in support of the bill;

(a)   If the claim is for costs only without any additional liability the papers to be filed, and the order in which they are to be arranged are as follows:

    (i)   instructions and briefs to counsel arranged in chronological order together with all advices, opinions and drafts received and response to such instructions;

    (ii)   reports and opinions of medical and other experts;

    (iii)   any other relevant papers;

    (iv)   a full set of any relevant pleadings to the extent that they have not already been filed in court.

    (v)   correspondence, files and attendance notes;

(b)   where the claim is in respect of an additional liability only, such of the papers listed at (a) above, as are relevant to the issues raised by the claim for additional liability;

(c)   where the claim is for both base costs and an additional liability, the papers listed at (a) above, together with any papers relevant to the issues raised by the claim for additional liability.

40.13   The provisions set out in Section 20 of this Practice Direction apply where the court disallows any amount of a legal representative's percentage increase, and the legal representative applies for an order that the disallowed amount should continue to be payable by the client in accordance with Rule 44.16.

40.14   The court may direct the receiving party to produce any document which in the opinion of the court is necessary to enable it to reach its decision. These *documents will in the first instance be produced to the court, but the court may ask the receiving party to elect whether to disclose the particular document to the paying party in order to rely on the contents of the document, or whether to decline disclosure and instead rely on other evidence.*

40.15 Costs assessed at a detailed assessment at the conclusion of proceedings may include an assessment of any additional liability in respect of the costs of a previous application or hearing.

40.16 Once the detailed assessment hearing has ended it is the responsibility of the legal representative appearing for the receiving party or, as the case may be, the receiving party in person to remove the papers filed in support of the bill.

[30.70]

The notice of commencement will have been served, followed by points of dispute, but the request for a detailed assessment will be the first occasion in which the court has been involved. The request must be filed within three months of the expiry of the period for commencing detailed assessment proceedings, which in effect means the receiving party has six months from the date of the award of costs in which to request a detailed assessment hearing. If the receiving party fails to file a request the paying party may apply under CPR 47.14(3) for an order with default provisions requiring the receiving party to request a hearing.

The request for a detailed assessment hearing helpfully lists the documents which should accompany it, which include the solicitor's client care letter or retainer where the receiving party alleges the indemnity principle is of relevance. Paragraph 40.12 of the Practice Direction specifies the supporting papers which should be filed. I understand that receiving parties rarely annotate the points of dispute in compliance with para 40.2(d), which probably explains why few court officers ever comply with para 40.6(2).

There are increasing reports and complaints about some provincial courts adopting protocols based on para 40.5 of the Practice Direction and their general case management powers, which create so many obstacles to obtaining a detailed assessment hearing that district judges no longer have to hear them! Such directions typically include a requirement that the parties' representatives shall confer and file a joint statement setting out the agreed and disputed issues.

Speaking at the IBC Annual Costs Conference, John Hocking, the then chairman of the Association of Law Costs Draftsmen, complained about practices which prolong the process, increase the costs, result in issues being re-visited and amount to a denial of the right to a fair hearing. He even impugned their parentage saying that in reality they are local practice directions and therefore *ultra vires* the CPR. He particularly objected to the practice of giving a short hearing in the morning with another in the afternoon. If the costs were not agreed in the morning the parties have to come back in the afternoon and are forbidden to leave the court precincts in the meantime. When I enquired whether the parties were tagged between the two hearings John Hocking said please don't suggest it.

The word 'may' in section 40.14 of the Costs Practice Direction confers a discretion on the costs judge to ask the receiving party to elect whether to disclose a particular document to the paying party in order to rely on the contents of the document, or whether to decline disclosure and instead rely on other evidence. No paying party can invariably and automatically compel the putting of the receiving party to his election simply by declining to deal with the matter on the usual informal basis. In *Gower Chemicals Group Litigation v Gower Chemicals Ltd* [2008] EWHC 735 (QBD), 17 April the defendants had, sensibly, accepted the informal procedure: it was only at the stage of the assessment of the costs of undisclosed experts' reports for which substantial costs were being claimed that they sought disclosure. The reports were potentially of substantial importance and there was a clear issue arising on this: there was clear justification for the defendants to seek to see the reports if they were relied on by the claimants.

Right of Audience

[30.71]

Section 27(2)(e) of the Courts and Legal Services Act 1990 provides that a person shall have a right of audience in chambers, except in reserved family proceedings, if '(i) he is employed (whether wholly or in part) or is otherwise engaged to assist in the conduct of litigation and is doing so under instructions given (either generally or in relation to the proceedings) by a qualified Litigator.'

Because since the commencement of the Human Rights Act 1998 hearings in chambers are no longer in private but in public, representatives of qualified litigators have a right of audience except in family and other specified proceedings where the permission of the court is required. In *Ahmed v Powell* [2003] EWHC 9011, SCCO 19 February the Senior Costs Judge ruled that although law costs draftsmen instructed by solicitors clearly came within the definition, costs negotiators instructed by an insurance company did not. However, although Fellows of the Association of Law Costs Draftsmen are classified as experts whose fees may be recovered by a litigant in person this classification has not previously extended to conferring rights of audience on them. They could, of course, attend a hearing as a McKenzie friend, or even be called as an expert witness, but this requires the attendance of the client and does not, in theory, enable the costs draftsman to act as an advocate. The ALCD sought to remedy the situation by applying for Fellows of the Association to be granted rights of audience and rights to litigate on all costs issues including appeals at first instance. The Association of Law Costs Draftsmen Order 2006 (SI 2006/3333) came into force on 1 January 2007, designating the Association as an authorised body for the purposes of ss27 and 28 of the Courts and Legal Services Act 1990. Fellows of the Association can now attend a course which includes conducting costs litigation, advocacy and the ALCD Accounts Rules. Upon successful completion of this course, they are granted rights of audience by the Association. Fellows with rights of audience may also act for litigants in person in costs proceedings including those under ss 70 and 71 of the Solicitors Act 1974. Not all costs draftsmen are members of the ALCD and there are no regulations, other than the Association's code of conduct, governing costs draftsmen. This grant of authorised body status is a boost for the Association as well as a step along the road towards regulation.

A company may only be represented by an officer or employee with the permission of the court.

A bankrupt has no right to be heard without an order under s 303 of the Insolvency Act.

Counsel may appear on their own behalf, but without a fee. Counsel's clerks have no right of audience but the SCCO Guide states they may be permitted to appear on the written request of counsel and permission of the costs judge or officer.

[30.72]

FORM N258

Request for detailed assessment hearing (general form)

In the	
Claim No.	
Claimant (include Ref.)	
Defendant (include Ref.)	

I certify that the attached Notice of Commencement was served on the paying party ....

(and give details of any other party served with the notice)

on .... *(insert date)*

I now ask the court to arrange an assessment hearing.

I enclose copies of *(tick as appropriate)*

☐ the document giving the right to detailed assessment;

☐ a copy of the Notice of Commencement;

☐ the bill of costs;

☐ the paying party's point of dispute, annotated as necessary in order to show (1) which items have been agreed and their value and (2) which items remain in dispute and their value;

☐ points in reply (if any);

☐ a statement giving the names, addresses for service and references of all persons to whom the court should give notice of the hearing;

☐ the relevant details of any additional liability claimed;

☐ a copy of all the orders made by the court relating to the costs of the proceedings which are to be assessed;

☐ any fee notes of counsel and receipts or accounts for other disbursements relating to items in dispute;

☐ [where solicitors' costs are disputed] the client care letter delivered to the receiving party or the solicitor's retainer.

I believe the hearing will take .... *(give estimate of time court should allow)*.

I enclose my fee of £ ....

Signed .... **Date** ....

(Claimant) (Defendant) ('s solicitor)

The court office at

is open between 10 am and 4 pm Monday to Friday. When corresponding with the court, please address forms or letters to the Court Manager and quote the claim number.

N258 Request for detailed assessment hearing (general form) (7.00)

[30.73]

SECTION V   INTERIM COSTS CERTIFICATE AND FINAL COSTS CERTIFICATE

CPR Rule 47.15: Power to issue an interim certificate

(1)   The court may at any time after the receiving party has filed a request for a detailed assessment hearing—

    (a)   issue an interim costs certificate for such sum as it considers appropriate;

    (b)   amend or cancel an interim certificate.

(2)   An interim certificate will include an order to pay the costs to which it relates, unless the court orders otherwise.

(3)   The court may order the costs certified in an interim certificate to be paid into court.

(4)   Where the court –

    (a)   issues an interim costs certificate; or

    (b)   amends or cancels an interim certificate,

in detailed assessment proceedings pursuant to an order under section 194(3) of the Legal Services Act 2007, the receiving party must send a copy of the interim costs certificate or the order amending or cancelling the interim costs certificate to the prescribed charity.

[30.74]

CPD Section 41 Power to issue an interim certificate: Rule 47.15

41.1

(1)   *A party wishing to apply for an interim certificate may do so by making an application in accordance with Part 23 (General Rules about Applications for Court Orders).*

(2)   *Attention is drawn to the fact that the court's power to issue an interim certificate arises only after the receiving party has filed a request for a detailed assessment hearing.*

[30.75]

In addition to the court's power to order costs on account in CPR Rule 44.3(8), this rule gives the court a complete discretion to award an interim certificate even though there has been no assessment or agreement on quantum. The points of dispute should enable the court to calculate the minimum amount the receiving party will eventually be awarded, but no doubt busy district judges would appreciate it if the calculations and the resulting minimum amount accompanied the application. The court may order that the amount in an interim certificate shall be paid either to the receiving party or into court.

[30.76]

CPR Rule 47.16: Final costs certificate

(1)   In this rule a completed bill means a bill calculated to show the amount due following the detailed assessment of the costs.

(2)   The period for filing the completed bill is 14 days after the end of the detailed assessment hearing.

(3)   When a completed bill is filed the court will issue a final costs certificate and serve it on the parties to the detailed assessment proceedings.

(4)   Paragraph (3) is subject to any order made by the court that a certificate is not to be issued until other costs have been paid.

(5)   A final costs certificate will include an order to pay the costs to which it relates, unless the court orders otherwise.

(6)   Where the court issues a final costs certificate in detailed assessment proceedings pursuant to an order under section 194(3) of the Legal Services Act 2007, the receiving party must send a copy of the final costs certificate to the prescribed charity.

(The Costs Practice Direction deals with the form of a final costs certificate)

[30.77]

CPD Section 42 Final costs certificate: Rule 47.16

42.1   At the detailed assessment hearing the court will indicate any disallowance or reduction in the sums claimed in the bill of costs by making an appropriate note on the bill.

42.2   The receiving party must, in order to complete the bill after the detailed assessment hearing make clear the correct figures agreed or allowed in respect of each item and must re-calculate the summary of the bill appropriately.

42.3   The completed bill of costs must be filed with the court no later than 14 days after the detailed assessment hearing.

42.4   At the same time as filing the completed bill of costs, the party whose bill it is must also produce receipted fee notes and receipted accounts in respect of all disbursements except those covered by a certificate in Precedent F(5) in the Schedule of Costs Precedents annexed to this Practice Direction.

42.5   No final costs certificate will be issued until all relevant court fees payable on the assessment of costs have been paid.

42.6   If the receiving party fails to file a completed bill in accordance with rule 47.16 the paying party may make an application under Part 23 (General Rules about Applications for Court Orders) seeking an appropriate order under rule 3.1 (The court's general powers of management).

42.7   A final costs certificate will show:

(a)   the amount of any costs which have been agreed between the parties or which have been allowed on detailed assessment;

(b)   where applicable the amount agreed or allowed in respect of VAT on the costs agreed or allowed.

This provision is subject to any contrary provision made by the statutory provisions relating to costs payable out of the Community Legal Service Fund.

42.8   A final costs certificate will include disbursements in respect of the fees of counsel only if receipted fee notes or accounts in respect of those disbursements have been produced to the court and only to the extent indicated by those receipts.

42.9   Where the certificate relates to costs payable between parties a separate certificate will be issued for each party entitled to costs.

42.10   Form N257 is a model form of interim costs certificate and Form N256 is a model form of final costs certificate.

42.11   An application for an order staying enforcement of an interim costs certificate or final costs certificate may be made either:

(1)   to a costs judge or district judge of the court office which issued the certificate; or

(2)   to the court (if different) which has general jurisdiction to enforce the certificate.

42.12   Proceedings for enforcement of interim costs certificates or final costs certificates may not be issued in the Costs Office.

[30.78]

FORM N257

Interim costs certificate

In the	
Claim No.	
Claimant (including ref.)	
Defendant (including ref.)	
Date	

To [Claimant] [Defendant] ['s Solicitor]

Upon application by the [claimant] [defendant] for [a detailed assessment hearing] [the issue of an interim Costs certificate by agreement].

[Master] [District Judge][   ]has ordered that you must pay £   to the [claimant] [defendant] [within 14 days from the date of this order] [on or before [   ] [[into court to await the issue of a final costs certificate].

───── Take Notice ─────

To the defendant (claimant)

If you do not pay in accordance with this order your goods may be removed and sold or other enforcement proceedings may be taken against you. If your circumstances change and you cannot pay, ask at the court office about what you can do

───── Address for Payment ─────

───── How to Pay ─────

• **PAYMENT(S) MUST BE MADE** to the person named at the address for payment quoting their reference and the court case number.
• **DO NOT** bring or send payments to the court. **THEY WILL NOT BE ACCEPTED.**
• You should allow <u>at least</u> 4 days for your payment to reach the claimant (defendant) or his representative.
• Make sure that you keep records and can account for all payments made. Proof may be required if there is any disagreement. It is not safe to send cash unless you use registered post.
• A leaflet giving further advice about payment can be obtained from the court.
• If you need more information you should contact the claimant (defendant) or his representative.

The court office at

is open between 10 am and 4 pm Monday to Friday. Address all communications to the Court Manager quoting the claim number

N257 Interim cost certificate

[30.79]

FORM N256

Final costs certificate

Name of court	Claim No.
Name of Claimant (including ref.)	
Name of Defendant (including ref.)	
[Defendant's][Claimant's] date of birth	
Date	

To [Claimant][Defendant]['s Solicitor]

In accordance with [identify the document giving the right to detailed assessment]

District Judge [   ] has assessed the total costs as £   [including £
for the costs of the detailed assessment]

[And £   already having been paid under the interim costs certificate issued on [   ]]

You must pay [the balance of]£   to the [claimant][defendant] [within 14 days from the date of this order] [on or before[   ]]

The date from which any entitlement to interest under this certificate is to run is:-

1. as to the amount of the bill as assessed excluding the costs of assessment, [the date of the order]

2. and as to [£   ] being the costs of assessment, the date of this certificate.

─────── **Take Notice** ───────

To the defendant (claimant)

If you do not pay in accordance with this order your goods may be removed and sold or other enforcement proceedings may be taken against you. If your circumstances change and you cannot pay, ask at the court office about what you can do.

Further interest may be added if judgment has been given for £5,000 or more or is in respect of debt which attracts contractual or statutory interest for late payment.

If you do not pay as ordered, this judgment may be registered on the Register of Judgments, Orders and Fines. This may make it difficult for you to get credit. **If you then pay in full within one month** you can ask the court to cancel the entry on the Register. You will need to give proof of payment. You can (for a fee) also obtain a Certificate of Cancellation from the court. If you pay the debt in full after one month you can ask the court to mark the entry on the Register as satisfied and (for a fee) obtain a Certificate of Satisfaction to prove that the debt has been paid.

─── **Address for Payment** ───

─────── **How to Pay** ───────

• **PAYMENT(S) MUST BE MADE to the person named at the address for payment quoting their reference and the court case number.**
• **DO NOT bring or send payments to the court. THEY WILL NOT BE ACCEPTED.**
• You should allow <u>at least</u> 4 days for your payment to reach the claimant (defendant) or his representative.
• Make sure that you keep records and can account for all payments made. Proof may be required if there is any disagreement. It is not safe to send cash unless you use registered post.
• A leaflet giving further advice about payment can be obtained from the court.
• If you need more information you should contact the claimant (defendant) or his representative.

The court office at

is open between 10 am and 4 pm Monday to Friday. Address all communications to the Court Manager quoting the claim number.

N256 Final cost certificate (04.06)

[30.80]

At the conclusion of the detailed assessment proceedings the receiving party must complete the bill by calculating the amounts due, filing the completed bill together with fee notes and receipted accounts for disbursements exceeding £500 and all outstanding court fees. A tip from Harry Birks:

> 'If there has not been time at the end of the detailed assessment hearing to agree the final total of the bill, it is a good idea for the solicitors for the parties (or their costs draftsmen) to communicate to agree the figures before the completed bill is filed. This can avoid the necessity for a further application to the court if the paying party disputes the figure on the final costs certificate.'

[30.81]

The final costs certificate will include an order to pay the costs, which, as ever, under Rule 44.8 must be complied with within 14 days unless an extension is obtained.

[30.82]

Section VI CPR Rule 47.17: Detailed assessment procedure for costs of a LSC funded client or an assisted person where costs are payable out of the Community Legal Service Fund

(1)   Where the court is to assess costs of a LSC funded client or an assisted person which are payable out of the Community Legal Services Fund, that person's solicitor may commence detailed assessment proceedings by filing a request in the relevant practice form.

(2)   A request under paragraph (1) must be filed within 3 months after the date when the right to detailed assessment arose.

(3)   The solicitor must also serve a copy of the request for detailed assessment on the LSC funded client or the assisted person, if notice of that person's interest has been given to the court in accordance with community legal service or legal aid regulations.

(4)   Where the solicitor has certified that the LSC funded client or that person wishes to attend an assessment hearing, the court will, on receipt of the request for assessment, fix a date for the assessment hearing.

(5)   Where paragraph (3) does not apply, the court will, on receipt of the request for assessment provisionally assess the costs without the attendance of the solicitor, unless it considers that a hearing is necessary.

(6)   After the court has provisionally assessed the bill, it will return the bill to the solicitor.

(7)   The court will fix a date for an assessment hearing if the solicitor informs the court, within 14 days after he receives the provisionally assessed bill, that he wants the court to hold such a hearing.

[30.82A]

CPD Section 43 Detailed assessment procedure where costs are payable out of the Community Legal Service Fund: Rule 47.17

43.1   *The provisions of this section apply where the court is to assess costs which are payable only out of the community legal service fund. Paragraphs 39.1 to 40.16* and 49.1 to 49.8 apply in cases involving costs payable by another person as well as costs payable only out of the community legal service fund.

43.2   The time for requesting a detailed assessment under rule 47.17 is within 3 months after the date when the right to detailed assessment arose.

(1)   The request for a detailed assessment of costs must be in Form N258A. The request must be accompanied by:

    (a)   a copy of the bill of costs;

    (b)   the document giving the right to detailed assessment (for further information as to this document, see paragraph 40.4 above);

    (c)   a copy of all orders made by the court relating to the costs which are to be assessed;

    (d)   copies of any fee notes of counsel and any expert in respect of fees claimed in the bill;

    (e)   written evidence as to any other disbursement which is claimed and which exceeds £500;

    (f)   the legal aid certificates, LSC certificates, any relevant amendment certificates, any authorities and any certificates of discharge or revocation and;

    (g)   a statement signed by the solicitor giving the solicitor's name, address for service, reference, telephone number, fax number, e-mail address where available and, if the assisted person has a financial interest in the detailed assessment and wishes to attend, giving the postal address of that person, to which the court will send notice of any hearing.

(2)   The relevant papers in support of the bill as described in paragraph 40.12 must only be lodged if requested by the costs officer.

43.4   Rule 47.17 provides that the court will hold a detailed assessment hearing if the assisted person has a financial interest in the detailed assessment and wishes to attend. The court may also hold a detailed assessment hearing in any other case, instead of provisionally assessing a bill of costs, where it considers that a hearing is necessary. Before deciding whether a hearing is necessary under this rule, the court may require the solicitor whose bill it is, to provide further information relating to the bill.

43.5   Where the court has provisionally assessed a bill of costs it will send to the solicitor a notice, in Form N253 annexed to this practice direction, of the amount of costs which the court proposes to allow together with the bill itself. The legal representative should, if the provisional assessment is to be accepted, then complete the bill.

43.6   The court will fix a date for a detailed assessment hearing if the solicitor informs the court within 14 days after he receives the notice of the amount allowed on the provisional assessment that he wants the court to hold such a hearing.

43.7   The court will give at least 14 days notice of the time and place of the detailed assessment hearing to the solicitor and, if the assisted person has a financial interest in the detailed assessment and wishes to attend, to the assisted person.

43.8   If the solicitor whose bill it is, or any other party wishes to make an application in the detailed assessment proceedings, the provisions of Part 23 (General Rules about Applications for Court Orders) applies.

43.9   It is the responsibility of the legal representative to complete the bill by entering in the bill the correct figures allowed in respect of each item, recalculating the summary of the bill appropriately and completing the Community Legal Service assessment certificate (Form EX80A).

[30.83]

CPR Rule 47.17A: Detailed assessment procedure where costs are payable out of a fund other than the community legal service fund

(1)   Where the court is to assess costs which are payable out of a fund other than the Community Legal Service Fund, the receiving party may commence detailed assessment proceedings by filing a request in the relevant practice form.

(2)   A request under paragraph (1) must be filed within 3 months after the date when the right to detailed assessment arose.

(3)   The court may direct that the party seeking assessment serve a copy of the request on any person who has a financial interest in the outcome of the assessment.

(4)   The court will, on receipt of the request for assessment, provisionally assess the costs without the attendance of the receiving party, unless it considers that a hearing is necessary.

(5)   After the court has provisionally assessed the bill, it will return the bill to the receiving party.

(6)   The court will fix a date for an assessment hearing if the party informs the court, within 14 days after he receives the provisionally assessed bill, that he wants the court to hold such a hearing.

[30.83A]

CPD Section 44 Costs of detailed assessment proceedings where costs are payable out of a fund other than the Community Legal Service Fund: Rule 47.17A

44.1   *Rule 47.17A provides that the court will make a provisional assessment of a bill of costs payable out of a fund (other than the Community Legal Service Fund) unless it considers that a hearing is necessary. It also enables the court to direct under rule 47.17A(3) that the receiving party must serve a copy of the request for assessment and copies of the documents which accompany it, on any person who has a financial interest in the outcome of the assessment.*

44.2

(a)   *A person has a financial interest in the outcome of the assessment if the assessment will or may affect the amount of money or property to which he is or may become entitled out of the fund.*

(b)   *Where an interest in the fund is itself held by a trustee for the benefit of some other person, that trustee will be treated as the person having such a financial interest.*

(c)   *'Trustee' includes a personal representative, receiver or any other person acting in a fiduciary capacity.*

44.3   *The request for a detailed assessment of costs out of the fund should be in Form N258B, be accompanied by the documents set out at paragraph 43.3(a) to (e) and (g) above and the following;*

(a)   *a statement signed by the receiving party giving his name, address for service, reference, telephone number, fax number and,*

(b)   *a statement of the postal address of any person who has a financial interest in the outcome of the assessment, to which the court may send notice of any hearing; and*

(c)   *in respect of each person stated to have such an interest if such person is a child or protected party, a statement to that effect.*

44.4   *The court will decide, having regard to the amount of the bill, the size of the fund and the number of persons who have a financial interest, which of those* persons should be served. The court may dispense with service on all or some of them.

44.5   Where the court makes an order dispensing with service on all such persons it may proceed at once to make a provisional assessment, or, if it decides that a hearing is necessary, give appropriate directions. Before deciding whether a hearing is necessary under this rule, the court may require the receiving party to provide further information relating to the bill.

44.6

(1)   Where the court has provisionally assessed a bill of costs, it will send to the receiving party, a notice in Form N253 of the amount of costs which the court proposes to allow together with the bill itself. If the receiving party is legally represented the legal representative should, if the provisional assessment is to be accepted, then complete the bill.

(2)   The court will fix a date for a detailed assessment hearing, if the receiving party informs the court within 14 days after he receives the notice in Form N253 of the amount allowed on the provisional assessment, that he wants the court to hold such a hearing.

44.7   Where the court makes an order that a person who has a financial interest is to be served with a copy of the request for assessment, it may give directions about service and about the hearing.

44.8   The court will give at least 14 days notice of the time and place of the detailed assessment hearing to the receiving party and, to any person who has a financial interest in the outcome of the assessment and has been served with a copy of the request for assessment.

44.9   If the receiving party, or any other party or any person who has a financial interest in the outcome of assessment, wishes to make an application in the detailed assessment proceedings, the provisions of Part 23 (General Rules about Applications for Court Orders) applies.

44.10   If the receiving party is legally represented the legal representative must in order to complete the bill after the assessment make clear the correct figures allowed in respect of each item and must recalculate the summary of the bill if appropriate.

[30.84]

SECTION VII   COSTS OF DETAILED ASSESSMENT PROCEEDINGS

CPR Rule 47.18: Liability for costs of detailed assessment proceedings

(1)   The receiving party is entitled to his costs of the detailed assessment proceedings, except where—

   (a)   the provisions of any Act, any of these Rules or any relevant practice direction provide otherwise; or

   (b)   the court makes some other order in relation to all or part of the costs of the detailed assessment proceedings.

(1A)   Paragraph (1) does not apply where the receiving party has pro bono representation in the detailed assessment proceedings but that party may apply for an order in respect of that representation under section 194(3) of the Legal Services Act 2007.

(2)   In deciding whether to make some other order, the court must have regard to all the circumstances, including—

   (a)   the conduct of all the parties;

   (b)   the amount, if any, by which the bill of costs has been reduced; and

   (c)   whether it was reasonable for a party to claim the costs of a particular item or to dispute that item.

[30.85]

CPD Section 45 Liability for costs of detailed assessment proceedings: Rule 47.18

45.1   *As a general rule the court will assess the receiving party's costs of the detailed assessment proceedings and add them to the bill of costs.*

45.2   *If the costs of the detailed assessment proceedings are awarded to the paying party, the court will either assess those costs by summary assessment or make an order for them to be decided by detailed assessment.*

45.3   *No party should file or serve a statement of costs of the detailed assessment proceedings unless the court orders him to do so.*

45.4   *Attention is drawn to the fact that in deciding what order to make about the costs of detailed assessment proceedings the court must have regard to the conduct of all parties, the amount by which the bill of costs has been reduced and whether it was reasonable for a party to claim the costs of a particular item or to dispute that item.*

45.5

(1)   *In respect of interest on the costs of detailed assessment proceedings, the interest shall begin to run from the date of the default, interim or final costs certificate as the case may be.*

(2)   *This provision applies only to the costs of the detailed assessment proceedings themselves. The costs of the substantive proceedings are governed by rule 40.8(1).*

[30.86]

The costs of the detailed assessment proceedings will generally be awarded to the receiving party unless at some previous hearing the court has ordered otherwise, or an offer made by the paying party under Rule 47.19 is taken into account, or the costs officer disallows all or part of the costs on the grounds of misconduct in relation to the detailed assessment proceedings. Such misconduct could be the inclusion of an unjustifiable item or amount in the bill. The amount of the costs of the detailed assessment proceedings will almost certainly be dealt with by way of summary assessment, although the costs officer could for good reason order a detailed assessment. The receiving party would be well advised to be prepared for a summary assessment even though the provisions of para 13.5 of the Practice Direction (para [29.3]) for a statement of costs do not apply to the receiving party, because he is already entitled to the costs of the assessment under the order for the costs being assessed (see paras 45.1 and 45.3 of the Practice Direction). Supplying the costs officer with your figures in writing is all part of the art of advocacy.

There is no expectation that a party who succeeds in dramatically reducing a bill will be entitled to their costs of attending the assessment in the absence of an offer which meets the requirements of rule 47.19(1) (*Horsford v Bird* [2007] UKPC 55, [2006] All ER (D) 20 (Dec)).

[30.87]

CPR Rule 47.19: Offers to settle without prejudice save as to costs of the detailed assessment proceedings

(1)   Where—

(a)   a party (whether the paying party or the receiving party) makes a written offer to settle the costs of the proceedings which gave rise to the assessment proceedings; and

(b)   the offer is expressed to be without prejudice$^{(GL)}$ save as to the costs of the detailed assessment proceedings,

the court will take the offer into account in deciding who should pay the costs of those proceedings.

(2)   The fact of the offer must not be communicated to the costs officer until the question of costs of the detailed assessment proceedings falls to be decided.

(The Costs Practice Direction provides that rule 47.19 does not apply where the receiving party is a LSC funded client or an assisted person, unless the court orders otherwise)

[30.88]

CPD Section 46 Offer to settle without prejudice save as to the costs of the detailed assessment proceedings: Rule 47.19

46.1   *Rule 47.19 allows the court to take into account offers to settle, without prejudice save as to the costs of detailed assessment proceedings, when deciding who is liable for the costs of those proceedings. The rule does not specify a time within which such an offer should be made. An offer made by the paying party should usually be made within 14 days after service of the notice of commencement on that party. If the offer is made by the receiving party, it should normally be made within 14 days after the service of points of dispute by the paying party. Offers made after these periods are likely to be given less weight by the court in deciding what order as to costs to make unless there is good reason for the offer not being made until the later time.*

46.2   *Where an offer to settle is made it should specify whether or not it is intended to be inclusive of the cost of preparation of the bill, interest and value added tax (VAT). The offer may include or exclude some or all of these items but the position must be made clear on the face of the offer so that the offeree is clear about the terms of the offer when it is being considered. Unless the offer states otherwise, the offer will be treated as being inclusive of all these items.*

46.3   *Where an offer to settle is accepted, an application may be made for a certificate in agreed terms, or the bill of costs may be withdrawn, in accordance with rule 47.10 (Procedure where costs are agreed).*

46.4   *Where the receiving party is an assisted person or an LSC funded client, an offer to settle without prejudice save as to the costs of the detailed assessment proceedings will not have the consequences specified under rule 47.19 unless the court so orders.*

[30.89]

The provision for the court to take into account offers by *either* party was a significant change. It means that receiving parties cannot afford to sit back, ignore offers they expect to beat and go along to the assessment hearing in the expectation that they will recover their full costs of the detailed assessment proceedings. Costs officers are now more likely to penalise the receiving party even when they beat the paying party's offer, if they have made little or no attempt to compromise – unless the offer is derisory and the bill demonstrably reasonable. In any event every paying party should make a Rule 47.19 offer, even where the receiving party is publicly-funded, and be prepared with a statement of costs to support his claim for costs of the assessment if the receiving party does not beat his offer. In *Wills v Crown Estate Comrs* [2003]

EWHC 1718 (Ch), [2003] All ER (D) 410 (Oct) the High Court judge on appeal upheld the deputy costs judge's refusal to deprive the receiving party of the costs of the assessment because the receiving party had failed to better an offer made shortly before the hearing. He said 'This appeal emphasises the need for paying parties who wish to protect themselves against the costs consequences of CPR 47.19 to make realistic settlement offers at the beginning of the detailed assessment proceedings and not at the end. The court is bedevilled by late settlements. The procedures in CPR 47.19 are designed to promote early reasonable offers and parties should bear this in mind in the future.'

Although negotiations on a 'without prejudice save as to costs' basis are obviously admissible on that question, negotiations on a completely 'without prejudice' basis are not. The parties may negotiate in the faith and expectation that such negotiations could not be used against them even on the question of costs. Although there were some exceptions to that rule, costs was not one of them (*Reed Executive Plc v Reed Business Information Ltd* [2004] EWCA Civ 887, [2004] 4 All ER 942, 14 July).

The costs of the substantive proceedings and of the assessment proceedings are quite different: *Crosbie v Munroe* [2003] EWCA Civ 350, [2003] 2 All ER 856, although a costs – only application under CPR Rule 44.12A, demonstrated that the 'costs of the proceedings' within the meaning of CPR 47.19 relate only to the costs leading up to the disposal (on this occasion by agreement) of the substantive claim. They are 'the proceedings which gave rise to the assessment proceedings', and the assessment proceedings cover the whole period of negotiations about the amount of costs payable through the Part 8 proceedings to the ultimate disposal of those proceedings, whether by agreement or court order.

If the receiving party seeks to recover the costs of negotiating the costs of the substantive proceedings, it should make clear that those negotiations will be dependant upon the paying party bearing the costs of the negotiations. Alternatively a claimant could accept the final offer for costs conditionally upon the defendant paying his costs of the negotiations. What must be avoided is what was described as the Russian doll analogy in the unreported case of *Longman v Feather and Black* (18 March 2008, unreported) in Southampton County Court where an appeal was allowed against an order that the defendant pay the claimant's costs of the costs negotiations to be assessed if not agreed. Under the order, if the defendant had opted to negotiate the costs of the costs negotiations, and if these were agreed, the claimant would have then been entitled to demand the costs of those negotiations, and so on *ad infinitum*. . . .'

[30.90]

CPD Section 49A: Costs payable by the trustee for civil recovery under a recovery order

49A.1   *In this section –*
'the Act' means the Proceeds of Crime Act 2002;
'the Order in Council' means the Proceeds of Crime Act 2002 (External Requests and Orders) Order 2005; and
'the Regulations' means the Proceeds of Crime Act 2002 (Legal Expenses in Civil Recovery Proceedings) Regulations 2005.

49A.2   *This section applies to the assessment of costs where the court has made a recovery order which provides for the payment by the trustee for civil recovery of a person's reasonable legal costs in respect of civil recovery proceedings. Such an order may be made under section 266(8A) of the Act or article 177(10) of the Order in Council. The procedure for obtaining a recovery order is set out in the Act and Order in Council, together with the Civil Recovery Proceedings Practice Direction.*

49A.3   *Where this section applies, costs are to be assessed in accordance with the procedure for detailed assessment under Part 47, subject to the modifications set out in Parts 4 and 5 of the Regulations.*

49A.4   *The detailed assessment will normally be made by a costs judge, even if the costs are within the authorised amounts specified in paragraph 30.1(1). The appropriate office for the purpose of rule 47.4(1) is the Costs Office.*

49A.5   *In detailed assessment proceedings to which this section applies –*
(1)   *the paying party is the trustee for civil recovery;*
(2)   *the receiving party is the person whose reasonable legal costs are payable pursuant to provision made in the recovery order under section 266(8A) of the Act or article 177(10) of the Order in Council; and*
(3)   *the relevant persons for the purpose of rule 47.6(2) include the enforcement authority or the appropriate officer as defined in paragraph 1.5 of the Practice Direction – Civil Recovery Proceedings in addition to the persons referred to in paragraph 32.10.*

49A.6   *On commencing detailed assessment proceedings, the receiving party must, in addition to serving the documents listed in paragraph 32.3 on the paying party and all other relevant persons, serve a statement giving the date, amount and source of all interim payments which have been released in respect of any of those costs under Part 3 of the Regulations.*

49A.7   *By virtue of regulation 13(2) of the Regulations, detailed assessment proceedings must be commenced not later than 2 months after the date of the recovery order, and a request for a detailed assessment hearing must be filed not later than 2 months after the expiry of the period for commencing the detailed assessment proceedings.*

49A.8   *The documents which must accompany the request for a detailed assessment hearing shall include copies of all exclusions from property freezing orders or interim receiving orders made by the court for the purpose of enabling the receiving party to meet the costs which are to be assessed, and of every estimate of costs filed by the receiving party in support of an application for such an exclusion.*

49A.9   *The receiving party's costs will be assessed on the standard basis, subject to Part 5 of the Regulations (and in particular regulation 17, which specifies the hourly rates which may be allowed). Attention is also drawn to regulation 14, which provides that the amounts of any interim payments released in respect of the receiving party's costs will be deducted from the costs allowed in accordance with Part 5 of the Regulations.*

(See also Part 48.)

Under the Proceeds of Crime Act 2002, as amended on 1 January 2006, a recovery order may provide that the trustee for civil recovery is to pay a person's reasonable legal expenses out of the recovered property. Regulation

13 of the Proceeds of Crime Act 2002 (Legal Expenses in Civil Recovery Proceedings) Regulations 2005 specifies that, if such costs cannot be agreed, the time for commencing detailed assessment is two months from the date of the recovery order, with a similar time for requesting a hearing following expiry of the period for commencement. Regulation 17(1) states:

> 'Subject to the following paragraphs of this regulation, remuneration for work done by a legal representative may only be allowed at the appropriate hourly rate shown in the Table below.'

The Table sets out 'standard' and 'higher' hourly rates for the usual four grades of fee earner, ranging from £225 for Grade A at the higher rate to £75 for Grade D at the standard rate, Higher rates may only be allowed where the case involves substantial novel or complex issues of law or fact.

What happens if the rate charged to the client is *less* than the prescribed rate for the fee earner instructed? The court *may only* allow the prescribed rate, no more, no less. This appears to be another example of the indemnity principle being of no effect – see [17.8].

[30.91]

CPR Rule 47.20: Right to appeal

See Chapter 31.

[30.92]

CPR Rule 47.21: Court to hear appeal

See Chapter 31.

[30.93]

CPR Rule 47.22: Appeal procedure

See Chapter 31.

[30.94]

CPR Rule 47.23: Powers of the court on appeal

See Chapter 31.

THE SUPREME COURT COSTS RULES 2009

[30.95]

Part 7 deals with costs in the Supreme Court accompanied by Practice Direction No 13.

Costs may be awarded on either the standard or the indemnity basis with the same definitions as in the CPR. There is provision for the paying party to file and serve points of dispute and for the receiving party to respond.

So, what is different?

Rule 47 provides that submissions as to costs are to be made *before* judgment unless before the close of oral argument a party applies to defer making submissions until after judgment. The court could direct oral submissions immediately after judgment, or the simultaneous or sequential filing of written submissions or written submissions followed by oral submissions.

Under rule 49 either party may request a *provisional assessment* of costs by the Registrar. If either or both parties are dissatisfied with the provisional assessment the registrar will try to resolve it in correspondence.

If that fails he will appoint an oral hearing before two costs officers, one of whom will be a taxing master and the other an appointee of the President – probably the Registrar.

And so it goes on. If you ascend to the dizzy heights of the Supreme Court you will no doubt read it all very carefully.

Enquiries about costs should be made to the Costs Clerk (tel: 020-7960 1990).

Enquiries about fees should be made to the Registry (tel: 020-7960 1991, 1992).

Drafts and cheques for fees, including assessment fees, should be made payable to 'The Supreme Court of the United Kingdom'.

Drafts and cheques for security money only should be made payable to 'UK Supreme Court Security Fund Account'.

CHAPTER 31

APPEALS AGAINST ASSESSMENTS

NO SPECIAL PROCEDURE

[31.1]

In the bad old days before the introduction of the Civil Procedure Rules, an appeal against a decision made on the taxation of costs, as detailed assessment was then called, was to the very person whose decision was being appealed against. The reasoning behind this apparently bizarre process was that, by the dissatisfied party taking in objections, as they were known, the original adjudicator was given a further opportunity to consider the decision away from the hurly-burly of the taxation. It was also an opportunity for him to give his considered reasons to be available if the matter proceeded to an appeal. The CPR removed this second bite of the cherry but CPR Rule 47.21 still required the dissatisfied party to obtain written reasons from the costs officer who had conducted the detailed assessment. Appeals from summary assessments were in accordance with the general rules relating to appeals. The remaining special provisions in respect of detailed assessments were removed by CPR Part 52 and now all costs appeals (except from authorised court officers, which are covered below from [31.9]) are dealt with in the same way as all other appeals.

REASONS

[31.2]

A difficulty now inherent in appeals against detailed assessments under Part 52 is that in order to succeed the appellant has to show that the costs judge was wrong either in law or in the exercise of his discretion, but the procedure for obtaining written reasons has gone and, often, the reasons uttered by the costs judge in the course of the assessment are incomplete.

In the rough and tumble of an assessment of costs, decisions are made on a number of disputed matters without the court delivering a reasoned judgment on each decision. It is now necessary for the court to enunciate its reasons and for the court and parties to keep a record of them for the purposes of any appeal. If the costs officer does not give adequate reasons and feels unable to provide them voluntarily, include lack of reasons in the application for permission to appeal. This should trigger the sequence of events as described in *English v Emery Reimbold & Strick Ltd* at para [16.13].

In *JemmaTrust Co Ltd v Liptrott & Forrester (No 2)* [20035] EWCA Civ 1476, [2004] 1 All ER 510 the first question was: 'Was the costs judge's judgment unsustainable for want of sufficient reasons?' The Court of Appeal held that it will often be impossible, and sometimes undesirable, for a costs judge to spell out the exact process of reasoning which led to the final figure. That will frequently be the result of triangulation, based very much on expert 'feel' between a variety of relatively unfixed possible positions. Despite the criticisms which could be made of the judgment for its lack of reasoning at the crucial point, the judge on appeal was not persuaded that it would be right to interfere with the judgment on those grounds.

GROUNDS

[31.3]

The only grounds of appeal are those prescribed in CPR 52.11(3): that the decision was (a) wrong, or (b) unjust because of a serious procedural irregularity.

'Wrong' may be an error of (i) law, (ii) fact or (iii) discretion. While the appellate court will readily entertain an appeal on a question of law it will need considerable persuasion to interfere with a finding of fact or the exercise of discretion.

The meaning of 'wrong' was considered in *Griffiths v Solutia UK Ltd* [2001] EWCA Civ 736, [2001] All ER (D) 196 (Apr), the relevant part of the judgment of the Court of Appeal being:

'[10]   The question before us is whether the deputy judge was entitled to conclude that the decision of the costs judge was wrong. The test which the deputy judge had to apply, in determining whether or not the costs judge's decision was wrong, was explained by this court in *Tanfern v Cameron-McDonald* [2000] 1 WLR 1311, para 32, where Brooke LJ says as follows:
"The first ground for interference speaks for itself. The epithet 'wrong' is to be applied to the substance of the decision made by the lower court. If the appeal is against the exercise of a discretion by the lower court, the decision of the House of Lords in *G v G (minors: custody appeal)* [1985] 1 WLR 647 warrants attention. In that case Lord Fraser of Tullybelton said, at page 652:

'Certainly it would not be useful to inquire whether different shades of meaning are intended to be conveyed by words such as "blatant error" used by the President in the present case, and words such as "clearly wrong", "plainly wrong" or "simply wrong" used by other judges in other cases. All these various expressions were used in order to emphasise the point that the appellate court should only interfere when they consider that the judge of first instance has not merely preferred an imperfect solution, which is different from an alternative imperfect solution which the Court of Appeal might or would have adopted, but has exceeded the generous ambit within which a reasonable disagreement is possible.'

[11]   The task that faces us is to apply that same test. Essentially the test requires the appellate court to consider whether or not, in a case involving the exercise of discretion, the judge has approached the matter applying the correct principles, has taken into account all relevant considerations and has not taken into account irrelevant considerations, and has reached a decision which is one which can properly be described as a decision which is within the ambit of reasonable decisions open to the judge on the facts of the case."'

In *Johnsey Estates (1990) Ltd v Secretary of State for the Environment, Transport and the Regions* [2001] EWCA Civ 535, [2001] 2 EGLR 128 the Court of Appeal held that an appellate court should not interfere with the judge's exercise of discretion merely because it takes the view that it would have exercised that discretion differently. This requires an appellate court to exercise a degree of self-restraint. It must recognise the advantage which the trial judge enjoys as a result of his 'feel' for the case which he has tried. Indeed, it is not for an appellate court even to consider whether it would have exercised the discretion differently unless it has first reached the conclusion that the judge's exercise of his discretion is flawed. That is to say, that he has erred in principle, taken into account matters which should have been left out of account, left out of account matters which should have been taken into account or reached a conclusion which is so plainly wrong that it can be described as perverse.

Sibley & Co v Reachbyte Ltd [2008] EWHC 2665 (Ch), [2008] All ER (D) 15 (Nov) was an appeal against the reduction of counsels' fees on a detailed assessment. It could not be said that the deputy master could not reasonably have come to the conclusion that he did based on the material before him. It is not the function of an appellate court to interfere with a decision without there being any valid criticism of the judge. To allow an appeal merely because a different view was entertained on the appeal on the same material that was before the judge would fail to give true effect to the primacy of the factual findings of the first instance tribunal.

ROUTE

[31.4]

Appeals from detailed or summary assessments of a district judge are to a circuit judge. Appeals from detailed and summary assessments of a costs judge and against summary assessments by a circuit judge are to a High Court judge. Appeals from summary assessments by a High Court judge are to the Court of Appeal. In an earlier edition, I said this would be an event for which they could sell tickets – but it has happened. See *1–800 Flowers Inc v Phonenames Ltd* at para [29.28], but they didn't charge for admission!

PERMISSION

[31.5]

Appeals against assessments are no longer as of right, but require permission either from the tribunal being appealed against or from the appellate court. An appeal does not act as a stay and it is likely that a court granting a stay will make it dependent upon at least the minimum amount conceded being paid forthwith.

The Court of Appeal has no jurisdiction to entertain an appeal against the refusal of a judge to grant permission to appeal against a decision of a costs judge. Nor has it any jurisdiction to review the judge's decision: *Riniker v University College London* [2001] 1 WLR 13, CA. Although permission to appeal is not normally required in insolvency proceedings, if the challenge is simply against a summary assessment of costs, then permission is required. (*Hosking v Michaelides* [2003] EWHC 3029 (Ch), (2003) Times, 17 December).

REVIEW, NOT RE-HEARING

[31.6]

Appeals against assessment decisions are no longer a full re-hearing (unless the appellate court so orders) but are limited to a review of the decision under appeal. Two cases in which there was a re-hearing were *U v Liverpool County Council* [2005] EWCA Civ 475, [2005] 1 WLR 2657 (whether to permit an appeal on an issue not raised on the detailed assessment) and *Rogers v Merthyr Tydfil County Borough Council* [2006] EWCA Civ 1134, [2007] 1 All ER 354 (the quantum of ATE insurance premiums affecting the insurance industry generally).

ASSESSORS

[31.7]

The costs rules used to provide for the appointment of assessors to sit with the judge on a review of taxation, usually a costs officer and a practising solicitor (or a barrister if counsel's fees were in dispute). Although there is now no such specific provision, judges hearing costs appeals may think it helpful to continue the practice by exercising their powers under the Supreme Court (now Senior Courts) Act 1981, s 70 or the County Courts Act 1984, s 63 as provided for in CPR 35.15. The costs of the assessors are not borne by the court, but by the parties. The traditional rate of pay is that of a deputy costs judge or district judge.

CPR Rule 35.15 introduced the new provision that an assessor's remuneration shall be determined by the court and shall form part of the costs of the proceedings. The court may order any party to deposit in the court office a specified sum in respect of assessor's fees and, where it does so, the assessor will not be appointed until the sum has been deposited; the SCCO has no knowledge of any such order having been made. CPR Practice Direction 35 provides that not less than 21 days before making any appointment, the court must notify each party of the names of the proposed assessors. Any objection must be filed with the court within seven days.

TIME FOR APPEALING

[31.8]

In *Kasir v Darlington & Simpson Rolling Mills Ltd* [2001] 2 Costs LR 228, QBD, at the end of a four-day detailed assessment in May 2000, it was left to the costs draftsmen to agree the calculations arising out of the costs judge's findings and submit to him the result. Unfortunately, they were unable to reach agreement which necessitated a further hearing in August which was followed by further correspondence lasting until a final figure was agreed in October. The claimant lodged an appellant's notice within 14 days from the date of the final agreement of the costs figure, which was some six months after the decisions on the items under appeal. The judge held that under CPR Rule 52.4, time runs from the decision of the lower court that the appellant wishes to appeal. The appeal was therefore out of time. It was pointed out to the judge that in long and detailed assessments spread over a period of time, a dissatisfied party might have to lodge several appellant's notices and further might not know until the end of the assessment whether the global result was such that he wanted to appeal. The judge suggested either the parties could agree, and the costs judge order, at the beginning of a long assessment that time for appeals should not start running until the last day or such an application could be made in the course of the assessment when a party received a decision that he was likely to want an appeal.

APPEALS FROM AUTHORISED COURT OFFICERS IN DETAILED ASSESSMENT PROCEEDINGS

[31.9]

CPR Rule 47.20: Right to appeal
(1)   Any party to detailed assessment proceedings may appeal against a decision of an authorised court officer in those proceedings.
(Part 52 sets out general rules about appeals)

[31.10]

CPD Section 47 Appeals from authorised court officers in detailed assessment proceedings — right to rule: Rule 47.20

47.1   *This Section and the next Section of this Practice Direction relate only to appeals from authorised court officers in detailed assessment proceedings. All other appeals arising out of detailed assessment proceedings (and arising out of summary assessments) are dealt with in accordance with Part 52 and the Practice Direction which supplements that Part. The destination of appeals is dealt with in accordance with the Access to Justice Act 1999 (Destination of Appeals) Order 2000.*
47.2   *In respect of appeals from authorised court officers, there is no requirement to obtain permission, or to seek written reasons.*

[31.11]

CPR Rule 47.21: Court to hear appeal
An appeal against a decision of an authorised court officer is to a costs judge or a district judge of the High Court.

[31.12]

CPR Rule 47.22: Appeal procedure

(1)   The appellant must file an appeal notice within 21 days after the date of the decision he wishes to appeal against.

(2)   On receipt of the appeal notice, the court will—

(a)   serve a copy of the notice on the parties to the detailed assessment proceedings; and

(b)   give notice of the appeal hearing to those parties.

[31.13]

CPD Section 48 Procedure on appeal from authorised court officers: Rule 47.22

48.1   *The appellant must file a notice which should be in Form N161 (an appellant's notice).*

48.2   *The appeal will be heard by a costs judge or a district judge of the High Court, and is a re-hearing.*

48.3   *The appellant's notice should, if possible, be accompanied by a suitable record of the judgment appealed against. Where reasons given for the decision have been officially recorded by the court an approved transcript of that record should accompany the notice. Photocopies will not be accepted for this purpose. Where there is no official record the following documents will be acceptable:*

(1)   *The officer's comments written on the bill.*

(2)   *Advocates' notes of the reasons agreed by the respondent if possible and approved by the authorised court officer.*

When the appellant was unrepresented before the authorised court officer, it is the duty of any advocate for the respondent to make his own note of the reasons promptly available, free of charge to the appellant where there is no official record or if the court so directs. Where the appellant was represented before the authorised court officer, it is the duty of his/her own former advocate to make his/her notes available. The appellant should submit the note of the reasons to the costs judge or district judge hearing the appeal.

48.4   *The appellant may not be able to obtain a suitable record of the authorised court officer's decision within the time in which the appellant's notice must be filed. In such cases, the appellant's notice must still be completed to the best of the appellant's ability. It may however be amended subsequently with the permission of the costs judge or district judge hearing the appeal*

[31.14]

CPR Rule 47.23: Powers of the court on appeal

On an appeal from an authorised court officer the court will—

(a)   rehear the proceedings which gave rise to the decision appealed against; and

(b)   make any order and give such directions as it considers appropriate.

SUMMARY ASSESSMENT

[31.15]

Appeals against summary assessment are in accordance with the general rules relating to appeals prescribed in CPR Part 52. Where an appeal is allowed and the appellate court makes an order for costs of the appeal and of the proceedings in the court below, the appellate court may, if it is appropriate, summarily assess the costs of the appeal but that court will probably not be in a position to deal with the costs in the court below, nor should the matter be remitted to the judge in the court below for summary assessment to be carried out. The whole purpose of summary assessment is that it should be carried out on the day of the hearing or very shortly after. The prospect of asking the judge at first instance to carry out an assessment months or perhaps years later is not sensible. In those circumstances the only option is to obtain an order for the detailed assessment of all the costs which the appellate court does not deal with.

Part IV

Sanctions and penalties

CHAPTER 32

WASTED COSTS

WASTED COSTS ORDERS

(a) The law

[32.1]

From 1 October 1991, s 4 of the Courts and Legal Service Act 1990 inserted a new s 51 in the Supreme Court (now Senior Courts) Act 1981 relating to both the High Court and the county courts introducing the concept of 'wasted costs', as follows:

> 6. In any proceedings mentioned in sub-section (1) [in the Court of Appeal, High Court and county court], the court may disallow or, (as the case may be) order the legal or other representative concerned to meet the whole of any wasted costs or such part of them as may be determined in accordance with Rules of Court.
>
> 7. In sub-section (6) 'wasted costs' means any costs incurred by a party: (a) as a result of any improper, unreasonable or negligent act or omission on the part of any legal or other representative or any employee of such a representative; or (b) which in the light of any such act or omission occurring after they were incurred, the costs considers it unreasonable to expect that party to pay.

[32.2]

CPR Rule 48.7: Personal liability of legal representative for costs—wasted costs orders

(1)   This rule applies where the court is considering whether to make an order under section 51 (6) of the Senior Courts Act 1981 (court's power to disallow or (as the case may be) order a legal representative to meet, 'wasted costs').

(2)   The court must give the legal representative a reasonable opportunity to attend a hearing to give reasons why it should not make such an order.

(4)   When the court makes a wasted costs order, it must—

    (a)   specify the amount to be disallowed or paid; or

    (b)   direct a costs judge or a district judge to decide the amount of costs to be disallowed or paid.

(5)   The court may direct that notice must be given to the legal representative's client, in such manner as the court may direct—

    (a)   of any proceedings under this rule; or

    (b)   of any order made under it against his legal representative.

(6)   Before making a wasted costs order, the court may direct a costs judge or a district judge to inquire into the matter and report to the court.

(7)   The court may refer the question of wasted costs to a costs judge or a district judge, instead of making a wasted costs order.

[32.3]

Although *Re Wiseman Lee (Solicitors) (wasted costs order) (No 5 of 2000)* [2001] EWCA Crim 707, (2001) 145 Sol Jo LB 119 was a criminal case the principle applies equally to civil matters. The court made a wasted costs order against the defendant solicitors in their absence with permission to make representations against the order by a given date. When no representations were received, the order was drawn up. The solicitors' appeal was allowed on the grounds that a legal representative must be allowed to make representations before a wasted costs order is made against him under CPR Rule 48.7(2).

Section 51(7) of the Supreme Court (now Senior Courts) Act 1981 defines wasted costs as 'any costs incurred by a party-(a) as a result of any improper, unreasonable or negligent act or omission on the part of any legal or other representative or any employee of such a representative . . . .'. In *R (on the application of Hide) v Staffordshire County Council* [2007] EWHC 241 (Admin), [2007] All ER (D) 402 (Oct) the claimant's solicitor advocate had engaged in behaviour which could properly be regarded as improper, unreasonable and/or negligent. The proceedings were completely unnecessary. They were doomed to failure and a reasonably competent solicitor should have known as much. Nevertheless, the judge reached the conclusion that he should not make an order against the solicitor. The reason for that conclusion related to the difficult financial circumstances in which the solicitor advocate found herself. The explanatory notes in the White Book under CPR 48.7 in relation to an application for wasted costs suggested that a three-stage test should be applied: (i) whether the legal representative had acted improperly, unreasonably or negligently; (ii) if so, whether such conduct had caused the applicant to incur unnecessary costs; and (iii) if so, whether it was in all the circumstances just to order the legal representative to compensate the applicant with the whole or part of the relevant cost. The third stage seemed to permit of a consideration of the effect of the order on the person against whom it was sought. In this case, the evidence was that an order for wasted costs would carry a significant risk of causing the solicitor to become bankrupt. That would be a disproportionate consequence of her unreasonable and negligent conduct in the litigation. On that discrete basis, a wasted costs order would not be made.

[32.4]

CPD Section 53 Personal liability of legal representatives for costs — wasted costs orders: Rule 48.7

53.1 Rule 48.7 deals with wasted costs orders against legal representatives. Such orders can be made at any stage in the proceedings up to and including the proceedings relating to the detailed assessment of costs. In general, applications for wasted costs are best left until after the end of the trial.
53.2 The court may make a wasted costs order against a legal representative on its own initiative.
53.3 A party may apply for a wasted costs order—
(1) by filing an application notice in accordance with Part 23; or
(2) by making an application orally in the course of any hearing.
53.4 It is appropriate for the court to make a wasted costs order against a legal representative, only if—

(1)   the legal representative has acted improperly, unreasonably or negligently;
(2)   his conduct has caused a party to incur unnecessary costs, and
(3)   it is just in all the circumstances to order him to compensate that party for the whole or part of those costs.

53.5   The court will give directions about the procedure that will be followed in each case in order to ensure that the issues are dealt with in a way which is fair and as simple a summary as the circumstances permit.

53.6   As a general rule the court will consider whether to make a wasted costs order in two stages—
(1)   in the first stage, the court must be satisfied—
    (a)   that it has before it evidence or other material which, if unanswered, would be likely to lead to a wasted costs order being made; and
    (b)   the wasted costs proceedings are justified notwithstanding the likely costs involved;
(2)   at the second stage (even if the court is satisfied under paragraph (1)) the court will consider, after giving the legal representative an opportunity to give reasons why the court should not make a wasted costs order, whether it is appropriate to make a wasted costs order in accordance with paragraph 53.4 above.

53.7   On an application for a wasted costs order under Part 23 the court may proceed to the second stage described in paragraph 53.6 without first adjourning the hearing if it is satisfied that the legal representative has already had a reasonable opportunity to give reasons why the court should not make a wasted costs order. In other cases the court will adjourn the hearing before proceeding to the second stage.

53.8   On an application for a wasted costs order under Part 23 the application notice and any evidence in support must identify—
(1)   what the legal representative is alleged to have done or failed to do; and
(2)   the costs that he may be ordered to pay or which are sought against him.

53.9   A wasted costs order is an order—
(1)   that the legal representative pay a specified sum in respect of costs to a party; or
(2)   for costs relating to a specified sum or items of work to be disallowed.

53.10   Attention is drawn to rule 44.3A(1) and (2) which respectively prevent the court from assessing any additional liability until the conclusion of the proceedings (or the part of the proceedings) to which the funding arrangement relates, and set out the orders the court may make at the conclusion of the proceedings.

(b) Client protection

[32.5]

Although neither s 51 nor Rule 48.7 specifically said so, the power of the court to disallow costs not only enables the court to order a legal representative to pay costs, it may also order him to indemnify his own client against a costs order against him, or to indemnify another party in respect of costs ordered against them, or order that the legal representative's costs against his own client be disallowed. If such a provision is not included in a wasted costs order against a legal representative, there would appear to be nothing to prevent him from charging his client for the work he had done in the proceedings giving rise to the wasted costs order.

(c) Privilege

[32.6]

In *Medcalf v Mardell* [2002] UKHL 27, [2003] 1 AC 120 the House of Lords rejected the argument that s 51 conferred no right on a party to seek a wasted costs order against any legal representative other than his own. It did, however, hold that in these circumstances if the party for whom the legal representative was acting refused to waive legal privilege thereby preventing the practitioner from telling the whole story the court should not make a wasted costs order unless it is (a) satisfied there is nothing the practitioner could say, if unconstrained, to resist the order and (b) it is in all the circumstances fair to make the order. However, it was held in *Brown v Bennett (wasted costs) (No 2)* [2002] Lloyd's Rep PN 242, ChD on a wasted costs application that it was permissible for the respondent barristers to be asked whether they saw or knew of non-privileged documents, provided that the purpose of the question was not to discover what was in the barristers' brief or instructions, even though answering the question might reveal the contents of the instructions or brief. That distinction might appear to be a very narrow and technical one. However, it was self-evident that it would be quite impermissible for the barristers to answer the question if the purpose of putting the question was to find out if a particular document was in his instructions, even if the document was open. But, it was by no means self-evident that if the purpose of asking the question was solely to discover whether the document was seen by or known to counsel that the question should not be answered. The question was permissible even if it happened to reveal that open documents, as opposed to privileged documents, were included in counsels' brief or instructions, provided that no prejudice was thereby caused to the client. In *Dempsey v Johnstone* [2003] EWCA Civ 1134, [2003] All ER (D) 515 (Jul), the claimant was a publicly funded bankrupt whose claim was dismissed at the trial on the grounds that he had no arguable prospect of success. The defendant sought and obtained a wasted costs order against the claimant's solicitors on the grounds that no reasonably competent legal representative would have continued with the action. The Court of Appeal held that the judge had applied the right test but had come to the wrong conclusion because he took the view that the facts pleaded could not support the claim made as a matter or law. The statement of claim settled by leading counsel was capable of supporting the claim, it was a matter for evidence. The question the judge should have asked was whether no reasonably competent legal adviser would have evaluated the chance of success as being such as to justify continuing with the proceedings. In determining that question, the judge could only come to a conclusion adverse to the solicitors if he had the opportunity of seeing counsel's advice which was privileged. In the absence of waiver of privilege, it could not be inferred that the evaluation of the claim was negligent in the relevant sense within s 51 of the Supreme Court (now Senior Courts) Act 1981.

(d) Satellite litigation

[32.7]

Applications under the wasted costs provisions started as a trickle which turned into a stream, consisting mainly of applications for orders against the legal representatives of unsuccessful state-funded claimants. It was becoming a new area of satellite litigation which the Court of Appeal was anxious to deter. Accordingly, they addressed all aspects of wasted costs applications in *Ridehalgh v Horsefield* [1994] Ch 205, CA, where, in appeals backed by the Bar Council, The Law Society and the Solicitors Indemnity Fund, the Court of

Appeal set aside wasted costs orders against two solicitors and a barrister and in the lead case declined to make an order in a case referred to them by a different division of the Court of Appeal. In delivering the judgment of the court, the Master of the Rolls said that while judges must not reject the weapon which Parliament intended to be used for the protection of those injured by the unjustifiable conduct of the other side's lawyers, they must be astute to control what threatened to become a new and costly form of satellite litigation.

Lord Bingham re-iterated this view in *Medcalf v Mardell*, approving the approach of the Privy Council in a New Zealand case that wasted costs orders should be confined to questions which are apt for summary disposal by the court, such as failures to appear; conduct which leads to an otherwise avoidable step in the proceedings; the prolongation of a hearing by gross repetition or extreme slowness in the presentation of evidence or argument. Such matters can be dealt with summarily on agreed facts or after a brief enquiry. Any hearing to investigate the conduct of a complex action is itself likely to be expensive and time-consuming. Compensating litigating parties who have been put to unnecessary expense is only one of the public interests to be considered.

In future, anyone considering applying for a wasted costs order should think twice.

The Practice Direction supplementing Rule 48.7 helpfully embodies the major findings of the Court of Appeal in *Ridehalgh*. Because wasted costs orders are made under the statute and Rule 48.7 and its supplementary Practice Direction govern merely the practice and procedure, not the principles, this is an area in which decisions made prior to 26 April 1999 are still of relevance and assistance.

(e) Three-stage test

[32.8]

In *Re Barrister (wasted costs order) (No 1 of 1991)* [1992] 3 All ER 429, CA, the Court of Appeal identified a three-stage test to be applied. It is incorporated in para 53.4 of the Practice Direction.

(f) Ridehalgh v Horsefield

(i) Improper, unreasonable or negligent conduct

[32.9]

The definitions of improper, unreasonable and negligent are as follows:
(1) 'Improper' covers, but is not confined to, conduct which would ordinarily be held to justify disbarment, striking off, suspension from practice or other serious professional penalty. It also covers conduct which according to the consensus of professional, including judicial, opinion could be fairly stigmatised as being improper whether it violated the letter of a professional code or not.
(2) 'Unreasonable' includes conduct which is vexatious, designed to harass the other side rather than advance the resolution of the case and it made no difference that the conduct was the product of excessive zeal and not

improper motive. Legal representatives cannot lend assistance to proceedings which are an abuse of process and they are not entitled to use litigious procedures for purposes for which they are not intended, as by issuing or pursuing proceedings for purposes unconnected with success in the litigation or pursuing a case known to be dishonest nor is he entitled to evade rules intended to safeguard the interests of justice as by knowingly failing to make full disclosure on an ex parte application or knowingly conniving at incomplete disclosure of documents. However, conduct is not unreasonable simply because it leads to an unsuccessful result or because other more cautious legal representatives would have acted differently. The acid test is whether the conduct permitted of a reasonable explanation. It is not unreasonable to be optimistic.

(3)   'Negligent' does not mean conduct which is actionable as a breach of the legal representative's duty to his own client. There is of course no duty of care to the other party. Negligence should be understood in an untechnical way to denote failure to act with the competence reasonably expected of ordinary members of the profession. However, the court firmly discountenanced any suggestion that an applicant for a wasted costs order needed to prove under the negligence head anything less than he would have had to prove in an action for negligence. It adopted the test in *Saif Ali v Sydney Mitchell & Co* [1980] AC 198, HL: 'advice, acts or omissions in the course of their professional work which no member of the profession who is reasonably well-informed and competent would have given or done or omitted to do'; an error 'such as no reasonably well-informed and competent member of that profession could have made'.

(ii)   Causation

[32.10]

The causal link must be established by the applicant and failure to do so will result in no award being made.

(iii)   Two-stage discretion

[32.11]

Jurisdiction to make the order depended upon the exercise of the court's discretion at two stages. First, on the initial application that the lawyer be given an opportunity to show cause. That was not something to be done automatically. The discretion was to be exercised judicially, but judges might not infrequently decide that further proceedings were not likely to be justified. Second, even if the court was satisfied that legal representatives had acted improperly, unreasonably or negligently so as to waste costs, the court was not bound to make an order, but would have to give sustainable reasons for the exercise of its discretion in that way. The Court of Appeal emphasised that judges should approach their task with caution and where possible consider the applicability of other sanctions of a disciplinary nature.

(iv) Threats

[32.12]

The threat of a wasted costs order should not be used as a means of intimidation. However, if one side considered that the conduct of the other was improper, unreasonable or negligent and likely to cause a waste of costs it was not objectionable to alert the other side to that view. There appears to be a fine line between 'threatening' and 'alerting'.

(v) Legal aid

[32.13]

It is incumbent on courts to bear prominently in mind the peculiar vulnerability of legal representatives acting for assisted persons. It would subvert the benevolent purposes of state funding legislation if such representatives were subject to any unusual personal risk and their advice and conduct was not to be tempered by the knowledge that their client was not their paymaster and so not, in all probability, liable for the costs of the other side. This was clearly a reference to what the Master of the Rolls called a new and costly form of satellite litigation arising out of attempts by successful litigants to obtain costs against counsel and solicitors for unsuccessful state-funded litigants on the grounds that the Legal Aid Board (now replaced by the Legal Services Commission) should have been advised either at the outset or after disclosure that the action had no realistic prospect of success.

(vi) Advocacy

[32.14]

Although the legislation intended to encroach upon the traditional immunity of the advocate by subjecting him to the wasted costs jurisdiction, full allowance must be made for the fact that an advocate in court often has to make decisions quickly and under pressure. Mistakes would inevitably be made, things done which the outcome showed to have been unwise. Advocacy is more an art than a science, it could not be conducted according to formulae. It was only when, with all allowances made, an advocate's conduct of court proceedings was quite plainly unjustifiable that it could be appropriate to make a wasted costs order against him. One of the appeals was *Antonelli v Wade Gery Farr (a firm)* [1994] Ch 205, CA in which the Court of Appeal had set aside an order that counsel should pay the costs of one day of a trial on the grounds that her acceptance of an unseen brief at very short notice was unreasonable and amounted to improper conduct as it was improbable that she had time to grasp properly the issues involved in the matter. She had been unclear about the issues involved, her submissions had been rambling, had contained many embarrassing pauses and she had failed to prepare written submissions when requested by the judge. The judge had failed to take into account para 209 of the Bar Code, known as the 'cab-rank' rule, which in the opinion of the Court of Appeal precluded the barrister from refusing the brief.

She did not then know how inadequate her instructions would be, but even if she had known, she would not have been entitled to refuse. Even when the inadequacy of her instructions became only too plain, para 506 of the Bar Code precluded her from returning the brief or withdrawing from the case in such a way or in such circumstances that the client may be unable to find other legal assistance in time to prevent prejudice being suffered by the client. There is no reason to think anyone else would have been better placed to conduct the case than she.

The question of an advocate's immunity from suit was re-visited by the House of Lords in *Arthur JS Hall & Co (a firm) v Simons* [2002] 1AC 615, HL when it was decided that advocates no longer enjoy immunity from suit in respect of their conduct of civil and criminal proceedings.

(vii)   Reliance on counsel

[32.15]

A solicitor did not abdicate his professional responsibility when he sought the advice of counsel. He had to apply his mind to the advice received. But the more specialist the nature of the advice the more reasonable it was likely to be for him to accept it.

(viii)   The application

[32.16]

The court agreed with the decision in *Filmlab Systems International Ltd v Pennington* [1994] 4 All ER 673, ChD that save in exceptional circumstances an application for a wasted costs order should only be made after the trial of the action. In the ordinary way applications were best left until after the end of the trial but it was impossible to lay down rules of universal application. In *Melchior v Vettivel* [2001] All ER (D) 351 (May) the court made a wasted costs order after the conclusion of the trial and the sealing of the costs order.

(ix)   Initiation

[32.17]

The court should be slow to initiate an enquiry itself because the court will be both the prosecutor and the adjudicator and difficult and embarrassing issues on costs could arise if an order were not made. The costs of the enquiry would have to be borne by someone and it would not be the court.

Judges should not make lawyers 'show cause' where the issue goes to the merits. That should be left to the parties. An example of a case where the court did intervene was *Abbassi v Secretary of State for the Home Department* [1992] Imm AR 349, CA where counsel and solicitors applied for judicial review of the decision of an immigration officer to refuse leave to their client, MrAbbassi, to enter the United Kingdom. Ordinarily, the correct course open to a person who disputed facts relied upon by the Home Office for refusing leave to enter was to appeal to a tribunal and not to apply for leave for judicial review. Although counsel and solicitors owed a duty to their clients, they also owed a duty to the courts. Not only had there been no possible prospect of the appeal succeeding, but it had been irresponsible to seek to advance arguments once it was clear that the court was not prepared to accept the evidence upon which the arguments were based.

The court adjourned to give counsel and the solicitors an opportunity to be heard and on hearing that the solicitors did not wish to take advantage of that opportunity the court ordered the costs thrown away by the appeal, of £500, should be borne equally by the counsel and solicitors, as agreed between them.

(x) Procedure

[32.18]

The application should be heard by the trial judge except where it is impracticable for the original judge to deal with the matter or where the parties agreed to another judge dealing with it. Any application for a wasted costs order in respect of proceedings at trial should be made to the judge at the conclusion of the trial. Although a wasted costs order could be made after the proceedings had been concluded, in practice a party would frequently ask for time and the court would make directions, those factors did not alter the fact that it was for the court that determined a case to make the order, and that court alone had jurisdiction (*Gray v Going Places Leisure Travel Ltd* [2005] EWCA Civ 189, [2005] All ER (D) 48 (Feb)).

The court should determine the procedure to be followed to meet the requirements of the individual case. The overriding requirements were that any procedure had to be fair and as simple and summary as fairness permitted. Elaborate pleadings should in general be avoided. No formal process of disclosure would be appropriate. The court could not imagine any circumstances in which the applicant should be permitted to interrogate the respondent lawyer. On the other hand, the respondent must be entitled to present a full defence and must be informed of the conduct complained of, the amount claimed and the alleged causal link between the two. Hearings should be measured in hours, not days or weeks (*Re P (Barrister) (wasted costs order)* [2001] EWCA Crim 1728, [2001] Crim LR 920).

(xi) Burden of proof

[32.19]

Although CPR Rule 48.7(2) provides that no order shall be made without giving the legal representative opportunity to give reasons why an order should not be made, that should not be understood to mean the burden is on the legal representative to exculpate himself. The burden of proving a wasted costs order should be made remains throughout on the applicant.

(g) Sheltering behind counsel

[32.20]

To what extent can a solicitor avoid personal liability by reliance on counsel? In addition to *Ridehalgh v Horsefield* (see above) a number of answers have been given, some more encouraging to solicitors than others. The low watermark was *Davy-Chiesman v Davy-Chiesman* [1984] Fam 48, CA, where counsel had advised in writing that the husband should not seek a lump sum payment from his wife payable directly to him as otherwise it would be taken immediately by his trustee in bankruptcy. At a subsequent conference, counsel advised that the husband should seek a lump sum payable to him direct and abandon all his other claims. It must have been glaringly apparent to any reasonable solicitor that the form of relief for which alone counsel was going to ask fell foul of the fundamental requirement that because of the bankruptcy any capital sum should not go direct to the husband. The duty the solicitor owed to inform the legal aid fund of any change of circumstances was not just to pass on any views expressed by counsel but to consider for himself the effect of any change of circumstances. The solicitor was at that stage guilty of 'a serious dereliction of duty' or 'serious misconduct' and it was not sufficient to absolve the solicitor that he acted in accordance with the advice of counsel. The solicitor was in many circumstances protected from personal liability if he had acted on the advice of experienced counsel properly instructed. The protection to the solicitor was not automatically total. The solicitor was highly-trained and expected to be experienced in his particular fields of law and he did not abdicate all responsibility whatever by instructing counsel. In this particular case, the solicitor had allowed his own skill and ability to be entirely subordinated to the dominant and forceful personality of counsel. Obviously, the Legal Aid Committee was not to be bombarded with notifications of every minute fluctuation in the estimate of the percentage prospects of success but only when it appeared, or should appear to a reasonable solicitor, that the assisted person no longer had any reasonable chance of success. The Law Society's application that the solicitor should pay both the husband's and wife's costs personally was allowed.

The culprit was counsel and yet it was the solicitors who were ordered to pay the costs of both parties. Counsel was not even named in the law report!

In *R v Oxfordshire County Council, ex p Wallace* [1987] NLJ Rep 542, QBD, the applicant commenced judicial review proceedings against the local education authority and the local health authority. On the first day of the hearing he was given leave to discontinue the proceedings against the health authority who at the end of the hearing applied for an order for their costs to be paid personally by the applicant's solicitors.

Counsel for the health authority argued that counsel's advice that the health authority should be joined as a party was based quite clearly on his stating the statutory position inaccurately and his advice that the decision of the health authority had been perverse was, or ought to have been, realised to be patently wrong by anyone with experience in this field, as had the applicant's solicitors. He relied on the decision in *Davy-Chiesman v Davy-Chiesman* that because the solicitors should have realised that there was not an arguable case for judicial review against the health authority they should be personally liable for costs in spite of the advice of counsel.

For the solicitors it was argued that they had obtained counsel's specific advice on the point as follows:

'I take the view that no reasonable health authority properly directing itself as to the law could possibly reach this decision (to provide no more speech therapy for the infant applicant than it was then providing) and that therefore there are good grounds for joining the health authority on an application for judicial review. This is the same sort of case as where a plaintiff is faced with two defendants, one blaming the other, and it is quite proper to join both defendants and let the unsuccessful defendant pay the costs.'

In addition it was contended for the solicitors that the single judge had granted leave to move against both authorities after hearing argument.

It was held that the case could be distinguished on its facts on *Davy-Chiesman*. In that case, counsel propounded a claim which he had earlier advised was bound to fail, as the solicitors in the case knew, and it was not the one for which, on his advice, the client had been granted legal aid. In *R v Oxfordshire County Council*, counsel had been specifically asked to advise against whom the proceedings should begin and the form they should take. A mere mistake or error of judgment is insufficient to attract liability of a solicitor for the costs of the other parties, for which purpose it was necessary to establish gross or serious negligence.

The case against the applicant's solicitors was not as strong as the authorities required it to be before any order for costs could be made against them. Accordingly an order for costs on behalf of the health authority against the solicitors was refused.

In striking out a copyright action in *Swedac Ltd v Magnet and Southerns plc* [1989] FSR 243, QBD, the trial judge criticised counsel and his solicitors. He refused to order the plaintiff's solicitors to pay the costs personally. It was held on appeal ([1990] FSR 89, CA) that although the solicitors could not automatically shelter behind counsel, in this particular case they had been justified in relying upon his advice.

However, in *Locke v Camberwell Health Authority* [1991] 2 Med LR 249, CA, it was held at first instance that the failure of a solicitor to ensure that pertinent information was before counsel advising on the merits in a negligence action constituted a gross dereliction of the solicitor's duty as an officer of the court and made him liable for the defendant's costs, thereafter thrown away. In advising on the merits, counsel did not have photocopies of the hospital notes, which it was his duty to request and the solicitor's duty to supply, as a result his advice was short and inadequate. However when it was established on appeal that the defendants had not in fact disclosed the relevant hospital notes, counsel and the solicitors were exonerated and the order set aside. As a general rule, a solicitor is entitled to rely upon the advice of counsel properly instructed but they must not do so blindly and must exercise their own independent judgment.

The pendulum swung back again in *Count Tolstoy-Miloslavsky v Lord Aldington* [1996] 2 All ER 556, CA) (after the decision in *Ridehalgh*), where the Court of Appeal in upholding an order that Count Tolstoy should pay 60% of Lord Aldington's costs of an action brought by Count Tolstoy to set aside on the grounds of fraud the monumental libel damages awarded against him, said that 'although the solicitors relied on fully instructed and very experienced, respected leading counsel who put his name to a statement of claim . . . counsel having extensive knowledge of the background of the case . . . this does not absolve the solicitors exercising their independent judgment nor allow them to close their eyes to the blindingly obvious . . . '. The document the solicitors were expected to overrule had been signed by both leading and junior counsel. Ouch!

(h) Against barrister for advice

[32.21]

In *Brown v Bennett* [2002] 2 All ER 273, ChD and *Medcalf v Mardell* [2002] UKHL 27, [2002] 3 All ER 721, it was submitted that a wasted costs order could only be made against a barrister by virtue of his conduct when actually exercising a right of audience, in other words, when actually conducting a case in court. The basis for this argument was that a wasted costs order could only be made as a result of inappropriate conduct on the part of any 'legal or other representative' which s 51(13) limited to 'any person exercising a right of audience or right to conduct litigation'. As a barrister, unlike a solicitor, did not 'conduct litigation' he could only be liable when he was exercising a right of audience. Rejecting this argument the court held that although it was true that the concept of conducting litigation would in many circumstances be understood to involve the traditional litigation activities of a solicitor, 'a right to conduct litigation' was not defined in the Act and it was quite permissible to give that expression a meaning which was less technical and more vernacular. There was no reason why it should not extend to such activities such as drafting or settling of documents and advising on prospects or procedure.

(i) Causation

[32.22]

The alleged conduct must in fact have led to identifiable wasted costs. Negligence alone does not suffice. However, in *Brown v Bennett* (above) the defendants contended that the court must be satisfied that there was a real prospect that the applicants would not have incurred all the costs that they did incur if the lawyers had not acted and advised as they did, and if the court were not so satisfied any uncertainty would have to be taken into account when assessing the level of costs or order against the lawyers. The court held that although there was a powerful argument in logic for awarding only a proportion of the total costs on the 'loss of chance' basis, that was not the appropriate approach to take. The court should ask itself whether, on the balance of probabilities, the applicant would have incurred the costs that he claimed from the lawyers if they had not acted or advised as they did.

(j) Orders made

[32.23]

Examples we have considered were the decisions in *Davy-Chiesman* (para [32.20]), *Tolstoy-Miloslavsky v Aldington* (para [32.20]) and *Abbassi v Secretary of State for the Home Department* (para [32.17]).

Re a Company (006798 of 1995) [1996] 2 All ER 417, ChD

A solicitor swore an affidavit in support of a winding-up petition, asserting on oath a belief that a company was insolvent on the ground that a debt was owing and that the company was unable to pay its debts as they fell due. There were in fact no grounds upon which a competent solicitor could have reached that view on the material available to him and he was ordered to pay the costs of the company personally.

General Mediterranean Holdings SA v Patel [1999] 3 All ER 673, QBD (Comm Ct)

The defendants denied an allegation of fraud until shortly before the trial when they admitted it. The action was compromised on terms that there be no order for costs, but the claimants obtained a wasted costs order against the defendants' solicitor on the grounds that the solicitor knew the defendants had admitted the existence of the fraud in other proceedings.

(k) Orders refused

[32.24]

Trill v Sacher (No 2) [1992] 40 LS Gaz R 32, CA

Where a statement of claim was struck out for want of prosecution the defendants sought wasted costs orders against the solicitors for the legally-aided claimant. The solicitors' explanation for the delay related to the difficulties experienced in complicated cases such as the present, where the plaintiffs had only a limited legal aid certificate. The solicitors' hands were tied in dealing with the Legal Aid authorities. The slow action by the authorities and by counsel in preparing written opinions had contributed to the delay. An order that they be personally liable for wasted costs was set aside.

[32.25]

Re a Solicitor (wasted costs order) [1993] 2 FLR 959, CA

In this case a solicitor who was having difficulty resolving the position regarding his client's Legal Aid certificate had not sought an adjournment until the day before the fixed hearing date, causing expense to the other side and to their witnesses. His failure to warn the court or his opponents in sufficient time was an error of judgment. However, the material now available showed that the Law Society accepted that the solicitor had found himself in an extremely difficult position. It would not be right to go further than to say the solicitor had been guilty of an error of judgment: he had not acted in dereliction of his duty. A wasted costs order against him personally was not warranted.

[32.26]

Wall v Lefever [1998] 1 FCR 605, CA

The wasted costs provisions of s 51 involve the tension between two important public interests. First, that lawyers should not be deterred from pursuing their client's interests by fear of incurring a personal liability to their clients' opponents, and second, that litigants should not be financially prejudiced by the unjustifiable conduct of litigation by their or their opponents' lawyers. Care should be exercised before launching an appeal against the refusal of a wasted costs order by a judge at first instance who had heard the evidence. If the judge concluded that the conduct complained of had not fallen within that proscribed by s 51 an appeal was only justified if some point of principle indicated that the judges approach had been wholly wrong. That was not the present case.

[32.27]

Re a Barrister (wasted costs order No 4 of 1993) (1995) Times, 21 April, CA

It is important for a judge considering making a wasted costs order, which is a draconian order, to remember that he is removed from the daily demands of practice and to make allowance for difficulties with time estimates. The appellant had accepted a brief for a two-day trial listed at Derby Crown Court immediately prior to another trial in which he was to appear at Nottingham Crown Court. The first trial was late starting and progressed more slowly than anticipated. In granting an adjournment of the second trial the judge ordered the barrister to pay the consequential wasted costs. In quashing the order, the court said that although the barrister had been over-optimistic in failing to anticipate delays in the first trial, his conduct could not be described as unreasonable.

[32.28]

Turner Page Music v Torres Design Associates Ltd (1998) Times, 3 August, CA

The ability of the court to make a wasted costs order can have advantages, but it will be of no advantage if it is going to result in complex proceedings which involve detailed investigation of fact. If the situation involves detailed investigation of facts and indeed allegations of dishonesty then it may well be that the wasted costs procedure is largely inappropriate to cover the situation, except in what would be an exceptional case. If the situation involved breach of a solicitor's professional duty to a client that too might make it unsuited to a summary procedure. The claimant's application for a wasted costs order against the defendant's solicitors was dismissed.

[32.29]

Regent Leisuretime Ltd v Skerrett [2006] EWCA Civ 1032, [2006] All ER (D) 34 (Jul), 4 July

Although an oral application in the course of a hearing is possible pursuant to paragraph 53, that is only likely to be sensible if the scope of the application to the costs said to have been wasted is narrow and clear; for example, if an adjournment is necessary because of a solicitor's or counsel's conduct, as regards the costs thrown away by the adjournment. In the present case, given that the scope and nature of the costs claimed was wholly unclear at the time of the hearing before the judge he should not have allowed the application to be made orally or to have considered it even at the first stage. He should have told the defendant litigants in person that if they wanted to apply for costs they should issue a Part 23 application notice supported by evidence as required by Paragraph 53.8. There could have then have been either a first stage hearing or, perhaps if paragraph 53.7 was satisfied, a hearing at which the first stage and if relevant the second stage were both considered.

The judge's approach was wrong and was outside the scope of the admittedly flexible discretion given to him as to how to proceed. He did not have enough material before him to form even a prima facie view, and had not formed such a view, that the solicitor had acted improperly, unnecessarily or negligently, and he had no material on which he could form a view as to whether any significant unnecessary costs had been caused to be incurred by reason of the solicitors' conduct. Nor could he save any time or money by proceeding to a first-stage assessment on that day even if he had had before him the necessary material. The judge was plainly wrong to order the defendants' claim for wasted be investigated because he was unable to be satisfied of either 53.4(i) or (ii) and on the further information that is available before the Court of Appeal it was clear that any costs lost by the defendants as litigants in person did not justify the time and expense of an investigation.

[32.30]

Byrne v South Sefton (Merseyside) Health Authority [2001] EWCA Civ 1904, [2002] 1 WLR 775

The solicitors had acted for the claimant in connection with his allegations of clinical negligence by the defendant, but ceased to act for the claimant before he instructed other solicitors, who commenced proceedings. When the action was dismissed as out-of-time the defendant applied for a wasted costs order against the solicitors on the grounds that its costs had been incurred as a result of the solicitors' failure to bring proceedings within the limitation period. Section 51(6) of the Supreme Court (now Senior Courts) Act 1981 empowers costs to be awarded against 'a legal or other representative', while s 51(13) defines a legal or other representative as a person who has issued proceedings, exercised rights of audience or performed ancillary functions in relation to the conduct of litigation. The defendant's case against the solicitors rested on the very fact that they had failed to do any of these things. Furthermore there was no causative link between the solicitors' conduct and the costs incurred by the defendant. The defendant's costs had not been incurred by the defendant's failure to act, but by the claimant's current solicitors' decision to bring an action outside the limitation period.

[32.31]

B v Pendlebury [2002] EWHC 1797, [2002] NLJR 1072

On an application for wasted costs in a case in which there has been no adjudication of the primary facts, the court should be reluctant to enquire into a state of affairs in which it has no solid foundation from which the process of analysis essential to the wasted costs procedure can proceed. The process and procedure envisaged in the Practice Direction is not readily to be equated with what was involved on a trial of issues. The phrases 'simple and summary as the circumstances will permit' and 'after giving the legal representative an opportunity to give reasons' did not lend themselves as appropriate to a disputed trial involving consideration and resolution *of complex* and disputed evidence. It is axiomatic that a solicitor is bound by the instructions of his client. He is not obliged to act as a filter between the instructions provided by the client and the opposing party. Quite simply, a solicitor owes no duty to the opposing party although he does, of course, owe such a duty to the court: *Orchard v South Eastern Electricity Board* [1987] QB 565, CA.

[32.32]

Persaud v Persaud [2003] EWCA Civ 394, [2003] All ER (D) 80 (Mar)

The court's jurisdiction to make a wasted costs order against a solicitor is founded on breach of the duty owed by the solicitor to the court to perform his duty as an officer of the court in promoting within his own sphere the cause of justice. There is no doubt that the jurisdiction under s 51 of the Supreme Court (now Senior Courts) Act 1981 to make a wasted costs order has now been extended to barristers, but before a wasted costs order can be made against a member of the Bar there must have been a breach of duty to the court by the barrister. It is not enough that the court considers the advocate has being arguing a hopeless case. The litigant is entitled to be heard; to penalise the advocate for presenting his client's case to the court would be contrary to constitutional principles. The position is different if the court concludes that there has been improper time-wasting by the advocate or the advocate has knowingly lent himself to an abuse of process. However it is relevant to bear in mind that, if a party is raising issues or is taking steps which have no reasonable prospects of success or are scandalous or an abuse of process, both the aggrieved party and the court have powers to remedy the situation by invoking summary remedies – striking out – summary judgment – peremptory orders etc. The making of a wasted costs order should not be a primary remedy; by definition it only arises once the damage has been done. It is a last resort. There must be something more than negligence for the wasted costs jurisdiction to arise; there must be something akin to an abuse of process if the conduct of the legal representative is to make him liable to a wasted costs order. In the present case the conduct of counsel did not involve any breach of duty to the court, nor was there an abuse of process.

[32.33]

Dempsey v Johnstone [2003] EWCA Civ 1134, [2003] All ER (D) 515 (Jul)

After reviewing the authorities relied on in *Persaud* (above) the court did not accept that the meaning of 'negligence' had been modified by those authorities as suggested in *Persaud*. Where it was alleged that the legal representative had pursued a hopeless case, the question was whether no reasonably competent legal representative would have continued with the action. It was difficult to see how that question could be answered affirmatively unless it could also be said that the legal representative acted unreasonably, which was akin to establishing an abuse of process. Negligence could be the appropriate word to describe the situation in which it was abundantly plain that the legal representative had failed to appreciate that there was a binding authority fatal to the client's case, but in practice it was difficult to envisage a case in which that situation would have persisted to trial without the other party having drawn it to the attention of his opponent. The statement of claim settled by leading counsel was capable of supporting the assertion on which the claimant's case was based that there was a joint venture agreement. Its existence was a matter for evidence. The question was whether no reasonably competent legal advisor would have evaluated the chance of success as being such as to justify continuing with the proceedings. In the absence of seeing counsel's advice, which was privileged, it could not be inferred that the evaluation of the claim was negligent in the relevant sense within s 51 of the Supreme Court (now Senior Courts) Act 1981.

I am grateful to Tony Girling for this analysis of the decisions in Persaud and Dempsey.

[32.34]

Koo Golden East Mongolia (A Body Corporate) v (1) Bank Of Nova Scotia (2) Scotia Capital (Europe) Ltd (3) Central Bank Of Mongolia (T/A Mongolbank) [2008] EWHC 1120 (Admin), QBD, 20 May

The defendant bank claimed a wasted costs order against the solicitors who had acted for the unsuccessful claimant in a claim to trace and recover missing gold. It contended that it was entitled to a wasted costs order because the solicitors' conduct was persistently negligent and unreasonable in making and continuing to have the Central Bank of Mongolia as a party to the action because the solicitors should have appreciated that the bank was immune from suit because of the provisions of the State Immunity Act 1978. In dismissing the claim the court gave the following reasons:

- a bill of costs should have been served before making the application;
- the claimant should have been given a proper opportunity to pay the costs;
- the absence of an application to strike out the claim was hardly consistent with the submission that it was misconceived;
- the suggestion that 'no reasonable solicitor could have been optimistic' was well below the threshold for sufficient negligence or unreasonableness to justify a wasted costs order;
- even a binding authority fatal, or almost fatal, to the client's case might not justify a wasted costs order.

[32.35]

Hallam-Peel & Co v Southwark London Borough Council [2008] EWCA Civ 1120, [2008] All ER (D) 200 (Oct)

A firm of solicitors had not acted unreasonably in raising a new point in possession proceedings, which led to further adjournments and its conduct did not involve a breach of duty to the court. Accordingly, a wasted cost order should not have been made against them and their appeal was allowed.

(l) Appeals

[32.36]

There have been numerous cautionary statements warning against appeals from judges who have refused to make a wasted costs order. It will only be in a very rare case that the Court of Appeal will interfere with the decision by the judge as to whether or not to make a wasted costs order. The judge who has conducted the trial will be fully aware of the conduct of legal representatives in the case before him. It was striking in the present case that the judge, despite the very severe criticisms made by him of the claims, nevertheless refused to make a wasted costs order (*Persaud v Persaud* (above)).

An appeal against a wasted costs order does not relate only, or indeed primarily, to costs: it relates to the conduct of the solicitor, and accordingly does not fall within the ambit of s 18(1)(*f*) of the Supreme Court (now Senior Courts) Act 1981 which prohibits appeals against orders for costs only, unless the judge has mis-exercised his discretion (*Wilkinson v Kenny* [1993] 3 All ER 9, CA).

(m) Non-parties

[32.37]

There is jurisdiction to make an order for wasted costs even though the applicant was not a party to the proceedings within s 51(6) and (7) of the Act (*Lubrizol v Tyndallwoods Solicitors* (8 April, 1998, unreported), where the applicants were directly interested in the subject matter of an application for judicial review). However, there is no power in the court to make a wasted costs order in favour of, or (by parity of reasoning) against, a person who elected to oppose an ex parte application for leave to apply for judicial review. Such a person is not a party for present purposes. The modern practice of the court in regularly hearing and sometimes inviting the participation of such persons could not make it otherwise; only legislation or a rule change could make it so (*R v Camden London Borough Council, ex p Martin* [1997] 1 All ER 307, QBD). The test for determining whether the court should exercise its power under the Supreme Court (now Senior Courts) Act 1981, s 51(1) and (3) to order a non-party firm of solicitors to pay the costs of an action is whether it would be just to do so. While ordering a non-party to pay the costs would not normally be merited in the ordinary case where a party was prosecuting or defending a claim for its own advantage through the medium of solicitors acting as such, in cases where one or both of those characteristics was missing, the issue would be one for the judge's discretion (*Globe Equities Ltd v Globe Legal Services Ltd* [1999] BLR 232).

(n) After judgment or stay

[32.38]

There is nothing to prevent an application for a wasted costs order being made and entertained after judgment for or against the claimant. Where the proceedings have been settled and stayed under a Tomlin order, there is no need to apply to lift the stay. This serves to emphasise the free-standing nature of an application for wasted costs (*Wagstaff v Colls* [2003] EWCA Civ 469, (2003) 147 Sol Jo LB 419).

WRONG COURT

(a) Reduction of costs

[32.39]

The second penalty introduced by the new s 51 of the Supreme Court (now Senior Courts) Act 1981 may be imposed by 'the person responsible for determining the amount which is to be awarded' and arises where, in the opinion of the court, a case brought in the High Court should have been brought in the county court. The costs officer may reduce the costs by an amount not exceeding 25%, this being a figure which may be varied by order of the Lord Chancellor.

(b) Striking out

[32.40]

Section 40 of the County Courts Act 1984 as amended by s 2(1) of the Courts and Legal Services Act 1990 provides:

> '(1)   where the High Court is satisfied that any proceedings before it are required by any provision of the kind mentioned at sub-section (8) . . . to be in a county court it shall – (a) order the transfer of the proceedings to a county court; or (b) if the court is satisfied that the person bringing the proceedings knew, or ought to have known, of that requirement, order that they be struck out.'

In *Restick v Crickmore* [1994] 2 All ER 112, CA the judge had followed a decision of Turner J in *Groom v Norman Motors (Wallisdown) Ltd* [1993] PIQR P215, Crown Ct in holding there was no discretion and they had no alternative but to strike out. This was because the word 'shall' in s 40(1) had been treated as being mandatory and governing paragraph (*b*) giving the court no option but to strike out when the relevant conditions were satisfied. That construction ignored the word 'or'. The use of the word 'shall', positioned where it was, did not require the court to adopt one course rather than the other, simply because the necessary precondition for exercising choice (*b*) was satisfied. The court was required to make a choice between two alternatives, but it could only strike out if the additional condition was satisfied, namely that the person bringing the proceedings knew or ought to have known, of the requirement to bring the case in the county court. Otherwise the choice or discretion was unfettered. That construction accorded with the policy of the courts that provided proceedings were started within the time permitted by the statute of limitations, were not frivolous, vexatious, or an abuse of the court and disclosed a cause of action, they would not as a rule be struck out because of a mistake in procedure on the part of the plaintiff or his advisers. The discretion to strike out might, for example, be exercised where there was a deliberate attempt to harass a defendant by running up unnecessary costs or in defiance of a warning of the defendants as to the proper venue or where a party persistently started actions in the wrong court.

Writing in the *Law Society Gazette* of 13 April 1994, Diana Bretherick identified some of the circumstances in which the court would exercise its discretion to strike out as being the persistent commencement of actions wrongly in the High Court, attempts to harass a defendant or where the claim is obviously below the threshold value. She observed that one of the temptations to commence in the High Court is that a generally endorsed writ may be issued and served without the need for a detailed statement of claim in cases where prognosis, and hence quantum, is uncertain. It is a temptation to be avoided unless the solicitor is prepared to swear an affidavit with calculations showing the claim appeared to be worth £50,000 or more in a personal injury claim and £25,000 or more in other claims.

TRIBUNALS

[32.41]

From 3 November 2008 the Tribunal Procedure (Upper Tribunal) Rules 2008 and the Tribunal Procedure (First-Tier Tribunal) (Health, Education and Social Care Chamber) Rules 2008 provide that a tribunal shall not make an order in respect of costs other than for wasted costs or if the tribunal considers that a party or its representative has acted unreasonably in bringing, defending or conducting the proceedings. The Upper Tribunal may also make an order in respect of cost in proceedings on appeal from another tribunal, to the extent and in the circumstances that the other tribunal had the power to make an order in respect of costs. Either tribunal may make an order for costs on an application or on its own initiative. The amount of cost to be paid may be ascertained by:

(a)   summary assessment;
(b)   agreement of a specified sum by the paying person and the person entitled to receive the cost;
(c)   assessment as the whole or a specified part of the costs incurred by the receiving person, if not agreed.

Following an order for assessment, the paying person or the receiving person may apply to the High Court in the Upper Tribunal and to the county court in the First-Tier Tribunal for a detailed assessment of costs in accordance with the Civil Procedure Rules 1998 on the standard basis or, if specified in the order, on the indemnity basis.

CHAPTER 33

MISCONDUCT

[33.1]

CPR Rule 44.14: Court's powers in relation to misconduct

(1) The court may make an order under this rule where—

    (a) a party or his legal representative, in connection with a summary or detailed assessment, fails to comply with a rule, practice direction or court order; or

    (b) it appears to the court that the conduct of a party or his legal representative, before or during the proceedings which gave rise to the assessment proceedings, was unreasonable or improper.

(2) Where paragraph (1) applies, the court may—

    (a) disallow all or part of the costs which are being assessed; or

    (b) order the party at fault or his legal representative to pay costs which he has caused any other party to incur.

(3) Where—

    (a) the court makes an order under paragraph (2) against a legally represented party; and

    (b) the party is not present when the order is made,

the party's solicitor must notify his client in writing of the order no later than 7 days after the solicitor receives notice of the order.

[33.2]

CPD Section 18 Court's powers in relation to misconduct: Rule 44.14

18.1 *Before making an order under rule 44.14 the court must give the party or legal representative in question a reasonable opportunity to attend a hearing to give reasons why it should not make such an order.*

18.2 *Conduct before or during the proceedings which gave rise to the assessment which is unreasonable or improper includes steps which are calculated to prevent or inhibit the court from furthering the overriding objective.*

18.3 *Although rule 44.14(3) does not specify any sanction for breach of the obligation imposed by the rule the court may, either in the order under paragraph (2) or in a subsequent order, require the solicitor to produce to the court evidence that he took reasonable steps to comply with the obligation.*

(a)   DURING ASSESSMENT

[33.3]

There has been a misunderstanding about the purpose of this rule. The misunderstanding is that the rule had been envisaged as providing a simple summary procedure to deal with misconduct without involving the sledgehammer procedure of a wasted costs inquiry under the Supreme Court (now Senior Courts) Act 1981, s 51. It was even proposed originally that an order could be made in the absence of the defaulting party, but it was appreciated that natural justice required the absent party to be heard on such an application and this was remedied in the Practice Direction. However, the misunderstanding has been to think that this provision applies to the court's powers generally in relation to misconduct, while in fact it relates solely to either during the course of a detailed assessment or in respect of misconduct before or during the main proceedings which only comes to light during the assessment. The heading should therefore be 'Court's Powers on Assessment in Relation to Misconduct'. Its primary object is to invest costs officers with disciplinary powers.

The misconduct may be either that of the legal representative of a party or of the party personally. If the allegation is in respect of the legal representative, all the factors relating to a wasted costs order under the Courts and Legal Services Act 1990, s 51 (see Chapter 32) will apply.

The investigation into misconduct can be initiated by the judge or costs officer or at the request of one of the parties.

(b) OWN CLIENT

[33.4]

An apparent omission from Rule 44.14 is that, unlike under the Supreme Court (now Senior Courts) Act 1981, s 51, it contains no provision to prevent the solicitor from rendering a charge to his client in respect of any between-the-parties costs which are being disallowed. The remedy may be to invite the solicitor to undertake not to render a charge to his client as the alternative to the court initiating an investigation under s 51. In any event, Rule 44.14(3) requires the solicitor to notify his client in writing of any order based upon his misconduct no later than seven days after the solicitor receives notice of the order if the party is not present when the order is made.

(c) CASES

[33.5]

Although one approaches pre-26 April 1999 decisions with caution, two earlier decisions cast some light on the meaning of the words 'unreasonable or improper'. In *Sinclair-Jones v Kay* [1988] 2 All ER 611, CA, the Court of Appeal held that the test was that a solicitor was liable to pay personally the costs of other parties to the proceedings where such costs had been incurred improperly or unreasonably or where they had been wasted by his failure to conduct the proceedings with reasonable competence and expedition. *Mainwaring v Goldtech Investments Ltd* (1991) Times, 19 February, CA, identified the following guidelines for making an order under the predecessor to Rule 44.14:

(i)   The criteria to be applied are those in *Sinclair-Jones* (above).
(ii)   Any order is purely compensatory.
(iii)   The court must be satisfied that the amount of costs claimed was caused by the impropriety.
(iv)   A high standard of proof is required because the order affects the solicitor's reputation.

(d)   PRE-ACTION MISCONDUCT

[33.6]

In *Hall v Rover Financial Services (GB) Ltd (t/a Land Rover Financial Services)* [2002] EWCA Civ 1514, [2003] 1 Costs LR 70 the claimant purchased a Range Rover for £38,000 which was subsequently seized and sold under the previous owner's hire purchase agreement. She succeeded in her claim against the hire purchase company for £38,000 damages for conversion but the judge refused to award her costs because he took the view that a reasonable person would have been suspicious at paying that amount for a three-month old car which sold originally for an amount exceeding £50,000. CPR Rule 44.3 provides that to deprive a successful party of his costs on the ground of misconduct, the misconduct had to relate to the proceedings themselves. The question was, therefore, whether the claimant's conduct was truly a part of, or extraneous to, the proceedings. While her conduct was relevant to credit it did not relate to the proceedings themselves and the claimant should not have been deprived of her costs. But, in *Groupama Insurance Co Ltd v Overseas Partners Re Ltd* [2003] EWHC 34 (Comm), [2003] All ER (D) 226 (Jan), the High Court held that *Hall v Rover* was no more than a matter of Commercial Court practice and CPR Rules 44.3(4)(a) and 44.3(5)(a) do not contain any limitation as would shut out reliance in an appropriate case of misconduct in and about the matters which triggered the litigation. It is difficult to imagine worse pre-action misconduct than in *McMinn v McMinn* [2003] 2 FLR 839 in which the husband had murdered his wife. The husband nevertheless succeeded in his claim against the executors of the wife's estate that because property had been held as tenants in common he was entitled to ownership of half of it. However, in view of the husband's pre-action misconduct the Court refused to award him his costs, but because of the executors' failure in the litigation, the Court was unable to order the husband to pay their costs, even though their conduct had been reasonable.

(e)   TRIBUNALS

[33.7]

In *Ramsay v Bowercross Construction Ltd* [2008] All ER (D) 131 (Aug) the Employment Tribunal found that the employee had acted unreasonably in bringing his claim and ordered him to pay the employer's costs in the sum of £10,000. It found that any costs attributable to the employer's solicitor were incurred "in relation to the proceedings" under the Employment Tribunal's (Constitution and Rules of Procedure Regulations 2004) and were therefore recoverable. Costs orders could be made under Schedule 1 paragraph 40 of the regulations where the receiving party had been legally represented at the hearing. "Legally represented" means having the assistance of a person who had a general qualification within the meaning of the Courts and Legal Services Act 1990, s 71. However, although the employer's counsel had a general qualification, their solicitor had not. The solicitors' fees were therefore recoverable only by way of a preparation time order, but Schedule 1 paragraph 46(1) precluded a tribunal from making both a preparation time order and a costs order in favour of the same party: *Agassi v Robinson (Inspector of Taxes) (Bar Council intervening)* [2005] EWCA Civ 1507, [2006] 1 All ER 900, [2006] 1 WLR 2126 could not be distinguished.

[33.8]

In *Deman v Victoria University of Manchester* [2008] All ER (D) 194 (Dec) the Employment Tribunal made a number of findings which were critical of the employee's conduct of the case. He had constantly made loud and aggressive interruptions and applications which had wasted time. His behaviour had been vexatious, abusive and disruptive, and had, at times, been scandalous and unreasonable. In the event, it ordered the employee to pay the employer's costs of the proceedings, limited to the sum of £8,000 and also to repay to the Secretary of State the whole of the allowances paid by the Secretary of State to two persons for their attendance before the tribunal. In dismissing the employee's appeal the Employment Appeal Tribunal held that a tribunal has a mandatory duty to consider making an order for the costs where it was of the opinion that any of the grounds for making a costs or preparation time order had been made out. The effect of that was that if a tribunal considered that there had been unreasonable conduct by a party or his representative or that the bringing or conducting of the proceedings had been misconceived it had actively to address the question of a possible award whether or not an application for costs had been made.

Part V

Particular People

CHAPTER 34

NON-PARTIES

[34.1]

CPR Rule 48.1: Pre-commencement disclosure and orders for disclosure against a person who is not a party

(1)   This paragraph applies where a person applies—

    (a)   for an order under—

        (i)   section 33 of the Senior Courts Act 1981; or

        (ii)   section 52 of the County Courts Act 1984,

(which give the court powers exercisable before commencement of proceedings); or

    (b)   for an order under—

        (i)   section 34 of the Senior Courts Act 1981; or

        (ii)   section 53 of the County Courts Act 1984,

(which give the court power to make an order against a non-party for disclosure of documents, inspection of property etc).

(2)   The general rule is that the court will award the person against whom the order is sought his costs—

    (a)   of the application; and

    (b)   of complying with any order made on the application.

(3)   The court may however make a different order, having regard to all the circumstances, including—

    (a)   the extent to which it was reasonable for the person against whom the order was sought to oppose the application; and

    (b)   whether the parties to the application have complied with any relevant pre-action protocol.

[34.2]

This is one of the few costs rules that does not have a supplementary Practice Direction.

This rule gives a party against whom an order for pre-commencement or non-party disclosure is made the general right to his costs but emphasises that the court may make some other order. Rule 48.1(3)(*a*) suggests that the court may well make different orders relating to the costs if an application is unsuccessfully opposed. Similarly, the person required to comply with a pre-action disclosure order will not only be awarded the costs of the application but the costs of complying with the order although, again, unreasonable behaviour, perhaps failure to comply with a pre-action Protocol, may result in the court making a different order.

In *Totalise plc v Motley Fool Ltd* [2001] EWCA Civ 1897, [2003] 2 All ER 872 Interactive Investor Ltd (Interactive) ran a website providing financial information to individual investors, on which subscribers could post information and opinions likely to be of interest to other investors. An investor under the name of 'Zeddust' posted defamatory statements questioning the competency and integrity of the claimants. When the claimants complained, Interactive removed the offending messages and suspended the account of Zeddust. However, they declined to reveal the identity of Zeddust on the grounds that, in the absence of a court order, they were precluded from disclosing personal details about any account to a third party under the provisions of the Data Protection Act 1998 and under the terms of the contract with their investors. The judge, in making the order sought by the claimants, ordered Interactive Investor to pay the costs of the application. Interactive's appeal against the order was allowed. 'Norwich Pharmacal' applications (see *Norwich Pharmacal Co v Customs* and *Excise Comrs* [1974] AC 133, HL) are not ordinary adversarial proceedings but are akin to proceedings for pre-action disclosure where costs are governed by CPR Rule 48.3. In general the costs incurred should be recovered from the wrongdoer rather than from an innocent party. Although there may be exceptions requiring a different order, these did not include cases where:

- the party required to make the disclosure had a genuine doubt that the person seeking the disclosure was entitled to it;
- the party was under an appropriate obligation not to reveal the information or where the legal position was not clear, or the party had a reasonable doubt as to the obligations; or
- the party could be subject to proceedings if disclosure was voluntary; or
- the party would or might suffer damage by voluntarily giving the disclosure; or
- the disclosure would or might infringe a legitimate interest of another.

If a party refusing disclosure had supported or was implicated in a crime or tort or sought to obstruct justice being done, the court would require that party to bear its costs and, if appropriate, pay the other party's costs.

In *Habib Bank Ltd v Customs* and *Excise Comrs* (28 January 1999, unreported, QBD), HM Customs and Excise had given an undertaking to indemnify third parties against expenses incurred in complying with a freezing order. The bank claimed that one provision contained within the order had been poorly drafted and caused some confusion. It had felt obliged to seek the advice of outside solicitors and the court held that as the applicant was unfamiliar with orders of the kind in question it was, therefore, reasonable for independent solicitors to be instructed for the purpose of interpretation and that the claimant should pay their costs of so doing.

[34.3]

CPR Rule 48.2: Costs orders in favour of or against non-parties

(1) Where the court is considering whether to exercise its power under section 51 of the Senior Courts Act 1981 (costs are in the discretion of the court) to make a costs order in favour of or against a person who is not a party to proceedings—

    (a)   that person must be added as a party to the proceedings for the purposes of costs only; and

    (b)   he must be given a reasonable opportunity to attend a hearing at which the court will consider the matter further.

(2) This rule does not apply—

    (a)   where the court is considering whether to—

        (i)   make an order against the Legal Services Commission;

        (ii)   make a wasted costs order (as defined in 48.7);

(b)   in proceedings to which rule 48.1 applies (pre-commencement disclosure and orders for disclosure against a person who is not a party).

[34.4]

Another Rule without a Practice Direction.

The approach of the court to making orders for costs against non-parties was set out in *Symphony Group plc v Hodgson* [1994] QB 179, CA and exemplified in subsequent cases.

THE GENERAL APPROACH

[34.5]

In *Symphony Group plc v Hodgson* the claimant obtained injunctive relief against the defendant who had left his employment to join Halvanto, a competitor, in breach of restrictive covenants in his contract of employment. The claimant did not add Halvanto as a defendant or initiate proceedings against it or tell Halvanto that it might seek to make it liable for costs. Halvanto's managing director gave evidence for the defendant. The defendant was protected by a legal aid certificate and the complainant successfully applied for an order that Halvanto should pay the claimant's costs of the action. In allowing Halvanto's appeal the court said that since *Aiden Shipping Co Ltd v Interbulk (No 2)* [1986] AC 965, HL the courts had entertained claims for costs against non-parties where a person had some management of or financed the action, where the person had caused the action, where the person was a party to a closely- related action which had been heard at the same time but not consolidated, and in group litigation. The court identified the following material considerations to be taken into account:

(a)   An order for the payment of costs by a non-party would always be exceptional. The judge should treat any application for such an order with considerable caution.

(b)   It would be even more exceptional for such an order to be made where the applicant had a cause of action against the non-party and could have joined him. Joinder as a party gave the person concerned all the protection conferred by the rules, eg the framing of issues, discovery and the knowledge of what the issues were before giving evidence. (Rule 48.2(1)(*a*) now requires that he must be added as a party.)

(c)   Even if the applicant could provide a good reason for not joining the non-party against whom he had a valid cause of action, he should warn the non-party that he might apply for costs against him.

(d)   An application should normally be determined by the trial judge.

(e)   The fact that the trial judge might have expressed views on the conduct of the non-party neither constituted bias nor the appearance of bias.

(f)   The procedure for the determination of costs is a summary procedure, not necessarily subject to all the rules that would apply in an action. Thus, subject to any statutory exceptions, judicial findings were inadmissible as evidence of the facts on which they were based in proceedings between one of the parties to the original proceedings and a stranger. Yet, in the summary procedure, for a solicitor to pay the costs of an action to which he was not a party, the judge's findings of fact might be admissible. That departure from basic principles could only be justified if the connection of the non-party with the original proceedings was so close that he would not suffer any injustice by allowing the exception to the general rule.

(g)   The normal rule was that witnesses in either civil or criminal proceedings enjoyed immunity from any form of civil action in respect of evidence given during the proceedings. In so far as the evidence of a witness in proceedings might lead to an application for costs against him or his company, it introduced an exception to a valuable general principle.

(h)   The fact that an employee or even a director or managing director of a company gave evidence in an action did not normally mean that the company was taking part in that action.

(i)   The judge should be alert to the possibility that an application for costs against a non-party was motivated by resentment or an inability to obtain an effective order for costs against a state-funded litigant.

An application for a non-party costs order should be made to the trial judge, even if he has expressed a view about the conduct of the non-party. It is not wrong for a judge to mention the possibility of an application for a non-party costs order at the outset of the trial (*Equitas Ltd v Horace Holman & Co Ltd* [2008] EWHC 2287 (Comm), [2009] 1 BCLC 662, [2008] All ER (D) 35 (Oct)).

In *Wiggins v Richard Read (Transport) Ltd* (1999) Times, 14 January, CA, David Wiggins, who was disabled, was suing by his brother and next friend. After a trial of a preliminary issue, the judge determined that the claimant did not have a cause of action, struck out the proceedings and ordered his parents to pay the costs of the defendant. In allowing their appeal, the court said that Note 62/2/7 in the White Book had misled the judge into thinking that the closeness of a third party to litigation on its own allowed a costs order to be made against the third party. The categories of case where an order could be made and the guiding principles were set out by Balcombe LJ in *Symphony Group plc v Hodgson* which was cited in the Note. Balcombe LJ had identified nine guidelines but the Note in relation to the sixth guideline did not include all the words of Balcombe LJ. Because of the omission of some of those words, the sixth principle was elided and misshapen. It could never be enough simply to show a close relationship or than an action was inspired by a parent for his disabled son in order for a costs order to be made against a parent. There must be something more. The judge did not ask whether it had been shown that the parent had consciously brought the action for his own benefit and not for his son's or whether he had consciously encouraged a hopeless action.

An application for an order to join a party for the purpose of seeking an order for costs against them would normally be expected to explain the nature of the claim against the intended party and the purpose to be served by joining that party. If it was clear that a joinder of the intended party was an abuse of process, then the court would be expected to dismiss the application. In *PR Records Ltd v Vinyl 2000 Ltd* [2007] EWHC 1721 (Ch), 18 July, the Master had been wrong to refuse to join the second defendant as a party to the proceedings and not to allow the matter to proceed to the second stage envisaged under CPR rule 48.2(1)(b). The application had not involved an abuse of process of the court. At the stage of joinder, it would not be inappropriate to attempt a preliminary assessment of the merits in order to see whether an application for a non-party cost order had a real prospect of success. The right order in the present case was to permit the joinder under CPR rule 48(1)(a) and to allow the matter to proceed to the second stage under CPR rule 48(1)(b).

Although funding took place in most of the reported cases, it is not, essential, in the sense of being a jurisdictional pre-requisite to the exercise of the court's discretion. If the evidence is that a respondent (whether director or shareholder or controller of a relevant company) has effectively controlled the proceedings and has sought to derive potential benefit from them, that will be enough to establish the jurisdiction. Whether such jurisdiction should be exercised is, of course, another matter entirely and the extent to which a respondent has, in fact, funded any proceedings may be very relevant to the exercise of discretion. There is a danger that the exercise of the jurisdiction to order a non-party to proceedings to pay the cost of those proceedings becomes over-complicated by reference to authority. Where a non-party director can be described as the "real party", seeking his own benefit, controlling and/or funding the litigation, then even where he has acted in good faith or without any impropriety, justice may well demand that he be liable in costs on a fact-sensitive and objective assessment of the circumstances (*Petromec Inc v Petroleo Brasileiro SA Petrobas* [2006] EWCA Civ 1038, 150 Sol Jo LB 984, 19 July.

In *Lingfield Properties (Darlington) Ltd v Padgett Lavender Associates* [2008] EWHC 2795 (QB), [2008] All ER (D) 162 (Nov) the court refused to join a company secretary personally as a party to the proceedings for the purposes of a non-party costs order. Although he was no longer a director he had been the principal person involved in managing the company's claims and the claim depended on his evidence. He was the only person through whom the company had acted. He had also arranged the funding of the claim, although he had not funded it personally. Nevertheless, it was clear he was not the real party to the claim. The board probably applied their minds independently to the matters to be decided in the litigation. The company risked its own assets and made arrangements for funding the litigation that did not materially depend upon the financial contribution of the company secretary. The company was the real party to the litigation.

NOTICE

[34.6]

It is relevant to the exercise of the discretion whether to make an order for costs against a non-party to consider whether the non-party had received notice, before or during the litigation that he may be made subject to an order for costs. It would be a denial of the fundamental right of non-parties to be heard on serious allegations if the court was to decide them on a summary application on the hearing of which it is not appropriate for the court to embark on an enquiry of the type that justice would require *(Barndeal Ltd v Richmond-upon-Thames London Borough Council* [2005] EWHC 1377 (QB), [2005] All ER (D) 369 (Jun), 30 June).

In *Oriakhel v (1)Vickers (2) Groupama Insurance Co Ltd (3) Khan (4) Graham Coffey & Co (A Firm)* [2008] EWCA Civ 748, 4 July the claimant in a fraudulent conspiracy with the first named defendant (V) brought a road traffic accident claim for damages against him. V's insurers contended that the claim was bogus and were joined as second defendant by G to contest the claim and to counterclaim. The judge dismissed the claim as fraudulent. At the trial a Mr Khan (K) gave evidence which the judge disbelieved concluding that he too was involved in the conspiracy. G then joined K as a party for the purpose of seeking a costs order against him, which the judge refused to make under the mistaken belief that it had to be shown that the non-party was a funder or controller of the litigation before a non-party costs order could be made. Nevertheless on appeal the Court of Appeal refused to make a non-party costs order against K on the grounds it would be exceptional for an order to be made against a non-party where the applicant had a cause of action against the non-party and could have joined him as a party to the original proceedings. Prior to the trial G contended that K was a dishonest conspirator. If he had been made a defendant to the counterclaim, he would have had a full opportunity of taking legal advice, adducing such evidence and documents as might support his defence and considering his own position. G remained free to sue K for his part in the dishonest conspiracy and if it succeeded, the costs of successfully defending the primary claim would be recoverable damages flowing from the conspiracy. K had not been given notice of the claim at any time when he could have taken legal advice and, if necessary, deployed further material by way of his defence and, if so advised, applied to be joined as a party. Where a non-party has, in effect, controlled the primary litigation it would be bound by the result. But K did not have such a close connection with the primary claim that he was bound by the result. Witness immunity was yet another reason why the court should not exercise its discretion to award costs against K.

INSURERS

[34.7]

Insurers who took over the defence of an action and conducted it for their own benefit could properly be said to have been the real defendants and were ordered to pay the costs although they were not a party to the action (*Pendennis Shipyard Ltd v Magrathea (Pendennis) Ltd (in liquidation)* [1998] 1 Lloyd's Rep 315, QBD. However, legal expenses insurers were not liable to pay more than the limit of their cover merely on the grounds that they had funded the litigation under a commercial agreement (*Murphy v Young & Co's Brewery plc* [1997] 1 All ER 518, CA).

In *TGA Chapman Ltd v Christopher* and *Sun Alliance* [1998] 2 All ER 873, CA, the Court of Appeal held that the defendant's negligence insurers were liable for the full amount of a judgment of £1,100,000 plus costs even though their liability under the insurance policy was limited to £1,000,000 inclusive of opponents costs. The insurers were in a different position from those in *Murphy* because, as in *Pendennis*, above, the litigation was funded, controlled and directed by the insurance company motivated entirely by its own interest. It was the same in *Plymouth and South West Co-operative Society Ltd v Architecture, Structure and Management Ltd* [2006] EWHC 3252 (TCC), 111 Con LR 189 where the insured had virtually no assets and had ceased trading but the insurers fought the claim to protect their own liability to the defendant of £2 million under the policy.

In *Palmer v (1) MIB; (2) PZ Products; (3) Royal & Sun Alliance* [2008] EWCA Civ 46, 6 February the appellant Royal & Sun Alliance (RSA) insured the second defendant(PZ) and had financed its unsuccessful liability defence to the claim. The other defendants had admitted liability and one of the co-defendants, the MIB, had made a Part 36 Offer to accept a contribution of £300,000 from PZ and to meet the whole of the remainder of the claim. This offer had been rejected.

PZ were ordered to pay the claimant's and defendants' costs of the liability proceedings. The damages were likely to exceed £2million. RSA's liability under the policy was limited to £500,000. which would be exhausted by the claims for damages and costs. PZ was in financial difficulties and would not be able to make a substantial contribution toward the sums claimed. and PZ's co-defendants would have to pay the balance. The MIB sought an order under s 51 of the Supreme Court (now Senior Courts) Act 1981, that RSA personally pay the costs incurred by the other parties which would free the whole of the £500,000 payable under the policy to be applied towards the damages.

HELD: The Part 36 offer ought to have been accepted to save PZ from further risk, but RSA had rejected that offer without consulting PZ, demonstrating that RSA had been motivated, either exclusively or at least predominantly, by its own interest in the manner in which it had conducted the defence, and that that was a circumstance that pushed the case into the exceptional type in which it was appropriate to make the order sought. RSA could be regarded as the true defendant in all but name. PZ had no commercial interest in pursuing the claim and RSA should have been aware of this. When the opportunity to settle had arisen RSA had turned it down without reference to PZ. The inference was that the defence of the claim was conducted on the basis that the only real interest being protected was that of RSA. On that basis it was proper to make an order for costs against RSA.

DIRECTORS

(a) Not summary

[34.8]

In *Robertson Research International Ltd v ABG Exploration BV* (1999) Times, 3 November, QBD (Pat Ct), after directions for trial had been given in a robustly-defended action, the defendant company gave notice that it was ceasing to trade, its solicitors came off the record and it consented to judgment for the entire sum claimed. By then it was an empty shell. The claimants joined as parties a director and the financial controller of the defendant company alleging that they had known there was no defence and seeking an order for costs against them. The defendants argued that in view of the strictures of the Court of Appeal in *Turner Page Music* (para [33.28]) in wasted costs matters that such applications will not be heard unless they can be dealt with summarily, the present applications should be dismissed. The master accepted these submissions, but on appeal, Laddie J held that unlike the wasted costs jurisdiction, applications against non-parties were solely compensatory and it was irrelevant whether there was any impropriety on the part of those responsible. Although such orders would always be exceptional, it was not necessary that the applications had to be capable of being dealt with summarily. The matter could be dealt with appropriately by, for example, limiting it to principle issues, limiting or disposing with cross examination and limiting the length of the hearing.

(b) Orders not made

[34.9]

In *Taylor v Pace Developments Ltd* [1991] BCC 406, CA, the Court of Appeal held that the controlling director of a one-man company should not be personally liable for the costs of defending an action even though he knew the company would not be able to meet the plaintiff's costs should the company prove unsuccessful. That would be far too great an inroad on the principle of limited liability, although the director might be made liable if the company's defence was not bona fide, as, for example, where the company had been advised that there was no defence.

Gardiner v FX Music Ltd [2000] All ER (D) 144, ChD confirmed that an order for costs against a non-party is always an exceptional order. In the case of a sole or guiding director of an insolvent company, such an order is not normally made unless it can be shown that the director caused the company to bring or defend proceedings improperly.

Re Land and Property Trust Co plc (No 4) [1994] 1 BCLC 232, CA provided a good illustration of the dangers inherent in treating an application for costs against a third party in the same manner as one against a party to the proceedings. On refusing a petition by a company for an administration order, the judge had ordered the costs incurred by a creditor to be paid by the directors personally. Although he had jurisdiction to make such an order for costs, he had refused the directors' application for an adjournment to enable them to have a proper opportunity of putting in evidence and his failure to do so caused him to err in principle. On the fresh evidence that was available before the Court of Appeal the order for costs ought not to have been made.

In *H Leverton Ltd v Crawford Offshore (Exploration) Services Ltd (in liquidation)* (1996) Times, 22 November, QBD, an application succeeded where a Mr Crawford was found to be the defendant company for all practical purposes. He had acted in bad faith by concocting false claims supported by forged documents, destroyed and suppressed documents, given false evidence, and had substantially financed the proceedings. These were exceptional circumstances making it appropriate to order costs against him.

(c) Orders made

[34.10]

In *Secretary of State for Trade and Industry v Backhouse* [2001] EWCA Civ 67, [2001] 1 BCLC 468, two companies were ordered to be wound up, the judge having found that no proper books of account had been kept, that the businesses of the companies were intertwined with the defendant personally, who treated the companies' moneys as his own and that a savings scheme marketed through the companies lacked intrinsic merit. After judgment, the Secretary of State warned the defendant for the first time that he intended to apply for a costs order against him personally. The judge ordered the defendant to pay the costs personally because he had defended to protect his own reputation and position without seriously considering the interests of the companies or their creditors. The crucial question was whether the relevant director held a bona fide belief that the company had an arguable defence and that it was in the companies' interests to advance that defence. If he did so believe, to make a non-party pay the costs would constitute an unlawful inroad into the principle of limited liability. However, on the facts, the defendant had not considered the companies' interests but only his own; there was ample evidence to justify the costs order despite the absence of an early warning concerning costs.

In *Bournemouth and Boscombe Athletic Football Club Ltd v Lloyds TSB Bank plc* [2004] EWCA Civ 935, [2004] All ER (D) 323 (Jun) the claimant football club was in severe financial trouble and was unable to meet its obligations to its bankers, the defendants who appointed administrative receivers. The club entered into a company voluntary arrangement and its business was sold to a new company. One of the directors initiated proceedings against the bank in the name of the company which were struck out. He then initiated further proceedings making the same allegations. That action too was struck out and an appeal against the striking out also failed. The director was ordered to be added as a defendant to enable an application to be made for a costs order against him pursuant to CPR Rule 48.2 (1). The director had sought to play fast and loose with the civil justice system by commencing and presenting hopeless claims and by presenting a hopeless appeal on behalf of an insolvent company. The circumstances were sufficiently exceptional to justify the court making him face the financial consequences of his conduct by ordering him personally to pay the costs of the company's unsuccessful appeal.

In *Goodwood Recoveries Ltd v Breen: Breen v Slater* [2005] EWCA Civ 414, 149 Sol Jo LB 509 Michael Slater controlled the claimant debt recovery company and was also a consultant solicitor in a firm which funded proceedings brought by the company under a conditional fee agreement. The costs of the litigation brought by the claimant company would not have been incurred without Mr Slater's involvement. He formulated the claim and brought it albeit in the name of the company. He was the real party for whose benefit the litigation was brought. He did not fund it, but only because it was funded under a CFA by the firm of solicitors for whom he acted as a consultant and in whose name he undertook the conduct of the litigation. A lack of *bona fides* is not necessarily a condition of claiming against a third party, if the third party was really the party for whose benefit the case was conducted, but in any event the whole of the costs of the litigation were caused by Mr Slater's dishonesty or impropriety, irrespective of whether he had any *bona fide* belief in the claim. Therefore it was not necessary to decide whether there to be a causal link between all the costs and the alleged impropriety, it was appropriate to order Mr Slater to pay the whole of the costs and not merely the additional costs which could be attributed directly to improper conduct on his part.

LIQUIDATORS AND RECEIVERS

[34.11]

Although the court has jurisdiction to order a liquidator as a non-party to proceedings brought by an insolvent company to pay costs personally, it will only exercise that jurisdiction in exceptional circumstances where there has been impropriety on the part of the liquidator, particularly in view of the fact that the normal remedy of obtaining an order for security for costs is available to the defendant. The caution necessary in all cases when attempt is made to render a non-party liable for costs would be the greater in the case of a liquidator having regard to public policy considerations (*Metalloy Supplies Ltd (in liquidation) v MA (UK) Ltd* [1997] 1 All ER 418, CA). However in *Apex Frozen Foods Ltd (in liquidation) v Abdul Ali* [2007] EWHC 469 (Ch), [2007] All ER (D) 158 (Mar) a freezing order was granted subject to the liquidator giving a personal undertaking to the effect that he would be liable for any loss to the claimant if the court found that the order had occasioned such loss and that the claimant should be compensated for it.

The freezing order was subsequently discharged on the basis that there had been improper disclosure of the material facts at the time that the freezing order was granted. The purpose of the undertaking was to ensure that a mechanism was available to make good any detriment suffered by the claimant through the grant of the freezing order if it was subsequently established that there should not have not been an injunction. The claimant had incurred costs in relation to the injunction proceedings as a result of the freezing order being obtained in the absence of proper disclosure of material facts. The fact that the liquidator was innocent of any personal conscious failure was insufficient to absolve him from liability when such absolution would produce precisely the injustice, which the undertaking was designed to guard against. Accordingly, the claimant was entitled to recover its costs as recoverable damages on the standard basis.

In *Dolphin Quays Developments Ltd (In Administrative and Fixed Charge Receivership) v Mills* [2007] EWHC 1180 (Ch), 17 May the applicant applied for an order that the receivers should pay the costs of unsuccessful litigation that had been brought by the claimant company against him. He was a substantial creditor of the claimant company's parent company, and contended that the receivers were the real parties to the unsuccessful litigation who had conducted the litigation for their benefit and the benefit of the Royal Bank of Scotland which had appointed them. The application was refused. Third party costs orders are only to be made in exceptional circumstances and this was an entirely normal case of receivers seeking to enforce a contractual right forming part of the security. The fact that the claim failed might be unusual but could hardly be classified as 'exceptional'. If an order were made in this case then it would have to be made in all such cases. There was no impropriety or unreasonableness in pursuing the litigation on which a third party costs order could be founded. Neither the receivers nor the bank could be viewed as the real parties to the litigation. Mr Mills could have applied for security for costs from the company when the litigation was first instigated.

In appropriate cases, a non-party costs order against a receiver or against the secured creditor might be made, especially where the non-party was the 'real party'. Costs orders against receivers would more readily be made where the company was in liquidation and the receiver's agency had terminated, or where the successful party had not been able to obtain security for costs. The availability of security was an important factor in the exercise of the discretion. *Mills v Birchall* [2008] EWCA Civ 385, 18 April was an entirely normal case of receivers seeking to enforce a contractual right forming part of the security. The absence of any element of impropriety or unreasonableness confirmed that the claim was not exceptional and also underlined the fact that it was not an alternative justification for making the order sought. The receivers had directed the proceedings on behalf of the company without any direction or interference by the bank and the funding of the proceedings by the company was derived from the realisations in the receivership. The receivers did not fund the claim, nor did they have any interest in the monies from which the claim was funded or in the outcome of the claim. Neither the receivers nor the bank were to be regarded as the real party. The position of receivers as agents was analogous to the position of directors and liquidators. In an ordinary case in which a director or liquidator caused the company to bring proceedings that were unsuccessful, a personal costs order would not be made. Some additional element was required. The judge did not place too much weight on the absence of an application the security of the costs. There were no factors that, in accordance with established principles, justified interference with the judge's exercise of discretion. The decision in *Aiden Shipping Co Ltd v Interbulk Ltd (The Vimeira) (No 2)* (1986) AC 965, HL did not justify the judicial creation of a substantive rule that receivers should be personally responsible for the costs of a successful party.

TRIBUNALS

[34.12]

The court has power to order costs against a tribunal whose decision was overturned on appeal, but only if the tribunal made itself a party by appearing on the appeal or taking steps to defend the determination (*Providence Capitol Trustees Ltd v Ayres* [1996] 4 All ER 760, ChD). Where in a successful appeal against a decision of the Pensions Ombudsman the ombudsman had appeared at the appeal and made representations in support of his determination, the costs recoverable from him were not limited to the amount by which they had been increased by his appearance but could, in principle, extend to the whole of the successful party's costs in making the appeal. The decisions in *Elliott v Pensions Ombudsman* [1998] OPLR 21, ChD and *University of Nottingham v Eyett (No 2)* [1999] 2 All ER 445, ChD that the ombudsman could be ordered to pay the costs of a successful appeal only to the extent that those costs were increased by his participation was wrong and would not be followed (*Moore's (Wallisdown) Ltd v Pensions Ombudsman* [2002] 1 All ER 737, ChD).

FUNDERS

[34.13]

Non-party costs orders are to be granted only in exceptional cases. In respect of costs against an insolvent company, costs can only be recovered from a third party if the funding provided by the non-party and the costs incurred by the claiming party have a causal link. Such an order would normally be appropriate only where a company officer stood to benefit from the litigation, controlled and directed it, or started and pursued it unreasonably or for an ulterior purpose not connected with the best interests of the company.

The relevant test for causation in an application for costs against a non-party under s 51 is whether or not the funding provided by the non-party caused the applicant to incur costs that he or she would not otherwise have incurred. It is simple logic that if the s 51 applicant would have incurred the relevant costs whether the funded party was funded by the non-party or not, then it would be wrong in principle to make a s 51 order (*Jackson v Thakrar* [2007] EWHC 626 (QB), [2007] NLJR 483).

(a) No order made

[34.14]

In *Shah v Karanjia* [1993] 4 All ER 792, ChD an application against a non-party failed both because he had been given no adequate warning of the application and because of lack of evidence that he had funded the proceedings.

Hamilton v Al Fayed (No 2) [2002] EWCA Civ 665, [2002] 3 All ER 641 distinguished between 'pure' funders who made donations in support of a litigant as an act of charity and 'professional' funders, such as insurers, who were almost always contractually bound to fund the litigation. An order for costs would rarely be made against a charitable, philanthropic, altruistic or merely sympathetic donor who, on the information before him, had reasonable grounds for believing that the litigant had reasonable grounds for asserting his right or a defence to the claim, and who wished to ensure that a genuine dispute was not lost by default or inadequately contested. If pure funders were regularly exposed to liability under s 51, such funds would dry up and access to justice would thereby on occasions be lost. They should not, however, ordinarily be held liable. So long as the law continued to allow impoverished parties to litigate without having to provide security for their opponents' costs, those sympathetic to their plight should not be discouraged from assisting them to secure representation.

In *Gulf Azov Shipping Co Ltd v Chief Humphrey Irikefe Idisi* [2004] EWCA Civ 292, [2004] All ER (D) 284 (Mar), the court allowed an appeal by a Nigerian lawyer against a costs order made against him for personally intervening on behalf of one of the defendants against whom damages had been awarded for the wrongful detention of the claimant's vessel. The defendant's assets were subject to a world wide freezing order in an attempt to enforce the award. The lawyer could not be criticised for assisting the defendant financially in instructing solicitors of high standing and for assisting the defendant in attempting to discharge his costs liabilities. There was no suggestion that the lawyers had been personally interested in the outcome of the litigation.

The benefit derived by the funder does not have to be a direct financial one and funding motivated by personal animosity could also justify a non-party costs order (*Vaughan v Jones and Fowler* [2006] EWHC 2123 (Ch), [2006] All ER (D) 62 (Aug)).

(b) Order made

[34.15]

In *Locabail (UK) Ltd v Bayfield Properties Ltd (No 3)* [2000] 2 Costs LR 169, ChD, the first husband of one of the defendants had given evidence on her behalf at the trial when he had been found to be an unsatisfactory witness, prone to exaggeration. He admitted to funding his former wife's action and recommending a solicitor to her. The complainants sought costs against him and he was joined in the action solely in relation to the claim for costs. It was not appropriate to punish the former husband by awarding costs solely on the basis of his funding the litigation of another and behaving unsatisfactorily as a witness. However he was ordered to pay the claimants' costs on the following bases:
(a) he had funded proceedings knowing that his former wife would be unable to satisfy a costs order if unsuccessful;
(b) his intense identification with his former wife's position in his own evidence;
(c) his indifference to the legal and factual issues in the case; and
(d) the court's rejection of the factual basis of his former wife's case.
In *Dymocks Franchise Systems (NSW) Pty Ltd v Todd* [2004] UKPC 39, [2004] NLJR 1325, 21 July, the Privy Council held that costs would be awarded against a non-party who had not merely funded the proceedings but had substantially controlled them, or was to benefit from them or who promoted and funded proceedings by an insolvent company solely or substantially for his own financial benefit.

Arkin v Borchard Lines Ltd, Zim Israel Navigation Co Ltd and Managers and Processors of Claims (Part 20 defendants) [2003] EWHC 2844 (Comm), [2004] 1 Lloyd's Rep 88, MPC, a professional funding company, entered into a funding agreement with the claimant, whereby it funded the employment of expert witnesses, the preparation of their evidence and the organisation of the enormous quantities of documents which became necessary to investigate before the trial.

In applying for a costs order against MPC the defendants laid stress on the very substantial proportion of any recoverable damages or settlement payments (25% of the first £5 million and 23% of any excess) which MPC was to receive under its funding agreement. The amount of the claim, including exemplary damages, eventually reached $160 million, which would have resulted in a benefit of some $40 million to the funders. The defendants also drew attention to the absence of any undertaking by MPC to pay the defendants' recoverable costs or to take out after the event (ATE) insurance cover in respect of such costs. They submitted that, in principle, professional funders, as distinct from pure funders, who are maintaining litigation for their profit, should be liable for the costs of the defendants if their claim fails, which in this case it did.

In resisting this application MPC submitted that conditional fee agreements with professional funders which have the purpose of enabling impecunious claimants to pursue claims of real substance which, but for such funding, they could not have done, should not be visited with costs orders against the funders if the claim fails.

The court held that in these circumstances the public policy objectives of the deterrence of weak claims and of the protection of the due administration of justice from interference by those who fund litigation must yield to the objective of making access to the courts available to impecunious claimants with claims of sufficient substance. An order for costs against MPC would, no doubt, operate as a strong deterrent to professional funders to provide support for impecunious claimants with large and complex claims.

On appeal the Court of Appeal held that a professional funder, who finances part of a claimant's costs of litigation, should be potentially liable for the costs of the opposing party *to the extent of the funding provided*. In its judgment the court said 'The effect of this will, of course, be that, if the funding is provided on a contingency basis of recovery, the funder will require, as the price of the funding, a greater share of the recovery should the claim succeed. In the individual case, the net recovery of a successful claimant will be diminished. While this is unfortunate, it seems to us that it is a cost that the impecunious claimant can reasonably be expected to bear. Overall justice will be better served than leaving defendants in a position where they have no right to recover any costs from a professional funder whose intervention has permitted the continuation of a claim which has ultimately proved to be without merit.' The decision may not please purists like me but it should have the practical effect of giving some protection to successful defendants without killing off professional funding.

In *Phillips v Princo* [2003] All ER (D) 99 (Sep), noted in the ALCD Journal October 2003, the judge went the whole way, holding there is a clear distinction to be drawn between disinterested, in the sense of commercially disinterested, funders on the one hand and those whose interests stood to be advanced by a successful outcome of the litigation on the other. Phillips commenced patent infringement proceedings against Aventi in respect of unlicensed discs made by Princo. Phillips made a deliberate decision not to join Princo in the litigation. Princo undertook payment of the costs of Aventi's defence which enabled Aventi to defend the action. Aventi went into insolvent liquidation and Phillips were permitted to join Princo as a party for the purpose of seeking an order for costs against them. It was clear that Princo was interested in the outcome of the proceedings and was not a pure funder. The action would not have been defended but for their funding. Even though Princo did not involve itself in the action and did not control it, Phillips ran up costs in an action which, but for Princo's funding of Aventi for its own commercial benefit, would not have needed to be incurred. Accordingly Princo was ordered to pay the costs of the action.

Similarly in *Gemma Ltd v Gimson* [2005] EWHC 69 (TCC), [2005] BLR 163 it was clear that the claimant company could not have funded its role in the litigation without the funding provided by the defendants and that funding directly led to the claimant incurring substantial costs. The defendants would have been the sole or principal beneficiaries of any recovery from the claimant and had failed to inform the company's professional advisors of material facts that, if disclosed, would have inevitably led to advice that the company's case was hopeless. The proceedings were only pursued out of the defendants' vendetta against the claimant. Fairness and justice required that a non-party costs order should be made against the defendants and accordingly they were joined in the proceedings and were made jointly and severally liable for all the costs the company was ordered to pay to the claimant.

Nevertheless, the court stressed that non-party costs orders are to be granted only in exceptional cases. In respect of costs against an insolvent company, costs could only be recovered from a third party if the funding provided by the non-party and the costs incurred by the claiming party have a causal link. Such an order would normally be appropriate only where a company officer stood to benefit from the litigation, controlled and directed it, or started and pursued it unreasonably or for an ulterior purpose not connected with the best interests of the company.

In *Total Spares & Supplies Ltd v Antares SRL* [2006] EWHC 1537 (CH), [2006] All ER (D) 314 (Jun), 27 June the main defendant had transferred most of its assets to a new company a week before the trial and then allowed itself to be struck off the Italian company register leaving the claimant unable to recover its costs. The claimants sought an order that Francisco Gargani, who controlled both companies, and the new company, Antares, should pay the costs. Since *Arkin v Borchard Line Ltd* (see above) it can no longer be said that causation is a necessary pre-condition to an order for costs against a non-party. Causation would often be a vital factor but there could be cases where, in accordance with principle, it was just to make an order for costs against a non-party who could not be said to have caused the costs in question. In the circumstances, it was just to make an order. The facts of the case were exceptional and justified the making of an order that Antares should pay 55% of the claimant's costs incurred after the transfer. Mr Gargani was directly responsible for the transfer and it was just that he should be responsible for the costs originally ordered to be paid by the defendant.

In *Adris v Royal Bank of Scotland (Cartel Client Review Ltd, additional parties)* [2010] EWHC 941 (QB), [2010] NLJR 767, [2010] All ER (D) 156 (May) the allegation was the more usual one of control, "real party " etc. in respect of the litigation itself, in which causation is still an important element which should be shown at least to some extent. Indeed it was hard to see how a party could "control" litigation without it following that such conduct had a bearing on the incurring of costs by the other side. The same was true of funding - funding was necessary and it followed that in its absence the litigation may not have started or continued - with the consequence that some or all of the costs would not have been incurred. On the facts, a non-party order was justified.

Petromec Inc v Petroleo Brasileiro SA Petrobras [2007] EWHC 1589 (Comm), [2007] All ER (D) 102 (Jul) held that actual funding by a third party is not a jurisdictional pre-requisite to the exercise of the court's discretion under s 51 of the Supreme Court (now Senior Courts) Act 1981. If the evidence is that a person, whether a director or shareholder or controller of a relevant company, had effectively controlled the proceedings and sought to derive potential benefit from them, that was enough to establish the jurisdiction. Whether the jurisdiction should be exercised is another matter, and the extent to which a person has, in fact, funded any proceedings might be very relevant to the exercise of discretion. In any event, the appellant had funded the proceedings throughout. The ability to obtain an order for security for costs and the existence of any security put up as a result of such an order were matters that a judge had to take into consideration and the judge had had those factors clearly in mind in this case. The fact that in the course of the proceedings, a judge had ordered security that, in the event, had turned out to be inadequate was not any reason for declining to exercise jurisdiction in an otherwise appropriate case. This was not case of a liquidator or director bringing proceedings for the benefit of the company. Accordingly, the judge had been right to join the appellant to the proceedings and make him jointly and severally liable for the costs of the successful defendants because he had controlled the proceedings, funded them, and would have benefited from them if they had been successful.

In *Thomson v Berkhamsted Collegiate School* [2009] EWHC 2374 (QB), [2009] NLJR 1440, [2009] All ER (D) 39 (Oct) the claimant was a 25-year-old unemployed university graduate who sued the private school he had attended between 1994 and 2002 for injury, loss and damages of nearly £1 million for failing to prevent him being bullied. He discontinued the proceedings two weeks into the trial. He was unable to meet any costs order and the defendants wished to seek a third party costs order against his parents. Pursuant to that application the school sought orders requiring the parents to file and serve disclosure statements setting out correspondence between them and their son's solicitors, experts and counsel, and orders against the son with respect to disclosure and his claim of legal professional privilege.

The parents were not merely funders but were directly concerned with the facts of the claim and played an active role in the litigation. It was doubtful that it would have been funded if the parents had not made funds available themselves. Accordingly, an application for third party costs had a reasonable prospect of success. The only doubt was over whether the parents gained a benefit from the litigation and sought to control its course. The defendant could only demonstrate the element of control if it knew what communications the parents had had with the solicitors, counsel and experts in the case. Accordingly the school was entitled to disclosure.

(c) Investment in litigation

[34.16]

The Civil Justice Council recommendation of building on the judgment of the Court of Appeal in *Arkin v Borchard Lines Ltd* para [34.15] by giving further consideration to the use of third party funding was overwhelmingly endorsed by those attending its last Costs Forum, and *Arkin* and other decisions having confirmed the validity of the commercial funding of litigation, there is now a market in investing in litigation. Chapter 41 is therefore devoted to Third Party Funding.

INTERVENORS

[34.17]

In the course of proceedings concerning children, the court gave directions for an assessment by a family centre. The father made a statement in intemperate terms attacking the personal and professional integrity of the social worker responsible for the family centre's report. The centre was granted leave to intervene in the proceedings in order to defend these allegations. The centre was formally joined in the proceedings for the purpose of a costs application in accordance with CPR Rule 48.2. The father's attack on the centre had gone far beyond the limits of toleration. The centre's intervention had been warranted and an order for their costs was made against the father: *Re A (family proceedings: expert witnesses)* [2001] 1 FLR 723, Fam.

FREEZING ORDERS

[34.18]

A freezing order is a special type of injunction, the very existence of which is controversial. A non-proprietary freezing injunction, unlike more classic interlocutory injunctions, does not relate to assets in which the applicant has any claim or interest at the time of grant. Indeed, unlike other sorts of interlocutory injunction, they create a right where none existed before. If a third party was detrimentally and unfairly affected by an interlocutory injunction his interest could either be put before the court by the defendant or he could himself make an application to the court, either to vary or discharge the injunction or to extend to him the benefit of the cross-undertaking. In respect of a freezing order, it was appropriate to make an order 'The applicant will pay the reasonable costs of anyone other than the respondent which had been incurred as a result of this order . . . if the court later finds that this order has caused such person loss, and it decides that such persons should be compensated for the loss, the applicant will comply with any order that the court may make'. It would not be appropriate to make the grant of an injunction, other than a freezing order, conditional on the claimant undertaking to pay the reasonable costs of any third party incurred as a result of the order (*Miller Brewing Co v Ruhi Enterprises Ltd* (2003) Times, 6 June, ChD).

WITNESSES

[34.19]

The claimant had issued and served a witness summons under CPR Part 34 on an employee of the Halifax Bank of Scotland plc requiring his attendance at the hearing of the action and the production of the bank's documentation. It was an anomaly that if the application had been made under s 34 of the Supreme Court (now Senior Courts) Act 1981, the rules would have provided that the person against whom the order had been made could recover the costs of compliance with the order, but there is no equivalent provision in Part 34 to enable a witness to recover his costs of complying with a summons. The courts of first instance have jurisdiction under CPR Rule 48.2 to award costs where it is just and reasonable and therefore it was inappropriate to order that the bank be joined to the proceedings for the purposes of costs and that the claimant be ordered to pay the costs incurred by the bank in complying with the summons (*Individual Homes Ltd v Macbream Investments Ltd* [2002] 46 LS Gaz R 32, ChD).

In *Phillips v Symes* [2004] EWHC 2330 (Ch), (2004) Times, 5 November a cost order was made against an expert witness who by his evidence had caused significant expense to be incurred in a flagrant reckless disregarded of his duties to the court.

The claimant in a fraudulent conspiracy with the first named defendant (V) brought a road traffic accident claim for damages against him. V's insurers contended that the claim was bogus and were joined as second defendant (G) to contest the claim and to counterclaim. The judge dismissed the claim as fraudulent. At the trial a Mr Khan (K) gave evidence which the judge disbelieved concluding that he too was involved in the conspiracy. G then joined K as a party for the purpose of seeking a costs order against him, which the judge refused to make under the mistaken belief that it had to be shown that the non-party was a funder or controller of the litigation before a non-party costs order could be made. Nevertheless on appeal the Court of Appeal refused to make a non-party costs order against K on the grounds it would be exceptional for an order to be made against a non-party where the applicant had a cause of action against the non-party and could have joined him as a party to the original proceedings. Witness immunity was another reason why the court did not exercise its discretion to award costs against K (*Oriakhel v (1) Vickers (2) Groupama Insurance Co Ltd (3) Khan (4) Graham Coffey & Co* [2008] EWCA Civ 748, [2008] All ER (D) 69 (Jul)).

SOLICITORS

(a) Funders

[34.20]

In a previous edition I wrote:

> 'In *Arkin v Borchard* the court did not suggest that it was in any way unlawful or against public policy for impecunious litigants to be funded in this way provided

there is a level playing field. The implications are wide-ranging. Is not a solicitor who invests his time, and perhaps funds disbursements, a 'commercial funder who is financing part of the costs of the litigation in a manner which facilitates access to justice and which is not otherwise objectionable'? Accordingly should not a solicitor who in return for a substantial success fee acts for an impecunious client without insurance cover for the defendant's costs if the claim fails be similarly liable? Otherwise lawyers acting under a CFA with a success fee can win the lottery without even buying a ticket.

I shall not be popular for again suggesting that lawyers entering into CFA agreements risk incurring personal liability. Quite simply, the financing of litigation by a solicitor is maintenance and because he seeks to profit out of it, it is champertous maintenance. Success fees are the solicitor's share of the proceeds of litigation. Champerty is unlawful and therefore a champertous retainer is unenforceable: that is why it was necessary in s 58(3) of the Courts and Legal Services Act 1990 to provide that a CFA should not be unenforceable for that reason alone. Section 58(3) did not purport to abolish a solicitor's liability to a third party as the maintainer of litigation.

Lawful, or justifiable, maintenance is no longer against public policy. In the words of Lord Scarman in *Wallersteiner v Moir (No 2)* [1975] 1 All ER 849. 'The maintenance of other people's litigation is no longer regarded as a mischief: trade unions, trade protection societies, insurance companies and the State do it regularly and frequently'. But, as was said by Lord Denning in *Hill v Archbold* [1968] 1 QB 686, and confirmed in case after case thereafter: 'It is perfectly justifiable and is accepted by everyone as lawful, *provided always that the one who supports the litigation, if it fails, pays the costs of the other side*'.

Hodgson v Imperial Tobacco Ltd [1998] 2 All ER 673 is often quoted as authority to the contrary. It is not. The court in *Hodgson* simply held that the existence of a CFA should not make a legal adviser's position as to costs any worse than in any other form of funding. The court was concerned with the solicitor's liability as a solicitor and not as a maintainer of litigation. The words 'maintenance' and 'champerty' are nowhere mentioned in the judgment, nor did the Court of Appeal consider any of the authorities. It did not say that a CFA put a solicitor in a better position than any other maintainer of litigation, and why should it? Why should a successful defendant be in a worse position against a maintainer of litigation because he is a member of the legal profession who, like other professional maintainers, is making a profit out of it? My advice to solicitors and clients alike is – keep taking out after-the-event insurance!'

And it came to pass in *Myatt v National Coal Board* [2007] EWCA Civ 307, [2007] 1 WLR 1559.

The Court of Appeal had dismissed the claimants' appeals against the finding of the costs judge that the conditional fee agreements they had entered into with their solicitors were unenforceable and therefore although the four claimants had each succeeded in their claim for damages for personal injuries the indemnity principle precluded them from recovering costs from the defendants.

The claimants had no insurance against any liability for costs because it was a condition precedent to the liability of the insurers under the claimants' ATE policies that enforceable CFAs were in place. In those circumstances the defendant sought an order for the costs of the appeals against the solicitors under s 51 of the Supreme Court (now Senior Courts) Act 1981.

There were 60 other cases where clients had entered into CFAs with the solicitors in similar circumstances who had a total a sum in the region of £200,000 at stake.

The four claimants also had a financial interest in the appeals because they were liable for their own disbursements which, including the ATE premium, averaged £2,500 to be paid out of their modest damages of £3,000–£4,000.

In his judgment in *Tolstoy-Miloslavsky v Aldington* [1996] 1 WLR 736 Rose LJ said at page 743:

'Sections 51(1) and (3) of the Supreme Court Act 1981 do not confer jurisdiction to make an order for costs against legal representatives when acting as legal representatives . . .

There are only three categories of conduct which can give rise to an order for costs against a solicitor:

1. It is within the wasted costs jurisdiction of section 51(6) and (7);
2. It is otherwise a breach of duty to the court, such as even before the Judicature Acts could found an order, eg if he acts even unwittingly without authority or in breach of an undertaking;
3. If he acts outside the role of solicitor, eg in a private capacity or as a true third party funder for someone else.'

Roch LJ in the same case put it in much the same way:

'The legal representative who acts as a legal representative does not make himself a quasi-party and no jurisdiction to make an order for costs against him under section 51(1) (3) arises. However, a legal representative who goes beyond conducting proceedings as a legal representative and behaves as a quasi party will not be immune from a costs order under section 51(1) and (3) merely because he is a barrister or a solicitor.'

The third category described by Rose LJ in *Tolstoy* should be understood as including a solicitor who is 'a real party . . . in very important and critical respects' and who 'not merely funds the proceedings but substantially also contributes, or at any rate, is to benefit from them'. The mere fact that a solicitor is on the record prosecuting proceedings for his or her client is not fatal to an application by the successful opposing party under s 51(1) and (3) of the Supreme Court (now Senior Courts) Act 1981, that the solicitor should pay some or all of the costs.

Suppose that the claimants had no financial interest in the outcome of the appeal at all because the solicitors had assumed liability for all the disbursements with no right of recourse against the clients. In that event, the only party with an interest in the appeal would be the solicitors. They would undoubtedly be acting outside the role of solicitor, as envisaged by Rose LJ.

In these circumstances it would be very surprising if the fact that the claimants had a modest financial interest meant that the solicitor's financial interest counted for nothing when deciding what order for costs it was just to make.

It was salutary to recall that Lord Brown said that the non-party need not be the only real party to the litigation, provided that he is 'a real party . . . in very important and critical respects'. There is no good reason why those observations should not apply with equal force to solicitors and non-solicitors.

There is no doubt that there is jurisdiction to make an order under s 51(3) against a solicitor where litigation is pursued by the client for the benefit or to a substantial degree for the benefit of the solicitor.

The authorities do not set out in definitive terms exactly what is the borderline between the case where a solicitor acts purely as such in the ordinary way on behalf of a client and is therefore immune from the jurisdiction of the court under ss 51(1) and (3), and on the other hand a case where the solicitor's acts are such that he is within the scope of that jurisdiction. Although the court in *Tolstoy* noted the enactment of the conditional fee provisions of the Courts and Legal Services Act 1990, it did not have occasion to consider the implications of those provisions in detail.

There may be cases of litigation funded on a conventional private basis where it may be said to be in the interests of the appellant's solicitor that an appeal be brought and succeed on question of costs, for example if the opponent is clearly able to pay, whereas the client would have greater difficulty in paying. Such a case would however be fundamentally different from this one as regards the profit cost element because here the claimants were and are not at risk at all for the profit costs.

Although the decision in favour of the respondents and against the solicitors in the present case is of wider relevance its relevance is limited to cases where the litigation is funded by a CFA and where the issue is as to the enforceability of the CFA.

It was correct to regard the solicitors in relation to the conduct of the appeal as having acted in part for the sake of their own benefit in a respect which was of no interest or concern to their clients, and as having acted as a matter of business to seek to establish their right to be paid, not by their own clients in practice, the profit costs on these four cases and all the others of which these were representative.

In those circumstances, which could be common in relation to cases where the enforceability of a CFA is at stake but would be most unusual in any other situation, it was proper to regard the solicitors as having acted in respect of the appeal in a dual capacity; acting for their clients, certainly and with a real interest of those clients to protect, but primarily acting for their own sake.

The fair and just order to make in this case was to order the solicitors to pay 50% of the defendant's costs of the appeal. In arriving at this percentage the court took into account the fact that the claimants had a real financial interest in the success of the appeals; their disbursements represented approximately one third of the total costs incurred by them before their claims were settled. It also took into account the fact that the solicitors were not given a warning until the appeals had been dismissed that an application for costs might be made against them.

(b) Lack of authority

[34.21]

Skylight Maritime SA v Ascot Underwriting [2005] EWHC 15 (Comm), [2005] NLJR 139, 18 January were proceedings brought against solicitors on the grounds of breach of warranty of authority in commencing proceedings on behalf of a one-yacht Panamanian company against insurance brokers without authority from the client to begin proceedings. In such circumstances the general rule is that the court has jurisdiction to make a summary order against the solicitor for the costs incurred by the opposite party caused by the solicitor's unauthorised conduct (*Yonge v Toynbee* [1910] 1 KB 215). However, in this case there were substantial issues of fact that could not be resolved in the course of the usual summary procedure and therefore the application for a summary determination was refused.

In *(1) David Warner (2) SMP Trustees Ltd v Merriman White (A Firm)* [2008] EWHC 1129 (Ch) a firm of solicitors issued a petition purporting to act on behalf of the two petitioners, when it had, in fact, only obtained instructions from one of them and the other had no knowledge of the proceedings until it was ordered to give security for costs. In striking the other party from the petition and ordering the solicitors to pay the costs of the other parties the court drew attention to the Guide to the Professional Conduct of Solicitors rule 2.01(1)(c) and rule 12.05 (now Rule 2.01 of the Solicitors' Code of Conduct 2007) which was explicit about a solicitor's duty to ensure that there were clear instructions from a client where instructions are given by someone else.

CHAPTER 35

COSTS PAYABLE UNDER A CONTRACT

[35.1]

Rule 48.3 and its supplementary Practice Direction deal with the amount of costs where costs are payable pursuant to a contract.

[35.2]

CPR Rule 48.3: Amount of costs where costs are payable pursuant to a contract
(1)   Where the court assesses (whether by the summary or detailed procedure) costs which are payable by the paying party to the receiving party under the terms of a contract, the costs payable under those terms are, unless the contract expressly provides otherwise, to be presumed to be costs which—
    (a)   have been reasonably incurred; and
    (b)   are reasonable in amount,
and the court will assess them accordingly.
(The Costs Practice Direction sets out circumstances where the court may order otherwise)
(2)   This rule does not apply where the contract is between a solicitor and his client.

[35.3]

CPD Section 50 Amount of costs where costs are payable under a contract: Rule 48.3

50.1   *Where the court is assessing costs payable under a contract, it may make an order that all or part of the costs payable under the contract shall be disallowed if it is satisfied by the paying party that costs have been unreasonably incurred or are unreasonable in amount.*
50.2   *Rule 48.3 only applies if the court is assessing costs payable under a contract. It does not—*
(1)   *require the court to make an assessment of such costs; or*
(2)   *require a mortgagee to apply for an order for those costs that he has a contractual right to recover out of the mortgage funds.*
50.3   *The following principles apply to costs relating to a mortgage—*
(1)   *An order for the payment of costs of proceedings by one party to another is always a discretionary order: section 51 of the Senior Courts Act 1981.*
(2)   *Where there is a contractual right to the costs the discretion should ordinarily be exercised so as to reflect that contractual right.*
(3)   *The power of the court to disallow a mortgagee's costs sought to be added to the mortgage security is a power that does not derive from section 51, but from the power of the courts of equity to fix the terms on which redemption will be allowed.*
(4)   *A decision by a court to refuse costs in whole or in part to a mortgagee litigant may be—*
    (a)   *a decision in the exercise of the section 51 discretion;*

(b)   a decision in the exercise of the power to fix the terms on which redemption will be allowed;

(c)   a decision as to the extent of a mortgagee's contractual right to add his costs to the security; or

(d)   a combination of two or more of these things.

The statements of case in the proceedings or the submissions made to the court may indicate which of the decisions has been made.

(5)   A mortgagee is not to be deprived of a contractual or equitable right to add costs to the security merely by reason of an order for payment of costs made without reference to the mortgagee's contractual or equitable rights, and without any adjudication as to whether or not the mortgagee should be deprived of those costs.

(1)   Where the contract entitles a mortgagee to—

(a)   add the costs of litigation relating to the mortgage to the sum secured by it;

(b)   require a mortgagor to pay those costs, or

(c)   both,

the mortgagor may make an application for the court to direct that an account of the mortgagee's costs be taken.

(Rule 25.1(1)(n) provides that the court may direct that a party file an account)

(2)   The mortgagor may then dispute an amount in the mortgagee's account on the basis that it has been unreasonably incurred or is unreasonable in amount.

(3)   Where a mortgagor disputes an amount, the court may make an order that the disputed costs are assessed under rule 48.3.

MORTGAGES

[35.4]

Many contracts, particularly mortgages, contain provisions to the effect that one or other party will be liable for the costs incurred pursuant to the contract. Under the terms of a mortgage deed, the mortgagee is usually entitled to add to his security his usual and proper costs of proceedings between himself and the mortgagor or any surety. He does not require an order from the court to do so. However, the court has an equitable jurisdiction to disallow all or part of a mortgagee's costs as being unreasonably incurred or of an unreasonable amount, in fixing the terms of redemption. In addition to his costs of proceedings between himself and the mortgagor, a mortgagee may recover the reasonable and proper costs of proceedings between himself and a third party where what is impugned is the title to the estate. But where a third party impugns the title to a mortgage or the enforcement or exercise of some right or power accruing to the mortgagee under it, the mortgagee's costs of the proceedings, even though reasonable and proper, are not recoverable from the mortgagor (*Parker-Tweedale v Dunbar Bank plc (No 2)* [1991] Ch 26, CA).

There is a presumption that costs payable under a mortgage or any other contract are reasonably and properly incurred and such costs are to be paid on the indemnity basis (*Gomba Holdings (UK) Ltd v Minories Finance Ltd (No 2)* [1993] Ch 171, CA).

Rule 48.3 is a summary of the law as I have explained it. There was, however, uncertainty arising out of the original Practice Direction which was para 50.1 only. This was interpreted by some as meaning that the court now had to assess the costs payable under a contract and that mortgagees had to obtain an order before they could add their costs to the mortgage debt. Accordingly the Practice Direction was expanded into its present comprehensive statement of the law and practice. But even that was not enough. Paragraph 13.2 of the Practice Direction supplementing Rule 44.7 provides that the general rule is that the court *should* make a summary assessment of the costs at the end of fast track trial or any hearing that has lasted not more than a day. That necessitated inserting a new para 13.3 as follows:

'The general rule in paragraph 1 does not apply to a mortgagee's costs incurred in mortgage possession proceedings or other proceedings relating to a mortgage unless the mortgagee asks the court to make an order for his costs to be paid by another party. Paragraphs 49.3 and 49.4 deal in more detail with costs relating to mortgages.'

The additional para 50.4 contains the useful provision for a mortgagor to apply for a direction that an account of the mortgagee's costs be taken and for any disputed costs to be assessed under Rule 48.3.

In the November 2003 update of his Review of the Law of Costs in England and Wales, the Senior Costs Judge, Peter Hurst, said the costs payable by a borrower to a mortgage lender had been giving rise to concern from the judiciary who have to deal with debt collection and repossession cases. He continued 'Recent experience shows that mortgage lenders are becoming far more aggressive in their repossession claims, demanding repossession in respect of debtors who have been prompt payers for many years but who then slip briefly into arrear. The lender is able to add a figure for costs to the mortgage debt which the debtor (having agreed to do so in the original deed) has no option but to pay. The amounts added to mortgage debt in this way are frequently out of all proportion to what is reasonable. In many cases the courts are effectively powerless to intervene.'

LANDLORD AND TENANT

[35.5]

Forcelux Ltd v Binnie [2009] EWCA Civ 1077, [2010] HLR 340, [2009] All ER (D) 234 (Oct)

The tenant had fallen into arrears with payment of ground rent and charges and the landlord obtained a default judgment against him. The landlord obtained an order for possession which a district judge set aside in the exercise of his discretion under CPR Rule 39.3 and granted relief from forfeiture on terms as to payment of outstanding monies. In the Court of Appeal confirmed the setting aside of the possession order. The landlord claimed to be entitled to its costs of the entirety of the proceedings on the basis that the tenant had covenanted in the lease to pay "all costs charges and expenses (including legal costs . . .) which may be incurred by the lessor in or in contemplation . . . of any steps or proceedings under Section 146 of the Landlord and Tenant Act 1925".

The Court of Appeal held that possession proceedings brought to enforce a right of re-entry following a notice under 146(1) of the Act were proceedings "under" that section. The possession action was within the scope of the words "any statutory proceedings" within the scope of the covenant. It followed that the application to set aside the possession order was as much an application as the application for relief and forfeiture coupled with it, and was also within the scope of those words. However, the tenant had been the substantial winner of the appeal. Even assuming that the contractual provisions in the lease covered the costs of the appeal, which was a matter of construction, the contractual right was not an absolute one and did not oust the jurisdiction of the court to make another order if there were good reason for doing so. In the circumstances, the tenant was entitled to a costs order which departed from the contract in the exercise of the court's discretion.

CONTRACTUAL COSTS

[35.6]

Venture Finance plc v Mead [2005] EWCA Civ 325, [2005] All ER (D) 376 (Mar)

Where the contractual obligation on each defendant was to pay all costs and expenses arising out of the recovery of monies under a deed of guarantee, the judge had erred by concluding that the only order for costs that gave effect to the parties' contractual rights was that each defendant should be liable for only 50% of the whole costs of the proceedings.

The claimant had obtained judgment by consent for less than one-third of the amount claimed but there was nothing that enabled the judge to decide why it had been willing to settle for that sum. It was impossible to say that one party had obviously won and the other had obviously lost. The judge had erred in principle. He had wrongly thought that the only order for costs that gave effect to the parties' contractual rights was that each defendant should be liable for only 50% of the whole costs of the proceedings. The contractual obligation on each defendant was to pay all costs and expenses arising out of the recovery of monies from that defendant under the guarantee. The right course for the judge was to consider, in relation to each defendant, the extent to which the whole costs of the proceedings could be said to arise out of the claim to recover under the guarantee obligations of that defendant. That approach might have led to a conclusion that a proper proportion of the whole costs of proceedings to be awarded against each defendant was 100%, or some lower proportion. It was difficult to see how the appropriate proportion could be as low as 50%. If the claimant could not recover 100% of its costs from the second defendant, it would be left with a shortfall as the first defendant was bankrupt.

The judge had also erred in thinking that he was required to apply CPR rule 48.3 (Amount of costs where costs are payable under a contract) when making the costs order. That rule applied only at the stage when the court was assessing costs and not when it was deciding by whom costs should be paid. The judge should have been exercising his discretion under CPR rule 44.3 and the Supreme Court (now Senior Courts) Act 1981, s 51(3).

CHAPTER 36

TRUSTEES AND PERSONAL REPRESENTATIVES

[36.1]

CPR Rule 48.4: Limitations on court's power to award costs in favour of trustee or personal representative

(1)   This rule applies where—
    (a)   a person is or has been a party to any proceedings in the capacity of trustee or personal representative; and
    (b)   rule 48.3 does not apply.

(2)   The general rule is that he is entitled to be paid the costs of those proceedings, insofar as they are not recovered from or paid by any other person, out of the relevant trust fund or estate.

(3)   Where he is entitled to be paid any of those costs out of the fund or estate, those costs will be assessed on the indemnity basis.

[36.2]

CPD Section 50A Limitation on court's power to award costs in favour of trustee or personal representative: Rule 48.4

50A.1   *A trustee or personal representative is entitled to an indemnity out of the relevant trust fund or estate for costs properly incurred, which may include costs awarded against the trustee or personal representative in favour of another party.*

50A.2   *Whether costs were properly incurred depends on all the circumstances of the case, and may, for example, depend on –*

    (1)   whether the trustee or personal representative obtained directions from the court before bringing or defending the proceedings;

    (2)   whether the trustee or personal representative acted in the interests of the fund or estate or in substance for a benefit other than that of the estate, including his own; and

    (3)   whether the trustee or personal representative acted in some way unreasonably in bringing or defending, or in the conduct of, the proceedings.

50A.3   *The trustee or personal representative is not to be taken to have acted in substance for a benefit other than that of the fund by reason only that he has defended a claim in which relief is sought against him personally.*

ENTITLEMENT TO COSTS OUT OF THE TRUST OR ESTATE

[36.3]

Trustees and personal representatives have a duty to protect the trust fund or the estate and are entitled to their costs on the indemnity basis of any proceedings undertaken in their capacity of trustee or personal representative out of the trust fund or estate, less, of course, any costs recovered from or paid by another party or source. Such costs are presumed to have been of a reasonable amount and properly incurred, unless they were incurred contrary to the duty of the trustees or personal representatives or the trustee or personal representative has acted for a benefit other than that of the fund or estate.

PRE-EMPTIVE ORDERS

[36.4]

If trustees or personal representatives are concerned that it might be suggested that they have acted unreasonably or in their own interests they may apply to the court before commencing or defending proceedings for an order that, win or lose, they will be entitled to their costs out of the property in dispute, before the facts have been fully investigated and before the law has been fully argued. Because, however, such an order could involve the expenditure of a substantial part of the funds or estate, there is a strong public interest in the Attorney-General being represented on the application (*Re Beddoe* [1893] 1 Ch 547, CA). It is known as a 'Beddoe application'.

PROSPECTIVE COSTS ORDERS

[36.5]

PRACTICE STATEMENT (TRUST PROCEEDINGS: PROSPECTIVE COSTS ORDERS)

1 May 2001 ([2001] 3 All ER 574, ChD)

(1)   This practice statement is about the costs of applications by trustees, or beneficiaries, or other person concerned, in relation to the administration of a trust including questions of construction, questions relating to the exercise of powers conferred by the trust, or questions as to the validity of the trust.

(2)   Where trustees have the power to agree to pay the costs of some other party to such an application, and exercise properly such a power, CPR Rule 48.3 applies. In such a case, an order is not required and the trustees are entitled to recover out of the trust fund any costs which they pay pursuant to the agreement made in the exercise of such power.

(3)   Where the trustees do not have, or decide not to exercise, a power to make such an agreement, the trustees or the party concerned may apply to the court at any stage of the proceedings for an order that the costs of any party to the application referred to in paragraph 1 above (including the costs of the trustees) shall be paid out of the fund (a 'prospective costs order').

(4)   The court, on an application for a prospective costs order, may (a) in the case of the trustees' costs, authorise the trustees to raise and meet such costs out of the fund; (b) in the case of the costs of any other party, authorise or direct the trustees to pay such costs (or any part of them, or the costs incurred up to a particular time) out of the trust fund to be assessed, if not agreed by the trustees,

on the indemnity basis or, if the court directs, on the standard basis, and to make payments from time to time on account of such costs. A model form of order is set out at the end of this practice statement.

(5)   The court will always consider whether it is possible to deal with the application for a prospective costs order on paper without a hearing and in an ordinary case would expect to be able to do so. The trustees must consider whether a hearing is needed for any reason. If they consider that it is they should say so and explain why in their evidence. If any party to the application referred to in paragraph 1 above (or any other person interested in the trust fund) considers that a hearing is necessary (for instance because he wishes to oppose the making of a prospective costs order) this should be stated, and the reasons explained, in his evidence, if any, or otherwise in a letter to the court.

(6)   If the court would be minded to refuse the application on a consideration of the papers alone, the parties will be notified and given the opportunity, within a stated time to ask for a hearing.

(7)   The evidence in support of an application for a prospective costs order should be given by witness statement. The trustees and the applicant (if different) must ensure full disclosure of the relevant matters to show that the case is one which falls within the category of case where a prospective costs order can properly be made.

(8)   The model form of order is designed for use in the more straightforward cases, where a question needs to be determined which has arisen in the administration of the trust, whether the claimants are the trustees or a beneficiary. The form may be adapted for use in less straightforward cases, in particular where the proceedings are hostile, but special factors may also have to be reflected in the terms of the order in such a case.

Sir Andrew Morritt

Vice Chancellor

COSTS AGAINST TRUSTEES

[36.6]

A trustee or personal representative who has acted outside his duty or has acted in his own interests or otherwise unreasonably not only will be unable to recover his costs out of the fund or estate, but he may be ordered to pay the costs of another party personally. Similarly, although trustees and personal representatives will generally be justified in making an application to obtain the opinion of the court on a matter of construction or difficulty, if they appeal against the court's decision unsuccessfully, they may expect to be ordered to pay the costs of the appeal personally (*Re Earl of Radnor's Will Trusts* (1890) 45 Ch D 402, CA). Only in exceptional circumstances, say, for example, where large interests are at stake or where the interests of unborn persons are affected, will the costs be ordered to be paid out of the estate.

[36.7]

CPR Rule 47.17A: Detailed assessment procedure where costs are payable out of a fund other than the community legal service fund

(1)   Where the court is to assess costs which are payable out of a fund other than the Community Legal Service Fund, the receiving party may commence detailed assessment proceedings by filing a request in the relevant practice form.

(2)   A request under paragraph (1) must be filed within 3 months after the date when the right to detailed assessment arose.

(3)   The court may direct that the party seeking assessment serve a copy of the request on any person who has a financial interest in the outcome of the assessment.

(4)   The court will, on receipt of the request for assessment, provisionally assess the costs without the attendance of the receiving party, unless it considers that a hearing is necessary.

(5)   After the court has provisionally assessed the bill, it will return the bill to the receiving party.

(6)   The court will fix a date for an assessment hearing if the party informs the court, within 14 days after he receives the provisionally assessed bill, that he wants the court to hold such a hearing.

[36.8]

CPD Section 44 Costs of detailed assessment proceedings where costs are payable out of a fund other than the Community Legal Service Fund: Rule 47.17A

44.1   *Rule 47.17A provides that the court will make a provisional assessment of a bill of costs payable out of a fund (other than the Community Legal Service Fund) unless it considers that a hearing is necessary. It also enables the court to direct under rule 47.17A(3) that the receiving party must serve a copy of the request for assessment and copies of the documents which accompany it, on any person who has a financial interest in the outcome of the assessment.*

(a)   *A person has a financial interest in the outcome of the assessment if the assessment will or may affect the amount of money or property to which he is or may become entitled out of the fund.*

(b)   *Where an interest in the fund is itself held by a trustee for the benefit of some other person, that trustee will be treated as the person having such a financial interest.*

(c)   *'Trustee' includes a personal representative, receiver or any other person acting in a fiduciary capacity.*

44.3   *The request for a detailed assessment of costs out of the fund should be in Form N258B, be accompanied by the documents set out at paragraph 42.3(a) to (e) and (g) above and the following—*

(a)   *a statement signed by the receiving party giving his name, address for service, reference, telephone number, fax number and,*

(b)   *a statement of the postal address of any person who has a financial interest in the outcome of the assessment, to which the court may send notice of any hearing; and*

(c)   *in respect of each person stated to have such an interest if such person is a child or protected party, a statement to that effect.*

44.4   *The court will decide, having regard to the amount of the bill, the size of the fund and the number of persons who have a financial interest, which of those persons should be served. The court may dispense with service on all or some of them.*

44.5   *Where the court makes an order dispensing with service on all such persons it may proceed at once to make a provisional assessment, or, if it decides that a hearing is necessary, give appropriate directions. Before deciding whether a hearing is necessary under this rule, the court may require the receiving party to provide further information relating to the bill.*

(1)   *Where the court has provisionally assessed a bill of costs, it will send to the receiving party, a notice in Form N253 of the amount of costs which the court proposes to allow together with the bill itself. If the receiving party is legally*

represented the legal representative should, if the provisional assessment is to be accepted, then complete the bill.

(2) The court will fix a date for a detailed assessment hearing, if the receiving party informs the court within 14 days after he receives the notice in Form N253 of the amount allowed on the provisional assessment, that he wants the court to hold such a hearing.

44.7 Where the court makes an order that a person who has a financial interest is to be served with a copy of the request for assessment, it may give directions about service and about the hearing.

44.8 The court will give at least 14 days' notice of the time and place of the detailed assessment hearing to the receiving party and, to any person who has a financial interest in the outcome of the assessment and has been served with a copy of the request for assessment.

44.9 If the receiving party, or any other party or any person who has a financial interest in the outcome of assessment, wishes to make an application in the detailed assessment proceedings, the provisions of Part 23 (General Rules about Applications for Court Orders) applies.

44.10 If the receiving party is legally represented the legal representative must in order to complete the bill after the assessment make clear the correct figures allowed in respect of each item and must recalculate the summary of the bill if appropriate.

CHAPTER 37

CHILDREN AND PROTECTED PARTIES

GLOSSARY

[37.1]

The useful umbrella description of a 'party under a disability' was perceived to be politically incorrect and has gone. The word 'minor', itself a recent replacement for 'infant', has now given way to the word 'child'– despite the irrefutable fact that we are all someone's child. CPR Rule 21.1(2) defines 'child' as a person under 18 and changes the description 'patient' to 'protected party', who it defines as a party, or an intended party, who lacks capacity to conduct the proceedings. The terms 'next friend' and 'guardian *ad litem*' were replaced by 'litigation friend' in civil litigation. Guardians *ad litem* are alive and well in Children Act 1989 proceedings.

LITIGATION FRIEND

[37.2]

A protected party must have a litigation friend to conduct proceedings on his behalf (CPR Rule 21.2(1)) and a child must have one unless the court permits the child to conduct his own proceedings (CPR Rule 21.2(3)). Where the child or protected party is a claimant, the litigation friend must give an undertaking to pay any costs which the child or protected party may be ordered to pay in relation to the proceedings, subject to any right he may have to be repaid from the assets of the child or protected party whether the litigation friend has become one without a court order (CPR Rule 2.3(1)(*e*)) or has been appointed under a court order (CPR Rule 3.4(4)). The litigation friend's liability for costs continues until the child or protected party serves notice that the litigation friend's appointment has ceased (giving his address for service and stating whether or not he intends to carry on the proceedings) or the litigation friend serves notice on the parties that his appointment to act has ceased (CPR Rule 21.9(6)).

DETAILED ASSESSMENT

[37.3]

CPR Rule 48.5: Costs where money is payable by or to a child or protected party
(1)   This rule applies to any proceedings where a party is a child or protected party and—

(a)   money is ordered or agreed to be paid to, or for the benefit of, that party; or

(b)   money is ordered to be paid by him or on his behalf.

('Child' and 'protected party' have the same meaning as in rule 21.1(2))

(2)   The general rule is that—

(a)   the court must order a detailed assessment of the costs payable by, or out of the money belonging to, any party who is a child or protected party; and

(b)   on an assessment under paragraph (a), the court must also assess any costs payable to that party in the proceedings, unless—

(i)   the court has issued a default costs certificate in relation to those costs under rule 47.11; or

(ii)   the costs are payable in proceedings to which Section II of Part 45 applies.

(3)   The court need not order detailed assessment of costs in the circumstances set out in the Costs Practice Direction.

(4)   Where—

(a)   a claimant is a child or protected party; and

(b)   a detailed assessment has taken place under paragraph (2)(a),

the only amount payable by the child or protected party is the amount which the court certifies as payable.

(This rule applies to a counterclaim by or on behalf of child or protected party by virtue of rule 20.3)

[37.4]

CPD Section 51 Costs where money is payable by or to a child or protected party: Rule 48.5

51.1   *The circumstances in which the court need not order the assessment of costs under rule 48.5(3) are as follows:*

(a)   *where there is no need to do so to protect the interests of the child or protected party or his estate;*

(b)   *where another party has agreed to pay a specified sum in respect of the costs of the child or protected party and the solicitor acting for the child or protected party has waived the right to claim further costs;*

(c)   *where the court has decided the costs payable to the child or protected party by way of summary assessment and the solicitor acting for the child or protected party has waived the right to claim further costs;*

(d)   *where an insurer or other person is liable to discharge the costs which the child or protected party would otherwise be liable to pay to his solicitor and the court is satisfied that the insurer or other person is financially able to discharge those costs.*

[37.5]

Rule 48.5 is designed to protect the interests of a child or protected party and to prevent exploitation by unscrupulous legal representatives or litigation friends. Generally, detailed assessment is required of any costs payable by a child or protected party to his solicitor and when such an assessment takes place the court must also assess any costs payable to that party in the proceedings, unless a default costs certificate has been issued.

The court is given the discretion to dispense with a detailed assessment where it is not needed to protect the interests of the child or protected party:

(a)   where another party has agreed to pay a specified sum in respect of the costs and the solicitor has waived the right to claim any further costs from the child or protected party;

(b)   where the court has decided the amount of costs payable by way of summary assessment; and

(c)   where an insurer or other person is liable to discharge the costs which the child or protected party would otherwise be liable to pay and the court is satisfied that the person liable is financially able to discharge the costs.

EXPENSES INCURRED BY A LITIGATION FRIEND

[37.6]

From 1 October 2005 CPR Rule 21.11A and section 8A.1 of the supplementary Practice Direction provide that a litigation friend who incurs expenses on behalf of a child or protected party in any proceedings is entitled to recover the amount paid or payable out of any money recovered or paid into court to the extent that it has been reasonably incurred and is reasonable in amount. Expenses may include all or part of an insurance premium, as defined by rule 42.2(1)(m) and interest on a loan taken out to pay an insurance premium or other recoverable disbursement. Here they are:

[37.7]

21.11A Expenses incurred by a litigation friend

(1)   In proceedings to which rule 21.11 applies, a litigation friend who incurs expenses on behalf of a child or protected party in any proceedings is entitled to recover the amount paid or payable out of any money recovered or paid into court to the extent that it –

(a)   has been reasonably incurred; and

(b)   is reasonable in amount.

(2)   Expenses may include all or part of –

(a)   an insurance premium, as defined by rule 43.2(1)(m); or

(b)   interest on a loan taken out to pay an insurance premium or other recoverable disbursement.

(3)   No application may be made under this rule for expenses that –

(a)   are of a type that may be recoverable on an assessment of costs payable by or out of money belonging to a child or protected party; but

(b)   are disallowed in whole or in part on such an assessment.

(Expenses which are also 'costs' as defined in rule 43.2(1)(a) are dealt with under rule 48.5(2)).

(4)   In deciding whether the expense was reasonably incurred and reasonable in amount, the court must have regard to all the circumstances of the case including the factors set out in rule 44.5(3).

(5)   When the court is considering the factors to be taken into account in assessing the reasonableness of expenses incurred by the litigation friend on behalf of a child or protected party, it will have regard to the facts and

circumstances as they reasonably appeared to the litigation friend or child's or protected party's legal representative when the expense was incurred.

(6)　Where the claim is settled or compromised, or judgment is given, on terms that an amount not exceeding £5,000 is paid to the child or protected party, the total amount the litigation friend may recover under paragraph (1) of this rule shall not exceed 25% of the sum so agreed or awarded, unless the Court directs otherwise. Such total amount shall not exceed 50% of the sum so agreed or awarded.

[37.8]

Section 8A. Expenses incurred by litigation friend

8A.1　*A litigation friend may make a claim for expenses under rule 21.11A(1) –*

(a)　*where the court has ordered an assessment of costs under rule 48.5(2), at the detailed assessment hearing;*

(b)　*where the litigation friend's expenses are not of a type which would be recoverable as costs on an assessment of costs between the parties, to the Master or District Judge at the hearing to approve the settlement or compromise under Part 21 (the Master or District Judge may adjourn the matter to the Costs Judge); or*

(c)　*where an assessment of costs under Part 48.5(2) is not required, and no approval under Part 21 is necessary, by a Part 23 application supported by a witness statement to a Costs Judge or District Judge as appropriate.*

8A.2　*In all circumstances, the litigation friend shall support a claim for expenses by filing a witness statement setting out –*

(i)　*the nature and amount of the expense;*

(ii)　*the reason the expense was incurred.*

SOLICITOR AND CLIENT

[37.9]

In *Scott v Harrogate Borough Council* (20 January 2003, unreported, Harrogate County Ct) the district judge ordered a deduction from the child's damages a conditional fee agreement administrative success fee of 10% and interest on a bank loan obtained to cover expenses, both of which were not recoverable from the defendant.

CHAPTER 38

LITIGANTS IN PERSON

THE STATUTE

[38.1]

The Litigants in Person Costs and Expenses Act 1975 provides that where any costs of a litigant in person (known affectionately as LIPs or 'lippies') are ordered to be paid by any other party to proceedings there may be allowed (subject to any rule of the court) on assessment or determination of the costs, sums in respect of any work done and any expenses and losses incurred by the litigant in or in connection with the proceedings. The provisions of the Act apply to all civil proceedings in the House of Lords, the Supreme Court, the Lands Tribunal and county courts in which any order is made that the costs of a LIP are to be paid by any other party to those proceedings or in any other way. Prior to the coming into force of the Act in April 1976, LIPs (other than those who were practising solicitors) whose costs were ordered to be paid were entitled to recover from the paying party no more than such out-of-pocket expenses as had been properly incurred. The Act enabled LIPs to recover the same category of costs as would have been allowed if the work had been done by a solicitor on the litigant's behalf, limited in amount to such sum as was required to compensate the litigant for the time he had reasonably spent on preparing and conducting his case, subject to any rules of court. Here are the Rule, as amended, and its supplementary Practice Direction:

RULE AND PRACTICE DIRECTION

[38.2]

CPR Rule 48.6: Litigants in Person

(1) This rule applies where the court orders (whether by summary assessment or detailed assessment) that the costs of a litigant in person are to be paid by any other person.

(2) The costs allowed under this rule must not exceed, except in the case of a disbursement, two-thirds of the amount which would have been allowed if the litigant in person had been represented by a legal representative.

(3) The litigant in person shall be allowed—

    (a) costs for the same categories of—

        (i) work; and

        (ii) disbursements,

    which would have been allowed if the work had been done or the disbursements had been made by a legal representative on the litigant in person's behalf;

(b)   the payments reasonably made by him for legal services relating to the conduct of the proceedings; and

(c)   the costs of obtaining expert assistance in assessing the costs claim.

(The Costs Practice Direction deals with who may be an expert for the purpose of paragraph (2)(c))

(4)   The amount of costs to be allowed to the litigant in person for any item of work claimed shall be—

(a)   where the litigant can prove financial loss, the amount that he can prove he has lost for time reasonably spent on doing the work; or

(b)   where the litigant cannot prove financial loss, an amount for the time reasonably spent on doing the work at the rate set out in the practice direction.

(5)   A litigant who is allowed costs for attending at court to conduct his case is not entitled to a witness allowance in respect of such attendance in addition to those costs.

(6)   For the purposes of this rule, a litigant in person includes—

(a)   a company or other corporation which is acting without a legal representative; and

(b)   a barrister, solicitor, solicitor's employee, manager of a body recognised under section 9 of the Administration of Justice Act 1985 or a person who, for the purposes of the Legal Services Act 2007, is an authorised person in relation to an activity which constitutes the conduct of litigation (within the meaning of that Act).

[38.3]

CPD Section 52 Litigants in person: Rule 48.6

52.1   *In order to qualify as an expert for the purpose of rule 48.6(3)(c) (expert assistance in connection with assessing the claim for costs), the person in question must be a*

(1)   *barrister,*

(2)   *solicitor,*

(3)   *Fellow of the Institute of Legal Executives,*

(4)   *Fellow of the Association of Law Costs Draftsmen,*

(5)   *law costs draftsman who is a member of the Academy of Experts,*

(6)   *law costs draftsman who is a member of the Expert Witness Institute.*

52.2   *Where a litigant in person wishes to prove that he has suffered financial loss he should produce to the court any written evidence he relies on to support that claim, and serve a copy of that evidence on any party against whom he seeks costs at least 24 hours before the hearing at which the question may be decided.*

52.3   *Where a litigant in person commences detailed assessment proceedings under rule 47.6 he should serve copies of that written evidence with the notice of commencement.*

52.4   *The amount, which may be allowed to a litigant in person under rule 46.3(5)(b) and rule 48.6(4), is £9.25 per hour.*

52.5   *Attention is drawn to rule 48.6(6)(b). A solicitor who, instead of acting for himself, is represented in the proceedings by his firm or by himself in his firm name, is not, for the purpose of the Civil Procedure Rules, a litigant in person.*

[38.4]

The Rules have always limited the costs recoverable by a litigant in person to two-thirds of the amount which would have been allowed to a legal representative. The reasoning behind this figure is that a solicitor's charges have usually included a 50% profit mark-up on his expense rate, but as an LIP may not make a profit out of the costs of litigation, the 50% is deducted, leaving two-thirds.

FINANCIAL LOSS

(a) Two categories

[38.5]

In previous editions I said the Rule was less than satisfactory. Although it was amended with effect from 2 December 2002 by the Civil Procedure (Amendment) Rules 2002 they provided that work done before 2 December 2002 is still governed by the previous Rule 48.6(3) and (4). Here they are:

(3)   Costs allowed to the litigant in person shall be—

(a)   such costs which would have been allowed if the work had been done or the disbursements made by a legal representative on the litigant in person's behalf;

(b)   the payments reasonably made by him for legal services relating to the conduct of the proceedings; and

(c)   the costs of obtaining expert assistance in connection with assessing the claim for costs.

(The Costs Practice Direction deals with who may be an expert for the purpose of paragraph (2)(c))

(4)   Subject to paragraph (2), the amount of costs to be allowed to the litigant in person for any item of work to which the costs relate shall, if he fails to prove financial loss, be an amount in respect of the time spent reasonably doing the work at the rate specified in the Costs Practice Direction.

[38.6]

The anomaly was that an LIP who could prove any financial loss, however small, crossed the threshold and was entitled to recover up to two-thirds of what a solicitor would have charged for all the work that he had done, whether or not it all caused a financial loss. Under the amended Rule 48.6(4)(a) the amount an LIP can now claim cannot exceed his financial loss. That is the first category. An LIP who cannot prove financial loss continues, under the new Rule 48.6(4)(b), to be able to recover for the amount of time reasonably spent at the prescribed rate, which is at present £9.25 an hour. That is the second category. But are the categories mutually exclusive? When the costs of an LIP in category 1 reach the limit of his financial loss, may he switch to category 2? Or may the wording of sub-Rule (4)(a) be interpreted as confining the LIP to category 1? I hope not, but if not, may an LIP jump from one category to the other for each item of work, depending on whether or not it resulted in financial loss, resulting in LIPs calculating which category would be most favourable to them at any particular stage? According to the senior costs judge, the SCCO spends a disproportionate amount of time dealing with the issue of financial loss, with 85% of LIPs failing to establish any relevant loss. He and the Civil Justice Council now propose that successful LIPs should be entitled to a simple flat (or a fixed fee in a scale scheme) whether or not they have sustained financial loss. A figure of £25 an hour has been mooted.

(b) Legal costs

[38.7]

Although a litigant may have acted in person without a solicitor on the record, he is nevertheless entitled to recover payments reasonably made for legal services relating to the conduct of the proceedings and the costs of obtaining expert assistance in connection with assessing the claim for costs, including representation on a detailed assessment. The categories of expert are identified in paragraph 5.1 of the Practice Direction.

The price of a LIP not using a solicitor was dramatically illustrated in *Agassi v Robinson (Inspector of Taxes)* [2005] EWCA Civ 1507, [2006] 1 All ER 900, 2 December. Former Wimbledon champion, Andre Agassi in his battle with the taxman retained a tax expert who was a member of the Chartered Institute of Taxation licensed to instruct counsel directly. No solicitors were involved. Mr Agassi was awarded his costs as a LIP. Were the tax expert's fees recoverable as costs under the general costs provisions of CPR rule 48.6? No. Although Mr Agassi could recover counsel's fee as a disbursement he was not entitled to recover as a litigant in person costs as a disbursement in respect of work done by the tax expert which would normally have been done by a solicitor. That meant he was not entitled to recover the costs of the tax expert providing general assistance to counsel. However, it could be appropriate to allow Mr Agassi at least part of the expert's fees as a disbursement. It might be possible to argue that the cost of discussing the issues with counsel, and assisting with the preparation of the skeleton argument etc was allowable as a disbursement, because the provision of that kind of assistance in a specialist esoteric area was not the kind of work that would normally be done by the solicitor instructed to conduct the appeals. Another way of making the same point is that it might be possible to characterise the specialist services as those of an expert.

The court observed that the solution to the problems raised by the case was for an organisation such as the Chartered Institute of Taxation to become an 'authorised body' within the meaning of s 28(5) of the Courts and Legal Services Act 1990, and for those members who wished to conduct litigation to become authorised litigators and thereby 'legal representatives' within the meaning of CPR rule 2.3(1).

The unhappy postscript for Mr Agassi was that the Revenue appealed on the merits and succeeded in the House of Lords, which awarded them their costs both in the House and in the Court of Appeal, so his inability to recover the tax expert's costs was in any event academic. Game, set and match to the Inspector of Taxes.

Agassi was followed in the SCCO in *Cuthbert v Gair* on 3 September 2008 reported in the Law Society Gazette of 16 October 2008 and the Journal of the Association of Law Costs Draftsmen of November 2008.

The claimant issued proceedings for damages for personal injuries suffered while attending an equestrian event, but served notice of discontinuance. On the detailed assessment of the defendants' costs, the defendants sought to recover payments made to a loss adjuster by the defendants' insurers, both before and after solicitors were instructed. The work of the loss adjuster under the first invoice included corresponding with the claimant's solicitor, investigating the accident, obtaining witness statements and dealing with documentation. That work was work that would normally be carried out by a solicitor and the defendants were not entitled to recover costs in respect of it.

In respect of a second invoice, for work done by the loss adjuster after solicitors had been instructed, it was necessary to assess the relationship between the defendants' solicitors and the loss adjuster. If the defendant's solicitors had sought assistance from the loss adjuster on an agency basis, then they would have been entitled to recover their costs, not as a disbursement, but as a profit cost, following *Crane v Canons Leisure Centre* [2007] EWCA Civ 1352, [2008] 2 All ER 931, [2008] NLJR 103. However no true agency agreement existed between the solicitors and the loss adjuster, there was no letter of instruction and no terms of engagement. On that basis, it was not possible for the defendants to recover the loss adjuster's fees after the solicitors had been instructed.

Furthermore, the work undertaken by the loss adjuster did not fall within the category of 'expert assistance' that otherwise might have rendered the costs recoverable (*Re Nossen's Letter Patent* [1969] 1 WLR 638. The present was a simple case of an insurer contracting out part of its work in order to investigate claims made against the insured. It was routine work, which many insurers would have undertaken in-house. The mere fact that the defendants' insurer chose to contract out that work did not render the costs recoverable.

Writing in the ALCD Journal, Roger Mallalieu observed that insurers do not normally seek to recover their own costs in subrogated claims, but do seek to recover the costs of solicitors who have been instructed. Subrogation merely allows the insurer to step into the insured's shoes and enjoy the insured's rights in relation to a third party. It does not create extra rights. The paying party is only liable for the insured's reasonable costs, not the insurers. To avoid this problem, a number of fictions are indulged in. First, the insured normally enters into a 'dual' retainer with the solicitor, alongside the insurer. Second, even if this does not happen, the court is happy to invent an 'implied retainer' between insured and solicitor to side step the indemnity principle. However here, there were no solicitors. This was no more than the insurer contracting out part of its own costs and it was no more recoverable than if the defendants had sought to claim the insurer's internal costs. There was no 'contractual nexus' which would have allowed the cost to be recovered in any event. Recovery would breach the indemnity principle. In the past, insurers did not seek to recover such costs, it being part of the administration costs and overheads they recouped through premiums. If recovery is now to be sought between the parties, Mr. Mallalieu suggested we are likely to see the instruction of solicitors at an earlier stage to ensure recoverability of such costs, which no doubt 'will in turn produce a variety of challenges on the basis of premature instruction, unreasonable conduct and the indemnity principle'.

(c) Fast track trial costs

[38.8]

The effect of the test of financial loss can become bizarre when applied to the fixed costs of fast track trials. Rule 46.3, which has not been amended, provides:

> (5) Where the party to whom fast track trial costs are to be awarded is a litigant in person, the court will award—
>
> (a) if the litigant in person can prove financial loss, two-thirds of the amount that would otherwise be awarded; or
>
> (b) if the litigant in person fails to prove financial loss, an amount in respect of the time spent reasonably doing the work at the rate specified in the costs practice direction.

This provision throws up a ludicrous anomaly. Rule 48.6(3) still provides that the costs allowed to a LIP shall be such costs as would have been allowed if the work had been done by a legal representative. Rule 46.2 provides that the court may not award less than the prescribed amounts and therefore any LIP who can show that he has suffered any financial loss, however small, must be awarded two-thirds of the prescribed amount. Surprisingly, it has not been possible to devise a means of circumventing this anomalous windfall to a LIP; the provision is clearly in breach of the indemnity principle, but, by their nature, no fixed costs take into account the receiving party's liability to his own solicitor.

(d) Re-appraisal

[38.9]

Despite the amendment of Rule 48.6(3) and (4) there is still a need for a full re-appraisal of the philosophy, practice and procedure relating to costs awarded to LIPs, which is now underway.

QUANTIFICATION

[38.10]

In *Law Society v Persaud* (1990) Times, 10 May, QBD, the defendant, who lived in South Africa, successfully contested proceedings brought by the Law Society and obtained an order for costs against them. On the assessment of his costs two items were disallowed: the cost of travelling from South Africa to England to defend the action in person of £1,391.25 and the cost of travelling between Birmingham and London of £74.

The claimants did not suggest that the defendant had been extravagant or acted in bad faith but that the disbursements did not come within the terms of Ord 62, r 18(1) (now Rule 48.6(3)) because no solicitor would have been allowed to charge as a disbursement the cost of travel from South Africa to England because the solicitor would already be in England and similarly the cost of travelling from Birmingham to London would not be incurred because the solicitor would already be in London.

The defendant justified his disbursements on the grounds that they were less than would have been the cost of instructing solicitors and counsel. The costs officer had assessed the costs of solicitors at £2,457 and allowed the defendant £1,643, being two-thirds of this, resulting in a saving to the claimants of £821 of the amount if the defendant had instructed solicitors. To this, the defendant argued, must be added the estimated cost of instructing counsel. The Law Society and the costs officer took the view that this was wrong, following the decision in *Hart v Aga Khan Foundation (UK)* [1984] 2 All ER 439, CA, where the Court of Appeal had held that the notional cost of counsel should not be allowed where counsel had not in fact been instructed. To apply that decision in *Persaud* was too literal an approach; it did not preclude the costs officer from allowing reasonable disbursements which had in fact been incurred. The costs sought to be recovered by the defendant did not exceed what would have been the actual cost and disbursements allowable to a London solicitor, including counsel's fees. There was still an overall saving to the other side as a result of the relevant party having chosen to represent himself, and therefore, both sets of disallowed disbursements were restored.

The *New Law Journal* of 1 July 1994, p 890 reported that a litigant in person who after a three-and-a-half-day hearing was granted leave to proceed under the Mental Health Act against seven defendants with the costs of the application awarded against those defendants, was allowed on taxation her costs in excess of £59,000 for obtaining legal assistance in the preparation and presentation of a case from solicitors who were not on the record.

In *R v Common Professional Examination Board, ex p Mealing-McCleod* (2000) Times, 2 May, CA it was held:

(a)   CPR Rule 48.6(4) suggests that more time should be allowed to a litigant in person than to a solicitor doing the same task.

(b)   When a litigant in person is restricted to the litigant in person charging rate of £9.25 per hour, it is likely that the costs of the other side, if legally represented are likely to be very much higher. The proportionality mentioned in CPR Rule 48.5 is that the costs incurred by a party must be proportionate to the amount of the claim and the litigation generally. It does not mean that the costs of a legally represented party must be reduced below a reasonable level of remuneration because the other side is a litigant in person restricted to payment over £9.25 per hour.

However, in *Greville v Sprake* [2001] EWCA Civ 234, [2001] All ER (D) 182 (Feb) the Court of Appeal, without referring to *Mealing-McCleod*, held that a litigant in person is limited to the time which would reasonably have been spent by a solicitor on the preparation of his or her case based on Rule 48.6(3)(*a*). This appears to be another demonstration of the urgent need for a complete overhaul of LIPs' costs.

[38.11]

The provision that a LIP may only recover two-thirds of what a notional solicitor would have charged limits the amount the LIP may claim for any particular item. The correct approach therefore for the assessment of a LIP claiming at the specified rate is to ascertain what the total of that item is. Then compare that with two-thirds of the notional solicitor's rate and allow the lower of the two items. This means that the bill of costs drawn by the LIP must be gone through in some detail, item by item (*Morris v Wiltshire & Woodspring District Council* (16 January 1998, unreported, QBD).

In *R (on the application of Wulfsohn) v Legal Services Commission* [2002] EWCA Civ 250, [2002] 3 Costs LR 341 a successful LIP produced a rough costs schedule purporting to show that he had been engaged for over 1,200 hours on research and he also gave oral evidence, which the court had no reason to disbelieve, that he had spent well in excess of 1,200 hours. In these circumstances the right course is to start with the cap imposed by CPR Rule 48.6(2) which provides that the costs of a litigant in person shall not exceed two-thirds of the amount which would have been allowed if the litigant in person had been represented by a legal representative. The litigant in person also produced a letter to him from a firm of solicitors saying: 'On the limited information that we have been provided by yourself and the Citizens Advice Bureau in the Royal Courts of Justice and having seen at a very preliminary stage the documentation with regards the matter we would estimate that the legal costs would be in the region of £15,000 to £20,000 plus VAT'. Doing the best it could on the information in front of it the court 'being extremely rough-and-ready' about it took the figure of £15,000 which resulted in a cap of £10,000. In addition to that the court allowed photocopying, postage and travelling totalling £460, resulting in a total award of costs of £10,460, instead of the £120 awarded by the trial judge.

WHO IS A LITIGANT IN PERSON?

[38.12]

Rule 48.6(6) provides that a litigant in person includes a company or other corporation which is acting without a legal representative, a barrister, solicitor, solicitor's employee or other authorised litigator who is acting for himself. This would preclude a solicitor acting on his own behalf, for example suing for unpaid costs, from recovering his normal charges. When this was appreciated, it was too late to change the rule so it was circumvented by paragraph 52.5 of the Costs Practice Direction providing that a solicitor, who, instead of acting for himself, is represented in the proceedings by his firm or by himself in his firm name (presumably even if he is a sole practitioner) is not a litigant in person. A classic example of a Practice Direction reversing a Rule! Accordingly, a solicitor who instead of acting for himself is represented in the proceedings by his firm, or by himself in his firm's name, is not, for the purposes of the Civil Procedure Rules, a litigant in person.

It was established in *London Scottish Benefit Society v Chorley* (1884) 13 QBD 872, CA that where an action was brought against a solicitor who defended it in person and obtained judgment, he was entitled to the same costs as if he had employed a solicitor, except in respect of items which the fact of his acting directly rendered unnecessary. Paragraph 52.5 means that the principle applies where a defendant solicitor does not expend his own time and skill in defending the claim, because the defence was undertaken by one of his partners and by others within his firm (*Malkinson v Trim* [2002] EWCA Civ

1273, [2003] 2 All ER 356). It is of course important for a solicitor litigant, especially if he is a sole practitioner, to make it clear that he is acting through his firm and not in person, for example by using his firm's, and not his private, notepaper.

In *Re Minotaur Data Systems Ltd, Official Receiver v Brunt* [1998] 4 All ER 500, ChD the judge had with some regret come to the conclusion that the Official Solicitor acting as an applicant in proceedings under the Company Director Disqualification Act 1986, s 6 without the aid of a solicitor was not a litigant in person and therefore not entitled to an allowance in respect of costs. The judge therefore would have been pleased that his decision was reversed by the Court of Appeal on 2 March 1999 ([1999] 3 All ER 122, CA), which held that although the Official Solicitor could not be said to be acting for the Crown as a litigant in person, he was himself a litigant in person for the purposes of recovering his costs.

PROFESSIONAL LITIGANTS IN PERSON

[38.13]

In *Re Nossen's Patent* ([1969] 1 WLR 638) it was held that when it was appropriate that a corporate litigant should recover, on a between-the-parties basis, a sum in respect of expert services performed by its own staff, the amount must be restricted to a reasonable sum for the actual and direct costs of the work undertaken, and not a proportion of the corporation's overheads, no part of such expenditure being occasioned by the litigation.

London Scottish Benefit Society v Chorley ((1884) 13 QBD 872) established the rule of practice that a litigant in person who was a solicitor could recover costs as if he had employed a solicitor, applied only in the context of litigants in person who were solicitors and that generally speaking, a litigant in person could not recover for his time. Although the decision was before the CPR, it would be an inadmissible extension of that case to treat the principle established by it to other professionals such as accountants. An accountant LIP could at most recover for work he had done himself, what the cost of obtaining the expert advice of an independent professional would have been, but he is not entitled to recover the costs of general assistance to the expert in the conduct of the litigation (*Sisu Capital Fund Ltd v Tucker* [2005] EWHC 2170 (Ch), [2005] All ER (D) 200 (Oct) (09 September 2005)).

CHAPTER 39

GROUP (MULTI-PARTY) LITIGATION ORDERS

[39.1]

CPR Rule 48.6A: Costs where the court has made a group litigation order

(1)　This rule applies where the court has made a Group Litigation Order ('GLO').

(2)　In this rule—

    (a)　'individual costs' means costs incurred in relation to an individual claim on the group register;

    (b)　'common costs' means—

        (i)　costs incurred in relation to the GLO issues;

        (ii)　individual costs incurred in a claim while it is proceeding as a test claim, and

        (iii)　costs incurred by the lead solicitor in administering the group litigation; and

    (c)　'group litigant' means a claimant or defendant, as the case may be, whose claim is entered on the group register.

(3)　Unless the court orders otherwise, any order for common costs against group litigants imposes on each group litigant several liability(GL) for an equal proportion of those common costs.

(4)　The general rule is that where a group litigant is the paying party, he will, in addition to any costs he is liable to pay to the receiving party, be liable for—

    (a)　the individual costs of his claim; and

    (b)　an equal proportion, together with all the other group litigants, of the common costs.

(5)　Where the court makes an order about costs in relation to any application or hearing which involved—

    (a)　one or more GLO issues; and

    (b)　issues relevant only to individual claims,

the court will direct the proportion of the costs that is to relate to common costs and the proportion that is to relate to individual costs.

(6)　Where common costs have been incurred before a claim is entered on the group register, the court may order the group litigant to be liable for a proportion of those costs.

Where a claim is removed from the group register, the court may make an order for costs in that claim which includes a proportion of the common costs incurred up to the date on which the claim is removed from the group register. (Part 19 sets out rules about group litigation.)

[(GL) Several liability: A person who is severally liable with others may remain liable for the whole claim even where judgment has been obtained against the others.]

There is no supplementary practice direction to this rule, but paragraph 16 of the second Practice Direction Supplementing CPR Part 19 (which deals with GLOs) provides that the costs judge shall apportion the amounts of common and individual costs, if the court has not already done so.

CODIFICATION

[39.2]

This Rule was introduced on 3 July 2000 in an attempt to codify the guidance in the authorities on some of the costs issues arising in group litigation. Some of the problems where a few claims are selected out of a large number as test cases are concerned with how the costs of those cases are to be apportioned among all of the claimants in a variety of circumstances, such as when a between-the-parties costs award in their favour is obtained which is less than the solicitor and client costs, or where there is an adverse costs order. A frequent complication is where some, but not all of the claimants are state-funded. In *BCCI v Ali* (13 April 2000, unreported, ChD) of some 300 claimants, five were chosen as test cases. They were not awarded any between-the-parties costs, although not ordered to pay any but the non-test case claimants argued that the solicitor and client costs should be paid solely by the test case claimants, on the grounds that they had lost because of their own dishonesty. Surprisingly, no costs sharing order or agreement had been made. The court found that when the test cases were chosen it was the common expectation of all the claimants that the test case costs would be shared equally, and it so ordered. In *Ochwat v Watson Burton (a firm)* [1999] All ER (D) 1407 the test case claimants won on the general issues of duty of care and breach of that duty, but failed on causation. The judge awarded the defendants 75% of their costs of which he ordered the test case claimants to pay 75% and the remaining claimants 25%. On appeal it was held that this was unfair to the test case claimants and that the costs awarded to the defendants should be paid by all the claimants.

Rule 48.6A provides that, unless the court orders otherwise, orders against group litigants impose several liability for an equal proportion of common costs and that a group litigant will be responsible for his own individual solicitor and client costs and an equal share of the common costs. The court may make provision for the costs contribution of a party who joins the group late, or leaves it early.

DISCONTINUANCE

[39.3]

In *Sayers v Merck SmithKline Beecham plc* [2001] EWCA Civ 2017, [2003] 3 All ER 631 appeals arose in relation to the details of costs-sharing in three separate multi-party actions. However likely it might be that, if common issues were directed at trial, the costs of those issues would be ordered to follow the determination of those issues rather than await the individual fate of each claimant's action, it would be wrong to say that that should always be the presumptive position. Parties who settle their cases did not usually need any presumptive order as to the incidence of costs since costs would be part of the discussion leading to a settlement in any event. Discontinuers, however, gave rise to a more difficult problem. The order usually made in these circumstances was too blunt an instrument and was unnecessarily favourable to defendants, at a stage of the proceedings when it was as yet unknown whether the claimants as a whole were to be successful in the common issues which were to be tried. The orders in the present case should be amended to read:

'If in any quarter a claimant discontinued his claim against any one or more of the defendants or it is dismissed by an order of the court whereby the claimant is ordered to pay such defendant's costs, then he will be liable for his individual costs incurred by such defendants up to the last day of that quarter; liability for common costs and disbursement to be determined following the trial of common issues, with permission to apply if such trial does take place.'

This form of order should in future be used in multi-party actions.

Michael Goldberg of Davies Arnold Cooper regarded the judgment as an opportunity lost to reinforce a restraint on claimants. In the New Law Journal of 22 March 2002 he wrote:

'Claimants ought to be able to leave a group action knowing their liability for costs, pay them, and then put the litigation behind them. Instead, claimants wishing to forget their unsuccessful foray into group litigation may have their claims re-examined. Quite how the court will be able to embark on such re-examination remains unanswered.

Group actions function as a cost-effective and administratively convenient way of ensuring that large numbers of claimants are able to have claims litigated with minimal delay. Whilst the judgment might be perceived by some as good news for the lawyers acting on both sides in group actions, who can now anticipate a drawn-out enquiry on costs at the end of each trial, one cannot help wondering whether justice is truly being served.

Ultimately, it is the litigants themselves who are being short changed.'

INDIVIDUAL CLAIM

[39.4]

In *O v Ministry of Defence* [2006] EWHC 990 (QB), [2006] All ER (D) 203 (May), 15 May the claimant in group litigation was awarded personal damages for clinical negligence the MoD sought to set off the claimant's proportionate share of the costs of trial of the generic issues, against either his costs of his individual action or against his damages. Although the claimant might have benefited in the pursuit of his individual action had the generic issues been resolved differently the fact remained that in his own individual action the claimant proved that he sustained injury and consequential loss and damage, as a consequence of negligent treatment. He would have succeeded in that action whether or not the generic issues had been litigated. The formation of the group litigation and his involvement in it, as to which he had no real choice, inevitably resulted in a very substantial delay in the resolution of his claim. The justice of the case required that neither the claimant's own order for costs nor his damages should be subject to a set-off of his share of the generic costs.

GENERIC COSTS

[39.5]

Where a client is a member of a group involved in litigation which is awarded costs against the other party he is entitled to recover the costs for which he would have been liable to his solicitor. He is liable to his solicitor for all costs properly incurred whether they were incurred solely on his behalf or whether they were incurred for the benefit of the group and he has only to pay an appropriate proportion. There is nothing fundamentally different or special about generic costs; they are simply costs that have been shared for the sensible purpose of keeping the costs of each claim down. A defendant's protection against an inflated claim is to be found in CPR 44.5(1)(a) where it provides that when assessing costs on the standard basis, the court has to consider whether, in the circumstances the costs are proportionately and reasonably incurred and are proportionate and reasonable in amount. That is an objective test. Further, any doubts about the reasonableness or proportionality of any item on the bill has to be resolved in favour of the paying party (CPR 44.4(2)(b)). The protection provided by detailed assessment under CPR 44.5(1) would not in any way be enhanced by the existence of a letter sent at the time of the retainer wherein the solicitor told the client that some of the costs would be expended for the benefit of other claimants besides himself, so that he would only be asked to pay a share of those costs. In the real world, that would be a statement of the obvious. In practice, it was highly likely that the claimant would be aware that there were others making similar claims, through the same solicitors. Why would the solicitor do anything other than share costs, which were capable of being shared and thereby save money?

It would be good practice for a solicitor to mention in a client care letter that some of the work to be done would be for the benefit of a group of clients and that individuals would be liable only for their share. It would be sensible for a firm to keep records of the number of clients for whom it was acting at any time. Such records would help to demonstrate, if need be, that the proportion claimed for any individual client was justified. Where solicitors intended to claim a share of costs incurred by other solicitors, it would be wise for them to ensure that the terms of the agreement between the solicitors were clearly defined, to demonstrate more easily that the bill under scrutiny was reasonable and proportionate. In short, such records were desirable because they would be an aid to proving the reasonableness of a bill; they were not required as a pre-requisite to the recovery of a share of generic costs.

Where the litigation has been funded under conditional fee agreements entered into by each client, standing alone it would only be necessary for the individual client to demonstrate that there was an agreement between him and his solicitor collateral to the CFA specifically relating to generic costs if generic costs were in some way different from costs incurred solely for the individual client. There is therefore no requirement for any additional or collateral agreement relating to generic costs in a CFA for a successful claimant to recover such costs in an action where no group litigation order has been made (*Brown v Russell Young & Co* [2007] EWCA Civ 43, [2007] 2 All ER 453).

COSTS CAPPING

[39.6]

In *Various Claimants v Corby Borough Council* [2008] EWHC 619 (TCC), 1 April, the claimants were children born to mothers who had lived in or close to Corby during the 1980s and 1990s. They alleged that as a result of negligent work, toxins had escaped and had affected pregnant women so as to cause birth defects in their offspring.

The parties accepted that an overall costs cap should be fixed. In fixing such a cap, the court had to have regard to the constituent elements making up each party's submitted costs estimates. It was impossible to predict with absolute precision or accuracy how much individual costs heads would ultimately cost and an overall costs cap allowed an element of flexibility. Each party had agreed a conditional fee agreement with their solicitors and the claimants had taken out litigation costs insurance. It was accepted that the costs capping should not be on the basis of what their CFA would allow the successful party. Nor was the claimants' insurance taken into account. It was necessary to take an informed but broad-brush approach to the amount of the costs cap to be fixed upon each of the parties.

The parties agreed that a contingency was a fair and sensible allowance to make given the nature of the litigation and the likely encountering of expenditure or increase in levels of expenditure which was probably inevitable even if it could not be specifically foreseen which the judge fixed at 5%. The parties had liberty to apply to the Court for adjustment of the costs caps if, unforeseeably and beyond the reasonable control of the party in question, circumstances so changed or new circumstances arose such that there was a genuine need to adjust the figures.

FUNDING

[39.7]

The Civil Justice Council recommends that in contentious business cases where contingency fees are currently disallowed, American style contingency fees requiring abolition of the fee shifting rule should not be introduced. However, consideration should be given to the introduction of contingency fees on a regulated basis along similar lines to those permitted in Ontario by the Solicitors' Act 2002 particularly to assist access to justice in group actions and other complex cases where no other method of funding is available.

As I comment in Chapter 42, there is no practical difference between contingency and conditional fees; this proposal is really a sophisticated attempt to abolish recoverability of the success fee between the parties – and as such, good luck to it. As the Law Society's Gazette commented on 6 October 2005, although the proposal envisages contingency fees playing a limited role in funding, once the door opens there is little chance of it being shut again.

The Civil Justice Council has also recommended that a generic collective action should be introduced with collective claims being brought by a wide range of representative parties on an opt-in or opt-out basis with full fee-shifting.

Part VI

Funding

CHAPTER 40

STATE-FUNDED COSTS

[40.1]

The quantification of state funded costs as between the provider and the Commission is not straightforward. It used to be governed by General Civil Contracts. Now it is governed by the Unified Contract. The Unified Contract for civil legal aid providers replaces the General Civil Contract and Family Mediation Contract. There is a myriad of different payment rates for different types of work for different years. Furthermore, as a review of *Cook on Costs 2006* observed, the former chapter that I had devoted to the quantification of state funded costs had become little more than an introductory guide. That was fair comment and an introductory guide is of little use in these days of preferred suppliers and discrete contracts. Since February 1999, only legal service providers with a contract with the LSC have been able to take on publicly-funded clinical negligence cases, and since 1 January 2000 only contracted organisations have been able to give initial help in any civil matter or provide any level of LSC-funded service in family and immigration cases, while from 1 April 2000 most personal injury cases (except clinical negligence) have been excluded from public funding. On 1 April 2001, the civil contracting scheme was extended to cover all levels of service for all types of case, which can now only be supplied under an LSC contract. In 2007 we witnessed the introduction of the Unified Contract. However, it has not been smooth running since 31 March 2010 when the Unified Contract came into force. On Friday 3 September, the LSC and the Law Society provisionally agreed to a one month extension of the current unified civil contract. This has been agreed following the Law Society's successful challenge by way of Judicial Review of the LSC's family tender process. Lord Justice Moses said the process was 'irrational'. He said it was 'contrary to the LSC's own ends' not to have given firms the details of the selection criteria regarding caseworker panel membership in time for solicitors to achieve accreditation. Lord Justice Moses said that, in failing to give selection details in time, the LSC had 'arbitrarily and unfairly' distinguished between providers, and deprived some of those most in need of the opportunity to obtain the services of well-qualified and experienced family lawyers. The impact on contracts is not yet known, with the court still to provide a decision on relief. The latest is that the contracts currently in place will now expire at midnight on Sunday, 14 November. The new civil contracts will start first thing on the morning of Monday, 15 November.

An important package of changes to the Funding Code received Parliamentary approval and came into effect on 1 April 2010. These follow from the recent consultation Legal Aid: Refocusing on Priority Cases. There are changes to the Criteria for judicial review, multi-party actions, public interest cases and claims against public authorities. The Code Procedures have been amended to set up a new power to seek representations on means in certain family cases (initially to be applied to a limited ranges of cases only - further guidance to follow) and set up new 'Special Controls' system and Review Panel (replacing PIAP and the MPA committee) for certain high cost and public interest cases.

The versions of the Code Criteria and Procedures set out below show all amendments which apply to new applications from 1 April 2010. Procedure changes apply to both existing and new cases from that date.

From August 2009 changes were made to the Family Graduated Fees for the Bar with the aim of saving a staggering £6.5m per year to the LSC budget requirements. Consultation on Best Value Tendering (otherwise known as BVT) in civil legal aid closed on 19 June 2009. Jack Straw, the then Justice Secretary, and Lord Bach, the then Legal Aid Minister, listened carefully to the representations made by the Law Society and by legal aid firms. They were persuaded that the scheme proposed was unlikely to lead to the efficient, re-structured legal services market envisaged by Lord Carter in his 2006 Review of Legal Aid procurement.

In the 2007 edition I reported on the LSC's decision to launch a preferred supplier pilot scheme which was intended radically to change the way in which the LSC interacts with legal aid providers. However, following consultation the LSC has decided to take key elements of the Preferred Supplier Scheme approach and integrate them into the LSC's legal aid reform programme. The LSC has concluded that there is no need to introduce a separate Preferred Supplier Scheme as originally proposed. That is not to say that quality and assurance are not high on the agenda. They clearly are. Independent Peer Review is now carried out by the Institute of Advanced Legal Studies and a team of experienced legal aid practitioners who assess stratified random sample files to determine levels of quality. In addition to that the LSC requires 'Quality Profiles' as a case progresses. These tools, together with 'Costs Compliance Audits' ensures that any solicitor aspiring to undertake civil or family legal aid work must now attain and maintain standards and specialisation considerably more demanding than anything this book could provide. Yet more change is on the way with the implementation of the report by Lord Carter and so we have reached the stage where I must leave the remuneration of solicitors out of public funds to the experts.

However, this does not mean that you or I can ignore the public funding of litigation, because Rule 2.03 of the Solicitors' Code of Conduct 2007 requires every solicitor to consider whether each client may be eligible and should apply for public funding. This was recently demonstrated in *David Truex (a firm) v Kitchin* [2007] EWCA Civ 618, [2007] Fam Law 903 which dismissed a solicitor's claim for costs against a client who was eligible for public funding on the grounds that solicitors are bound at the outset to consider whether a client might be eligible for public funding, rather than continue to take instructions and run up costs while they gathered information before considering public funding eligibility. Accordingly this chapter is still compulsory reading for all.

A NATIONAL LEGAL SERVICE?

[40.2]

In 1945 the new Labour government gave the legal and medical professions the alternatives of either being nationalised, or of voluntarily coming up with proposals for providing their services free to those who could not afford to pay for them. The medical profession came up with nothing, and they got the National Health Service. The legal profession avoided the creation of a National Legal Service by proposing the Legal Aid Scheme, funded by a 15% reduction in lawyers' fees to those clients who qualified for legal aid, subject to contributions. Prior to that a key concept in the running of a solicitors' practice had been 'cross-subsidisation' – whereby the more profitable work (mainly probate and conveyancing) subsidised the less profitable or unprofitable work (such as crime and litigation), with work being done *pro bono* for deserving clients who could not afford to pay anything. It was contemplated that the new Legal Aid Scheme would embrace this philosophy and that all firms of solicitors would offer legal aid as a method of funding to those who qualified for it. The National Health Service may or may not be in a mess, but the Legal Aid Scheme, as originally envisaged, is dead. It went wrong at both ends of the spectrum. It was not obligatory for firms of solicitors to undertake legal aid work, and not all of them did. Over the years, the number of firms not accepting legal aid work, and, indeed, not now being allowed to accept it because they have neither a public-funding contract nor franchise, has increased from a trickle to a flood. At the other end of the spectrum are firms of solicitors seeking to make a living out of publicly-funded work, much of which had previously been done at a loss or *pro bono*. The result is that instead of legal aid being provided by the legal profession as a whole – which was the consideration for not being nationalised – we have the present polarisation, with legal aid being provided by a diminishing number of specialist firms and the majority of the profession being unwilling, and now unable, to undertake publicly-funded work.

DISENCHANTMENT

[40.3]

A survey by the Law Society's *Gazette*, supported by the Legal Aid Practitioners Group, among 150 firms of solicitors throughout the country, found that:
- 57% had given up legal aid contracts or were considering doing so.
- 21% had dropped more than one area of work or were considering doing so in the future.
- 15% of firms had stopped, or were stopping, doing all publicly-funded family work, as were 14% in respect of crime and 11% in respect of housing.
- 85% of firms had no intention of taking on new areas of publicly-funded work.
- 54% said they had given up the work because it was unprofitable.
- 23% could not meet the supervisory requirements governing the amount of work they needed to do to get a contract.
- 20% blamed bureaucracy.

The Legal Aid Practitioners Group in a consultation paper refers to an 'unimaginable crisis' ahead unless the problems in recruiting and maintaining senior staff, trainees and support staff are rapidly addressed. The report went on:

'Where there is no private work to subsidise the legal aid sector, it is difficult to make a reasonable living. Where there is, those partners doing private work increasingly resent having their income so significantly reduced by the comparative lack of income from the legal aid parts of the firm.'

No concept of cross-subsidisation or *pro bono* there. It may be the object of the Legal Services Commission to achieve efficiency and economy by having fewer and larger specialist firms providing state-funded litigation services, but we have come a long way from the vision of 1945, and perhaps a step closer to a National Legal Service.

THE LEGAL SERVICES COMMISSION

[40.4]

On 1 April 2000, the Legal Aid Board was replaced by the Legal Services Commission (LSC). The LSC runs two schemes, the civil scheme working with those legal service providers (solicitors and not-for-profit agencies) who are members of the Community Legal Service (CLS) and the criminal scheme, the Criminal Defence Service. Both schemes deliver services primarily through contracts with legal service providers who have satisfied the LSC's prescribed standards, which entitles them to display the CLS civil logo.

Article 4 of the Community Legal Service (Funding) Order 2000 preserved reg 107 of the Civil Legal Aid (General) Regulations 1989 so that it applies to cases funded under a Community Legal Service funding certificate as well as to those cases still funded under a Legal Aid certificate. Article 6 made similar provision in respect of family proceedings

THE SERVICES PROVIDED BY THE LSC

[40.5]

Section 4 of the Access to Justice Act 1999 describes the services to be provided by the CLS as:
(a)   The provision of general information about the law and legal system and the availability of legal services.
(b)   The provision of help by the giving of advice as to how the law applies in particular circumstances.
(c)   The provision of help in preventing, settling or otherwise resolving, disputes about legal rights and duties.
(d)   The provision of help in enforcing decisions by which such disputes are resolved.
(e)   The provision of help in relation to legal proceedings not relating to disputes.

THE SERVICES EXCLUDED BY THE LSC

[40.6]

Schedule 2 to the Access to Justice Act provides that the following services may not be funded as part of the CLS:
(a)   Allegations of negligently caused injury, death or damage to property, apart from allegations relating to clinical negligence.
(b)   Conveyancing.
(c)   Boundary disputes.
(d)   The making of wills.
(e)   Matters of trust law.
(f)   Defamation or malicious falsehood.
(g)   Matters of company or partnership law.
(h)   Other matters arising out of the carrying on of a business.

THE LEVELS OF SERVICE

[40.7]

The LSC funds various levels of service under the CLS in various categories. Here they are.

(a) Help

[40.8]

Help comes in the form of Legal Help and Help at Court.

Legal Help provides initial advice and assistance and is the equivalent of the Legal Advice and Assistance formerly provided under the Green Form Scheme.

Help at Court replaces the former Assistance by Way of Representation, known as ABWOR, authorising legal representation for the purposes of a particular hearing, but not in the proceedings generally.

These two levels of service provide help from a legal service provider up to an amount of £500 (with a higher figure for immigration asylum cases). Once the cost limit is reached the solicitor or adviser can only carry out further work at this level with the authority of the LSC regional office. Legal Help cannot be applied for retrospectively.

(b) Legal representation

[40.9]

There are two forms of Legal Representation which are equivalent to the former Civil Legal Aid.

(i) Investigative help

[40.10]

This is similar to a former Legal Aid Certificate limited to making enquiries, obtaining counsel's opinion and issuing, but not serving, proceedings. It is intended for fast track and multi-track claims where substantial investigative work is necessary to assess the strength of a proposed claim. It is only available where the prospects of success are not clear and the investigation is likely to be expensive. Its purpose is to enable the prospect of success to be assessed for the purposes of a conditional fee agreement or for full CLS funding. All certificates for Investigative Help will contain a cost limitation. It would be unusual for the initial certificate for Investigative Help to have a costs limitation exceeding £1,500. Investigative Help will be refused unless damages are likely to exceed £5,000.

(ii) Full representation

[40.11]

This is the equivalent of a former full Legal Aid Certificate and is the main form of legal representation. Although the LSC may impose limitations and conditions on the extent of funding, in principle, full representation can cover all work needed to take legal proceedings to trial and beyond.

(c) Support funding

[40.12]

This is a new concept of mixed funding, which previously was not allowed, with part of the costs being financed by the state and the balance privately with the assistance of a conditional fee agreement. When support funding is granted, the LSC does not take over general responsibility for funding the costs of the proceedings. The case will continue on a private basis with the solicitor being paid limited payments by the LSC during the case towards the overall legal costs. It again comes in two forms.

(i) Investigative support

[40.13]

This provides limited funding for the investigation of the strength of a proposed claim with a view to proceeding under a conditional fee agreement. It covers only work done in investigating the strength of the claim and does not cover other investigative work, for example the amount of the claim. As soon as sufficient investigative work has been carried out to estimate prospects of success and to decide whether to proceed under a conditional fee agreement, this must be reported to the LSC and no further work will be funded. It is only available where the reasonable costs of investigation are exceptionally high, ie disbursements, such as experts' reports, are likely to exceed £1,000 or the solicitor's fees to investigate the case are likely to exceed £3,000. Other merits criteria apply to this level of funding, including a requirement that the likely damages exceed £5,000.

(ii)   Litigation support

[40.14]

This is any type of Support Funding other than Investigative Support. It is intended to provide partial funding support for high-cost litigation already proceeding under a conditional fee agreement. It is only available where the reasonable costs of the litigation are exceptionally high, ie disbursements such as experts' reports, are likely to exceed £5,000 or the solicitor's costs and the barrister's fees together are likely to exceed £15,000 calculated at the rate of £70 an hour. The other merits criteria apply to this level of funding. Litigation Support has its own prescribed rates: £70 an hour for solicitors, £90 an hour for senior counsel, £50 an hour for junior counsel. Travelling time is paid at 25% of those rates.

(d) Family

[40.15]

In addition to Legal Help and Legal Representation there are additional services in respect of family matters.

(i)   Approved family help

[40.16]

Approved Family Help provides help in family cases short of Full Representation in contested proceedings. It includes the services covered by Legal Help, but also includes issuing proceedings and representation where necessary to obtain disclosure of information from another party, or to obtain a consent order following an agreement of matters in dispute. It is also available in two forms.

1.   Help with mediation

[40.17]

This is only available to those who are actually participating in Family Mediation or have successfully reached an agreement or settlement as a result of Family Mediation, and are in need of legal advice or assistance. It may be provided only by solicitors with a contract with the LSC in family law. The charges for the work may not exceed £150 where mediation relates to children issues only; £250 for financial issues only; and £350 where mediation covers both. These limits can be extended where necessary by the LSC regional office. The result of all work properly carried out under this level of service is exempt from the statutory charge.

2.   General family help

[40.18]

General Family Help covers negotiations in a family dispute where no mediation is in progress, although it will not usually be granted unless the suitability of the case for mediation has been considered by a mediator. It also includes representation in proceedings where this is necessary to obtain disclosure of information (for example, about their finances) from another party. It is only available from solicitors with a family law contract. The solicitor or adviser's charges are limited to an initial £1,500, which can be extended where necessary on application to a LSC regional office. The statutory charge will apply to any money or property recovered or preserved under this level of service.

(ii) Family mediation

[40.18A]

Family Mediation provides funding for mediation of a family dispute for couples who qualify financially. The dispute may relate to children, money and property. It is important to remember that a mediator does not make decisions for the parties but helps them to reach their own decisions in a neutral environment. It is an alternative to reaching agreements or obtaining court orders, although it does not replace legal or other advice. Those eligible for mediation can obtain legal advice and assistance from a solicitor to support them during mediation either through Legal Help or Help with Mediation.

FINANCIAL ELIGIBILITY

[40.18B]

I am grateful to the Community Legal Service for their permission to reproduce the following quick reference card, known to those at the LSC as Keycard No. 46 issued in April 2010. It provides a handy quick reference guide which I hope will be of use:

General

This card is intended as a quick reference point only when assessing financial eligibility for those levels of service for which the supplier has responsibility: Legal Help, Help at Court; Legal Representation before the Asylum and Immigration Tribunal, and before the High Court in respect of an application under s.103A of the Nationality, Immigration and Asylum Act 2002; Family Mediation; Help with Mediation, and Legal Representation in respect of Specified Family Proceedings before a Magistrates' Court (other than proceedings under the Children Act 1989 or Part IV of the Family Law Act 1996). Full guidance on the assessment of means is set out in Part F of Volume 2 of the Legal Services Commission Manual. References in this card to volume and section numbers e.g. volume 2F-section 1 are references to the relevant parts of that guidance. Suppliers should have regard to the general provisions set out in guidance volume 2F-section 2, particularly those set out in sub paragraphs 3–5 regarding the documentation required when assessing means. This keycard and the guidance are relevant to all applications for funding made on or after 6 April 2009.

Level of Service	Income Limit	Capital Limit
All Levels of Service*	Gross income not to exceed £2,657** per month	Disposable Capital not to exceed
- Legal Help		
- Help at Court	Disposable income not to exceed £733 per month.	£3,000 (CLR immigration matters)
- Family Mediation		
- Family Help (Lower), and	Passported if in receipt of Income Support, Income Based Job Seekers' Allowance, Income Based Employment and Support Allowance or Guarantee Credit	£8,000 (all other levels of service)
- Legal Representation before the Asylum and Immigration Tribunal; and before the High Court in respect of an application under s.103A of the Nationality, Immigration and Asylum Act 2002;		Passported if in receipt of Income Support, Income Based Job Seekers' Allowance Income Based Employment and Support Allowance or Guarantee Credit
- Legal Representation in respect of Specified Family Proceedings before a Magistrates' Court (other than proceedings under the Children Act 1989 or Part IV of the Family Law Act 1996).	[Also passported for Legal Help, Help at Court and Legal Representation (asylum and immigration matters only), if in receipt of NASS Support].	[Also passported for Legal Help, Help at Court and Legal Representation (asylum and immigration matters only), if in receipt of NASS Support].

*   may be subject to contribution from income and/or capital (see volume 2F-section 3.2 paras 1 to 5

**   A higher gross income cap applies to families with more than 4 dependent children. Add £222 to the base gross income cap shown above for the 5th and each subsequent dependent child.

Additional information regarding the financial eligibility criteria is also provided in guidance volume 2f-section 3.

Step 1: Determine whether or not the client has a partner whose means should be aggregated for the purposes of the assessment (see guidance in volume 2F-section 4.2 paras 1–5)

Step 2: Determine whether the client is directly or indirectly in receipt of a 'passporting' benefit in order to determine whether the client automatically satisfies the relevant financial eligibility test as indicated by the 'passported' arrangements stated in the table above.

Step 3: For any cases which are not 'passported' determine the gross income of the client, including the income of any partner, (see guidance in volume 2F-section5). Where that gross income is assessed as being above £2,657 per month, then the client is ineligible for funding for all levels of service and the application should be refused without any further calculations being performed. Certain sources of income can be disregarded and a higher gross income cap applies to families with more that 4 dependent children

Step 4: For those clients whose gross income is not more than £2,657 per month, assess disposable income. Fixed allowances are made for dependents and employment expenses and these are set out in the table below. Other allowances can be made for: tax, national insurance, maintenance paid, housing costs and childminding. If the resulting disposable income is above the relevant limit then funding should be refused across all levels of service without any further calculations being necessary.

Fixed rate allowances (per month) from 10 April 2006

Work related expenses for those receiving a wage or salary	£45

Dependants Allowances:

Partner	£162.08
Child aged 15 or under	£250.16
Child aged 16 or over	£250.16
Housing cap for those without dependants	£545

Step 5: Where a client's disposable income is below the relevant limit then it is necessary to calculate the client's disposable capital (see guidance in volume, 2F-section 7). If the resulting capital is above the relevant limit, then the application should be refused.

Step 6: For those clients whose disposable income and disposable capital have been assessed below the relevant limits then for all levels of service other than Legal Representation in Specified Family Proceedings, the client can be awarded funding.

Step 7: For legal Representation in Specified Family Proceedings, it is necessary to determine whether any contributions from either income or capital (or both) should be paid by the client (see guidance in volume 2F-section 3.2 paras 1 to 5). For ease of reference the relevant income contribution table is reproduced below. Such contributions should be collected by the supplier (see guidance in volume 2F-section 3.2 para 4).

Band	Monthly disposal income	Monthly contribution
A	£316 to £465	¼ of income in excess of £311
B	£466 to £616	£38.50+ ⅓ of income in excess of £465
C	£617 to £733	£88.85 + ½ of income in excess of £616

ELIGIBILITY ON MERITS

(a) Costs-benefit

[40.19]

The CLS General Funding Code prescribes a costs-benefit matrix for deciding whether a case merits the grant of funding. Where the prospects of success are very good (80% or more) the anticipated damages must exceed the costs. Where the prospects of success are classified as good (60–80%) the estimated damages must exceed the costs by a ratio of two to one. Moderate prospects of success (50–60%) require that the estimated damages must exceed the costs by a ratio of four to one. Poor prospects of success (less than 50%) will not qualify for funding in the absence of specified circumstances.

(b) The merits criteria

[40.20]

The *Legal Aid Handbook* was replaced by the *Legal Services Commission Manual* with effect from 1 April 2000. The manual now fills four large ring binders, the whole of the contents of which I could not even summarise in a work of this nature. One of the aspects on which I have concentrated is eligibility for state funding, which is based on the three criteria of financial eligibility(see para 41.18B], prospects of success and cost-benefit. The latter two criteria are covered comprehensively in Part 1 of the Legal Services Commission's Funding Code, which apart from the introductory sections, I am reproducing in full below.

THE FUNDING CODE: PART 1 – CRITERIA

[40.21]

Section 1 – Levels of Service

1.1. Levels of Service Available

The Commission will fund only the following levels of service as part of the Community Legal Service, subject to the provisions of the Act, orders regulations and directions made under the Act, these criteria and the Funding Code Procedures:
(1)   Legal Help.
(2)   Help at Court.
(3)   Approved Family Help – this can be either General Family Help or Help with Mediation.
(4)   Legal Representation – this can be either Investigative Help or Full Representation.
(5)   Support Funding – this can be either Investigative Support or Litigation Support.
(6)   Family Mediation.
(7)   Such other services as are authorised by specific orders or directions from the Lord Chancellor.

1.2 Representation

Legal Representation and Help at Court will be funded only in relation to proceedings for which advocacy may be funded in accordance with section 6(8) of and paragraph 2 of Schedule 2 to the Act.

1.3 Disbursements

Contracts or guidance may specify what items may or may not be charged as disbursements under each level of service. The following may not be charged under any level of service unless authorised by a specific order or direction from the Lord Chancellor:
(i)   All costs or expenses of or relating to the residential assessment of a child;
(ii)   All costs or expenses of or relating to treatment, therapy, training or other interventions of an educative or rehabilitative nature.

[40.22]

Section 2 – Definitions

2.1 Levels of Service

Note: Nothing in these definitions limits the power of the Commission to place conditions or limitations on any grant.

'Legal Help' is a level of service the grant of which authorises services falling within Section 4(2) of the Access to Justice Act 1999 other than:

(i)   The provision of general information about the law and legal system and the availability of legal services (except where such provision is incidental to the provision of help in a specific case).

(ii)   Issuing or conducting court proceedings.

(iii)   Advocacy or instructing an advocate in proceedings.

(iv)   The provision of mediation or arbitration (but this does not prevent legal help being given in relation to mediation or arbitration or covering payment of a mediator's or arbitrator's fees as a disbursement).

'Help at Court' is a level of service the grant of which authorises help and advocacy for a client in relation to a particular hearing, without formally acting as legal representative in the proceedings, unless this is authorised by the Commission.

'Family Help' is a level of service the grant of which authorises help in relation to a Family Dispute including assistance in resolving that dispute through negotiation or otherwise. Family Help does not include the provision of mediation services but covers help and advice in support of Family Mediation. Family Help covers all services within the scope of either Legal Help or Legal Representation other than preparation for or representation at a contested final hearing or appeal.

'Family Help (Lower)' means Family Help which is limited to exclude issue of proceedings or representation in proceedings other than help in obtaining a consent order following settlement of a Family Dispute.

'Family Help (Higher)' means a grant of Family Help other than Family Help (Lower).

'Legal Representation' is a level of service the grant of which authorises legal representation for a party to proceedings or for a person who is contemplating taking proceedings. This includes the following:

(i)   Litigation services.

(ii)   Advocacy services.

(iii)   All such help as is usually given by a person providing representation in proceedings, including steps preliminary or incidental to proceedings.

(iv)   All such help as is usually given by such a person in arriving at or giving effect to a compromise to avoid or bring to an end any proceedings.

Legal representation does not include the provision of mediation or arbitration (but this does not prevent help being given in relation to mediation or arbitration, or the payment of a mediator's or arbitrator's fees as a disbursement).

'Investigative Help' means Legal Representation which is limited to investigation of the strength of a proposed claim. Investigative Help includes the issue and the conduct of proceedings only so far as necessary to obtain disclosure of relevant information or to protect the client's position in relation to any urgent hearing or time limit for the issue of proceedings.

'Full Representation' means a grant of Legal Representation other than Investigative Help.

'Family Mediation' is a level of service the grant of which authorises mediation of a family dispute, including assessing whether mediation appears suitable to the dispute and the parties and all the circumstances.

2.2 Case categories

'Clinical Negligence Proceedings' means proceedings which include:

(i)   a claim for damages in respect of an alleged breach of duty of care or trespass to the person committed in the course of the provision of clinical or medical services (including dental or nursing services); or

(ii)   a claim for damages in respect of alleged professional negligence in the conduct of such a claim.

'Family Dispute' means a legal dispute arising out of a family relationship, including disputes concerning the welfare of children or which may give rise to Family Proceedings.

'Family Proceedings' means proceedings which arise out of family relationships, including proceedings in which the welfare of children is determined (other than judicial review proceedings). Family Proceedings also include all proceedings under any one or more of the following:

(a)   the Matrimonial Causes Act 1973;

(b)   the Inheritance (Provision for Family and Dependants) Act 1975;

(c)   the Adoption Act 1976;

(d)   the Domestic Proceedings and Magistrates' Courts Act 1978;

(e)   Part III of the Matrimonial and Family Proceedings Act 1984;

(f)   Parts I, II and IV of the Children Act 1989;

(g)   Part IV of the Family Law Act 1996;

(h)   the Adoption and Children Act 2002;

(i)   the Civil Partnership Act 2004; and

(j)   the inherent jurisdiction of the High Court in relation to children.

'Special Children Act Proceedings' means proceedings under the Children Act 1989 (other than appeal proceedings) where Legal Representation is applied for on behalf of:

(i)   a child in respect of whom an application is made for an order under:

    (a)   Section 31 (a care or supervision order);

    (b)   Section 43 (a child assessment order);

    (c)   Section 44 (an emergency protection order); and

    (d)   Section 45 (extension or discharge of an emergency protection order);

(ii)   any parent of such a child or person with parental responsibility for the child within the meaning of the 1989 Act;

(iii)   a child who is brought before a Court under Section 25 (use of accommodation for restricting liberty) who is not, but wishes to be, legally represented before the Court.

'Other public law children cases' means public law proceedings concerning the welfare of children other than Special Children Act Proceedings or related proceedings (see Section 11.8) but including:

(i)   Appeals (whether interim or final) from orders made in Special Children Act Proceedings;

(ii)   Other proceedings under Part IV or V of the 1989 Act;

(iii)   Adoption proceedings, including freeing for adoption;

(iv)   Proceedings under the inherent jurisdiction of the High Court in relation to children.

'Private Law Children Cases' means proceedings concerning residence, contact and other private law issues concerning children other than issues of financial provision.

'Public Law Family Proceedings' means Special Children Act Proceedings, Related Proceedings (see Section 11.8) and Other Public Law Children Cases.

2.3 Merits, Costs and Damages

'Prospects of Success' means the likelihood of the client obtaining a successful outcome in the proceedings, assuming the case was determined at trial or other final hearing. Guidance may give examples of what may constitute a successful outcome for different types of proceeding.

Different categories of Prospects of Success have the following meanings:

'Very Good' means 80% or more;

'Good' means 60%–80%;

'Moderate' means 50%–60%;

'Borderline' means that Prospects of Success are not Poor, but because there are difficult disputes of fact, law or expert evidence, it is not possible to say that Prospects of Success are better than 50%;

'Poor' means clearly less than 50% so that the claim is likely to fail;

'Unclear' means that the case cannot be put into any of the above categories because further investigation is needed;

'Likely Costs' means an estimate of the likely total gross costs to be incurred on behalf of the client to disposal of the proceedings. This includes counsel's fees, disbursements and any enhancement or uplift on costs. Where appropriate, costs should be calculated by reference to standard or prescribed remuneration rates set by the Lord Chancellor or the Commission. Likely Costs and all cost thresholds specified in the Code are exclusive of VAT;

'Likely Damages' means a realistic estimate of the size of any money award the client would receive if substantially successful at trial or final hearing, after allowing for any likely reduction through contributory negligence or otherwise. Likely Damages should be discounted (by anything up to 100%) if there is doubt as to whether the opponent will be able to pay the money award.

2.4 Other Definitions

'the Act' means the Access to Justice Act 1999 and terms defined in the Act have the same meaning in the Code.

'Asylum and Immigration Tribunal' means the tribunal established under section 81 of the Nationality, Immigration and Asylum Act 2002.

'Central Budget' means the budget set by the Lord Chancellor for the funding of very expensive cases in accordance with Code Procedures.

'Conditional Fee Agreement' or 'CFA' means a conditional fee agreement or any other private funding arrangement authorised under the provisions of Part II of the Access to Justice Act 1999.

'Contract' means a contract with the Commission under which services are provided which are funded as part of the Community Legal Service.

'Discrimination' means discrimination on the grounds of age, disability, gender reassignment, marriage and civil partnership, pregnancy and maternity, race, religion or belief, sex or sexual orientation.

'Excluded Services' means services which are excluded under Schedule 2 of the Act and are not covered by any direction or authorisation under section 6(8) of the Act.

'Guidance' means guidance published by the Lord Chancellor or the Commission for the purpose of making decisions under the Code.

'Hague Convention' means the convention defined in section 1(1) of the Child Abduction and Custody Act 1985.

'European Convention' means the convention defined in section 12(1) of that Act.

'Hague Convention Countries' has the same meaning as in the Reciprocal Enforcement of Maintenance Orders (Hague Convention Countries) Order 1979.

'Maintenance Orders (Reciprocal Enforcement) Act 1972' means the Act as applied with such exceptions, adaptations and modifications as are specified in the 1979 Order.

'Immigration Adjudicator' and 'Immigration Appeal Tribunal' mean the adjudicators and Tribunal referred to in Part IV of the Immigration and Asylum Act 1999.

'Mental Health Tribunal' means the First-tier Tribunal (established under the Tribunals, Courts and Enforcement Act 2007) acting under any provision of the

Mental Health Act 1983 or Paragraph 5(2) of the Schedule to the Repatriation of Prisoners Act 1984, or the Mental Health Review Tribunal for Wales;

'Multi-Party Action' or 'MPA' means any action or actions in which a number of clients have causes of action which involve common issues of fact or law arising out of the same cause or event.

'the 1989 Act' means the Children Act 1989.

'Overwhelming importance to the client' means a case which has exceptional importance to the client, beyond the monetary value (if any) of the claim, because the case concerns the life, liberty or physical safety of the client or his or her family, or a roof over their heads.

'Prescribed' means either set out in Regulations or specified by the Commission.

'Proceedings' means legal proceedings before any court, tribunal, arbitrator or panel in England and Wales, but mediation and any form of dispute resolution which cannot make a determination which is binding on the client do not count as proceedings.

'Public Authority' has the meaning given in section 6 of the Human Rights Act 1998.

'Regulations' means orders or regulations under the Access to Justice Act 1999.

'Residential Assessment' means any assessment of a child, whether under section 38(6) of the Children Act 1989 or otherwise, in which the child, alone or with others, is assessed, on a residential basis, at any location other than his or her normal residence. It also includes an assessment or viability assessment, whether residential or not, preparatory to or with a view to the possibility of a residential assessment.

'Special Cases Unit' means a unit established by the Commission under the Code Procedures whose functions include administering the central budget and issuing contracts in very expensive cases.

'Upper Tribunal' means the Upper Tribunal established under the Tribunals, Courts and Enforcement Act 2007.

'Wider Public Interest: a case shall be regarded as having Wider Public Interest only if the Commission is satisfied that:

(i) the case has means the potential of the proceedings to produce real benefits for individuals other than the client (other than benefits to the public at large which normally flow from proceedings of the type in question); and

(ii) the case is considered on its particular facts to be an appropriate case to realise those benefits.

[40.23]

Section 3 – Case Categories

3.1 The General Funding Code

Applications for funding will be considered under the General Funding Code except to the extent that different criteria are specified for specific categories of case or proceeding. Definitions and criteria for specific categories are given in sections 6–14 of these Criteria.

3.2 Disputed Categories

Where any issue arises as to which category a case falls into, the Commission will apply the criteria which appear to it to be most relevant to the substance of the application.

3.3 Mixed Claims

Where it appears to the Commission that an application for Legal Representation or Support Funding relates to proceedings covering more than one category, the Commission may apply the criteria which appear to it most appropriate to the proceedings as a whole. If proceedings have not been started, the Commission may consider each aspect of the case under the criteria relevant to it and may apply appropriate restrictions on any grant.

3.4 Excluded Proceedings
The Commission will refuse an application for Legal Representation if, in the view of the Commission, effective representation cannot be provided in the proceedings without the provision of excluded services.

3.5 Guidance
Guidance may give examples of descriptions of proceedings in particular case categories.

3.6 Foreign Orders and Judgments
Cases within the scope of section 11.14 shall be subject only to the criteria in that section (whether or not the proceedings in question are Family Proceedings).

[40.24]

Section 4 – Standard Criteria

4.1 Scope of this section
The criteria in this section apply to all applications under the Code.

4.2 English Law
An application will be refused if it relates to law other than that of England and Wales, save where this is permitted by or under section 19 of the Act.

4.3 Excluded Services
An application for the provision of excluded services will be refused.

4.4 Directions on Scope
Where an application relies upon a direction or authorisation under section 6(8) of the Act the application will be refused if any conditions specified in the direction or authorisation are not satisfied.

4.5 Identity of Client
An application will be refused unless it is for the benefit of a client who is an individual and who satisfies such other conditions as are specified in the Code Procedures.

4.6 Identity of Supplier
An application will be refused unless the proposed supplier of services is of a description specified in the Code Procedures.

4.7 Contract Scope
Where an application is for services which under the Code Procedures can be provided only under contract, the application will be refused unless the supplier has a contract and is permitted to provide those services under the terms of the contract.

4.8 Procedures

An application may be refused or rejected if any Code Procedures have not been complied with.

4.9 Financial Eligibility

An application will be refused unless the client is assessed as financially eligible under regulations, except where:

(i)   under Regulations services are available without reference to means:

or

(ii)   Regulations or Code Procedures authorise services to be provided before completion of the financial assessment.

4.10 Conduct

An application may be refused if it appears unreasonable to grant funding in the light of the conduct of the client in connection with this or any other application or in connection with any proceedings.

[40.25]

Section 5 – The General Funding Code

5.1 Application of General Funding Code

This section applies, in addition to the criteria in section 4, to any application for funding, save to the extent that different criteria are applied for specific categories of case or proceedings in sections 6 to 14.

5.2 Criteria for Legal Help

5.2.1 Sufficient Benefit Test

Help may only be provided where there is sufficient benefit to the client having regard to the circumstances of the matter, including the personal circumstances of the client, to justify work or further work being carried out.

5.2.2 Funding as part of CLS

Help may only be provided if it is reasonable for the matter to be funded out of the Community Legal Service Fund, having regard to any other potential sources of funding.

5.3 Criteria for Help at Court

5.3.1 Criteria for Legal Help

The criteria for Legal Help apply to an application for Help at Court, in addition to the following two criteria.

5.3.2 The Need for Representation

Help at Court may only be provided if the nature of the proceedings and the circumstances of the hearing and the client are such that advocacy is appropriate and will be of real benefit to the client.

5.3.3 Legal Representation

Help at Court may not be provided if the contested nature of the proceedings or the nature of the hearing is such that, if any help is to be provided, it is more appropriate that it should be given through Legal Representation.

5.4 Standard Criteria for Legal Representation

5.4.1 Scope of this Section

The following criteria apply to all applications for Legal Representation or Support Funding, in addition to the criteria relevant to the specific level of service applied for.

5.4.2 Alternative Funding

An application may be refused if alternative funding is available to the client (through insurance or otherwise) or if there are other persons or bodies, including those who might benefit from the proceedings, who can reasonably be expected to bring or fund the case. For the purpose of this criterion only, alternative funding does not include funding by means of a conditional fee agreement.

5.4.3 Alternatives to Litigation

An application may be refused if there are complaint systems, ombudsman schemes or forms of alternative dispute resolution which should be tried before litigation is pursued.

5.4.4 Other Levels of Service

An application may be refused if it appears premature or if it appears more appropriate for the client to be assisted by some other level of service under the Code, such as Legal Help or Help at Court.

5.4.5 The Need for Representation

An application may be refused if it appears unreasonable to fund representation, for example in the light of the nature and complexity of the issues, the existence of other proceedings or the interests of other parties in the proceedings to which the application relates.

5.4.6 Small Claims

An application will be refused if the case has been or is likely to be allocated to the small claims track.

5.5 Emergency Representation

5.5.1 Urgency

Legal Representation may only be granted as a matter of urgency where it appears in the interests of justice to do so.

5.5.2 Limited Information

Where only limited information is available to determine whether the criteria for Legal Representation are satisfied, emergency representation may be granted only if it appears likely on the information available that those criteria would be satisfied.

5.6 Criteria for Investigative Help

5.6.1 Potential for a Conditional Fee Agreement

Investigative Help may be refused if the nature of the case and circumstances of the client are such that investigative work should be carried out privately with a view to a conditional fee agreement or that funding should take the form only of Investigative Support.

5.6.2 The Need for Investigation

Investigative Help may only be granted where the prospects of success of the claim are uncertain and substantial investigative work is required before those prospects can be determined. Guidance may indicate what constitutes substantial investigative work for this purpose.

5.6.3 Damages

If the client's claim is primarily a claim for damages and has no significant wider public interest, Investigative Help will be refused unless the damages are likely to exceed £5,000. For the purposes of this criterion, if the claim is part of a Multi-Party Action, the claim may only be regarded as having a significant wider public interest if it is a lead claim within that action.

5.6.4 Prospects after Investigation

Investigative Help may only be granted if there are reasonable grounds for believing that when the investigative work has been carried out the claim will be strong enough, in terms of prospects of success and cost benefit, to satisfy the relevant criteria for Full Representation.

5.7 Criteria for Full Representation

5.7.1 Conditional Fee Agreements

If the nature of the case is suitable for a CFA, and the client is likely to be able to avail himself or herself of a CFA, Full Representation will be refused.

5.7.2 Prospects of Success

Full Representation will be refused if:
(i)   Prospects of success are unclear;
(ii)   Prospects of success are borderline and the case does not appear to have a significant wider public interest or to be of overwhelming importance to the client; or
(iii)   Prospects of success are poor.

5.7.3 Cost Benefit – Quantifiable Claims

If the claim is primarily a claim for damages by the client and does not have a significant wider public interest, Full Representation will be refused unless the following cost benefit criteria are satisfied:
(i)   If prospects of success are very good (80% or more), likely damages must exceed likely costs;
(ii)   If prospects of success are good (60%–80%), likely damages must exceed likely costs by a ratio of 2:1;
(iii)   If prospects of success are moderate (50%–60%), likely damages must exceed likely costs by a ratio of 4:1.

5.7.4 Cost Benefit – Unquantifiable Claims

If the claim is not primarily a claim for damages (including any application by a defendant or a case which has overwhelming importance to the client), but does not have a significant wider public interest, Full Representation will be refused unless the likely benefits to be gained from the proceedings justify the likely costs, such that a reasonable private paying client would be prepared to litigate, having regard to the prospects of success and all other circumstances.

5.7.5 Cost Benefit – Public Interest Cases

If the claim has a significant wider public interest, Full Representation may be refused unless the likely benefits of the proceedings to the applicant and others justify the likely costs, having regard to the prospects of success and all other circumstances.

5.7.6 Multi-Party Action Damages

If the claim is part of a Multi-Party Action, is primarily a claim for damages and has no significant wider public interest, Full Representation will be refused unless the damages are likely to exceed £5,000. For the purposes of this criterion the claim may only be regarded as having a significant wider public interest if it is a lead claim within that action.

5.8 Criteria for Other Services

5.8.1 Orders and Directions

Levels of service other than those provided for in the General Funding Code or elsewhere in these criteria may be funded only if a specific order or direction from the Lord Chancellor so provides, and then only in accordance with the terms of the order or direction.

5.8.2 Reasonableness

An application for such services may be refused if it appears unreasonable in all the circumstances to grant it.

[40.26]

Section 6 – Special Cases Unit Very Expensive Cases

6.1 Scope

This section applies to applications or certificates for Legal Representation which have been referred to the Special Cases Unit in accordance with Code Procedures.

6.2 Relevant Criteria

All Criteria relevant to the level of service and category of case in question shall apply, as modified in this section, in addition to the Criteria set out in this section.

6.3 The Costed Case Plan

Funding may be refused if the proposals put forward for progressing the litigation including proposals as to cost do not appear to the Commission to be satisfactory.

6.4 Affordability

Subject to 6.5 below, funding will be refused or deferred unless it appears reasonable for funding to be granted in the light of the resources available in the Central Budget and likely future demands on those resources.

6.5 Top Priority Cases

The Affordability criterion in 6.4 shall not apply to:
(i)   Special Children Act Proceedings;
(ii)   judicial review proceedings under section 7 of the Criteria in which funding is to continue by virtue of criterion 7.5.2;
(iii)   other proceedings in which the life or liberty of the client is at risk.

[40.27]

Section 7 – Judicial Review

7.1 Scope

This section applies to applications for Legal Representation in relation to court proceedings concerning public law challenges to the acts, omissions or decisions of public bodies, including in particular challenges by way of judicial review or habeas corpus and proceedings under Part VII of the Housing Act 1996.

7.2 Criteria for Investigative Help

7.2.1 *General Funding Code Criteria*

Criteria 5.6.1 (potential for a conditional fee agreement) and 5.6.3 (minimum damages level) do not apply to applications for Investigative Help under this section.

7.2.2 *Is Judicial Review Available?*

An application may be refused if the act or decision complained of in the proposed proceedings does not appear to be susceptible to challenge.

7.2.3 *Administrative Procedures*

Investigative Help may be refused if there are administrative appeals or other procedures which should be pursued before proceedings are considered.

7.2.4 *Client Interest*

Investigative Help will be refused unless the proceedings have the potential to produce real benefits for the applicant, for the applicant's family or for the environment. However funding will not automatically be withdrawn if the applicant ceases to have a direct personal interest during the course of the proceedings.

7.3 Criteria for Full Representation

If, at the time the application for funding is made, the court has not granted permission to bring the proceedings or if according to rules of court such permission is not required, the criteria in section 7.4 apply. If at the time the application is made the court has granted permission, the criteria in 7.5 apply.

7.4 Pre-Permission Criteria

7.4.1 General Funding Code
The following criteria replace those in section 5.7 of the General Funding Code.

7.4.2 Is Judicial Review available?
An application may be refused if the act or decision complained of in the proposed proceedings does not appear to be susceptible to challenge.

7.4.3 Administrative Procedures
Full Representation may be refused if there are administrative appeals or other procedures which should be pursued before proceedings are considered.

7.4.4 Client Interest
Full Representation will be refused unless the proceedings have the potential to produce real benefits for the applicant, for the applicant's family or for the environment. However funding will not automatically be withdrawn if the applicant ceases to have a direct personal interest during the course of the proceedings.

7.4.5 Notification to Respondent
Full Representation will be refused unless the proposed respondent has been given a reasonable opportunity to respond to the challenge or deal with the applicant's complaint, save where this is impracticable in the circumstances.

7.4.6 Prospects of Success
Full Representation will be refused if the prospects of successfully obtaining the substantive order sought in the proceedings are:
(i)   unclear;
(ii)   borderline and the case does not appear to have significant wider public interest, to be of overwhelming importance to the client or to raise significant human rights issues; or
(iii)   poor.

7.4.7 Cost Benefit
Full Representation may be refused unless the likely benefits of the proceedings justify the likely costs, having regard to the prospects of success and all other circumstances.

7.5 Post-Permission Criteria

7.5.1 General Funding Code
The following criteria replace those in section 5.7 of the General Funding Code.

7.5.2 The Presumption of Funding
If the case has a significant wider public interest, is of overwhelming importance to the client or raises significant human rights issues, then, provided the standard criteria in Section 4 Section 5.4 are satisfied, funding shall be granted save where, in light of information which was not before the court at the permission stage or has subsequently come to light, it appears unreasonable for Legal Representation to be granted.

7.5.3 *Refusal on the Merits*
Where the case does not appear to have a significant wider public interest, to be of overwhelming importance to the client or to raise significant human rights issues, Legal Representation will be refused if:
(i)   prospects of success are borderline or poor; or
(ii)   the likely costs do not appear to be proportionate to the likely benefits of the proceedings having regard to the prospects of success and all the circumstances.

[40.28]

Section 8 – Claims Against Public Authorities Alleging Serious Wrong-doing etc

8.1 Scope
This section applies to applications for Legal Representation in relation to proceedings or proposed proceedings against public authorities concerning serious wrong-doing, abuse of position or power or significant breach of human rights, other than cases falling within the scope of section 7 (Judicial Review) or section 10 (Housing).

8.2 Criteria for Investigative Help

8.2.1 *Potential for a Conditional Fee Agreement*
Criteria 5.6.1 does not apply to applications under this section unless the application relates to a multi-party action.

8.2.2 *Police and Prison Complaints*
Without prejudice to criterion 5.4.3 Investigative Help may be refused if it is more appropriate for the client to pursue the police, prison or probation complaints, or to refer the matter to the Prisons and Probation Ombudsman, than to pursue procedure than litigation.

8.2.3 *Damages*
Criterion 5.6.3 (minimum damages level) only applies does not apply to applications for Investigative Help under this section if:
(i)   the application relates to a Multi-Party Action; and
(ii)   the Multi-Party Action is not based upon allegations of abuse of children or vulnerable adults or allegations of Discrimination.

8.3 Criteria for Full Representation

8.3.1 *General Funding Code*
Subject to 8.3.5 and 8.3.6 below, the following criteria replace the criteria in section 5.7 of the General Funding Code in applications to which this section applies.

8.3.2 *Prospects of Success*
Full Representation will be refused if:
(i)   Prospects of success are unclear;
(ii)   Prospects of success are borderline and the case does not appear to have a significant wider public interest, to be of overwhelming importance to the client or to raise significant human rights issues;

    (iii)   Prospects of success are poor.

8.3.3 Cost Benefit
Legal Representation may be refused unless the likely benefits of the proceedings justify the likely costs, having regard to the prospects of success and all other circumstances.

8.3.4 Police and Prison Complaints
Without prejudice to criterion 5.4.3, Full Representation may be refused if it is more appropriate for the client to pursue the police, prison or probation complaints or to refer the matter to the Prisons and Probation Ombudsman, than to pursue procedure than litigation.

8.3.5 Conditional Fee Agreements
Criterion 5.7.1 does not apply to applications under this section unless the application relates to a multi-party action.

8.3.6 Multi-Party Action Damages
Criterion 5.7.6 applies to applications under this section unless the Multi-Party Action is based upon allegations of abuse of children or vulnerable adults or allegations of Discrimination.

[40.29]

Section 9 – Clinical Negligence

9.1 Scope
This section applies to applications for Legal Representation in Clinical Negligence Proceedings.

9.2 Criteria for Investigative Help

9.2.1 Potential for a Conditional Fee Agreement
Criterion 5.6.1 does not apply to applications under this section, unless the application relates to a multi-party action.

9.2.2 The Complaints Scheme
Investigative Help may be refused if it is more appropriate for the client to pursue the NHS complaints procedure than litigation.

9.3 Criteria for Full Representation

9.3.1 Conditional Fee Agreements
Criterion 5.7.1 (refusal on grounds that the case is of a type suitable for a CFA) does not apply to applications under this section, unless the application relates to a multi-party action.

[40.30]

Section 10 – Housing

10.1 Scope
This section applies to applications for legal representation for a client in proceedings which concern possession of the client's home, the client's legal status in the home, or the obligations of a landlord or other person to keep the client's home in good repair and allow quiet enjoyment of the property. However, this section does not apply to cases within the scope of section 7 (Judicial Review).

10.2 Criteria for Investigative Help

10.2.1 Potential for a Conditional Fee Agreement
Criterion 5.6.1 does not apply to applications under this section.

10.2.2 Damages
In applications under this section the figure for minimum damages in criterion 5.6.3 shall be £1,000.

10.3 Criteria for Full Representation – Possession Cases

10.3.1 General Funding Code
The following criteria replace those in section 5.7 of the General Funding Code for proceedings which concern possession of the client's home.

10.3.2 Prospects of Success
Full Representation will be refused if the client has no substantive legal defence to the proceedings or the prospects of successfully avoiding an order for possession (or, if the client is bringing proceedings, the prospects of obtaining such an order) are poor.

10.3.3 Cost Benefit
Full representation may be refused unless the likely benefits of the proceedings to the client justify the likely costs, having regard to the prospects of success and all other circumstances.

10.4 Criteria for Full Representation – Other Housing Cases

10.4.1 General Funding Code
The following criteria replace the criteria in section 5.7 of the General Funding Code in applications within the scope of this section other than possession cases.

10.4.2 Notification to Landlord
Where the client is applying for Full Representation to bring proceedings the application may be refused unless the landlord or other person responsible for dealing with the matters complained of has been notified of the client's complaint and given a reasonable opportunity to respond and put matters right, save where this is impracticable in the circumstances.

10.4.3 Prospects of Success
Full Representation will be refused if:
(i)   Prospects of success are unclear;

(ii)   Prospects of success are borderline and the case does not appear to have a significant wider public interest or to be of overwhelming importance to the client;

(iii)   Prospects of success are poor.

10.4.4 Cost Benefit

Full Representation may be refused unless the likely benefits of the proceedings to the client justify the likely costs, having regard to the prospects of success and all other circumstances.

[40.31]

Section 11 – Family

11.1 Scope

This section applies to applications for Family Help, Family Mediation and Legal Representation in Family Proceedings.

11.2 Help at Court

Help at Court is not available in relation to Family Disputes.

11.3 Criteria for Family Help

11.3.1 Significant Family Dispute

Family Help may only be provided where the client requires ongoing help in relation to a significant Family Dispute. Guidance may specify what constitutes a significant Family Dispute for this purpose.

11.3.2 Cost Benefit

Family Help will be refused unless the benefits to be gained from the help provided justify the likely costs, such that a reasonable private paying client would be prepared to proceed in all the circumstances.

11.3.3 Other Levels of Service

Family Help will be refused if it is more appropriate for the client to be assisted by way of Legal Help or Legal Representation.

11.4 Criteria for Family Help (Higher)

11.4.1 Family Help Criteria

An application for Family Help (Higher) must satisfy the following criteria, in addition to the criteria for Family Help at 11.3 above.

11.4.2 Referral to Family Mediation

Family Help (Higher) will be refused if, in accordance with Code Procedures, the case must first be referred to a mediator for a determination as to whether mediation is suitable to the dispute and the parties and all the circumstances.

11.4.3 Suitability for Mediation

Family Help (Higher) may be refused if mediation is more appropriate to the case than Family Help (Higher).

11.4.4 Attempts at Settlement

Family Help (Higher) may be refused unless reasonable attempts have been made to resolve the dispute without recourse to contested proceedings, through negotiation or otherwise.

11.4.5 Public Law Cases

Family Help (Higher) is not available for Public Law Family Proceedings.

11.5 Criteria for Family Mediation

11.5.1 The Assessment Meeting

An assessment of whether mediation is suitable to the dispute and the parties and all the circumstances ("an assessment meeting") may only be provided if the standard criteria in Section 4 are satisfied.

11.5.2 Substantive Mediation

Mediation beyond the assessment meeting may be provided only where the mediator is satisfied that mediation is suitable to the dispute and the parties and all the circumstances.

11.6 Legal Representation in Family Proceedings

11.6.1 Investigative Help

Investigative Help is not available in Family Proceedings. Legal Representation in Family Proceedings shall take the form only of Full Representation.

11.6.2 Standard Criteria

The criteria at Section 5.7 of the General Funding Code (criteria for Full Representation) and criterion 5.4.6 (small claims) do not apply to applications for Legal Representation in Family Proceedings.

11.6.3 Legal Representation Criteria

The criteria at Sections 11.7 to 11.14 below apply only to applications for Legal Representation.

11.7 Criteria for Special Children Act Proceedings

Legal Representation shall be granted in Special Children Act Proceedings (as defined in Section 2) provided the relevant criteria in Section 4 and criterion 5.4.5 (the Need for Representation) are satisfied. The other standard criteria in Section 5.4 of the General Funding Code shall not apply.

11.8 Related Proceedings

Where Legal Representation has been granted to a person in Special Children Act Proceedings, Legal Representation may also be granted for that person in related proceedings which are being heard together with those proceedings or in which an order is being sought as an alternative to an order in those proceedings.

11.9 Criteria for other Public Law Children Cases

11.9.1 Standard Criteria

The standard criteria for Legal Representation in Section 5.4 of the General Funding Code do not apply in other public law children cases, save for the following criteria:–

(i)   5.4.2 (refusal on the ground of the availability of alternative sources of funding);

(ii)   5.4.5 (refusal on the ground that representation is not necessary).

11.9.2 Prospects of Success

Where Legal Representation is sought on behalf of a client who is making or supporting an application or appeal, Legal Representation will be refused if the prospects of the application or appeal being successful are poor.

11.9.3 Reasonableness

An application for Legal Representation may be refused if it appears unreasonable for funding to be granted, having regard to the importance of the case to the client and all other circumstances.

11.10 Domestic Violence Cases

11.10.1 Scope

These criteria apply to proceedings seeking an injunction, committal order or other orders for the protection of a person from harm (other than public law children proceedings).

11.10.2 Prospects of Success

Legal Representation will be refused if the prospects of obtaining the order sought in the proceedings are poor.

11.10.3 Cost Benefit

Legal Representation will be refused unless the likely costs are proportionate to the likely benefits of the proceedings, having regard to the prospects of obtaining the order sought and all other circumstances.

11.11 Private Law Children Cases

11.11.1 Scope

These criteria apply to applications for Legal Representation in Private Law Children Cases, other than cases covered by sections 11.13 or 11.14

11.11.2 Referral to Family Mediation

Legal Representation will be refused, if in accordance with Code Procedures, the case must first be referred to a mediator for a determination as to whether mediation is suitable to the dispute and the parties and all the circumstances before Legal Representation can be provided.

11.11.3 Suitability for mediation

Legal Representation may be refused if mediation, supported if necessary by Family Help, is more appropriate to the case than Legal Representation.

11.11.4 *Attempts at settlement*

Legal Representation may be refused unless reasonable attempts have been made to resolve the dispute without recourse to contested proceedings, through negotiation or otherwise.

11.11.5 *Prospects of Success*

Legal Representation will be refused if prospects of success are poor.

11.11.6 *Cost Benefit*

Legal Representation will be refused unless the likely benefits to be gained from the proceedings for the client justify the likely costs, such that a reasonable private paying client would be prepared to take or defend the proceedings in all the circumstances.

11.12 Financial Provision and Other Proceedings

11.12.1 *Scope*

These criteria apply to ancillary relief and other family proceedings concerning financial provision, and to all other family proceedings which are not covered by criteria elsewhere in this section.

11.12.2 *Referral to Family Mediation*

Legal Representation will be refused if, in accordance with Code Procedures, the case must first be referred to a mediator for a determination as to whether mediation is suitable to the dispute and the parties and all the circumstances before Legal Representation can be provided.

11.12.3 *Suitability for mediation*

Legal Representation may be refused if mediation, supported if necessary by Family Help, is more appropriate to the case than Legal Representation.

11.12.4 *Attempts at settlement*

Legal Representation may be refused unless reasonable attempts have been made to resolve the dispute without recourse to contested proceedings, through negotiation or otherwise.

11.12.5 *Prospects of Success*

Legal Representation will be refused if prospects of success are:–
(i)   borderline or unclear, save where the case has overwhelming importance to the client or a significant wider public interest;
(ii)   poor

11.12.6 *Cost Benefit*

Legal representation will be refused unless the likely benefits to be gained from the proceedings for the client justify the likely costs, such that a reasonable private paying client would be prepared to take or defend the proceedings in all the circumstances.

11.12.7 *Private Funding*

Legal Representation may be refused if it appears reasonable in all the circumstances for the proceedings to be funded privately, having regard to the financial circumstances of the client and the value of the assets in dispute.

11.13 Child abduction cases

Subject only to Section 4, Legal Representation shall be granted to a person whose application under the Hague Convention or the European Convention has been submitted to the central authority in England and Wales pursuant to Section 3(2) or Section 14(2) of the Child Abduction and Custody Act 1985 and on whose behalf a legal representative has been instructed in England and Wales in connection with the application.

11.14 Registration of foreign orders and judgments

11.14.1 Scope

This section applies to a person who;
(i) appeals to a Magistrates' Court against the registration of or the refusal to register a maintenance order made in a Hague Convention country pursuant to the Maintenance Orders (Reciprocal Enforcement) Act 1972 or;
(ii) applies for the registration of a judgment under Section 4 of the Civil Jurisdiction and Judgments Act 1982.
and who satisfies the criterion set out below.

11.14.2 Legal aid abroad

Legal representation under this provision shall be granted if the standard criteria in Section 4 are satisfied and if the client benefited from complete or partial legal aid, other public funding or exemption from costs or expenses in the country in which the maintenance order was made or the judgment was given.

[40.32]

Section 12 – Mental Health

12.1 Scope

This section applies to applications for Legal Representation in proceedings before a Mental Health Review Tribunal under the Mental Health Act 1983 on behalf of a person whose case or whose application to the Tribunal is or is to be the subject of the proceedings.

12.2 Investigative Help

Investigative Help is not available in applications under this section. Applications for Legal Representation under this section shall take the form of Full Representation.

12.3 General Funding Code

The criteria in Sections 5.4 and 5.7 of the General Funding Code shall not apply to applications under this section (but this should not be taken as restricting the scope of the reasonableness criterion below).

12.4 Reasonableness

An application may be refused if it is unreasonable in the particular circumstances of the case for Legal Representation to be granted.

[40.33]

Section 13 – Immigration

13.1 Scope
This section applies to applications for Legal Representation for a client whose case is before:
(i)   the Immigration and Asylum Tribunal;
(ii)   the High Court, in relation to applications under section 103A of the Nationality, Immigration and Asylum Act 2002;
(iii)   an Upper Tribunal in relation to any appeal or review arising from an Immigration and Asylum Tribunal.

13.2 Investigative Help
Investigative Help is not available in applications under this section. Applications for Legal Representation under this section shall take the form of Full Representation.

13.3 General Funding Code
The standard criteria for Legal Representation in Section 5.4 of the General Funding Code apply to applications under this section, save for criterion 5.4.6 (small claims). The criteria for Full Representation under Section 5.7 of the General Funding Code do not apply to applications under this section.

13.4 Prospects of Success
Legal Representation will be refused if the prospects of achieving a successful outcome for the client are:
(i)   unclear or borderline, save where the case has a significant wider public interest, is of overwhelming importance to the client or raises significant human rights issues; or
(ii)   poor.

13.5 Cost Benefit
Save where the case has a significant wider public interest, Legal Representation will be refused unless the likely benefits to be gained from the proceedings justify the likely costs, such that a reasonable private paying client would be prepared to take the proceedings, having regard to the prospects of success and all other circumstances.

[40.34]

Section 14 – Quasi-Criminal Proceedings

14.1 Scope
This section applies to applications for Legal Representation in proceedings in which the client may be subject to orders or penalties which are (or which the client is reasonably contending are) criminal penalties within the meaning of article 6 of the European Convention on Human Rights.

14.2 Investigative Help
Investigative Help is not available in applications under this section. Applications for Legal Representation under this section shall take the form of Full Representation.

14.3 General Funding Code

The criteria in Section 5.7 of the General Funding Code shall not apply to applications under this section (but should not be taken as restricting the scope of the interests of justice criterion below).

14.4 Interests of Justice

An application may be refused unless it is in the interests of justice for Legal Representation to be granted.

[40.35]

Section 15 – Withdrawal of Funding

15.1 Scope

This section applies where funding has already been granted under the Code Criteria. Funding may be withdrawn in accordance with the following criteria and the Code Procedures. Code Procedures may in particular specify the grounds for withdrawal of emergency representation.

15.2 Criteria No Longer Satisfied

Funding may be withdrawn where the criteria under which funding was originally granted are no longer satisfied.

15.3 Reasonableness

Funding may be withdrawn where it is unreasonable for funding to continue in all the circumstances of the case, taking into account the interests of the client, any wider public interest and the interest of the Community Legal Service Fund.

15.4 Investigations

Investigative Help or Investigative Support will cease where it appears that sufficient work has been carried out to enable prospects of success to be determined. Investigative Support will also cease when a conditional fee arrangement is entered into.

15.5 Other Grounds

Without prejudice to any of the above criteria, funding may be withdrawn:
(i)   where the client has died;
(ii)   where the client has had a bankruptcy order made against him or her;
(iii)   on financial grounds, in accordance with Code Procedures and Regulations;
(iv)   with the consent of the client;
(v)   where the case has been disposed of or all work authorised by the Commission has been completed;
(vi)   where, in accordance with Code Procedures, it is unreasonable for funding to continue in the light of the conduct of the client.

ALTERNATIVE FUNDING

[40.36]

As paragraph 5.4.2 of the Criteria list above demonstrates, an application for LSC funding may be refused if alternative funding is available for the client (through insurance or otherwise). Similarly there may be other third parties, persons or bodies, who can reasonably be expected to bring or fund the claim. If the client has insurance which would cover the legal costs of the proposed proceedings, CLS funding will almost inevitably be refused. If the client is a member of a trade union which provides legal services to its members, funding will normally be refused. The mere fact that a union may refuse to cover a case does not mean that LSC funding will be available. The test to apply is whether the union "can reasonably be expected" to fund the case. We were all recently reminded of the importance of checking the availability of any before the event insurance and alternative forms of funding: *Garrett v Halton Borough Council; Myatt v National Coal Board* [2006] EWCA Civ 1017, (2006) Times, 25 July.

THE STATUTORY CHARGE

[40.37]

Regulations 43–53 of the Community Legal Service (Financial) Regulations 2000 provide that where any money or property is recovered for a client in a relevant dispute or proceedings, the amount of the statutory charge shall be the aggregate of the sums referred to in s 10(7)(*a*) and (*b*) of the Access to Justice Act 1999. These are sums expended by the LSC in funding the services and other sums payable by the individual by virtue of regulations which shall constitute a first charge on any property recovered or preserved by an individual (whether for himself or any other person) in any proceedings or in any compromise or settlement of any dispute in connection with which the services were provided. The charge does not cover sums expended by the LSC in funding (a) Legal Help; (b) Help at Court; (c) Family Mediation or (d) Help with Mediation, except (a), (c) and (d) do not apply where the funded services were given in relation to family, clinical negligence or personal injury proceedings or a dispute which may give rise to such proceedings.

Solicitors have a duty to explain the operation of the statutory charge before their clients apply for legal aid. The LSC guidance also provides that 'Clients should also be given an opportunity to comment on the amount of their solicitors costs before they are assessed.' According to LSC figures at the end of September 2006 there were just over 60,000 such charges on homes in England and Wales.

(a) The law

(i) Cases under the Legal Aid Act 1988

[40.38]

Where a client has received advice and assistance under Part II of the Legal Aid Act 1988, the relevant law is in s 11 of that Act and regs 31–33 and Sch 4 of the Legal Advice and Assistance (Scope) Regulations 1989. Where a certificate was granted for representation under the Legal Aid Act 1988, the relevant law is in s 16 of that Act and Part XI of the Civil Legal Aid (General) Regulations 1989.

(ii)   Cases under the Access to Justice Act 1999

[40.39]

Where the Commission funds a service for a client as part of the Community Legal Service, unless regulations provide otherwise, the unrecovered cost of funding the service gives rise to a first charge on any property recovered or preserved by the client in any proceedings, or in any compromise or settlement of any dispute, in connection with which the services were funded – see the Access to Justice Act 1999, s 10(7).

(b) Extent

[40.40]

The charge does not arise in respect of the cost to the Commission of:
(a)   Legal Help, except in relation to family, clinical negligence or personal injury disputes or proceedings
(b)   Help at Court, except in relation to family, clinical negligence or personal injury disputes or proceedings
(c)   Family Mediation, or
(d)   Help with Mediation
The charge consists of:
(a)   the amount of money the Commission has spent on funding services at all levels in connection with the proceedings or dispute; (note: when a contract does not distinguish the costs of the client's individual case and other cases, the cost is what the Commission specifies in writing);
(b)   less any costs recovered by the client in the proceedings or dispute;
(c)   less any payment by the client by way of contribution or otherwise; see s 10(7) of the Access to Justice Act 1999 (*LSC Manual*).

(c) Amount

[40.41]

For the purposes of calculating the amount of the charge, the cost of funding services does not include the costs of assessment proceedings under the CPR, or taxation proceedings in the House of Lords. The costs of drawing up a bill are not part of the costs of assessment proceedings. Those costs will therefore form part of the deficiency to the fund: reg 40(4) of the Community Legal Service (Financial) Regulations 2000.

When a client had a certificate under the 1988 Act, the Commission treated the value of the charge as the value of the property recovered or preserved, or the net deficiency, whichever was less. Regulation 99(6) of the Civil Legal Aid (General) Regulations 1989 supported this approach. But s 10(7) of the 1999 Act and reg 43 of the Community Legal Service (Financial) Regulations 2000 do not permit the Commission to value the charge in this way. The charge is always the cost of the funded services, less costs and contributions actually received, even if the property to which it attaches is worth less on recovery or preservation.

If the client pays off the charge at the end of the case, the changed approach to valuation is unlikely to make any difference. The Commission cannot seek more than the value of the charged property in satisfaction of the deficiency to the Fund. But if we agree to defer enforcing the charge by securing it on the client's home, and the home increases in value before the client pays off the charge, we may enforce the charge up to its full amount, depending on how much the property is worth at the time.

In determining the value of the property at the time the charge is enforced, the £2,500 or £3,000 exemption in most family proceedings will take effect to the extent that it has not already been used up on any other asset or assets (*LSC Manual*).

(d) Exemptions

[40.42]

Regulation 44(1) provides that the charge shall not apply to any of the following:
(a)   any periodical payment of maintenance;
(b)   other than in circumstances which are exceptional having regard in particular to the quantity or the value of the items concerned, the client's clothes or household furniture or the tools or implements of his trade;
(c)   any sum or sums ordered to be paid under s 5 of the Inheritance (Provision for Family and Dependants) Act 1975 or Part IV of the Family Law Act 1996;
(d)   the first £2,500 (£3,000 if the charge arose, is in existence or is discharged on or after 3 December 2001) of any money or the value of any property recovered or preserved in most family proceedings.
(e)   one-half of any redundancy payment within the meaning of Part XI of the Employment Rights Act 1996 recovered by the client;
(f)   any payment of money made in accordance with an order made by the Employment Appeal Tribunal (excluding an order for costs);
(g)   where the statutory charge is in favour of the supplier, the client's main or only dwelling, or
(h)   any sum, payment or benefit which, by virtue of any provision of or made under an Act of Parliament, cannot be assigned or charged (which generally covers state benefits and pensions).
(i)   the former matrimonial home as long as it is the client's main or only dwelling where the funded service was only Legal Help or Help at Court. Where the client recovers or preserves the home in family proceedings after the Commission has granted a certificate in the same matter, the exemption does not apply.

(e) Waiver

[40.43]

The LSC may grant a supplier authority, either in respect of individual cases or generally, to waive either all or part of the statutory charge where its enforcement would cause grave hardship or distress to the client or would be unreasonably difficult because of the nature of the property.

The LSC may, if it considers it equitable to do so, waive some or all of the amount of the statutory charge in respect of proceedings which it considers have a significant wider public interest and the Commission considers it cost-effective to fund those services for a specified claimant or claimants, but not for other claimants or potential claimants who might benefit from the litigation. 'Wider public interest' is defined as meaning that the potential of the proceedings to produce real benefits for individuals other than the client (other than any general benefits which normally flow from proceedings of the type in question) (reg 47).

(f) Enforcement

[40.44]

The LSC may enforce the statutory charge in any manner which would be available to a chargee in respect of the charge given between parties (reg 51). Since the introduction of the Land Registration Act 2002 on 13 October 2003 the Legal Services Commission has been unable to render a caution against dealings with a property where it has not been possible to obtain the consent of all joint proprietors to register a contractual charge in the Commission's favour. In these circumstances solicitors for a funded client are urged by the LSC to make arrangements with their client's joint proprietor(s) to agree to a contractual charge in the Commission's favour at the time the case settles or otherwise concludes. If such consent is not forthcoming the Commission would only agree to postpone enforcing the statutory charge if the funded client agrees to the matter being referred to its Debt Recovery Unit for immediate enforcement. This will enable the DRU to obtain a charging order which is capable of being registered as a restriction against the property which will provide adequate security for the Commission. However, the extra costs of taking these steps will be borne by the funded client.

(g) Deferment

[40.45]

The Commission may postpone the enforcement of the statutory charge where (but only where):
(a)   by order of the court or agreement it relates to property to be used as a home by the client or his dependants, or, where the relevant proceedings were family proceedings, to money to pay for such a home;
(b)   the LSC is satisfied that the property in question will provide such security for the statutory charge as it considers appropriate;
(c)   as soon as it is possible to do so, the LSC registers a charge under the Land Registration Act 1925 to secure the amount in reg 43 or, as appropriate, takes equivalent steps to protect its interests in the property.
Where the client wishes to purchase a property in substitution for the property over which a charge is registered under paragraph (c) the Commission may release the charge if the conditions in paragraph (b) and (c) are satisfied. Where the enforcement of the statutory charge is postponed, interest shall accrue to the Commission from the date on which the charge is first registered at the rate of 8% calculated on the lesser of the amount of the statutory charge outstanding from time to time or where the value of the client's interest in the property at the time it was recovered was less than the amount of the statutory charge, such lower sum as the LSC considers equitable in the circumstances. All conveyances and acts done to defeat or operate to defeat any charge shall,

except in the case of a bona fide purchaser for value without notice, be void as against the LSC, without prejudice to the provisions of the Land Registration Act 1925 and the Land Charges Act 1972 (Regulations 52 and 53).

PROPERTY AND COSTS RECOVERED FOR A FUNDED CLIENT

[40.46]

There are strict rules to ensure that a funded client meets all his obligations to the CLS Fund before he receives the benefit of the litigation. The provisions are contained in Part III of the Community Legal Service (Costs) Regulations 2000 as follows:

[40.47]

COMMUNITY LEGAL SERVICE (COSTS) REGULATIONS 2000 (SI 2000/441)

PART III   PROPERTY AND COSTS RECOVERED FOR A FUNDED CLIENT

14 Application of this Part

(1)   In this Part:

'the awarded sum' means the amount of costs to be paid in accordance with a client's costs order or a client's costs agreement;

'client's costs order' and 'client's costs agreement' mean, respectively, an order and an agreement that another party to proceedings or prospective proceedings pay all or part of the costs of a client;

'Fund' means the Community Legal Service Fund established under section 5 of the Act;

'the funded sum' means the amount of remuneration payable by the Commission to a supplier for the relevant work under a contract or any other arrangements that determine that supplier's remuneration, including those that apply by virtue of article 4 of the Community Legal Service (Funding) Order 2000; and, where funding is provided by the Commission under a contract which does not differentiate between the remuneration for the client's case and remuneration for other cases, means such part of the remuneration payable under the contract as may be specified in writing by the Commission as being the funded sum;

'relevant work' means the funded services provided in relation to the dispute or proceedings to which the client's costs order or client's costs agreement relates;

'remuneration' includes fees and disbursements and value added tax on fees and disbursements;

'statutory charge' means the charge created by section 10(7) of the Act.

15 Amount of costs under client's costs order or client's costs agreement

(1)   Subject to the following paragraphs of this regulation, the amount of the costs to be paid under a client's costs order or client's costs agreement shall, subject to regulation 16, be determined on the same basis as it would be if the costs were to be paid to a person who had not received funded services.

(2)   Subject to paragraph (3), the amount of the awarded sum shall not be limited to the amount of the funded sum by any rule of law which limits the costs recoverable by a party to proceedings to the amount he is liable to pay to his legal representatives.

(3)　Paragraph (2) applies only to the extent that the Commission has authorised the supplier under section 22(2)(b) of the Act to take payment for the relevant work other than that funded by the Commission.

16　Costs of serving notices and other documents

The amount of costs to be paid under a client's costs order or client's costs agreement may include costs incurred in filing with the court, or serving on any other party to proceedings, notices or any other documents in accordance with these Regulations, the Financial Regulations or the Funding Code.

17　Application of regulations 18 to 24

(1)　Regulations 18 to 24 apply only where funded services have been provided under a certificate.

(2)　If the client is no longer being represented by a solicitor, all money to which regulation 18(1) applies shall be paid (or repaid) to the Commission, and all references in regulations 18(1) and 19 to the client's solicitor shall be construed as references to the Commission.

18　Money recovered to be paid to solicitor

(1)　Subject to the following paragraphs of this regulation, and to regulation 17(2), all money payable to or recovered by a client in connection with a dispute by way of damages, costs or otherwise, whether or not proceedings were begun, and whether under an order of the court or an agreement or otherwise, shall be paid to the client's solicitor, and only the client's solicitor shall be capable of giving a good discharge for that money.

(2)　Paragraph (1) shall not apply to:

　(a)　any periodical payment of maintenance; or

　(b)　any money recovered or preserved by a client in any proceedings which:

　　(i)　has been paid into, or remains in, court, and is invested for the client's benefit; and

　　(ii)　under regulation 50 of the Financial Regulations, is not subject to the statutory charge.

(3)　Where the client's solicitor has reason to believe that an attempt may be made to circumvent the provisions of paragraph (1), he shall inform the Commission immediately.

19　Notice to third parties

(1)　Where money is payable under regulation 18, and that money is payable by a trustee in bankruptcy, a trustee or assignee of a deed of arrangement, a liquidator of a company in liquidation, a trustee of a pension fund or any other third party ('the third party') the client's solicitor shall send to the third party notice that funded services have been funded for the client by the Commission.

(2)　Notice under paragraph (1) shall operate as a request by the client that money payable under regulation 18 be paid to his solicitor, and shall be a sufficient authority for that purpose.

20　Solicitor to pay money recovered to commission

(1)　The client's solicitor shall forthwith:

　(a)　inform the　.　.　.　Director of any money or other property recovered or preserved, and send him a copy of the order or agreement by virtue of which the property was recovered or preserved;

　(b)　subject to the following paragraphs of this regulation, pay to the Commission all money or other property received by him under regulation 18.

(2)   Paragraph (1)(b) shall not apply to any money or other property to which the statutory charge does not apply, by virtue of the Financial Regulations.

(3)   Where he considers it essential to protect the client's interests or welfare, the . . . Director shall pay, or direct the client's solicitor to pay, to the client any money received by way of any interim payment made in accordance with an order made under CPR rule 25.6, or in accordance with an agreement having the same effect as such an order.

(4)   The . . . Director may direct the client's solicitor to:

    (a)   pay to the Commission under paragraph (1)(b) only such sums as, in the . . . Director's opinion, should be retained by the Commission in order to safeguard its interests; and

    (b)   pay any other money to the client.

(5)   Where the solicitor pays money to the Commission in accordance with this regulation, he shall identify what sums relate respectively to:

    (a)   costs;

    (b)   damages;

    (c)   interest on costs; and

    (d)   interest on damages.

21 Postponement of statutory charge

(1)   In this regulation:

'conveyancer' means a solicitor or any other person who lawfully provides conveyancing services;

'family proceedings' means proceedings which arise out of family relationships, including proceedings in which the welfare of children is determined. Family proceedings also include all proceedings under any one or more of the following:

    (a)   the Matrimonial Causes Act 1973;

    (b)   the Inheritance (Provision for Family and Dependants) Act 1975;

    (c)   the Adoption Act 1976;

    (d)   the Domestic Proceedings and Magistrates' Courts Act 1978;

    (e)   Part III of the Matrimonial and Family Proceedings Act 1984;

    (f)   Parts I, II and IV of the Children Act 1989;

    (g)   Part IV of the Family Law Act 1996;

    (ga)   the Adoption and Children Act 2002;

    (h)   the inherent jurisdiction of the High Court in relation to children; and

    (i)   the Civil Partnership Act 2004;

'purchase money' means money recovered or preserved by the client in family proceedings which, by virtue of an order of the court or an agreement, is to be used to purchase a home to be used by the client or the client's dependants, and 'the purchased property' means the property purchased or to be purchased with that money.

(2)   The following paragraphs of this regulation apply, and (subject to paragraph (6)) regulation 20(1)(b) does not apply, where the Commission decides to postpone enforcement of the statutory charge under regulation 52 of the Financial Regulations.

(3)   The solicitor may release the purchase money to the seller or the seller's representative on completion of the purchase of the purchased property; and shall as soon as practicable provide the Commission with sufficient information to enable it to protect its interest in accordance with regulation 52(1)(c) of the Financial Regulations.

(4)   The client's solicitor may release the purchase money to a conveyancer acting for the client in the purchase of the purchased property, if he is satisfied that adequate steps have been, or will be, taken to protect the interests of the Commission.

(5)   The steps referred to in paragraph (4) shall include, but are not limited to, the securing of an undertaking from the conveyancer referred to in that paragraph to:

(a)   provide the information referred to in paragraph (3); and

(b)   repay the purchase money under paragraph (6).

(6)   Where the purchase of the purchased property has not been completed within 12 months after the date of the Commission's decision referred to in paragraph (2), or such longer period as the Commission considers reasonable, regulation 20(1)(b) shall apply and the purchase money shall accordingly be repaid to the Commission.

22 Retention and payment out of money by the commission

(1)   The Commission shall deal with the money paid to it under this Part in accordance with this regulation.

(2)   The Commission shall retain:

(a)   an amount equal to the costs incurred in taking steps under regulation 23;

(b)   an amount equal to that part of the funded sum already paid to the supplier in respect of the relevant work; and

(c)   where costs are paid to the Commission together with interest, an amount equal to that interest, less the amount of any interest payable to the supplier under paragraph (3)(b)(ii).

(3)   The Commission shall pay to the supplier:

(a)   any outstanding amount of the funded sum payable to him in respect of the relevant work;

(b)   where costs are ordered or agreed to be paid to the client, and those costs are received by the Commission, and those costs (less any amount retained under paragraph (2)(a) or payable under paragraph (5)) exceed the funded sum:

(i)   an amount equal to the amount of the excess; and

(ii)   where those costs are paid to the Commission together with interest, an amount equal to the interest attributable to the excess referred to in sub-paragraph (i).

(4)   Paragraph (5) applies where a solicitor has acted on behalf of the client in proceedings before that client receives funded services in respect of the same proceedings, or has a lien on any documents necessary to proceedings to which a client is a party, and has handed them over subject to the lien, but applies only so far as is consistent with the express terms of any contract between the Commission and the solicitor.

(5)   Where the solicitor referred to in paragraph (4) gives the Commission written notice that this paragraph applies, the Commission shall pay to that solicitor the costs to which that solicitor would have been entitled if those costs had been assessed on an indemnity basis.

(6)   Where the amount of costs payable under paragraph (5) have not been assessed by the court, they may instead be assessed by the Commission.

(7)   Where the amount received by the Commission, less any amount retained under paragraph (2)(a), is insufficient to meet the funded sum and any sum payable under paragraph (5), the Commission shall apportion the amount received proportionately between the two.

(8)   The Commission shall pay all the money paid to it under this Part, which is not paid or retained under paragraphs (2) to (5), to the client.

23 Enforcement of orders etc in favour of client

(1)   Where, in relation to any dispute to which a client is a party, whether or not proceedings are begun:

(a)   an order or agreement is made providing for the recovery or preservation of property by the client (whether for himself or any other person); or

(b)   there is a client's costs order or client's costs agreement

the Commission may take any steps, including proceedings in its own name, as may be necessary to enforce or give effect to that order or agreement.

(2)   A client may, with the consent of the . . . Director, take proceedings to give effect to an order or agreement under which he is entitled to recover or preserve money or other property.

(3)   Subject to paragraph (4), the client's solicitor may take proceedings for the recovery of costs where a client's costs order or a client's costs agreement has been made.

(4)   Where the client's costs order or client's costs agreement relates wholly or partly to costs incurred in carrying out work which is remunerated, or to be remunerated, in the funded sum, but those costs have not been reimbursed by payment from any other party in favour of the client, the solicitor shall require the consent of the . . . Director before taking proceedings to which paragraph (3) refers.

(5)   Where the Commission takes proceedings, it may authorise any person to make a statement, file a proof or take any other step in the proceedings in its name.

(6)   The costs incurred by the Commission in taking any step to enforce an order or agreement where paragraph (1) applies shall be a first charge on any property or sum so recovered.

24 Interest on damages

(1)   Where the Commission receives damages paid in favour of a client it shall, subject to the following paragraphs, pay to the client a sum representing gross interest earned while the damages are being held by the Commission.

(2)   Without prejudice to its other powers to invest money, the Commission shall maintain and may deposit damages to which this regulation refers in one general account at a deposit taker.

(3)   The rate of interest payable to the client under this regulation shall be 0.5% per annum less than the rate payable on damages deposited in the general account.

(4)   The Commission shall not be required to pay interest where the damages received do not exceed £500 or where the period during which they are held by the Commission is less than 28 days.

(5)   Interest shall be payable for the period beginning on the third business day after the date on which damages are received by the Commission to and including the date on which the Commission determines the amount to be paid under regulation 22(8).

(6)   In this regulation:

'business day' means a day other than a Saturday, a Sunday, Christmas Day, Good Friday or a bank holiday under the Banking and Financial Dealings Act 1971;

'deposit taker' means the Bank of England, or the branch, situated in England or Wales, of either—

(a)　a person with permission under Part 4 of the Financial Services and Markets Act 2000 to accept deposits, or

(b)　an EEA firm of the kind mentioned in paragraph 5(b) of Schedule 3 to that Act, which has permission under paragraph 15 of that Schedule (as a result of qualifying for authorisation under paragraph 12(1) of that Schedule) to accept deposits;

'general account' means an interest bearing account opened in the name of the Commission, the title of which does not identify any client.

(7)　The definition of 'deposit taker' in paragraph (6) must be read with—

(a)　section 22 of the Financial Services and Markets Act 2000;

(b)　any relevant order under that section; and

(c)　Schedule 22 to that Act.

OBTAINING PAYMENT

[40.48]

The Legal Services Commission has provided the following helpful charts and guidance. I am again grateful for their permission to reproduce them.

REGULATION	TIME LIMIT APPLICABLE
Retainer determined before proceedings begun – costs must be assessed by LSC (reg 105(2)).	Within three months of determination of the solicitor's retainer
Proceedings begun, costs not more than £500 – costs must be assessed by LSC	All other cases
	If the certificates revoked or discharged within three months of the termination of the retainer.
	Otherwise within the period CPR 47.7 would have specified (reg 105(2A)); or
Proceedings begun and costs not more than £1,000 costs must be assessed by LSC (Reg 105(3)(2), or	
Special circumstances (Reg 105(3)(c) or	
Following direction/order for detailed assessment recovery costs are incurred Reg 105(3)(d)	
SOURCE OF RIGHT TO DETAILED ASSESSMENT	TIME BY WHICH DETAILED ASSESSMENT PROCEEDINGS MUST BE COMMENCED
Judgment, direction, order, award or other determination.	Three months after the date of the judgment etc, but where detailed assessment is stayed pending an appeal, three months after the date of the order lifting the stay.

REGULATION	TIME LIMIT APPLICABLE
Discontinuance under Part 38.	Three months after the date of service of notice of discontinuance under Rule 38.3 or three months after the date of the dismissal of any application to set the notice of discontinuance aside under Rule 38.4.
Acceptance of an offer to settle or a payment into court under Part 36.	Three months after the date when the rights to the cost arose.

(i) Late claims sanctions

[40.49]

I am grateful to the Legal Services Commission for this summary.

The Legal Services Commission has powers to sanction those who delay in submitting costs claims for assessment under Public Funding Certificates. Pursuant to reg 105 of the Civil Legal Aid (General) Regulations, an application for an assessment shall be made within three months of the termination of the solicitor's retainer where the certificate is revoked or discharged or otherwise within the period specified by CPR Rule 47.7 for the commencement of detailed assessment proceedings if the costs fall to be determined by way of detailed assessment. The Civil Legal Aid (General)(Amendment No 2) Regulations 2002, which came into force on 31 December 2002, provided that for reg 105(10) there shall be substituted:

'Where a solicitor or counsel has failed to comply with the time limit (3A) the costs shall be assessed and the Area Director shall consider what, if any, reduction is reasonable and proportionate in all the circumstances; provided that costs shall not be reduced unless the solicitor or counsel has been allowed a reasonable opportunity to show cause in writing why the costs should not be reduced.'

The LSC guideline deductions are:

- Bills submitted up to 9 months late   5%
- Bills submitted between 9 and 18 months late   10%
- Bills submitted between 18 and 27 months late   15%
- Bills submitted between 27 and 35 months late   20%
- Bills submitted between 36 and 45 months late   30%

The percentage reductions are a guide only, so if the solicitor provides an explanation that justifies the delay, the regional office will consider what is an appropriate reduction in the circumstances. Where, for example, a bill submitted up to three months out of time has been delayed through no fault of the solicitor, no deduction would be applied. Where circumstances are outside the firm's control, it is less likely that a penalty will be imposed. In deciding what, if any, deduction to make the tests are reasonableness and proportionality. Examples of where it may be reasonable for some delay to have been incurred are linked to related actions awaiting final disposal; where conveyancing or other work by the conducting solicitor is necessary to implement an ancillary leave order; the court has delayed in sending the final order; counsel has failed to submit a fee note, despite reasonable steps by the solicitor to obtain it; delays in drafting by a law costs draftsman; awaiting the conclusion of the case transferred from the magistrates' to the county court before assessment; intervention of insolvency, illness or injury to the conducting solicitor; and damage to files through office fire or flood. The test of proportionality applies to the size of the claim. If the cost claim is above average, ie over £2,500, it may be appropriate for a lesser deduction to be applied than that in the guidelines. Deductions are based on the solicitor's profit cost. The deductions will be made from the solicitor unless counsel has been responsible for the delay. Even where profit is disallowed in full, the solicitor is still bound to discharge any experts' fees that have been incurred.

(ii) Point of principle CLA 29

[40.50]

The Association of Personal Injury Lawyers Newsletter for October 2003 reported that solicitor Stephen Irving wrote to his publicly funded client requesting him to contact him within 14 days. Six months later the solicitor requested the client to contact him within the next four weeks. He heard nothing, closed his file and submitted a request for discharge of the certificate and a claim for payment. The LSC rejected the claim on the grounds that it was out of time, on the view that the retainer had been terminated 14 days after the first letter. Stephen Irving's appeal was allowed by the Costs Appeal Committee on the grounds that the original letter was intended to spur the client into making contact and was not a termination of the retainer. In publicly funded cases the retainer is not usually considered terminated until the certificate is discharged. The appeal resulted in the publication of a new Point of Principle CLA 29 as follows:

For the purpose of the three-month time limit in reg 105(3A)(a) and (b)(i), whether the parties have terminated the retainer is a matter of general contract law, and depends on the parties' intentions, as evidence by their acts. The following factors may be relevant to when the retainer should be treated as having ended:

(1)   Where the solicitor represents the client in proceedings, termination of the retainer can be inferred if the solicitor has applied to be removed from the court record.

(2)   Where no proceedings were issued the solicitor must have completed the work he or she was instructed to do, or if not, either the solicitor or the client must have made a conscious decision, which the other party acknowledges as being effected, that the solicitor should no longer act for the client.

(3)   Mere inactivity by the solicitor for a period of time, however long, does not in itself terminate the retainer.

(4)   A letter from the solicitor warning that in the absence of a response by a stipulated time, he or she will no longer act for the client, does not necessarily demonstrate either that the solicitor intended to terminate the retainer, nor that the client regarded it as at an end, when the stipulated period expired.

(5)   Where other facts and circumstances show that the retainer is terminated, an application for discharge of the certificate or a letter from the client to the solicitor is not evidence that it still subsists.

(iii) Guidance

[40.51]

While a letter to his or her client may state that the solicitor is seeking instructions and, in the event of a non-reply may consider closing his file, the letter does not necessarily terminate the retainer on the expiry of any warning period given. If a solicitor has had difficulty obtaining instructions or there have been long periods of inactivity before the application for discharge was made the solicitor should be asked to provide evidence to establish when the retainer did actually terminate.

CHAPTER 41

THIRD PARTY FUNDING

DEFINITIONS

Third party funding (TPF)

[41.1]

TPF is a relatively recent development in the funding of litigation in the English courts (having developed in Australia and Germany before finding its way over here in the past ten years), albeit it that it has been permitted in matters arising out of insolvencies since *Seear v Lawson* (1880) 15 Ch D 426.

TPF is the funding of litigation, throughout its life, by individuals or companies who have no previous connection with the litigation with a view to making a profit out of it. TPF involves a direct arrangement between a party to litigation and a funder whereby the funder receives a share of the proceeds of the litigation if it succeeds in return for funding the case as it proceeds, taking full liability for all of the costs it has agreed to cover (which can include opponent's costs) of the action if it fails.

Section 2.03 of the Solicitor's Code of Conduct 2007, further requires solicitors to discuss with their clients how they will pay for the costs of their claim, including whether there are funding or insurance options available to them to cover such costs

However, it is the combination of a policy steer by the Civil Justice Council, the Court of Appeal judgment of *Arkin* in 2005 (see para [41.9]) and crucially the impact of the Jackson Report, which for the first time in a report produced at that level, devoted an entire chapter to TPF (see para [41.2]).

The effect of this is to recognise the role of TPF as a permanent part of the costs funding landscape and a matter of which all practitioners should make sure they are aware to avoid falling foul of the Solicitors Code of Conduct 2007.

It is important to remember that TPF is not just for the impecunious client and practitioners are reminded to ensure they discuss funding options with all clients.

THE JACKSON REPORT – IMPACT ON FUNDING

[41.2]

Jackson's conclusions were generally positive about the presence of TPF as an option for funding litigation costs. He said 'I remain of the view that, in principle, third party funding is beneficial and should be supported. He compared TPF favourably with CFAs and ATE because TPF does not involve recovering an 'additional liability' from the losing party which he is seeking to have abolished. He also considered that TPF 'filters out unmeritorious claims' and provides Access to Justice'.

The recommendations he made were:

(1) not to abolish champerty and maintenance;
(2) that it is too soon in the development of this 'nascent industry' to introduce formal regulation into TPF;
(3) that he supported a Voluntary Code of Conduct ('the Code') and suggested the existing draft be re-visited to address:

- Capital Adequacy requirements for funders, given that it is critical that a funder is adequately funded to fund all the cases it is funding to completion.
- The basis on which a funding agreement might be terminated should be re-considered and if possible, expanded, in the Code.

A group of funders have therefore re-worked the Code in the light of these observations, and the new draft was the subject of a consultation process managed by the Civil Justice Council, which ended on 3rd December 2010 (http://www.civiljusticecouncil.gov.uk/files/TPF_consultation_paper_ (23.7.10).pdf).

At present the bulk of funding occurs in commercial litigation. If there are new entrants who operate solely consumer based litigation, there may well need to be a separate code to deal with the issues arising there. In the meantime of course, the consumer has the protection of the Consumer Credit Act.

In addition, an Association of Litigation Funders has been formed as a forum for funders and non-funders alike to discuss matters relating to funding and provide a contact point for those using funding. This body will also be responsible for future developments of the Code.

The developments in funding generally, the arrival of new entrants and the endorsement of TPF by Jackson help see funding enter its teenage years of development. Its wholesale acceptance and understanding by the profession is still to be seen.

THE FUNDING AGREEMENT

[41.3]

A Third Party Funder covers all the costs (or such costs as the funded party seeks to have covered by the funder) of the litigation in return for a share of the proceeds of the action, including its own legal costs, expert's and court fees and any adverse costs orders.

There is no need for a conditional fee agreement (though funders will no doubt look more favourably on cases where the solicitor is prepared to act on at least a partial conditional fee agreement as a demonstration of their belief in the merits of the case in question) or after-the-event insurance. The price is typically 20%–50% of the amount recovered, depending on how long this takes. This form of funding is not champertous provided the funder does not (and is not entitled to) control the conduct of the action by the client.

Agreements must be structured so that the client retains full control over the way in which they conduct their action. This includes the funder not being permitted to set minimum settlement levels when signing up a case, or interfering in the day to day conduct of the matter.

Withdrawal of funding if the claim's merits plummet does not amount to interference.

Once the case is signed up, the client is then left to run his litigation in the usual way. The funding agreement sets out the responsibilities and liabilities of the parties. If at any stage the claim's merits suffer a 'material adverse decline' (which will include the ability of any successful judgment to be enforced against the defendant, the position on liability or claim value, or the conduct of the claimant, amongst others), the funder has the right to terminate the funding, while retaining the liability for all own side and adverse costs up to that date. The fact that investors in litigation are only interested in funding good claims also sends the powerful message to the opponent that a dispassionate and commercially focused third party also thinks the claim is good. The role of funders in accelerating settlement discussions has inevitably been a welcome development for third party funded claimants.

THE LITIGATION FUNDER'S CRITERIA

[41.4]

TPF is not for everyone. There are at the time of writing four major funders (not to be confused with litigation funding brokers who seek to introduce the litigants to the funders) and their minimum sizes of claim they will fund ranges from £350,000 to £3,000,000.

Additional eligibility criteria for considering funding a claim are:
* a defendant who can pay the amount claimed;
* good legal merits (60%-70% prospect of success), with a demonstrable minimum claim value;
* where the costs of pursuing the matter are proportionate to the size of the claim; and
* the lawyer who it is proposed will run the claim is demonstrably experienced in the area to which the claim relates.

TPF OR CFA AND ATE?

[41.5]

In my view this is a no-brainer. IF the client can find lawyers willing to act under a conditional fee agreement and insurers willing to provide after-the-event insurance he should grab them before they change their minds – if only because on these terms under the law as it stands if he wins he will recover his claim free of all costs and recover the insurance premium, while under a TPF agreement he will have to share the spoils of victory with his funder.

But you will note it is a big IF. Not all lawyers are prepared to underwrite the costs of substantial litigation, and while specialist insurers may offer ATE, the premium may be prohibitive. In addition, ATE is not always deemed adequate security for costs. Funders can provide a payment into court or purchase the extra deed of indemnity which can accompany ATE to help defeat such security for costs applications.

If you cannot afford to litigate, 50% under a TPF agreement is a lot better than nothing. Critically ATE does not provide funding for payment of bills throughout the life of the case, it only pays out if the case is lost.

What is clear therefore is that TPF is typically more suited to larger more complex claims where such cash flow requirements need to be covered. Where an expert witness is required, they cannot be paid on a conditional fee basis and their fees must be paid in full. The good news is that funders are happy to fund all or any of the costs of a case, so a pick and mix approach is possible, to achieve the most cost effective outcome for the client.

This means an opponent can be confronted with an opponent with the formidable combination of a third party funder, and the prospect of paying a 100% success fee and a huge ATE premium if he has the temerity to oppose the claim and loses.

What is certain is that in all substantial litigation, whatever the financial position of the client, the solicitor now has a duty to advise on this new method of finance.

EVOLUTION

[41.6]

The evolution of TPF into a respectable and acceptable method of funding civil litigation has been impeded since the middle ages by the doctrines of maintenance and champerty. Here is the story.

Maintenance

[41.7]

'Maintenance is the procurement, by direct or indirect financial assistance, of another person to institute, or carry on or defend civil proceedings without lawful justification' (The Law Commission 1966). Or, if you prefer the classic definition: 'Maintenance is the wanton and officious intermeddling with the disputes of others in which the maintainer has no interest whatever, and where the assistance he renders to the one or other party is without justification or excuse' (*British Cash and Parcel Conveyors Ltd v Lamson Store Service Co Ltd* [1908] 1 KB 1006, 77 LJKB 649, CA). Or, going back even further, there was Lord Loughborough LC in *Wallis v Duke of Portland* in 1798: ' . . . maintenance is not *malum prohibitum*, but *malum in se*: that parties shall not by their countenance aid the prosecution of suits of any kind: which every person must bring upon his own bottom and at his own expense'.

Champerty

[41.8]

'Champerty is an aggravated form of maintenance. The distinguishing feature of champerty is the support of litigation by a stranger in return for a share of the proceeds' (Steyn LJ in *Giles v Thompson* [1994] 1 AC 142, [1993] 3 All ER 321, HL). In other words, those of Lord Mustill also in *Giles v Thompson*, 'Champerty is maintenance with the addition of a division of the spoils of the litigation'.

These doctrines developed because, according to Professor Winfield one of the abuses which afflicted mediaeval administration of justice was the practice of assigning doubtful or fraudulent claims to royal officials, nobles or other persons of wealth and influence, who could in those times be expected to receive a very sympathetic hearing in the court proceedings. The agreement often was that the assignee would maintain the action at his own expense, and share the proceeds of a favourable outcome with the assignor.

Gradually the conditions which led to the emergence of maintenance and champerty disappeared. Jeremy Bentham wrote in 1843:

'A mischief, in those times it seems but too common, though a mischief not to be cured by such laws, was, that a man would buy a weak claim, in hopes that power might convert it into a strong one, and that the sword of a baron, stalking into court with a rabble of retainers at his heels, might strike terror into the eyes of a judge upon the bench. At present, what cares an English judge for the swords of a hundred barons? Neither fearing nor hoping, hating nor loving, the judge of our days is ready with equal phlegm to administer, upon all occasions, that system, whatever it be, of justice or injustice, which the law has put into his hands.'

By 1908 an English judge, Fletcher Moulton LJ in *British Cash* (above) was able to say:

'The truth of the matter is that the common law doctrine of maintenance took its origin several centuries ago and was formulated by text-writers and defined by legal decisions in such a way as to indicate plainly the views entertained on the subject by the courts of those days. But these decisions were based on the notions then existing as to public policy and the proper mode of conducting legal proceedings. Those notions have long since passed away, and it is indisputable that the old common law of maintenance is to a large extent obsolete.'

Nevertheless in 1963 Lord Denning MR in *Re Trepca Mines (No 2)* [1963] Ch 199 explained that the reason the common law still condemned champerty was 'because of the abuses to which it may give rise. The common law fears that the champertous maintainer might be tempted, for his own personal gain, to inflame the damages, to suppress evidence, or even to suborn witnesses. These fears may be exaggerated; but, be that so or not, the law for centuries has declared champerty to be unlawful, and we cannot do otherwise than enforce the law . . . .'.

PUBLIC POLICY

[41.9]

Both maintenance and champerty were criminal offences and torts until the Criminal Law Act 1967 abolished them as such (together with the crimes of eavesdropping, scolding and challenging an enemy to a fight!) but section 14(2) preserved 'any rule of that law as to the cases in which a contract is to be treated as contrary to public policy or otherwise illegal'. The common law restrictions on maintenance and champerty therefore remain, and the courts still have to decide on the facts of each litigation funding agreement whether the contract is unenforceable on the grounds of public policy.

Public policy was considered in *Arkin v Borchard Lines Ltd, Zim Israel Navigation Co Ltd and Managers and Processors of Claims (Part 20 defendants)* [2003] EWHC 2844 (Comm), [2004] 1 Lloyd's Rep 88, both in the High Court and the Court of Appeal. The second defendants (MPC), a professional funding company, entered into a funding agreement with the claimant, whereby it funded the employment of expert witnesses, the preparation of their evidence and the organisation of the enormous quantities of documents which it became necessary to investigate before the trial.

In applying for a costs order against MPC the defendants laid stress on the very substantial proportion of any recoverable damages or settlement payments (25% of the first £5 million and 23% of any excess) which MPC was to receive under its funding agreement. The amount of the claim, including exemplary damages, eventually reached $160 million, which would have resulted in a benefit of some $40 million to the funders. The defendants also drew attention to the absence of any undertaking by MPC to pay the defendants' recoverable costs or to take out after-the-event (ATE) insurance cover in respect of such costs. They submitted that, in principle, professional funders, as distinct from pure funders, who are maintaining litigation for their profit, should be liable for the costs of the defendants if their claim fails, which in this case it did.

In resisting this application MPC submitted that funding agreements with professional funders which have the purpose of enabling impecunious claimants to pursue claims of real substance which, but for such funding, they could not have done, should not be visited with costs orders against the funders if the claim fails.

The court held that in these circumstances the public policy objectives of the deterrence of weak claims and of the protection of the due administration of justice from interference by those who fund litigation must yield to the objective of making access to the courts available to impecunious claimants with claims of sufficient substance. An order for costs against MPC would, no doubt, operate as a strong deterrent to professional funders to provide support for impecunious claimants with large and complex claims.

[41.10]

On appeal the Court of Appeal held that a professional funder, who finances part of a claimant's costs of litigation, should be potentially liable for the costs of the opposing party *to the extent of the funding provided*. In its judgment the court said:

'The effect of this will, of course, be that, if the funding is provided on a contingency basis of recovery, the funder will require, as the price of the funding, a greater share of the recovery should the claim succeed. In the individual case, the net recovery of a successful claimant will be diminished. While this is unfortunate, it seems to us that it is a cost that the impecunious claimant can reasonably be expected to bear. Overall justice will be better served than leaving defendants in a position where they have no right to recover any costs from a professional funder whose intervention has permitted the continuation of a claim which has ultimately proved to be without merit.'

The decision may not have pleased purists like me (because the issue of causation should be the key: if a funder, or indeed a solicitor running a case on a full CFA, causes an opponent to incur costs and subsequently loses the case, then they should be liable to pay all costs recoverable by their opponent, since but for that funding, the opponent would not have incurred the costs in question) but it was a step in the right direction of a commercial funder of litigation being liable for *all* of the costs awarded against the fundee if the claim fails.

Over recent years the courts have indicated that the overriding need for claimants to have access to justice makes third party funding acceptable, subject to certain safeguards and protections. The present attitude of the judiciary to third party funding was exemplified by Lord Phillips in *Gulf Azov Shipping Co Ltd v Idisi* [2004] EWCA Civ 292 when he said: 'Public policy now recognises that it is desirable, in order to facilitate access to justice, that third parties should provide assistance designed to ensure that those who are involved in litigation have the benefit of legal representation.

In June 2007, the Civil Justice Council, as part of its wider consideration of 'Access to Justice', considered a range of funding options and, endorsed the decision in *Arkin* in stating TPF was a legitimate mechanism for paying for litigation costs. See http://www.civiljusticecouncil.gov.uk/files/future_funding_litigation_paper_v117_final.pdf.

LANDMARKS

[41.11]

Here is a chronological summary of some landmark decisions in the TPF journey.

[41.12]

Stocznia Gdanska v Latreefers [2001] 2 SCLC 116 (CA). Funders agreed to finance commercial litigation in exchange for 55% of the proceeds. They agreed to pay the between-the-parties costs if the litigation failed. They also had a prior commercial interest in the litigation because they were already owed money under an agreement which successful litigation would enable them to recover. The defendants sought a stay of the proceedings on the ground of champerty relying on the disproportion between the value of the funders' prior interest (about $7m) and the value of their 55% share if the case were successful (about $40m). Although the Court of Appeal did not have to decide whether or not the agreement was champertous, it was strongly of the view that it was not, because the alleged disproportion was more theoretical than real, the funders were undertaking a very substantial potential costs liability, they had a pre-existing interest in the subject-matter of the claim and they would not be able to influence the conduct of the litigation because that, including any negotiations, was in the hands of experienced solicitors.

[41.13]

The Eurasian Dream (No 2) [2002] 2 Lloyd's Rep 692 (Commercial Court). Marine claims assessors had carried out work for the claimants on the basis of a no-win, no-fee agreement providing for 5% of recoveries. The judge rejected an argument that the agreement was champertous, saying it was necessary to consider the role played by the consultants to see whether the nature of their interest in the outcome carried with it any tendency to sully the purity of justice. The opportunity for the consultants to influence the outcome was limited, as solicitors and counsel were instructed. It was relevant that it was the practice in this market to be remunerated on a similar basis.

[41.14]

R (on the application of Factortame) v Secretary of State for Transport, Environments and the Regions (No 2) [2002] EWCA Civ 932, [2003] QB 381. Impecunious Spanish trawler owners had obtained judgment against the British Government for damages for breaches of their fishing rights but they could not afford to proceed with the assessment of damages. Accountants agreed to provide litigation support in the form of handling documents and programming services, as well as undertaking to pay the fees of expert witnesses, in exchange for 8% of any amount recovered. The Court of Appeal held that the agreement was not champertous, saying:

> 'Where the law expressly restricts the circumstances in which agreements in support of litigation are lawful, this provides a powerful indication of the limits of public policy in analogous situations. Where this is not the case, then we believe one must today look at the facts of the particular case and consider whether those facts suggest that the agreement in question might tempt the allegedly champertous maintainer for his personal gain to inflame the damages, to suppress evidence, to suborn witnesses or otherwise to undermine the ends of justice.'
>
> [36]

> ' . . . .it is necessary to look at the agreement under attack in order to see whether it tends to conflict with existing public policy that is directed to protecting the due administration of justice with particular regard to the interests of the defendant.'
>
> [44]

> 'The greater the share of the spoils that the provider of legal services will receive, the greater the temptation to stray from the path of rectitude. The 8% that was agreed between Grant Thornton and the claimants was not extravagant.'
>
> [85]

> 'Although the prospect of receiving 8% of recoveries would have provided a motive to inflame the damages, the court was entitled to take into account that the accountants were members of a respectable and regulated profession. No reasonable

onlooker would seriously have suspected that they would be tempted by the percentage to deviate from the honest performance of their duties.'

[87]

'Although the accountants played an important role in the preparation of the computer model on which the damages claims were based, this was subject to checking by the other side and was transparent. No lack of objectivity on the part of the accountants could be expected to impact on the assessment of damages.'

[88–89]

'The claimants were represented by highly experienced solicitors and counsel, and the solicitors had very properly insisted on remaining in control of the conduct of the litigation. It was unrealistic to suggest that the accountants might have attempted to procure a settlement on terms which were at odds with their appreciation of the merits.'

[90]

I am grateful to Jeremy Morgan QC for this summary.

[41.15]

Campbells Cash and Carry Ltd v Fostif Pty [2006] HCA 41. This is a much quoted seminal Australian case (known as '*Fostif*'). I am grateful to the Civil Justice Council for the following summary.

Fostif involved the attempted recovery of payments of state based licence fees for tobacco that had been found to be unconstitutional. Firmstones, a firm of accountants, wrote to tobacco retailers seeking their authority to act on their behalf to recover fees paid. They offered to fund the litigation, and protect the retailers from adverse costs in the event that they lost the claim, in return they would take one third of any recovery, plus any recovered costs. Firmstones instructed solicitors to 'front' the action, on terms of instruction that severely limited access to their clients, who to all intents and purposes were represented by Firmstones. The claim was set down as a 'representative proceeding' (there are no group litigation or class action proceedings in New South Wales), with only one single identified claimant, but with an opt-in provision intended to permit other parties, once identified and willing to participate, to join the proceedings. At first instance the defendant (Campbells) applied to have the proceedings dismissed or stayed on the grounds that (i) the proceedings were not properly constituted; due to lack of common interest the action was not sufficiently representative, and (ii) that the third party funding arrangements amounted to an abuse of process because of intermeddling, and the degree of control exercised over the proceedings by the funders (Firmstones).

The first instance judge, Einstein J, decided that the funding arrangements were contrary to public policy and that the proceedings as constituted did not meet the requirements of a representative action. He entered a stay. The decision was successfully appealed to the Court of Appeal of New South Wales which rejected both grounds of the stay. On further appeal, the High Court (Australia's final appeal process) decided by a majority of 5:2 that the case did not meet the procedural requirements to become a representative proceeding, and stayed the case, allowing that limb of the appeal. However, the Court also removed the stay on the basis of the second limb of the appeal by a majority of 5:2 (a differently constituted majority decision) that the third party funding arrangements did not constitute an abuse of process, and that the arrangements were not contrary to public policy. The appeal therefore succeeded on this ground, giving strengthened legitimacy to third party funding in Australia.

[41.16]

London & Regional (St George's Court) Ltd v Ministry of Defence [2008] EWHC 526 (TCC). Coulson J summarised the present state of the authorities as:

- the mere fact that litigation services have been provided in return for a promise in the share of the proceeds is not by itself sufficient to justify that promise being held to be unenforceable;
- in considering whether an agreement is unlawful on grounds of maintenance or champerty, the question is whether the agreement has *a tendency to corrupt public justice*, and such a question requires the closest attention to the nature and surrounding circumstance of a particular agreement;
- the modern authorities demonstrate a flexible approach where courts have generally declined to hold that an agreement under which a party provided assistance with litigation in return for a share of the proceeds was unenforceable;
- the rules against champerty, so far as they have survived, are primarily concerned with the protection of the integrity of the litigation process by the limitation of control of the conduct of the action by a third party.

PERSONAL INJURY CASES

[41.17]

Jeremy Morgan QC has drawn attention to a particular difficulty in third party funding of personal injury claims. He says:

'Solicitors need to be aware of it and the Law Society needs to eradicate it if modern third party funding is to play any role in providing access to justice in personal injury litigation. Given that Legal Aid is now very hard to get for group actions the current situation precludes the use of modern third party funding in important areas such as pharmaceutical litigation. The problem arises as follows.

In its recent wholesale revision of the rules governing the practice of solicitors, the Council of the Law Society decided to retain the old Practice Rule 9. It now appears as Rule 9.01(4) of the Solicitors Code of Conduct 2007 which reads:

'You must not, in respect of any claim arising as a result of death or personal injury, either:

(a)   enter into an arrangement for the referral of clients with; or
(b)   act in association with any person whose business, or any part of whose business, is to make, support or prosecute (whether by action or otherwise, and whether by a solicitor or agent or otherwise) claims arising as a result of death or personal injury and who, in the course of such business, solicits or receives contingency fees in respect of such claims.'

Clearly the Rule affects any solicitor who works with a third party funder in a personal injury case where the funder has stipulated for a contingency fee.

Rules made under the Solicitors Act 1974, such as this one, have the force of law (*Awwad v Geraghty* [2001] QB 570). The prohibition in the Rule is not one which bites on the agreement between the funder and the funded party, but only on the association with the solicitor. Accordingly it should not render the agreement itself unlawful, particularly as there is nothing in the provisions brought into force under the Compensation Act 2006 to preclude claims management companies from entering into such agreements. It is only the Law Society that has a problem with them. Nevertheless it is a trap for solicitors, who face disciplinary action if they breach the rule, and several prosecutions for the breach of the predecessor of this rule are being brought by the Solicitors Regulation Authority.'

[41.18]

There have been a number of rule 9 prosecutions resulting in at least two convictions by the Solicitors Disciplinary Tribunal, mainly arising from the Miners' Respiratory Disease Litigation where it may be that unions receive a percentage of the damages in return for funding cases. There are other cases going through the system

The draft Solicitors' Code of Conduct 2007 had not originally included an equivalent of the previous practice rule 9 concerning claims assessors. That practice rule (broadly) prohibited solicitors from accepting referrals from introducers who solicited or received contingency fees in claims arising out of personal injury or death.

A decision was made to omit the provision because the government had announced its intention to regulate claims managers, and it was thought that would in effect legitimise and regulate claims assessors.

[41.19]

Solicitors are able, by virtue of conditional fee agreements, to charge clients on a contingency fee basis (to a maximum of 200% of their hourly rate) because these arrangements are sanctioned through legislation, and clients' interests are protected by various safeguards. There are no equivalent protections for clients who enter contingency fee arrangements with claims assessors – indeed such agreements may be contrary to the common law. Clients suffered as a result of entering into agreements with some unscrupulous claims assessors, which resulted in the clients paying over a significant proportion of their damages.

In all the circumstances, it was considered that unless and until there was clarity about the regulation of the activities of claims assessors in this area, the new Code of Conduct should maintain the previous *status quo* and contain a similar prohibition.

Rule 9 needs urgent revision now that claims management companies are regulated.

WORD OF WARNING

[41.20]

The largest claim that is known to have been commercially funded, a £69.5 million professional negligence claim in *Stone & Rolls Ltd (in liquidation) v Moore Stephens (A Firm)* [2009] UKHL 39, [2009] 3 WLR 455,

[2009] NLJR 1218 gives insight into the inherent risks and high stakes of litigation funding. It failed in the Court of Appeal and failed again in the House of Lords by a 3–2 majority. TPF is not for the faint-hearted.

Part VII

Conditional Fees

CHAPTER 42

THE BACKGROUND

CONTINGENCY FEES

(a) A change of attitude

[42.1]

Since the Statute of Westminster in 1275 it has been inculcated into each generation of English lawyers as a tenet of professional ethics that contingency fees (payment by results) for litigation are not merely unlawful but, in the words of the judges, 'inherently immoral', 'deeply corrupting' and 'definitely sinister'. They are the scarlet women of the law. They might make suitable consorts for brash American lawyers, but no respectable clean-living English barrister or solicitor should associate with, let alone embrace, them. Yet in 1989 a Scottish Presbyterian Lord Chancellor published a Green Paper on contingency fees inviting English lawyers seriously to consider getting into bed and cohabiting with this method of funding litigation. What had happened? Was it that contingency fees were not as bad as they had been painted over the centuries? Had it been a case of mistaken identity? Could they even now be redeemed and reformed? Had our moral values changed? Or was it simply that to keep the purse strings tight on the Legal Aid Fund the Treasury was able to view with equanimity the prospect of the legal profession living on immoral earnings? The change was as sudden as it was dramatic, two converts being the Law Society and the government. In 1979, the government had accepted the view of the Royal Commission on Legal Services that in a contingency fee system 'the lawyer is exposed to strong temptation to settle the claim before incurring the heavy expense of preparing for trial, and of trial itself, although it may not be in his client's interest to do so. Alternatively, the client, having nothing to lose, may insist that a hopeless or irresponsible claim be pursued to litigation in the hope some profit will result'. ('Having nothing to lose' overlooked the possibility of between-the-parties costs being awarded against the client.)

In July 1987, a Law Society working party (in its report 'Improving Access to Civil Justice') agreed with the views of the Royal Commission and added 'we would go further and say that conflict of interest between solicitor and client is inherent in contingency fee arrangements' and 'it would be impossible to overcome the ethical and consumer protection problems'.

However in its Green Paper, the government believed 'that it is appropriate to consider the introduction in England and Wales of speculative actions on the Scottish model' (para 5.3), while the Law Society's working party in its second report advised the Council of the Law Society 'to seek an opportunity to remove the statutory bars on contingency fees . . . and that if they are removed the Council should immediately permit "speculative" funding of all types of case'.

(b) For and against

[42.2]

The arguments propounded in favour of contingency fees included: greater access to justice; avoiding the client funding litigation during its currency; protection against costs on failure; an incentive to lawyers; assurance to clients of their lawyer's motivation and extra work for lawyers with higher rewards for success. Furthermore there had never been any problem with contingency fees in non-contentious business (see para [43.42]), not even in the Employment Tribunal (see para 21.1]).The arguments against were that contingency fee agreements would conflict with a lawyer's duty to the court; be a temptation for unprofessional conduct; lead to unmeritorious 'blackmailing' actions; remove lawyer's objective independence from their clients; afford clients no protection against between-the-parties costs, expert fees and other disbursements; result in lawyers sharing in their client's awards and being paid by results leading to conflicts of interest between the lawyer and the client. Some of these arguments were raised again in 2004 in *King v Telegraph Group Ltd* para [10.12], in respect of an impecunious claimant in defamation proceedings, in which the Court of Appeal attempted to control the costs consequences of the CFA regime. However, in *Kellar v Williams* [2004] UKPC 30, [2004] All ER (D) 286 (Jun) the message from the Privy Council was:

' . . . their Lordships wish to make it plain that they are not to be taken as accepting without question the traditional doctrine of the common law that all such agreements are unenforceable on grounds of public policy. The content of public policy can change over the years, and it may now be time to reconsider the accepted prohibition in the light of modern practising conditions.'

(c) Still unlawful

[42.3]

The 1989 Green Paper was followed by a White Paper which was a triumph of semantics. Contingency fees were still an abhorrence, but conditional fees were given cautious approval. It was a distinction without a difference. A contingency agreement provides that the successful lawyer will receive a direct share of the proceeds, while under a conditional fee agreement (CFA) with a success fee the lawyer receives a higher fee than normal – paid, of course, out of the proceeds. The end result is the same under both regimes – the client gets less and the lawyer gets more. Conditional fees were described as 'contingency fees by the back door'. Nevertheless, semantics apart, contingency fee agreements were and still are, unlawful maintenance and champerty. The prohibition does not apply to members of other professions who may provide services in support of litigation on a contingency fee basis, that is, in return for a direct share of the proceeds, without being champertous. This was the decision of the Court of Appeal in *R (on the application of Factortame) v Secretary of State for Transport, Environment and the Regions (No 2)* [2002] EWCA Civ 932, [2003] QB 381, [2002] 4 All ER 97 which concluded that an agreement to pay accountants 8% of the final settlement received was not contrary to the common law nor was it governed by the Courts and Legal Services Act 1990. However, the court expressly disapproved of any such arrangement with expert witnesses (see para [45.3]).

However, in *Benaim (UK) Ltd v Davies Middleton & Davies Ltd* [2004] EWHC 737 (TCC), [2004] NLJR 617, [2004] All ER (D) 531 (Mar), the court accepted a CFA in which the determination of the amount of the solicitor's uplift, subject to its maximum of 100%, was by reference to the amount recovered.

The Court of Appeal further countenanced what may have been perceived as maintenance and champerty in *Arkin v Borchard Lines* [2005] EWCA Civ 655, [2005] 3 All ER 613, by accepting an arrangement by a commercial funder to fund expert evidence and document management on a contingency basis although holding that such a funder had a potential liability for the costs of the opponent limited to the sum it had funded (see para [34.14]).

Going the other way is the decision in the Court of Appeal in *Farrell v Birmingham City Council* [2009] EWCA Civ 769, [2009] All ER (D) 172 (Jun)that a car hire company had by its hire terms and a collective CFA both instigated and then controlled the litigation with the consequence that they were liable for costs as a third party. The SCCO decision in *Dix v Townend* [2008] EWHC 90117 (Costs) raised the profile of champerty where a solicitor undertook to indemnify the client against adverse costs. That risk was uninsured. The retainer was successfully challenged. Even if not champertous it was in any event contrary to public policy as explained by Lord Phillips MR in *R (on the application of Factortame) v Secretary of Sate for Transport, Environment and the Regions (No 2)* [2002] EWCA Civ 932, [2003] QB 381, [2002] 4 All ER 97. Dix was not followed however in the decisions of MacDuff J in *Morris v London Borough of Southwark* [2010] EWHC B1 (QB) and of Master O' Hare in *Murray Lewis v Tennats Distribution Ltd* [2010] EWHC 90161 (Costs). In the former the risk to the solicitor in having to pay opponent's costs under the arrangement made with their client was small and far outweighed by the advantages of the arrangements as a whole. In the latter it was simply not accepted that an agreement to shoulder the risk of adverse costs orders ought to be regarded as threatening the integrity of any solicitor.

(d) Damages based agreements

[42.3A]

The Ministry of Justice issued a consultation paper on 1 July 2009 'Damages based agreements' (known as 'DBA's), which are of course contingency fees. Consultation ended on 25 September 2009. We now have S58 AA of the Courts and Legal Services Act 1990, inserted via the Coroners and Justice Act 2009, permitting damages based agreements in employment matters that are, or could become, the subject of proceedings before an employment tribunal. Such agreements are governed by the Damages-Based Agreements Regulations 2010 (SI 2010 No 1206) which came into force on 9 April 2010. The Regulations permit an agreement to require a "payment" of a part of the sum recovered in respect of the claim or damages awarded that the client agrees to pay and excludes expenses. The amount of the payment, including VAT, must not exceed 35% of the sum recovered. Having said all that, Regulation 3(b) then goes on to require a DBA to set out the circumstances in which the representative's payment, expenses and costs, or part of them, are payable – in other words it treats the "payment" as being separate not only from expenses but also from own costs. Costs means the hourly rate and it will only apply where the DBA is terminated such that the 'payment' is replaced by the hourly rate.

On 27 May 2010 the Law Society issued a practice note advising on the relevant legislation, the content of the Regulations themselves and relevant rules and guidance already contained within the Solicitors Code of Conduct 2007, together with additional guidance to assist with compliance. You will find it at http://www.lawsociety.org.uk/productsandservices/practicenotes/da magesbasedagreement/4526.article

CATEGORIES OF CONDITIONAL FEE

[42.4]

All CFAs allow a lawyer to act for a client on the basis he will not charge his client, or charge a lower amount, if an agreed result is not achieved. Most agreements allow the solicitor to charge a success fee if the agreed result is achieved. Any fee agreement whereby the solicitor is to be paid different sums in different circumstances constitutes a CFA under s 58 of the Courts and Legal Services Act 1990 as substituted by s 27 of the Access to Justice Act 1999.

Harrington v Wakeling [2007] EWHC 1184 (Ch), 151 Sol Jo LB 744, [2007] 5 Costs LR 710 was a dispute between the claimant and his solicitor about the solicitor and client costs of successful litigation. The dispute between them was settled on terms that the solicitor would not seek any further costs from Mr Harrington but the solicitor would be paid any further costs recovered from the defendant. On the detailed assessment of the between-the-parties costs the defendant argued that the agreement constituted an unenforceable CFA and therefore under the indemnity principle no costs were payable at all. The court held:

> '(1) An agreement that costs are payable only to the extent that they are recovered from a third party does not offend the indemnity principle: there is no conceptual difficulty with a liability which is payable only if funds are first recovered from another source. (2) Such an agreement reached after the underlying litigation is concluded is not a CFA or otherwise contrary to public policy. There is no element of futurity.'

(a) CFAs with no success fee

[42.5]

These have also been variously known as contingent fee agreements; no-win, no-fee agreements; *Thai Trading* agreements and conditional normal fee agreements (CNFAs). In *Thai Trading Co (a firm) v Taylor* [1998] QB 781, [1998] 3 All ER 65, CA, Lord Justice Millett summarised the position in common law as follows:

' . . . there is nothing unlawful in a solicitor acting for a party to litigation to agree to forego all or part of his fee if he loses, provided that he does not seek to recover more than his ordinary profit costs and disbursements if he wins.'

Unfortunately, a QBD Divisional Court subsequently held in *Hughes v Kingston upon Hull City Council* [1999] QB 1193, [1999] 2 All ER 49, following *Swain v Law Society* [1983] 1 AC 598, [1982] 2 All ER 827, HL (which had been overlooked in *Thai Trading*), that because such an agreement contravened the Solicitors' Practice Rules, which had the force of statute, this rendered the agreement illegal. The 1990 Act was then amended by the Access to Justice Act 1999 to make unenforceable any CFA that did not comply with the statute. So not even the common law could save a simple 'no win – no fee' agreement.

(b) CFAs with success fee

[42.6]

If the case is won, the lawyer is not only entitled to charge his normal fee, he may also charge a success fee calculated as a percentage of his normal charges, to recompense him for the risk he has run of not being paid and of having to fund the litigation. The Lord Chancellor's Department's consultation paper of March 1998 said 'Conditional fees ensure that the risks of litigation are shared between the lawyer and the client: clients do not pay their lawyer's fees unless they win; and lawyers when they win receive a level of fees that recognises the risk they have taken'.

(c) Discounted CFAs

[42.7]

On this basis, the lawyer receives payment whatever the result, but at a discounted rate if a specific result is not achieved. Tony Girling suggests two options. An example of the first is an agreement that provides for charges of £300 an hour if the case is won and an order for costs is secured, but only £200 an hour if the prescribed result is not achieved. His other option is an attractive variation on the lines of '£300 an hour if the case is won with a success fee of *(for example)* 50%; if the case is lost, this fee arrangement be discounted to £200 an hour'. This formula gives the solicitor and the client the best of both worlds. Justifying the various figures in such arrangements will need care. In particular, account must be taken of the fact that by no means all of the solicitor's fees are being risked so that the success fee needs to reflect the real level of risk. The question then arises 'Do discounted fee arrangements constitute a success fee?'. In *Dunn v Glass Systems (UK) Ltd* [2007] EWHC 1901 (QB), [2007] All ER (D) 369 (Jul) it was argued that the agreed base rate of £265 with a lower rate of £90 if the case was lost amounted to a success fee in excess of the statutory limit of 100% (see para [43.6]) but the point was left open.

(d) Speccing agreements

[42.8]

This is where a solicitor speculates by acting for an impecunious client who has no prospect of paying the solicitor's fees unless the proceedings are successful. The solicitor in effect agrees to act for such costs as are recovered from the opponent. English law has had considerable difficulty in dealing with this everyday reality. In *British Waterways Board v Norman* (1993) 26 HLR 232, [1993] NPC 143, QBD, the court implied an understanding between the solicitors and their impecunious client that they would not look to her for costs if she lost which was an unlawful contingency fee agreement. An agreement of this type became lawful from 2 June 2003 by an amendment to the CFA Regulations creating what are known as 'simplified' CFAs (see para [42.40]). More recently the Competition Appeal Tribunal in *Albion Water v Water Services Regulation Authority* [2007] CAT 1 refused to conclude that there was a CFA only on the ground that the client was paying a small monthly sum but was receiving legal services of far higher value.

(e) Variable rate agreements

[42.9]

These are success fees determinable by reference to the amount recovered, as in *Benaim (UK) Ltd v Davies Middleton & Davies Ltd* (para [42.3]).

OPEN TO ALL

[42.10]

In *Campbell v MGN Ltd* [2005] UKHL 61, [2005] 4 All ER 793, [2005] 1 WLR 3394 the House of Lords rejected the contention that a litigant who was sufficiently wealthy to fund her litigation but who nevertheless had entered into a CFA should not be entitled to recover the success fee. The impracticality of requiring a means test and the small number of individuals who could be said to have sufficient resources to provide them with access to legal services entitled Parliament to lay down a general rule that CFAs are open to everyone. It was a deliberate policy of the Access to Justice Act 1999 to impose the cost of all CFA litigation, successful or unsuccessful, upon unsuccessful defendants as a class. In a similar vein was the decision in *Sousa v Waltham Forest London Borough* [2010] EW Misc 1 (EWCC).

The defendant contended that the claimant should not recover a success fee under his CFA because he was never at risk as to costs because he was indemnified under his insurance policy. Allowing the CFA would be a windfall for the insurer or their solicitors. The district judge agreed, holding that "It was incumbent on the court to look at and reflect the reality of the situation. The claimant was never at risk as to costs and it was unreasonable to allow him to rely on a CFA. Accordingly the success fee could not be recovered." He was wrong. The Court of Appeal held it is inherent in the concept of subrogation that an insurer is entitled to benefit from the same rights as the insured. The defendant could not rely on the fact of the insurer funding the claim as a defence to the policy holder's claim for a success fee when the claim succeeded: the insurer would be on a worst position than the policy holder would have been. The decision would lead to an anomaly that an insurer with an assigned cause of action could take advantage of a CFA but an insurer with a subrogated claim could not. The appeal was allowed.

CHAPTER 43

THE LEGISLATION

THE STATUTES

Courts and Legal Services Act 1990

[43.1]

Statutory provision for CFAs with or without a success fee was first made by the Courts and Legal Services Act 1990, s 58. It authorised the Lord Chancellor to permit CFAs in respect of all categories of work except criminal and family proceedings by Order after consultation with the designated judges, the General Council of the Bar, the Law Society and such other authorised bodies he thought appropriate. All of this took time, and it was not until 5 July 1995 that the Conditional Fee Agreements Order 1995 and accompanying regulations came into force. At first they were restricted to a few specified proceedings, but on 30 July 1998 the Conditional Fee Agreements Order 1998 extended the categories to all work except that prohibited by the Act.

Access to Justice Act 1999

(a)   New sections 58 and 58A

[43.2]

On 1 April 2000, s 27 of the Access to Justice Act 1999 substituted a new s 58 of the Courts and Legal Services Act 1990 and introduced a new s 58A:

[43.3]

27 Conditional Fee Agreements
    (1)   For section 58 of the Courts and Legal Services Act 1990 substitute—
    '58 Conditional fee agreements
        (1)   A conditional fee agreement which satisfies all of the conditions applicable to it by virtue of this section shall not be unenforceable by reason only of its being a conditional fee agreement; but (subject to subsection (5)) any other conditional fee agreement shall be unenforceable.
        (2)   For the purposes of this section and section 58A—
            (a)   a conditional fee agreement is an agreement with a person providing advocacy or litigation services which provides for his fees and expenses, or any part of them, to be payable only in specified circumstances; and
            (b)   a conditional fee agreement provides for a success fee if it provides for the amount of any fees to which it applies to be increased, in specified circumstances, above the amount which would be payable if it were not payable only in specified circumstances.

(3)   The following conditions are applicable to every conditional fee agreement—

(a)   it must be in writing;

(b)   it must not relate to proceedings which cannot be the subject of an enforceable conditional fee agreement; and

(c)   it must comply with such requirements (if any) as may be prescribed by the Lord Chancellor.

(4)   The following further conditions are applicable to a conditional fee agreement which provides for a success fee—

(a)   it must relate to proceedings of a description specified by order made by the Lord Chancellor;

(b)   it must state the percentage by which the amount of the fees which would be payable if it were not a conditional fee agreement is to be increased; and

(c)   that percentage must not exceed the percentage specified in relation to the description of proceedings to which the agreement relates by order made by the Lord Chancellor.

(5)   If a conditional fee agreement is an agreement to which section 57 of the Solicitors Act 1974 (non-contentious business agreements between solicitor and client) applies, subsection (1) shall not make it unenforceable.

Advocacy or Litigation Services

[43.4]

Section 58(1) applies to the provision of litigation services which are defined in s 119(1) as 'any services which it would be reasonable to expect a person who is exercising, or is contemplating exercising, a right to conduct litigation in relation to any proceedings, or any contemplated proceedings, to provide'. In *Gaynor v Central West London Buses Ltd* [2006] EWCA Civ 1120, [2007] 1 All ER 84, [2007] 1 WLR 1045 the retainer letter included the provision: 'If your claim is disputed by your opponent and you decide not to pursue your claim then we will not make a charge for the work we have done to date'. The claim was pursued and the client awarded her costs. Did this provision make the agreement a CFA and thus unenforceable because it did not comply with the CFA regulations? 'No' said the Court of Appeal. The work done before a decision was made not to pursue the claim was pre-litigation work which did not constitute the provision of litigation services under section 119(1). The solicitors were not exercising their right to conduct litigation and could not be said to be contemplating exercising that right until the potential defendant disputed the claim. Advising on the merits and writing a letter before action did not amount to litigation services. Therefore the agreement was not a CFA and the costs were recoverable. It is possible to make either too much or too little of this decision. Clearly the use of the disputed provision does not render a retainer unenforceable. Although pre-proceedings work is by definition non-contentious business this does not prevent the parties entering into a CFA in respect of it at the outset. Most CFAs are entered into at the non-contentious business stage and many of them relate to claims which are settled without the issuing of proceedings, which would retrospectively convert the work into contentious business (see Chapter 21). The curiosity of this decision is that although the work in question was converted into contentious business by the subsequent commencement of proceedings it was not litigation services for the purposes of s 119(1). The Court of Appeal appears to have identified the new category of 'pre-litigation contentious business'. In the absence of a valid CFA the successful claimant cannot of course recover any success fee between the parties, nor of course may a success fee be recovered for non-contentious business which has not been converted into contentious business by the commencement of proceedings.

More recently the decision in *Roche v Newbury Homes Ltd* [2009] EW Misc 3 (EWCC) that a CFA in Law Society Model terms does not cover a pre-action application for disclosure, has been rejected by a district judge in *Billy Mae Smith v McDonalds* (Liverpool CC 9LV31641) (2009), unreported taking the view that a CFA would generally cover costs throughout, including preparation and specifically in this case a pre-action application resulting from an opponent's failure to comply with the protocol.. As to whether the client had a liability to pay the costs of a pre-action application for disclosure, the standard Law Society wording is as follows:

> 'If on the way to winning or losing you are awarded any costs by agreement or Court order, then we are entitled to payment of those costs together with a success fee on those charges if you win overall.'

That was accepted by Master Haworth in *Connaughton v Imperial College Healthcare NHS Trust* [2010] EWHC 90173 (Costs) as giving rise to a liability in the client and there was therefore no breach of the indemnity principle in ordering the opponent to pay the costs of a pre-action application. As to the argument that pre-action work was not covered by the CFA a lay-person's reasonable expectation would be that non-compliance with a pre-action protocol which was part of the pre-litigation process and necessitated an application to the Court, would be covered under the terms of this CFA.

A final twist in this case was that the Claimant was not now proceeding against the Defendant, but against another party – the Defendant's cleaner. Did that mean the PAD application cannot be 'within the claim' by virtue of the fact that proceedings have now been brought against another party? No. The fact that proceedings had not been issued against the Defendant, did not mean that the Claimant was not claiming against the Defendant in accordance with the definition of 'claim' within the CFA.

Section 58 also applies to the exercise of a right of audience and in *Fosberry v Revenue & Customs Comrs* [2006] EWHC 90061 (Costs) the parties conceded that the VAT Tribunal was a Court for the purposes of the section. It was held that the tribunal had granted a non-legal professional advisor a right of audience and the right to conduct litigation. Accordingly his fee arrangement was governed by s 58, and was, unhappily, an invalid CFA, a decision upheld on appeal to the High Court. This reasoning does not apply to Employment Tribunals because, despite arguments to the contrary, their proceedings continue to be classified as non-contentious business (see para [21.1]).

[43.5]

58A Conditional fee agreements: supplementary

(1)   The proceedings which cannot be the subject of an enforceable conditional fee agreement are—

(a)   criminal proceedings, apart from proceedings under section 82 of the Environmental Protection Act 1990; and

(b)   family proceedings.

(2)   In subsection (1) "family proceedings" means proceedings under any one or more of the following—

(a)   the Matrimonial Causes Act 1973;

(b)   the Adoption and Children Act 2002;

(c)   the Domestic Proceedings and Magistrates' Courts Act 1978;

(d)   Part III of the Matrimonial and Family Proceedings Act 1984;

(e)   Parts I, II and IV of the Children Act 1989;

(f)   Parts 4 and 4A of the Family Law Act 1996;

(fa)   Chapter 2 of Part 2 of the Civil Partnership Act 2004 (proceedings for dissolution etc of civil partnership);

(fb)   Schedule 5 to the 2004 Act (financial relief in the High Court or a county court etc);

(fc)   Schedule 6 to the 2004 Act (financial relief in magistrates' courts etc);

(fd)   Schedule 7 to the 2004 Act (financial relief in England and Wales after overseas dissolution etc of a civil partnership); and

(g)   the inherent jurisdiction of the High Court in relation to children.

(3)   The requirements which the Lord Chancellor may prescribe under section 58(3)(c)—

(a)   include requirements for the person providing advocacy or litigation services to have provided prescribed information before the agreement is made; and

(b)   may be different for different descriptions of conditional fee agreements (and, in particular, may be different for those which provide for a success fee and those which do not).

(4)   In section 58 and this section (and in the definitions of "advocacy services" and "litigation services" as they apply for their purposes) "proceedings" includes any sort of proceedings for resolving disputes (and not just proceedings in a court), whether commenced or contemplated.

(5)   Before making an order under section 58(4), the Lord Chancellor shall consult—

(a)   the designated judges;

(b)   the General Council of the Bar;

(c)   the Law Society; and

(d)   such other bodies as he considers appropriate.

(6)   A costs order made in any proceedings may, subject in the case of court proceedings to rules of court, include provision requiring the payment of any fees payable under a conditional fee agreement which provides for a success fee.

(7)   Rules of court may make provision with respect to the assessment of any costs which include fees payable under a conditional fee agreement (including one which provides for a success fee).

(b)   Base costs

[43.6]

The amended s 58 refers to a fee which is 'above the amount which would be payable if it were not payable only is specified circumstances', while its predecessor defined a success fee as 'an amount above the amount which would be payable if it were not a conditional fee agreement'. For nineteen years I have been trying to discover what the 'amount that would be payable' is. In 1990 I asked the Lord Chancellor's Department (as it then was) and the Law Society what they thought it meant. The Lord Chancellor's Department replied: 'The uplift will fall upon the fees which the solicitor would charge his client under the normal remuneration procedure. As you point out in your letter, the solicitor and client can agree any amount as the fee'. Precisely. No two firms of solicitors have exactly the same rates and system of charging; some firms have different rates for different classes of work and different charges for different clients, depending on such factors as the level of fee earner, the difficulty, complexity, importance, expertise and urgency involved. A solicitor may charge all red-headed clients 100% more than other clients, if they agree his charges. Similarly a solicitor could charge 100% more for personal injury work than for other types of litigation, if he and the client so agree. Solicitors do not even have to quote hourly rates – they may agree to litigate for a fixed fee.

The Law Society replied:

> The answer to your question is that the uplift does indeed relate to the amount that would indeed have been charged in the individual case on the ordinary basis. If the client believes that the solicitor has falsely stated the hourly rate which would otherwise be charged, he or she can challenge the rate on [*assessment*]. If the basic rate seemed unusually high, the [*assessing*] authorities might no doubt expect the solicitor to demonstrate that there were other clients, instructing the solicitor on the ordinary basis, who were charged roughly the same as the rate the solicitor was seeking to uphold as the basic rate for the conditional fee client'.

A difficult proposition for the client to establish. This was well illustrated by the decisions in *Dunn v Glass Systems* (at para [42.7]) and *Crook v Birmingham City Council* [2007] EWHC 1415 (Admin), [2007] NLJR 939, [2007] 5 Costs LR 732 where it was agreed with a number of clients of modest means in housing litigation that if they recovered damages of £3,000 or less but no costs they would be charged at the solicitors' usual hourly rate with a cap of £1,000. The defendants contended that the reduced level of fees represented what the market would bear and therefore the increment amounted to a success fee. It was held that there was no success fee but simply a discount from the 'normal fee'. If the defendant's analysis were right it could be argued in every case and would obliterate the distinction in conditional fee agreements between the 'base fee' and the 'success fee'.

In *Gloucestershire County Council v Evans* [2008] EWCA Civ 21, [2008] 1 WLR 1883, [2008] NLJR 219 the local authority had a Collective CFA providing for an hourly rate of £95 payable irrespective of outcome and a rate of £145 for a win. A success fee of 100% was to apply to the higher rate in the event of a win. It might be assumed that the % increase is an increase on base costs – model CFAs take that approach. But the statute talks not of the base costs you are charging in the CFA but a fee that you would have charged had there been no CFA at all – of course no one ever states what that fee would have been. The CFA in question referred to 'basic charges' (£145) and 'discounted charges' and applied the success fee only to the former.

It was argued that the success fee sought by the local authority really amounted to 290% based on the fact that the costs at risk were only £50 per hour. (Clearly even referring to the £90 rate would have left a success fee in excess of 100% anyway but that was not the argument run.) The Court held that the success fee applied to the base charges and did not offend the statute: the Agreement provided for basic charges of £145 per hour. That was the amount of the fees that would be payable if the Agreement was not a CFA.

A similar result was reached in the SCCO case of *Morris v Dennis* [2008] EWHC 90112 (Costs) where the CFA defined the base charges to which a 100% success fee was applied plus an administration charge of £150. It was held that the charge was not part of the uplift which accordingly did not exceed the 100% maximum.

[43.7]

The impact of the provision between the parties was lessened by the introduction of the recoverability of the success fee because, in effect, the success fee will be applied to the between-the-parties costs that have been allowed. It is inconceivable that on an assessment the paying party would be ordered to pay a success fee on base costs he has not been ordered to pay, even though the CFA applies the success fee to the whole of the base costs payable by the client.

There is, in principle, no need for a success fee. There is no reason why solicitors should not charge CFA rates which recognise that a proportion of the cases they handle on a conditional fee basis fail. Different types of litigation may also give rise to different levels of 'ordinary' charging rates. Success fees have survived mainly because they are recoverable between the parties and a modest hourly charging rate with a success fee is more likely to be recovered in full than a high hourly charging rate without a success fee. In any event s 58 is now worded to preclude the simpler approach.

(c)   Recoverability

(i)   Success fees

[43.8]

Section 58A included the revolutionary, but long-awaited, provision that success fees payable to the receiving party's lawyer under a CFA should be recoverable from the paying party.

(ii) Insurance premiums

[43.9]

Section 29 of the Access to Justice Act 1999 made provision for rules to allow the court to order the party ordered to pay the costs in litigation to pay the premium on any after-the-event insurance policy taken out by the receiving party in respect of costs, whether or not the receiving party has entered into a CFA.

(d) Fee shifting

(i) The vital difference

[43.10]

The vital difference between the system of funding litigation in the USA and in this country is not that the former is on a contingency basis and the latter is on a conditional basis. That is a distinction of semantics and not substance. The real difference is between-the-parties costs, fee- shifting. In the USA the client has a free ride if he loses. He has no liability to his own lawyer and no liability to the other party. In the UK (it applies to Scotland as well) there is a double whammy – the unsuccessful litigant is not only liable for his own lawyer's costs but usually also for the costs of the other side. A CFA protects a losing client against his own lawyer's costs but not against those of the other side. 'The good news is that you are only going bankrupt for the other party's costs, not for your own costs as well' has a hollow ring to it.

(ii) Accident Line Protect

[43.11]

The Law Society resolved the dilemma and made CFAs workable for personal injury and road traffic accident claims by a brilliant stroke. They negotiated 'after-the-event insurance' (known by the irreverent as 'the morning after pill') with Accident Line Protect whereby after a CFA had been entered into the client could for a mere £85 insure himself against an order for between-the-parties costs up to £100,000. He was also insured against his own disbursements. Such a low premium was achieved by limiting the availability of the policy to clients whose solicitors were members of the Accident Line Scheme and who entered into CFAs similar to the Law Society's Model. It was an experiment that seemed to have worked. However . . .

(iii) The Gatekeepers to justice

[43.12]

The low premium – high cover did not last long. After two years the premiums had to be dramatically increased. In 1997 premiums for personal injury policies almost doubled to £161.20 and in respect of road traffic accidents to

£95.68 and by April 2005 to £375 for road traffic cases, £815 for other personal injury claims and £1,175 for occupational disease cases. This is in respect of work in which the chances of success are high and the work involved is reasonably clear from the outset. But how are the chances of success to be evaluated in a medical negligence claim and who is to finance the gathering of the evidence and reports upon which that evaluation is to be based? Flat rate premiums appear to be out of the question. The state is now only prepared to finance litigation where there is more, often much more, than a 50% chance of winning. Are commercial insurance companies going to accept any longer odds, and if so, at what price the premiums? If it does not make sense to have non-profit-making state funding is it likely to make any more sense to profit-making insurance companies? And what amount of cover will be on offer? £100,000 will cover the cost of virtually any road traffic accident case, but what about medical negligence cases with heavy experts' fees, and defamation actions? When he was Chairman of the Bar, Robert Owen QC, referred to a medical negligence case in which he was involved in which the client had to pay a premium of £15,000 to obtain £100,000 of cover. In one of the cases in the *RSA Test Cases* [2005] EWHC 90003 (Costs) the insurer wanted a £153,378 premium for a claim worth £250,000. The premium allowed was £41,708. Will that insurer be prepared in future to insure similar cases at that reduced level of premium? Who will insure the 60/40 case, let alone the 50/50 case, even if a firm of solicitors and a barrister can be found to act on a CFA basis? The lawyers and the insurers are now the gate-keepers to justice. They decide not only who is to be admitted through the portals of justice, but the price of admission. Will there now be a substantial class of litigants whom no one will back – not the state, not the lawyers and not the insurers because they are not racing certainties? These are some of the questions to which answers must be found before conditional fee agreements become a realistic way of financing all forms of litigation.

(iv) The insurers

[43.13]

There has been no shortage of companies offering after-the-event insurance (known as ATE or AEI), although the nature of the cover and the terms vary considerably. Here is a recent list taken from *Litigation Funding*. Movement into and out of this market means that by the time you read this, the list will be neither up-to-date nor comprehensive.

1st Class Legal (0845 241 2076)	Abbey Legal Protection (0870 607 8999)
Access Legal Solutions (0800 077 8498)	Allianz Legal Protection (0870 243 4340)
Amicus Legal Ltd (01206 731 950)	Amtrust Europe Legal (0844 815 8501)
ARAG (0117 917 1680)	ATE (0117 917 1680)

Benchmark Insurance (NAH) (01536 527 500)	Box Legal (0870 766 9997)
Capita Assistance (0870 523 4597)	Collegiate (0207 459 3469)
Compass Costs (1051 481 4444)	Complete Claims (0161 817 7764)
Composite Legal Expenses (0870 2208 516)	Egate (01604 715 768)
8oe (DAS) (0117 934 0087)	Elite Litigation Services (0845 601 1221)
Financial and Legal (0161 603 2230)	First Legal Indemnity (020 7977 1408)
First Assist Insurance Services (020 8652 1437)	Guardian Legal Services (0844 414 2124)
Ibex Legal (0161 860 4945)	Keystone Legal Benefits (01252 354100)
Law Assist (01903 881182)	Law Link (0161 707 1102)
LPS Commercial (0800 1777 402)	Litigation Protection (01903 889966)
LSL (01444 451752)	Motor Accident Solicitors Society (MASS) (0117 925 9604)
Mount Grace Insurance (01670 528295)	QBE (0207 105 5169)
QLP Legal (020 7626 0191)	Special Risk Solutions (0151 649 9199)
Temple Legal Protection (01483 577 877)	Westongate Associates (01625 667 165)

(e)   Prescribed bodies – s 30

[43.14]

Section 30 of the Access to Justice Act 1991 enables a prescribed body which has undertaken to meet the adverse costs liabilities of a party to recover an additional sum for having provided the facility and made provision for recovery by such body as follows:

(1)   This section applies where a body of a prescribed description under-takes to meet (in accordance with arrangements satisfying prescribed conditions) liabilities which members of the body or other persons who are parties to proceedings may incur to pay the costs of other parties to the proceedings.

(2)   If in any of the proceedings a costs order is made in favour of any of the members or other persons, the costs payable to him may, subject to subsection (3) and (in the case of court proceedings) to rules of court, include an additional amount in respect of any provision made by or on behalf of the body in connection with the proceedings against the risk of having to meet such liabilities.

(3)   But the additional amount shall not exceed a sum determined in a prescribed manner; and there may, in particular, be prescribed as a manner of determination one which takes into account the likely cost to

the member or other person of the premium of an insurance policy against the risk of incurring a liability to pay the costs of other parties to the proceedings.

(4)   In this section 'prescribed' means prescribed by regulations made by the Secretary of State by statutory instrument; and a statutory instrument containing such regulations shall be subject to annulment in pursuance of a resolution of either House of Parliament.

(5)   Regulations under subsection (1) may, in particular, prescribe as a description of body one which is for the time being approved by the Secretary of State or by a prescribed person.

[43.15]

The Access to Justice (Membership Organisations) Regulations 2000 which came into force on 1 April 2000 defined the bodies which are prescribed for the purpose of s 30 as able to recover a sum as part of legal costs from unsuccessful opponents to reflect the provision of legal help for members and their families. The definition is now contained in the Access to Justice (Membership Organisation) Regulations 2005. CPR Rule 44.3B(1)(*b*) at para [44.9] provides that any provision for an additional liability by a membership organisation which exceeds the likely cost of an after-the-event insurance premium shall not be recoverable between the parties.

The Lord Chancellor has approved as prescribed bodies all trade unions listed by the Certification Office for Trade Unions and Employers Organisations and:

RAC Motoring Services
Defence Police Federation
Engineering Employer's Federation
Police Federation of England and Wales
The Automobile Association

The Lord Chancellor's Department published guidance in April 2000 relating to applications for approval as a prescribed body.

(f)   Indemnity Principle Disapplied – s 31

[43.16]

In order to avoid the operation of the indemnity principle (see Chapter 17), the Access to Justice Act 1999 (Commencement No 10) Order 2003 on 2 June 2003 brought into force s 31 of the Access to Justice Act 1999. This section amended s 51(2) of the Supreme Court (now Senior Courts) Act 1981, allowing rules of court to be made 'for securing that the amount awarded to a party in respect of the costs to be paid by him to [legal or other] representatives is not limited to what would have been payable by him to them if he had not been awarded costs'. In other words, rules which limit or regulate the indemnity principle: s 31 does not abolish the indemnity principle but delegates its curtailment to the CPR. The first change to the CPR was the recognition of the simplified form of CFA (see para [43.30]). We now have fixed costs under CPR 45 which do not depend upon a valid retainer and are in effect a further departure from the indemnity principle – see para [44.53]. Wholesale removal of the indemnity principle would certainly simplify collective CFAs and pave the way for more transparent arrangements for guaranteeing that damages will be retained by the client without even the complication of using the simplified CFA. More importantly, removal would leave the funding arrangements where they ought to be – between the solicitor and the client.

THE ORDER

(a) The Conditional Fee Agreements Order 2000

[43.17]

1 Citation, Commencement and Interpretation
(1) This Order may be cited as the Conditional Fee Agreements Order 2000 and shall come into force on 1st April 2000.
(2) In this Order 'the Act' means the Courts and Legal Services Act 1990.

2 Revocation of 1998 Order
The Conditional Fee Agreements Order 1998 is revoked.

3 Agreements Providing for Success Fees
All proceedings which, under section 58 of the Act, can be the subject of an enforceable conditional fee agreement, except proceedings under section 82 of the Environmental Protection Act 1990, are proceedings specified for the purposes of section 58(4)(a) of the Act.

4 Amount of Success Fees
In relation to all proceedings specified in article 3, the percentage specified for the purposes of section 58(4)(c) of the Act shall be 100%.

(b) All agreements

[43.18]

For the purposes of s 58(4)(*a*) of the Courts and Legal Services Act 1990 provision for a success fee may be made in all enforceable conditional fee agreements except in proceedings under the Environmental Protection Act 1990, s 82.

(c) The maximum uplift

[43.19]

The maximum percentage increase of costs in a success fee permitted under the amended s 58(4)(*c*) of the Courts and Legal Services Act 1990 was set at 100%, despite at one time it being contemplated that there should be no limit for proceedings in the Commercial, Technology and Construction and Admiralty Courts. In such cases the prospect of reflecting in a success fee both the risk of losing and the cost of the substantial delay in payment within the 100% maximum seems to be a hopeless task.

The Department for Constitutional Affairs commissioned research to ascertain whether the setting and assessment of success fees is a science or an art. Scientifically we now have the statistics to support the fixed success fee regime for road traffic cases and employer liability cases which are on the costs debate page of the Civil Justice Council's web site at: http://www.civiljust icecouncil.gov.uk. The more artistic approach of the Court of Appeal is appa rent in the several decisions at para [45.1] ff.

(d) Profit increased by more than 100%

[43.20]

In the House of Lords debate, Baroness Hamwee, a practising solicitor, pointed out that a 100% increase in a solicitor's charges amounted to considerably more than a doubling of the profit, because hourly rates include overheads. A charge-out hourly rate which is calculated on the basis of the direct cost of doing the work plus a 50% profit mark-up comprises two-thirds cost and one third profit. Accordingly a success fee of 100% on the total base costs is in fact a 300% increase of the profit element, whilst even a modest 10% success fee results in a 30% increase in the profit.

THE REGULATIONS BEFORE 1 NOVEMBER 2005

(a) Conditional Fee Agreements Regulations 2000

[43.21]

The Access to Justice Act was followed, eventually, by the Conditional Fee Agreements Regulations 2000 and the Collective Conditional Fee Regulations 2000 which also came into force on 1 April 2000, replacing the Conditional Fee Agreements Regulations 1995. The Regulations were amended by the Conditional Fee Agreements (Miscellaneous Amendments) Regulations 2003 with effect from 2 June 2003 to provide for a simplified CFA in Regulation 3A (see para [43.33]). However, on 1 November 2005 both Regulations were revoked by the Conditional Fee Agreements (Revocation) Regulations 2005 and now there are no regulations for CFAs made on or after that date. I consider the reasons for this and the new regime at paras [43.43] ff, However, because the revocation was not retrospective the Regulations and decisions arising from them will be relevant for some years to come where the CFA was entered into before 1 November 2005. Here they are:

[43.22]

1 Citation, commencement and interpretation
　(1)　These Regulations may be cited as the Conditional Fee Agreements Regulations 2000.
　(2)　These Regulations come into force on 1st April 2000.
　(3)　In these Regulations—
　　'client' includes, except where the context otherwise requires, a person who—

    (a)   has instructed the legal representative to provide the advocacy or litigation services to which the conditional fee agreement relates, or

    (b)   is liable to pay the legal representative's fees in respect of those services; and

'legal representative' means the person providing the advocacy or litigation services to which the conditional fee agreement relates.

[43.23]

2 Requirements for contents of conditional fee agreements: General

(1)   A conditional fee agreement must specify—

    (a)   the particular proceedings or parts of them to which it relates (including whether it relates to any appeal, counterclaim or proceedings to enforce a judgement or order),

    (b)   the circumstances in which the legal representative's fees and expenses, or part of them, are payable,

    (c)   what payment, if any, is due—

        (i)   if those circumstances only partly occur,

        (ii)   irrespective of whether those circumstances occur, and

        (iii)   on the termination of the agreement for any reason, and

    (d)   the amounts which are payable in all the circumstances and cases specified or the method to be used to calculate them and, in particular, whether the amounts are limited by reference to the damages which may be recovered on behalf of the client.

(2)   A conditional fee agreement to which regulation 4 applies must contain a statement that the requirements of that regulation which apply in the case of that agreement have been complied with.

[43.24]

3 Requirements for contents of conditional fee agreements providing for success fees

(1)   A conditional fee agreement which provides for a success fee—

    (a)   must briefly specify the reasons for setting the percentage increase at the level stated in the agreement, and

    (b)   must specify how much of the percentage increase, if any, relates to the cost to the legal representative of the postponement of the payment of his fees and expenses.

(2)   If the agreement relates to court proceedings, it must provide that where the percentage increase becomes payable as a result of those proceedings, then—

    (a)   if—

        (i)   any fees subject to the increase are assessed, and

        (ii)   the legal representative or the client is required by the court to disclose to the court or any other person the reasons for setting the percentage increase at the level stated in the agreement,

    he may do so,

    (b)   if—

        (i)   any such fees are assessed, and

        (ii)   any amount in respect of the percentage increase is disallowed on the assessment on the ground that the level at which the increase was set was unreasonable in view of facts which were or should have been known to the legal representative at the time it was set,

that amount ceases to be payable under the agreement, unless the court is satisfied that it should continue to be so payable, and

(c)   if—

    (i)   sub-paragraph (b) does not apply, and

    (ii)   the legal representative agrees with any person liable as a result of the proceedings to pay fees subject to the percentage increase that a lower amount than the amount payable in accordance with the conditional fee agreement is to be paid instead,

the amount payable under the conditional fee agreement in respect of those fees shall be reduced accordingly, unless the court is satisfied that the full amount should continue to be payable under it.

(3)   In this regulation 'percentage increase' means the percentage by which the amount of the fees which would be payable if the agreement were not a conditional fee agreement is to be increased under the agreement.

[43.25]

3A Requirements where the client's liability is limited to sums recovered

(1)   This regulation applies to a conditional fee agreement under which, except in the circumstances set out in paragraphs (5) and (5A), the client is liable to pay his legal representative's fees and expenses only to the extent that sums are recovered in respect of the relevant proceedings, whether by way of costs or otherwise.

(2)   In determining for the purposes of paragraph (1) the circumstances in which a client is liable to pay his legal representative's fees and expenses, no account is to be taken of any obligation to pay costs in respect of the premium of a policy taken out to insure against the risk of incurring a liability in the relevant proceedings.

(3)   Regulations 2, 3 and 4 do not apply to a conditional fee agreement to which this regulation applies.

(4)   A conditional fee agreement to which this regulation applies must—

    (a)   specify—

        (i)   the particular proceedings or parts of them to which it relates (including whether it relates to any appeal, counterclaim or proceedings to enforce a judgment or order); and

        (ii)   the circumstances in which the legal representative's fees and expenses, or part of them, are payable; and

    (b)   if it provides for a success fee—

        (i)   briefly specify the reasons for setting the percentage increase at the level stated in the agreement; and

        (ii)   provide that if, in court proceedings, the percentage increase becomes payable as a result of those proceedings and the legal representative or the client is ordered to disclose to the court or any other person the reasons for setting the percentage increase at the level stated in the agreement, he may do so.

(5)   A conditional fee agreement to which this regulation applies may specify that the client will be liable to pay the legal representative's fees and expenses whether or not sums are recovered in respect of the relevant proceedings, if the client—

    (a)   fails to co-operate with the legal representative;

    (b)   fails to attend any medical or expert examination or court hearing which the legal representative reasonably requests him to attend;

    (c)   fails to give necessary instructions to the legal representative;

    (d)   withdraws instructions from the legal representative;

    (e)   is an individual who is adjudged bankrupt or who enters into an arrangement or a composition with his creditors, or against whom an administration order is made; or

    (f)   is a company for which a receiver, administrative receiver or liquidator is appointed.

(5A)   A conditional fee agreement to which this regulation applies may specify that, in the event of the client dying in the course of the relevant proceedings, his estate will be liable for the legal representative's fees and expenses, whether or not sums are recovered in respect of those proceedings.

(6)   Before a conditional fee agreement to which this regulation applies is made, the legal representative must inform the client as to the circumstances in which the client or his estate may be liable to pay the legal representative's fees and expenses, and provide such further explanation, advice or other information as to those circumstances as the client may reasonably require.

[43.26]

4 Information to be given before conditional fee agreements made

(1)   Before a conditional fee agreement is made the legal representative must—

    (a)   inform the client about the following matters, and

    (b)   if the client requires any further explanation, advice or other information about any of those matters, provide such further explanation, advice or other information about them as the client may reasonably require.

(2)   Those matters are—

    (a)   the circumstances in which the client may be liable to pay the costs of the legal representative in accordance with the agreement,

    (b)   the circumstances in which the client may seek assessment of the fees and expenses of the legal representative and the procedure for doing so,

    (c)   whether the legal representative considers that the client's risk of incurring liability for costs in respect of the proceedings to which agreement relates is insured against under an existing contract of insurance,

    (d)   whether other methods of financing those costs are available, and, if so, how they apply to the client and the proceedings in question,

    (e)   whether the legal representative considers that any particular method or methods of financing any or all of those costs is appropriate and, if he considers that a contract of insurance is appropriate or recommends a particular such contract—

        (i)   his reasons for doing so, and

        (ii)   whether he has an interest in doing so.

(3)   Before a conditional fee agreement is made the legal representative must explain its effect to the client.

(4)   In the case of an agreement where—

    (a)   the legal representative is a body to which section 30 of the Access to Justice Act 1999 (recovery where body undertakes to meet costs liabilities) applies, and

> > (b)   there are no circumstances in which the client may be liable to pay any costs in respect of the proceedings,
> paragraph (1) does not apply.
> (5)   Information required to be given under paragraph (1) about the matters in paragraph (2)(a) to (d) must be given orally (whether or not it is also given in writing), but information required to be so given about the matters in paragraph (2)(e) and the explanation required by paragraph (3) must be given both orally and in writing.
> (6)   This regulation does not apply in the case of an agreement between a legal representative and an additional legal representative.

[43.27]

5 Form of Agreement
> (1)   A conditional fee agreement must be signed by the client and the legal representative.
> (2)   This regulation does not apply in the case of an agreement between a legal representative and an additional legal representative.

[43.28]

6 Amendment of Agreement
> Where an agreement is amended to cover further proceedings or parts of them—
> > (a)   regulations 2, 3, 3A and 5 apply to the amended agreement as if it were a fresh agreement made at the time of the amendment, and
> > (b)   the obligations under regulation 4 apply in relation to the amendments in so far as they affect the matters mentioned in that regulation.

(i)   Definitions — 'client', 'legal representative' and 'proceedings'

[43.29]

Regulation 1 includes in the definition of 'client' a person who is liable to pay for litigation services under a CFA, for example an insurance company or trade union. The same regulation specifies that a 'legal representative' is the person providing the advocacy or litigation services – a definition of considerable importance when applying the requirements to provide information to clients, as was demonstrated in *Accident Group Test Cases* Tranche 2 [2003] NLJR 790, 147 Sol Jo LB 657, where TAG's use of unqualified representatives to carry out the obligations on the legal representative was challenged. The Court of Appeal held that the obligations can be delegated to an unqualified person ('out-sourced'), provided there is adequate supervision by a solicitor. The issue of the adequacy of supervision has not yet been considered by a court.

Regulation 2 applies to all pre-November 1 2005 CFAs and paragraph (a) of reg 2 requires them to specify 'The proceedings, or parts of them, to which it relates and particularly whether it relates to any counterclaim or proceedings for enforcement'. This paragraph caused difficulty in *Roche v Newbury Homes* (see para [43.4] with respect to pre-action work. In *Blair v Danesh* [2009] EWCA Civ 516 the CFA referred to a claim for refund of monies given under undue influence but four years later the action ranged widely. Costs were awarded for the successful undue influence claim but it was argued that the

CAF was invalid because the proceedings as they turned out were not specified. The Court of Appeal refused leave on that point seemingly because the costs had only been awarded for undue influence and the consumer protection purpose of the Regulations had been satisfied. The law Society Model CFA includes appeal brought against the client. The Court of Appeal in *Bexbes LLP v Beer* [2009] EWCA Civ 628, [2009] All ER (D) 273 (Jun) where BexBes had given notice before trial of funding by means of a conditional fee under a CFA, which provided for a success fee was required to consider whether notice of the CFA had been given in relation to the appeal. The conclusion, having consulted with the Senior Costs Judge, was that there was no separate requirement for giving notice of a CFA in an appeal and opponents and advisers should know that a standard CFA would continue if the opponent brings an appeal.

[43.30]

Section 58(1) of the Courts and Legal Services Act 1990 provides that a CFA shall not be unenforceable only if it satisfies the conditions contained in regulations 2 and 3.

(ii)   No win – no fee

[43.31]

Regulation 2 requires the CFA to specify:
(a)   The proceedings, or parts of them, to which it relates and particularly whether it relates to any counterclaim or proceedings for enforcement.
In *Brierley v Prescott* 2006 (SCCO Ref: 0504718) the CFA referred to a claim against an insurer. In the proceedings the driver's name was later substituted for that of the insurer. On assessment it was argued that there was no liability under the CFA in respect of the claim against the driver and that therefore the driver could not be liable to indemnify those costs. It was held that the CFA covered a claim arising out of the accident and costs were therefore payable by the client and recoverable. A similar decision was reached in *Scott v Transport for London* (December 2009 unreported) (Hastings County Court) where the CFA named a local authority and not the defendant. No harm was done because the CFA Regulations did not require the defendant to be named in the CFA.
(b)   The circumstances in which the legal representative's fees and expenses, or part of them are payable. In other words, what is a 'win'?
As to paragraph (b) 'no-win, no-fee' is an attractive sound-bite, but it is too simplistic. In the House of Lords, the Lord Chancellor warned that 'it would be wise' for lawyers and clients to discuss at the outset the likely proceeds from the enterprise and that 'it might be possible to meet the point by putting in some requirement about the situation that should obtain with regard to the net amount that the client could expect to recover as a measure of success in terms of the agreement'. In *Milne v David Price Solicitors* 2005 (SCCO) 04/P8/340) the client agreed a settlement with his opponent that did not amount to a win defined in the CFA as settlement at a specified sum. His acceptance of the settlement was held to be a termination of the CFA with the result that he had to pay his base costs. There are snags also once an opponent becomes a paying party. In *Hanley v Smith and MIB* [2009] EWHC 90144 (Costs) the CFA was

made two years after a standard retainer and by then the first defendant had admitted liability albeit not its extent. It was argued that the definition of win in the Law Society model had already been satisfied. That argument failed with the court holding that the claim against the MIB was an essential ingredient of the claim, a reasonable person would have understood that the central purpose of the litigation would not be satisfied merely by obtaining a worthless (but necessary) judgment against the driver. A win though, (however defined) is surely not enough. What if none, or only part of, the damages awarded and between-the-parties costs are recovered because, for example, the defendant is, or becomes, insolvent? Unless the formula is 'No recovery, no pay' the empty-handed client will have nothing to pay with. The lawyers will be entitled to their costs and success fee, so the client will, in fact, be substantially worse off than if he had lost the action! And what effect is a successful counterclaim, perhaps arising out of an allegation of contributory negligence, to have on the specified circumstances? The Law Society's Model CFA for Personal Injury defines a win in terms only of a final decision on the claim in the client's favour. Until the indemnity principle is removed there may be difficulty with a definition of 'win' in terms of actual recovery. A simplified CFA can achieve that aim and indeed the Senior Costs Judge expressed the view in *The Accident Group Test Cases* Tranche 2 [2003] NLJR 790 that a standard CFA could define win in terms of recovery. Some argue that the lawyer is not a guarantor of the solvency of the client's opponent and is entitled to his success fee whether or not the judgment is paid. But surely the lawyer is being rewarded for taking the risk, which includes the risk of the client not recovering his award – if not, where is the sharing of risk?

(a)   What payment is due, if any, for only partial success; or on termination of the agreement for any reason, for example the failure of the client to co-operate, or if his evidence has been fabricated.

(b)   The amount of the fees payable or the method used to calculate them, and whether they are capped with reference to the damages.

It is surprising to find a reference to such a limit in respect of a non-success fee agreement. When CFAs were first introduced there was concern that a 100% success fee might swallow up most or all of the damages leading to a justifiable public outcry. To avoid this the Law Society recommended a cap on the uplift of 25% of the amount recovered, while the Bar suggested a modest 10%. Now that success fees are recoverable between the parties the cap has gone and the June 2000 edition of the Law Society model agreement provides '*If you win your claim, you pay our basic charges, our disbursements, and a success fee. The amount of these is not based on or limited by the damages.*' Indeed the indemnity principle would again cause problems were a standard CFA to limit the success fee to a percentage of the damages.

The agreement must also confirm that the information required by regulation 4 has been supplied to the client.

(iii)   With success fee

[43.32]

Regulation 3 contains the extra requirements for CFAs which provide for a success fee (see para [43.6]). These could be tricky. The agreement must give brief reasons for setting the success fee at the agreed percentage. What if the reasons are that the client is extremely demanding or difficult, or that he and his witnesses are of doubtful credibility? That will require tactful wording, but you cannot afford to be too tactful because the reasons given will have to be relied upon if the percentage increase is challenged. Following *Bray Walker Solicitors v Silvera* [2010] EWCA Civ 332, [2010] 15 LS Gaz R 18, [2010] All ER (D) 261 (Mar) it appears that 'brief reasons' can be very brief indeed. In that case merely stating that the reasons were the unspecified sufficed. The client must consent in the agreement to the reasons being disclosed if required by the court, which, of course, it will do if there is a dispute between the parties. It was held in *Brennan v Associated Asphalt* 2006 (SCCO 0507905) that failure to specify that the postponement element was nil was a breach of Regulation 3. On the basis however that no postponement fee could therefore be charged there was no materially adverse effect on the protection of the client. Nor was there a materially adverse effect on the administration of justice. A similar result was arrived at in *Hughes v George Major Skip Hire* [2009] EWHC 90147 (Costs) where the client had been certain from the solicitor's explanation of the CFA that she would not be liable for any costs not recovered from the defendant. The CFA had a confusing reference to the postponement element such that reg 3 had been breached but no material adverse effect was shown because of the client's certainty from the explanation given. Also under 'brief reasons' the agreement must provide that any between-the-parties reduction of the success fee shall be binding on the solicitor unless the court orders otherwise. The court will only 'order otherwise' if the solicitor can show that there were exceptional circumstances. The conflict between a solicitor and his client could not be more starkly illustrated. The client is unlikely to have been separately advised before entering into the agreement; will he be separately advised when the solicitor seeks to recover the shortfall? For the procedure see CPR Rule 44.16 at para [44.30].

(iv)   Simplified CFAs

1.   Simplification

[43.33]

From 2 June 2003 the Conditional Fee Agreements (Miscellaneous Amendments) Regulations 2003 amended the Conditional Fee Agreements Regulations 2000 by inserting reg 3A to provide that a CFA is still enforceable even though the client is liable to pay his legal representative's fees and expenses only if, and to the extent that, he recovers damages or costs in the proceedings. These are sometimes referred to as 'CFAs Lite'. Amendments made to the Civil Procedure Rules 1998 provide that costs payable under such a CFA are recoverable under Parts 44 to 48 of those Rules. Thus the indemnity principle is in effect abrogated in relation to this type of CFA.

2. Contents

[43.34]

A client's liability for his own solicitor's 'fees and expenses' under a simplified CFA is limited to 'sums recovered . . . whether by way of costs or otherwise' – not just to 'costs' recovered. The limitation does not include the client's liability for any after-the-event insurance premium. Simplification is achieved because regulations 2, 3 and 4 do not apply to simplified CFAs, although they must still state the circumstances in which fees and expenses are payable – they must define a 'win'. Brief reasons for the percentage success fee must still be given and the client should in the agreement waive his privilege in those reasons should the court order disclosure. Regulation 3A(5) permits the solicitor to include a provision imposing liability on the client for fees and expenses in specified circumstances of non-cooperation or misbehaviour by the client or the death or insolvency of the client.

3. Not so simple

[43.35]

The problem with Rule 43.2(3) is the words 'or otherwise'. These envisage circumstances in which a solicitor deducts his solicitor and client costs from the damages. Their inclusion was influenced by the belief of Lord Phillips MR that they were needed to produce a logical scheme. He said that as a matter of principle there was no reason why one should allow this kind of agreement and then limit the client's liability to costs recovered. It is still leaving the client better off than having a liability to pay the solicitor simply because the claim succeeded, even though nothing is recovered where, for example, damages are recovered but not costs. Is that what is intended and, if so, does the client understand that? If the damages are intended to be protected, the CFA should use the word 'costs' only, provided the solicitor is willing to write off the disbursements if they are not recovered. If costs are to be taken out of the damages, the Law Society recommends they should be limited to 25% of the damages. The Law Society also takes the view that global settlements which do not distinguish between damages and costs are incompatible with simplified CFA s. In the next paragraph I consider the problem where the client fails to beat a Part 36 offer.

4. No recovery

[43.36]

Where the client has won, the simplified CFA rules allow a solicitor to say to the client that he will keep his damages. But that does not deal with the situation where the client has lost or has failed to beat a Part 36 offer. In these situations the simplified CFA produces a very different result. Where the client loses and recovers nothing he may have no liability at all, not for fees, not for disbursements and not for counsel. If he has no liability at all he has no insurable interest on which to base an after-the-event insurance policy –

therefore the whole risk lies with the solicitor. Where there is a failure to beat a Part 36, a sum will be recovered and the client can therefore be liable for his own solicitor's costs and disbursements up to the amount of the sums recovered. Presumably that amount is what will be left after the client has paid his opponent's costs since the Part 36 payment was made. If it is intended to protect the client's damages, the client's liability for his opponent's costs after the Part 36 payment must be insured against under a policy which covers such costs without setting off the pre-Part 36 payment own costs recovered. Otherwise any shortfall must either come out of the client's damages or be borne by his solicitor. The regulations may be simpler, but explaining them to a client is certainly not.

5.   Between-the-parties costs

[43.37]

CPR Rule 43.2(3) and (4) provide that costs whose recovery is limited by a simplified CFA as in para [43.33] are nevertheless recoverable from an opponent for the purposes of CPR Parts 44 to 48.

(v)   Client information

[43.38]

Regulation 4 sets out the information to be given to clients before they enter into a CFA. It is important to appreciate that this provision applies to all clients entering into a CFA, including family, friends and employees. The temptation to avoid going to the trouble of doing this must be firmly resisted because on a dispute the solicitor must be able to prove compliance. The regulation contains the unusual requirement that four elements of information, while they may be given in writing, must also be given *orally*: what is a win; the right to a detailed assessment; has the client pre-purchased legal expenses insurance and what other methods of financing the costs are available. The solicitor's views and advice on any particular method of funding and insurance together with an explanation of the effect of the agreement and a disclosure if there is an interest in recommending the policy must be given to the client both *orally* and *in writing*. There must clearly be some careful drafting and record keeping (perhaps even literally an audio recording of the oral advice, or perhaps a tape recording to be played to each client?!) to ensure that compliance with these provisions can be proved when necessary. An accurate oral explanation failed to cure an inaccurate written one in *Bevan v Power Panels Electrical Systems Ltd* [2007] EWHC 90073 (Costs). All of this must be given by the 'legal representative' which by Regulation 1 means the 'person' providing the advocacy or litigation services. In *The Accident Group Test Cases* the explanations were given by non-legally qualified persons not directly employed by the solicitor. The Court of Appeal held that the regulations did permit delegation, the important safeguard being supervision by the solicitor. No one, surely, would suggest that the validity of a CFA depends upon successfully explaining it, whoever attempts that explanation.

The dire consequences of failure to comply with Regulation 4 are illustrated by the cases at paras [43.40]-[43.42].

(vi) Signature

[43.39]

Regulation 5 requires the agreement to be signed by both parties except between one legal representative and an additional legal representative. This usually means counsel although it includes any other person providing advocacy or litigation services such as a solicitor advocate or agent. Following the draconian decision in *Garrett* [43.42] failure of one or both parties to sign will be regarded as a material breach – in *Fenton v Holmes* [2007] EWHC 2476 (Ch), [2008] 2 Costs LR 238, [2007] All ER (D) 12 (Jun) the client had not signed and in *Preece v Caerphilly* (2007) Cardiff CC 15/8/2007 the solicitors had not signed. In each case the CFA was invalid. In *Dunn v Mici* [2008] EWHC 90115 (Costs) the CFA stated that the agreement covered Mr Dunn's claim for damages and personal injury 'by his mother and litigation friend'. The issue for decision was whether Mr Dunn alone was the client; if so, did he receive advice which complied with reg 4; if not and he and his mother were both clients, what was the effect on the enforceability of the CFA if one had received compliant advice but the other had not? Master Campbell held that no formal appointment under CPR 21 as litigation friend was ever made and therefore Mrs Dunn was not, and could not, have been the client. As to the reg 4 BTE enquiry the solicitors discharged the tasks which the Regulations required them to undertake in relation to Mr Dunn, there being no requirement that these should be repeated in relation to Mrs Dunn.

(b) Validity

(i) Spot the breach

[43.40]

To be lawful a pre- 1 November 2005 CFA must comply not only with the statute but also with the CFA Regulations, and this requirement coupled with the indemnity principle (see Chapter 17) resulted in a torrent of satellite litigation based on the game of 'spot the breach'. If a CFA is unenforceable by the solicitor against his client the indemnity principle precludes the recovery of any between-the-parties costs which have been awarded. The paying party becomes a non-paying party. The technical points raised to invalidate CFAs have nothing to do with justice or merit, nor indeed with the protection of the client for which they were designed. In *Hollins v Russell* [2003] EWCA Civ 718, [2003] 4 All ER 590, [2003] 1 WLR 2487) the Court of Appeal considered some of these points, which they described 'as unattractive as they were unmeritorious' and held that a departure from the regulations did not affect the validity or enforceability of a CFA unless the departure was both material and adversely affected the client or the administration of justice. None of the challenges considered by the Court of Appeal were successful. The court summarised its 228-paragraph judgment as: 'The court should be watchful when it considers allegations that there have been breaches of the regulations. The parliamentary purpose is to enhance access to justice, not to impede it, and to create better ways of delivering litigation services, not worse ones. These purposes will be thwarted if those who render good service to their clients under CFAs are at risk of going unremunerated at the culmination of the bitter trench warfare which has been such an unhappy feature of the recent litigation scene.'

In *Burstein v Times Newspapers Ltd* [2002] EWCA Civ 1739, [2003] 03 LS Gaz R 31, (2002) Times, 6 December Latham LJ ended the judgment of the court with these words:

> ' . . . The deputy costs judge is to be commended for ensuring that the detailed assessment did not become an excuse for further expensive litigation at the behest of a disappointed but persistent litigant. Satellite litigation about costs has become a growth industry, and one that is a blot on the civil justice system. Costs Judges should be astute to prevent such proceedings from being protracted by allegations that are without substance. In future district judges and costs judges must be equally astute to prevent satellite litigation about costs from being protracted by allegations about breaches of the CFA Regulations where the breaches do not matter. They should remember that the law does not care about the very little things, and that they should only declare a CFA unenforceable if the breach does matter and if the client could have relied on it successfully against his solicitor.'

(ii)   Satellite litigation

[43.41]

Rightly or wrongly the profession interpreted *Hollins* as heralding the end of technical challenges unless the client had suffered some material detriment. The euphoria did not last long.

In *Spencer v Gordon Wood t/a Gordons Tyres (a firm)* [2004] EWCA Civ 352, 148 Sol Jo LB 356, [2004] 3 Costs LR 372 reg 3(1)(b) was breached because the CFA failed to specify how much of the 75% success fee related to postponement. There was a separate risk assessment on file which included an item 'Deferment of costs until conclusion of case . . . .50%', but, as the circuit judge commented, '50% of what? Of the success fee? Of the profit costs? How is the postponement charge reflected in the overall success fee of 75%? The risk assessment is silent as to that, as are the agreement and the schedule.' The Court of Appeal agreed. The breach materially affected the client because he did not know how much of the 75% would be recoverable from the defendant and the punishment (no fees at all) was not objectionable — the words 'shall be unenforceable' meant what they said.

A CFA in Law Society Model form for 2000 caused similar problems but a different outcome in *Hughes v George Major Skip Hire* [2009] EWHC 90147 (Costs). The CFA referred to a 50% success fee. Schedule 1 to the CFA stated that the postponement element was 50%, that risk elements amounted to 50% and that the total success fee was 50%. That confusion and breach of reg 3 was rescued by the oral explanation that left the client certain that they would not be paying any costs out of damages so there was no material breach. Burnton J in *Re Palmier plc (in liquidation); Sandhu v Sidhu* [2009] EWHC 983 (Ch), [2009] All ER (D) 93 (May) upheld a CFA that stated there was no charge for postponement although the schedule risk assessment made no reference to postponement. That absence of postponement in the schedule made it clear that there was no charge for that element.

Several cases in the Supreme Court Costs Office (now the Senior Courts Costs Office) ended in tears for the solicitors:

In *Samonini v London General Transport Services Ltd* [2005] EWHC 90001 (SCCO) the client said he had no existing legal expenses cover and the solicitor took his word for it without further enquiry. The client was correct — had no BTE and however diligently the solicitor had searched he would have found nothing because there was nothing to find. Nevertheless, the Senior Costs Judge held that the solicitor's failure to comply with reg 4(2)(d) (which required him to 'consider' the availability of legal expenses insurance) was a material breach invalidating the CFA.

In *Oyston v Royal Bank of Scotland* [2006] EWHC 90053 (Costs) a CFA provided for a 100% success fee and a £50,000 bonus if over £1 million was recovered. A deed of variation that removed the reference to the bonus payment was then made to try to avoid invalidity.. The ubiquitous senior costs judge held against them: No retrospective rectification, the breach would inescapably have a materially adverse effect on the proper administration of justice and no severance.

Hughes v Newham London Borough Council 2005 SCCO 0502314 were housing disrepair cases where legal aid was available and the clients would have been eligible. The failure of the solicitors to consider legal aid was a material breach of reg 4(2)(d) fatal to the CFA.

In *Jones v Caradon Catnic Ltd* [2005] EWCA Civ 1821, [2006] 3 Costs LR 427 the Court of Appeal held that a statement in the risk assessment to a CFA of a 120% success fee was such a stark departure from the 100% maximum specified in paragraph 4 of the Conditional Fee Agreements Order 2000 that the CFA could not be saved by a 100% cap elsewhere in the agreement even though no one would be the loser. If this breach were held to be immaterial, all breaches would be held to be immaterial. The robust language of the judgment was quoted with approval in *Garrett* (below).

(iii) 'Guidance'

[43.42]

In *Garrett v Halton Borough Council; Myatt v National Coal Board* [2006] EWCA Civ 1017, [2007] 1 All ER 147, [2007] 1 WLR 554, the Court of Appeal gave what it described as 'guidance' on CFAs concerning a solicitor's duty to consider existing litigation expenses insurance under CFA reg 4(2)(c) and to disclose any interest in any insurance policy he was recommending under reg 4(2)(e). However, as both regulations were revoked on 1 November 2005, the decisions were not so much guidance but more of a checklist for those wishing to embark on satellite litigation. The enforceability of a CFA was to be determined at the date of its commencement and not in the light of its consequences. It was not necessary for there to any actual material detriment to the client or to the administration of justice to constitute a breach. The language of s 58 of the Courts and Legal Services Act 1990 was clear and uncompromising. The statutory scheme provided that if any of the conditions were not satisfied, the CFA would not enforceable and the solicitor would not be paid. That was clear and stark. Such a policy was tough but not irrational: it was designed to protect clients and to encourage solicitors to comply with the statutory requirements. *Hollins* [43.40] had done no more than deal a fatal blow to challenges on the grounds of literal but trivial and immaterial departures from the statutory requirements.

In *Garrett* the solicitors were members of a panel which referred work to them provided they recommended a particular policy of insurance. This was clearly an interest disclosable under reg 4(2)(e) and it did not suffice merely to inform the client of membership of the panel without explaining its implications. Further consideration has been given to reg 4(2)(e) in the context of the Accident Line Protect (ALP) insurance scheme. In *Tankard v John Fredricks Plastics Ltd* [2008] EWCA Civ 1375, [2009] 1 WLR 1731, (2009) Times, (2009) Times, 16 January the court said a solicitor has an interest if a reasonable person with knowledge of the relevant facts would think that the existence of the interest might affect the advice given by the solicitor to his client. The ALP scheme did not involve such an interest. But, their Lordships decided to make obiter statements about what level of disclosure would be required where a solicitor did have an interest. The client should have been told what the nature of the interest is – it was not enough to say that there was an interest. This decision concentrated on the word 'interest' in reg 4 almost to the exclusion of any consideration of the word 'whether'. The regulation actually says the solicitor must when recommending insurance inform the client 'whether he has an interest in doing so'. As a matter of statutory interpretation it is hard to see how this means 'and go on to tell the client what the nature of that interest is'. I fear this further retrospective guidance is once more a green light to validity challenges.

The court in *Garrett* did not dissent from its decision in *Hollins* that it is not necessary to state that a solicitor has no interest in the insurance he is recommending – it is only necessary to state when he has.

In *Myatt* the solicitor asked the wrong question in her attempt to comply with reg 4(2)(c). She should not simply have asked unsophisticated clients whether they had credit cards, household or motor insurance policies or trade union membership which would entitle them to legal expenses insurance in respect of the contemplated claim. The solicitor is required to take reasonable steps to ascertain whether the client's risk for costs is already insured and those steps will depend on a variety of circumstances such as the nature of the client, the circumstances in which the solicitor is instructed, the nature of the claim, the cost of the ATE premium may be a relevant factor (the court did not explain how) and whether a referring body has already investigated the availability of BTE. The requirement in *Sarwar v Alam* [45.28] that the client should be invited to bring all relevant policy and other documents to the first interview should be treated with considerable caution in high-volume low-value litigation – in which the solicitor might never have a first interview. In any event, *Sarwar* related not to reg 4 but to the reasonableness of entering into a CFA or ATE insurance.

In the light of this 'guidance' it seemed inevitable that the spate of satellite costs litigation would continue unabated for so long as the indemnity principle survived. It did survive and there was no abatement for some time. A robust approach was taken in *David Smith v Countrywide Farmers plc* (11 February 2010, unreported), QBD Judge Seys-Llewellyn QC sitting as a deputy judge of the High Court declaring that it was in principle and in practice wrong for a judge to trawl through a CFA to check compliance. Dare one say that in the last twelve months the flow has almost dried up? Here is a sample of the cases on breach of the regulations. In *Bevan v Power Panels Electrical Systems Ltd* [2007] EWHC 90073 (Costs) both *Garrett* and *Myatt* points were taken. *Myatt* also tripped up solicitors in *Andrews v Dawkes* (2006) (QBD Birmingham) where the solicitors did not check that their client was unlikely to have access to before the event insurance (BTE). In *Berry v Spousals* (2007) Birmingham CC BM 309007 solicitors did not at any time check claims management company arrangement to see if it would cover costs rather than use a CFA. *Myatt* featured in *Choudhury v Kingston Hospital Trust* [2006] EWHC 90057 (Costs) but there the client consultant anaesthetist wrote to the solicitors confirming she had no BTE – a sophisticated client answering the *Myatt* ultimate question. The same result occurred in *Kashmiri v Ejaz* [2007] EWHC 90074 (Costs) with a commercial client able to provide all the *Myatt* answers himself. BTE has caused particular difficulties in cases involving buses with no consistency in the lower courts as to whether a solicitor before 2005 could have been expected to check the bus company's insurance to see if it covered injured passengers. Paying parties should consult *Tranter v Hansons* [2009] EWHC 90145 (Costs), receiving parties *Dole v ECT* (17 September 2007, unreported).

Membership of Accident Line was the basis of a *Garrett* challenge in *Myers v Bonnington* [2007] EWHC 90077 (Costs). The firm had received 24 referrals over six years – a de minimis factor and not enough to amount to an interest. Finally, in *O'Driscoll v Liverpool City Council* (2007) (Liverpool County Court) there had been no 'positive averment' that solicitors would lose TAG panel membership if their client had not taken a policy with TAG, and therefore no basis for an inference to be drawn as that in *Myatt* that the solicitors had an interest in recommending an insurance policy. With such ingenuity by the judiciary and the profession it is probable that unless the indemnity principle is disapplied the rewards for successful challenges are such that the satellite litigation will continue even for CFAs entered into after the removal of the Regulations on 1 November 2005, to which we now turn.

THE REGULATIONS FROM 1 NOVEMBER 2005

(a) Consultation

[43.43]

The situation with costs in general and CFAs in particular deteriorated so alarmingly that with increasing frequency more costs were incurred in disputes about the costs than on the substantive litigation itself, which had often been resolved by agreement. Costs had become a hydra-headed monster ('unhelpful turbulence' is how the Minister for Civil Justice put it) which the judiciary alone was unable to control, and indeed some of the decisions of the lower echelons of the judiciary positively encouraged satellite litigation. So, the Department for Constitutional Affairs, stepped in with a consultation paper, '*Simplifying Conditional Fee Agreements and Proposals for Reform*', inviting views on how CFAs could be made simpler and more transparent, and what levels of consumer protection were needed for the future. In June 2004 the

DCA summarised the responses to the consultation paper in another one entitled '*Making Simple "No Win No Fee" Arrangements a Reality*' and in August 2005 published a summary of the responses to the paper and its proposals.

(b) The concerns

[43.44]

The DCA paper of August 2005 identified four areas of concern:
(1)   The regulations were too complex and extensive
(2)   The indemnity principle encouraged technical challenges by the paying party
(3)   The regulations were difficult to understand and impossible to explain
(4)   The regulations over-lapped the Solicitors Practice Rules and Client Care Code.

(c) The solution

[43.45]

The radical answer to prevent problems arising from breaches and alleged breaches of the regulations was to revoke the regulations!

The Conditional Fee Agreement and Collective Conditional Fee Agreement Regulations were neither necessary nor effective and they were revoked from 1 November 2005. The primary legislation (s 27 of the Access to Justice Act 1999) provides the minimum legislative framework for the use of CFAs. Primary responsibility for client care, contractual and guidance matters was transferred to the Law Society (now the SRA) and is now focused on solicitors by the SRA Code of Conduct, supporting costs guidance and new model CFAs. The Membership Organisation Regulations 2000 have been simplified as far as primary legislation allow. The Law Society and other relevant stakeholders have developed an appropriate model CFA to support the new regime, to ensure the professional rules can effectively regulate and/or guide solicitors' use of CFAs and their obligations to their clients. The Law Society had been expected to introduce amended rules and new model agreement at the same time as the CFA regulations were repealed but we waited until July 2007 and the new rules make no substantive change. Minor consequential amendments to the Civil Procedure Rules to take account of the reforms to the CFA regulations have been made.

In the debate during the early 1990s I am thought to have opposed the introduction of CFAs, but I did not. I welcomed them. What I was opposed to were the accompanying convoluted rules and regulations as being unnecessary. There was no need for the contortions of the Conditional Fee Agreements Orders, Regulations and Rules to regulate the position between the solicitor and his client under a no win, no fee agreement.

There has never been any problem about no win, no fee agreements in non-contentious business, which are frequently entered into, for example, in domestic and commercial conveyancing, management buy-outs and acquisitions. Why should a litigation client require any additional protection?

(d) What was left?

[43.46]

Sections 58 and 58A of the Courts and Legal Services Act 1990 (see paras [43.3] and [43.5]) and the Civil Procedure Rules 1998 and their supplementary practice directions (see paras [44.3] ff) still provide the basis and overall framework for conditional fee agreements, with minor consequential amendments to the CPR introduced in 2006. The only remaining statutory provisions are that the CFA must be in writing, must state the percentage success fee to be applied and the use of CFAs in criminal and family proceedings is prohibited. There is no requirement for signature

(e) What was new?

(i) Solicitors' Practice (Client Care) Amendment Rule 2005

[43.47]

The Solicitors' Practice (Client Care) Amendment Rule 2005 added at the end of paragraph 5 of the Solicitors' Costs Information and Client Care Code 1999 (*'Additional Information for particular clients'*) (para [2.25]):

Clients represented under a conditional fee agreement (including a collective conditional fee agreement)

(d)   Where a client is represented under a conditional fee agreement, the solicitor should explain:

 (i)   the circumstances in which the client may be liable for their own costs and for the other party's costs;

 (ii)   the client's right to assessment of costs, wherever the solicitor intends to seek payment of any or all of their costs from the client; and

 (iii) any interest the solicitor may have in recommending a particular policy or other funding.

Only para (i) will apply if the client is to be harmless as to costs and the solicitor has no interest in the funding. Simplicity itself.

The rule came into force on 1 November 2005 and remained so until 1 July 2007.

(ii) Solicitor's Code of Conduct 2007 Rule 2.03 (from 1 July 2007)

[43.48]

2.03

(1)   You must give your client the best information possible about the likely overall cost of a matter both at the outset and, when appropriate, as the matter progresses. In particular you must:

 (a)   advise the client of the basis and terms of your charges;

 (b)   advise the client if charging rates are to be increased;

 (c)   advise the client of likely payments which you or your client may need to make to others;

(d)   discuss with the client how the client will pay, in particular:
   (i)   whether the client may be eligible and should apply for public funding; and
   (ii)   whether the client's own costs are covered by insurance or may be paid by someone else such as an employer or trade union;
(e)   advise the client that there are circumstances where you may be entitled to exercise a lien for unpaid costs;
(f)   advise the client of their potential liability for any other party's costs; and
(g)   discuss with the client whether their liability for another party's costs may be covered by existing insurance or whether specially purchased insurance may be obtained.

(2)   Where you are acting for the client under a conditional fee agreement, (including a collective conditional fee agreement) in addition to complying with 2.03(1) above and 2.03(5) and (6) below, you must explain the following, both at the outset and, when appropriate, as the matter progresses:
   (a)   the circumstances in which your client may be liable for your costs and whether you will seek payment of these from the client, if entitled to do so;
   (b)   if you intend to seek payment of any or all of your costs from your client, you must advise your client of their right to an assessment of those costs; and
   (c)   where applicable, the fact that you are obliged under a fee sharing agreement to pay to a charity any fees which you receive by way of costs from the client's opponent or other third party.

(3)   Where you are acting for a publicly funded client, in addition to complying with 2.03(1) above and 2.03(5) and (6) below, you must explain the following at the outset:
   (a)   the circumstances in which they may be liable for your costs;
   (b)   the effect of the statutory charge;
   (c)   the client's duty to pay any fixed or periodic contribution assessed and the consequence of failing to do so; and
   (d)   that even if your client is successful, the other party may not be ordered to pay costs or may not be in a position to pay them.

(4)   Where you agree to share your fees with a charity in accordance with you must disclose to the client at the outset the name of the charity.

(5)   Any information about the cost must be clear and confirmed in writing.

(6)   You must discuss with your client whether the potential outcomes of any legal case will justify the expense or risk involved including, if relevant, the risk of having to pay an opponent's costs.

(7)   If you can demonstrate that it was inappropriate in the circumstances to meet some or all of the requirements in 2.03(1) and (5) you will not breach 2.03.

In Thomas v Butler T/A Worthington's Solicitors [2009] EWHC 90153 (Costs) the defendant firm took over a case that had run with a different firm under a CFA. The first firm had declined to continue because of poor prospects. The client thought the new firm was acting under a CFA and that he was covered for adverse costs by BTE insurance. There had been discussion with the new firm about a CFA but the matter was not confirmed either way. This was the main failing of the firm and was a breach of the Solicitors' Costs Information and Client Care Code 1999 (similar provisions are contained in the current SRA Code). The client had become liable for own costs on a private paying basis and was left with an adverse costs bill not covered by the BTE. The court had power to deal with the own cost side and assessed it at nil on the basis that those costs had been "unreasonably incurred". The court had no power in respect of the adverse costs but made clear what it thought the firm ought to do.

(iii) Law Society Model CFA Agreement

[43.49]

For use on or after 1 November 2005

For use in personal injury and clinical negligence cases only..

This agreement is a binding legal contract between you and your solicitor/s. Before you sign, please read everything carefully. This agreement must be read in conjunction with the Law Society document "What you need to know about a CFA".

Agreement date

[. . . .]

I/We, the solicitor/s [. . . .]

You, the client [. . . .]

What is covered by this agreement

– Your claim against [. . .] for damages for personal injury suffered on [.].(if either the name of the opponent or the date of the incident are unclear then set out here in as much detail as possible to give sufficient information for the client and solicitor to understand the basis of the claim being pursued)

– Any appeal by your opponent.

– Any appeal you make against an interim order.

– Any proceedings you take to enforce a judgment, order or agreement.

– Negotiations about and/or a court assessment of the costs of this claim.

What is not covered by this agreement

– Any counterclaim against you.

– Any appeal you make against the final judgment order.

Paying us

If you win your claim, you pay our basic charges, our disbursements and a success fee. You are entitled to seek recovery from your opponent of part or all of our basic charges, our disbursements, a success fee and insurance premium as set out in the document "What you need to know about a CFA."

It may be that your opponent makes a Part 36 offer or payment which you reject on our advice, and your claim for damages goes ahead to trial where you recover damages that are less than that offer or payment. If this happens, we will *[not add our success fee to the basic charges]* *[not claim any costs]* for the work done after we received notice of the offer or payment.

If you receive interim damages, we may require you to pay our disbursements at that point and a reasonable amount for our future disbursements.

If you receive provisional damages, we are entitled to payment of our basic charges our disbursements and success fee at that point.

If you lose you remain liable for the other sides costs.

The Success Fee

The success fee is set at [. . . . . .]% of basic charges, where the claim concludes at trial; or [. . . . . .] % where the claim concludes before a trial has commenced. In addition [. . . . . .]% relates to the postponement of payment of our fees and expenses and can not be recovered from your opponent. The Success fee inclusive of any additional percentage relating to postponement cannot be more than 100% of the basic charges in total.

Other points

The parties acknowledge and agree that this agreement is not a Contentious Business Agreement within the terms of the Solicitors Act 1974.

Signatures

Signed by the solicitor(s): ....

Signed by the client: ....

Conditional Fee Agreements: what you need to know

Definitions of words used in this document and the accompanying CFA are explained at the end of this document.

What do I pay if I win?

If you win your claim, you pay our basic charges, our disbursements and a success fee. The amount of these is not based on or limited by the damages. You can claim from your opponent part or all of our basic charges, our disbursements, a success fee and insurance premium.

It may be that your opponent makes a Part 36 offer or payment which you reject on our advice, and your claim for damages goes ahead to trial where you recover damages that are less than that offer or payment. Refer to the "Paying Us" section in the CFA document to establish costs we will be seeking for the work done after we received notice of the offer or payment.

If you receive interim damages, we may require you to pay our disbursements at that point as well as a reasonable amount for our future disbursements.

If you receive provisional damages, we are entitled to payment of our basic charges, our disbursements and success fee at that point. If you win overall but on the way lose an interim hearing, you may be required to pay your opponent's charges of that hearing.

If on the way to winning or losing you are awarded any costs, by agreement or court order, then we are entitled to payment of those costs, together with a success fee on those charges if you win overall.

What do I pay if I lose?

If you lose, you pay your opponent's charges and disbursements. You may be able to take out an insurance policy against this risk. If you lose, you do not pay our charges but we may require you to pay our disbursements.

Ending this agreement

If you end this agreement before you win or lose, you pay our basic charges and disbursements. If you go on to win, you also pay a success fee.

We may end this agreement before you win or lose.

Basic charges

These are for work done from now until this agreement ends. These are subject to review.

How we calculate our basic charges

These are calculated for each hour engaged on your matter. Routine letters and telephone calls will be charged as units of one tenth of an hour. Other letters and telephone calls will be charged on a time basis. The hourly rates are:

Grade of Fee Earner	Hourly Rate
1 Solicitors with over 8 years experience after qualification	
2 Solicitors with over four years' experience after qualification	
3 Other solicitors and legal executives and other staff of equivalent experience	
4 Trainee solicitors and other staff of equivalent experience	

We review the hourly rate on [review date] and we will notify you of any change in the rate in writing.

Road Traffic Accidents

[If your claim is settled before proceedings are issued, for less than £10,000, our basic costs will be £800; plus 20% of the damages agreed up to £5,000; and 15% of the damages agreed between £5,000 and £10,000.] [If you live in London, these costs will be increased by 12.5%]. These costs are fixed by the Civil Procedure Rules.

Success fee

The success fee percentage set out in the agreement reflects the following:
(a)   the fact that if you lose, we will not earn anything;
(b)   our assessment of the risks of your case;
(c)   any other appropriate matters;
(d)   the fact that if you win we will not be paid our basic charges until the end of the claim;
(e)   our arrangements with you about paying disbursements.

Value added tax (VAT)

We add VAT, at the rate (now [. . . . . .]%) that applies when the work is done, to the total of the basic charges and success fee.

The Insurance Policy

In all the circumstances and on the information currently available to us, we believe, that a contract of insurance with [. . .] is appropriate to cover your opponent's charges and disbursements in case you lose.

This is because

You do not have an existing or satisfactory insurance that would cover the costs of making this claim. The policy we recommend will pay:
(a)   *the costs of the other party in the event that the claim fails, to a maximum of £X;*
(b)   *all your disbursements if your claim fails.*
(c)   *[add other key features where necessary such as, our costs and the other side's costs (without deduction from your damages) if you fail to beat an (Part 36) Offer to Settle your claim, which you rejected following our advice].*
or:

[We cannot identify a policy which meets your needs but our recommended policy is the closest that we can discover within the products that we have searched. It does not meet your needs in the following respects:
(a)   *it has an excess of £Z*
(b)   *the maximum cover is £ZZ]*
or:

[We cannot obtain an insurance policy at this stage but we shall continue to look for one and if we are successful in our search then we shall advise you at that stage of the benefits of the policy and purchasing it]

[NB. The italicised reasons in set out are examples only. Your solicitor must consider your individual circumstances and set out the reasons that apply].

Law Society Conditions

The Law Society Conditions below are part of this agreement. Any amendments or additions to them will apply to you. You should read the conditions carefully and ask us about anything you find unclear.

Our responsibilities

We must:

- always act in your best interests, subject to our duty to the court;
- explain to you the risks and benefits of taking legal action;
- give you our best advice about whether to accept any offer of settlement;
- give you the best information possible about the likely costs of your claim for damages.

Your responsibilities

You must:

- give us instructions that allow us to do our work properly;
- not ask us to work in an improper or unreasonable way;
- not deliberately mislead us;
- co-operate with us;
- go to any medical or expert examination or court hearing.

Dealing with costs if you win

- You are liable to pay all our basic charges, our disbursements and success fee.
- Normally, you can claim part or all of our basic charges, our disbursements success fee and insurance premium from your opponent.
- If we and your opponent cannot agree the amount, the court will decide how much you can recover. If the amount agreed or allowed by the court does not cover all our basic charges and our disbursements, then you pay the difference.
- You will not be entitled to recover from your opponent the part of the success fee that relates to the cost to us of postponing receipt of our charges and our disbursements. This remains payable by you.
- You agree that after winning, the reasons for setting the success fee at the amount stated may be disclosed: (i) to the court and any other person required by the court; (ii)to your opponent in order to gain his or her agreement to pay the success fee.
- If the court carries out an assessment and reduces the success fee because the percentage agreed was unreasonable in view of what we knew or should have known when it was agreed, then the amount reduced ceases to be payable unless the court is satisfied that it should continue to be payable.
- If we agree with your opponent that the success fee is to be paid at a lower percentage than is set out in this agreement, then the success fee percentage will be reduced accordingly unless the court is satisfied that the full amount is payable.

- It may happen that your opponent makes an offer of one amount that includes payment of our basic charges and a success fee. If so, unless we consent, you agree not to tell us to accept the offer if it includes payment of the success fee at a lower rate than is set out in this agreement.
- If your opponent is receiving Community Legal Service funding, we are unlikely to get any money from him or her. So if this happens, you have to pay us our basic charges, disbursements and success fee.

As with the costs in general, you remain ultimately responsible for paying our success fee.

You agree to pay into a designated account any cheque received by you or by us from your opponent and made payable to you. Out of the money, you agree to let us take the balance of the basic charges; success fee; insurance premium; our remaining disbursements; and VAT.

You take the rest.

We are allowed to keep any interest your opponent pays on the charges.

If your opponent fails to pay

If your opponent does not pay any damages or charges owed to you, we have the right to take recovery action in your name to enforce a judgment, order or agreement. The charges of this action become part of the basic charges.

Payment for advocacy

The cost of advocacy and any other work by us, or by any solicitor agent on our behalf, forms part of our basic charges. We shall discuss with you the identity of any barrister instructed, and the arrangements made for payment.

Barristers who have a conditional fee agreement with us

If you win, you are normally entitled to recover their fee and success fee from your opponent. The barrister's success fee is shown in the separate conditional fee agreement we make with the barrister. We will discuss the barrister's success fee with you before we instruct him or her. If you lose, you pay the barrister nothing.

Barristers who do not have a conditional fee agreement with us

If you win, then you will normally be entitled to recover all or part of their fee from your opponent. If you lose, then you must pay their fee.

What happens when this agreement ends before your claim for damages ends?

(a) Paying us if you end this agreement

You can end the agreement at any time. We then have the right to decide whether you must:

- pay our basic charges and our disbursements including barristers' fees but not the success fee when we ask for them; or
- pay our basic charges, and our disbursements including barristers' fees and success fees if you go on to win your claim for damages.

(b) Paying us if we end this agreement

(i) We can end this agreement if you do not keep to your responsibilities. We then have the right to decide whether you must:

- pay our basic charges and our disbursements including barristers' fees but not the success fee when we ask for them; or
- pay our basic charges and our disbursements including barristers' fees and success fees if you go on to win your claim for damages.

(ii) We can end this agreement if we believe you are unlikely to win. If this happens, you will only have to pay our disbursements. These will include barristers' fees if the barrister does not have a conditional fee agreement with us.

(iii) We can end this agreement if you reject our opinion about making a settlement with your opponent. You must then:
- pay the basic charges and our disbursements, including barristers' fees;
- pay the success fee if you go on to win your claim for damages.

If you ask us to get a second opinion from a specialist solicitor outside our firm, we will do so. You pay the cost of a second opinion.

(iv) We can end this agreement if you do not pay your insurance premium when asked to do so.

(c) Death

This agreement automatically ends if you die before your claim for damages is concluded. We will be entitled to recover our basic charges up to the date of your death from your estate.

If your personal representatives wish to continue your claim for damages, we may offer them a new conditional fee agreement, as long as they agree to pay the success fee on our basic charges from the beginning of the agreement with you.

What happens after this agreement ends

After this agreement ends, we may apply to have our name removed from the record of any court proceedings in which we are acting unless you have another form of funding and ask us to work for you.

We have the right to preserve our lien unless another solicitor working for you undertakes to pay us what we are owed including a success fee if you win.

Explanation of words used

(a) *Advocacy*

Appearing for you at court hearings.

(b) *Basic charges*

Our charges for the legal work we do on your claim for damages.

(c) *Claim*

Your demand for damages for personal injury whether or not court proceedings are issued.

(d) Counterclaim

A claim that your opponent makes against you in response to your claim.

(e) Damages

Money that you win whether by a court decision or settlement.

(f) Our disbursements

Payment we make on your behalf such as:
- court fees;
- experts' fees;
- accident report fees;
- travelling expenses.

(g) *Interim damages*

Money that a court says your opponent must pay or your opponent agrees to pay while waiting for a settlement or the court's final decision.

(h) *Interim hearing*

A court hearing that is not final.

(i) Lien

Our right to keep all papers, documents, money or other property held on your behalf until all money due to us is paid. A lien may be applied after this agreement ends.

(j) Lose

The court has dismissed your claim or you have stopped it on our advice.

(k) Part 36 offers or payments

An offer to settle your claim made in accordance with Part 36 of the Civil Procedure Rules.

(l) Provisional damages

Money that a court says your opponent must pay or your opponent agrees to pay, on the basis that you will be able to go back to court at a future date for further damages if:

- you develop a serious disease; or
- your condition deteriorates;

in a way that has been proved or admitted to be linked to your personal injury claim.

(m) Success fee

The percentage of basic charges that we add to your bill if you win your claim for damages and that we will seek to recover from your opponent.

(n) Trial

The final contested hearing or the contested hearing of any issue to be tried separately and a reference to a claim concluding at trial includes a claim settled after the trial has commenced or a judgment.

(o) Win

Your claim for damages is finally decided in your favour, whether by a court decision or an agreement to pay you damages or in any way that you derive benefit from pursuing the claim.

'Finally' means that your opponent:

- is not allowed to appeal against the court decision; or
- has not appealed in time; or
- has lost any appeal.

(f) The symptoms and not the disease?

[43.50]

Many of the problems with CFAs are attributable to the introduction of recoverability of additional liabilities between the parties (they should be simply a matter between the solicitor and the client) and the continued existence of the perfidious indemnity principle. Unfortunately, they both survive these reforms, which appear to address the symptoms and not the disease. It is supremely optimistic to hope that transferring regulation to the SRA will put an end to future costs satellite litigation. If the solicitor contravenes the code of conduct, which has the same statutory force as the revoked regulations (see para [42.5], cannot the client still contend that the retainer is unenforceable, or at least that the solicitor's costs entitlement is reduced, thereby enabling the paying party to rely on the indemnity principle to avoid liability for payment? These arguments were addressed in *Garbutt v Edwards* [2005] EWCA Civ 1206, [2006] 1 All ER 553, [2006] 1 WLR 2907, when the Court of Appeal confirmed that the practice rules and care code did have statutory effect, but held that their breach did not make the agreement unenforceable. The word 'shall' in this context in Rule 15 was not mandatory. The sanctions for non-compliance are disciplinary and a client cannot be penalised for not initiating disciplinary proceedings against his own solicitor. Between the parties the costs judge should consider whether and, if so, to what extent the costs claimed would have been significantly lower had an estimate been given. It remains to be seen whether other breaches of Rule 15 and of the Solicitors Code of Conduct 2007 are held to be so innocuous. All the arguments based on the indemnity principle alleging that the costs claimed between the parties exceed those payable by the client to the solicitor will remain. Because the government could not countenance making the new regime retrospective it appears matters must get worse before they get better because the costs warfare will for the foreseeable future be waged on two fronts – the old and the new. What also will be the effect of a breach of the Solicitors Financial Services (Conduct of Business) Rules 2001 in respect of ATE insurance? See para [43.42].

(i)   Disclosure of a CFA

[43.51]

The Court in *Hollins* (para [43.40]) said that it should become normal practice for a CFA to be disclosed for the purpose of costs proceedings in which a success fee is claimed, subject to the provision in paragraph 40.14 of the Costs Practice Direction that the judge may ask the receiving party to elect whether to disclose the CFA to the paying party in order to rely on it or whether to decline disclosure and instead rely on other evidence. If the CFA contains confidential information relating to other proceedings, it may be suitably redacted before disclosure takes place. A party given that option who then consistently refuses to provide the CFA or sufficient other evidence of compliance will suffer the consequences of failing to recover costs, the exact outcome in *David Smith v Countrywide Farmers plc* (unreported 11 February 2010 QBD Cardiff District Registry). Attendance notes and other correspondence should not ordinarily be disclosed, but the judge conducting the assessment may require the disclosure of material of this kind if a genuine issue is raised. A genuine issue is one in which there is a real chance that the CFA is unenforceable as a result of failure to satisfy the applicable conditions (*Pratt v Bull, Worth v McKenna* [2003] EWCA Civ 718, [2003] 1 WLR 2487). With the removal of the Regulations from 1 November 2005 a CFA needs only to be in writing (seemingly it need not be signed) but that did not stop an application for disclosure in *Ashley Cole v News Group* (2006) October 18 SCCO. That application failed simply because no points of dispute had been served hence CPR 47.14 and CPD 40.14 did not apply. The applicability of *Hollins* to post 1 November 2005 CFAs was considered in *Findlay v Cantor Index Ltd* [2008] EWHC 90116 (Costs) where disclosure was sought of the CFA, the reasons for the success fee and counsel's opinion. Master Campbell held that Costs Practice Direction 32.5 could have no application to post 1 November 2005 CFAs (where there is no requirement to state reasons for the success fee) and thus the paying party has no right to information concerning the setting of the success fee, and presumably no proof other than the solicitor's assertion as to what it was! As to the CFA, *Hollins* still required it to be disclosed at the costs stage although counsel's opinion was privileged despite being referred to in a disclosed risk assessment. If the focus of attention now turns to compliance with Solicitors Practice Rule 15 and the Client Care Code or the Solicitors' Code of Conduct 2007 since 1 July 2007 we have the prospect of applications for disclosure of a variety of documents other than the CFA. We are in danger of having opened yet another Pandora's box.

COLLECTIVE CONDITIONAL FEES

Collective Conditional Fee Agreements Regulations 2000

[43.52]

(as amended by the Conditional Fee Agreements (Miscellaneous Amendments) Regulations 2003 and the Conditional Fee Agreements (Miscellaneous Amendments)(No 2) Regulations 2003). As with individual CFAs these regulations were revoked from 1 November 2005 but many cases in the future will be governed by them. As for individual cases taken on since revocation but under a CCFA made before revocation see below at para [43.63].

[43.53]

1 Citation, commencement and interpretation
(1)   These regulations may be cited as the Collective Conditional Fee Agreements Regulations 2000, and shall come into force on 30th November 2000.
(2)   In these Regulations, except where the context requires otherwise—
'client' means a person who will receive advocacy or litigation services to which the agreement relates;
'collective conditional fee agreement' has the meaning given in regulation 3;
'conditional fee agreement' has the same meaning as in section 58 of the Courts and Legal Services Act 1990;
'funder' means the party to a collective conditional fee agreement who, under that agreement, is liable to pay the legal representative's fees;
'legal representative' means the person providing the advocacy or litigation services to which the agreement relates.

[43.54]

2 Transitional provisions
These Regulations shall apply to agreements entered into on or after 30th November 2000, and agreements entered into before that date shall be treated as if these Regulations had not come into force.

[43.55]

3 Definition of 'collective conditional fee agreement'
(1)   Subject to paragraph (2) of this regulation, a collective conditional fee agreement is an agreement which—
    (a)   disregarding section 58(3)(c) of the Courts and Legal Services Act 1990, would be a conditional fee agreement; and

(b)   does not refer to specific proceedings, but provides for fees to be payable on a common basis in relation to a class of proceedings, or, if it refers to more than one class of proceedings, on a common basis in relation to each class.

(2)   An agreement may be a collective conditional fee agreement whether or not—

(a)   the funder is a client; or

(b)   any clients are named in the agreement.

[43.56]

4 Requirements for contents of collective conditional fee agreements: general

(1)   A collective conditional fee agreement must specify the circumstances in which the legal representative's fees and expenses, or part of them, are payable.

(1A)   The circumstances referred to in paragraph (1) may include the fact that the legal representative's fees and expenses are payable only to the extent that sums are recovered in respect of the proceedings, whether by way of costs or otherwise.

(2)   A collective conditional fee agreement must provide that, when accepting instructions in relation to any specific proceedings the legal representative must—

(a)   inform the client as to the circumstances in which the client or his estate may be liable to pay the costs of the legal representative; and

(b)   if the client requires any further explanation, advice or other information about the matter referred to in sub-paragraph (a), provide such further explanation, advice or other information about it as the client may reasonably require.

(3)   Paragraph (2) does not apply in the case of an agreement between a legal representative and an additional legal representative.

(4)   A collective conditional fee agreement must provide that, after accepting instructions in relation to any specific proceedings, the legal representative must confirm his acceptance of instructions in writing to the client.

[43.57]

5 Requirements for contents of collective conditional fee agreements providing for success fees

(1)   Where a collective conditional fee agreement provides for a success fee the agreement must provide that, when accepting instructions in relation to any specific proceedings the legal representative must prepare and retain a written statement containing—

(a)   his assessment of the probability of the circumstances arising in which the percentage increase will become payable in relation to those proceedings ('the risk assessment');

(b)   his assessment of the amount of the percentage increase in relation to those proceedings, having regard to the risk assessment; and

(c)   the reasons, by reference to the risk assessment, for setting the percentage increase at that level.

(2)   If the agreement relates to court proceedings it must provide that where the success fee becomes payable as a result of those proceedings, then—

(a)   if—

(i)   any fees subject to the increase are assessed, and

(ii)   the legal representative or the client is required by the court to disclose to the court or any other person the reasons for setting the percentage increase at the level assessed by the legal representative,

he may do so,

(b)   if—

    (i)   any such fees are assessed by the court, and

    (ii)   any amount in respect of the percentage increase is disallowed on the assessment on the ground that the level at which the increase was set was unreasonable in view of facts which were or should have been known to the legal representative at the time it was set that amount ceases to be payable under the agreement, unless the court is satisfied that it should continue to be so payable, and

(c)   if—

    (i)   sub-paragraph (b) does not apply, and

    (ii)   the legal representative agrees with any person liable as a result of the proceedings to pay fees subject to the percentage increase that a lower amount than the amount payable in accordance with the conditional fee agreement is to be paid instead,

the amount payable under the collective conditional fee agreement in respect of those fees shall be reduced accordingly, unless the court is satisfied that the full amount should continue to be payable under it.

(3)   In this regulation 'percentage increase' means the percentage by which the amount of the fees which would have been payable if the agreement were not a conditional fee agreement is to be increased under the agreement.

(4)   Sub-paragraphs (b) and (c) of paragraph (2) do not apply to a collective conditional fee agreement under which, except in the circumstances set out in paragraphs (6) and (7), the client is liable to pay his legal representative's fees and expenses only to the extent that sums are recovered in respect of the proceedings, whether by way of costs or otherwise.

(5)   In determining for the purposes of paragraph (4) the circumstances in which a client is liable to pay his legal representative's fees and expenses, no account is to be taken of any obligation to pay costs in respect of the premium of a policy taken out to insure against the risk of incurring a liability in the relevant proceedings.

(6)   A collective conditional fee agreement to which paragraph (4) applies may specify that the client will be liable to pay his legal representative's fees and expenses whether or not sums are recovered in respect of the relevant proceedings, if the client—

    (a)   fails to co-operate with the legal representative;

    (b)   fails to attend any medical or expert examination or court hearing which the legal representative reasonably requests him to attend;

    (c)   fails to give necessary instructions to the legal representative;

    (d)   withdraws instructions from the legal representative;

    (e)   is an individual who is adjudged bankrupt or enters into an arrangement or a composition with his creditors, or against whom an administration order has been made; or

    (f)   is a company for which a receiver, administrative receiver or liquidator is appointed.

(7)   A collective conditional fee agreement to which paragraph (4) applies, may specify that, in the event of the client dying in the course of the relevant proceedings, his estate will be liable for the legal representative's fees and expenses, whether or not sums are recovered in respect of those proceedings.

[43.58]

6 Form and amendment of collective conditional fee agreements

(1)   Subject to paragraph (2), a collective conditional fee agreement must be signed by the funder, and by the legal representative.

(2)   Paragraph (1) does not apply in the case of an agreement between a legal representative and an additional legal representative.

(3)   Where a collective conditional fee agreement is amended, regulations 4 and 5 apply to the amended agreement as if it were a fresh agreement made at the time of the amendment.

[43.59]

7 Amendment to the Conditional Fee Agreements Regulations 2000

After regulation 7 of the Conditional Fee Agreements Regulations 2000 there shall be inserted the following new regulation:—

'8 Exclusion of collective conditional fee agreements

These Regulations shall not apply to collective conditional fee agreements within the meaning of regulation 3 of the Collective Conditional Fee Agreements Regulations 2000.'

(a) Bulk purchase

[43.60]

Collective conditional fee agreements (CCFAs) were a response to concerns expressed during the passage of the Access to Justice Act 1999 that the individual CFA regime was not administratively suitable for the bulk purchase of legal services. In particular commercial organisation and membership organisations such as the AA and RAC and the trade unions were not able to use the existing CFA provisions because of the practical and physical difficulties of administering the rules on an individual basis. As with individual CFAs the Regulations were revoked from 1 November 2005.

(b) Two categories

[43.61]

The CCFA Regulations 2000 made provision for all CCFAs irrespective of the context in which they were to be used. The regulations apply to bulk purchasers of legal services, such as the legal department of a multi national company, and to bulk providers of legal services such as the legal representatives retained by a trade union to act for its members. There is a crucial difference between these two categories in that the bulk purchaser is also the client, whereas the bulk provider will involve numerous clients who are not funding the litigation. The regulations, however, apply consumer protection provisions to all CCFAs, including those where the client is also the funder. The regulations are not set out so as to have provisions applying according to whether the CCFA is for a bulk purchaser or not.

(c) Disclosure

[43.62]

A CCFA is governed in the same way as an individual CFA in terms of the CPR and Costs Practice Direction. The rules for the disclosure of funding arrangements apply to CCFAs in the same way as for individual CFAs. Form N251 may be used for the giving of this information.

(d) The indemnity principle

[43.63]

There are no provisions in the CPR for CCFAs and no changes have been made following the commencement of s 31 to disapply the indemnity principle. There was therefore a question as to the validity of CCFAs where the party to the proceedings is not also the funder. Two explanations of CCFAs have so far emerged from costs assessments. In *Gliddon v Lloyd Maunder Ltd* (SCCO-JOH 0211064), [2003] NLJR 318 Master O'Hare took the view that the CFA Regulations did not abrogate the indemnity principle. He found, however, that there was a link between the individual client and the solicitor such that there was a retainer between them. In *Thornley v Lang* [2003] EWCA Civ 1484, [2004] 1 All ER 886, [2004] 1 WLR 378, the Court of Appeal reviewed the line of authorities dealing with trade union funding and held that the member here was liable on the basis of the CCFA. It reached that result by alternative routes. Either the union agreed with the authority of its member or the member ratified the union's agreement. On either footing there was a contract under which the member was liable and that contract was a CCFA. The Court expressly rejected the argument that the member had entered into a CFA on an individual basis which would be subject to the CFA Regulations.

Several challenges to a trade union CCFA were made in *Duffy v Port Ramsgate* (2004) SCCO (SCCO JOH 0306901). It was argued that because the member's liability was, under the terms of the CCFA, limited to the liability of the losing opponent the whole agreement was invalid – an indemnity principle argument. It was also argued that a member represented under such a CCFA still requires the same explanation as to costs under Rule 15 of the Law Society Rules as a private client. Both arguments were rejected. The CCFA also covered work done on the case before 30 November 2000 when CCFAs were introduced. No success fee was claimed in respect of the earlier work and the court rejected the argument that this earlier work had been conducted under an invalid agreement. The challenge in *Various Claimants v Gower Chemicals* (2007) SCCO CW05054225 failed where Field J sitting in the county court held that Regulation 5(1) is complied with where the CCFA contains a requirement to prepare and retain a risk assessment – actual performance is not a further requirement.

As for the use of CCFAs after 1 November 2005 the position is intriguing. To take the typical case of a trade union there will be in place between it and its solicitors a CCFA dated long before 2005 but intended to govern cases run today. Does the Court of Appeal's analysis in *Thornley* make for difficulty? Assume that a pre- 1 November 2005 CCFA is the only one and that it is invalid for breach when made. What is the effect in 2006 or 2010 when it is still being used? Has the member adopted an invalid CCFA? Did an invalid CCFA suddenly become valid on 1 November 2005?

(e) Simplified CCFAs

[43.64]

The Conditional Fee Agreements (Miscellaneous Amendments) Regulations 2003 from 2 June 2003 introduced a simplified version of a CCFA which restricts own costs liabilities to sums recovered. Where a CCFA is being used by a membership organisation it is probable that the member is intended to retain all damages even under a standard CCFA. The difference is that now the agreement can actually say so, but it is subject to the same wording as the simplified individual agreement 'sums are recovered . . . whether by way of costs or otherwise'.

As with the individual version, a simplified CCFA can still impose an own costs liability where the client fails to co-operate, attend a medical or expert examination or court hearing, fails to give instructions or withdraws instructions and upon the death or insolvency of the client. The burden of explanation in the case of CCFAs was always rather less than for individual CFAs and no changes were made to the level of explanation required.

The revocation of the Regulations from 1 November 2005 means that a CCFA made after 1 November 2005 need only comply with s 58 Courts and Legal Services Act 1990 (see [43.60] and it can of course be worded to achieve the result intended by the simplified regulations. On the basis of *Duffy* (para [43.63]) Rule 15 plays no significant role, at least where the CCFA relates to a Trade Union and the realistic position is that the member receives free legal services.

MEMBERSHIP ORGANISATIONS

[43.65]

By s 30 of the Access to Justice Act 1999 and the Access to Justice (Membership Organisations) Regulations 2000 provision is made for the recoupment of a sum no greater than the equivalent of the cost to a member of taking out a personal insurance policy covering adverse costs only. The Access to Justice (Membership Organisation) Regulations 2005 replaced the 2000 Regulations from 1 November 2005. This regulatory scheme still leaves the organisation responsible for the administration of the litigation and for ensuring that an agreement with the member exists which can give rise to the recoupment of the costs. It also leaves own costs in lost cases with the organisation. A collective CFA can then be used to transfer the own costs risk to its lawyers who can seek to cover that risk by success fees in successful cases. Whether any membership organisations will seek to make use of CCFAs with an after-the-event policy is likely to depend on the administrative load of that route rather than the s 30 route. On the basis of *Thornley v Lang* (above) the individual has a costs liability for own costs as well as opponent's costs and could therefore insure by use of an individual ATE policy and seek then to recover the premium under s 29. Such a route deals with own disbursements where the case loses, s 30 does not. It is possible that a membership organisation may fund the ATE premium or could negotiate deferred premiums. If the organisation were to take out its own insurance the premium would be the 'provision' made by the organisation but that would lead to seemingly insurmountable problems in apportioning any part of such provision to an individual case.

THE STATUTORY REQUIREMENTS

[43.66]

The 2000 regulations (applicable to any arrangements made before 1 November 2005) are based upon the individual CFA Regulations, a matter which itself may give rise to some difficulties. The basis of the recovery of the amount representing the 'self-insurance cost' to the organisation is a provision which enables the member himself to recover such an amount, not for the organisation to recover it directly. The regulations make no requirement that the member is under any liability to account to the organisation any amount recovered. Under the 2000 regulations the organisation must give a written undertaking to the member or other person who is a party to the proceedings to meet an order for adverse costs. Provisions are made for the giving of a written statement to the member of the circumstances in which the member may be liable for costs, but the recovery of the sum intended to reflect the cost to the organisation is a recovery by the member. As to the costs actually incurred by the organisation in 'self-insuring', the relevant figure appears to be that at which an individual could have obtained insurance.

The 2005 regulations differ from their predecessors only by removing the references to the detailed circumstances in which the member is liable to pay the costs of the proceedings – those are the words taken from the individual CFA regime and which were inappropriate for the arrangements with membership organisations. But, the 2005 regulations still require the arrangements to contain a statement specifying the circumstances in which the member may be liable to pay costs of the proceedings and it is difficult to see how in real terms this is any different to the former regulations. The requirement to give a copy of the arrangements to the member has been removed in the 2005 regulations.

Access to Justice Act 1999

[43.67]

30 Recovery where body undertakes to meet costs liabilities

(1) This section applies where a body of a prescribed description undertakes to meet (in accordance with arrangements satisfying prescribed conditions) liabilities which members of the body or other persons who are parties to proceedings may incur to pay the costs of other parties to the proceedings.

(2) If in any of the proceedings a costs order is made in favour of any of the members or other persons, the costs payable to him may, subject to subsection (3)

and (in the case of court proceedings) to rules of court, include an additional amount in respect of any provision made by or on behalf of the body in connection with the proceedings against the risk of having to meet such liabilities.

(3) But the additional amount shall not exceed a sum determined in a prescribed manner; and there may, in particular, be prescribed as a manner of determination one which takes into account the likely cost to the member or other person of the premium of an insurance policy against the risk of incurring a liability to pay the costs of other parties to the proceedings.

(4) In this section 'prescribed' means prescribed by regulations made by the Lord Chancellor by statutory instrument; and a statutory instrument containing such regulations shall be subject to annulment in pursuance of a resolution of either House of Parliament.

(5) Regulations under subsection (1) may, in particular, prescribe as a description of body one which is for the time being approved by the Lord Chancellor or by a prescribed person.

[43.68]

Sub-section (1) of s 30 makes it clear that the provision which can lead to the recovery of an additional amount is a provision to meet a member's liability for opponent's costs, not his own costs. The 'provision' made by the organisation is therefore an 'additional liability' which can be claimed by the individual and may be included in a costs order. Section 30(2) can be taken to mean that there has to be evidence of the making of such a provision. The assumption will be made that where a body such as a trade union or motoring organisation is providing an indemnity to its membership for their own and their opponent's costs (ie their costs liability if the case is lost), there is a clear provision in the accounts to enable such indemnity to be financed. If that is the case then there are insurmountable difficulties where the organisation does not formally make a 'provision' in its accounts but nonetheless does indemnify the member. If the organisation makes global provision for prospective liabilities in its future accounting year then the problem is in apportioning that provision in respect if any individual case. The section perhaps assumes that the organisation makes an individual provision against each case it takes on but in most cases such a formal process is unlikely. By sub-s (3) the amount claimed cannot exceed the 'likely' cost to an individual in purchasing an insurance policy to provide cover only for opponent's costs. That is more restrictive than the provisions of s 29 which permit the recovery by an individual of a premium paid in respect not only of opponent's costs but own disbursements and costs. The wording of s 30(1) does not however appear to mean that such an equivalent sum can be recovered, only that the 'provision' made can be recovered subject to a cap. Some trade unions are now using the ATE insurance route, perhaps to avoid these complications.

Access to Justice (Membership Organisations) Regulations 2000

[43.69]

1 Citation, commencement and interpretation

(1) These Regulations may be cited as the Access to Justice (Membership Organisations) Regulations 2000.

(2) These Regulations come into force on 1st April 2000.

[43.70]

2 Bodies of a prescribed description

The bodies which are prescribed for the purpose of section 30 of the Access to Justice Act 1999 (recovery where body undertakes to meet costs liabilities) are those bodies which are for the time being approved by the Lord Chancellor for that purpose.

[43.71]

3 Requirements for arrangements to meet costs liabilities

(1)   Section 30(1) of the Access to Justice Act 1999 applies to arrangements which satisfy the following conditions.

(2)   The arrangements must be in writing.

(3)   The arrangements must contain a statement specifying—

   (a)   the circumstances in which the member or other party may be liable to pay costs of the proceedings,

   (b)   whether such a liability arises—

   (i)   if those circumstances only partly occur,

   (ii)   irrespective of whether those circumstances occur, and

   (iii)   on the termination of the arrangements for any reason,

   (c)   the basis on which the amount of the liability is calculated, and

   (d)   the procedure for seeking assessment of costs.

(4)   A copy of the part of the arrangements containing the statement must be given to the member or other party to the proceedings whose liabilities the body is undertaking to meet as soon as possible after the undertaking is given.

[43.72]

4 Recovery of additional amount for insurance costs

(1)   Where an additional amount is included in costs by virtue of section 30(2) of the Access to Justice Act 1999 (costs payable to a member of a body or other person party to the proceedings to include an additional amount in respect of provision made by the body against the risk of having to meet the member's or other person's liabilities to pay other parties' costs), that additional amount must not exceed the following sum.

(2)   That sum is the likely cost to the member of the body or, as the case may be, the other person who is a party to the proceedings in which the costs order is made of the premium of an insurance policy against the risk of incurring a liability to pay the costs of other parties to the proceedings.

Access to Justice (Membership Organisation) Regulations 2005

[43.73]

1 Citation, commencement and interpretation

(1)   These Regulations may be cited as the Access to Justice (Membership Organisation) Regulations 2005 and shall come into force on 1st November 2005.

(2)   In these Regulations a reference to a section by number alone is a reference to the section so numbered in the Access to Justice Act 1999.

[43.74]

2 Revocation and transitional

(1)   Subject to paragraph (2), the Access to Justice (Membership Organisation) Regulations 2000 (the "2000 Regulations") are revoked.

(2)   The 2000 Regulations shall continue to have effect for the purposes of arrangements entered into before 1st November 2005 as if these Regulations had not come into force.

[43.75]

3 Bodies of a prescribed description

The bodies which are prescribed for the purpose of section 30 (recovery where body undertakes to meet costs liabilities) are those bodies which are for the time being approved by the Secretary of State for that purpose.

[43.76]

4 Requirements for arrangements to meet costs liabilities

(1)   Section 30(1) applies to arrangements which satisfy the following conditions.

(2)   The arrangements must be in writing.

(3)   The arrangements must contain a statement specifying the circumstances in which the member may be liable to pay costs of the proceedings.

[43.77]

5 Recovery of additional amount for insurance costs

(1)   Where an additional amount is included in costs by virtue of section 30(2) (costs payable to a member of a body or other person party to the proceedings to include an additional amount in respect of provision made by the body against the risk of having to meet the member's or other person's liabilities to pay other parties' costs), that additional amount must not exceed the following sum.

(2)   That sum is the likely cost to the member of the body or, as the case may be, the other person who is a party to the proceedings in which the costs order is made of the premium of an insurance policy against the risk of incurring a liability to pay the costs of other parties to the proceedings.

DISCLOSURE OF THE EXISTENCE OF A S 30 ARRANGEMENT

[43.78]

A s 30 arrangement is a 'funding arrangement' within the meaning of CPR Rule 43.2(1). It follows that the rules concerning the disclosure of funding arrangements apply to s 30 arrangements.

CHAPTER 44

THE CIVIL PROCEDURE RULES AND PRACTICE DIRECTIONS

[44.1]

Here are the provisions relating exclusively to CFAs with their supplementary Practice Directions:

DEFINITIONS AND APPLICATION TO CFAS

[44.2]

CPR Rule 43.2 had sub-paragraphs (*k*) to (*o*) added to the list of definitions. To save you looking in Chapter 9, here it is again:

[44.3]

CPR Rule 43.2: Definitions and Application

(1) In Parts 44 to 48, unless the context otherwise requires—

    (a) 'costs' includes fees, charges, disbursements, expenses, remuneration, reimbursement allowed to a litigant in person under rule 48.6, any additional liability incurred under a funding arrangement and any fee or reward charged by a lay representative for acting on behalf of a party in proceedings allocated to the small claims track;

    (b) 'costs judge' means a taxing master of the Senior Courts;

    (ba) 'Costs Office' means the Senior Courts Costs Office;

    (c) 'costs officer' means—

        (i) a costs judge;

        (ii) a district judge; and

        (iii) an authorised court officer;

    (d) 'authorised court officer' means any officer of—

        (i) a county court;

        (ii) a district registry;

        (iii) the Principal Registry of the Family Division; or

        (iv) the Costs Office;

whom the Lord Chancellor has authorised to assess costs.

    (e) 'fund' includes any estate or property held for the benefit of any person or class of person and any fund to which a trustee or personal representative is entitled in that capacity;

    (f) 'receiving party' means a party entitled to be paid costs;

    (g) 'paying party' means a party liable to pay costs;

    (h) 'assisted person' means an assisted person within the statutory provisions relating to legal aid;

 (i) 'LSC funded client' means an individual who receives services funded by the Legal Services Commission as part of the Community Legal Service within the meaning of Part I of the Access to Justice Act 1999;

 (j) 'fixed costs' means the amounts which are to be allowed in respect of solicitors' charges in the circumstances set out in Part 45.

 (k) 'funding arrangement' means an arrangement where a person has—

  (i) entered into a conditional fee agreement or a collective conditional fee agreement which provides for a success fee within the meaning of section 58(2) of the Courts and Legal Services Act 1990;

  (ii) taken out an insurance policy to which section 29 of the Access to Justice Act 1999 (recovery of insurance premiums by way of costs) applies; or

  (iii) made an agreement with a membership organisation to meet that person's legal costs;

 (l) 'percentage increase' means the percentage by which the amount of a legal representative's fee can be increased in accordance with a conditional fee agreement which provides for a success fee;

 (m) 'insurance premium' means a sum of money paid or payable for insurance against the risk of incurring a costs liability in the proceedings, taken out after the event that is the subject matter of the claim;

 (n) 'membership organisation' means a body prescribed for the purposes of section 30 of the Access to Justice Act 1999 (recovery where body undertakes to meet costs liabilities);

 (o) 'additional liability' means the percentage increase, the insurance premium, or the additional amount in respect of provision made by a membership organisation, as the case may be;

 (p) 'free of charge' has the same meaning as in section 194(10) of the Legal Services Act 2007;

 (q) 'pro bono representation' means legal representation provided free of charge; and

 (r) 'the prescribed charity' has the same meaning as in section 194(8) of the Legal Services Act 2007.

(2) The costs to which Parts 44 to 48 apply include—

 (a) the following costs where those costs may be assessed by the court—

  (i) costs of proceedings before an arbitrator or umpire;

  (ii) costs of proceedings before a tribunal or other statutory body; and

  (iii) costs payable by a client to his solicitor; and

 (b) costs which are payable by one party to another party under the terms of a contract, where the court makes an order for an assessment of those costs.

(3) Where advocacy or litigation services are provided to a client under a conditional fee agreement, costs are recoverable under Parts 44 to 48 notwithstanding that the client is liable to pay his legal representative's fees and expenses only to the extent that sums are recovered in respect of the proceedings, whether by way of costs or otherwise.

(4)   In paragraph (3), the reference to a conditional fee agreement is to an agreement which satisfies all the conditions applicable to it by virtue of section 58 of the Courts and Legal Services Act 1990.

[44.4]

CPD SECTION 2 SCOPE OF COSTS RULES AND DEFINITIONS: RULE 43.2

2.1   *Where the court makes an order for costs and the receiving party has entered into a funding arrangement as defined in rule 43.2, the costs payable by the paying party include any additional liability (also defined in rule 43.2) unless the court orders otherwise.*

2.2   *In the following paragraphs—*

'funding arrangement', 'percentage increase', 'insurance premium', 'membership organisation' and 'additional liability' have the meanings given to them by rule 43.2.

* *A 'conditional fee agreement' is an agreement with a person providing advocacy or litigation services which provides for his fees and expenses, or part of them, to be payable only in specified circumstances, whether or not it provides for a success fee as mentioned in section 58(2)(b) of the Courts and Legal Services Act 1990.*

'base costs' means costs other than the amount of any additional liability.

2.3   *Rule 44.3A(1) provides that the court will not assess any additional liability until the conclusion of the proceedings or the part of the proceedings to which the funding arrangement relates. (As to the time when detailed assessment may be carried out see paragraph 27.1 below.)*

2.4   *For the purposes of the following paragraphs of this practice direction and rule 44.3A proceedings are concluded when the court has finally determined the matters in issue in the claim, whether or not there is an appeal. The making of an award of provisional damages under Part 41 will also be treated as a final determination of the matters in issue.*

2.5   *The court may order or the parties may agree in writing that, although the proceedings are continuing, they will nevertheless be treated as concluded.*

[44.5]

'Additional liability' is the compendium description of a success fee, an after-the-event insurance premium, or both. Paragraph 2.2 defines costs other than the amount of any additional liability as 'base costs', while the Law Society model agreement refers to them as 'basic charges'. It is important not to confuse either definition with 'direct cost', which is the basic cost of doing the work before adding a profit mark-up.

ASSESSMENT

[44.6]

CPR Rule 44.3A: Costs Orders relating to Funding Arrangements
(1)   The court will not assess any additional liability until the conclusion of the proceedings, or the part of the proceedings, to which the funding arrangement relates.

('Funding arrangement' and 'additional liability' are defined in rule 43.2)

(2)   At the conclusion of the proceedings, or the part of the proceedings, to which the funding arrangement relates the court may—

    (a)   make a summary assessment of all the costs, including any additional liability;

    (b)   make an order for detailed assessment of the additional liability but make a summary assessment of the other costs; or

    (c)   make an order for detailed assessment of all the costs.

(Part 47 sets out the procedure for the detailed assessment of costs)

[44.7]

CPD SECTION 9 COSTS ORDERS RELATING TO FUNDING ARRANGEMENTS: RULE 44.3A

    9.1   Under an order for payment of 'costs' the costs payable will include an additional liability incurred under a funding arrangement.

    9.2

(1)   If before the conclusion of the proceedings the court carries out a summary assessment of the base costs it may identify separately the amount allowed in respect of: solicitors' charges; counsels' fees; other disbursements; and any value added tax (VAT). (Sections 13 and 14 of this Practice Direction deal with summary assessment.)

(2)   If an order for the base costs of a previous application or hearing did not identify separately the amounts allowed for solicitor's charges, counsel's fees and other disbursements, a court which later makes an assessment of an additional liability may apportion the base costs previously ordered.

[44.8]

This provision is necessary because the barrister and the solicitor may have agreed different success fees. Even where there is not an additional liability it is good practice for the judge to separately assess the barrister's and solicitor's awards, so that it is clear what has been allowed to each.

RECOVERY

[44.9]

CPR Rule 44.3B: Limits on Recovery Under Funding Arrangements
(1)   Unless the court orders otherwise, a party may not recover as an additional liability—

(a)   any proportion of the percentage increase relating to the cost to the legal representative of the postponement of the payment of his fees and expenses;

(b)   any provision made by a membership organisation which exceeds the likely cost to that party of the premium of an insurance policy against the risk of incurring a liability to pay the costs of other parties to the proceedings;

(c)   any additional liability for any period during which that party failed to provide information about a funding arrangement in accordance with a rule, practice direction or court order;

(d)   any percentage increase where that party has failed to comply with—

      (i)   a requirement in the costs practice direction; or

      (ii)   a court order,

to disclose in any assessment proceedings the reasons for setting the percentage increase at the level stated in the conditional fee agreement;

(e)   any insurance premium where that party has failed to provide information about the insurance policy in question by the time required by a rule, the practice direction or court order.

(Paragraph 9.3 of the Practice Direction (Pre-Action Conduct) (para [44.28]) provides that a party must inform any other parties as soon as possible about a funding arrangement entered into before the start of proceedings.)

(2)   This rule does not apply in an assessment under rule 48.9 (assessment of a solicitor's bill to his client).

(Rule 3.9 sets out the circumstances the court will consider on an application for relief from a sanction for failure to comply with any rule, practice direction or court order)

[44.10]

CPD SECTION 10 LIMITS ON RECOVERY UNDER FUNDING ARRANGEMENTS: CPR RULE 44.3B

10.1   *In a case to which rule 44.3B(1)(c) or (d) applies the party in default may apply for relief from the sanction. He should do so as quickly as possible after he becomes aware of the default. An application, supported by evidence, should be made under Part 23 to a costs judge or district judge of the court which is dealing with the case. (Attention is drawn to rules 3.8 and 3.9 which deal with sanctions and relief from sanctions.)*

10.2   *Where the amount of any percentage increase recoverable by counsel may be affected by the outcome of the application, the solicitor issuing the application must serve on counsel a copy of the application notice and notice of the hearing as soon as practicable and in any event at least 2 days before the hearing. Counsel may make written submissions or may attend and make oral submissions at the hearing. (Paragraph 1.4 contains definitions of the terms 'counsel' and 'solicitor'.)*

[44.11]

CPR Rule 3.9: Relief from sanctions

(1)   On an application for relief from any sanction imposed for a failure to comply with any rule, practice direction or court order the court will consider all the circumstances including –

    (a)   the interests of the administration of justice;

    (b)   whether the application for relief has been made promptly;

    (c)   whether the failure to comply was intentional;

    (d)   whether there is a good explanation for the failure;

    (e)   the extent to which the party in default has complied with other rules, practice directions, court orders and any relevant preaction protocol (GL);

    (f)   whether the failure to comply was caused by the party or his legal representative;

    (g)   whether the trial date or the likely trial date can still be met if relief is granted;

    (h)   the effect which the failure to comply had on each party; and

    (i)   the effect which the granting of relief would have on each party.

(2)   An application for relief must be supported by evidence.

[44.12]

In *Tait v Cataldo* [2010] EWHC 90166 (Costs) a Notice of Funding served in February 2008 referred only to a CFA made in November 2006 with no reference to two earlier CFAs or to an ATE policy. In respect of the ATE the failure was an error in transcribing a written N251 into the typed version sent to the defendants. As to the two earlier CFAs those had come to an end by the time the notice had to be given and the solicitor took the view that those earlier CFAs, being spent, did not need to be referred to. That understanding was not however relied upon before Master O'Hare who took the view that counsel was right not to argue that the earlier CFAs need not be referred to. The explanations given for the mistakes did not count in favour of granting relief but Master O'Hare did grant relief in all respects based on the view that the CFA mistakes were of little significance, the ATE mistake had caused no prejudice to the defendants and the mistakes had in terms of substance been remedied informally before the settlement process commenced.

In *Supperstone v Hurst* [2008] EWHC 735 (Ch), [2008] 4 Costs LR 572, [2008] BPIR 1134 Floyd J said that relief from sanctions should not be granted lightly and a party who fails to comply with the CPR runs a significant risk that he would be refused relief. If a party does not have a very good explanation, or the other side is prejudiced by his failure, relief from sanctions would usually be refused. That decision was followed in *Kutsi v North Middlesex University Hospital NHS Trust* [2008] EWHC 90119 (Costs). Contrary to CPR 44.15 and CPR 44.3B, the defendant had not been notified of the existence of the policy until after the claim was settled, as a result of which the claimant needed the court to grant relief from sanctions before she could attempt to recover the premium of £80,325.00 from the defendant on detailed assessment. Held right to be critical of the firm's failure to be aware of rudimentary CPR principles and there was no good explanation for the complete failure to give any notice of the premium at all. It followed that irrespective of any prejudice to the paying party relief from sanction would be refused.

[44.13]

Any element of a success fee which relates to the funding of the litigation by the solicitor because of his inability to receive payments on account is not recoverable between parties. It is recoverable from the client and must therefore be shown separately (See *Spencer v Wood* para [43.41])

[44.14]

CPR 44.12B Costs-only proceedings – costs in respect of insurance premium in publication cases

(1) If in proceedings to which rule 44.12A applies it appears to the court that—
  (a) if proceedings had been started, they would have been publication proceedings;
  (b) one party admitted liability and made an offer of settlement on the basis of that admission;
  (c) agreement was reached after that admission of liability and offer of settlement; and
  (d) either—
    (i) the party making the admission of liability and offer of settlement was not provided by the other party with the information about an insurance policy as required by the Practice Direction (Pre-Action Conduct); or
    (ii) that party made the admission of liability and offer of settlement before, or within 42 days of, being provided by the other party with that information,

  no costs may be recovered by the other party in respect of the insurance premium.
(2) In this rule, "publication proceedings" means proceedings for—
  (a) defamation;
  (b) malicious falsehood; or
  (c) breach of confidence involving publication to the public at large.

FACTORS TO BE TAKEN INTO ACCOUNT IN DECIDING THE AMOUNT OF COSTS

[44.15]

CPR Rule 44.5 is to be found in Chapter 21 at para [21.4].

[44.16]

CPD SECTION 11 FACTORS TO BE TAKEN INTO ACCOUNT IN DECIDING THE AMOUNT OF COSTS: RULE 44.5

11.1 *In applying the test of proportionality the court will have regard to rule 1.1(2)(c). The relationship between the total of the costs incurred and the financial value of the claim may not be a reliable guide. A fixed percentage cannot be applied in all cases to the value of the claim in order to ascertain whether or not the costs are proportionate.*

11.2 *In any proceedings there will be costs which will inevitably be incurred and which are necessary for the successful conduct of the case. Solicitors are not required to conduct litigation at rates which are uneconomic. Thus in a modest claim the proportion of costs is likely to be higher than in a large claim, and may even equal or possibly exceed the amount in dispute.*

11.3 *Where a trial takes place, the time taken by the court in dealing with a particular issue may not be an accurate guide to the amount of time properly spent by the legal or other representatives in preparation for the trial of that issue.*

11.4 *Where a party has entered into a funding arrangement the costs claimed may, subject to rule 44.3B include an additional liability.*

11.5 *In deciding whether the costs claimed are reasonable and (on a standard basis assessment) proportionate, the court will consider the amount of any additional liability separately from the base costs.*

11.6 *In deciding whether the base costs are reasonable and (if relevant) proportionate the court will consider the factors set out in rule 44.5.*

11.7 *When the court is considering the factors to be taken into account in assessing an additional liability, it will have regard to the facts and circumstances as they reasonably appeared to the solicitor or counsel when the funding arrangement was entered into and at the time of any variation of the arrangement.*

11.8

(1) *In deciding whether a percentage increase is reasonable relevant factors to be taken into account may include:*
  (a) *the risk that the circumstances in which the costs, fees or expenses would be payable might or might not occur;*
  (b) *the legal representative's liability for any disbursements;*
  (c) *what other methods of financing the costs were available to the receiving party.*
(2) *Omitted.*

11.9 *A percentage increase will not be reduced simply on the ground that, when added to base costs which are reasonable and (where relevant) proportionate, the total appears disproportionate.*

11.10 *In deciding whether the cost of insurance cover is reasonable, relevant factors to be taken into account include:*

(1) *where the insurance cover is not purchased in support of a conditional fee agreement with a success fee, how its cost compares with the likely cost of funding the case with a conditional fee agreement with a success fee and supporting insurance cover;*
(2) *the level and extent of the cover provided;*
(3) *the availability of any pre-existing insurance cover;*
(4) *whether any part of the premium would be rebated in the event of early settlement;*
(5) *the amount of commission payable to the receiving party or his legal representatives or other agents.*

11.11 *Where the court is considering a provision made by a membership organisation, rule 44.3B(1)(b) provides that any such provision which exceeds the likely cost to the receiving party of the premium of an insurance policy against the risk of incurring a liability to pay the costs of other parties to the proceedings is not recoverable. In such circumstances the court will, when assessing the additional liability, have regard to the factors set out in paragraph 11.10 above, in addition to the factors set out in rule 44.5.*

[44.17]

The Practice Direction was considerably simplified from the original draft, 14 factors having been reduced to five. A late addition was the amount of any commission payable to the client, the client's agent or legal representative. Costs Practice Direction 14.9(3) requires the risk assessment prepared at the time the funding arrangement was made to be included in the summary assessment bundle. Such an assessment was required by reg 3 of the now revoked 2000 Regulations but thus far the practice direction has not been amended. CPD 35.2 on the same point but in respect of detailed assessment does not apply to post 1 November 2005 CFAs – see para [43.51]. Where there is a claim for a success fee in costs only proceedings CPD 11.8(2) provided that the costs judge or district judge should have regard to the time when and the extent to which the claim had been settled and to the fact that the claim has been settled without the need to commence proceedings. 11.8(2) has been removed. So too has CPD 17.8(2) which provided that in costs only proceedings regard should be given to the time when and the extent to which the claim has been settled and to the fact that the claim has been settled without the need to commence proceedings. What is left is CPD 11.7 which provides that when the court is considering the factors to be taken into account in assessing an additional liability, it will have regard to the facts and circumstances as they reasonably appeared to the solicitor or counsel when the funding arrangement was entered into and at the time of any variation of the arrangement.

In *U v Liverpool City Council* [2005] EWCA Civ 475, [2005] 1 WLR 2657, (2005) Times, 16 May (see para [45.17]) the Court of Appeal held that where the CFA as a matter of contract did not provide for different success fees for different periods in the proceedings, the costs practice direction was wrong at 11.8(2) in suggesting that the court had power to order differential rates. That provision has now been removed but it appears to leave open the possibility of the CFA itself as a matter of contract providing for different rates at different stages, increasing as the litigation progresses, although it may be argued that this does not comply with the requirement of s 58 of the Courts and Legal Services Act 1990 to specify the percentage increase.

Information

[44.18]

CPR Rule 44.15: Providing information about funding arrangements

(1)   A party who seeks to recover an additional liability must provide information about the funding arrangement to the court and to other parties as required by a rule, practice direction or court order.

(2)   Where the funding arrangement has changed, and the information a party has previously provided in accordance with paragraph (1) is no longer accurate, that party must file notice of the change and serve it on all other parties within 7 days.

(3)   Where paragraph (2) applies, and a party has already filed—

   (a)   an allocation questionnaire; or

   (b)   a pre-trial check list (listing questionnaire),

he must file and serve a new estimate of costs with the notice.

(The costs practice direction sets out—

the information to be provided when a party issues or responds to a claim form, files an allocation questionnaire, a pre-trial check list, and a claim for costs;

the meaning of estimate of costs and the information required in it) (Rule 44.3B sets out situations where a party will not recover a sum representing any additional liability)

[44.19]

CPD SECTION 19 PROVIDING INFORMATION ABOUT FUNDING ARRANGEMENTS: RULE 44.15

19.1

(1)   A party who wishes to claim an additional liability in respect of a funding arrangement must give any other party information about that claim if he is to recover the additional liability. There is no requirement to specify the amount of the additional liability separately nor to state how it is calculated until it falls to be assessed. That principle is reflected in rules 44.3A and 44.15, in the following paragraphs and in Sections 6, 13, 14 and 31 of this Practice Direction. Section 6 deals with estimates of costs, Sections 13 and 14 deal with summary assessment and Section 31 deals with detailed assessment.

    (2)   In the following paragraphs a party who has entered into a funding arrangement is treated as a person who intends to recover a sum representing an additional liability by way of costs.

    (3)   Attention is drawn to paragraph 57.9 of this Practice Direction which sets out time limits for the provision of information where a funding arrangement is entered into between 31 March and 2 July 2000 and proceedings relevant to that arrangement are commenced before 3 July 2000.

Practice Direction (Pre-action Conduct)

[44.20]

Information about funding arrangements

9.3   Where a party enters into a funding arrangement within the meaning of rule 43.2(1)(k), that party must inform the other parties about this arrangement as soon as possible and in any event either within 7 days of entering into the funding arrangement concerned or, where a claimant enters into a funding arrangement before sending a letter before claim, in the letter before claim.
(CPR rule 44.3B(1)(c) provides that a party may not recover certain additional costs where information about a funding arrangement was not provided.)

The Senior Master sitting as a judge within the High Court in *Arroyo v BP Exploration Co (Columbia) Ltd (Case No HQ08X00328)* (May 2010, unreported), QBD) having heard full argument on the matter, concluded that contrary to the decisions in *Henry v BBC* [2005] EWHC 2503 (QB), [2006] 1 All ER 154, [2006] 1 All ER 154 and *Barr v Biffa Waste Services Ltd* [2005] NLJR 1780 a court has no power to order a party to disclose an ATE policy of insurance. The Costs Practice Direction at 19.4 (1) requires information about an ATE policy to be given "unless the court otherwise orders". That enabled a court to relieve a party of the obligation to give some or all of that information – it did not provide a power to require greater disclosure. The Senior Master went on to decide that the policy was covered by litigation privilege it having come into existence for the purposes of proceedings.

In *Henry v BBC* [2005] EWHC 2503 (QB), [2006] 1 All ER 154 in an application for a costs capping order in defamation proceedings it was held that where there was a legitimate concern as to the level of indemnity and exclusions in an ATE policy it was to be hoped that in future the terms of the policy would be disclosed at an early stage in the proceedings. Had earlier disclosure been made a timely application for a costs capping order could have been made. In *Barr v Biffa Waste Services Ltd* [2009] EWHC 1033 (TCC), [2010] Lloyd's Rep IR 428, [2009] All ER (D) 218 (May) the ATE Insurance policy was a disclosable document pursuant to CPR 31.14 was relevant and not privileged. It enabled the defendant to a GLO to assess the costs risk it faced. It seems that the level of premium is not relevant in those circumstances and would be redacted from the disclosed policy. These two decisions were reviewed in Arroyo and departed from on the basis that full argument had not been heard in those earlier cases. The next case was not referred to in Arroyo.

In *R (on the application of Buglife, The Invertebrate Conservation Trust) v Thurrock Thames Gateway Development Corpn* [2008] EWCA Civ 1209, [2008] 45 EG 101 (CS), (2008) Times, 18 November the Court of Appeal held that although the provisions of 44 PD do not say in terms that the level of a success fee should be disclosed, in the context of an application for a costs capping order, there was no doubt that this information should be supplied.

[44.21]

Method of giving information
19.2
(1)   In this paragraph, 'claim form' includes petition and application notice, and the notice of funding to be filed or served is a notice containing the information set out in Form N251.

(2)
   (a)   A claimant who has entered into a funding arrangement before starting the proceedings to which it relates must provide information to the court by filing the notice when he issues the claim form.
   (b)   He must provide information to every other party by serving the notice. If he serves the claim form himself he must serve the notice with the claim form. If the court is to serve the claim form, the court will also serve the notice if the claimant provides it with sufficient copies for service.

(3)   A defendant who has entered into a funding arrangement before filing any document
   (a)   must provide information to the court by filing notice with his first document. A 'first document' may be an acknowledgement of service, a defence, or any other document, such as an application to set aside a default judgment;
   (b)   must provide information to every party by serving notice. If he serves his first document himself he must serve the notice with that document. If the court is to serve his first document the court will also serve the notice if the defendant provides it with sufficient copies for service.

(4)   In all other circumstances a party must file and serve notice within 7 days of entering into the funding arrangement concerned.

(Practice Direction (Pre-Action Conduct) (para [42.111]) provides that a party must inform any other party as soon as possible about a funding arrangement entered into prior to the start of proceedings.)

Form N251

Notice of funding of case or claim

Notice of funding by means of a conditional fee agreement, insurance policy or undertaking given by a prescribed body should be given to the court and all other parties to the case:
- on commencement of proceedings
- on filing an acknowledgment of service, defence or other first document; and
- at any later time that such an arrangement is entered into, changed or terminated.

In the	
The court office is open between 10 am and 4 pm Monday to Friday. When writing to the court, please address forms or letters to the Court Manager and quote the claim number.	
Claim No.	
Claimant (include Ref.)	
Defendant (include Ref.)	

Take notice that in respect of

☐ all claims herein

☐ the following claims

☐ the case of *(specify name of party)*

[is now][was] being funded by:

(Please tick those boxes which apply)

☐ a conditional fee agreement
   ┌Dated────

   which provides for a success fee

☐ an insurance policy issued on
   ┌Date────   ┌Policy no.────

   ┌Name and address of insurer────

   Level of cover

   Are the insurance premiums staged?
   ☐ Yes   ☐ No

   If Yes, at which point is an increased premium payable

☐ an undertaking given on
   ┌Date────

   by
   ┌Name of prescribed body────

   in the following terms

The funding of the case has now changed:

☐ the above funding has now ceased

☐ the conditional fee agreement has been terminated

☐ a conditional fee agreement
   ┌Dated────

   which provides for a success fee has been entered into;

☐ an insurance policy
   ┌Date────

   has been cancelled

☐ an insurance policy has been issued on
   ┌Date────   ┌Policy no.────

   ┌Name and address of insurer────

continued over the page ➪

N251 Notice of funding of case or claim (09.09) © Crown Copyright. Reproduced by permission of the Controller of Her Majesty's Stationery Office. Published by LexisNexis.

Factors to be taken into account in deciding the amount of costs **44.21**

Level of cover

☐ an undertaking given on
Date

has been terminated

Are the insurance premiums staged?

☐ Yes   ☐ No

☐ an undertaking has been given on
Date

Name of prescribed body

If Yes, at which point is an increased
premium payable

in the following terms

Signed

Dated

Solicitor for the (claimant) (defendant)
(Part 20 defendant) (respondent) (appellant)

[44.22]

Notice of change of information

19.3

(1)   *Rule 44.15 imposes a duty on a party to give notice of change if the information he has previously provided is no longer accurate. To comply he must file and serve notice containing the information set out in Form N251. Rule 44.15(3) may impose other duties in relation to new estimates of costs.*

(2)   *Further notification need not be provided where a party has already given notice:*

    (a)   *that he has entered into a conditional fee agreement with a legal representative and during the currency of that agreement either of them enters into another such agreement with an additional legal representative; or*

    (b)   *of some insurance cover, unless that cover is cancelled or unless new cover is taken out with a different insurer.*

(3)   *Part 6 applies to the service of notices.*

(4)   *The notice must be signed by the party or by his legal representative.*

[44.23]

Information which must be provided

19.4

(1)   *Unless the court otherwise orders, a party who is required to supply information about a funding arrangement must state whether he has—*

entered into a conditional fee agreement which provides for a success fee within the meaning of section 58(2) of the Courts and Legal Services Act 1990;

taken out an insurance policy to which section 29 of the Access to Justice Act 1999 applies;

made an arrangement with a body which is prescribed for the purpose of section 30 of that Act;

or more than one of these.

(2)   *Where the funding arrangement is a conditional fee agreement, the party must state the date of the agreement and identify the claim or claims to which it relates (including Part 20 claims if any).*

(3)   *Where the funding arrangement is an insurance policy, the party must—*

    (a)   *state the name and address of the insurer, the policy number and the date of the policy and identify the claim or claims to which it relates (including Part 20 claims if any);*

    (b)   *state the level of cover provided by the insurance; and*

    (c)   *state whether the insurance premiums are staged and, if so, the points at which an increased premium is payable.*

(4)   *Where the funding arrangement is by way of an arrangement with a relevant body the party must state the name of the body and set out the date and terms of the undertaking it has given and must identify the claim or claims to which it relates (including Part 20 claims if any).*

(5)   *Where a party has entered into more than one funding arrangement in respect of a claim, for example a conditional fee agreement and an*

*insurance policy, a single notice containing the information set out in Form
N251 may contain the required information about both or all of them.*
19.5 *Where the court makes a Group Litigation Order, the court may give
directions as to the extent to which individual parties should provide information in
accordance with rule 44.15. (Part 19 deals with Group Litigation Orders.)*

Transitional Provision

19.6 *The amendments to the parenthesis below paragraph 19.2 and to
paragraph 19.4(3) do not apply where the funding arrangement was entered into
before 1st October 2009 and the parenthesis below paragraph 19.2 and
paragraph 19.4(3) in force immediately before that date will continue to apply to that
funding arrangement as if those amendments had not been made.*

1. Disclosure between the parties

[44.24]

This is another section of the Practice Direction which was drastically altered
from the original draft. The concern was that it could be prejudicial to a party
if the success fee percentage and insurance premium were revealed to another
party during the currency of the litigation. An early draft proposed that the
success fee and insurance premium should be fixed at the outset by the court
at a between-the-parties hearing. It disappeared after I pointed out the scenario
would be the claimant arguing that his case had little chance of success and
was purely speculative, justifying a 100% success fee, with the defendant
contending that the claim was cast iron and certain to succeed, that the defence
was only a delaying tactic and therefore no success fee was warranted! The
information to be provided was reduced to a minimum: the date and existence
of a CFA; the date and existence of after-the-event insurance, and the name of
the insurer; the name of any trade union or other funding body and the terms
of their undertaking together in all cases with an indication of the claim or
claims to which the funding relates are all that were required to be revealed.
Two additions from 1 April 2004 are the address of the insurer and the policy
number. All of this information can be given by completing form N251 which
is reproduced after para [44.20]. The amount of the success fee percentage or
of the insurance premium does not have to be disclosed until after the final
order for costs and any appeal has been disposed of or the time for seeking
permission to appeal has expired. Langley J held in *Montlake v Lambert Smith
Hampton Group* [2004] EWHC 1503 (Comm), [2004] 4 Costs LR 650,
[2004] NPC 112 that there was no requirement to inform an opponent of the
existence of a policy of insurance covering the opponent's costs. The reasoning
was that the notice requirements refer to the funding of the fees of the party
giving the notice and insurance is not funding. Nevertheless, the combined
effect of Rule 44.15 and the Costs Practice Direction 19.2 and 19.4 appears to
require notice to be given of any funding arrangement which will give rise to
an additional liability. That does include a policy covering opponent's costs.
On the facts of *Montlake* the claimant had not taken out insurance but neither
had form N251 been used. While use of that form is not compulsory, where it
is used the recipient of the notice will see by default that there is no insurance
policy. As it was, Langley J held that in any event the paying party had not

been prejudiced, mainly because they had been aware that the case was being run on a CFA even though the strict terms of the Practice Direction had not been followed.

Concern has been expressed that the paucity of information to be disclosed defeats the avowed aim of the CPR to provide transparency as to costs throughout the course of the litigation (see [para 42.103]). It is an aspect which does not sit well with the aims of the fixed costs schemes now in place. While success fees are set there is no guide on insurance premiums with the result that the total additional liabilities are still not known in advance. If after the time for appeal has expired details of the additional liabilities have been disclosed to the paying party, this would be strong grounds for resisting an application for permission to appeal out of time, and it may therefore be good tactics to pre-empt such an application by making voluntary disclosure as soon as the time for appeal has expired!

The amount of information required to be disclosed changed from 1 October 2009. Costs Practice Direction 19.4(3)(b) introduced a new requirement as to disclosing the 'level of cover' There was seemingly no consultation on this change and it is difficult to see what was so important about this piece of information that justified a change which has the consequence of rendering a premium irrecoverable if that information is not given. The prospect for more disputes over costs rather than fewer seems to me to look large. It is not known what is meant by 'level of cover' but judging by the amended form N251 (see para [42.105]) it simply means the financial limit of cover.

The Senior Master sitting as a judge within the High Court in *Arroyo & Ors v BP Exploration Co (Columbia) Ltd* (unreported QBD Case No HQ08X00328 May 2010)) held that a court has no power to order a party to disclose an ATE policy of insurance. The Costs Practice Direction at 19.4 (1) requires information about an ATE policy to be given "unless the court otherwise orders". That enabled a court to relieve a party of the obligation to give some or all of that information – it did not provide a power to require greater disclosure. The Senior Master went on to decide that the policy was covered by litigation privilege it having come into existence for the purposes of proceedings.

It is important to note that Rule 44.3B provides that no success fee is recoverable in respect of any period during which Rule 44.15 has not been complied with, although relief from this sanction was granted under Rule 3.9 in *Wilkins v Plymouth Community Services NHS Trust* [2003] CLY 337. Relief was also granted in *Montlake* on the basis that the paying party had suffered no prejudice as a result of the breach of the Costs Practice Direction. See further at para [44.10].

2. Disclosure to the court

(a) Summary assessment

[44.25]

CPD 14.9 provides:

In order to facilitate the court in making a summary assessment of any additional liability at the conclusion of the proceedings the party seeking such costs must prepare and have available for the court a bundle of documents which must include –

(1)   a copy of every notice of funding arrangement (Form N251) which has been filed by him;

(2)   a copy of every estimate and statement of costs filed by him;

(3)   a copy of the risk assessment prepared at the time any relevant funding arrangement was entered into and on the basis of which the amount of the additional liability was fixed.

(b)   Detailed assessment

[44.26]

CPD 32.4 provides:

If the detailed assessment is in respect of an additional liability only, the receiving party must serve on the paying party and all other relevant persons the following documents:

(a)   a notice of commencement;

(b)   a copy of the bill of costs;

(c)   the relevant details of the additional liability;

(d)   a statement giving the name and address of any person upon whom the receiving party intends to serve the notice of commencement.

(c)   CPD 32.5

[44.27]

The relevant details of an additional liability are as follows:

(1)   In the case of a conditional fee agreement with a success fee:

    (a)   a statement showing the amount of costs which have been summarily assessed or agreed, and the percentage increase which has been claimed in respect of those costs;

    (b)   a statement of the reasons for the percentage increase given in accordance with reg 3(1)(a) of the Conditional Fee Agreements Regulations or reg 5(1)(c) of the Collective Conditional Fee Agreements Regulations 2000. [Both sets of regulations were revoked by the Conditional Fee Agreements (Revocation) Regulations 2005 but continue to have effect in relation to conditional fee agreements and collective conditional fee agreements entered into before 1 November 2005.]

(2)   If the additional liability is an insurance premium: a copy of the insurance certificate showing whether the policy covers the receiving party's own costs; his opponents costs; or his own costs and his opponent's costs; and the maximum extent of that cover, and the amount of the premium paid or payable.

(3)   If the receiving party claims an additional amount under s 30 of the Access of Justice Act 1999: a statement setting out the basis upon which the receiving party's liability for the additional amount is calculated.

Where the detailed assessment is in respect of base costs and an additional liability the details required in 32.5 must be provided (CPD 32.7).

In *Findlay v Cantor Index Ltd* [2008] EWHC 90116 (Costs) it was held that CPD 32.5 could have no application to post 1 November 2005 CFAs given the revocation of the Regulations.

CPD 35.2(1)(b) requires a statement. That statement must be complete, its purpose being to enable the paying party to know the basis of the uplift when it was set. Where reasons given in reply to points of dispute differed from those in the CFA that was not a complete statement. In any event a statement must be given at commencement not in reply to points of dispute – *Middleton v Vosper* (2009) Southampton CC 6SO05696.

In *Wooldridge v Hayes* (2005) unreported SCCO Case No: HQ 0100072 the claimant disclosed an insurance schedule that described the cover as being 'subject to the policy wording'. The policy wording had not been served but in any event it did not provide the information required by the CPD 32.5(2). Under CPR 44.3B (1) (c) a party may not recover any additional liability for any period in the proceedings during which he failed to provide information about a funding arrangement in accordance with a rule, practice direction or court order. It was held that in the case of an insurance premium it was the full premium which fell within CPR 44.3B since it does not accrue (unlike a success fee) on a daily basis. On the facts relief from sanction was granted.

In the case of an additional liability in the form of a success fee, CPR 44.3B(1)(d) disentitles a receiving party to recover any success fee at all if there is a failure to provide the relevant details of the success fee as required by paragraph 32.5 of the Costs Practice Direction. In *Middleton v Vosper Thornecroft UK Ltd and others* (unreported 2009 on appeal to Winchester CC Claim No 6SO 05696) it was held in respect of a CFA governed by the CFA Regulations 2000 that CPD 35 means the paying party is entitled to have the statement of reasons as included in the CFA and in full and to know that that is what he is being given. That information must be proved at commencement of detailed assessment and no later. Here all that the paying party had been given were answers to points of dispute that gave some but not all of the reasons contained in the CFA. That was not compliant with the CPD.

In validity challenges (see para [43.51]) further disclosure has often been sought with varying degrees of success in the SCCO and county courts resulting in a variety of non-binding conflicting decisions in support of most arguments. A decision of precedent value from the High Court or above would be welcome.

PRACTICE DIRECTION (PRE-ACTION CONDUCT)

[44.28]

Information about funding arrangements

9.3 Where a party enters into a funding arrangement within the meaning of rule 43.2(1)(k), that party [should]* must inform the other parties about this arrangement as soon as possible and in any event either within 7 days of entering into the funding arrangement concerned or, where a claimant enters into a funding arrangement before sending a letter before claim, in the letter before claim.

(CPR rule 44.3B(1)(c) provides that a party may not recover certain additional costs where information about a funding arrangement was not provided.)* Note: From 1 October 2009 the word "should" becomes "must" but not retrospectively.

[44.29]

From 1 October 2009 the new Practice Direction (Pre-Action Conduct) has required disclosure of funding agreements pre-issue – see above [42.111]. Before that date to answer the question 'Do I have to disclose funding arrangements pre-issue' the unsatisfactory position was that there were no fewer than four documentary sources plus recent case law to consider. The Protocols Practice Direction stated that it was to apply whether or not there was a relevant protocol and said you 'should' disclose. It seemingly contradicted the Costs Practice Direction which recommended, but did not expressly require, pre-issue disclosure. The Civil Procedure Rules only make provision for disclosure at the time of issue. The revised Personal Injury Protocol in force from 1 April 2005 requires the letter of claim to disclose the existence of any funding arrangement. Those are the four documents you had to consult. There is also *Rogers v Merthyr Tydfil County Borough Council* [2006] EWCA Civ 1134, [2007] 1 All ER 354, [2007] 1 WLR 808 which requires disclosure of the fact that an ATE policy has a stepped premium (see para [45.31]. In *Metcalfe v Clipstone* (2004) unreported the Costs Judge held that the recommendation in the Protocols PD there was not a requirement to give notice pre-issue. Accordingly the success fee was recoverable even though the defendants were not informed of the existence of the CFA until 5 months after the pre-issue settlement and some 20 months since the CFA was made. All that changed on 1 October 2009. CPR Rule 45.5(3) also requires the court to have regard to pre-issue conduct and that under that rule the success fee may have been vulnerable.

DISALLOWANCE

[44.30]

CPR Rule 44.16: Adjournment where legal representative seeks to challenge disallowance of any amount of percentage increase

(1)   This rule applies where the Conditional Fee Agreements Regulations 2000 or the Collective Conditional Fee Agreements Regulations 2000 continues to apply to an agreement which provides for a success fee.

(2)   Where –

    (a)   the court disallows any amount of a legal representative's percentage increase in summary or detailed assessment proceedings; and

    (b)   the legal representative applies for an order that the disallowed amount should continue to be payable by his client,

the court may adjourn the hearing to allow the client to be –

    (i)   notified of the order sought; and

    (ii)   separately represented.

[44.31]

(Regulation 3(2)(b) of the Conditional Fee Agreements Regulations 2000, which applies to Conditional Fee Agreements entered into before 1 November 2005, provides that a conditional fee agreement which provides for a success fee must state that any amount of a percentage increase disallowed on assessment ceases to be payable unless the court is satisfied that it should continue to be so payable. Regulation 5(2)(b) of the Collective Conditional Fee Agreements Regulations 2000, which applies to Collective Conditional Fee Agreements entered into before 1 November 2005, makes similar provision in relation to collective conditional fee agreements.)

[44.32]

CPD Section 20 Procedure where legal representative wishes to recover form his client an agreed percentage increase which has been disallowed or reduced on assessment: Rule 44.16
20.1

(1)   *Attention is drawn to Regulation 3(2)(b) of the Conditional Fee Agreements Regulations 2000 and to Regulation 5(2)(b) of the Collective Conditional Fee Agreements Regulations 2000, which provide that some or all of a success fee ceases to be payable in certain circumstances. [Both sets of regulations were revoked by the Conditional Fee Agreements (Revocation) Regulations 2005 but continue to have effect in relation to conditional fee agreements and collective conditional fee agreements entered into before 1st November 2005]*

(2)   *Rule 44.16 allows the court to adjourn a hearing at which the legal representative acting for the receiving party applies for an order that a disallowed amount should continue to be payable under the agreement.*
20.2   *In the following paragraphs 'counsel' means counsel who has acted in the case under a conditional fee agreement which provides for a success fee. A reference to counsel includes a reference to any person who appeared as an advocate in the case and who is not a partner or employee of the solicitor or firm which is conducting the claim or defence (as the case may be) on behalf of the receiving party.*

[44.33]

Procedure following summary assessment
20.3

(1)   *If the court disallows any amount of a legal representative's percentage increase, the court will, unless sub-paragraph (2) applies, give directions to enable an application to be made by the legal representative for the disallowed amount to be payable by his client, including, if appropriate, a direction that the application will be determined by a costs judge or district judge of the court dealing with the case.*

(2)   *The court that has made the summary assessment may then and there decide the issue whether the disallowed amount should continue to be payable, if:*
(a)   *the receiving party and all parties to the relevant agreement consent to the court doing so;*
(b)   *the receiving party (or, if corporate, an officer) is present in court; and*
(c)   *the court is satisfied that the issue can be fairly decided then and there.*

[44.34]

Procedure following detailed assessment

20.4

(1)   Where detailed assessment proceedings have been commenced, and the paying party serves points of dispute (as to which see Section 34 of this Practice Direction), which show that he is seeking a reduction in any percentage increase charged by counsel on his fees, the solicitor acting for the receiving party must within 3 days of service deliver to counsel a copy of the relevant points of dispute and the bill of costs or the relevant parts of the bill.

(2)   Counsel must within 10 days thereafter inform the solicitor in writing whether or not he will accept the reduction sought or some other reduction. Counsel may state any points he wishes to have made in a reply to the points of dispute, and the solicitor must serve them on the paying party as or as part of a reply.

(3)   Counsel who fails to inform the solicitor within the time limits set out above will be taken to accept the reduction unless the court otherwise orders.

20.5   Where the paying party serves points of dispute seeking a reduction in any percentage increase charged by a legal representative acting for the receiving party, and that legal representative intends, if necessary, to apply for an order that any amount of the percentage disallowed as against the paying party shall continue to be payable by his client, the solicitor acting for the receiving party must, within 14 days of service of the points of dispute, give to his client a clear written explanation of the nature of the relevant point of dispute and the effect it will have if it is upheld in whole or in part by the court, and of the client's right to attend any subsequent hearings at court when the matter is raised.

20.6   Where the solicitor acting for a receiving party files a request for a detailed assessment hearing it must if appropriate, be accompanied by a certificate signed by him stating:

(1)   that the amount of the percentage increase in respect of counsel's fees or solicitor's charges is disputed;

(2)   whether an application will be made for an order that any amount of that increase which is disallowed should continue to be payable by his client;

(3)   that he has given his client an explanation in accordance with paragraph 20.5; and,

(4)   whether his client wishes to attend court when the amount of any relevant percentage increase may be decided.

20.7

(1)   The solicitor acting for the receiving party must within 7 days of receiving from the court notice of the date of the assessment hearing, notify his client, and if appropriate, counsel in writing of the date, time and place of the hearing.

(2)   Counsel may attend or be represented at the detailed assessment hearing and may make oral or written submissions.

20.8

(1)   At the detailed assessment hearing, the court will deal with the assessment of the costs payable by one party to another, including the amount of the percentage increase, and give a certificate accordingly.

(2)   The court may decide the issue whether the disallowed amount should continue to be payable under the relevant conditional fee agreement without an adjournment if:

    (a)   the receiving party and all parties to the relevant agreement consent to the court deciding the issue without an adjournment,

    (b)   the receiving party (or, if corporate, an officer or employee who has authority to consent on behalf of the receiving party) is present in court, and

> (c)   the court is satisfied that the issue can be fairly decided without an adjournment.
>
> (3)   In any other case the court will give directions and fix a date for the hearing of the application.

FIXED SUCCESS FEES

(a) RTA

[44.35]

The first fixed costs provisions related to costs only proceedings in RTA cases and did not initially fix the success fee. From 1 March 2004 the success fee in such cases is fixed at 12.5%. The Civil Procedure (Amendment) Rules 2004 introduced a new Section III to Part 45 with effect from 1 June 2004, implementing an industrial agreement in respect of other fixed success fees in RTA cases (other than costs only) where the accident occurred after 5 October 2003. From 30th April 2010 in respect of road accidents occurring on or after 30th April 2010 where there is a claim that includes personal injury, the total claim is for less than £10,000 and if proceedings were started they would not be in the small claims track, then a new pre-action protocol applies supported by a new Section VI of Part 45.

[44.36]

III   FIXED PERCENTAGE INCREASE IN ROAD TRAFFIC ACCIDENT CLAIMS

CPR Rule 45.15: Scope and interpretation

(1)   This Section sets out the percentage increase which is to be allowed in the cases to which this Section applies.

(Rule 43.2(1)(l) defines 'percentage increase' as the percentage by which the amount of a legal representative's fee can be increased in accordance with a conditional fee agreement which provides for a success fee)

(2)   This Section applies where –

     (a)   the dispute arises from a road traffic accident; and

     (b)   the claimant has entered into a funding arrangement of a type specified in rule 43.2(k)(i).

(Rule 43.2(k)(i) defines a funding arrangement as including an arrangement where a person has entered into a conditional fee agreement or collective conditional fee agreement which provides for a success fee)

(3)   This Section does not apply if the proceedings are costs only proceedings to which Section II of this Part applies.

(4)   This Section does not apply –

     (a)   to a claim which has been allocated to the small claims track;

     (b) ·   to a claim not allocated to a track, but for which the small claims track is the normal track; or

     (c)   where the road traffic accident which gave rise to the dispute occurred before 6th October 2003.

(5)   The definitions in rule 45.7(4) apply to this Section as they apply to Section II.

(6)   In this Section –

     (a)   a reference to 'fees' is a reference to fees for work done under a conditional fee agreement or collective conditional fee agreement;

(b)   a reference to 'trial' is a reference to the final contested hearing or to the contested hearing of any issue ordered to be tried separately;

(c)   a reference to a claim concluding at trial is a reference to a claim concluding by settlement after the trial has commenced or by judgment; and

(d)   'trial period' means a period of time fixed by the court within which the trial is to take place and where the court fixes more than one such period in relation to a claim, means the most recent period to be fixed.

[44.37]

CPR Rule 45.16: Percentage increase of solicitors' fees

Subject to rule 45.18, the percentage increase which is to be allowed in relation to solicitors' fees is –

(a)   100% where the claim concludes at trial; or

(b)   12.5% where –

    (i)   the claim concludes before a trial has commenced; or

    (ii)   the dispute is settled before a claim is issued.

[44.38]

CPR Rule 45.17: Percentage increase of counsel's fees

(1)   Subject to rule 45.18, the percentage increase which is to be allowed in relation to counsel's fees is –

(a)   100% where the claim concludes at trial;

(b)   if the claim has been allocated to the fast track –

    (i)   50% if the claim concludes 14 days or less before the date fixed for the commencement of the trial; or

    (ii)   12.5% if the claim concludes more than 14 days before the date fixed for the commencement of the trial or before any such date has been fixed;

(c)   if the claim has been allocated to the multi-track –

    (i)   75% if the claim concludes 21 days or less before the date fixed for the commencement of the trial; or

    (ii)   12.5% if the claim concludes more than 21 days before the date fixed for the commencement of the trial or before any such date has been fixed;

(d)   12.5% where –

    (i)   the claim has been issued but concludes before it has been allocated to a track; or

    (ii)   in relation to costs-only proceedings, the dispute is settled before a claim is issued.

(2)   Where a trial period has been fixed, if –

(a)   the claim concludes before the first day of that period; and

(b)   no trial date has been fixed within that period before the claim concludes,

the first day of that period is treated as the date fixed for the commencement of the trial for the purposes of paragraph (1).

(3)   Where a trial period has been fixed, if

(a)   the claim concludes before the first day of that period; but

(b)   before the claim concludes, a trial date had been fixed within that period, the trial date is the date fixed for the commencement of the trial for the purposes of paragraph (1).

(4)　　Where a trial period has been fixed and the claim concludes –

　　(a)　　on or after the first day of that period; but

　　(b)　　before commencement of the trial,

the percentage increase in paragraph (1)(b)(i) or (1)(c)(i) shall apply as appropriate, whether or not a trial date has been fixed within that period.

(5)　　For the purposes of this rule, in calculating the periods of time, the day fixed for the commencement of the trial (or the first day of the trial period, where appropriate) is not included.

[44.39]

In *Sitapuria v Khan* (10 December 2007, unreported) on the day fixed for the final hearing, before the case was opened, the judge made a consent order in the terms of an agreement reached by the parties. Were the claimant's solicitors and counsel entitled to a 100% success fee?

No, held Judge Stewart:

> 'CPR rule 45.15(6)(b) clearly refers to the words "contested hearing". Of course, if the trial commences – by which, in any normal sense of the word, it means that the case has been called on and has at least begun to be opened as a contested hearing – and the parties then settle the matter, then the trial has commenced and either that settlement which takes place after the case has been called on, and therefore has commenced, or judgment of the court in those circumstances entitles both solicitors and counsel to 100 percent. However, it seems to me that the trial has not commenced in the sense that there is no contested hearing which has commenced, if the parties conclude a settlement prior to the case being called on as a contested hearing and the opening has commenced of such a contested hearing. That is where Rules 45.15(6) and 45.16 seem inexorably to lead.'

Accordingly the success fee allowed was 12.5% for the solicitors and 75% for counsel in relation to the assessed base costs

The judge disagreed with the SCCO decision of Master Haworth in *Dahele v Thomas Bates & Son Ltd* [2007] EWHC 90072 (Costs), Judgment 17 of April 2007 in which he found that the rules in relation to counsel's success fees include an intermediate stage not available to solicitors where the claim concludes 21 days or less before the date fixed for commencement of the trial.

That case settled after the time fixed for the hearing to begin – namely, at around 11.10 a.m. If a trial does not commence for the purposes of the rules until the case is called on, and the reaching of agreement before that happens were to count as conclusion of the claim, there would be a lacuna in the rules. Counsel would get 75% if the case settled up to the night before the hearing, or 100% if the judge tells the parties to go and settle as soon as the case has been called into court, but no figure is prescribed if it settles in the few hours in between. He held that the solicitors should be treated the same as counsel and awarded them 100% each.

Both the virtue and the vice of fixed costs are illustrated in these cases – certainty on the one hand and inflexibility on the other. In *Sitapuria* all the pre-trial work intended by the predictable costs scheme to trigger a 100% success fee had been done by the solicitors and counsel and they were deprived of it by the technicality that the case had not been formally opened. Should the claimant's solicitors have refused to settle unless a 100% success fee was agreed? Failing this should they have waited until their case had been opened and then accepted the offer? The lower courts are discouraged from adopting a purposive approach to interpretation but the appellate courts at times have shown no such inhibition.

In the previous edition I expressed the hope that this important disagreement between two respected costs authorities would receive the attention of the Court of Appeal. It has. In *Thenga v Quinn* [2009] EWCA Civ 151 it was argued that a summary assessment hearing following a settlement of the substantive claim constituted a trial and therefore gave rise to an uplift of 100%. Not so, said the Court of Appeal. It was plain beyond serious argument that, in drafting Rule 45.15(6)(b), the rule-makers had not thrown out the conventional notion of a 'trial' and 'final contested hearing' related to the substantive claim, albeit including a hearing referable to a disputed claim for an award of costs in principle, ie subject to quantification. However the single Court of Appeal judge in referring to *Sitapuria* and *Dahele* said 'as to whether the announcement to the court of a settlement on the day fixed for the trial of the action but prior to the opening of the contested case to the court means that the claim concluded at trial or before a trial has commenced seems to me to be in principle a much nicer — by which I mean a much finer — point than the point raised in the present proceedings. So, the jury is still out.

[44.40]

CPR Rule 45.18: Application for an alternative percentage increase where the fixed increase is 12.5%

(1)   This rule applies where the percentage increase to be allowed –

    (a)   in relation to solicitors' fees under the provisions of rule 45.16; or

    (b)   in relation to counsel's fees under rule 45.17,

is 12.5%.

(2)   A party may apply for a percentage increase greater or less than that amount if –

    (a)   the parties agree damages of an amount greater than £500,000 or the court awards damages of an amount greater than £500,000; or

    (b)   the court awards damages of £500,000 or less but would have awarded damages greater than £500,000 if it had not made a finding of contributory negligence; or

    (c)   the parties agree damages of £500,000 or less and it is reasonable to expect that, but for any finding of contributory negligence, the court would have awarded damages greater than £500,000.

(3)   In paragraph (2), a reference to a lump sum of damages includes a reference to periodical payments of equivalent value.

(4)   If the court is satisfied that the circumstances set out in paragraph (2) apply it must –

    (a)   assess the percentage increase; or

    (b)   make an order for the percentage increase to be assessed.

[44.41]

CPR Rule 45.19: Assessment of alternative percentage increase

(1)   This rule applies where the percentage increase of fees is assessed under rule 45.18(4).

(2)   If the percentage increase is assessed as greater than 20% or less than 7.5%, the percentage increase to be allowed shall be that assessed by the court.

(3)   If the percentage increase is assessed as no greater than 20% and no less than 7.5% –

(a)   the percentage increase to be allowed shall be 12.5%; and

(b)   the costs of the application and assessment shall be paid by the applicant.

Illustration The standard success fees of 50%, 75% and 100% apply retrospectively to all the work done in the case from the commencement of the case to its conclusion at the stage to which the particular standard success fee applies. By way of illustration only, the industrial agreement included the following table summarising the agreement:

	Stage 1	Stage 2		Stage 3 Trial
Solicitor's success fee		12.5%		100%
Counsel's success fee	12.5%	Multi Track: From 21 days pre-trial	Fast Track: From 14 days pre-trial	
		75%	50%	100%

Example:

In a Fast Track Case settling 7 days before trial:

Solicitor's success fee: 12.5% for all the Solicitor's work.

Counsel's success fee: 50% for all Counsel's work.

VI   PRE-ACTION PROTOCOL FOR LOW VALUE PERSONAL INJURY CLAIMS IN ROAD TRAFFIC ACCIDENTS

[44.42]

(This protocol, which includes success fees where appropriate, is in Chapter 27.)

(b) Employers Liability Accident Cases

[44.43]

In May 2004 even more industrial agreement, known as the Montagu House Agreement, was reached in respect of success fees in employers liability accident claims and these were incorporated in a new Section IV of CPR Part 45 on 1 October 2004. They are based on Part III with variations and apply where the accident occurred after 30 September 2004. They apply whether or not substantive proceedings are issued.

IV   FIXED PERCENTAGE INCREASE IN EMPLOYERS LIABILITY CLAIMS

[44.44]

45.20 Scope and interpretation

(1)   Subject to paragraph (2), this Section applies where—

    (a)   the dispute is between an employee and his employer arising from a bodily injury sustained by the employee in the course of his employment; and

    (b)   the claimant has entered into a funding arrangement of a type specified in rule 43.2(1)(k)(i).

(2)   This Section does not apply—

    (a)   where the dispute—

        (i)   relates to a disease;

        (ii)   relates to an injury sustained before 1st October 2004; or

        (iii)   arises from a road traffic accident (as defined in rule 45.7(4)(a)); or

        (iv)   relates to an injury to which Section V of this Part applies; or

    (b)   to a claim—

        (i) which has been allocated to the small claims track; or

        (ii)   not allocated to a track, but for which the small claims track is the normal track.

(3)   For the purposes of this Section—

    (a)   'employee' has the meaning given to it by section 2(1) of the Employers' Liability (Compulsory Insurance) Act 1969(2); and

    (b)   a reference to 'fees' is a reference to fees for work done under a conditional fee agreement or collective conditional fee agreement.

[44.45]

45.21 Percentage increase of solicitors' and counsel's fees

In the cases to which this Section applies, subject to rule 45.22 the percentage increase which is to be allowed in relation to solicitors' and counsel's fees is to be determined in accordance with rules 45.16 and 45.17, subject to the modifications that—

    (a)   the percentage increase which is to be allowed in relation to solicitors' fees under rull 45.16(b) is—

        (i)   27.5% if a membership organisation has undertaken to meet the claimant's liabilities for legal costs in accordance with section 30 of the Access to Justice Act 1999; and

        (ii)   25% in any other case; and

    (b)   the percentage increase which is to be allowed in relation to counsel's fees under rule 45.17(1)(b)(ii), (1)(c)(ii) or (1)(d) is 25%.

('membership organisation' is defined in rule 43.2(1) (n))

[44.46]

45.22 Alternative percentage increase

(1)   In the cases to which this Section applies, rule 45.18(2)–(4) applies where—

    (a)   the percentage increase of solicitors' fees to be allowed in accordance with rule 45.21 is 25% or 27.5%; or

    (b)   the percentage increase of counsel's fees to be allowed is 25%.

(2)   Where the percentage increase of fees is assessed by the court under rule 45.18(4) as applied by paragraph (1) above—

    (a)   if the percentage increase is assessed as greater than 40% or less than 15%, the percentage increase to be allowed shall be that assessed by the court; and

     (b)   if the percentage increase is assessed as no greater than 40% and no less than 15%—

          (i)   the percentage increase to be allowed shall be 25% or 27.5% (as the case may be); and

          (ii)   the costs of the application and assessment shall be paid by the applicant.

(c) Employers Liability Disease Cases

[44.47]

From 1 October 2005 fixed success fees apply to disease claims following a mediated agreement under the auspices of the Civil Justice Council. The agreed level is 27.5% in asbestos cases, 62.5% for deafness, vibration white finger and all other diseases except for stress or repetitive strain injury when the level is 100%. It was incorporated in a new Section V of CPR Part 45:

V FIXED RECOVERABLE SUCCESS FEES IN EMPLOYER'S LIABILITY DISEASE CLAIMS

[44.48]

45.23 Scope and Interpretation

    (1)   Subject to paragraph (2), this Section applies where –

        (a)   the dispute is between an employee (or, if the employee is deceased, the employee's estate or dependants) and his employer (or a person alleged to be liable for the employer's alleged breach of statutory or common law duties of care); and

        (b)   the dispute relates to a disease with which the employee is diagnosed that is alleged to have been contracted as a consequence of the employer's alleged breach of statutory or common law duties of care in the course of the employee's employment; and

        (c)   the claimant has entered into a funding arrangement of a type specified in rule 43.2(1)(k)(i).

    (2)   This Section does not apply where –

        (a)   the claimant sent a letter of claim to the defendant containing a summary of the facts on which the claim is based and main allegations of fault before 1st October 2005; or

        (b)   rule 45.20(2)(b) applies.

    (3)   For the purposes of this Section –

        (a)   rule 45.15(6) applies;

        (b)   'employee' has the meaning given to it by section 2(1) of the Employers' Liability (Compulsory Insurance) Act 1969;

        (c)   'Type A claim' means a claim relating to a disease or physical injury alleged to have been caused by exposure to asbestos;

        (d)   'Type B claim' means a claim relating to –

           (i)   a psychiatric injury alleged to have been caused by work-related psychological stress;

           (ii)   a work-related upper limb disorder which is alleged to have been caused by physical stress or strain, excluding hand/arm vibration injuries; and

        (e)   Type C claim' means a claim relating to a disease not falling within either type A or type B.

(The Table annexed to the Practice Direction supplementing Part 45 contains a non-exclusive list of diseases within Type A and Type B).

[44.49]

45.24 Percentage increase of solicitors' fees

(1)   In the cases to which this Section applies, subject to rule 45.26, the percentage increase which is to be allowed in relation to solicitors' fees is –

    (a)   100% if the claim concludes at trial; or

    (b)   where –

        (i)   the claim concludes before a trial has commenced; or

        (ii)   the dispute is settled before a claim is issued,

to be determined by rule 45.24(2).

(2)   Where rule 45.24(1)(b) applies, the percentage increase which is to be allowed in relation to solicitors' fees is –

    (a)   in type A claims –

        (i)   30% if a membership organisation has undertaken to meet the claimant's liabilities for legal costs in accordance with section 30 of the Access to Justice Act 1999; and

        (ii)   27.5% in any other case;

    (b)   in type B claims, 100%; and

    (c)   in type C claims –

        (i)   70% if a membership organisation has undertaken to meet the claimant's liabilities for legal costs in accordance with section 30 of the Access to Justice Act 1999; and

        (ii)   62.5% in any other case.

('Membership organisation' is defined in rule 43.2(1)(n)).

[44.50]

45.25 Percentage increase of counsel's fees

(1)   In the cases to which this Section applies, subject to rule 45.26, the percentage increase which is to be allowed in relation to counsel's fees is –

    (a)   100% if the claim concludes at trial; or

    (b)   where –

        (i)   the claim concludes before a trial has commenced; or

        (ii)   the dispute is settled before a claim is issued,

to be determined by rule 45.25(2).

(2)   Where rule 45.25(1)(b) applies, the percentage increase which is to be allowed in relation to counsel's fees is –

    (a)   if the claim has been allocated to the fast track, the amount shown in Table 6; and

    (b)   if the claim has been allocated to the multi-track, the amount shown in Table 7.

(3)   Where a trial period has been fixed, rules 45.17(2) to 45.17(5) apply for the purposes of determining the date fixed for the commencement of the trial.

Table 6 Claims allocated to the fast track

	If the claim concludes 14 days or less before the date fixed for commencement of the trial	If the claim concludes more than 14 days before the date fixed for commencement of the trial or before any such date has been fixed
Type A claim	50%	27.5%
Type B claim	100%	100%
Type C claim	62.5%	62.5%

Table 7 Claims allocated to the multi-track

	If the claim concludes 21 days or less before the date fixed for commencement of the trial	If the claim concludes more than 21 days before the date fixed for commencement of the trial or before any such date has been fixed
Type A claim	75%	27.5%
Type B claim	100%	100%
Type C claim	75%	62.5%

[44.51]

45.26 Alternative percentage increase

(1)   In cases to which this Section applies and subject to paragraph (2) below, rules 45.18(2) to (4) apply where the percentage increase is the amount allowed under rules 45.24 and 45.25.

(2)   For the purposes of this section, the sum of £250,000 shall be substituted for the sum of £500,000 in rules 45.18(2)(a) to (c).

(3)   Where the percentage increase of fees is assessed by the court under rule 45.18(4), as applied by paragraph 1 above, the percentage increase to be allowed shall be the amount shown in Table 8.

(4)   The percentage increase cannot be varied where the case concludes at trial.

Table 8

Type of claim	Amount Allowed	
A	If the percentage increase is assessed as greater than 40% or less than 15%, the percentage increase that is assessed by the court.	If the percentage increase is assessed as no greater than 40% and no less than 15%–
		(i) 27.5%; and
		(ii) the costs of the application and assessment shall be paid by the applicant.

Type of claim	Amount Allowed	
B	If the percentage increase is assessed as less than 75%, the percentage increase that is assessed by the court.	If the percentage increase is assessed as no less than 75%–
		(i) 100%; and
		(ii) the costs of the application and assessment shall be paid by the applicant.
C	If the percentage increase is assessed as greater than 75% or less than 50%, the percentage increase that is assessed by the court.	If the percentage increase is assessed as no greater than 75% and no less than 50%–
		(i) 62.5%; and
		(ii) the costs of the application and assessment shall be paid by the applicant.

CPD SECTION 25B FIXED RECOVERABLE SUCCESS FEES IN EMPLOYER'S LIABILITY DISEASE CLAIMS

25B.1   *The following table is a non-exclusive list of the conditions that will fall within Type A and Type B claims for the purposes of Rule 45.23.*

Claim type	*Description*
A	*Asbestosis*
	Mesothelioma
	Bilateral Pleural thickening
	Pleural Plaques
B	*Repetitive Strain Injury/WRULD*
	Carpal Tunnel Syndrome caused by Repetitive Strain Injury
	Occupational Stress

(d) Summary

Road traffic cases

[44.52]

Date rule in force	Date of accident	Costs only/substantive proceedings	Base Costs	Success fee
06.10.03	On or after 06.10.03	Costs only proceedings	Fixed	Agreed or assessed (not fixed)
01.03.04	On or after 06.10.03	Costs only proceedings	Fixed	Fixed at 12.5%
01.06.04	On or after 06.10.03	Substantive proceedings	Not fixed	Fixed according to stage proceedings reach

Employer liability accident cases

Date rule in force	Date of accident	Costs only/substantive proceedings	Base Costs	Success fee
1 October 2004	On or after 1 October 2004	Both	Not fixed	Fixed according to stage proceedings reach

Employer liability disease cases

Date rule in force	Date of accident	Costs only/substantive proceedings	Base Costs	Success fee
1 October 2005	Before 1 October 2005	Both	Not fixed	Fixed according to type of disease and stage proceedings reach

(e) The indemnity principle

[44.53]

Nizami v Butt [2005] EWHC 159 (QB), [2006] 2 All ER 140, [2006] 1 WLR 3307 confirmed that the intention underlying CPR 45.7-14 (see Chapter 27) was to provide an agreed scheme of recovery that was certain and easily calculated by providing fixed levels of remuneration, which might over-reward in some cases and under-reward in others, but which were regarded as fair when taken as a whole. There was a change in the law effected by the amendment to s 51(2) of the Supreme Court (now Senior Courts) Act 1981 which significantly modified the indemnity principle and permitted changes in the rules to give effect to the modification.

It was clear that it was intended that the indemnity principle should not apply to the figures that were recoverable, and accordingly there is little reason why the indemnity principle should have any application to Rules 45.9 and 45.11, and good reasons why it should not:

(i)   the overriding objective of the CPR included saving expense and dealing with cases in ways that were proportionate to the amount of money involved.

(ii)   The range of fixed costs recoverable under rule 45.9 was £800 to £2,550 with the resultant range of success fee under rule 45.11 being £100 to £318.75 and it was hardly consistent with the overriding objective for those figures to be subjected to the sort of scrutiny proposed by the defendants.

(iii)   The whole idea underlying Part 45 (II) was that it should be possible to ascertain the appropriate costs payable without the need for further recourse to the court.

The decision is also interesting in the context of whether or not primary legislation is required to abolish the indemnity principle. The court held that the CPR had successfully disapplied the indemnity principle in relation to the predictable costs scheme. The result in *Nizami* was that the validity of the CFA was not relevant (to the indemnity principle argument) while the result in *Wetzel v KBC FIDEA* [2007] EWHC 90079 (Costs) was that the reasonableness of using a CFA rather than BTE was also irrelevant. Taking *Nizami* to its logical conclusion, if the CFA was in fact invalid, although the claimant recovered the predictable costs he had no liability to the solicitor for them – costs belong to the client!

DETAILED ASSESSMENT OF SUCCESS FEE BETWEEN SOLICITOR AND CLIENT

[44.54]

CPR Rule 48.8: Basis of detailed assessment of solicitor and client costs (continued from para [5.30])

(3)   Where the court is considering a percentage increase, whether on the application of the legal representative under rule 44.16 or on the application of the client, the court will have regard to all the relevant factors as they reasonably appeared to the solicitor or counsel when the conditional fee agreement was entered into or varied.

(4) In paragraph (3), 'conditional fee agreement' means an agreement enforceable under section 58 of the Courts and Legal Services Act 1990 at the date on which that agreement was entered into or varied.

[44.55]

CPD Section 54 Basis of detailed assessment of solicitor and client costs: Rule 48.8 (continued from para [5.31])

54.5

(1)   Attention is drawn to rule 48.9(1) as amended by the Civil Procedure (Amendment No 3) Rules 2000 (SI 2000/1317) with effect from 3 July 2000. Rule 48.9 applies only where the solicitor and the client have entered into a conditional fee agreement as defined in section 58 of the Courts and Legal Services Act 1990 as it was in force before 1 April 2000. A client who has entered into a conditional fee agreement with a solicitor may apply for assessment of the base costs (which is carried out in accordance with rule 48.8(2) as if there were no conditional fee agreement) or for assessment of the percentage increase (success fee) or both.

(2)   Where the court is to assess the percentage increase the court will have regard to all the relevant factors as they appeared to the solicitor or counsel when the conditional fee agreement was entered into.

54.6   *Where the client applies to the court to reduce the percentage increase which the solicitor has charged the client under the conditional fee agreement, the client must set out in his application notice:*

(a)   the reasons why the percentage increase should be reduced; and
(b)   what the percentage increase should be.

54.7   *The factors relevant to assessing the percentage increase include—*

(a)   the risk that the circumstances in which the fees or expenses would be payable might not occur;
(b)   the disadvantages relating to the absence of payment on account;
[(c)   whether the amount which might be payable under the conditional fee agreement is limited to a certain proportion of any damages recovered by the client;] (c) whether there is a conditional agreement between the solicitor and counsel;
(d)   the solicitor's liability for any disbursements.

54.8   *When the court is considering the factors to be taken into account, it will have regard to the circumstances as they reasonably appeared to the solicitor or counsel when the conditional fee agreement was entered into.*

CHAPTER 45

CONDITIONAL FEES IN PRACTICE

LEGAL EXPENSES INSURANCE

[45.1]

A client does not have to enter into a CFA to benefit from litigation insurance. There is of course the traditional legal expenses insurance (LEI) – known also as before-the-event (BTE) insurance. Premiums for before-the-event policies are not recoverable, but neither are they significant. Most people do not take out specific BTE insurance because they do not expect to be involved in litigation and most policies are simply add-ons to other policies such as car and house insurance. It is also true to say that many who do have BTE insurance do not even know that they have it, a fact which has caused difficulties with recoverability of the after-the-event premium under reg 4 (see para [43.38]) and on the grounds it was unreasonable ((see *Sarwar v Alam* [45.27]). A client who does not wish to enter into a CFA may still insure himself against paying between-the-parties costs if he loses by taking out an after-the-event insurance policy. Indeed he could insure himself against his own legal costs as well. Many of the after-the-event providers have just such a policy.

THE BAR

[45.2]

The Bar has never been comfortable with CFAs. A former chairman said:

'There is a very real danger of abuse. There is a conflict of interest at the very heart of these conditional fee agreements which could lead to the public being ripped-off. Ordinary people have no way of knowing whether the risk assessment on which lawyers increase their fees was accurate. The blunt truth is that people will end up paying more to lawyers and we do not think that is a satisfactory arrangement in the public interest.'

The current guidance from the Bar Council has this introduction from John Foy QC:

'When John Grace Q.C. wrote the original introduction to this Guidance in January 2001 he said "It will be apparent to anyone reading this Guidance that conditional fees and the legislation governing them are complex, that they raise novel practical problems, and that they have significant potential pitfalls for the Bar, whose risk profile is different from that of solicitors". That is no less true now than it was then.'

Paul Shrubsall, a Vice-President of the Institute of Barristers' Clerks, speaking at the Bar Conference 1999 asked: 'Would any barrister take a CFA by choice?' and answered his own question: 'No'. His reply to his next question, 'Is there a choice?', was: 'Ultimately, no'. The Bar had advocated a Contingency Legal Aid Fund – CLAF to its friends – a self-financing fund into which litigants put a slice of their winnings and in his speech to the 2005 Bar Conference the Chairman re-iterated the proposal. This is what was envisaged in the provision for litigation funders in the Access to Justice Act 1999, s 28, a section of the Act still not in force. Barristers are also concerned at what role they will play in risk assessment – and whether they will be paid for reading papers and evaluating the prospects of success. What if there is a dispute between the barrister, the solicitor and the client about how a case is to be conducted and funded or over whether or not an offer is to be made or accepted? The bar is also concerned about the problem of returned briefs – if a barrister who has entered into a CFA cannot appear at the hearing, will another barrister be willing to take over on the same terms? Some chambers have now made arrangements to ensure that there will be another barrister available for returned briefs. A recent report of the Bar Council's CFA working party argued that it is against the public interest for barristers to work under CFAs, and instead their fees should be treated as disbursements. It continued: 'Most barristers' fees are earned at or near trial when the risks are likely to be at their highest. Barristers are increasingly avoiding – or being more selective in taking on – CFA work. CFAs give solicitors, barristers and insurers the same interest in cases, but the client would be far better served if the barrister were in a position to give independent advice, free of personal financial interest in the result of the litigation. Paying barristers as disbursements would preserve their independence, while the cab-rank rule could be enforced because barristers would be less picky about cases.' The severe criticism by Brooke LJ of the amount of counsel's success fee in *Begum v Klarit* [2005] EWCA Civ 234, (2005) Times, 18 March, [2005] 3 Costs LR 452 for a hearing of an appeal is unlikely to encourage the increased involvement of the Bar in CFAs. With barristers being less than enthusiastic about entering into CFAs, solicitors will have to grasp the problem of who is to pay counsel's fees. Or is this where solicitor High Court advocates will come into their own?

EXPERTS

[45.3]

I once saw an advertisement by an expert in an American law journal proclaiming 'Never been on the losing side!'. I was only slightly less horrified when I read recently an attempted justification for expert witnesses in this country entering into CFAs. That would be an end to their role as independent advisers to the court and would seriously undermine and devalue their written and oral evidence. The Court of Appeal made this very point in *R (on the application of Factortame) v Secretary of State for Transport, Environment and the Regions (No 2)* [2002] EWCA Civ 932, [2003] QB 381, [2002] 4 All ER 97. It is also likely that the professional body to which the expert belongs prohibits such arrangements. An expert entering into such an agreement would have no protection against charges of maintenance and champerty and could well be personally liable for any unpaid costs as maintainers of litigation. But there is still the question of how experts are to be financed under a CFA; some are not willing to wait until the end of the case for payment or to limit their fees to the amount allowed on assessment between the parties.

SUCCESS FEES

(a) Warning

[45.4]

I cannot stress too strongly that the funding of CFAs is an industry with many players using highly sophisticated techniques of risk assessment and cash-flow monitoring, way beyond the concept of the non-specialist lawyer and most members of the judiciary. What follows is no more than a general outline. The Rules and Practice Directions are there to protect the naive and the innocent. If you enter into CFAs or make after-the-event (ATE) insurance arrangements without studying those rules you are inviting catastrophe. Guidance from the Court of Appeal together with fixed success fees in some cases have not removed the need for this warning.

(b) Prospects of success

[45.5]

When betting at the racecourse the search is for value for money, a horse at 6/1 or 7/1 may give better value than either an odds-on favourite or a 100/1 outsider. The search for value may be helpful on a racecourse but it is a disastrous guide to deciding whether or not to act under a CFA. That decision must be on the merits alone. There must be a sophisticated system for evaluating the prospects of success. You cannot increase the prospects of success by increasing the success fee. Do not let fear of losing work cloud your judgement. And do not take on a no-hoper on the grounds that the case is bound to settle as soon as the other side learn that it is you who is acting against them. It is a matter of risk assessment. How many firms of solicitors keep records of their success rate in different types of litigation — for example, in commercial cases, and actions involving estate agents, boundary disputes, building contracts, etc? How many solicitors record the amount of their solicitor and client and between-the-parties profit costs in the different categories? What are your average profit costs and average disbursements in a personal injury action and a medical negligence action? There are various formulae for assessing the risk and calculating the appropriate success fee based on that risk. It requires information, experience and expertise to evaluate the prospects of success. The success fee must be expressed in terms of percentage and so should the prospects of success.

An aspect of success fees to which not enough attention is given, is the prospect of recovery. This is not usually a problem where the other party is backed by an insurance company, but as CFAs spread to all forms of litigation there will be cases where the victory will prove to be Pyrrhic because the loser cannot pay the damages or costs. Defendants as well as claimants can enter into CFAs, and they may obtain judgment against a claimant who is a man of straw, or has the protection of a funding certificate. The agreement should not be 'no win, no fee', it should be 'no recovery, no fee (or 'no pay')', with the risk of not recovering the amount that has been awarded or the between-the-parties costs in appropriate cases, being reflected in the risk assessment and the resultant success fee, Because of the indemnity principle the Law Society Model for standard CFAs CFA cannot take this approach, but a simplified CFA could refer to the amount recovered rather than to the amount awarded.

(c) Calculating the risk

[45.6]

The fee can be calculated in two parts, one to reflect the risk of losing the litigation and one to cover the cost of funding it. The former is recoverable between the parties, the latter is not.

It is first necessary to express the risk as a percentage and then to convert it into a success fee, also in percentage terms.

The Law Society's publication *Conditional Fees – A Survival Guide* (2nd edn, 2001) by Michael Napier, Fiona Bawdon and Gordon Wignall provides the following method of calculating a success fee:

F divided by S multiplied by 100 equals SF, where:
F = chances of failure
S = chances of success
SF = success fee
For example:

You assess the chances of success in a particular case as 75%. This gives you a success fee of 33.3%. In other words, out of every 4 cases, 1 is going to lose. In order to pay for that losing case the costs on the other 3 must each yield an additional 1/3 in costs.

The calculation comes out as follows:

A case with a 75% chance of success has a 25% chance of failure so: 25 divided by 75 equals 0.333 multiplied by 100 equals 33.3%.

Ready Reckoner

Chance of winning	Success Fee	Chance of winning	Success Fee
50	100%	75	33%
51	96%	76	32%
52	92%	77	30%
53	89%	78	28%
54	85%	79	27%
55	82%	80	25%
56	79%	81	23%
57	75%	82	22%
58	72%	83	20%
59	69%	84	19%
60	67%	85	18%

Chance of winning	Success Fee	Chance of win-ning	Success Fee
61	64%	86	16%
62	61%	87	15%
63	59%	88	14%
64	56%	89	12%
65	54%	90	11%
66	52%	91	10%
67	49%	92	9%
68	47%	93	8%
69	45%	94	6%
70	43%	95	5%
71	41%	96	4%
72	39%	97	3%
73	37%	98	2%
74	35%	99	1%

[45.7]

The authors expressed a caveat about the assumption made in the ready reckoner that costs earned in won cases will be at the same level as those in lost cases.

(d) Cost of delay in payment

[45.8]

The payment of fees (and, in some cases, disbursements) will be postponed until the (successful) outcome of the case. The cost of this delay is carried by the solicitor and if a charge for this is included in the success fee it does not form part of the additional liability recoverable from an unsuccessful opponent (CPR Rule 44.3B. It remains the liability of the client if the case is successful and is lost to the firm if the case fails. (For pre-1 November 2005 CFAs reg 3(1)(b) required the delay element to be separately stated – see [43.32]).

The client may challenge the percentage of the success fee in the usual way under Part 48. The percentage of the success fee relating to waiting for payment will on the face of the CFA apply to the base costs actually incurred in the litigation. Those costs will have been incurred over a period of time accumulating to a total to which the percentage of the success fee is then applied. Using the success fee as the mechanism for this recovery of cost will, therefore, have a tendency to inflate the amount recovered because the success fee in effect assumes all the costs were incurred from day one. This tendency can be accounted for when setting the percentage figure. The difficulty in an individual case is accurately to predict the length of time during which the solicitor is waiting for payment.

The use of the success fee as the mechanism for recovering the cost of waiting for payment calls for an accurate prediction of the length of time which will elapse before the conclusion of the case. The following table illustrates the percentage of a success fee which would be called for to obtain the annual interest rates in the table but remember that the costs to which it applies will not have been outstanding for the whole of the time that the case runs.

Interest Rate (%) Month	6.0	8.0	10.0	Interest Rate (%) Month	6.0	8.0	10.0
9	4.5	6.0	7.5	23	11.5	15.3	19.2
10	5.0	6.7	8.3	24	12.0	16.0	20.0
11	5.5	7.3	9.2	25	12.5	16.7	20.8
12	6.0	8.0	10.0	26	13.0	17.3	21.7
13	6.5	8.7	10.8	27	13.5	18.0	22.5
14	7.0	9.3	11.7	28	14.0	18.7	23.3
15	7.5	10.0	12.5	29	14.5	19.3	24.2
16	8.0	10.7	13.3	30	15.0	20.0	25.0
17	8.5	11.3	14.2	31	15.5	20.7	25.8
18	9.0	12.0	15.0	32	16.0	21.3	26.7
19	9.5	12.7	15.8	33	16.5	22.0	27.5
20	10.0	13.3	16.7	34	17.0	22.7	28.3
21	10.5	14.0	17.5	35	17.5	23.3	29.2
22	11.0	14.7	18.3	36	18.0	24.0	30.0

(e) Disbursement liability

[45.9]

Section 11.8(1)(*b*) of the Costs Practice Direction expressly states the legal representative's liability for any disbursements is a factor to be taken into account in assessing the reasonableness of the success fee. The success fee is applied to the fees charged and not to the disbursements. If the solicitor is carrying the liability for disbursements if the case is unsuccessful, the only mechanism for reflecting that risk lies in increasing the percentage of the success fee. The increase attributable to this liability will be recoverable from a losing opponent and can therefore be challenged as being set at an unreasonable level. The test is whether the percentage increase was reasonable having regard to the circumstances as they reasonably appeared at the time the percentage was set (para 11.7).

As with the percentage for waiting for payment the difficulty is in accurately predicting the level of disbursements to be reflected in a percentage of the success fee which is a multiplier to the fees incurred throughout the life of the case. In order to calculate the percentage success fee to recover disbursement liability it is first necessary to express the disbursements as a percentage of costs. That percentage is then multiplied by the percentage figure representing the risk of the case losing since that is also the risk value in relation to losing the disbursements. This element of the success fee is vulnerable to inaccuracy in predicting the level of costs and/or disbursements with a risk of over or underestimating.

Illustration of the calculation of the disbursement element of a success fee

A	B	C	D	E
Disburse-ments	Costs	Ratio D to C	% Confi-dence	Disburse-ment
			success fee	success fee %
£500	£10,000	5%	33.3	1.66

The formula:
A ÷ B × 100 = C
C × D ÷ 100 = E
E is then added to the success fee D

(f) Assessment by the court

(i) *The Court of Appeal*

[45.10]

The long-awaited judgment of the Court of Appeal in *Callery v Gray* [2001] EWCA Civ 1117, [2001] 3 All ER 833; *Callery v Gray (No 2)* [2001] EWCA Civ 1246, [2001] 4 All ER 1 was delivered in two parts on 17 and 31 July 2001. The court emphasised that the information before it was sketchy and it was dealing only with a routine road traffic accident (RTA) case.

The categories

[45.11]

The Court of Appeal identified three categories of CFA with different principles applying to the success fees for each category, as follows:

Category A – Off-the-peg: In RTA cases the success fee should not exceed 20% of the costs. This is based upon the overall success rate being in the region of 90%. No guidance was given on cases other than RTA cases. The court allowed 20% on these facts on the grounds of a global success fee for all RTA cases undertaken by firms of solicitors handling bulk quantities of RTA cases.

[45.12]

Category B – Bespoke: Where there are at the outset factors suggesting the case may fail, then a higher success fee than the standard 20% is reasonable but it is likely that the figure cannot be set until a response has been obtained to a letter before action.

Category C – Two-stages: Where it is expected that the case will not settle until at least the end of the Protocol period, it would be reasonable to set a higher success fee, but to provide for a significant rebate if the case unexpectedly settles within the Protocol period. The court gave no guidance as to how the two figures should be calculated but it envisaged both figures being set at the outset. If the case settles in the Protocol period the lower fee would apply to the whole case; if the case does not settle, the higher figure applies to the whole case. The court gave an example of a 100% fee rebated to 5% if the claim settled within the Protocol period.

(ii)   The House of Lords

[45.13]

The costs industry held its collective breath and 150,000 cases were put on hold awaiting the certainty of an authoritative ruling by the House of Lords on appeal from the decisions of the Court of Appeal ([2002] 3 All ER 417). They did not get one. In the view of the House the appropriate forum to monitor the new funding regime and resolve its teething problems was the Court of Appeal, not the House of Lords, so they dismissed the appeal. a Their Lordships did comment, however, that a 20% success fee for simple cases looked too high and that two-stage success fees might be the way ahead.

(iii)   The Court of Appeal again

1.   5%?

[45.14]

In *Halloran v Delaney* [2002] EWCA Civ 1258, [2003] 1 All ER 775, [2003] 1 WLR 28 Lord Justice Brooke stunned the costs industry when he said:

> 'After taking advice from our assessor, and after considering the arguments in the present case, we consider that judges concerned with questions relating to the recoverability of a success fee in claims as simple as this which are settled without the need to commence proceedings should now ordinarily decide to allow an uplift of 5% on the claimant's lawyers' costs (including the costs of any costs only proceedings which are awarded to them) pursuant to their powers contained in CPD 11.8(2) unless persuaded that a higher uplift is appropriate in the particular circumstances of the case. This policy should be adopted in relation to all CFAs, however they are structured, which are entered into on and after 1st August 2001, when both *Callery* judgments had been published and the main uncertainties about costs recovery had been removed.'

2.   Clarification

[45.15]

So, no sooner had the ink dried on the House of Lords decision not to interfere in *Callery*, than the Court of Appeal had not only replaced the 20% success fee benchmark with 5%, but also backdated its effect to 1 August 2001. In the 2004 edition I asked 'How can anyone run a business among such shifting sands? How will it work?' Some of the headlines were less complimentary: 'Which Court of Appeal do we believe?' (Mark Harvey, New Law Journal),

'*Halloran* leaves PI unworkable' (Editorial, Solicitors' Journal), 'Are conditional fees finished?' (Kerry Underwood, Solicitors' Journal). All was not, however, as it seemed. Lord Justice Brooke in *Claims Direct Test Cases* [2003] EWCA Civ 136, [2003] 4 All ER 508, [2003] 2 All ER (Comm) 788 provided the following 'clarification' of his judgment in *Halloran*:

> 'Subsequent events have shown that I should have expressed myself with greater clarity. The type of case to which I was referring was a case similar to *Callery v Gray* and *Halloran v Delaney* in which, to adopt the "ready reckoner" in *Cook on Costs* (2003), p 545, the prospects of success are virtually 100%. The two-step fee advocated by the court in *Callery v Gray (No 1)* is apt to allow a solicitor in such a case to cater for the wholly unexpected risk lurking below the limpid waters of the simplest of claims. It did not require any research evidence or submissions from other parties in the industry to persuade the court that in this type of extremely simple claim a success fee of over 5% was no longer tenable in all the circumstances. The guidance given in that judgment was not intended to have any wider application.'

The provision in CPD 11.8(2) that a costs judge might substitute different success fees for different periods for the amount contractually agreed between the solicitor and client was subsequently held to be *ultra vires* the statutory scheme in *U v Liverpool City Council* (para [45.17]) and revoked.

(iv)   *Gloucester v Evans – what is a success fee?*

[45.16]

The court of appeal in *Gloucestershire County Council v Evans* [2008] EWCA Civ 21, [2008] 1 WLR 1883, [2008] NLJR 219 considered a CFA that provided for an hourly rate of £95 payable irrespective of outcome and a rate of £145 for a win. It was argued that the success fee sought by the local authority really amounted to 290% based on the fact that the costs at risk were only £50 per hour. It was held that the success fee applied to the base charges and did not offend the statute: the CCFA defined basic charges at £145 per hour. The court rejected the argument that it should look at the costs at risk in order to decide whether the success fee amounted to more than 100%. That said, the case is not authority that a 100% uplift is reasonable and therefore recoverable where only part of the costs are being risked. The case was not at all concerned with whether the success fee sought was reasonable – see further [43.6]].

(v)   *Staged success fees*

[45.17]

Yet more clarification and further encouragement for two-stage success fees was provided in *Atack v Lee* [2004] EWCA Civ 1712, [2005] 1 WLR 2643, [2006] RTR 127 and *Ellerton v Harris* [2004] EWCA Civ 1712, [2005] 1 WLR 2643, [2006] RTR 127. In *Atack* the Court upheld the reduction of a success fee from 100% to 50% in a case which went to trial and then settled for £30,000 after a finding of liability. In *Ellerton* the court reduced the success fee from 30% to 20% on the basis that it was a straight forward case and therefore 20% was the maximum to be awarded. The only significant risk was the possibility of the claimant accepting her solicitor's advice and then not beating a payment-in, which was just one of the rare risks which justified a success fee set as high as 20% in the simplest of claims

The ubiquitous Lord Justice Brooke provided this summary:

'Because there seems to be some lingering uncertainty about the combined effect of *Callery v Gray* and *Halloran v Delaney* we feel that we ought to restate for the benefit of district judges and costs judges the principles in cases governed by the old regime The reasonableness of the success fee has to be assessed as at the time the CFA was agreed. It is permissible for any CFA to include a two-stage success fee, and this is to be encouraged. In other words the success fee may be a higher percentage (up to 100% in an appropriate case) in the event that a claim does not settle within the protocol period, and a lower success fee (down to 5% in the very simplest of cases) in claims which do settle within that period. Further statistical evidence is now available to which it will be legitimate for parties to refer in relation to success fees agreed in an old regime case after the date of this judgment.'

The reference to the 'old regime' was to cases which do not fall into the fixed success fee rules (see paras [44.30]-[44.46].)

U v Liverpool City Council [2005] EWCA Civ 475, [2005] 1 WLR 2657 (This case started life as *Ungi v Liverpool City Council*; it then became *KU (through her mother PU) v LCC* and even *Ku v LCC* before settling on the title I have used. Good luck in finding it in the reports) considered the reasonableness of a single stage success fee of 100% set in October 2001 in a personal injury claim involving a four year old child who had stepped into a hole in a grass verge. The Court allowed 50% as a single stage success fee but set out the reasoning behind the use of two stage fees:

[21] 'When deciding upon a success fee [the claimant's solicitor] had two choices. He could have taken the view that this claim would probably settle without fuss at a reasonably early stage, but he wished to protect himself against the risk that the claim might go the full distance and might eventually fail. In those circumstances he could select the two-stage success fee discussed by this court in *Callery v Gray* [2001] EWCA 1117 at [106]–[112], [2001] 1 WLR 2142. In this situation he would be willing to restrict himself to a low success fee if the case settled within the protocol period – or within such other period, perhaps until the service of the defence, as he might choose – and to have the benefit of a high success fee for the cases that did not settle early. As things turned out, he would have benefited on the facts of this case if he had adopted this course: a high two-stage success fee would have been more readily defensible in a case which did not settle until proceedings were quite far advanced.'

[22] 'Alternatively, he could have selected, as he did in fact, a single-stage success fee, being a fee which he would seek to recover at the same level however quickly or slowly the claim was resolved. In those circumstances it would not be possible to justify so high a success fee.'

The judgment endorsed Lord Woolf's encouragement to lawyers in *Callery v Gray* to take seriously the possibility of agreeing an initial success fee of, say 100%, on the basis that if the claim settled within the protocol period (or some other period identified by the parties to the CFA) a lower success fee would be recoverable under the CFA. At the assessment of costs attention would then be paid to the reasonableness of the success fee which was recoverable as things turned out, and this type of arrangement would lead to a greater chance of establishing the reasonableness of a higher success fee given that the claim did not settle within the agreed period.

Costs judges should therefore be more willing to approve what appear to be high success fees in cases which have gone a long distance towards trial if the maker of the CFA has agreed that a much lower success fee should be payable if the claim settles at an early stage. *Re Claims Direct Test Cases* [2003] EWCA Civ 136 at [101], [2003] 4 All ER 508 was an earlier exposition of this principle.

The message from the Court of Appeal was that where the CFA was entered into before the *Callery* judgment on1 August 2001 the guidance given in Callery applies so that even a simple road traffic case will attract a single step success fee of 20%. Where the CFA is made after 1 August 2001 and a two stage fee is provided, then, again in simple cases, the lower figure should be 5%. There has been repeated encouragement to use a two-stage fee and the carrot of the award of a substantially higher second stage fee has been dangled.

But, even the Court of Appeal since then has not fully embraced those messages. In *C v W* [2008] EWCA Civ 1459, [2009] RTR 199, [2009] NLJR 73 the court decided that a 20% success fee in a road traffic passenger claim where liability had been admitted was about right. No two stage fee there. The court did say that if a solicitor agrees to forgo all fees post Part 36 if the offer is not beaten then the success fee could be reviewed during the life of the CFA – quite how that is achieved was not explained. The statute requires the percentage to be stated. A two stage fee states the percentage for each stage – how a reviewed fee would fit the statutory requirement must be in some doubt.

For an example of a staged success fee in defamation see *Peacock (Matthew) v MGN Ltd* [2010] EWHC 90174 (Costs). The success fee was in three stages: 100% of the basic charges, where the claim proceeds to 28 days after service of the defence; 50% if the case settles after proceedings are issued but before 28 days after the defence is served; or 25% if the case settles before proceedings are issued. Given MGN continued with a reasoned defence to stage three Master Campbell allowed the 100% success fee.

(vi) Delayed CFA is not analogous to a two stage success fee

[45.18]

It was argued in *Hennessy v Burger King* (2005) SCCO JOH0502087 that by entering into a CFA following two months on a conventional retainer and after a denial of liability was analogous to a two stage success fee given that for the first two months there was no success fee at all. Master O'Hare rejected that argument. The Claimant's solicitor had not agreed that 'a much lower success fee would be payable if the claim settles at an early stage', the words from *U v Liverpool*, and was indistinguishable from *Atack v Lee*.

(vii)   Statistics

[45.19]

We also now have the assistance of statistics. Lying behind the fixed success fee regime is a set of statistics produced for the Civil Justice Council and available on the costs debate page of its website — http://www.civiljusticecouncil.gov.uk. The Court of Appeal made it clear in *Atack v Lee* [45.15] that the fixed success fees themselves cannot be used for cases that do not fall under that regime but the underlying statistics can be used as guidance.

The Court of Appeal in *U v Liverpool City Council* [44.17] referred to other statistical material obtained by the Association of Personal Injury Lawyers. A full table was published in *Litigation Funding* of August 2003, but here is a summary:

SUCCESS RATES – PERSONAL INJURY CASES CRU STATISTICS

	RTA	EMPLOYER	PUBLIC	CLIN NEG
2001-2	89%	74%	61%	46%
2002-3	87%	77%	60%	46%

(viii)   Routine or straight forward cases

[45.20]

In *Bensusan v Freedman* [2001] All ER (D) 212 (Oct), SCCO the Senior Costs Judge equated a simple clinical negligence case, which involved a dental tool being dropped in the claimant's mouth who then swallowed it, with a personal injury action arising out of a rear-end shunt. (The analogy escaped me!) While the costs judge accepted that the risk of failure in a clinical negligence action can be greater than in a personal injury case, this particular case was 'simple and straightforward'. In *Callery v Gray* the Court of Appeal indicated that in a routine road traffic accident action the success fee should not exceed 20% and the Senior Costs Judge took the same view in this case, reducing a success fee of 50% to 20%. Using *Callery* as 'no more than a starting point', he said the effect of the Costs Practice Direction was to prevent excessive claims for success fees in cases which settle without the need for proceedings when it was clear, or ought to have been clear, from the outset that the risk of having to commence proceedings was minimal. In *Edwards v Smiths Dock Ltd* [2004] EWHC 1116 (QB), [2004] 3 Costs LR 440, [2004] All ER (D) 181 (May), the court, in approving an 87% success fee, distinguished a complicated assessment of quantum from a simple claim as in *Callery*. These early case can be contrasted with the decision in *C v W* where a 20% success fee was allowed in a road traffic claim where liability had been admitted –see [45.17].

(ix)   CFAs at an early stage

[45.21]

The essence of *Callery v Gray* was that a client could be offered a CFA at the outset of a case. The question then arises as to how the success fee is to be calculated when at such an early stage little is known about the risks of the case. According to the judgment *McCarthy v Essex Rivers Healthcare NHS Trust (Case No HQ06X03686)* (13 November 2009, unreported) QBD is the fourth case in which the same clinical negligence firm's CFA has been reviewed by a court. This time the point taken was that the CFA (as do most) provided that it could be terminated ' . . . if we believe that you are unlikely to win'. That, said Mackay J, was relevant to the level of a single stage success fee (claimed at 100%). Also relevant was the fact that this was not a two stage success fee. The success fee had been reduced to 80% and this appeal against that decision failed. It was accepted that the case was, at the time taken on, a 50:50 risk. Mackay J took the view that the termination clause meant that at a fairly early stage cases below a 50% chance can be removed leaving claims falling into the range of 50% to 80% prospects. In *Oliver (executor of the estate of Oliver) v Whipps Cross University Hospital NHS* [2009] EWHC 1104 (QB), 108 BMLR 181, 153 Sol Jo (no 21) 29, John Frederick Oliver had died of septicaemia in a hospital run by the defendants. The same solicitors agreed to act under the same conditional fee agreement as in *McCarthy* with a success fee of 100%, which represented a notional 50% prospect of success in the action. The agreement noted that the solicitors had not yet had the opportunity to test the credibility of the evidence or assess the relevant facts of expert witnesses. Accordingly the prospects of success were uncertain and it was impossible to assess the percentage chance of success with any mathematical precision. The proceedings were settled. The costs judge reduced the success fee to 67% which represented a 60% chance of success on the grounds that the solicitors must have thought there was more than a 50% chance of success, otherwise the claim would not have been accepted. On appeal, the judge held that the claim was of a kind that faced difficulties and had uncertain prospects, and based on what the solicitors knew when the conditional fee agreement was made, it was one that could easily have been assessed as having chances of success lower than 50%. Accordingly, the costs judge was wrong to take the view that he did. The judge also rejected the view that there had to be a two stage fee if a 100% figure was ever to be approved. The result was he approved a single stage 100% fee.

(x)   Liability admitted cases

[45.22]

C v W (see para [45.17] considered the success fee that could be set where liability had been admitted prior to the CFA being made. The figure arrived at was 20%. In *Hanley v Smith and MIB* [2009] EWHC 90144 (Costs) the CFA was made two years after a standard retainer and by then the first defendant had admitted liability. The extent or liability, quantum and the liability of the MIB were all still live. The solicitor had a 100% success fee of which 90% was for risk. It was held that apart from a double counted element in the risk assessment the risks were properly assessed and 82% was allowed. Leading counsel whose CFA was made after the MIB had admitted liability but before quantum was agreed had sought a success fee of 82% but it was reduced to 54%. The court said that there was a Part 36 risk and the earlier an offer was likely to be made the greater the risk was, but not great enough to justify 82%.

(xi)   High value

[45.23]

In *Cox v MGN* [2006] EWHC 1235 (QB), [2006] All ER (D) 396 (May), a media privacy action, the solicitor claimed a 95% success fee and the paying party offered 5%. Unfortunately for the solicitor, leading counsel's pre-CFA opinion was 'bullish' and the success fee was reduced on assessment to 40%, a figure held on appeal to be within the range of reasonable assessments. The CFA was entered into in 2002 at a time when the law on privacy was not as clear as it is now. Today the success fee allowed would probably be lower.

(xii)   Retrospective success fees

[45.24]

Forde v Birmingham City Council [2009] EWHC 12 (QB), [2010] 1 All ER 801, [2009] 1 WLR 2732 was an appeal from the decision of Master Campbell that a CFA can be retrospective but the success fee, following the decision of the Senior Costs Judge in *King v Telegraph Group Ltd* [2005] EWHC 90015 (Costs), could not. On appeal Christopher Clarke J took a different view. Retrospective success fees are permitted. There were at least three situations where such fees might arise: an ordinary retainer later turned into a CFA with a success fee; a CFA on no win, no fee terms and, after the work has converted after some time to include a success fee; CFA with a success fee at x % initially and later change it, retrospectively to y %. The only limit then appears to be that a following *Harrington v Wakeling* [2007] EWHC 1184 (Ch), 151 Sol Jo LB 744, [2007] All ER (D) 317 (May) the CFA must be made before the close of the case – otherwise there is no element of futurity.

(xiii)   Multiple claims and global success fees

[45.25]

In *Bray Walker Solicitors (a firm) v Silvera* [2010] EWCA Civ 332, [2010] 15 LS Gax R 18, 154 Sol Jo (no 13) 29 one CFA covered two claims. The first claim was for the costs of litigation negligently pursued by solicitors. The prospects there were 70% to 80%. The second claim was for loss of chance of success in that negligently pursued litigation. There the prospects were rather lower. The CFA provided for a single success fee of 70% triggered if any recovery at all was made. Wilson LJ took the view (obiter) that the global success fee had to reflect the split on risk and that 70% was too high. The level of the success fee did not fall to be determined but these observations leave the very difficult question of how to set a success fee where different heads of claim carry different risks. If such a case gets to an assessment and if (and it is a big 'if') an issues based costs order has been made, then presumably a reasonable success fee can be allowed a different rates for the different issues, even though a single rate is stated in the CFA.

(xiv) Fixed success fees

[45.26]

It should be kept in mind that costs belong to the client. Part 45 fixes the success fee which can be ordered against a paying party. The CFA will govern the level of fees payable to the solicitor and thought must be given to drafting the CFA to reflect the fixed fee steps. These multiple variations are not easy to explain to the client but if they are not included then the client will keep the difference between the costs allowed and those specified in the CFA. In this respect even the use of a simplified CFA which provides that the client's liability for costs will be limited to the costs recovered from the opponent will not avoid the complexities of the variable success fee because it is s 58 of the 1990 Act that requires the CFA to state the percentage by which fees are to be increased. Debate about whether a variable success fee can satisfy that requirement will no doubt continue but the fixed costs rules make no sense unless the variations can be incorporated into the CFA. The Law Society Model CFA sets out the success fee in steps for fixed success fee cases.

AFTER-THE-EVENT INSURANCE

(a) BTE or ATE?

[45.27]

Although in *Myatt* [43.42] the Court of Appeal held that in considering whether contemplated low-value litigation was covered by an existing insurance policy it was not necessary strictly to follow the procedure commended in *Sarwar v Alam* [2001] EWCA Civ 1401, [2001] 4 All ER 541 it is still of importance in considering whether ATE is preferable to an existing BTE policy.

Lord Justice Brooke provided the following helpful summary:

'This is another appeal concerned with the new arrangements for financing the costs of personal injury litigation which came into effect last year. Legal Aid is now no longer available for most litigation of this type. In *Callery v Gray*, the Court of Appeal was concerned two months ago with issues relating to the appropriate size of a success fee in a conditional fee agreement made in connection with a small claim for personal injuries suffered in a road traffic accident which was settled quite quickly without any need to bring court proceedings. In that case a passenger in a car had made a claim against the driver of the car involved in an accident. The court was also concerned with the appropriateness of taking out 'after the event' ('ATE') insurance in connection with such a claim, and the reasonableness of the ATE premium claimed in that case.

The present appeal is concerned with a similar claim brought by a passenger against the driver of the car in which he was travelling. The court below had disallowed the recovery of an ATE premium on the grounds that the claimant ought to have enquired into the availability of 'before the event' ('BTE') legal expenses insurance which formed part of the cover provided by the driver's insurance policy, and then made use of that cover. This policy covered the costs and expenses of both sides in a claim brought by a passenger in the car against the insured driver himself up to a limit of £50,000.

The Court of Appeal allowed the appeal on the grounds that the policy did not provide the claimant with appropriate cover in the circumstances of this case. Representation arranged by the insurer of the opposing party, to which the claimant had never been a party, and of which he had no knowledge of the time it was entered into and where the opposing insurer through its chosen representative reserved to itself the full conduct and control of the claim, was not a reasonable alternative to representation by a lawyer of the claimant's own choice, backed by an ATE policy.

The court suggested that the position might be different if BTE insurers financed some transparently independent organisation to handle such claims, and made it clear in the policy that this is what they were doing.

The court said, however, that if a claimant making a relatively small (ie less than about £5,000) claim in a road traffic accident had access to pre-existing BTE cover which appeared to be satisfactory for a claim of that size, that in the ordinary course of things he/she should be referred to the relevant BTE insurer'

The court gave guidance as to the nature of the enquiries a solicitor should make in this class of case into the availability of BTE cover and the insurance policies and other documents the solicitor should ask the client to produce. A solicitor should normally invite a client, by means of a standard form letter, to bring to the first interview any relevant motor and household insurance policy, as well as any stand-alone LEI policy belonging to the client and/or spouse or partner. However, regard has always to be had to the amount at stake, and a solicitor was not obliged to embark upon a treasure hunt. The court emphasised that this guidance should not be treated as an inflexible code, and that the overriding principle was that the claimant, assisted by his/her solicitor, should act in a manner that was reasonable.

(b) BTE guidance

[45.28]

The Law Society was disappointed that in *Sarwar v Alam* the Court of Appeal did not accept the Society's contention that there is a strong public interest in maintaining the client's freedom of choice, which should prevail over any implied requirement to use before-the-event insurance even if held in the claimant's name, at least unless certain minimum conditions were met. It has not generally been the case hitherto that a method of funding is rendered unreasonable by the fact that individual claimants may have an alternative available. In the view of the Law Society the availability of a BTE policy should be taken into account only in limited circumstances and cannot be regarded as a suitable alternative unless:

- the claimant has a reasonable choice of solicitor (for example, any Law Society personal injury panel member);

- the BTE insurer pays reasonable fees (that is, normal between the party rates); and
- the policy provides for the freedom for the instructed solicitor to conduct the litigation on its merits rather than being subject to direction by the BTE insurer.

(c) Collateral benefits

[45.29]

The Court of Appeal in *Callery v Gray No 2* held that s 29 of the Access to Justice Act 1999 should be interpreted so as to treat the words 'insurance against the risk of incurring a costs liability' as meaning 'insurance against the risk of incurring a costs liability that cannot be passed on to the opposing party'. This dealt with any argument about allowing a premium in costs-only proceedings, a point not pursued in the House of Lords. On the facts the court in *Callery* held that the premium of £350 was reasonable. Annexed to the judgment (but not part of it) was a report from Master O'Hare, the main points of which are:

- High limit of indemnity does not itself indicate unreasonable premium
- Block risk policies not unreasonable
- Allowed premium is total not the pure underwriting risk premium
- Assessment fees and profit costs of complying with policy recoverable
- Receiving party need not have made the best choice – must be reasonable choice
- Can be reasonable to insure before sending letter to opponent
- Also reasonable to wait until defendant's reaction known
- If premium at or above top of range of other policies – purchaser must explain

(d) Challenging the premium

[45.30]

There are two challenges which can be made to premiums: first, that not all of the sum paid was in fact premium and, second, that the premium paid is unreasonably high. The first type of challenge featured in In *Re Claims Direct Test Cases* [2002] All ER (D) 76 (Sep) and in challenges to the scheme known as The Accident Group (TAG) see *The Accident Group (TAG) test cases* 2003 SCCO Case No: PTH 0204771 15 May.

Most challenges are however to the level of premium itself. The provisions of CPR 44.4(1) and (2) and 44.5(3) (the seven pillars of wisdom) and paras 11.1, 11.5, 11.7 and 11.10 of the Costs Practice Direction are especially relevant to the assessment of premiums. CPR 44.12A applies to costs-only proceedings.

In the *RSA Pursuit Test Cases* [2005] EWHC 90003 (Costs) the Senior Costs Judge set out the test:

'... the court should look both at the costs risks and at the size of the claim when considering the premium' [261]

On the basis that no other ATE policy had been obtainable, exceptionally high premiums were allowed once the insurer's flawed method of calculation had been corrected. Master Hurst concluded that the method was flawed because it was based on flawed estimates of costs with no provision for reflecting true costs. A formula based on the opponent's actual costs was accepted.

General guidance has also been provided by the Court of Appeal as to how a costs assessor can hope to approach the question of the level of premium. Brooke LJ had this to say in *Rogers v Merthyr Tydfil County Borough Council* [2006] EWCA Civ 1134, [2007] 1 All ER 354, [2007] 1 WLR 808:

> 'District Judges and Costs Judges do not as Lord Hoffmann observed in *Callery v Gray (Nos 1 and 2)* [2002] 1 WLR 2000 para 44 have the expertise to judge the reasonableness of a premium except in very broad brush terms and the viability of the ATE market will be in peril if they regard themselves (without the assistance of expert advice) as better qualified than the underwriter to rate the financial risk the insurer faces. Although the Claimant very often does not have to pay the premium himself this does not mean that there are no competitive or other pressures at all in the market. The evidence before this court shows it is not in an insurer's interest to fix a premium at a level which will attract frequent challenges.' [117]

That passage is now often cited in decisions on recovery of premium and was the focus of the judgment of Simon J in *Kris Motor Spares Ltd v Fox Williams* [2010] EWHC 1008 (QB), [2010] All ER (D) 87 (May) who made it clear that without reversing the burden of proof the paying party must produce some evidence that the premium is unreasonable, remembering that doubt must be resolved in its favour. He provided the following guidance:

> ' . . . challenges must be resolved on the basis of evidence and analysis, rather than by assertion and counter-assertion. The issue should be identified promptly and, where necessary, there should be directions for the proper determination of specific issues. This may involve the Costs Judge looking at the proposal; and in the receiving party providing a note for a one-off ATE premium and not just for a staged premium.' [46]

The requirement for 'a note' is a reference to the decision in *Rogers v Merthyr Tydfil County Borough Council* [2006] EWCA Civ 1134, [2007] 1 All ER 354, [2007] 1 WLR 808 (see para [42.167]). Simon J also dismissed the argument that taking ATE insurance late in the proceedings was unreasonable. The solicitor defendants had insured their increasing down side only days before a hearing.

(e) Staged premiums

[45.31]

In *Rogers v Merthyr Tydfil County Borough Council* [2006] EWCA Civ 1134, [2007] 1 All ER 354, [2007] 1 WLR 808 the court considered the stepped premium model offered by the DAS 80e policy. The court allowed the premium in full, even though it was twice the amount of the damages in a simple tripping claim. There was no objection to staged premiums in principle. The evidence showed that it was necessary for solicitors to sign up to provide products from particular insurers. DAS imposed such an obligation. The solicitor explained why he chose DAS as a provider, and his reasons were legitimate. Although the premium appeared disproportionate to the damages, the *Lownds v Home Office* **[11.39]** test of necessity was to be applied. Given the need for the solicitor to subscribe to DAS in all of his cases, it was therefore necessary to incur the premium in the present claim. Therefore it was not in fact disproportionate. 'Necessity . . . . may be demonstrated by the application of strategic considerations which travel beyond the dictates of the particular case. Thus it may include the unavoidable characteristics of the market in insurance of this kind. It does so because this very market is integral to the means of providing access to justice in civil disputes in what may be called the post-legal aid world.' It was wrong to consider proportionality only with reference to size of the damages. The court had to take 'all the circumstances' into account (CPR 44.5(1)), and this included the risk to which the insurer was exposed. Here the costs exposure of about £6,500 justified the premium claimed in any event, even though the damages claimed did not exceed half this amount.

The court gave the following guidance:

(a) A party who has an ATE insurance policy incorporating two or more staged premiums should inform its opponent that the policy is staged, and should set out accurately the trigger moments at which the second or later stages will be reached. If this is done, the opponent has been given fair notice of the staging, and unless there are features of the case that are out of the ordinary, his liability to pay at the second or third stage a higher premium than he would have had to pay if the claim had been settled at the first stage should not prove to be a contentious issue.

(b) If an issue arises about the size of a second or third stage premium, it will ordinarily be sufficient for a claimant's solicitor to write a brief note for the purposes of the costs assessment explaining how he came to choose the particular ATE product for his client, and the basis on which the premium is rated – whether block rated or individually rated.

In a letter to the New Law Journal an ATE provider wrote:

> 'It is not true that staged-after-the-event premiums are more expensive than single premium policies. Obviously, a third-stage premium might prove more expensive than a policy with a single flat rate, in an individual case, but in the majority of settled cases, staged premiums offer a far cheaper alternative to single premiums. In fact, it was noted in *Rogers v Merthyr Tydfil County Borough Council* that our average premiums compared favourably to competitors using a single premium model'.

The challenge to a staged premium in *Parker (Kenneth Ronald) v Seixo (Joel Carlos)* [2010] EWHC 90162 (Costs) came in the context of a £120,000 personal injury claim where the staged premium began at £551 with an additional £9,550 if the case reached service of a defence. The challenge failed again on the basis that without expert evidence the court was in no position to second guess the underwriter.

(f) ATE and Counsel's CFA

[45.32]

ATE policies frequently include counsel's fees where counsel is not acting under a CFA. In *Hennessy v Burger King* (2005) JOH0502087 Master O'Hare held it was reasonable to instruct counsel under a CFA with success fee where the ATE policy did include counsel's fees but had a low limit of indemnity of £15,000

(g) Percentage and issues based orders

[45.33]

In *Kew v Bettamix Ltd (formerly Tarmac Roadstone Southern Ltd)* [2006] EWCA Civ 1535, [2009] PIQR P210, (2006) Times, 4 December the successful claimant, who had failed on two important issues, contended that the making of issues- based costs orders would have great consequences for access to justice because lawyers would be faced with difficult decisions as to whether to take a point and risk costs, even if ultimately successful in the action, or not take the point and risk an allegation of professional negligence. If the court made either an issues-based order for costs or a percentage costs order, severe consequences could result. For example, ATE insurers were likely to become even more reluctant to back claims or will significantly raise premiums and claimant's solicitors may become even more cautious as to what claims they take on or how they run them thereby increasing the conflict of interest with their clients and having a detrimental effect on access to justice. ATE insurers would not provide insurance to claimants if the only point they were arguing on limitation was for an extension pursuant to Section 33. It was in order to obtain such insurance that rather weak points on Section 14 had been run. A claimant is entitled to put his case at its highest.

Nevertheless, the court accepted the contentions of the defendant that a percentage costs order encourages the parties to concentrate on those issues on which they are likely to succeed. The issue had nothing to do with funding criteria, but everything to do with not taking plainly bad points on the available evidence. Because the claimant was determined to pursue an argument that proceedings had been issued before the preliminary limitation period had expired, there was a very much lengthier hearing than would otherwise have been the case. It was incumbent on all those involved in litigation to ensure that they carefully reflect on those issues that they seek to put before the court and it would be no bad thing if that leads to the reduced pursuit of bad points. Although, making an adverse order for costs in circumstances such as these (overall success albeit following failure to make good a significant alternative formulation of the case) could impact on premiums and might well have a detrimental effect on a number of aspects of funding in this field, the same argument does not apply to percentage costs orders, which can be fashioned to ensure that a party does not profit from his failure on a substantial point, which resulted in a real increase of the overall costs. The ATE insurers would simply not be engaged on the basis that no adverse order for costs would result. There is a distinction between putting the case at its highest (for example, in relation to many heads of damage in a personal injuries claim) and advancing a basis for relief that fails (especially if it is entirely unsupportable). There was no reason why the defendants should bear the costs (enhanced to reflect the risk in a conditional fee agreement) in relation to an issue on which they had succeeded. Although the claimant should not be ordered to pay any costs to the defendant, in order to reflect the way in which the issues were resolved, (but taking account of the evidence that would have been necessary in any event on the facts of the case) the defendants were ordered to pay 65% of the claimant's costs.

(h) ATE policies and third party rights

[45.34]

In *Persimmon Homes Ltd v Great Lakes Reinsurance (UK) Plc* [2010] EWHC 1705 (Comm), [2010] All ER (D) 114 (Jul) a claim was brought under the Third Parties (Rights against Insurers) Act 1930 where an insured under an ATE policy had become insolvent. No reference is made to *Tarbuck v Avon Insurance plc* [2002] QB 571, [2002] 1 All ER 503 or to the Law Commission (Law Com No 272) each of which states that the 1930 Act has no application to legal expenses insurance. Odder still is the fact that the Third Parties (Rights against Insurers) Act 2010 will replace the 1930 Act and one of the intended changes is to now include legal expenses insurance. As it was, in Persimmon the insurer avoided the policy on grounds of misrepresentation.

BACKDATING OF CFAS

[45.35]

On 15 June 2000, the claimant instructed solicitors to act in his personal injury claim against the defendants under a conditional fee agreement with no success fee. On 25 August 2000 a new agreement was entered into providing for a 25% success fee, backdated to 15 July 2000. The claim was settled on the basis that the defendants would pay the claimant's costs. The agreement provided that the basic charges were 'for work done from now until this agreement ends' and as it was clear that the claimant understood the agreement would not operate retrospectively it was enforceable (*Holmes v Alfred McAlpine Homes (Yorkshire) Ltd* [2006] EWHC 110 (QB), [2006] 3 Costs LR 466, [2006] All ER (D) 68 (Feb); SJ 3 March).

RETROSPECTIVE CFAS

[45.36]

Birmingham City Council v Forde [2009] EWHC 12 (QB), [2009] All ER (D) 64 (Jan) accepted not only that a CFA can be retrospective but so can a success fee. A retrospective CFA is not however a backdating exercise but a CFA dated on the day it is made but specifying an earlier date from which it is to cover the legal services provided. The CFA in *Holmes* was not a retrospective agreement but one that had simply been backdated. The agreement was made in August but had been dated July. That was not a permissible means of providing retrospective effect and such was not given in *Holmes*.

ASSIGNMENT AND CANCELLATION OF CFAS

[45.37]

In *Jenkins v Young Brothers Transport Ltd* [2006] EWHC 151 (QB), [2006] 2 All ER 798, [2006] 1 WLR 3189; NLJ 10 March the claimant instituted proceedings funded by a CFA and took out after the event insurance. When the solicitor acting for him changed firms, the CFA was assigned from the first firm to the second. The solicitor changed firms again and once again the CFA was assigned. The case was settled on terms of damages of £445,000 with costs to be agreed. The defendant challenged the lawfulness of the CFA on the basis that it could not be assigned. The court held that it would be a novel approach to the administration of justice were the court seek on its merits to interfere with a professional relationship whose proprietary and worth had never been challenged. In these circumstances the benefit and burden of the CFA could be assigned as an exception to the general rule.

Cancellation of a CFA was held not to terminate the retainer in *Kris Motor Spares Ltd v Fox Williams LLP* [2009] EWHC 2813 (QB), [2009] All ER (D) 156 (Nov), with very significant consequences for the client. The client misled the solicitors as to the independence of an expert witness whose evidence was crucial. The solicitors terminated the CFA on terms that they would continue to provide services to conclude the case on ordinary fee terms, the opponents having offered a "drop hands" outcome. The CFA provided for full fees to be paid in the event of such termination. Had the solicitors not terminated at that stage the case would have concluded as a loss under the CFA and the solicitors would have only recovered 70% of their fees. It was held that the CFA had been validly terminated, the retainer remained and therefore the client was not left unrepresented but had a liability for costs.

MOTOR INSURERS BUREAU LEGAL EXPENSES SCHEME

[45.38]

Where a claim is made under the MIB Uninsured Drivers Agreement on or after 13 November 2003 the MIB Legal expenses scheme is available if the claimant does not have BTE insurance. The MIB view is that it will not pay a success fee nor an ATE premium in such cases. This then is another alternative which has to be considered in road traffic cases albeit only where the driver is uninsured. The scheme provides legal expenses and does not restrict the client to a panel of solicitors. It is not based on a CFA. To use the scheme solicitors must register with the MIB which can be simply done via the MIB website (http ://www.mib.org.uk).

CFAS AND GROUP LITIGATION

[45.39]

The claimants in *A v Tui* 2005 SCCO (HQ04X03737) were holiday makers. In many group situations the claimants will now expect to be represented cost free. It is inevitable that a CFA will be expected. There are difficulties in the construction of a CFA for a group that are well beyond the scope of this work. In *Brown v Russell Young & Co* 2006 SCCO ref: 53R/2005 no group litigation order ('GLO') or other costs sharing order had been made, and there had been no specific order for the defendant to pay generic costs. CFAs existed in conventional Law Society form, which made no special mention of generic costs. The Senior Costs Judge held on appeal that where claims are settled before proceedings have been issued, and therefore before the opportunity to make such an order has arisen, common or generic costs are, in principle, recoverable either under CPR 36.13(1) or under the terms of the CFA, The CFA words 'our charges for the legal work we do on your claim for damages', are wide enough to incorporate generic or common costs. In the *Tui* case itself the Senior Costs Judge made this observation:

> 'There is a very real danger that in litigation of this type, where many Claimants would not think it worth risking their own money in order to sue for very modest damages, the funding regime created by the Access to Justice Act 1999 has provided a vehicle for litigation to be conducted for the benefit of the lawyers by generating costs rather than for benefit of the clients. This is a criticism frequently levelled against the contingency fee system in the United States in respect of class actions.'[para 79]

The relevance of success fees and ATE premiums to freezing orders in group actions was considered in *Guerrero v Monterrico Metals plc* [2009] EWHC 2475 (QB), [2009] All ER (D) 191 (Oct) where Glsoter J was prepared to make an assumption that it was legitimate to allow for the 100% uplift and for an ATE premium although in the case of the latter only 50% of the estimated cost would be reflected in the order. It would be unfair that the defendant would otherwise in effect be providing security for their own costs, effectively putting the preponderance of risk onto the defendant.

CFAS/ATE AND SECURITY FOR COSTS

[45.40]

Akenhead J reviewed the authorities relating to security for costs in *Michael Phillips Architects Ltd v Riklin* [2010] EWHC 834 (TCC), [2010] NLJR 943, [2010] All ER (D) 164 (Jun) where the claimant had an ATE policy and the defendant sought security for costs. Holding that *Keary Developments Ltd v Tarmac Construction Ltd* [1995] 3 All ER 534, [1995] 2 BCLC 395, CA governed such applications Arkenhead set out the following common sense guide to ATE in security for cots cases:
(a)   There is no reason in principle why an ATE insurance policy could not provide some or some element of security.
(b)   It will be a rare case where the ATE insurance policy can provide as good security as a payment into court or a bank bond or guarantee.
(c)   A claimant must demonstrate that the policy actually does provide some security: there must not be terms pursuant to which or circumstances in which the insurers can readily but legitimately and contractually avoid liability to pay out for the defendant's costs.

(d)   There is no reason in principle why the amount fixed by a security for costs order could not be somewhat reduced to take into account any realistic probability that the ATE insurance would cover the costs of the defendant.

In *Al-Koronky v Time-Life Entertainment Group Ltd* [2006] EWCA Civ 1123, [2006] All ER (D) 447 (Jul) the court held that the existence of a CFA was not relevant to an application for security for costs. However, a satisfactory ATE policy helps in resisting an application. But in *Al-Koronky* the policy did not pay out if the claimant had been untruthful, and as this was a libel claim where the only real issue was the truthfulness of the claimant the policy was in effect worthless. In *Monarch Energy Ltd v Powergen Retail Ltd* [2006] CSOH 102, 2006 SCLR 824, OH there was a high risk that the ATE policy had been obtained without disclosure of material facts, therefore the court would not accept it as security under s 726(2) Companies Act 1985. More generally applicable views were expressed by the court of appeal in *Belco Trading Co v Kondo* [2008] EWCA Civ 205 that it was most unlikely that any standard form of ATE insurance could provide a suitable alternative to the standard form of order for security for costs.

CFAS AND INTEREST ON COSTS

[45.41]

In *Eiles v Southwark London Borough Council* [2006] EWHC 2014 (TCC) costs were awarded in exercise of the discretion under CPR 36.1(2) and interest on those costs was awarded under CPR 36.21 on the basis of when the work was done, notwithstanding that under the CFA the work was not yet paid for. (It is instructive here to note that the Law Society Model CFA states that interest can be retained by the solicitors.)

ATE AND COSTS CAPPING

[45.42]

In *Barr v Biffa Waste Services Ltd* [2009] EWHC 2444 (TCC), [2009] NLJR 1513, [2009] All ER (D) 176 (Oct) Coulson J thought it entirely random to link the amount at which a claimant's costs could be capped to the amount that a defendant could recover against the claimants under an ATE policy, particularly where the latter figure was outside the control of the defendant and, at least directly, outside the control of the court. What mattered were the criteria in CPR, r 44.18(5) and:
(1)   Is there a risk that costs will be disproportionately incurred (sub rule (5)(b));
(2)   If so, can that risk be adequately controlled by case management and/or detailed assessment of cost (sub rule (5)(c)); and
(3)   In all the circumstances, is it in the interests of justice to make a costs capping order?
No costs capping order was made.

CHAPTER 46

THE FUTURE

RECOVERABILITY

[46.1]

CFAs had settled down by 1999 and had become a useful method of funding routine litigation. It all started to go wrong when it was perceived that CFAs could not be regarded as a substitute for state funding (which the government was anxious to curtail) if the client had to pay part of the money he recovered to his solicitor as a success fee, and part to the insurers as a premium for after-the-event indemnity against the other party's costs. Politics apart, many of us also thought that it was fairer for the loser in litigation to pay the additional liabilities, as they are called, than the winner. Where recovery of CFA additional liabilities went wrong was it breaches a fundamental tenet of English law that the costs of funding litigation are not recoverable between the parties. There are many ways of funding litigation, including the loss of interest on investments; the realisation of assets at a loss; the borrowing of money at high interest and the forgoing of holidays or other enjoyments to finance the litigation. These receive no compensation for the very good reason that it would be impossibly complicated to try to justify and quantify them, yet that is precisely what we are trying to do in respect of additional liabilities, with the spectacularly disastrous results I have outlined earlier in this chapter. As I said in an article in The Times, we opened Pandora's Box and look what flew out, is flying out and has yet to fly out. It is also unfair to successful litigants that one form of funding litigation is recoverable while no other is. The recoverability of additional liabilities also destroys the control, certainty and transparency which the new costs regime was designed to achieve. In addition, not the least of the problems is that there is no incentive for the client to keep the solicitor and client costs down, because he is not going to pay them whatever the outcome.

The Jackson Report recommends that success fees and ATE insurance premiums should cease to be recoverable from unsuccessful opponents in civil litigation, explaining: 'If this recommendation is implemented, it will lead to significant costs savings, whilst still enabling those who need access to justice to obtain it. It will be open to clients to enter into "no win, no fee" (or similar) agreements with their lawyers, but any success fee [and ATE insurance premium] will be borne by the client, not the opponent.'

FUNDING

(a) CLAF and SLAS

[46.2]

In 'The Future Funding of Litigation- Alternative Funding Structures', the second of its Series of Recommendations to the Lord Chancellor on the Development of Improved Funding Structures the Civil Justice Council (CJC) on June 2007 recommended a Supplementary Legal Aid Scheme (SLAS) should be established to introduce a form of self-funding mechanism into the public funding whereby, if a case was won, costs would be recovered and an additional sum would be payable to the fund by means of a levy to be paid as a percentage of damages recovered, or out of recovered costs. Lord Justice Jackson considered this proposal in his report and concluded: 'However, one of the critical matters for any CLAF (Contingency Legal Aid Fund) or SLAS is whether a self-funding scheme is economically viable for any significant number of cases. The information I have reviewed during the Costs Review does not provide any strong indication of financial viability. I would, nevertheless, recommend that the use of CLAFs and SLASs as a form of legal funding for civil litigation be kept under review.'

(b) Third Party Funding

[46.3]

The CJC also recommended that properly regulated third party funding should be recognised as an acceptable option for mainstream litigation. It should be encouraged, subject to (i) the constraints laid down by *Arkin* and (ii) suitable regulation of commercial third party funders to ensure consumer protection particularly in the retainer relationship between funder, lawyer and client, and who has control of the litigation. Because of the small number of funders and the nascent stage of third party funding a voluntary code was the most appropriate regulatory step, a view which was supported in the Jackson Report. A series of meetings under the auspices of the CJC resulted in the formation of the Association of Litigation Funders (ALF to its friends) which in June 2010 produced drafts of a constitution and a code of conduct.

(c) Contingency fees

[46.4]

Another CJC recommendation was that in multi party cases where no other form of funding is available, regulated contingency fees should be permitted to provide access to justice. The Ministry of Justice should conduct thorough research to ascertain whether contingency fees can improve access to justice in the resolution of civil disputes generally. The introduction of properly regulated contingency fees would simplify the funding system reducing satellite litigation and the role of costs intermediaries. This would save costs for those who ultimately pay for the litigation and for the lawyers involved in the litigation. There would also be a saving in the disproportionate amounts of time, cost, and Government resource spent on the Courts role in resolving costs disputes. Transparency and simplicity for the consumer clients would be a significant benefit under a contingency fee regime.

The Jackson Report goes much further and recommends that lawyers should be able to enter into contingency fee agreements with clients for all contentious business, provided that:

(1)   the unsuccessful party in the proceedings, if ordered to pay the successful party's costs, is only required to pay an amount for costs reflecting what would be a conventional amount, with any difference to be borne by the successful party; and

(2)   the terms on which contingency fee agreements may be entered into are regulated, to safeguard the interests of clients. They should not be valid unless the client has received independent advice.

DEFAMATION

[46.5]

In a consultation paper 'Conditional Fee Agreements in Publication Proceedings. Success Fees and After the Event Insurance' the Ministry of Justice agreed with what is known in the industry as the Theobald's Park Plus Agreement mediated by the Civil Justice Council between leading claimant and media lawyers. It is based on the agreement in principle achieved at Theobalds Park and also includes a draft protocol regarding the behaviour of parties to defamation litigation. The agreement sets out the variance in levels of success fees recoverable at different stages of a claim, including a nil recoverable additional liabilities if cases are settled and amends agreed within 14 days, with a 100% recoverable success fee if the case reaches trial or settles within 45 days before the start of a trial. This may be the way ahead for controlling success fees in other categories of litigation, but the difficulties inherent in such negotiations were illustrated by the midnight oil spent on the 'Hutton House Near Agreement'.

Having announced the reduction of maximum success fees in defamation proceedings from 100% to 10%, having reduced the customary consultation period to a mere four weeks, having survived opposition in the House of Lords from Lords Woolf and Scott, and having announced that an amendment by Statutory Order would be introduced in April 2010, the Labour government dropped the proposal. A spokeswoman for the Ministry of Justice said that Harriet Harman, the Leader of the House of Commons, had simply "announced that the motion on the order paper is not being brought forward". Whether this was because the government ran out of time as a result of dissolution of parliament prior to the general election or because all parties on the Commons Delegated Legislation Committee voted against the proposal despite the committee having a government majority, or because the association of claimant libel lawyers, Lawyers for Media Standards, had threatened a judicial review, or for all these reasons was not clear.

BLUEPRINT

[46.6]

No wonder there are those, including Lord Scott, who are looking across the Atlantic for the answer to our problems. Mistakenly, they say they are attracted to contingency fees, but contingency fees are virtually the same as conditional fees – they both come out of the proceeds of the litigation. The fundamental difference between the two systems is not contingency fees, but fee-shifting. In the USA they do not have between-the-parties costs – and it is the absence of fee-shifting that the proponents of contingency fees are really attracted to.

But there is no need for such a drastic remedy as the abolition of between-the parties costs. The culprits are recoverability and the indemnity principle. The solution is to get back to the basic principle of not looking behind the solicitor and client screen, of ignoring the method of funding the litigation and removing additional liabilities from the arena of party and party costs. My blueprint for the costs recoverable between the parties, which assumes the abolition of the indemnity principle, continues to be simply: 'Such sum as is reasonable and proportionate having regard of the subject matter of the litigation (on the fast track such amount to be determined and predictable), regardless of the terms under which the legal services have been provided'.

I was much encouraged when Lord Phillips, then Master of the Rolls, said at an Association of Personal Injury Lawyers conference, that he was now converted to the proposition that an end to the recoverability between the parties of CFA additional liabilities and the introduction of a limited form of contingency fee, could go some way to relieving the present funding mess and the unproductive and wasteful satellite costs litigation. Lord Phillips recalled that before recoverability was introduced in 1999 there was in effect a form of restricted contingency fee capped at 25% and paid by the client out of the damages. He was inclined to think that what has gone wrong since then is the shifting of this recovery element to the defendant. In his view the more satisfactory system is one whereby you recover your costs in the normal way but if lawyers were acting on a conditional fee basis, that liability will not be transferred to the defendant. The senior costs judge, Peter Hurst, has endorsed this view and I respectfully concur. I also entirely agreed with Patrick Allen when, as President of APIL, he said 'In its obsession with pre-action costs the Civil Justice Council is fiddling while Rome burns. The real confusion surrounding recent costs litigation lies with success fees, insurance premiums and recoverability, not base costs. The system of costs as a whole is falling apart for reasons that are nothing whatsoever to do with base costs.'

Such is the gathering momentum to abolish between-the-parties costs altogether, and to replace them with out-and-out American style contingency fees I am concerned that if we cannot get litigation costs back on an even keel, we may find that the alleged simplification of CFAs has been merely re-arranging the deck chairs on the Titanic.

RESEARCH

(a) Contingency fees in the USA

[46.7]

A research paper "Contingency fees-a study of their operation in the United States of America" by Professor Richard Moorhead and senior costs judge Peter Hurst commissioned by the Civil Justice Council concluded that so long as the present costs system in England and Wales continues to operate, there is no pressing need to introduce any other type of costs system. The problems inherent in the present system are such, however, that it has to be accepted that the system may breakdown and policy needs to be developed to respond to that eventuality should it occur.

Fears that damages-based contingency fees would lead to an Americanisation of our civil justice system are almost certainly overstated. Any excesses in the American system appear to be driven by levels of damages and jury awards in particular rather than contingency fees.

Whilst, it is possible for contingency fees to operate without fee shifting, our working assumption is that if CFAs collapse, it will be because of failure of the ATE market. In that event, it is likely that the basic cost rules would have to be adapted, with loser pays perhaps being abolished or a move towards one-way costs shifting. Even under abolition, there is the potential for fee-shifting to be introduced in partial form through the offers to settle process, which may improve the effectiveness and efficiency of the claims process.

If fee shifting is done away with and contingency fees are permitted, the evidence suggests that, properly regulated, the new regime would operate satisfactorily and without the satellite litigation which bedevils the current system in this jurisdiction. Contingency fees would also be likely to introduce greater proportionality in the system.

It has to be accepted however that such a change might have a significant effect on which cases are brought (particularly low value cases) and thus access to justice could be adversely affected. Similarly, cases which hinge on non-monetary remedies or where monetary remedies are low relative to legal costs would not be well-served by a damages-based contingency fees system. A partial solution to this dilemma would be the increase in the level of the small claims jurisdiction, so that such cases could be litigated informally without the need for the lawyers or with more packaged, limited cost support (again perhaps through contingency fees).

Were contingency fees to be introduced, consideration would also need to be given to consumer protection measures around the setting and charging of such fees (including disbursements; VAT and recoupment deductions); and settlement clauses. Broader regulation of fees in high value cases might also be considered, but it is important to bear in mind that restricting the levels of fee as a significant detrimental effect on access to justice.

In a letter in the Law Society Gazette Professor Moorhead wrote that the evidence is not that contingency fees present no problems, but that those problems are more modest than many assume. They are neither the source of, nor the solution to, all of the justice system's problems. Properly regulated, he believed they can help, but only a little.

The Law Society Gazette has described the rights and wrongs of contingency fees as being one of the great debates. One side sees them egging on unscrupulous lawyers to fuel a crazed litigation culture, as in the US. The other says they reward lawyers for the results achieved for their clients, rather than the work put in, and ensure 'costs are proportionate to damages'. Referring to concerns over possible conflicts of interest between the solicitors and their clients when it comes to settlement, the editorial continued: 'But every form of charging has a conflict inherent in it-conditional fees, like contingency fees encourage the lawyer to settle and ensure they are paid; the hourly rate pushes the lawyer to keep going. The reality is that, with conditional fees and fixed costs for road traffic cases-where fees are to a degree related to damages-we are some way down the road to a contingency fees. Dissatisfaction with the system is now greater than ever and these reports indicate that contingency fees probably combined with the abolition of cost-shifting, are a radical reform worth consideration'.

Contingency Fees in Tribunals

[46.8]

This study was also co-authored by Professor Richard Moorhead.

It found that the use of contingency fees in employment tribunals throws up few major concerns and marginally improves access to justice, but needs better regulation to protect clients over issues such as transparency of charging. Professor Moorhead said he had conducted the study because of growing talk about 'How terrible and American-like the system was becoming'.

He concluded: 'There is nothing particularly to worry about, which is quite an important message for people who bang on about how bad contingency fees are'.

Index

A

A factor
charging for time, and 22.12
Abuse of power
indemnity basis, and 11.55
Acceptance of payment in
generally 14.18
one or more, but not all, defendants,
by 14.23
Practice Direction 14.33
Accident Line Protect
recovery of insurance premiums,
and 43.11
Accounts rules
liens, and 6.21
Additional liability
see also CONDITIONAL FEE AGREEMENTS
costs estimates, and 10.5
definition 9.1
summary assessment, and
generally 29.11
Practice Direction 29.16
SCCO Guide 29.17
Administrations
routine work, and 23.23
Admission
security for costs, and 13.20
Adrenalin
non-routine factors, and 23.4
Adverse costs orders
costs information, and 2.10
Advisory Committee on Civil Costs
generally, 22.27
Advocacy
summary assessment,
Counsel 29.26
solicitors 29.25
wasted costs orders, and 32.14
After-the-event (ATE) insurance
challenging the premium 45.30
collateral benefits 45.29
cost capping, and 45.42
counsel's fees 45.32
generally 45.27

After-the-event (ATE) insurance – *cont.*
issues based orders 45.33
percentage orders 45.33
security for costs, and
generally 13.47
introduction 45.40
selection issues 45.27
staged premiums 45.31
third party rights, and 45.34
Agreed costs
detailed assessment, and
generally 30.56
Practice Direction 30.55
Rule 30.54
summary assessment, and 29.6
Agreed damages
road traffic accidence claims 27.42
Agreed fees
value added tax, and 4.6
Agreements with clients
between-the-parties cap 2.30
client care
Code of Conduct 2007 2.35
deficiencies in letters 2.42
introduction 2.36
terms and conditions of retainer 2.38
conditional fees
and see CONDITIONAL FEE AGREEMENTS
introduction 2.34
contentious business agreements 2.29
costs information
adverse costs orders 2.10
best information possible 2.5
Code of Conduct 2007 2.3
escape clause 2.13
fixed fees 2.15
funding 2.8
Guidance 2.3
increases 2.6
lien 2.9
payment in kind 2.12
payment to others 2.7
pre-1 July 2007, and 2.1
sanctions 2.14

851

Index

Index

Index

Index